KODANSHA
ENCYCLOPEDIA OF
JAPAN

Distributors
JAPAN: KODANSHA LTD., Tokyo.
OVERSEAS: KODANSHA INTERNATIONAL LTD., Tokyo.
   U.S.A., Mexico, Central America, and South America: KODANSHA INTERNATIONAL/USA LTD.
     through HARPER & ROW, PUBLISHERS, INC., New York.
   Canada: FITZHENRY & WHITESIDE LTD., Ontario.
   U.K., Europe, the Middle East, and Africa: INTERNATIONAL BOOK DISTRIBUTORS LTD.,
     Hemel Hempstead, Herts., England.
   Australia and New Zealand: HARPER & ROW (AUSTRALASIA) PTY. LTD., Artarmon, N.S.W.
   Asia: TOPPAN COMPANY (S) PTE. LTD., Singapore.

Published by Kodansha Ltd., 12-21, Otowa 2-chome, Bunkyo-ku, Tokyo 112 and Kodansha
International/USA Ltd., 10 East 53rd Street, New York, New York 10022.
Copyright © 1983 by Kodansha Ltd.
All rights reserved.
Printed in Japan.
First edition, 1983.

LCC 83-80778
ISBN 0-87011-625-8 (Volume 5)
ISBN 0-87011-620-7 (Set)
ISBN 4-06-144535-9 (0) (in Japan)

Library of Congress Cataloging in Publication Data
Main entry under title:

Kodansha encyclopedia of Japan.

   Includes index.
   1. Japan—Dictionaries and encyclopedias. I. Title:
Encyclopedia of Japan.
DS805.K633 1983   952'.003'21   83-80778
ISBN 0-87011-620-7 (U.S.)

KODANSHA
ENCYCLOPEDIA OF
JAPAN

5

KODANSHA

L

libraries

In Japan today a full range of libraries and library activities exists, including public and private libraries, information centers sponsored by public and private bodies, central and local governmental libraries, children's and school libraries, and academic and special libraries. Library associations, educational and training programs, and cooperative exchanges among libraries enrich the profession and assist it in fulfilling its social objectives. Japan is also meeting the challenge of the ever-increasing amount of information available, which has necessitated sophisticated methods of storing and retrieving library records through electronic and mechanical devices. Development of nationwide networks of information sharing, particularly of scientific and technological data, is foremost among the country's current library concerns.

History —— The history of Japanese libraries can be traced back to even before the Nara period (710–794). In early Japan strong clan chiefs and noblemen collected records that kept alive the memory of ancestors, local events, and important religious precepts and rituals. These materials later came to be housed in what were usually designated as *bunko* (libraries, or literary storehouses), repositories of religious, literary, and family documents, rigidly guarded and controlled for a fixed clientele. Materials used in religious study were gathered together in the Yumedono (Hall of Dreams), believed to be the earliest library in Japan, located on the grounds of the temple HŌRYŪJI near Nara. After promulgation of the TAIHŌ CODE of 701, the court established the ZUSHORYŌ (Bureau of Books), the earliest known archival library, in which Buddhist scriptures, images, and books were stored.

From the earliest times the growth of *bunko* in the houses of wealthy families, such as the FUJIWARA FAMILY, was often tied to support of the schools founded by the aristocracy to educate their members. These libraries, known as *kuge bunko*, housed Buddhist scriptures, Chinese classics, family genealogies, local histories, and so forth, and were not unlike the libraries that were built in the West in ancient and medieval times. One such library, the UNTEI, built by ISONOKAMI NO YAKATSUGU (729–781), was open to scholars upon application. In subsequent generations the archetypical library became the *buke bunko* (warrior library), reflecting the dominance of the military in the affairs of the country. Some of these libraries were closely guarded, for they were in fact repositories of family secrets, histories, military stratagems, and scientific knowledge. The best known *buke bunko*, however, was open to scholars and priests. This was the KANAZAWA BUNKO, established in 1275 by Hōjō Sanetoki (1224–76) in what is now Kanagawa Prefecture. Here Chinese and Japanese books were collected, controlled, and made available to *samurai* qualified to use them. Today a portion of this *bunko* is maintained in the Kanagawa Prefectural Library. In 1432, another historically significant library, the Ashikaga Gakkō Bunko (Ashikaga School Library) was revived by UESUGI NORIZANE (1411–66). His collections are among the few dating from this period to survive and are today maintained at the school's site in the city of Ashikaga (see ASHIKAGA GAKKŌ ISEKI TOSHOKAN). The first Tokugawa shōgun, TOKUGAWA IEYASU (1543–1616), built a strictly guarded library within the shogunal palace grounds in Edo (now Tōkyō), which was known first as the Fujimitei Bunko and later as the Momijiyama Bunko. After the fall of the Tokugawa shogunate in 1867–68, members of the Tokugawa family assembled a collection of shogunate documents and books at Ieyasu's former retreat Sumpu (now the city of Shizuoka). This collection is now known as the AOI LIBRARY (Aoi Bunko) and is maintained by the Shizuoka Prefecture Central Library.

During the Edo period (1600–1868) the various *daimyō* built their own collections for the use of their educated retainers. Notable among them were the SONKEIKAKU LIBRARY built by the Maeda family of the Kaga domain (now Ishikawa Prefecture); the first ASAKUSA BUNKO, built in Edo by Itazaka Bokusai; the Awa no Kuni Bunko, in the Tokushima domain (now Tokushima Prefecture); and the Aoyagi Bunko in the Sendai domain (now Miyagi Prefecture). Although these collections were primarily intended for the use of the ruling classes, in principle some of them were open to the reading public. It was not until after the Meiji Restoration of 1868, however, that the concept that libraries should be open to all, regardless of social status, was fully realized.

During the Meiji period (1868–1912), prominent national figures such as FUKUZAWA YUKICHI (1835–1901) and TANAKA FUJIMARO (1845–1909) provided the stimulus for Japanese public library development based on their observations of library activities overseas. Their ideas quickly took hold and in 1872 the first modern public libraries, the Shojakukan in Tōkyō and the Shūshoin in Kyōto, were built. Laws were promulgated to establish the legal and economic bases for libraries, and many institutions began to appear throughout the country. The Japan Library Association was founded in 1892, and in 1907 the first library journal, *Toshokan zasshi*, was published.

Principal concerns of the growing profession of *shisho* (librarians) were the training of librarians, the development of technical processing of library materials, and the expansion of services to library users. The Library Law of 1950 established the legal standards for a full and meaningful library service to the entire nation. Fulfillment of the goals envisioned in this legislation will depend upon the economic support of government at all levels, and the political support of the people of Japan.

Roles and Functions of Modern Japanese Libraries —— After 1868, when Japan came under strong Western influence, concepts of the value of libraries were introduced as part of the general "modernization" of Japanese society. Since the rationale for public libraries in Western countries has been the need for the electorate to understand political and social issues, with the library serving as a common source of community information, library development in Europe and America has been evolutionary. In Japan, on the other hand, libraries were introduced over the short period of a few decades by educators and politicians, and were not created by the will and interest of the people who were expected to use them. The highly structured social system, the educational framework, the emphasis on book ownership over book borrowing, and the peculiarities of the Japanese language all must be taken into account when studying the modern Japanese library and its social role.

Academic libraries serve the teaching and research needs of colleges and universities but are hampered by physical, organizational, and economic problems. Specialized scientific and technological libraries have been notably forward-looking and innovative in response to the needs of government agencies, corporations, banks, factories, economic research institutes, and other institutions.

Types of Library —— Libraries in Japan are classified both by the source of their major support, such as national, prefectural, or municipal, and by the nature of the clientele they are designed to serve, such as public, school, special, academic, and children's.

National government funds support the largest library in Japan, the NATIONAL DIET LIBRARY, which together with its many branches forms the nation's single most important library system. Aside from directly operating libraries, the role of the government is also significant in that it provides the funding for national university libraries and shares in the expenses of operating other quasi-governmental institutions, such as the Japan Information Center for Science and Technology. About half of the 55 braille libraries in Japan are government sponsored, and libraries located in national hospitals, prisons, military establishments, and research institutes also benefit from national funding. The various executive, judicial, and legislative arms of the government which maintain libraries, most of which are branches of the National Diet Library, are also national libraries. Under the provisions of the Library Law of 1950, the national government lends some support to local public libraries.

All 47 prefectures in Japan sponsor public library services. Prefectural libraries are usually located in the chief city or prefectural capital and provide some form of outreach service, especially to inhabitants of rural areas. Bookmobiles, reading clubs, and interlibrary loans form the basis of these services. Within the average prefectural library, exhibits, lectures, films, and other cultural activities complement the core of reading-centered services. Many prefectures offer more than one facility and help pay for municipal library services as well.

Local public libraries in cities, towns, and villages receive support from all levels of government in Japan according to the provisions of the Zaisei Hō (General Finance Law). Despite the firm legal basis for public libraries and the detailed budgeting formulae which provide funding for them, the levels of service, staffing, and collection building have not kept pace with the growth of other social education institutions such as museums and citizens' public halls. As of 1976 about 73 percent of the 666 cities and 10 percent of the 2,613 towns and villages in Japan, including Okinawa, provided public library service. While the quality of service varies, outstanding examples of public libraries can be seen in the cities of Hino, which has a high rate of circulation of books, Nagoya, which has an extensive system of branches serving the metropolitan area, and Kōchi, which provides innovative services for the general public and the handicapped.

Libraries for children in the elementary, middle, and high schools are provided for by the School Library Law of 1953, which also seeks to establish levels of collections and size of staff. As of 1978 school libraries were close to 41,000 in number. Grade school libraries stock an average of 6 to 9 books per pupil, and secondary school libraries somewhat more. School libraries are partially funded by the national government in order to assure attainment of the minimum standards prescribed by law. Separate from school libraries are children's libraries, which are generally found either in public libraries or as independent operations maintained by individuals, who often set up small collections in their homes for use by neighborhood preschoolers.

Academic institutions as of 1976 reported about 780 libraries, over half of which were privately sponsored. The national government supports some 295 libraries in its 81 universities. Local governments, mostly prefectures, have libraries in about 50 universities. There are also over 300 junior colleges which maintain libraries. With no national law calling for uniformity of organization, library functions within academic institutions vary widely. Some colleges have strong centralized collections, but in most large universities library services are scattered among the academic departments, or faculties, and libraries on such campuses are subject to little central control. The largest national university library is the Tōkyō University Library, dating from 1877. The combined collections there exceed 3.5 million volumes, with annual increases in excess of 120,000 volumes. Important private university libraries include those of the International Christian University, noted for its service innovations, and Keiō University, noted for its range of specialized collections. The TENRI CENTRAL LIBRARY, in Tenri, Nara Prefecture, though not a university library, is noted for its treasures of early Japanese, Chinese, and Western literature.

Special libraries have assumed the role of innovators in the development of practical and effective library services suited to the needs of a country whose general priorities have been economic growth and political stability. Government and corporate special libraries have assumed the major burden of the informational needs of technological Japan. The Japan Special Libraries Association has helped coalesce an otherwise highly competitive group of enterprises into a model system of cooperation, information dissemination, and computerized applications in libraries, especially in the field of scientific information. Leading specialized information centers are the Japan Information Center for Science and Technology, the Ajia Keizai Kenkyūjo (Institute of Developing Economies), and the Nomura Sōgō Kenkyūjo (Nomura Research Institute of Technology and Economics). Various branches of government ministries and agencies, the national institutes of social and humanistic studies, medical libraries, and local chamber of commerce libraries have also served private enterprise in developing the best specialized library services possible, not only in Japan but throughout the world.

The Profession —— A shisho (librarian) is anyone who works in a library who has met certain training, educational, or experience-level requirements prescribed by article 5 of the Library Law of 1950. Depending on the type of work performed or the type of library one works in, a professional librarian might also be referred to as an archivist, documentalist, teacher librarian, or information scientist. There are also shishoho (assistant librarians), who perform nonprofessional tasks in libraries. The education of Japanese librarians has consistently relied on models of library development in the West, and the professional lexicon is filled with terms borrowed from Europe and America. Many colleges and universities offer courses in librarianship, and most institutions supporting libraries provide some training toward certification of librarians. Continuing education is provided by national and regional associations as well as by opportunities for international travel and participation in conferences and educational programs abroad. The principal professional associations include the Japan Library Association, the School Library Association, councils of private, public, and national university libraries, the Nippon Documentation Association, and the Japan Medical Library Association. The most widely read general professional journals are Toshokan zasshi, Toshokan kenkyū, and Gendai no toshokan.

Technical Processing —— As in other countries where librarianship has developed as a profession, Japan has endeavored to meet the many challenges relating to the organization of library collections. The development of bibliographies, construction of classification schemes, rules for cataloging, and lists of subject headings have formed the traditional focuses of processing activity. During the past decade, great concern has been given to automated alternatives to manual processing. Japan has taken the lead in Asia and is equal to many of her Western counterparts in the application of computer technology in libraries.

In the area of classification Japan was influenced by Western approaches. Although some large libraries such as the National Diet Library and the Tōkyō University Library have developed their own classifications, most libraries today use the Nippon Jisshin Bunruihō (Nippon Decimal Classification, NDC), a modified version of the Dewey Decimal Classification, altered to meet the different range of topics covered by Sino-Japanese publications. The NDC is now in its seventh edition and has served as the basis of the standard classification used by all school libraries, as well as most university and public libraries. Special libraries generally use the Universal Decimal Classification.

The development of a standardized approach to cataloging has involved problems of choice of entry, filing of cards, description of works, and separation of Western works from Chinese and Japanese publications. Unlike the traditional emphasis on authorship in the West, the Chinese-Japanese tendency has been to place importance on the title of a work. Whether to enter the record, be it a catalog card or a bibliography entry, under the name of the author or the title has been a controversial issue from the beginnings of modern cataloging development. Because of the prevailing interest in Western cataloging principles and the need for a unified approach, the first edition of the standard tool for cataloging, Nippon Mokuroku Kisoku (Nippon Cataloging Rules, NCR), published in 1943, emphasized the feasibility of author main entry for all works, both oriental and Western. The NCR in all its subsequent revisions, the latest of which was in 1965, has attempted to reconcile the problems inherent in cataloging both Western and Sino-Japanese books. Because Western books often form a major part of a Japanese library's holdings, collections have tended to be physically divided between foreign and domestic publications. This division has required separate catalogs for each, thus doubling the technical effort and multiplying the cataloging problems associated with maintaining separate classified, author, and title coverage for each division of the collections. Related to the rationale for maintaining separate cataloging files are the language-oriented principles underlying each: the Western alphabet does not lend itself to interfiling with Chinese characters and the Japanese syllabary, unless the latter are romanized. Romanization has worked only to a limited degree because of the nonstandardization of romanization schemes and because of difficulties in establishing a division system for Japanese words.

The assignment of subject headings is both the most difficult and least developed technical problem throughout the world of librarianship. In Japan, likewise, emphasis in the past upon classification has tended to draw effort away from assignment of subjects to the records of library holdings. This is due, in part, to the reliance in Japan upon classified catalogs and, in part, to the nature of the title-dominated interest in books. Titles of Sino-Japanese books tend to be very descriptive and to adequately indicate the subject coverage of their contents. Nevertheless, the development of subject headings lists has formed a part of the scholarly concern of the library profession since the 19th century. The standard work, compiled in 1930 by Katō Shūkō, is a table of subjects known as the Nihon kemmei *hyōmokuhyō* (Japan Subject Headings), which, although not widely in use, is a substantial guide to those libraries which find this problem important enough to devote attention to it in their technical processing efforts.

Advances in the development of data bases, specialized bibliographies, and the retrieval of catalog information in a variety of ways have led the Japanese library world, headed by the National Diet Library and other leading research institutions, to develop new standards, services, and products in the field of documentation. This work centers on the capabilities òf the computer to produce the growing accumulations of records generated by postindustrial societies. While these efforts have largely focused on scientific and technological information, the call for standardization, both nationally and internationally, is having great impact on the nature, staffing, and budgets of all libraries throughout the country. Thus these efforts, designed to result in a national scientific information network in Japan, will also affect libraries in the fields of humanities and social sciences in the years ahead.

Problems Peculiar to Libraries in Japan——Public libraries in Japan compete with several significant traditions of society in the struggle for their very existence. The high regard for private book ownership and the relatively low cost of books until recently have fostered the tendency of personal indifference toward public library collections. Bookstores far outnumber public libraries. Public libraries also compete with publicly supported *kōminkan* (community centers), many of which provide library collections and reading rooms. Their existence represents an overlap of function with the public library, thus increasing the duplication of effort and competition for the small-user base. Because public libraries have not kept up with the demands and needs of users, meaningful support for them is lacking. *Kashihon'ya* (book rental shops) outnumber libraries in some areas of the country by as much as five to one. Their appeal is directed mainly to the recreational reading habits of high school students and others who borrow books for a small fee.

Libraries for children are few in number and poorly supported. Their problems lie less in the provision of books and materials, which are numerically adequate in most cases, than in the provision of qualified library personnel who are able to organize and service their collections in ways which go beyond the present limitations of clerical support in response to the needs of the classroom.

Academic libraries suffer from a lack of organizational cooperation both within and among institutions of higher education. Chief librarians are generally faculty members who serve in the post for a few years on a rotating basis, and it is difficult for career librarians to reach the top post, thereby using to best advantage their years of experience in the profession.

The interlibrary loan of materials in Japan succeeds best between libraries which enjoy close affiliation, such as medical libraries of universities and research libraries which do not otherwise compete with each other in their search for new knowledge.

Given the advanced state of technological development in Japan, the problems surrounding the identification, storage, and retrieval of the ever-expanding stock of information differ little from those in other countries. Japan's unique challenge relates to the way information is recorded in both Western and oriental languages, especially to the way Chinese and Japanese characters are manipulated by machine. Problems of the latter kind are being confronted and solved through national leadership and through international exchange of technical ideas and standards. The Japanese are not only meeting the challenge but exhibit the potential of becoming a world leader in the computerized control of information.

📖——Verner W. Clapp, "National Diet Library of Japan," *Science* 107 (1948). Robert L. Gitler, "Education for Librarianship Abroad: Japan," *Library Trends* 12 (1963). Kokuritsu Kokkai Toshokan, ed, *Zenkoku tokushu korekushon yōran* (1977). Nihon Toshokan Kyōkai, ed, *Toshokan handobukku* (1966). Nihon Toshokan Kyōkai, ed, *Nihon no toshokan* (1976). Okada Narau et al, ed, *Nihon bunko meguri* (1964). Ono Noriaki, *Nihon toshokan shi* (1970). Takahisa Sawamoto, "Post-War Developments in Japanese Academic Libraries," *Library Science* 2 (1964). Louise Watanabe Tung, "Library Development in Japan," *The Library Quarterly* 26 (1956). Takeo Urata and Takeshi Ogawa, ed, *Toshokan Hō seiritsu shi shiryō* (1968). Theodore F. Welch, *Toshokan: Libraries in Japanese Society* (1977).

Theodore F. WELCH

Liefde

The first Dutch ship to reach Japan. The *Liefde*, belonging to a Rotterdam trading firm, was disabled and blown off course while sailing across the Pacific and arrived in Usuki Bay in Bungo Province (now Ōita Prefecture) on 19 April 1600 (Keichō 5.3.6). Of the original crew of 110, only 24 survived, including Captain Jacob Quaeckernaeck, the English pilot William ADAMS, and Second Mate Lodenstijn JAN JOOSTEN. They were received at Ōsaka Castle by the future shōgun TOKUGAWA IEYASU and queried about Europe and trade conditions. Adams and Jan Joosten later became trusted advisers to Ieyasu, and through the efforts of Adams trade was initiated between Japan and the Netherlands. See also NETHERLANDS AND JAPAN.

life cycle

Society's schedule of stages for an individual's life. The life cycle is generally thought to extend from birth to death, although the individual becomes a social entity before birth, and most religions posit the continued existence of the soul after death. Conception and ancestorhood thus can be considered the beginning and culmination of life's cycle. The stages of growth of an individual mark his or her readiness to participate in social roles and institutions. As we progress through these stages, we gain and later may lose the qualities that entitle us to act as adult members of society—as "whole persons" (*ichinimmae* in Japanese). Along the way, we pass through lesser arcs of socialization that teach us to conduct ourselves appropriately for each substage and position in the schedule. The schedule itself evolves over time, adjusting to historical changes in demography and in the patterning of society's institutions. During the centuries when Japan was an agrarian society the schedule altered gradually, but in the decades of concentrated industrial development in the 20th century, the schedule has been radically rearranged.

Age Reckoning and Life Stages——In Japan as elsewhere personal age is reckoned variously for social purposes. Relative age is most often set by order of birth—seniors, peers, juniors—though a person may be judged immature or precocious relative to normal conduct at his or her stage in life. Some observers claim that seniority rules are more pervasive in Japan than in other industrialized societies, but these claims may be the result of selective perception, with one society stressing seniority in domains of behavior where another deems it irrelevent or unimportant.

Absolute age may be measured by biological events such as the eruption of permanent molars or the onset of menstruation, but the most important measure is that of years since birth. Premodern Japanese custom counted age by calendar years. That is, a child was one in the year of his or her birth, and on 1 January a year was added to every person's age. Technically, an infant born on the last day of December would be two years old the very next day. Since World War II, Japanese most often reckon age from the day of one's birth, and it is becoming common to celebrate birthday anniversaries.

Certain years of life have traditionally been considered favorable, others dangerous. The favorable years cluster in old age—60, 70, 77, and 88—and mark success in achieving longevity. The danger years (*yakudoshi*) come earlier, the most serious being 19 and 33 for women, 25 and 42 for men. Why these years should be considered risky remains a mystery. Folk etymologies explain them by word-play. For example, 42 can be pronounced *shini* (going to die) and 33 *sanzan* (painful childbirth). Scholars speculate that the traditional life path took a major turn at or near these ages; e.g., typically, a man would have been about 42 when his eldest son married.

Though most Japanese today scorn the danger years as superstition, many continue to observe them. Some still obtain protective amulets or blessings from Shintō shrines to ward off the danger. Others avoid new ventures during the year. Parents may symbolically "abandon" a child born in its mother's 33rd year or its father's 42nd year in order to prevent it from being contaminated by the danger. Though this custom is no longer common, births are still avoided during these years.

The outline below depicts life stages as a typical individual might pass through them. Done for the sake of simplicity, this distorts a major social fact that must be kept in mind. We do not make the journey of our life cycle alone but in company. Our age mates enter each stage at about the same time we do. Our life cycle companions also include two or more generations of seniors and juniors, each moving through stages different from the one we are in. Their progress affects ours, and vice versa. The birth of a first child, for example, promotes a married couple into parenthood and may promote two other couples into grandparenthood. Seen in its fullest form, the life cycle is a cluster of connected schedules for persons copresent in society at different levels of growth.

Infancy ——— It is common for Japanese mothers to present expectant daughters with an abdominal sash in the fifth month of pregnancy; this is the first overt recognition of the child by society. In some areas it is the custom for the expectant mother to return to her parental home during the final weeks of pregnancy. Prayers are offered to JIZŌ (Buddhist guardian deity of children) or to *ubugami* (infant deity). Prospective parents give much thought in advance to naming the newborn, and they may delegate this task to a senior relative as a mark of honor.

In premodern Japan a birth was generally not officially registered until the child had survived to a certain age. Age seven was the norm during the Edo period (1600–1868), and villages often had a separate cemetery for those who died before their seventh year. Today births tend to be registered promptly. However, because of the widespread belief that the year signs of the East Asian zodiac shape one's personality, registration of birth may be shifted to another year. The most striking example is that of girls born under the combined fire element and horse year, which comes every 60 years; they are said to be troublesome mates, or are even believed to be capable of killing their husbands. The number of recorded female births usually drops during this year, but increases during the years immediately before or after.

About a month after birth, infants are generally taken to the local Shintō shrine to become an *ujiko* (parishioner) of the community's guardian diety. This excursion, usually with the mother's mother in attendance and the infant elaborately clothed, marks the entrance of the infant into the community. In the first year, 3 March for girls (DOLL FESTIVAL) and 5 May for boys (CHILDREN'S DAY) are celebrated with relatives in attendance. Ages three, five, and seven are marked in November when children of these ages don fancy traditional clothes for excursions to Shintō shrines to receive blessings and lucky arrows (see SHICHIGOSAN).

Childhood (about 7–13 years) ——— Children over seven traditionally began to help their parents by acquiring skills such as weaving, sewing, weeding, or picking tea leaves. A child became a responsible participant in society as a member of the local children's group (*kodomogumi*) or as a student in school. The *kodomogumi* continue to operate in some communities, helping to pull carts or carry portable shrines (MIKOSHI) at local festivals. They also carry out minor public duties, such as driving away birds from the fields or warning people to be careful with fire on early winter evenings.

Six years of education were made compulsory in the Meiji period (1868–1912) and nine years, after World War II. The first day of elementary school is marked by the family with gifts and picture-taking. Becoming a student involves wearing a student uniform, acquiring a study desk at home, and reckoning one's life by years in school more than by years since birth. Participation in school ceremonies or sports days gives public evidence of one's progress toward maturity.

Children's groups are loosely organized and supervised, and they rarely hold rites for incoming or departing members. Modern schools, on the other hand, are large institutions with matriculation and graduation ceremonies, elaborate rules of conduct, and well-defined standards for promotion. Thus, in addition to knowledge, they impart the social skills that will be needed later in the vast institutions that now order most sectors of the society.

Confucian norms called for the separation of the sexes after age seven, but this has not been practiced rigorously in Japan. The children's groups include both girls and boys. Modern elementary schools have always been coeducational, as have most higher schools since 1945. At home it is quite common for children to sleep and bathe together or with parents well into the school years. See also CHILDHOOD AND CHILD REARING.

Youth (about 13–25 years) ——— Coming of age was celebrated in premodern Japan between the ages of 13 and 17. A *samurai* youth was presented with a particular kind of headgear, and a common youth might be given a loincloth. A girl was given an underskirt as an addition to her wardrobe, and in some parts of the country she started to color her teeth black; this practice was later observed only by married women (see COSMETICS). Often a sponsor bestowed coming-of-age gifts and in so doing acknowledged a lifelong obligation to look after the welfare of his "child." All of these rituals indicated the transition to a marriageable age.

Young people were considered full-fledged members of society. They were considered capable of performing a full day's work on communal projects. Youth groups had major functions in premodern villages. Young men's groups were particularly well organized. Their most common task was to provide dances, dramas, and other services during local festivals, and they also taught literacy skills, protected community property, and fought fires. Some young men's groups owned and operated their own fields or other productive property.

There were dormitories for young men *(wakamono yado)* and women in villages in the southwest, particularly in coastal areas, and in cities for apprentices. Youth groups and dormitories were sex-segregated, but interaction was not severely restricted except among samurai. Today other institutions have taken over most of the functions of the youth groups, though in some communities the groups may still organize for festival services. Agricultural cooperatives, religious organizations, and various other groups have developed youth leagues of their own. See also YOUTH.

Over 90 percent of Japanese children continue in school for at least three years beyond the compulsory nine. Many middle-school students attend special tutoring academies (JUKU) after their regular classes, in preparation for high school entrance examinations. Students in high school and college may take part-time jobs; the modern word for this is *arubaito* (work, from German *Arbeit*). But they are expected to concentrate on their studies, and the keen competition for entry into prestigious high schools and universities helps enforce the norm. Pressures from the "examination hell" *(shiken jigoku)* drastically alter the daily lives not only of the students but also of their families and acquaintances. At prestigious colleges only a fraction of the entering class will come directly from high school. The rest will have taken the examinations at least twice before succeeding. See ENTRANCE EXAMINATIONS.

Today legal maturity and the right to vote are attained at age 20, and most municipalities hold Coming-of-Age Day (Seijin no Hi) ceremonies for new citizens on 15 January, a national holiday. Until 1945, however, a term of compulsory military service for men starting at 20 had probably been a more significant mark of maturity.

Job placement has become formalized in the industrial age. Usually, before graduation from college or high school, a job will have been secured, often through recruitment at schools. Mate selection by contrast, is primarily a task for informal social networks, and usually happens after the potential husband is firmly established in a job. "Love marriage"—mutual self-selection—is the modern ideal, and about 6 couples in 10 say that theirs is a love marriage and not an arranged one. But parents, peers, teachers, and employers are widely consulted and asked for help in the process. In premodern Japan relationships were nurtured by the young men's and women's associations, and communal village activities such as those at New Year's, the BON FESTIVAL, local festivals, and rice-planting were times for courtship. Go-betweens (NAKŌDO) play an important role in urban industrial society, where young people lack the social networks of villages. Even when a go-between has not actually arranged the marriage interview (MIAI), at the marriage ceremony someone (often an important business or social contact of the parents) always acts as an honorary go-between and later may help the couple in difficulties.

The marrying age, as well as the age of full-fledged adulthood (*ichinimmae*), has steadily risen in Japan. The increase in number of years of education has delayed the entrance of many into adult society, and the economic burden of maintaining a household separate from one's parents means that many young people work and save for years before getting married. The average marrying age is around 24 or 25 for women and 28 or 29 for men, with many marrying later.

Formerly, engagement required a ceremony and exchange of gifts, and WEDDINGS were religious ceremonies enacted in homes. After the elaborate Shintō wedding of the Emperor Taishō in 1900, Shintō ceremonies became popular. Nowadays there is a great diversity in wedding ceremonies, which are scheduled on auspicious days and require extravagance unsurpassed at any other time of life. No ceremony is required by law; a union becomes legal simply by being entered in the family registers. Honeymoons have become very popular. See also MARRIAGE.

Maturity (about 26–60 years) ——— Most Japanese move through the adult stages of the life cycle at about the same pace, establishing households, rearing children, and looking after aging parents. Schedules for occupational careers, however, are as diverse as is the industrial division of labor. A *sumō* wrestler may be "old" at 35, but a Diet member "young" at 45. Male and female schedules diverge more greatly during the mature years than in any other stage of the life cycle, and the gap between them appears to have widened in the modern century. Before, a man could gradually yield craft tasks and household leadership to his eldest son, and a woman could train her son's wife in domestic duties and slowly shift to her the responsibility for them. Today men are expected to work full-time throughout their years of maturity, and for all but a fraction of men who have farms, crafts, or small shops, this means paid employment away from home. A man's pace of life and focus of ambition are caught up in promotions, raises, and occupational skills, and less in the family dynamics.

Most Japanese women obtain paid employment on leaving school, but few sustain full-time occupational careers throughout the adult years. A woman is expected to leave the labor force either when she gets married or when she becomes pregnant, and to devote her energies to housekeeping and childrearing at least until her children have entered school. In contrast to a century ago, however, today the typical woman gives birth to only two or three children, spaced closely together, so that she has completed the period of intensive child care within about a decade after marriage. Many women later take up paid employment, though they are at a disadvantage in the labor market. Lately the trend toward "lifelong learning" has expanded educational opportunities for adults, and women may become busy with many such activities outside the home.

In general, during the first decade of adulthood, one concentrates on proving competence at work and at home. After that one should enter a phase of the "flowering of working skills" (hataraki-zakari), and begin to show the full "dignity" (kanroku) of maturity. One is responsible, in these years of middlehood, for the life passage of aging seniors and growing juniors. Much of one's own life passage is marked by events in those other lives, such as the retirement of a parent or the school graduation of a daughter.

Old Age (61 and over) —— The 60th year of life, when the signs of the East Asian zodiac complete one full cycle, was the traditional beginning of old age in Japan. In the Edo period samurai were usually retired from office at age 60, and commoners were freed from the obligation to perform a full day's work on collective village tasks. Today some Japanese privately celebrate 60 as the coming of seniority, but the year no longer has major social significance. Compulsory RETIREMENT from paid employment typically occurs at age 55 in most large enterprises and government bureaus, and retired employees often receive pensions in a lump sum at the time of retirement. Since government social-security benefits are not paid until age 60 or later, most men and some women must seek reemployment after retirement to maintain an income. Typically, they remain in the labor force for another 10 years.

The Japanese heritage includes norms of strong respect for seniors and elders. The Tokugawa domains often held annual ceremonies honoring the aged. This was revived in most municipalities in 1963 when Respect-for-the-Aged Day (Keirō no Hi) became a national holiday (15 September). The state annually designates a number of senior craftsmen and artists as Living National Treasures, and state decorations are usually only presented to persons over 70.

In recent years, the number of elderly in the population has increased so dramatically that old-age welfare has become a major national issue. Most elderly Japanese can rely upon offspring for support and care; 7 in 10 are living with a lineal descendant. But there is a rising demand that society at large assume a greater responsibility for caring for the increasing number of old people who are chronically ill, frail, indigent, or kinless. See also INKYO; OLD AGE AND RETIREMENT.

Postmortem —— Social recognition continues well after death in Japan. Birth or death anniversaries of the famous may be widely celebrated, and every household continues to honor its departed family members for many years.

At death an individual is given a posthumous name by the priest of the family temple. This is inscribed on his or her tombstone and on a personal memorial tablet (ihai) kept in the home. The ihai receive frequent, if not daily, offerings and reports of family events. The deceased are welcomed home at the midsummer Bon Festival and on several other festivals during the year.

During the first year after a death, rites are held weekly and monthly for the comfort of the soul. Later, death-day anniversaries are honored for periods of upwards of 50 years—differing from sect to sect and family to family—or as long as anyone who can remember the departed personally remains alive. After that one's individuality dissolves into the collective otherness of the household ancestors.

Change and Conflict —— Under the impact of modernization different parts of the life cycle schedule have changed in ways that may

often be contradictory. Legal maturity is granted at age 20, but popular opinion regards anyone as immature until married or embarked on a working career. Family versus work is a serious issue for many men and women. Retirement at 55 seems unduly early when life expectancy now exceeds 70 years.

Options have widened at some stages of the cycle and narrowed at others. There are now no legal barriers to the choice of spouse or occupation, but schooling and retirement have become compulsory at fixed times. Japanese social critics in the 1970s began calling on individuals and the state to build into all institutions and programs a life-cycle perspective relevant to the changes in modern society. See also FAMILY; LIFESTYLES.

■——George A. DeVos and Hiroshi Wagatsuma, "Status and Role Behavior in Changing Japan: Psychocultural Continuities," in *Socialization for Achievement: Essays on the Cultural Psychology of the Japanese* (1973). Christie Kiefer, "The Life Cycle in Traditional Japan and in America," in *Changing Cultures Changing Lives* (1974). Morioka Kiyoma, *Kazoku shūki ron* (1973). Murakami Yasuke et al, *Shōgai sekkei (raifu saikuru) keikaku* (1975).　　David W. PLATH

life insurance

(seimei hoken). The life insurance business in Japan started in 1881 with the establishment of the Meiji Mutual Life Insurance Company. Subsequently, numerous companies were established. Despite the disastrous blow suffered in World War II, the life insurance business recovered quickly after the war and expanded accordingly during the years of rapid economic growth. At the end of 1979, the value of life insurance policies held by private life insurance companies totaled ¥521 trillion (about $2.37 trillion), second in the world after the United States. The ratio against national income was also a remarkable 293 percent, the highest in the world.

Two chief reasons for the expansion of life insurance in Japan are the utilization of some 300,000 canvassers, mostly women, and the innovative types of insurance coverage. The kind of life insurance most popular in past years was regular endowment insurance, used to buffer expenses such as encountered in old age and for education. In general this type reflected the strong tendency of the Japanese to save. As defined in Japan, standard endowment insurance provides equal benefits upon term expiration to the insured, or to the beneficiary in case of death. In recent years, however, the most popular variety has become endowment insurance with prescribed terms, that is, the payment of benefits upon death. The increase in popularity of this type of life insurance is supposedly related to rising numbers of traffic accidents and changes in people's perception of life insurance. Among company employees group insurance with prescribed terms is popular. Sickness and annuity insurance are becoming increasingly common as a supplement to social security, reflecting the rising costs of medical treatment and growth in the number of the aged. There are 21 Japanese and 2 foreign life insurance companies in Japan today. In addition, there is postal insurance begun in 1916 and operated by the Ministry of Posts and Telecommunications' Post Office Life Insurance Bureau, as well as life insurance under the various agricultural cooperative associations begun in Hokkaidō in 1948 and extended nationwide in 1951. See also INSURANCE SYSTEM.　　MOCHIDA Minoru

lifelong learning

(shōgai kyōiku). An alternative term for adult education that has gained wide currency in Japan since the concept was discussed by UNESCO in 1965. With increasing longevity, shorter working hours, and expanding leisure time, the idea of lifelong learning has become a subject of great interest, not only among the Japanese public but also within the government.　　TAKAMURA Hisao

lifestyles

In the past century the dominant lifestyle in Japan has changed from a rural, agrarian, village-centered way of life to an urban industrial lifestyle, in which social life is focused on the work place and the nuclear family. Although perhaps 20 percent of the Japanese lived in towns and cities even two centuries ago, urbanization was accelerated with the industrialization that began after the Meiji Restoration of 1868. Not only do the majority of Japanese live in urban areas today, but by the mid-1970s nearly two-thirds of those Japanese who still farmed obtained more of their family income from nonfarming activities than from agriculture. However, most Japanese still hold many of the traditional values concerning family, groups, education, and work. This, combined with the survival of many traditional aspects of life, provides a strong thread of continuity, lending stability to Japanese society.

Housing —— Today approximately half of the Japanese live in the urban corridor stretching from Tōkyō in the east to Nagoya, Kyōto, Ōsaka, and Kōbe in the west, and a large proportion of the rest of the population lives in towns and cities located in the few plains areas on this mountainous island nation. Space is at a premium, today even more than in the past; most of these city dwellers live in small units in high-rise apartment buildings or in tiny houses squeezed together along narrow streets. Since housing is expensive and hard to come by, people move infrequently, commuting long distances to school or to work. The suburbs surrounding Tōkyō are now spread over several prefectures, and the people living in them spend an average of over two hours every day commuting.

Houses in Japan are flimsy by Western standards. Traditionally they were built mostly of wood and paper without substantial foundations or basements. Because the climate is damp and the islands prone to earthquakes, this is actually the healthiest and safest type of construction. Houses usually face south to obtain maximum sunlight, and the sliding doors are opened in the daytime to air out the rooms. Verandas extend for several feet on the sunniest side of both homes and apartments, blurring the distinction between house and garden. The Japanese do distinguish between inside and outside, but, instead of designating walls to perform this function, they take off their shoes when entering a house.

Houses and apartments are also considered small by Western standards. By the mid-1970s the average family had just over four rooms for an average of three-and-one-half family members. Much of the increase in space per family member is due to the boom in housing construction in the past several decades, but part of it is due to the decrease in the average number of family members, which fluctuated around five from the 18th century through World War II, then dropped to the present three-and-one-half. However, because of the high cost of land, especially in the areas surrounding the major cities, most Japanese live in small apartments of from one to four rooms or in houses only slightly larger.

Small one-room apartments in modern ferroconcrete high-rises are built with the same lifestyle in mind as the traditional multiroom middle-class house. Since Japan has long been a crowded nation, architects have maximized the use of space by designing rooms with multiple functions. The traditional room has little furniture except for storage chests and a low table that can be removed at night to be replaced by the heavy quilts *(futon)* used for sleeping. The floors are not made of wood but rather of frames of woven rush matting (TATAMI), which, when spread with quilts or cushions, are comfortable for both sleeping and sitting. Thus a single room can serve as a living room, a dining room, and a bedroom.

Rooms are usually small, with the most common size a six-mat room (about 2.7 by 3.7 m or 9 by 12 ft), but the divisions between them are sliding paper doors. This enables the Japanese to create one large room from several small ones for a party or funeral. These paper partitions permit visual separation, but sounds easily penetrate, resulting in little privacy for family members. Japanese families spend their evenings together around the television set in the main room, and many families all sleep in one room when the children are small, even when there is sufficient space to provide separate bedrooms. Only when a child reaches the age that requires him to study long hours for entrance exams for high school or university do parents try to provide a separate room for study. See HOUSING PROBLEMS.

Use of Time and Space —— The familiar Japanese reputation for neatness is perhaps a habit arising from necessity. A family with two small children living in a two- or three-room apartment must sleep, eat, play, relax, study, and carry out household chores in a very limited space. In most apartment dwellings, before dinner can be served the table must be cleared of school books, sewing projects, and the like. The kitchen is often only a corner of a small apartment, and laundry is done on the small balcony and hung out to dry on lines strung above the railings, on which the bedding is aired.

Because it is impossible to tuck away all the hundreds of gadgets and appliances gathered even in these small apartments, one's home is a very personal space. All but the most intimate guests are entertained outside the home in the hundreds of thousands of restaurants, bars, and coffee shops. Naturally, those who can afford larger homes have special rooms for entertaining guests. Before World War II these rooms, called *ōsetsuma,* were apt to be formal, West-

ern-style parlors, but as general living has gradually shifted more and more to Western-style rooms, the formal guest room in a high-income home is often now the only traditional, rush-matted, Japanese room in the house.

Living quarters are cramped, and only the mother with very small children and the elderly spend much time at home. Men who are white-collar workers spend most of their day at work and in the evening often entertain clients or relax with their colleagues at a bar. This is especially the case for those who are climbing the corporate or government ladder. Time spent with colleagues strengthens the company bonds among workers, many of whom stay in the same firm for the duration of their working life. For these salaried workers there is no real distinction between work and play. Added to the hours spent at work and with colleagues is often a long ride by train, bus, or combination of the two. Consequently, many children only see their fathers briefly in the morning and on Sundays and holidays.

Education —— Children first attend nursery school at the age of three or four and then formally enter grade school at age six. The postwar school system is patterned after the American system, with six years of primary school, three of middle school, three of high school, and four of college. But here most of the resemblance ends. The career pattern and the degree of success are determined to a large extent by the university one attends. Thus there is tremendous competition to be admitted to the most prestigious university in the country, Tōkyō University, or to another of the top-ranking national or private schools.

In the early postwar period, the intense competition was concentrated at the level of university entrance exams. But gradually, performance on entrance exams for high school, junior high school, and even elementary school and kindergarten assumed more and more importance in determining a man's ultimate career and a woman's prospects for marriage. Now mothers spend months preparing their children for the entrance exams to the "right" kindergartens, which will ensure their entering a prestigious primary school that will start them up the ladder to the university that has the best record of placing its graduates in high government posts. Thus it is quite common for mothers to feel that their children are "failures" in life if they are not admitted to the best primary school in town. Children, too, feel great pressure to perform in school, and their young lives are dominated by this goal. By 1975, just over half of all sixth graders attended a special preparatory school (JUKU) on top of their regular school schedule to help them prepare for the entrance exams to junior high school. Since school is compulsory through the ninth grade, and since more than 92 percent of Japanese youth go to high school and 37 percent of these go to college, admission into a school is not the problem—it is getting into the "right" school that is the obsession.

The Life of Schoolchildren —— In addition to long hours in school and the accompanying long hours of homework from the primary grades on, Japanese children study a variety of other subjects outside school hours: English conversation, the abacus, calligraphy, and so on. Many children study a different subject every day of the week and go to preparatory school to take practice exams on Sundays.

The life of the child thus centers around school and study. At home, children are usually studying or relaxing around the television set. Surveys show that very few children help around the house. They do not spend much time enjoying themselves outside or with friends of the opposite sex. The 12 years from first grade to high school graduation are full of hard work and stress, and this is reflected in the fact that the suicide rate among children, though still very low, has risen in recent years; most suicides seem to be related to failure in school. Release from academic pressures is found in school athletic events, large school outings, and trips by the graduating classes, plus the usual social events of shopping, movies, television, and time spent with friends, but altogether, students spend far more hours at their desk than in these pursuits. See also CHILDHOOD AND CHILD REARING.

Women —— Just as their husbands spend most of their time at work and their children at school-related activities, wives, too, have a focus: the home and the welfare of their families. Except for the wealthy, very few women have outside help with the housework. Just as it is the husband's role to earn the family income and to represent the family in the world outside, it is the wife's duty to care for the family, manage the budget, and maintain social relationships with relatives and neighbors. Women take their household and child-rearing responsibilities very seriously. Most wives are expected not only to take full responsibility for running the house, including the handling of the family finances, but also to fix tea and snacks for individual family members at any hour of the day and to minister to the personal needs of their husbands and children. A wife customarily waits for her husband's return, no matter how late, and many men are so dependent on their wives that they do not know where their socks or underwear are kept, much less how to prepare a meal for themselves. The expectations of the wife's role are rigorous to a degree that many Western women would find unbearable.

Most Japanese women marry between the ages of 23 and 25, and usually have two children within three or four years. While their children are young, they stay at home and care for them with rarely any time off, since the only babysitters in Japan are grandparents. A common sight on Japanese intraurban trains is a woman with one child strapped to her back and a second, older child at her side. However, before the average mother is 35, her youngest child has entered primary school, and after a decade of being tied to the house, and with educational expenses looming ahead for their children, many mothers decide to go back to work.

Most women work between leaving school and getting married, many at dead-end office or sales jobs, and quit either at marriage or on the birth of their first child. Apart from women who have to work to make ends meet or the very few women with professional careers, few work while they have young children at home. But since so many return to work in their thirties and forties, women in these age groups now constitute 57 percent of the female work force. Many return to part-time jobs as clerks in supermarkets, tutors of English, or factory workers. Few are able to obtain positions that will give them prestige and high salaries, but they are able to supplement the family income.

The Elderly —— Both men and women feel a pressure to work hard and save money because retirement comes early in Japan; in most companies it is at age 55 for men who do not become executives and even sooner for women, despite their life expectancy of over 75 years. Thus Japanese perceive old age as beginning when most Westerners consider themselves middle-aged, and a whole new style of life begins. Men often try to find second careers, and if they have good reputations, technicians and government officials can obtain positions with small companies, while teachers can join preparatory schools. Many fall back on the small amounts of farmland they have inherited and manage to cultivate enough rice and vegetables to feed the family. Grandmothers often care for grandchildren so that their daughters can work. Middle-aged and older women also make up a large part of the farm work force. Nearly three-quarters of the Japanese aged 65 and over live with their families or relatives, and they usually perform a useful function in the family. They must rely on their children for much of their support, since retirement pensions, though rising, are still inadequate. See also OLD AGE AND RETIREMENT.

The Standard of Living and Leisure Time —— The change in work patterns in the postwar period from farm-dominated employment to jobs away from home for both men and women, combined with the long hours of school and lessons that children face, has radically altered the life of the small neighborhood communities, particularly in rural areas. Instead of the majority of residents staying within the village during the day, only the elderly and mothers with their very young children are at home. And instead of visiting with neighbors over a cup of tea for relaxation, Japanese now relax around the color television set.

Many Japanese regret the loss of community life that has accompanied the new way of life, but most of them think they are better off now. Whereas many were malnourished at the end of World War II and remained at a standard of living below that of the mid-1930s until the early 1950s, today the Japanese enjoy a standard of living higher than that of Italy and Great Britain, although still lower than that of West Germany and the United States. Housing is the major area in which Japan lags behind its Western counterparts, and the Japanese seem to make up for this lack by purchasing consumer goods and by investing in LEISURE-TIME ACTIVITIES, including travel. The number who travel abroad increases yearly, with Hawaii, Guam, Hong Kong, and Taiwan ranking as favorite vacation spots. Many companies sponsor special group or honeymoon trips, and this is one of the reasons for the international reputation the Japanese have for traveling in groups.

As the economy began to grow after the Korean War, the Japanese eagerly acquired consumer durables. From the late 1950s to the early 1960s, the "three sacred items of consumption" were the three

S's: *sempūki* (electric fan), *sentakuki* (washing machine), and *suihanki* (electric rice cooker). Soon these became standard items in every household, and in the 1960s the status symbols switched to the three C's: car, color television, and cooler (room air conditioner). By the 1970s everyone was racing for the three J's: jewels, "jetting" (overseas air travel), and *jūtaku* (a private house). Whereas during the mid-1950s, among the major consumer durables only sewing machines, bicycles, and Japanese-style chests were owned by more than 50 percent of the households, by the mid-1970s more than 80 percent owned sewing machines, color television sets, and vacuum cleaners; and over 95 percent owned refrigerators, electric fans, washing machines, and Western-style wardrobes. Despite the high price of gasoline, crowded highways, and the great difficulties in finding a place to park, 40 percent of families had private cars. See also CONSUMPTION AND SAVING BEHAVIOR.

Because the small living quarters can accommodate only so many goods, and because people find themselves in each other's way at home on a Sunday or holiday, many families prefer to go out to spend their leisure time. Any Sunday will find the trains packed with families on outings, carrying picnic lunches and thermos bottles, all heading for a day of play or shopping. If the destination is a department store, some of the family will head for the roof, where there is generally a playground, amusement center, and, often, musical entertainment. Families with cars head for the country. In summer, most beaches and swimming pools are so packed that one can only get wet; there is no room to swim.

Japanese engage in their leisure-time activities with the same enthusiasm and professional approach they have toward work. Beginning tennis students will purchase complete outfits and the best rackets; those studying tea ceremony or calligraphy will buy the necessary materials, usually the best available. Men prefer such pastimes as SHŌGI (Japanese chess), MAH-JONGG, PACHINKO (pinball), betting on the races, or golf and fishing; while women, especially in the years before marriage, attend concerts, go to movies, or study flower-arranging, tea ceremony, or cooking; the elderly prefer gardening and visiting hot springs. And, of course, everyone watches television, and most play card games, either Western or traditional Japanese.

Home Life —— Because of the long hours spent away from home, Japanese think of it as a private place where they can completely relax rather than as a place where they can bring friends and business associates. When a man comes home from work, the first thing he does is to change into a casual *kimono* or another garment not suitable for outside wear. He will then relax with beer or hot *sake* (Japanese rice wine) in front of the television, but usually his return is so late that he will not be in time to eat dinner with the family or even to see his youngest children before they go to bed. Women with jobs rarely work such long hours, but they will still have to rush home to shop, prepare dinner, and wash clothes. The most relaxing activity at home is the hot bath, which most Japanese take daily, washing first outside the tub and then soaking up to the neck in very hot water. Adult members of the family share the bath in turn or are accompanied by the youngest children.

Guests are usually family and relatives. A formal party for male business associates is a major undertaking at which the wife will have to act as cook and maid with no chance to join the group until everyone has finished eating. Unexpected guests will be treated to SUSHI (various kinds of raw fish served on rice) and other dishes that have been ordered by phone and delivered to the house. A party for married couples is almost unheard-of. Unless the house is large and the family well-to-do, a man will prefer the comfort and convenience of entertaining business associates (and foreigners) at a good restaurant without having to worry about being bothered by children or forcing extra work on his wife. See also FOOD AND EATING.

Modern and Traditional Elements in Japanese Life —— Japanese life today is a mixture of the traditional and modern. Virtually everybody owns at least one television set and reads at least one of the national daily newspapers, as well as weekly magazines and books, often on the commuter train. Despite the difficulty of the written language, the literacy rate is one of the highest in the world. Japanese enjoy reading, and even history books are occasionally best sellers. The constant exposure to the written word and to other mass media such as television and radio means that new ideas, fashions, and fads are communicated quickly across all social classes.

The mixture of old and new, East and West is sometimes manifested in ways that are surprising to the Western viewer. For example, one in four young women study *ikebana,* traditional Japanese flower arrangement; but equally popular for young children is the

r2e

study of a Western musical instrument: the organ, piano, or violin. Similarly, in any large city one can find traditional noodle shops side by side with McDonald's hamburgers and Kentucky Fried Chicken.

Movies, baseball, concerts, and coffeehouses outdraw the traditional *kabuki*, Nō, and puppet theater, but the traditional entertainments still survive. SUMŌ (wrestling) is even more popular than it used to be, because it is now nationally televised, and avid fans can follow all the tournaments wherever they are held.

Language, too, provides many contrasts. English is taught as a second language in Japan, and is so widely used in advertisements and in conveying popular new ideas that it is virtually impossible to find a page in a weekly magazine that does not have at least one word borrowed from English. At the same time, traditional Japanese calligraphy, which is taught to all schoolchildren, is a favorite hobby of adults, particularly women, who have the time to study the traditional arts of Japan.

Just as traditional cultural and leisure activities remain alongside the modern, so it is true with the material aspects of Japanese life. Western dress now predominates, with the *kimono* having become a status symbol, partly because a handmade silk kimono is far more expensive than most of the exclusive Paris fashions. Inconvenient for street wear and difficult to put on by oneself, the kimono is reserved for very formal occasions, and its cotton counterparts such as the *yukata* serve as casual or sleep wear.

The traditional diet, maintained long after industrialization, has undergone rapid changes since World War II, particularly among young people, who prefer French pastry to sweets made of rice and beans, and coffee to green tea. However, despite the increased consumption of meat and dairy products, Japanese in the mid-1970s still consumed, on the average, only 20.7 kilograms (45.6 lb) of meat per capita, compared to the American average of 115.7 kilograms (255.1 lb), and more than five times as much fish as did Americans. Few people now eat rice three times a day, and many consume a "Western-style" breakfast of ham and eggs, toast, milk, coffee or tea, plus a green salad. For lunch they eat noodles or a sandwich, and in the evening, a Japanese-style dinner is served in which the main food is steamed white rice eaten with a variety of side dishes, which have as their main seasoning soy sauce or *miso* (soybean paste). While the wife may prepare broiled fish, *miso* soup, and several side dishes of vegetables for her husband when he returns home, earlier in the evening she is likely to have fed her children spaghetti, hamburgers, or pork cutlets, as the more Western-style dishes are their preference. When she is in a hurry, there are numerous frozen foods to serve. Since beef is outrageously expensive, *sukiyaki,* the famous beef dish, is reserved for guests or special occasions.

Household furnishings also reflect the traditional and the modern. Most Japanese possess at least one or more items of Western furniture, including a child's study desk. *Tatami* rooms are gradually becoming fewer, as the rush matting has become exorbitantly expensive, but many people spread carpeting either on top of the mats or on wooden flooring, and proceed to use the room in traditional fashion, with everyone sitting on cushions on the floor around a low table. Although central heating is available in new homes, on the cold winter evenings many families gather cozily around the *kotatsu,* a low covered table with a built-in space heater, sharing a physical closeness that is often missing in Western culture. Today one would be hard put to find either an all-Western style or a completely traditional house in Japan.

The majority of Japanese are engaged neither in agriculture nor in the high-prestige, white-collar occupations—the segments of society that we have particularly focused on here—but work in factories, own small shops, engage in the transportation or service industries, or in traditional crafts, the mass media, or any one of hundreds of other occupations. Clearly, a Japanese family who owns a small shop lives a different kind of life from that of an office worker's family. A couple who run a dry-cleaning establishment will find themselves on call from mid-morning until 9:00 at night, and customers who call at the dinner hour will find the owner or his wife running out to the front of the shop from the kitchen-dining room at the rear, where they have been trying to grab a bite to eat.

Although the lifestyle of the individual will certainly vary according to occupation and to whether the family lives in a farmhouse, an apartment in a major city, or a tract home in the suburbs, there are more similarities than differences among the lifestyles of all of these groups. A remarkably homogeneous people, all Japanese use the same language, belong to the same racial group, share a common culture, read national newspapers, watch nationally televised programs, and follow similar school curricula. Japanese will

make much of the differences in dialect, customs, and climate in various parts of their country, but though a family born and bred in Tōkyō may feel uncomfortable moving to Nagoya, to the non-Japanese the similarities are far more striking than any differences that exist.

Class and status differences still persist, but they are comparable to those in the United States and far weaker than those in Great Britain. Although class boundaries were rigid in the pre-1868 period and determined not only a person's occupation but also where he lived, how he talked, what he wore, and how he spent his leisure time, this has changed considerably in the past century. The educational system has had a strong ameliorating effect on status and class, particularly in the period of upheaval immediately following World War II, when a bright boy could pass the entrance exam to a prestigious national university and go on to a career in an influential government ministry or a large corporation. One's ancestry and family economic position continue to be status symbols, but they count for little if the family heir is not successful in his own right.

With the importance of the after-hour cram schools, money and socioeconomic background have become more important for success in the school system; but the mass media, the complete diffusion of Western clothing, which makes it difficult to discern class differences, and the homogeneity of the population have all contributed to making nearly 90 percent of the people feel that they belong to the middle class.

Thus one's sex, family role, and stage in the life cycle are far more important determinants of one's lifestyle than class, occupation, or place of birth and upbringing. Statistically, a woman between the ages of 25 and 30 is almost certain to be married and caring for small children in the home, and this will determine how she will spend her time more than any other fact in her life at the moment. On the other hand, it is quite likely that she will go back to work once her children reach school age. Well over 50 percent of women between the ages of 30 and 60 work in Japan, a far higher proportion than in the United States, Sweden, or France. Family size, too, is highly predictable. Nearly all children are one of only two siblings; in 1972, 84 percent of all children born were either the first or second child in the family. Thus, when one speaks of "averages" in regard to the Japanese, one is apt to find more people who actually behave as the statistics suggest than in most other countries.

In conclusion, despite the conspicuous changes brought about in lifestyles through the industrialization prior to World War II and the rapid economic growth that followed it, one finds many aspects of Japanese life that can be traced back to the 18th and 19th centuries, if not further. First, Japanese life is remarkably oriented around the groups to which one belongs: originally the small farm community (and now the company or government bureau where one works) and the immediate neighborhood. Social life centers on school or on the place of work, and family members generally lead rather separate social lives compared to families in many Western countries. Home life retains many of the characteristics it has always had, in spite of the physical changes wrought by the introduction of a multitude of consumer goods. The Japanese continue to place the same value on education and on working for the good and honor of the family, and retain the same enthusiasm for such new pastimes as golf and travel that was previously shown in the community festivals celebrated seasonally. People in every society retain many of their distinctive values and attitudes even in the midst of rapid social change, but this tendency is particularly pronounced among the Japanese. It is this which has helped them to preserve their lifestyles and traditions in the midst of the modern transformation of the physical environment.

■——Robert E. Cole, *Japanese Blue Collar: The Changing Tradition* (1971). Ronald P. Dore, *City Life in Japan: A Study of a Tokyo Ward* (1967). David W. Plath, *The After-Hours: Modern Japan and the Search for Enjoyment* (1969). Edwin O. Reischauer, *The Japanese* (1977). Robert J. Smith, *Kurusu: The Price of Progress in a Japanese Village, 1951–1975* (1978). Ezra P. Vogel, *Japan's New Middle Class: The Salary Man and His Family in a Tokyo Suburb* (1963). Susan B. HANLEY

lighting equipment

The oldest traditional lighting sources in Japan were the hearth, the torch, and the bonfire. In addition to providing light and heat, fire had religious significance in its association with purification. When a death or other contamination occurred in a house, the fire was always made anew from an outside source. This respect for fire is

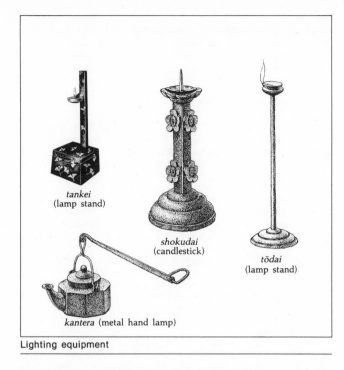

tankei
(lamp stand)

shokudai
(candlestick)

tōdai
(lamp stand)

kantera (metal hand lamp)

Lighting equipment

sene lamps in 1872. Gas lamps were used for a time during the Meiji period (1868–1912). The modern electric lamp is generally known as *denki sutando* ("electric stand"), while electric ceiling lights are variously known as *denki* or *akari*.

Li Hongzhang (Li Hung-chang) (1823–1901)

(J: Ri Kōshō). Chinese statesman and diplomat who dominated China's foreign relations in the last quarter of the 19th century. Having emerged into prominence during the suppression of the anti-Manchu anti-Western Taiping (T'ai-p'ing) Rebellion (1850–64), Li Hongzhang's period of greatest power was from 1870 to 1895, when he was governor-general of the capital district of Zhili (Chihli) and superintendent of trade for the north. Standing between the inertia of conservatives at the Manchu court and the threat of foreign encroachment, Li promoted the development of economic enterprises and the adoption of Western technology. He also attempted to counter foreign pressures with diplomacy as China was forced to move its traditional tributary system toward a system of modern international relations.

In the late 1860s Li, who admired Japan's technological reforms, suggested that the Chinese government try to keep Japan oriented toward China to prevent Japan's alignment with the West. The first modern treaty between the two countries was negotiated by Li with Date Munenari (1818–92) in 1871. It provided for the exchange of diplomatic representatives, though China failed to send a consul to Japan until after Japan's annexation of the Ryūkyū (Liuqiu or Liuch'iu) Islands (1874). In the treaty China refused to concede "most-favored nation" status to Japan or to allow Japan's request for trade in the Chinese interior.

In the spring of 1885 Li met ITŌ HIROBUMI, the Japanese leader, in Tianjin (Tientsin) to discuss disturbances in the tribute state of Korea, where Japan was pushing for modern commercial and diplomatic relations. The TIANJIN (TIANTSIN) CONVENTION of 1885 provided that China and Japan both abstain from stationing troops and advisers in Korea, give prior notice should it become necessary to send troops into Korea temporarily, and agree on military advisers from a third power to train the Korean army. China, in effect, acknowledged equality with Japan in relation to Korea.

After China's defeat in the SINO-JAPANESE WAR OF 1894–1895, a war that had grown out of a domestic rebellion in Korea and that Li had opposed, Itō insisted that no one less than Li come to Shimonoseki to negotiate an armistice. He presented the Chinese statesman with terms so harsh that Li was forced to refuse them. On 24 March 1895 a Japanese fanatic shot and wounded Li, and amidst the public reaction, Itō granted an armistice on 30 March. Li's nephew and adopted son, Li Jingfang (Li Ching-fang; d 1934) continued the negotiations. The terms of the Treaty of SHIMONOSEKI went far beyond what Japan had hoped to achieve in the two earlier agreements. The treaty also marked Japan's entry into the struggle for spheres of influence in China. Li died shortly after signing the protocol concluding the antiforeign BOXER REBELLION (1900–1901). Despite being in disgrace since the Treaty of Shimonoseki, he was still the only man at that time capable of dealing with foreign powers.

lilies

(*yuri*). *Lilium* spp. In Japanese *yuri* is a general term for plants of the family Liliaceae, genus *Lilium*. Bulbous perennials which grow wild in mountain fields and on coastal cliffs, they are also cultivated as ornamentals. More than 100 species are found in the northern hemisphere, of which 15 are indigenous to Japan.

The *yamayuri* (*L. auratum*) grows to a height of 100–150 centimeters (39–59 in). Its funnel-shaped flowers, which measure 15–20 centimeters (6–8 in) in diameter, are white with purplish brown spots. It is known for its fragrance and also valued for its edible bulb.

The *sakuyuri* (*L. platyphyllum*) generally resembles the *yamayuri* but grows to a greater height with broader leaves and larger yellow-spotted flowers.

The *teppōyuri* (*L. longiflorum*) has white or pale red trumpet-shaped flowers valued for their beauty and scent. There are many varieties, including the popular Easter lily.

The *himeyuri* (*L. concolor*) grows to a height of 30 to 50 centimeters (12–20 in), with soft leaves. The flower is 5 centimeters (2 in) in diameter and gracefully shaped, hence its name, "princess lily" (*himeyuri*) or "maiden lily" (*otomeyuri*).

demonstrated today in certain local festivals and in the custom of KIRIBI, or striking sparks with flint and steel for good luck.

Fire was traditionally made by striking flintstone against metal, or by rotating a device with a long wooden stick in a hole bored into a flat wooden base (*hikiri*). The fire was transferred with strips of folded paper or wood that had been dipped in sulfur (*tsukegi*).

With the introduction of Buddhism to Japan in the 6th century, various kinds of oil lamps and candles came into use, at first for temples but later for homes and public buildings. The earliest lamps in Japan burned plant oil, generally derived from rapeseed, perilla, camellia, or cottonseed. The oil was placed in a saucer with a wick of hemp or cotton and was either used as is or placed in a lamp stand (*tōdai*). The simplest lamp stands were made of three poles tied together in tepee fashion, with the oil cup balanced in the crook. An early lamp stand known as *tankei* consisted of a single pole attached to a large base, often made of metal. To this was added a reflector, at first a round shield affixed behind the oil cup, later a movable piece allowing control over the direction of the light. These basic forms and their many variations have been in use since at least the Nara period (710–794). One popular type employed a large box with a drawer in it as the base and a square, wooden frame covered with white paper as the reflector. The famous *nezumi tankei* had a metal, rat-shaped vessel atop the pole, dripping oil from its mouth to keep the oil cup full.

The first Japanese candles (*rōsoku*) were made of hardened pine resin wrapped in bamboo leaves. Later, candles were made of the wax of a kind of sumac. Wicks were made of twisted paper, then cotton, and later rush. Candlestands and candlesticks (*shokudai*) were generally similar in shape to the oil-lamp stands and were much used in temples. Many candlestick designs employed Buddhist symbols. One well-known type consisted of an image of a tortoise with a crane standing on its back holding a lotus leaf, the candleholder, in its mouth. Other Buddhist candlestands had multiple candlesticks for worshipers to add their own candles. Candlestands for use in the home could be secured to the wall or stood on the floor.

Perhaps the best-known and most artistically developed traditional Japanese lighting devices are LANTERNS (*tōrō*). Standing lanterns for outdoor use, generally for temple grounds or for gardens, are made of stone or metal. Hanging lanterns are made of metal or paper. During the Edo period (1600–1868), the most widespread light source for the home was the *andon*, a small standing lantern.

With Western influences reaching Japan during the Edo period, a metal or ceramic lamp called *kantera* (a name derived from the Portuguese or the Dutch word for candle) became popular. *Kantera* had a thick wick and burned plant oil and later kerosene. At the end of the Edo period, kerosene lamps were imported and the English word "lamp" (*rampu*) came into use. Japan started manufacturing kero-

The *oniyuri (L. lancifolium)*. The petals of the flower, which measures about 10 centimeters (4 in) in diameter, curl backward toward the base of the flower. The stem is mottled with purplish brown spots and has white hairs. Blackish scaly bulbils form in the axils, and the blossoms are a deep red with blackish purple spots. The *oniyuri* is widely cultivated for its edible roots. A similar but smaller variety is called *kooniyuri*.

The *kanokoyuri (L. speciosum)* has oblong pale green leaves, somewhat rounder than those of other lily species. The flowers, measuring 10 centimeters (4 in), are white, blending into pink at the center, with red spots. The petals curl backward toward the base of the flower. Cultivated extensively as an ornamental with many varieties, it is exported abroad on a large scale.

The *sukashiyuri (L. elegans)*. Flowers measure 10 centimeters (4 in) in diameter and grow erect, the petals narrowing at the base. Its alternate leaves grow densely. Many horticultural varieties have been developed.

The *kurumayuri (L. medeoloides)* is a small species with verticillate leaves. Its deep red flowers measure 5–6 centimeters (2–2.4 in).

Apart from these native species, lilies of foreign origin are also cultivated in Japan, including the *takeshimayuri (L. hansonii)* from Korea, with orange yellow flowers and dark red spots; the *kikanokoyuri (L. henryi)* from China, with yellow orange flowers; and the *takasagoyuri (L. formosanum)* from Taiwan, with flowers that are milky white on the inside and purplish brown on the outside. See also DAY LILIES.

■——Asayama Eiichi et al, *Genshoku zufu engei shokubutsu* (1977). Shimizu Motoo, *Nihon no yuri* (1971). MATSUDA Osamu

limited liability company

(yūgen kaisha). A type of association incorporated for the purpose of profit making under the provisions of the Limited Liability Company Law (Yūgen Kaisha Hō) of 1938. The capital of a limited liability company consists of many equal contribution units, and all its members are obliged to contribute to the capital of the company. Individual members are not personally liable, however, for corporate obligations. Corresponding to the English private company and the closed corporation in the United States, the *yūgen kaisha* is a corporate form suitable for enterprises, especially small and medium ones, that are not in need of contributions of capital from the general public and wish to avoid many of the onerous requirements imposed on joint-stock companies (see JOINT-STOCK COMPANY).

Next to the joint-stock company, the limited liability corporation is the most common corporate form in Japan. In 1975 there were about 360,000 *yūgen kaisha*, which operated over 400,000 establishments, employed over 2.25 million people, and had a total capital of about ¥1.1 trillion ($3.3 billion). The overwhelming majority of these companies have a capital fund of less than ¥14.8 million ($49,865); only one has a capital fund in excess of ¥1.48 billion ($5 million).

The articles of incorporation of a *yūgen kaisha* are to be prepared and executed by all those who will become members of the company. Only one corporate director need be appointed, and there is no functional distinction between the BOARD OF DIRECTORS and the representative director. OVERSEERS are not mandatory; one or more may be appointed as provided for in the articles of incorporation. The procedure for calling a members' general meeting is simplified, and a resolution may be carried on written consent of all members without a formal meeting.

Stressing mutual confidence of the members, the law limits the number of members of a *yūgen kaisha* to fewer than 50, restricts transfers of shares, and prohibits public offerings of shares and debentures. The principle of disclosure is also relaxed, and public notification of the company's FINANCIAL STATEMENTS is not required. To prevent any abuse of the limited liability privilege, however, the liability of members is intensified in one way. When a limited liability company is established or its capital increased, if there is an unreasonable disparity between actual market value and the valuation claimed for payment in kind for shares or property in a takeover contract to be delivered to the company, or if the members' contribution is unpaid, the members at the time of the formation of the company or the members who have agreed to the increase in capital are jointly and severally liable to pay the difference between the valuation and the market value or the as-yet-unpaid portion of the contribution. See also LIMITED PARTNERSHIP COMPANY; UNLIMITED PARTNERSHIP COMPANY.

NAGAHAMA Yōichi

limited partnership company

(gōshi kaisha). A type of company incorporated under the COMMERCIAL CODE that is composed of both limited and unlimited liability partners. It is similar to a limited partnership in Anglo-American law. Unlimited partners not only have a duty to contribute a specified amount of capital to the company but also jointly and severally bear direct and unlimited liability to the company's creditors in the event that its assets are insufficient to meet its obligations. Limited partners jointly and severally bear direct and limited liability to the company's creditors up to the specified amount of their contributions. Limited partners may only make contributions of cash or other property and are not allowed to contribute services or credit. Limited partners, being exposed to less liability than unlimited partners, do not, as a general principle, have the right to administer the affairs of the company or to represent it, although they do have certain rights of supervision. For this reason, a limited partner is not prohibited from engaging in business activities that compete with the partnership. Fundamental company matters such as amendment of the articles of incorporation, mergers, and dissolution of the company require the consent of all partners.

Articles of incorporation containing the purpose of the company, its trade name (which must expressly state that the company is a limited partnership), and other information must be prepared and registered with the appropriate registry office. In addition to court-ordered liquidation, voluntary liquidation is also permitted under certain conditions.

In 1978 there were more than 82,000 limited partnerships, making the limited partnership company the third most common of Japan's four corporate forms, the others being the JOINT-STOCK COMPANY, the LIMITED LIABILITY COMPANY, and the UNLIMITED PARTNERSHIP COMPANY. See also PARTNERSHIP.

KITAZAWA Masahiro

Lion Corporation

Leading producer of toothpaste and detergent. Also manufactures and markets a diversified line of products, including household and personal care products, pharmaceuticals, food products, and industrial chemicals. The company was established by the merger in January 1980 of two sister companies, Lion Dentrifrice Co, Japan's largest manufacturer of toothpaste and toothbrushes, and Lion Fat & Oil Co, a leading manufacturer of household cleaning products. The companies were both founded by the entrepreneur Kobayashi Tomijirō in 1891 and 1919, respectively. Lion Corporation is engaged in joint ventures in Japan with such companies as Bristol–Meyers Co, McCormick & Co, and Cooper Laboratories, Inc, of the United States and Akzo Chemie b.v. of the Netherlands. It has subsidiaries and affiliated companies in Southeast Asia. It provides technical and manufacturing expertise about detergent and toothpaste to several leading companies in Europe and elsewhere, and exports finished or intermediate products and specialty chemicals to more than 40 countries. Total 1981 sales were ¥227 billion (US $1 billion), distributed as follows: detergent 41 percent; toothpaste and toothbrushes 23 percent; cosmetics and toiletries 12 percent; other household products 12 percent; and foods, pharmaceuticals, chemicals, and others 12 percent. It was capitalized at ¥7.7 billion (US $34.4 million) in 1981. Corporate headquarters are in Tōkyō.

Lions Club

Lions Club activities in Japan began in 1952 when the Tōkyō chapter was organized. The national headquarters was established in Tōkyō in 1958. The club, as in other countries, is an organization for businessmen and professionals devoted to providing community services and promoting international relations. The international conference of the Lions Club was held in Tōkyō in 1969. As of 1979, 2,331 chapters existed with a total membership of 134,409.

HOMMA Yasuhei

literacy rate

Japan achieved a relatively high rate of literacy during the premodern Edo period (1600–1868) through the proliferation of educational institutions such as the domain schools for the military class and TERAKOYA for commoners. By 1870, two years after the Meiji Restoration, 40 to 45 percent of boys and 15 percent of girls were found able to read and write Japanese and to solve simple mathematical problems. A modern educational system was instituted under the EDUCATION ORDER OF 1872, and within 30 years the school attendance rate had reached 90 percent. In recent years, the attendance rate has been about 99.9 percent; the literacy rate is not currently measured in Japan, but it is assumed to closely parallel the school attendance rate.

HORIUCHI Mamoru

literary criticism, modern

In considering the history of modern Japanese literary criticism, we face a number of basic questions. Where should one draw the line to demarcate modern from premodern criticism? How did modern criticism originate? Who should be called the first modern Japanese literary critic? In political history the Meiji Restoration of 1868 is generally made the starting point of Japan's modernization. However, this is an arbitrary division for the sake of convenience; in recent years historians have been increasingly concerned with the true origin and process of Japan's modernization. They have pointed out that it was in fact in the Edo period (1600–1868), hitherto considered feudalistic and unmodern, that modernization began its course. Literary history is even more complicated than political history, and the basic concept of modernity and how it applies to literature is difficult to define clearly.

Since the Meiji Restoration a great number of critics have written on modernity and modernization; they have criticized old conventions and traditions, emphasized individualism, and expressed their fervent hopes for social reform alongside their attraction to the sensual delights of hedonism. During the middle of the 19th century, when Japan was exposed to the military and political pressure of the Western powers, the term "modernization" was, in fact, synonymous with "Westernization." The Japanese looked up to Western systems as models and set up the ideal of rebuilding their country by adopting them. Literary criticism became one of the areas in which Western impact was clearly and strongly felt. Naive but serious attempts were made to learn the terms, framework, and standards of Western literary criticism and to apply them to Japanese literary works. However, works of literature cannot be made to order in accordance with the theories of critics, nor is it possible to overhaul the traditions of a country's literature. These attempts to criticize literary works in Japan by Western standards were not reasonable, because literary traditions in Japan were in many ways quite different from those in the West. As a result, the attempts at criticism of early literary critics in the modern period were frequently filled with empty slogans and generally ended up as procrustean beds, completely unrelated to the actual literary works and the psychology of their authors.

We must not conclude, however, that criticism was always a hasty imitation of that of the West, an unfruitful product born of an imperfectly learned alien theory. For centuries there had existed in Japan a wide stratum of readers who could appreciate literature and who formed an audience for good criticism closely connected with the actual work under consideration. In other words, the general standard of critical appreciation was already high in Japan. There were numerous examples of literary criticism in the early modern period that attested to a sensitive appreciation of literature. Much criticism, even in the early period, was outstanding in its delicacy, sharpness, and keen aesthetic sense, though its theoretical structures were borrowed from the West. With self-reflection and a reaction against hasty Westernization there appeared critics who began to place great emphasis on the reevaluation of Japan's own literary traditions. It became gradually clear that the fundamental problem of Japan's modern literature lay in the relationship between modernity and native traditions. Efforts were made to discover a point of contact between the literature of the West and Japan and to take a detached view of the merits and weaknesses of Japanese literature.

The First Modernists —— As for the starting point of modern criticism, a majority of literary historians would no doubt agree that it was TSUBOUCHI SHŌYŌ's (1859–1935) *Shōsetsu shinzui* (1885–86, The Essence of the Novel). This critical pamphlet, written in Tsubouchi's mid-twenties, not long after his graduation from Tōkyō University, had a great effect on the literary world of the time, perhaps much more than it deserved. Tsubouchi's literary scholarship was neither wide nor deep and his critical judgment was frequently shallow. However, his youthful passion and serious commitment to literature were genuine, and the goals which he set for himself were quite suited for the demands of the time. We may say that Tsubouchi's *The Essence of the Novel* was the first piece of Japanese criticism stressing the modernity of literature. Tsubouchi stated clearly that the novel is the leading genre of modern literature, a prophetic assertion in terms of the subsequent development of Japanese literature. According to Tsubouchi, "Human nature is the nucleus of the novel, and social conditions and popular morals are the next important." He defined human nature as "human desire" and declared that the "duty of the writer" was to "dig deeply into human desire." He emphasized that the depiction of character should be based on psychological reasoning. Tsubouchi should be given credit for his sensitivity and quickness in recognizing modern realism as it was accepted in the West and for his championing of the novel as an art form at a time when theoretical criticism of the genre of novel was only developing even in the West.

Tsubouchi's basic standpoint was antitraditionalist, laying stress on the present, a standpoint typical of a young man. His criticism was directed especially at the celebrated writer of the Edo period, BAKIN (1767–1848), whose works were full of Confucian didacticism. Since the young Tsubouchi was a great reader of the works of Bakin, his criticism was in a way an attempt to reform something in himself under the strong impact of the West. There is a sentence in *The Essence of the Novel* that reads: "I would like to improve my immature novels and historical romances into perfect ones comparable to those of the West."

Another pioneering young "Westernizer" who first became active in the late 1880s was MORI ŌGAI (1862–1922). He studied in Germany for four years as a medical student, and on his return to Japan expressed his views on numerous topics as one of the very few Japanese who had had personal contact with the West. When Tsubouchi praised Shakespeare for what he called the latter's "rejection of ideals" *(botsu risō)*, Ōgai severely criticized his view and engaged him in a lively dispute. The term *botsu risō* is ambiguous; it would surely be a mistake to say there are no ideals in Shakespeare's plays. What Tsubouchi intended was to draw attention to Shakespeare's dramatic objectivity, but Ōgai misunderstood this and attempted to refute him from the standpoint of German idealist aesthetics. One might say that Ōgai attacked Tsubouchi's interpretation of English realism and empiricism from his own standpoint of German philosophical idealism, in other words, that this was merely a literary proxy war. In viewing the literary career of Ōgai after his controversy with Tsubouchi, it is difficult to say that he remained always an idealist. If one were to name the most idealistic literary critic of the period it would have to be KITAMURA TŌKOKU (1868–94).

Kitamura, who killed himself in his mid-twenties, was a born romantic who moved young authors and readers of the day with his passionate eloquence. As a young man he participated in the FREEDOM AND PEOPLE's RIGHTS MOVEMENT, which in those days was synonymous with political radicalism. He was also strongly attracted to the American transcendentalist Ralph Waldo Emerson, of whom he wrote an excellent critical biography. As a critic, Kitamura attacked the Edo-period idea of sensual love in favor of the Western ideal of romantic love. On the other hand, he was quick to criticize Western utilitarianism, which was coming into vogue in Japan at the time. Though his activity as a literary critic was very brief, Kitamura's influence on his friends and readers was considerable.

Advent of Traditionalists —— The first major wave of Westernization in Japan, which began in the 1880s, lasted about 20 years. However, from the early 1890s, a nationalistic reaction had already begun to emerge in various fields. The most notable reactions appeared in the magazine *Nihonjin* and the newspaper *Nihon*. SHIGA SHIGETAKA (1863–1927), the editor of *Nihonjin*, wrote an essay entitled "Nihon fūkei ron" (1894), in which he described the beauty of the Japanese landscape in a vigorous emotional style. This essay was welcomed by a wide range of readers. The study of traditional Japanese literature, which had for a time fallen into a decline, became more popular, and the reprinting of classical Japanese literature in such collections as *Nihon bungaku zenshū* and *Nihon kagaku zenshū* was a great success. The popularity of Bakin, who had been so severely criticized by Tsubouchi, waned, but SAIKAKU (1642–93) and UEDA AKINARI (1734–1809) were rediscovered and reevaluated. The style of Saikaku influenced the novels of OZAKI KŌYŌ (1867–1903) and HIGUCHI ICHIYŌ (1872–96), both important novelists of the period.

There was also a revival of the traditional Japanese short-verse forms HAIKU and TANKA. The leading organizer and critic of this movement was MASAOKA SHIKI (1867–1902). Shiki, who had been a reporter during the Sino-Japanese War of 1894–95, was afflicted with tuberculosis and spent a long period battling the disease. Even during these painful days, Shiki continued his activities as a poet-critic and exerted a strong influence. His contributions as a critic were paradoxical in that he was both traditionalist and iconoclastic. He was a traditionalist in the sense that he revived short-verse forms such as haiku and *tanka,* but he was an iconoclast in the sense that he challenged conventional viewpoints by severely criticizing BASHŌ (1644–94), who had been admired for a long time as a "poet-saint" of haiku. Instead Shiki acclaimed the works of BUSON (1716–84), who had been largely ignored. Stimulated by the Western-style painters of his day, Shiki insisted on a realistic photographic element *(shasei)* in poetry, an important theme in the modern haiku and *tanka* movement.

TAKAYAMA CHOGYŪ (1871–1902) was another traditionalist literary critic, though different in critical emphasis from Shiki. Takayama was also a victim of tuberculosis and died young. He lived a flamboyant life, and though he was simple and naive as a critic, he was by nature exceedingly sentimental and romantic and wrote in a flowery style, qualities that appealed particularly to young readers. Takayama attacked Tsubouchi's advocacy of a literature free from moralizing. He also attacked Tsubouchi's "realism" as "antinationalistic" and called for a nationalist literature and a nationalist criticism. He criticized the "pessimistic" Kitamura as "effeminate" and praised the poet DOI BANSUI (1871–1952) as masculine, saying that Doi was close to an ideal national poet. Takayama was later attracted to Friedrich Wilhelm Nietzsche; in 1901 he published the essay "Biteki seikatsu o ronzu" (Essay on the Aesthetic Life), in which he claimed that the objective of life was the fulfillment of the instincts, and he thus cannot be categorized as a simple-minded nationalist.

Another type of traditionalist literary critic was OKAKURA KAKUZŌ (1862–1913). His important books, originally written in English, are *The Ideals of the East* (1903) and *The Book of Tea* (1906), through which Okakura attempted to explain and clarify what he thought of as the superior characteristics of oriental arts and Japanese culture to readers in English-speaking countries. Okakura's aim was to demonstrate the hidden superiority of Asian cultures to the culture of the West, which in terms of economic and military might was so overwhelmingly superior to Japan and other Asian countries. He attempted particularly to clarify the significance of the cultural role Japan played in Asian history. Bold generalizations can be found in his writings, but his perspective was wide and his style of writing, with its striking paradoxes and skillful anecdotes, appealed greatly to his readers. Okakura was a traditionalist critic in that he never doubted the real value of Japanese traditions. However, he did try to carry on a dialogue with readers in the West and in that sense he was a cosmopolitan rather than a narrow-minded nationalist.

Second Wave of Westernization ———— Japan's victory in the Russo-Japanese War of 1904–05 resulted in another wave of Westernizing. The "national goal" of learning from the West and catching up with it was seen to have been realized, at least in military prowess. Foreign countries were astounded that this "great progress" had been achieved by Japan in only a generation. While the Japanese were exhilarated and self-satisfied over this victory, it took some time before this overconfidence became evident in literature. The achievement of the "national goal" resulted in creating feelings of relief and dispelling the tension brought forth by the Meiji Restoration of 1868. However, it is not easy to say what sort of influence this atmosphere had on literature and literary criticism. Japanese literature immediately following the Russo-Japanese War was characterized by the popularity of the novels of so-called Japanese NATURALISM and the appearance of socialist writers, both focusing on the dark and seamy side of society. But in parallel with this trend there appeared young writers and critics who leaned toward aestheticism and decadence.

There also appeared the so-called SHIRAKABA SCHOOL, whose members glorified the artistic geniuses of the West, acclaiming them as the representatives of mankind. Their motto was to imitate such geniuses and develop their own individuality to the utmost. The literary theories and practices of this school seem quite different from those of the other two groups, but, from a historical perspective, it can be seen that each of the three groups took as its point of departure new movements and vogues current in the West. This was, therefore, a second period of Westernization, when cosmopolitanism flourished. This second period is different from the first, the early part of the Meiji period (1868–1912), in that a wide range of interests from socialist ideology to aesthetics was observed. Undoubtedly, it was Japan's victory in the war with Russia that led the Japanese to believe that instead of merely learning from the West, they could now pursue Western thoughts and interests themselves.

Among the representative literary critics of this period were SHIMAMURA HŌGETSU (1871–1918), UEDA BIN (1874–1916), NATSUME SŌSEKI (1867–1916), and ISHIKAWA TAKUBOKU (1886–1912). Shimamura was originally a scholar and professor of Western aesthetics; his *Shin bijigaku* (1902) was a manual, rich in examples, concerning the rhetorics of Japan, China, and the West. Numerous editions of the book were published; however, one does not find keen critical insight in it. The year the book was published, Shimamura went to Europe and attended lectures in universities both in England and Germany for three years. He saw many plays in the two countries. It was due to these experiences that Shimamura, after his return to Japan, became an active literary critic with great influence. His experience of the theater in Europe inspired him to become a committed leader in establishing a new theater in Japan. Immediately after his return from Europe, Shimamura wrote an essay entitled "Torawaretaru bungei," in which he showed a great interest in European symbolism and mysticism while discussing the relationship between Christianity and Western literature. Later, however, after reading SHIMAZAKI TŌSON's (1872–1943) *Hakai* (1906; tr *The Broken Commandment,* 1974) and TAYAMA KATAI's (1872–1930) *Futon* (1907), he came to appreciate the realism of the Japanese naturalists. In regard to Tayama's *Futon,* Shimamura wrote: "This is a bold confession of a man of the flesh *(niku no hito),* a confession of the naked self . . . One aspect of the naturalist school has fully matured in this book, that is, where the earlier naturalists depicted both the beautiful and the ugly, we now have concentration exclusively on something ugly."

It is extremely doubtful whether "the man of the flesh" was fully described in *Futon* as Shimamura says, or whether the "ugly side" of human nature was fully exposed, but the combination of shock and enthusiasm aroused in readers and critics by Tayama's boldness in those days when Confucianism still imposed strong moral restraints can be easily imagined today. We can appreciate the excitement created by the advent of a novel which both authors and readers believed to be on the same level with contemporary Western literature in thought and techniques. At the same time it is interesting as an example of the dangers of oversubjectivity.

Ueda Bin was a voracious reader and sensitive appreciator of Western literature. He was also a brilliant translator of the works of such French symbolists as Baudelaire, Mallarmé, and Verlaine. He was such a skillful and refined writer of Japanese that his translations of modern Western poems gave a great stimulus to young poets in Japan. His stance was a "dilettantism" similar to that of Walter Pater. Ueda, who studied English literature under Lafcadio HEARN (1850–1904), was one of the first generation of Japanese who could truly appreciate Western literature.

Natsume Sōseki, also a member of that generation but different from Ueda, was a more systematic literary theoretician. His *Bungakuron* (1907, Theory of Literature) was the first systematic and comprehensive literary criticism in modern Japan and revealed a sharp analytical mind. It contains psychological interpretations that could be said to anticipate those of I. A. Richards. However, this work was too ambitious and schematic, and ended up resembling a colossal building with many unfinished rooms. Sōseki was more famous and important as a writer of novels than as a critic, but even his *Bungaku hyōron* (1909, Lectures on English Literature) showed his sharp intuition and observational power as a creative writer. In one of his occasional essays, entitled "Gendai Nihon no kaika" (1910, The Enlightenment of Modern Japan), he pointed out the shallowness of Japan's culture in the Meiji period and warned his countrymen not to become too impatient in catching up with the West. In another essay, "Watashi no kojin shugi" (1915, My Version of Individualism), he wrote in retrospect about his intellectual growth, giving a vivid personal case history of the modern ego in Japan.

Ishikawa Takuboku was a brilliant poet who died young; his *tanka,* which utilized unconventional colloquialisms to the utmost, are still popular despite their sentimentalism and self-pity. His literary criticism was on the whole fragmentary; however, some of it, particularly his essays on the Japanese naturalist novelists of his time and his social criticism, contained sharp observations. Although Ishikawa recognized the importance of these so-called naturalists in Meiji intellectual history, he complained that their actual novels dealt with only their own private lives and failed to analyze and solve social problems. Of course, it must be pointed out that Ishikawa's own social philosophy was naive and ambiguous and that his incipient socialism has been overemphasized by later leftist literary critics.

Practical Critics —— In Japan a long tradition of criticism by novelists and other creative writers became particularly important from about 1920 in the occasional criticism of such novelist-critics as MASAMUNE HAKUCHŌ (1879–1962), TANIZAKI JUN'ICHIRŌ (1886–1965), HIROTSU KAZUO (1891–1968), UNO KŌJI (1891–1961), and SATŌ HARUO (1892–1964). A little later there were KAWABATA YASUNARI (1899–1972) and NAKANO SHIGEHARU (1902–1979). Most of this criticism was impressionistic, and although it lacked theoretical consistency, its informal style was easy and enjoyable to read. The comments were full of irony and wit and even the personal biases of the writers were interesting to readers. Particularly perceptive is Masamune's *Bundan jimbutsu hyōron* (1932), a collection of appreciative essays on practically all major Japanese novelists since the Meiji period. It is a masterpiece of modern Japanese literary criticism, as is Masamune's *Shizen shugi seisuishi* (1948, Rise and Fall of Japanese Naturalism), a literary retrospect of his youth. Satō's *Taikutsu dokuhon* (1926) and *Kindai Nihon bungaku no tembō* (1950) are still readable and illuminating because of their historical perspective, based on the author's personal experiences and tastes, and their informal style. Tanizaki, a much more important novelist than Satō, wrote essays on traditional Japanese culture, most notably those on the contrasts between the cultures of Tōkyō and Ōsaka and those on BUNRAKU, the traditional puppet theater. Also important was his dispute on the novel with AKUTAGAWA RYŪNOSUKE (1892–1927). Kawabata, a winner of the Nobel Prize for literature, for many years wrote monthly criticism about the current literary scene. This has been reprinted in a four-volume set. Considering the fact that Kawabata was essentially a lyrical novelist, his wide range of appreciation, sharp critical intuition, and sensitivity are astounding. This type of appreciative criticism was not limited to the novel. KŌDA ROHAN (1867–1947), who had been a formidably well-read young writer in the 1890s, wrote an essay (1919–47) on verse of the Bashō school of haiku that was a masterpiece of literary scholarship and appreciation of this elusive genre. The brilliant *tanka* poet SAITŌ MOKICHI (1882–1953) wrote a study of the 7th century WAKA poet KAKINOMOTO NO HITOMARO (Kakinomoto no Hitomaro, 5 vols, 1934–40), which was quite impressive in its attention to detail and passionate erudition.

Professional Critics —— The first professional critics in modern Japan were SAITŌ RYOKUU (1867–1904) and UCHIDA ROAN (1868–1929). Saitō wrote light parody and satirical criticism with something like the flavor of Edo-period literature. Uchida was the first Japanese translator of Dostoevsky's *Crime and Punishment* (his translation was based on an English version of the book). He was not only active in introducing foreign literature to Japanese readers but also wrote satirical novels himself. A brilliant writer of light essays and a bibliophile, he was especially good at presenting personal impressions of various writers in an attractive style. Other literary critics who were active during the late 1880s were ISHIBASHI NINGETSU (1865–1926), who was active only for a short period; YAMAJI AIZAN (1864–1917), who wrote impressive literary biographies; and HASEGAWA TENKEI (1876–1940), who was an active supporter of Japanese naturalism and also a pioneer in psychoanalytical criticism.

Criticism as an independent profession, however, did not really emerge in Japan until the field of professional journalism was firmly established by a corps of seriously committed critics who were well-read in Western literary criticism. It was in the late 1920s and early 1930s, when these conditions were met, that a group of particularly brilliant critical talents appeared on the literary scene. The most brilliant of all was KOBAYASHI HIDEO (1902–83), whose uncompromising courage, sharp critical eye, and provocative style of writing imparted a great stimulus and influence on the writers of his period. Kobayashi was attracted to French symbolist poets and read eagerly the criticism of Sainte-Beuve and Valéry. Although he did not possess an especially wide literary scholarship or a consistent theory of his own concerning Japanese literary history, Kobayashi has been the most influential and widely read modern Japanese literary critic. For Kobayashi, criticism became an individualistic, living medium for self-expression. His essays of the 1940s concerning the Japanese classics are short and fragmentary, but wonderfully evocative and poetic. His collected essays have been published and republished, a rare occurrence in the case of a critic. His most important works are *Kindai kaiga* (1958, Modern Painting) and *Motoori Norinaga* (1965–76).

Among the other critics of Kobayashi's time were KAWAKAMI TETSUTARŌ (1902–80) and KAMEI KATSUICHIRŌ (1907–66), as well as the leftist critic AONO SUEKICHI (1890–1961). Kawakami wrote a book of literary reminiscences, *Watashi no shi to shinjitsu* (1953),

and *Yoshida Shōin* (1966–68), a biography of YOSHIDA SHŌIN, in which he expressed his sympathy toward Confucianist and *samurai* traditions. Kamei began his career as a leftist, but soon turned traditionalist, writing lyrical, evocative essays on ancient temples he had visited in Nara. His study of Buddhism culminated in the ambitious, unfinished *Nihonjin no seishinshi kenkyū* (4 vols, 1959–66; Studies in the Spiritual History of the Japanese).

The two men who were most influential in reevaluating Japanese literary traditions were the poet-scholar ORIKUCHI SHINOBU (1887–1953) and the folklorist YANAGITA KUNIO (1875–1962). Among the critics who also pursued this theme in regard to modern literature were YASUDA YOJŪRŌ (1910–81), Karaki Junzō (1904–80), and YAMAMOTO KENKICHI (b 1907). Yasuda was a passionate romantic and an ultranationalist during World War II. His *Nihon no bungakushi* (1972, History of Japanese Literature) appealed to readers because of its aesthetic intuition, sensitive style, and original perspective. Yamamoto wrote a detailed commentary on Bashō and discussions on modern haiku. He also threw new light on poetic traditions springing from the 8th-century poetry anthology the MAN'YŌSHŪ.

Critics who made their appearance a little later than Kobayashi were NAKAMURA MITSUO (b 1911) and HIRANO KEN (1907–78). Maintaining the attitude of an orthodox Westernizer and using the modern European novel as his criterion, Nakamura sharply criticized the weakness and distortion of Japan's modern novels, which made him frequently the center of controversy in literary disputes. Hirano was faithful to native elements; he studied the I-NOVEL, a peculiarly Japanese genre, with strong sympathy. His most important work involves a sensitive analysis of the often intricate relationship between the works of modern Japanese writers and their private lives.

Among other critics who were noted for their unconventional point of view and flowery rhetoric were FUKUDA TSUNEARI (b 1912) and HANADA KIYOTERU (1909–74). With the rapid economic growth period that began in the 1960s, the literary market in Japan expanded, and the demand for literary criticism increased considerably, at least in quantity. The number of critics active in the late 1970s far surpassed that of any previous period, and it would be impossible to name all of them here. The standards of criticism have been diversified and the tendency to look toward Western literature for models has weakened. Instead, there is a tendency to reevaluate the traditions of Japanese literature and discover new significance in them. There is also an interest in examining Japanese literature from the viewpoint of comparative literature. Modern Japanese criticism seems to have emerged finally from the awkward transition of the Meiji period, ready to enter a period of maturity.

——Hisamatsu Sen'ichi, *Nippon bungaku hyōron shi—Kinsei saikinsei hen* (1936). Isoda Kōichi, *Sengo hihyōka ron* (1969). *Kinsei bungaku hyōron taikei*, 10 vols (Kadokawa Shoten, 1971–75). *Shōwa hihyō taikei*, 10 vols (Banchō Shobō, 1968–78). Tanizawa Eiichi, *Taishōki no bungei hyōron* (1962). Yoshida Seiichi, *Kindai bungaku hyōron shi—Meiji hen* (1976), *Taishō hen* (1980).

Saeki Shōichi

literary criticism, premodern

Literary criticism in premodern Japan comprises critical and theoretical writings on WAKA, *haikai* (see RENGA AND HAIKAI), NŌ, and other literary forms that evolved over a span of more than 10 centuries. Major critics were in general not philosophers or rhetoricians but were themselves poets, playwrights, and novelists. Consequently their thoughts on literature tended to be unsystematic, yet provided advice of a practical nature to fellow artists. For ideas and terms they often resorted to Buddhism, Confucianism, and Shintoism, but in dealing with the peculiarities of their specific literary forms, they also cultivated a number of unique aesthetic concepts on their own. Some of these aesthetic ideals, like YŪGEN and SABI, permeated the arts and helped to establish the identity of Japanese culture. Insofar as literature occupied a high place in premodern Japanese society, literary criticism functioned as an important determinant of the cultural climate in each age.

Early Thoughts on Literature —— The MAN'YŌSHŪ (mid-8th century), the earliest anthology of Japanese poetry, already includes indications that poets thought about their craft. The headnote "Allegorical Poem" indicates the conscious use of the technique of allegory, while prefatory notes like "Pouring Forth My Emotion" and "Expressing My Thoughts by Allusion" suggest an underlying concept of poetry as emotional expression. Other notes refer to the purpose of verse writing: in one case the poet explains that he wrote his poem to admonish an acquaintance, and in another instance poetry is said to "console the deep gloom of a lonely traveler and relieve the melancholy of a languishing lover." All these ideas and attitudes originated in China, where literary criticism had developed early. The Confucian classics, particularly the poetic anthology *Shijing (Shih ching)* and the expressive theory of literature expounded therein, exerted considerable formative influence on early Japanese literary attitudes. Evidence of thorough familiarity with the particulars of Chinese versification is provided in KŪKAI's *Bunkyō hifuron,* a detailed and voluminous study in Chinese of the poetic theory of the Six Dynasties period (220–618) and the early part of the Tang (T'ang; 618–907) period.

The first treatise on Japanese poetics appeared in 772. Written in Chinese, *Kakyō hyōshiki* by Fujiwara no Hamanari (724–790) discussed the origin, form, style, prosody, and purpose of Japanese poetry. Hamanari drew heavily on Chinese poetics, speaking even of rhymes that do not exist in Japanese verse, and attempted to apply Chinese-style designations of poetic styles and "diseases" (defects) to *waka.* Although his direct application of Chinese poetics to Japanese verse was less than successful, Hamanari's work, as the first systematic attempt to apply critical standards to native verse, provided a precedent for later generations of theorists.

Ideals of Heian Court Poetry —— Japanese poets became increasingly aware of their national identity in the Heian period (794–1185). Following the 9th-century vogue for Chinese verse, *waka* began to enjoy renewed popularity and prestige, and the first major piece of literary criticism written in Japanese, the Kana Preface to the KOKIN-SHŪ by KI NO TSURAYUKI (872?–945), appeared in the early 10th century. Though the author was once again indebted to Chinese poetics, he nonetheless stressed the native tradition of Japanese poetry, discussing its basic nature, tracing its origin and history, classifying its styles, and commenting on the works of the Six Poetic Geniuses (see ROKKASEN). As poetic principles, spontaneity of verse writing and harmony between emotion *(kokoro)* and expression *(kotoba)* were highly valued. In arguing his points, Tsurayuki made great use of vegetation imagery, partly to compare verse writing to the natural growth of plants, and partly to hint at a harmonious vision of the world which encompassed both the animate and the inanimate. Harmony was also a guiding principle for appraising poetic styles: the most desirable was a well-balanced style, a style neither overly emotional nor overly intellectual.

The ideals of poetry advanced by Tsurayuki provided the standard norms for *waka* criticism throughout the rest of the Heian period, with later refinements and elaborations by FUJIWARA NO KINTŌ (966–1041) and MINAMOTO NO TOSHIYORI (1055?–1129). In general, poetics grew more and more aesthetically oriented, valuing the creation of beauty more highly than the expression of emotion. Freshness and novelty were increasingly stressed, since *waka,* confined within the boundaries of court life, tended to become hackneyed in theme. Furthermore, later critics preferred indirection and understatement (YOJŌ) in diction. Kintō, for example, placed poems embodying this technique in the highest rank in his *Waka kuhon* (Nine Stages of Waka). Admiration of obliquity helped pave the way for medieval poetics, which attached high value to brevity, terseness, and suggestive overtones.

Defense of Fiction —— With the rise of MONOGATARI BUNGAKU in the Heian period, appraisals, generally negative, of the nature of prose fiction began to appear in various writings. Fictional tales were considered primarily for the amusement and entertainment of court ladies who had many tedious hours to kill. Filled with unearthly characters and fanciful events, an entertaining tale was thought to include any number of "lies." From both the Confucian and Buddhist points of view, such tales were deficient in moral purpose.

The first major attempt to defend fiction occurs in the greatest of all Heian tales, the TALE OF GENJI. Using the hero of the tale as her mouthpiece, the author MURASAKI SHIKIBU convincingly refuted contemporary charges against prose fiction. In her view, "lies" found in a good tale are different from ordinary lies because they embody imaginative truth. Characters and events which appear in fiction originate in the factual world, but are all recast and rearranged so as to support the purpose of the tale. A fictional story can be more valuable than a book of history because it deals with the internal, rather than external, realities of human life. In this respect it resembles a religious parable which features persons and events that have no place in history but nevertheless embody truth and help the reader to distinguish between good and evil. In Murasaki Shikibu's argument, then, a tale can have a moral purpose not unlike the Buddhist scriptures, since it is able to present truth in an imaginative guise.

Because Murasaki Shikibu's defense of fiction appears unobtrusively in her tale, her argument had little effect on literary criticism in the centuries that immediately followed. Attacks on *monogatari* from a moralistic viewpoint persisted and even intensified as Buddhism grew more influential in the Kamakura (1185–1333) and Muromachi (1333–1568) periods. Murasaki Shikibu herself was popularly believed to be suffering in hell for having told many "lies" in the *Tale of Genji.* On the other hand, some medieval admirers of *monogatari* deified Murasaki Shikibu in the belief that she had written the famous tale by divine inspiration, dreaming of the story as she dozed at a temple.

Serious studies of *monogatari* were produced by some of Murasaki's admirers. Certain poets who felt that a careful reading of Heian tales was a prerequisite for writing respectable *waka* annotated the *Tale of Genji* and other classics of fiction. Historians, who considered themselves storytellers as well, sometimes presented discussions of *monogatari,* as witnessed in the ŌKAGAMI (ca 1119?) and IMAKAGAMI (1170), two narrative historical tales. This tradition also produced the MUMYŌ-ZŌSHI, a discussion of many classical tales which dates from the early years of the Kamakura period. Its approach is largely impressionistic and emotional, with an underlying sense of longing for the lost glory of Heian culture. The discussion of the *Tale of Genji* is the most detailed, describing the reader's response to each chapter and expressing likes and dislikes for the leading characters.

Medieval Waka Aesthetics —— The main subject of medieval literary criticism, however, was not prose fiction but *waka,* with Fujiwara no Shunzei (FUJIWARA NO TOSHINARI; 1114–1204) as its central figure. A court noble who personally witnessed the collapse of the Heian aristocracy, Shunzei evolved a poetic aesthetic distinguished by its underlying pessimism. Some of the poetic ideals he advocated, such as *aware* ("gentle melancholy," see MONO NO AWARE) and SABI ("loneliness") reflect disillusionment with the sad realities of contemporary society; while others, such as *take takashi* ("lofty seriousness") and *yūgen* ("mystery and depth"), suggest romantic longing for the glory that had long passed. Shunzei was also attracted to the scheme of salvation offered by Buddhism, and his literary aims often acquired religious overtones.

Shunzei's poetics was adopted by his son, Fujiwara no Teika (FUJIWARA NO SADAIE; 1162–1241), with some significant modifications. Teika had a penchant for a more colorful, albeit unearthly, beauty. In his early years he favored the poetic ideal of *en* or *yōen* ("ethereal charm"), a dreamy beauty that lay far beyond terrestrial realities of human life. Where his father was religious, Teika was aesthetic. His prime concern was sensory beauty. Though he later advocated the ideal of *ushin* ("conviction of feeling") in his major critical work *Maigetsushō,* Teika stressed aesthetic sensitivity to poetic subjects over expression of personal emotion, thus contributing to the general trend away from Tsurayuki's advocacy of poetry as the vehicle of personal lyricism.

This same tendency can be observed in the literary theory of another major critic, KYŌGOKU TAMEKANE (1254–1332), Teika's great-grandson. In an essay on poetry known as *Tamekane Kyō wakashō* he urged that a poet at work should "become one with the subject, discover its true essence and feel its manifestations; when his mind responds to it, he should submerge this response deep in his soul, then give words to it." Clearly this is an antilyrical type of creative process minimizing the role of personal emotion in verse writing. Though Tamekane was known as an admirer of the *Man'yōshū,* he did not escape the influence of the contemporary trend against lyricism.

In addition to Shunzei, Teika, and Tamekane, a number of other medieval critics wrote treatises on the art of *waka.* Notable among them were Emperor GO-TOBA (1180–1239), who favored more lyrical poetry than Teika; KAMO NO CHŌMEI (1156?–1216), who advocated *waka* with rich overtones; and SHŌTETSU (1381–1459), who prized the mysterious beauty of *yūgen.* Altogether their critical writings rendered the Japanese concept of poetry markedly more complex and subtle than before, especially in defining the aesthetic effects created by *waka.* The overabundance of poetic criticism, however, inevitably led to academicism, idol worship and factional rivalries. Coupled with the decline of *waka* as a literary genre, *waka* poetics as such no longer held a central position in literary criticism by the 16th century.

Valuational Criticism in Poetry Contests —— The UTA-AWASE, or "poetry contest," is a unique form of literary criticism which began in the early Heian period and reached its peak in the early Kamakura period. In a usual contest, two *waka* written on the same theme were paired in a round, which was then refereed by a judge or team of judges. The number of rounds in a contest ranged from 10 to 1,500. In the early phase of its history the *uta-awase* was a kind of game played in a lighthearted mood, but it grew more serious with time, and winning a match came to be considered a great honor. Critics of high prestige were invited to serve as judges, and respected poets like Toshiyori, FUJIWARA NO MOTOTOSHI (ca 1056–1142?), Shunzei and Teika all served as referees at one time or another and wrote comments on the poems they judged. Such comments reflected their conceptions of the ideal poem; moreover, under the circumstances they had to be specific in justifying their judgment, which in turn helped to sharpen their critical acumen. If the end of all literary criticism is evaluation, the *uta-awase* by its very nature demanded that a critic do just that.

In some instances a competing poet felt dissatisfied with the judge's verdict and wrote a letter of protest. The most famous case is that of KENSHŌ (fl 1161–1207), a participant in a large contest held in 1195. His long letter, addressed to the presiding judge Shunzei, focused on the love poems he had contributed, including one verse with the ocean "where whales are hunted" as its principal image. Shunzei had passed an unfavorble verdict on the poem, saying that the image of the whale was too frightening for inclusion in court poetry. Kenshō vehemently protested, arguing that no reader would be frightened by a whale in a poem, and that, indeed, poems in the *Man'yōshū* contained such imagery. The controversy had in part to do with factional rivalries; still, such an instance as this well illustrates the danger of subjectivism in impressionistic criticism. Poetry contests did, however, contribute a great deal to the scrutiny of the nature of poetic beauty which critics often discussed only vaguely in their treatises.

The history of *uta-awase* reached a high point when Emperor Go-Toba, then in retirement, sponsored a contest known as the *Sen gohyakuban uta-awase* in 1201. Three thousand *waka* by 30 leading contemporary poets were gathered and paired in 1,500 rounds with Go-Toba, Shunzei, Teika, Kenshō, and 5 others serving as judges. The result was a large collection of excellent poems with critical commentary by eminent poets which casts light on the state of contemporary poetry criticism.

Uta-awase declined in the late medieval period as they became ever more institutionalized. Later, when *haikai* became popular, HAIKU contests began to be held, but as literary criticism they never matured to the extent *waka* competitions did. Poetry competition as a form of literary criticism had exhausted much of its potential by the 13th century.

Renga and Structural Principles —— In the 14th and 15th centuries poetic criticism began to focus more on the newly popular *renga* (linked verse) than on *waka*. By its very nature *renga* promoted literary criticism: a verse form with multiple authorship, it required that every participant be a poet as well as a critic, scrutinizing his colleagues' contributions to their joint poem. A number of rules on composition were formulated to curb the poets' individuality and guarantee their teamwork, and these rules constituted the framework of *renga* criticism.

The most distinctive feature of *renga* criticism arises from the art of progression—the method of linking one stanza to another. Since two successive stanzas of a *renga* were normally composed by two different poets, there had to be some agreement between participants on the principle of linking lest the poem lose its structural unity. Various techniques of linkage were included in the standard repertory, each with a specific designation such as "Explicative Linking," "Allusive Linking," "Narrative Linking," "Linking through Words," or "Linking through Unusual Association." Rule makers supplied examples to define and illustrate each method. Artful progression was most highly appreciated in *renga*, and no other type of literary criticism in Japan explored the problem of structural unity in such detail.

Aesthetic ideals of *renga* differed somewhat among the major critics. NIJŌ YOSHIMOTO (1320–88), who prized the graceful beauty of Heian *waka*, advocated elegance in both subject matter and style. SHINKEI (1406–75), a Buddhist monk, emphasized the poet's ability to appreciate the aesthetic impact of desolate scenery, and he favored verses that evoked a lonely, tranquil beauty. SŌGI (1421–1502), a versatile *renga* poet, seemed to admire a variety of aesthetic styles of *waka* from the *Man'yōshū* to the SHIN KOKINSHŪ (1205). In general, *renga* critics' ideals resembled, with slight modifications, those of earlier *waka* poetics. They made extensive use of

the latter's vocabulary, employing such terms as *miyabi* (courtly elegance), *yūgen,* and *yojō.* If *renga* was an outgrowth of *waka* in form, it was so in terms of literary aesthetics as well.

The Art of the Nō —— Theoretical and critical remarks on drama began to appear for the first time during the 14th century, when the Nō attained its maturity as a theatrical art. A number of treatises were written by actors who wished to hand down the secrets of their trade to their heirs. The works of ZEAMI (1363–1443) and KOMPARU ZENCHIKU (1405–70?) are the most outstanding examples, though from the standpoint of literary criticism they include a number of marginal materials. While Zeami tended to be either excessively pedagogic or technical, Zenchiku, going to the opposite extreme, at times became excessively abstract. Yet, particularly in their concern with the aesthetic effects of acting, Zeami and Zenchiku approached the views of medieval *waka* critics concerned with the affective aspects of poetry.

Zeami's massive writings on the art of the Nō centered on three basic principles: imitation, *yūgen,* and sublimity. Holding the view that acting is basically mimicry *(monomane),* he heavily emphasized the importance of verisimilitude in the Nō. Yet he was also concerned with the aesthetic effect of mimicry, which he termed the "flower." In Zeami's terminology, the purpose of a Nō performance is to cause a beautiful flower to bloom on the stage. Of the many kinds of "flowers," he most highly admired the flower of *yūgen,* which, at least in his early years, implied a lovely, graceful beauty. An actor impersonating an old man is urged to do so in such a way as to create a lovely impression; Zeami suggests such beauty by the metaphor "blossoms on a dead tree." Zeami's concept of *yūgen* changed over time, so much so that he later employed a different word, sublimity, in his advocacy of the beauty of age, dignity, austerity, and mystery.

Because in his day leading actors also composed the plays in which they performed, Zeami wrote on the art of the playwright as well. For the material of a play he recommended Heian tales. Some of the heroines of the *Tale of Genji* were considered particularly suitable as leading characters in the Nō. As for structure, Zeami favored the format of "introduction" *(jo),* "development" *(ha),* and "finale" *(kyū),* a three-part pattern borrowed from GAGAKU court music. A play was also required to have two climaxes, one literary and the other theatrical. Zeami's unique concept of the denouement is related to the double nature of the Nō as both literature and a performing art.

The treatises of Zenchiku, Zeami's son-in-law, are characterized by his attempt to integrate the art of the Nō with Buddhism on the one hand and *waka* poetics on the other. From Buddhism he derived the scheme of "the six wheels and one drop of dew," which he used to explain the way in which the invisible essence of the Nō would manifest itself in visible form through the actor's body. In his opinion, a Nō performance of the highest quality is as transparent and as tasteless as water, yet inclusive of all the colors and tastes on earth, much like the Buddhist concept of the void. Zenchiku's idea of the Nō resembled *waka* poetics in that he considered the actor's bodily movement a form of emotional expression. In his view, a person with an intense feeling normally vented it in poetry, but when the emotion became even more intense he began to move his hands and feet in a dancelike motion. "*Waka* is formless dance, and dance is wordless *waka,*" remarked Zenchiku in *Kabu zuinō ki.* Moreover, since a Nō play usually included both *waka* and dance, he urged young actors to become well versed in the 31-syllable verse form. All in all, Zenchiku's scheme to explain the art of the Nō in terms of Buddhism and poetics was, while not entirely successful, a daring experiment rarely attempted before or since.

Neither Zeami nor Zenchiku said much about the art of KYŌGEN, a comic interlude performed between two Nō plays. Ōkura Toraakira (1587–1662; see ŌKURA SCHOOL), himself a *kyōgen* actor, tried to fill the gap in a treatise which dealt exclusively with that art form. His famous remark, "Nō transforms the unreal into the real; *kyōgen,* the real into the unreal," tersely suggests the difference between the Nō as symbolic drama and *kyōgen* as satirical comedy. He stressed the importance of the "real" in *kyōgen* and warned against the actor's attempt to solicit the audience's laughter through unnatural gestures. He made that point particularly well in a didactic *waka*:

> Making an odd gesture
> To catch the spectator's eye
> Is an ugly act, indeed.
> It is like a normal man's
> Temporarily becoming a cripple.

Ōkura's discussion of the comic theater consequently says less about the comic than about theater, and often resembles the theories of Zeami, whom he highly admired.

Poetics of Haikai and Haiku——Soon after *haikai* became independent of *renga* in the 16th century, remarks on its nature and art began to appear. With its popularization in the subsequent centuries, an enormous number of books and essays were written by *haikai* masters who gave instruction in the craft. Many of these writings were either pedagogic guidebooks explaining rules and techniques, or polemical treatises defending a given school or faction within the *haikai* circle. Although *haikai* critics had a tendency to become overly concerned with trivial details, some dealt squarely with the fundamental problems of poetics, borrowing extensively from *waka* and *renga* criticism at first, but gradually advancing new theories of their own. By the middle of the Edo period (1600–1868) the poetics of *haikai* had become well established as a branch of literary criticism.

BASHŌ (1644–94) laid the foundation for the poetics of *haikai* and haiku, though he himself wrote no elaborate treatise. According to his disciple MUKAI KYORAI (1651–1704), Bashō's central poetic principle was built around a lonely beauty called *sabi*, which entails a sad but resigned recognition of man's mortality against the background of nature's everlasting cycle. In his last years Bashō proposed another poetic ideal, *karumi* ("lightness"), a more lighthearted mood arising from verses on the ordinary lives of ordinary men. A Buddhistic endeavor for spiritual detachment while living amidst the mire of this world was latent in Bashō's aesthetic. Poetics and religion were closely interrelated in Bashō's literary thought, though his eagerness to unite the two resulted in a painful dilemma at times.

While demonstrating high regard for Bashō's poetics, BUSON (1716–84) chose to place poetry in a sphere far removed from actual life. His ideal of poetry was distinguished by his insistence on *rizoku*, or "detachment from the mundane." In Buson's opinion, this detachment was best attained by reading the classics of China and Japan, for through books the poet would be able to roam a world distant in time and space, forgetting the frustrating realities of life. Buson, too, failed to write any lengthy essay on poetics, but his practice in verse writing well supported his idea of *rizoku* and helped propagate it among his followers.

Other notable *haikai* critics include UEJIMA ONITSURA (1661–1738), who valued sincerity in verse writing; HATTORI TOHŌ (1657–1730), who helped to interpret and propagate Bashō's teachings; KAGAMI SHIKŌ (1665–1731), who did the same in a markedly more dogmatic manner; MORIKAWA KYOROKU (1656–1715), who was interested in the juxtapositional technique of haiku; and ISSA (1763–1827), who considered *haikai* largely a vehicle for emotional expression. Some interesting insights into the art of haiku also appear in the works of lesser or unknown masters. One such work, *Haikai uya-muya no seki* (1764), of unknown authorship, explains by specific examples the "correct" way of composing a haiku:

> False: The string snapped.
> The paper kite
> Became a cloud.
> True: The string snapped.
> The paper kite
> Fell from the clouds.
> Correct: The string snapped.
> The paper kite
> Did not become a cloud.

Since haiku is such a brief verse form, critics were able to cite a number of instructive examples like the above, to support their contentions, thus avoiding vague or abstract argument.

Jōruri and Kabuki Criticism——Dramatic criticism in the Edo period dealt almost exclusively with JŌRURI and KABUKI. Writings on the art of these plebeian theaters did not on the whole, however, attain a high level of sophistication as literary criticism. Unlike the Nō, *jōruri* and kabuki were primarily entertainment for the masses and required less artistic finesse. In the case of kabuki, spectators were interested less in the literary qualities of the play than in the actors' physical appeal. As printing techniques advanced, there appeared many booklets (*yakusha hyōbanki*) evaluating famous actors and their recent performances, but these are not very interesting as literary criticism. More valuable are records of casual remarks made by actors and playwrights.

One of the famous instances of the latter is the case of the playwright CHIKAMATSU MONZAEMON (1653–1724), whose random comments on the art of *jōruri* have been recorded in the preface to a book annotating puppet plays, *Naniwa miyage* (1738). Chikamatsu's observation that "art lies in the thin margin between the real and the unreal" well expressed his stand on the question of literary verisimilitude. Chikamatsu's remarks also demonstrate his use of *giri* (obligation) as a dramatic principle. He thought that a high dramatic tension could be created when the play's main character was torn between love *(ninjō)* and social obligation (see GIRI AND NINJŌ). Although Chikamatsu elaborated on neither of these points, his remarks are highly instructive when viewed in connection with his oeuvre.

In the field of kabuki criticism, *Yakusha rongo* (1776; tr *Actors' Analects*, 1969), compiled by Hachimonjiya Jishō (d 1745), includes some revealing comments and accounts concerning kabuki acting. The concept of realism in the kabuki is suggested, for instance, in a remark by the actor SAKATA TŌJŪRŌ (1647–1709) that a performer should copy the real-life model in all cases except when cast in a beggar's role, in which case he should do the copying "roughly." How eager Tōjūrō himself was in his attempt to copy reality is revealed in an episode in which the famous actor, cast in an adulterer's role, tried to commit adultery in real life just to see how an unfaithful husband would feel.

Gezairoku (1801), by Nyūgatei Ganyū, probably to be identified with Namiki Shōzō II (d 1807), contains various pieces of advice for the kabuki playwright. On composing a play based on an actual love suicide, for instance, the playwright is advised to go to the scene of death and talk to witnesses, but to incorporate a bit of groundless rumor in his plot as well. In discussing the writing of a historical play, Nyūgatei introduced the concepts of "vertical" and "horizontal" plots, the former providing the historical setting and the latter supplying the dramatic action. In other matters as well, the author's advice is more practical than theoretical, a factor which is at once the book's strength and weakness.

Jōruri and kabuki, together with other genres of Edo popular literature (see GESAKU), gave birth to several new aesthetic ideals. Most notable were the aesthetics of IKI AND SUI, referring to a chic, urbane, sensual type of beauty deeply rooted in contemporary urban life. Although theater critics did not elaborate on abstract aesthetic notions, their reviews of kabuki performances and actors were informed by these popular values. Edo townsmen took pride in being unpretentious; writing a formal treatise perhaps seemed a bit too conceited an act to them.

Didactic Theories——Didactic views of literature gained prominence in the Edo period, mainly due to the government's endorsement of Neo-Confucianism (see SHUSHIGAKU) as its official school of thought. From early times Confucian scholars had considered literature a means of admonishing rulers and spreading virtue among the ruled. This notion was espoused by most Neo-Confucian followers in Japan, in whose view the merit of a literary work was in direct proportion to the amount of moral edification it offered the reader. At the hands of didactic theorists, literature came to be viewed solely as a means to an end.

A typical Neo-Confucian view of literature is embodied in Andō Tameakira's (1659–1716) study of the *Tale of Genji*. Tameakira viewed all the amorous adventures ascribed to the novel's characters as counterexamples of proper conduct; the sad destiny of the characters in the novel demonstrated to the reader why he should refrain from similar romantic pursuits. Other Neo-Confucian scholars who had more respect for the famed Heian classic attempted to justify its content. Some, like HAYASHI RAZAN (1583–1657), recognized a redeeming virtue in the beauty of Murasaki Shikibu's prose style, while others, like KUMAZAWA BANZAN (1619–91), suggested that the amorous episodes could be viewed as a means of elucidating the workings of human emotion. In general, scholars belonging to more humanistic factions of Neo-Confucianism took the latter attitude and were consequently more understanding of the *Tale of Genji* as a work of literature.

Many writers of popular fiction in the late Edo period themselves sided with the didactic viewpoint. Most representative was BAKIN (1767–1848), who once remarked that in prose fiction the writer's aim lies "simply in presenting the truth about human feelings so as to promote virtue." Indeed, the eight heroic *samurai* described in his masterpiece NANSŌ SATOMI HAKKENDEN symbolize eight Confucian virtues. Another writer of popular fiction, SHIKITEI SAMBA (1776–1822), prefaced his *Ukiyoburo* with the remark "The most efficient way to teach moral lessons is to record the accounts of people at the public bath." Samba's idea may have derived more from SHINGAKU ("Heart Learning") than from Neo-Confucianism, for Shingaku teachers liked to expound their messages by telling entertaining stories. "If you look closely," said one Shingaku leader, "you will find a moral even in a popular song." Whatever their orientation, popular writers of the Edo period knew full well that the masses liked to be entertainingly edified, and they gladly embraced a literary theory which conveniently accommodated their profession.

Kokugaku Scholars and Their Literary Theories —— KOKU-GAKU (National Learning), which arose in the 17th century and reached its peak in the century that followed, profoundly affected the evolution of literary criticism in Japan. Two main contributions resulted from this movement. First, Kokugaku scholars' intense interest in the ancient Japanese classics promoted a study of historical linguistics, which in turn helped develop textual criticism. They annotated such books as the KOJIKI and the Man'yōshū with a degree of exacting scholarship unknown in the previous age. Second, their predilection for primitive culture led them to emphasize the role of emotion in creative writing. Ardent nationalists, they disliked Chinese thinkers who placed so much emphasis on the intellect; a literary work seemed best to them when it bared the author's inmost heart in unadorned language. Under the influence of Kokugaku, literary criticism became noticeably more humanistic.

KEICHŪ (1640–1701) was the earliest major scholar who viewed literature from a Kokugaku vantage point. A monk of the Shingon sect, he studied Japanese classics with an ascetic's rigor and produced voluminous textual studies. Their value is mainly linguistic and bibliographical, but critical comments scattered throughout suggest he sought in the ancient classics spontaneous manifestations of human nature unrefined by latter-day culture. This view was further elaborated by later Kokugaku scholars.

KAMO NO MABUCHI (1697–1769) also wrote a number of textual commentaries on the Japanese classics and helped promote historical linguistics. His main contribution lay, however, in his theoretical writings centering on makoto ("sincerity") and masuraoburi ("manliness"). In his aesthetics makoto meant the straightforward expression of true feeling unhampered by intellectual or moral concerns. Masuraoburi, as opposed to taoyameburi ("femininity"), sprang from the vigorous, stout heart of primitive man as expressed in the poetry of the Man'yōshū. According to Mabuchi, later poets lost sight of manliness and wrote verses which were predominantly feminine, a tendency which to him represented a degradation of poetry.

MOTOORI NORINAGA (1730–1801), a disciple of Mabuchi, modified his teacher's theory by de-emphasizing masculinity. He thought human feelings were ultimately effeminate: even the bravest samurai, he said, would think of his wife and children as he lay dying on the battlefield. Norinaga's famous concept of mono no aware is noticeably more feminine than Mabuchi's masuraoburi in its implications. Norinaga's stand also enabled him to effectively defend the Tale of Genji from its Neo-Confucian attackers, since all the amorous episodes in the tale could be interpreted as a means to demonstrate the workings of mono no aware. He also defended the artifice of Heian and post-Heian waka against Mabuchi's attack by remarking that later poets, who had lost sight of makoto, were justified in trying to compensate for this loss by means of verbal artistry. Norinaga's literary theory was at once more comprehensive and more complex than Mabuchi's. His extensive study of the Kojiki also supplied a more philosophical flavor.

FUJITANI NARIAKIRA (1738–79), primarily a linguist, contributed to Japanese literary criticism by introducing an unusually analytical approach. Analyzing the psychological process of writing a poem, he identified four phases: "the realm," "the theme," "the form," and "the finish." The first phase was subdivided into "subjective" and "objective" realms; the second phase, into "major" and "minor" themes. He combined these concepts with many other original ideas in his study of waka, departing radically from traditional poetics. He died, however, before he had time to present his unique approach in a systematic form.

KAGAWA KAGEKI (1768–1843) resembled Mabuchi in his high regard for makoto, but differed from the latter in his attempt to equate truth with beauty. According to him, hidden truth was transformed into beauty when it embodied itself in words with beautiful rhythm. Thus in Kageki's poetics rhythm assumed primary importance, for it was an agent which made intangible truth accessible to the human senses. Unlike most Kokugaku scholars, Kageki was a poet of considerable talent, and his waka theory exerted a measure of influence on practicing poets of his time.

Among other Kokugaku scholars who wrote on the nature of literature were OZAWA ROAN (1723–1801), who advocated realistic poetry which expressed plain feelings in plain words; HIRATA ATSUTANE (1776–1843), who extended Norinaga's theory in a direction more extremely Shintoistic; and FUJITANI MITSUE (1768–1823), Nariakira's son, who elaborated on his father's theory with more emphasis on Shintoism and on the cathartic function of poetry. Some Kokugaku scholars engaged in literary controversies, producing numerous polemical tracts in the process. They were, however, in basic agreement in recognizing the importance of premoral human feelings as the basic material of literature. In their opinion, the inmost feelings of a man as a free individual were to be given the highest regard, and literary works which depicted these feelings could make an invaluable contribution to society. A trend toward modern humanism is evident in Kokugaku views of literature.

Conclusion —— The history of literary criticism in premodern Japan can be broadly viewed as a movement from primitive expressionism in the early centuries to various types of aestheticism in the medieval period, then to humanistic expressionism in the late Edo period. In ancient times lyric poetry was the dominant literary mode, and as a result those who wrote on the nature of literature paid close attention to the relationship between the poet and the poem. During the late Heian and medieval times, literary artists aimed at the creation of beauty by means of waka, renga, or Nō. Literary criticism of this time inevitably focused on the aesthetic impact created by a work of art. With the approach of the modern age, however, men of letters became newly aware of the expressive function of literature and began to harbor a romantic yearning for the primitive age when people voiced their powerful emotion in simple language.

Premodern Japanese concepts of literature share many basic assumptions with Western literary theories. The Platonic concept of the muse, the Aristotelian idea of mimesis, and the Horatian notion of the function of poetry are all present in different guises. Literary aesthetics in premodern Japan, however, does possess several distinguishing features. One such characteristic is an antirealistic tendency: partly due to the influence of Buddhism, mimetic theories in Japan tended to encourage a representation of the invisible essence rather than the visible surface, and that trend continued even after the decline of Buddhism. Another feature is antirationalism. Lacking the Hellenist tradition of the West, Japanese theorists were apt to adopt a mystical approach toward literature. Medieval aesthetic ideals in particular centered around vague, ethereal qualities. The penchant for ambiguity also resulted in a fondness for brevity of form and expression, and clear delineation became almost synonymous with shallowness of perception. As regards structural methods, Japanese theorists abhorred a logically conceived structure, favoring instead a unity achieved through tone, imagistic association, and mood. As a result, literary criticism often became impressionistic in both the complimentary and derogatory senses of the term. These and other features of literary aesthetics in premodern Japan, developing independently of the Western tradition, form a unique contribution to the transcultural definition of literature.

■ —— Robert Brower and Earl Miner, Japanese Court Poetry (1961). Hisamatsu Sen'ichi, Nihon bungaku hyōron shi (1936–50). Hisamatsu Sen'ichi, The Vocabulary of Japanese Aesthetics (1963). Kitazumi Toshio, Nihon no bungei ishiki (1962). Makoto Ueda, Literary and Art Theories in Japan (1967). Saitō Kiyoe, Nihon bungei shichō zenshi (1963). Yasuda Ayao, Nihon no geijutsu ron (1965, 1972).　　　　　Makoto UEDA

literary groups

PREMODERN PERIOD

The first literary groups in Japan were groups of poets of linked verse (renga; see RENGA AND HAIKAI), which formed from the latter half of the 13th to the 14th century. In linked poetry sessions, especially of long renga, from two to ten persons participated in the composition of a chain renga. This kind of group art required that participants share, to some extent, common cultural refinements, interests, artistic temperaments, and a sense of camaraderie. Consequently, renga practitioners organized into various literary groups by place of residence (Kyōto, Kamakura, Nara, etc) or by class standing (aristocrats, monks, warriors, commoners, etc); within these groups they formed still smaller social groups. Since each individual group drew up its own peculiar literary rules for renga composition, they were exclusivist by nature, and since social intercourse between classes was limited, these literary groups were, in the beginning, quite small.

In the 14th century, the priest GUSAI (1281?–1375?), who belonged to the commoner poets, and the aristocrat poet NIJŌ YOSHIMOTO (1320–88) joined together and cooperated in forming a *renga* poetry group that crossed class lines, with themselves at the center. Its charter members were a group of *renga* practitioners who numbered upwards of 450 poets. The group has been anthologized in the TSUKUBASHŪ (1356, Tsukuba Collection) compiled by Gusai and Nijō Yoshimoto. By the time of the compilation of the SHINSEN TSUKUBASHŪ (1495, New Tsukuba Collection), over a century later, it had developed into a large group, led by such *renga* masters as Ōuchi Masahiro (d 1495), SŌGI (1421–1502), SHŌHAKU (1443–1527), and SŌCHŌ (1448–1532). With the decline of *renga*, a companion form of linked poetry, *haikai no renga* (comic linked verse, which eventually developed into HAIKU) became the mainstream literary art form. *Haikai* was also a group art, with the same essential elements as *renga*. *Haikai* poets proceeded to form new literary groups.

MATSUNAGA TEITOKU (1571–1653) is regarded as the originator of *haikai,* and the so-called Teimon school of *haikai* with Teitoku at its center was the most prestigious literary group in the country from the 1620s to the 1680s. Its adherents included YASUHARA TEISHITSU (1610–73), Kaedei Ryōtoku (1585–1679), Yamamoto Saimu (1606–78), KITAMURA KIGIN (1624–1705), Takase Baisei (1613–1701), Saitō Tokugen (1559–1647), Sugiki Moichi (d 1667), MATSUE SHIGEYORI (1602–80), NONOGUCHI RYŪHO (1595–1669), and others. The school was centered in Kyōto; there were branches in Ōsaka, Edo (now Tōkyō), and other cities and towns. The *Enokoshū* (Puppy Collection), a collection of *haikai* verse by Teimon school devotees published in 1633, included pieces by 178 poets; the *Gyokkaishū* (Jeweled Sea Collection) of 1651 contained verses by 658 poets from 74 different areas.

The next major school of *haikai* was the DANRIN SCHOOL. It was established by NISHIYAMA SŌIN (1605–82) and had many followers. These included Ihara SAIKAKU (1642–93), better known for his prose fiction, and OKANISHI ICHŪ (1639–1711) in Ōsaka; Tashiro Shōi (dates unknown) in Edo; and Sōhonji Takamasa (dates unknown) and Tanaka Tsunenori (d 1682) in Kyōto. Branches were also established in Ise (now part of Mie Prefecture), Sakai (now in Ōsaka Prefecture), and elsewhere. The *daimyō* of the Iwaki Taira domain (now part of Fukushima Prefecture), Naitō Yoshiyasu (d 1685), was fond of *haikai* and enjoyed associating with poets of both the Teimon and Danrin schools. He invited Sōin, Shigeyori, Kigin, and others to his house on several occasions. Naitō was a patron of other literary pursuits as well. The salon of writers and poets centered around him constituted a new form of literary group.

The Danrin school was in turn succeeded by the Bashō school, organized by Matsuo BASHŌ (1644–94) about 1677. The so-called Ten Disciples of Bashō, including such early stalwarts of the Bashō style as TAKARAI KIKAKU (1661–1707) and HATTORI RANSETSU (1654–1707) in Edo and MUKAI KYORAI (1651–1704) in Kyōto, firmly established themselves as poets. Two other Bashō disciples, Yamamoto Kakei (1648–1719) in Nagoya and Esa Shōhaku (1650–1722) in Ōmi Province (now Shiga Prefecture), also possessed considerable influence. The Bashō school, according to the *Bashō shosei zenden* (compiled 1818–29 and edited by Endō Hakujin), numbered some 430 disciples.

In the latter half of the 18th century the publishing industry, which had been developing slowly since the late 17th, grew rapidly. New kinds of literary groups were formed, centering around publishers and printers. Tsutaya Jūzaburō (1750–97), who published a popular line of illustrated fiction and picture books including SHAREBON, KIBYŌSHI, and NISHIKI-E, was the foremost publisher in Edo. Around him formed what might be called the Tsutaya group of writers and artists. Among its principal members were ŌTA NAMPO (1749–1823), KOIKAWA HARUMACHI (1744–89), SANTŌ KYŌDEN (1761–1816), Tegara no Okamochi (1735–1813; see HŌSEIDŌ KISANJI), Takizawa BAKIN (1767–1848), and JIPPENSHA IKKU (1765–1831). It also included such woodblock printmakers (UKIYO-E artists) as Kitagawa UTAMARO (1753–1806), Tōshūsai SHARAKU (active mid-1794–early 1795), and Katsushika HOKUSAI (1760–1849). Their works were published by Tsutaya, and they in turn furnished him with new ideas.

Another such group composed of both writers and artists revolved around the artist Suzuki HARUNOBU (1725?–70). Harunobu produced somewhere between 600 and 800 woodblock prints in a six-year period toward the end of his life. Behind him was a literary support group that included some 30 artists and writers, among them HIRAGA GENNAI (1728–80). These people supplied Harunobu

with ideas. The literary groups that supported these artists and printmakers competed for ideas and through exchanges and symposiums formed larger literary groups.

Scholars of traditional Chinese learning and practitioners of poetry and prose in Chinese also organized groups. Disciples of such representative figures as HATTORI NANKAKU (1683–1759), GION NANKAI (1677–1751), and YANAGAWA SEIGAN (1789–1858) in Edo and Emura Hokkai (1713–88), Minagawa Kien (1734–1807), and RAI SAN'YŌ (1781–1832) in Kyōto established literary groups. Similar groups appeared in outlying areas as well, like those established by the followers of KAN SAZAN (1748–1827) in Hiroshima and of HIROSE TANSŌ (1782–1856) in what is now Ōita Prefecture in Kyūshū. The disciples of Kien are said to have exceeded 3,000. Though the book and painting distribution gatherings held by writers like Bakin, Ōkubo Shibutsu (1767–1837; a writer of verse in Chinese), and Kikuchi Gozan (1776–1859), with their publishers acting as promoters, were chiefly a means of earning a livelihood, those who regularly attended the meetings constituted a group of men of letters and amateurs of art. There were some groups that assembled at eating and drinking establishments who were more interested in the pursuit of pleasure and amusement than in literature as a serious art. There was, for example, a group of painters and writers centered around SAKAI HŌITSU (1761–1828), younger brother of the lord of Himeji Castle, who was himself an accomplished painter and devotee of *haiku*. Associated with the district in which his Edo residence was located, they were known as the Shitaya group. They included the Confucian scholar KAMEDA BŌSAI (1752–1826), the writer-poet Ōta Nampo, and the painter TANI BUNCHŌ (1763–1840). Another group met regularly at the Shin Umeyashiki (today known as the Hyakkaen) in a garden opened by the antique dealer Sawara Kikuu (1762–1831). It included the popular fiction writer SHIKITEI SAMBA (1776–1822), the two National Learning (Kokugaku) scholar-poets KATŌ CHIKAGE (1735–1808) and MURATA HARUMI (1746–1811), and the poet Ōkubo Shibutsu.

MODERN PERIOD

Fiction —— The first literary group to appear after the collapse of the Tokugawa shogunate and subsequent establishment in 1868 of the Meiji government was the KEN'YŪSHA (Friends of the Inkstone). With the modernizing of Japan, literary circles came under the influence of newspapers and publishing companies, and many groups began to reflect the political and social changes of the time.

In fiction, the Ken'yūsha was the most influential literary group of the period. Founded in 1885 by a group of writers headed by OZAKI KŌYŌ (1867–1903), it soon gained influence over the literary policies of the YOMIURI SHIMBUN, a large national daily newspaper known for its authoritative literary section, and the HAKUBUNKAN and Shun'yōdō, two established Tōkyō publishing houses. Among the important early members of the Ken'yūsha were YAMADA BIMYŌ (1868–1910), KAWAKAMI BIZAN (1869–1908), and HIROTSU RYŪRŌ (1861–1928). The group was opposed to the use of fiction as a political medium and called for a return to popular prose styles of the late 18th and early 19th centuries. They deplored the superficial Westernization of Japanese literature and sought to revive interest in traditional Japanese forms. Eventually some 200 popular writers participated in Ken'yūsha literary activities, including IZUMI KYŌKA (1873–1939), TOKUDA SHŪSEI (1871–1943), TAYAMA KATAI (1872–1930), and NAGAI KAFŪ (1879–1959). The influence of this group reached its peak in the late 1890s. With the ascendancy of the Japanese school of naturalism in the early 1900s, the Ken'yūsha gradually lost strength, and with the death of its leader, Ozaki Kōyō, it finally dissolved.

In 1880, five years prior to the founding of the Ken'yūsha, the Seinen Bungaku Kai, a group led by journalist-critic TOKUTOMI SOHŌ (1863–1957), which advocated romanticism, had been formed. With the conclusion of the Russo-Japanese War of 1904–05, new literary groups formed in rapid succession. The Bungei Kyōkai was formed in 1905 by TSUBOUCHI SHŌYŌ (1859–1935) and SHIMAMURA HŌGETSU (1871–1918). It had as its goal the reformation of literature, the fine arts, religion, and the theater and was especially active in drama. In 1906 the so-called Mokuyōkai (Thursday Club) was established by disciples of the novelist NATSUME SŌSEKI (1867–1916) and met once a week at the home of their teacher. In 1908, in addition to the neo-romantic group Seichōkai, centered around OGAWA MIMEI (1882–1961), the PAN NO KAI (Pan Society), a band of aesthete artists, writers, and poets who were attracted to French symbolism, was organized. Among its early members were Ishii Hakutei (1882–1958), Yamamoto Kanae (1882–1946), KITAHARA HAKUSHŪ (1885–1942), and YOSHII ISAMU (1886–1960). In 1909 the

Bungei Kakushin Kai was formed as part of a growing antinaturalist movement. It was headed by Sasakawa Rimpū (1870–1949), Anezaki Chōfū (1873–1949), and MIYAKE SETSUREI (1860–1945). That same year the SHIRAKABA SCHOOL was founded by the Gakushūin (Peers' School; now Gakushūin University) group, a band of young writers, mostly aristocrats, who attacked naturalism and embraced a kind of Tolstoyan humanism. Led by MUSHANOKŌJI SANEATSU (1885–1961), the group included SHIGA NAOYA (1883–1976), NAGAYO YOSHIRŌ (1888–1961), SATOMI TON (b 1888), Kojima Kikuo (1887–1950), and YANAGI MUNEYOSHI (1889–1961). For over 10 years the group published the prestigious literary magazine Shirakaba. Eventually, with the growing popularity of the socialist movement, it gradually lost its appeal; however, during its heyday the Shirakaba school had great influence on young writers.

In the Taishō period (1912–26), around 1914–15 a group of writers associated with the magazine SHINSHICHŌ (New Currents of Thought), including AKUTAGAWA RYŪNOSUKE (1892–1927), KIKUCHI KAN (1888–1948), and HIROTSU KAZUO (1891–1968), became known as the "neorealist" school (it is sometimes referred to as the intellectual school). In 1919 the Kokumin Bungei Kai was organized. Members included OSANAI KAORU (1881–1928), KUBOTA MANTARŌ (1889–1963), and Miyake Shūtarō (1892–1967). In 1924 the literary magazine BUNGEI JIDAI (Literary Age) was launched. The writers who started it were called the SHINKANKAKU SCHOOL (School of New Sensibilities Impressions). Two of its better known members were YOKOMITSU RIICHI (1898–1947) and KAWABATA YASUNARI (1899–1972). Like the neorealist school, it is generally regarded as a kind of literary group rather than a close-knit school of writers. Finally, in 1926, the pupils of Tokuda Shūsei organized the Arakurekai.

At the beginning of the Shōwa period (1926–), Marxism was flourishing and dominated creative letters, but in 1930 an anti-Marxist group, following in the footsteps of the Shinkankaku school and calling itself the SHINKŌ GEIJUTSU HA (New Art school), vociferously declared a "new literary art movement" and formed a kind of writer's club called the Jūsan Kurabu. This group included Kawabata Yasunari, Nakamura Murao (1886–1949), IBUSE MASUJI (b 1898), and Yoshiyuki Eisuke (1906–40). In 1935 NAKANO SHIGEHARU (b 1902) and KUBOKAWA TSURUJIRŌ (1903–74) formed the Sancho Kurabu, which favored satiric literature. That same year the coterie known as the NIHON RŌMANHA (Japanese Romantic school), including KAMEI KATSUICHIRŌ (1907–66), YASUDA YOJŪRŌ (1910–81), and Haga Mayumi (b 1903), began publishing a magazine by the same name. With the rise of nationalism following the Manchurian Incident, the revival of National Learning (Kokugaku) in the next decade paved the way for the promotion of a "Japanist" literature. In 1937, following a proposal by Minister of Agriculture and Forestry ARIMA YORIYASU (1884–1957), Wada Tsutou (b 1900), SHIMAKI KENSAKU (1903–45), and others organized the Nōmin Bungaku Konwa Kai for the promotion of a Japanese agrarian literature in conformance with increasingly nationalist government policies. In 1939 the Shin'yōkai, led by HASEGAWA SHIN (1884–1963), was formed to perform the same function for popular literature. Meanwhile, two groups opposed to this government-led literary movement were formed, the Seinen Geijutsu Ha (Youth Art School) in 1940 and the Machine Poetiku (Matinée Poétique) in 1942. The former was led by Noguchi Fujio (b 1911) and Minamikawa Jun (1913–55), the latter by KATŌ SHŪICHI (b 1919) and FUKUNAGA TAKEHIKO (1918–79). They were totally without influence in the face of the overwhelming strength of militarism at the time.

After World War II new literary groups began forming in reaction to wartime events. In 1945 writers of the PROLETARIAN LITERATURE MOVEMENT established the Shin Nihon Bungaku Kai (New Japan Literature Society), which proclaimed a policy of noncooperation in war in the future. Among its central figures were Akita Ujaku (1883–1962), KURAHARA KOREHITO (b 1902), Nakano Shigeharu, and MIYAMOTO YURIKO (1899–1951). Also included as members at the beginning were Shiga Naoya, NOGAMI YAEKO (b 1885), Hirotsu Kazuo, MASAMUNE HAKUCHŌ (1879–1962), and MUROO SAISEI (1889–1962). Later, because of internal rifts among members and the Communist Party, some members withdrew and others split off into factions. In 1946 the Nihon Jidō Bungakusha Kyōkai, a national organization of writers and critics of children's literature, was established. By 1955 it had 296 members and the name was changed to Nihon Jidō Bungeika Kyōkai. About 1948 a group of sharply self-critical, rebellious, anti-establishment writers that included ISHIKAWA JUN (b 1899), DAZAI OSAMU (1909–48), SAKAGUCHI ANGO (1906–55), and ODA SAKUNOSUKE (1913–47) became known as the

Shin Gesaku Ha (New Burlesque School). This was not a consciously organized literary group (all were individualists) but a name bestowed on them collectively by literary critics and historians because of a certain shared element in their works—the theme of irreverence for established order, values, and ethics and a search for new identity in the turmoil of the postwar era. In 1955 the Kiroku Geijutsu no Kai, the first literary group to include writers, dramatists, artists, musicians, filmmakers, and even media broadcasters, was established. Among its writer members were NOMA HIROSHI (b 1915), ABE KŌBŌ (b 1924), HANADA KIYOTERU (1909–74), and Sasaki Kiichi (b 1914). In 1959 the Kindai Bungaku Kondan Kai, a friendship society of modern writers, was formed with over 120 members.

Tanka——In the field of TANKA poetry, a great many associations and societies came into existence, subdivided, and dissolved during the course of the Meiji period. Among these, some of the major early groups and the central poets associated with them were as follows: the Kagakukai (1892) and Asakasha (1893), both led by OCHIAI NAOBUMI (1861–1903); the Kagakukai (1896) headed by SASAKI NOBUTSUNA (1872–1963); the Negishi Tanka Kai (Negishi Tanka Society, 1898) founded by MASAOKA SHIKI (1867–1902), one of the principal figures in the development of modern tanka and haiku; the Ikazuchi Kai (1898) led by Ochiai Naobumi and ONOE SAISHŪ (1876–1957); and the Chikuhakukai (1898) also led by Sasaki Nobutsuna. In 1900 Ochiai formed yet another tanka group, the Akebonokai. That same year MYŌJŌ (Bright Star), the literary magazine of the Shinshisha (New Poetry Society) founded by YOSANO TEKKAN (1873–1935) in November 1899, began publishing.

The so-called Myōjō school flourished during the first decade of the new century, its romanticism greatly affecting poets such as YOSANO AKIKO (1878–1942), ISHIKAWA TAKUBOKU (1886–1912), and Kitahara Hakushū. In 1903 came the Shiragikukai, headed by Kaneko Kun'en (1876–1951). The Shazensōsha, led by Onoe Saishū, WAKAYAMA BOKUSUI (1885–1928), and MAEDA YŪGURE (1883–1951), and the Jūgatsukai, led by KUBOTA UTSUBO (1877–1967), were formed in 1905. In 1907, through the good offices of MORI ŌGAI (1862–1922), tanka poets from various fraternal associations started the Kanchōro Kakai. Among the participants were poets ITŌ SACHIO (1864–1913), Sasaki Nobutsuna, and SAITŌ MOKICHI (1882–1953).

In 1908 the followers of Masaoka Shiki under the leadership of Itō Sachio and Saitō Mokichi founded the ARARAGI school of tanka, upholding Shiki's dictum of "realism" (shajitsu shugi) and his preference for the straightforward, direct style of the 8th century poetry anthology MAN'YŌSHŪ. The mainstream Araragi realists, which numbered among their ranks KOIZUMI CHIKASHI (1886–1927), Ishihara Jun (1881–1947), SHIMAKI AKAHIKO (1876–1926), NAKAMURA KENKICHI (1889–1934), and TSUCHIYA BUMMEI (b 1890), were the most influential tanka group throughout the Meiji and Taishō periods and maintained this position into the postwar years of the Shōwa period.

The Kadankai, the first organization of tanka poets in Japan to cut across fraternal and school lines, was formed in 1918. It was headed by Saitō Mokichi, Sasaki Nobutsuna, Yoshii Isamu, and TOKI ZEMMARO (1885–1980). In 1925 the first colloquial language tanka association, the Shin Tanka Kyōkai (New Tanka Society) led by Ishihara Atsushi and Nishimura Yōkichi (1892–1959) was formed. In 1927 a new organization of tanka poets, the Nihon Kajin Kyōkai, was formed, which succeeded the already disbanded Kadankai. It had some 70 members, most of whom had been affiliated with the Kadankai, but it had negligible success and dissolved within about 10 years. In 1935, calling for a tanka revolution, the Shinkō Kajin Remmei, headed by Gotō Shigeru (b 1900), Maekawa Samio (b 1903), and Watanabe Junzō (1894–1972), was formed; it too dissolved within less than a year because of ideological infighting. That same year Kitahara Hakushū organized the Tama Tanka Kai, advocating a revival of the romantic spirit and a new symbolism; this group ended with Hakushū's death in 1942.

In 1936 the Nihon Kajin Kyōkai dissolved, and soon afterward the Dai Nihon Kajin Kyōkai was newly organized with Kitahara Hakushū, Tsuchiya Bummei, Toki Zemmaro, Kawada Jun (1882–1966), and Shaku Chōku (1887–1953; see ORIKUCHI SHINOBU) as its leading members. It had as its goal the development and elevation of the tanka establishment and the cultivation of mutual aid and friendship among members. In 1940 a splinter group of member poets with pronationalist tendencies provoked a split in the group, which caused it to disband. In 1941 the Dai Nihon Kajin Kai, centered around Tsuchiya Bummei, Kawada Jun, and Handa Ryōhei (1887–1945), was established, with the aim of promoting the war effort. In 1942 it was absorbed by the *tanka* division of the government-sponsored Nihon Bungaku Hōkoku Kai.

In 1945 the Shin Nihon Kajin Shūdan was established. It was opposed to factions and master-pupil relationships and advocated the popularization of *tanka* and elevation of the creative spirit of the common people. It was headed by Watanabe Junzō and Akagi Kensuke (b 1907) and began publishing the *Jimmin tanka,* a literary organ later renamed the *Shin Nihon tanka.* In 1946 an association of Tōkyō-area *tanka* poets known as the Tōkyō Kawa Kai was formed. It included Kubota Shōichirō (b 1908), Gotō Shigeru, SATŌ SATARŌ (b 1909), and Abe Shizue (b 1899). A group of centrist *tanka* poets, led by Kondō Yoshimi (b 1913) and Miya Shūji (b 1912), likewise organized the Shin Kajin Shūdan. Both groups dissolved two or three years later. In 1947 the Nihon Kajin Kurabu was established. It is the largest of the postwar *tanka* poet friendship associations and has some 2,000 members.

Haiku —— Among Meiji-period *haiku* circles, first was the Tsukubakai, a group of haiku poets and scholars formed in 1894, which included Ōno Shachiku (1872–1913), Sassa Seisetsu (1872–1917), and Sasakawa Rimpū (1870–1949). It was succeeded in 1895 by the Shūseikai under the leadership of Tsunoda Chikurei (1856–1919), Ōno Shachiku, and Itō Shōu (1859–1943). With the start of publication of HOTOTOGISU, a haiku magazine founded by Masaoka Shiki and TAKAHAMA KYOSHI (1874–1959) in 1899, the Hototogisu school was established. Early disciples included KAWAHIGASHI HEKIGOTŌ (1873–1937) and Naitō Meisetsu (1847–1926). This literary group continued through the Taishō and Shōwa periods and was still active in the early 1980s. It helped launch many prominent haiku poets on successful careers and has been one of the most powerful forces in the haiku world since its inception. It later spawned many Hototogisu-affiliated haiku societies.

In 1915 IIDA DAKOTSU (1885–1962) became editor of a successful local haiku magazine called *Ummo.* In 1920 a "new-style" haiku organization, the Kyōdai Haiku Kai, was formed. Its members included Hino Sōjō (1901–56), Suzuka Noburo (1887–1971), YAMAGUCHI SEISHI (b 1901), and MIZUHARA SHŪŌSHI (1892–1981). Kyōdai Haiku Kai poets later participated in the modern haiku movement of the late 1920s and early 1930s; the group eventually dissolved in 1940 under the growing military oppression of the period.

In 1928 a group of poets under the leadership of Mizuhara Shūōshi, who were opposed to the simple, unadorned objectivism and conservatism of the Hototogisu school, advocating instead subjective lyricism, broke from Hototogisu ranks and formed their own coterie. It took its name, Ashibi, from the name of the group's haiku magazine. A number of talented poets who shared Shūōshi's views, like Yamaguchi Seishi, joined the group, and though the group went its own separate way, it held to the fixed-season form and aesthetic tendency of haiku. Like Hototogisu, it spawned numerous Ashibi-affiliated groups. In 1946 poets from various prewar haiku societies like the Kyōdai Haiku Kai came together and formed the Shin Haikujin Remmei, one of whose primary goals was democratic haiku. It was headed by Ishibashi Tatsunosuke (1909–48) and Kuribayashi Issekiro (1894–1961). In 1947 a group of poets, critics, and scholars active at the forefront of haiku circles established the Gendai Haiku Kyōkai. Members included such highly regarded poets as Hino Sōjō, Yamaguchi Seishi, Akimoto Fujio (b 1901), and ISHIDA HAKYŌ (1913–69). It functioned to assist members in earning a living, provide recognition for new poets, and publish the group's literary organ.

Modern Poetry —— In the field of modern poetry in the Meiji period, the previously mentioned Shinshisha (New Poetry Society), founded by Yosano Tekkan in 1899, was a literary group of major importance. Its magazine *Myōjō,* with its European and romantic tendencies, was, as in the field of *tanka,* one of the most influential modern poetry journals of the period; it nurtured the poets who created Japanese modern poetry and carried its development into the Taishō period, in particular such poets as KAMBARA ARIAKE (1876–1952), SUSUKIDA KYŪKIN (1877–1945), TAKAMURA KŌTARŌ (1883–1956), and HAGIWARA SAKUTARŌ (1886–1942). The Shinshisha had branches throughout the country and lasted until 1949. In 1906 NOGUCHI YONEJIRŌ (1875–1947), newly returned from the United States, issued a call for a union of poetry groups and founded the Ayamekai, which brought together poets like DOI BANSUI (1871–1952; also known as Tsuchii Bansui), KAWAI SUIMEI (1874–1965), Kambara Ariake, and UEDA BIN (1874–1916). This group dissolved after less than a year, but its coterie magazine, *Aya-*

megusa, listed William Butler Yeats (1865–1939), Arthur Symons (1865–1945), and Thomas Hardy (1840–1927) as participating members. Among Japanese literary groups, the Ayamekai was probably the only one in which foreign writers and poets participated.

In 1907 Kawai Suimei, Kambara Ariake, and Ueda Bin founded the Shisōsha, and it became one of the bases of the colloquial language poetry movement. That same year a group of poets affiliated with Waseda University formed the Waseda Shisha. Among its members were Sōma Gyofū (1883–1950), MIKI ROFŪ (1889–1964), and Noguchi Ujō (1882–1945). It dissolved in 1909, and out of it was newly created the Jiyūshisha (Free Verse Society), whose early members included Hitomi Tōmei (1883–1924), YAMAMURA BOCHŌ (1884–1924), Fukuda Yūsaku (1886–1948), and Katō Kaishun (1885–1946).

The Taishō period saw modern poetry come to full development, and poets grouped and regrouped as various movements swept over the literary world. At the urging of Sangū Atsushi (1892–1967) and others, in 1917 the Shidankai was established as a literary cooperative comprised of poets unhindered by the tendency to factionalize. Its members included poets Kitahara Hakushū, KAWAJI RYŪKŌ (1888–1959), and HINATSU KŌNOSUKE (1890–1971). In all some 70 poets belonged to the Shidankai, and it was the largest association of poets in the Taishō period. In 1921 it broke up, and the Shinshikai was newly created. Shinshikai members included Sangū Atsushi, Kitahara Hakushū, Miki Rofū, HORIGUCHI DAIGAKU (1892–1981), and Taketomo Sōfū (1891–1954).

The first postwar modern poetry association was the Nihon Gendai Shijin Kai (Japan Modern Poets Society) established in 1950. It was a general association of poets with no ideological orientation and had as a goal the realization of cooperative activities by native and international poets. Among its more than 400 members were poets KITAGAWA FUYUHIKO (b 1900), KUSANO SHIMPEI (b 1903), MIYOSHI TATSUJI (1900–1964), and MURANO SHIRŌ (1901–75). That same year, at the suggestion of Sangū Atsushi and Masatomi Ōyō (1881–1967), the Nihon Shijin Kurabu was established, having as a goal the betterment of poetry and the promotion of international exchanges among poets.

Women's Groups —— Among specialized literary associations, a number of women's groups are worthy of mention. In 1928 a new women's magazine called *Nyonin geijutsu* began, which published only works by women writers. Its leading contributors, who were regarded as a kind of literary group, were Hasegawa Shigure (1879–1941), Okada Yachiyo (1883–1962), Miyamoto Yuriko, and HIRATSUKA RAICHŌ (1886–1971). It cultivated the talents of younger writers like HAYASHI FUMIKO (1903–51) and Ōta Yōko (1906–63). After it ceased publication in 1933 a group known as the Kagayaku Kai centered around Hasegawa Shigure was formed. It included writers, artists, and critics. Among its members were ENCHI FUMIKO (b 1905), Masugi Shizue (1905–55), Mori Mari (b 1903), and Ōta Yōko. During the Sino-Japanese War of 1937–45 the Kagayaku Kai was supportive of the Japanese military.

Politically Oriented Groups —— Numerous groups with wide-ranging political and ideological leanings formed from the first decade of the century down to the postwar era. One such early group was the Kabenkai, a socialist youth literary association formed in 1905. Its leading members were Kodama Kagai (1874–1943), Shirayanagi Shūko (1884–1950), Yamaguchi Koken (1883–1920), NAKAZATO KAIZAN (1885–1944), and UCHIDA ROAN (1868–1929). The Kabenkai was a forerunner of proletarian literary groups of later years. In 1921 the Tanemakisha, an organization advocating pacifism and internationalism, was founded under the leadership of Komaki Ōmi (1894–1979) and Kaneko Yōbun (b 1894). It published the very influential literary magazine TANE MAKU HITO (The Sowers) and also participated in the Esperanto movement.

In 1925 the first proletarian literary organization in Japan, the Nihon Puroretaria Bungei Remmei (Japan Proletarian Literary League), was formed. Led by AONO SUEKICHI (1890–1961), Hayashi Fusao, and others, it included an anarchist faction. The following year it disbanded, with the anarchist faction splitting off. The league was reorganized and renamed the Nihon Puroretaria Geijutsu Remmei. Two years later, in 1928, the Nihon Sayoku Bungeika Sōrengō (General League of Japan Left-wing Literary Artists) was founded. It was an organization of leftist critics and writers having a united common front, and its leading members were KURAHARA KOREHITO (b 1902), Aono Suekichi, Nakano Shigeharu, Eguchi Kiyoshi (1887–1975), and Miyoshi Jūrō (1902–58). However, it disintegrated only a few days after it was formed because of the mass arrest of communist sympathizers in the MARCH 15TH INCIDENT. In its place

a Communist Party support group, led by Nakano Shigeharu, Kurahara Korehito, KOBAYASHI TAKIJI (1903–33), TOKUNAGA SUNAO (1899–1958), and MURAYAMA TOMOYOSHI (1901–77), newly established the Zen Nihon Musansha Geijutsu Remmei (All Japan Proletarian Art League). Its name was later changed to Zen Nihon Musansha Geijutsu Shūdan Kyōgikai; it was better known by the acronym NAPF from the initials of its Esperanto name Nippona Artista Proleta Federacio.

In 1928 the first proletarian *tanka* poets' association, the Musansha Kajin Remmei, was formed, headed by Watanabe Junzō (1894–1972) and Asano Jun'ichi (1902–76), but was disbanded within a year. In 1929 the literature division of the All Japan Proletarian Art League became independent and established the Nihon Puroretaria Sakka Dōmei (Japan Proletarian Writers' League). Among its members were Nakano Shigeharu, Kobayashi Takiji, Tokunaga Sunao, Hayashi Fusao, FUJIMORI SEIKICHI (1892–1977), and Tateno Nobuyuki (1903–71). It later became part of the lower organizational structure of NAPF. The Puroretaria Kajin Dōmei (Proletarian Tanka Poets' League) was also created in 1929. It too was absorbed into the organizational structure of NAPF. Members included Watanabe Junzō, Asano Jun'ichi, Maekawa Samio, and Gotō Miyoko (1898–1978). In 1930 the Puroretaria Shijin Kai (Proletarian Poets' Society) was created as the poetry division of NAPF, headed by Itō Shinkichi (b 1906) and Ōe Mitsuo (b 1906).

In 1931 NAPF was dismantled. Its six constituent groups recombined into six new groups to found the Nihon Puroretaria Bunka Remmei (Japan Proletarian Culture League), commonly referred to as KOPF from its Esperanto name Federacio de Proletaj Kultur Organizo Japanaj. However, KOPF disbanded in 1934 because of increasing militarist pressure. In 1934 a group of worker-writers, including HAYAMA YOSHIKI (1894–1945), MAEDAKŌ HIROICHIRŌ (1888–1957), and Satomura Kinzō (1902–45), founded the Puroretaria Sakka Kurabu; it disbanded two years later. In 1935 a group of writers seeking a unification of proletarian camps established the Dokuritsu Sakka Kurabu. This group included Hayashi Fusao, Eguchi Kiyoshi, Aono Suekichi, HIRABAYASHI TAIKO (1905–72), and Matsuda Tokiko (b 1905). It dissolved in 1938, and with its demise all pre–World War II proletarian literary groups disappeared.

In the postwar era, a small band of proletarian writers who were dismissed from the previously mentioned Shin Nihon Bungaku Kai (founded in 1945) as a result of an internal dispute surrounding the valuation and succession of proletarian literature formed the Nihon Minshu Shugi Bungaku Dōmei in 1965. Its leading members were Eguchi Kiyoshi, Shimota Seiji (b 1913), Nishino Tatsukichi (b 1916), and Tsuda Takashi (b 1930).

Other Special-Purpose Groups —— In the category of specialized literary vocational organizations, there have been a number of important groups. In 1920 the Gekisakuka Kyōkai, an association of playwrights, was established. It was followed in 1921 by the Shōsetsuka Kyōkai, a writers' association. In 1926, at the insistence of Kikuchi Kan, the Bungeika Kyōkai, an association of literary artists, was founded. In addition to the goal of promoting mutual friendship and aid among members, it issued a series of books by association members and published a yearbook. As ultranationalism grew in strength from the 1930s onward, increasing pressure was put on literary groups by the government. In 1934 the Bungei Konwa Kai was established under the direction of Matsumoto Manabu, chief of the Metropolitan Police Security Bureau, as a kind of literary watchdog to oversee regulation of literary groups. It was headed by NAOKI SANJŪGO (1891–1934), Kikuchi Kan, and YOSHIKAWA EIJI (1892–1962). Other participants included KISHIDA KUNIO (1890–1954), Kawabata Yasunari, Yokomitsu Riichi, and SHIMAZAKI TŌSON (1872–1943). Besides participating as observers of military maneuvers, the group instituted the Bungei Konwa Kai Prize. It was later absorbed by the Teikoku Geijutsuin (Imperial Art Academy).

In 1935 the JAPAN P.E.N. CLUB was founded as part of the International Association of Poets, Playwrights, Editors, Essayists, and Novelists, with Shimazaki Tōson as president. In 1942 the NIHON BUNGAKU HŌKOKUKAI (Patriotic Association for Japanese Literature) was created to promote the war effort and help raise the patriotic consciousness of the people through literature. Presided over by Tokutomi Sohō, it had eight divisions and over 4,000 members, including KUME MASAO (1891–1952), Nakamura Murao, Nagayo Yoshirō, and Kikuchi Kan. It sponsored bi-annual Great Asian Literary Congresses, public lectures, and the publication of collections of nationalistic poems and war novels. The Nihon Bungaku Hōkokukai was the literary group most supportive of the war effort.

In 1945, following the end of World War II, the Bungeika Kyōkai, which had been absorbed by the Nihon Bungaku Hōkokukai, was reestablished. It was renamed the Nihon Bungeika Kyōkai and sponsored a wide variety of literary activities and publications. It is currently the largest literary organization in the country, having over 1,000 members. In 1947 the Japan P.E.N. Club, which had disbanded during the war, was likewise reestablished with Shiga Naoya as president.

In the early 1980s, if such special vocational organizations as the Nihon Bungei Kyōkai and Japan P.E.N. Club are excluded, there were virtually no other literary groups of major importance. The various large national and local newspapers had core groups of writers and critics who contribute to their literary sections on a regular basis, but there were no exclusivist groups like the Ken'yūsha of the Meiji period, which exerted control over the literary sections of a number of popular newspapers of the period. Literary magazines published by the major publishing houses such as BUNGEI SHUNJŪ and BUNGAKUKAI (by BUNGEI SHUNJŪ, LTD), CHŪŌ KŌRON and *Umi* (by CHŪŌ KŌRON SHA, INC), *Shinchō* (by SHINCHŌSHA COMPANY), and *Gunzō* (by KŌDANSHA, LTD) have their regular contributors, and each of them employs groups of writers for other projects. These groups may be referred to as the "such and such school," but they are by no means literary groups with a particular literary commitment. As for groups that do advocate a particular literary stand, it is possible to cite various small coteries. There are thousands of them around the country, but if we read the little magazines they publish, we find that many of them are little more than literature appreciation groups with no significant major differences among them. Their prime contribution can be seen as providing an outlet for aspiring writers.

The major universities also issue literary magazines such as *Akamon bungaku* (Tōkyō University), WASEDA BUNGAKU (Waseda University), and MITA BUNGAKU (Keiō University). The editors of these magazines are affiliated with the universities, but this is not always so in the case of contributors. Neither can the contents of these magazines be said to subscribe to one particular school of literary thought. Some groups are referred to by such names as the "Kamakura men of letters" or the "Chūō Line writers" because they live in the same general locale, but the implication is not that of the Bloomsbury group, for example; it simply means that they sometimes share the same pastime activities and live in the same general area.　　　　　　　　　　　　　　　　　　　　　　　TAMAI Kensuke

literary magazines

Literary magazines and periodicals *(bungei zasshi)* have played a significant role in the history and development of modern Japanese literature. Japanese literary critics and historians attach considerable importance to them for several reasons. First, journals can be used to identify changing literary trends, especially broad movements like proletarian, naturalist, and romantic literature. Vague categories can thus be made more precise and workable; one can speak, for example, of the differing romantic traditions of BUNGAKUKAI (The Literary World, 1893–98), MYŌJŌ (Bright Star, 1900–1908), and NIHON RŌMANHA (The Japanese Romantic School, 1935–38). Second, journals are central to the closely knit inner circle of the Japanese literary establishment (the BUNDAN). This network of personal relationships not only reflects the literary power structure but also provides an extra-literary context for a fuller understanding of writers and their works. Finally, when viewed historically, journals also reveal many of the broad changes that have taken place in Japan since the Meiji Restoration of 1868. The steady expansion of the reading public, the growth of the publishing industry, and the intermittent periods of censorship and political repression are a few of the developments reflected in the journals discussed below.

Types of Magazine —— The first periodicals appeared in the 1870s and contained literature written in classical Japanese or Chinese. They were usually either small private affairs run by established writers or larger satirical magazines. By the late 1880s a number of journals had become involved in developing the new "modern" literature. Most were small, a few were connected to universities, and all were staffed by very young men. Daily newspapers and larger magazines devoted to the propagation of "enlightened" thought were the first to publish the new literature on a wider scale. In 1895, when the HAKUBUNKAN publishing house inaugurated Japan's first mass-audience general-interest magazines *(sōgō zasshi)*, journals publishing modern literature were established as an important sector of the growing publishing industry. Since this time, such large commercial ventures have generally served to popularize writers and literary trends developed in the smaller literary journals.

One type of small magazine, the literary coterie magazine or *dōjin zasshi,* has been particularly significant. *Dōjin zasshi* are organized along cooperative lines, with members *(dōjin)* generally sharing in all aspects of the writing, editing, and financing. Members can thus express themselves freely while working together with a group of like-minded associates. In a society which places considerable importance on group affiliation, *dōjin* literary magazines provide a supportive group identity free of the usual set of hierarchical relationships. Their circulation rarely exceeds a few thousand, but they receive attention far out of proportion to their size. Although some *dōjin zasshi* are in fact united as much by friendship and school affiliation as by any shared literary philosophy, they do often embody shared principles or attitudes and are used extensively by critics and historians as tools to help identify or predict the changing currents which shape Japan's complex literary history.

Another type of magazine is the literary "organ" *(kikanshi),* put out by political or literary groups. Leftist organizations have extensively utilized this type of magazine, as have schools of Japanese *tanka* and *haiku* poetry.

Early Development (1868–1885) —— In the mid-1870s, the renaissance of literature written in the Chinese idiom and the introduction of movable type to replace the traditional woodblock printing made it possible for popular writers to publish their own small pamphletlike journals, the most notable being NARUSHIMA RYŪHOKU's *Kagetsu shinshi* (The Flower Moon Journal, 1877–84). This early type of literary magazine was particularly influential because it was widely read by the educated youth of its time, the group that has historically played the central role in forwarding new literary modes and ideas. The 1870s also witnessed the development of the mass appeal satirical magazine, a prime example of which was the weekly lampoon *Maru-maru chimbun* (The Dumpling Lampoon, 1877–1907). These heavily illustrated journals, written in classical Japanese, competed for the broad mass audience with the entertainment-oriented "little newspapers" of the time, so it is not surprising that their literary level was quite low. Nevertheless, they were the first in a long line of magazines to disseminate popular literature to a mass audience and can be seen as forerunners of the comprehensive journal.

The Development of Modern Literature (1885–1895) —— *Garakuta bunko* (Library of Odds and Ends, 1885–89), the first *dōjin* literary magazine, is also conventionally regarded as Japan's first modern literary magazine, though its teenage authors, which included OZAKI KŌYŌ and YAMADA BIMYŌ, wrote their light-hearted essays in a classical Japanese style. In the fall of 1888, the 20-year-old Bimyō was asked by the Kinkōdō publishing house to become editor of *Miyako no hana* (Flower of the Capital, 1888–93). Whereas *Garakuta* had been a slender amateurish affair, *Miyako* was thick, beautifully illustrated, and filled with works written in the new colloquial style. If it lacked anything, it was a clear critical stance, an articulate sense of which direction the new literature should take. This was provided within a year's time by the advent of *Shigarami zōshi* (Weir of Words, 1889–94), the first of MORI ŌGAI's many journalistic ventures, which emphasized book reviews and critical articles. At the same time, a number of young and talented writers were writing for two large and influential magazines, JOGAKU ZASSHI (Magazine of Women's Learning, 1885–1904) and KOKUMIN NO TOMO (The Nation's Friend, 1887–98). Neither *Kokumin no tomo,* which was primarily concerned with political and social enlightenment, nor *Jogaku zasshi* were literary journals, but they nurtured the young new writers and, by placing literary works and criticism side by side with articles on educational and philosophical issues, helped give the new literature a stature and scope it had lacked before. In 1893 a number of writers, including KITAMURA TŌKOKU and SHIMAZAKI TŌSON, broke away from *Jogaku zasshi* to establish *Bungakukai,* which launched a new romantic tradition. Together with TSUBOUCHI SHŌYŌ's WASEDA BUNGAKU (Waseda Literature, 1891–98), these journals were the focus of intense critical activity. An example of this was a protracted debate on the role of aesthetics in literature pitting Ōgai's German-influenced romanticism *(Shigarami-zōshi)* against Shōyō's British-influenced realism *(Waseda bungaku).* This was the first famous *ronsō,* theoretical jousts that set writer (or group of writers) against writer, journal against journal.

Development of Large Literary and Comprehensive Magazines (1895–1900) —— As modern literature grew, so did the number of people educated enough to read it, and the resulting market opened a whole new range of commercial possibilities for the expanding

publishing industry. In 1895 the Hakubunkan publishing house decided to merge 13 of its smaller journals into 3 large magazines. One of these, TAIYŌ (The Sun, 1895–1928) was Japan's first truly general-interest magazine, with articles on two dozen general topics ranging from literature to science, politics to home economics. Created in the same amalgamation was BUNGEI KURABU (Literary Club, 1895–1933),·which also staked out a new field, that of the large-scale commercial literary magazine. The initial success of *Bungei kurabu* prompted Shun'yōdō, the dean of Japan's 19th-century publishing houses, to resurrect a literary journal named SHINSHŌSETSU (New Fiction, 1896–1926) that it had tried putting out briefly in 1889–90, and to reorganize it along similar lines. The same year, a *dōjin* magazine called *Shinsei* (New Voice, 1896–1910) appeared. Within five years its circulation had reached a remarkable 12,000, and in 1904 some of its members left to form a new and larger magazine, SHINCHŌ (New Currents, 1904–). To do this, they formed the Shin-chōsha publishing company, which quickly became, along with Shun'yōdō and Hakubunkan, one of the three leading publishing houses of the Meiji period. Another important general-interest magazine still surviving today is the CHŪŌ KŌRON (The Central Review, 1899–). Like *Shinchō, Chūō kōron* had its roots in a small *dōjin* magazine—in this case, one put out by students of a Kyōto Buddhist school calling for alcoholic abstinence and moral rectitude—and like *Shinchō* it formed its own publishing house. Unlike its competitor *Taiyō, Chūō kōron* was soon emphasizing literature and literary criticism, an unusual policy for a general-interest magazine. By the turn of the century, therefore, a number of large literary and general-interest magazines had established themselves as cornerstones of the growing publishing industry and were setting about to expand and popularize modern literature.

The turn of the century also marked the beginning of a brief but important renaissance in both traditional and modern poetry. Two journals central to this poetic revival were organs of poetry associations. *Myōjō* was the organ of the New Poetry Association (Shin-shisha) formed by YOSANO TEKKAN and YOSANO AKIKO, a group which stressed poetic innovation and developed the lyrical romantic tradition established by *Bungakukai.* As with most journals stressing bold new literary ideas, however, *Myōjō* was relatively short-lived. The longevity of HOTOTOGISU (Cuckoo, 1897–), the organ of MASAOKA SHIKI's Negishi Tanka Association, has much to do with the fact that its roots were in the traditional world of haiku, though it developed new styles and even published novels for a while. Not only is the Negishi Tanka Association still putting out *Hototogisu,* it has also published the influential *tanka* journal *Araragi* (Yewtree) continuously since 1908. This stability is the rule rather than the exception with organs of haiku and *tanka* groups—the *tanka* journal *Kokoro no hana* (Flower of the Heart), for example, has been headed by four successive generations of the same family since 1898.

Magazines and the Development of Naturalist Literature (1905–1910) —— Four magazines were of central importance in the development of the so-called naturalist literary movement (see NATURALISM). One of these was the general-interest magazine *Taiyō,* which had published some of the foundational naturalist works in the years before it became a movement. The other three journals, all launched in 1906, were *Bunshō sekai* (The World of Literary Style, 1906–20), *Shumi* (Taste, 1906–10), and a revival of *Waseda bungaku. Waseda bungaku* and *Shumi* were both connected with the Waseda University Literary Association, and the new literary current quickly became associated with this prestigious school. With the intellectuals of *Waseda bungaku,* particularly SHIMAMURA HŌGETSU and HASEGAWA TENKEI, providing the theoretical base, and a number of new and established writers producing a string of successful novels, naturalism developed into a dominant movement in just two or three years.

Bunshō sekai's success in introducing new writers had much to do with the fact that it utilized an "open-door" editorial policy, considering any and all manuscripts submitted for publication. This system was quite common during the late Meiji and early Taishō periods and served to help writers lacking the usual connections gain access to the rather closed and cliquish literary establishment of the time.

Journals Opposing Naturalism (1910–1915) —— Naturalism peaked in 1909 and was already fading by the end of 1910. These were years of intense critical debate, and accordingly new magazines emerged to speak for the various groups involved. The four most important journals opposing naturalism were SUBARU (The Pleiades, 1909–13), MITA BUNGAKU (Mita Literature, 1910–), SHINSHICHŌ (New Currents of Thought, 1907–70), and *Shirakaba* (White Birch,

1910–23; see SHIRAKABA SCHOOL). *Subaru* was a continuation of *Myōjō*, which had broken up following a succession of factional disputes. Literary elder Mori Ōgai stepped in to reconcile the quarreling members and help them organize this new journal, but as *Subaru's* young poets were united primarily by their opposition to naturalism, they disbanded again when that movement had subsided. *Mita bungaku* was launched by the Keiō University Department of Letters, which was piqued at the success of rival Waseda University's *Waseda bungaku*. They offered the editorship first to Ōgai, then to UEDA BIN. Both declined but recommended NAGAI KAFŪ, who quickly brought *Mita bungaku* to the front lines of the anti-naturalist movement. One of Kafū's young associates, 24-year-old TANIZAKI JUN'ICHIRŌ, was a member of the second version of *Shinshichō* (1910–11), and writers from the two journals moved quite freely from one to the other. While *Subaru*, *Mita bungaku*, and *Shinshichō* formed one phalanx of the attack on naturalism, the young members of *Shirakaba* formed another. Generally speaking, the former group disliked the introspective and colorless quality of naturalist literature, calling for a return to beauty and sensuality, whereas the *Shirakaba* group attacked the naturalists' gloomy defeatism, emphasizing instead a kind of optimistic humanism.

Most of these journals were connected to schools in one way or another. Waseda University had *Waseda bungaku* and *Shumi*, Tōkyō University was represented by *Shinshichō* and *Teikoku bungaku* (Imperial Literature, 1895–1920), Keiō had *Mita bungaku*, and the members of *Shirakaba* were mostly graduates of the aristocratic Peers' School. The success and longevity of the members of these journals, many of whom continued as central figures in the literary establishment well into the postwar era, served to embed the importance of school affiliation even more deeply into the modern literary world. Though this helped establish great and lasting literary traditions at universities like Waseda and Keiō and gave many writers an almost familial closeness, it also provoked strong resentment from those left on the outside and added to literature's reputation as the province of a university elite.

Journals of the Mid- and Late Taishō Period (1915–1925)

Though the last years of Meiji had been a time of literary ferment, once the Taishō period was well underway things settled down. With theoretical and factional warfare at an ebb, and a plethora of young writers sufficiently established to publish in the large-circulation literary and general-interest magazines, chances for *dōjin* journals to break into the establishment were very slight. Thus, though the Taishō period was an era of great literary productivity, instances of new journals making a deep literary mark were notably scarce. There were, of course, exceptions. One was *Shinshichō*, whose third and fourth revivals (in 1914 and 1916, respectively) introduced a number of important new writers, including KIKUCHI KAN and AKUTAGAWA RYŪNOSUKE. The latter's controlled intellectual style of writing soon became the trademark of the *Shinshichō* group. Another exception was *Kiseki* (Miracle, 1912–13), but though its members went on to become writers of stature, their writing style and connection with Waseda University marked them more as innovators within the naturalist tradition than as a really new movement. The biggest exception was a string of quasi-political literary journals influenced by or connected to the budding socialist movement, journals that laid the groundwork for the PROLETARIAN LITERATURE MOVEMENT that was to follow. In the world of poetry, though the golden age of the late Meiji period had ended, *Araragi* established a new "realistic" style of modern *tanka*, and poetry magazines like *Zamboa* (The Shaddock Fruit, 1911–13) and *Kanjō* (Sentiment, 1916–19) continued to develop the lyrical "romantic" tradition of *Myōjō* and *Subaru*.

Journals of the Leftist Literary Movement (1925–1935)

The year 1926 happened to fall near the midpoint of a major leftward shift in Japan's intellectual and literary establishment. The destruction caused by the Tōkyō Earthquake of 1923, the delayed impact of the Russian revolution, the increased proximity to contemporary Western culture—all helped give Japan's young intellectuals a strong conviction that a new era was at hand. In the literary world, the earthquake's decimation of the city and its publishing houses coupled with the widely shared belief that the predominant I-NOVEL genre of the Taishō period had reached an impasse to create a vacuum into which new writers with fresh ideas could move. These writers, most of whom were very young, formed a remarkable number of small *dōjin* journals in the years immediately following the earthquake. By 1928, however, most of these journals, *Roba* (Donkey, 1926–28) and *Tsuji basha* (The Hansom Cab, 1925–27) being but two examples, had been torn apart by the political polarization

brought about by the rapid growth of the proletarian literature movement. This movement, which grew steadily throughout the 1920s only to collapse in a morass of factionalism and government repression in the early and mid-1930s, had its roots in the small but active radical movement of late Meiji period. The first leftist literary magazines were *Kaben* (Whip of Fire, 1905–06) and *Seinembun* (Youth Literature, 1895–97). *Kaben*, which functioned as the literary organ for the young anarchists clustered around KŌTOKU SHŪSUI, can be seen as the progenitor of the later Marxist "organs." When political repression of all socialist ideas followed the 1911 executions of Kōtoku and his associates for treason, journals like *Hechima no hana* (The Snake-gourd Flower, 1914–15) and *Seikatsu to geijutsu* (Life and Art, 1913–16) provided a forum where frustrated radicals could discuss their ideas within a safer (i.e. literary) context. Proletarian literature came into being as a self-conscious, though still heterogenous, literary movement with the publication of TANE MAKU HITO (The Sowers, 1921–23). Three comprehensive magazines, KAIZŌ (Reconstruction, 1919–55), *Kaihō* (Emancipation, 1919–33), and *Warera* (We, 1919–30), all launched within a month of each other, helped spread the new literature and the political theories which supported it. Soon all the major literary journals were filling their pages with works by the young leftist writers. After the Tōkyō Earthquake of 1923, which wiped out *Tane maku hito* and the commercial leftist literary journal *Shinkō bungaku* (New Literature, 1922–23), governmental repression increased and the proletarian movement itself began to move into a more politicized and dogmatic stage of development. By the late 1920s, most young writers were members of one or another of the leftist "artists' leagues," each of which ran its own literary organ. Of these journals, BUNGEI SENSEN (Literary Front, 1924–32) was of the greatest literary significance, while SENKI (Battle Flag, 1928–31), with a circulation of over 20,000, probably achieved the greatest political impact. Though issues of these leftist organs were frequently banned by the authorities, copies were circulated and discussion groups formed through an extensive political network that reached out into the schools and factories of working-class communities and even into the farming areas. Great efforts were made to develop writers from working-class backgrounds as well, so that these politicized journals, though of dubious literary value, broadened participation in what had previously been an extremely exclusive literary establishment.

Nonleftist Journals——Proletarian literature, dominant though it was during the late 1920s and early 1930s, did not hold a monopoly on new literary trends and developments. Young writers like YOKOMITSU RIICHI and KAWABATA YASUNARI were inspired more by contemporary French literature than by Marxist ideology and developed a new literary style loosely termed "neoimpressionism" in their *dōjin* journal BUNGEI JIDAI (Literary Age, 1924–27). Lamenting that the literary world had been polarized into neoimpressionist and proletarian camps, another group of young writers published their own *dōjin* journal, aptly named *Fudōchō* (Noncooperation, 1925–29), to provide a third alternative. When the expansion of proletarian literature continued unabated, with young writers abandoning *dōjin* literary journals in droves to join the various leftist writers' leagues, magazines like *Shinchō* and *Fudōchō's* successor *Kindai seikatsu* (Modern Living, 1929–32) tried to stem the leftist tide by supporting the creation of counter-organizations like the short-lived SHINKŌ GEIJUTSU HA. Of greater long-term effect on the literary world, however, was the development of new packaging, promotional, and pricing techniques by the major publishing houses of the day. Starting with the prestigious Kaizō House, publisher of the comprehensive journal KAIZŌ, publishers drastically reduced book prices while increasing the amount of advertising and the number of copies printed. The success of this campaign not only rescued most publishers from grave economic difficulties, but further expanded a reading public already being widened by the proletarian movement. Large-scale literary and comprehensive magazines of high literary quality like *Kaizō*, *Shinchō*, *Chūō kōron*, and Kikuchi Kan's remarkable BUNGEI SHUNJŪ (Literary Annals, 1923–) all flourished in the wake of these new developments. In 1933, concurrent with the forced decline of the proletarian movement, three new influential journals ushered in what is termed a period of "literary revival": *Bungakukai* (Literary World, to be distinguished from the noted Meiji journal of the same name, 1933–), BUNGEI (The Literary Arts, 1933–44), which was published by the Kaizō Press, and *Kōdō* (Action, 1933–35).

Journals and the War (1935–1945)——As political repression increased, Japan's literary and comprehensive journals reacted in a variety of ways. *Kōdō* and *Jimmin bunko* (The People's Library,

1936–38) tried to swim against the growing nationalist-militarist tide but quickly sank. The latter was particularly critical of a new literary movement which emphasized the "Japanese Spirit," thus fitting nicely with the increasingly chauvinistic atmosphere. Journals such as *Kogito* (1932–44), *Nihon rōmanha* (The Japanese Romantic School, 1935–38), and *Bungei seiki* (The Literary Century, 1939–46) were important in the development of this so-called romantic movement, which grew more and more jingoistic as the hostilities progressed. At the same time, large magazines like *Chūō kōron, Kaizō,* and *Bungei shunjū* were sending writers to report on the war and the success of Japan's colonizing effort. The strategy used by the governmental authorities to control the contents of these reports can be seen in the case of ISHIKAWA TATSUZŌ, winner of the first Akutagawa Prize for literature. *(Bungei shunjū created both the Akutagawa and Naoki prizes in 1935.)* Tried and convicted of "disturbing public peace and order" for his piece describing the conduct of Japanese soldiers in China in the March 1938 issue of *Chūō kōron,* Ishikawa was sent back to China by the same journal to write a "correct" essay less than a year later. When the war began to turn against Japan, however, editors were forced to plead with the authorities not just on behalf of their writers but for the very existence of the journals themselves. Particularly vulnerable were the comprehensive magazines which, by their very nature, had political as well as literary overtones. The mere name of a journal like *Kaizō* (Reconstruction) was a problem in itself. After 1940, periodicals were gradually reduced in size by as much as 80 percent, and legislation requiring the "rationalization" of the publishing industry did further damage; some magazines were forced to discontinue publication by the authorities. By the end of the war, the combination of paper rationing brought on by severe shortages and the destruction of publishing plants and offices in the bombing raids had forced practically every journal, literary and otherwise, to suspend publication.

Postwar Journals (1945–1955) —— When the war ended Tōkyō was in ruins. Just as had happened after the earthquake of 1923, a flood of small but energetic magazines rose from the ashes to try to fill the physical and psychological vacuum that resulted, and lead the way into the new era. This time, however, many of the new journals were staffed not by inexperienced students but by men in their thirties and forties who had suffered through the collapse of the proletarian movement and subsequent decade of repression. Some hoped to create a new leftist literary movement. Within months of the surrender, they had organized the New Japanese Literature Society, and by March 1946 they were publishing a monthly literary journal, *Shin Nihon bungaku* (New Japanese Literature, 1946–). They were opposed by another group of former leftists determined to resist a return to politicized literature. This group formed *Kindai bungaku* (Modern Literature, 1946–64). Immediately, the two journals began to debate a number of issues, including writers' responsibility for the war and the proper relationship between politics and literature. These journals were primarily devoted to criticism. Another group of older writers, including Kawabata Yasunari and KUME MASAO, were more interested in writing literature. When they launched *Ningen* (Humanity, 1946–51), they were surprised to find long queues of people waiting outside their bookstore to buy copies. Despite the hordes of prospective readers, the wartime paper shortage was still not to be remedied for several years, and all these journals were forced to print on whatever they could find. Actually, only a handful of the many small journals and publishing companies established right after the war lasted for more than a few years. Many of these had been highly tenuous affairs, especially the lurid pulp magazines *(kasutori zasshi),* which often lasted a matter of weeks. Most of the old publishing houses survived, however, for they had both tradition and experienced staff to build from, and soon the large and growing reading public was buying record numbers of old favorites like *Bungei shunjū, Shinchō, Bungakukai,* and *Chūō kōron,* as well as a variety of new journals whose fiction did not fit into the old "pure literature" and "popular literature" categories. Starting in the mid-1950s, publishing houses began packaging this new semipopular fiction—which had previously been published only in newspapers—in weekly magazines.

Modern Developments (1955–1975) —— In 1956, when an unknown student, ISHIHARA SHINTARŌ, was catapulted into public stardom by the publication of a single work that made up in energy and public appeal what it lacked in literary polish, it was obvious that a new era was at hand. Literature was developing into the child of the growing mass media, and public taste was replacing the opinions of a narrow literary circle in determining the literary direction

of the nation. Now money and status could come quickly to the writer whose work found public favor, and the publishing houses, forced into greater and greater competition as the scale of the industry grew, were only too happy to help a likely prospect along. Literary prizes, a common way for new writers to get noticed since the 1930s, were made into a media event. This growth in the literary influence of the mass media has correspondingly diminished the traditional influence of small *dōjin* and school-affiliated journals. The public is much less concerned with new literary movements and philosophies than the old literary circle was. Neither is the public overly impressed with school affiliations or personal connections, though of course writers possessing these still have certain advantages. Whereas the literary circle of the past shaped literary developments, now it must respond to them. As a result, few literary journals since 1955 have aspired to create new literary movements or presented themselves as the embodiment of some group mission. Even the literary leftists, deprived of their vanguard status when communism shifted from an intellectual to a mass political movement, have muted their old rhetoric. Though small literary journals have lost some of their former influence, thousands are still published yearly in Japan. They offer young writers a chance to get noticed (entries for literary prize competitions, for example, are usually drawn from *dōjin* journals) and also provide established writers with a chance to write how and what they want. The literary quarterly has been revived and serves, as it did during the late 1920s and early 1930s, to explore new literary ideas, especially those from the West. Tradition is also a source of strength for today's journals. A number of the famous literary journals of the past have recently been reprinted in their original form—that thousands of these expensive series are purchased illustrates the abiding respect and affection Japanese have for them. See also MAGAZINES.

——Joseph K. Yamagiwa, ed, *Japanese Literature of the Shōwa Period* (1959), contains a list of magazines of the Shōwa period and a convenient survey of modern literary history. James Morita, "Garakuta Bunko," "Shigarami Zōshi," *Monumenta Nipponica* 24 (1969), the only articles in English on specific literary magazines. *Nihon kindai bungaku daijiten* (Kōdansha, 1977), vol 5 contains information on all major journals including bibliographical references. Edited by the Nihon Kindai Bungakukan in Tōkyō, where copies of all the magazines and information concerning them are kept. Another library, the Meiji Shimbun Zasshi Bunko at Tōkyō University, specializes in Meiji journals. Inagaki Tatsurō, "Taishō no bungaku zasshi," *Kindai Nihon bungaku no fūbō,* discusses Taishō literary magazines. Takami Jun, "Genryūkō to iu isshō," *Shōwa bungaku seisui shi* (1958), discusses the literary magazines of the early Shōwa period. *Theodore W.* GOOSSEN

literary prizes

Literary prizes awarded in various categories by publishing companies, newspapers, and literary organizations. Given once, or in some cases, twice a year, the selections are made by committees of leading writers, critics, and scholars.

The best-known awards are those for writers of fiction. Many, such as the Akutagawa Ryūnosuke Shō (the Akutagawa Prize), the Naoki Sanjūgo Shō (the Naoki Prize), and the Dazai Osamu Shō (the Dazai Prize) are specifically designated for new talent, while the Nihon Geijutsuin Shō (the Japan Art Academy Award), the Noma Bungei Shō (the Noma Literary Prize), and the Mainichi Geijutsu Shō (the Mainichi Art Award) are given in recognition of a writer's lifelong contribution to literature. The Shinchō Bungaku Shō (the Shinchō Literary Prize) and the Tanizaki Jun'ichirō Shō (the Tanizaki Prize) are given to active leading writers. The Naoki Prize may sometimes be awarded on this basis as well. There are also prizes for companies which have published works of outstanding literary value.

The number and categories of Japanese literary prizes have proliferated greatly since the early 1950s, and now total over 50. The Akutagawa and Naoki prizes are generally regarded as the most prestigious; receipt of one of these serves to establish an author's reputation and often helps to increase the sales of his or her work. The former was established in 1935 by the writer KIKUCHI KAN (1888–1948) in memory of his colleague AKUTAGAWA RYŪNOSUKE (1892–1927) and is awarded for works of serious fiction. Suspended after World War II, it was revived in 1949 and served to introduce the so-called second and third waves of postwar writers. The Naoki Prize, also established in 1935 by Kikuchi Kan, is for works of popular fiction. Like the Akutagawa Prize, it is awarded once in the spring and again in the fall. Winning works for both of these prizes are frequently short stories or novellas rather than full-length novels.

The oldest and most prominent of the several annual poetry awards is the H-Shi Shō (H-Shi Prize), established in 1951 to recognize new poets. Other annual prizes honor outstanding authors of children's books, essayists, critics, playwrights, women writers, and *haiku* and *tanka* poets. A few, including the prestigious Yomiuri Bungaku Shō (the Yomiuri Literary Prize) are awarded in several of the above categories. ———————————————————— ASAI Kiyoshi

literati painting → bunjinga

literature

introduction
early literature
Heian literature
medieval literature
Edo literature
modern fiction
modern poetry
modern drama

INTRODUCTION

Japanese literary art has received foreign influences since its beginning in the 6th century. It has always been in a condition of "chemical combination," so to speak, with foreign cultures. Before the middle of the 19th century, the sources of influence were the cultures of China and India. Since Indian influences came via China, we can speak of them as if they were part of Chinese culture. After the middle of the 19th century, the impact of modern Western culture became predominant, Chinese culture gradually receding into the background. The ratio of these "chemical combinations" has varied depending on the period and situation: sometimes the foreign element increased, while at other times indigenous culture prevailed. Even so, when one compares Japanese and foreign literary art, one finds qualities in Japanese art that are different from either Chinese or modern Western literary art. These qualities can be thought of as distinctly Japanese.

Period of Chinese Influence ——— In the 1300-year period under Chinese influence, we find the following distinct characteristics.

Form. Japanese literary art has a strong proclivity for brevity. It is most noticeable in poetry, whose shortest forms are the 17-syllable HAIKU and *senryū* (see ZAPPAI AND SENRYŪ). These short forms became increasingly popular and reached their peak between the 17th and 19th centuries. Even in the 20th century there have been a vast number of haiku poets. No epic developed in Japan. In prose, too, long fiction was exceptional. The TALE OF GENJI is long, but, lacking in structure and unity, it is more like a collection of middle-length stories than a novel. The *Pillow Book (Makura no sōshi)* of SEI SHŌNAGON and the *Essays in Idleness (Tsurezuregusa)* of YOSHIDA KENKŌ, regarded as representative works of Japanese classical literary art, are miscellanies, consisting of short essays without continuity.

Chinese poems, on the other hand, whether *shi* (shih; lyrical poetry) or *fu* (narrative poetry), are rarely very extensive, but are much longer than Japanese poems.

Content. In Japanese literary art there is no polarity between man and nature, individual and group, author and audience. Nature is handled as part of human life, hostile feelings never recognized. An individual's views and feelings are expressed as representing those of his group; hence strong individuality is absent. The author often works by identifying with the consciousness of the audience. The author is then "expressive-affective."

In China, by contrast, ancient and medieval poetry only sang of man and society. Even when nature entered later, there was distance between nature and man. While less manifest than in postromantic Europe, the independence of individuals from their groups can be recognized in Chinese literary art considerably more than in the Japanese case. The absence of a strong polarity between the author and audience, however, is similarly observed in China. This is, then, not exclusively Japanese, yet it is a dominant characteristic of Japanese literary art.

Tone. Japanese literary art generally has a negative tone: sorrow rather than joy, escape rather than aggression. Of the love songs collected in the 21 IMPERIAL ANTHOLOGIES, none expresses the joy of consummated love. Only 1 among the 250 or so extant NŌ dramas contains humor. In the technique of description, too, the indirect and ambiguous are preferred to the direct and clear.

In China, the negative tone of Buddhism was offset by the positive stance of Confucianism, Taoism representing a midpoint. Japan did not adopt this positive Confucian tone. The *Satomi and the Eight "Dogs" (Nansō Satomi hakkenden)* of BAKIN which is Confucian, is considered exceptional and outside the main stream.

Period of Western Influence ——— Since the latter half of the 19th century, Japanese literary art has undergone remarkable changes under the influence of modern Western cultures. But deep underneath, it has maintained indigenous characteristics.

Form. The greatest influence came from modern Western fiction. The composition of long novels with unity and structure became possible only due to the impact from the West. However, Japanese authors seem to lack the qualities necessary to succeed with genuine long novels, and it is probably pointless for the time being to expect "river" novels *(romans-fleuves)* from them. They have been successful with middle-length stories or with full-length novels like *The Makioka Sisters (Sasameyuki)* of TANIZAKI JUN'ICHIRŌ, which are essentially collections of episodes. In poetry traditional short forms like haiku and TANKA still flourish.

Content. The kinds of polarity mentioned as lacking in the past have begun to be present in the modern period. This represents a weakening of one indigenous characteristic. However, such polarities are not yet as strong as in the West. In the works of outstanding authors, for example Tanizaki Jun'ichirō and NAGAI KAFŪ, the harmony of man and nature is still preserved.

Tone. Modern Japanese works began to contain a positive tone due to the impact of modern Western literary art. However, the so-called Japanese NATURALISM of the early 20th century, which marked an attempt to imitate European naturalism, resulted in the peculiarly Japanese and escapist I-NOVEL. Again, such authors as DAZAI OSAMU who find beauty in destruction remain popular, an indication of the degree to which the Japaneseness of modern Japanese literature still persists. ———————————————— KONISHI Jin'ichi

EARLY LITERATURE

The term early literature *(kodai bungaku)* is customarily applied in Japanese literary history to a wide variety of materials which were composed, sung or recited, and eventually written down over a long period of time. Unlike certain convenient labels accorded to other major phases of Japanese literary history, it is not really delimited by any one geographical area, nor by the predominance of any single group or class within Japanese society. It is most easily applied to the 8th century and the Nara period (710–794), a time when the major texts achieved their final form. Within its bounds, however, may also be included later collections of stories and songs which borrow their material or characters from the 8th and earlier centuries. In addition, the term must comprehend the now lost written and oral traditions that the Nara-period texts were themselves dependent upon, and these traditions may extend back to the 6th and 5th centuries and even beyond.

Sources ——— For our knowledge of Japan's early literature, oral or written, we are chiefly indebted to three documents, each of considerable size, different in plan and in execution, and each of varying interest to the student of literature. In some respects the KOJIKI (Records of Ancient Matters) and the NIHON SHOKI (also known as the *Nihongi;* Chronicle of Japan) are perhaps best characterized as the political scriptures of early Japan: the former was submitted to the throne in 712, the latter in 720. Their overall aim is to present the story of imperial preeminence and authority from the age of ancestral gods who created and pacified the islands, through generations of legendary monarchs when the divine mission to rule all Japan is said to have been accomplished; they continue on into a historical period of real emperors and empresses when contacts with Korea and China and the increased power of the main native lineage groups had begun to transform a primitive island kingdom into an imitation, on a smaller scale, of the Chinese empire.

In telling this story, the *Kojiki* and *Nihon shoki* draw upon a wide range of older materials: Chinese literature and history, native myths and legends, genealogies of the imperial line and more important lineage groups, brief stories of romance and intrigue, and also tales and myths that, for all the political coloration of these works, seem rooted in the oral traditions of an agrarian peasant culture. Inserted into this varied and episodic prose matrix, we find songs and poems—from calls to battle, magical incantations accompanying court ritual, scraps of reworked folksong—as well as a style of dramatic lyricism which highlight many otherwise bare narratives. The *Kojiki* and *Nihon shoki* have preserved a literary heritage whose age and complexity only a handful of nations can rival. Moreover, within this body of literature we can see that many of the features of classical Japanese letters had already begun to take shape.

The third major source is the MAN'YŌSHŪ (Collection for Ten Thousand Generations or Collection of Ten Thousand Leaves), the oldest extant anthology of Japanese verse. The continued popularity of this collection, greatly increased by the inexpensive and readable editions of recent decades, suggests that the title was indeed well chosen. The *Man'yōshū* contains some 4,500 poems, many of them from the 7th century. However, its final poem is dated New Year's Day 759, and we know that the whole of the anthology was only put together some years after that date.

Several other works supplement the testimony of these three sources. In 713 provincial officials were ordered to compile and submit gazetteers—geographical reference books—dealing with the territories under their administrations. In these FUDOKI (literally, "records of wind and earth") the officials were to transcribe known place names, using auspicious-sounding Chinese characters, to record natural and agricultural resources, to account for the etymologies of old place names, and to include traditional lore about ancient and noteworthy matters. The last two categories of information would not have been solicited by a court unconcerned with regional or folk literature, and they have provided the modern-day student with an intriguing batch of legends, anecdotes and songs.

A knowledge of Chinese was important to the educated courtiers of the day, and they often composed poetry in that language. The KAIFŪSŌ (Fond Recollections of Poetry), dated 751 is Japan's oldest anthology of Chinese verse. While the literary value of its 120 poems may seem slight, it allows us a glimpse at poets of the 7th and 8th centuries, some best known for works in their native language, trying their hands at a continental art that was as essential to the Asian courtier as was a handsome sword to his European counterpart. This collection stands as the precursor of the Chinese verse anthologies which would proliferate in the Heian period (794–1185).

The KOGO SHŪI (Collected Remnants of Ancient Stories) is a prose work from the beginning of the Heian period. It was compiled by one Imbe no Hironari and, according to his preface, submitted to the throne in 807. This collection of myth and legend gives some interesting variants of *Kojiki* and *Nihon shoki* tales, which are used to champion the cause of the Imbe family, whose fortunes were on the decline. From this same time comes the NIHON RYŌIKI (tr *Miracle Stories of Japan*, 1973). This collection of 116 Buddhist-inspired, moralistic tales was assembled by the priest Kyōkai, probably by around 822. This collection belongs most properly to the field of Buddhist literature particularly the type of moralistic tales known in Japan as SETSUWA BUNGAKU. Finally, we should mention a collection called the *Kinkafu* (Scores for Koto Songs) that has come down to us in a copy dated 981. Despite the late date, it is a valuable source of information as to how some of the songs of the *Kojiki* and *Nihon shoki* continued to be performed at the Heian court.

Recording and Transmission ——— As noted above, the *Kojiki, Nihon shoki* and *Man'yōshū* date from the 8th century, the brief but spectacular age when the city of Nara was the political and cultural capital of Japan.

However, the dates we attribute to these documents mark the end rather than either the beginnings or mature age of ancient traditions. They stand as summations of the past, looking backwards from the vantage point of a sophisticated society that seems in many ways to have prefigured the following age of classical Heian culture.

In order to see just how far back these sources may take us, we need to consider briefly how Japan came to borrow and adapt the Chinese written language. Traditional accounts in the *Kojiki* and *Nihon shoki* claim that as early as the 3rd century Japanese rulers were bringing Korean scribes and scholars to their country (see KIKAJIN). These Korean teachers were learned in the language and writings of China and were also prized for their wisdom and their knowledge of the Confucian classics, much as later Korean and Chinese Buddhist priests would be revered for their command of the sutras. Certainly from the 4th and 5th centuries, Japanese monarchs had need not only of record keepers but of scribes who could handle diplomatic correspondence with Korean kingdoms and China itself.

Chinese and Japanese are fundamentally unrelated languages, so native students faced a tremendous task merely in learning to read the Chinese language, to say nothing of actually composing in it. Yet well before the Nara period some of them had not only gained a certain mastery over literary Chinese, they had begun to bend and shape its writing system into a tool, clumsy and imperfect, for recording their own language.

The Japanese faced many difficulties in using Chinese characters (graphs) to write their own language, and a truly Japanese written language was only achieved well after the dates of our texts. Nevertheless, the prose of the *Kojiki,* though written with Chinese characters, is essentially in a sinicized form of the Japanese language and would make little sense to anyone attempting to read it as Chinese. The semantic value of some Chinese characters is meant to be read out as the corresponding native Japanese word (much the same thing as reading the symbol "5" as "five," rather than "cinq" or "cinco"). At the same time other graphs are used solely for their one-syllable Chinese sound value in the phonetic transcription of Japanese words. The style of the *Nihon shoki* leans more heavily upon continental models and is accordingly closer to pure classical Chinese. But it, too, as a matter of course, often uses the foreign medium to express either the semantic or sound values of the Japanese language. The *Kojiki* and *Nihon shoki* contain several hundred songs and poems (some 50 found in both), which are transcribed entirely in Chinese characters used phonetically. As for the *Man'yōshū,* many of its older poems are written with a complex mixture of Chinese characters, sometimes read for meaning and sometimes read for sound, but all standing clearly for Japanese words. The bulk of the verse is written wholly with characters used phonetically. Because of its predominance in the anthology, this phonetic script is usually referred to as *man'yōgana* (see the section on the *man'yō* writing system in the article on the MAN'YŌSHŪ). This creation would in time make possible the development of the Japanese phonetic syllabary called *kana*. The invention of this Sino-Japanese system of writing meant that, perhaps by the 6th century, Japanese and naturalized Koreans could capture some of the flavor of native stories and songs in a form approximating the native spoken word. As might be imagined, however, length and freedom of expression were still severely limited and controlled by the very medium employed.

No doubt behind much of this Sino-Japanese written material lie oral traditions of song and verse, myth and legend. Fragments of these traditions may transmit to us an echo from the first centuries of the Christian era when wet-rice agriculture with its village settlements became established over most of the islands. Their roots may reach back and intertwine with the traditions of Korea, South China, and Southeast Asia, and even in some instances with those of the far-off cultures of Polynesia. Easier to detect are groups of legends and songs which were popular at the emperors' courts in more recent centuries. Added to the difficulties of deciphering its writing system, a work such as the *Kojiki* presents us with another problem: tales and incidents at times seem jumbled together with little care for any artistic effect or even logical progression. We might then conclude that some of these stories, whether out of antiquarian or political motives, were only recorded by official scribes at a time, well into the 7th century, when they were already half-forgotten and no longer part of a living narrative tradition.

It is hard to know who exactly transmitted the early literature before the era of our main texts. It is generally assumed that lineage groups involved in ritual matters at the early court, like the Imbe family or Nakatomi family, were also responsible for the preservation of royal genealogies and myths. We can suppose that a similar if less official function would have been carried out by professional singers and reciters both at the court and within the houses of individual lineage groups and subgroups. Such a group of transmitters seems to be indicated by the term KATARIBE, often translated "reciters' guild." The particular word *kataribe* does not appear in the literary texts of this period, but on occasion there do appear people's names containing the element *katari* (recitation, storytelling). There is also evidence of a group called *amagataribe* ("fishermen-reciters"), who rendered menial service at the emperor's table, and who offered song and story at court long before the Nara period. The name *kataribe* does appear on census records of the 8th century and in Heian accounts of court ritual. Here it seems that rather than specialists in myth or genealogy, the *kataribe* were peasant singers who would be brought in to perform songs of their provinces at the investiture ceremony of a new emperor. By scattered references in the early texts to talented peasant singers and musicians being summoned to court we may guess that folk songs and folktales continued to play some role in shaping the literature of the upper classes. It should be added that performances given by such a *kataribe*, like those said to have been presented by the Kume family, the people of Kuzu, or the Hayato soldiers, were not simply a matter of entertaining an idle king and his retainers. In the autocratic society of early Japan, just as the farmers had to deliver up their produce and labor, the warriors their service and might, so too did these families practice the arts of submission: in song, dance, or in story they presented their performing skills as symbol and pledge of loyalty to their ruler.

Kojiki and Nihon Shoki —— The *Kojiki* is made up of a preface and three sections, or books. The first section covers the age of the gods, from the appearance of the very first deities, the creation of the islands and the pacification of hostile spirits by divine imperial ancestors, to the birth of the first legendary emperor, Jimmu. The second book follows Jimmu to the East on his conquest of the central Yamato region and ends with the reign of Emperor Ōjin. The latter is said to have ruled during the late 3rd and early 4th centuries, but he is more likely a legendary composite of the powerful monarchs that governed from the area of present-day Ōsaka in the 4th and 5th centuries. The last book continues with the reign of Ōjin's son Nintoku and ends with Empress Suiko (r 593–628). The reign-by-reign accounts of the last section grow increasingly brief and factual. It is probably no accident that the *Kojiki* stops with Suiko, since it was during her age that Buddhism and other new influences of mainland culture gained a particularly strong foothold in Japan.

The longer *Nihon shoki* is divided into 30 short books covering much the same span of time. The first two are devoted to the mythological age, with subsequent books usually treating a single ruler, though as many as eight fictional, nondescript emperors may be crowded into one section. Its narrative extends some 70 years beyond that of the *Kojiki* and concludes with the reigns of Emperor Temmu (r 672–686) and his wife Jitō (r 686–697). These last books provide us with crucial information about the 7th century when both these chronicles were being formed.

The *Nihon shoki*'s reliance upon Chinese writings (and some Korean histories of questionable authenticity), combined with a manifest concern for international and lineage-group politics, works against its literary appeal. The title itself, "Chronicle of Japan," reflects a consciousness of other nations with their own chronicles that is largely absent from the *Kojiki*. Its historical and political value was immediately recognized, and soon after its presentation to the throne in 720 it became a kind of bible for the central bureaucracy. The influence of the *Nihon shoki* is clear in the *fudoki*, and later writers and scholars were very familiar with it.

In contrast, the testimony of history is strangely silent about the *Kojiki*. It was cited by notes in the text of the *Man'yōshū*, but no sign of it appears in later official histories, including the *Nihon shoki*. For a long time it seems to have been copied and transmitted by families of Shintō priests, but its real study was only established with the antiquarian researches of MOTOORI NORINAGA (1730–1801). And yet despite its episodic nature and difficult script, it is the *Kojiki* which holds an abiding interest for the student of Japanese literature.

The preface to the *Kojiki*, written in Chinese, is signed by a minor official named Ō no Yasumaro (d 723). He writes that when Emperor Temmu came to the throne after defeating the allies of his brother, Emperor Tenji (r 661–672), he was dismayed by all the errors and falsifications that had made their way into the legends and imperial genealogies kept by various lineage groups. Determined that they be rectified, he called upon one Hieda no Are to produce a new, authoritative account of Japan's past. The project lapsed with his death but was seen to its conclusion by Empress Gemmei (r 707–715), Temmu's daughter-in-law and daughter of Tenji.

Whether this Hieda no Are was a male scribe or a female storyteller, and whether he or she was employed to interpret difficult Sino-Japanese records, or to produce an oral version of the Kojiki that Yasumaro was then to write down are questions that have occasioned much scholarly debate. As unlikely as the oral theory seems, those who piece the slender evidence together in support of Hieda no Are's being a woman remind us that as poets and storytellers, as shamanic priestesses and as empresses, women played a major role in the growth of Japanese letters well before the days of *The Tale of Genji*.

Both the *Kojiki* and *Nihon shoki* begin with a complex set of creation myths. In addition to its main account, the *Nihon shoki* includes, here and elsewhere, a number of variant versions of the narrative which commence with the notice "according to another

text . . ." Compared to the continuous, simpler flow from episode to episode of the *Kojiki*, this gives the already sinicized *Nihon shoki* a rather choppy, almost academic look. What seems like a minus from a literary point of view is, however, very much a plus for the student of comparative mythology or the history of religions.

Content of the Kojiki —— Among the mythological stories in the earlier parts of the *Kojiki*, particularly well told are the creation story concerning the male deity Izanagi and the female deity Izanami; the story of the conflict between Amaterasu Ōmikami (the sun goddess and imperial ancestress) and her unruly brother Susanoo no Mikoto; and the story of the Izumo deity Ōkuninushi. For detailed synopses of these and other early myths, see MYTHOLOGY.

Emperor Jimmu. The middle book of the *Kojiki* contains the story of the legendary Emperor Jimmu. Most of his conquests on the way to becoming Japan's first emperor are not carried out by pitched battle, but usually through subterfuge. For example, Jimmu invites the chieftain Yaso Takeru and his men to a banquet at the hollowed-out grotto of Omuro. To his own men, who are to act as servants, he distributes swords and tells them to attack when he gives the signal. When ready, he sings: "To the grotto of Omuro many have come and entered in, many have entered in. Bold Kume boys, with your round-pommelled, rock-pommelled swords, now is the time to strike!" Another time, about to surprise a different enemy, he sings a song likening the foe to leek and ginger-plant: "Bold Kume boys. In the millet field, there's a single stalk of leek. Tear out its stalk, bulb and roots! Strike them down!" "Bold Kume boys. There's ginger planted by the fence. Mouth tingles [i.e., memory of harm done us still rankles]. I'll not forget! Strike them down!" The *Nihon shoki* informs us that these and other songs, along with an accompanying dance, were performed at court by members of the Kume family. Although the Kume were no longer a powerful family by the 7th century, and their arts of submission were eventually taken over by other families, in these vigorous war songs we can gain some idea of how a family might use song both to pledge loyalty to their ruler and to assert the antiquity of their cooperation in his family's cause.

Jimmu's love affairs are also related. Ōkume, a famed Kume ancestor, has told Jimmu about a maiden called Isukeyori, whom one day they encounter amidst a group of girls in a field. Ōkume and Jimmu exchange songs, Ōkume asking which girl his lord would like to sleep with, and Jimmu replying, the older one there in front. When Ōkume approaches Isukeyori, she sings making fun of his big-eyed expression: "Swift, wagtail, plover, or bunting—why the wide-open eyes?" To this he replies, "So wanting to meet the girl— that's why my wide-open eyes!"

It has been pointed out that the way in which the characters of this episode toss songs back and forth seems to prefigure the style of witty repartee found already in poetry exchanges of the more urbane poets of the *Man'yōshū*. By the time of the lords and ladies of the Heian period, the poetry exchange, be it between friends, lovers, or strangers, had long become a staple means of coquetry and courtly communication. It also shaped a major portion of the Japanese poetic tradition.

Yamatotakeru. One of the best remembered *Kojiki* tales is that of the hero Yamatotakeru: his name means the bold one of Yamato. His legend is at times episodic and disconnected, but he himself is, along with being a fierce fighter, as close to a tragic figure, complete with hubris, as anyone in the early literature. His father, Emperor Keikō, learns that after he had asked Yamatotakeru to admonish his older brother for being absent from their meals, Yamatotakeru had "grabbed and crushed him, ripped off his limbs, wrapped him up in matting, and tossed him away." Even though this brother had previously insulted Keikō by stealing away two of his women, Keikō is astonished by such ferocity. He hurriedly dispatches Yamatotakeru to subdue hostile tribesmen in the west, and once that is accomplished, packs him off to the east to do the same.

On his way east, Yamatotakeru stops at the Ise Shrine, where his aunt serves as priestess. Here his bravado melts from him as he laments that his own father seems to want him dead. But he carries on, defeating men and spirits alike, and even finds time to court a few princesses. He next goes off to battle the god of Ibukino Mountain with his bare hands, leaving behind him with his new bride the sword given him by his aunt. Climbing the mountain, he comes across a huge white boar. He disdains to stop and kill it, thinking it only the god's lackey. However, it is in fact the god in animal form. Yamatotakeru soon finds himself lost and disoriented, poisoned by the baleful power of the mountain spirit. Yamatotakeru descends the mountain and, feeling better after resting beside a spring, tries to return to Yamato, but soon grows weak again. He declares prophetically that always in his heart he had wished to soar through the skies, yet now he can barely shuffle his feet. Hobbling on a stick, he at last comes to a plain called Nobono. Here, in praise and longing for his home, he sings: "Yamato, fine and high-rising land. Piled-up green fence of mountain. Mountain-secluded Yamato, so beautiful!" Then he focuses on the scene of a single mountain: "You with your lives ahead of you, take oak leaves from Heguri Mountain and wear them in your hair. You, children!" Two brief songs later, still far from home, he dies. When the wife and the children he had left behind in Yamato come forth to build him a tomb and sing songs of mourning, his spirit changes into a great white bird and flies off and away.

The blending of prose and song, or of prose and verse, was well developed in this period, as we have seen. It had always been an important technique for supplying mood and context to the brief poetic forms favored by the Japanese and also for supplying a narrative with dramatic or lyric highlights. This song-story style would be carried on and elaborated in the poetry and tales of later centuries. The story of Yamatotakeru is only one example of how well it was already being used by the 7th century.

Man'yōshū —— The 4,516 poems of this anthology are arranged in 20 books. Included are the works of many eras and many poets (some 450 are named, and many of the poems are anonymous), and also a number of different organizational schemes (such as chronological, topical, and seasonal). In contrast to this variety, the verse forms actually used are few. The *tanka* ("short poem") accounts for over 90 percent of the total. This is a 31-syllable form, metrically patterned in syllable groups as 5-7-5-7-7, which was to remain the mainstay of Japanese courtly lyric or WAKA. *Chōka* ("long poem") make up the bulk of the remainder. These are made up of a series of 5- and 7-syllable units rounded off by a final 7-syllable line. Often they are followed by one or more *tanka*. In this instance, the short poem is termed *hanka*, a Chinese literary term usually translated as "envoy."

Tanka do appear in older works like the *Kojiki*, and many of its longer songs approximate the *chōka* form. However, in these earlier songs and in some of the older pieces of the *Man'yōshū*, we most often see no strict adherence to 5–7 phrases but rather, a general and consistent alternation of short plus long phrases. Why a 5–7 combination and, in particular, the fixed 31-syllable *tanka* seem to have become so dominant by the mid-7th century are questions that have never been satisfactorily answered.

The *Man'yōshū* opens with a poem said to be the work of Yūryaku, a late 5th-century emperor: "A basket, carrying your basket, with a trowel, carrying your trowel, you, girl, gathering greens upon this hill—I want to know where you're from, I want to learn your name! The land of Yamato it is I overconquering, me over-ruling. Shall it be me who tells them, your home and your name?" The setting is spring, the season later imperial anthologies would choose to begin with. The second poem is attributed to Emperor Jomei (r 629–641), best known as the father of Tenji and Temmu: "In Yamato are crowds of mountains, but it is well-shielded, heaven's Kagu Mountain that I ascend, and when I view the land, from the land-plains vapor rising climbs, from the sea-plains gulls rising, climb. This rich land! Dragon-fly island, land of Yamato!" Jomei seems simply to be describing a grand natural vista, yet the tiny Kagu Mountain on which he stands was then as now situated in a rather small basin surrounded by other hills and rings of high mountains that completely block the Yamato Plain from the ocean. More than just describing, he is evoking and arousing with his language the bounty and fertility of the whole realm.

One of the finest of the early poets is NUKATA NO ŌKIMI (Princess Nukata; ca 630?–after 690). Some of her *tanka* are vividly dramatic: "Ready to embark from Nikita Harbor, we wait for the rise of the moon. Now the tide is just right, now let us row out!" "As I long for you to come, rustling the blinds, the autumn wind." Tradition has it that she was loved by both Tenji and Temmu, the most powerful men of the 7th century. Certainly she established a worthy beginning for the long line of great women poets in Japanese literature.

Surprisingly little is known about the most famous *Man'yōshū* poet, KAKINOMOTO NO HITOMARO (fl ca 685–705). He was active toward the end of the 7th century, and his legend and reputation are based not only on his more personal lyrics, but on the many *chōka* he composed in praise of, or lamenting for, members of the imperial family. Also much esteemed are several long laments he made for his wife, and one for a stranger whose body he found on the lonely

shore of an island in the Inland Sea. Hitomaro's wife has turned her back on the world of the living, "and whenever the baby she left me as keepsake wails and cries, there is nothing I can give him. So I, a man, tuck him under my arm and carry him to the room where my love and I together slept, and where my days are spent in grieving, my nights in sighs." Even when he addresses the dead stranger, his thoughts turn to the image of the man's wife: "Sprawled on a hard bed, you have a beach full of the waves' roar for a pillow. If I knew your home, I'd go and tell them. If she knew, she would come seek you. Not knowing where to go, she must wait longing and anguished, your beloved wife." And said to be his death poem is: "Not knowing that I lie here on the rocks of Kamo Mountain, my love will be waiting, waiting." After a century or two, when they could only puzzle out some of the difficult *Man'yōshū* writing system, Japanese poets still remembered and looked back to Hitomaro as their spiritual and artistic ancestor.

YAMABE NO AKAHITO (d ca 736) wrote during the second quarter of the 8th century. By the time of his generation, the poetry of imperial praise had become a mere formality, and a poet like Akahito was more inclined to give his real attention to the description and evocation of the natural scene: "Passing out of Tago Bay, I see the snow fallen pure white on the high peak of Fuji." "On the tips on the branches in a fold of Kisa Mountain at Yoshino, the cry of the birds." "Black night goes on deepening, and on the pure tree-grown riverbank, plover keep up their call." Another noted nature poet was TAKECHI NO KUROHITO (fl ca 690–710), probably a contemporary of Hitomaro: "The cranes cry out crossing over toward Sakurada. The tides will have ebbed at Ayuchi Beach. The cranes cry out crossing over."

Finally, some of the very best examples of Japanese love poems are found in this anthology. For their directness, their forcefulness, later poets tended to substitute wit and word play, and this loss was a major one for the tradition of court poetry. The best poetry of the *Man'yōshū* takes us a long way from the feel of myth and ritual, war song, and folktale. It suggests, too, how very modern Japan's early literature can sound and how its appeal still reaches out to us from this ancient culture and this long gone age.

——Works in English: Translated texts: Michiko Y. Aoki, tr, *Izumo Fudoki* (1971). W. G. Aston, *Nihongi* (1896). Noah Brannen and William Elliott, tr, *Festive Wine: Japanese Poems from the Kinkafu* (1969). Genchi Katō and Hikoshirō Hoshino, tr, *Kogoshūi* (1926). Kyoko Motomochi Nakamura, tr, *Miraculous Stories from the Japanese Buddhist Tradition* (1973). Nippon Gakujutsu Shinkōkai, tr, *The Man'yōshū: One Thousand Poems* (1940, repr 1965). Donald L. Philippi, tr, *This Wine of Peace, This Wine of Laughter* (1968). Donald L. Philippi, tr, *Kojiki* (1969). General works: Michiko Y. Aoki, *Ancient Myths and Early History of Japan* (1974). Roy Andrew Miller, *The Japanese Language* (1967). George Sansom, *Japan: A Short Cultural History* (1943). Ryūsaku Tsunoda et al, ed, *Sources of Japanese Tradition*, vol 1 (1958).

Works in Japanese: Texts: the most convenient texts are those in the *Nihon koten bungaku taikei* published by Iwanami Shoten: *Kojiki, norito* (1958), *Nihon shoki* (1965–67), *Man'yōshū* (1957–62), *Fudoki* (1958), *Kodai kayōshū* (1957), *Nihon ryōiki* (1967). To these may be added Iida Sueharu, ed, *Kogoshūi shinkō* (1940). General works: Matsumura Takeo, *Nihon shinwa no kenkyū* (1954–58). Nakanishi Susumu, *Man'yō no sekai* (1973). Ōbayashi Taryō, *Nihon shinwa no kigen* (1973). Ōkubo Tadashi, *Jōdai Nihon bungaku gaisetsu* (1972). Saigō Nobutsuna, *Kojiki no sekai* (1967). Tsuchihashi Yutaka, *Man'yōshū: Sakuhin to hihyō* (1956). Tsuchihashi Yutaka, *Kodai kayō no sekai* (1968). Ueda Masaaki, *Nihon shinwa no sekai* (1967). Ueda Masaaki, *Nihon shinwa* (1970).   *Mark* MORRIS

HEIAN LITERATURE

For the purposes of literary history the Heian period (794–1185) may be divided into three parts. The initial period extends from the foundation of the city of Heian in 794 to the commissioning of the KOKINSHŪ, (also known as the *Kokin wakashū*) the first imperial anthology of WAKA (classical Japanese poetry) in 905. This stretch of a little over 100 years is characterized by two trends—an intense interest in the composition of works in Chinese, especially Chinese poetry (*kanshi*; see POETRY AND PROSE IN CHINESE), and the renascence of *waka* after a few decades of neglect early in the 9th century. The 10th century constitutes in many ways a new epoch. In addition to the basically poetry-oriented activity of the earlier period, it saw the emergence of a variety of prose genres in the native language. *Waka* continued to be very important, and in fact its prestige as the most admired of the literary arts was never challenged after the *Kokinshū*. Chinese writings went into a relative decline, though they too continued to be practiced. But the century after 905 stands out as the time when Japan first developed a prose literature. The trends in this direction came to a climax early in the 1000s with the composition of one of Japan's greatest works, the *Genji monogatari* (TALE OF GENJI). The remainder of the Heian period, a long epoch extending over nearly 200 years, is less easily characterized. Strong and varied interest in prose literature continued to be in evidence, with new genres beginning to emerge late in the period. Poetry, especially *waka*, flourished, but with peaks and valleys of talent and enthusiasm. Poetic styles began to change in the late 11th century, and by the beginning of the 13th the art of *waka* was enjoying its palmiest days, as an extraordinarily large number of talented poets appeared on the scene, their activity benefiting from vigorous imperial patronage. No third work comparable in stature and significance to the *Kokinshū* and the *Tale of Genji* appeared before the end of the Heian age in 1185, and so it might be best to ignore this political demarkation and for literary purposes extend the period to 1205, by which time the SHIN KOKINSHŪ, the eighth and perhaps greatest of the imperial *waka* anthologies, had been compiled. Thus the period from about 1020 to 1205 can be seen as one of consolidation and growth, dominated by the examples of the *Kokinshū* and the *Genji* in poetry and prose fiction respectively, but with important new developments in each area toward the close of the age.

I. CHINESE WRITINGS AND THE REVIVAL OF WAKA (794–905)

At first glance it may seem strange that Japanese poets should have written in a foreign language, Chinese, but this can be understood as a perfectly normal feature of the culture of East Asia at that time. During the Tang (T'ang) dynasty (618–907), and indeed generally throughout premodern times, down at least until the middle of the 19th century, China served as the cultural focus of the East Asian world, and Chinese was the language of learning in peripheral countries such as Korea and Japan. By composing in Chinese, Japanese literati were showing themselves to be civilized men, the use of the language being in this respect somewhat similar to the employment of Latin among scholars of medieval and Renaissance Europe. As in Europe, the development of the native vernacular as a literary medium took place in a context where the prestige of learning belonged to a foreign classical tongue.

Poetry in Chinese —— Certain developments in early 9th-century Japan were particularly favorable to literary activity in Chinese. Composition of Chinese poetry by Japanese poets had begun in the late 7th century, and by 751 the first anthology had been compiled. This was the KAIFŪSŌ (Fond Recollections of Poetry), a collection of over a hundred poems put together by an unknown compiler, and the oldest extant poetic anthology of any kind in Japan. It was nevertheless dwarfed by the gigantic anthology MAN'YŌSHŪ (Collection for Ten Thousand Generations or Collection of Ten Thousand Leaves), whose lengthy compilation process was also going on during the 8th century and whose over 4,500 poems are with a few exceptions in Japanese. The *Man'yōshū*, whose last dated poem is from 759, commemorates the age of the first full flowering of Japanese poetry. On the basis of surviving evidence, it seems that composition in Chinese was of relatively minor importance. During the first few decades of the 9th century the situation was essentially reversed. Three imperially commissioned anthologies of Chinese poetry appeared in rapid succession, while there was no official anthology of *waka* for over a hundred years. The cumulative effect of longer exposure to Chinese civilization may have had something to do with the change, and it is important to remember that the writing of national histories in Chinese continued unbroken from early in the 8th until late in the 9th century, evidence of well-established sinocentric procedures in an area peripheral to literature. But more was involved in the new popularity of Chinese verse. The motivation for the removal of the capital from Nara (Heijōkyō) in 784 and its eventual reestablishment in Heiankyō 10 years later is to be sought in the attempt by a series of emperors, beginning with KAMMU (737–806, r 781–806), to strengthen the throne vis-à-vis both the Buddhist clergy and the noble clans. One method they used to this end was to model the bureaucracy more closely on that of China, i.e., to make it a meritocracy subservient to the monarch rather than letting it be a function of hereditary clan power. The emperors eventually lost out in this attempt, but they enjoyed some initial success early in the 9th century. In order to train officials, they set up a university whose curriculum consisted of the Confucian classics and whose course of study inculcated some modicum of skill

in the composition of both Chinese prose and Chinese poetry. Officially sponsored poetry-composing parties were held, and ability to turn out an acceptable verse was at the least no detriment to a successful career. The first emperors of the Heian epoch were ardent sinophiles, and the native *waka* had little prestige at their courts. Emperor SAGA (786–842, r 809–823) ordered two anthologies of Chinese verse, the *Ryōunshū* in 814 and the BUNKA SHŪREISHŪ in 818. In 827 a third, the KEIKOKUSHŪ, was presented to Emperor Junna (786–840, r 823–833).

The principal compiler of the *Ryōunshū* or "Cloud-borne Collection" was Ono no Minemori (778–830). The work contains 90 poems in the form known in Chinese as *shi* (shih), the most common form of classical Chinese poetry, with lines either five or seven characters in length. The *Bunka shūreishū* or "Collection of Literary Masterpieces" is somewhat longer, containing 140 *shi*. It was compiled principally by FUJIWARA NO FUYUTSUGU (775–826). The third and last of the imperial anthologies of Chinese verse, the *Keikokushū* or "Collection for the Ordering of the State," was larger still. It originally comprised 20 chapters, of which only 6 are extant. In addition to *shi*, it contains poems in the long and more loosely constructed *fu* form and a section of answers to civil-service examination questions. Its principal compiler was Yoshimine no Yasuyo (785–830).

The most prominent characteristic of early Heian *kanshi* or (Chinese poetry) is its diligent imitativeness. The Japanese poets writing in Chinese at this time took their inspiration in direct and for the most part undiluted form from the poetry produced on the Chinese mainland. This may be regarded as natural and inevitable at what was still a fairly early stage of schooling in Chinese literature. Of more interest is the fact that the Japanese imitated not the poetry of the contemporary Tang dynasty, but that of a precedent phase of Chinese history, the Six Dynasties (222–589), and especially that of the 6th century, the late, decadent phase of the Six Dynasties. Much of the Chinese poetry that the Japanese were acquainted with at this time was preserved in the great 6th-century anthologies *Wenxuan* (Wen-hsüan; J: Monzen), *Gujin shiyuan yinghua* (Ku-chin shih-yüan ying-hua), and *Yutai xinyong* (Yü-t'ai hsin-yung). The first two were compiled by Xiao Tong (Hsiao T'ung; 501–531) and the last by Xu Ling (Hsü Ling; 507–583). Much of this poetry exemplifies a phase in Chinese taste which was characterized by delight in artifice, a delight that was later scorned as excessive and degenerate, but that the Japanese of the 7th and 8th centuries regarded as the height of literary style. This style avoided direct statement in favor of oblique formulations involving reasoning as to cause and effect, heavy use of ornate metaphor, "elegant confusion" (pretended inability to discern differences between similar phenomena), and an obtrusively insistent employment of antithetical parallelism. Most Japanese *kanshi* from the period under discussion also embody these qualities. They read like exercises in an artful game of words—which they are. This is not to say that there are not poems expressing a poet's real feelings, ones in which a degree of sobriety restrains technique from becoming an end in itself. But they are merely a leavening of the flat, sugary confection of early Heian *kanshi*.

Prose Works in Chinese —— Another notable work written in Chinese at this time presents an entirely different picture. It is *Nihonkoku gempō zen'aku ryōiki* (Miraculous Stories of Karmic Retribution of Good and Evil in the Land of Japan), more briefly known as NIHON RYŌIKI (tr *Miraculous Stories of Japan*, 1973). This collection of 116 short anecdotes was put together by the Buddhist monk Kyōkai around 822. It is the earliest example of the genre known as *setsuwa* ("tale" or "anecdote"; see SETSUWA BUNGAKU). Buddhist *setsuwa* already had a history in China, and the content of *Nihon ryōiki* draws on such Chinese collections as the 7th-century *Mingbaoji* (Ming-pao-chi). Anecdotes were used to enliven and illustrate the sermons of Buddhist preachers, and collections of such oral material were made in China, and later in Japan. The stories in *Nihon ryōiki* are meant to show, through supposedly true examples, how good and evil deeds are infallibly rewarded and punished in this life and lives to come—to illustrate the principle of karma. The stories are arranged in chronological order, from the reign of Emperor Yūryaku in the 5th century to that of Emperor Saga in the 9th. They foster a sense of factuality by giving exact names of people and places involved, as well as specifying the historical period. Straightforwardly moralistic and blunt, the narratives are lacking in artistry but do present a vivid picture of piety and credulous faith. Thus the state of storytelling and versification in Japan in the third decade of the 9th century presents an interesting contrast of naiveté and effete pseudosophistication.

In addition to the members of the secular aristocracy, the literate population at this time included the Buddhist clergy, one of whose number, Kyōkai, was as we have seen the compiler of the first *setsuwa* collection. Other monks took part in the composition of Chinese verse, and specifically Buddhist poems were included in the anthologies discussed above. The beginning of the Heian period coincided with major developments in Buddhism, as two new sects, Tendai and Shingon, were introduced from China early in the 9th century, supplementing and eventually overshadowing the established sects of Nara. The men who brought these two new sects to Japan, the rival monks SAICHŌ (767–822) and KŪKAI (774–835), are among the most important figures in Japanese religious and cultural history. Kūkai in particular possessed a broad and powerful intellect. In addition to the establishment of esoteric Buddhism in Japan, for which he must share credit with Saichō, Kūkai left a variety of writings in Chinese, both doctrinal and literary. He combined the qualities of mystic, organizer, linguist, recluse, and man of affairs. Broadly learned in secular as well as sacred texts, he was a favorite of the sinophilic emperor Saga and as much as any one man the central cultural figure of his day. He was in particular a student of Chinese poetry and the author of an important study in this field, *Bunkyō hifu ron* ("The Secret Treasure House of the Mirrors of Poetry"). Some of his own poetry and other writings have been preserved in a collection entitled *Henjō hakki seirei shū* ("The Collected Works of the Universally Illuminating Soul-Inspiring One").

Thus far it would seem that the history of Heian literature was to be a history of writings in Chinese. The plausibility of a prolonged Chinese dominance is not to be dismissed lightly, in view of the literary histories of countries like Korea and Vietnam, also on the periphery of China. But Japan was farther off, an island state in a position to control the degree of Chinese influence in accordance with its own preferences. By the middle of the 9th century the rage for Chinese modes of expression was on the wane, though paradoxically the most notable exponent of such modes had yet to make his appearance. This was SUGAWARA NO MICHIZANE (845–903), the best of the early Japanese poets in Chinese, whose life coincided with a *waka* revival.

Resurgence of Japanese Poetry —— *Waka* had never vanished, even in the early decades of the 9th century. It was simply not prized as a public art: for public themes and occasions *kanshi* was preferred. The preempting of the formal and the public by *kanshi* left *waka* with the informal and private. This state of affairs is what KI NO TSURAYUKI (872?–945) later alluded to when he referred to *waka* being reduced to something hidden in the houses of the pleasure-loving, not something to present openly on formal occasions. The political and cultural climate of the late 8th and early 9th centuries was as we have seen favorable to expression in Chinese, and it can hardly be merely coincidental that it was precisely during this time span that the CHŌKA, the "long poem" that had been the glory of the *Man'yōshū*, vanished as a major literary vehicle. A few *chōka* continued to be written in the Heian period and even later, but the art was lost, and the results are far removed indeed from the work of KAKINOMOTO NO HITOMARO (fl ca 685–705), YAMANOUE NO OKURA (660–ca 733), and ŌTOMO NO YAKAMOCHI (718?–785), or even, more significantly, from the average anonymous *chōka* of the *Man'yōshū*. For some centuries extended poetic expression meant expression in Chinese. What was left was the 31-syllable TANKA ("short poem"), and the tradition of amorous exchanges between men and women.

Women indeed never learned in any appreciable number to write in Chinese; the university and the world of scholarship were male territory. But the position of women in court society at large was by no means without its advantages, especially compared to what it became in the later feudal period. Women could own and inherit property in their own right, had their own houses, and had to be wooed. And the wooing was done with poetry. It had always been thus, from earliest times. Archaic Japan in fact had elements of a matriarchal society. Women and men addressed each other in song from the earliest chronicles on, and amorous repartee was a highly developed mode long before the Heian period began. For this reason, if for no other, *waka* did not die out even at the height of the "Chinese" period. And the two most remarkable poets of the *waka* revival were also famous as lovers.

Toward the middle of the 9th century a political change began to take place at the Japanese court which had far-reaching implications for literature and culture as a whole. In brief, the emperors lost their struggle with the FUJIWARA FAMILY. In a series of successful moves the Fujiwara closed in on the imperial house, assuming the powers of regent, marrying their daughters to the occupants of the throne, and then forcing early abdication and installing a new, immature sovereign who was half Fujiwara in blood. As a result of such marriage politics, strong, assertive emperors such as Kammu and Saga gradually became a rarity, and the policy they had favored of fostering Chinese studies—for political as well as cultural purposes—languished. Under Fujiwara hegemony, traditional hereditary aristocratic patterns reasserted themselves, and a Japan- rather than China-oriented culture gradually grew and flourished. The way was open for revival of official interest in *waka*.

The earliest Heian *waka* poets were the same men who were active in the production of *kanshi*. Not much of their work has been preserved, and practically nothing of that of the women with whom they undoubtedly exchanged poems. But what remains, along with the increasingly copious production of the mid and late 9th century, shows a shift in the direction of that very obliquity which characterized so fully the Chinese poetry of the Six Dynasties and of its Japanese imitators. Ornate and deliberate metaphor (see x as y), "elegant confusion," hyperbole, questioning of logic and sense experience, reasoning, pretended paradoxes, archness, and plays on double meanings—all these began to crop up in *waka*. In aggregate they constitute the so-called "Kokinshū style," since they characterize much of the poetry later collected in that anthology. This style marks a significant change in *waka* away from the more direct and wholehearted declarations of Man'yō poetry, though it is a mistake to conceive of Man'yō poetry as being all of a piece. Metaphor in the *Man'yōshū* is usually handled through the technique of the *jo* or "preface," where a natural object is presented for implied or overt comparison with a human condition. This technique goes back to the beginning of Japanese metrical utterances and continued on into Heian poetry, though with decreased frequency after the early phase. The new style, based on the multifaceted artifice of Six-Dynasties poetry, superseded the archaic simplicity of viewpoint of Man'yō *tanka* at the same time as it turned away from the majestic cadences and rich ironies of the *chōka*. The transition to the "Kokinshū style" happened during the half century from roughly 810 to 860, and it was brought about by *waka* poets adapting admired Chinese techniques to composition in their own language. The process was probably inevitable, as often the same poets wrote in both languages.

By the middle of the 9th century, *waka*, newly revived but limited to the *tanka* form, existed in intertwining strands. There were the traditions going back to the *Man'yōshū*, a love tradition of passionate avowal, sometimes directly declarative and sometimes metaphorical, and a nature tradition that already emphasized the beauties of the different seasons. And there was the newly evolved "Kokinshū style," which added elements of intellectual play, indirectness, and a courtly distancing from common life. Around this time there began to appear a number of poets of unusual ability, including at least two who rank with the greatest of any age. These two, a woman known as ONO NO KOMACHI, and a courtier named ARIWARA NO NARIHIRA (825–880), came to stand in the minds of later Japanese as the very embodiments of the Heian ideal of courtly love and of its expression in poetry. Komachi is a figure of a remote and mysterious glamor about whose life practically nothing is known, but who became in time the center of a large number of legends emphasizing her supposed beauty, cruelty to her lovers, and miserable old age. She may have served at court at some point during her life, but all that we really know is that she left a small body of about a hundred poems of an unprecedented passion and melancholy beauty. They are love poems and imply that she experienced in full measure desire, yearning, and despair. Komachi deals often with the theme of meeting in dreams a lover impossible to find in life. Her poetry is rich in word play and in highly inflected verbs expressing the fine gradations of feeling and perception of which the language is capable. She belongs to the tradition of amorous women poets, forthright in declaration of passion, but brings to it a dark intensity and a sadness all her own. Not an exponent of the more effete ranges of the "Kokinshū style," she nevertheless draws effectively from the heightened delight in double meanings which was one of its hallmarks.

More is known about the life of Ariwara no Narihira. He was the son of an imperial prince who had been demoted to nonroyal status and taken the Ariwara family name. His grandfather was Emperor Heizei (774–824; r 806–809), son and successor of Emperor Kammu. Narihira had little wordly success as a courtier and functionary in the Heian bureaucracy, but left a name as the beau ideal of the gallant lover, and as a poet of unusual ability. His poetry shows wit, a characteristic of much Heian verse, and an intense questioning of reality in what may be called the style of passionate confusion, a deeper version of that "elegant confusion" that mistakes plum blossoms for snow. Narihira's best poems imply a search for truth which imbues them with a seriousness beyond the *jeu d'esprit*, the acrostic and punning poems at which he was also adept.

Another poet of some interest, a contemporary of Komachi and Narihira, was the man known as Sōjō HENJŌ, or Bishop Henjō (816–890). He was the grandson of Emperor Kammu. He had the lay name Yoshimine no Munesada until he "abandoned the world" and took Buddhist orders on the death of Emperor Nimmyō (810–850; r 833–850), in whose service he had been. Henjō presents a curious mixture of deep loyalty, piety, and a spirited delight in the most playful and frivolous expressions of the "*Kokinshū* style." A typical poem asks why dewdrops on lotus leaves (sacred in Buddhism) practice deceit by making us think them pearls. Another expresses Henjō's coy confusion at having fallen off his horse into a patch of "lady flowers"(*ominaeshi*, a common wildflower).

Revived interest in *waka* and the appearance of a number of talented poets culminated late in the 9th century in the advent of a new literary phenomenon, the UTA-AWASE or poem contest. This was a social and literary occasion when a group of poets, readers, supporters, and a judge gathered to match poems one against another and decide which were superior. The participants were divided into teams of the left and right, and rivalry was keen. The first known *uta-awase* was held between 884 and 887 at the home of Ariwara no Yukihira (818–893), Narihira's elder brother. Another, held a few years later (between 889 and 893), was the *Kampyō Ōntoki no Kisai no Miya no uta-awase*, "The Poem Contest of the Empress of the Kampyō Era." Consisting of 200 poems in 100 rounds, it drew on the works of the galaxy of poets flourishing at the end of the century, as well as on that of earlier poets, and undoubtedly served as source material for the *Kokinshū*. It should be noted that many of the early *uta-awase* combined matching poems with matching other things, such as flowers (especially chrysanthemums), roots, shells, perfumes, pictures, fans, and even stories and riddles. Such matching games were among the chief amusements of the Heian court.

Sugawara no Michizane: Scholar and Poet ——— Amidst the flurry of activity centered on *waka*, the composition of Chinese poetry still went on. In fact, the greatest Heian *kanshi* poet, Sugawara no Michizane, lived precisely at this time, in the second half of the 9th century. His death came just a few years before the compilation of the *Kokinshū*. He was a scholar and statesman as well as a poet; after his death he was considered a god. Michizane was born in 845 of a scholarly family, did brilliantly at the university, and pursued a career as teacher and official. He was recognized for his scholarship by Emperor UDA (867–931; r 887–897), who was still trying to fight off Fujiwara control, and became an intimate adviser of this monarch, and eventually minister of the right under his son, Emperor DAIGO (885–930; r 897–930). It was almost unprecedented for a mere scholar to rise so high. Michizane's Fujiwara rivals, especially Tokihira (871–909), the minister of the left, engineered his downfall in 901, when he was charged with treason and dismissed from office. He ended his days in exile, dying two years later in Kyūshū in the post of provisional governor-general of the ancient defense headquarters at Dazaifu. A series of calamities and early deaths among his enemies ensued, leading to attempts by the court to placate what was believed to be his angry spirit. Eventually he was deified as the god Tenjin, and a shrine was erected in his honor at Kitano in the capital in 947. He remains the object of a Shintō cult to this day.

Judging from his surviving writings, Michizane seems to have been a compassionate, humanistic scholar-poet in the best Chinese tradition, perhaps as close an approximation of this ideal as Japan was to produce. He served as governor of Sanuki Province (now Kagawa Prefecture) and wrote feelingly about the lives of the local peasants. He also wrote about his children, including an account of his grief for a son he lost, and recorded his reaction to downfall and disgrace. Michizane in fact reveals more of his personality in his Chinese writings than most poets who wrote in their own language. In a way he is the successor of the *chōka* poets of the *Man'yōshū*, especially of Ōtomo no Yakamochi and Yamanoue no Okura, to the latter of whom his Confucian outlook and strong family feeling bear a striking resemblance. Michizane wrote much verse in the artificial Six-Dynasties mode, but is remembered best for his poems showing the influence of the great Tang poet Bo Juyi (Po Chü-i; 772–846; known in Japan as Haku Rakuten from an alternate name, Ch: Bo

Letian or Po Le-tien) whom he admired and in some respects resembled. The plain, direct, and quiet voice of this Chinese poet is effectively echoed in the finest *kanshi* that had yet been composed in Japan. Michizane was also the author of a small surviving body of *waka*, as well as of a history and various scholarly writings. He left two collections of his works, the *Kanke bunsō* or *Literary Works of the House of Sugawara* and the *Kanke kōshū* or *Later Collection of the House of Sugawara*, which contains his poems of exile. He is also sometimes credited with a curious work entitled *Shinsen man'yōshū* (Newly Selected Man'yōshū), which appeared in 893. *Shinsen man'yōshū* is a collection of *waka* which is based principally on the *Kampyō Ōntoki no kisai no miya no uta-awase* and also on the *Koresada no Miko no ie no uta-awase* (Poem Contest at the Home of Prince Koresada) of 893 or earlier. The "poems of the left" in these contests are found arranged under categories in volume 1 of *Shinsen man'yōshū*, while the "poems of the right" are in volume 2. What makes this work something other than the earliest Heian *waka* anthology, however, is the fact that four-line Chinese poems accompany each *waka* (in the original version, only in volume 1). The *kanshi* are not translations of the *waka*, but independent treatments of the same themes, using some of the same imagery. It has been thought since at least the end of the 10th century that Michizane wrote the *kanshi* and served as the editor of the work. The juxtaposition of *waka* and *kanshi* on the same topics was to be taken up again later in the Heian period.

As the 9th century drew to a close (an event of which the Japanese were of course unaware), *waka* was thus in a period of renewed efflorescence, while Chinese writings had found their greatest exponent in the early period of their practice in Japan. In the realm of prose fiction nothing remains after *Nihon ryōiki*, though Kūkai had referred to a no longer extant humorous work in KAMBUN (Chinese prose) entitled *Suikakuki* or "A Record of Waking from Sleep," written by a Japanese named Hi no Obito. It is possible that other early *setsuwa* have been lost, and that the origins of *monogatari* (tale) fiction go back before the beginning of the 10th century. In particular, the work known as *Taketori monogatari* (see below) is supposed to have had 9th-century origins. But practically nothing remains of what may have been in existence at this early period. For a long time prose was not regarded with the same seriousness as poetry and was not preserved as well.

The First Imperial Anthology of Poetry ——— The year 905 marks the culmination of the first period of Heian literature. A date in the fourth month of that year is mentioned in each of the two prefaces attached to the *Kokinshū* or *Kokin wakashū*, though it has long been unclear as to whether the reference is to the issuance of the commission for the anthology bearing that name, or to the submission of the completed product. In either case, the date is a handy one on which to hang the single most important work in purely literary terms in the history of *waka* between the 8th and 13th centuries, and the most influential compilation in the entire history of the art. The *Kokinshū*, whose name means "Collection from Ancient and Recent Times," was the first of what became a string of 21 "imperial anthologies" (*chokusenshū*) stretching on into the 15th century. It was either ordered or received (current opinion favors the latter) by Emperor Daigo in 905. Daigo gave the commission for its compilation to four accomplished poets of the day, charging them to select poems of their own and old poems not included in the *Man'yōshū*. The four compilers were Ki no Tsurayuki (872?–945), Ki no Tomonori (fl ca 900), ŌSHIKŌCHI NO MITSUNE (fl ca 900), and MIBU NO TADAMINE (fl ca 910). They produced a book containing 1,111 poems in 20 volumes, with prefaces both in Chinese and Japanese. The 20-volume format became standard for later imperial anthologies. It grouped the seasonal poems at the beginning, with two volumes devoted to spring, one to summer, two to autumn, and one to winter. The other major category, the love poems, began the second half of the anthology, occupying 5 volumes, 11–15. Other minor categories such as poems of parting or of grief took up 1 volume each, and miscellaneous poems 2 volumes. Within these broad groupings poems were arranged in meaningful patterns of association and progression to give the order of a season or a love affair, and to provide the aesthetic pleasure of linked images. The content includes a large number of anonymous poems whose atmosphere and technique suggest they represent the older ranges of the anthology's coverage. There are also a very large number of poems by the compilers and their contemporaries, the poets of the early 10th century. A third group of poets represented are those known by name from the previous century, notably Komachi, Narihira, and Henjō, as discussed above. These three and three other poets of lesser importance are mentioned by name in both the Japanese and Chinese prefaces, and have for this reason become known as the ROKKASEN or Six Poetic Geniuses. Since each is made the subject of a derogatory comment, it is rather ironic that they should have come to be so known. However, it was of course an honor to be mentioned at all. The Chinese preface (J: "Manajo"), by Ki no Yoshimochi (d 919), was probably written first; the Japanese preface ("Kanajo") is an adaptation by Ki no Tsurayuki. Together the prefaces, though derivative to a degree from the "Great Preface" of the Chinese anthology *Shijing* (*Shih ching*), the ancient *Classic of Poetry,* as well as other Chinese works on poetics, constitute a landmark in Japanese views of *waka.* Serious *waka* poetics may be said to begin with the "Kana Preface" (*kana* being the Japanese phonetic script), which describes Japanese poetry as the spontaneous creation of the human heart when faced with life's tangle of events. The "Kana Preface" is also the first extended piece of pure Japanese prose, a sign that in this respect too the native language had come of age for literary purposes and could assume the dignity of scholarship. Its author, Tsurayuki, implies a preference for a classical balance of form (*kotoba;* literally, "words") and content (*kokoro;* literally, "heart"), and the anthology itself sets a standard of limited, courtly diction. As the *Kokinshū* became elevated into poetic scripture, these tendencies were to have a profoundly conservative effect on the tradition.

II. THE BIRTH OF PROSE LITERATURE (905–1020)

The period of roughly a hundred years after the *Kokinshū* was one of the most creative in the entire history of the Japanese literature. It was a time of new growth, as many potentialities of Japan's unique courtly culture began to be realized. Poetry continued to flourish, with sponsorship at the highest level, producing two more imperial anthologies. But it was in the evolution of fictional, semifictional, and intimately personal genres of prose writing that the century left its mark. These too, however, grew out of and existed in symbiotic relationships with *waka.*

Poetry contests continued to be held both at court and in private mansions. Fourteen are recorded from the decade following 905, with a falling off thereafter, and another spurt after midcentury. A particularly notable occasion was the *Teiji no In no uta-awase* (Poem Contest at Teiji Palace) of 913, presided over and judged by ex–Emperor Uda, the former patron of Sugawara no Michizane. The prose description of the contest which serves as a preface is credited to the poetess Lady Ise (ca 877–940). It not only lists the contestants and other participants (who included Ki no Tsurayuki and other *Kokinshū* poets), but specifies the costumes worn and the decor of the site. Indeed, the early *uta-awase* were as much social as literary events. The poetry presented on these occasions was naturally formal, and the existence of the contests and such galas as Emperor Uda's outing to the river Ōigawa in 907 tended to preserve the distinction between formal verse and what was being exchanged in the private lives of these same courtiers. Tsurayuki was called on again to write a brief and elegant preface for the Ōigawa poems, the "Ōigawa gyōkō waka jo" or "Preface to the Waka for the Imperial Progress to Ōi River."

Ki no Tsurayuki was the most considerable literary figure of his day, and after the death of Michizane in 903 undoubtedly the greatest writer in Japan. Like Michizane, he served a period as a governor of a province in Shikoku, but unlike the great master of *kanshi,* he was safely ensconced in the middle ranks of the bureaucracy and never ran afoul of Fujiwara ambitions. The Ki family, like the Sugawara, was a scholarly one, but after Michizane no scholar was elevated to power again. Tsurayuki was in the first place an accomplished *waka* poet, as accomplished as any of his day, and has left about 800 of his own poems. His authorship of the "Kana Preface" to the *Kokinshū* and his work as chief compiler of that anthology are equally important, for they enabled him to help mold the taste of later generations. But Tsurayuki has still another claim to fame. A true pioneer, even if a very elegant one, he wrote the first travel diary, indeed the first literary diary of any sort, in Japanese literature. And the diary was to become a staple mode of expression throughout the Heian period and beyond. During the years 930–934, by which time he was quite an elderly man, Tsurayuki was sent out to govern the province of Tosa (now Kōchi Prefecture) on the south coast of Shikoku. This was a normal event in the life of a middling member of the Heian bureaucracy, which is what Tsurayuki was, for all his literary *éclat.* At the end of 934 Tsurayuki's term expired, and he returned to the capital with his family and entourage. The voyage was by boat, long and perilous, taking about two months due to bad weather. Storms and pirates were much on

the minds of the travelers. In 935, on reaching home safely, Tsurayuki wrote up the experience in a work known as *Tosa nikki* or *Tosa Diary.* The ancestor of the literary diary and its variant the travel record, *Tosa nikki* stands at the beginning of Japanese prose literature. It is the longest piece of Japanese prose up to its time, and like the "Kana Preface" was written in the phonetic script known as *kana.* Other than for *waka,* this comparatively simple script was used mostly by women, while men, educated in Chinese, wrote prose in that language. Thus Tsurayuki in his old age was popularizing the use of Japanese not only for poetry, but for an emergent prose literature. But the idea was still so new that he chose to create a female narrator, one who remarks self-consciously at the beginning that she will try and see if a woman can do what she understands men do—write a diary. The male diaries to which she alludes, which survive in considerable numbers from the Heian period, were written in *kambun* and are not literary works. The *Tosa Diary* is very literary, however. The use of a fictitious narrator enables the author to distance himself from the work for ironic purposes, and to experiment with a feminine point of view. The *Tosa* is full of day-by-day incidents, of pathos, excitement—and of poetry. It is a "poetic diary," with *waka* composed by the people in it to express emotions and to react to the various scenes along the way. In all these matters it was a forecast of things to come.

The Record of Masakado —— The travelers in Tsurayuki's "diary" were justified in their fear of pirates on the Inland Sea. Just a few years later the area was terrorized by the depradations of the pirate chieftain FUJIWARA NO SUMITOMO (d 941), and the court was obliged to send an expedition to suppress him. As ill luck would have it, danger and insurrection threatened from the opposite direction at the same time. Late in 939 TAIRA NO MASAKADO (d 940), a landholder in Shimōsa Province (now part of Chiba and Ibaraki prefectures) in eastern Japan, suddenly rebelled against the central government and in rapid succession took over the eight provinces of the Bandō region, an immense area stretching in all directions from what is now the city of Tōkyō. Masakado appointed his own provincial governors and seems to have intended to set up a separate kingdom. The whole affair was over in two months, as Masakado was killed in a battle with one of his relatives in March 940, but the sudden military threat he posed had caused alarm in the capital. In the 10th century the Bandō region was already a hotbed of feuding families, military offshoots of the Taira and Minamoto families. Masakado was but one of many jostling warlords in the area, an area out of which two and a half centuries later the nemesis of the whole court system of rule emerged. The 10th-century courtiers of Heian could not know that Masakado was only a small taste of things to come. His revolt was important for literary purposes because it produced an account—written in Chinese—entitled SHŌMONKI, which is the first of what became a major genre, the war tale or GUNKI MONOGATARI. Also referred to as *Masakadoki*—both titles mean "Record of Masakado"—the work details how Masakado fought shifting alliances of other warlords for a number of years, when he suddenly found himself almost at a stroke the master of the entire east. According to the account he was seized with megalomaniac ambitions, and proclaimed himself New Emperor over a separate kingdom. There is no independent verification for this claim. As he emerges from the awkward, rather Japanized Chinese text, Masakado has something of the quality of a tragic hero, but the narrative goes by fits and starts and does not build a consistent image. The author is unknown but is thought to have been a man of some education (as in later war tales, there are many references to Chinese parallels) who was close to the action. The work was probably completed in 940, less than a year after the climactic events.

The Tale of the Bamboo Cutter —— It was probably about this time or a little later that there emerged into the form in which we know it now the earliest remaining fictional narrative written in Japanese, TAKETORI MONOGATARI or *The Tale of the Bamboo Cutter.* This is the story of Kaguyahime, a magical infant found by an old bamboo cutter in the bole of a bamboo, and of how she grew up to set tasks for her numerous suitors. The suitors all fail, and the emperor himself has a try at winning the maiden's hand but is foiled when people descend from the moon to take Kaguyahime away. It turns out that she is an exile from the moon, reborn on earth to expiate for a time some lunar misdemeanor. The story draws on worldwide fairy tale motifs—magic birth, tasks for suitors, origin myths—which relate it to sources outside Japan. There is, for instance, a Tibetan story which contains the motifs of a girl born from bamboo who imposes tasks on five suitors, the same number as in *Taketori monogatari.* It is not known when or how the tale entered

Japan, but it is obviously very ancient in Tibet. Stylistic characteristics of *Taketori* suggest that the present text may have been reworked from a *kambun* original or originals, perhaps going back to the 9th century. In any case, the work as it ultimately came to be realized close to the middle of the 10th century successfully exploits the humor and pathos inherent in the story of the ridiculous tasks set the suitors, and Kaguyahime's regard for her aged foster parents.

Prose and Poetry as Complementary Genres ——— The second half of the 10th century saw literary works appear with increasing frequency. The second imperial *waka* anthology, the GOSEN WAKASHŪ (also known as the *Gosenshū*; Later Waka Collection) was ordered in 951. Like the *Kokinshū*, it was compiled by a committee, this time of five—MINAMOTO NO SHITAGAU (911–983), ŌNAKATOMI NO YOSHINOBU (921–991), Ki no Tokibumi (dates unknown), Kiyohara no Motosuke (908–990), and Sakanoue no Mochiki (d 975). These are the "Five Gentlemen of the Pear Chamber," so called from the room where they held their deliberations in the palace. In addition to compiling the *Gosenshū*, they were charged with the exegesis of the *Man'yōshū*, which by then had become something of a problem to read because of orthographic and linguistic changes. The *Gosenshū* does not maintain as high a poetic level as the *Kokinshū*, but is notable for the long headnotes to many of its poems, prose settings which amount to little stories.

Another important type of literary work that had started to appear by this time was the personal poetry collection (SHIKASHŪ or *ie no shū*). Such had already existed in pre-Heian times, but are known only from their subsumed content in the *Man'yōshū*. The extant collections of the 9th-century poets Komachi, Narihira, and Henjō are thought to be *ex post facto* compilations by later hands. The earliest extant poetry collection put together by the poet himself is the *Kudai waka* of Ōe no Chisato, dated to 894. This is a formal arrangement of poems on the topics of lines of Chinese poetry, which is what *kudai* means. Other *shikashū* followed chronological arrangements, maintained a greater informality, and combined poetry with extended prose headnotes, as in the *Gosenshū*. The *Iseshū*, a collection of the poetry of Lady Ise, was of this nature. It features detailed settings for the first 33 of its poems in *monogatari* or storytelling style, employing the third person. A similar 10th-century *shikashū* is that of Fujiwara no Koretada (or Koremasa; 924–972), the *Ichijō Sesshō gyoshū* (Collection of the Regent from the First Ward). This is also known as *Toyokage,* because the opening section embeds its poems in a fictionalized context about a young courtier of low rank dubbed Kurahashi no Toyokage. Both formal and informal *shikashū* served as source material for the imperial anthologies, and were sometimes put together to that end.

Uta Monogatari ——— The combination of *waka* and prose contexts seen in the *Gosenshū* and some *shikashū* is a product of the same trend toward poem-stories that led to the appearance of three anonymous works toward the middle of the 10th century that are now grouped under precisely that genre designation—*uta monogatari* (see MONOGATARI BUNGAKU) or "poem tale." The most admired and widely read of these works, both in its own day and since, is the one known as ISE MONOGATARI or *Tales of Ise*. This work has no connection with the *Iseshū*, the poetry collection of Lady Ise mentioned above. The title probably derives from one of the most sensational of the 125 episodes making up the book, in which the anonymous hero has an affair with the sacrosanct priestess of the Ise Shrine. The stories, each centered on one or more poems, are brief and use a formulaic opening, beginning, *"Mukashi otoko . . ."* ("Once a man . . ."). Most of them describe a love situation, usually with a sad ending. It was always believed that the hero was Ariwara no Narihira, the 9th-century poet, and indeed the work contains all 30 of the poems attributed to Narihira in the *Kokinshū*. Some of the tales allude to affairs with which his name has always been associated; others are about noncourtly types or other people who cannot reasonably be identified with him. The anonymous author apparently drew on various sources, one of which may have been an early collection of Narihira's poems, for verses to make the subject of explanatory anecdotes. In some cases the prose is no longer than a headnote, in others it amounts to a story a few pages in length. There is a distinct overlap with the *Kokinshū*, and it is plausible that the latter and the *Ise* may have drawn on the same sources. In any case, *Ise monogatari* contributed to the formation of the ideal of Heian courtly love, with its emphasis on the superiority of romantic feelings to all other considerations. It also contains among its 209 verses some of the best early Heian poetry and preserves the legend of the poet-lover Narihira in its classic form.

It is possible that *Ise monogatari* took shape gradually as its materials were worked over by a number of hands, and reached its present form by the middle of the 10th century. The same process has been suggested as that which created another work in the genre, HEICHŪ MONOGATARI, in this case with terminal dates of about 960–965. As *Ise* refers in veiled fashion to Narihira, so does *Heichū* to another famous poet-lover, Taira no Sadabun (also known as Taira no Sadabumi; d 923). But whereas Narihira was renowned for success in love, Sadabun (known by his nickname Heichū) was notorious as a failure, ever eager but usually rejected. The 39 episodes of this work, like *Ise* probably based partially on a lost personal poetry collection, focus more exclusively on the activities of a hero (here also anonymous) who is obviously the same person throughout, which is to say that *Heichū* is a more tightly knit work than *Ise*. Its stories are also more highly developed, with extended prose passages not tied to poems. The work employs a kind of gentle irony in depicting its failed hero, a quality which lifts it to a higher level of literary sophistication than *Ise*. The level of poetic content is not as high, however. Sadabun was a less accomplished poet than Narihira, though by no means to be despised. As a poet he was simply one of the lesser lights in the galaxy of the *Kokinshū* period.

The third of the midcentury poem-tale collections is different in at least two respects from the other two. Known as *Yamato monogatari*, and probably completed by 952, it consists of 173 episodes which constitute anecdotes of a variety of people, their love adventures, and the poems they composed. There is no unification around the figure of one lover. In addition, the anonymity preserved in *Ise* and *Heichū* is for the most part abandoned here. Many of the stories are simple anecdotes explaining how a certain poem came to be written. But others are devoted to developing a fictional plot situation, are several pages in length, and constitute a step toward the long fictional *monogatari* which began to appear before the end of the 10th century. The title means "Tales of Yamato," but its significance is not known; since Yamato is an old name for Japan, it might simply mean "Japanese Stories."

Another work of uncertain authorship and date, which may have been written during 962, though different from the *uta monogatari* discussed above in not being made up of separate little love stories, is similar in that it treats the life of a real person, interweaving poetry and prose. This is *Tōnomine Shōshō monogatari* (The Tale of the Minor Captain of Tōnomine). The person named in the title is Fujiwara no Takamitsu (d 994), a highly placed young nobleman who abandoned the world and took Buddhist orders at an early age in 962. The work consists of 30 short episodes in which Takamitsu exchanges poems with his grief-stricken family. It covers only six months and ends before his final retirement to his mountain retreat at Tōnomine.

Diaries ——— The first literary diary or *nikki* had been written by Ki no Tsurayuki after his return from Tosa in 935. It is highly fictionalized and written in the third person. An experimental work, it had no immediate followers. The next literary diary, an entirely different kind of work, appeared after the middle of the 10th century. This was KAGERŌ NIKKI. The author of *Kagerō nikki* was a woman, and with her begins the succession of prose works by women which were to be the glory of Heian literature. Previously women writers had been limited to the role of poet, though Lady Ise had written several prose introductions (also interestingly enough called *nikki*) to the records of poem contests, as well as the story-like opening of her personal poetry collection. Curiously, the opening of *Kagerō* is similarly cast in the third person, though this section is limited to only a few sentences. *Kagerō* is a substantial piece of writing, a work in three volumes, amounting to well over 200 pages in a modern printed edition. It is in fact the earliest Japanese autobiography. Probably written after most of the events it records had occurred, but perhaps contemporaneously with them for the last few years, it describes a period of 21 years from 954 to 974 in the life of the author, who is known from her only child as the Mother of Michitsuna (Fujiwara no Michitsuna no Haha). She was a Fujiwara noblewoman married to FUJIWARA NO KANEIE (929–990), one of the politically dominant men of his day. Her autobiography is a thematic one—to tell her side of an unhappy marriage and let her readers decide if this was the sort of thing she should have had to expect. The book is by way of being an indictment of Heian polygamy (she was a secondary wife), a cry from the heart of an abused woman. Psychologically interesting, it is also important as the first piece of social realism. Highborn women, the educated leisure class of Heian, were to produce its best writing, a phenomenon probably unique in world literature.

Utsubo Monogatari and Ochikubo Monogatari —— The second half of the 10th century is also notable as the probable time of composition of the first attempts at a Heian novel. Of the larger number of long *monogatari* which circulated at this time, two survive. In both cases the date and authorship are unknown, but both have been attributed on no discernible evidence to Minamoto no Shitagau, the scholar and poet who was on the committee that compiled the *Gosenshū*. The fairy tale *Taketori monogatari* has likewise been attributed to him. Skepticism is justified in regard to all these attributions. Japanese scholars do hold the opinion, however, that the two novels are the work of a man rather than a woman. They are entitled UTSUBO MONOGATARI (The Tale of the Hollow Tree) and OCHIKUBO MONOGATARI (The Tale of the Lower Room).

Utsubo monogatari may or may not be the earlier of the two. The author of *Genji monogatari*, writing early in the 11th century, thought of it as "new" in contrast to *Taketori monogatari*, which was "old." *Utsubo* is an extremely long work, the longest of the Heian *monogatari* except for *Genji* itself. Like *Genji*, its story extends over three generations. An attempt at a thematic novel, it suffers from extreme unevenness of style and a jerky story line, which indicate that it may be the product of more than one hand and that the manuscript has suffered damage and disordering. The story falls into four parts, beginning with an opening chapter of fantastic happenings which introduces the theme of the magic music and one of the main characters. This chapter is a self-contained *monogatari* as supernatural and whimsical as *The Tale of the Bamboo Cutter*. Taking place partially in Japan and partially in a magical realm beyond the seas called Hashikoku ("Persia"), it has among its characters child prodigies of genius and filial piety, demons, sages, angels, the Buddha, the emperor, innocent young lovers, brigands, and a family of bears. These last live in a hollow tree, the same that gives its name to the entire work. The second part of the novel describes the wooing of Atemiya, a beautiful young girl who finally rejects all her suitors and marries the crown prince. This section is extremely romantic, but ultimately antiromantic, as the agonies of the rejected suitors go beyond the believable into the satirical. The third section is a piece of social realism in Heian terms—the account of a power struggle between factions at court for the prize of succession to the throne. It is marriage politics as it in fact functioned at the time. In the final section the losing side recoups its glory by substituting art for mere mundane power, and the theme of the magic music is reasserted.

Ochikubo monogatari is more down-to-earth and much better unified. A shorter work, about 200 pages in a modern edition, it is totally devoid of supernatural elements. It is nevertheless realistic only in detail: it is in fact a Cinderella story of an abused stepdaughter and her devoted and determinedly monogamous Prince Charming. Belonging to what was once a larger group of stepdaughter stories, it tells of how the lovely, innocent heroine is taken advantage of by her cruel stepmother and obliged to live as a servant in a lower room. The heroine is rescued by a dashing young officer at court with the aid of some clever servants, but not before truly harrowing adventures. The hero marries her and then takes protracted revenge on the evil old woman, only to forgive her in the end at his wife's insistence. The book has a happy ending, an anomaly in Japanese fiction. It also has suspense and a great deal of racy and often scatological humor. Certain scenes read like slapstick versions of tragic scenes in the *Tale of Genji*. The work is thought to belong to the 960s or 970s.

Another work of prose fiction of the period belongs not to secular *monogatari* but to religious *setsuwa*. It is *Sambōe* (also called *Sambō ekotoba*), a collection of 62 stories written by Minamoto no Tamenori (d 1011) in 984 for the edification of the young Princess Takako, who died the next year at just under 20 years of age. The stories are arranged in three volumes, each devoted to one of the "Three Treasures" (Sambō) of Buddhism: the Buddha, the Law, and the Priesthood. They originally contained pictures (*e*) and text (*kotoba*). There is some overlap with the content of *Nihon ryōiki*, but *Sambōe* unlike the earlier collection is written in Japanese, as it was intended for a lady.

The Golden Age of Heian Literature —— With the advent of the 990s, Heian literature entered its heyday. It was the period when FUJIWARA NO MICHINAGA (966–1028) began his long dominance of the court, when his son-in-law, the boy emperor ICHIJŌ (980–1011; r 986–1011), was on the throne, and when Ichijō's consorts set up rival coteries of talented literary ladies. It was the age that produced *The Pillow Book* and *Tale of Genji*. *The Pillow Book* or *Makura no sōshi* is the journal-sketchbook of a court lady known as SEI SHŌNAGON.

Shōnagon (that was her nickname; "Sei" indicates she was a member of the Kiyohara family) was in service to Ichijō's first empress, Sadako (976–1001), during the 990s, and even after the death of her imperial mistress in 1001 she seems to have remained a well-known character at court. Over the course of her years of service she wrote down her observations and thoughts in a book that has made her famous as the epitome of the Heian aristocratic lady. Actually, she was unique, very much an individual, all sharp angles and sharper opinions. She was also one of the most talented writers Japan has produced. Her most admirable traits are her economy and deftness in rendering a scene. In these qualities she is unexcelled. Her book is referred to as a ZUIHITSU or collection of random jottings rather than a *nikki* or diary. It is made up of four types of content: lists, eyewitness accounts, stories she passes on, and short fictional sketches. Helter-skelter in organization, vivid in description, and uncompromising in its opinionatedness, it is the liveliest document left by the golden age of Heian letters.

Another lively author of the time was IZUMI SHIKIBU, the most talented poet living at the end of the 10th century. Also a court lady, she was as famous for her ardor as Sei Shōnagon was for her wit. The many men in her life included two husbands and an indefinite number of lovers, most notably two imperial princes, brothers, who both died young in the full tide of their passion for her. The boldness of much of her poetry reflects this side of her character. Like Ono no Komachi she belongs to the tradition of the passionate poetess. Much more is known of her, however, since about 1,500 of her poems have been preserved. She is also the subject of a curious and controversial work known variously as *Izumi Shikibu nikki* and *Izumi Shikibu monogatari*. This is a third-person account of the beginning of her relationship with one of her lovers, Prince Atsumichi (981–1007). Since the work is not a "diary," but a piece of imaginative fiction—based closely on the facts, no doubt—it has for some time been debated whether or not Izumi Shikibu wrote it herself. The question is impossible to answer. Analogies can be drawn to two different works—to *Tōnomine Shōshō monogatari*, also a poem-studded account of several months in the life of a real person, presumably written by someone other than the main character, Takamitsu; and to *Iseshū*, the collected poems of Lady Ise, which begins with a third-person narrative, presumably written by the poetess herself. It has also been argued that *Izumi Shikibu nikki* was modeled on the love sequences of the imperial *waka* anthologies. Whatever may be the truth of the matter, the work presents a distinctly more melancholy picture of Izumi Shikibu than is to be derived from her collected poems, from which she emerges as a multifaceted individual with brash and witty moods offset against moments of intense passion, courtly languor, and a desire for the peace of Buddhist renunciation. In all these things she handled the language with consummate skill. Like Sei Shōnagon and most other court ladies, her birth and death dates are unknown. The crucial period in her life dealt with in *Izumi Shikibu nikki* fell in 1003–1004, and it is known that she was still living in 1027.

Aside from the work of Izumi Shikibu, the poetry of the late 10th and early 11th centuries is known more for its competence than its brilliance. It was primarily an age of prose, though the prose was always interwoven with the omnipresent *waka*. After the *Gosenshū*, at midcentury poetry as an official and social art continued to flourish—indeed the number of poetry contests increased. The most renowned was held in 960, a grand affair at the Imperial Palace sponsored by Emperor Murakami (926–967, r 946–967), the same sovereign who had ordered the compilation of the *Gosenshū* nine years earlier. One of the more interesting poets of the second half of the century was SONE NO YOSHITADA (fl ca 985). Yoshitada left a reputation as an eccentric, including an anecdote of perhaps questionable reliability that he was once literally booted out of a poetry party he had tried to crash. The thing that attracted censure to Yoshitada's poetry was that he introduced imagery not sanctioned by the authority of the *Kokinshū*, such as hair drenched with sweat, forests of mugwort, and fields planted with melons. The rough country images and some of his diction hark back to the *Man'yōshū*; they are also said to owe a debt to the plain style of the much admired Chinese poet Bo Juyi. Yoshitada was ahead of his time in his interest in descriptive poetry divorced from the "*Kokinshū* style," and he was admired and anthologized extensively later in the tradition. But he did not succeed in altering the courtly nature of that tradition. Probably he did not intend to, for he himself was a practitioner of the standard style, and his earthier poems remained experiments.

Three important poetic anthologies bracket the beginning of the 11th century. The first was *Kokin waka rokujō* (also called *Kokin rokujō*; Six Volumes of Ancient and Recent Waka), an extensive collection of about 4,500 poems arranged by topics as an encyclopedia-like reference work for poets. There are large overlaps with the content of *Man'yōshū*, *Kokinshū*, and *Gosen wakashū*. The compiler is unknown, but may have been either Prince Kaneakira (914–987) or Minamoto no Shitagau. *Kokin rokujō* is assigned to the 970s or 980s. The next major anthology of the period was the SHŪI WAKASHŪ (also called *Shūishū*; "Collection of Gleanings"), the third imperial *waka* anthology. Of all the imperial anthologies, the *Shūishū* is the one whose origins are surrounded with the most uncertainties. It seems to have been commissioned by ex–Emperor KAZAN (968–1008; r 984–986), and compiled at least in its initial stages by FUJIWARA NO KINTŌ (966–1041). Kintō's draft, known as the *Shūishō* (literally, "Selections from *Gleanings*"), was probably in existence by 999; the complete *Shūishū* may be an expanded version by Kazan, perhaps datable between 1005 and 1007. Kintō was the most highly regarded poet of his day, though later ages rightly preferred Izumi Shikibu, whose brilliance and originality he lacked. He was also the author of two brief works on poetics, *Shinsen zuinō* (Newly Selected Essentials) and *Waka kuhon* (The Nine Levels of Waka). The former provides examples of good and bad poems; the poet is instructed to avoid repetitions—synonyms and homophones. These faults are known as "poetic diseases" (*uta no yamai*). The Buddhist-influenced nine-level analysis in *Waka kuhon* takes as its highest level that of "excess of heart" (*amari no kokoro*), a phrase that Tsurayuki had used in a sense usually taken to be pejorative in the "Kana Preface" to the *Kokinshū*. Kintō's aesthetic is more mystical.

Kintō was also the compiler of the third of the three anthologies mentioned above, this a collection of Japanese and Chinese verse for oral recitation, which is the meaning of its title WAKAN RŌEISHŪ. Compiled either in 1013 or 1018, it arranges its content under topical headings, with at least one Japanese and one Chinese verse for each topic. The Japanese verses are complete *waka*, but the Chinese are usually couplets from longer poems. There are 217 of the former and 587 of the latter. The Chinese verses draw from the work of both Chinese and Japanese poets. *Rōei*, the intoning of poetry, sometimes to musical accompaniment, was one of the artistic accomplishments cultivated at the Heian court.

The Tale of Genji —— The most astonishing work produced at that court was a novel of great length entitled *Genji monogatari (Tale of Genji)*. It was written over a period of several years during the first two decades of the 11th century by a woman in service to Empress Akiko (also called Shōshi, 988–1074), the second and more successful of the two principal consorts of Emperor Ichijō. This lady is known as MURASAKI SHIKIBU, a court nickname like Izumi Shikibu and Sei Shōnagon. As with them, her birth and death dates are unknown. What we do know of her life stems almost exclusively from the diary she kept at court during 1008–10. This is a very interesting short work entitled *Murasaki Shikibu nikki*. It reveals that *Genji monogatari* was at least partly written during those years and was circulating at court. It also includes eyewitness accounts in the manner of *The Pillow Book*, but the most fascinating sections are those in which Murasaki analyzes her own character and the characters of the men and women around her. Sei Shōnagon and Izumi Shikibu were both known to her, and she displays a devastating condescension toward them both. She also confesses that she herself is generally disliked as a sour and hypercritical person, but claims that people who really get to know her find to their surprise that she belies her distasteful reputation.

This defensive introvert created the great work of Japanese literature, a long and multifaceted novel covering three generations and immortalizing once and for all the world it depicts, a somewhat idealized version of Heian society. It is the story of Genji, a dashing and amorous young hero, and of his gradual aging; of the women and children in his life, and the lives of his descendants. Genji is one of the most problematical characters in world literature. Readers often react violently to him in one way or another—which may be taken as evidence that the characterization has brought him to life. As a young man he is all charm and handsomeness, talent and ardor. A very attractive figure, the author makes us feel. But at the same time she is showing his self-centeredness, rashness, his insensitivity to the feelings of others. He brings pain and disaster to some of the many women he loves—all the while of course having meant only the best. Lover, man of taste, accomplished beyond all others in the various arts, intensely alive, feelingful, generous—Genji is also lech-

erous, hypocritical, a master of self-deceit. In him the author has created a figure somewhat larger than life, but endowed with a believable human complexity. And he is only one of a vast gallery of characters. Most of the major characters are women, each a distinct personality understood from the inside. The most beloved—both to Genji and to the author—is Murasaki, the character from whom the author takes her nickname. Murasaki is the fully realized portrait of a woman, from petulant and bashful childhood to the moment of her death as a wise, sad, and loving wife. The author ranges over many personality types, from the healthy to the highly disturbed, and each is allowed to exist in all of his or her simplicity, complexity, or contradictoriness. The work is in fact a psychological novel, something for which nothing in the tradition from which it emerged quite prepares us. The social realism of *Kagerō nikki* was a step on the way, and the minute examination of emotion in *waka* also tended toward fostering fine-grained sensibility, but Murasaki Shikibu went beyond into depth of discovery and thematic resonance for which the only explanation is genius. The work as a whole, though rich with memorable scenes of sensuous beauty, is deeply and bitterly pessimistic. At the end Genji is long dead, the world is in decline, the main characters have shallow or neurotically ineffectual personalities, and love—the search for which is the novel's grand theme—is seen as an illusory dream.

III. FROM GENJI MONOGATARI TO SHIN KOKINSHŪ (1020–1205)

The 11th Century —— The first corroboration of the existence and popularity of *Genji* outside Murasaki Shikibu's own diary is provided by another autobiographical work, SARASHINA NIKKI. This is a work comparable to *Kagerō nikki* in that it covers decades of the author's life and deals with a selection of the experiences that the author seems to have found most significant. But whereas the Mother of Michitsuna was obsessed with her marriage and talks endlessly about it, marriage was precisely the one subject which (although she was in fact married) the Daughter of Takasue (Sugawara no Takasue no Musume; b 1008), the author of *Sarashina nikki*, chose to ignore. She was far more interested in her dreams and her books—especially *Tale of Genji*, which she read in its entirety and for which she is the first known enthusiast. She lived in fact in that world of romance which her aunt the *Kagerō* authoress bitterly dismisses in her opening sentences. Her autobiography begins in 1020 when she was 12 years old, recounting her trip back to the capital in the company of her father, Sugawara no Takasue (b 973), who had been serving as vice-governor of the eastern province of Kazusa (now part of Chiba Prefecture). This travel record, though no doubt written much later, recaptures the sense of a child's wonder, and establishes the author as a sensitive and romantic person, much taken with stories and the beauties of nature. The balance of the work describes her life in the capital, which was quiet and bookish. She read the *Tale of Genji* at an early age, and fantasized herself as the heroine of such a story. Eventually, in her thirties, she went into court service, and still later married. She was left a widow in 1058, and seems to have spent a gloomy old age. The title of her memoirs assumes its significance in this regard, as Sarashina is a place associated with an old story of an aged woman taken into the mountains and abandoned (see OBASUTEYAMA).

Toward the end of her autobiography the Daughter of Takasue repeatedly bemoans the time she wasted on romantic stories in her youth. This gives a peculiar ambiguity to the fact that she is credited with having written two such stories herself. FUJIWARA NO SADAIE (also known as Fujiwara no Teika; 1162–1241), the scholar-poet who made a copy of *Sarashina nikki* about a century and a half later, added a colophon in which he states that she was the author of four *monogatari*. Two of the works he names are no longer extant; the other two are *Yowa no nezame* and *Mitsu no hamamatsu*. These are in fact probably the two earliest post-*Genji* novels, and if the Daughter of Takasue wrote both of them in addition to *Sarashina* she is indeed one of the major authors of the Heian period.

Yowa no nezame (Waking at Midnight), also known as *Yoru no nezame* (Waking at Night), is a highly introspective account of frustrated love derivative from *Genji monogatari*, and especially from the last ten chapters of that novel, the "Uji jūjō." The work has come down to us in fragmentary condition, with only parts one and three of an original four intact, though the outline of some of the missing sections can be reconstructed from references in other sources. The central figure is a woman, beautiful and desirable, but cursed with unhappiness, and the plot has to do with her loves and those of her rivals and her children. She is the daughter of "the Genji Minister," i.e., an imperial prince who has relinquished princely status and taken the Minamoto clan name, and become a minister in the government—in all these respects like the hero of the *Tale of Genji*. In a typical bit of Heian mistaken identity, she is ravished by the hero, a young aristocrat who eventually rises to Palace Minister. He discovers her in a country setting, therefore thinking her a woman of low rank, not realizing she is the sister of his own bride. Deeply in love with the woman on whom he has forced himself (like Prince Niou in the *Tale of Genji*), the hero pursues her through the first three sections of the book—finally making her his wife only when she is pregnant with her third child by him! She meanwhile has married a kind old man, been left a widow, and busied herself with looking after both her stepchildren and her own. Amorously pursued by the emperor as well, she flees back to the hero, and is finally reconciled to him, though still unhappy, as he himself is now married to a jealous second wife. The dominant theme of unhappiness in love is no doubt derived in some degree from the *Tale of Genji*, as is the scene where the hero (like Kaoru in the earlier novel) falls in love with the heroine as a result of peeping at her as she plays music in a house in the country. But whereas the author of *Genji* lets her characters' fates emerge from their own inner natures, the author of *Nezame* has a heavenly being come down at the beginning to tell the heroine that she is fated to be unhappy in love. *Nezame* is also almost entirely concerned with the inner lives of its characters, lacking those descriptions of nature and public events that shed a kind of splendor over *Genji* and balance its psychological aspect. *Nezame* is claustrophobic, and one wonders about the attribution to the Daughter of Takasue in this regard, for her autobiography, although also very private, contains many lyrical descriptions of nature. In the lost fourth part of *Nezame* apparently there was a startling passage in which the heroine either feigns death or actually dies and comes back to life, before becoming a nun. The echoes of the story of Ukifune in *Genji* are fairly clear.

The other extant novel attributed by Teika to the Daughter of Takasue, *Mitsu no hamamatsu* (The Pine on the Beach at the Royal Port), is more commonly known as *Hamamatsu Chūnagon monogatari* (The Tale of the Hamamatsu Middle Counselor). There is evidence suggesting that it was written after 1064, at which time the Daughter of Takasue, if still living, would have been in her 57th year. The many dream sequences, and the faith put in dreams as motivating forces, are qualities shared with *Sarashina nikki*, lending a certain credibility to the attribution. Some opinion holds that differences in manner make it unlikely that the same person wrote both *Nezame* and *Hamamatsu*. As with *Nezame*, the manuscript has not survived intact. Of an original six chapters the first and last had been lost by the Edo period (1600–1868), but the last was rediscovered in 1930, and the outline of the still-missing first chapter can be reconstructed from various sources. The plot of *Hamamatsu Chūnagon monogatari* is based largely on an exploitation of the theory of reincarnation. An unbelievably tangled web of liaisons, births, and rebirths across generations, of all extant late-Heian *monogatari* it displays the greatest interest in the exotic. The story takes place partly in China, where the hero is welcomed by the Tang court, and consummates an affair with the Chinese empress. He has gone to China in the first place in search of his deceased father, revealed in a dream to have been reincarnated as the third son of the Tang emperor. The hero's widowed mother has meanwhile started a relationship with another man, and the son's resentment at this and the subsequent vision of his dead father are fairly striking evocations of the Hamlet theme. In China, the hero meets not only the prince who was once his father, but the half-Japanese, half-Chinese empress, whose attraction to him leads to a liaison and the birth of a son. Thus he becomes the stepfather of his own father. Taking his infant son, the hero returns to Japan. There he delivers a letter from the Empress of China to her Japanese mother, now a nun living in the mountains of Yoshino with her daughter by another man. This daughter, the half-sister of his lover the Empress, is fated to be the hero's wife, thus enabling the Empress to fulfill her filial desire to reestablish bonds with the mother from whom she has long been parted. But fate has decreed that misfortune will befall the young woman if she becomes pregnant before her twentieth year. In the meantime hero and son are informed by a disembodied voice that the empress has died and been reborn in heaven. Further complications ensue when a prince kidnaps the hero's bride-to-be, for whose coming of age he has been patiently waiting, and impregnates her. But this too is fate: the dead empress comes to the hero in a dream and informs him that his longing for her has caused her to come to earth once more, and dwell in the womb of her half-sister. The prince whose seed has caused this new conception is elevated to

crown prince of Japan, and news arrives from China confirming that the empress is indeed dead, and that her first child, the hero's reincarnated father, is now crown prince of China. The hero experiences a strange mixture of joy and sorrow. A novel such as this obviously represents a step away from the realism of *Genji*. The use of reincarnation as the basic device of the plot, and the bold decision to set part of the story in China, give individuality to this work, but at the same time take it further in the direction of fantasy. The dominant role played by pregnancy in the mechanics of the plot is inevitable given the theme, but also suggestive of the preoccupations of a society dominated by marriage politics. Such realism as the book possesses is to be found here.

A third novel probably stemming from the late 11th century is *Sagoromo monogatari*. Its author was a court lady variously known as Senji, Seshi, and Seji (d 1092), an attendant to Princess Baishi (1039–96), daughter of Emperor Go-Suzaku (1009–45, r 1036–45), and an important patron of poetry and prose fiction. Estimates of the novel's date tend to center on the 1070s. The "Sagoromo" ("Narrow Cloak") of the title refers to the hero, a nickname derived from an image in one of his poems. Faithful to the by now venerable tradition of the court novel, *Sagoromo* has as its theme the search for love, and the griefs and frustrations inevitably attendant thereon. The story is full of echoes. The hero, for instance, is in love with his foster sister, Genji no Miya. There is a reference to *The Tales of Ise* in this connection, but an even closer parallel is with the incestuous love of Nakazumi for his sister Atemiya in *The Tale of the Hollow Tree*. As with Nakazumi, Sagoromo's passion remains frustrated and rebuked by his sister. Like Toshikage and Nakatada in the same novel, Sagoromo too plays music so magically that heavenly beings descend. If he had been willing, they would have whisked him away like Kaguyahime in *The Tale of the Bamboo Cutter*. Another of Sagoromo's loves is for a mysterious young woman, Asukai, whose character and fate contain elements reminiscent of Yūgao, Tamakazura, and Ukifune in the *Tale of Genji*. As with Genji and Yūgao, Sagoromo and Asukai meet in a secret humble abode, and conceal their identities from each other. Asukai is abducted and carried away in a boat, a fate that Tamakazura just barely escaped. And like Ukifune, Asukai tries to end her life by drowning. There is also a series of events modeled on the love affair of Genji and Fujitsubo. A child born to an imperial princess is passed off as the emperor's son, although fathered by Sagoromo. The substitution motif so prominent in *Genji* also has its place in this highly derivative novel. Toward the end the hero marries a cousin of his first love Genji no Miya, who bears a strong resemblance to her. Contrary to the pattern of *Genji*, however, Sagoromo finally mounts the throne as emperor, making the substitute figure his consort, and the illegitimate child his heir. The book, in four chapters, has survived intact.

The literary circle of Princess Baishi was the source of at least one other piece of Heian fiction. This is the short story entitled "Ausaka koenu gonchūnagon" ("The Provisional Middle Counselor Who Didn't Cross Meeting Hill"), one of ten stories and a fragment making up the collection known as TSUTSUMI CHŪNAGON MONOGATARI. The record of a poem contest which took place in 1055 at Baishi's court includes a poem from this story, the story's name, and the name of the author, Koshikibu. Who this court lady was is not known, but she is not in any case to be identified with the daughter of Izumi Shikibu who was known by the same nickname. The occasion for the story's composition seems to have been a story contest, where Baishi's ladies-in-waiting wrote and matched stories. The dates and authors of the other stories are not known, but are generally thought to be later, with one story perhaps dating from after the end of the Heian period. The stories are brief, and their content is sometimes ironic or in some way a travesty on the usual courtly tastes and situations. An elaborate abduction plot is foiled in one story when the would-be lover carries off an aged nun by mistake. The best known of the stories, "Mushi mezuru himegimi" (tr "The Lady Who Loved Insects," 1929), presents a striking comical sketch of a young lady who revels in a menagerie of crawling things, refuses to have herself made up, and writes in mannish script on stiff paper. Her disdain for Heian courtly norms and her pretentious seriousness link her in one comic type with the scholarly young woman portrayed in the second chapter of the *Tale of Genji*. As short stories these brief pieces of fiction differ from the poem-tales (*uta monogatari*) of the 10th century in that they are not based on factual or legendary material about real people, incorporating poems already in circulation, but to all appearances are original compositions made up for a specific literary occasion, with poems composed to fit the story, rather than the other way around. The poems, none of very striking quality, are not central to the stories.

Historical Literature —— Thus the techniques and conventions of the court novel and short story were worked out during the 10th and 11th centuries; not all of the production in these genres over this time span has survived. During the 11th century those techniques and conventions came to be turned to different purposes as well—to the narration not of fiction but of history. The earliest such work, EIGA MONOGATARI (A Tale of Flowering Fortunes), deals in its 30-chapter main section with the period from 887 to 1028; a 10-chapter continuation brings the narrative of events down to 1092. The two sections are by different authors, in both cases unknown. The most common ascription, probably acceptable, assigns the main section to the court lady and poet AKAZOME EMON (ca 957–1041), a contemporary of Murasaki Shikibu, with whose work she was no doubt familiar. The date for this section is somewhere between 1028 and midcentury. Whoever wrote the work had a court lady's eye for colorful detail, and interest in recording anecdote. *Eiga monogatari* takes as its theme the glory of the Fujiwara family, and indeed a large part of its significance is to be found in the fact that it is Japan's first thematic history. The earlier National History (see RIKKOKU-SHI) series had degenerated into a mere chronology of the official acts of government before its demise at the end of the 9th century. The author of *Eiga* seems to have wished above all else to impress her readers with the splendor of her central character, Fujiwara no Michinaga, the epitome of Fujiwara political skill and cultural display. The greatest density of description concerns him, his deeds, and his immediate family. He may in fact be said to be the hero, the "shining Genji" of a work that treats history as if it were a series of episodes in an episodic novel. As in *Genji*, the chapters have poetic or flowery titles, and the focus of attention is on the ceremonial and intimate sides of history—what a court lady would have had available to her observation. Ironically or otherwise, the overtly fictional predecessor goes more deeply into the complexities of human motivation than does its historiographical analogue. The work is largely uncritical, even adulatory when it deals with Michinaga and other favored figures, and in this connection it may be significant that Akazome Emon was in service to Michinaga's wife, and spent her life as a dependant of his family. The aim of the narration—to give a vivid picture of the splendors of a splendid age—is largely achieved, but at the expense of an understanding in depth of the events described. Nevertheless, *Eiga monogatari* is discussable as literature because of its concentration on the emotional lives of its characters, and its interest in a wealth of anecdote. The 10-chapter continuation is deficient in these areas where the first 30 chapters are rich, and is of distinctly inferior interest.

Eiga monogatari turned out to be a trend-setting work, and was soon imitated by other lively historical narratives that used a storytelling style. The first and most notable of these is ŌKAGAMI (The Great Mirror), a work about one-third the length of *Eiga,* which probably dates from the late 11th century. Its author is unknown; it has been attributed to Minamoto no Akifusa (1026–94) among others. It runs parallel to *Eiga monogatari,* covering the period from 850 to 1025, and it too concentrates on the fortunes of the major Fujiwara figures, especially Michinaga. The most important difference between the two works is that *Ōkagami* attempts to explain why things happened, not just to describe what in fact did happen. If *Eiga* is the first thematic history of Japan, *Ōkagami* with its attempt to dig into the mechanisms of event may be called the first critical one. Its set of values is also different—the author sets great store by shrewdness, nerve, and ability to handle practical political situations. These qualities seem to reflect something of the masculine world seen only from a distance in feminine writings such as *Eiga*. To the author of *Ōkagami* a degree of unscrupulousness was acceptable as a trait of character if it led to worldly success. The author of *Eiga monogatari* preferred to ignore and gloss over such matters. The character of Michinaga, rich in unscrupulousness, thus posed contrary problems for the two historians. The two histories also differ in narrative technique. *Eiga* employs basically impersonal narration, though this lapses into first-person eyewitness accounts when the author quotes or adapts a source such as *The Diary of Murasaki Shikibu*. *Ōkagami* on the contrary has a dramatic framework. It takes the form of the recollections of a preternaturally old man, Yotsugi, who entertains the crowd gathered to hear a preacher at a temple in the environs of the capital. Yotsugi at 190 has lived through most of the events he describes, and has opinions on them

as well. Another oldster pipes up from time to time, and there are further comments and objections from a first-person narrator and another member of the congregation. All this makes room for a critical, investigatory approach to history, as well as for liveliness of narrative. Nevertheless, it must be said that the presentation of the period dealt with is slanted strongly in favor of Michinaga and his clique. *Eiga monogatari* and *Ōkagami* mark the beginning of a genre of Japanese writing, the *rekishi monogatari* or "historical tale," one that continued on into the Kamakura period (1185–1333).

Other Literary Genres of the 11th Century —— In the meantime, the stream of courtly autobiographical writing continued. The mid-10th century saw two notable works in this genre, *Shijōnomiya Shimotsuke shū* and *Jōjin Azari no Haha shū*. The former is the poetic memoir of a lady known as Shijōnomiya Shimotsuke, in the service of the consort of Emperor Go-Reizei (1025–68, r 1045–68). It consists of 211 poems with long headnotes arranged in chronological order, covering the years 1051–71. According to the author it was rewritten from memory after having been burned. *Jōjin Azari no Haha shū* (The Collection of the Mother of Jōjin Azari) is a unique work. It is the testament of the bitter and possessive love of an octogenarian woman for her son, the prominent Tendai cleric Jōjin Azari (1011–81), who in his sixties decided to make a pilgrimage to Buddhist sites in China. His mother did not wish to let him go, and poured out her grief in a poetic memoir covering the years 1067–73. Jōjin left nevertheless in 1072. He never saw his mother again, nor did he read her testament, for he died in China without returning to Japan. The work remains as an expression of a different kind of love from the usual court lady's diary, but of an intensity unsurpassed by any of the others.

About the middle of the 11th century vastly different events led to the compilation of an account that foreshadowed literary developments of the feudal period. The situation in eastern and northern Honshū was increasingly unstable as central authority declined in that remote region, and war with the Ezo, semi-independent aborigines, broke out repeatedly in the 1050s and later. One series of these campaigns, known as the EARLIER NINE YEARS' WAR, went on sporadically between 1055 and 1063, and was recorded in a short work known as *Mutsu waki* (A Tale of Mutsu). Written in Chinese by an aristocrat in the capital, it centers on the heroic figures of Minamoto no Yoriyoshi (988–1075) and his son Yoshiie (1039–1106), who succeeded after hard campaigning in destroying the rebel Abe family. It was written probably soon after the events it describes. The lineaments of the warrior hero and of the feudal ethic are already discernible in this work, which anticipates the war tales *(gunki monogatari)* of the 13th century and later. In these respects, and in narrative skill, it shows a marked advance over the *Shōmonki* account of the rebellion of Taira no Masakado a century earlier. Each of these works stands as a milestone on the way to a new heroic literature, a literature which was to come into maturity only after the end of the Heian period.

The 11th century was not on the whole a time of outstanding creativity in the Chinese language in Japan. Official contacts between the two countries had ended in the 9th century, and though unofficial ones continued, the level of Chinese scholarship in Japan at this period was not high. The many *kambun* diaries of Japanese court officials show some lapse in control of the language. Nevertheless interest in Chinese belles-lettres continued, as exemplified by the anthology known as HONCHŌ MONZUI (Literary Essence of Our Land), compiled by FUJIWARA NO AKIHIRA (989–1066) around the year 1060. This work contains 427 items of prose and poetry by Japanese authors, from the early 9th to the early 11th century. In 14 volumes, its organization is modeled to some extent on that of the *Wenxuan*. It has relatively few poems in the *shi* form, and no "regulated *shi*." The relative informality of its content is delightfully exemplified by such compositions as Minamoto no Shitagau's poem, "Song of the Tailless Ox," and the prose piece "Record of the Pond Pavilion" ("Chiteiki"), by YOSHISHIGE NO YASUTANE (ca 931–1002), not to mention a few pieces of erotica.

The last two thirds of the 11th century was not a great age of *waka* either. After the *Shūishū* early in the century there were no more imperial anthologies for about 80 years, and no poets comparable in talent to Izumi Shikibu emerged during this period. Nevertheless, *waka* was a firmly established art, and poetry contests continued to be held with frequency throughout the century, peaking in the 1050s. The "Kokinshū style" continued regnant, but a gradual reevaluation of purely descriptive nature poetry began to show results, leading to one of the major styles of the next century and after. The formal context of the *uta-awase* tended to act as a conservative force, poems being subject to criticism for violating technical rules of diction and decorum. Experimental poems were composed mostly outside such contexts. One of the most experimentally-minded poets of the late 11th century was MINAMOTO NO TSUNENOBU (1016–97). Tsunenobu was particularly fond of a lofty style of natural description having echoes of the *Man'yōshū*, and was the senior poet of his day when the fourth imperial *waka* anthology, the *Goshūi wakashū* (Later Collection of Waka Gleanings; also known as *Go shūishū*) was commissioned by Emperor Shirakawa (1053–1129, r 1073–87) in 1075. He was nevertheless passed over as compiler in favor of a younger, more conservative poet, FUJIWARA NO MICHITOSHI (1047–99), who brought the anthology to completion in 1086. Tsunenobu lashed back with a critique entitled *Nan goshūi*, "Censuring the *Go shūishū*." The anthology does nevertheless reflect the nascent trend of its time in including a considerable amount of descriptive poetry. It also gives official recognition of the preeminence in her day of the long-dead Izumi Shikibu. She leads all other poets in the anthology with 67 poems.

The 12th Century —— Although it is fallacious to impose a Western concept of centuries on premodern Japanese history, the hundred years or so from 1104 to 1205 does seem to work out well as a unit in a discussion of Japanese poetry. It was a time of new trends, new talents, and strongly revived interest in the art of *waka*. It begins with the *Horikawa hyakushu* and culminates with the compilation of the SHIN KOKINSHŪ. The *Horikawa hyakushu* were a set of 100-poem sequences *(hyakushu)* ordered by Emperor Horikawa (1079–1107, r 1087–1107) and submitted to him in 1104. About 15 or 16 poets took part. The 100-poem sequence was an art form, which gained increasing popularity from this time, in which a poet composed poems on a number of set topics, arranged often in the manner of a miniature imperial anthology. Such sequences were often commissioned in fact to provide material for such anthologies. In the case of the Horikawa sequences, each poem had an individual, precisely defined topic. These topics and the poems they called forth were much emulated later. The excitement created by this literary event was considerable, and did much to breathe new life into the somewhat static *waka* scene. At least two important trends emerged—an increased attention to expressing the very essence of the *dai* or topic, and some fairly bold experimentation with colloquial and archaic diction.

Of the participants in the *Horikawa hyakushu*, the most renowned and the most eager to experiment was MINAMOTO NO TOSHIYORI, better known as Minamoto no Shunrai, (1055?–1129). Shunrai was the son of Tsunenobu, the disappointed author of *Nangoshūi*. Despite his championing of unconventional diction by the example of his poetry, he could on occasion act the conservative as a judge at a poem contest, disqualifying his own verses with perhaps tongue-in-cheek severity. An extraordinarily accomplished as well as various poet, he was more successful than his father in securing imperial patronage, being appointed compiler of the fifth imperial anthology, the KIN'YŌ WAKASHŪ (Waka Collection of Golden Leaves; also known as *Kin'yōshū*) by ex-Emperor Shirakawa in 1124. He was obliged to revise the manuscript twice, however, probably to increase its acceptability to conservatives. It was finally approved in 1127. The *Kin'yōshū* and the next imperial anthology, the *Shikashū*, are the only two that depart from the standard 20-volume format, each consisting of only 10 volumes. Shunrai's personal poetry collection, *Samboku kikashū*, itself contains about 1,600 poems, and is important as an early example of the careful structuring of such a collection along the categorical lines of the various topics of classical poetry. In addition to this formal aspect, it has personal sections such as 58 poems on the death of his father Tsunenobu. After Shunrai's time many of the personal poetry collections (*shikashū* or *ie no shū*) became increasingly formal. *Samboku* in the title is a humble reference to Shunrai's court office, and *kikashū* means "Collection of Strange Poems." Shunrai is also the author of a work on poetics, *Toshiyori* (or *Shunrai*) *zuinō* ("Toshiyori's Essentials"). It is less radical than his poetic practice.

The sixth imperial *waka* anthology, the SHIKA WAKASHŪ (Waka Collection of Verbal Flowers; also known as *Shikashū*), was compiled by FUJIWARA NO AKISUKE (1090–1155) in ca 1151–54 at the behest of ex-Emperor Sutoku (1119–64, r 1123–42). Akisuke was the son of Akisue (1055–1123), founder of the Rokujō branch of the Fujiwara clan. The Rokujō became known for their scholarship—of a highly pedantic nature—in poetic matters, and for a conservative position in poetry. It is easy to overestimate and misunderstand this conservatism, since Rokujō scholarship held a high opinion of the

Man'yōshū, hardly a bastion of the "*Kokinshū* style," and the new trend toward descriptive poetry was shared by all schools. Nevertheless, in practice they opposed Shunrai's type of experimentation as well as the more radical styles that emerged at the end of the 12th century. The division of the poetic scene into conservative and innovating factions had begun in the late 11th century with Michitoshi and Tsunenobu. Shunrai too had had his archconservative opponent in FUJIWARA NO MOTOTOSHI (ca 1056–1142?). From the mid-12th century the Rokujō became the conservative champions for several decades. Akisuke himself, however, was broadminded enough to include poets such as Sone no Yoshitada and Shunrai in the *Shikashū*.

Prose Literature —— The first half of the 12th century was not without its prose works. Nothing remains of courtly *monogatari* definitely assignable to this period, but an interesting work of the autobiographical type has come down to us. This is SANUKI NO SUKE NO NIKKI (The Diary of Sanuki no Suke). The author was Fujiwara no Nagako (b ca 1079), a lady-in-waiting to Emperor Horikawa, with whom she took service in 1100. Her brief memoir is concerned exclusively with the years 1107 and 1108. Emperor Horikawa took sick in the summer of 1107, and this work describes in detail his final month of life. This intimate account provides its chief interest. The author was recalled to serve Horikawa's son, the five-year-old Emperor Toba (1103–56, r 1107–23), whose coronation is also described in her memoir. Her work is in two volumes, the first an eyewitness account of Horikawa's final illness, direct and devoid of poems, and the second a more reflective series of flashbacks and vignettes in the style of the poetic diary.

The other major prose work probably assignable to the early 12th century is the great collection of *setsuwa* tales known as *Konjaku monogatari shū* (also known as KONJAKU MONOGATARI). The title means, "Collection of Konjaku Tales." *Konjaku* is an alternate pronunciation of the Chinese characters used to write the opening formula of each of the more than 1,000 stories, *ima wa mukashi* ("at a time now past"). The bulk and variety of this collection make it the dominant work of the *setsuwa* tradition. A date of about 1120 has been proposed for the compilation of *Konjaku*, but opinions vary widely. The author/compiler is also unknown. Since the collection is so large, it may be the product of more than one hand. The language employed is Japanese, but of a peculiar sort. Linguistically and stylistically very remote from the pure Yamato speech of Murasaki Shikibu and other classical writers, *Konjaku* represents a way station between the Chinese in which the first *setsuwa* were written, and a new kind of Japanese evolved from reading a Chinese text into the native language. This phenomenon took place over a broad spectrum, yielding texts with a heavy seasoning of Chinese loan words, grammatical peculiarities derived from Chinese, and a very different texture and flow from old Japanese in its undiluted purity. That purity was ultimately preserved only in the *waka* tradition; *Konjaku* with its harsher, more masculine quality, is a milestone on the way to modern Japanese. The style of *Konjaku* also differs from courtly writings in being determinedly explanatory, paradoxically at once terse and prolix, but never vague and misty. *Konjaku* is a highly structured work: stories of India, China, and Japan are subdivided (except in the case of India) into religious and secular stories, which are further subdivided and grouped in thematic ways and linked associationally. Thus the material of *Konjaku* is extremely varied, but the work as a whole is the product of a shaping intelligence. Many of the tales teach piety and faith in Buddhism, but there are many others that delight in exposing credulity and ecclesiastical fraud. The secular stories draw their material from a broader spectrum of social classes than is true of courtly *monogatari*, and give a much more down-to-earth and varied picture of life in the Heian period. A good many are also unblushingly sexual or scatological in content, or interested in crime, the supernatural, or the merely grotesque. Traditional folktales and legends about historical figures are also included. Each story is framed by a formulaic opening and closing sentence, the latter often pointing out the moral or message to be derived from the narrative.

It was also at about this time that Fujiwara no Mototoshi, the conservative opponent of Minamoto no Shunrai, compiled the *Shinsen rōeishū* (Newly Selected Collection for Recitation), an anthology of Chinese and Japanese verse modeled on the *Wakan rōeishū* put together by Fujiwara no Kintō early in the 11th century. In two books, it contains 203 *waka* and 542 Chinese selections, and gives testimony to the continued popularity of pairing Chinese and Japanese poetry for oral recitation. As in the earlier anthology, Bo Juyi is the single best represented poet in either language.

Poetry: 1150–1188 —— The last half of the 12th century was a time of cataclysmic change in Japan, when latent socioeconomic forces intertwined with disputes within the ruling house to bring bloodshed to the streets of the capital, and ultimately to bring the Heian period to an end. These changes had nothing to do with literature in the first instance, though they were to affect it profoundly in the long run. They certainly had nothing to do with the gentle art of poetry; nevertheless, they caught the lives of many a poet in midstream. One of those poets, one whose life was singular by the standards of his day, and yet may be taken to point in the direction of a new age, was the monk-poet SAIGYŌ (1118–90). Saigyō was a young imperial guardsman named Satō Norikiyo when he abandoned the secular life in 1140. He spent the rest of his long life either in seclusion in some Buddhist retreat or on pilgrimages that took him to parts of the country, such as the far north, never seen by most of the court poets of the day. To later ages he became the image of the wandering poet, free of all earthly ties and seeking only the truth. As such he has exercised a permanent hold over the Japanese imagination, and was emulated by the *haikai* master BASHŌ (1644–94) in the 17th century. Saigyō's most characteristic verse speaks from a direct experience of the things of nature, and preserves a sense of genuineness that has been much valued. His adoration of cherry blossoms borders on the childlike, but his art has deeper, more somber tones as well, reflections on vanished glory, and a sense of being torn between Buddhist renunciation and a clinging to the world of natural beauty. An outsider by choice, he was nevertheless on close terms with some of the leading established poets of the day, who much admired his work. The eighth imperial *waka* anthology included more poems by Saigyō than by any other poet. His personal poetry collection is entitled *Sankashū* (Collection of the Mountain Hermitage).

Ultimately the best established of all the poets of the 12th century was a man who followed a quite conventional career in the lower and middle ranks of the court bureaucracy, but whose long life of dedication to poetry drew the almost unanimous respect of his contemporaries and the reverence of later generations. FUJIWARA NO TOSHINARI, better known as Fujiwara no Shunzei, was born in 1114, and by the time of his death at 90 in 1204 was universally recognized as the grand old man of poetry, treated with deference even by ex-Emperor GO-TOBA (1180–1239; r 1183–98). He more than any other guided, criticized, and presided over the great renascence of *waka* that took place during his lifetime. Shunzei sought a middle way between the innovators and the conservatives, a way that would be true to the essence of *waka* at its finest. He hit upon the formula "old words, new heart," i.e., a fidelity to classical diction as defined by the first three imperial anthologies, combined with a fresh integrity of conception. Although his branch of the Fujiwara clan, the Mikohidari family, came to be thought of as the liberal faction in contrast to the Rokujō conservatives, Shunzei himself insisted on adherence to classical decorum in the vital context of the poem contest, and by the seriousness of his dedication to poetry as an art ultimately rose above the discord of the clashing schools. He often served as a judge at poetry contests in his later life, and as such introduced positive criteria into his judgments, instead of confining himself as had been the custom to finding disqualifying faults. Scrupulously fair-minded, he earned for himself a deserved respect, which is not to overlook the fact that his jugments were attacked on occasion by poets with opposing views. In his own poetry he is said to have valued the quality of YŪGEN, a deep and suggestive allusiveness, often somber in tone, that came to be a major aesthetic ideal of succeeding generations. He was a close personal friend of Saigyō, who sent to him for criticism one of his own major poetic efforts, the *Mimosusogawa uta-awase* or "Poetry Contest at Mimosuso River" of 1187 in which Saigyō matched his own poems against each other. Shunzei's own personal collection is entitled *Chōshū eisō* (Seaweed of Poetic Composition of Long Autumns). "Seaweed" is used in somewhat the same sense as "grass" in Whitman's *Leaves of Grass*, and "Long Autumns" is the Chinese style of the court office which was Shunzei's sinecure.

The seventh imperial *waka* anthology was ordered by ex-Emperor Go-Shirakawa (1127–92, r 1155–58) in 1183. The honor went to Shunzei, who completed the task in 1188. SENZAI WAKASHŪ (Waka Collection of a Thousand Years; also known as *Senzaishū*) was the title chosen. Shunzei seems to have labored hard on the anthology to make it representative. Of its 1,285 poems, 52 are by Minamoto no Shunrai, the innovator of the generation before Shunzei, who thus occupies first place, but the poets of the rival Rokujō house are also included with quite respectable numbers for each.

Saigyō has 18 poems. Shunzei originally included only 10 or 11 by himself, but increased the number to 36 at the behest of his imperial patron. Earlier poets such as Izumi Shikibu (21) are also well represented. The younger poets of the *Senzaishū* included many who were to create the poetry distinguishing the next imperial anthology, the *Shin kokinshū* of 1205.

A number of poems in the *Senzaishū* which are listed as anonymous are known to have been written by members of the Taira clan. The Taira ruled the capital during the period from 1160 to 1180, having emerged victorious from the disturbances of 1156 and 1159. TAIRA NO KIYOMORI (1118–81), their leader, was feared and hated. He ruled as the Fujiwara had done by intermarrying with the imperial family, but controlled the city with a brutal hand. The scion of a warrior family, he had armed men and spies everywhere, and his rule marks the real end of the Heian period as it had been. But Taira dominance proved to be short-lived. A rival military clan, the Minamoto, overthrew them in a bloody and fiercely contested civil war which raged from one end of the country to the other from 1180 to 1185. The result was not a restoration of imperial and aristocratic privilege, but the substitution of more sophisticated and lasting means of military control. Power had permanently passed out of the hands of the court by the end of the 12th century. Kiyomori himself died of illness in 1181, and his family was driven out of the capital two years later in 1183. The Taira who retreated from the capital included more than one who had become devoted to the gentler arts of peace during the years of their supremacy. One of these was the poet TAIRA NO TADANORI (1144–84), a younger brother of Kiyomori. According to an anecdote recorded in *The Tale of the Heike* (HEIKE MONOGATARI), the medieval saga of the civil war, Tadanori returned with a small band of men into the enemy-infested capital to deliver to Shunzei a scroll of his poems, asking him to select just one for the new imperial anthology. Moved by Tadanori's plea, Shunzei included one of his poems in the *Senzaishū*, but listed it as anonymous, as the Taira were officially rebels.

Prose Literature: 1150–1200 —— The wars of the late 12th century were soon described in texts which bore some resemblance to earlier military accounts such as *Shōmonki* and *Mutsu waki*. These written texts provided sources for oral recitations of the deeds of the war heroes, and through a process of evolution produced a new literary genre, the *gunki monogatari* or war tale. But this development, while of absorbing interest, lies outside the purview of Heian Literature and cannot be entered into here. Historiography continued to skirt the borders of literature in further examples of the *rekishi monogatari* or historical tale such as IMAKAGAMI (The Mirror of the Present), author unknown (perhaps by Minamoto no Michichika [1149–1202]), and *Mizukagami* (The Water Mirror) by Nakayama Tadachika (1132–95). The former, completed in 1170, covers the years 1025–1170, picking up where *Ōkagami* leaves off. The latter goes back to deal with the period before *Ōkagami*, from the first emperor down to the year 850. Its date is not known. Thus *Ōkagami* served as the inspiration for a series of works known as *kagami-mono* or "mirror pieces," one which continued on into the 13th century.

The stream of courtly *monogatari* had seen its best days, but was not exhausted. Such stories as *Sagoromo* and the *Tale of Genji* were themselves in the process of becoming classics, and *Genji* at least would eventually be the beneficiary of a whole critical and exegetical literature. MUMYŌ-ZŌSHI (The Nameless Booklet), the first critical work devoted to *monogatari*, appeared early in the 13th century. It is attributed to "the Daughter of Shunzei," a poetess and adopted child of Shunzei who was actually his granddaughter. *Mumyō-zōshi* mentions a curious work which appears to be the last of the surviving long *monogatari* of the Heian period. It is entitled *Torikaebaya*, a word which means "If only I could exchange them," and is a novel based on sex-role reversal. It appears from *Mumyō-zōshi* to have existed in two versions, an earlier and a later. The old (*furu*) version is no longer extant; what we have is that which *Mumyō-zōshi* calls *Imatorikaebaya monogatari*, the "present" version. The author of *Mumyō-zōshi* praises this latter as superior—lacking offensive scenes said to have existed in the original version. For better or worse, what has come down to us may be a bowdlerization. Date and authorship of both versions are unknown. Opinion holds that *Furutorikaebaya* was written after *Sagoromo monogatari*, i.e., late 11th century or later; *Imatorikaebaya* is probably a 12th-century, perhaps late 12th-century work. The story is about a boy and girl, half-siblings, who show marked preference for the dress and manners of the opposite sex. The boy is shy and refined, and dresses as a girl; the girl is correspondingly boyish and outgoing, and is allowed to dress as a boy. Before long only the family knows the truth. Both go into service at court, the young man becoming a lady-in-waiting to an imperial princess, and his sister cutting a dashing figure as a guards officer. To complicate matters further, the guards officer (a woman) takes a wife, and the lady-in-waiting (a man) establishes a secret sexual relationship with the princess. By this time the two central characters and those intimately involved with them are experiencing a predictable degree of tension between their social roles and their true sex. The novel's exploration of this tension is both sensitive and humorous, as if the author were aware of the possibilities for farce inherent in his (or her) trick plot, but at the same time faithful to the sentimental and affective tradition of courtly fiction. The stasis of the plot is broken by another of the main characters, a friend of the guards officer who, in the role of the Heian amorist descended from Prince Niou in *The Tale of Genji*, rapes his friend's wife and gets her pregnant. After this event the situation starts to unravel. The "friend" discovers the true sex of his supposed colleague in the guards, and starts an affair with her too, so that both husband and wife are pregnant by the same lover. Consternations and embarrassments abound in this delicate pass, and the novel achieves some of its best effects in describing them. In the end the brother and sister revert to their true sexes and exchange roles at court, leading to further delicious confusion on the part of those not privy to the secret. The brother becomes regent, the sister empress, and the "friend" is left baffled as to just what has happened. *Torikaebaya* has been condemned as decadent, the nadir of late Heian taste for the improbable, but it is equally possible to regard it as that rarity in the tradition of sensibility, an achieved comic novel.

Two further examples of the court diary-autobiography deal in part with the last years of the 12th century. One is *Kenju Gozen nikki*, a record of the experiences of a daughter of Fujiwara no Shunzei known as Kenju Gozen (b 1157), who served two imperial ladies, Kenshun Mon'in (1142–76), the consort of ex-Emperor Go-Shirakawa, and Princess Hachijō In (1136–1211), the daughter of Emperor Toba. Kenju Gozen's memoir relates incidents and impressions of her life at court from 1168 to 1211. The other work parallels *Kenju Gozen nikki* closely in time, but belongs to that stream of writing which is half memoir, half collected poems. It is KENREI MON'IN UKYŌ NO DAIBU SHŪ, the collection of a lady known by the court nickname Ukyō no Daibu, who was in service to Taira no Kiyomori's daughter, the empress Kenrei Mon'in, as a young woman. The main theme of her memoir is her grief over the loss of her lover, Taira no Sukemori (1161?–85), a grandson of Kiyomori who died in the Taira defeat at Dan no Ura. The span of her work is from 1174 to 1213. With its interweaving of poetry and prose it exemplifies the survival to the end of the period of a major mode of Heian writing. Such works by court ladies continued to be written into the succeeding Kamakura period, but eventually died out with the impoverishment and decline of the court.

Poetry: 1193–1205 —— It is no doubt ironic that the fall of Heian should have coincided with the greatest flowering of its choicest art, that of poetry. The decades immediately following the civil war which established military power saw the culmination of the poetic revival which had been going on throughout the 12th century. The new overlords were content to preserve the court and its traditional culture, and, in the matter of poetry, things continued to depend more on an active imperial or noble patron than on major shifts in real political power. Poetry in fact became more important to the nobility than ever, a badge and warranty of their superiority at least in cultivation. Ex-Emperor Go-Shirakawa, the wiliest maneuverer on the Heian scene in the late 12th century, became the sponsor of the *Senzaishū* in 1183, perhaps, it has been suggested, less out of his own interest in *waka* than at the urging of Shunzei. It was probably not lost on Go-Shirakawa's subtle mind that the exercise of this unique imperial prerogative could be a useful political assertion in his then delicate situation. That Go-Shirakawa was interested more personally in other kinds of poetry is implied by his compilation of a collection of Buddhist hymns and popular songs entitled RYŌJIN HISHŌ, fragments of which have survived. The title, "Secret Selections of Rafter Dust," alludes to an old Chinese anecdote about a singer whose voice raised motes of dust from the rafters. *Ryōjin hishō* is especially noted for containing the texts of *imayō* ("up-to-date") songs, very popular at that time and often accompanied by dances executed by young women performers known as *shirabyō-shi*, a predecessor of the later *geisha*.

An important group of other patrons of poetry appeared before and after the turn of the century. Two of these were Fujiwara no Kanezane (also known as KUJŌ KANEZANE; 1149–1207) and his son Go-Kyōgoku Yoshitsune (also known as FUJIWARA NO YOSHI-TSUNE; 1169–1206), who for a time held what political power remained with the court. Both were accomplished poets and energetic sponsors of poetic events. One of the most prodigious of these events was the "Poetry Contest in 600 Rounds" (*Roppyakuban uta-awase*) of 1193, the largest such event ever staged up until that time. This contest, sponsored by Yoshitsune, drew together twelve poets—four of the conservative Rokujō school, four innovators, and four neutrals. Each poet composed a 100–poem sequence, with each poem on a different specified topic, as in the Horikawa sequences of 1104. Then the resultant 1,200 poems were matched against each other in 600 rounds. Shunzei was called upon to judge. He insisted on strict standards of poetic decorum, showing more tendency than usual to disqualify poems on technical grounds. As usual, he aimed for a middle position between the conservatives who argued for *Man'yōshū* diction—a radical position a hundred years earlier—and the truly radical experiments in syntax of younger poets like his son Teika. Shunzei's own position remained depth of poetic conception expressed in *Kokinshū* diction. His judgments drew the fire of one disgruntled contestant, the priest KENSHŌ (fl 1161–1207), a Rokujō poet who issued counterarguments in the form of a *chinjō* or "appeal." All in all, the occasion was an important testing ground for the different schools, a highly successful attempt on the part of its sponsor to discover the state of the art.

It was only a few years later, in 1197, that Shunzei wrote his most extended disquisition on Japanese poetry, the work known as *Korai fūtei shō* (Notes on Poetic Style through the Ages). This is a short survey of *waka* history accompanied by instructional comments written for Princess Shokushi (also known as Princess SHIKISHI; d 1201), a daughter of ex-Emperor Go-Shirakawa who was one of the leading poets of her time. Shunzei is at pains to show the variety that has characterized *waka* over the course of its long history, and to demonstrate his familiarity with the *Man'yōshū*, detailed knowledge concerning which had been the pride of his poetic rival and critic Kenshō. But more importantly he argues for the deep seriousness, even the religious significance of a devotion to poetry as a way of life, drawing parallels to doctrines of the Buddhist faith. The insistence on depth and search for the essence of poetic truth was Shunzei's final contribution to the art he so prized.

Although the Heian period must be regarded as officially over at this point, at least three events of the first decade of the 13th century must be mentioned to round off the narrative insofar as it concerns Japanese poetry. All three were owing to the appearance of a new patron, one of the most vital in the entire history of *waka*, namely the young ex-emperor Go-Toba, aged 21 by Japanese count in the year 1200. In that year this ambitious and vigorous newly retired sovereign, an important poet in his own right, showed his interest in sponsoring lively activity in *waka* by twice calling on the leading poets of the day to submit 100–poem sequences. The first of these sets, the *Shōji ninen shodo hyakushu* (First Hundred-Poem Sequences of the Second Year of Shōji) occupies a key position in *waka* history because of the relation to it of Shunzei's son, Fujiwara no Teika (also known as FUJIWARA NO SADAIE; 1162–1241). Teika is the pivotal figure in the entire development of *waka*, the one man through whose hands the tradition flowed, and from whom all later schools branched out. The remarkable son of a remarkable father, he was an even greater poet as well as a more systematic thinker. But one thing he lacked was his father's equable temperament. Teika was a moody and irascible man, in and out of favor at court. He was the particular enemy of the Rokujō faction of poets, who had gained political ground at this time, and who influenced Go-Toba to exclude him from participation in the new sequences. For Teika, whose career was stymied and who had been out of favor for two years, this was a serious blow. He badly needed official recognition. The situation was saved by the intervention of his father Shunzei, who successfully appealed to the ex-Emperor. Teika was added to the list at the last moment, and eventually became one of Go-Toba's poetic intimates. This put him in a position to participate in the most important literary activity of the age, the compilation of the eighth imperial *waka* anthology, the *Shin kokinshū*.

Go-Toba already had in mind the announcement of a new anthology, and the sponsorhip of activity among the poets was designed partially to provide material for it. Many of the poems from the sequences of 1200 were in fact included. The next year, 1201, Go-Toba announced the establishment of a Poetry Bureau (Wakadokoro), appointing 11 prominent poets as members. Of these, six were selected to start work on compiling an imperial anthology which would represent all times from the ancient past to the present—the *Shin kokin wakashū* (New Collection of Ancient and Recent Waka; also known as SHIN KOKINSHŪ). A title which makes clear Go-Toba's intent to emulate the *Kokin wakashū* of three hundred years before. In order to provide even more new poems for consideration, in 1201 the ex-emperor held still another grandiose poetic event, a "Poetry Contest in 1,500 Rounds" *(Sengohyakuban uta-awase)*, thus putting in the shade even the contest in 600 rounds of eight years earlier. Thirty poets submitted 100 poems each, yielding a total of 3,000 poems, matched in 1,500 rounds and judged by nine different judges, a process that went on in stages into the following year. The *Shin kokinshū* gradually took shape over a number of years, Go-Toba himself taking an active part in the compilation. The official completion banquet was held in 1205, but further refinement went on for some years after that, and Go-Toba even continued revision of the text in exile after 1221, following his defeat in an attempt to overthrow the new military government. The official text, however, stems from a copy made in 1216. Go-Toba's great interest in arranging the poems making up the *Shin kokinshū* resulted in an anthology which in its very structure is a work of art, the fruition of centuries of practice in the techniques of association and progression. The arrangement of the *Shin kokinshū* is regarded as the ultimate in smoothness, subtlety, and refinement.

The six compilers of the *Shin kokinshū* (other than Go-Toba) were FUJIWARA NO IETAKA (1158–1237), Minamoto no Michitomo (1171–1227), Fujiwara no Ariie (1155–1216), ASUKAI MASATSUNE (1170–1221), the priest JAKUREN (ca 1139–1202), and Fujiwara no Teika. All of them were accomplished poets—in an age when talent seems to have been more plentiful than ever—but Teika can be singled out as both the representative and the dominant figure among them. Unlike his father, for whom depth and fineness were all, Teika was a daring experimenter, at least in his youth. A fad of the time, for which he was in good measure responsible, was to reach for new effects by the dislocation of normal linkages between subject and predicate, as in "the wind grows late" instead of "the night grows late," and "spread the moonlight" rather than "spread the sleeping mat." Opinion varied on the merit of such experiments; many condemned them as *daruma uta*—"zen" poems, i.e., nonsense verse. Another of Teika's preferences in his youth was for a style of shimmering, diaphanous beauty called *yōen* ("ethereal charm"). The effect of many of the poems in this style is almost magical, but the use of language is compressed and difficult. After a dry period following his father's death, Teika in his later years came to prefer a simpler, less obviously lovely style, that known as USHIN or "conviction of feeling." In this he was undoubtedly coming closer to what Shunzei had prized as the essence of *waka*. In addition to his work as a poet, Teika wrote many essays in poetics, and the later history of this field of scholarship is greatly indebted to him. And besides all this, he interested himself in Japanese literature in the broad sense, collecting, preserving, and copying out manuscripts of many of the classical works. Through his hands much of the richness of Heian literature reached later generations.

📖 ——Works in English: Jennifer Brewster, tr, *The Emperor Horikawa Diary: Sanuki no Suke no Nikki* by Fujiwara no Nagako (1977). Robert H. Brower, tr, *Fujiwara Teika's Hundred-Poem Sequence of the Shōji Era, 1200* (1978). Robert H. Brower and Earl Miner, *Japanese Court Poetry* (1961). Edwin A. Cranston, tr, "Atemiya: A Translation from the *Utsubo monogatari*," *Monumenta Nipponica* 24.3 (1969). Edwin A. Cranston, tr, *The Izumi Shikibu Diary: A Romance of the Heian Court* (1969). Yoshito S. Hakeda, tr, *Kūkai: Major Works* (1972). Phillip Tudor Harries, *The Poetic Memoirs of Lady Daibu* (1980). Carol Hochstedler, tr, *The Tale of Nezame: Part Three of Yowa no Nezame Monogatari* (1979). Donald Keene, ed, *Anthology of Japanese Literature* (1955). Donald Keene, tr, "*Taketori Monogatari*: The Tale of the Bamboo Cutter," *Monumenta Nipponica* 11.4 (1956). Konishi Jin'ichi, "The Genesis of the *Kokinshū* Style," tr Helen C. McCullough, *Harvard Journal of Asiatic Studies* 38.1 (1978). William R. LaFleur, tr, *Mirror for the Moon: A Selection of Poems by Saigyō, 1118–1190* (1977). Helen Craig McCullough, tr, "A Tale of Mutsu," *Harvard Journal of Asiatic Studies* 25 (1964–65). Helen Craig McCullough, tr, *Tales of Ise: Lyrical Episodes from Tenth-Century Japan* (1968). Helen Craig McCullough, tr, *Okagami: The Great Mirror: Fujiwara Michinaga (966–1027) and His Times* (1980). William H. and Helen Craig McCullough, tr, *A Tale of Flowering Fortunes: Annals of Japanese Aristocratic Life in the Heian Period*, 2 vols (1980), a translation of *Eiga monogatari*. Earl Miner, tr, *Japanese Poetic Diaries* (1969) contains a translation of *Tosa nikki*. Robert Alfred Mintzer, "*Jōjin Azari no*

haha shū: Maternal Love in the Eleventh Century—An Enduring Testament," PhD dissertation, Harvard University (1978). Ivan Morris, tr, *The Pillow Book of Sei Shōnagon*, 2 vols (1967). Ivan Morris, tr, *As I Crossed a Bridge of Dreams* (1971), a translation of *Sarashina nikki*. Kyoko Motomochi Nakamura, tr, *Miraculous Stories from the Japanese Buddhist Tradition: The Nihon ryōiki of the Monk Kyōkai* (1973). Judith Rabinovitch, "*Shōmonki*: The Earliest Japanese War Tale," PhD dissertation, Harvard University (1981). John M. Rosenfield, Fumiko E. Cranston, and Edwin A. Cranston, *The Courtly Tradition in Japanese Art and Literature: Selections from the Hofer and Hyde Collections* (1973). Clifton Wilson Royston, Jr., "The Poetics and Poetry Criticism of Fujiwara Shunzei, 1114–1204," PhD dissertation, University of Michigan (1974). Edward G. Seidensticker, tr, *The Gossamer Years: The Diary of a Noblewoman of Heian Japan* (1964), a translation of *Kagerō nikki*. Edward G. Seidensticker, tr, *The Tale of Genji*, 2 vols (1976). Mildred Tahara, tr, *Tales of Yamato: A Tenth-Century Poem-Tale* (1980). Marian Ury, tr, *Tales of Times Now Past: Sixty-Two Stories from a Medieval Japanese Collection* (1979), translations from *Konjaku monogatari*. Susan Downing Videen, "*Heichū monogatari* and the Heichū Legend," PhD dissertation, Stanford University (1979). Arthur Waley, tr, *The Pillow-Book of Sei Shōnagon* (1929, repr 1960). Arthur Waley, tr, *The Tale of Genji* (1935, repr 1960). Janet A. Walker, "Poetic Ideal and Fictional Reality in the *Izumi Shikibu nikki*," *Harvard Journal of Asiatic Studies* 37.1 (1977). Burton Watson, tr, *Japanese Literature in Chinese*, vol 1 (1975). Wilfred Whitehouse, tr, *Ochikubo monogatari: or The Tale of the Lady Ochikubo* (rev ed 1965).

Works in Japanese: Abe Akio, Akiyama Ken, and Imai Gen'ei, ed, *Genji monogatari*, 6 vols, Nihon koten bungaku zenshū 12–17 (Shōgakukan, 1970–76). Akiyama Ken, ed, *Nihon bungaku shi: Chūko* (1978). Endō Yoshimoto and Kasuga Kazuo, ed, *Nihon ryōiki, Nihon koten bungaku taikei (NKBT)* 70 (Iwanami Shoten, 1967). Hagitani Boku, ed, *Heichū zenkō* (1959). Hisamatsu Sen'ichi, ed, "Karonshū," in Hisamatsu and Nishio Minoru, ed, *Karonshū, nōgakuron shū, NKBT* 73 (1961). Hisamatsu Sen'ichi et al, *Shimban Nihon bungakushi nempyō* (1973). Ikeda Kikan, Kishigami Shinji, and Akiyama Ken, ed, *Makura no sōshi, Murasaki Shikibu nikki, NKBT* 19 (1958). Kajihara Masaaki, ed, *Shōmonki*, 2 vols (1975–76). Kawaguchi Hisao, ed, *Kanke bunsō, Kanke kōshū, NKBT* 72 (1966). Kawaguchi Hisao and Shida Nobuyoshi, ed, *Wakan rōeishū, Ryōjin hishō, NKBT* 73 (1965). Kōno Tama, ed, *Utsubo monogatari*, 3 vols, *NKBT* 10–12 (1959–62). Kubota Utsubo, ed, *Izumi Shikibu shū: Ono no Komachi shū* (Asahi Shimbunsha, 1958). Kubota Utsubo, ed, *Kambon shin kokin wakashū hyōshaku*, 3 vols (1964–65). Matsuda Takeo, ed, *Shinshaku kokin wakashū*, 2 vols (Kazama Shobō, 1968). Matsumura Hiroji, ed, *Ōkagami, NKBT* 21 (1960). Matsumura Hiroji and Yamanaka Hiroshi, ed, *Eiga monogatari*, 2 vols, *NKBT* 75–76 (1964–65). Matsuo Satoshi, ed, *Ochikubo monogatari, NKBT* 13 (1957). Matsuo Satoshi, ed, *Hamamatsu Chūnagon monogatari*, in Endō Yoshimoto and Matsuo Satoshi, ed, *Takamura monogatari, Heichū monogatari, Hamamatsu Chūnagon monogatari NKBT* 77 (1964). Mitani Eiichi and Sekine Yoshiko, ed, *Sagoromo monogatari, NKBT* 79 (1965). Saeki Umetomo, Murakami Osamu, and Komatsu Tomi, ed, *Izumi Shikibu shū zenshaku* (1959). Saeki Umetomo, Murakami Osamu, and Komatsu Tomi, ed, *Izumi Shikibu shū zenshaku: Zokushūhen* (1977). Sakakura Atsuyoshi, ed, *Yoru no nezame, NKBT* 78 (1964). Sakakura Atsuyoshi, Ōtsu Yūichi, Tsukishima Hiroshi, Abe Toshiko, and Imai Gen'ei, ed, *Taketori monogatari, Ise monogatari, Yamato monogatari, NKBT* 9 (1967). Suzuki Tomotarō, Kawaguchi Hisao, Endō Yoshimoto, and Nishishita Kyōichi, ed, *Tosa nikki, Kagerō nikki, Izumi Shikibu nikki, Sarashina nikki, NKBT* 20 (1957). Tamagami Takuya, ed, *Genji monogatari hyōshaku*, 14 vols (1964–69). Tamai Kōsuke, *Nikki bungaku no kenkyū* (1965). Watanabe Shōkō and Miyasaka Yūshō, ed, *Sangō shiiki, Seireishū, NKBT* 71 (Iwanami Shoten, 1965). Yamada Yoshio, Yamada Tadao, Yamada Hideo, and Yamada Toshio, ed, *Konjaku monogatari shū*, 5 vols, *NKBT* 22–26 (1959–63).

Edwin A. CRANSTON

MEDIEVAL LITERATURE

Japanese scholars disagree on the time frame of the term "medieval" *(chūsei)* as applied to Japanese literature. Its seems best for our purpose to treat the medieval period in literature as occurring between approximately 1200 and 1600, i.e., roughly between the beginning of the Kamakura period (1185–1333) and the end of the Azuchi-Momoyama period (1568–1600). We acknowledge, however, that some "medieval" characteristics appear before and some "Heian" characteristics continue to appear after 1200, while the early stages of Edo-period (1600–1868) popular literature in many ways continue developments begun well before 1600. Some scholars have even argued that since Japan remained essentially a feudal country until the Meiji Restoration (1868), late Edo literature can still be regarded as belonging to the Middle Ages. Again, some regard medieval literature as beginning as early as the middle of the Heian period (794–1185). Even among those who date it from the eclipse of the Heian court nobility and the rise of military government in the 12th century, there are still several possible starting points, e.g. the Hōgen and Heiji disturbances of 1156 and 1160, the formal institution of the Kamakura shogunate in 1192, and the Jōkyū Disturbance of 1221. Of course, changes in the content and style of literature can almost never be as abrupt and easily dated as some of these arguments would suggest.

Of the new literary forms that emerged within the period from 1200 to 1600, the *renga* or "linked verse" (see RENGA AND HAIKAI) and the NŌ drama are two developments from very down-to-earth and sometimes plebeian forms of entertainment or pastimes, yet their perfected form leans heavily toward the classical aristocratic tradition of poetry and embraces distinctly unpopular canons of taste and refinement. Another form, the GUNKI MONOGATARI or "war chronicles" such as HEIKE MONOGATARI, tells of a side of human activity that found no place in Heian court prose literature; yet these chronicles too are by no means devoid of episodes of a courtly, romantic, and sentimental type, and their poetic elements hark back to the court tradition of poetry. At the same time, it is a most significant feature of war chronicles that they were chanted or recited by itinerant performers; thus, unlike Heian prose romances, they became well known to and appealed to a wide range of people from all social classes all over the country. Nor were war chronicles by any means the only form of text propagated by itinerant performers. Along with the blind priests who recited the *Heike monogatari*, many other types of performers were active, some of them of very low status, including even prostitutes and beggars. These people traveled around making a living by narrating tales. A consideration of the material they propagated shows that the emergence of popular prose literature in the 17th century was not a sudden new phenomenon, but owed much to earlier developments.

Classical Poetry and the Evolution of Renga —— One important Heian literary genre, the prose romance, of which *Genji monogatari* (TALE OF GENJI) is such an outstanding example, had already gone into decline before the end of the Heian period, though until well into the Kamakura (1185–1333) and Muromachi (1333–1568) periods writers continued to produce stereotyped works of this kind. The literary genre in which Heian traditions were not only preserved but continued to produce great art was WAKA poetry; one of the finest in the series of 21 IMPERIAL ANTHOLOGIES from the early 10th-century KOKINSHŪ to the *Shin zoku kokin wakashū* of 1439, and in some ways the culmination of the classical poetic tradition, was the eighth in the line, the SHIN KOKINSHŪ, compiled in 1205. Poetry had for several centuries been dominated by the standards of the *Kokinshū*, and although certain individual poets had from time to time attempted to compose along original lines, the *Kokinshū* tradition remained very strong. For Fujiwara no Shunzei (FUJIWARA NO TOSHINARI; 1114–1204) and his son Fujiwara no Teika (FUJIWARA NO SADAIE; 1162–1241), one of the compilers of the *Shin kokinshū*, the watchword was "old words, new treatment," and the poetic achievements were remarkable.

The qualities of the poetry of Shunzei that are particularly characteristic of the time are SABI, literally "loneliness," and YŪGEN, "mystery and depth." The latter term denotes something like the YOJŌ ("residual feeling," "overtones") so prized in the *Kokinshū* style. Here, however, the feelings referred to are more profound, akin perhaps to Wordsworth's "thoughts that do often lie too deep for tears." In the intellectual, religious, and political climate of the day, the tone of the poetry of deep feeling (one term for this is USHIN, literally "having heart") tended to be melancholy or at least somber; beauty could be found as much in a scene of chilling bleakness as in a colorful scene. Two poems, one by Teika (tr Donald Keene) and the other by his father (tr Robert H. Brower and Earl Miner), perfectly illustrate this:

Miwataseba	In this wide landscape
Hana mo momiji mo	I see no cherry blossoms
Nakarikeri	And no crimson leaves—
Ura no tomaya no	Evening in autumn over
Aki no yūgure	A straw-thatched hut by the bay.

Yū sareba	As evening falls,
Nobe no akikaze	From along the moors the autumn wind
Mi ni shimite	Blows chill into the heart,
Uzura naku nari	And the quails raise their plaintive cry
Fukakusa no sato	In the deep grass of secluded Fukakusa.

Given the limitations of the tradition in which they were working, the *Shin kokinshū* poets felt the need of an elaborate technique in the attempt to give life to old and well-worn themes. Some critics find the verbal techniques over-elaborate and the symbolism of the poetry sometimes overdone and obscure. However, certain developments contributed significantly to the range of suggestion and to the flexibility of the 31-syllable *waka*. One was the technique of HONKADORI, "allusive variation," by which the emotional range of a poem could be immeasurably widened through explicit allusions to well-known poems of earlier times. There was also an increasing tendency to place a caesura after the third line of a poem, or even after the first line. Coupled with this was sometimes a reversal of the normal order of syntax, the second half of the poem belonging grammatically before the first. Another common technique that was clearly conducive to the impressionistic effect of the whole poem was that of ending the last line with a noun instead of the inflected form (verb or adjective) with which normal Japanese sentences end.

It is at least a tenable view that *Shin kokinshū* poetry represents the peak of Japanese court poetry. Yet the limitations of the *waka* form are such that there was little scope for further development, and most critics consider that in the subsequent imperial anthologies the level of poetry steadily declines. The way forward was to be found not in the *waka* form but in linked verse.

Courtiers in the Heian period delighted in capping verses produced by others; in the first story in the Heian collection of short stories TSUTSUMI CHŪNAGON MONOGATARI, for instance, after one guards officer, moved by the sight of falling cherry petals, composes the first three lines of a *waka*: "When I see the flowers falling before I have gazed my fill at them, how keenly I feel that . . ." A fellow officer adds a final couplet: "In the same way I too have withered and faded" so that the two together make a 31-syllable, 5-line poem. The joining of couplets like this had no deep artistic motive, it was simply fun. Greater fun still, of course, was the practice that gradually developed of stringing a whole series of half-poems together— 5-7-5, 7-7, 5-7-5, 7-7, and so on. The aim was to link each of these to the preceding, so that each pair (a-b, b-c, c-d and so on) made a kind of *waka* poem on its own. The links could be in the actual subjects of the separate verses, but they could be established also in a more trivial way, by word associations or wordplays. In fact, the whole business developed very much as a game, governed by elaborate rules as to the intervals at which certain subjects could be mentioned or certain words repeated. In their ordinary and no doubt at times uproarious forms the sequences were known as *haikai no renga*, "unconventional (or amusing) linked verse." Out of this unpromising party game there developed by the 14th century an art which at times came to be treated with an almost religious solemnity and became the bearer of the true artistic tradition in Japanese poetry.

The seeds of this development were already to be found in *Shin kokinshū* poetry. In their book *Japanese Court Poetry*, Robert H. Brower and Earl Miner draw attention to the fact we have already noted, that the *waka* was becoming increasingly fragmented, and they point out that this very fragmentation tended to facilitate the integration of *waka* poems into longer forms, such as the hundred-poem sequence. They also discuss at some length the rediscovery by Japanese scholars of the principles of association and progression which underlie the arrangement of poems in imperial anthologies from the *Kokinshū* onward, but which are particularly highly developed in the *Shin kokinshū*. Undoubtedly the aesthetic principles underlying the arrangement of poems in these anthologies bear a close resemblance to those governing the sequences to be aimed at in the artistic *renga*. Particularly interesting is the fact that the associations between adjacent poems in later imperial anthologies like *Gyokuyōshū* or *Fūgashū* (1313 or 1314 and 1344–46 respectively) become much looser and more subtle, and also that the innovators among poets of this period tended to compose "distantly related verses"; that is, poems divided grammatically, and often in meaning as well, into two logical parts, as opposed to verses that flowed smoothly from beginning to end. The latter tendency is clearly conducive to the development of the *renga* sequence. As used by SHINKEI (1406–75), the medieval practitioner and critic of *renga*, the term "distantly related verses" refers to couplets in a *renga* sequence which are not linked in any obvious or superficial way. Such links he considered to be the best type; at the highest level of artistic composition, the poet had really to think himself so deeply into the mood of the preceding verse that his own linking verse would be determined as it were by intuition, not by a conscious effort to make surface links of subject matter or wording. Thus poetic inspiration required a contemplative, almost religious frame of mind, not unlike the attitude that Shunzei and Teika considered necessary in the composition of waka, a kind of mystical identification with the topic by means of intense concentration and meditation. The same quality of "mystery and depth" that had characterized Shunzei's poetry is typical of artistic renga.

The religious doctrine that had influenced Shunzei was that of shikan (concentration and insight), an aspect of TENDAI SECT Buddhism. The Buddhist influence on renga came largely from ZEN, which had been introduced to Japan at the very beginning of the medieval period. By the 14th century Zen Buddhism had come to play a significant part in Japanese life, both in the practical (Zen priests served Ashikaga shōguns as political advisers) and cultural spheres. There grew up, for instance, a genre of literature practiced by Zen priests which consisted of prose and poetry in Chinese. Known as Gozan bungaku (literally, "literature of the five monasteries"; see GOZAN LITERATURE) it was produced by priests of the most important Zen temples in the country. These works patterned on Chinese models are not of the first importance in Japanese cultural history, though the poetry is perhaps most worthy of attention. But Zen literary influence extended far beyond the boundaries of Zen monasteries. The attitude toward the composition of renga called for by Shinkei owes much to Zen, with its emphasis on intuition. Moreover the descriptive verses he prefers are those in which there are no sharp, clear outlines and all is hazy or indistinct; such verses have much the same appeal as a typical Zen painting, a scene depicted with a few bold and vigorous strokes shading off into mist or cloud or simply into nothing—suggesting much more than it shows.

The Nō —— Another example of Zen influence is to be found in the Nō plays, which became prominent and reached their perfected form under the patronage of that great enthusiast of Zen culture, the Ashikaga shōgun Yoshimitsu (1358–1408), who had incidentally received instruction in court ceremonial and accomplishments from NIJŌ YOSHIMOTO, a leading figure in the history of renga, and fostered in his own palace in Kyōto a cultural life unprecedented in the world of the buke or warrior class. The dramas created by his protégés KAN'AMI (1333–84) and ZEAMI (1363–1443) had their ultimate origin in a low-level type of popular entertainment of several centuries earlier, which even included such things as juggling. Out of this there had evolved simple playlets of a comic or even farcical nature known as SARUGAKU (written with characters that literally mean "monkey music," but in fact a corruption of the earlier name sangaku, "scattered music"), which still later came to be performed at shrines and temples. Comic pieces survived and continue to be performed to this day as KYŌGEN, the farces interspersed in a Nō program between the serious plays. The growth of serious Nō drama is associated with the use of plays to explain the significance of religious rites or to depict religious legends. By the 14th century various troupes of performers were operating outside a religious environment, and their repertoire came to include pieces with broader artistic aims, incorporating song and dance. Kan'ami was the leader of one such troupe. Under the patronage of Yoshimitsu, he and his son Zeami elevated the Nō (originally sarugaku no nō) into the highly serious, aristocratic art form that we know today.

The influence of Zen aesthetics can be seen in the very externals of Nō—the bare stage and the rudimentary props—but also in the slow and stylized action and the total lack of "dramatic effect" in the conventional Western sense. In most plays there is little action on stage, much of the story, being unfolded in narrative as having happened in the past. Often the climax of a play is a dance. Characters, some of whom wear masks, are not depicted as rounded individuals; the aim is to present the essence of the character type—the mother seeking her lost son only to find that he is dead, the young aristocrat reliving the scene of the battle in which he was killed, the hunter suffering in hell for the sin of having killed birds in life. The subject matter of the plays is very diverse, being taken from the whole range of Chinese and Japanese history, literature, or legend; two particularly important sources are the court literature of the mid-Heian period and the chronicles that had been developing since the end of the Heian period from tales about the civil wars between the Minamoto and the Taira families. The same basic theme, however, is common to a large majority of the plays, i.e., the sinful nature of attachment to the things of the world. Typical examples are the

plays of the second of five groups into which Nō plays are conventionally classified; in these we see a warrior suffering torments in the afterlife being helped by the power of Buddhism to lose his hatred for his former enemies, to achieve reconciliation, to break the chains of passion that still bind him to earthly things and thus to achieve salvation. Some Nō plays do deal entirely with the "real" world, but the majority have as the main character an apparition; typically, he or she appears in some earthly guise in the first part of the play, but reappears later in true form as the spirit of some dead person. This interaction between the world of the supernatural and the "real" world gives the plays an atmosphere of profound mystery, indeed there is much about the Nō that makes it seem on occasion like some religious rite. Though Zeami in his writings on Nō uses the word yūgen to mean elegance or grace in the acting and dancing, the plays undoubtedly have the quality of yūgen in the sense in which we have used it before, of mystery and depth both in content and in language, which is in poetical passages of quite astonishing complexity, full of allusions, quotations from earlier literature, and above all of puns or pivot words, by which one statement is made to lead directly into another.

The Zen influence on Nō, both on its artistic form and on its treatment of themes, is undeniable. But we must not overlook the fact that the basic religious doctrine expressed in the plays is that of PURE LAND BUDDHISM; in most cases, reconciliation and salvation are achieved through prayers to the Buddha AMIDA. The fact is that the Amidist faith had grown immensely in importance and popular appeal, particularly from the late Heian period onward. Indeed, the first notable prose work of the medieval period, Hōjōki, is a clear assertion of the need for such a faith on the part of suffering mankind.

Hōjōki and Heike Monogatari —— In the work Hōjōki (An Account of My Hut), written in 1212, a former courtier, KAMO NO CHŌMEI (1156?–1216), explains his reasons for having done as many men of the time were doing, i.e., for having abandoned the secular world and devoted himself as a hermit to the worship of Amida. The lasting fame of the Hōjōki owes much to its beauty of style. It also gives a moving picture, first of the miseries caused by natural disasters such as fire, whirlwinds, or famine (which emphasizes the futility of so much human endeavor), and then of the solace afforded by religion. Buddhist teaching always had expounded the transitoriness of human life and the pointlessness of human activity. In this period that doctrine received ever-increasing emphasis, since it was believed that Japan had entered the so-called Latter Age of the Law (mappō; see ESCHATOLOGY), a time when Buddhist Law would decline, the world would grow ever more chaotic and wicked, and man would have no hope without reliance on the saving grace of Amida. One of the major works of the medieval period, the war chronicle Heike monogatari, begins with just such a statement of the futility of human pride and endeavor: "The sound of the bell of Gionshōja echoes the impermanence of all things. The hue of the flowers of the teak tree declares that they who flourish must be brought low. Yea, the proud ones are but for a moment, like an evening dream in springtime. The mighty are destroyed at the last, they are but as the dust before the wind" (tr A. L. Sadler). This chronicle does not relate the early stages in the rise of the Taira through the succession disputes of 1156–60; they are told in two similar though less important works, HŌGEN MONOGATARI (Tale of the Hōgen Disturbance) and HEIJI MONOGATARI (Tale of the Heiji Disturbance). Heike monogatari begins with TAIRA NO KIYOMORI (1118–81) at the height of his power and arrogance and sets out to portray him in the blackest of terms. The fall of his house is thus seen as inevitable retribution. When the Taira are utterly defeated in the final battle at sea and his wife is about to leap into the water with her grandson, the young emperor Antoku, she says to him, "Turn to the east and bid farewell to the deity of the Great Shrine of Ise and then to the west and say the nembutsu, that Amida and the Holy Ones may come to welcome you to the Pure Western Land. Japan is small as a grain of millet, but now it is a vale of misery. There is a pure land of happiness beneath the waves, another capital where no sorrow is."

Uji Shūi Monogatari —— It is curious that in his catalogue of disasters in the Hōjōki Chōmei refers only indirectly to the Gempei (Taira-Minamoto) wars which had so devastated the country at the time of which he was writing. The same is true of a collection of tales compiled about the same time as Hōjōki which in other respects gives us as good a picture of the ordinary life of Japan as one can find anywhere, namely UJI SHŪI MONOGATARI. Here we find not only tales of religion and superstition—for benefits in this life people looked to KANNON, for intercession on behalf of sinners in hell they prayed to JIZŌ, for rebirth in paradise they prayed to

Amida, for protection against all manner of evil influences they recited spells associated with Fudō (see MYŌŌ), and so on—we can find also what amused people, their gaiety and often ribald humor as well as their hopes and fears. Some collections in this genre of SETSUWA BUNGAKU, "tale literature," are exclusively secular, others exclusively Buddhist, e.g. Hosshinshū, also written by Chōmei. It should be stressed that these collections do not belong to the world of fairy tales or folk literature, though they of course contain many terms of folkloristic interest; many of the tales in Uji shūi monogatari are about the everyday life of ordinary people of all classes, curiously mixed, however, with edifying religious exemplary tales. A similar and even more puzzling combination is found in the collection known as KONJAKU MONOGATARI, with which Uji shūi has a close but not satisfactorily explicable connection; this work may have had some connection with preaching, but how we do not know. Though compiled about 1120, it is of interest to us here as very much a transitional work. Stylistically, much of it anticipates the language of the medieval war chronicles (it even includes a few items which in a minor way are early examples of war tales), while many of its stories give us sidelights on the changing attitudes and structure of society in the late Heian period. Paradoxically one can find already in Konjaku monogatari that nostalgia for "the old days" of court culture which becomes such a prominent characteristic of later collections.

Tsurezuregusa——Equally nostalgic is the second most famous medieval work by a hermit, the Tsurezuregusa (ca 1330; tr Essays in Idleness, 1967) by YOSHIDA KENKŌ (ca 1283–ca 1352). This collection of random jottings of that peculiarly Japanese type known as ZUIHITSU (literally, "following the pen") contains diverse anecdotes and observations on life and manners that give us a most intriguing picture of the attitudes of an educated man of the 14th century—his mind embracing a variety of doctrines, including Confucianism and Taoism as well as the more conventional Buddhist sentiments (and the occasional Zen idea)—who clearly regretted the decline in artistic and other standards. A slightly worldly cleric, Kenkō does not disapprove, for instance, of drinkers or romantic lovers—provided they observe what seems to him important in all activities, i.e., moderation. Deeply conscious of the transitoriness of human activity, he yet prizes the very fact of life's uncertainty. Aesthetically, he is drawn by the imperfect, the withered, the incomplete, and in this he is very much the medieval cultivated man; he comments, for instance, on the pleasure to be derived, not only from actually seeing the moon and cherry blossoms, but from longing for the moon on a rainy night or from sitting under an almost bare cherry tree and reflecting on the now faded glory of the blossoms. This statement greatly impressed Shinkei, and one can well imagine that it is to just such a person as Kenkō that certain qualities praised by Shinkei in renga poetry—hiesabi, "frosty loneliness," or yasesamushi, "thin and cold"—would appeal. Moreover, just as Chōmei does not comment on the Gempei wars, so Kenkō does not refer to the political troubles of his own time, the wars that resulted from the emperor Go-Daigo's (1288–1339; r 1318–39) attempt around 1330 to restore the long-lost supremacy of imperial rule.

War Chronicles and Tales of Heroes——We must now, however, turn to that major category of medieval literature in which these cataclysmic events do find expression, indeed expression of an epic kind, i.e., the war chronicles. Apart from two (to be mentioned later) which deal not with whole campaigns but with a single hero or a pair of heroic brothers, the most important are Hōgen monogatari, Heiji monogatari, Heike monogatari, and the TAIHEIKI (Chronicle of the Great Peace; tr Taiheiki, 1959), dealing with Go-Daigo's wars in the 14th century. The outstanding work among all these is beyond doubt the Heike monogatari. Another work which is technically a war chronicle, the GEMPEI SEISUIKI (The Rise and Fall of the Genji and Heike), tells essentially the same story as Heike, but differs fundamentally in kind. Whereas Gempei seisuiki is the product of a line of written texts, meant to be appreciated by the eye and not the ear, Heike monogatari, like the other chronicles named above, is a katari-mono, i.e., a narrated text, chanted or recited dramatically for an audience. There is evidence that a written form of the Heike story, probably composed by a court nobleman, came into being early in the 13th century. But alongside the line of written texts, of which Gempei seisuiki represents an advanced stage, another development took place. The details of this are obscure but we know that for well over a century and a half the tale of the Taira clan was chanted by itinerant blind minstrels known as BIWA HŌSHI (literally, "lute priests"). It was not a fixed text, but was constantly created and recreated in the course of recitation, by the same kind of formulaic process thought to have led to the development of the Homeric

epics. In this way, not only did the wording fluctuate but the content of the episodes themselves was constantly being revised or added to; the version now regarded as standard is that committed to writing in 1371 as the version of a famous reciter, Kakuichi.

The written chronicle Gempei seisuki is certainly not without interest, but it lacks the stirring qualities of Heike monogatari. How audiences must have thrilled to the latter's account of the fearful death of Taira no Kiyomori, consumed even on his deathbed by the fires of hatred for the Minamoto, and to the subsequent overthrow of the Taira at the hands of Kiso Yoshinaka (also known as MINAMOTO NO YOSHINAKA; 1154–84) and MINAMOTO NO YORITOMO's (1147–99) younger brother MINAMOTO NO YOSHITSUNE (1159–89)! How they must have been moved by the heroic vigor and grandeur of the battle scenes, with their accounts of bravery, nobility of mind, loyalty, and self-sacrifice! The tale has pathos, too, in the fate of Yoshinaka and Yoshitsune, both victims of Yoritomo's suspicion, and in the more romantic tales of sad lovers. Its most lasting effect was to glorify, almost to create, the image of the warrior (samurai). However, it is not reliable as history; what in one case ends up as a valiant fight to the death began in an early version as a somewhat ignominious rout. It has grown to be looked on as a kind of "national epic," inspiring countless Japanese ever since, and firing the imagination of many writers and playwrights—as indeed have numerous incidents and characters in other war chronicles, for instance the mighty Minamoto no Tametomo (1139–70) in Hōgen monogatari, or Kusunoki Masashige (d 1336) in Taiheiki, who gave his life fighting for his emperor, Go-Daigo.

It would be wrong, however, to look at these works so strictly from the literary point of view that we overlook another aspect of at least some of them, i.e., that in the early stages of their development they may have had a religious function. It is not simply a question of their embodying a religious moral, as Heike monogatari so obviously does. The fact is that in medieval Japan the recitation of accounts of battles and the manner in which heroic figures died sometimes constituted a kind of religious ritual undertaken partly to comfort the spirits of the departed and partly to pacify them and ward off any evil and vengeful influences that they might bring to bear (see GORYŌ). It is highly probable that early accounts of this kind about the Gempei wars contributed to the development of Heike monogatari. Certainly there is ample evidence that such practices played a major part in the genesis and growth of SOGA MONOGATARI, the story of the revenge exacted by the Soga brothers in 1193 for the murder of their father at the instigation of a man who by the time of the revenge was a retainer of Yoritomo. An examination of this work sheds considerable light not only on the process by which such chronicles evolved but also on the whole situation of popular tales in medieval Japan. For instance, there is a remarkable connection between the earliest extant version of Soga monogatari in pseudo-Chinese dating from the late 13th or early 14th century, and the Shintōshū, a collection probably made about 1350 of tales relating the origin of deities at certain Shintō (in reality syncretic-Buddhist) shrines. Not only do some passages in the early Soga monogatari, particularly passages relating to the origin of deities and shrines, show exact correspondence of wording with Shintōshū, but the two works resemble each other in certain peculiarities of script. The compilation of Shintōshū seems to have been undertaken by the Agui branch of Tendai Buddhism, which is known to have specialized in popular preaching. In the early medieval period Agui gained control of the Hakone Shrine, a religious center which figures prominently in the story of the Soga brothers. All the evidence points to the Soga story having been propagated as part of the Agui's repertory by proselytizing storytellers connected with the Hakone Shrine; indeed this link with the activities of Agui in Eastern Japan is thought to have in places influenced the very content of Soga monogatari. Again, some 80 years after the revenge and death of the brothers in 1193, we find a work of history, AZUMA KAGAMI (Mirror of Eastern Japan), naming as an actual historical personage one Tora Gozen, mistress of the elder of the Soga brothers. Modern research suggests, however, that the name of this character in the Soga story almost certainly comes from a generic term for a kind of itinerant female performer of religious rituals (a kind of MIKO). What seems to have happened is that the original record was reshaped to include a character created by the narrators. The mention of Tora Gozen in Azuma kagami suggests that this apparently documentary record at least in this case derived material from popular tales current at the time.

Undoubtedly many storytellers in medieval Japan had close connections with religion. Besides the Agui preachers, there were the holy men of the JI SECT of popular Buddhism, whose influence is detected in *Soga monogatari*. There were also blind women known as GOZE, who told tales to the accompaniment of a hand drum (a picture exists of one of these reciting *Soga monogatari*) and the blind minstrels known as *biwa hōshi* (literally, "lute priests," though the word *hōshi* here should not be taken in too formal a sense) who chanted *Heike monogatari;* the reciters of *Taiheiki*, incidentally, were known as *monogatarisō*, "narrator priests." In addition there were several kinds of *etoki* or "picture explainers." Among the male *etoki,* some performed in temples, explaining the history of the institution in question or the lives of famous priests; others were peripatetic (though some of these were lay performers). There were also women *etoki* known as Kumano nuns, originally representatives of the particular form of popular Buddhism associated with the KUMANO SANZAN SHRINES not far from Ise. In later times these women degenerated into entertainers who were not above acting as prostitutes. Their early activities, however, consisted in showing pictures, e.g., scenes of hells *(jigoku),* and telling stories to explain the illustrations. Though no direct evidence connects this particular group with *Soga monogatari,* it seems certain that women of such a type played a part in developing the Soga story. Indeed, its propagation by women (*goze* and perhaps Kumano nuns) undoubtedly brought about the introduction (or at least an emphasis) into later versions of the story of certain elements such as a love interest. The origin of such features in medieval stories is sometimes that a narrator has recounted personal experiences as an encouragement to religious faith, giving the narratives a distinctly confessional or penitential flavor. As time went on, however, and the purpose of storytelling tended more and more toward entertainment, it is only natural that features such as love interest were introduced for their own sake.

An intriguing accretion of this kind takes place in the development of legends about Minamoto no Yoshitsune, perhaps Japan's greatest hero. By the early 16th century we find evidence suggesting that the repertory of blind minstrels called ZATŌ (a type of *biwa hōshi*) included a tale about a love affair between Yoshitsune as a youth and Lady Jōruri, daughter of a rich man of Yahagi (in what is now Aichi Prefecture), where Yoshitsune stayed on his way to northeastern Japan. In late medieval Japan this chanted *Jōruri hime monogatari* (or *Jūnidan sōshi;* Tale of Jōruri in Twelve Sections) gained such popularity that the whole type of entertainment that it represents (which later, with the addition of puppets and *shamisen* accompaniment, developed into the puppet drama) came to be known as JŌRURI. Quite apart from its love interest, a feature of this story is its inclusion of utterly fantastic magical elements.

Ballad-Drama and Otogi-Zōshi —— As a subject of tales, Minamoto no Yoshitsune was outstandingly popular. Of the 50 extant KŌWAKA—a medieval form of ballad-drama which at one time rivaled Nō in popularity and consisted of a kind of dance (though the dance element is minimal today) performed to a rhythmical drum accompaniment while a narrator told the story—about two-fifths concern him (in fact, by far the majority of *kōwaka* deal with events of the period between 1160 and 1193, seven of them relating episodes in the Soga story). One important body of tales about Yoshitsune, though it does not contain the Jōruri legend, is the probably 15th-century war chronicle GIKEIKI (tr *Yoshitsune*, 1966). We shall look in vain in it, however, for the historical Yoshitsune, for it is little more than a group of legends brought together in a work permeated through and through by the sentiment of *hōgan-biiki*, "sympathy for the *hōgan*," i.e., for Yoshitsune; it is an account of a romantic and heroic but also, in the end, pathetic figure.

One more story of Yoshitsune, even more fantastic than that of his encounter with Lady Jōruri, brings us to the last category of medieval literature to be considered. This is "Yoshitsune's Voyage Among the Islands," in which he journeys, calling in at such places as the Island of Horse-headed People, or the Island of the Naked, or the Island of Dwarfs, in quest of a secret military treatise in the possession of a demon king 160 feet tall. The demon's daughter falls in love with him, and, though it costs her her life, she enables him to steal and copy the treatise (which then becomes blank paper) and escape. This tale is an example of the OTOGI-ZŌSHI, (companion booklets or entertainment booklets) of which some 500 are extant. Until comparatively recently they were almost entirely neglected by scholars as intended only for children or women. This contempt for them stems from the fact that the very existence of such a large corpus of tales was unknown until modern times. Previously they were known from a group of 23 tales (including the Yoshitsune story) published as a volume specifically for women in the early 18th century. Given the nature of some of these stories, *otogi-zōshi* were thought to be little more than fairy tales. Certainly the genre does include some fairy tales (e.g., *Issumbōshi*, a Japanese Tom Thumb story). It is clear that however naive and artless many of the tales may be, they were definitely not just children's books, but appealed also to adults, including men. The range of subjects is wide. There are, for instance, popular versions of the kind of love stories found in Heian court literature. There are tales of wicked stepmothers, heroes, and the achievement of fame and fortune. Fantastic elements abound, as the Yoshitsune tale shows. There are stories in which animals fall in love with and marry humans, and even burlesques of the famous war chronicles where the characters are all animals, or even, in one case, plants and trees. However wide the range of subjects, though, there is nothing that cannot lend itself to religious propaganda. Miracle tales abound, of course, but even the most unlikely stories can be rounded off with statements to the effect that such-and-such a character eventually became a Buddhist divinity at some temple or a Shintō deity at some shrine. All this would suggest that at least some of the tales may have been used in preaching or derived from material used in preaching. (It has been suggested that these little books served as talismans distributed by Kumano nuns.) How else the tales may have been used for public narration we do not know. Certainly there is evidence in the phraseology of some stories that people listened to as well as read them. We should not forget also, particularly in view of the suggestion that the books were talismans, that many of these tales are known to have appeared as Nara *ehon*, picture books produced in large quantity from the mid-Muromachi to mid-Edo periods and drawn in a naïve—although increasingly gorgeous—style originating among priests in the Nara area.

From the point of view of literary art, this corpus of popular tales has no great importance. Its significance lies elsewhere, in that it shows how far the dissemination of popular literature had already progressed even before the burst of activity in this field in the 17th century. Artistically, the achievements of the medieval period in literature lie predominantly in the fields of drama and poetry, and the aesthetic criteria governing them have continued to exercise an influence on Japanese life down to the present day (though of course the Edo period saw the growth of different forms of drama, with a more popular appeal, in KABUKI and JŌRURI, and of a more popular form of poetry, the HAIKU, which evolved from the late medieval period onward from the opening verses of *renga* sequences). It must be noted that the standards set in serious drama and poetry were aristocratic standards, owing little to the politically dominant warrior caste, who produced no literature worth speaking of that was peculiarly their own. On another level we must of course recognize the achievement of the best among the war chronicles. At the same time, as tales with a wide popular appeal, they are also part of the great mass of popular literature, including both chanted or recited literature *(katari-mono)* and printed books such as *otogi-zōshi*, which played a significant role in laying the groundwork for the development of prose literature in the Edo period. Speaking of *etoki*, and Kumano nuns, along with other wandering proselytizers and "jongleurs," Barbara Ruch says, "First, they built a body of vocal literature, a repertory of heroes and themes that permeated all genres and became Japan's first national literature. This literature was performed for people on all levels of society and served basic needs that were shared by all classes equally . . . Second, as more and more of their stories were transcribed and circulated, books became a familiar part of Japanese life." In this sense, even the humblest of medieval literature has an importance out of all proportion to its strictly artistic value.

■——James T. Araki, *The Ballad-Drama of Medieval Japan* (1964). Robert H. Brower and Earl Miner, *Japanese Court Poetry* (1961). Earle Ernst, *Three Japanese Plays from the Traditional Theatre* (1959). Donald Keene, *Nō, The Classical Theatre of Japan* (1973). Kokusai Bunka Shinkōkai, ed, *Introduction to Classic Japanese Literature* (1948). Earl Miner, *Japanese Linked Poetry* (1979). P. G. O'Neill, *A Guide to Nō* (1954). Shio Sakanishi, *Japanese Folk-Plays: The Ink-smeared Lady and Other Kyōgen* (1960). *Uji shūi monogatari,* tr D. E. Mills as *A Collection of Tales from Uji* (1970). *Gikeiki,* tr Helen C. McCullough as *Yoshitsune* (1966). *Heiji monogatari,* tr Edwin O. Reischauer, in Edwin O. Reischauer and Joseph K. Yamagiwa, *Translations from Early Japanese Literature* (1951). *Heike monogatari,* tr Hiroshi Kitagawa as *The Tale of the Heike* (1975). *Heike monogatari,* tr A. L. Sadler, *Transactions of the Asiatic Society of Japan* 46 (1918), 49 (1921), excerpts as well as a translation of *Hōjōki* are in *The Ten Foot Square Hut and Tales of the Heike* (1928, repr 1972). *Hōgen monogatari,* tr William Ritchie Wilson as *The Tale of the Disorder in Hōgen* (1971). *Hōjōki,* tr D. L. Keene as "*An Account of My Hut,*" in Donald Keene, ed, *Anthology of Japa-*

nese Literature (1955), a partial translation. *Konjaku monogatari*, tr Bernard Frank as *Histoires qui sont maintenant du passé* (1968). D. E. Mills, "Medieval Japanese Tales," *Folklore* 84 (Spring 1973). D. E. Mills, "*Soga monogatari, Shintōshū* and the Taketori Legend," *Monumenta Nipponica* 30.1 (1975). Jacqueline Pigeot, *Histoire de Yokobue (Yokobue no sōshi): Étude sur les récits de l'époque Muromachi, Bulletin de la Maison Franco-Japonaise, Nouvelle série* 9.2 (1972). Barbara Ruch, "Origins of *The Companion Library*: An Anthology of Medieval Japanese Stories," *Journal of Asian Studies* 30.3 (1971). Barbara Ruch, "Medieval Jongleurs and the Making of a National Literature," in John W. Hall and Takeshi Toyoda, *Japan in the Muromachi Age* (1977). *Taiheiki*, tr Helen McCullough (1959). *Tsurezuregusa*, tr Donald Keene as *Essays in Idleness* (1967). Marian Ury, *Poems of the Five Mountains: An Introduction to the Literature of the Zen Monasteries* (1977).   Douglas E. MILLS

EDO LITERATURE

Literature of the period when the Tokugawa family ruled Japan from Edo (now Tōkyō); also known as Tokugawa literature. The term Edo literature is somewhat misleading because much of the literature emanated from Kyōto and Ōsaka. Japanese literary historians often use a term equivalent to "recent literature" (*kinsei bungaku*).

The period was one of general peace and isolation, characterized by the transfer of cultural activity from aristocratic, warrior, and priestly classes to that of the merchants and townsfolk (see CHŌNIN), and by the commercial printing and publication of works of fiction and poetry, production of plays with live actors and puppets, and popular art in the form of woodblock prints, reaching a public greater than ever before. The date 1724 marks a division between an early, initiative period and a later one of steady development.

I. EARLY PERIOD

Pre-Genroku Literature —— The GENROKU ERA (1688–1704) saw a flowering of artistic production in Japan, and the years 1600–1687 can be seen as a preparation for this. Pre-Genroku literature started with a fairly low level of attainment; however, printing spread from religious texts to general books and illustrations, encouraging an interest in old literature. A 1608 edition of ISE MONOGATARI (ca mid-10th century) is often mentioned as a masterpiece of book production. Commercial printing started in 1609 (see PRINTING, PREMODERN). Reading and participation in literature thus changed from an élitist to a popular pursuit.

Prose fiction. A group of miscellaneous tales known under the general name of OTOGI-ZŌSHI (stories to divert) were printed around 1720. These had already existed for some time in manuscript form and were often works of considerable calligraphic and illustrative art. Their subjects are varied, including fairy tales, tales of animals in human form, tales imitating the prose of the Heian period (794–1185), love stories (sometimes homosexual), Buddhist tales, and folktales. Though not strictly of the Edo period, they were undoubtedly read widely and gave inspiration to story writers. Another influence from earlier years was that of the Jesuit missionaries in Nagasaki; a printing press had been set up in Amakusa which had produced at the close of the 16th century a romanized version of HEIKE MONOGATARI, the 13th-century war romance (see JESUIT MISSION PRESS). A translation into romanized Japanese of *Aesop's Fables* appeared in 1593, but it was only natural that this did not have a wide readership, since very few Japanese could have read it in roman letters. A new translation appeared in the early 17th century in Japanese script, under the title ISOHO MONOGATARI. It was widely read and is now considered an important title on the list of KANA-ZŌSHI, i.e., books for reading *(sōshi)* written in KANA, the Japanese syllabary. The prose works of these years (1600–1682) are so called, but their linguistic accessibility to readers of the time is almost the only thing *kana-zōshi* have in common, apart from a tendency to division into short anecdotal sections, for their subject matter varies widely and is by no means always fictional. For example, most varieties of *otogi-zōshi* are found and in addition, there appear parodies of old literature (derived ultimately from comic verse and cartoon-like picture scrolls), didactic and utilitarian works such as guides for growing rich and for traveling the great roads of Japan, and *hyōbanki*, or critical appraisals of KABUKI actors and prostitutes. Although depth of characterization or development of plot are minimal, *kana-zōshi* were often closely in touch with contemporary life and were no longer escapist tales of the past. Few names of authors emerge, but ASAI RYŌI (d 1691) is still remembered, particularly for his *Ukiyo monogatari* (ca 1660, Tales of the Floating World), an early use of the term *ukiyo*, which was to be widely used later. Ryōi wrote *kana-zōshi* of various sorts, some criticizing social conditions. He was also a Buddhist scholar of note, conversant as well with the prevailing Confucian ethic. He can be thought of as the first professional prose writer, writing and producing books in editions large enough to provide him with an income.

Drama. Literary production was still generally restricted to the Kyōto–Ōsaka (Kansai) area, for the Tokugawa capital, Edo, was as yet too new and brash to support a culture of its own. Kabuki drama had appeared in Kyōto at the beginning of the 17th century with female performers, who were banned by government decree in 1629, a ban that in 1652 was extended to young male actors taking women's parts. Rather than a literary form the kabuki was at this time more a vulgar dance theater, or a front for brothels, though it used a stage derived from that of the NŌ theater, and realistic comic interludes from the same source. The same is not true of the puppet theater (BUNRAKU), established in Kyōto at about the same time as kabuki; in *bunraku*, chanters, SHAMISEN players, and puppeteers, all practitioners of independent arts, united to form a new drama. With a series of popular chanters this new theater, performing plays of violence with mythical military heroes, caught on in Edo, the abode of often idle *samurai*. The plays were not high literature, but the texts, often printed with lively illustrations, can be thought of as a sort of prose fiction. Texts for narrative chanting though they were, they must often have been read for themselves (see JŌRURI).

After the great fire of 1657, which temporarily interrupted theater performances, some Edo chanters moved to the Kyōto–Ōsaka area. The cross-fertilization of the "soft" Kansai style and the "rough" Edo style brought about more refined puppet plays with chanters like Sakurai Tamba no Shōjō (fl 1660–1700) in Ōsaka and Uji Kaga no Jō (1635–1711) in Kyōto. (The second elements [Tamba no Shōjō; Kaga no Jō] in these names are honorary titles traditionally conferred on chanters and other performers.) The latter's plays tended to be more truly dramatic under the influence of Nō plays, which, along with another medieval dance and narrative form, the KŌWAKA, had become an official entertainment for warriors; texts of the *kōwaka* were a source of material for the puppet theater.

Poetry. The other great literary category of the period, which later came to be known as HAIKU, developed from *renga* or "linked verse" (see RENGA AND HAIKAI). Haiku took the first 17 syllables of the *renga* form and created a new verse form. Nearly everyone with artistic aspirations composed haiku, and every kabuki actor, for example, possessed a special name for this purpose. Whereas writers of drama and fiction wrote for a living, many wrote haiku for literary glory, or to maintain their position as teachers. The popularity of haiku produced much disputation, creating division into a number of schools. In the 17th century before 1680, a traditionalist, intellectual school, named Teimon after MATSUNAGA TEITOKU (1571–1653) and continued by YASUHARA TEISHITSU (1610–73), was opposed by the DANRIN SCHOOL led by NISHIYAMA SŌIN (1605–82), who favored a witty style and made shocking use of vulgarisms and sometimes indecent words. The purpose of the *haikai* (the contemporary name for haiku) was to draw word pictures of momentary events in nature. Some effective early examples from the thousands written still survive. For sheer performance, if not quality, Ihara SAIKAKU (1642–93; see below concerning his prose) is remembered for his 1684 record of composing 23,500 verses in 24 hours in his eccentric "Dutch style."

Genroku Literature —— The Genroku era in literature is dominated by three great figures: the prose writer Saikaku, the poet Matsuo BASHŌ (1644–94), and the dramatist CHIKAMATSU MONZAEMON (1653–1724). They were at the peak of achievement in a period which saw great flourishing of all the arts, when the townsfolk of Kyōto, Ōsaka, and Edo were rivaling the warriors as patrons of the arts. One reason for this brilliance was the increased prosperity among merchants arising from the stability of Tokugawa rule; this made resources available for ostentatious expenditure on pleasures. Another was the availability of talent from the national stock of intellects hitherto confined to military and administrative duties but now seeking, as RŌNIN (masterless samurai), to earn a living. Bashō and Chikamatsu were two such *rōnin*, and there were hundreds more in all professions.

Bashō. Bashō was a lowly samurai, employed in the castle at Ueno in Iga Province (now part of Mie Prefecture) as companion to the young lord. He benefited there from excellent teachers, including a follower of Teitoku, KITAMURA KIGIN (1624–1705), who taught both of them *haikai*. Bashō's first poems appeared in print in 1664. The young master died, and Bashō moved to Edo in 1672. His reputation rests on his poetry, collected by his pupils, and his travel diaries. He was influenced by the Teitoku and Danrin schools of *haikai*, older Japanese poets like SAIGYŌ (1118–90), and Chinese poets like Li Bo (Li Po; 701–762), whom he studied avidly. He enjoyed great success but probably lived largely on gifts from pupils and friends. He brought *haikai* verse, both the 17-syllable *hokku* (haiku) and the linked poetry *renku*, to a level which it had not reached before, his best works having a breathtaking poignancy in descriptions of nature, couched in a language deceptively simple and lacking in ornament. Bashō's style became supreme, and for some time after his death his pupils, such as TAKARAI KIKAKU (1661–1707), MUKAI KYORAI (1651–1704), and MORIKAWA KYOROKU (1656–1715), carried on his methods, with differing degrees of individuality. Bashō's writing may owe something to his study of Zen Buddhism, with its preference for plain speech and its preoccupation with the moment of enlightenment; in many of Bashō's poems an instant of movement occurs against a featureless background.

Saikaku. Bashō's activity, though centered in Edo, extended over much of Japan. Saikaku and Chikamatsu confined their work almost entirely to Ōsaka and Kyōto. In Ōsaka an active commercialism was developing and preoccupation with manufacturing and trading characterized it then as today. In contrast, Kyōto, for all its lack of real power, was still the seat of the emperor, court aristocrats, and many Buddhist priests who were preoccupied with the pursuit of elegance and taste, which did not necessarily bring in much money. Although few details of Saikaku's life are known, it is certain that he was an Ōsaka shopkeeper. Toward the end of his career he may have earned a considerable amount from his writing, but it is doubtful whether his early prowess as a high-speed verse-writer brought him anything more than fame. In 1682 he wrote a work of fiction, the first of a new genre, namely UKIYO-ZŌSHI (books of the floating world), which was to replace the earlier *kana-zōshi*. Its immediate success rested on Saikaku's genius in bringing together influences from Ryōi and other writers of fiction compounded with his mastery of a racy style derived from his *haikai*. This work, *Kōshoku ichidai otoko* (1682; tr *The Life of an Amorous Man*, 1964) is in 54 chapters, each a year in the life of Yonosuke in his quest for sexual enjoyment. His two other masterpieces of this sort, *Kōshoku gonin onna* (1686; tr *Five Women Who Loved Love*, 1956) and *Kōshoku ichidai onna* (1686; tr *The Life of an Amorous Woman*, 1963), extend his work to a much more real world. The five unfortunates in the former work, all based in real life, remained some of the archetypes of tragic lovers; the second novel describes the rise and decline of a courtesan and documents not only methods used by an unmarried woman to make a living but also the complicated hierarchy of prostitution at the time. Saikaku also wrote stories styled as folk legends and stories of love and revenge among the samurai. Another successful variety was works treating merchant life, not the erotic aspect but the ways of making, keeping, and losing money. Two examples are *Nippon eitaigura* (1688; tr *The Japanese Family Storehouse*, 1959) and *Seken munesan'yō* (1692; tr *Worldly Mental Calculations*, 1976). Saikaku seldom became involved with his characters, customarily maintaining a cynical distance. His writing, apparently dashed off at high speed, has a vividness and wit that cannot help but suffer in translation.

Chikamatsu. In drama the Genroku era is dominated by the writer Chikamatsu Monzaemon and the chanter Takemoto Gidayū I (1651–1714), who exerted a strong influence on all his collaborators. Chikamatsu probably became acquainted with the *jōruri* chanter Uji Kaga no Jō while in service to a noble family in Kyōto. The first play to be presented by Kaga no Jō for which Chikamatsu is credited with the authorship is *Yotsugi Soga* (1683), a novel drama built around the widely known 14th-century tale of revenge, SOGA MONOGATARI, though he may have collaborated on a number of earlier plays. At this point Gidayū was just beginning his career, and the older established chanters reacted to the stimulus of his new methods. Among them was Kaga no Jō, who on his only excursion to Ōsaka in 1685 presented the puppet play *Koyomi* (1685, The Calendar), Saikaku's one certain *jōruri*. Gidayū successfully countered this challenge for the favor of his audience with a rewrite by Chikamatsu of an old play. Thereafter Saikaku wrote no more plays and Kaga no Jō stayed in Kyōto, often putting on versions of Gidayū's Ōsaka productions. Chikamatsu stayed on with Gidayū for a while, and wrote for him *Shusse Kagekiyo* (1686, Kagekiyo Victorious), the first of the "new *jōruri*," so called because of the innovative style they established. In 1686 Chikamatsu's name began to appear as author on puppet playbooks, an indication of the improved status of playwrights. In 1693 his association with SAKATA TŌJŪRŌ I (1647–1709), a kabuki actor who played handsome lovers with great success, commenced and until 1705 most of Chikamatsu's writing was devoted to writing kabuki plays for Tōjūrō in Kyōto. Chikamatsu's collaboration with Tōjūrō ended in 1702, and he returned to writing exclusively for the puppet stage and collaborating with Gidayū. Tōjūrō's skill as an actor had given kabuki 10 years of dominance in Kyōto, but now it was to give way to the puppet theater. Edo dramatists meanwhile produced plays performed in a vigorous style known as *aragoto* ("rough business"); however, there was some exchange of actors and thus they were not completely isolated from developments in Kyōto and Ōsaka.

There has been much speculation about the reasons for the relative fortunes of kabuki and the puppet theater at this time. It is not clear whether it was because Chikamatsu transferred his allegiance back to *jōruri* that kabuki went into decline, or whether he transferred because he realized a decline was coming. Complete texts of his kabuki plays do not survive, so their literary value cannot be known. His return to writing for Gidayū was marked by a development in 1703 which seems more significant than the earlier change from "old" to "new" *jōruri*, i.e. the introduction of plots based on contemporary incidents, often suicides for love. Such stories could be treated with a realism of language and truth of sentiment which made them comparable, for their tragic poetry and dramatic skill, to the best European plays of the time. The dominant theme of late *jōruri* was the conflict between GIRI AND NINJŌ ("loyalty and human affection"), for example, between a man's love for a prostitute and his duty to his family. Chikamatsu excelled also in composing *michiyuki* (the travel-dance section of a play), usually a scene of travel under stress, using allusive language and purple passages all of which displayed the varied skills of the chanter to best advantage. Given their concern for the individual, modern-day readers tend to think of Chikamatsu's domestic plays *(sewa-mono)* as his masterpieces, but he by no means abandoned historical plays *(jidai-mono)*, and the success of *Kokusen'ya kassen* (1715; tr *The Battles of Coxinga*, 1951), a long, spectacular, and fantastic play about events in China and Japan at the fall of the Ming dynasty (1368–1644), is indicated by the fact that it ran for an unprecedented 17 months, at a time when a complete program change was expected at least every month. An *ukiyo-zōshi* of the same title came out in 1716, and kabuki versions were soon being produced in Kyōto, Ōsaka, and Edo.

In 1703 a pupil of Gidayū took the name Toyotake Wakatayū, set up a rival theater, and employed his own playwright, KI NO KAION (1663–1742). Although Kaion's work is far from negligible, it lacks Chikamatsu's warmth of feeling, and his style is at times so decorative that one wonders how the audiences could have understood the chanting, although still delivered in the GIDAYŪ-BUSHI style. Nevertheless, Kaion's plots have survived in later adaptations. His play *Yaoya Oshichi* (ca 1711–15, Oshichi the Greengrocer's Daughter), for example, is based on a true story elaborated by Saikaku in *Gonin onna* about the love of a girl for a young priest, and her subsequent execution for arson. Although Kaion survived Chikamatsu by almost 20 years, he wrote no plays after his rival's death.

II. LATER PERIOD

The early peak of literary production ends with the deaths of the three great figures, Bashō, Saikaku, and Chikamatsu. For the remainder of the Edo period, it seems more convenient to take the various genres separately, and indicate interrelationships as they occur. Developments took place in poetry, in response to a continuing desire for self-expression and improvement of the art; in drama and prose fiction, in an effort to maintain audiences and sales, and sometimes to educate, by exploring new fields and improving old styles. Writers, artists, and publishers had to contend not only with waning enthusiasm, but also with changing attitudes and capricious controls on the part of the government. Although much literature of value was produced, one senses nevertheless an inability to reach the heights attained in the Genroku era and a definite decline toward the end of the Edo period.

Poetry —— *Haikai and haiku.* Haiku poetry continued to be written throughout the Edo period and even today hardly suffers any quantitative decline. It maintained its ability to engender controversy, and although many illustrated books of *haikai*, still highly valued as works of art, were produced, in general, haiku poetry remained the pursuit of those who earned a living in other fields. Writers of *haikai* continued to write diaries, essays, and other *belles lettres*, in which Chinese influence was strong. *Fūzoku monzen* (1705), a miscellaneous collection by several authors, including Bashō, based in form on the Chinese *Wenxuan (Wen-hsüan)*, seems to belong to a period of decline because of efforts to achieve literary effect and ornamentation, far removed from Bashō's masterly simplicity.

After Bashō's death various manneristic styles arose among his followers, and as the 50th anniversary of his death (an important time in Buddhist belief when the spirit merges with its collective ancestors) approached, a conservative movement calling for a return to Bashō's style arose in Edo. However, it was Yosa BUSON (1716–84) who, working chiefly in Kyōto, achieved excellence and originality as a painter as well as a haiku poet. His paintings and poems often appear together. Whereas Bashō made few explorations into the past, concentrating instead on what lay before his eyes, Buson liked historical themes. Moreover, it is often possible to detect the eye of the painter in his poems. Buson also showed more human affection in his poetry than Bashō, who tended to write mainly about his relationship with nature. After him, both in Kyōto and in Edo, the tendency was toward a romantic, if not sentimental and popularizing, attitude. The outstanding writer in this vein is the third of the great haikai writers of the period, Kobayashi ISSA (1763–1827), who studied haikai in Edo. His life was dogged with misfortune and his poetry reflects his loneliness; in it he transferred to small things like sparrows and flies the friendly thoughts that he would have welcomed from others. His many prose writings also reflect a similar sentiment, interspersed with a whimsicality that reminds one that haikai is fundamentally a comic art. After Issa haikai declined into a vulgarity not to be relieved until after the Meiji Restoration of 1868.

Waka. It should not be thought that the 31-syllable poem, the WAKA, had been completely replaced by haikai. It is characteristic of Japanese artistic forms that although the main development may shift from one form to another, hardly any form is ever totally abandoned. The imperial court in Kyōto maintained literary conventions for nearly a millennium; for example, the court aristocrat KARASU-MARU MITSUHIRO (1579–1638), who was a pioneer of kana-zōshi, was also a composer of waka. In general, throughout the period, the motivation for composing waka was an interest in the Japanese past. Early poetry collections like the MAN'YŌSHŪ, the oldest extant anthology of Japanese classical verse dating from the mid-8th century, and KOKINSHŪ (ca 905), the first imperial waka anthology, were carefully studied, and many attempts were made to compose waka in the archaic styles. Much work was also done in the area of poetics. Students of National Learning (KOKUGAKU) like KAMO NO MABUCHI (1697–1769) and MOTOORI NORINAGA (1730–1801) left a few classical waka but these were clearly not the vehicle for the expression of spontaneous feeling, being bound not only by a restricted vocabulary but also by a restricted field of reference. From about 1800 a reform movement flourished whose object was to make everyday contemporary life a fit subject for waka poetry; it included poets like KAGAWA KAGEKI (1768–1843), the priest RYŌKAN (1758–1831), and TACHIBANA AKEMI (1812–68). The first was active in Kyōto, the other two worked in the country.

Senryū and kyōka. Two comic verse forms in which many writers also composed were the 17-syllable senryū (see ZAPPAI AND SENRYŪ) and the 31-syllable KYŌKA. Senryū shows slight technical differences from haikai, such as the lack of a word indicating season, and concentrates on satirical, comic, or sympathetic commentary on the life of the common folk, mainly of Edo. Its initiator was Karai Hachiemon (1718–90), also known as Karai Senryū (hence the name of the form), who in 1757 published a first volume of senryū; by 1838 a total of 167 volumes had appeared, an indication of the form's great popularity. They are read today both for pure enjoyment and also because they are a storehouse of information about Edo popular culture. The form is by no means dead, and volumes of senryū still appear. Senryū are typical of an age in which Japanese writers found their fellow countrymen to be absorbing objects of observation, and, being simple in expression, they are still relatively comprehensible to modern readers. The same cannot be said of kyōka, or "mad verse," which is much more intellectual and full of obscure references and ornamentation. Seventeenth-century kyōka are usually parodies of classical verse. They appeared in collections such as Gogin wagashū (ca 1650, My Collection of Poems Written by Myself) by ISHIDA MITOKU (1587–1669), an atrocious pun on Kokin wakashū (formal title of the Kokinshū). The late 18th and early 19th centuries saw a revival of kyōka in Edo, which added satire and comedy to parody. Writers from all classes indulged in writing kyōka, even samurai, and collections with illustrations appeared which have now become collectors' items. Kyōka embodied a spirit of irreverence which had long been an undercurrent in Japanese culture.

Fiction ——— *Ukiyo-zōshi.* Scholars of Japanese literature tend to consider prose fiction after that of the 17th-century master Saikaku in terms of types of work rather than authors; characteristically one author works in various genres, not only of prose writing, but also verse. It is perhaps symptomatic that the ukiyo-zōshi writer NISHIZAWA IPPŪ (1665–1731), who was strongly influenced by Saikaku, was of a publishing family, for from this point on ukiyo-zōshi are linked with the Kyōto bookseller Hachimonjiya (see HACHIMON-JIYA-BON). This firm had been selling playbooks and actors' critiques (hyōbanki) and employed EJIMA KISEKI (1666–1735) to write the latter, which became very popular with readers. Ejima also wrote a series of collections of anecdotes about prostitutes and their clients, starting in 1701 with Keisei irojamisen (The Courtesan's Amorous Shamisen), and continued in this vein for a decade. His masterpiece in this genre is generally considered to be Keisei kintanki (1711, Courtesans Forbidden to Lose Their Temper), which has an elaborate construction and is partly in the form of a Buddhist debate. Credit for authorship, however, was taken by Hachimonjiya Jishō (d 1745), Kiseki's employer. These works were derived to some extent from Saikaku, but a newer vein was tapped from 1711, when Kiseki set up his own establishment and started to publish a series of "character sketches" (katagi-mono), such as Seken musuko katagi (1715, Characters of Worldly Sons), no longer involving exclusively the inhabitants of brothels but extending as well to the respectable world. Kiseki later returned to Hachimonjiya, continuing to write for them until his death. Ukiyo-zōshi in the form of character sketches continued to be written for some years, but were in a state of decline.

Yomihon. Another important genre of Edo period narrative prose fiction (see GESAKU) was the YOMIHON, literally, "books for reading," in which, unlike KUSAZŌSHI (see below), the illustrations were subordinate to the text, serving only to highlight the climaxes. The first important writer of yomihon was UEDA AKINARI (1734–1809), a professional scholar whose activities also included haikai, classical Japanese studies, and Chinese studies (and the attendant practice of Chinese medicine). His prose fiction included some pieces classified as ukiyo-zōshi, but his tales of the supernatural, recognized yomihon masterpieces, have outlasted all his other work. A traditionalist, he lived and worked in the Kyōto-Ōsaka area. His writing style is carefully worked and didactic, depending for its ornamentation more upon works of the past and their literary devices than the witty juxtapositions and unconventional grammar of the haikai-inspired writers of ukiyo-zōshi. In some of his stories the influence of Chinese is strong, and a considerable knowledge of Chinese characters is necessary to read them, in contrast to kana-zōshi and ukiyo-zōshi, where the phonetic kana orthography was predominant. For a long time his only masterpiece was thought to be Ugetsu monogatari (1776; tr Tales of Moonlight and Rain, 1974), but with the publication for the first time in 1951 of the complete text of Harusame monogatari (completed 1808; tr Tales of the Spring Rain, 1975), it was realized that his fame should not rest on one work. Only a few of his stories are derived from Chinese sources; most have a Japanese setting and carry on a tradition, also strong in kana-zōshi, which harkened back to the dawn of Japanese literature, to that of spirits and the supernatural. The widespread belief in, and fear of, ghosts and malevolent spirits was given further credence by their role in popular Buddhism, with its preoccupation with the other world. His tales are written with a vigor and an economy that make them effective even today.

In the 19th century, Edo became the center of yomihon production. SANTŌ KYŌDEN (1761–1816) and his erstwhile pupil Takizawa (or Kyokutei) BAKIN (1767–1848) profited from renewed interest in translations from the Chinese and started writing long romances more or less inspired by similar lengthy continental models. A favorite among these was Shuihuzhuan (Shui-hu chuan; J: Suikoden; Water Margin) of which every yomihon author seems to have produced a version. Kyōden's version, Chūshin suikoden (1799), was his introduction to the genre, but after a while he abandoned yomihon for other varieties of gesaku fiction to be mentioned later. Bakin, however, is best known for his yomihon. He was of a samurai family, and, like Akinari, studied Chinese medicine, but, in the old Japanese apprentice tradition, he went to the successful author Kyōden to learn the trade of fiction writing, and in 1796 wrote his first yomihon. Many of Bakin's works are very free translations of famous Chinese novels, and some are adaptations into a Japanese environment of Chinese themes. His style does not have the simplicity of Akinari; it is convoluted and sometimes virtually impenetrable. The theme of his yomihon is the advancement of virtue and repression of evil, expressed in the unswerving loyalty of his warrior heroes and heroines to their superiors, with none of the human sentiment of a Chikamatsu, for example, and no characterization beyond the stereotype. Much of the swashbuckling popular literature of samurai tales in modern Japan derives from Bakin but rarely attains his high tone and seriousness.

Kibyōshi and gōkan. These two genres of *gesaku* fiction are in form and origin very different from *yomihon.* It is a tribute to the standard of education of the readers and to their teachers (often *rōnin*) that many of them could read *yomihon,* and even more people could read the books printed mainly in phonetic *kana* syllables, in spite of their often extremely crabbed script. KIBYŌSHI ("yellow covered books") are in a line known generally as *kusazōshi,* which may mean "smelly books" because of the inferior materials used to produce them, though there are other explanations such as that the meaning is "miscellaneous books." Similar to modern comics in being fundamentally picture books with a minimum of continuous text, these very short books were named according to the color of their covers. Obviously written for the illiterate and children, they had some affinity with the old *otogi-zōshi,* but possessed little of their elevation. The early illustrations were crude and violent, related to those of *kimpira jōruri* playbooks, which catered perhaps to similar audiences. *Kusazōshi* were a purely Edo phenomenon. *Kibyōshi,* however, advanced in sophistication, but retained the format in which pictures were important for advancing the story, and not, as in *yomihon,* merely illustrating it. Conversations among characters were written as part of the pictures, separate from the main text, which was often arranged on the page to fit round the pictures, sometimes making it difficult to follow the sequence of the passages. By the end of the 18th century *kibyōshi* had advanced so that it became worthwhile for authors to sign their names to their works. More and more the contents were taken from contemporary life, with an emphasis on sexual and other pleasures. Although most writers active in Edo tried their hand at *kibyōshi,* including Bakin, Kyōden was the master. It is a world of young rakes dreaming of conquest, preparing to charm all women who come their way, and often failing, to the unconcealed delight of their acquaintances. It is all far removed from the seriousness of *yomihon.* The style is racy, colloquial, and full of slang and cant words. The illustrations, often by the author, as with Kyōden, are lively and attractive.

The last phase of *kusazōshi* was the GŌKAN, "collected volumes" in *kibyōshi* form, but drawn out in successive fascicles into long novels. The outstanding work is *Nise Murasaki inaka Genji* (1829–42, Rustic Genji, Imitation Murasaki) by RYŪTEI TANEHIKO (1783–1842). *Inaka Genji* is a rework of the great TALE OF GENJI, which it transfers to the Muromachi period (1333–1568) and transforms into a tale of loyalty and revenge, in an elevated tone, but not as heavy and pompous as that of a *yomihon,* which Tanehiko had abandoned in the face of competition from Bakin. It is a lavish production, with color illustrations by UTAGAWA KUNISADA (1786–1864), the prolific UKIYO-E artist.

Sharebon. Another genre of *gesaku* fiction produced contemporaneously with *yomihon* and *kibyōshi* in the late 18th century was the SHAREBON. The content of the *sharebon* was similar to the *kibyōshi* in that they focused almost exclusively on goings-on in the pleasure quarters; the form, however, was not that of picture books. They derived from adaptations of Chinese erotica and developed into accounts, in an elegant, often pseudo-Chinese, style, exalting the dandy who knew how to make his way through the pleasure quarters with style and mocking the crudeness of the uninitiated. This sophisticated way of life can be termed *share* in Japanese, hence *sharebon.* A famous example shows Confucius, Laotze, and the Buddha amusing themselves in Li Bo's house of assignation. The best *sharebon* are those of Santō Kyōden written between 1785 and 1790. Their fairly explicit love scenes, however, got him and his publisher into trouble with the policies of the Edo reformist MATSU-DAIRA SADANOBU (1758–1829) under whose direction the government proscribed the publication of salacious literature in 1790. Kyōden had to give up writing *sharebon,* turning for a short period to *yomihon* and then later concentrating on writing *gōkan.*

Kokkeibon. The KOKKEIBON, or "humorous books," derived in part from guide books for the great roads of Japan, which were produced in large quantities for pilgrims and other travelers. A professional writer of comic satire, JIPPENSHA IKKU (1765–1831), who also excelled in *kibyōshi* on the theme of revenge, struck a gold mine with a series of *kokkeibon* involving two typical Edo townies named Yajirobei and Kitahachi. He follows their travels through the Japanese countryside and relates their comic and scabrous, one might even say Chaucerian, adventures in which their urban sense of superiority over rustics often leads to humiliation. Their do-

ings along the road from Edo to Ōsaka as told in Ikku's *Tōkaidōchū hizakurige* (1802–22; tr *Shank's Mare,* 2nd ed, 1960) are the most amusing, but tend to be rather repetitive. Another style, rather like that of some latter *ukiyo-zōshi* was used by SHIKITEI SAMBA (1776–1822) in *Ukiyoburo* (1809–13) and *Ukiyodoko* (1813–14), conversations of clients of bathhouses and hairdressers respectively reported with unrelenting accuracy.

Ninjōbon. NINJŌBON, or "human affection books," complete the list of the principal categories of prose fiction that vied for popularity in the Edo period. *Ninjōbon* were partly descended from *sharebon,* but in place of the superficial polish and *savoir faire* of the *sharebon,* they substituted stories of sentiment, largely with the brothel as background, but depicting true passion rather than mercenary license. One *ninjōbon* that is outstanding for the brilliant realism of its conversations and for the three-dimensional characters it displays is *Shunshoku umegoyomi* (1832–33, Colors of Spring: the Plum Calendar) by TAMENAGA SHUNSUI (b 1789). It is similar in spirit to the kabuki of that time, and in fact the work is structured more like a play, with conversations prefixed with the name of the speaker. Shunsui was a publisher turned writer, and when the success of *Shunshoku umegoyomi* aroused a demand for more and more *ninjōbon* he had to employ assistants. Both *ninjōbon* and *kokkeibon* were to survive the Meiji Restoration, forming a nostalgic substratum to the literature of the new age.

Drama —— *Puppet theater.* When Chikamatsu died, his rival and potential successor, Ki no Kaion, also disappeared from the scene. The puppet theater, however, embarked on a period of accelerated technical development. The increasing intricacy of the puppets' movement appealed to audiences, as did the developing skills of the chanters. The new plays that emerged were either modifications of previous masterpieces or long, involved dramas with many subplots and standardized situations. Chikamatsu's domestic dramas tended not to be performed in their original form, but were modified to make their plots consistent and more theatrically effective. In their original form, Chikamatsu's plays were more like literature for reading than for the stage. Playwrights like CHIKAMATSU HANJI (1725–83), who took the name in honor of his great predecessor, specialized in these text revisions, but also wrote skillful plays of his own which have survived.

The typical puppet plays of the post-Chikamatsu period, however, are those written by committees of writers. In the Takemoto theater there was an old family of puppet technicians and stage managers called Takeda, and one of them (the name was handed on from father to son, so identities are not always clear), Takeda Izumo II (1691–1756; see TAKEDA IZUMO), was to be Chikamatsu's successor as provider of plays, and it was he who organized the joint works. These include *Sugawara denju tenarai kagami* (1746; tr *Sugawara's Secrets of Penmanship,* 1959) and *Kanadehon chūshingura* (1748; tr *Chushingura: The Treasury of Loyal Retainers,* 1971). The first is a long and fantastic account of the disgrace and exile of the 10th-century statesman SUGAWARA NO MICHIZANE, written in cooperation with Takeda Izumo I (d 1747), Miyoshi Shōraku (1706?–1772?), and NAMIKI SŌSUKE (1695–1751?). The sentiment is that of the 18th century, with an emphasis, even stronger than in Chikamatsu's works, on the conflict between duty and affection, with a protracted self-disembowelment scene and a scene in which the life of a retainer's son is sacrificed to save the life of his lord's son. As a result of the joint authorship, the various acts sometimes seem disconnected; this led to the practice of staging single acts or scenes. *Chūshingura,* a tale of revenge based on the FORTY-SEVEN RŌNIN INCIDENT, is a famous play shown even now in near entirety. By the early 18th century, Edo theatergoers had been won over by chanters of the Gidayū school, so that the puppet theaters in all the main centers were showing similar programs. After Izumo and Hanji, the novelty of advanced puppetry having faded, and kabuki, finally released from earlier governmental controls, having taken over the whole of the puppet theater repertory, puppets went into decline and their theater virtually disappeared around 1765. Their survival was due mainly to an entrepreneur who established the Bunrakuza in Ōsaka in the early years of the 19th century, and partly to performances continued in the provinces by traveling groups or country amateurs.

Kabuki. The literary value of kabuki is tenuous. It is a theater for actors, with costume, make-up and special effects, with dance and acrobatics, struck poses and quick changes. Even in Chikamatsu's time the author was subordinate to the actors who were free to improvise. The texts of the 18 plays (KABUKI JŪHACHIBAN) of the ICHIKAWA DANJŪRŌ acting family, although not finally selected until 1840, are typical of pure kabuki unaffected by *jōruri.* Three or four of them are still in the repertory. However, they have undergone, and continue to undergo, changes of text, indicating that they only really exist as plays on the stage.

With the puppet theater in decline, and its repertory and music (and acting devices) taken over by kabuki, the latter entered from the mid-18th century upon a prosperous period in Edo, with Kyōto and Ōsaka clearly in second place. Namiki Shōzō I (1730–73) operated in both regions, and wrote kabuki plays that contained jōruri elements. His pupil NAMIKI GOHEI (1747–1808) showed some tendency toward realism, and Tsuruya Namboku IV (1755–1829; see TSURUYA NAMBOKU) continued this trend. However, the plays of these three writers are more rewarding seen on the stage, with all its available techniques utilized to the full, than read as literary texts. Kabuki had in Kawatake MOKUAMI (1816–93) one of the few authors, along with one or two kokkeibon and ninjōbon writers, whose works would survive into modern Japan. His plays certainly show great dramatic skill, humor and some realism in depicting urban life. Apart from the inclusion of some Western stage props, however, he showed little sign of appreciating that Japan had entered a new era.

Didactic Writing—— This account of Edo literature has given a picture of frenzied activity and competition in the production of entertaining, frivolous, or sentimental works written for the purpose of making money, and the predominantly merchant-class readers were well satisfied with this situation. There were, of course, many serious-minded men who wrote at great length, but little of their writings can be classified as true literature. There was, for example, much writing on Buddhist matters, some written in an arcane, simulated-Chinese style, some more approachable. CONFUCIANISM was the official philosophy of the Tokugawa rulers, and much was written in the way of theoretical discussion by various schools. Apart from these can be mentioned people such as ARAI HAKUSEKI (1657–1725), a man of extensive interests, ultimately interested in writing history, who also left an excellent autobiography, *Oritaku shiba no ki* (1716; tr *Told Around a Brushwood Fire*, 1979). OGYŪ SORAI (1666–1728) and his pupil DAZAI SHUNDAI (1680–1747) are representative of those who were not only Confucianists but also experts on Chinese matters. Although professing to despise Japanese culture, they nevertheless encouraged the study of antiquity, an interest which was taken up by those in the National Learning school. Of these, Motoori Norinaga, linked with the revival of Shintō, had the most influence on literature, not so much for creative writing, but for his literary studies, such as those of the KOJIKI (712, Record of Ancient Matters), imperial poetry collections, and the *Tale of Genji*. His work on literary aesthetics was of seminal importance, and, with his attempts to write pure Japanese (as distinct from a language heavily influenced by Chinese), however prolix and repetitive it may seem, he nevertheless was a pioneer of the attempt, continued by, for example, FUKUZAWA YUKICHI (1835–1901), to write for the purpose of communication rather than for showing skill in ornamentation.

Edo literature, though largely written for pleasure, does not reflect the whole of Japanese society at the time. It was kept in check by government administrators, religious and philosophical persuaders, social historians, and moralists. After the Edo period had come to an end in 1867 one or two authors, such as Mokuami, survived, but for the most part there was a clean break with the past. The influences on prose fiction writing came from the West, new practical forms were introduced, and the traditional drama went through a period of decline. Since World War II, the literature of the Edo period has been reassessed, and is now quite highly appreciated for its historical value.

■ ——Joyce Ackroyd, tr, *Told Around a Brushwood Fire* (1979). Wm. Theodore de Bary, tr, *Five Women Who Loved Love* (1956). Ben Befu, tr, *Worldly Mental Calculations* (1976). R. H. Blyth, *Haiku*, 4 vols (1949–52). R. H. Blyth, *Japanese Life and Character in Senryu* (1960). James Brandon, *Kabuki: Five Classic Plays* (1975). F. J. Daniels, ed, *Selections from Japanese Literature* (1975). Charles J. Dunn, *The Early Japanese Puppet Drama* (1966). Charles J. Dunn, *Everyday Life in Traditional Japan* (1969). Charles J. Dunn and Bunzō Torigoe, *The Actor's Analects* (1969). Earle Ernst, *The Kabuki Theater* (1956). Earle Ernst, *Three Japanese Plays from the Traditional Theater* (1959). Masakatsu Gunji, *Kabuki*, tr John Bester (1969). Kenji Hamada, tr, *The Life of an Amorous Man* (1964). Harold G. Henderson, *An Introduction to Haiku* (1958). Howard Hibbett, *The Floating World in Japanese Fiction* (1959). Barry Jackman, tr, *Harusame Monogatari* (1975). Donald Keene, ed, *Anthology of Japanese Literature: From the Earliest Era to the Mid-Nineteenth Century* (1955). Donald Keene, *The Battles of Coxinga* (1951). Donald Keene, *Major Plays of Chikamatsu* (1961). Donald

Keene, *Bunraku: The Art of the Japanese Puppet Theatre* (1965). Donald Keene, *Chushingura: The Treasury of Loyal Retainers* (1971). Donald Keene, *World Within Walls* (1976). Ivan Morris, tr, *The Life of an Amorous Woman* (1963). G. W. Sargent, tr, *The Japanese Family Storehouse* (1959). Thomas Satchell, tr, *Shank's Mare* (1960). A. C. Scott, tr, *Genyadana: A Japanese Kabuki Play* (1953). Leon M. Zolbrod, *Takizawa Bakin* (1967). Leon M. Zolbrod, tr, *Ugetsu Monogatari* (1974).   *Charles DUNN*

MODERN FICTION

The history of modern Japanese fiction may be said to begin after the MEIJI RESTORATION of 1868 (for a history of poetry and drama of the period see LITERATURE: modern drama and LITERATURE: modern poetry). Arbitrary as all such distinctions between "modern" and "premodern" may seem, the fact is that in the case of Japanese fiction, what is modern can be defined with reasonable assurance.

Western readers acquainted with translations of premodern Japanese fiction will be aware of its long and distinguished history. Yet it is a sad fact that at the time of the Restoration, fiction in Japan had deteriorated to such an extent that it was generally regarded, with justification, as a low, popular form of entertainment, not worthy of the attention of the serious-minded.

That following so soon after this decline fiction in Japan should have attained the distinction it did is one of the more remarkable aspects of modern Japanese history. For, toward the end of the 19th century, in response to the challenges of a quickly changing society, a new kind of fiction began to appear which, without being entirely imitative of Western fiction, expressed the new self-awareness or individualism and the accompanying confusion and loneliness of the modern Japanese; and by the first decade of this century, novels were written that for their subtlety of psychological delineation and power of language are still read with admiration.

In attempting a definition of what precisely was new about these novels, what it was that clearly distinguished them from their predecessors, one cannot help resorting to seemingly arbitrary judgments about degrees of truthfulness and intelligence, about "psychological realism," and so on. Yet it is certain that in their careful depiction of contemporary society and the conflicts between the old and the new, between individual values and accepted convention; in their unabashedly contemplative tone; in their concern for delineation of the inner workings of the human mind; in their rejection of standards and explanations of conduct that were approved by tradition and convention; in the seriousness of their purpose and intended readership; and in the precision, the modernity of their language, the more distinguished works of fiction of the late 19th and early 20th century showed a considerable difference from their predecessors. In brief, fiction was raised from the status of low or popular entertainment to that of serious art.

This new fiction was a marked departure not only from the fiction of the immediately preceding period of decline, but from the more distinguished works of the Edo period (1600–1868) which, for all their elegance, imaginativeness, erudition, or vigor, were nevertheless expressly popular in their appeal, even if it sometimes took a highly literate reader to enjoy them, and were not accorded a place of distinction in the literary hierarchy; whereas in the history of modern Japanese literature as a whole, the rise of the realistic novel dwarfs all other considerations.

Although the Western model had a great deal to do with the emergence of the modern realistic novel in Japan (by the 1880s a surprising amount was known about major Western literatures), the distinction it so quickly attained would not have been possible had the impulse to write and read novels which described the complexities of modern life not grown out of deeply felt needs in the Japanese.

The Development of a New Literary Language—— It was in 1885–86 that TSUBOUCHI SHŌYŌ (1859–1935) published his remarkable treatise *Shōsetsu shinzui* (Essence of the Novel), in which he expressed with great articulateness his sense of the need for a new kind of fiction that depicted the realities of modern life. He was a scholar trained in English, so that he was better acquainted with both English literature and English criticism than most of his contemporaries. But what gave his treatise authority was not only his familiarity with foreign literature but his thorough knowledge of Edo period fiction and his respect for it. His argument, then, was not really that traditional Japanese fiction was inferior to Western fiction; rather, it was that the former, encrusted as it was with habits and expectations of a different era, had little to bequeath to a generation faced with new challenges, new freedoms, new relationships (whether between individuals or between the individual and society), and new knowledge. He was not, as is commonly imagined, critical of the didacticism of BAKIN (1767–1848), say, whose romances were inspired by Neo-Confucian moralism; rather, he believed that a more probing, more self-consciously intellectual and sceptical genre of fiction was needed if modern life and people were to be depicted realistically. "Realism" meant for him not something that remains unchanged in its mode of expression through different ages, but a way of expressing and describing the aspirations and perceptions of a particular time which is appropriate for that time. And so he did not question the "realism" of MURASAKI SHIKIBU (fl ca 1000) or of TAMENAGA SHUNSUI (b 1789); what he did question, however, was the validity of their conceptions of fiction for his own time.

Shōyō discusses at great length and with admirable clarity a major problem facing the would-be modern Japanese novelist, which was that he had to create a new written language with the vigor and universal comprehensibility of the spoken language, and with at the same time the versatility, the precision, and the dignity appropriate for a serious modern work of fiction. That is, the Japanese writer then had not only to learn to write a new kind of novel, but to fashion a new literary language that was far closer to the spoken language than any of the various literary languages his predecessors had used. Unlike his Western counterpart, the Japanese writer of Shōyō's time had not inherited a standardized "modern" colloquial style: what he had at his disposal was a selection of various combinations of decorative, "classical" styles with their time-honored imagery, highly allusive vocabulary, restrictive rhythmic patterns, all containing at the same time colloquial usages in varying degrees.

The colloquial language in Japan, then, had no history of literary standardization as the principal medium for the writer of fiction. Yet the modern realistic novel called for a language that would be free of the restrictions of the various "classical" literary styles and that would provide the flexibility, precision, and vigor necessary for the description of modern conditions and perceptions; and, of course, it had to be aesthetically pleasing.

The trouble, as Shōyō pointed out, was that even in the spoken language, there was no one standard form. Not only were there a great many dialects in Japan at the time; but also, even in one particular region, there were many kinds of speech, depending on the class of the speaker and, moreover, on whom one was speaking to. The writer had the problem of deciding which of these different styles would be appropriate for his purpose, even before he confronted the problems involved in the very attempt to give literary shape to what was fundamentally a nonliterary language.

What is almost incredible is that by the turn of the century, a highly developed and versatile modern colloquial style had evolved, and writers such as KUNIKIDA DOPPO (1871–1908), SHIMAZAKI TŌSON (1872–1943), and NATSUME SŌSEKI (1867–1916) were beginning to write in what is essentially the standard colloquial style today. This was less than two decades after Shōyō's treatise was published. When Shōyō himself wrote Tōsei shosei katagi (1885–86, Manners of Contemporary Students) a somewhat confused novel which amusingly describes various types of college students to be found in contemporary Tōkyō and their numerous escapades, he was still resorting to a style which, for all his effort, is farther removed from the style of the later Doppo than Jane Austen's, say, is from Saul Bellow's.

Given the fact, then, that the Japanese writer in the 1880s was still groping for something so basic as a modern writing style, it is truly impressive that a novel of the maturity of FUTABATEI SHIMEI's (1864–1909) Ukigumo (Drifting Clouds; tr Ukigumo, 1965) should have appeared as early as 1887–89. Futabatei's style is more modern than Shōyō's in Tōsei shosei katagi, but it is still encumbered with traditional mannerisms and cadences, and even where his colloquial style is sustained, the tentativeness and the strain are obvious. The prose, it seems, is that of a man whose imagination and sensitivity simply cannot find easy expression through the language at his disposal: it falters, it is inconsistent, on occasion it becomes incongruously tasteless. Yet for all that, the novel is a brilliant achievement, and, historically at least, it remains one of the great landmarks of modern Japanese literature. It has been called, surely with justification, "the first modern Japanese novel," and to appreciate its significance is to go a long way toward understanding the difference between the modern and the premodern in Japanese fiction.

Futabatei was a student of Russian language and literature. His command of Russian was considerable, and he is as much remembered for his translations from the Russian as he is for Ukigumo. That his knowledge of Russian fiction had much to do with his work

as a novelist, that he was initially inspired by it, is undeniable. Yet Ukigumo is an authentic Japanese novel, with a life and conviction all its own.

The story is about a minor government clerk, unremarkable in all respects except in his adherence to old-fashioned virtues (perhaps all virtues by definition are). His family had been samurai before the Restoration, and he is by upbringing and nature unsuited to survive in a changing society. He cannot flatter, he is stubborn, he is clumsy when others behave unpredictably, he is proud yet timid, he is suspicious of facile people, he is honest to the point of idiocy. He is a man who might have been loved or at least tolerated by his equals and superiors in a different time; but now his virtues, lacking as they do the support of initiative and resourcefulness, render him a pathetic, indeed contemptible figure in the eyes not only of his more opportunistic colleagues and superiors, but, in time, of his female cousin and presumed fiancée, in whose home he lives as a boarder and whom he loves. An ordinary man, he cannot afford the luxury of his virtues in a society that has done away with the traditional order and the protection it had once given such men as he. He is fired from his job when there is a shake-up in the government; and when this becomes known to his ambitious aunt and his superficially liberated cousin much confused by a "modern" education, he finds himself alone and unwanted in his cousin's house. His mother, still living in the provinces, loves him. But she has so far depended entirely on the meager allowance he has been sending her. How can he face her now? And how would they survive even if he did go home to her? The novel leaves him in this forlorn state, the only hope in him being that perhaps his cousin will decide to like him again.

In many plays and novels of the Edo period we find ordinary or ineffectual enough heroes whose most noteworthy characteristic seems to be their capacity to fall in love with women of the demimonde, so that the ordinariness of the hero in Ukigumo is not in itself necessarily modern. What is strikingly modern about the novel, however, is Futabatei's conception of his hero's plight within the social context—his implicit commentary on the moral problems of a quickly changing society, his handling of the psychological confusion of an ethical man faced with having to live in a highly pragmatic society, where old-fashioned ethical values no longer afford him protection or even self-respect. It is in the acuteness and complexity of his implicit social commentary and in the subtlety of the psychological examination of his undistinguished yet intelligent enough hero that we find Futabatei's pioneering modernity as a novelist.

It is a mark of his brilliance that for over a decade no one in Japanese letters appeared who showed anything like his level of understanding of what a modern psychological novel ought to be. The freshness of his language—his contribution to the general development of a modern writing style was considerable—and indeed the novelty of the content of his novel were immediately perceived by the more sensitive of educated readers; yet the subtlety of his understanding of the characters and of the implicit social commentary must have been lost on many. He was too far ahead of his time, and his decision to stop writing novels (though he did write two more many years later) must in some measure have reflected a feeling that he was yet without his reading public.

In other words, the distinction of Futabatei's novel reflects not so much the general state of Japanese letters at the time as the eccentric and isolated genius of its author. It seemed to leave no legacy, no heirs. Romances which in spirit were akin to their predecessors of the Edo period, albeit dressed in modern clothes, continued to appear; but none of them had the intellectual content, or the psychological acumen, or the daring absence of melodrama, of Ukigumo.

The concern for the plight of the uprooted in a society undergoing great changes, the concern for personal identity and personal values in a world where without them there seemed to be little meaning and order to those who questioned the new pragmatism of the successful and the ambitious—these concerns, which later were to provide the impetus for the new realistic fiction in Japan, found early, tentative, and, in a sense, premature expression in Futabatei's novel.

It was in the 1890s that young writers began to appear who, inspired partly by an unlikely combination of English romantic poetry, Protestant Christianity, and Western individualism and scepticism, but mostly by their own emotional and intellectual needs and expectations as young Japanese brought up in the Meiji period (1868–1912), would write fiction which, unlike Ukigumo, spoke to and for the younger generation.

Writers of the Bungakukai Group

The yearnings and the frustrations of a generation who saw alternatives unrecognized by their predecessors were perhaps most typically expressed by a coterie who published the famous literary journal, BUNGAKUKAI (The Literary World, 1893–98). The intellectual leader of this group was KITAMURA TŌKOKU (1868–94), poet, essayist, and critic. A passionate and brilliant man, he saw Japan of his own time as "the graveyard of the young," ruled by philistines who understood nothing of the new Romantic awakening. But it was a younger colleague of Bungakukai, Shimazaki Tōson, who would later write fiction that expressed the new emotions of their generation and who would find in the novel the most congenial medium, because it was the most free, for that expression. It is in this transformation of the "romantic" poet into the "realistic" novelist that we find the origins of one mainstream of modern Japanese fiction, where the freed spirit sought an escape from the historical confinements of the Japanese poetic language through the novel, with its promise of far greater freedom of language and form. That the desire to assert the awareness of one's identity and to describe the alternatives made possible by that awareness should find expression first in romantic poetry and then in the realistic novel would seem a natural progression, for the new realism in Japanese literature, whatever the degree of its fictionality, was indeed the inevitable outcome of the need to assert the distinctness and authenticity—thus the reality—of the individual personality.

Perhaps the most famous work of fiction published by Bungakukai is the novella "Takekurabe" (1895–96; tr "Growing Up", 1956) by HIGUCHI ICHIYŌ (1872–96). She was really not of the coterie that ran the journal, and, unlike Tōkoku or Tōson, she had not had their exposure to Western thought and literature. She was, however, steeped in traditional Japanese literature, and we find in her writings a degree of debt to it that we do not find in Tōson's fiction. Her language is still heavily classical in diction and imagery, and lacks the terseness and directness of the major writers who, some years after her untimely death, would begin to publish their realistic novels. It would therefore be very easy for the reader of "Takekurabe" to be distracted by the beauty and complexity of her classical style and overlook the extraordinary modernity of the content.

In this story about adolescents living in or near the old pleasure quarter of Yoshiwara, Ichiyō describes, as no one had done before, the loneliness of adolescence, the pain and the confusion in the growing awareness of sex, and the callousness of the adult world, which soon must be theirs. What is modern about Ichiyō's treatment of the characters is that she conceives them as people apart, made lonely by their own misunderstanding of each other and the adults' misunderstanding of them, as people capable of a kind of suffering that is peculiar to them. These are not "incomplete" versions of adults who in time will become more real. Rather, they are different from the adults in their sensibility and vulnerability, in their poignant individuality, which sets each apart in his or her own pain and pride; and it is in Ichiyō's perception of adolescent dignity, her sensitivity to their special kind of loneliness, and the subtlety and seriousness of her handling of their psychology that we find something very new in her vision.

But Ichiyō died too young, and her works were too fragile to have much effect on the general development of modern Japanese fiction. It is doubtful that even those young men who published "Takekurabe" were quite aware of the profound intelligence and modernity that lay beneath the neoclassical beauty of Ichiyō's lyricism. They responded to the romantic celebration of loneliness in Ichiyō, to the special kind of poignancy which we have later come to associate with Japan of the 1880s and the 1890s; but what Ichiyō lacked was their explicit intellectuality and their forceful modern language. It was only when in 1906 Tōson published his first novel, Hakai (tr The Broken Commandment, 1974) that the romantic movement symbolized by Bungakukai of the 1890s can be said to have found its expression in realistic fiction.

Shimazaki Tōson

Hakai is considered a landmark in the history of modern Japanese realism, and with justification. In this novel about a BURAKUMIN (a minority group traditionally subject to discrimination) schoolteacher who hides his origin from his fellows until he realizes that his only salvation as a man lies in divulging his secret, we see perhaps for the first time in Japanese literature such themes as bigotry and self-hatred, guilt, and isolation treated with such intensity of feeling, psychological sophistication, and social awareness. Moreover, the language of Hakai is absolutely modern. Any ordinarily literate man today would be able to read it with no difficulty whatsoever. The language is marvelously clear and precise; and such is Tōson's mastery that even now one marvels at the articulateness with which he depicts the burakumin hero's conflicting emotions about his origin, his abjectness and pride, and the provincial community's careless bigotry, which begins to be shared even by its victims. In its depth of psychological delineation, then, in its intelligent and lively examination of the milieu, in its opposing of personal integrity to the values of an entire community (for the final decision of the hero to divulge his secret is an assertion of the self as the ultimate standard), Hakai is a truly modern novel, and a triumph of the new Japanese realism.

What is remarkable about Tōson's later career as a novelist is that after Hakai, he retreated into his own private world, and began to write that genre of autobiographical or semiautobiographical novel known in Japan as the watakushi shōsetsu (I-NOVEL). The vigorous presence of the outside world acting on the fictional hero, the drama of imagined characters acting out their fates in imagined circumstances, the explicit social criticism—these disappear from his later works. The characters turn inward, away from the reality of others, and the novels become records of the survival of the author's identity.

Perhaps the political and social climate of early 20th-century Japan did not encourage the extension of "realism" to include the examination in fiction of society as a force and the articulation of the relation and opposition of the self to it; or perhaps the newly awakened sense of self was yet too fragile to include the realization of "other selves" in fiction. At any rate, the move of Tōson from the social realism and explicit psychological delineation in Hakai to the more contained, mundane, and implicit world of the self-contemplating writer was more than idiosyncracy on his part; for it helped to establish a genre in 20th-century Japan that for years nearly dominated its literary scene. And if anything gave the "naturalism" of Tōson and his colleagues a bad name, it was its identification with fiction so private and literal-minded in its adherence to "realism" that it seemingly discounted the place of imagination. It was as though the awareness of a world of alternatives, which gave Hakai its vitality, drama, and potential tragic significance, and which gave its hero his full humanity, had lost its meaning and become replaced by a mood of resignation, of bare survival of individual identity in a world of limited alternatives.

Natsume Sōseki and Mori Ōgai

For all that Tōson accomplished in Hakai, it was not through him but through NATSUME SŌSEKI (1867–1916) that the development of the modern Japanese realistic novel was sustained and brought to full maturity. Sōseki shared none of the later Tōson's lack of confidence about fiction per se and reluctance to entertain. With an extraordinary flair for the dramatic, full confidence in his own intellectual powers, and a literary skill that led to the fashioning of a whole new language which combined lyrical beauty, descriptive vigor, and analytical capacity, he wrote a series of novels which still are among the most probing and imaginative fictional accounts of the vicissitudes of modern middle-class life in Japan. His heroes, almost always university-educated men made vulnerable by the new "egoism" (the word Sōseki himself uses) and a too keen perception of their own separation from the rest of the world, are all destined to live out their lives in isolation. They may try to find solace in religion or in love, but neither is possible, given their incapacity to love themselves or to surrender their trust in their own rationality. In Kokoro (1914, The Heart, tr Kokoro, 1957), perhaps the most popular of his later novels, the hero, unable to overcome his guilt for having unwittingly yet cruelly driven a friend to suicide because of their love of the same woman, and unable to bear the loneliness brought about by the guilt, finally kills himself. In Mon (1910, The Gate, tr Mon, 1972), the hero, again burdened with the memory of having betrayed a friend, tries to escape from his loneliness through religion, but fails. There is a bond between him and his wife, who had shared in the betrayal, but that is not enough to assuage his extreme loneliness. Even the coming of spring at the end of the novel, which offers his wife a brief moment of cheer, is for the hero only a prelude to the inevitable return of winter. In Kōjin (1912–13; tr The Wayfarer, 1967), the hero, an academic, is driven to near-madness by his fear of betrayal, even by his wife and his younger brother.

Guilt, betrayal, and isolation—these are for Sōseki inevitable consequences of the liberation of the self and all the uncertainties which have come with the advent of Western culture. The benefit of modernity for the young intellectual in Japan may have been the awakening of the self, Sōseki seems to be saying in his novels; but without the safeguards that Western society has in the course of centuries developed for the nurture and protection of the individual, the liberated, conscientious Japanese intellectual who asserts his ego is doomed. It is not so much that the others destroy him as that he destroys himself, for he has no inherited psychological or moral protection against his own self-centeredness.

Sōseki was the first Japanese writer to probe with precision and with confidence in his own daring, tragic imagination the plight of modern man in Japan. The tools and advantages that Futabatei had lacked when he wrote *Ukigumo*, Sōseki had in abundance 20 years later: a fully developed modern language with a vocabulary adequate for explicit psychological and sociological analysis; the intellectuality of a highly trained academic mind (he was teaching at Tōkyō University when he decided to become a professional writer); full identification with modern Japan and the critical stance that accompanied that identification; a confidence in the novel as a medium for serious comment and in the legitimacy of fiction; and the assurance that his novels would be read by many with full understanding of his intentions. In other words, by the end of the first decade of this century, there appeared in Japan a novelist whose claim to world recognition still seems legitimate; whose intelligence, dramatic sense, social vision, and language appear even in translation to belong undeniably to a writer of the first rank.

Yet the very daring and imaginativeness of Sōseki, his capacity to entertain, which have won him many admirers in the West, ironically have made him slightly suspect in the eyes of purists in Japan, who sometimes see in his writings the excesses of a "popular" writer; and for many of them, it is MORI ŌGAI (1862–1922), rather than Sōseki, who is *the* great modern Japanese writer. Doctor, general (he became the head of the army medical corps), German scholar, translator, master stylist, critic, historian, and novelist, he was the versatile intellectual par excellence of his time. The apparent severity of the man, the sometimes ponderous antiquarianism and intrusive scholarship, the deliberate pace of his style, the almost perverse detachment of his stance as a writer in his mature years—qualities which in the West would not be found particularly endearing in a writer of fiction—have in Japan won him the kind of reverence accorded to no other writer.

His reputation in Japan is a literary phenomenon of much significance, for it tells us something about the ambivalence the serious Japanese reader feels towards fiction. While admitting Sōseki's genius as a novelist, he sees Ōgai's own nonnovelistic tendencies even when writing novels (or something akin to them) as somehow the mark of a greater artist. In the hierarchy of traditional Japanese literary values, the imaginative and the playful aspects of fiction, which help give it its dramatic tension and rhetorical power, its sheer entertainment value, cannot, perhaps because of their very seductiveness, take precedence over the static contemplativeness of the essayist. And so, even the great fictional skills of Sōseki, directed as they are to serious goals, give him perhaps an air of irresponsibility. His tragic vision sometimes seems excessive and self-indulgent, his metaphors seem too rich, his characters too much the creatures of his passion. Whereas Ōgai at his most mature seems to some Japanese as the better writer *because* the manipulative aspects of the novelist's craft are reduced to the very minimum in his writings.

Ōgai first won public acclaim through the publication of three very romantic short stories set in Germany, each with a Japanese character involved. The most popular of these, "Maihime" (1890; tr "The Dancing Girl," 1964), deals with the doomed love affair of a young Japanese studying in Berlin with a German dancing girl of humble circumstances. Though it is written in a language which today may seem too ornate, it is nevertheless a remarkably effective story, honest in its depiction of the hero's fear of a misalliance and of his ignoble, though understandable, desertion of the young woman for the sake of respectability. The hero's confusion when offered the chance to return home to respectable employment, the young woman's trust and its betrayal, the smugness of Japanese officialdom—these are described with an admirable lack of sentimentality. If the story still carries conviction despite the semiclassical ornateness of the language, it is because even here Ōgai is fully aware of the realistic implications of the romantic affair between two young people of different races and different social backgrounds. His great intelligence and scepticism, which characterized his later fiction and which helped form modern Japanese realism, are already present in his early fiction.

Perhaps because Ōgai's reputation for austerity is so formidable, and perhaps because this reputation rests primarily on his historical and biographical pieces, there has been a tendency, both in Japan and the West, to underrate his works of fiction which came before them. True, his major novels with contemporary settings are not as

dramatic as Sōseki's, nor are they as rich in explicit social commentary. It must be admitted, they suffer from what one can only call a tentativeness in the author's commitment to fiction, so that they lack the purposefulness of Sōseki's best works. Yet, in such works as *Seinen* (1910–11, Young Man), a novel about a young provincial intellectual who arrives in Tōkyō to pursue a writer's career, and *Gan* (1911–13; tr *The Wild Geese*, 1959), a novel about a usurer's mistress who falls in love with a student, we find an unprecedented sureness and a new complexity in the psychological delineation of some of the characters. The austerity of his demeanor and the dignity of his official position notwithstanding, Ōgai was the first serious Japanese novelist to treat awakening sexuality in a proud and dignified woman (the heroine of *Gan*) with subtlety and without euphemistic coyness, or to see humor in the seduction of a young provincial (the hero of *Seinen*) by the sophisticated widow of a distinguished professor of law. (After watching an inane production of Ibsen she invites the young man, who happens to be sitting next to her, to come and make use of her late husband's library some time.) Unlike the hero of Sōseki's *Sanshirō* (1908; tr *Sanshiro*, 1977), whose respect for his own virginity never seems in doubt, Ōgai's young man succumbs readily to temptation in the older woman's house, then returns to his own house to record his fall in his diary. The seductress in *Seinen* is unique in Japanese fiction of the time, for in her civilized indifference she seems to reflect Ōgai's very un-Victorian acceptance of female sexuality. She is an extremely attractive woman, who retains through the dalliance, which quickly becomes a bore for her, composure and good manners. The usurer in *Gan*, too, is subtly drawn. He has as little of the stereotype of the usurer as the woman in *Seinen* has of the ubiquitous femme fatale of Japanese fiction: he is a nasty enough man, yet when we see him bickering with his unattractive wife, who grows even more unattractive as he becomes richer, we begin to see the pathos of their lives, and forgive a little of his mean, helpless attempt to buy the love of a younger, prettier woman. And *Wita sekusuarisu* (1909; tr *Vita Sexualis*, 1972), though without the humanity of *Gan*, is an extraordinarily candid and often funny account of the role that sex has played in the narrator's life, in boyhood, in college, and after. What resourcefulness he has is put fully to the test at college, where he must devote much of his time and energy to devising ways of avoiding being sodomized by his more highly sexed fellow students. The book was put out of circulation immediately after publication by Ōgai's presumably incredulous and more proper fellow employees in the government. It is true that no Japanese mother, after reading the book, would have sent her son to a college dormitory without very serious reservations.

Ōgai's treatment of sex in such novels is but one facet of this towering figure of the modern Japanese enlightenment. He and Sōseki, in their different ways, brought to Japanese literature a new kind of confidence in modern intellectuality and liberation. However different their novels may have been, one thing they did have in common: a singular awareness of their role as mentors in the new enlightenment. That they both had been exposed in depth to foreign cultures, that they both had received the best education Meiji Japan could provide, had much to do with the intellectual confidence and liberality they brought to Japanese fiction. But they were great writers also because they were men who were thoroughly grounded in their own traditions, who were supreme masters of their own language, and who saw themselves as embodying the ambiguities of Japanese modernity.

The interesting thing about Ōgai is that unlike Sōseki, who articulated these ambiguities through increasingly complex, meditative, and pessimistic psychological novels which assumed the signficance of the modern individual personality, he seems in his later years to have questioned the very validity of such an assumption, in other words, the very basis of the sort of fiction he had been writing, and to have sought solace from the ambiguities of Westernized, modern experience through reliving, as it were, the past.

The most representative works of Ōgai's later career are essentially fictionalized studies in history and biography. Indeed, such a piece as "Sakai jiken" (1914; tr "The Incident at Sakai," 1977), in which he describes the execution by enforced self-disembowelment of 11 footsoldiers who had shot some raucous French sailors just before the Restoration, has hardly any element of fiction in it at all. It is a grim and grisly tale, made all the more so by the author's unrelenting detachment. It is not as a modern interpreter of the incident that Ōgai shows his skill. No one would know from the manner of the narration that the author had ever been a skilled novelist. Rather, what effectiveness the story has—and if the horror evoked in the reader is the measure of its effectiveness, then it is totally successful—is owing to the very absence of explanation, to Ōgai's refusal to impose his modern understanding on the story. He betrays no horror at the pain and cruelty of the bloodletting as one footsoldier after another kneels before the authorities and disembowels himself. If he thinks the punishment unjust, he does not say so; or if he thinks the conduct of the soldiers courageous or touched by bravado, he does not tell us either. It is as though by simply telling the story as objectively as possible, he feels that he might achieve a level of understanding quite beyond the reach of the educated modern mind or, one might add, of the modern psychological novelist; it is as though he is trying to surrender himself to a ritual, the meaningfulness of which defies modern rationalization.

In another famous historical piece, "Abe ichizoku" (1913; tr "The Abe Family," 1977), a story of the destruction of a distinguished samurai family in the 17th century, Ōgai allows the events to take over, to overwhelm the characters so that here too they begin to seem helpless participants in a great ritualistic process. By a whim of fate, as it were, the family is forced out of honor to take one self-destructive action after another, until they are ultimately destroyed by the forces of their domainal lord. It is a violent story, in which many innocent people as well as the more culpable die by the sword, not because of choice but because they simply must if they are to remain faithful to their way of life.

Perhaps surpassing these historical stories in reputation is Ōgai's life of a doctor of the late Edo period, Shibue Chūsai (1916). This is a work so full of seemingly irrelevant detail that it would take a measure of devotion to read it all the way through. Here Ōgai the antiquarian seems to take over from Ōgai the storyteller, so much so that Chūsai, the subject of the biography, is often buried under quantities of only remotely relevant information which the author feels duty bound to give us. Yet in the end, the work does emerge as a literary work of distinction. Ōgai's pedantry, if it is that, has power to seduce, so that the reader begins to discard his preconceptions about what is and is not relevant in a biography, what constitutes rational selection of material in such a study, and finds himself being persuaded by the stateliness of the pace and the ritualistic recounting of detail after detail.

Ōgai's later works are indeed a challenge to all our preconceptions about proper narrative technique, whether in historical fiction or in biography. They are in a sense acts of faith carried out in literature, attempts to transcend the dictates of Western rationalism as applied to literature and to find a deeper sense of identification with one's heritage. There is meaning for Ōgai, one feels certain, in the mere act of recording the names of ancestors of even his secondary characters, of the places they were associated with, for to do so increases his participation in their existence and their world.

We admire Sōseki for his commitment as a modern novelist to the reality of the present, no matter how dark the vision of that commitment. But we admire Ōgai, too, for his later austere rejection of his role as a modern novelist and for his search for meaning and harmony in ritual and in the moral order of the past, no matter how cruel or irrational such an order might seem to the modern mind.

Sōseki's tragic vision of his own times, Ōgai's immersion in the past, or Tōson's retreat into the privacy of his own experience—these represent some of the various ways in which modern Japanese fiction, in its first phase of maturity and distinction, developed. The richness of Japanese fiction after Sōseki is such that it would be unrealistic to suggest that it developed in any particular way through the 1920s and 1930s. It was a period when, with a new assurance partially made possible by the efforts of their predecessors, such writers as SHIGA NAOYA (1883–1971), TANIZAKI JUN'ICHIRŌ (1886–1965), and AKUTAGAWA RYŪNOSUKE (1892–1927)—to mention only a few—brought new dimensions to the art of fiction. The naturalists, too, retained their vigor, and produced works notable for their attention to detail and suppression of the more flamboyant aspects of story-telling.

Naturalist Writers and the I-Novel ——— For some years now, the reputation of the naturalists has not fared well. Yet despite their prosaic qualities, such novels as Tōson's Ie (1910–11; tr The Family, 1976) and Shinsei (1918–19, New Life), and TOKUDA SHŪSEI's (1871–1943) Kabi (1911, Mold), Ashiato (1910, Footprints), and later works do represent in different ways certain peaks of modern Japanese literary expression. Ie, perhaps the most famous of Japanese naturalistic novels is a complex, carefully constructed autobiographical account of the decline of two provincial families unable to cope with changing circumstances. The emotions here are so suppressed, the author is so careful to maintain the appearance of objectivity,

that the reader is constantly in danger of missing the implications of the blandly described gestures and silences of the characters. With careful reading, however, one becomes aware that beneath the prosaic surface, there is dignity and poetry in Tōson's perception of the fate of the two families.

Shūsei was probably the most gifted of the naturalists. His best works are so relentlessly and conscientiously prosaic that one wonders at their strange power over the reader's attention. But as one reads Ashiato, say, which traces the life of a young provincial girl of no extraordinary merit, except perhaps survival power, as she grows to womanhood in Tōkyō, one begins to see beauty in the purity of Shūsei's art, in his determination to paint a picture of a young woman and her milieu that makes real to the reader all the subtleties and contradictions in the seemingly ordinary. In his hands, even the sordid aspects of a life of poverty gain dignity, if only because he depicts them with such lack of sentimentality.

Such naturalistic writing, especially when it achieves the perfection of Ashiato, does exhaust the reader eventually; and it is no wonder that while the naturalists continued to enjoy some esteem through the 1920s, and while the watakushi shōsetsu, so closely identified with them, has to this day continued to thrive in its various guises, the Japanese literary scene of the post-Sōseki era can be said to have been more typically represented by writers who extended the notion of realism to include more fanciful aspects of storytelling.

The writers of that generation whom we associate with the Taishō (1912–26) and early to middle Shōwa (1926–) periods, rather than with Meiji (though of course Sōseki and Ōgai lived into the Taishō period), could seemingly more easily than their predecessors reconcile with serious intent the bizarre, the exotic, the overtly erotic, and even the grotesque; and while the best of Japanese fiction written in the 1920s and 1930s or later is not necessarily more distinguished than the fiction of Ōgai or Sōseki, it does indeed touch on a greater range of human experience.

Even Shiga Naoya's highly acclaimed novel An'ya kōro (1921–37; tr A Dark Night's Passing, 1976), which is so conventional on the surface, so reticent in its diction, and so reminiscent in presentation of the standard watakushi shōsetsu, probes far more deeply into the subconscious than any of Sōseki's novels, so that not only do the hero's fantasies and dreams (erotic and otherwise) occupy a substantial part of the narrative, but the author's own fantasies are raised to the level of historical reality. The distinction between fantasy and reality, between the subconscious and the conscious becomes blurred in this work, in a way it never had even in Sōseki's novels; intuition, superstition, myth, and dreams all are legitimate motivating forces in Shiga's world, having as much substance as, and inseparable from, other facets of reality.

Tanizaki Jun'ichirō ——— For all Shiga's originality of vision, his one great work (he wrote no other full-length novel) seems staid, though considerably more distinguished, when compared to Tanizaki Jun'ichirō's more playful earlier excursions into the world of blurred distinctions. In such early novels as Chijin no ai (1924–25, A Fool's Love), and Manji (1928–30, Whirlpool), the author's manipulations of the plot become as bizarre as the characters themselves, and the reader comes to feel that however intelligent may be Tanizaki's implied statements about the fragility of so-called normality and of our hold on reality, their significance becomes lost in the maze of tricks the author plays on us. But in these two stories of sexual infidelity and abandon, of deceptions within deceptions, of sanity destroyed by obsessions, of reality lost in fantasy, Tanizaki is introducing a whole new awareness of the complexities of fiction itself, where the deceptions of the characters within the novel are metaphors for the deceptiveness of fiction. And however tricky and playful Tanizaki may be at his most frivolous, there is in him a constant mindfulness of the writer's responsibility to entertain, and the reader's pleasure in being manipulated and deceived (within reason). The solemnity of his predecessors was for Tanizaki not a necessary ingredient of good fiction-writing; and it is a measure of the fast development of modern Japanese fiction that by the Taishō period, serious Japanese writers had already begun to go far beyond the conventions of earlier realism.

There was, too, in Tanizaki a rare capacity to articulate through allegory the cultural confusions of modern Japan. If the blurring of sanity and insanity, or fantasy and reality, is treated with too much levity in his earlier novels to merit serious consideration by the reader, his later novel, Kagi (1956; tr The Key, 1961) is certainly rich in serious allegorical meaning. In this stark novel written in the form of diaries of a middle-aged and sexually obsessed professor and of his wife (at first conventionally demure then startlingly wanton), the reader finds himself not knowing what to believe in what the diarists say, any more than they themselves seem to know. It can be read as an interesting psychological study of an obsessive middle-aged man trying to postpone inevitable old age and impotence. But it seems also to be an allegory about a twilight world which has lost its bearing, a world in which conventions and traditional values have so lost their hold that even objective reality, which is given shape and meaning by such values, becomes a plaything of the mind.

Tanizaki, having started as an enfant terrible of the post-Sōseki literary scene, impresses us by remaining mischievous even in his last substantial work, *Fūten rōjin nikki* (1961–62; tr *Diary of a Mad Old Man*, 1965). There is extraordinary vitality in this novel about an old man not far from death (presumably Tanizaki himself for the most part) who is still lively enough to find his daughter-in-law's feet irresistible. It is a novel about dying, but Tanizaki holds on to life, however mad and graceless the world may have become.

The novel for which Tanizaki may best be remembered, however, is the most conventional of his major works, *Sasameyuki* (1943–48, Light Snow; tr *The Makioka Sisters*, 1957). In its leisurely pace, attention to detail, and historical concern, it reads almost like a classic naturalist novel. A chronicle about sisters born to a patrician merchant family in its last stages of decline just prior to the outbreak of World War II, it is a beautiful, elegiac account of the final passing of all that remained in Kansai (the Kyōto–Ōsaka–Kōbe area) of the older, more elegant world. There is no mischief here, no virtuoso manipulation of fictional possibilities. Yet however different in style, however more sombre this major work of Tanizaki's may be than some of his earlier or later works, it does share with these others his concern for cultural values, his preference for articulating historical reality.

Akutagawa Ryūnosuke——Superficially similar to Tanizaki in his fictional manipulativeness, yet fundamentally different, was Akutagawa Ryūnosuke who, of all the Taishō writers, has probably most captured the Japanese public's imagination. He is the most famous of Japan's short-story writers, though one can question whether his short stories are indeed better than those of Shiga Naoya, who wrote several distinguished ones, or Tanizaki. He certainly was a brilliant writer, a virtuoso stylist with a masterly understanding of his chosen form. With a penchant for the bizarre and the exotic, he sought an outlet for his subtle and devious imagination by typically placing his stories in the past, which through its remoteness seemed to offer him the freedom the present could not. His interest in the past was quite different from Ōgai's. Ōgai's search was for truth in history; whereas Akutagawa's was for the exotic and the manipulable. Such stories as "Hana" (1916; tr "The Nose," 1961), "Rashōmon" (1915; tr "Rashōmon," 1952), "Jigokuhen" (1918, tr "The Hell Screen," 1961), or "Yabu no naka" (1922; tr "In a Grove," 1952) are brilliantly told, combining psychological subtlety and modern cynicism with a fancifulness that delights in the grotesque. For all his genius, Akutagawa's hold on reality seems at best to have been tenuous. His own awareness of this is made movingly clear in his "Haguruma" (1927; tr "Cogwheels," 1965) written just before his suicide, where images of the hallucinating mind begin to erase reality. Modern ghosts dressed in shabby raincoats appear, far more haunting and threatening than any figure dressed in period costume. If Akutagawa can in any meaningful sense be called a representative figure of the Taishō period, he is so because of his tenuous sense of reality, the fragility that seems to have come with the sophistication of the freed imagination.

To say that the sophistication, the subtlety, the playfulness of such writers as Akutagawa and Tanizaki was accompanied by a weakening sense of identity, whether cultural or personal—or that with the growing sense of freedom in fiction came greater ambivalence—would perhaps be too pat. But it is true that Tanizaki consciously sought a sense of continuity by leaving Tōkyō, his birthplace, and settling down in the Kansai area, where he thought more of the past remained, and where the scenes of his best sustained works are set; and the best of his earlier novels is *Tade kuu mushi* (1928–29; tr *Some Prefer Nettles*, 1955), in which the hero, an indecisive, Westernized man living in Ōsaka, his marriage turned loveless, slowly begins to discover beauty in the traditional arts (such as the puppet theater), to which his antiquarian father-in-law introduces him. And without a place to identify with, no matter how self-consciously, he could not have written his finest novel, *Sasameyuki*.

The problem of identity, or of belonging, is after all what all or most major Japanese writers have had to confront, living as they do

in a culture which is nothing if not a symbol of cultural ambiguity. It seems no accident that those writers who come to terms with the question, whatever their means of doing so, survive best.

Shiga was an entirely different kind of writer from Tanizaki. He was less prolific, less popular, more austere, and, if his one novel is to be taken as the standard of comparison, less quick of wit. Yet like Tanizaki he had tenacity, the power to survive as a writer.

Shiga's novel *An'ya kōro* shows none of Tanizaki's self-conscious reference to old cultural values. In a sense Shiga is much more at home in the modern world. But the search for identity is the theme of his novel. The hero, born of an incestuous liaison between his mother and her father-in-law and kept ignorant of this ugly fact until his maturity, suddenly finds himself without a sense of identity when he is told about it. In the course of the novel, as he comes to terms with his dead mother's "unclean" act, with his own wife's adultery with her cousin, with the death of his child, and finally with himself and with nature, we see Shiga expressing his own sense of participation in all that his ancestors had experienced before him. The stress on intuition found in this novel, the descriptions of religious ceremony, the acceptance of superstition, the hero's final succumbing to the seduction and embracement of nature—these represent Shiga's affirmation of his inheritance.

Nagai Kafū——What seems to give the more representative Japanese writers of modern times much of their authority is their sense of geographical place. It was Sōseki's sense of place that Akutagawa coveted; it is Tanizaki's sense of place, even as an exile in Kansai, which gives *Sasameyuki* its conviction; and it is NAGAI KAFŪ's (1879–1959) which gives his writings their unique beauty. Much as Kafū abhorred the changes taking place in Tōkyō (always for the worse as far as he was concerned), he remained loyal to the streets and shadows of the city at night, and in his hands, the shabby and even the sordid scenes acquire a haunting beauty. The old man in *Bokutō kidan* (1937; tr *A Strange Tale from East of the River*, 1965), wandering alone through the streets, is paradoxically not a rootless figure but one firmly placed in surroundings which, however changed, retain for him their historical context. What reality the characters have in his works is acquired from being where they are; and it is the where that matters so much to Kafū, that gives his writings their lyrical power.

Ibuse Masuji——If anybody in modern Japanese letters has this sense of geographical place, it is IBUSE MASUJI (b 1898), whose finest work is *Kuroi ame* (1965–66; tr *Black Rain*, 1969), a novel about the atomic bombing of Hiroshima. The greatness of this novel, told in the form of diaries of ordinary people, lies in its ability to take us through all the frightening details of the event and yet leave us with a sense of affirmation, not explicitly stated, of humanity. Amid the horror, people carry on their common civil customs of burying the dead, of worshiping, of helping others. The most mundane matters of day-to-day living are described by the diarists with as much care as are events of greater magnitude; for it is Ibuse's intention to show that through such observation of ordinary custom communities survive and continue, and retain their civility. What clothes to wear, what food to eat, whether or not to show up at one's place of work, what trains are still running—these are questions the diaries ask, as well as questions of familial significance, such as whether the young woman, the niece of the main diarist, has escaped radiation poisoning and may marry. Nothing so grand as forgiveness gives the novel its dignity; rather, it is Ibuse's faith in the capacity of ordinary people to survive, in the power of civil customs rooted in a community. From Ibuse's book one could almost draw a map of Hiroshima, because it is about that city and its rural environs, as well as the people who live there. For Ibuse, the place and the people are inseparable.

Kawabata Yasunari——It is this sense of inseparability of place and people that writers otherwise so different from each other as KAWABATA YASUNARI (1899–1972) and MISHIMA YUKIO (1925–70) seem to have lacked. Ironically, it is partly because of their fragile sense of place that their novels have had such great universal appeal. In Kawabata's case at least, this fragility led to the writing of novels of great beauty, such as *Yukiguni* (1935–48; tr *Snow Country*, 1956). Yet beneath the beauty and delicacy of his juxtapositions of images, there is a feeling of threat. There is no world more ambiguous in human terms, no life more vulnerable to the sudden intrusions of silences, depersonalized voices, and the relentless, arbitrary acts of nature, than what he describes in *Yukiguni*, in which life seems terribly precarious, as if it had nowhere to put itself. But, undeniably, his voice is authentically Japanese, echoing voices of the Japanese past; and the placelessness he expresses is perhaps not so new. Surely modern Japanese fiction has needed such a voice, so different, often so much more poignant, than the firmer voices of those writers with a stronger sense of place.

See also DAZAI OSAMU; INOUE YASUSHI; ABE KŌBŌ; ŌE KENZABURŌ; SHŌWA LITERATURE; WAR LITERATURE; POSTWAR LITERATURE; LITERARY CRITICISM, MODERN; BUNDAN; LITERARY MAGAZINES; PROLETARIAN LITERATURE MOVEMENT; POPULAR FICTION; SCIENCE FICTION; MYSTERY STORIES; FŪZOKU SHŌSETSU; CHŪKAN SHŌSETSU.

📖 ——Translations of original works cited in the text: Akutagawa Ryūnosuke, "Rashōmon" (1915), tr Takashi Kojima as "Rashomon" in *Rashomon and Other Stories* (1952). "Hana" (1916), tr Takashi Kojima as "The Nose" in *Japanese Short Stories* (1961). "Jigokuhen" (1918), tr Takashi Kojima as "The Hell Screen" in *Japanese Short Stories*. "Yabu no naka" (1922), tr Takashi Kojima as "In a Grove" in *Rashomon and Other Stories*. "Haguruma" (1927), tr Beongcheon Yu as "Cogwheels," in *Chicago Review* 18.2 (1965). Futabatei Shimei, *Ukigumo* (1887–89), tr Marleigh Grayer Ryan in *Japan's First Modern Novel: Ukigumo of Futabatei Shimei* (1967). Higuchi Ichiyō, "Takekurabe" (1895–96), tr Donald Keene as "Growing Up," in *Modern Japanese Literature* (1956). Ibuse Masuji, *Kuroi ame* (1966), tr John Bester as *Black Rain* (1969). Kawabata Yasunari, *Yukiguni* (1935–48), tr Edward Seidensticker as *Snow Country* (1956). Mori Ōgai, "Maihime" (1890), tr Richard Bowring as "The Dancing Girl," in *Monumenta Nipponica* 30.2 (1975). Mori Ōgai, *Wita sekusuarisu* (1909), tr Kazuji Ninomiya and Sanford Goldstein as *Vita Sexualis* (1972). Mori Ōgai, *Gan* (1911–13), tr Kingo Ochiai and Sanford Goldstein as *The Wild Geese* (1959). Mori Ōgai, "Abe ichizoku" (1913), tr David Dilworth as "The Abe Family," in David Dilworth and J. Thomas Rimer, ed, *The Incident at Sakai and Other Stories* (1977). Nagai Kafū, "Bokutō kidan" (1937), tr Edward Seidensticker as "A Strange Tale from East of the River" in *Kafū the Scribbler: The Life and Writings of Nagai Kafū, 1879–1959* (1965). Natsume Sōseki, *Sanshirō* (1908), tr Jay Rubin as *Sanshiro* (1977). Natsume Sōseki, *Mon* (1910), tr Francis Mathy as *Mon* (1972). Natsume Sōseki, *Kōjin* (1912–13), tr Beongcheon Yu as *The Wayfarer* (1967). Natsume Sōseki, *Kokoro* (1914), tr Edwin McClellan as *Kokoro* (1957). Shiga Naoya, *An'ya kōro* (1921–37), tr Edwin McClellan as *A Dark Night's Passing* (1976). Shimazaki Tōson, *Hakai* (1906), tr Kenneth Strong as *The Broken Commandment* (1974). Shimazaki Tōson, *Ie* (1910–11), tr Cecilia Segawa Seigle as *The Family* (1976). Tanizaki Jun'ichirō, *Tade kuu mushi* (1928–29), tr Edward Seidensticker as *Some Prefer Nettles* (1955). Tanizaki Jun'ichirō, *Sasameyuki* (1943–48), tr Edward Seidensticker as *The Makioka Sisters* (1957). Tanizaki Jun'ichirō, *Kagi* (1956), tr Howard Hibbett as *The Key* (1961). Tanizaki Jun'ichirō, *Fūten rōjin nikki* (1961), tr Howard Hibbett as *Diary of a Mad Old Man* (1965).

Anthologies: Howard Hibbett, ed, *Contemporary Japanese Literature* (1977). Donald Keene, ed, *Modern Japanese Literature* (1956). Ivan Morris, ed, *Modern Japanese Stories* (1962).

Selected secondary sources in English: Francis Mathy, *Shiga Naoya* (1974). Edwin McClellan, *Two Japanese Novelists: Sōseki and Tōson* (1969). Masao Miyoshi, *Accomplices of Silence: The Modern Japanese Novel* (1974). Mitsuo Nakamura, *Contemporary Japanese Fiction: 1926–68* (1969). Mitsuo Nakamura, *Modern Japanese Fiction: 1868–1926* (1968). John Nathan, *Mishima: A Biography* (1974). J. Thomas Rimer, *Mori Ōgai* (1975). Marleigh Grayer Ryan, *The Development of Realism in the Fiction of Tsubouchi Shōyō* (1975). William Sibley, *The Shiga Hero* (1979). Kinya Tsuruta and Thomas E. Swann, ed, *Approaches to the Modern Japanese Novel* (1976). Makoto Ueda, *Modern Japanese Writers and the Nature of Literature* (1976). Janet A. Walker, *The Japanese Novel of the Meiji Period and the Ideal of Individualism* (1979). Beongcheon Yu, *Akutagawa: An Introduction* (1972). Beongcheon Yu, *Natsume Sōseki* (1969).
                                                    Edwin McCLELLAN

MODERN POETRY

Modern Japanese poetry, called *shi* to distinguish it from TANKA and HAIKU, has a relatively short history. *Shi* has always played a leading role in the development of modern Japanese literature, introducing or creating and propagating new language, movements, and ideas, though it has hardly occupied the dominant position among other literary arts. Some of the most sensitive and original minds applied themselves to *shi*, and several outstanding poets created voices and forms of their ages and beyond in the carefully wrought language which is modern Japanese. These poets usually belonged to one or more poetic societies or coteries and published their works in their own journals, commercial poetry journals, general magazines, and daily papers. They further published books of poetry,

both privately and commercially. Today, there are at least 3,500 publishing poets, excluding *tanka* and haiku specialists; the number of poetry societies and their magazines has reached 1,000, spreading geographically from Hokkaidō to the islands southwest of Kyūshū. As many as 600 individual books of *shi* are produced annually. Furthermore, well-organized poetry readings and lectures are frequently held for the public as well as for coterie members, and they are, despite usual admission charges, generally well attended. Round-table discussion-style criticism of poetry is also common; an impressive number of poets are good scholars of contemporary and classical poetry as well. It is difficult, therefore, to generalize or extract a particular trend or single out one school among the many in modern poetry, which may be best compared to innumerable streams of different shape and size not yet forming a great river. Like most poets their concern seems to lie, however, in pursuing existence by assessing man's past and his anxiety for the future through the extreme exploration of the potentiality of language. By varying uses of the language, some reveal that they are fundamentally lyricists, while others have established a poetic world which is often dark, cold, and primeval, detached from reality yet deeply rooted in the unstable nature of the age. Quite a few indicate their awareness of the issues of the times, but few write overtly political poetry. Having exhausted poetical forms, many resort to prose poems; virtually none use the traditional prosodic technique of alternating lines of 5 and 7 syllables. Here is but one example, called "The Egg," translated by Hiroaki Satō, from *Seibutsu* (1955, Still Life) by Yoshioka Minoru (b 1919):

> When God too was absent
> When no shadows of living things were
> And no smells of death rose
> At the summer noon of deep stupor
> Out of a crowded zone
> Tearing apart nebulous matter
> Flooding viscous matter
> In a place dead quiet
> A thing was born
> A thing that indicated life:
> Polished with dust and light
> An egg occupies the earth

The main stimulus which changed Japanese poetry from the classical "flower, bird, wind, and moon" themes to such as this was Western culture. When the Westerners came and Emperor Meiji was enthroned in 1868, poetry, like the novel, was in a sorry condition. No poet of distinction was writing, and *tanka* and haiku were saddled with old phraseology and hackneyed imagery. As modern technology and new thought penetrated into all areas, writers felt a need to deal with diverse subjects and to express emotions in a form and style more suitable than those they had known. The first important such work was *Shintaishi shō* (1882, Collection of New Style Poetry), produced by three professors (of sociology, biology, and philosophy). Containing 14 translated English and American poems, 1 French poem from an English version, and 5 original poems, *Shintaishi shō* was written in a new long form, equipped with lineation and stanzas like most poems in the West, while retaining the centuries-old practice of alternating five and seven syllables. The term *shintaishi*, in general, came to denote new poetry in such form and style. Early *shintaishi*, though lacking necessary grace due in part to prosaic subjects like the principles of sociology or the concept of liberty, nevertheless demonstrated that *shi* cannot be restricted to what was commonly deemed "poetic" in classical poetry. Not to be dismissed in this connection was the influence of Christian hymns. The New Testament having been translated in 1879, Christianity and the rhythm of its hymns were a source of inspiration for enthusiastic poets, including Yuasa Hangetsu (1858–1943), who wrote *Jūni no ishizuka* (1885, Twelve Stone Tablets) on Old Testament themes.

The strength of the traditional poetic spirit, which was that poetry is essentially the expression of a sincere heart, had not died out. MORI ŌGAI (1862–1922) introduced Goethe, Heine, and other German and English poets and, along with them, romanticism as manifested in his translations, *Omokage* (1889, Vestiges). Almost simultaneously, KITAMURA TŌKOKU (1868–94), feeling isolated from the growing bureaucracy, wrote a dramatic poem in the style of Byron. And romanticism was brought to maturity by SHIMAZAKI TŌSON (1872–1943), who took literature as a serious means by which to pursue life. *Shi* was once again realized as something that rises from within a poet's heart, as in "A Fox" in his *Wakanashū* (1897,

Collection of Young Herbs), which is written in the alternating five and seven syllable form:

Niwa ni kakururu/ kogitsune no
Hito naki toki no/ yoru idete
Aki no budō no/ ki no kage ni
Shinobite nusumu/ tsuyu no fusa

Kimi wa kitsune ni/ arane domo
Kimi wa budō ni/ arane domo
Hitoshirezu koso/ shinobi ide
Kimi o nusumeru/ waga kokoro

A little fox in hiding
Appears at night no one sees
To steal the dew of the grape
In the shade of the autumn vine

You are not the fox
Nor are you the grape
It is my secret heart
That has gone astray to catch your heart

Form, style, and language remained problems with poetry longer than with the novel which, by the turn of the century, was adopting colloquialism and learning from the naturalist novel in the West. For example, UEDA BIN's (1874–1916) *Kaichōon* (1905, Sound of the Tide), a notable collection of translations of English, Italian, French, and German poems, was filled with classical expressions, though its symbolist techniques greatly influenced contemporary poetry. However, the symbolist poems of KAMBARA ARIAKE (1876–1952), MIKI ROFŪ (1889–1964), and others, though written in classical language, broke away from the rigid form and style of *shintaishi* to develop into free verse. NAGAI KAFŪ's (1879–1959) translations from Baudelaire, Verlaine, and others, called *Sangoshū* (1913, Coral Collection), were also instrumental in stabilizing the French influence and, especially, in advancing free verse in the colloquial language. Symbolist free verse, appealing to the readers' liking for suggestiveness and their familiarity with the ambiguous character of the language, formed a lasting lineage of significance in the development of *shi*. It was HAGIWARA SAKUTARŌ (1886–1942) who was most successful in using the colloquial language to produce a truly modern poetic vision. In his free verse, symbolism was merged with his innate lyricism to create a world of almost neurotic, haunted beauty. In doing so, Hagiwara insisted on the aesthetic value of poetry and objected to coarse, socialist or realist poetry which was also gaining popularity. His "Voluptuous Grave" of 1923 reads:

A breeze passes through the willows.
Where can there be
a gloomy scene of graves like this.
A slug creeps up the fence.
From seaward comes the scent
of the lukewarm tide.
Why have you come,
mysterious shadow,
pale and tender like a blade of grass.

You are no shell nor bird nor cat
—lonely spirit.
Your wandering shadow
smells like an old fish
left in the alley of a paltry town,
guts rotted by the sun
—the smell of sorrow
painful, pathetic and unbearable.

Ah, lukewarm like this spring night
you wander, wearing a red bright dress,
as tender as my sister.
Neither moon over the graves
nor phosphorus nor shadow nor truth
but only pity, an absolute pity.
My soul and body rot:
look, behind this faded scene of NIHIL
they melt—syrupy, voluptuous.

Surrealism had made its way to young poets, many of whom rejected conventional values and concepts. Some wrote Dadaist poems, while others were vehement Marxists. There were self-proclaimed anarchists who vigorously tried to carry out their revolution in art and life. Poets' activities were spread to overseas Japanese territories: An avant-garde magazine, *A* (Asia), exerted influence from Manchuria on the poets at home. High-caliber poets, including Hagiwara and MIYOSHI TATSUJI (1900–1964), launched an influential journal, *Shiki* (Four Seasons), in 1934 and opposed both intellectualism and socialism. TAKAMURA KŌTARŌ (1883–1956), a poet of dignity and rare stoicism, led many lyricists in the journal *Rekitei* (Historical Course), and he himself published virile, yet tender poems of his life's exaltation. Numerous societies, their magazines, and their frequent formations and dissolutions are indicative of the abundance of poets and their tendency to group together, the relatively short lives of such groupings, and the basically homogenous character of both the poets and their groups. This might also imply that there was less individuality or prominence. It is remarkable, however, that the traditional function of poetry as an active agent for self-cultivation—social cultivation was added with *shi*—has not changed much.

During the period in which the military controlled the government and censored publication, some poets moved further into surrealism, while others published propaganda works in collaboration with the war efforts. Many turned reticent. Unlike the French poets, few resisted the power that suppressed poetry. In the confusion of the social and economic collapse of the post–World War II period, some poets sank into despair; new writers set out in search of human values in poetry. Resistance movements in Europe were studied and poets' war crimes were discussed. Poems on the atomic bomb were read, and leftists were quick to revive proletarian *shi*, attracting a membership from broad political and literary spectrums. Members of the *Arechi* (Wasteland) group, some nearer Sartre and Camus, compared the times to T. S. Eliot's post–World War I Europe and expressed a sense of spiritual vacuum and futility. By publishing his wartime poems, KANEKO MITSUHARU (1895–1975) revealed a self undisturbed by the contemporary conditions. NISHIWAKI JUNZABURŌ (1894–1982), who had led intellectuals with his theories and surrealism in the 1930s, published his major work, expanding his poetic realm by means of flashing haiku-like techniques. New magazines were launched and discontinued magazines resumed. Now highly educated, many poets have turned to criticism; others continue to keep abreast of contemporary foreign poetry. And female poets dot every group or stand alone. They write about family, sexuality, and what it means to be female, and present a vision of a tomorrow with much intricacy and despair like their male counterparts. Younger poets, male and female, some influenced by American beat poetry, show no sign of war wounds or shadow of the wasteland, and seem to write with intensity, less about themselves and their country than about world issues, cast in the last glow of the 20th century.

■——*Gendai Nihon shijin zenshū,* 16 vols (Sōgensha, 1953–55). *Sengoshi taikei,* 4 vols (San'ichi Shobō, 1970–71). A. R. Davis, "Introduction," in James Kirkup, tr, *Modern Japanese Poetry* (1978). Harry Guest, Lynn Guest, and Kijima Shōzō, ed and tr, *Postwar Japanese Poetry* (1972). Hinatsu Kōnosuke, *Meiji Taishō shi shi* (1948). Donald Keene, "Modern Japanese Poetry," in Donald Keene, *Landscapes and Portraits* (1971). Kijima Hajime, ed, *The Poetry of Postwar Japan* (1975). Ichirō Kōno and Rikutarō Fukuda, ed and tr, *An Anthology of Modern Japanese Poetry* (1957). *Kōza Nihon gendaishi shi,* 4 vols (1973). *Meiji Taishō Shōwa shi shi,* vol 12 of *Gendaishi kanshō kōza* (1969). Takamichi Ninomiya and D. J. Enright, *The Poetry of Living Japan* (1957). J. Thomas Rimer and Robert Morrell, *Guide to Japanese Poetry* (1975). Hiroaki Satō and Burton Watson, ed and tr, *From the Country of Eight Islands: An Anthology of Japanese Poetry* (1981). Hiroaki Satō, *Ten Japanese Poets* (1973). "Toward a Modern Japanese Poetry," special issues of *Literature East and West,* 19.1–4 (1975). James R. MORITA

MODERN DRAMA

The drama of the Meiji (1868–1912) and Taishō (1912–26) periods is characterized by a fluctuating relationship between playwrights and the practical theater. Far from there being a stable symbiosis of plays and stage, at different times during these years plays existed at one extreme only in the closed world of the traditional KABUKI theater and at the other only in the sparsely read pages of small coterie magazines. The major problem faced by the serious modern playwright in Japan has been how to achieve a satisfactory, working cooperation with theater companies, without sacrificing artistic integrity if they were commercially oriented, or a chance of fame if they were not. Some wrote for the commercial theater (kabuki and SHIMPA, the latter being Japan's earliest form of modern theater, still heavily influenced by the kabuki tradition) and found fulfillment there; others wrote for it reluctantly, hoping the day would come when their plays might receive the treatment that they merited; still others wrote exclusively for small, semiprofessional SHINGEKI (modern theater as known in the West) groups which would only occasionally attract any attention; and there were some who wrote plays merely to amuse themselves.

Very few of the plays written for the kabuki and puppet (BUNRAKU) theaters in the 200 years before the Meiji Restoration of 1868 have ever been accorded serious treatment as literature. Plays only existed within the theater, and even these were only granted a low status by the preeminent actors, who altered them at will. Most plays were never written out in full. Few names of playwrights active at the time of the Meiji Restoration of 1868 are remembered, but one exception is Kawatake MOKUAMI (1816–93). Mokuami cooperated with actors who were genuinely trying to reform kabuki during the 1870s and 1880s, but, although in terms of kabuki history his achievements were considerable, in general his contribution to the development of a modern dramatic literature in Japan was not very significant.

It required the importation of Western drama to awaken the intellectuals of the time to the literary potential of the play. In the decade beginning in 1877, many Western plays (mostly Shakespeare) were either partially or wholly translated into Japanese, and under this stimulus serious discussion of drama by literary men began to appear in print.

Pre–World War II Drama ——— The pioneer work of modern Japanese literary criticism was TSUBOUCHI SHŌYŌ's (1859–1935) *Shōsetsu shinzui* (1885–86, The Essence of the Novel) and drama is mentioned in this book, if only to support Tsubouchi's arguments concerning the novel. Over the next 10 years a number of literary men took up the subject of drama, notably MORI ŌGAI (1862–1922), who returned to Japan from Germany in 1888. Disagreeing with those who thought that reform should begin in the physical theater itself, Ōgai argued authoritatively for a drama which should first of all have literary merit. After an important debate between Ōgai and Shōyō on the place of idealism in literary works, a debate which began with a discussion of *Macbeth*, drama's right to be considered an essential part of a new Japanese literature was generally recognized.

Stimulated by this, several writers (often referred to as "outsiders" because they were not employed as scriptwriters by theater managements of the time) published plays in the 1890s and early 1900s. Most of these plays were historical dramas, and the influence of kabuki—the playwrights' only practical yardstick—was unmistakable. Guided, however, by Tsubouchi Shōyō's theories, especially as expressed in *Waga kuni no shigeki* (1893, Japan's Historical Drama), and having benefited from a translation of *Hamlet* (also by Tsubouchi), there was a general move toward placing emphasis on characterization rather than situation. Tsubouchi's own plays *Kiri hitoha* (1894–95, Paulownia Leaf) and *Maki no kata* (1896, The Lady Maki) can be seen as typical of this trend.

During the 1890s and the first decade of the 20th century many writers experimented with different forms of plays and different techniques of playwriting, and it is impossible to assess what the individual contribution of each of these experiments was to the general development of modern Japanese drama. The romantic poet KITAMURA TŌKOKU (1868–94) wrote a dramatic poem entitled *Hōraikyoku* (1891, Ballad of Mount Hōrai), which he never intended for the stage. By contrast Tsubouchi Shōyō in the early 1900s believed that the only way forward for Japanese theater was through a new type of dance drama, and he wrote and produced several. Others, meanwhile, were content to work gradually for change within the established commercial theater. While little was accomplished inside *shimpa*, already monopolized by popular melodrama, OKAMOTO KIDŌ's (1872–1939) *Shūzenji monogatari* (1909, tr *The Mask Maker*, 1928), with its more realistic characterization and new view of human commitment to ideals, typifies the new kabuki (*shin kabuki*) of the era.

Entertainment was now big business, and it was to be expected that the commercial theater would discourage radical innovation on the part of its playwrights. An anticommercial drama movement (later known as *shingeki*) was developing, however, and with the large-scale importation of the latest European dramas in the 1900s a new type of play—to which the adjective "modern" is often applied—began to appear. The major influence was Ibsen. From about the time of his death (1906) there was an Ibsen boom in Japan. He was the harbinger of naturalism, and Japanese intellectuals and writers discussed him avidly. The first Ibsenesque plays were published in the late 1900s and seemed to prove that if the concept of social drama (*shakaigeki*) had been accepted, the necessary playwriting technique had not yet been acquired. These early Japanese naturalists persisted, however, and during the first years of the Taishō period their efforts were seen to be bearing fruit. *Kamisori* (1914, tr *The Razor*, 1923) by Nakamura Kichizō (1877–1941), and *Kikatsu* (1915, Starvation) by Nagata Hideo (1885–1949) are generally regarded as representing the peak of naturalist achievement. Romanticism and symbolism also had their followers among aspirant playwrights. The plays of Maurice Maeterlinck and Hugo von Hofmannsthal had been introduced by no less a figure than Mori Ōgai, who in 1910 wrote the tragically romantic *Ikutagawa* (River Ikuta). KINOSHITA MOKUTARŌ's (1885–1945) mood piece *Nambanji monzen* (1909, Before the Gates of the Namban Temple) and his more realistic *Izumiya somemonomise* (1911, Izumiya Dyers) with its clash between old conventions and new ideals demonstrated the possibilities afforded by this type of drama.

Like novelists and poets, playwrights were categorized as belonging to one or another literary school. Several moved between them, as, for example, Akita Ujaku (1883–1962) and IWANO HŌMEI, who both left romanticism for naturalism. Others were clearly committed, such as the members of the SHIRAKABA SCHOOL, whose leader MUSHANOKŌJI SANEATSU (1885–1976) was an important playwright. His play *Sono imōto* (1915, tr *The Sister*, 1936) was hailed for its portrayal of a war-blinded artist struggling to find a new life as a novelist and established Mushanokōji's reputation in modern Japanese theater.

The overall standard of playwriting remained low during the first half of the Taishō period. Circumstances were not generally favorable to the development of a new drama. On the one hand, as journalism began to take more notice of the theater as a part of Japan's modern culture, the opportunities for publishing plays increased greatly. However, relatively few of these new plays were actually performed. The commercial theater preferred certain box-office successes, and these were seldom achieved with new plays. *Shingeki* groups for their part concentrated on translated Western plays. All but one of the plays individually mentioned above were seen by audiences, but they were the exception; the combination of easy publication and rare performance had an unhealthy effect on young playwrights. Referred to in Japan by the German term *Lesedrama*, lifeless dramatic essays proliferated during this period and created the unfortunate impression that playwriting was not as rigorous a literary exercise as the writing of novels.

The situation slowly improved during the second half of the Taishō era, and performances of new Japanese plays gradually became more frequent. The more serious of the playwrights were encouraged, and an unqualified commercial success by one of them served to confirm the trend. This was provided in 1920 by the performance (by kabuki actors) of KIKUCHI KAN's (1888–1948) *Chichi kaeru* (tr *The Father Returns*, 1925). The play, which displays considerable technical mastery in construction and characterization, depicts the superior power of family affection over rationally conceived hatred and proved to Japanese audiences of the time that new plays could affect them as deeply as their best-loved classics.

Six years were to pass before the end of the Taishō period, and other types of plays made their appearance. In retrospect, however, most of what was produced during this time can be seen as forming a prelude to the bitter division in early Shōwa drama. By the end of the Taishō period the Western models had largely been assimilated and the difficulties of practical playwriting appreciated. Some remarkable plays had been written, and in 1926 the first performances of Japanese plays by the only theater dedicated entirely to modern drama (Tsukiji Shōgekijō, opened in 1924) gave hope for the future.

From the beginning of the Shōwa period (1926–) the world of *shingeki* was split by the advent of "proletarian drama." In very general terms Japanese playwrights had been groping toward what one may call common-sense realism, in contrast to the obvious exaggerations of kabuki. The exponents of proletarian literature dismissed any realism that was not structured by a Marxist world view. See PROLETARIAN LITERATURE MOVEMENT.

A number of new playwrights adopted this viewpoint. FUJIMORI SEIKICHI (1892–1977), after a promising start as a sensitive writer of romantic fiction, produced in the mid-1920s several plays of varying left-wing content. The most famous and successful of these (later even taken up by the commercial theater) was *Nani ga kanojo o sō saseta ka?* (1927, What Made Her Do It?), whose heroine is goaded into an instinctive act of destruction by the pressures of an evil society. MURAYAMA TOMOYOSHI (1901–77) had been, with Akita Ujaku, a major exponent of expressionism in Japanese drama, and, like Fujimori, he too turned to the new realism. In 1929 he wrote the most famous proletarian play of all, *Bōryokudan ki* (Record of a Gang of Thugs), which described a strike, ultimately unsuccessful, by workers on the Beijing (Peking)–Hankou (Hankow) Railway in 1923.

For a brief period proletarian drama dominated *shingeki*, but opposition to it was determined, and during the late 1920s some outstanding plays were written by playwrights who could not accept the premises on which left-wing theater was based. KUBOTA MAN-TARŌ's (1889–1963) *Ōdera gakkō* (1927, Ōdera School) shows a headmaster trying, and failing, to save his own small school by relying on traditional sentiments to which others no longer subscribe. Although *Ōdera gakkō* is Kubota's own adaptation of an earlier novel of his, it stands in its own right as one of the technically most accomplished *shingeki* plays of the prewar period. A second playwright who remained implacably opposed to proletarian drama was KISHIDA KUNIO (1890–1954), later to lead the group of playwrights associated with the magazine *Gekisaku* (Playwriting). Emphasizing the primary role of words in drama, he published in 1929 *Ushiyama hoteru* (Hotel Ushiyama), a finely detailed evocation of the life of some expatriate Japanese in French Indochina. If *Ōdera gakkō* was compelling in its realism, *Ushiyama hoteru* fascinated with its atmosphere.

The rapidly changing political conditions of the 1930s affected the theater at least as much as, if not more than, other art forms. Overt left-wing drama was no longer possible, and some playwrights formerly associated with proletarian drama turned to "socialist realism," which in Japan meant a full and accurate exposition of socially signficant subjects without any political beliefs being openly expressed. Such plays as *Hokutō no kaze* (1937, Northeast Wind) by HISAITA EIJIRŌ (1898–1976) and *Kazan baichi* (1937–38, Ash-Earth of the Volcano) by KUBO SAKAE (1901–58) achieved new standards of characterization within very broad canvases over which the playwrights seemed to maintain a tight control. There was, however, a tendency toward wordiness which slowed down the action. Much later drama, in aiming at a similar mixture of detailed precision and universality, could not avoid long passages of static, undramatic dialogue. Other left-wing writers renounced their political beliefs and turned to the more conventional subjects of modern Japanese literature. MIYOSHI JŪRŌ (1902–58) based his play *Bui* (1940, Buoy) on his own life during the last phase of his wife's fatal illness, and he has left a memorable account of the human spirit's resilience under extreme adversity. During the same period there was a resurgence of comedy, now more thoughtful than before, and melodrama, now technically better. The lyricism and incipient satire of Ima Uhei or (Ima Harube; b 1908) and the sentimental but sensitive portrayal of the hero in HŌJŌ HIDEJI's (1902–77) *Kakka* (1940, Honored Sir), grand spectacle though the play is, pointed to a new richness in modern Japanese drama that was to come when normal times returned.

In general, realism in the conventional (preproletarian drama) sense made great strides during the 1930s. No playwright evinced this quality more than MAYAMA SEIKA (1878–1948), whose early naturalism and long apprenticeship in *shimpa* flowered into a mastery of the historical play in the years before the outbreak of World War II. His long re-creation of the story of the FORTY-SEVEN RŌNIN INCIDENT, *Genroku chūshingura* (serialized between 1934 and 1941), was still frequently being performed in the 1970s.

The political circumstances of Japan in the later 1930s and during World War II put severe constraints on the majority of serious playwrights. There was an attempt to foster a national drama more in consonance with the times and, as the war progressed, there was a call for morale-boosting plays which could be performed on tour throughout Japan. Surprisingly, a few plays with satirical content were written during this period, notably by Ima Uhei and IIZAWA TADASU (b 1909). The latter was severely reprimanded by the authorities for his play *Chōjū kassen* (1944, Battle of Birds and Beasts).

Post–World War II Drama —— The end of the war and the Occupation gave Japanese playwrights, especially those connected with *shingeki*, a freedom they had never known before. There were still constraints (increasingly so after the so-called RED PURGE of 1950), but in general a long-standing taboo was lifted from a whole range of social and political topics. In the midst of the desperate dislocation of the early postwar years, playwrights could hope for a new age in the theater. In the later 1940s plays such as *Onna no isshō* (1945, tr *A Woman's Life*, 1961) by MORIMOTO KAORU (1912–46) and *Reifuku* (1949, Dressed for the Occasion) by AKIMOTO MA-TSUYO (b 1911) chilled by their penetrating exposure of what personal desolation could be caused and what violent feelings repressed by the much lauded traditional family system.

Theater historians note the continuity of personalities in the prewar and postwar theater. Many playwrights who were already established before the war, such as Hisaita Eijirō, Kishida Kunio, Kubo Sakae, and Miyoshi Jūrō, continued writing in the late 1940s and 1950s and with their experience provided a much needed sense of stability in a time of rapid change.

Though the postwar achievements of these writers were considerable, most of what has been recognized as new in postwar drama has come from the work of young playwrights, some still in their infancy when the war ended. A host of new playwrights emerged from a wide variety of backgrounds. Amateur theater and high-school dramatics enjoyed great popularity in the first postwar decade, and both needed, and produced, their own playwrights. A somewhat different trend was encouraged by Kishida Kunio, who persuaded a number of novelists, MISHIMA YUKIO (1925–70) and ABE KŌBŌ (b 1924) among them, to turn to writing for the stage.

As might be expected, the range of subject matter and dramatic method has been considerable in the postwar period. Several former members of Kishida Kunio's prewar Gekisaku group have found success as playwrights with plays which combine intensity of subject with distinctive stage language. In *Kyōiku* (1954, Education) TANAKA CHIKAO (b 1905) used three conversations consisting of dialogue that alternates between the poetic and the prosaic, the abstract and the concrete, to present the self-delusion and mutual distrust of his characters. KOYAMA YŪSHI (1906–82) set the antiatomic bomb theme of *Taisamboku no ki no shita de* (1962, Under the Taisan Tree) in a beautifully evoked Inland Sea atmosphere.

Other playwrights sought their subject matter in traditional Japan. KATŌ MICHIO's (1918–53) poetic *Nayotake* (1946, Young Bamboo) was based on the 10th century TAKETORI MONOGATARI (Tale of the Bamboo Cutter) and hauntingly re-creates the mood of the original classic with its skillful blending of reality and fantasy. Very different in style was Mishima Yukio's series of adaptations of Nō plays. Here prominence is given to the characters' probing of their own and each other's psychology.

KINOSHITA JUNJI (b 1914) used an experimental language, a traditional theme, and a regional location for his *Yūzuru* (1949; tr *Twilight Crane*, 1952, 1956). The region, however, in this and all Kinoshita's *minwageki* (folk-tale plays) is indeterminate, and Kinoshita hopes for a universal appeal free from any particular reference. *Yūzuru* and Mayama Miho's (b 1922) *Dorokabura* (1952, Muddy Turnip) are Japan's most performed plays and, though different in many respects, the one being pessimistic and the other optimistic about human nature, they both portray in their main characters a naive innocence to which audiences seem to respond naturally.

Abe Kōbō by contrast shows his audiences a frighteningly real world by a process of apparently antirealistic disorientation. Illogical and "absurd" though many of his plays seem, there is an internal logic to *Tomodachi* (1967; tr *Friends*, 1969), which is compelling in its simplicity. A similar process is evident in *Idō* (1971; tr *The Move*, 1979), by Betsuyaku Minoru (b 1937), in which an encounter in a desert between billposters and a family on the move invites the audience to contemplate humanity with misgiving.

Betsuyaku was one of the leaders of the underground (*angura*) theater that burst into life at the end of the 1960s. The works of *angura* playwrights such as KARA JŪRŌ (b 1941) and Satō Makoto (b 1943) are characterized by jumbles of images, visual and auditory, modern and traditional, familiar and alienating, and they may also incorporate any element from any part of Japan's long and varied tradition of performing arts. The audience may reel from the assault on its senses by, for example, Satō's *Nezumi Kozō Jirōkichi* (1970; tr *Nezumi Kozō, The Rat*, 1970), but the playwright seems to intend his various themes to rise later in the audience's consciousness.

Japan's postwar drama is thus bewildering in its vitality and variety. The search continues for a new dramaturgy that will link the contemporary theater with its rich past but also provide a basis for the future. Kinoshita Junji recently sought it in *Shigosen no matsuri* (1978, The Dirge of the Meridian), a combination of choral speaking and dialogue which quotes liberally from a medieval classic. Others will have very different answers. No one can doubt that the search will be long and exciting.

📖 ——Akiba Tarō, *Nihon shingeki shi,* 2 vols (1955). Itō Sei et al, ed, *Gendai Nihon gikyoku senshū,* 12 vols (Hakusuisha, 1955). Iwata Toyoo, ed, *Nihon gendai gikyoku shū,* 5 vols (Shinchōsha, 1951). Kawatake Shigetoshi, ed, *Sōgō Nihon gikyoku jiten* (Heibonsha, 1971). Nagahira Kazuo, *Kindai gikyoku no sekai* (1972). Ochi Haruo, *Meiji Taishō no gekibungaku* (1971). Ōyama Isao, *Kindai Nihon gikyoku shi,* 4 vols (1973). J. Thomas Rimer, *Toward a Modern Japanese Theatre* (1974). J. Thomas Rimer, "Four Plays by Tanaka Chikao," *Monumenta Nipponica* 31.3 (1976). San'ichi Shobō henshūbu, ed, *Gendai Nihon gikyoku taikei,* 8 vols (San'ichi Shobō, 1971–72). Ted T. Takaya, *Modern Japanese Drama: An Anthology* (1979).   Brian POWELL

Liutiaogou (Liu-t'iao-kou) Incident

(Ryūjōkō Jiken). A bombing incident staged by the Japanese military at Liutiaogou just north of Mukden (now Shenyang), Manchuria, in September 1931; it was used as a pretext for Japan's subsequent seizure of Manchuria in what is known as the MANCHURIAN INCIDENT.

As planned by Colonel ITAGAKI SEISHIRŌ and Lieutenant Colonel ISHIWARA KANJI of the Japanese GUANDONG (KWANTUNG) ARMY, a contingent of Japanese troops detonated a bomb on the South Manchuria Railway on the night of 18 September. Only one length of rail was displaced, and the southbound train crossed the damaged track without falling behind schedule. Nevertheless, Itagaki accused the Chinese troops in Mukden of planting the bomb, seized the Mukden army barracks and arsenal, and by dawn on 19 September was in control of the city. The General Staff of the army in Tōkyō knew in advance of the plot but, thinking it premature, sent General TATEKAWA YOSHITSUGU to prevent it. However, HASHIMOTO KINGORŌ cabled Itagaki and Ishiwara to speed up their plans, and it is believed that Tatekawa purposely delayed delivering his message after his arrival on the evening of 18 September.

Liu Yongfu (Liu Yung-fu) (1837–1917)

(J: Ryū Eifuku). A Chinese bandit leader in Tonkin (North Vietnam), most famous for commanding the "Black Flags" irregulars against the French seizure of Annam (Vietnam). Liu Yongfu led local Taiwanese resistance against the Japanese occupaton of Taiwan after China's defeat in the SINO-JAPANESE WAR OF 1894–1895. After the cession of Taiwan in the Treaty of SHIMONOSEKI, the Taiwanese elite, including such figures as Qiu Fengjia (Ch'iu Feng-chia; 1864–1912), established a short-lived, independent Taiwan Republic in May 1895. With the arrival two months later of the Japanese governor-general, KABAYAMA SUKENORI, and Japanese troops, the republic collapsed. Portions of its volunteer militia continued to fight the Japanese under Liu, who attempted to reestablish the republic in the city of Tainan. Tainan fell to the Japanese in October 1895, and Liu escaped to the Chinese mainland.

Livelihood Protection Law

(Seikatsu Hogo Hō). A law based on the provisions of article 25 of the constitution which provides for the right to life, whereby the state is to provide necessary care to all citizens living in poverty, according to the extent of their impoverishment. The objective of the law is to ensure a minimum means of livelihood while promoting the independence of the aid recipients. The original law was enacted in 1946 and the present law in 1949.

The basic principles are as follows. (1) All citizens who fulfill the requirements of the law may receive the care provided (principle of equality without prejudice). (2) A healthy civilized minimum standard of living is guaranteed (guarantee of minimal lifestyle). (3) In order that impoverished recipients may receive the care provided in the law, it is necessary that they take self-help measures using their own resources and abilities. Furthermore, support by parties obliged under the Civil Code to provide support and other aid provided by other laws must precede any care provided by this law (principle of supplementary care).

Care is provided as follows: (1) Application for care: care is given after an application is filed by the person requiring care, by parties under obligation to provide support to the potential recipient, or by other parties of the same residence as the potential recipient; but in urgent cases, the state of its own authority may initiate matters. (2)

Standards and extent of care: the minister of health and welfare, considering the age, sex, household composition, residence of the potential recipient, and the type of care required, may establish a standard of care which is adequate to meet the needs of a minimum standard of living and which does not exceed such a level. The extent of care shall be limited to that sufficient to make up for a deficiency which the recipient cannot fulfill out of his own financial resources, and is based on the above standard of care established by the minister. (3) Conformance with needs: care shall meet the actual needs of individuals or households requiring it. (4) Household unit: taking the household as the unit, decisions are made whether or not to grant care and if so, how much. In exceptional cases it is permissible to consider individuals units.

Although the state undertakes the obligation to provide the care, in fact, the actual decisions concerning the care and its provision are made by the prefectural governors and the mayors of towns and villages together with the local welfare commissioners (Minsei Iin Hō; Welfare Commissioners Law). Concerning the varieties of care available, there is livelihood assistance, educational assistance, housing assistance; medical assistance, maternity assistance, employment assistance, funeral assistance and so forth. As a general rule, these types of assistance are made by cash payments, but payment in kind is permissible in certain cases. Medical assistance is generally in kind. Livelihood assistance is given at the place of residence, but it can also be received at care facilities. Local public bodies may establish relief facilities, rehabilitation facilities, medical facilities, vocational aid facilities, and facilities offering lodging, but other facilities may be established only by social welfare juristic persons and the Japanese Red Cross. Medical and maternity institutions that provide medical and maternity assistance are designated by the minister of health and welfare or by prefectural governors.   KATŌ Shunpei

livestock → agriculture

Living National Treasures

(Ningen Kokuhō). Term popularly used to refer to the men and women in the fields of traditional crafts and performing arts who have been designated Bearers of Important Intangible Cultural Assets (Jūyō Mukei Bunkazai Hojisha) by the government. These designations are part of a government plan administered by the Agency for Cultural Affairs of the MINISTRY OF EDUCATION since 1950 to preserve and pass on to future generations cultural skills necessary for the preservation of certain traditional arts.

Important art objects had been protected in a preservation program initiated in the Meiji period (1868–1912) and expanded in 1929 by the Preservation of National Treasures Law (Kokuhō Hozon Hō). In the immediate post–World War II years a new effort to nurture traditional crafts and performing arts on a national basis resulted in the promulgation of the 1950 Law for the Protection of Cultural Assets (Bunkazai Hogo Hō), amended and expanded in 1954 and 1970. The 1950 law covered certain intangible assets *(mukei bunkazai)* as well as tangible objects. The criteria set forth in 1954 for preserving the intangible were implemented, and by 1979, 75 individuals in the fields of NŌ, BUNRAKU, KABUKI, traditional music, and *buyō* (see DANCE, TRADITIONAL) had been singled out for their particular skills in the performing arts. In traditional crafts, by that year, 65 individuals had been designated for their work in CERAMICS, weaving, stenciling, and dyeing (see TEXTILES; DYES AND DYE COLORS), lacquer, metal, wood and bamboo, DOLLS, and paper (WASHI).

The first list of 31 persons designated by the government for 28 categories of skills was made known on 15 February 1955 and the public immediately transferred the word *kokuhō,* meaning national treasure, from the 1929 law referring to the preservation of important objects, to the individuals named in this first list, calling them Ningen Kokuhō (Human National Treasures). The term has been used ever since, despite protestations on the part of the Ministry of Education and the designees themselves that the program is designed not to honor individuals, but to ensure that certain traditional skills will be transmitted for future generations.

Sixty-five specific skills under the general heading of traditional performance or craft have been recognized under this program, with an updated list usually appearing each spring. However, particular skills are not selected beforehand for recognition; thus, if one Living National Treasure dies, another in his or her particular field will not necessarily be selected. In general, the number of designees in the same field is limited.

The designation Living National Treasure is not inherited or passed on; successors or heirs may, however, be designated Ningen Kokuhō in their own right. Thus the size of the list of Living National Treasures, as well as the range of crafts and performances it covers, changes each year.

Only those performing arts and crafts deemed to be of outstanding artistic and historical worth are considered. Although crafts and performances that preserve strong regional characteristics are given special consideration (especially ceramics and music), they are usually honored by designating groups rather than individuals. The lacquerers of Wajima and some Okinawan dancers in Naha are examples: no one member or single troupe is considered a Ningen Kokuhō. Individuals may be named Bearers of Intangible Cultural Assets on a regional, prefectural, and municipal basis, but only the national designees are considered Ningen Kokuhō.

To be considered for the honor of Ningen Kokuhō, a person must display skill and artistry that is traditionally and technically correct. In the field of crafts, the objects produced must fall within the definition of a craft, rather than an art object, and therefore must have a functional, not merely decorative, value. Dolls are considered necessary for the tokonoma (alcove); SWORDS also qualify, for historical reasons; paper stencils are still required for certain types of textile dyeing. Painters, printmakers, and others in the fine arts are not eligible for the designation Ningen Kokuhō but may be honored for their creative accomplishments by appointment to the JAPAN ART ACADEMY (Nihon Geijutsuin) or by the bestowal of the Order of Culture (Bunka Kunshō). Some Ningen Kokuhō also receive this appointment or decoration.

The designation Ningen Kokuhō, then, results from an indefinable balance of artistry, technique, historical position, and even personality. A candidate is proposed by the Committee for the Protection of Cultural Assets, which is appointed by the Agency for Cultural Affairs and is composed of a ministry official, scholars, writers, historians, curators, and other professionals in the arts. To follow up a proposal, the agency initiates investigations and is advised by a committee of examining experts for either crafts or performing arts, each composed of 15 persons serving two-year terms. These committees include scholars and critics in art, history, drama, and dance, as well as practicing experts in specific fields like ceramics or classical dance. Responsibility for the final choice lies with the Ministry of Education, and it is the minister himself who presents the list of Ningen Kokuhō to a full cabinet meeting for approval; the designation is made by the national government and is therefore a national honor.

The honor carries with it responsibilities as well as distinction and acclaim. A stipend of one and a half million yen (about US $6,000) is granted annually to enable the Ningen Kokuhō to maintain a high level of skill and to engage in the training of others. There is no specific teaching requirement, but the honored individual is expected to find and train apprentices and successors, as well as to teach those who come for brief periods of study. It often involves sharing knowledge with artisans and performers in study groups, research centers, or at the national theater or regional meetings, as well as appearing professionally in various demonstrations throughout Japan. In addition, recipients are expected to leave written, recorded, taped, or filmed records of their accomplishments, including not only what they learned from their predecessors, but also what they have developed individually.

The Ningen Kokuhō program serves to provide honors and incentives for traditional craftspeople and performers and to focus the attention of a large segment of the Japanese public on its rich national cultural heritage.

■——Barbara Adachi, *The Living Treasures of Japan* (1973). Masataka Ogawa, *The Enduring Crafts of Japan* (1968).

Barbara C. ADACHI

loanwords

(gairaigo). Foreign loanwords and phrases that are extensively used in Japanese and normally written in the *katakana* syllabary (see KANA) are called *gairaigo*. Loanwords from China are not normally treated as *gairaigo*, since they are not only numerous but written in Chinese characters and hence are not easily distinguishable from native words. The most important *gairaigo* are American and European loanwords. According to a 1956 survey conducted by the NATIONAL JAPANESE LANGUAGE RESEARCH INSTITUTE, *gairaigo* constitute approximately 10 percent of the language, a rate that is increasing. Arakawa Sōbei's *Gairaigo jiten* (Dictionary of Foreign Loanwords) contains 25,000 headings.

The high proportion of foreign loanwords can be attributed to several factors. First, foreign words were introduced along with new things and new ideas from foreign cultures; many of these, such as the large number of technical terms, had no adequate Japanese equivalent. Second, even when Japanese had equivalent expressions, foreign words were in many cases employed more for their novelty or the sense of prestige they gave the speaker rather than for their usefulness in communication. For example, the English word "young" (which is used in Japanese in the sense of "youth" or "the young") sounds more contemporary to young Japanese ears than the Japanese *wakamono* (youth), and its use is especially common in the fashion world. Third, a foreign word is often substituted as a euphemism for a Japanese word, as in the case of "WC" and *toire* (from "toilet"). For such reasons, the Japanese use of foreign loanwords, aside from technical terms, tends to be rather emotional and vague, and they are often used with meanings and in grammatical contexts quite different from their original ones.

The earliest foreign loanwords are hardly recognized as such by present-day Japanese speakers. Some of them are written in Chinese characters rather than *katakana*. Many of them were introduced quite early in Japanese history, and often refer to things closely associated with everyday Japanese life. *Kawara* (rooftile) comes from Sanskrit, as do Shaka (from Śākya, Buddha) and other Buddhist terms; *sake* (salmon) comes from Ainu and *miso* (bean paste) from Korean. After the arrival of the Portuguese in 1543, Christian and commercial terms were borrowed from Portuguese: *kirishitan* (from *Christão*, Christian), *kurusu* (from *cruz*, cross), *pan* (from *pão*, bread), *tabako* (from *tabaco*, tobacco), *rasha* (from *raxa*, woolen cloth), and so on. When Christianity was banned and the NATIONAL SECLUSION policy adopted in 1639, borrowing from Portuguese stopped. Many of the Portuguese words already introduced became obsolete. Among those which remain current are *kappa* (from *capa*, raincoat), *juban* (from *gibao*, undershirt), *tempura* (from *tempero*, batter-fried foods). These words are often written in Chinese characters and most Japanese people believe they are original Japanese words.

The Spanish also entered Japan about the same time as the Portuguese, but the number of Spanish words that remained in Japanese is limited. *Meriyasu* (from *medias*, knit material), and *shabon* (from *jabón*, soap) are among them.

The Dutch arrived in 1600 and continued to have limited access to Japan even during National Seclusion, bringing a number of Dutch words into the language. Some commercial, scientific, and nautical terms are still widely employed: *gomu* (from *gom*, rubber), *gasu* (from *gas*, gas), *garasu* (from *glas*, glass), *koppu* (from *kop*, cup or glass), *kōhī* (from *koffie*, coffee), *bīru* (from *bier*, beer), *arukōru* (alcohol), *renzu* (lens), *mesu* (from *mes*, knife), *korera* (cholera), *dekki* (from *dek*, deck), *masuto* (mast), *dokku* (from *dok*, dock).

In the latter part of the Edo period (1600–1868), French, English, and Russian words began to arrive. *Gētoru* (garters), *shappo* (cap), and *zubon* (trousers) are from the French *guêtres*, *chapeau*, and *jupon*. At present English loanwords outnumber other loanwords. French words are especially numerous in fashion (*pantalon*, *haute couture*, *négligé*), art (*atelier*, *palette*, *dessin*, *objet*), cooking (*mayonnaise*, *cognac*, *restaurant*, *potage*, *bifteck*), foreign affairs and politics (*agrément*, *communiqué*, *coup d'état*). Russian words include, besides food (*vodka*, *pirozhki*, *ikra*) and things Russian (*pechka*, *tundra*, *tzar*), such modern terms as *kolkhoz*, *kombinat*, and *sputnik*. After Japan reopened to foreign countries in the second half of the 19th century, a great number of German words also entered. They are most numerous in medicine and the humanities and among mountaineering and skiing terms: *arerugī* (from *Allergie*, allergy), *tsuberukurin* (from *Tuberkulin*, tuberculin), *noirōze* (from *Neurose*, neurosis), *rentogen* (from *Röntgen*, x-ray), *karute* (from *Karte*, chart), *tēze* (from *These*, thesis), *zairu* (from *Seil*, rope), *hyutte* (from *Hütte*, hut), *gerende* (from *Gelände*, ski slope). Italian words were also introduced beginning in the Meiji period (1868–1912). Besides musical terms like *soprano*, *tempo*, and *finale*, such words as *spaghetti*, *macaroni*, and *gondola* are in common use. Other foreign words include *mazurka* (Polish), *fjord* (Norwegian), and in philosophy, *a priori*, *ego* (Latin), *chaos* (Greek), and so on.

Foreign loanwords are often introduced as nouns. The verb form can be made by attaching *suru* (to do) at the end of the foreign noun. Further, by suffixing *na* and *ni*, a loanword can be used respectively as a noun modifier (i.e., an adjective) and an adverb.

Some loanwords are transformed when they enter Japanese. Most obvious is a change in pronunciation. In Japanese, the English words "bus," "bath," and "bass" are pronounced the same: *basu.* "Right" and "light" likewise fall together in Japanese. On the other hand, the word "gesture" is pronounced in two different ways, *zesuchua* and *jesuchā.* Since Japanese syllables are open syllables, "strike," which is monosyllabic in English, becomes five syllables as either *su-to-ra-i-ku* or *su-to-ra-i-ki.* (While the former is used as a baseball term, the latter signifies "work stoppage." The two-syllable abbreviation *su-to* is also used in the latter meaning.) Since the first *a* in "American" is an unstressed syllable in English, it was dropped when the word was first imported in the Meiji period, becoming shortened in Japanese as *meriken.* (This shortened form is obsolete except in a few compounds such as *merikenko,* "wheat flour," and words derived from "America" now keep the *a.*) Among shortened forms *ketto* (blanket) and *maito* (dynamite) have omitted the first half of the English word, while the last half is dropped in *toire* (toilet), *demo* (demonstration), *depāto* (department store). Head portions of two words are sometimes combined to make a new word, as in *mobo* (modern boy), *torepan* (training pants, i.e., sweatpants), and *hansuto* (hunger strike).

Grammatical license is frequent. A word that is one part of speech in the original language is often used as a different part of speech in Japanese (for example, *avec* in French is a preposition but is used in Japanese as a noun meaning "a man and a woman keeping company"). Another type of license is the dropping of English suffixes such as *-s, -ed,* and *-ing,* as in *sangurasu* (sunglasses), *onzarokku* (on the rocks), *kondensu miruku* (condensed milk), *karē raisu* (curried rice), *furai pan* (frying pan), and *wōmu appu* (warming up). An entire word is dropped in *hamu eggu* (ham and eggs). Often compounds are created by combining a foreign word with a native Japanese word or a Japanese word of Chinese origin: *batakusai* (butter-reeking, i.e., Westernized), *denki sutando* (electric lamp stand), and *haiki gasu* (exhaust gas).

Differences in meaning are also observed in some cases. The word *ofisu* (office) refers to a room in a company and is not used for a professor's office. *Saidā* (from cider) refers not to apple juice but to a kind of carbonated soft drink. *Bosu* means a gang leader, not one's boss at work. When expressions of foreign and domestic origin exist side by side, the Japanese term often has the most general and broad meaning. Foreign loanwords tend to have a limited meaning, often with elite connotations. The Japanese word *yasumi* is used for anything from a five-minute break to a long summer vacation. The French word *vacances,* pronounced *bakansu,* is often used to refer to a deluxe overseas trip. *Raisu* (rice), as opposed to the Japanese word *gohan,* is used by some only to mean rice on a plate (instead of in a bowl in the Japanese manner). *Raisu, bakēshon* (vacation), *bakansu,* and other such words are felt to be modern and upper-class.

Some argue that the borrowing of foreign words enriches the Japanese vocabulary and makes foreign languages more accessible. Others find it a symbol of cultural backwardness, or object to it on the grounds that enlarging a vocabulary insufficiently comprehensible to them reinforces the Japanese people's indifferent or ambiguous attitude toward the meaning of words.

■——Arakawa Sōbei, *Gairaigo gaisetsu* (1943). Arakawa Sōbei, *Gairaigo jiten* (1967). Umegaki Minoru, *Gairaigo* (1975). Yoshizawa Norio and Ishiwata Toshio, *Gairaigo no gogen* (Kadokawa Shoten 1979). *KAWAMOTO Takashi*

local autonomy

The concept of local autonomy in government involves the right of local entities such as prefectures, cities, towns, and villages to decide and administer a range of public policies on their own initiative with relative freedom from supervision ("corporate autonomy") and the right of local citizens to participate, directly or indirectly, in the formation of such policies ("civic autonomy"). Although the term *chihō jichi* (local autonomy) had been widely used ever since the Meiji period (1868–1912), little local autonomy in either of these two senses existed before 1945. The 1947 constitution contains a chapter on "local autonomy," implemented by the Local Autonomy Law (Chihō Jichi Hō) of the same year. The HOME MINISTRY, which had been the fulcrum of centralization, was also abolished in 1947, but in 1949 a successor, the Local Autonomy Agency (Chihō Jichi Chō), was created, and it became a full-fledged ministry (see MINISTRY OF HOME AFFAIRS) again in 1960. Its supervision is somewhat limited, and existing restrictions of local autonomy are not only due to this

supervision. The main problems are rather in the areas of functions and finances. Education and police, decentralized under the OCCUPATION, were recentralized to some extent thereafter. Beyond this, many functions, which could be considered local, are governed by national laws. In many cases the administration of these laws is delegated to governors and mayors as agents of the national government, subject to supervision by the appropriate ministries. In these cases the relevant function lies outside the jurisdiction of local assemblies.

The types and standard rates of local taxes are determined by the Local Tax Law (Chihōzei Hō). Local taxes account only for about one third of total local revenues, so that the phrase "30 percent local autonomy" has become current. Most of the remaining revenues come from transfers of funds by the national government, which dominates the major tax sources. Some of these transfers are made according to fairly objective standards. But in cases of categorical grants-in-aid, the transfers often fall short of local requirements, leading to an "excess financial burden" for local governments. Financial dependence and financial stringency limit local autonomy. Demands for reforms in the direction of a fuller implementation of the constitutional "principle of local autonomy" have increased with the emergence of progressive governors and mayors since the late 1960s. Thus the actual extent of local autonomy has now become a significant political issue.

■——Ide Yoshinori, *Chihō jichi no seijigaku* (1972). Isomura Eiichi and Hoshino Mitsuo, *Chihō jichi tokuhon* (1961). Katō Kazuaki, Katō Yoshitarō, and Watanabe Yasuo, *Gendai no chihō jichi* (1975). Terry E. MacDougall, *Localism and Political Opposition in Japan* (1981). Kurt Steiner, *Local Government in Japan* (1965). Kurt Steiner, Scott Flanagan, and Ellis Krauss, ed, *Political Opposition and Local Politics in Japan* (1980). *Kurt STEINER*

local government

Since the MEIJI RESTORATION (1868), the forms of local government have undergone a number of changes as national and community leaders have attempted to arrange for the provision of basic services to localities, on the one hand, and for the building of a unified and integrated state in which policies determined by the central government would be implemented throughout the nation, on the other. During most of the years since 1868, the system has been constituted so as to permit citizens to participate in local government affairs through election of officials and members of local assemblies.

Viewed in broad perspective, the trends in modern local government have been toward the expansion of local decision-making authority in areas of local concern and toward the fuller participation of citizens in the local political process. The World War II years stand out as an interlude during which these trends were reversed in order to effect total mobilization of the populace for war, but since 1945 change has mostly followed the prewar trends.

The system of local government has been called the "local autonomy system" (*chihō jichi seido*) from the time of the promulgation of codes for city, town, and village organization in 1888 and codes for prefectural (*ken*) and district (*gun;* also translated as county) organization in 1890. Autonomy is a misleading word, however, for localities have never enjoyed more than partial self-government. Much of the business conducted by local governmental organs in fact has been delegated business, that is, work assigned to the locality and its officers by some central government organ. The question of the proper balance of power and responsibility between the nation and the locality has yet to be resolved.

Local Government at the Time of the Restoration——At the time when the last shōgun, TOKUGAWA YOSHINOBU, returned the political mandate to the throne in late 1867, Japan was administratively divided into territory ruled directly by the shogunate (*tenryō*) and some 260 domains (*han*) governed by *daimyō* and their separate domainal governments (see BAKUHAN SYSTEM). Although there was some variation in the structure of local government, we can identify a typical pattern. Ordinarily the daimyō's financial affairs office had supervisory power over district commissioners and intendants (*kōri bugyō* or DAIKAN) or town commissioners (MACHI BUGYŌ). These magistrates were *samurai*-status officials who were charged with general responsibility for tax collection and administration of justice in an area encompassing many villages, usually one or more geographical districts (*kōri* or *gun*), or one city or town. Below these samurai administrators were commoner officials. In some parts of Japan commoner offices were hereditary, while elsewhere commoner officials were elected. Some domains had peasant officials (*ōjōya*) who managed the tax and judicial affairs of several tens of villages; other domains, following the pattern of the Tokugawa shogunal domain, had no such headmen of groups of villages. Virtually every village and town ward in Japan had its own headman, and in this commoner office was located the interface between the authority of the shogunate or domain, above, and the concerns of the bulk of the populace, below.

Within the village or town ward, it was largely up to the commoners and their officials to determine regulations of behavior and participation in community activities, amounts of taxes to be paid by individual commoners, and the like. Samurai administrators routinely dealt with the village or ward as a unit and left the details of local governance to the peasants and townsmen. Shogunal and domainal governments required the remittance of certain amounts of taxes and the maintenance of law and order, but considerable latitude remained for villages and wards in traditional Japan to determine the forms and functions of their own political, economic, social, and religious management (see GŌSON SYSTEM). Authority over the countryside was not only fragmented among the various domains but was also diversely organized at lower levels. This was the situation the leaders of the group around the Meiji emperor inherited when they proclaimed the restoration of imperial rule on 3 January 1868.

Early Meiji Period (1868–1878) —— Initially the leaders of the new Meiji government paid scant attention to subnational government, being preoccupied with subduing forces loyal to the Tokugawa. Domains that acknowledged imperial authority were allowed to go on administering their own affairs much as before, even in the critical areas of military and financial affairs. Domains of the Tokugawa and their supporters who had resisted Meiji rule were confiscated by the state and reconstituted as prefectures (ken) with appointees of the new central government as chief executives. The urban centers of Tōkyō, Ōsaka, and Kyōto were likewise placed directly under the new government and were designated urban prefectures (fu). Centrally appointed administrators took office as fu governors.

It quickly became apparent that these arrangements contained too much diversity to permit central leaders to build the kind of unified nation-state that seemed necessary if Japan were to survive in a competitive world. The first major step toward national unification was taken in July 1869, when the daimyō were "permitted" to return the registers of land and people of their domains to the emperor (hanseki hōkan). Thereupon the imperial government appointed the daimyō as domainal governors. Although they continued to hold authority over their old domains, in legal terms the former daimyō were now governors who held office conferred by imperial appointment, rather than lords of hereditary fiefs.

An even more momentous change in the local government system was effected with the abolition of domains and the creation of prefectures (haihan chiken; see PREFECTURAL SYSTEM, ESTABLISHMENT OF), proclaimed in 1871. Domainal governors were ordered to relinquish office and move to Tōkyō, and the central government appointed new officers, nearly always men from other parts of Japan, to take over as chief prefectural executives (KENREI, later chiji). Another change, intended to streamline administration and strengthen the position of the national government in its relations with localities, was the reduction of the number of prefectures from 302 to 72, in addition to the three big urban prefectures. Below the level of the prefecture, the nation was divided into census districts (daiku, shōku) to administer the Family Registration Law of 1871 (see JINSHIN KOSEKI). At first the persons appointed to implement this law had no function except as registrars, but gradually they came to act as local officials in various community affairs. When the old positions of village and ward headman were abolished by law in 1872, what had been registration districts became regular administrative districts, and the chiefs of these districts became the most important subprefectural officers.

The central government established the HOME MINISTRY (Naimushō) in November 1873 and vested it with supervisory power over local affairs. The home minister had the power to oversee and to sanction or disapprove the actions of prefectural governors, who had the same power over the actions of the district chiefs. This pattern of supervision tended in practice to inhibit the growth of grassroots initiative in the local government system. However, some, but not all, prefectures and some lower units of government created assemblies during the first decade of the Meiji period.

The Three New Laws System (1878–1888) —— Changes in local government in the first decade of the Meiji period had proceeded

according to trial and error, and at different rates in different places. Home Minister ŌKUBO TOSHIMICHI wanted more coherence in the system and desired also to devolve some of the responsibility of government to localities so that the central government would not be blamed for everything that went wrong. His ideas were embodied in three laws promulgated on 22 July 1878, three months after he himself had been assassinated. Known as the "Three New Laws" (SANSHIMPŌ), this legislation defined the local government system for over a decade, until the implementation of the Meiji Local Autonomy System.

Districts, wards, towns, and villages. The first of the Three New Laws introduced the gun (district; also translated as county) as administrative unit and created, in populous cities, wards (ku) at the same level as gun. These new units replaced the large districts that had been set up after 1872. Within the gun, towns (machi or chō) and villages (mura or son) became the basic governmental units, and the small districts were abolished. Town and village definitions adopted under the Three New Laws came closer to pre-Meiji "natural" lines than the small census districts, which in many cases had disregarded customary boundaries and notions of community. The chief officers of gun and ku were appointed and supervised by the prefectural governors and paid out of prefectural funds. A national administrative law stipulated their duties in terms that made clear that they must be more attentive to their bureaucratic superiors than to the ordinary folk of the gun or ku.

The law of 1878 treated towns and villages as having a "dual nature"; they were at once units of the state administrative apparatus and units of local citizens' self-government. The state delegated much business to towns and villages. At the same time, however, the law provided that citizens should select their own town and village chiefs. In many localities elections were thereby made a feature of the governmental system for the first time, although autonomous actions by such bodies rarely exceeded a modest scale.

To broaden participation in public affairs and increase citizens' sense of responsibility, the government in 1880 enacted the Law on Ward, Town, and Village Assemblies (Ku-Chō-Son Kai Hō). Through voting for, or participation in, such assemblies, citizens gained a greater say in local politics. The cause of local self-rule was set back in 1884, however, when the positions of town and village chiefs were made appointive, and the appointed chiefs were made the presidents of the local assemblies. The central government at the same time stepped up the rate of amalgamation of towns and villages, a process that had been advancing slowly since the Restoration and would accelerate dramatically after 1888. The 1884 law also strengthened the hierarchy of supervision over local assembly actions, requiring the prefectural governor's approval for a larger number of actions than before.

Prefectural assemblies. The second of the Three New Laws established representative assemblies in all prefectures. Less than 5 percent of the population was enfranchised to vote for these deliberative bodies, and fewer still were eligible for election, but the creation of these assemblies was nevertheless epoch-making. For the first time, elective representative institutions became a regular feature of government, and prefectures acquired some autonomous standing. Yet the power to originate bills was vested in the governor alone—assembly members could not introduce legislation—and the governor and home minister had other powers intended to keep assemblies in check, culminating in the authority to prorogue or dissolve these bodies.

Local taxes. The Local Tax Regulations (Chihōzei Kisoku), the third of the Three New Laws, laid down uniform rules for the collection of taxes at the prefectural and subprefectural levels. The ratio of central government, prefectural, and subprefectural spending for local government was roughly 1:3:3 through the second Meiji decade.

In the early 1880s prefectural assemblies in several areas became tinderboxes of protest against the amounts of taxes and the policies that the taxes were being used to support, but such opposition died down or was suppressed by 1885. For much of the Three New Laws period it appears that the central government's priorities suited most citizens as well as the oligarchs (genrō) in Tōkyō.

The Meiji Local Autonomy System —— In the 1880s government leaders began a reexamination of the local government system at the same time that they commenced the investigation of models for a Japanese constitution. As home minister from 1883, YAMAGATA ARITOMO headed the inquiry into local government institutions. In part because he believed that Japan must have a comprehensive, codified system of local rule as well as a written constitution in order to gain revision of the Unequal Treaties (see UNEQUAL TREATIES, REVISION OF), Yamagata steered the investigation to Western codes. He found the Prussian example the most attractive, and in 1886 he added a jurist from Berlin, Albert MOSSE, to the Home Ministry investigatory committee on local government law.

The government appended a commentary to the Municipal Code (Shisei) and Town and Village Code (Chōsonsei) when it issued them in 1888. Closely based on a draft by Mosse, it explained that the purpose of the new laws was "to implement the principles of self-rule and division of powers" (jichi bunken); within its boundaries, a city, town, or village was to stand independent and govern its own affairs. It added, however, that "the locality is fundamentally a part of the state, and must discharge its duties under the jurisdiction of the state."

Municipal code and town and village code. The laws expressly defined cities, towns, and villages as juristic persons and stated that they should administer their own affairs "subject to the supreme control of the central government." The codes distinguished between "residents" (jūmin), that is, all who lived in a locality, and "citizens" (kōmin), male residents who met several criteria of age, financial and familial condition, and taxpaying status. Citizens had the right to participate in city, town, or village elections and were eligible or even obliged to serve in honorary local office.

The first organ of self-government treated in the codes of 1888 was the Assembly (Shikai). The Assembly had the power to make and alter city, town, or village bylaws, to decide matters to be defrayed out of local revenues, to make the local budget, to levy local taxes and impose fees for use of local facilities or services, and to enter lawsuits or arbitrations for the locality. The Assembly was to elect the city, town, or village officials. The mayor of a city was chosen by the home minister from a list of three candidates submitted by the Assembly and formally appointed by the emperor. An assembly's choice of a town or village chief needed the approval of the prefectural governor, but not of the home minister. For voting in Assembly elections, citizens were divided into electoral classes on the basis of their taxpaying status. Cities had three electoral classes, each of which elected one-third of the Assembly members. Towns and villages had two classes of electors, each of which chose half of the Assembly members.

Executive authority, according to the Municipal Code, belonged to the City Council (Shisanjikai), made up of the mayor, his assistants, and between 6 and 12 honorary councilmen. Created in imitation of a Prussian institution, the council executed the Assembly's decisions; it could also suspend execution of an Assembly action, make the Assembly reconsider it, and if the Assembly failed to alter its decision, submit the matter to a higher authority for a ruling. Towns and villages had no councils. According to the Town and Village Code, the chief had the same powers and responsibilities in his locality as the mayor and council in the city.

The burden of delegated business was not lightened by the local autonomy codes. Town and village amalgamations occurred with dizzying speed between the promulgation and the implementation of the new local government laws. These were made for administrative and economic rationalization in local government and to make it easier for central government authorities to monitor local bodies' activities. Amalgamations probably contributed to a general improvement in local services around the nation, but they also deprived many communities of independence and local identity; further, they resulted in the loss of certain properties that had traditionally been held communally.

Prefectural code and district code. Drafts of the codes governing prefectural and district (gun; also translated as county) organization underwent more extensive revision at the hands of the Chamber of Elders (GENRŌIN) than had the municipal and town and village codes, and most of these revisions strengthened the position of the state and restricted the self-government of prefectures and counties. Although they were issued in 1890, it was not until 1899 that the Prefectural Code (Fukensei) and District Code (Gunsei) were in force in all prefectures (except Okinawa, which did not implement them for another nine years). The number of prefectures did not change under the new system, the last of a series of changes having taken place in 1888 with the separation of Ehime and Kagawa. From that date until the end of World War II there were 46 prefectures (3 fu and 43 ken) and one administrative province (dō), Hokkaidō.

Still under the executive stewardship of a centrally appointed governor, the prefecture by no means ceased to be a unit of the national administrative mechanism. The system allotted considerable power to the governor. The governor continued to be answerable to the home minister and, in matters falling within their purviews, to the other state ministers. On the other hand, it was implicit in the Meiji Local Autonomy System that the prefecture was also a unit of self-government and a juridical person, with certain powers, rights, and responsibilities.

In the area of legislative power, the 1890 code added a new body, the Prefectural Council (Ken Sanjikai). The Prefectural Council handled business delegated to it by the Assembly, acted for the Assembly in emergencies when the Assembly was not in session, and examined the prefectural budget before the governor submitted it to the Assembly. Two high-ranking prefectural officials appointed by the home minister and several honorary councillors named by the Prefectural Assembly joined the governor on the council. The role of the Prefectural Assembly was much the same under the Meiji Local Autonomy System as it had been under the Three New Laws.

Establishing the county as a unit of self-government on the model of the Prussian Kreis was one of Yamagata Aritomo's pet projects. Cities were provided for by their own code, but all towns and villages came under district jurisdiction, according to the District Code. The district executive was the chief (gunchō), an appointee of the governor. In the hierarchy of bureaucratic supervision, the district chief was above the town and village chiefs and under the prefectural governor.

Comparable in its function to the Prefectural Council, a District Council made up of the district chief and four unpaid councillors was created by the 1890 code. Three of the honorary councillors were chosen by the District Assembly and a fourth by the prefectural governor.

Another new organ in the Meiji system was the District Assembly (Gunkai). In principle each town and village in a district sent one representative, and the wealthiest landowners in the district (those with holdings worth at least ¥10,000) selected several representatives. One-third of the total membership was to be chosen by the rich landholders, the rationale being that the prudent representatives of the well-to-do would countervail any capricious impulses of town and village delegates.

Fiscally, districts were in straitened circumstances from the outset. They could not assess direct taxes, but had to get along on revenues from district properties and facilities and from contributions that towns and villages were required to make in proportion to their national and prefectural taxes.

Administrative justice. Article 61 of the Meiji CONSTITUTION (1889) provided for an Administrative Court (Gyōsei Saibansho), separate from the Judicial Court (Shihō Saibansho). French and German law similarly separated administrative and judicial courts. An 1890 law assigned to the Administrative Court exclusive jurisdiction over suits relating to "rights alleged to have been infringed by illegal measures of the administration authorities." Critics of the Meiji system, including OCCUPATION authorities after World War II, maintained that the Administrative Court did not provide adequate protection for citizens against bureaucratic abuses of power.

Reforms of the Local Autonomy System —— Although its basic structure endured until 1940, the Meiji Local Autonomy System underwent a number of changes during its half-century of existence. In 1899 the Diet passed complete revisions of the prefectural and county codes. The revised Prefectural Code explicitly stated that the prefecture was a juridical person. It provided for direct elections of prefectural assembly members. The governor could still prorogue the assembly, but the home minister had to obtain imperial approval before ordering dissolution. The governor's power to create, supervise, and discipline officials was broadened. The amended District Code provided that District Council members be selected by and from District Assembly members and allowed districts to join together in public corporations to provide common services. After 1899 all male residents who had paid three yen in direct national taxes within the county in the year before the election could vote.

A major reform of the city, town, and village regulations was enacted in the New Municipal Code and New Town and Village Code of 1911. For cities, the most important change was that the mayor became the executive organ, instead of the whole City Council, as had been the case under the 1888 law. Together, the two new codes clarified the limits of power and responsibility of cities, towns, and villages and allowed them to enter into associations for joint undertakings. In general, the 1911 revisions removed ambiguities from the language of the codes but did not decrease the volume of delegated business or substantially increase the sphere of local decision making.

Some scholars have portrayed the modifications of 1899 and 1911 as the Japanization of Western-style institutions. This interpretation probably overestimates the reach of these late-Meiji reforms.

Local government —— Table 1

Local Government Expenditures, 1891–1944		
	Local expenditures (millions of yen)	Index
1891	45	100
1906	174	387
1920	963	2,140
1925	1,429	3,176
1930	1,775	3,944
1935	2,229	4,953
1940	3,123	6,940
1944	4,232	9,404

SOURCE: Fujita Takeo, *Gendai Nihon chihō zaisei shi* (1976).

But one alteration of the Meiji Local Autonomy System does stand as evidence that not all Prussian local government forms could be successfully adapted to Japan. In 1921 the Diet revoked the District Code, the revocation effective from 1923. The district was stripped of the structure and functions of a local self-governing body and made an administrative unit of the state only. Towns and villages came directly under prefectures. Districts had not been self-governing before the Restoration, and so this step represented in a sense a realignment of the local autonomy system to make it accord more closely with Japanese tradition. The last vestiges of the district as an administrative organ were swept away when legislation of June 1926 concerning local government officials took effect. District chiefs and district offices were eliminated. Their bailiwicks became mere geographic designations.

The Universal Manhood Suffrage Law (Futsū Senkyo Hō), adopted for national elections in 1925, became the rule for local elections the following year. Other 1926 revisions expanded local power. Town and village assemblies, in "special circumstances," were allowed to choose their own presidents instead of automatically having the town or village chiefs in the chair. City Council powers were diminished, to the advantage of the City Assembly, which theoretically should have been more responsive to citizens' opinions. Perhaps the most remarkable change was that the role of the home minister in appointing mayors, and that of the governor in approving town and village chiefs, were done away with. A vote of the local assembly became sufficient to choose a mayor or chief. A number of provisions of the 1926 law loosened the net of state supervision of localities. Central government approval was no longer required for certain local actions, nor the governor's approval for others.

The year 1929 was a banner year for advocates of local power. The home minister was divested of power to make peremptory cuts in prefectural budgets. The list of local actions requiring higher authorities' approval was shortened. A change in the procedure for delegating tasks to local government officials made it necessary for the national government to obtain a law passed by the Diet or an imperial rescript; all that had been needed before was an administrative order (gyōsei meirei). Prefectural assemblies gained power to legislate and to delegate powers, not just to deliberate on governors' proposals. Local assembly and council members acquired the power to originate bills, except budgetary bills. The system contained more democratic potential after the 1929 reform, but it was not a fully realized democracy.

A Home Ministry investigation of local government expenditures in fiscal year 1934 showed that 74 percent of all prefectural spending and 42 percent of city, town, and village spending went to pay for delegated business. In 1936 the central government began providing "temporary relief" to towns and villages. The following year it greatly expanded the temporary relief payments program, extending it to prefectures and cities as well as towns and villages. Central government assistance payments continued through the war years (1937–45), finally becoming institutionalized in 1940. Although they redressed some of the inequalities in services between rich and poor localities, these grants came with strings attached: the central government scrutinized the budgets of localities receiving aid, and local governments lost some of their autonomy. After the outbreak of the Sino-Japanese War in 1937, the central government required localities to take on more and more war-related duties, so that even with national assistance grants, local governments were often hard pressed for funds.

Wartime Local Government —— The China conflict produced new difficulties for Japan. In order to mobilize the people for a concerted national effort, in September 1940 the Home Ministry ordered the creation of community councils (CHŌNAIKAI) in city block areas and villages and placed them under the leadership of mayors and town and village chiefs. These councils were made up of neighborhood associations (TONARIGUMI) responsible for the policing and welfare of their areas. Regular monthly meetings of these neighborhood associations were ordered after July 1941. In 1942 the cabinet decided to tighten the national grip on community councils by placing liaison officers of the IMPERIAL RULE ASSISTANCE ASSOCIATION in them.

The pinnacle of wartime centralization was attained in 1943. Revised prefectural laws reduced the powers of the Assembly and enlarged the powers of the governor. The home minister had to sanction assemblies' choices of mayoral candidates, and formal appointment of a mayor again became an imperial act. Mayors and town and village chiefs took on new powers also. The government reverted to the practice of using orders instead of laws or imperial rescripts for delegating tasks to local authorities.

Long-contemplated changes in the local government of Japan's biggest city came about with enactment of the Tōkyō Metropolitan Area Ordinance (Tōkyō To Sei) in June 1943. Tōkyō was given a structure different from Kyōto and Ōsaka. The position of mayor of Tōkyō was abolished. The 35 wards of the city became autonomous bodies, standing in the same relation to the governor of the metropolis as did other cities, towns, and villages in the metropolitan area. In a move consonant with other recent centralizing policies, the government reserved the power of appointment of Tōkyō ward chiefs for the home minister. Attempting to coordinate local administration even more closely, the TŌJŌ HIDEKI cabinet in July 1943 created nine Regional Administrative Councils (Chihō Gyōsei Kyōgikai) in major cities around the nation. They had the power to direct almost everything in their regions. Striving to strengthen the sinews of war through centralization and authoritarianism, Japan had all but extinguished local autonomy.

The Heritage of Prewar Local Government —— Between the Meiji Restoration and World War II, local government in Japan expanded enormously. This is suggested by expediture figures compiled for the period 1891–1944 (see Table 1). Military spending aside, national government expenditures did not grow nearly as much. Locally provided services multiplied, especially in education, health, social welfare, and gas and electric utilities. As it got bigger, local government became more important to the functioning of the nation.

Through participation in local affairs and by sharing the burden of paying for the widening range of local government services, citizens experienced the responsibility of self-administration in prewar Japan; the term *jichi*, autonomy, was not entirely a misnomer. But for the majority of Japanese during most of the prewar period local autonomy remained an unrealized notion. The legacy of the recent past to postwar Japan was a system of local execution of national directives, not of local self-government.

■ ——Harumi Befu, "Village Autonomy and Articulation with the State," in John W. Hall and Marius B. Jansen, ed, *Studies in the Institutional History of Early Modern Japan* (1968). Fujita Takeo, *Nihon chihō zaisei seido no seiritsu* (1941). Fujita Takeo, *Gendai Nihon chihō zaisei shi,* vol 1 (1976). Thomas R. H. Havens, *Valley of Darkness* (1978). Ishii Ryōsuke, ed, *Meiji bunka shi,* vol 2 of *Hōsei hen* (1953), tr William J. Chambliss as *Japanese Legislation in the Meiji Era* (1958). Jichi Shinkō Chūō Kai, ed, *Fuken seido shiryō* (1941, repr 1973). Kikegawa Hiroshi, *Jichi gojūnen shi,* ed, Tōkyō Shisei Chōsa Kai (1941, repr 1977). Kikegawa Hiroshi, *Chihō seido shōshi* (1962). Walter W. McLaren, ed, "Japanese Government Documents," *Transactions of the Asiatic Society of Japan,* 1.42 (1914). Ōishi Kaichirō, "Chihō jichi," in *Iwanami kōza: Nihon rekishi,* vol 16 (Iwanami Shoten, 1967). Ōshima Mitsuko, *Meiji no mura* (1977). Kurt Steiner, *Local Government in Japan* (1965). Ukai Nobushige et al, ed, *Nihon kindai hō hattatsu shi* (1958). Yamagata Aritomo, "Chōheisei oyobi jichi seido kakuritsu no enkaku," in Kokka Gakkai, ed, *Meiji kensei keizai shiron* (1919).

James C. BAXTER

The Allied Occupation and Local Government —— Decentralization of governmental authority and the enhancement of the autonomy of local governmental bodies emerged in the early months of the Allied OCCUPATION as a central goal of the democratization program of the headquarters of the Supreme Commander for the Allied Powers (SCAP). With the establishment of the Government Section on 2 October 1945, a branch of SCAP was officially commissioned to make recommendations for the decentralization of the Japanese government and the encouragement of local responsibility. Opinion within SCAP, however, was divided on the merits of decentralization. Many reformers felt that strong central controls would be necessary for restoring the economy and for developing programs of public health, public safety, social security, and resource extraction. Despite such reservations, the establishment of local autonomy became a central goal of SCAP, and one clearly supported by General Douglas MACARTHUR, who subscribed to a theory of local government as "a schoolhouse for democracy."

In making their recommendations for local governmental reform, members of the Government Section of SCAP were not merely imposing a new and alien conception of democracy on Japan. The period of TAISHŌ DEMOCRACY in the 1920s had witnessed important advances for local autonomy, including enhanced authority for the big cities and a loosening of hierarchical controls over the selection of mayors (see above). And Japanese reformers had long hoped for curtailment of central bureaucratic controls over local governments, the direct election of governors, and a strengthening of local assemblies. Thus, the local government reforms of the Allied Occupation carried on the liberalizing trends of the 1920s rather than imposing a wholly new system on Japan, although important new elements were added.

Decentralization began with dismantling of what SCAP saw as a monolithic and authoritarian administrative structure with the Home Ministry at its pinnacle and neighborhood associations at its base. Immediate prewar and wartime innovations, like the neighborhood associations and regional administrative councils, were abolished. The Home Ministry, which had been second in prominence and power only to the war ministries, successively lost its police, fire, election management, public works, and supervisory functions and was finally abolished on 27 December 1947. Over the years several of its functions were reconsolidated in the Local Autonomy Agency (later the MINISTRY OF HOME AFFAIRS). Although this ministry has become increasingly important, it lacks the breadth of legal powers of the earlier Home Ministry and is now as much a defender of local autonomy as a supervisor of local governments.

The Occupation's goal of decentralization was most notably achieved in respect to the police and educational systems. Reforms in these areas were motivated by a desire to dismantle structures believed to have contributed to prewar indoctrination and thought control, rather than by a judgment that these functions would be handled best at the local level. The Police Law (Keisatsu Hō) of 17 December 1947 established a national rural police and, for communities with a population of at least 5,000, municipal police forces. Administrative control of the national police was vested in the six-member NATIONAL PUBLIC SAFETY COMMISSION, appointed by the prime minister with the consent of the Diet. Operational control was assigned to prefectural public safety commissions. Municipal police were put totally under the control of their own public safety commissions. Similarly, Occupation authorities sought to free education from the direct control of the Ministry of Education while keeping it independent of local administration. With the passage of the Board of Education Law (Kyōiku Iinkai Hō) on 15 July 1948, popularly elected prefectural and municipal boards of education (to which were added single members selected by the local assemblies) were put in charge of all public schools and invested with significant budgetary authority. In addition, the Fire Defense Organization Law (Shōbō Soshiki Hō) decentralized fire adminstration previously controlled by the police.

New system of local government. The CONSTITUTION of 1947 put local government on an entirely different footing from that of the prewar years. Chapter VIII (arts. 92–95) provided a fundamental guarantee of "the principle of local autonomy" and such basic features of the new system as the separation of local from national administration and the direct popular election of chief executives (governors and mayors), as well as assembly representatives. Further provisions for the organization and operation of local government were consolidated in the Local Autonomy Law (Chihō Jichi Hō) of 17 April 1947, which has undergone yearly revision as the functions of local governments have expanded. Other aspects of the system were eventually elaborated in the Local Finance Law (Chihō Zaisei Hō; July 1948), Public Office Election Law (Kōshoku Senkyo Hō; April 1950), Local Tax Law (Chihōzei Hō; July 1950), Local Public Service Law (Chihō Kōmuin Hō; December 1950), and Local Public Enterprise Law (Chihō Kōei Kigyō Hō; August 1952).

The new system of local government was intended to break up concentrated bureaucratic power revolving around the appointed governors, increase citizen participation and control, assure fairness in the conduct of local affairs, and expand the scope of autonomous local jurisdiction. Executive authority was deconcentrated by the creation of prefectural and municipal commissions in charge of public safety, election management, and inspection of local administration. Citizens were invested with the right to recall public officeholders and to make direct demands for the enactment of by-laws and inspection. Their representative assemblies were strengthened vis-à-vis the chief executive by the right to approve his appointments to the commissions and certain other offices, to override his veto with a two-thirds majority, and to seek his resignation through a vote of no confidence. The chief executive, in turn, could choose to dissolve the assembly and take a dispute directly to the people. And, in keeping with the constitutional principle of local autonomy, a clear division of work was to be made between local and national administration, except when national interest required central ministry guidance over local governmental execution of delegated national work.

Problems of the new system. For several reasons these reforms did not provide as solid a base for local autonomy as intended by Occupation authorities, and the new system more closely resembled prewar antecedents, derived largely from centralized European (chiefly Prussian) models of administration, than an American model of decentralized local government. From the outset there was strong bureaucratic resistance to administrative and financial decentralization, skepticism on the part of conservative governments, and failure by the occupying authorities themselves to tackle early and strongly enough problems of local finance and division of administrative functions among the three levels of government. SCAP's draft constitution, for example, provided for a kind of local home rule through the right of municipalities to enact their own "charters," but this was revised by Japanese authorities to read "regulations." Much of the national work previously assigned to appointed governors was directly transferred to the popularly elected governors who, in carrying it out, acted as agents of the national ministries and remained subject to their guidance. In fact, this practice of agency delegation (kikan inin jimu) was extended to the municipalities as well. To enforce it, provisions were included in the Local Autonomy Law (Chihō Jichi Hō) for dismissal of chief executives (after recourse to the courts) if they failed to carry out these responsibilities or otherwise violated the laws under which the delegations were made. Adequate measures were not taken to create an autonomous financial base for local governments, leaving them dependent upon taxes redistributed through national offices. Moreover, such reforms as those establishing municipal police forces or requiring the building of a vast number of junior high schools for the new educational system created financial strains for local governments. Thus, when the thrust of Occupation policies turned decisively from democratization to economic stabilization with the so-called DODGE LINE, local governments were thrown deeply into debt by a drastic decrease in the local redistribution tax received from the national government.

These developments finally forced Occupation authorities to address the difficult financial and administrative problems. A tax mission led by Carl S. Shoup of Columbia University (see SHOUP MISSION) presented its report in September 1949 spelling out the difficulties: the lack of a clear tax structure or separation of functions by level of government; insufficient local tax sources and their control by central authorities; tight limits on local borrowing authority; unpredictability of national grants and subsidies; and inadequate means to correct discrepancies between rich and poor areas. The Shoup Report recommended a package of reforms to correct these problems. The newly appointed Local Administration Investigation Committee under Kambe Masao (1877–1959) of Kyōto University elaborated these recommendations in a report to the government that called for a concerted effort to strengthen local institutions through a clear demarcation of functions by level of government, a tax structure adequate for each level of government to support its own work from general funds, the assignment of each function to the lowest appropriate level of government, and the near-elimination of agency delegation. In time, some of these recommendations led to more adequate means to remedy regional discrepancies in wealth and to regularize the dispersement of national grants and subsidies; but most of them came to naught. The need for administrative efficiency and economic recovery and a strong skepticism about the level of local skills led Japanese authorities to strengthen national controls, which had been so useful in Japan's earlier modernization.

Local government————Table 2

	1953	1956	1966	1975	1980	1981
Number of Local Governments in Selected Years						
Prefectures[1]	46	46	46	47[2]	47	47
Large cities[3]	5	5	6	9	9	10
Other cities	281	486	554	634	637	636
Towns and villages	9,582	4,285	2,812	2,614	2,609	2,609
Total	9,914	4,822	3,418	3,304	3,302	3,302

[1] Including Tōkyō and Hokkaidō.
[2] Okinawa was returned to Japan in 1972.
[3] For 1953, Ōsaka, Nagoya, Yokohama, Kyōto, and Kōbe. For 1966, includes Kita Kyūshū; for 1975 and 1980, includes Sapporo, Kawasaki, and Fukuoka; for 1981, includes Hiroshima.

SOURCE: Jichishō (Ministry of Home Affairs), ed, *Chihō zaisei hakusho* (annual): 1982.

Post-Occupation Evolution of Local Government———The legacy of the Occupation's local governmental reforms was a mixed system combining aspects of prewar centralized administration with postwar norms of local autonomy, a measure of institutional separation between levels of government, and an intensified need for local governmental responsiveness to popular constituencies. It has proved to be a flexible and dynamic system, adjusted constantly over the past three decades as a result of the efforts of political and administrative elites, organized interests, and the general public to use it as a means to meet changing social needs. Considerable recentralization, sometimes of a highly controversial sort, has taken place. But many localities have learned how to use the system for their own advantage. Japanese municipalities today have considerable leverage in setting their policy priorities.

The issue agenda of Japanese local government have evolved through four overlapping phases, each with rather distinct central themes, at intervals of about a decade. They are political questions involving the deconcentration of administrative authority and its recentralization during the first postwar decade; economic development efforts from the mid-1950s through the late 1960s; revitalization of local government and growing citizen activism in response to severe environmental, urban, and social problems; and adjustment to less rapid economic growth through internal reform, reallocation of administrative authority, and community building.

Administrative recentralization. Even before the end of the Occupation, Japan's conservative national leaders began to assess the utility of the new decentralized institutions established in the early postwar years. In general they were skeptical about local administrative skills, concerned that autonomous local institutions might be unduly influenced by oppositional groups, and convinced that Japan's economic recovery depended on establishing greater central administrative controls. Although the most politically explosive aspects of administrative recentralization were legislated by the mid-1950s, the process continued in other respects during the next two decades.

Recentralization of the police and education systems stirred strong opposition from the socialists, labor unionists, and intellectuals fearful of a reversion to prewar authoritarianism. As early as June 1951 the Police Law was amended to allow towns and villages to abolish their police forces and put themselves under the jurisdiction of the national rural police, thereby alleviating a major financial strain. Fundamental reform, however, was delayed by political protest until the establishment of a new Police Law on 15 May 1954. This law created a single "autonomous" prefectural-level police system, replacing the earlier dual system. It was coordinated by the National Police Agency. The National Public Safety Commission, whose head was now to be a cabinet member, appointed the chief of the National Police Agency, with the consent of the prime minister, and the chiefs of the prefectural police forces, with the consent of the prefectural public safety commissions and, in the case of Tōkyō, of the prime minister. Similarly, in 1956 the Board of Education Law was replaced by the Law concerning the Organization and Management of Local Educational Administration (Chihō Kyōiku Gyōsei no Soshiki Oyobi Un'ei ni Kansuru Hōritsu), which provided for the appointment of regular members of education boards by the gover-

nors and mayors with the approval of their local assemblies. Prefectural superintendents of education had to be approved by the minister of education, and municipal superintendents by the prefectural boards. The boards' role in budgetary matters was reduced to that of consultation with local authorities, while the Ministry of Education could provide guidance in matters like curriculum and textbook selection. Prefectural boards were vested with authority to hire and fire municipal elementary and junior high school as well as prefectural high school teachers. The new law achieved its desired political effect of reducing the influence of the Japan Teachers' Union (NIKKYŌSO) on educational administration and policy. It also recentralized and standardized education. Although these systems are sometimes criticized for their excessive uniformity, the above legal changes undoubtedly contributed to the development of high-quality education and police services. See POLICE SYSTEM; EDUCATION: modern education.

Recentralization also resulted from the efforts of central elites to achieve administrative efficiency and to facilitate economic recovery and development. Administrative efficiency was pursued through the time-honored practice of encouraging amalgamations of municipalities. Even before the 1953 Law for the Promotion of the Amalgamation of Towns and Villages (Chōson Gappei Sokushin Hō) and the 1956 Law for the Promotion of Construction of New Cities, Towns, and Villages (Shin Shichōson Kensetsu Sokushin Hō), prefectural governors were authorized to draw up amalgamation plans, while national authorities provided financial incentives for their implementation. Amalgamations were seen as a means to avoid waste of scarce resources, to upgrade the overall quality of public administration, and to facilitate the implementation of economic plans and national functions delegated to local authorities. The effect of these efforts on the total number of local governments can be seen in Table 2.

Additional plans for replacing the prefectures with broader administrative regions were never realized because of entrenched prefectural interests and oppositional political concerns over excessive centralization. But regional blocs were created for the implementation of economic development policies, and cooperation among localities was facilitated by national legislation. For example, the Local Autonomy Law provided for partial (single-function) associations of municipalities for joint performance of fire, sanitation, welfare, and other functions. Financial incentives were also provided for coordinated development among neighboring municipalities.

By the 1960s, administrative recentralization proceeded at a rapid pace. Revision of certain laws, like that concerning waterways, resulted in effective jurisdiction being reabsorbed by the national ministries, from which local authorities would now have to seek permission for related projects. Branch offices of the central ministries were newly established or strengthened in their role of guiding and checking on local government. Moreover, with the creation of a wide range of centrally funded public corporations, like the Japan Housing Corporation (see HOUSING AND URBAN DEVELOPMENT CORPORATION) and the JAPAN HIGHWAY PUBLIC CORPORATION, local authorities often lost the initiative and control over public investment and development in their areas. By 1975 the agency-delegated work performed by local governments under central guidance had doubled for municipalities and increased by nearly two and a half times for prefectures over what it had been in 1952.

Despite these developments, the designation of local governmental units remained relatively unchanged from the prewar years. Collectively, the prefectures are known as *todōfuken*. Tōkyō is the sole *to* (metropolis; i.e., metropolitan prefecture), Hokkaidō the only *dō* (region), and Kyōto and Ōsaka the *fu* (urban prefectures); the remaining prefectures are *ken*. The legal jurisdiction of prefectures is the same, except for Hokkaidō which lost some of its autonomy with the creation of the Hokkaidō Development Agency in the Prime Minister's Office in 1951. Municipalities are known as *shichōson*, with the *shi* (cities) having somewhat greater functions than the *chō* or *machi* (towns) and *son* or *mura* (villages). Two classes of cities, however, differ from the rest. First, cities of over 500,000 population may be designated by the Diet to a special status *(shitei toshi)* combining the normal functions of a city with many of those performed by the prefectures—for example, in planning and welfare. These cities also establish administrative and electoral wards *(ku)*. The initially designated cities were Yokohama, Nagoya, Kyōto, Ōsaka and Kōbe. In subsequent years several others have been added: first, Kita Kyūshū, then Sapporo, Kawasaki and Fukuoka, and finally Hiroshima. This status may be seen as the culmination of the prewar movement among big cities for expanded autonomy to address their special needs. Second, in addition to its outlying municipalities, Tōkyō contains 23 wards *(ku)* corresponding roughly to the prewar Tōkyō City. These wards are separate municipalities known as *to-kubetsu ku* (special wards), which are less autonomous from the prefectural administration than are other cities. Although the term *gun* (district) is still used for contiguous groupings of municipalities, no local governmental functions are attached to these units.

Economic development. By the mid-1950s, Japan's central economic elites had reorganized themselves sufficiently for close cooperation with the still powerful central bureaucracy and the newly unified LIBERAL DEMOCRATIC PARTY (LDP) in a concerted effort for economic development. Thus, national planning by this time had turned from resource development, guided by the COMPREHENSIVE NATIONAL LAND DEVELOPMENT PLAN (Kokudo Sōgō Kaihatsu Keikaku; adopted 1962 in conformity with a 1950 law), to industrial development, facilitated by the establishment of the JAPAN DEVELOPMENT BANK and several regionally oriented industrial development laws. These provided mechanisms for public financing and investment in new industrial sites, water resources, transportation, roads, harbors, and other industrial infrastructures needed by industry. Local authorities joined this effort at industrial expansion by passing ordinances to attract industry. The number of these ordinances, which provided tax incentives, public services to industry, and even subsidies, grew rapidly: in 1955 there were 9 such ordinances on the prefectural level and 102 on the municipal level; in 1969 there were 41 and 1,303, respectively. Meanwhile, major industries continued to concentrate in the large metropolitan areas with their skilled labor forces and relatively high stock of social overhead capital. Growth in the Tōkyō area was to be coordinated by national authorities through the 1956 Capital Region Development Law (Shutoken Seibi Hō) and in the Nagoya and Ōsaka metropolitan areas by similar laws.

Significant regional development was spurred, however, by a series of new laws in the early 1960s that reversed the tendency of Prime Minister Ikeda Hayato's INCOME-DOUBLING PLAN to concentrate industrial development in the industrial belt between Tōkyō and Ōsaka. Pressure exerted by local authorities through their LDP representatives in the Diet led to legislation like the 1961 Law for the Promotion of Industrial Development of Less Developed Areas (Teikaihatsu Chiiki Kōgyō Kaihatsu Sokushin Hō), the 1962 Comprehensive Land Development Plan (Zenkoku Sōgō Kaihatsu Keikaku) and the Law for the Promotion of the Construction of New Industrial Cities (Shin Sangyō Toshi Kensetsu Sokushin Hō), and the 1964 Law for the Promotion of Industrial and Regional Adjustment (Kōgyō Seibi Tokubetsu Chiiki Seibi Sokushin Hō). Local authorities now competed with each other to receive national government designation as target areas, and industries such as petroleum refining, petrochemicals, steel, nonferrous metals, machinery, and other heavy and chemical products spread throughout the country.

Local control. By the late 1960s many Japanese local governments had begun to rethink their priorities. Most had not invested sufficiently in local roads, sewers, parks, housing, and other expensive social infrastructure. Instead, they had been absorbed in providing the minimum required educational, sanitation, and welfare facilities and promoting the local economy. Rapid economic growth, however, led to depopulation of the countryside and excessive urban crowding. One result was the spiraling of urban land prices that made the provision of an adequate social infrastructure all the more difficult. Another was the proliferation of new urban problems like environmental pollution, traffic congestion and accidents, and uncontrolled urban sprawl. Moreover, social changes lessening the solidarity of the family and local communities created new needs for social services. The intensity of such problems in many areas led to social unrest and efforts by ordinary citizens to seek ameliorative policies from local government. Under these circumstances, many local authorities began to pioneer in new forms of communications with residents, pollution control measures, social welfare, and planning mechanisms. Local priorities diverged significantly from national ones and contributed to a shift in the national consensus from economic growth to establishing a higher quality of life.

National authorities turned to similar corrective policies by the early 1970s, significantly upgrading the national SOCIAL WELFARE system and laying a strong legal basis for pollution control (see POLLUTION COUNTERMEASURES BASIC LAW). In some cases, like pollution control, free medical care for the aged, and childhood allowances, these measures were clearly modeled on local precedents. By and large such laws did not preempt local action but rather nationalized certain minimum standards which only the richer local governments could have achieved on their own. Local governments could still call for higher standards or provide supplementary

Local government —— Table 3

	Net, all local governments[1]	Prefectures[2]	Large cities[3]	Other cities	Towns and villages
Local Government Revenue Sources, Fiscal Year 1979 (in percentages)					
Local taxes	32.5	31.3	36.9	36.0	16.9
Shared tax	17.9	18.0	9.9	12.0	29.6
National treasury disbursements	22.5	26.9	17.5	17.3	12.2
Prefectural disbursements	—	—	1.9	4.6	10.8
Local bonds	11.8	10.0	12.3	12.5	14.6
Other	15.3	13.8	21.5	17.6	15.9
Total	100.0	100.0	100.0	100.0	100.0

[1] Minus accounts duplicated between prefectures and cities, towns, or villages.
[2] Including Tōkyō.
[3] Sapporo, Yokohama, Kawasaki, Nagoya, Kyōto, Ōsaka, Kōbe, Kita Kyūshū, and Fukuoka.
SOURCE: Prime Minister's Office, Statistics Bureau, *Japan Statistical Yearbook* (annual): 1982.

benefits to those required by national law. Local governments were called upon to implement much of this new legislation. Thus, for example, they were delegated responsibility to negotiate emission levels with the specific industries within their territory.

Adjusting to stable growth. After the OIL CRISIS OF 1973 and the advent of an era of stable, rather than rapid, economic growth, local governments found it more difficult to pioneer in the costly new programs. Instead, they turned to the tasks of improving their efficiency, redeveloping community life, and upgrading the delivery of services. By the late 1970s many prefectures had devolved considerable administrative authority to their municipalities, strengthening the level of government closest to the people.

Local finance: The extent and limits of dependency. The structure of Japanese local finance is set by national laws that regulate the kinds and, in many cases, rates of local taxes and other revenue sources and designate many categories of obligatory expenditure. A series of revisions of the Local Finance Law and Local Tax Law in the early 1950s, in response to the recommendations of the Shoup and Kambe commissions, set the basic structure of postwar local finance. In place of the earlier local surcharge on national taxes, independent local tax sources were expanded. Prefectures collect individual and corporate inhabitants' and business taxes; vehicle, eating and drinking, real estate, and tobacco excise taxes; and other special purpose taxes. Municipalities collect individual and corporate inhabitants' taxes, based on both flat rates and income levels, and taxes on fixed assets such as land and residences. They also have tobacco, electricity, gas, and other special purpose taxes. In place of the earlier arbitrary national efforts at financial equalization, a new shared (or equalization) tax was established as a fixed share of the nationally collected income, corporate, and liquor taxes to be redistributed according to a complex formula that reflected the financial capacity and needs of localities. Such changes provided a modicum of local financial autonomy. The shared-tax system has proved to be the single most effective means for bringing public facilities and programs in the rural and other poor areas of the country up to the national standard. See TAXES.

But even this system fell short of what the Shoup and Kambe reports envisioned as the minimum financial base necessary for local autonomy. And, for several reasons, it has been criticized as "30-percent local autonomy." (The 30-percent figure represents the approximate share of local governmental revenue that came from local taxes. See Table 3.) National authorities still control most tax revenues, collecting two-thirds of them, even though prefectural and municipal governments outspend the national government two-to-one in their general account (tax-funded) budgets. The difference is made up by large-scale transfers of funds from national to local government in the form of both categorical (tied) grants—including partial or complete subsidies for compulsory and optional work—and noncategorical (untied) grants like the shared tax. But since new tasks may be assigned unilaterally by national legislation to local government, often mandating significant local contributions, local

Local government———Table 4

Division of Total Public Expenditures between National and Local Governments, 1979 (in percentages)			
Area of expenditure	Share of total public expenditures	Local governments' share	National government's share
Administrative			
General	} 13.0	79.0	21.0
Courts and police		77.0	23.0
Defense	3.1	0.0	100.0
Land policy			
Land conservation		71.0	29.0
Land development	} 19.6	78.0	22.0
Disaster relief		73.0	27.0
Economic development			
Agriculture	} 9.2	34.0	66.0
Commerce		69.0	31.0
Education			
School education	} 18.6	85.0	15.0
Other education		95.0	5.0
Social security			
Public welfare		50.0	50.0
Sanitation	} 21.8	92.0	8.0
Housing		78.0	22.0
Other			
Pensions		12.0	88.0
Bonds	} 14.7	38.0	62.0
Other		5.0	95.0
Total	100.0	64.0	36.0

NOTE: Based on the national General Account Budget, the Special Account for Allotment of the Local Allocation Tax and Transferred Tax, nine other special accounts, and the local government general account budgets.
SOURCE: Jichishō (Ministry of Home Affairs), ed, *Chihō zaisei hakusho* (annual): 1981.

governments have found their discretionary funds extremely limited. Moreover, they have complained of an "excess financial burden" caused by inadequate reimbursement from some national authorities for agency-delegated work and by unrealistically low estimates of material costs as the basis of national subsidies in such crucial areas as school construction. Moreover, local authorities must still seek national permission before floating bonds.

The picture of local dependence that grows out of this description of local-national financial ties and the earlier description of recentralization, however, can be overdrawn. Japanese local governments do not have a European-style prefect scrutinizing their budgets, and their revenue sources are relatively greater than those in many European democracies. During the years of rapid economic growth, in particular, they found ample funds to pass supplementary budgets implementing a wide range of new programs. Moreover, the picture of central tutelage does not take adequate account of the fact that the central ministries present a large selection of optional programs and subsidies to local authorities. Over time, local governments, particularly in the medium-size and large cities and prefectures, have upgraded their local public services to the level where they can compete with their national counterparts in expertise and salary. And with the development of local planning departments since the 1960s, local authorities have found a powerful new instrument to shape their developmental destinies according to local priorities, determined by their own political processes. Finally, the fact that local governments continue to administer most public programs, whether delegated to them or of their own choosing, means that implementation is largely in their hands (see Table 4). It is no wonder that, when questioned on their political interests, Japanese tend to find local (especially municipal) government and politics more relevant and responsive than national politics.

Local Politics——*Prewar local politics.* In the prewar years politicization of local government proceeded despite national control of the local administrative structure. By the turn of the century, prefectural assemblies were almost as politicized as they are today, with over three-quarters of the seats won by party-endorsed candidates. Municipal assemblies remained far less politicized (as they still are), although after the passage of the Universal Manhood Suffrage Law in 1925 assembly seats in many of the larger cities went mainly to party representatives. Although nonpartisanship remained the norm of local politics, particularly in small municipalities and for executive officers, parties made significant inroads. This partisan activity was dominated by the two major parties (RIKKEN SEIYŪKAI and RIKKEN MINSEITŌ) which later formed the basis of the postwar Liberal Democratic Party. Parties of the Left, on which the postwar JAPAN

SOCIALIST PARTY (JSP) was built, were active in certain areas from the late 1920s, but, with the exception of the major urban centers and occasional villages, their assembly representation was very low. See also POLITICAL PARTIES.

The two major parties, particularly the Seiyūkai, sought to penetrate the administration system at virtually every level. Through their control of the Home Ministry, which appointed governors and supervised local administration and public works, and their growing strength in the larger local assemblies, these parties gained influence with local executives and sought to channel government subsidies, investments in new projects, and agricultural and industrial bank loans to local interests that would support them. A positive policy of government spending on new schools, parks, roads, dams, railroads, and other public works permitted party expansion by "pork barrel." Local and national politics became intimately connected because politicians could no longer afford to ignore local interests and because of party penetration of the centralized administrative apparatus that allocated resources. Despite the relative decline of party influence in the years preceding World War II, many of these practices were continued and extended, in altered form, in the postwar years, providing a solid basis for conservative dominance of local politics and the underpinnings of their national control as well.

Postwar local politics: Institutions and practices. Executive dominance has continued into the postwar years despite efforts by the Occupation to strengthen assemblies vis-à-vis the mayors and governors. Almost all bylaws, as well as the budget, are drafted by bureaucrats and proposed by the chief executive. Mayors and governors set the tone for local governments. Most of them spend considerable time in Tōkyō or delegate aides to negotiate for public works, subsidies, bond allocations, permission to carry out various projects, or designation to receive developmental grants. Mayors of the smaller municipalities have extensive contact with community groups and intervene at virtually every stage of the policy process. They participate in long-term planning, setting budget priorities, discussing specific projects, and negotiating with interest groups and assembly members. In the larger cities and prefectures, chief executives intervene more selectively in the policy process because of the complexity of bureaucratic organization and other demands. Still, they may have a considerable impact on policy if they clarify their priorities, develop political and popular support for these policies, and put in the time and effort needed for developing administrative mechanisms and training personnel to deal with such concerns. More often, they will endorse bureaucratic proposals to meet widely recognized needs and intervene in the final stages of budget making to save politically important programs.

Local government ──── Table 5

Prefectural and Municipal Assembly Seats by Party, April 1979					
	Prefectural assemblies[1]	Large city assemblies[2]	Other city assemblies[3]	Tōkyō ward assemblies	Town and village assemblies	Total seats
Liberal Democratic Party	1,528	193	1,878	498	209	4,306
New Liberal Club	38	9	57	35	2	141
Independents	398	40	11,988	50	20,989	33,465
Minor parties	54	8	90	0	5	157
Democratic Socialist Party	109	61*	597	51	47	865
Kōmeitō	197	108	1,654	179	638	2,776
United Social Democratic Party	6	0	27	11	0	44
Japan Socialist Party	411	101	1,938	107	546	3,103
Japan Communist Party	138	87	1,477	156	744	2,602
Total	2,879	607	19,706	1,087	23,180	47,459

[1] Three vacancies. Includes Tōkyō Metropolitan Assembly.
[2] Sapporo, Yokohama, Kawasaki, Nagoya, Kyōto, Ōsaka, Kōbe, and Fukuoka.
[3] Includes Kita Kyūshū.
SOURCE: *Asahi shimbun*, 10, 23, and 24 April 1979.

Local bureaucrats draft most policy proposals. Many of these simply reflect nationally delegated responsibilities. Other programs are developed by local bureaucrats to attract public works, subsidies, or special designation for receiving preferential national funding. Prefectures and large municipalities often place in key positions national bureaucrats on loan, especially in financial and public works sections, but these special personnel are seen less as an instrument of central control than as an avenue of access to the center. With the upgrading of their education and expertise, development of professional associations, and increased informal lateral communications with different locales, local bureaucrats have become more competent. Within their internal bureaucratic processes of decision making, they feel pressure from clientele groups and assembly members, but they look primarily to the leadership of the chief executive.

Local assembly members exercise considerable influence in the policy process, although not necessarily in ways anticipated by early postwar reformers. They have been concerned foremost with bringing concrete benefits—a new school, road, bridge, or developmental loans, subsidies, or favorable regulatory decisions—to the communities and functional (for example, commercial and agricultural) groups that support them. In the smaller municipalities this is achieved largely through direct access to the functional departments of the bureaucracy rather than through assembly deliberations. These assemblies are not normally divided along partisan lines, since local politics in such areas is largely equated with community representation. Major decisions, such as those affecting the industrial character of a municipality, may sometimes divide assemblies, usually between pro- and anti-mayoral groupings. In larger cities and prefectures partisan programs and politics may influence the character of assembly proceedings, but here too, assembly members tend to seek special favors for their constituents through direct access to the functional departments of the bureaucracy.

Local residents normally influence the policy process through election (and occasional recall) of assembly representatives and chief executives, using community associations, organized interest groups, and civic groups as intermediaries with local bureaucracy and, in recent years, through mechanisms like consultation booths or representation on pollution control boards at city halls. Traditional agricultural and commercial interests predominate in the towns and villages, but they have been joined or superceded in the cities by industrial, labor, professional, and numerous other special-interest groups. Civic groups concerned with the environment, prices, and social welfare became particularly influential in the late 1960s and early 1970s.

Postwar local politics: Partisan competition. Postwar local politics exhibited greater continuity with prewar developments in respect to partisan activity than was the case at the national level. Local conservatives, whether descendants of the two major prewar parties or independents, continued to dominate local politics. The left showed some early strength in the big cities and selected provincial areas where labor and tenant movements were particularly strong; but such areas were highly circumscribed, and leftist (largely socialist) strength floundered in the wake of the collapse of the KATAYAMA TETSU cabinet in 1948, the RED PURGE, the full imple-

mentation of the LAND REFORMS OF 1946, and the conservative resurgence in national politics. The prewar legacy of a lack of leftist grass-roots organization put them at a competitive disadvantage with the conservatives, who continued to dominate local social and economic organization. Even members of labor unions were disinclined to introduce partisan ideology into community matters. Although they fought recentralization of police and education, both the labor and socialist movements in practice neglected local politics in favor of issues concerning international political alignment and the national constitutional order.

Partisanship played a much more important role from the start in city mayoral, gubernatorial, and prefectural assembly elections, since leftist party and labor union organization was more easily mobilized in these large constituencies. But conservatives continued to dominate these elections as well because of the dearth of leftist candidates who could appeal to broad constituencies and the widely accepted notion that governors should be persons of administrative experience with "pull" in Tōkyō, and mayors should be persons above partisan loyalties. Thus candidates for prefectural assemblies generally ran with party endorsements (kōnin), while party backing was less obtrusive in the form of recommendations (suisen) or support (shiji) for executive candidates.

Conservative dominance did not significantly erode until the mid-1960s, when independent progressives backed by the Japan Socialist Party, alone or in coalition with other opposition parties, began to win the mayorships of the largest and of many medium-size cities, and MINOBE RYŌKICHI, who was backed by the socialists and communists, was elected as governor of Tōkyō Prefecture. At the same time, LDP and conservative independent dominance in these crucial urban assemblies was displaced by a more fluid situation in which no single party or political orientation prevailed.

In most of the country, however, conservative strength in local politics remains impressive (see Table 5). After the local elections in 1979, conservatives still held close to two-thirds of all prefectural assembly seats. Independents predominate in city, town, and village assemblies; but most of them are conservative in orientation, if not in formal affiliation. In fact, they are the vital local links in the support groups of LDP Diet members. In 1979 Liberal Democrats, New Liberals, and independents held 70 percent of all city assembly seats and were even more dominant at the town and village level. In most urban areas, however, conservative strength is less pronounced—somewhat over 50 percent in the ward assemblies of Tōkyō and under 40 percent in the assemblies of the other large cities.

Gubernatorial and mayoral elections exhibit similar patterns. Most of these are ostensibly nonpartisan in character, but at the gubernatorial and city mayoral levels it is possible to distinguish over 90 percent of the candidates by their partisan backing. In 1975, at the peak of progressive strength in these elections, approximately 72 percent of the prefectural governors and the same percentage of small- and medium-size city mayors could be considered "conservatives" and another 8 percent "neutrals." Only 20 percent were "progressives," including 9 of the 47 governors and 132 of the 634 mayors of small- and medium-size cities. But 6 of the 9 large city mayors were progressives. These progressive executives, however, were more important than their numbers since they governed over 40 percent of the nation's populace.

The emergence of progressive local government was the result of the rapid economic growth politics of the conservative national leadership. Growth produced both wealth and a new poverty of the living environment. It also undermined community solidarity, which had been the pillar of conservative dominance. The new urban, environmental, and social concerns of the late 1960s and early 1970s provided a nucleus of issues around which local opposition parties could coalesce and spawned highly competitive and increasingly partisan-related local governments that contrasted sharply with national authorities, which were still lethargic about such problems. Rapid economic growth provided the budgetary surpluses to experiment; local bureaucratic expertise provided the tools; and strong popular demands in a competitive political environment furnished the political incentive for local leaders of varying partisan orientations to respond creatively to the challenge.

Party involvement in local politics has continued to expand, for example, in the form of KŌMEITŌ and DEMOCRATIC SOCIALIST PARTY backing for executive candidates, even after the economic slowdown of the mid-1970s made costly local policy innovations more difficult. The earlier conservative-progressive split has been replaced by more complex patterns of alliances that in part reflect national political trends. The rapid diffusion of policy innovations among local governments also has made it more difficult to identify most policies on a partisan basis. The former disinterest of most of the political parties in local affairs has been replaced by an appreciation of the importance of local government in allocating desired resources, implementing most of the nation's public policies, and keeping in touch with the pulse of the people.

———— Akimoto Ritsuo, Gendai toshi no kenryoku kōzō (1971). Gary D. Allinson, Japanese Urbanism (1975). Gary D. Allinson, Suburban Tokyo: A Comparative Study of Politics and Social Change (1979). Scott Flanagan, Ellis Krauss, and Kurt Steiner, ed, Political Opposition and Local Politics in Japan (1980). Hoshino Mitsuo, Chihō jichi no riron to kōzō (1970). Jichi Daigakkō Kenkyūbu, ed, Sengo jichi shi, 7 vols (1977). Jichishō, ed, Chihō jichi no dōkō (1978). Yasumasa Kuroda, Reed Town, Japan: A Study in Community Power Structure and Political Change (1974). Terry E. MacDougall, Localism and Political Opposition in Japan (1981). Narita Noriaki et al, Kuni to chihō no atarashii kankei (1977). Nihon Toshi Sentā, ed, Toshi keiei no genjō to kadai (1978). Noguchi Yukio et al, "Chihō zaisei ni okeru ishi kettei no bunseki," Keizai bunseki 3.71 (1978). Kurt Steiner, Local Government in Japan (1965). James W. White and Frank Munger, ed, Social Change and Community Politics in Urban Japan (1976). Terry Edward MacDougall

local history

(chihōshi). The generic term for historical studies of a region and its people, as opposed to more conventional studies of the rule of a centralized state. Full-scale research into local history in Japan began after World War II, and its empiricism has contributed greatly to advances in the understanding of many historical issues, the MEIJI RESTORATION prominent among them.

Before World War II an author's historical account of his native place (kyōdoshi) served to chronicle and explain the national government's relation with a particular region and the characteristics peculiar to that region's political history. The underlying values found in such studies included an agrarian nationalism (NŌHON SHUGI), which idealized the community (kyōdōtai) and advocated a system of small family farms; a belief in the wisdom of people following their natural ways; and a strong work ethic extolling diligence as the best way to rise from poverty. In contrast, local history had its start from criticism of this kind of agrarian thinking and attempted to restructure the historical study of the state's relationship with its people from the local area up. Local history also sought to protect and better the lives of the inhabitants of the region studied.

Forerunners of Local History

We can gain an understanding of the tradition of the genre of local history in Japan by examining regional gazetteers and documents. The tradition of the "old" Nara-period (710–794) FUDOKI (accounts of local traditions and conditions) was followed by the compilation of geographical records in the manner of the Chinese Da Ming yitongzhi (Ta Ming i-t'ung-chih; ca 1450, Comprehensive Gazetteer of the Great Ming Empire). Both of these genres constituted source compilations intended to

relay information on local areas to the central government. Gazetteers, financed privately or by domainal governments, first appeared as a genre in the Edo period (1600–1868). They too helped the government to rule and control the people. A further development was the compilation of new records such as the Shimpen Hitachi kokushi (1836, printed 1894–1901; Newly Edited Gazetteer of Hitachi Province), and private editing of "new" fudoki, such as Uchiyama Matatsu's Tōtōmi no Kuni fudoki den (1789, printed 1900). Kōno Michiharu wrote (and Shinjō Michio later amended) the Suruga shin fudoki (1830, amended 1834; New Annals of Suruga). The Tokugawa shogunate also sponsored and published gazetteers between 1804 and 1844, most notably the Shimpen Musashi no Kuni fudoki kō (Newly Compiled Materials on Musashi Province). This tradition influenced the form of such modern gazetteers as the government-sponsored Kōkoku chishi (1872, Geographical Gazetteer for the Empire).

Modern Japan and Birthplace History

The tendency for Japanese to view their native place as a "homeland" with familiar sights and a unique natural beauty was influenced ironically by Prussian gazetteers (Heimatkunde), introduced during the Meiji period (1868–1912). The writing of state-centered history promoting patriotism was increasingly encouraged and regional characteristics disregarded. Japanese viewed native places as "homelands" and regarded them emotionally in terms of the traditions they preserved. This view, which distinguished state from homeland, gave rise to a "science of homeland" (kyōdo kagaku), which stressed the area's Wissenschaft, or the scientific study of its natural history, on the one hand, and, on the other, to a short-lived movement to put control of the locale back into the hands of its inhabitants and to develop it differently than planned by the central government. Despite these efforts, the "homelands" lost their local autonomy and were made mere units of the central state. This evolution has been the overriding trend in the local regions' relation to the central government throughout modern Japanese history.

The "Study of the Lore of Rural Localities"

Together with NITOBE INAZŌ, YANAGITA KUNIO attempted to create the "study of the lore of rural localities" (jikatagaku) to oppose state-sponsored rural improvement programs. With a firm belief in the energy and spiritual resources of the rural villagers, he labored to unearth the thinking of what he called the "jōmin" (the unchanging, or everyday, people), whom he considered to be the source of the nation's productive energy. He also considered it crucial for these people to continue to transmit their traditional wisdom.

Thus, FOLKLORE STUDIES (minzokugaku) began in Japan as a discipline centered on preserving the collective wisdom of the common people. Its early practitioners wished to make it the study of governing in the original sense of "saving the people" (keisei saimin) and so form a new view of history. The high-growth economic policies of the Japanese government in the 1960s rearranged the local structures. It is the task of local history to take these changes into consideration as it refines its conceptual schemes and to encompass every group, however marginal. HAGA Noboru

local ordinances

(jōrei). In a broad sense, the word jōrei refers to any law enacted under the authority of a local public body (chihō kōkyō dantai), but it more usually refers to laws enacted by vote of the assembly of a local public body.

The 1947 constitution of Japan emphasizes local self-government and commits a wide range of matters to the management of local public bodies. The subject matter of local ordinances is accordingly broad, and, because the Local Autonomy Law (Chihō Jichi Hō) permits punishment including imprisonment for up to two years for violation of a local ordinance, the importance of local ordinances has increased. Moreover, citizens have the right to seek the reform or repeal of local ordinances as distinguished from statutes (HŌRITSU) passed by the national Diet. An ordinance may not conflict with a statute or an order (meirei) and, in this sense, ordinances occupy the bottom rank among laws, but, in fact, a large part of a citizen's daily life is regulated by ordinances. Examples of important ordinances include those that determine the specific policies for preventing noise, air and water pollution, those that regulate the quality of products and otherwise protect consumers, those that for the sake of public safety regulate marches and demonstrations, and those that protect minors from harmful books and movies. ITŌ Masami

Lo Chen-yū → Luo Zhenyu (Lo Chen-yū)

Lockheed Scandal

A political scandal that occurred in 1976 with the purchase by a Japanese civil airline of planes manufactured by Lockheed Aircraft Corporation. Involving bribes and kickbacks, it led to the prosecution of businessmen and high-level politicians, including former Prime Minister TANAKA KAKUEI.

In February 1976 the US Senate subcommittee on multinational industries announced that Lockheed Aircraft had spent large sums of money in efforts to sell its military and civilian aircraft in several foreign countries, including the Netherlands, Italy, and Japan. The stunned Japanese public demanded clarification of the affair, and an investigation, aided by evidence gathered in the United States, led to the prosecution of 16 people, including 3 politicians.

Investigations revealed first, that the collusion between the Liberal Democratic Party (LDP; Jiyū Minshutō) and business sectors had resulted in corruption within the government, and second, that with the high growth rate of the Japanese economy during the 1960s, a kind of plutocracy (kinken seiji) had emerged within the LDP, of which Tanaka took advantage. This prevailing tendency and Tanaka's own colorful personality had allegedly brought about the act of bribery. The Lockheed scandal was only a small part of an international scandal caused by collusion between multinational industries and politicians in the respective countries. As of 1982 the final judgment had yet to be rendered.   TAKAHASHI Naoki

locusts

(inago). A general term for insects of the family Acrididae, genus Oxya. From about July to September, the adult insects, about 4 centimeters (1.6 in) long, appear in rice paddies and feed on rice plants, but the damage is insignificant. Crop failure said to be caused by locusts is often caused by plant hoppers (unka) and other harmful insects. Locusts are often eaten in farm villages. They are rapidly decreasing because of the wide-spread use of insecticide.
                                              TSUKUBA Hisaharu

Loew, Oscar (1844–1941)

German agricultural chemist. Twice instructor at what is now Tōkyō University between 1893 and 1907. Succeeding Oscar KELLNER, he taught agricultural chemistry at the university. Among his students were SUZUKI UMETARŌ and many other Japanese agrochemists. He is known for various outstanding research studies including his work on the effect of lime on acid soils. Together with Kellner he rendered distinguished service in introducing agricultural chemistry to Japan.   KATŌ Shunjirō

London, Jack (1876–1916)

Real name John Griffith London. American author of 50 books ranging from stories of adventure to essays on cultural and political ferment. Born in San Francisco on 12 January 1876, he early began a career of odd jobs, travel, and self-education. At 17 he joined a sealing expedition to the Pacific, which provided the material for his first published story, "A Typhoon Off the Coast of Japan" (1893). London achieved fame with his novel The Call of the Wild in 1903, and that same year he established his socialist credentials with The People of the Abyss, a study of London slums. Despite his socialist principles, he helped William Randolph Hearst exploit fear of the "YELLOW PERIL" as a correspondent during the Russo-Japanese War of 1904–05. Novels like The Sea Wolf (1904), White Fang (1906), and The Iron Heel (1907) reveal the contradictory influences of Darwin, Marx, and Nietzsche, especially in London's assertion of the white race's superiority, while the more autobiographical works The Road (1907), Martin Eden (1909), and John Barleycorn (1913) describe his aspirations and defeats. He committed suicide on 22 November 1916.

⬛——Joan London, Jack London and His Times (1939). Richard O'Connor, Jack London: A Biography (1964). Irving Stone, Sailor on Horseback (1938).   Joseph W. SLADE

London Naval Conferences

Conferences held in London in 1930 and 1935–36 to extend the Five-Power naval arms limitation system established at the WASHINGTON CONFERENCE (1921–22). The first conference imposed limits on submarines and auxiliary surface craft. The second ended in failure with Japan's withdrawal.

Article 21 of the WASHINGTON NAVAL TREATY OF 1922 provided for subsequent meetings to revise and update the original limitation agreement on a 10:10:6 ratio for the United States, British, and Japanese navies. In 1927 Japan sent Admiral SAITŌ MAKOTO and Ambassador ISHII KIKUJIRŌ to Geneva to seek a 10:10:7 ratio in auxiliary surface craft, 70,000 tons in submarines, and a pledge to reduce naval armaments overall. The Geneva meeting degenerated into an Anglo-American quarrel over respective strengths in cruisers and ended in failure. Following talks between the British prime minister and the American president, it was agreed to convene a new conference at London. In preparation for that meeting the Japanese Navy Ministry lobbied for a 10:10:7 strength ratio, claiming that this figure would leave the Imperial Japanese Navy "a menace toward none, with security for all." Former Prime Minister WAKATSUKI REIJIRŌ, Navy Minister Admiral TAKARABE TAKESHI, and Ambassador Matsudaira Tsuneo were chosen to represent the Japanese government. They were given instructions by the HAMAGUCHI OSACHI cabinet to press for a 10:10:7 ratio.

At the conference, which opened on 21 January 1930, it soon became apparent that the Japanese proposals were unacceptable to the American and British delegates. A Japanese effort to secure neutralization of the Philippine Islands also ended in failure. United States Senator David Reed and Ambassador Matsudaira arrived at a complex compromise, reluctantly agreed to by Admiral Takarabe and accepted by the Hamaguchi cabinet on 14 March 1930. By its terms the Imperial Japanese Navy was limited to a 10:10:6 ratio in eight-inch gun cruisers but given the desired 70 percent strength ratio in other cruisers and destroyers together with parity in submarines. The treaty embodying these terms was to last for five years and was signed on 22 April 1930.

Although the treaty more nearly matched Japanese than Anglo-American desires, it generated bitter opposition in Tōkyō. Admiral KATŌ HIROHARU, chief of the Naval General Staff, charged the Hamaguchi cabinet with having violated the right of supreme command in disregarding his protests against the ratio compromise (see TŌSUI-KEN). Although Prime Minister Hamaguchi overcame opposition within the Supreme War Council and Privy Council and Katō Hiroharu resigned, ratification of the treaty on 2 October 1930 came at a heavy cost. Hamaguchi had to support major naval budget increases, and Admiral Takarabe resigned. His successor presided over changes in naval administration that enhanced the influence of those who had opposed the treaty.

Over the next four years opposition within the navy to the Washington and London treaties mounted. In July 1934 the navy minister, Admiral Ōsumi Mineo (1876–1941), threatened to resign if the OKADA KEISUKE cabinet did not agree to end the Washington Naval Treaty and seek parity with the United States and Great Britain. Foreign Minister HIROTA KŌKI promised to terminate the treaty but persuaded the navy to seek parity in stages in cooperation with Washington and London. In September 1934 the efforts of Ambassador Matsudaira and Rear Admiral YAMAMOTO ISOROKU to secure Anglo-American acceptance of this scheme failed. On 30 December 1934 the Okada cabinet announced its intention to abrogate the Washington Naval Treaty of 1922.

In an effort to prevent complete collapse of the naval arms-limitation system, the British government invited American, French, Italian, and Japanese delegates to meet at London in December 1935. Japan's representatives, Ambassador Nagai Matsuzo (1877–1957) and Admiral NAGANO OSAMI, sought full parity with the American and British navies and an agreement to expand fleets to a common upper limit. When this proposal was rejected, Japan withdrew from the conference. The remaining delegates then concluded an agreement that preserved limits on the size and armament of individual vessels and required exchange of information on building programs. While it did not immediately touch off a naval arms race, the failure of the second London conference ended an arms control system that had for 15 years moderated naval rivalry in the Pacific.

⬛——Bōeichō Bōei Kenshūjo Senshishitsu, ed, Daihon'ei kaigunbu rengō kantai, vol 1 (1975). Kajima Heiwa Kenkyūjo, ed, Nihon gaikō shi, vol 16 (1973). Kobayashi Tatsuo, "Kaigun gunshuku jōyaku," in Tsunoda Jun, ed, Taiheiyō sensō e no michi, vol 1 (1963).

Raymond G. O'Connor, *Perilous Equilibrium* (1962). Stephen E. Pelz, *Race to Pearl Harbor* (1974). *Roger* DINGMAN

Long-Term Credit Bank of Japan, Ltd

(Nippon Chōki Shin'yō Ginkō). Private bank that specializes in long-term credit loans to businesses. There are three banks of this kind, the other two being the INDUSTRIAL BANK OF JAPAN, LTD, and NIPPON CREDIT BANK, LTD. The Long-Term Credit Bank of Japan was founded in 1952 and now ranks second in the nation among such banks. Its aim was to provide financial aid for the Japanese economy, seeking recovery from its devastation after World War II through modernization of its core industries. Initially the bank financed chiefly the steel, coal, electric, and ocean transport industries, but, keeping pace with the rapid growth of the economy, it provided long-term loans to the electric machinery and shipbuilding industries and to the chemical and other heavy industries for investment in equipment and factories. In the 1970s the bank expanded its operations to include real estate, wholesale, retail, service, and other tertiary industries. It has also offered assistance to the housing and communications industries and to urban, maritime, and space development projects. It is renowned for its market research facilities.

The demand for long-term funds for equipment investment has declined since the oil crisis of the 1970s, but the bank has provided short-term loans, similar to those offered by general commercial banks, to tertiary industries. The bank has wholly owned subsidiaries in the United Kingdom, Switzerland, Hong Kong, and Curaçao, and joint financial institutions in Belgium, Thailand, and other countries, and is active in the international long-term capital investment market. At the end of March 1982 it had funds of ¥10.3 trillion (US $42.8 billion), 68 percent of which was raised through the issuance of bank debentures. In the same year it was capitalized at ¥100 billion (US $415.4 million). Corporate headquarters are in Tōkyō.

looms

The earliest evidence of spinning and weaving in Japan is found in textile imprints on pottery of the latter part of the Jōmon period (ca 10,000 BC–ca 300 BC) and early part of the Yayoi period (ca 300 BC–ca AD 300). Fibers from tree bark and plants were made into yarn by hand knotting and twisting. Garments were made by netting, twining, braiding, and weaving with simple looms.

The primitive loom used for weaving bast fibers (fibers taken from tree bark, plant stems, and so forth) is still extant in the form of the Ainu backstrap loom used to weave *attush* in Hokkaidō. At this primitive stage the loom had no framework. Ends of the warp yarn were stretched between a stable peg and a cloth beam attached to the weaver's waist with a backstrap. A reed placed on the peg end of the warp to keep the yarns evenly apart distinguished this loom from primitive backstrap looms of other countries. The *kappeta* loom, extant in Izu on the island of Hachijōjima, is also of primitive construction. This loom weaves silk double-faced twill by the addition of multiple heddle sticks to facilitate pattern weaves with geometric designs.

During the Kofun period (ca 300–710) new techniques of weaving and dyeing were introduced from China and Korea. The type of ancient backstrap loom with foot rope which was brought from Korea at that time and which is called *jibata* or *izaribata* is still used in Japan. The *jibata* has a framework; a large, swordlike shuttle-beater; and a paddle-shaped cloth beam. The opening of the shed is operated by means of a foot rope, and the weaver takes a low seated position. Until the floor loom became dominant in the 19th century, the *jibata* was used all over Japan for weaving hemp, ramie, banana fiber, homespun silk, and cotton fabrics for household use as well as for tax payment.

The floor loom and the technique of weaving fine silk are said to have been brought to Japan in the 4th century. Although there are no records describing the floor looms of this time, the structure of later floor looms can be seen in *Kishoku ihen*, compiled by Ōzeki Masunari (1782–1845) in 1820. These floor looms (*takahata, kinubata*, and so forth) resemble Western hand looms.

Compound silk weaving using intricate patterns was done on a draw loom (*hanabata*). The draw loom features an apparatus built above the floor loom, on which one or two heddle boys (*monhiki*) sit and control the pattern by pulling on an array of strings arranged so as to raise individual warp yarns in the order that the pattern is to appear. In the early part of the Meiji period (1868–1912) the first Jacquard loom was introduced. The Jacquard loom uses a mechanical punch-card system which eliminates the need for heddle boys.

Other types of looms used in Japan are twining frames for matting, frames for braiding (KUMIHIMO), and a vertical loom with a heavy beater-heddle used for making straw mats.

■ ——Gotō Shōichi, *Kosho ni miru kinsei Nihon no senshoku* (1963). Miki Yokichirō, *Awa ai fu* (1963). Miyamoto Tsuneichi (text) and Sonobe Kiyoshi (photographs), *Nihon no mingu*, vol 2 (1965). Nishimura Hyōbu, *Shōsōin no aya* (1960). Nishimura Hyōbu, *Orimono*, no 12 of *Nihon no bijutsu* (April 1967). Nishimura Hyōbu, *Shōsōin no ra* (1967). Okamura Kichiemon, *Aratae no sho* (1970). Tahara Hisashi, *Mingu*, no 58 of *Nihon no bijutsu* (March 1971). Tsunoyama Yukihiro, *Nihon senshoku hattatsu shi* (1968). *Junco Sato* POLLACK

lord keeper of the privy seal → naidaijin

Loti, Pierre (1850–1923)

Pen name of Louis Marie Julien Viaud, French naval officer and novelist, whose delicate, sensual portrayals of exotic characters and settings won great popularity in the late 19th and early 20th centuries. Loti's visits to Japan in 1885 and 1900–1901 provided him with material for several books, including *Madame Chrysanthème* (1887) and *Japoneries d'automne* (1889); the former is particularly notable as one of the earliest successful treatments of Japan as a setting by a Western author.

Lotte Co, Ltd

Leading confectioner. Founded in 1948. Initially producing chewing gum, the firm expanded operations to include the production of chocolate, ice cream, and cookies. With its entry into the field of fruit drinks in recent years, it has become a comprehensive manufacturer of confections. Lotte has five factories in Japan and controls a sales firm, Lotte Shōji Co, Ltd, and a firm engaged in the restaurant business, Lotteria Co, Ltd. It has a factory in the United States for the production of chewing gum. Stock in the company has not been offered for public sale. Sales for the fiscal year ending March 1982 totaled ¥140 billion (US $581.6 million) and capitalization stood at ¥217 million (US $0.9 million). The head office is in Tōkyō.

lotteries, public

(*takara kuji*). Public lotteries were introduced in 1945 in order to cope with inflationary conditions in the economy and provide a source of revenue for the national and local governments. Both the central and local governments operated public lotteries until 1954; since then only local governments (prefectural governments and specified city governments) have done so. Under the law, these local governments are required to appropriate the proceeds from public lotteries to public works projects. (Prefectural governments are authorized to use the proceeds as subsidies to the public works projects of cities, towns, and villages.) Banks are allowed to bid for the concession of operating public lotteries; however, since 1966 the Nippon Kangyō Bank (now Dai-Ichi Kangyō Bank)—an operator from 1945—has operated all such lotteries in Japan. The proportion of monies from public lotteries in local government finance is only 0.2 percent, however, and it has been declining. UDAGAWA Akihito

lotus

(*hasu*). *Nelumbo nucifera*. A perennial water plant of the family Nymphaeaceae found in ponds, marshes, and paddy fields throughout Japan. Its flowers are admired for their beauty, and its rhizomes (underground stems) are used for food. This species of lotus is found in Japan, India, China, Iran, and Australia. It is believed to have originated in India and to have come to Japan from China in ancient times. The white, multiple-jointed rhizomes lie in mud underwater. At the end of fall, the tip of the rhizome grows large enough to be harvested for the food called *renkon*. Leaves grow from these rhizomes and have long petioles which grow straight up to the surface of the water. The leaf blades are nearly round in shape. In summer, the lotus produces large fragrant flowers about 20 centimeters (8 in) across on long, straight stalks rising above the water surface; they are red, pink, or white in color. In some varieties multiple flowers bloom on a single stem. The flowers bloom for four days, opening each day at dawn and closing in mid-afternoon.

The fruit has an oval shape and its receptacle, which contains the seeds, looks like a beehive. The seeds are long-lived; some believed to be more than 2,000 years old, discovered in a peat deposit by Ōga Ichirō (1883–1965), have been successfully germinated.

The lotus is first mentioned in the *Kojiki* (712), the earliest Japanese collection of legends and chronicles. Its flower has been appreciated since ancient times, and many varieties were cultivated during the Edo period (1600–1868). The lotus flower is an important symbol in the Buddhist tradition. Because it rises above the mud to bloom, the lotus symbolizes the human capacity to rise above the world's impurities and attain enlightenment. It is also the symbol of the world of Vairocana Buddha (see DAINICHI) and of the Pure Land. In Buddhist art, the lotus appears frequently on statues and ritual objects. To represent the Pure Land in miniature, a pond with lotus flowers was frequently created within temple precincts. See also WATER LILY. *Matsuda Osamu*

Lotus Sutra

(J: *Hokekyō; Hokkekyō*). A key early Mahāyāna sutra which provided a doctrinal basis for Buddhist devotional cults of the 1st and 2nd centuries AD. The Lotus Sutra (Skt: *Saddharmapuṇḍarīka-sūtra*) advocates simple devotion (even that shown by a child piling sand in the shape of a stupa or pagoda dedicated to the Buddha) as a means of enlightenment, praises those who preach its teachings, and tells of paradigmatic bodhisattva saviors who answer men's prayers. The sutra attempted to subsume the two contending traditions among the Hīnayāna (Lesser Vehicle) of disciples or "listeners" and self-enlightened ones and the Mahāyāna (Greater Vehicle) of the BODHISATTVA (J: *bosatsu*)—under the Ekayāna (J: *Ichijō*) or One Vehicle.

The authoritative Chinese translation of the Lotus Sutra, the *Miaofalianhuajing* (*Miao-fa-lien-hua-ching*; J: *Myōhō renge kyō*) or in abbreviated form *Fahuajing* (*Fa-hua-ching*; J: *Hokekyō* or *Hokkekyō*), was made by Kumārajīva in 406. This sutra was deemed by the Tiantai (T'ien-t'ai; J: Tendai) patriarch Zhiyi (Chih-i; 538–597 [J: Chigi]) the final, most comprehensive, and perfect teaching. Zhiyi emphasized the advocacy by the Lotus Sutra of the universality of the Buddha-nature and considered its teaching of the continued existence of the Buddha after his "final extinction" (Skt: *parinirvāṇa*) as an intimation of the *dharmakāya* (eternal body of law) or eternal, formless aspect of Buddhahood.

The Lotus Sutra was influential in Japan from an early date, as its inclusion among commentaries on three sutras (see SANGYŌ GISHO) by Prince SHŌTOKU (574–622) indicates. Later SAICHŌ introduced the teachings of Zhiyi on the Lotus Sutra and established the Japanese TENDAI SECT with this sutra as its canonical basis. Employed in the Heian period (794–1185) for practical and this-worldly benefits such as the protection of the nation, the Lotus Sutra gained wide popularity. The 25th chapter of this translation, which exalts the salvific grace of the bodhisattva Avalokiteśvara (J: KANNON), has often been treated independently as *Kannon-gyō* and has promoted the worship of Kannon. In the Kamakura period (1185–1333) it was the sutra of primary importance to DŌGEN and to NICHIREN, who defended the Lotus Sutra and advocated chanting its *daimoku* (title), the invocation NAMU MYŌHŌ RENGE KYŌ, as the ultimate act of devotion. The Lotus Sutra has remained a major influence in Japanese Buddhism, serving as the canon for such modern lay religious movements as SŌKA GAKKAI, RISSHŌ KŌSEIKAI, and REIYŪKAI. *Whalen Lai*

Lowell, Percival (1855–1916)

American astronomer and writer. Born in Boston; brother of the poet Amy Lowell. After graduating from Harvard College in 1876, he entered business. From 1883 to 1893 he traveled extensively in Asia and related his experiences in a series of books. *The Soul of the Far East* (1888) was praised by Lafcadio HEARN for its insights into the thought of the Orient. In *Occult Japan* (1895), he described practices and rites of SHINTŌ, in which he became interested following a trip up the sacred mountain Ontakesan. Lowell developed an interest in astronomy and founded the Lowell Observatory in Flagstaff, Arizona, in 1894. He began observations of Mars and came to the conclusion that Mars was inhabited by intelligent beings. From 1902 he was nonresident professor of astronomy at the Massachusetts Institute of Technology.

low-pollution engines

Automobile engines developed to comply with emission control standards set by government agencies. The first EXHAUST GAS

Lotus Sutra

Detail of a lavishly decorated copy of the sutra. Shown are two Heian-period noblewomen praying before an altar. Known as the *Heike nōkyō*, this copy consists of 33 decorated handscrolls. Ink, colors, gold, and silver on dyed paper. 1164. Height 25.8 cm. Itsukushima Shrine, Hiroshima Prefecture. National Treasure.

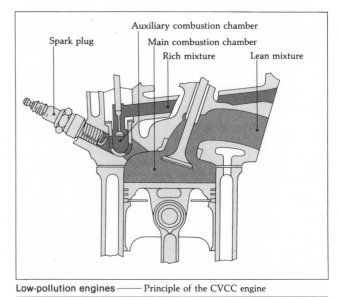

Low-pollution engines —— Principle of the CVCC engine

The engine has an auxiliary combustion chamber containing the spark plug and is otherwise similar to a conventional engine. A small amount of rich air-fuel mixture is ignited in the auxiliary chamber, and this in turn ignites a lean mixture in the main chamber.

REGULATION in Japan was established in 1966 after air pollution in urban areas had developed into a serious social problem (see ENVIRONMENTAL QUALITY). Regulations have become increasingly stringent since then, and the latest emission standards issued by the Ministry of Transport and the Environment Agency in 1976 are among the most exacting in the world. Carbon monoxide and nitrogen oxides are the primary targets of control.

Japanese auto manufacturers have developed a number of low-pollution engines that comply with environmental quality standards. These include stratified charge combustion engines, exhaust gas recirculation engines, and engines equipped with catalytic converters. In addition, research is being conducted on electric and hydrogen-powered automobiles.

The combined vortex controlled combustion (CVCC) engine. This stratified charge combustion engine developed by HONDA MOTOR CO, LTD, accomplishes more complete combustion of harmful gases by decreasing the richness of the fuel mixture. Theoretically, 15.2 grams of air are required for the complete combustion of 1 gram of gasoline. This air-fuel mixture is said to have a mixture ratio of 15.2, which is used as the standard in measuring excess air factors and is expressed as 1.

Analysis of exhaust shows that combustion with an excess air factor of 1.2–1.3 (or a mixture ratio of 18.2–19.7) produces almost no carbon monoxide and very little nitrogen oxide. However, gas vapor can only be ignited by an electric spark if it has a mixture ratio in the 9–18 range. To solve this problem, the CVCC engine uses a stratified charge. The engine has a main combustion chamber with ordinary intake and exhaust valves and an auxiliary combustion chamber with an auxiliary intake valve and a spark plug. The two chambers are connected with a torch nozzle. A rich air-fuel mixture is directed into the auxiliary chamber, while the main chamber is filled with a lean mixture. The rich gas is ignited and then gushes through the torch nozzle into the main chamber. The lean gas then burns, creating exhaust that is very low in carbon monoxide and nitrogen oxides.

The exhaust gas recirculation (EGR) engine. The amount of nitrogen oxide contained in exhaust gas increases as the temperature of the combustion rises. To reduce this temperature, some exhaust gas can be redirected into the intake manifold to mix with the air-fuel mixture in amounts controlled by a check valve. However, the use of EGR results in reduced combustion speed and thermal efficiency. In order to surmount these problems, TOYOTA MOTOR CORPORATION, developed a turbulence-generating pot (TGP) engine. As in the CVCC engine, an auxiliary combustion chamber is used, but here the purpose is different. When the burning gas flows from the torch nozzle into the main chamber, it ignites the gas in the main chamber at the beginning of the downstroke of the piston. A turbulence flow is thus created that prevents a reduction in combustion speed. A method using two spark plugs for the same purpose has been developed.

Treatment of exhaust by catalytic converter. Exhaust gas can also be purified by routing it through a catalytic converter installed between the exhaust pipe and the muffler. The catalyst is a platinum-coated ceramic or aluminum ball with a diameter of about 5 millimeters (0.2 in) that is contained in an insulated chamber. It converts hydrocarbons and carbon monoxide to water vapor and oxygen.

Electric automobiles. The weight of conventional lead and nickel-cadmium batteries has hampered efforts to develop an efficient electric automobile, since the loads such cars can carry and the distance they can be driven on one charge are limited. The uses of such vehicles are few and specialized. Fuel cells offer a possible alternative source of power. Two types have been developed, using hydrogen and oxygen or air, and hydrazine and oxygen or air, as fuel. Research has been conducted on these possibilities since 1972, and they have a promising future, although the high cost of hydrogen will remain a problem.

Hydrogen engines. Engines fueled by liquid hydrogen are very efficient, but the fuel must be transported at low temperatures and high pressures. Musashi Institute of Technology has experimented with these vehicles, while a methanol-hydrogen engine that uses methanol as the primary fuel with a small amount of hydrogen has been the focus of efforts at Kōgakuin University. See also AUTOMOTIVE INDUSTRY.

——Esso Research and Engineering Co, ed, *Evaluation of Exhaust Recirculation for NO$_x$ Control* (1975). W. R. Marshall, *Engine Performance Test of the Honda CVCC* (1969).　SONE Ken'ya

loyalty

The Confucian concept of loyalty (*chūsei, chūgi,* or *chū*) was introduced to Japan from China early in the historical period. The concept attained social and ideological significance in the feudal period, when it provided an ideological basis for the relationship of a warrior to his lord. Loyalty required service to one's lord, even at the risk of death, in return for rewards such as land titles that the lord gave or was expected to give. One's immediate superior was the primary object of loyalty in feudal Japan, so that large-scale organizations involving hundreds or thousands of people, such as the Kamakura or Tokugawa governments, were actually constructed from smaller groups that were tied together through an ascending series of loyalty relationships. The concept was later applied to the rela-

tionship between apprentices or disciples and their master in commercial or artistic fields. In the Meiji period (1868–1912), the concept of loyalty was extended to apply to the emperor and to the state as a nonpersonal entity. This was an innovation, in that this form of loyalty was not based on personal ties; it represented an attempt to adapt feudal relationships to the modern world of nation-states. See also FILIAL PIETY.　*Harumi* BEFU

loyalty to the emperor

Before the Meiji Restoration (1868), which resulted in the political reorganization of Japan as a nation state based on the principle of imperial absolutism, no principle upon which the Japanese could develop the notion of loyalty (*chū*) to the emperor (*tennō*) had been clearly articulated. Warrior society, which had predominated from the Kamakura period (1185–1333) to the time of the Restoration, had centered on the lord-vassal relationship. This relationship was seen as a reciprocal one, in which the vassal received favor (ON) in the form of property rights or grants of land in return for selfless service to his lord. With the establishment of the Tokugawa political system (see BAKUHAN SYSTEM) in the Edo period (1600–1868), the warrior class strengthened its feudalistic dominance over all segments of society. It absolutized the feudal ethics that had emerged from this medieval lord-vassal relationship, claiming that such morality had been preordained by heaven, and looked to the Zhu Xi (Chu Hsi; see SHUSHIGAKU) school of Confucianism for further ideological justification.

When the leaders of the Meiji government endorsed the virtues of loyalty and filial piety as the twin pillars of national morality, and especially when they elevated loyalty to the emperor to the level of religious belief, the feudal notion of loyalty to one's lord was in effect transformed into loyalty to the emperor, and by extension, to the nation as embodied in the emperor. Accordingly, government leaders strove to minimize the power of Buddhism and to promote Shintō as the state religion (see HAIBUTSU KISHAKU), since in Shintō the emperor was regarded as a descendant of AMATERASU ŌMIKAMI, the sun goddess and divine founder of Japan. In such a society, the people owed loyalty to the emperor, a living KAMI (god) who bestowed divine favors. In several documents issued by the Meiji government, such as the 1889 CONSTITUTION, the IMPERIAL RESCRIPT TO SOLDIERS AND SAILORS, and the IMPERIAL RESCRIPT ON EDUCATION, the new ideological basis of loyalty to the emperor was given formal articulation.　SAITŌ *Shōji*

Lucky Dragon Incident

(*Daigo Fukuryū maru* Jiken). Nuclear incident that sparked a massive outcry in Japan against American testing of nuclear weapons. On 1 March 1954 a 90.7-ton Japanese fishing boat, the *Daigo Fukuryū maru* (Lucky Dragon V), while operating in the central Pacific, was sprayed by a cloud of radioactive ash. This accident was caused by a US thermonuclear weapon test on Bikini Island (part of the Marshall Islands), 135 kilometers (85 mi) to the west of the boat. Earlier that year, US authorities had issued a general warning defining a danger zone around Bikini, but no specific warning had been given regarding the timing or location of the various tests. The Japanese crew apparently knew of the warning and assumed that they were operating outside the danger area. Their tuna trawler was in fact about 32 kilometers (20 mi) outside the zone.

Early that morning several members of the crew had noticed a bright light in the sky to the west, and about six to seven minutes later they heard a loud explosion, which they speculated might have been caused by a *pikadon*, as the atomic bomb was popularly called. Nearly three hours later sandy ash rained down on their boat. Soon most of the 23 crew members had begun to suffer nausea, pain, and skin inflammation, but they did not associate these symptoms with the explosion and made no radio report of the incident.

After returning to their home port of Yaizu in Shizuoka Prefecture on 14 March, they reported their ailments to a local doctor. An observant student passed the news to a *Yomiuri shimbun* reporter; as a result, the Tōkyō office of the newspaper scored a major scoop with its report of the incident and of the treatment of the two crew members who had been sent to Tōkyō University Hospital for examination.

The condition of the crew members and the circumstances of their injuries became matters of worldwide interest and intense concern in Japan for months to come. All of the crew members were hospitalized in Tōkyō. Several were in poor condition for some time, and one, Kuboyama Aikichi, the radiotelegraph operator, died on 23 September 1954. The precise cause of his death was disputed, some experts claiming that it was due primarily to radioactive damage to the liver and others arguing that the prime cause was infectious hepatitis brought on by frequent blood transfusions. The United States donated ¥1 million (US $2,800) to the widow as a gesture of sympathy. The remaining crew members all recovered with no apparent aftereffects despite their exposure to powerful doses of radiation aboard ship while returning to Japan.

Following extended negotiations, the United States made a payment of $2 million to the Japanese government on 4 January 1955, without admitting legal liability, to compensate for all the injuries and damages caused as a result of the five nuclear tests it had conducted in the Marshall Islands, including the damages and injuries sustained by the crew of the *Daigo Fukuryū maru*. In a statement made on 31 March 1954, the chairman of the United States Atomic Energy Commission noted that the power of the 1 March test had been about double that calculated. Experts estimate that the actual yield was the equivalent of about 15 megatons of TNT, one thousand times the power of the atomic bomb exploded at Hiroshima on 6 August 1945, and that this bomb had evidently been of a new type combining fission and fusion processes.

The *Lucky Dragon* Incident touched on several sensitive issues in Japan: the atomic legacy of World War II; disruption in the supply of fish, a principal food item; curtailment of fishing rights on the high seas; and a deep-rooted concern that the United States was insensitive to the feelings and sufferings of the Japanese people and unduly preoccupied with the development of weapons for mass destruction. See ATOMIC WEAPONS, MOVEMENT TO BAN.   *Richard B.* FINN

Lu Hsün → Lu Xun (Lu Hsün)

Luo Zhenyu (Lo Chen-yü) (1866–1940)

(J: Ra Shingyoku). Eminent Chinese classical scholar, antiquarian, and bibliographer. Luo Zhenyu was a Manchu loyalist who served in the government of the Japanese-sponsored puppet state of MAN-CHUKUO during the 1930s. Having promoted the translation of works from Japanese into Chinese, as well as Japanese language studies in China in the 1890s, Luo first visited Japan in 1901 to study its educational system. After the collapse of the Manchu (Qing or Ch'ing) dynasty (1644–1912) in 1911, he went to Kyōto, where he lived for eight years and did research on Chinese archaeology. Returning to Tianjin (Tientsin) in 1919, Luo became one of three main advisers to PUYI (P'u-i), the dethroned Manchu emperor.

In 1928, after a Manchu restoration had been suggested to Japan by Puyi's supporters, Luo went to live in Dairen (Ch: Dalian or Talien), in Japanese-controlled Guandong (Kwantung). He frequently disagreed on policy with ZHENG XIAOXU (Cheng Hsiao-hsü), Puyi's other main adviser. Zheng's acceptance of Japan's proposal for the creation of a republic in Manchuria prevailed over Luo's insistence on a monarchy, and Manchukuo was established on 1 March 1932 with Puyi as chief executive.

After serving as an official in the Manchukuo government from 1933, Luo retired to his home in Dairen in 1938, disappointed by Japanese control of the Manchukuo government.

Lutheran Church

The history of the Lutheran churches in Japan began in 1892 with the arrival of missionaries from the United States and later from Finland. After World War II, joined by other groups, they formed the Japan Evangelical Lutheran Church. There are, in addition, the Japan Lutheran Church established by the Lutheran Church–Missouri Synod and two groups in the Kansai (Kyōto–Ōsaka–Kōbe) area established by mission societies from Norway. The church has its own educational and social service institutions including the Japan Lutheran Theological College and Seminary. There is also a Lutheran publishing house, Seibunsha, which is producing a Japanese translation of the collected works of Luther in 36 volumes (1963–). In the early 1980s there were about 25,000 Lutheran church members in Japan.   *Tokuzen Yoshikazu*

Lu Xun (Lu Hsün) (1881–1936)

(J: Ro Jin). The most influential writer and social critic in modern China. Real name Zhou Shuren (Chou Shu-jen). Lu Xun was noted for his iconoclastic attacks on traditional China and for his uncompromising exposure of the inhumanity of contemporary China.

Lu Xun went to Japan in 1902 to study medicine at Sendai Medical College and remained there until 1909. Extensive reading of Western literature in Japanese translation together with distance from China enabled him to clarify his attitudes toward his own country. In 1906 he gave up his medical studies, a decision described in "Tengye Xiansheng" (Teng-yeh Hsien-sheng, 1926; tr "Mr. Fujino," 1956). Convinced that only a basic alteration of the Chinese spirit could effect the changes necessary in China, he spent the next three years in Tōkyō writing and translating and trying to introduce the literature of other oppressed countries to China through the unsuccessful journal, *Xin Sheng (Hsin Sheng*; New Life; founded 1907).

Lu Xun's most productive period lay between the literary revolution of the second decade of the 20th century (see MAY FOURTH MOVEMENT), when his first vernacular story "Kuangren riji" (K'uang-jen jih-chi, 1918; tr "A Madman's Diary," 1954) appeared in the radical monthly *Xin qingnian (Hsin ch'ing-nien*; New Youth), and the repression of leftists which came with the 1927 coup by the right wing of the Guomindang (Kuomintang; Nationalist Party). Lu Xun was a leading figure, as was his brother, ZHOU ZUOREN (Chou Tso-jen), in the Wenxue Yenjiu Hui (Wen-hsüeh Yen-chiu Hui; Literary Research Society; founded 1921) and the Yusi She (Yü-ssu She; Tatler Society; founded 1924); these groups encouraged humanism and realism in literature against the romanticism of the Chuangzao She (Ch'uang-tsao She; Creation Society), which had been founded by GUO MORUO (Kuo Mo-jo) in 1921.

After 1927 Lu Xun continued to write satirical essays and translated Russian works on literary theory. Though never a thorough or devout student of Marxism, he lent his name and prestige to the radical Zuoyi Zuoji Lianmeng (Tso-i Tso-chi Lien-meng; League of Left-Wing Writers, founded in 1930).

◼——Lu Xun (Lu Hsün), *Lu Xun Xiansheng quanji (Lu Hsün hsien-sheng ch'uan-chi*; 1938, supp. 1946, 1952). Yang Hsien-yi and Gladys Yang, tr, *Selected Stories of Lu Hsün* (1963). Yang Hsien-yi and Gladys Yang, *Selected Works of Lu Hsün* (1956, 1957, 1959, 1960).

Lyman, Benjamin Smith (1835–1920)

American geologist. Born in Massachusetts. In 1872 he was invited by the Japanese government to survey the coal and oil fields in Hokkaidō and along the Sea of Japan coastline. Until his return to the United States in 1881, he educated many Japanese and introduced them to modern techniques for the survey of natural resources. He published the first geologic map of Hokkaidō, called *Nihon Ezo chishitsu yōryaku no zu* (Geological Sketch Map of the Island Yesso, Japan), in 1876.

Lytton Commission

Commission appointed by the League of Nations in December 1931 to determine the causes of the incident near Mukden (now Shenyang) on 18–19 September 1931 that led to Japan's seizure of Manchuria (see MANCHURIAN INCIDENT). After visiting government leaders in Japan and China, the five-man commission, headed by the second Earl of Lytton, spent six weeks in Manchuria in the spring of 1932. In September the Japanese government recognized MANCHUKUO, the puppet state created by the GUANDONG (KWANTUNG) ARMY in Manchuria, despite the probable negative effect of such action on the league's deliberations. On 2 October the commission made public its conclusion that Japan had in effect been the aggressor in Manchuria. When in February 1933 the General Assembly of the League of Nations adopted the Lytton Report, the Japanese delegate, MATSUOKA YŌSUKE, walked out in protest. In March Japan announced its withdrawal from the organization, thus destroying all hope of a Chinese-Japanese accord. See also LEAGUE OF NATIONS AND JAPAN.

M

ma

A term widely used in traditional arts—especially music, dance, and the theater—to designate an artistically placed interval in time or space. By its very absence of sound or color, *ma* helps accentuate the overall rhythm or design. A musical term in origin, it initially meant a rest or rhythmic silence but later assumed metaphorical meanings and came to be used in many other arts as well.

Japanese music uses various types of *ma*, such as *homma* (whole rest), *hamma* (half rest) and *hayama* (quick rest), to create desired effects roughly in the same way that Western music does. Traditionally, however, Japanese musicians have had a greater liberty in lengthening or shortening a rest according to their interpretation of a given composition. In dance and drama also, performers have considerable freedom to insert or extend a pause in their singing, speech, and bodily movement, even when doing a time-honored classical piece. Especially in Nō drama, an actor is expected to attain highly dramatic expression when he stops all motion momentarily amidst an act. ZEAMI (1363–1443), an actor and theorizer of the Nō, once inferred that soundless and motionless moments in the Nō performance were most appealing to a seasoned spectator because it was in those moments that the performer's heart was revealed. In KABUKI, too, actors pay great attention to an interval between words or gestures and act it out in such a way that the effect of stillness may be maximized. One such interval has been codified as *mie,* a moment of emotional intensity when the actor stops all motion and turns toward the audience without speaking a word. Even in more popular forms of entertainment like RAKUGO and MANZAI, *ma* plays an important role in achieving the intended comic effect.

The concept of *ma* is also utilized outside the performing arts. Traditional Japanese painters try to create a "meaningful void" by the deliberate use of blank space. In landscape gardening, open space is placed at a strategic spot in order to enhance the effect of the whole design. In poetry, such ideas as YOJŌ ("overtones") and YŪGEN ("mystery and depth") can be seen as variations of the same concept. Among modern novelists, KAWABATA YASUNARI (1899–1972) was considered a master in the use of *ma,* as he skillfully inserted a pause or a one-sentence paragraph to create an effective caesura in the narrative flow. *Makoto UEDA*

Mabechigawa

River in Iwate and Aomori prefectures, northern Honshū. It originates in northeastern Iwate Prefecture, flows north between the Kitakami Mountains and the Ōu Mountains and enters the Pacific Ocean at the city of Hachinohe, Aomori Prefecture. Rice and apples are cultivated in the river's basin. The water is used by Hachinohe for industrial purposes. Length: 142 km (88 mi); area of drainage basin: 2,676 sq km (1,032 sq mi).

Mabe Manabu (1924–)

Painter. Born in Kumamoto Prefecture, Mabe emigrated with his parents to Brazil in 1934. While working as a farmer in a remote area of the state of São Paulo, he devoted himself to painting. He eventually became internationally known. He has held individual exhibitions in Europe and America and won a number of prizes. His works are characterized by a lyrical romanticism expressed in the French *informe* style. *SAITŌ Hiroshi*

MacArthur, Douglas (1880–1964)

Commander of the US Army forces in the Far East and supreme commander of the Allied powers (SCAP) during the Allied OCCUPATION of Japan until his dismissal in April 1951 by President Harry S.

Douglas MacArthur

MacArthur landing at Atsugi Air Base near Tōkyō on 30 August 1945 to head the Allied Occupation of Japan.

Truman of the United States. MacArthur was the son of Arthur MacArthur (1845–1912), a prominent army general who served in the Philippines and Mary Pinckney Hardy MacArthur. Born near Little Rock, Arkansas, MacArthur graduated first in his class from West Point in 1903 and served extensively in the Philippines and East Asia (once with his father, as an observer during the Russo-Japanese War of 1904–05). He was wounded twice in World War I and participated in the American occupation of the German Rhineland. After service as superintendent of West Point between 1919 and 1922 and five years in the Philippines, MacArthur achieved notoriety as commander of the forces that evicted the "Bonus Army" of unemployed World War I veterans from Washington, DC, on 28 July 1932. Chief of staff from 1930 to 1935, MacArthur next was sent back to the Philippines as chief military adviser to the new commonwealth. He resigned his US Army commission on 31 December 1937 in order to remain in the Philippines and complete his work of reorganizing the Philippine Army.

MacArthur's second career began on 28 July 1941, when President Franklin D. Roosevelt recalled him to active duty and appointed him commander of the US Forces in the Far East. In view of the rapidly deteriorating relations between the United States and Japan, the move was doubtless designed to warn the Japanese of the American determination to fight if provoked. On the same day as the attack on Pearl Harbor, American planes near Manila were destroyed on the ground by Japanese bombers. Because the attack came six hours after Pearl Harbor, many thought it should have been anticipated, and there was criticism also of MacArthur's defense of the Philippines. Ordered to leave the doomed forces at Bataan in March 1942 and retreat to Australia, MacArthur dramatically proclaimed "I shall return." He fulfilled this promise when he landed on Leyte in October 1944 after directing a counteroffensive of "island-hopping" campaigns that skillfully combined air, sea, and land forces. By the war's end, MacArthur, despite Soviet probes for a joint command, was the logical choice to be appointed supreme commander of the Allied forces. On 2 September 1945 he accepted the surrender of Japan on the USS *Missouri*.

As supreme commander, MacArthur commanded troops initially numbering some 500,000 and supervised over 5,500 military and civilian bureaucrats engaged in remodeling Japanese society. Proud of his understanding of what he called the "Oriental mind," MacArthur was deliberately aloof and grandiloquent in his pronouncements on the progress that Japan was making toward American-style democracy. Intensely anticommunist, he nevertheless favored complete disarmament, vigorous land reforms (see LAND REFORMS OF 1946), and the partial dissolution of the ZAIBATSU (financial combines). He also pressed for women's rights, a new constitution, and education for the masses. His goals were often expressed in what sounded like 19th-century classical liberal theories of freedom and rugged individualism. Underlying his programs was his intense belief, founded on his experiences in the Philippines and the Rhineland, that democracy could take hold in Japan only if the Japanese themselves implemented reform without foreign dictation and under full national sovereignty.

With the outbreak of the KOREAN WAR on 25 June 1950, MacArthur's attention was diverted from Japan to the Korean battlefield. He again proved a brilliant strategist, staging a massive amphibious landing at Inch'ŏn, behind North Korean lines, on 15 September 1950. But he misjudged the intentions and abilities of the Chinese communists and seemed surprised when they entered the war. MacArthur openly disagreed with the American administration's policy of limited response to the Chinese and insisted on retaliatory action against China. On 11 April 1951, MacArthur was relieved of his command by President Truman. Upon his return to the United States he was greeted as a hero. In speeches before Congress, at West Point, and the Republican National Convention, MacArthur appealed to patriots, and it was thought that he might become a candidate for president; however, he ended his life in retirement, keeping his rank as a five-star general.

In Japan, where he was generally respected, MacArthur's dismissal was received with shock. Ironically, the subordination of the general's military individualism to the broader dictates of civilian needs was not only the last, but in many respects the most crucial of the lessons in democracy that he was so eager to teach the Japanese people.

■ ——Douglas MacArthur, *Reminiscences* (1964). Dorris Clayton James, *The Years of MacArthur*, 3 vols (1970–). William Manchester, *American Caesar* (1978).

Peter FROST

MacDonald, Ranald (1824–1894)

Adventurer who went to Japan in the 1840s. Born in Astoria, Oregon, the son of Archibald MacDonald, a trader for the Hudson's Bay Company, and Princess Sunday, the daughter of a Chinook Indian chief. During his childhood in British Columbia his interest in Japan was aroused when he heard that three Japanese had been cast ashore near Cape Flattery. After finishing school in 1839, MacDonald served for two years as an apprentice clerk at a bank in St. Thomas, Ontario. The life did not agree with him, however, and for the next five years he traveled about the world as a seaman. It was a time of awakening American interest in the Far East, and MacDonald too wanted to visit Japan. In 1847 he left the Hawaiian Islands in the whaler *Plymouth* bound for the Sea of Japan. On 27 June 1848 he jumped ship off the western coast of Hokkaidō and made his way alone by boat to the islands of Yagishiri and Rishiri. Under the NATIONAL SECLUSION policy, no foreigners were allowed to enter Japan, and he was accordingly arrested and sent to Nagasaki. From mid-October until the following April MacDonald was held captive in a small room (he called it his "cage") in a Nagasaki temple. During that time he taught English to MORIYAMA TAKICHIRŌ and other official Dutch-language interpreters (Oranda *tsūji*), and he is regarded as the first instructor of English in Japan. He left Japan at the end of April 1849 abroad the US naval vessel *Preble*, which had come to Nagasaki to pick up 13 Western castaways. From Japan he went to Australia to join the gold rush. He returned to British Columbia in 1853, and for the next three decades he engaged in several trades, wandering from place to place. In 1885 he finally settled in Fort Colville, Washington, and spent his last years working on his memoir, *Japan: Story of Adventure*, with the help of a friend. He died before it reached print. His manuscript, edited by William S. Lewis and Murakami Naojirō, was published as *Ranald MacDonald, 1824–1894*, in 1923.

TOMITA Torao

machi bugyō

(city commissioners). Officials of the Tokugawa shogunate (1603–1867) responsible for urban commoners' (CHŌNIN) affairs, they had administrative, judicial, and police duties. The term *machi bugyō* is commonly used to mean the EDO MACHI BUGYŌ, the commissioners of Edo (now Tōkyō), the shogunal capital. Several other *machi bugyō*, collectively known as *ongoku bugyō* (commissioners of distant places), were stationed in Kyōto, Ōsaka, and other cities and major towns under direct shogunate control. The commissioners of Ōsaka and Kyōto were influential officials responsible for the governing of their large city populations and for affairs in adjoining areas. The commissioners of Fushimi, Nara, Sakai, Uji Yamada, Nagasaki, Uraga, Nikkō, Niigata, and Sado were less important. All were drawn from families of HATAMOTO rank and had staffs, office procedures, and functions roughly analogous and proportional to those of the Edo city commissioners. The *machi bugyō*, the KANJŌ BUGYŌ (commissioners of finance), and the JISHA BUGYŌ (commissioners of temples and shrines) where known collectively as the *sambugyō* (three commissioners). See also SADO BUGYŌ; URAGA BUGYŌ; BUGYŌ.

Conrad TOTMAN

machibure

Official notices issued by the shogunate or by *daimyō* to townsmen (CHŌNIN) during the Edo period (1600-1868). The shogunate issued them in Edo (now Tōkyō), Kyōto, Ōsaka, and other towns under direct shogunate control; daimyō issued them in their own castle towns. In Edo *machibure* were issued in written or oral form by the MACHI BUGYŌ (city commissioners) to ward heads (*nanushi* or *machi-doshiyori*) and monthly representatives (*tsuki gyōji*), who then relayed them to *yanushi* (house heads) under their jurisdiction. In the case of important notices, written or oral statements of receipt were required at each stage of distribution. Notices were issued in a similar manner in Ōsaka and Kyōto and in a simpler form in castle towns. See also MACHI YAKUNIN.

Conrad TOTMAN

Machida

City in southern Tōkyō Prefecture, Machida developed in the 12th century as a POST-STATION TOWN on the highway connecting the shogunal seat of Kamakura with outlying provinces. It is now principally a residential suburb, with many housing complexes. Pop: 295,354.

machine tool industry

(*kōsaku kikai sangyō*). The machine tool industry has experienced extreme ups and downs over the years, but in 1977 production totaled ￥322.2 billion (US $1.2 billion), placing Japan fourth in the world after the United States, the Soviet Union, and West Germany. Exports accounted for 37 percent of total production, with a large proportion exported to South Korea, the United States, and the Soviet Union. Imports consisted primarily of high-grade tools from West Germany, the United States, and Switzerland, and they amounted to ￥15.6 billion (US $58 million) in the same year. There are about 2,000 enterprises in the Japanese machine tool industry, most of them small to medium in size. Japanese machine tool enterprises deal primarily in medium-grade machine tools. Numerical control has been widely applied in the industry, especially to small- and medium-sized machine tools.

MATSUNAGA Seiji

machishū

Townspeople of the Muromachi period (1333–1568) and the Azuchi-Momoyama period (1568–1600), primarily those of Kyōto. The term is also used, but less frequently, to denote the inhabitants of SAKAI, ISHIYAMA HONGANJI, and other urban areas. A *machi* consists of the rows of houses facing each other across a street, but this topographical entity in the course of the 15th and 16th centuries assumed a social role, integrating several different sectors of society into a communal aggregate, the *machishū*. As the authority of the Muromachi shogunate declined after the Kakitsu Disturbance of 1441 (Kakitsu 1), these communities took on the responsibility for internal security and defense against the incursions of armed peasants (TSUCHI IKKI) into Kyōto; between 1532 and 1536, a confederation of townsmen and temples of the Nichiren sect, the Hokke Ikki, was the effective power in the city (see TEMMON HOKKE REBELLION), ruling it through "assemblymen" *(shūe no shū)*; by the middle of the 16th century, several extended associations *(machigumi)*, each comprising some dozen *machi*, had appeared. These were institutions of self-government; that does not mean, however, that they operated in a democratic manner or that they were entirely free of external control.

George ELISON

machi yakko

Also known as *otokodate*. A type of town rowdy or hoodlum of the Edo period (1600–1868). In contrast to HATAMOTO YAKKO, who claimed association with particular *hatamoto* houses, *machi yakko* had no formal affiliation with feudal authorities. *Machi yakko* congregated in organized groups *(kumi)* in Edo (now Tōkyō), Ōsaka, and other large cities. They often assumed the responsibility for, and profits from, providing *daimyō* and *hatamoto* houses with day laborers from the ranks of the urban unemployed. *Machi yakko* were bound by a code of honor and usually recognized by their dandified attire. They were given to fighting, especially with *hatamoto yakko*; the shogunate sometimes used stern measures to check them, although it did not hesitate now and then to use their services in hunting down criminals. The adventures of Banzuiin Chōbei (1622–57) have been celebrated in *kabuki* plays and popular literature. See also KYŌKAKU.

Yoshiyuki NAKAI

machi yakunin

City and town officials of commoner (CHŌNIN) status during the Edo period (1600–1868). During those centuries cities and towns under direct shogunate control were administered by officials called MACHI BUGYŌ (city commissioners). The *machi bugyō* had a small staff to administer the commoners' section of town *(machi yashiki)*, but because it was so small, he relied heavily on the cooperation of *machi yakunin*. The titles and remuneration of these officials, their manner of selection (sometimes hereditary, more often by some sort of election), and their specific functions varied from town to town, but their basic character as minor functionaries and intermediaries between the rulers and urban populace was everywhere the same.

In the case of Edo (now Tōkyō), *machi yashiki* affairs were administered by officials titled *nanushi* (or *machi-doshiyori*; ward elders), *tsuki gyōji* (monthly representatives who were chosen from among the GONINGUMI), and *yanushi* (or *iemochi*; house heads). *Nanushi* acted as the senior spokesmen representing city wards, dealing directly with the *machi bugyō* and communicating downward through monthly representatives to the heads of houses. Through this hierarchy they helped the Edo *machi bugyō* to supervise a multiplicity of urban affairs: maintaining censuses (NIMBETSU ARATAME), guard patrols (JISHIMBAN AND TSUJIBAN), and firefighting organizations (HIKESHI); communicating and enforcing governmental notices (MACHIBURE); helping to resolve disputes, ease hardships, and collect irregular tribute (GOYŌKIN); and overseeing the plethora of festivals and other social activities that punctuated *chōnin* life.

—— Matsudaira Tarō, *Edo jidai seido no kenkyū* (1921). Nomura Kentarō, *Edo* (1966).

Conrad TOTMAN

mackerel

(saba). The *saba* or Pacific mackerel *(Scomber japonicus)* is a littoral migratory fish of the class Osteichthyes, order Perciformes, family Scombridae. It grows to over 40 centimeters (16 in) in length. It is thought to be distributed roughly in the temperate to subarctic zones of the northern Pacific Ocean and adjoining waters. With a typical spindle-like form, it moves north and south along the continental shelf in large schools. Unlike the common Atlantic mackerel, it has air bladders. A closely related form, *S. tapeinocephalus*, caught commercially in Japan, is called either *saba* or *gomasaba*. The two are used for food, either raw, cooked, canned, or dried, and are among the cheapest fish in Japan. They are caught by angling, purse seine, and scoop net.

ABE Tokiharu

Madre de Deus Incident

An international incident of the early 17th century that resulted from rivalry in the Southeast Asian sea trade and helped to harden the attitude of the Tokugawa shogunate (1603–1867) against European traders and their religion. In 1608 the crews of two ships belonging to the Christian *daimyō* ARIMA HARUNOBU became involved in a fracas with the Portuguese at Macao. The disturbance was forcibly suppressed by the governor, André Pessoa, who had one of the Japanese ringleaders executed. When Pessoa came to Nagasaki in July 1609 as captain-major of the carrack *Madre de Deus,* his explanation of the imbroglio was at first accepted by the local authorities and by TOKUGAWA IEYASU, then semiretired at Sumpu. But when Arima took up the case of his men and Pessoa fell afoul of the influential Hasegawa Sahyōe (or Fujihiro, 1568–1617), commissioner of Nagasaki, Ieyasu's attitude gradually changed. Finally he gave orders for Pessoa to be seized, dead or alive. The *Madre de Deus* beat off successive attacks by Arima's flotilla for three days and nights. When it was finally boarded on the night of 6 January 1610 (Keichō 14.12.12), Pessoa decided to blow it up rather than surrender. The Portuguese from Macao were eventually allowed to renew their trade by a shogunal edict promulgated in the autumn of 1611. See also VERMILION SEAL SHIP TRADE.

—— C. R. Boxer, *The Christian Century in Japan, 1549–1650* (1951, repr 1974). Michael Cooper, S. J., *Rodrigues the Interpreter* (1974).

C. R. BOXER

Maebara Issei (1834–1876)

Samurai activist of the Chōshū domain (now Yamaguchi Prefecture). An official in the early Meiji government and later leader of the HAGI REBELLION of 1876. Like ITŌ HIROBUMI, KIDO TAKAYOSHI, and other leaders of the MEIJI RESTORATION (1868), Maebara attended the private school of YOSHIDA SHŌIN, the antishogunate intellectual and activist. He held several high offices in the new government, including army vice-minister, but resigned in 1870 due to illness. Maebara returned to Chōshū and became increasingly dissatisfied with the government's dismantling of samurai privileges (see SHIZOKU). This had produced widespread discontent among former samurai and provoked a series of insurrections in southwestern Japan. In October 1876 Maebara organized a group of former Chōshū samurai and led them in armed revolt. This uprising, known as the Hagi Rebellion, was quashed by government forces, and Maebara was caught and executed.

Maebashi

Capital of Gumma Prefecture, central Honshū; on the river Tonegawa. A provincial center since the 8th century, in the Edo period (1600–1868) it developed as a castle town and as a distribution center for silk cocoons and raw silk. Besides silk spinning, its main industries are transport machinery, electrical appliances, and lumber. The remains of an 8th-century provincial temple (KOKUBUNJI) and the mounded tombs (KOFUN) at Futagoyama and Hachiman'yama are of historic interest. Maebashi is the birthplace of the poet HAGIWARA SAKUTARŌ. Pop: 265,171.

Maeda Construction Co, Ltd

(Maeda Kensetsu Kōgyō). Firm engaged in general construction and public works projects. Founded in 1919. Noted particularly for its superior technology in the field of major public works projects, such as dams and tunnels. In recent years the firm has been developing its general construction division. Since its advances into Hong Kong in 1963, the company has been involved in the construction of roads and subways in Southeast Asia. In the fiscal year ending November 1981 revenue was ¥250.5 billion (US $1.1 billion) and capitalization stood at ¥8.1 billion (US $36.2 million). Corporate headquarters are located in Tōkyō.

Maeda family

Daimyō family of the Edo period (1600–1868). Rising from obscure origins, MAEDA TOSHIIE was awarded Noto Province (now part of Ishikawa Prefecture) by ODA NOBUNAGA in 1581, and the family rapidly increased its power and wealth through later alliances with the national unifiers TOYOTOMI HIDEYOSHI and TOKUGAWA IEYASU. Based at Oyama Castle in the city of Kanazawa, the Maeda controlled the provinces of Kaga (now part of Ishikawa Prefecture), Noto, and Etchū (now Toyama Prefecture). The income from these lands, more than 1,200,000 *koku* (see KOKUDAKA), was the greatest of any daimyō domain, and the Maeda were renowned throughout Japan as the masters of the "million *koku* of Kaga" (Kaga *hyaku-man-goku*). The Maeda daimyō, especially MAEDA TSUNANORI, encouraged Confucian scholarship and such arts as gardening and pottery, striving to make their castle town of Kanazawa into a "little Kyōto."

Maedakō Hiroichirō (1888–1957)

Author. Active member of Japan's PROLETARIAN LITERATURE MOVEMENT in the 1920s and early 1930s. Born in Sendai, Miyagi Prefecture, the illegitimate son of a carpenter. His parents separated soon after his birth, and he was adopted and raised by his mother's elder brother, a physician. He studied at a middle school in Sendai but dropped out to go to Tōkyō, where he became a disciple of the eccentric Tolstoyan writer TOKUTOMI ROKA. After a few petty jobs, including one as messenger for *Shin kigen*, a Christian socialist magazine published by ISHIKAWA SANSHIRŌ and FUKUDA HIDEKO, Maedakō left for the United States in 1907 with moral and some financial support from his mentor, Tokutomi Roka.

Maedakō first lived in Chicago with two Japanese friends, socialist anarchists who had come to America a year before him. Supporting himself by taking numerous odd jobs, he became acquainted with the Japanese socialist Kaneko Kiichi (1876–1909) and his wife, Josephine Conger KANEKO, who were joint publishers of the socialist feminist paper the *Progressive Woman*. Through them he met their friend Floyd Dell (1887–1969), the author of the novel *Moon-Calf* (1920), who was at the time editor of the *Friday Literary Review* supplement of the *Chicago Evening Post*. With the help of these people Maedakō published a few literary pieces (in English) in the *Progressive Woman*, the *Friday Literary Review*, the *Coming Nation*, and the *International*. One of these pieces was "The Hangman" (1912), a short story on the theme of the Japanese HIGH TREASON INCIDENT OF 1910, in which the radical thinker KŌTOKU SHŪSUI and 11 other socialists and anarchists were executed for an alleged conspiracy to assassinate the Japanese emperor.

Late in 1915, following the example of Floyd Dell, Maedakō moved to New York City to further try his luck with writing. He wrote a few essays, three of which, entitled "Phantasies," were published in *Bruno's Weekly*, a small Greenwich Village literary magazine. However, he was frustrated by a general lack of success and gave up writing in English. He worked as a clerk for a Japanese organization in New York and later for *Nichibei shūhō,* a Japanese language newspaper, as the editor of its yearbook. Having earned enough money from the latter job, Maedakō returned to Japan in 1920 at the age of 32. The following year he wrote the short story "Santō senkyaku" (The Steerage Passengers) for the magazine *Chūgai*, of which he had become the editor. The dynamic depiction in this story of a group of Japanese returning home from America, where they had gone to make money, contrasted strongly with the monographic, autobiographical writing of the naturalist school (see NATURALISM; I-NOVEL), and set the pattern for the emerging Japanese proletarian fiction. In 1923 Maedakō joined the coterie that published the magazine TANE MAKU HITO, a forerunner of Japan's proletarian literature movement, and the following year he joined the magazine BUNGEI SENSEN, the stronghold of proletarian writers in the early years of the movement. By 1928 Maedakō had become a leading polemicist as well as the most prolific writer of the movement. During these years he wrote several novels, plays, and numerous short stories, almost all of which were based on his experiences in the United States. From 1928 to 1929 he traveled in China, where he became acquainted with LU XUN (Lu Hsün), YU DAFU (Yü Ta-fu), and other Chinese writers; several of his stories reflect his interest in China. After the mid-1930s, when the proletarian literature movement declined, he devoted his energies to writing biographical accounts of Tokutomi Roka, autobiographical novels, and autobiographies. During his career Maedakō translated many English works, most notably those of Upton Sinclair and Sinclair Lewis. His major works include *Daibōfūu jidai* (1924, The Age of Storm), a novel; *Jūnenkan* (1930, The Ten Years), a collection of critical essays; *Ningen* (1938, Human Being), an autobiographical novel; and *Seishun no jigazō* (1958, Self-Portrait as a Young Man), an autobiography which was published posthumously. His early stories and plays are collected in *Akai basha* (1923), *Shinsen Maedakō Hiroichirō shū* (1928), and *Shinsen Maedakō Hiroichirō shū zokuhen* (1928).   KOKUBO Takeshi

Maeda Magoemon (1818–1864)

Samurai from the Chōshū domain (now Yamaguchi Prefecture) active in the movement to overthrow the Tokugawa shogunate (see MEIJI RESTORATION). An inspector in the domainal government, he associated with the ideologue YOSHIDA SHŌIN and his disciples KUSAKA GENZUI and TAKASUGI SHINSAKU and supported the proimperial, antishogunate movement in Chōshū. With the ascendancy of conservative forces within the domain following the first shogunate expedition against Chōshū (see CHŌSHŪ EXPEDITIONS) in 1864, Maeda was imprisoned and executed.

Maeda Seison (1885–1977)

Japanese-style painter. Real name Maeda Renzō. Born in Gifu Prefecture; went to Tōkyō in 1901. Studied painting with Kajita Hanko (1870–1917), a popular newspaper and magazine illustrator trained in the MARUYAMA–SHIJŌ SCHOOL. Under the influence of OKAKURA KAKUZŌ he studied ancient Japanese art. He was a member of the artist group Kōjikai, along with IMAMURA SHIKŌ, YASUDA YUKIHIKO, KOBAYASHI KOKEI, and HAYAMI GYOSHŪ, and of the reorganized JAPAN FINE ARTS ACADEMY (Nihon Bijutsuin). In 1922 and 1923 he visited Europe. In 1935 he was appointed to the Imperial Fine Arts Academy (Teikoku Bijutsuin). Three years later he traveled to China; his visit to the Buddhist cave temple sites near Datong (Ta-t'ung) inspired several paintings, including *The Stone Buddha of Datong (Daidō no sekibutsu)*. In 1944 he was appointed as a court artist *(teishitsu gigeiin)* and in 1946 as a judge of the Nitten, successor to the Ministry of Education's prewar exhibitions, or BUNTEN. He also became a professor of art at the Tōkyō Bijutsu Gakkō (now Tōkyō University of Fine Arts and Music) where he taught until 1959. When fire damaged the 8th-century wall paintings in the main hall of the temple HŌRYŪJI in Nara in 1949, Maeda led a team of art experts and painters in the task of restoration. He was honored with the Order of Culture in 1955.   *Aya Louisa* McDONALD

Maeda Tamon (1884–1962)

Bureaucrat and politician. Viewed as one of Japan's leading "internationalists," Maeda served in many public and private offices, both national and international. Born in Ōsaka, he graduated from Tōkyō University in 1909. He worked for the Home Ministry from 1909 until 1920, when he was appointed deputy mayor of Tōkyō under GOTŌ SHIMPEI. In 1923 he served as the Japanese government's delegate to the International Labor Organization (ILO). From 1928 to 1938 he was an editorial writer for the newspaper *Tōkyō asahi shimbun,* and in 1938 he went to New York to head the Japan Culture Center, established to familiarize Americans with Japanese culture. When the Pacific War broke out in 1941, he was repatriated, and during the war years he served as governor of Niigata Prefecture.

Maeda is best remembered for his activities as minister of education just after the war (August 1945–January 1946). Working closely with Prime Minister SHIDEHARA KIJŪRŌ, he worked on the draft of the rescript in which the emperor renounced his divinity (see EMPEROR, RENUNCIATION OF DIVINITY BY). Maeda hoped that this rescript would put an end to the influence of State Shintō and its ideology which placed Japan above other nations because of the emperor's divine origins. He urged that the people be told the truth and exhorted to work together to build a peaceful nation, open to foreign cultural influences. Soon after the rescript was issued, however, Maeda was "purged" by Allied OCCUPATION authorities for having served as a governor during the war. He was rehabilitated in 1950, and until his death in 1962, he engaged in various civic and international causes, most notably UNESCO and the movement for "clean elections." In all such activities, he tried to set an example of what he called "civic-mindedness," a central concern throughout his life. During his student days he was a disciple of the Christian leaders UCHIMURA KANZŌ and NITOBE INAZŌ and after the war became a Quaker.   *Akira* IRIYE

Maeda Toshiie (1538?–1599)

Prominent *daimyō* of the Azuchi–Momoyama period (1568–1600). The son of a petty baron of Owari Province (now part of Aichi Prefecture), Toshiie became a page of the presence (KOSHŌ) of ODA NOBUNAGA in 1551, the year of the future hegemon's succession to the lordship of Nagoya Castle. Except for an interlude between 1559 and 1561, when he was dismissed for killing a fellow court attendant, Toshiie remained in Nobunaga's service until his lord's violent death, rising to become one of Nobunaga's principal captains and daimyō over a province. In his later career, he became an intimate confidant of the national unifier TOYOTOMI HIDEYOSHI.

Toshiie took part in most of Nobunaga's major military operations. He fought for Nobunaga at the Battle of OKEHAZAMA in 1560, as a *rōnin* (masterless *samurai*); in the conquest of Mino Province (now part of Gifu Prefecture) between 1561 and 1567; in the campaigns against ASAI NAGAMASA and ASAKURA YOSHIKAGE from 1570 to their destruction in 1573; in the struggle against the "religious monarchy" of the Buddhist True Pure Land sect (see JŌDO SHIN SECT) and its armed confederations (IKKŌ IKKI) on the Ōsaka, Ōmi (now Shiga Prefecture), and Ise Nagashima fronts from 1570 to 1574; and at the Battle of NAGASHINO in 1575, where he distinguished himself as a commander of musketeers *(teppō ashigaru)*.

In 1575 Nobunaga reconquered Echizen (now part of Fukui Prefecture) from the Ikkō *ikki* and assigned the province to SHIBATA KATSUIE, at the same time appointing Toshiie, Fuwa Mitsuharu (d 1581), and Sassa Narimasa (d 1588), to act as inspectors *(metsuke)* of Shibata's conduct of affairs. Toshiie thereby attained a daimyō's income and status; and he became a daimyō in his own right in 1581, when Nobunaga allotted him Noto Province (now part of Ishikawa Prefecture), a vital outpost in the Oda regime's war against UESUGI KAGEKATSU, the daimyō of Echigo (now Niigata Prefecture). Toshiie was engaged in that war when Nobunaga was assassinated in 1582 (see HONNŌJI INCIDENT). In the ensuing succession struggle, Toshiie tried to mediate between Shibata Katsuie, his close associate since his youth, and Toyotomi Hideyoshi; when that effort failed and the two rivals confronted each other in 1583 at the Battle of SHIZUGATAKE, Toshiie deserted Katsuie, thereby ensuring Hideyoshi's victory and Shibata's destruction. Rewarded by Hideyoshi with the addition of two districts in Kaga Province (now part of Ishikawa Prefecture) to his Noto holdings, Toshiie that year moved his residence to Kanazawa, thus becoming the founder of the great Kanazawa domain. Apart from the shōgun's own holdings, the Kanazawa fief, assessed at 1 million *koku* (see KOKUDAKA), was the largest domain of the Edo period (1600–1868).

In the course of Hideyoshi's conflict with the future shōgun TOKUGAWA IEYASU and Nobunaga's son Oda Nobukatsu (or Nobuo; 1558–1630) in 1584, Toshiie was given the mission of protecting the northern flank of Hideyoshi's realm. The Maeda domain was invaded by Sassa Narimasa, by then daimyō of Etchū (now Toyama Prefecture); with Narimasa's defeat in 1585, most of Etchū was transferred to Toshiie. He participated in Hideyoshi's ODAWARA CAMPAIGN against the Later Hōjō family (see HŌJŌ FAMILY) in 1590 and in the ensuing sweep through Japan's northernmost provinces, which concluded the next year with the entire country subjected to Hideyoshi's authority.

Toshiie was bound to Hideyoshi by close family ties: two of his daughters, Kiku (1578–84) and Gō (1574–1634), were adopted by Hideyoshi; another, Maa (Kaga-dono; 1572–1605), was Hideyoshi's concubine. Toshiie himself ranked as one of Hideyoshi's intimate companions (OTOGISHŪ) and remained close by his side throughout the 1590s, sharing his elegant pastimes and rising to the post of provisional great counselor *(gon dainagon)* and the second rank *(ju nii)* in the imperial court through his patronage. When Hideyoshi in 1595 instituted his council of "Five Great Elders" (Gotairō), Toshiie became a member of this topmost group in Japan's governing structure. Upon Hideyoshi's death in 1598, Toshiie assumed the principal responsibility for protecting the interests of his young heir, TOYOTOMI HIDEYORI. Toshiie's own death the next year removed one of the chief pillars of the Toyotomi house and a powerful restraining influence on the ambitions of those who hoped to exploit what amounted to an interregnum. The loss of this counterpoise helped to set in motion the dramatic conflict that culminated in 1600 with the Battle of SEKIGAHARA, where Tokugawa Ieyasu won the hegemony over Japan.

◾——Iwasawa Yoshihiko, *Maeda Toshiie*, in *Jimbutsu sōsho*, vol 136 (Yoshikawa Kōbunkan, 1966).　　　　*George* ELISON

Maeda Tsunanori (1643–1724)

Daimyō of the Kanazawa domain (now Ishikawa Prefecture). He became daimyō at the age of two following the sudden death of his father and ruled his domain until his retirement in 1723. Guided first by his grandfather Maeda Toshitsune (1593–1658) and later by his father-in-law, HOSHINA MASAYUKI, he initiated reforms in his domain, especially stressing agricultural policy with a view to increasing domainal control over the peasantry. This he accomplished by converting all *samurai* fiefholders into salaried (see KIRIMAI) samurai-bureaucrats and placing all land under direct domainal administration, carrying out rigorous cadastral surveys and holding

each village responsible for a fixed amount (JŌMEN) of taxes, and strengthening village organization by giving more responsibility to peasant officials (see also KAISAKUHŌ). Tsunanori was fond of scholarship and was associated with outstanding Confucian scholars of his day. He invited one of them, KINOSHITA JUN'AN, to collect, preserve, and edit old books and documents; these materials formed the core of what is now the SONKEIKAKU LIBRARY, a collection of more than 100,000 Japanese and Chinese works.

Maeda Yoshinori (1906–)

Newspaper and broadcast journalist. Born in Hokkaidō, he graduated from Tōkyō University of Foreign Studies. After studying political science at the University of Rome, Maeda became a correspondent in Rome for the newspaper ASAHI SHIMBUN. In 1947 he left his position at the *Asahi* as general manager of the foreign news department. He joined the Nihon Hōsō Kyōkai (NHK; Japan Broadcasting Corporation) in 1950 and succeeded ABE SHINNOSUKE as chairman (1964–1973).　　　　*GOTŌ Kazuhiko*

Maeda Yūgure (1883–1951)

WAKA poet. Real name Maeda Yōzō. Born in Kanagawa Prefecture. After dropping out of middle school, he went to Tōkyō to study, and there he began to write *waka*. Associating with writers of the naturalist school such as TAYAMA KATAI and SHIMAZAKI TŌSON, he established his name around 1910 as a *waka* poet of the same school (see NATURALISM). His poems, some written in free verse, are fluid and impressionistic. His principal collections are *Shūkaku* (1910) and *Suigen chitai* (1932).

Maehata Hideko (1914–)

Swimmer. Married name Hyōdō Hideko. She was born in Wakayama Prefecture. When she was in the 5th grade, she set the Japanese record in the 50-meter breaststroke. Maehata took the silver medal at the 1932 Olympics in Los Angeles. In the 1936 Berlin Olympics she won the women's 200-meter breaststroke and was the first Japanese woman swimmer to receive a gold medal.　　　　*TAKEDA Fumio*

Maejima Hisoka (1835–1919)

Founder of the Japanese postal service. Born Ueno Fusagorō in the village of Shimo Ikebe in Echigo Province (now part of Niigata Prefecture), the second son of a farmer. His father died seven months later, leaving the boy and his mother almost destitute. A passion for education carried him through a succession of schools in Echigo, Edo (now Tōkyō), Hakodate, and Nagasaki, studying medicine, classical Chinese literature, military science, naval engineering, and English. Two long trips through most of Japan in the decade after 1854 made him acutely aware of the nation's backwardness in communications and transportation, the two fields in which his later career was concentrated. His ambition for a post in the shogunal government was blocked by his family's low status until 1866, when he was adopted as heir to a minor shogunal retainer, Maejima Jōjirō, taking first the name Raisuke and later Hisoka. (Romanized signatures on numerous documents in the 1870s show that he pronounced the surname Maeshima, not Maejima.)

As a minor official of the Tokugawa shogunate in its last days, he had some difficulty in transferring to the new Meiji government, but on 29 January 1870 he obtained a low-ranking appointment to the Mimbushō (Ministry of Popular Affairs), where his ability brought him to the favorable attention of two younger men who were rising stars in the new government, ŌKUMA SHIGENOBU and ITŌ HIROBUMI. By the summer of 1870 Maejima held the concurrent positions of vice-chief of the Taxation Office and of a fledgling Postal Communications Office. On 30 June 1870 he proposed something he had first conceived in 1862: creation of a national postal service to replace the costly, inadequate, and uncoordinated official and private courier services of the feudal era. The new service began operations in April 1871 with daily mail linking 65 post offices along the Tōkaidō highway between Tōkyō, Kyōto, and Ōsaka. There were 1,160 post offices by the end of 1872, and 5,099 spread all over Japan by 1881, when Maejima resigned as chief of the postal service.

He was also determined to open an international mail service and to induce the governments of Britain, France, and the United States to close the post offices they had opened in the 1860s in Yokohama,

Kōbe, Nagasaki, and Hakodate under the provisions of the ANSEI COMMERCIAL TREATIES. He hired an American, Samuel M. Bryan of Cadiz, Ohio, to negotiate a postal exchange treaty with the United States (ratified 18 April 1874). It was the first treaty of any kind in which a Western power dealt with Japan as an equal. The next step was the admission of Japan to the Universal Postal Union (effective 1 June 1877). Maejima was then able to persuade reluctant British (1879) and French (1880) officials to close their post offices in Japan, completing the first substantive step toward abolishing extraterritoriality.

Maejima was also a leader in organizing postal savings (1874) and money order (1875) systems, revising weights and measures (1871) and the land tax (1878), and holding the first National Industrial Exhibition (1877). In 1872 he founded one of the first successful daily newspapers, the YŪBIN HŌCHI SHIMBUN (renamed Hōchi shimbun in 1894, combined with Yomiuri shimbun in 1942). To encourage other papers, he received approval for reduced postage rates for newspapers (from 1872 on) and free postage (from 1873 to 1882) for manuscripts mailed to newspaper editors.

He was also the earliest advocate of simplifying the Japanese writing system. He urged the last Tokugawa shōgun in 1866, and the Meiji government in 1869, to replace Chinese characters with KANA syllabics in order to reduce the time and effort required for becoming literate. In 1872 he founded another newspaper, the Mainichi hiragana shimbun, written entirely in syllabics. This lasted only three months, but Maejima remained active in the writing reform movement until his death. See JAPANESE LANGUAGE REFORMS.

When his close friend Ōkuma was ousted from the government in the POLITICAL CRISIS OF 1881, Maejima also resigned. He aided Ōkuma in founding the Tōkyō Semmon Gakkō (renamed Waseda University in 1901), and served as its second president (1886–90). He was also associated with Ōkuma in founding the RIKKEN KAISHINTŌ (Constitutional Reform Party), but after 1884 his energies were devoted chiefly to a business career as president or director of five private railway companies, a mining company, a life insurance company, and the Tōyō Kisen Kaisha (Oriental Steamship Co). He was also active in organizations for seamen's aid, education for the blind and the mute, and the study of electricity.

He served as vice-minister of communications (1888–91) and as a member of the House of Peers (1904–10).

📖——Maejima Hisoka, Kōsōkon (1920, repr 1955), autobiography. Hagiwara Itaru, Nippon yūbin no chichi: Maejima Hisoka (1947).   Robert M. SPAULDING

Maekawa Kunio (1905–   )

Architect and community center designer of international recognition. Born in the city of Niigata. Upon graduation from Tōkyō University in 1928, he studied in Paris under the French architect Le Corbusier. Two years later he returned to Japan and worked in the office of Antonin RAYMOND before starting his own firm in 1935. Known for his architectural use of concrete learned from Le Corbusier, Maekawa first worked to offset the pompous style of architecture of the Japanese militarist regime of the 1930s. Since 1931, when he knowingly disregarded the rule specifying a Japanese design in the competition for the Ueno Imperial Household Museum and submitted instead an international style entry, Maekawa has been known as one of the foremost advocates of modern architecture in Japan. His representative works include the Harumi Apartment House (1959), the Setagaya Community Center (1959), the Tōkyō Metropolitan Festival Hall (1961), the Saitama Prefectural Museum (1971), and the Tōkyō Kaijō Building (1974).   WATANABE Hiroshi

Maeno Ryōtaku (1723–1803)

Physician and scholar of WESTERN LEARNING. Born in Edo (now Tōkyō). He began his medical career as a doctor of Chinese medicine (kampō) in the Nakatsu domain (now part of Ōita Prefecture) but in his late forties developed an interest in Western medicine and studied Dutch as a means of gaining access to that field. In 1771, along with SUGITA GEMPAKU and other scholars, Maeno observed a human dissection (at the time only those of the lowest classes handled corpses), using a Dutch anatomy text, Ontleedkundige Tafelen (1734, Anatomical Tables), as a reference. Impressed by the accuracy of the Dutch book, which was a translation of the German work Anatomische Tabellen (1722) by Johann Adam Kulmus (1689–1745), the group decided to translate it. The translation was completed three years later under the title Kaitai shinsho (New Book of Anat-

omy); it was the first competent translation of a Western anatomy text into Japanese. Maeno's own writings include discussions and translations of astronomy, geography, natural sciences, and architecture.

Mafune Yutaka (1902–1977)

Playwright. Born in Fukushima Prefecture; studied English literature at Waseda University but left before graduating. He was influenced by Irish theater and began to write one-act plays. His leftist leanings led him to join the agrarian movement in the late 1920s. A number of his plays, such as Itachi (1934, Weasel), have rural settings and depict the distortions of human nature among the peasant class. The play Hadaka no machi (1936, Naked City) focuses on city life and was made into a movie by director UCHIDA TOMU. After World War II, Mafune turned to comedy and farce as a means of exploring what it means to be Japanese. He also wrote scripts for radio broadcasts, and his published work includes a five-volume collection entitled Mafune Yutaka senshū (1948–50).

magatama → beads, ancient

magazines

(zasshi). Since the first Japanese magazines were published in the years following the Meiji Restoration in 1868, periodicals have had a major, independent role in shaping ideas and behavior. They have provided a vital forum for the debate of political and social ideas, and their diversity has reflected the broad range of thought in Japan. After a period of suppression before and during World War II, postwar magazine publishing experienced an explosive boom; magazine circulation doubled in the 1960s and has continued to grow in the 1970s. The history of Japanese magazines can be divided into three stages: the emergence of the first magazines of opinion and general readership in the Meiji period (1868–1912); the growth of commercial publishing during the Taishō (1912–26) and early Shōwa (1926–) periods; and the post-World War II period of mass communications.

Meiji-Period Magazines —— The first periodical in Japan to use the word zasshi (literally, "miscellaneous writings") in the modern sense of magazine was Seiyō zasshi (The Western Magazine), which appeared in 1867 under the editorship of YANAGAWA SHUNSAN. It consisted primarily of translations from Dutch magazines. After the Meiji Restoration a number of political and enlightenment periodicals appeared. The Meiroku zasshi, begun in 1874 by a group of intellectuals called the MEIROKUSHA, and NARUSHIMA RYŪHOKU's Kagetsu shinshi (1877–84, The Flower and Moon Journal) were two of these. Several other periodicals supporting the FREEDOM AND PEOPLE'S RIGHTS MOVEMENT were begun but soon ceased publication as a result of government controls on freedom of the press.

In the following decades, opinion magazines in the true sense of the word began to appear. In 1887 TOKUTOMI SOHŌ, leader of the Min'yūsha group, founded KOKUMIN NO TOMO (The Nation's Friend), the first of a genre known as sōgō zasshi, or general interest magazines. In the same year Nihonjin (The Japanese), the journal of the nationalistic SEIKYŌSHA group, also made its appearance. Its name was later changed to Nihon oyobi nihonjin (Japan and the Japanese). Taiyō (The Sun), a magazine begun by the HAKUBUNKAN publishing company in 1895, established the standard format for the sōgō zasshi and led the publishing world during the Meiji years and on into the early Taishō period. The journal Hanseikai zasshi (1887, Magazine of the Self-Examination Society), established by the temperance movement, changed its name to CHŪŌ KŌRON (Central Review) in 1899 and set a new standard for editorial practices. The magazine's literary columns were under the direction of TAKITA CHOIN and provided a springboard for many new writers in the early 20th century. In the world of belles lettres, the Ken'yūsha literary group led by OZAKI KŌYŌ began Garakuta bunko (Library of Odds and Ends), the first of Japan's LITERARY MAGAZINES.

Taishō and Early Shōwa Periods —— The Taishō years marked the beginning of intense competition among magazines in the areas of entertainment, arts, women's topics, and children's interests. The 1920s saw the commercialization of magazine publishing. KŌDANSHA, LTD, began Kōdan kurabu (Story Club) in 1911. In 1915 Hakubunkan put out Kōdan zasshi (Story Magazine). As for children's periodicals, Kōdansha introduced SHŌNEN KURABU (Boys' Club) in 1914 with the editorial slogan "interesting and useful." Its serialized stories made it the most popular children's magazine of the early

Shōwa years. In the midst of the TAISHŌ DEMOCRACY movement, YAMAMOTO SANEHIKO founded KAIZŌ (Reconstruction) in 1919. Together with *Chūō kōron*, this magazine played an important role in disseminating democratic and socialist ideas. KIKUCHI KAN's BUNGEI SHUNJŪ (Literary Annals), begun in 1923, cultivated literary talent. Kōdansha's KINGU (King) offered a varied content of serialized fiction, moralistic stories, and practical information. It reached a record circulation of over one million. Magazines aimed at a female readership included SHUFU NO TOMO (The Housewife's Friend), which was begun in 1917 and concentrated on informative articles and serialized novels. It became the model for later WOMEN'S MAGAZINES. In addition to the above publications, the Taishō years saw the start of weekly magazines and magazines directed toward children of different ages.

As Japan embarked on an imperialist course and militarists gained influence on politics, restrictions were imposed on free speech. Magazines were called on to promote patriotism, and those that took a critical stance toward the authorities, such as *Chūō kōron* and *Kaizō*, were forced to discontinue publication.

Post–World War II —— With the end of World War II, *Chūō kōron*, *Bungei shunjū*, and *Kaizō* reappeared, and several other *sōgō zasshi* were inaugurated. These included *Sekai* (World), *Ningen* (Humanity), *Tembō* (Outlook), *Nippon hyōron* (Japan Critic), and *Chōryū* (Currents). In addition, there was a veritable flood of low-grade, "pulp" magazines (*kasutori zasshi*); but this proved to be a momentary phenomenon. The appearance of *Ōru yomimono* (All Reading Matter) in 1945 and *Shōsetsu shinchō* (New Currents in Novels) in 1947 marked the start of a class of magazines concentrating on light fiction with an emphasis on entertainment. A new term, CHŪKAN SHŌSETSU (middlebrow fiction), was coined to describe such reading matter. *Heibon* (Ordinary) began in 1945 and *Myōjō* (Bright Star; not be to confused with the former literary magazine of the same name) in 1952; dealing with gossip on singers and movie stars, they were closely allied with the broadcasting and screen industries and were widely read by teenagers. The biggest development in the publishing world, however, was the sudden growth in WEEKLY MAGAZINES.

Current Trends —— In recent years magazines such as *Chūō kōron*, *Bungei shunjū*, *Sekai*, *Tembō*, *Jiyū* (Freedom), and *Taiyō*, which serve an educated readership, have been losing their popularity. In their place have appeared magazines that cater to a specific readership, such as *Heibon panchi*, *Pureibōi* (Playboy) and *Goro* for young men; *An-an* and *Non-no* for young women; and adult comics like *Manga akushon*. The young people's magazines are also directed at specific audiences: *Shōnen magajin* (Youth Magazine), *Shōnen jampu*, *Shōjo furendo* (Girl's Friend), and *Māgaretto* are examples (see COMIC MAGAZINES). Large publishing houses have also put out a wide selection of sports magazines. These magazines put great emphasis on lavish illustrations.

The spread of television has prompted magazines to emphasize the individual interests and concerns of the reading public. This tendency will probably become stronger in the future as magazines seek out new ways of attracting readers. See also PUBLISHING.

■ —— Fukushima Jūrō, *Sengo zasshi hakkutsu* (1972). Ozaki Hotsuki and Munetake Asako, *Zasshi no jidai* (1979). Saitō Seiichi, *Zasshi dai kenkyū* (1979). Shimizu Tetsuo, *Gendai zasshi ron* (1973).
SHIMIZU Tetsuo

magemono

Round or oval containers made from slips of cypress or Japanese cedar that are shaved from logs following the grain about the circumference. The slips are held over flame or softened in water and bent into shape. Joints are bound with strips of cherry bark and slats of thicker wood are used to make the bottom. Lacquer is applied to some *magemono*; others are fashioned to serve as ladles, food steamers, or containers for meals. *Magemono* are distinguished from OKE, receptacles made with wooden staves held fast with twisted bamboo hoops.
INOKUCHI Shōji

mago

(packhorsemen). Men who led packhorses carrying freight or passengers. After the establishment of POST-STATION TOWNS (*ekisei*) under the RITSURYŌ SYSTEM in the 8th century, the peasants were required to furnish horses and labor. In the middle of the Heian period (794–1185), with the development of private landed estates (SHŌEN) and the need to transport tax grain (NENGU) from the prov-

inces to the capital, larger numbers of *mago* became necessary. From the late Kamakura period (1185–1333), they were called BASHAKU (teamsters) and became the principal transporters of rural products to the towns. By the Muromachi period (1333–1568), they virtually monopolized haulage on the highways through the well-organized associations they formed. These groups became known for uprisings (BASHAKU IKKI) in protest against the erection of toll barriers and for involvement in peasant revolts (TSUCHI IKKI), as well as for terrorizing travelers. In the Edo period (1600–1868), the term *mago* referred to those packhorsemen permanently assigned to post stations (*shukuba*). *Mago* songs (*mago uta*) are an important genre of Japanese FOLK SONG.
INAGAKI Shisei

Magome Pass

(Magome Tōge). Located in southwestern Nagano Prefecture, central Honshū. The nearby post-station town of Magome prospered during the Edo period (1600–1868) because of its location on the highway Nakasendō, but declined with the opening of state roads and a railway line over the pass. Vestiges of the post-station town still remain, and the area has many historical relics. Altitude: 801 m (2,627 ft).

Magoshi Kyōhei (1844–1933)

Businessman. Born in Bitchū Province (now part of Okayama Prefecture). In 1873 Magoshi entered a Tōkyō trading company established by the influential businessman MASUDA TAKASHI; the firm was reorganized as the MITSUI Trading Company (Mitsui Bussan Kaisha) in 1876, with Magoshi as Yokohama branch manager and a company director. In 1896 he left Mitsui to become managing director of the Nippon Brewery Company. After it absorbed two other breweries, the company changed its name in 1906 to Dai Nippon Brewery Company; it soon became the largest brewery in Japan, with 72 percent of the market. A leading business figure and popularly referred to as the "King of Beer," Magoshi was associated with over 100 companies, including Tōkyō Electric and the SOUTH MANCHURIA RAILWAY. He was named to the House of Peers in 1924.

magusaba

Term used in the Edo period (1600–1868) for areas, usually fields and mountains, designated for collecting grass, foliage, and other vegetation to be used as fertilizer and fodder. Most of these areas were collectively owned, with their use restricted to a certain village or group of villages. For the right to collect, which became increasingly important with the intensification of rice cultivation, supplementary taxes (*komononari*) were usually paid to the shogunal or domainal government. See also IRIAI.

Mahiru no ankoku

(1956, Darkness at Noon). A film directed by IMAI TADASHI. (It bears no relation to the Arthur Koestler novel of the same title.) The film offers a sympathetic portrayal of a group of young working-class men who are framed by the police and pressured into confessing to a murder they did not commit. Despite a disclaimer at the film's opening that it was not based on fact, it was obvious to all at the time that *Mahiru no ankoku* depicted an actual event (see YAKAI INCIDENT). The film achieved notoriety precisely because it was released while the courts were trying a murder case involving the boys on whom the heroes of the film were based. The film clearly advocated acquittal by demonstrating that the boys could not possibly have committed the crime. TŌEI CO, LTD, the film company for which *Mahiru no ankoku* was made, refused to distribute the film soon after it was released on the grounds that it had been threatened by high government officials.

Imai's theme in the film is that Uemura, the young protagonist, had been framed because he was poor and lived on the periphery of Japanese society. Such people are portrayed as frequent targets of the police. According to Imai, the real-life Uemura and his friends had been watched by the police for some time, and when an unsolved murder presented itself, the boys were framed and sentenced to death. Their conviction was later overturned by the Supreme Court.

Imai is concerned here, as in his other films, with exposing the injustice that persists in Japanese society. Yet the plot of the film ultimately turns on fortuitous circumstances that place final responsibility on no one, as in the sequence where a policeman sees the boys at a time and place that makes their guilt impossible, yet fails to testify in their favor because he fears the loss of an imminent promotion. The finest sequence is the surreal, satiric enactment of the murder in a flashback that employs a variety of cinematographic techniques to make a mockery of the case against the boys. The judge, bored, cleans his glasses, as Imai borrows a moment from Soviet director Pudovkin's *Mother*. Finally, melodrama takes over as Uemura, sentenced to death, yells instructions to his mother: "Supreme Court! Not yet!" Critic Iwasaki Akira called the film "the Japanese Sacco-Vanzetti, Tom Mooney, and Rosenberg cases all rolled into one," although Imai has contended that the film was not intended as a political statement. *Joan* MELLEN

Mah-Jongg

(J: *mājan*). Game of Chinese origin usually played by four persons competing with 136 pieces called tiles. The two Chinese characters from which the trade name Mah-Jongg was derived literally mean "house sparrow," and it is said that the game received this name because the shuffling of the tiles sounds like the twittering of sparrows. It is thought that the game itself derives from tarot cards introduced to China from Europe. Mah-Jongg is similar to the Western card game of rummy in that the object is to collect combinations of sequences and sets of identical tiles, but the possible combinations in Mah-Jongg are much more complex. Although it takes considerable concentration and practice to learn to play well, the game may on occasion be won by a beginner, because of the element of chance involved.

Mah-Jongg was introduced to Japan early in the 20th century. By the 1920s, it had become especially popular in urban areas. Following Japanese military intervention in China in 1931, the game lost many adherents, but after World War II it achieved an unprecedented level of popularity. Today there are over 60,000 Mah-Jongg parlors in the country and more than 15 million players. Mah-Jongg has traditionally been a man's game, but in recent years the number of women players has sharply increased, and they now make up about 10 percent of the total number of players. The increase in the number of women players and its acceptance in rural areas is probably due to the fact that Mah-Jongg has begun to be perceived more as a parlor than as a gambling game.

Initially Mah-Jongg tiles were made of paper or bamboo, and later of bone or ivory. In Japan bone and ivory tiles were commonly used until about 1960, when the use of plastics became customary. There are three suits, known in Japanese as *suotsu* (called bamboos in the American version), *tontsu* (circles), and *mantsu* (characters). Each suit consists of four identical sets of tiles each numbered one to nine, making 36 tiles per suit. In addition, there are four tiles for each of the following categories: *chun* (red dragons), *paku* (white dragons), *hatsu* (green dragons), *ton* (east wind), *nan* (south wind), *sha* (west wind), and *pei* (north wind). The eight flower and season tiles, once customary in the American game, are not generally used in Japan.

Play begins by shuffling the tiles and arranging them face down in four walls 17 tiles long and 2 tiles high. Each of the four players then throws the dice; the highest scorer becomes the east wind. Thereafter each player draws 13 tiles which he places on a rack facing himself, with the east wind drawing 14 and discarding 1. Play then rotates, with a turn consisting of the drawing of one tile, either the discard of an opponent or an unturned tile, and the return face up of an unwanted tile to the table. Any player may claim the discarded tile if he has a pair in his hand of the same suit as that discarded, even if it is not his turn, but he must place these tiles face up on the table, while play continues with the person on his left. Elaborate rules are used to determine who has precedence if two or more players make a claim. Players attempt to collect various combinations of tiles, usually in numerical series or of identical kinds, with different combinations awarded different point values. Scores are settled at the end of each hand by exchanging tokens, with special sets and combinations earning different scores. A round consists of four hands, each player becoming east for one hand, and a game is completed after four rounds. KATA Kōji

Maihara

Also known as Maibara. Town in northeastern Shiga Prefecture, central Honshū, on the eastern bank of Lake Biwa. A port town since the early 17th century, it is served by several highways and lines of the Japanese National Railways. Agriculture is the main industry. The Samegai district is known for its trout fisheries. Pop: 12,633.

Maiko

Also known as Maikonohama. Coastal district in Tarumi Ward, in the city of Kōbe, Hyōgo Prefecture, western Honshū, along the Akashi Strait. Maiko was formerly famous for its pine trees, but they have largely been destroyed by automobile exhaust fumes and by land development.

Mainichi Broadcasting System, Inc

(Mainichi Hōsō). An Ōsaka-based commercial radio and television broadcasting company serving the Kinki (west central Honshū) region. Established in 1950 with backing from the MAINICHI SHIMBUN, one of Japan's largest national daily newspapers, as the New Japan Broadcasting Company (Shin Nippon Hōsō), it was one of the first commercial radio stations to operate in Japan. In 1956 it joined with ASAHI BROADCASTING CORPORATION (ABC) to form the Ōsaka Broadcasting Corporation (Ōsaka Terebi). Later it withdrew its capital funds from Ōsaka Broadcasting and founded the present Mainichi Broadcasting System in 1958. Although under the aegis of the *Mainichi shimbun*, for many years it shared a network affiliation with Nippon Educational Television (now known as ASAHI NATIONAL BROADCASTING CO, LTD), a Tōkyō-based television company affiliated with the ASAHI SHIMBUN, another leading newspaper. In 1975 it switched affiliation to the Japan News Network (JNN) belonging to the *Mainichi shimbun*-affiliated TŌKYŌ BROADCASTING SYSTEM, INC (TBS) group. It has operated since then as a secondary affiliate. NAKASA Hideo

Mainichi shimbun

One of Japan's leading national daily newspapers. The history of the *Mainichi* dates back to the *Nihon rikken seitō shimbun,* an early political news organ of the Rikken Seitō (Constitutional Government Party), a spin-off of the JIYŪTŌ (Liberal Party), which began publishing in 1882. In 1888 the name was changed to the *Ōsaka mainichi shimbun,* and the paper emerged as a general news publication aimed at the Ōsaka merchant community. MOTOYAMA HIKOICHI, who took over as company president in 1903, was responsible for transforming the *Mainichi* into a first class national news publication. A fervent believer in the commercial newspaper business, Motoyama bought up the *Dempō shimbun* in Tōkyō in 1906 and changed its name to the *Mainichi dempō.* In 1911 he merged the *Mainichi dempō* with the *Tōkyō nichinichi shimbun* which, having been founded in 1872, was Tōkyō's first daily newspaper. The *Tōkyō nichinichi shimbun* and the *Ōsaka mainichi shimbun* were placed under joint management but continued to be published under separate banners. The *Mainichi shimbun* regards the year 1911 as marking the beginning of its official publication. In 1943 the *Tōkyō nichinichi shimbun* and the *Ōsaka mainichi shimbun* were consolidated under the present *Mainichi shimbun* banner. Along with the ASAHI SHIMBUN and YOMIURI SHIMBUN, it ranked as one of Japan's three largest national newspaper companies.

In the early 1970s the *Mainichi* fell into a crippling business slump and in 1977 was forced into virtual bankruptcy. The company was completely reorganized with new capital investments. In addition to its regular daily edition, the *Mainichi* publishes special newspapers for primary and middle-school students, the English language *Mainichi Daily News,* and numerous periodicals and books. It has four main offices located in Tōkyō, Ōsaka, Nagoya, and Kita Kyūshū and a regional office in Sapporo. News is gathered from local bureaus all across the country and 23 overseas bureaus. It is a participating member of international wire services in conjunction with United Press International, Agence France Presse, and Tass and has special contractual arrangements with foreign newspapers such as *Le Monde, Le Figaro,* and the *Christian Science Monitor.* In 1979 it was capitalized at ¥4 billion. Circulation: 4.6 million (1980).

Maisaka

Town in western Shizuoka Prefecture, central Honshū, on the southeastern bank of Lake Hamana. Maisaka developed as a post-station town on the highway TŌKAIDŌ. Its main industry is fishing; eel, *nori* (a seaweed), and snapping turtle *(suppon)* are raised. The town is also noted for its musical instrument industry. Attractions include the Bentenjima Hot Spring and the Hamanako boat races. Pop: 11,151.

Maitreya → Miroku

Maizuru

City in northern Kyōto Prefecture, central Honshū, on the Sea of Japan. A castle town and port in the Edo period (1600–1868), it has been the site of a naval base since 1901. After World War II it handled Japanese repatriates from overseas. It is still an important port for trade with the Soviet Union, South Korea, and Southeast Asia. The naval base has been taken over by the Self Defense Forces. Principal industries are spinning, lumbering, shipbuilding, plate glass, and chemicals. Pop: 97,579.

Majima Toshiyuki (1874–1962)

Organic chemist known for his extensive research on urushiol, the chief component of Japanese lacquer (urushi), safflower (benibana) and other vegetable pigments, and alkaloids. Born in Kyōto, he graduated from Tōkyō University. He studied in England, Germany, and Switzerland from 1907 to 1911 and, returning to Japan, became professor at Tōhoku University in 1911. He moved to Ōsaka University in 1932 and served as its president from 1943 to 1946. He was influential in founding the Tōkyō Institute of Technology (Tōkyō Kōgyō Daigaku) and in establishing the faculties of science at Tōhoku and Ōsaka universities. He received the Order of Culture in 1949.

maki

(pasture land). Little is known about the regulation of pasturage for horses and cattle until the TAIKA REFORM of 645, when they were put under the control of the Ministry of Military Affairs (Hyōbushō). Provincial governors (kokushi) were made responsible for the raising of these animals, which were used for transportation, farming, and military purposes. The ENGI SHIKI (927) lists 71 pastures scattered throughout Japan, some of which sent more than 50 horses a year to the capital. As the power of the central government declined from the 9th century onward, such official pasture lands were increasingly absorbed by private estates (shōen) and sometimes converted to farmland; horses raised on these estates were sent to the proprietors rather than the government. Horses and pasture land became vitally important during the wars of the 12th and later centuries; one reads of conflict between proprietors and the rural populace who wished to graze their own animals in these areas or, because of growing population, attempted to farm there. Pasture land was again strictly regulated under the Tokugawa shogunate (1603–1867); the eighth shōgun, TOKUGAWA YOSHIMUNE, established major government-controlled pasture areas at Kogane and Sakura in Shimōsa Province (now part of Chiba Prefecture), and many daimyō followed suit in their own domains.

maki-e

(literally, "sprinkled picture"). Term for a class of decorative techniques used in LACQUER WARE, all employing sprinkled powders or filings, usually of gold or silver. The powder is applied to lacquered designs while the lacquer is still damp. Maki-e techniques are a distinctive feature of Japanese lacquer ware. The first record of their use in Japan dates from the 8th century AD, when the technique of decorating lacquer with coarse gold filings was referred to as makkinru. During the Heian period (794–1185), maki-e became the dominant method of Japanese lacquer decoration, combining silver and gold in complex pictorial designs of exceptional beauty.

By the Kamakura period (1185–1333), three major maki-e techniques had evolved. The earliest to appear was togidashi maki-e, ("polished-out sprinkled picture") in which a design is polished with abrasives such as charcoal to produce a clearly defined pattern and an absolutely even surface. Hiramaki-e ("level sprinkled picture"), is a simpler technique in which the sprinkled design may be coated with thin, translucent lacquer for protection, but not polished down to the surface. In takamaki-e ("relief sprinkled picture"), certain areas are built up in relief by using lacquer in admixture with other materials, prior to final decoration of the surfaces. Takamaki-e, which first appears in lacquer ware of the Kamakura period, may produce a design only slightly raised from the surface of an object or may create three-dimensional designs with a sculptural or molded quality.

An important related technique first appearing in the Kamakura period is nashiji ("pear-skin ground"), in which larger particles of gold are irregularly sprinkled on layers of translucent, amber-colored lacquer to produce an effect similar to aventurine glass. In the Edo period (1600–1868), materials other than silver and gold were incorporated in maki-e designs. Powdered colored lacquers and powdered charcoal were used in the togidashi maki-e technique to render designs similar to colored or monochromatic paintings.

The principal maki-e techniques were often used in combination with each other or with other techniques. Cut gold leaf (KIRIKANE), silver leaf, or sheet silver might be applied as an accent. Sheet lead elements are often applied to maki-e designs associated with the RIMPA artists. Raden (MOTHER-OF-PEARL INLAY), a technique introduced from China in the Nara period (710–794), is often combined with maki-e techniques and is seldom used alone in Japanese lacquer ware.

Maki-e is virtually synonymous with Japanese lacquer ware and constitutes the most highly developed Japanese decorative tradition in this medium. Historically, maki-e shows a strong interaction with other Japanese pictorial and decorative arts, and with Japanese literary themes as well.

——Arakawa Hirokazu, Maki-e, no. 35 of Nihon no bijutsu (March 1969). Yoshimura Motoo, Maki-e, 3 vols (1976).
Ann YONEMURA

Maki Fumihiko (1928–   )

Architect and urban designer. Born in Tōkyō. After graduation from the architecture department of Tōkyō University in 1952, he pursued advanced studies at Cranbrook Academy and Harvard University. He has since taught sporadically in Japan and the United States and is known for his study of urban morphology entitled, "Investigations in Collective Form" (1960). Maki began his career with the Toyota Memorial Auditorium at Nagoya University (1960). His designs, which demonstrate a concern for relating building to context, include the Risshō University Kumagaya campus (1968), the Daikan'yama Hillside Terrace Apartments (1969–73), Katō Gakuen Elementary School (1972), Ōsaka Prefectural Sports Center (1972), and the Okinawa Aquarium (1975). WATANABE Hiroshi

Makiguchi Tsunesaburō (1871–1944)

Religious leader and educator. Founder and first president of the SŌKA GAKKAI, a lay organization of the Nichiren Shōshū sect of Buddhism. Born in Niigata Prefecture, he moved to Hokkaidō in 1885 and graduated from the Sapporo Normal School in 1893. He worked as an elementary school teacher in Hokkaidō for eight years before moving in 1901 to Tōkyō, where he again became a teacher and later a principal at several elementary schools. A prolific writer, he was the author of several books, including Jinsei chirigaku (1901, The Geography of Human Life), Kyōdoka kenkyū (1912, Studies in Folk Culture), and Sōka kyōikugaku taikei (1930, The System of Value-Creating Pedagogy). In his writings Makiguchi strongly emphasized his concept of value creation (kachiron) and asserted that true happiness can be attained through the creation of values. In 1928 he became an active member of Nichiren Shōshū, and through his study of Buddhist teachings he became convinced that Buddhist ideas were exactly what he had been striving to achieve in the classroom.

In 1930 he formed the Sōka Kyōiku Gakkai (Value-Creating Educational Society; renamed Sōka Gakkai in 1945) as a vehicle for his ideas of educational reform and the spread of Nichiren Shōshū's teachings. It grew slowly during the 1930s and early 1940s. In July 1943 Makiguchi and other top officials of his organization were jailed and charged with violating the 1941 version of the PEACE PRESERVATION LAW OF 1925 (Chian Iji Hō) for their opposition to the government's war policies and to enforced belief in STATE SHINTŌ. Makiguchi died in prison in Tōkyō on 18 November 1944, but after World War II the Sōka Gakkai developed into the largest of Japan's NEW RELIGIONS.

——Dayle Bethel, Makiguchi: The Value Creator (1973).

Maki Itsuma → Hayashi Fubō

Maki Izumi (1813–1864)

Activist in the antiforeign, antishogunate movement in the last years of the Edo period (1600–1868); also known as Maki Yasuomi. The son of a Shintō priest of the Kurume domain (now part of Fukuoka Prefecture), Maki went to Edo (now Tōkyō) and then to the Mito domain (now part of the Ibaraki Prefecture), where he was strongly influenced by the proimperial MITO SCHOOL of historical studies. Returning to Kurume, he made several recommendations to the domain government on internal reform, but was ordered into domiciliary confinement for speaking out of turn. During his confinement he wrote imperial-loyalist pamphlets. In 1862 Maki secretly left Kurume for Satsuma (now Kagoshima Prefecture) to establish contact with other antishogunate activists but was captured during the TERADAYA INCIDENT, in which several imperial loyalists clashed with Satsuma samurai. Confined again in Kurume, he was released in 1863 and returned to Kyōto, where he taught at the Gakushūin, a school for the nobility that had become a center of the antishogunate movement. He fled Kyōto after the COUP D'ETAT OF 30 SEPTEMBER 1863, in which forces from Aizu (now part of Fukushima Prefecture) and Satsuma expelled proimperial extremists led by Chōshū (now Yamaguchi Prefecture). Finding refuge in Chōshū, he continued to provide ideological support for the antishogunate cause by writing pamphlets. In the summer of 1864 he joined an army of Chōshū loyalists in an attempt to retake Kyōto (see HAMAGURI GOMON INCIDENT). After a bloody engagement on 20 August (Genji 1.7.19), the insurgents were forced to retreat; two days later Maki committed suicide.

Makino Eiichi (1878–1970)

Scholar of criminal law and legal theory; prominent advocate of reform in the theory and practice of the administration of Japan's Penal Code (see CRIMINAL LAW) and CRIMINAL PROCEDURE. Born in Takayama, Gifu Prefecture, Makino graduated from the law department of Tōkyō University in 1903 and subsequently secured appointments there as lecturer and assistant professor. From 1910 to 1913 he studied abroad in Germany, England, and Italy; he was particularly inspired by a seminar on the theory of modern criminal law given by the German jurist Franz von Liszt at Berlin University. Makino returned to Japan having been strongly influenced by the theories and procedures of criminal law of the modernist school that were then sweeping Europe. In 1913 he was appointed professor at Tōkyō University, a position he held for 25 years. Even after his retirement in 1938, he continued vigorously to contribute to the development of modern legal science in Japan. During his long career he actively sought the adoption of modernist criminal law and theory. He served on a number of legal reform advisory committees and was outspoken in advocating a freer, philosophical view of penal law than the strongly entrenched narrow viewpoint which characterized the traditional interpretation of Japan's Penal Code. Makino held that crime is shaped by character and environment and that criminal law is a utilitarian, purposeful, systematic body of law to be used as a device for protecting organized society from crime. Therefore he stressed the importance of the educative view of punishment, directed toward treating and rehabilitating the criminal, as opposed to the retributive view. He based this theory on legal evolutionism, calling for liberal legal interpretation of criminal law in conformity with society's development, and rejected the excessive emphasis on the principle of nulla poena, nullum crimen sine lege ("no punishment, no crime without a law"). He asserted a theory of subjectivism in interpretive method as applied to the Penal Code in opposition to objectivism. Makino's theory of criminal law interpretation derived from an optimism vis-à-vis the nation as "the trinity of authority, technology, and goodwill." This principle of subjectivity did not necessarily find many supporters among later generations of Japanese legal scholars, but it did exert considerable influence, both tangible and intangible, on the practice of criminal procedure. Makino served as longtime editor-in-chief of Kikan keisei (Quarterly Journal of Criminal Law and Criminology) and was himself a prolific writer. His published works number over 100 volumes, including Nihon keihō (1916, The Penal Code of Japan) and the 20-volume series Keihō kenkyū (1919–67, Studies in Criminal Law). In 1950 he was awarded the Order of Culture. TAMIYA Hiroshi

Makinohara

Upland on the west bank of the river Ōigawa, southern Shizuoka Prefecture, central Honshū. An elevated fan formed by deposits from the Ōigawa. Partially covered by dense forests. It became known for its extensive cultivation and production of tea during the Edo period (1600–1868). Elevation: 60–280 m (197–918 ft); length: 25 km (16 mi); width: 10 km (6.2 mi).

Makino Masahiro (1908–   )

Film director. One of the primary creators of period films during the most fruitful period of their production in the 1920s and 1930s, and a leading director of action films until the 1970s. His father, MAKINO SHŌZŌ, was one of the pioneers of early Japanese cinema. Young Makino grew up in Kyōto movie studios. He directed his first film at age 18 and made his first masterpiece when he was only 20.

That first masterpiece is still considered one of the classics of Japanese cinema: Rōningai (1928, Street of Masterless Samurai), a devastating look at the decadent society of the Edo period (1600–1868). His period films have always been vehicles for comment on contemporary society and as such they have expressed a certain degree of nihilism. This has carried over into his later films about gamblers and gangsters. His films have usually featured heroes who are loners, often masterless samurai or outlaws, who find themselves compelled to right an injustice simply out of a sense of personal obligation. These heroes are usually opponents of conventional society. Along with ITŌ DAISUKE, Makino is the director most responsible for creating the ethos of this film genre, which gained wide following especially among the youth of the 1960s as part of the counterculture's expression of disillusionment with conventional society. Makino's themes and heroes have been imitated by other directors in film and television.

He directed 235 films in a career that stretched from 1926 to 1972, involving every major studio and several small ones. Most of his recent films were made for TŌEI CO, LTD. David OWENS

Makino Nobuaki (1861–1949)

Also known as Makino Shinken. Politician and diplomat. Born in the Satsuma domain (now Kagoshima Prefecture), the second son of ŌKUBO TOSHIMICHI, a leading statesman of the early part of the Meiji period (1868–1912); adopted by the Makino family. In 1871 Makino went abroad with his father on the IWAKURA MISSION and remained in the United States for three years. He entered the Ministry of Foreign Affairs in 1880 and served in a variety of posts, including ambassador to Italy, minister of education in the first SAIONJI KIMMOCHI cabinet (1906–08), and minister of foreign affairs in the first YAMAMOTO GONNOHYŌE cabinet (1913–14), before attending the Paris Peace Conference (see VERSAILLES, TREATY OF) in 1919 as one of Japan's representatives. Beginning in 1921, first as imperial household minister and then as lord keeper of the privy seal (both extra-cabinet posts), Makino assisted the last Meiji oligarch (GENRŌ), Prince Saionji, in mediating among the competing elites (the political parties, the military, the bureaucracy, and big business). With the rise of military influence in the early 1930s, Makino came under heavy criticism from the military and the right wing for his support of a cooperative, nonexpansionist foreign policy and was forced to leave office in 1935. He narrowly escaped assassination in the FEBRUARY 26TH INCIDENT of 1936, an aborted coup by young officers. Prime minister YOSHIDA SHIGERU was his son-in-law.

Makino Shin'ichi (1896–1936)

Novelist. Born in Kanagawa Prefecture. Graduate of Waseda University. While working as a magazine editor in Tōkyō, he gained recognition as a writer in the autobiographical style (see I-NOVEL) with his short-story collection Chichi o uru ko (1924). Progressive alcoholism and emotional exhaustion, however, forced him to return in 1927 to his rural hometown. There he developed the style peculiar to him—a combination of dream and reality, of Greek mythological figures and fantasized landscapes. Often bohemian in flavor and ironic in tone, such short stories as "Mura no stoa ha" (1928) and "Zēron" (1931) reveal his antipathy toward his family. Suffering from severe depression, he eventually committed suicide in 1936. His other works include a collection of short stories, Kinada mura (1936).

Makino Tomitarō

Makino photographed at home in the early 1950s.

Makino Shinken → Makino Nobuaki

Makino Shōzō (1878–1929)

Director, producer. Born in Kyōto. Considered the father of Japanese film. Makino was manager of a small theater owned by his mother when he met Yokota Einosuke, head of the company that later became NIKKATSU CORPORATION. Yokota hired him to produce films, the first of which was *Honnōji-gassen* (1908). Later, on a visit to Okayama, Makino saw ONOE MATSUNOSUKE performing at a small rural theater. Completely taken by Onoe's remarkable agility and lightness, Makino went on to produce 60 to 80 films a year for the next 10 years with Onoe as his leading man. These films had immediate popular appeal—thrilling tales of masterful swordsmen and nonsensical, absurd monster stories. However, the sheer number of films caused him such dissatisfaction that he left Nikkatsu in 1921 and worked independently. In 1925 he built a studio in the Omuro section of Kyōto and established Makino Productions. He popularized realistic period dramas, starring actors like BANDŌ TSU-MASABURŌ. His son MAKINO MASAHIRO followed in his footsteps, becoming a director of period films. *ITASAKA Tsuyoshi*

Makino Tomitarō (1862–1957)

Plant taxonomist. Born in Kōchi Prefecture. After dropping out of elementary school, he studied botany on his own. In 1893 he became an assistant instructor at Tōkyō University and later an instructor. He helped publish *Shokubutsugaku zasshi* (The Botanical Magazine) and wrote *Nihon shokubutsu zukan* (1940, Illustrated Flora of Japan). He contributed greatly to the development of plant taxonomy in Japan and identified as many as 1,000 new species of plant. He was posthumously awarded the Order of Culture. *SUZUKI Zenji*

Maki Ryōko (1777–1843)

Calligrapher of the latter part of the Edo period (1600–1868). He was born in Echigo (now Niigata Prefecture) in a post-station town called Maki, from which he took his surname. He took his art name Ryōko from a nearby lake full of water chestnuts (*ryōko*). His parents died when he was young, so he traveled to Edo (now Tōkyō), where he became the pupil of KAMEDA BŌSAI. Ryōko quickly established a reputation as a poet and calligrapher, and in the latter art was considered one of the two leading masters of his day, along with

ICHIKAWA BEIAN, in Edo. In contrast to Beian, who attracted many followers from the governing elite, Ryōko, like his teacher Bōsai, appealed to Edo townsmen, but their influence on succeeding generations was equal.

While Ryōko's calligraphic style follows that of Bōsai, it is less dynamic and imaginative, being closer to the fluid style and grace of the Chinese masters Zhao Mengfu (Chao Meng-fu) and Dong Qichang (Tung Ch'i-ch'ang). He suffered from palsy in his late years and his line began to tremble, but this quality too was admired and widely imitated. *Stephen ADDISS*

Maki Yasuomi → Maki Izumi

Maki Yūkō (1894–   )

Pioneer of modern Japanese mountain climbing. Born in Miyagi Prefecture. In 1921, after graduating from Keiō University, Maki made the first ascent of the east face of the Eiger in the Bernese Alps. Four years later he made the first ascent of Mt. Alberta in the Canadian Rockies. In 1956 he led the first Japanese party to ascend Manaslu (Nepal). Member of the Japan Alpine Club; honorary member of the British Alpine Club. *TAKEDA Fumio*

makoto

(sincerity; Ch: *cheng* or *ch'eng*). *Cheng* is the cardinal virtue and metaphysical principle underlying the Five Virtues of Confucian teaching. Expounded as a central concept in the Confucian classic, *Doctrine of the Mean* (Ch: *Zhongyong* or *Chung-yung*; J: *Chū-yō*), it came to mean both the essence of humanity and the Way of Heaven. The unchanging principle that rules all things in heaven and on earth was thus taken to be the manifestation of *cheng*. The school of the Chinese Neo-Confucian philosopher Zhu Xi (Chu Hsi; J: Shushi) revered the *Zhongyong* and emphasized *cheng*, interpreting it as truthfulness and equating it with the universal principle *li* (J: *ri*). In order to approximate *cheng* with regard to personal conduct, the school enjoined seriousness of attitude (*jing* or *ching*; J: TSUTSU-SHIMI).

In Japan, ITŌ JINSAI and other nonorthodox Confucian thinkers interpreted *cheng* or *makoto* as sincerity of mind or heart that should rule relationships between individuals and take priority over *li*. At the same time, in the native SHINTŌ tradition, *makoto* (*ma*, true or genuine; and *koto*, words or conduct) was considered an essential virtue that underscored purity and honesty of mind or heart. Thus the term *makoto* was often used by Shintoists and KO-KUGAKU (National Learning) scholars of the Edo period (1600–1868); to some of the latter, it was considered to be the spirit of WAKA composition. *ŌNISHI Harutaka*

Maksimovich, Kark Ivanovich (1827–1891)

Russian botanist. Born near Moscow, the son of a doctor. Studied medicine and botany at the university in Dorpat (now Tartu). In 1853 he studied the flora of the Amur River region, and in 1860 he came to Japan, where he studied the distribution of plants in various areas of the country. He is said to have been consulted by many Japanese botanists of the time, and his findings influenced subsequent Japanese plant taxonomy. *SUZUKI Zenji*

makura kotoba

("pillow words"). Conventional epithets used in Japanese poetry to modify certain fixed words. *Makura kotoba* were used for images or tonal elevation and usually occupied one five-syllable line, modifying the first word in the following line. For example, in the following poem (GOSEN WAKASHŪ no. 659) by Taira no Sadabumi (also called Taira no Sadafun; d 923), *chihayaburu* ("mighty") is a *makura kotoba* modifying *kami* ("gods"):

Nanigoto o	What remains
Ima wa tanoman	On which I might rely?
Chihayaburu	Abandoned, I
Kami mo tasukenu	Find even mighty gods refuse
Waga mi narikeri	To lend a helping hand.

Makura kotoba appear in the poetry of the 8th-century chronicles, the KOJIKI and NIHON SHOKI, and were popular in the MAN'YŌSHŪ (compiled ca 759). Afterward, the technique of KAKEKOTOBA, or "pivot words," gained predominance, and the original meanings of many makura kotoba were lost. The device continued to be used by later poets, however, to elevate the language of a poem by recalling the glories of bygone days.   *Susan Downing* VIDEEN

Makura no sōshi → Sei Shōnagon

Makurazaki

City in southern Kagoshima Prefecture, Kyūshū. A well-known base for bonito fishing, it also produces tea. A government tea experimental station is located here. The ancient port of BŌ NO TSU is nearby. Pop: 30,063.

Malayan Campaign

Japanese invasion and conquest of the Malay Peninsula and the British territory of Singapore at the beginning of World War II. Commanding officers were Lieutenant General YAMASHITA TOMOYUKI and Vice Admiral Ozawa Jisaburō. The main military units that participated were the army's 25th Division and 3rd Aircraft Group and the navy's Southern Fleet. A surprise landing made on 8 December 1941 at the base of the Malay Peninsula, together with landings in southern Thailand, caught the British forces off guard. Japanese troops swiftly moved down the western coast of the peninsula through territory considered impassable and captured Singapore on 15 February 1942. At sea, in the Battle of the SOUTH CHINA SEA on 10 December, the major defending forces of the British Royal Navy were destroyed. See also WORLD WAR II.   *Kondō Shinji*

Malaysia and Japan

One of the first contacts between Japan and the Malay Peninsula dates back to the mid-16th century, when the Jesuit missionary Francis XAVIER arrived at Kagoshima on 15 August 1549. Xavier was accompanied by Anjirō, a *samurai* from Satsuma (now Kagoshima Prefecture) who had escaped to Malacca after having committed murder. After the Tokugawa shogunate established the NATIONAL SECLUSION policy in 1636, there was little intercourse between Japan and Malaya except through traders from the Ryūkyū Islands who called annually at Malacca, where they exchanged the products of Japan and China for the merchandise of the cosmopolitan port.

Only after the Meiji Restoration in 1868 did Japanese arrive and settle in Malaya. At the end of the Meiji period (1868–1912) there were more than 2,300 Japanese, of whom 1,700 were KARAYUKI SAN (women sold into prostitution and sent abroad). Most of them were sent back to Japan in 1920 when the British colonial authorities issued a decree abolishing prostitution. An increasing number of Japanese were attracted to economic opportunities in Malaya, and the rubber boom marked the beginning of Japanese economic interests in Malaya. The fluctuations in the rubber industry during and after World War I caused some Japanese to look for other fields of investment. The commercial and strategic importance of iron mining attracted a few farsighted Japanese. Iron mining soon became a Japanese monopoly, most actively carried on in Johore and Trengganu by two Japanese companies, Ishihara Sangyō and Kuhara Kōgyō. The last of the three major industries in which the Japanese asserted a dominant control was the local fishing industry.

During the 1930s Chinese in peninsular Malaya were actively engaged in the anti-Japanese boycott movement and helped the CHIANG KAI-SHEK government with financial and material contributions. When the Japanese army invaded Malaya in 1941–42, the *kempeitai* (military police) executed many people suspected of anti-Japanese activity in the Chinese community. Japanese atrocities committed during the military occupation period (1942–45) developed into the "BLOOD DEBT" INCIDENT between Japan and Malaysia in 1962. The Japanese occupation spurred the rise of the postwar Malay communist movement. Communist leaders of the anti-Japanese nationalist movement went into the jungle following the fall of Singapore in February 1942 and organized the Malayan People's Anti-Japanese Army (MPAJA). Aided by the British, the MPAJA harassed the Japanese. The communists, primarily Chinese, murdered Malay collaborators, contributing to the outbreak of bitter and bloody racial strife between the two ethnic groups in the postwar years. Following Japan's capitulation, the MPAJA emerged from the jungle as national heroes but had to fight the British for the

control of Malaya, which led local British authorities to declare an "emergency" in 1948. The communists were suppressed by the mid-1950s. Another legacy of the Japanese occupation was the emphasis on the spiritual training of Malay youths, a central value of Japanese militarism, at schools in Malaya and Japan. The indoctrination strengthened anticolonialism in Malay youths and fostered a spirit of self-discipline and self-confidence, which helped the young trainees in the difficult task of nation building following independence in 1957.

In postwar years Japanese have been engaged in a wide range of activities from investment in manufacturing to natural resources exploitation, construction of dams and irrigation projects, Youth Volunteer Corps assistance, educational support in Japanese language and studies, as well as agricultural and vocational training. Most Japanese activity dates from late 1966, when a yen credit for $50 million worth of goods and services was granted to the country (renamed Malaysia after 1963) for project aid in its first five-year plan. More than 200 Japanese firms are operating in Malaysia, mostly in joint ventures. One of the largest joint ventures is the Malayawata steel mill in Prai, opposite Penang, which began operating in late 1967.

Malaysia, with rich natural resources such as rubber, tin, palm oil, lumber, copper, and petroleum, is important to Japanese industry; Japan is of importance to Malaysia's five-year plans, which are aimed at industrializing the nation. Mutual interdependence in Japanese-Malaysian relations is indicated by trade figures. In 1980 Malaysia's exports to Japan were valued at $3.47 billion, an increase of 6.6 percent compared with the figure of 1979, while Japan's exports to Malaysia were estimated at $2.06 billion, an increase of 36.8 percent over the 1979 figure. Also, the Japanese government has signed a treaty with the government in Kuala Lumpur to guarantee safe passage in the Malacca Strait and has contributed $3 million toward the revolving funds set up by the Malaysian government. Malaysia is one of the nations receiving aid under the so-called Fukuda Doctrine (Japan's commitment to economic aid for ASEAN, the Association of Southeast Asian Nations) toward the construction of a fertilizer factory.

Each year the Japanese government offers 12 Mombushō (Ministry of Education) scholarships for Malaysian students to study for two to four years in Japan with a monthly stipend of ¥160,000 (about $640 in 1982). Approximately 150 Malaysians have graduated from Japanese universities and have organized an alumni association in Kuala Lumpur. The JAPAN FOUNDATION also has been assisting the University of Malaya's Japanese program for more than 10 years by sending professors and Japanese language teachers. The Japan–Malaysia Association in Tōkyō is active in promoting friendship and mutual understanding between the two nations.

📖——Yōji Akashi, "Japanese Military Administration in Malaya—Its Formation and Evolution in Reference to Sultans, the Islamic Religion, and the Moslem Malays, 1941–1945," *Asian Studies* (April 1969). Yōji Akashi, "The Japanese Military Administration of Malacca, 1941–1945," *Melaka* (1982). Yōji Akashi, "The Kōa Kunrenjo and Nampō Tokubetsu Ryūgakusei: A Study of Cultural Propagation and Conflict in Japanese Occupied Malaya, 1942–1945," *Shakai kagaku tōkyū* (March 1978). Chin Kee Onn, *Malaya Upside Down* (1976). Yuen Choy Leng, "Japanese Rubber and Iron Investments in Malaya, 1900–1941," *Journal of Southeast Asian Studies* (March 1974). Yuen Choy Leng, "The Japanese Community in Malaya before the Pacific War: Its Genesis and Growth," *Journal of Southeast Asian Studies* (September 1978).   AKASHI *Yōji*

Mamiya Rinzō (1775–1844)

Early 19th century explorer who discovered Sakhalin's insularity and made the first recorded voyage by a Japanese up the Amur River. Born the son of a barrel maker in Hitachi (now Ibaraki Prefecture), Rinzō (he is referred to by his given name) studied cartography under the geographer INŌ TADATAKA and from 1800 worked as a surveyor for the shogunal administration in EZO (now Hokkaidō) and the southern Kuril Islands. In 1807 he fought and was wounded in a Russian raid on Etorofu (Iturup). Ordered to reconnoiter Karafuto (Sakhalin), he explored its southern periphery with Matsuda Denjūrō (b 1769) in 1808. The following year, on his own initiative, he traveled alone up the west coast and discovered that, contrary to prevailing Japanese and Western theories, Sakhalin was separated from the continent by a strait. Without returning for further instructions, he crossed over to the mainland, ascended the Amur River, and made contact with Manchu officials at Deren (Te-jen), a tribute collection post located about 128 kilometers (80 mi) downstream from the present Soviet city of Komsomolsk. Rinzō's reports, *Kita Ezo zusetsu* (An Illustrated Account of Sakhalin) and *Tōdatsu kikō* (Travels in Tartary), made important ethnographic as well as geographic contributions to knowledge. The last half of Rinzō's career proved anticlimactic and in some ways tragic. He became a shogunal spy and informer and is thought to have been instrumental in bringing about the arrest of the cartographer TAKAHASHI KAGEYASU in 1828, after the latter had secretly exchanged some maps with the Bavarian naturalist Philipp Franz von SIEBOLD during Siebold's visit to Edo as a member of the Dutch mission. Rinzō died alone, impoverished, and ostracized by many former colleagues. After returning to Europe, Siebold publicized Rinzō's discoveries ("Mamiya Straits") which were duly recorded on Western maps.

📖 —— Hora Tomio, *Mamiya Rinzō* (1960).   John J. STEPHAN

Mampukuji

Head temple of the ŌBAKU SECT of ZEN Buddhism located in Uji, Kyōto Prefecture. Founded by the Chinese monk INGEN (1592–1673), the temple complex is especially noted for the pervasive stylistic influence of Ming-dynasty (1368–1644) China to be found in its architecture, decorative art, and statuary. Groundbreaking took place in 1661 on land contributed several years earlier by the shōgun TOKUGAWA IETSUNA. The dharma hall *(hattō),* built with a donation by the former chief elder *(tairō)* Sakai Tadakatsu (1587–1662), was dedicated in 1662, and construction of the entire complex was virtually complete by 1669. An important contributor to Ingen's effort to establish the Ōbaku sect as an independent branch of Zen in these early years was Ryūkei Shōsen (1602–70) of the temple MYŌSHINJI. Chinese monks exclusively held the abbacy at Mampukuji until 1740, when Ryūtō Gentō (1663–1746) became the first Japanese to be appointed as its 14th abbot. Thereafter Chinese and Japanese monks alternated as superiors of the monastery until 1786; since then only Japanese have succeeded to the abbacy at Mampukuji.

Most of the present temple buildings date from the time of its founding. No other temple in Japan preserves so well the Ming style of BUDDHIST ARCHITECTURE brought from China. Its four primary structures, consisting of a *sammon* (main gateway), *tennōden* (heavenly kings hall), *butsuden* (Buddha hall), and *hattō,* lie in a straight line at the center of the temple compound. Arranged to the left and right are various meditation and residence halls connected by corridors.

Mampukuji is likewise widely known for its carvings, calligraphy, and paintings also executed in the Ming style. Many of the carvings among its large statuary collection were done by the Chinese craftsman Han Dōsei (Ch: Fan Daosheng or Fan Tao-sheng). Best known are statues of the eccentric monk Hotei (see SEVEN DEITIES OF GOOD FORTUNE) and Idaten (Skt: Skanda), a guardian deity of monks. His work is also represented by statues of the 16 RAKAN (Skt: *arhat*), or worthy ones. Other statues, some anonymous, include carvings of the Shitennō (Four Heavenly Kings), Śākyamuni Buddha, Anan (Skt: Ānanda), and Kashō (Skt: Mahā-kāśyapa). The most famous specimens of calligraphy preserved at Mampukuji are by the so-called Ōbaku *sampitsu,* the three calligraphy masters of Ōbaku (Ōbakusan Mampukuji being the formal name of the temple). These three masters were its founder Ingen, Mokuan (1611–84), and Sokuhi (1616–71). Among its celebrated paintings are a portrait of Ingen done by the NAGASAKI SCHOOL master Kita Genki; also preserved at Mampukuji are paintings by such renowned artists as KANŌ TAN'YŪ (1602–74), IKE NO TAIGA (1723–76), and ITSUNEN (1601–68).   Hoyu ISHIDA

Manabe Akifusa (1667–1720)

Adviser to the sixth and seventh Tokugawa shōguns, TOKUGAWA IENOBU and Ietsugu (1709–16; r 1713–16). Born in Oshi, Musashi Province (now Saitama Prefecture). Manabe, the son of a retainer to Ienobu, was appointed Ienobu's page in 1684. He quickly became a favorite of his master and when Ienobu was made shogunal heir, Manabe accompanied him to Edo Castle. His responsibilities and personal wealth increased rapidly, as he proved himself a talented administrator. Appointed SOBAYŌNIN (grand chamberlain) in 1709, he had direct access to the shōgun at all times. When Ienobu died in 1712, he was succeeded in 1713 by the four-year-old Ietsugu. Manabe conducted governmental affairs during the short reign of the child shōgun, but in 1716 the capable TOKUGAWA YOSHIMUNE became shōgun, and Manabe lost his position of power. In 1717 he

was transferred to Murakami (in what is now Niigata Prefecture), where he died a few years later.

Manabe Akikatsu (1804–1884)

Senior councillor *(rōjū)* of the Tokugawa shogunate; supporter of the great elder *(tairō)* II NAOSUKE and a leading figure in the suppression of critics of the shogunate (see ANSEI PURGE). Manabe was *daimyō* of the small Sabae domain (now part of Fukui Prefecture); he held several important offices in the shogunate bureaucracy before his appointment in 1840 as Nishinomaru *rōjū* (Nishinomaru senior councillor), i.e., as assistant to the shōgun's chosen successor. He resigned this post in 1843 following disagreements with his fellow councillor MIZUNO TADAKUNI. Thereafter, he developed an interest in foreign affairs and associated with scholars of WESTERN LEARNING. When Ii Naosuke became *tairō* in 1858, Manabe was appointed senior councillor *(rōjū)* and given the difficult task of obtaining imperial approval for the signing of the ANSEI COMMERCIAL TREATIES, which opened Japan to relations with Western countries. Having initiated a wide-scale purge of critics of the shogunate, Manabe managed to obtain imperial sanction in 1859 but only on the condition that the treaties be abrogated in the near future. Soon afterward Manabe lost Ii's favor and was forced into retirement.

management

With few exceptions, large Japanese enterprises are now managed by professional managers. The origins of the professional manager go back to pre–World War II Japan. As the ZAIBATSU (the large prewar financial combines) expanded and diversified, the families began to turn over the management of their vast enterprises to capable, qualified professional managers. Family control was, of course, indispensable, but by the 1930s, professional managers came to assume the major management responsibilities. This trend became firmly established in the postwar era, as the *zaibatsu* were dissolved and stock ownership became widely disbursed.

Entry into a managerial career is based almost entirely on education rather than ownership. A study of 1,500 senior executives of major Japanese enterprises revealed that only 6 percent of the sample attained their present positions through ownership, and the remaining 94 percent through other means. A college education has become all but essential. Of the 1,500 sample executives, 90 percent had college degrees or the equivalent. Moreover, as many as 60 percent of these men (there are virtually no women among Japan's top managers) had graduated from one of the six best-known universities. Since the best universities are publicly supported, the cost of education is low, and opportunities for obtaining the best education are widely available. In this respect, Japan is among the most upwardly mobile societies in the world.

Personnel Practices —— One of the most prominent features of the Japanese managerial system is the practice of so-called lifetime employment. Management trainees are recruited directly from colleges yearly to begin work in April and are expected to stay with the company for their entire working careers. In other words, at least among large enterprises, there is virtually no inter-company managerial mobility. One is not dismissed for any reason short of serious moral misconduct. Incompetence or poor performance do not usually constitute grounds for dismissal (see also EMPLOYMENT SYSTEM, MODERN).

The practice of lifetime employment has a number of managerial implications. First, the recruitment of managerial personnel is a very important matter to a Japanese corporation. To the college graduate, the choice of the first job is even more important, since once the decision is made it is almost irreversible. Of course, a few do switch jobs in their lifetime, but they usually must be prepared to pay a rather high price for doing so. Second, under such an arrangement, it is impractical to recruit college graduates for specific positions. Individuals are rotated throughout the corporation from time to time. Thus, what is sought at the time of recruiting is not particular know-how; rather, the individual's personal attitudes and attributes are the most carefully examined traits. Third, though the commitment to employees is not, of course, legal in character, the ingrained tradition that it will not dismiss employees short of drastic circumstances reduces the flexibility of a corporation. However, the system is not without advantages, the most important of which is that the practice encourages organizational loyalty and commitment. Moreover, management training and career planning are somewhat facilitated.

Another distinct characteristic of Japanese employment practices is the reward system. The most critical criterion is seniority, and ability and performance are considered only within the overriding framework of seniority. One's degree of seniority is determined by the year in which one joined the company, and ties between those who joined in the same year are strong. Career progress in Japanese corporations is highly predictable, well paced, and meticulously controlled. At least up through the middle management ranks, advancement is almost automatic, and progress is highly orderly. However, one should not conclude from this that ability and performance are completely ignored. While they do play a part in career advancement, the Japanese style differs from that commonly found in large American enterprises in two major ways. One is that the time span over which one is evaluated is much longer and the reward is not immediately forthcoming. Excellent ability and performance are rewarded almost imperceptibly at first; then, only after 10 or more years, are they slowly translated into tangible rewards.

The second distinction from common American practice is that performance evaluation tends to be less formalized. One is watched constantly by his superiors, peers, and subordinates over a period of time, and the reward manifests itself only when there is a consensus that special recognition is deserved. Even then, this is done within the framework of seniority. By the time one reaches the middle management rank, advancement is accelerated for those with proven capacity and performance. For example, such an individual may be advanced to a managerial position, such as chief of a section, a year or two ahead of his less distinguished colleagues. Moreover, he is likely to be placed in charge of more important functions. By the time one reaches the upper middle management ranks, differences in advancement patterns become quite notable. Promotion to the top management ranks is highly selective and competitive.

The lifetime commitment and seniority-reward system requires mechanisms to ensure a regular turnover. For this reason, compulsory retirement for all but top management comes fairly early, usually between 55 and 60. Another mechanism frequently employed is transfer to the company's subsidiaries, related firms, and suppliers, where the employee will often work fewer hours for less pay. For some workers, such a transfer is not possible, and many of them will look for postretirement work elsewhere (see RETIREMENT). For high-ranking financial, corporate, and government officials, it is sometimes possible to find well-paying jobs with other institutions after retirement (see AMAKUDARI).

Just as career advancement is carefully paced within the overriding framework of seniority, so is compensation. Compensation consists of cash payment and fringe benefits, the latter being an important element. Major fringe benefits may include housing, recreational facilities, and liberal expense accounts. The cash compensation consists of base salaries and semiannual bonuses. The bonuses have become a regular part of the compensation system and are sometimes as high as 50 percent of the total annual salary. While the bonus is basically tied to the monthly salary, performance factors are considered to a limited degree. The fact that bonuses and benefits account for such a large percentage of one's yearly income helps to account for the low degree of mobility between companies.

Managerial compensation has been growing steadily during the past two decades. In 1978 the monthly average salary was ¥235,000 (about US $1,180). It is, however, still considerably lower than the American counterpart. Starting monthly salary (cash component) averages about $500. Likewise, the compensation for top management is substantially lower than in major American corporations.

Organizational Structure and Decision Making—— The organizational structure of a large Japanese corporation closely resembles—in outward appearances—its American counterpart. Beyond this superficial similarity, however, the manner in which the organization is structured and, more importantly, the manner in which it functions differs markedly from American organizational concepts and practices.

The basic unit of an organization is the group. A task is assigned to and performed by a group rather than by individuals. It is no exaggeration to state that the individual, at least historically, existed only as a member of the group and not as a strong, clearly identifiable and distinct entity. The task is defined on the basis of the group, the assignment is carried out by the group, and the responsibility is shared by all. What is required of a leader under such an organizational arrangement is to first create and then maintain a climate in which every member of the organization can work together harmoniously.

The ringi system. Closely related to the organizational structure is the decision-making pattern. The decision-making process commonly followed in a large bureaucratic organization is known as the *ringi* system. It has often been described as the approval-seeking process whereby the proposal, known as the *ringisho,* is prepared by a lower functionary, works its way up through the organizational hierarchy in a highly circuitous manner, often at a snail's pace, and at each step is examined by the proper officials, whose approval is indicated by affixing a seal. Somehow, out of this process, a decision emerges. Such a description, while partially true, does not capture the essence of the system but represents only the procedural aspect whereby the decision already reached is formally approved.

The substance of the *ringi* system is far more dynamic. Indeed, the *ringi* system defies a neat and clear definition. It is characterized as a from-the-bottom-up, group-oriented, and consensus-seeking process, and in fact possesses all these elements, but its essence is found in their dynamic interaction. The *ringi* system is intricately related to the strong emphasis the Japanese have traditionally placed on implicit understanding. One consequence of this is an aversion to the explicit definition of organizational goals and policies, and a strong preference for dealing with each major decision on an individual basis as the need arises, evaluating it on its own merits. It is from-the-bottom-up in the sense that the need for decision is first recognized by those at the operating level—typically middle management. It is group-oriented and consensus-seeking in that various interest groups which may be affected by a decision, as well as those who must implement it, participate in the decision making. A final decision emerges from this process of group interaction, rather than being made explicitly by an individual who occupies the formal leadership role. This consensus-building process is carried out through such subtle and informal interpersonal interaction as discussion, consultation, persuasion, bargaining, or arm-twisting.

The dynamic but informal interaction that characterizes every stage of decision making is the very essence of the *ringi* system. From the very early stage during which a decision is first being shaped, various ideas and alternatives are explored, albeit very informally. Different interests are accommodated and compromises are sought. At the same time, the process of education, persuasion, and coordination among various groups takes place. Thus, by the time the final decision is made, virtually all the major elements of decision making except implementation have been completed.

Another elusive element in the *ringi* system is the role of the formal leader. In this system the formal leader is not a decision maker in the classical sense. In the Japanese organization, while the status of a leader is meticulously defined, his role in the decision-making process is little differentiated from that of other members of the organization. In other words, the leader participates with his subordinates in the decision-making process. Thus, the degree to which the leader's view is incorporated into a decision depends largely on how well he is accepted and respected by his subordinates and on the kind of relationships he enjoys with them.

For the *ringi* system to operate effectively, certain conditions must prevail. First, as observed earlier, there must be heavy reliance on informal personal relations. Much of the discussion, negotiation, bargaining, and persuasion is performed through mobilization of personal networks. To make this possible, the organizational and physical setting must be such as to encourage regular and frequent face-to-face interaction. Moreover, not only are such opportunities necessary for the process of making a specific decision, but, more importantly, they are essential to building and maintaining the personal relations upon which the system is based. The need for frequent and close contacts is further reinforced by the very nature of interpersonal relationships in the Japanese cultural setting.

Another basic condition for making the *ringi* system effective is the need for a high degree of shared understanding and values among the participants. Moreover, participants are expected to be totally familiar with the climate of an organization and to have unswerving loyalty to it. Since anything important is not likely to be explicitly defined, participants in the system are expected to have a good feel for what is acceptable and possible within a given organizational context, how a decision is to be presented, who must be consulted, and how each must be approached. Moreover, communications often take the most subtle forms. In a system where individuals are bound to an organization for their entire working career, disagreements and conflicts on a particular issue must be managed in such a way as not to disturb subsequent relationships. Communications under these circumstances must be subtle, discreet, and indirect. Participants are required to understand the implications of the most oblique cues. They must be able to read the real meaning into what for outsiders may seem to be a most casual comment. To be able to do so requires a strong sense of shared understanding and common interest. In large Japanese corporate organizations, such shared understanding and organizational commitment are developed in a most elaborate manner.

This development process begins with the recruiting system, and is reinforced through subsequent personnel practices. Young men are carefully selected from among the graduates of outstanding universities and have thus already survived a series of rigorous screening processes and are highly homogeneous in their ability, training, background, and values. From their very first day in the company, they go through an intensive socialization process during which they are indoctrinated with the values of the particular firm. After a number of years, as one goes through the well-structured advancement system, he develops a high degree of shared understanding and commitment.

In the *ringi* system, there is no explicit control mechanism whereby the outcome of a particular decision is closely monitored and measured. The eventual outcome of a particular decision becomes known to virtually everyone concerned with that decision through their shared understanding and commitment. Such knowledge becomes, without doubt, an important input to subsequent decisions proposed by that particular group. Through their shared understanding and organizational commitment, the participants are assured of a reasonable degree of certainty that a decision, once made, will be implemented in the best interests of the organization.

Japanese practices are by no means static and are undergoing gradual change, but nevertheless the patterns described above are today commonly found in almost every large Japanese corporation.

Michael Y. YOSHINO

management of affairs

(jimu kanri). Legal term referring to the administration of the affairs of another in the absence of a legal or contractual duty to do so. Paying off a friend's obligatory duty to a third person and repairing a neighbor's broken fence during the neighbor's absence are two examples of management of affairs. Although management of affairs is undertaken in good faith for the sake of another, the CIVIL CODE contains several provisions recognizing the right of the person undertaking such a task to, for example, claim reimbursement for expenses incurred (Civil Code, art. 702). It is unusual for such rights and duties to arise in the absence of a contractual relationship, but these provisions were intended to enable the person undertaking the management of the affairs of another to recover at least those expenses which resulted in a benefit to the other party.

Persons undertaking the management of the affairs of another usually are not deemed to have any right to claim a fee for the work. However, in the case of the recovery of a lost article, the finder has been given, as an incentive, the right to claim a finder's reward of between 5 to 20 percent (usually 10 percent) of the value of the article recovered.

KATŌ Ichirō

managerial careers

Management as an identifiable career for talented individuals has at least as long a history in Japan as in any Western country. Large family concerns during the Edo period (1600–1868) allowed capable head clerks *(bantō)* to rise to significant responsibilities, often adopting the clerk into the family through marriage to a daughter. In the late 19th century, graduates of the newly established universities were even recruited into firms as professional managers. Following World War II, organizations such as the Japan Committee for Economic Development (Keizai Dōyū Kai) promoted the concept of professional management with public responsibilities, thereby furthering acceptance of the notion that ownership and control of a firm ought to be separated—the so-called managerial revolution.

Most large firms recruit only male college graduates as managers. Recruitment often begins late in the junior year, with recommendations from professors, standardized examinations, and personal interviews used as screening devices. Many firms recruit primarily from just a few universities, thereby using the university admissions process as a preliminary screen.

A job offer is typically seen as a lifetime commitment—high stakes for both the company and recruit. All the persons hired in a given year enter the firm on the same date, often 1 April, the beginning of Japan's fiscal and academic year. On this date there is usually a formal ceremony, attended by top management, to induct recruits into the firm's "family."

After a training period, a prospective manager is usually assigned to a section *(ka),* consisting of about six members. The section has responsibility for a set of tasks, and is headed by a section chief *(kachō),* who often has a very paternalistic relationship with the members of the section. The section chief is usually judged on ability to train young members as well as on ability to accomplish the section's tasks.

Although a young prospective manager may transfer among several sections, it usually takes at least 10 years before he is promoted to the level of section chief, or even assistant section chief. During this period, pay raises are largely a result of automatic seniority provisions, though merit pay differentials may also exist.

After promotion to section chief, the next major promotion may take as long as another 10 years. Usually several section chiefs report to a department head *(buchō).* At the rank of department head, perceived merit plays a much larger role in determining reward and future promotions. Department heads have usually been with a firm for two decades, and are thus widely known among their colleagues. A department head's status roughly equals the prestige associated with the title of vice president of a company in the United States.

Depending on the firm, a variety of titles may or may not exist beyond the level of department head. For most firms, top management consists of those who have been promoted to the board of directors. Japanese firms usually have a board of directors composed almost entirely of their own managers, unlike those in the United States, where outside directors play a major role. Japanese boards average around 40 members, twice the size of American boards. For a Japanese manager, promotion to the board of directors usually is an extremely important culmination of a successful career.

Managers who do not reach this level must retire around the age of 55, receiving a retirement allowance of a few years' salary. Some retirees may be rehired by the firm on yearly contracts at reduced salaries. Members of the board are usually given several extra years of employment. Since the reward system is based on seniority, these last years are relatively lucrative, and may even be considered a form of deferred compensation for earlier work done at lower wages.

The top spot of company president *(shachō)* is often given to someone who can act as a unifier and consensus-builder for the company. In many firms when a new president is appointed, all the managers older than he must retire, so that the president will have more seniority than everyone else. In some firms, however, the position of chairman of the board is even more powerful than the president's.

A few very astute and powerful older managers may continue to serve the firm as advisers or consultants following their retirement from the highest levels. These managers, drawing on the experience and personal contacts of a lifetime, commonly act as elder statesmen for the firm. See also COMPANY WELFARE SYSTEM; SENIORITY SYSTEM.

■———Thomas A. Rohlen, *For Harmony and Strength* (1974). M. Y. Yoshino, *Japan's Managerial System* (1968).

Thomas B. LIFSON

managerial ideology

Managerial ideology, in the limited sense used here, refers to ideas and values which attempt to legitimize the power of industrial managers, elicit the cooperation of the work force, and provide a defense against outside intervention into labor relations. The extent to which individual managers in Japan actually accept these values and practice what they preach are separate issues that must be treated elsewhere (see EMPLOYMENT SYSTEM, MODERN).

Prewar Ideology———In Japan prior to World War II, managerial ideology was based upon service to the nation, the *samurai* spirit, paternalism *(onjō shugi)* or familism *(kazoku shugi)* within an enterprise, and a sense of the uniqueness of Japanese culture.

The emphasis on service to the nation and the samurai spirit emerged early in the Meiji period (1868–1912) when influential business spokesmen like SHIBUSAWA EIICHI (1840–1931) sought to disassociate themselves from the old merchant class, which was allegedly too selfish and parochial to contribute significantly to Japan's economic progress. In contrast, it was claimed, the modern businessman (*jitsugyōka*, "man of enterprise") deserved government support and public trust precisely because he, like the public-spirited samurai heroes of the past, was willing to put the national interest before self-interest. Shibusawa often took the extreme view that the quest for private profit had no place in properly motivated business management. Even in milder statements of these themes in subsequent decades, Western doctrines of economic individualism and the centrality of the profit motive were implicitly or explicitly rejected.

PATERNALISM and Japan's cultural uniqueness became central themes only at the turn of the 20th century when industrial managers faced the threat of government intervention into labor relations. In countering proposals for factory laws aimed at regulating working conditions and mandating welfare benefits, most business spokesmen did not depend upon the standard Western ideological arguments, which stressed the sanctity of private property, laissez-faire economic principles, or social Darwinist notions of individual responsibility. The Japanese businessmen claimed that foreign models of labor legislation would be harmful to national progress and social stability, given Japan's particular circumstances. Executives from the emerging ZAIBATSU (financial and industrial combines) and other employers insisted that the government should not place restrictions on Japanese industry when it was still in its infancy, because survival in the international arena depended upon keeping labor costs low. They also claimed that such government intervention would never be necessary since Japanese managers—unlike Western capitalists—were motivated by a deep concern for the well-being of their workers, with whom they enjoyed a familylike relationship within the company enterprise. This stress on paternalism was soon developed into a full-blown defense of what came to be conceived of as a uniquely Japanese cultural heritage. Factory laws or other labor legislation were thus opposed on the grounds that legalistic intervention would jeopardize the traditional work ethic and destroy harmonious relations in the workplace. Unless weakened by the needless imitation of Western models of industrial relations, this cultural tradition would provide Japan with a natural immunity against the dreaded disease of class conflict, which had accompanied industrialization in the capitalist West.

The same appeals to cultural uniqueness and the special character of Japanese managers were intensified in the 1920s to counter criticism by left-wing political activists and labor union organizers. In the 1930s the primary threat to business interests came not from the left but from the right, which included both terrorist agitators, who resorted to assassination attempts on business executives, and the more respected advocates of national military strength, who attempted to harness industry to a new political order. Once again business spokesmen responded by asserting that their samurai-like commitment to the national purpose distinguished them from foreign capitalists and the proponents of economic liberalism among Japan's Western enemies, and thus made reform of Japanese industry unnecessary.

▰——R. P. Dore, "The Modernizer as a Special Case: Japanese Factory Legislation, 1882–1911," *Comparative Studies in Society and History* 11.4 (1969). Byron K. Marshall, *Capitalism and Nationalism in Prewar Japan: The Ideology of the Business Elite, 1868–1941* (1966).
Byron K. MARSHALL

Postwar Ideology——Postwar managerial ideology has retained many of the tenets of prewar ideology at the same time that private enterprise has accepted a place within a pluralistic institutional framework. This framework includes a widespread, powerful labor movement, comprehensive regulatory legislation, and cooperative business-government planning of industrial structure and investment. In this context, the basic elements of postwar ideology have taken shape as follows.

Two well-known practices of Japanese management are career-long employment and the age-based wage and SENIORITY SYSTEM. These practices are deeply rooted in the Japanese understanding of the individual in society, where the position of the individual is determined by the nature of his context, as in a family. The Japanese tend to accentuate the interdependence of human relationships. Thus, the idea of contract, though legally comparable to that in the West, receives quite different treatment. The unstated common recognition of the status and stability of relationships, as within a family, can often override the stated articles of contract. Therefore, although the owners of a business contractually retain the right to discontinue employment, an employee is fired only if he violates the rules of society and disgraces the company family. By the same

token, seniority, with its historical legitimacy, has been reinforced in the postwar period. The policy of paying more to older employees who have larger families to support and less to younger, single employees was a rational way to allocate limited resources while retaining a hierarchical structure.

Employee identification with the company in Japan is often evidenced by reference to "my company." This sense of ownership can be traced to traditional conceptions of PROPERTY RIGHTS. Although these rights have historically been held by the head of the family, the father, and passed from him to his eldest son, the family head was not normally allowed to sell the property. In a sense, he was not so much owner of the property as its consignee: property was passed on from ancestors for caretaking and was not to be used up or disposed of, but rather kept, protected, improved, and passed along to descendants. Property ownership was essentially in the hands of the family as a whole, not one generation or a single individual.

This sense of property rights influences the concept of ownership in Japanese enterprises today. The firm is felt to be the property of all its members. The "public" character of ownership was reinforced during the period of rapid economic growth during the 1950s and 1960s, during which most business expansion was financed through borrowing rather than issuing of shares. Corporate leadership is also not, in reality, controlled by shareholders. The company president is generally the one who holds the strongest balance of influence among the members of a firm. Once he assumes office, he plays the role of the eldest son who has succeeded the family head; he is even expected in many cases to choose his own successor upon retirement.

Although acquisition of another company is entirely legal, to take over another company or force it into bankruptcy is regarded as somewhat immoral and often considered the equivalent of burglary. This does not mean that competition is not intense: enterprises are always struggling for a larger share of the market. Yet competitiveness is accompanied by an equally strong sense of cooperation, especially in relation to Japan's international competitive position.

The close relationship between business and government in Japan has given rise to the term JAPAN INCORPORATED. The government's primary role is that of coordinating and reconciling different interests and developing a continuing consensus. ECONOMIC PLANNING by the government is often the product of discussions between government and business leaders, and those plans which are not the result of such a consensus are not likely to be carried out. In some senses, the government role in nurturing new industries (such as the computer industry) and overseeing the development of growing industries can again be compared to the role of the father: the government-business relationship might better be expressed as the "Japanese family."

Given the stigma attached to the nationalism and feudal spirit of prewar ideology, much of the expression of managerial ideology has been toned down and the importance of democratic institutions is recognized. Continuity with the past, however, remains strong, especially within the context of the corporate "family." See also CORPORATE CULTURE.
USHIRO Masatake

man and vegetation in prehistoric Japan

A recent major focus in the archaeological sciences has been to reconstruct past environmental conditions in relation to man's cultural activities. Fossils and remains found in bog and lake sediments tell us about the ancient environment; in particular, fossil pollen and spores are extraordinarily resistant to decay once they are embedded in the sediments. The study of the different types of pollen and spores found in various sediments (the science of pollen analysis or paleopalynology) provides indispensable information concerning man and his plant environment, such as which types of vegetation existed in what climates, which plants were cultivated, when agriculture began and so on.

Paleolithic Period——This period extends from the last interglacial to the late-glacial period, spanning approximately 90,000 years from about 100,000 to 12,000 years ago. The last interglacial vegetation in the Japanese archipelago differed only slightly from that found today. In terms of pollen assemblage, the last interglacial period corresponds to what palynologists call Pollen Zone I-3 (which stands for the third or the last major interglacial period). Cool-temperate forest species, such as umbrella pine (*Sciadopitys verticillata*), montane hemlock (*Tsuga sieboldii*), montane fir (*Abies firma*), beeches (*Fagus crenata* and *F. japonica*), boreal conifers, and birches (*Betula platyphylla* and *B. ermanii*) flourished in the northeast and in the highlands of the archipelago. The southwestern part of the archipelago was covered by evergreen oak-laurel forests (laurilignosa; J: *shōyō jurin;* see SHŌYŌ JURIN BUNKA), together with cool-temperate montane fir and hemlock forests. There is also evidence that Indian crape-myrtle *(Lagerstroemia indica)*, whose natural distribution is confined today to the hot and warm regions of Asia, grew along the coastline of southwestern Japan.

During the subsequent glacial (Pollen Zone G-4) period, there was a decrease of 6–8° C in mean annual temperature; the above species and some other warm-temperate species disappeared from the archipelago. Yeddo spruce *(Picea jezoensis)*, Hondo spruce *(P. jezoensis* var. *hondoensis)*, subalpine hemlock *(Tsuga diversifolia)*, Japanese larch *(Larix leptolepis)*, Korean pine *(Pinus koraiensis)*, and other boreal plants now found only in the mountains of central Japan and Hokkaidō covered the lowlands of northeastern Japan and mountainous regions from the Chūgoku region to Shikoku and Kyūshū. However, even during this glacial period, a warm interstadial occurred from time to time, and temperate plant species, such as umbrella pine, Japanese cedar *(Cryptomeria japonica)*, and beeches often migrated northward.

The present Inland Sea region became land throughout the last glacial period and was covered with parklike vegetation as a result of the relatively dry climate created by the rain shadow effect of the Chūgoku and Shikoku mountains. These dry regions south of Honshū became the habitat of the so-called Huangt'u fauna, the animal assemblage originating from the parkland vegetation zone of China. During the last glacial maximum from about 25,000 to 15,000 years ago, Hokkaidō was characterized by tundra in the north and coniferous taiga in the south, making ideal environments for the woolly mammoth *(Mammuthus primigenius)*, which probably crossed over from the Eurasian continent by the northern landbridge. Boreal forests extended as far south as the highlands of the Chūgoku region; deciduous hardwood forests species were scattered along the coastal zones south of about 37° N latitude.

Paleolithic people lived in these environments, but the origin and chronology of their cultural remains in Japan have not been fully understood. What is clear, however, is that Japan, located at the easternmost reaches of the Eurasian continent, was the last region to which man and culture came from the continent. Although the early paleolithic era, ostensibly from about 100,000 to 30,000 years ago, covered a relatively long span of time, there are only a few archaeological sites that can be assigned to this period. This has been viewed as evidence of the extremely small size of population at that time. By estimating probable population densities in primitive living conditions and the carrying capacity of a given ecosystem, and by extrapolating back from the earliest possible known census data from the Edo period (1600–1868) as a control, the population about 40,000 years ago has been estimated at several hundred people at most. However, remains of the late paleolithic culture between 30,000 to 12,000 years ago have been excavated at approximately 1,000 sites, indicating that late paleolithic man maintained discrete cultures at widely scattered places in the Japanese archipelago.

Late-Glacial Period——The latest paleolithic period of about 14,000 to 12,000 years ago coincides roughly with the early late-glacial period (15,000 to 10,000 years ago) and the beginning of a rapid warming trend. Following characteristics of pollen assemblage, this period is divided into two zones, L I (15,000 to 12,000 years ago) and L II (12,000 to 10,000 years ago). The L I zone includes boreal conifers, haploxylon pines *(Pinus parviflora, P. koraiensis,* and *P. pumila)*, and birches (mainly *Betula platyphylla* var. *japonica* and *B. ermanii)* in the region to the north of Japan and temperate conifer species (e.g., *Abies firma, Picea polita,* and *Tsuga sieboldii)* in lowlands of southwestern Japan.

At the onset of the L II period, the Chūbu and Tōhoku regions remained covered with boreal forests, and deciduous broadleaf forests flourished only along the coastal zones south of the Kantō region. With the rapid warming of the climate, boreal species began to retreat to the north or the uplands and were replaced by deciduous broadleaf forests. These forests provided an abundance of foods which included varieties of acorns, horse chestnuts, chestnuts, walnuts, beechnuts, and hazelnuts. This was a fortunate turn of events, in view of the fact that the number of animals available for food was on the decrease. A spurt in population and advances in hunting techniques, together with climatic conditions, led to the extinction of numerous animals, such as the woolly mammoth, Naumann's elephant *(Paleoloxodon naumannii)*, giant elk *(Megaloceros yabei)*, bison *(Bison occidentalis* in the Inland Sea region and *Leptobison Kinryuensis* in the Tōhoku region), horse *(Equus nipponicus)*,

wild boar *(Sus nipponicus)*, tiger *(Panthera tigris)*, leopard *(Panthera pardus)*.

L II corresponds to the mesolithic or transitional period between the paleolithic and Jōmon cultures (sometimes referred to as Incipient Jōmon). The mesolithic is clearly separated from the paleolithic culture by the existence of earthenware pottery which was most likely used for the collection, storage, and cooking of plant foods that were increasingly available from this period onward. No drastic increase in the population was evidenced during this period, however, and the total probably numbered no more than several thousand.

Postglacial Period——The postglacial period or Holocene epoch began with some rise of temperature. Pollen zones of postglacial Japan are known as R I, R II, and R III (R = recent). R I (10,000 to 7,000 years ago) is a transitional period from the plant life of the late-glacial to the warmest phase of the mid-postglacial R II period, the so-called hypsithermal interval or climatic optimum. As the climate further warmed, the vegetation migrated from south to north. During the R II period (7,000 to 4,000 years ago), the archipelago was covered for the first time with stable climax forests. R III (from about 4,000 years ago) shows a slight cooling trend and some changes in vegetation. The timing of the chronology of these pollen zones differs by one thousand years or so depending on the locality.

R I. The distribution of vegetation in the Japanese archipelago during the R I period can be briefly summarized as follows. Areas of northern Kyūshū and southern Shikoku were covered with laurilignosa forests; the interior of the Shikoku, Chūgoku, and southern Tōhoku regions, with deciduous broad-leaved forests; and northern Tōhoku to Hokkaidō, with birch-dominated forests. From the Chūgoku region to the Kantō Plain, where the laurilignosa predominates today, the R I zone can be subdivided into R Ia and R Ib. The R Ia/R Ib zonal boundary is placed at the first sign of some increase of trees of the genus *Cyclobalanopsis* (cyclic cup oak), although cool-temperate elements (mainly *Fugus* and *Lepidobalanus* or scaly cup oak) were still dominant during the R Ib period. An average date for the boundary was about 8,500 years ago, but the opening of the R Ib period was time-transgressive in a northerly direction because *Cyclobalanopsis* together with other laurilignosa species were migrating northward.

By far the largest concentration of archaeological sites is found in the Kantō region, followed by the mountainous regions of Tōkai and Chūbu, and next, Kyūshū. This is explained by the abundance of such foods as chestnuts, walnuts, and acorns in Kantō and Chūbu and of horse chestnuts and acorns in Kyūshū. In either case, the people preferred to live in somewhat montane regions rather than along the coast, since wild boar, deer, bear, and other animals made their homes in these forested areas. But as time passed, these animals became so scarce because of overhunting that people turned to birds and to fish and other marine organisms for animal protein. Dependency on shellfish is particularly noticeable in the period from the end of R I to R II. Conjecturing on the basis of the carrying capacity of the ecosystem and the population of the Yayoi period (ca 300 BC–ca AD 300), during this period (corresponding to the Earliest Jōmon [ca 7500 BC–ca 5000 BC]) the population is estimated to have been several thousand. By the end of the period (about 7,000 years ago) the population rose to some 40,000 people.

R II. The average annual temperature was about 2.0° C higher than today. It was also a period of stable climatic conditions, permitting the development of climax forests in all regions. Southwestern Japan and the Kantō Plain were covered with laurilignosa, and the Chūbu and Tōhoku regions with deciduous broadleaf forests. Japanese cedar *(Cryptomeria japonica,* one of the excellent indicators of plentiful rainfall) began to spread rapidly by the end of the R II period in all of the San'in region and the Izu Peninsula.

The continuing warming trend, coupled with the subsidence of the coastal plains, pushed the sea farther inland, raising the sea level; it reached the present level by about 5000 BC. The transgression continued further, and during the period from about 4000 BC to 3000 BC, the sea level was a few meters higher than it is today. This is known as the Jōmon transgression. The Sendai, Kantō, and Ōsaka plains, along with other areas, were partially submerged (see SHELL MOUNDS). The shallow ocean waters provided outstanding feeding and breeding grounds for shellfish, and the people of the Early and Middle Jōmon periods (ca 5000 BC–ca 2000 BC) clustered along coastal areas and the edges of lakes. Shell mounds are especially numerous on the coast along the Pacific Ocean from the Tōkai to Tōhoku regions, where the difference between high and low tide is as much as one meter. Midden deposits at these sites also yield

Man and vegetation in prehistoric Japan

Correlations between Cultural, Geological, and Vegetational Events over the Last 100,000 Years in Japan				

Years Before Present	Geological Epoch and Glacial Period		Pollen Zones[1]	Vegetation	
				Southwestern Japan	Northeastern Japan
400 500 600 700 800 900 1,000	Holocene	Postglacial	R IIIb	Japanese red pine and herbs (including rice paddy and farmland weeds)	Japanese red pine and herbs (including chiefly farmland weeds) *Intensified forest clearance begins*
1,500 2,000 2,500 3,000			R IIIa	Intensified forest clearance begins Laurilignosa (with some spreading of beech and deciduous oaks)	Deciduous hardwood forests (with some expansion of boreal forests and Japanese cedar)
4,000 5,000 6,000 7,000			R II	Laurilignosa (Japanese cedar begins to spread)	Deciduous hardwood forests
8,000 9,000			R Ib R Ia	Deciduous hardwood forests (with early Holocene pioneering species)	Deciduous hardwood forests (with birch in the Tōhoku region)
10,000 12,000	Late Pleistocene	Late glacial	L II	Temperate conifers (with haploxylon pines and birches[2])	Boreal pines and birches
15,000			L I		Boreal conifers, haploxylon pines, and birches
20,000		Maximum glacial	MG or FG	Temperate conifers (including haploxylon pines[3])	Boreal conifers (tundra in northern Hokkaidō)
30,000 40,000 50,000 60,000 70,000		Middle and early glacial	G-4 EG	Temperate conifers (with some deciduous broadleaf species)	Boreal conifers (with some beech and deciduous oaks)
80,000 90,000 100,000		Third interglacial	I-3	Laurilignosa	Temperate forest species

[1] R = Recent (Holocene); L = Late glacial; EG = Early glacial; G = Glacial; I = Interglacial.
[2] Ca 12,000 years ago, beech and deciduous oak began to increase south of 38° N latitude.
[3] In Kyūshū, *Picea bicolor,* a lower subalpine species, grew above altitudes of 200–300 m.

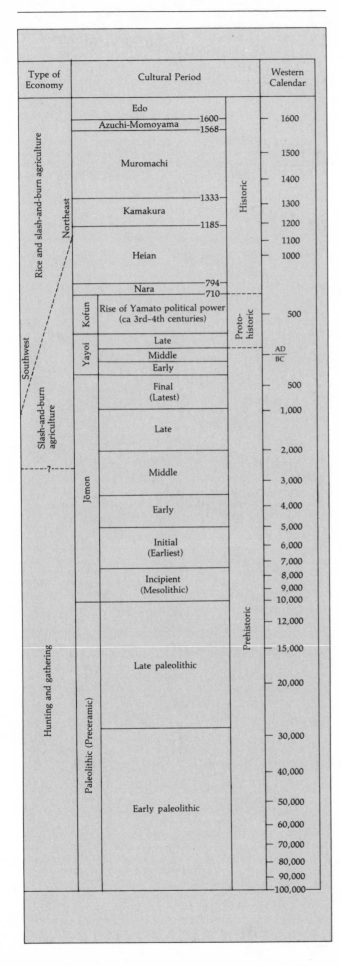

Type of Economy	Cultural Period		Western Calendar
	Edo		1600
	Azuchi-Momoyama —1600— —1568—		
	Muromachi	Historic	1500
			1400
	Kamakura —1333—		1300
	—1185—		1200
			1100
	Heian		1000
	Nara —794— —710—		
	Rise of Yamato political power (ca 3rd–4th centuries)	Proto-historic	500
	Late		AD / BC
	Middle		
	Early		
	Final (Latest)		500
			1,000
	Late		2,000
	Middle	Prehistoric	3,000
	Early		4,000
			5,000
	Initial (Earliest)		6,000
			7,000
	Incipient (Mesolithic)		8,000 / 9,000 / 10,000
			12,000
	Late paleolithic		15,000
			20,000
			30,000
	Early paleolithic		40,000 / 50,000 / 60,000 / 70,000 / 80,000 / 90,000 / 100,000

great quantities of fishing gear and fish bones—salmons (*Oncorhynchus gorbuscha, O. nerka, O. masou,* and so on), sea bream (*Pagrus major*), tuna (*Thunnus orientalis*), bonito (*Katsuwonus pelamis*)—teeth of sharks (*Plagiostomi*), and so on. The warming of climate also made for a rich plant food supply, mainly acorns of evergreen oaks in southwestern Japan and walnuts and acorns of deciduous oaks in northeastern Japan, and the population enjoyed a steady increase. The population was about 40,000 at the beginning of the Early Jōmon period (ca 5000 BC–ca 3500 BC), and was likely between 250,000 to 390,000 by the end of this period.

R III. A variety of evidence indicates the emergence of a moist and cooler environment from approximately 2000 BC or slightly earlier. Boreal conifers and beech trees descended about 300 meters (1,000 ft) in their growing altitude during the R II period. It is also the period when the mountain glaciers of the world descended and the oceans began to recede. Swamp plants invaded the newly exposed seafloor after this marine regression and began to form peat in cool coastal regions. Thus along the coasts of the Tōhoku region and Hokkaidō, the sedimentary profile shows a change from brackish to freshwater swamp sediments; the bottom of peaty swamp sediment, the product of incipient accumulation after the sea receded, is dated almost always at about 2000 BC.

The people of the Late and Final Jōmon periods (ca 2000 BC–ca 300 BC) both in the mountain and coastal regions were annually faced with a changing natural environment and a rapidly diminishing food supply. The number of Jōmon sites in northeastern Japan show a notable decrease, a trend which became even more marked toward the Final Jōmon (ca 1000 BC–ca 300 BC) period. With the exception of groups dependent on fishing along the Pacific coast in northeastern Japan and those in Kyūshū living close to forests abundantly producing acorns and nuts, the number of habitation sites decreased. It is very likely that maintaining a stable population was virtually impossible. Around this period, there was a sudden change of vegetation. The first intensified agriculture came into existence; people cut and burned primeval forests for the first time. Japanese red pine (*Pinus densiflora*) spread explosively, starting from southwestern Japan at the beginning of the Christian era and reaching the Chūbu and Kantō regions about AD 500 and the Tōhoku region by 1200. At the onset of pine rise, R III is divided into two pollen zones, R IIIa and R IIIb. See also JŌMON CULTURE.

Anthropogenic Period——Man's deforestation, however sporadic, began as early as 1500 BC. The initial cultivation of buckwheat, a plant easily grown on freshly exposed barren soil after clearing the forest, coincides with this early forest disturbance during the Late Jōmon period (ca 2000 BC–ca 1000 BC). Abundant cereal pollen (species unknown, but not the rice plant) are also found in Lake Nojiri and many other sites at this time. The emergence of buckwheat and other cereal cultivation was then undoubtedly inseparable from the clearing of climax forests and thus from early slash-and-burn agriculture. The burning of forests resulted in the lowering of nitrogen and organic content and an increase in calcium in the soil, thus prohibiting long-term field use. Japanese red pine and other weedy herbs soon invaded the abandoned fields and agriculturally inaccessible slopes. In most of the palynologically studied sites, the beginning of the Japanese red pine period (R IIIb) is well correlated with the first continuous occurrence of buckwheat pollen, indicating that pine expansion was caused by slash-and-burn farming. The shifting agriculture was intensified after the Kofun period (ca 300–710).

Soon after the initiation of slash-and-burn farming practice, the cultivation of the most important staple crop throughout Asia for the last several millennia was introduced to the Japanese archipelago directly from mainland China. Two reasons have been given for the introduction of a southern strain of rice seed not indigenous to Japan: the absence of an adequate food supply to support a population of several hundred thousand during the Late Jōmon period due to the gradual deterioration of the climate; and an increasingly moist climate, creating natural swamps and wetlands suitable for rice cultivation.

Palynological studies, which concentrate on the precise identification of fossil rice pollen by means of electron and phase-contrast microscopy, have determined when rice cultivation began: at the Itazuke site of northern Kyūshū, around 1200 BC; the Tsukazaki site, Kagoshima Prefecture, around 900 BC; the Jōtō site, Okayama Prefecture, about 1000 BC; and so on. These facts suggest that the beginning of rice agriculture was time-transgressive, starting from northern Kyūshū, the entry for cultural exchange with mainland Asia, and arriving at the Tōhoku region by the 5th century.

The Yayoi agriculturists migrated northward in search of wetlands for rice cultivation, clearing swamps with their primitive stone axes. Pollen profiles show a sudden decrease in swamp trees (mainly *Alnus japonica* and *Fraxinus mandshurica*). The undisturbed original swamp peat containing stumps and twigs of these and other wetland species can still be found deep underneath modern rice paddies. Following the adoption of the rice plant by the Final Jōmon people, there was a dramatic transition from a food-gathering and hunting economy to one based on intensified agricultural production (see YAYOI CULTURE). During the Middle Yayoi period (ca 100 BC–ca AD 100) when both slash-and-burn and wet-rice agricultures were practiced in southwestern Japan, the population underwent a marked growth. The size of the entire Yayoi population is posited between one to two million.

In sum, man depended solely on natural foods throughout most of his long history and began destroying the primeval climax forest for his agricultural needs only a few thousand years ago. Vegetational destruction was accelerated from the beginning of the Yayoi period. Abandoned fields, roadsides, and even cultivated fields were invaded by weeds. Man left his mark on nature, and it is for this reason that scholars refer to the last 3 millennia or so as the Anthropogenic period. See also HISTORY OF JAPAN: prehistory.

——Nihon Daiyonki Gakkai, ed, *Nihon no daiyonki kenkyū* (1977). Numata Makoto, ed, *The Flora and Vegetation of Japan* (1974). Tsukada Matsuo, *Koseitaigaku II: Ōyōron* (1974). Tsukada Matsuo, *Sugi no rekishi: Kako ichiman gosen nenkan* (1980). Watanabe Tadayo, *Ine no michi* (1977). *Matsuo TSUKADA*

Manase Dōsan (1507–1595)

Also known as Ikkei Dōsan. Physician of the Sengoku (1467–1568) and Azuchi–Momoyama (1568–1600) periods. Orphaned at the age of nine, he became an acolyte *(kasshiki)* at the great Zen monastery Shōkokuji in Kyōto in 1519. In 1528 he was sent to study Confucianism at the Ashikaga Gakkō, medieval Japan's only secular institution of higher learning, in the eastern province of Shimotsuke (now Tochigi Prefecture). Three years later, however, he became a disciple of TASHIRO SANKI, a physician trained in China in the medical tradition of the Yuan- (Yüan) period (1279–1368) scholars Li Dongyuan (Li Tung-yüan) and Zhu Danxi (Chu Tan-hsi). In 1545 Dōsan returned to Kyōto and the next year abandoned the Buddhist priesthood to concentrate on the practice of medicine. His patients included members of the imperial family, the shōgun Ashikaga Yoshiteru (1536–65), and a number of major *daimyō*; but it was his pioneering role as medical educator rather than his prominent clientele that earned Dōsan an honored place in the history of Japanese medicine. In his private academy, the Keitekiin, Dōsan trained several hundred students in Li-Zhu medicine; his writings, including *Keitekishū* (1574, Enlightening Teachings) and 17 other extant medical treatises, confirmed the Li-Zhu school's preeminence in Japan. Dōsan practiced the arts as well as science: he was an accomplished amateur of the tea ceremony, scholar of Chinese classics, and rhetorician. In 1584 he became a Christian, being baptized Belchior. It was an important conversion, for he was widely regarded as a leading intellect.

Ikkei Dōsan is not to be confused with his nephew and adopted son Gensaku (d 1632), also a famous physician, to whom he passed on the name Dōsan in 1583. This second Dōsan's son Genkan, known as Manase Dōsan III, was granted the name Imaōji by the imperial court, and internists bearing that name continued the family's medical tradition well into the 19th century. *George ELISON*

Manazuru

Also known as Manatsuru. Town in southwestern Kanagawa Prefecture, central Honshū. Situated on the Manazuru Peninsula, it is an important fishing port. Mandarin oranges are grown in the foothills to the north. The entire peninsula forms a natural park with recreational facilities and camping grounds. Pop: 9,968.

Manchukuo

(J: Manshūkoku). The puppet state established by the Japanese GUANDONG (KWANTUNG) ARMY after its conquest of Manchuria in 1931 (see MANCHURIAN INCIDENT). The military takeover began on 18 September 1931, when elements of the Guandong Army attacked the Chinese garrison in Mukden (now Shenyang). For 13 years, until

Japan's surrender in World War II in August 1945, Manchukuo remained a dependency of Japan.

The Land and People —— Geographically, Manchukuo comprised all of Manchuria and a portion of Inner Mongolia. At the time of its founding in 1932, it consisted of China's "three northeastern provinces," Liaoning, Jilin (Kirin), and Heilongjiang (Heilungkiang). The province of Rehe (Jehol) was added by annexation in 1933. Subsequently these four provinces were redivided until by 1943 there were 19 provinces and two special municipalities. The land area totaled about 1.4 million square kilometers (550,000 sq mi).

The land was populated mainly by Manchus, Chinese, and Mongolians. There were also many Koreans settled in the regions bordering on the Yalu River and some White Russian communities around the city of Harbin. Far fewer in numbers were the Japanese, Tibetans, and people of Central Asian stocks. Its population was estimated at about 43.2 million in the early 1940s. To represent this union of people with varied backgrounds, a flag consisting of horizontal bands of red, yellow, indigo, white, and black was chosen as the national emblem of Manchukuo.

Formation of the Puppet State —— In order to legitimize the newly founded regime, PUYI (P'u-i), who had been the last emperor of the Qing (Ch'ing) dynasty of China (1644–1912), was brought out of seclusion by DOIHARA KENJI of the Guandong Army and installed as the regent of Manchukuo in March 1932. Changchun was selected as the site for the new capital and renamed Xinjing (Hsinking; J: Shinkyō).

The United States was strongly opposed to Japan's seizure of Manchuria. Thus, Secretary of State Henry L. STIMSON applied a NONRECOGNITION POLICY to Manchukuo. Japan also ran into difficulties at the League of Nations in Geneva. The LYTTON COMMISSION report of October 1932, which in effect condemned Japan's action as aggressive, was unacceptable to Japan, and in the spring of 1933 it withdrew from the league.

Even in Japan itself, formal government recognition of Manchukuo did not come about readily. Premier INUKAI TSUYOSHI resented the arbitrary acts of the Guandong Army, which had been perpetrated in defiance of the Japanese government, and hoped to delay recognition. His views were shared by members of officialdom who were wary of the adverse turn of world opinion toward Japan. In May 1932, however, the premier met his death at the hands of young extremist officers. The succeeding premier, SAITŌ MAKOTO, had no alternative but to recognize Manchukuo for fear that any further delay might cause more terrorist acts on the part of Japanese extremists.

There were, however, further complications. Before recognition could be effected, the future respective roles of the SOUTH MANCHURIA RAILWAY, taken over by Japan following the Russo-Japanese War (1904–05), Japan's consulate general in Mukden, and the government of the GUANDONG (KWANTUNG) TERRITORY, leased from China after the Russo-Japanese War, had to be defined. As representatives of the Japanese government in Manchuria, each had assumed certain areas of responsibility over the course of 30 years. It was eventually (in 1934) decided that the commanding general of the Guandong Army, who was also governor of the leased territory, would arbitrate any differences that might arise among the three. His title was also upgraded to that of ambassador plenipotentiary to Manchukuo to reflect his increased authority.

The Protocol between Japan and Manchukuo (Nipponkoku Manshūkoku Kan Giteisho; usually called Nichiman Giteisho) was concluded on 15 September 1932. It was agreed that the Japanese government would be solely responsible for the internal security and defense of Manchukuo. However, it was the Guandong Army that actually directed the affairs of Manchukuo through the General Affairs Board. All policies, laws and ordinances, and rescripts of the new state required the prior consent of this all-important body. Represented on the board were the chief of the Fourth Section of the Guandong Army and the vice-ministers of the various Manchukuo ministries. These officials were invariably Japanese, although the respective ministries were nominally under Chinese ministers. This indirect mode of governing was referred to as "internal guidance" *(naimen shidō)*. Plans and decisions made by the General Affairs Board were coordinated with the Japanese government's Manchurian Affairs Board in Tōkyō.

While the provisions in the Japan–Manchukuo protocol were being reviewed, the CONCORDIA SOCIETY was formed by the Japanese in July 1932. Ostensibly established to promote harmony among the various ethnic groups, the society had as its main purpose the stifling of partisan politics through its network of offices in the provinces. These offices also served as centers for gathering intelligence.

In March 1934 Puyi was made emperor. Manchukuo received recognition from about a dozen countries, principally the Axis powers and their allied or occupied nations in Central Europe: Italy, Germany, Hungary, Czechoslovakia, Romania, and Bulgaria. The others were El Salvador, Spain, Finland, Thailand, and the Vatican.

Immigration—— Prior organized Japanese immigration to Manchuria from the turn of the century had invariably failed because of the harsh climate, Chinese officials' opposition, and the immigrants' inability to compete with the local peasants. After 1932, however, it became essential for Japan to populate the outlying areas to guard against the incursion of Russian and Outer Mongolian troops. Between 1932 and 1935 five contingents recruited from among Japanese army reservists settled in the regions of the Sungari River and the Russian Maritime Province. The Guandong Army also initiated a 20-year project for the immigration of one million households from Japan, with each Japanese prefecture serving as a basic unit for recruitment in a nationwide drive. However, with the onset of the second Sino-Japanese War in China proper in 1937 the project virtually came to a standstill because of the shortage in manpower (see SINO-JAPANESE WAR OF 1937–1945). As of 1940, fewer than 20,000 Japanese households had settled in Manchukuo with a total area of about 73,250 hectares (181,000 acres) under cultivation.

At the same time, supervised Korean immigration was promoted by the Manchukuo government and the Japanese-dominated Government-General of Korea in order to increase production of rice as well as to pave the way for Japanese colonists. Consequently, the Korean population, which had been about 800,000 in the late 1920s, grew to over 2 million by 1945, or about 5 percent of the total population.

Industries—— Since the Russo-Japanese War the South Manchuria Railway Company had spearheaded the penetration and expansion of Japan's interests in Manchuria. The company's holdings and operations reached the vast proportions of an empire. Its varied interests ranged from public transportation, mining, and agriculture to administration of areas near the railway over which it gradually gained control. Future expansion appeared limitless. However, in the 1930s, as the Tōkyō government became increasingly influenced by the military, the South Manchuria Railway came under the domination of the Guandong Army. The Control Law of May 1937 stipulated the integration of major industries in Manchuria into Japan's five-year program toward national mobilization.

The outbreak of Japan's war with China in 1937 further hastened the dissolution of the railway empire. Many of its affiliated companies, which numbered over 80, were combined with AIKAWA YOSHISUKE's Nissan combine to form the Manchuria Heavy Industry Company (Manshū Jūkōgyō Kaihatsu Kaisha). With the backing of the Guandong Army, this company emerged as the leading industrial force in Manchukuo. By 1943, with Japan's fortunes in World War II steadily on the decline, the combine was in financial straits, and its relationship with the military, the bureaucracy, and the old-line zaibatsu deteriorated.

"Bandits" and Border Skirmishes—— Marauding bands of armed men continually posed problems for Manchukuo. Although loosely referred to by the Japanese as "bandits," they varied in purpose. Many of them were the remaining followers of the deposed warlord ZHANG XUELIANG (Chang Hsüeh-liang) of Manchuria. Others were bands of religious fanatics, anti-Japanese guerrillas, antigovernment dissidents, and dispossessed peasants. At the time of the founding of Manchukuo they numbered as many as 360,000, but their numbers were reduced to 65,000 by the end of 1933. Nonetheless, following Japan's invasion of China in 1937, there was an increase in guerrilla raids, especially in the outlying areas.

In 1932 Japan had rejected Russia's offer to negotiate a nonaggression treaty, but in 1935 negotiations for the transfer of Russia's shares in the CHINESE EASTERN RAILWAY to Manchukuo were successfully concluded. Nevertheless, border clashes with the forces of Outer Mongolia and the Soviet Union became more frequent. Several encounters between the Guandong Army and Russian troops escalated into "pocket wars." These included the artillery duel at Changgufeng (Ch'ang-ku-feng) in July 1938 and the fierce air and tank battle at Nomonhan in May 1939 (see CHANGGUFENG [CH'ANG-KU-FENG] INCIDENT; NOMONHAN INCIDENT).

The War in the Pacific—— When Japan opened hostilities against the United States and the United Kingdom on 7 December 1941 (8 December, Japanese time), Manchukuo reduced imports from Japan and increased production of minerals as well as metal and agricul-

tural products to aid Japan's war effort. Assaults on Manchuria by American bombers began in the summer of 1944 and continued intermittently through mid-December. By the summer of 1945, superior divisions of the Guandong Army had been transferred to the Pacific front or to Japan's homeland. At daybreak on 9 August the Soviet Union invaded Manchukuo. Xinjing was hastily abandoned and the capital moved to Dunhua (Tun-hua). On 18 August 1945 Puyi abdicated. He was captured by the Russians the following day at the Mukden airport as he was attempting to flee to Japan. The period of Japan's dominance over Manchuria and a portion of Inner Mongolia had come to an end.

Hugh Borton, *Japan's Modern Century* (1970). Marius B. Jansen, *Japan and China from War to Peace, 1894–1972* (1975). F. C. Jones, *Manchuria since 1931* (1949). Roger Pelissier, *The Awakening of China, 1793–1949*, ed and tr Martin Kieffer (1970). Kungtu C. Sun, assisted by Ralph W. Huenemann, *The Economic Development of Manchuria in the First Half of the Twentieth Century* (1969). Kokusai Zenrin Kyōkai, *Manshū kenkoku no yume to genjitsu* (1975). Manshū Kaihatsu Yonjūnen Shi Kankō Kai, *Manshū kaihatsu yonjūnen shi*, 3 vols (1964–65). Takikawa Masajirō, Etō Shinkichi, et al, *Manshū kenkoku jūnen shi* (1969).

Takehiko YOSHIHASHI

Manchurian Incident

(Manshū Jihen). The conquest and pacification of Manchuria by the GUANDONG (KWANTUNG) ARMY, Japan's field army in Manchuria, from September 1931 to January 1933 or, more narrowly, the initial attack on the Chinese garrison in Mukden (now Shenyang) on the night of 18–19 September 1931 by elements of the Guandong Army (see LIUTIAOGOU [LIU-T'IAO-KOU] INCIDENT).

Background—— The origins of the Manchurian affair lay in the intensifying struggle in the late 1920s between Japan and China to gain a predominant position in Manchuria. Although Manchuria had been integrally linked with China since the beginning of the 17th century, Chinese control over the region had begun to be eroded at the end of the 19th century by the political and economic encroachments of tsarist Russia. This penetration, into southern Manchuria in particular, included the development of numerous commercial enterprises, the acquisition of mining concessions, the construction of major rail systems, and eventually the granting by China to Russia of a leasehold on the Liaodong (Liaotung) Peninsula, known as the Guandong Leased Territory. In the Treaty of PORTSMOUTH, which concluded the RUSSO-JAPANESE WAR of 1904–05, these interests, concessions, and territories in southern Manchuria were ceded to Japan (see GUANDONG [KWANTUNG] TERRITORY), though Manchuria outside the Guandong Leased Territory was still considered to be under the nominal control of China.

In the quarter century that followed, as Japanese colonists in southern Manchuria, growing in numbers and militancy, urged their government to assert a more visible role in Manchurian affairs, the various agencies of the Japanese presence in the region sought to expand their interests and jurisdiction. The SOUTH MANCHURIA RAILWAY Company, which operated the major rail line running north and south through Manchuria, not only came to control "attached lands"—ill-defined rights-of-way on either side of the railway—but also began to exercise jurisdiction over adjacent towns and villages, resulting in no little antagonism between Japanese and local Chinese officials. The Japanese Foreign Ministry, too, through its network of consulates and consular police scattered throughout Manchuria, sought to exercise influence far beyond the normal representational function for foreign-service posts abroad. But no Japanese in southern Manchuria caused more friction and bitterness than the Japanese railway guards and military garrisons whose presence along the South Manchuria Railway and in the "attached lands" had been authorized both by the Portsmouth treaty and a subsequent Sino-Japanese protocol. After 1919 these units came under the control of the Guandong Army, the Imperial Japanese Army's field command in Manchuria, with headquarters at PORT ARTHUR (Ch: Lüshun, now part of Lüda) in the Guandong Leased Territory. As the overall Japanese military command in southern Manchuria, the Guandong Army was responsible for the defense of the leased territory and the protection of Japanese lives and property outside the territory, including the South Manchuria Railway and its "attached lands." Elements of the Guandong Army, essentially a division and some miscellaneous garrison and artillery units, were stationed at several key cities and towns along the railway, including Mukden, the political center of southern Manchuria. Of all the Japanese elements in Manchuria it was the Guandong Army that became the most determined to consolidate Japanese control over the area to the point where southern Manchuria could be separated from China proper.

By 1920 Chinese authority in southern Manchuria had also begun to be eroded by political factionalism within the region itself. After the collapse of the Qing (Ch'ing) dynasty in 1911, Manchurian warlord elements had begun to exercise political power independent of China. For most of the decade of the 1920s this power was consolidated under a single warlord, Marshal ZHANG ZUOLIN (Chang Tso-lin). But by 1928 the Guandong Army staff had grown so jealous of his influence in southern Manchuria that it contrived to assassinate Zhang by blowing up his train outside Mukden. Zhang was succeeded by his son, "the Young Marshal," ZHANG XUELIANG (Chang Hsüeh-liang).

By this time the great tide of Chinese nationalism, the reunification drive by Chiang Kai-shek and the Guomindang (Kuomintang; Nationalist Party), had begun to approach the borders of Manchuria. By 1930, under pressure from the Chinese government in Nanjing (Nanking), which was determined to recover China's lost rights and interests in Manchuria and to diminish the Japanese presence in the region, Zhang Xueliang formally acknowledged the authority of the government of Nationalist China.

By 1931, therefore, the stage was set for a confrontation in Manchuria between China and Japan—the Chinese in an effort to reclaim actual as well as nominal control of Manchuria as an integral part of China, and the Japanese in an attempt to preserve their rights and properties in southern Manchuria by separating Manchuria from China once and for all. Among the leading Japanese elements in Manchuria it was the middle-echelon staff officers of the Guandong Army, in particular, who were the most stridently determined to bring about a violent rather than a negotiated solution to the "Manchurian problem." Their hope, moreover, was that possession of the territory and resources of Manchuria would provide Japan with strategic security and economic self-sufficiency as Japan moved into a dangerous period in its foreign relations.

The Takeover —— Led by two aggressive and energetic colonels, ISHIWARA KANJI and ITAGAKI SEISHIRŌ, the Guandong Army staff over a two-year period laid careful plans for the conquest of Manchuria by a modest contingent (slightly more than a division) in the face of Chinese forces that were vastly superior in numbers—particularly those of Zhang Xueliang at Mukden. These plans were conceived without the direction or authorization of central headquarters or the civilian government in Japan, though apparently with the knowledge and tacit approval of certain middle-echelon officers on the General Staff. The planning by Ishiwara and Itagaki culminated in a sudden attack by elements of the Guandong Army on the main Chinese garrison at Mukden on the night of 18–19 September 1931. The Guandong Army justified the assault as retribution for a supposed Chinese attempt to destroy the tracks of the South Manchuria Railway just north of the city, an act that had in fact been secretly perpetrated by Guandong Army staff officers.

This initial attack set in motion a runaway campaign for the conquest of southern Manchuria and the annihilation or intimidation of regional Chinese armies, despite the efforts of the Japanese civilian government and military high command in Tōkyō to limit the field initiatives of the Guandong Army staff. In this first, breakaway phase of "the Manchurian Incident," from September to December 1931, the most important operations were the seizure of Mukden and Changchun (18–19 September); the unauthorized entry into Manchuria of units of the Korea Army (the Guandong Army's sister field command in Korea) to support operations already under way (20–21 September); the seizure of Jilin (Kirin), capital of Jilin Province (22–24 September); the bombing of Jinzhou (Chinchou), a rail center on the Peking–Mukden line (8 October); the advance to the Nonni River in Heilongjiang (Heilungkiang) Province in northern Manchuria (2–4 November) on the pretext of repairing certain rail bridges destroyed by the northern warlord Ma Zhanshan (Ma Chanshan; 1884–1950); the battles around Daxing (Ta-hsing), just north of the bridges, (4–6 November); the rout of Ma's forces south of Qiqihar (Tsitsihar), the capital of Heilongjiang Province (18–19 November), after which the Guandong Army's "Nonni Force" entered Qiqihaer (20 November); and the abortive drive on Jinzhou (26–30 November) by which the Guandong Army intended to push through to Shanhaiguan (Shan-hai-kuan) at the border between Manchuria and China and thus link up with the Japanese garrison at Tianjin (Tientsin)—an act that was, however, prevented by the General Staff.

Manchurian Incident —— Manchukuo

During this critical first phase of the Manchurian campaign, the civilian government, concerned about the worsening image of Japanese aggression in world opinion, and the military high command, fearful of possible Soviet intervention in Manchuria, continually sought to limit the wide-ranging and unauthorized operations of the field command in Manchuria. However, by the beginning of December 1931 the Guandong Army was in possession of most of southern Manchuria and controlled the capitals of all three Manchurian provinces. Denied authorization to annex Manchuria formally as a Japanese territory, the Guandong Army staff, during the autumn of 1931, negotiated with suitably eminent and pliable Chinese leaders in Manchuria to establish an "autonomous" satellite state, eventually dubbed MANCHUKUO. These political maneuvers had also been undertaken over the express opposition of the political and military establishment in the home islands.

December 1931 witnessed two critical developments that affected the nature of the operations of the Guandong Army. The first of these was a resolution by the League of Nations that urged restraint on the military activities of both Japanese and Chinese forces in Manchuria pending the establishment of a neutral commission of inquiry (the LYTTON COMMISSION) but permitted Japanese operations against "bandits" and other "lawless elements." The second development was a sudden and distinct change in the political and military climate in the home islands: the downfall of the more liberal cabinet of Premier WAKATSUKI REIJIRŌ, its succession by that of INUKAI TSUYOSHI, less adamant in his opposition to the maintenance of Japanese interests in Manchuria by force, and a personnel shift in the high command, which now actively supported the Guandong Army's effort to occupy all of Manchuria.

With these developments the Manchurian Incident entered its final stage, which was characterized by aggressive operations—backed by increasingly powerful reinforcements from Japan—against the remaining Chinese resistance, now invariably termed "banditry." This "mopping-up" stage in the subjugation of Manchuria, from mid-December 1931 to January 1933, saw the conquest of Jinzhou and the occupation of southwestern Manchuria down to Shanhaiguan (December 1931); the occupation of Harbin (February 1932); mopping-up operations in eastern Jilin and along the Sungari River (April–May); the final destruction in June of the forces of the warlord Ma Zhanshan in Heilongjiang; pacification of northern and western Manchuria in the summer; and the conquest of northwestern Manchuria as far as Manzhouli (Manchuli) in the autumn of 1932. By January 1933 the Guandong Army had, for all practical purposes, completed the conquest of Manchuria and the incident can be said to have ended, though the aspirations of the Guandong Army Staff for the occupation of neighboring Rehe (Jehol) led to the invasion of that province early in 1933.

Significance —— Some have seen the Manchurian Incident as inextricably linked to the surge of "militarism," "facism," "imperial absolutism," and "government by assassination" in Japan during the 1930s. Others have concluded that the affair started Japan on a path of rampant expansion in Asia that led inevitably to a collision with the United States and to World War II. Setting aside the questions of whether such terms are very enlightening in analyzing the political and military complexities of Japan in the interwar period or whether historical processes are ever inevitable, it is possible to make a few generalizations concerning the major implications of the affair in the perspective of modern Japanese and world history.

To begin with, the inability of the political and military establishment in Japan to deal summarily and effectively with the undisciplined Guandong Army staff in the autumn of 1931 exposed the dangerous ambiguities not only within the chain of military command but within the whole political structure of modern Japan as well. The failure of Premier Wakatsuki's cabinet to rally any widespread support behind its efforts to control the headlong aggression of the field command in Manchuria indicated the degree to which civilian leaders and the public had lost confidence in attempts to solve Japan's foreign problems through international cooperation and diplomatic negotiation. Thus the Manchurian Incident may be linked not only to increasingly strident extremist elements in Japan who called for radical and violent solutions to Japan's foreign problems but also to the emergence of a widely shared conviction that the survival of the nation in a divided and unstable world depended on the forceful and unilateral creation of hegemony in East Asia to the exclusion of all other national and international interests there. Given, on the one hand, the Japanese insistence that mastery in East Asia was to be based on control of a Manchuria forever separated from China, and on the other, the resurgence of Chinese nationalism and irredentism, the Manchurian affair so inflamed Sino-Japanese animosities that there could be little hope of resolution short of war. From a global perspective Japan's grab in Manchuria further isolated and alienated it from the major powers. The Lytton Commission's verdict in 1932 that Japanese political and military restructuring of Manchuria was unjustified led to Japan's withdrawal from the league amid international condemnation of its actions. Worse still for Japan, its occupation of Manchuria up to the Amur River impelled the Soviet Union to undertake a vast strengthening of military forces in Siberia and the Maritime province. This new threat necessitated a counter build-up of Japanese military power to defend the newly won territory. In sum, the Guandong Army's adventure in Manchuria in 1931–32 brought Japan neither the military security nor the economic self-sufficiency its advocates had hoped for but instead propelled the nation along a perilous new path of foreign confrontation. See also SINO-JAPANESE WAR OF 1937–1945.

■ ——Sadako N. Ogata, *Defiance in Manchuria: The Making of Japanese Foreign Policy, 1931–32* (1964). Mark R. Peattie, *Ishiwara Kanji and Japan's Confrontation with the West* (1975). Richard Storry, "The Mukden Incident of September 18–19, 1931," *St. Antony's Papers 2/ Far Eastern Affairs 1* (1957). Takehiko Yoshihashi, *Conspiracy at Mukden: The Rise of the Japanese Military* (1963).

Mark R. PEATTIE

Manchurian-Mongolian Independence Movement

(Mammō Dokuritsu Undō). Name given to a series of Japanese plans during the first two decades of the 20th century to detach Manchuria and Mongolia from China by promoting separatist movements. In 1911 leaders in the Japanese General Staff saw the recent Chinese revolution overthrowing the Manchu dynasty as an opportunity to strengthen Japan's strategic and political position in Northeast Asia. Kawashima Naniwa, a Japanese adventurer (see TAIRIKU RŌNIN) in China, and elements in the General Staff decided to form a Manchu state in Manchuria. They brought their candidate for ruler, Prince SU, to the Japanese GUANDONG (KWANTUNG) ARMY headquarters in PORT ARTHUR. They also persuaded some Mongol princes from Inner Mongolia to agree to Japanese dominance of their country in exchange for military and financial aid. Word of their plans, however, reached the foreign ministry in Tōkyō. Kawashima was recalled to Japan, and the plans came to nothing.

In 1916, responding to an announcement by President Yuan Shikai (Yüan Shih-k'ai) of his intention to declare himself emperor of China, General TANAKA GIICHI, then deputy chief of staff, decided to resurrect Kawashima's plans. He had munitions, funds, and troops sent to Manchuria and Inner Mongolia in the hope that Yuan,

surrounded by enemies, would give up his monarchical ambitions. Plans were once again abandoned when Yuan died in June 1916.

mandala

(J: *mandara;* from Skt: *maṇḍala*). A symmetrically arranged symbolic diagram used in Hinduism and ESOTERIC BUDDHISM to express fundamental religious doctrine for the purposes of ritual and meditation. Buddhist mandalas range from simple geometric diagrams or arrangements of sacred words to complex configurations in which many Buddhas and bodhisattvas are depicted.

The word mandala, the central symbol of esoteric Buddhism, has many meanings, and no translation can do it justice. The original Sanskrit word *maṇḍala* meant circle, group, collection, company. It was interpreted in the esoteric Buddhist scripture *Mahāvairocana-sūtra* (J: *Dainichikyō*) and in commentaries on the scripture as consisting of *maṇḍa* (essence) and *la* (possession or attainment), essence being taken to mean supreme enlightenment, the state of inner enlightenment (J: SATORI) achieved by the Buddha. This state of enlightenment cannot be described verbally; it can only be said to be "not this, not that." This line of speculation resulted in the theory of emptiness (J: *shinkūron;* Skt: *śūnyatā-vāda*) and in the theory of the positive affirmation of wondrous existence (J: *myōuron;* Skt: *tathatā-vāda*). Parallel with these philosophical lines of development—and parallel to the use of the mandala—was the use in Buddhism, as a means of encouraging the faith, of various devices such as religious images; mystical syllables, words, or phrases (Skt: MANTRA; J: *shingon*); symbols, signs, or gestures (Skt: *mudrā;* J: *inzō*); symbolic scripts (Skt: *bija;* J: *shūji*); and even elements from non-Buddhist folk beliefs. Such devices were used to lead ordinary people to the great compassion of the Buddha. The mandala was a symbolic representation of *satori,* the state of enlightenment, meant to be used as an object of contemplation. It came to be expressed two- and three-dimensionally, that is, as painting and sculpture.

In Tibetan Buddhism the word *maṇḍala* was translated into Tibetan by a word meaning "circle," but in Chinese Buddhism it was not translated by a Chinese word but instead transliterated by use of Chinese characters whose sound approximated the sound of the Sanskrit word. The Japanese word *mandara* is also a transliteration based on the Japanese pronunciation of the Chinese characters. In Chinese commentaries the word was chiefly interpreted as "assembly," "assembly of the divine," or "place of assembly of the divine," in contrast with the Indian meaning of an expression of the state of enlightenment. In India a mandala was originally an earthen platform, built for the ordination rite, which was destroyed after the ceremony was completed; in China the mandala was a graphic representation on silk, often depicting Buddhas and bodhisattvas, which was hung on the wall or spread on the floor, and it was thus seen as an "assembly of the divine." In Japan, too, this interpretation generally prevailed. Although among Japanese esoteric Buddhist priests during and after the Kamakura period (1185–1333) the term was interpreted as *rin'en gusoku* ("wholly satisfied round wheel," i.e., perfect circle), this ambiguous meaning was not understood by most people.

Types of Mandalas —— As the path to enlightenment is manifold, so is its expression. Esoteric Shingon scriptures tell of many types of mandalas in which the state of enlightenment is visualized. These mandalas can be divided into two categories: those depicting (according to the prologue of a sutra) when and where which Buddha, surrounded by which bodhisattvas, preached; and those depicting the content of the teaching. They can also be divided into four types: (1) *dai mandara* (Skt: *mahā-maṇḍala*), in which Buddhas and bodhisattvas are diagrammatically represented with iconographically prescribed hand gestures *(mudrā)* and attributes; (2) *sammaya mandara* (Skt: *samaya-maṇḍala*), in which objects (e.g., sword, wheel, or lotus) symbolic of the nature and vows of different Buddhas and bodhisattvas are depicted; (3) *hō mandara* (Skt: *dharma-maṇḍala*), in which Buddhas and bodhisattvas are symbolically represented by the Sanskrit script; and (4) *kuyō* or *katsuma mandara* (Skt: *karma-maṇḍala*), a three-dimensional mandala in which various actions of divinities are depicted. Mandalas of these four types can be further classified under three Japanese terms as *besson, bue,* and *toe.* In *besson mandara* one central divinity and his retinue are depicted; examples of this type are the *Shaka mandara* and the *Amida mandara.* In *bue mandara* divinities belonging to the same family are depicted. For example, in *butchō mandara* various manifestations of the historical Buddha presiding over the Buddha family (J: *butsubu;* Skt: *tathāgata-kula*) are depicted; in the *Jūichimen Kannon mandara*

(Eleven-headed Kannon Mandala) various manifestations of Kannon presiding over the lotus family (J: *rengebu;* Skt: *padma-kula*) are depicted. In *toe mandara* all families of divinities are depicted, as in the *Taizō mandara* (Womb Mandala) and *Kongōkai mandara* (Diamond Realm Mandala). *Besson* and *bue* mandala can be classified more concretely according to the type of religious practice (*kyōbō*) or divinity depicted. Among the various divinities are Buddhas, bodhisattvas, MYŌŌ (Skt: *vidyārāja;* mostly fierce-natured deities), and *ten* (Skt: *deva;* heavenly beings; see TEMBU). *Kyōbō mandara,* which are used in religious practices, can be hung on the wall (*kake mandara*) or spread out on the floor or a platform (*shiki mandara*), the latter being so composed as to permit contemplation from all four sides.

Among all the different mandalas, the most fundamental are the *Taizō mandara* and *Kongōkai mandara,* both of which are of the *toe* type and which can be said to subsume all other mandalas. In orthodox esoteric Buddhism the great Buddha Mahāvairocana (J: DAINICHI) is the central symbol of the whole universe and of all beings and things; each individual being lives in and is given life by the whole, while the whole exists eternally through each being at each moment. This whole is the true figure of *satori;* and it is the two fundamental mandalas (the *Taizō mandara* and *Kongōkai mandara*) that most systematically express this relationship between the individual and the whole.

The *Taizō mandara* or formally *Daihi taizōshō mandara* (Skt: *Mahā-karuṇā-garbha-udbhava-maṇḍala;* Mandala of the Womb of Great Compassion; sometimes referred to in Japanese as the *Taizōkai* or Womb Realm Mandala) is based on the fundamental esoteric Buddhist scripture *Dainichikyō* (Skt: *Mahāvairocana-sūtra*). It symbolizes enlightenment in its depiction of Dainichi seated in the center on an eight-petaled lotus, surrounded by four Buddhas and four bodhisattvas, each on one petal, expressing the dualities of destruction of evil and encouragement of justice; great wisdom and deep compassion; altruism and self-interest. The *Taizō mandara* is also known as the *Renge mandara* or Lotus Mandala (the lotus being the fundamental symbol of great compassion) and as the *Sambu mandara* or Tripartite Mandala (its inner circle being composed of the Buddha family, the lotus family, and the diamond or thunderbolt family; J: *kongōbu;* Skt: *vajra-kula*).

The *Kongōkai mandara* (Skt: *Vajradhātu-maṇḍala;* Mandala of the Diamond [or Thunderbolt] Realm) is based on the first part of the scripture *Kongōchō-gyō* (Skt: *Vajraśekhara-sūtra*). It is an aggregate of nine mandalas symbolizing the ultimate reality, which is as eternal and indestructible as a diamond or thunderbolt, the actualization of this reality, and the wondrous interrelationship and interaction between the whole and individual phenomena. See also RYŌBU MANDARA.

These two fundamental mandalas, based on the two most important sutras of esoteric Buddhism, were transmitted to Japan, along with the religious doctrines of which the two are expressions, by the monk KŪKAI (774–835). These religious doctrines became the basis of the SHINGON SECT (as an alternate name, Himitsu Mandara Kyō or Esoteric Mandala Teaching, indicates); and the transmitted mandalas were successively copied as the fundamental mandalas of the true Shingon faith and circulated as *genzu mandara* ("reality illustration" mandalas). As Shingon took hold in Japan and was adapted to native conditions, mandalas also took on Japanese characteristics.

Mandalas that Developed in Japan —— Paintings of a type called *hensō mandara* ("transformed configuration" mandala), in which an assembly of one or more Buddhas and one or more bodhisattvas is depicted, illustrating the Pure Land of the Blessed (Jōdo; see PURE LAND BUDDHISM), were produced in large numbers during the Nara period (710–794) and early part of the Heian period (794–1185). The term mandala was used because of the similarity of composition to a mandala; the paintings came to be known as *Jōdo mandara* (Pure Land mandalas) during the mid-Heian period. The best-known types of *hensō* or *Jōdo mandara* are the *Chikō mandara,* the *Taima mandara,* and the *Seikai mandara.*

Mandalas of the type called *Amida gōshō mandara* (now known as Amida RAIGŌZU), which depicted the Buddha AMIDA (Skt: Amitābha) descending to welcome the dying faithful in fulfillment of his vow, were produced from the mid-Heian to the Kamakura periods. The Pure Land faith within the Shingon school, influenced by Tendai Pure Land Buddhism, also produced Amida mandalas.

In the Kamakura period, as new Buddhist movements arose, the use of the term *mandara* spread. The *Shōju fusha mandara* of Pure Land Buddhists who believed that the simple repetition of *Namu Amida Butsu* ("I place my faith in Amida Buddha"; see NEMBUTSU)

was sufficient for salvation is a mandala that depicts Amida Buddha with his salvific light shining only upon those who chant *Namu Amida Butsu.* Other Buddhists objected to this mandala on the grounds of its exclusivity and it ceased to be produced. The JŌDO SHIN SECT produced the *kōmyō honzon,* a type of mandala in which the phrase *Namu Amida Butsu* is written in large characters with the lineage of Indian, Chinese, and Japanese Pure Land Buddhist masters on both sides, as if they were receiving light from the central formula. Influenced by this mandala was the type called *dai mandara* or, more popularly, *hige mandara* ("beard" mandala) of the NICHIREN SECT. In the center are written the seven characters for the phrase NAMU MYŌHŌ RENGE KYŌ ("I take my refuge in the Lotus Sutra"), flanked by the names of various divinities named in the Lotus Sutra.

Mandalas were produced also by the older sects during the Kamakura period. The *Kegon kaie zenchishiki mandara* of the KEGON SECT, preserved at the temples TŌDAIJI and KŌZANJI, is one such example. In the upper center is depicted Birushana Buddha (Skt: Vairocana) of the sutra *Kegonkyō* (Skt: *Avataṃsaka-sūtra*); the rest of the mandala illustrates the encounters of the sutra's young protagonist Zenzai Dōji (Skt: Sudhana-śreṣṭhi-dāraka) with numerous wise men and the bodhisattvas Miroku (Skt: Maitreya) and Fugen (Skt: Samantabhadra), the Kōzanji version depicting only the wise men. The *Shōō mandara,* which arose out of the cult of Prince SHŌTOKU, has in its center the prince, the emperor Yōmei, and the empress SUIKO, all surrounded by various figures historically associated with the prince. Similarly, the *Kusha mandara* of the KUSHA SCHOOL has Śākyamuni Buddha and the two bodhisattvas Monju (Skt: Mañjuśrī) and Fugen surrounded by masters of the sect. The *Hossō mandara* of the HOSSŌ SECT depicts the bodhisattva Miroku and sect masters. The *Goshō mandara* of the temple Kōzanji, attributed to the monk MYŌE (1173–1232), depicts Taizō Dainichi Buddha surrounded by the four bodhisattvas Fugen, Monju, Kannon (Skt: Avalokiteśvara), and Miroku. Myōe is also responsible for the remarkable popularization of the *Kōmyō shingon mandara,* which has the sacred Sanskrit syllable *oṃ* in the center surrounded by Sanskrit words meaning "holy utterance of light" (J: *kōmyō shingon*) written in SIDDHĀM script.

Beginning in the Muromachi period (1333–1568), many *Jūsambutsu mandara* (13-Buddha mandalas), based on the then popular belief in the 10 Lords (Jūō) presiding over the nether world, were produced. In this mandala, each of the 13 most popular Buddhas and bodhisattvas of esoteric Buddhism is worshiped on behalf of the deceased on a different commemorative day counting from the day of death: for example, on the seventh day, Fudō Myōō (Skt: Acalanātha; see MYŌŌ); on the 14th day, Śākyamuni Buddha; on the 21st day, the bodhisattva Monju; and so on. Fudō Myōō is in the lower right-hand corner of the mandala and the bodhisattva Kokūzō (Skt: Ākāśagarbha)—who is worshiped on the 33rd anniversary of death (the 32nd anniversary by Western reckoning)—at the top, with rows of Buddhas and bodhisattvas in between.

In contrast to these mandalas, which were more or less in the Buddhist spirit, from the late Heian period mandalas based on indigenous beliefs began to appear. The most numerous of this category were *suijaku mandara* (mandalas of the manifestation), based on the syncretist HONJI SUIJAKU belief that a particular indigenous SHINTŌ deity is a reincarnation of a corresponding Buddha or bodhisattva. Various combinations of *miya mandara* (mandalas depicting shrines), *honji mandara* (mandalas depicting the primary source Buddhas of the *honji suijaku* belief), and *suijaku mandara* also existed. Also popular were mandalas depicting symbols, animals, and so on, sacred to various shrines, for example, the *Kasuga mandara* of the Kasuga Shrines, the *Hie Sannō mandara* of the HIE SHRINE of Mt. Hiei (Hieizan), the *Kumano mandara* of the Kumano Shrines, and the *Hachiman mandara* of the Hachiman Shrines.

For many centuries the word mandala held the utmost significance for followers of esoteric Buddhism. Although it is no longer a familiar word for most people today, the truth that the mandala expresses still exists deep within our subconscious.

▬——Lokesh Chandra, *The Esoteric Iconography of Japanese Mandalas* (1971). Hamada Takashi, *Mandara no sekai* (1971). Ishida Hisatoyo, *Mandara no kenkyū* (1975). Ryūjun Tajima, *Les deux grands maṇḍalas et la doctrine de l'ésotérisme Shingon* (1959). Toganoo Shōun, *Mandara no kenkyū* (1927).   TOGANOO *Shōzui*

mandarin duck

(*oshidori*). *Aix galericulata.* Waterfowl of the family Anatidae, a relative of the North American wood duck (*A. sponsa*), 45 centime-

Manekineko

A typical *manekineko*. This particular example was sold as a souvenir near the temple Gōtokuji in Tōkyō. Pottery. Height 28.5 cm.

Manga

A drawing by Hokusai placing a cyclops and two figures with elongated necks into ordinary domestic surroundings. Two facing pages from the 12th volume, published in 1834, of a set of 13 picture books of Hokusai's mainly comic sketches. Book size 22.7 × 15.7 cm. Private collection.

ters (18 in) in length. The breeding plumage of the drake is exceptionally colorful, with a pair of orange yellow fan-shaped wings ("sails") rising at the lower back. The hen is a dull gray brown with white rings around its eyes and a black bill. The male's bill is red, but both male and female have red legs. Living in streams, ponds, and marshes, they nest in the hollows of old tree trunks and perch on branches. Some breed in boxes specially set aside for them beside park ponds. Although commonly regarded as a symbol of conjugal fidelity, mandarin ducks actually change their partners each year. They are distributed throughout China, Japan, and the Ussuri region of southwestern Siberia; they have also been successfully introduced to Europe. *Takano Shinji*

Influenced by Chinese literary works, including the poem "Chang henge" ("Ch'ang hen-ko") by Bo Juyi (Po Chü-i), the Japanese have traditionally viewed pairs of mandarin ducks as a symbol of marital harmony. Mandarin ducks have also been celebrated for their faithfulness in popular legends, such as the story from the 13th-century anthology *Kokon chomonjū*, in which a hunter takes

holy orders after discovering that the mate of a drake he killed has died of grief. The legend was retold in English in Lafcadio HEARN's *Kwaidan*. The beauty and color of the birds have inspired many notable paintings; those by Ogata KŌRIN and ITŌ JAKUCHŪ are particularly famous. *Saitō Shōji*

Mandokoro

Originally, private administrative offices established by great noble houses of the Heian period (794–1185) to deal with family business, especially the administration of their extensive private estates (SHŌEN). Temples, shrines, and individual *shōen* also established such offices. The Mandokoro of the FUJIWARA FAMILY in its heyday was virtually a private government; it included a KUMONJO, which handled documents, and a KURŌDO-DOKORO or secretariat. Early in the Kamakura period (1185–1333), MINAMOTO NO YORITOMO established a Mandokoro or Administrative Board (this absorbed the functions of the existing Kumonjo, or Public Documents Office) in Kamakura, appointing ŌE NO HIROMOTO as its first administrator (*bettō*). It dealt with general matters of administration, especially shogunal finance, control of the city of Kamakura, and the settlement of lawsuits. As the HŌJŌ FAMILY took control of the shogunate, however, the duties of the Mandokoro were restricted to financial matters. The Muromachi shogunate (1338–1573) established a Mandokoro as well. *G. Cameron Hurst III*

manekineko

(literally, "beckoning cat"). A figurine in the shape of a sitting cat with one paw upraised, as though making the customary Japanese gesture used in beckoning to people. It is often found displayed in a prominent place at the front of shops and businesses that rely on heavy customer traffic, like eateries and drinking establishments. Traditionally regarded as a kind of mascot by shopkeepers and businessmen, it is believed to "beckon" good fortune and business success. Usually constructed of papier-mâché or pottery, some *manekineko* have the right front paw raised and some the left front paw. Some temples and shrines give out miniature replicas of *manekineko* as a protective amulet (GOFU) to those making their first shrine or temple visit of the new year. *Manekineko* are not only kept as good luck objects but nowadays are also sold commercially as coin banks. *Tsuchida Mitsufumi*

Man'en Kembei Shisetsu → United States, mission of 1860 to

manga

(comic pictures). The word *manga,* which originally meant "random sketches," has become a general term for comic or satiric pictures, cartoons, or comic strips.

Ancient Period——The oldest and most famous examples of Japanese comic art are found in the SHŌSŌIN repository in Nara. There one finds drawings of funny faces on cloth with the eyes cut out; called *fusakumen,* these depict a variety of facial expressions. Another item from the Shōsōin is a caricature called the *Daidairon,* representing a pop-eyed, bearded man (see GRAFFITI). This is drawn on the corner of a document dated 745.

In addition to such caricatures, comic drawings have been found on the ceilings of the *kondō* (main hall) in the 7th-century Buddhist temple HŌRYŪJI and on the platforms for the wooden figures of Brahma and Indra in the 8th-century temple TŌSHŌDAIJI. Among these are drawings used to drive away evil spirits, indicating that there were religious elements in the comic-picture tradition. Also, in the Phoenix Hall of the temple BYŌDŌIN, noted for its Heian period (794–1185) architecture, numerous caricatures of the lower court officials of the time are found.

We are told that during the Heian period the *oko-e,* a kind of comic drawing, was popular as a hobby of the aristocracy. Toward the end of the period, the caricatures of the CHŌJŪ GIGA picture scroll were drawn, probably by the illustrious monk TOBA SŌJŌ. Considered one of the finest examples of Japanese comic art, these depictions of birds and animals done in skilled brushwork are thought to be satires of the covetous nobles and monks of the time, eager for political power. The SHIGISAN ENGI EMAKI and the BAN DAINAGON EKOTOBA, both outstanding picture scrolls from the same period, contain comic elements in their vivid portrayal of scene and exaggerated depiction of the people. See also EMAKIMONO.

Middle Ages—— With the spread of Buddhism in Japan in the Kamakura period (1185–1333), illustrated scrolls depicting Buddhist teachings and scenes of suffering, such as the JIGOKU-ZŌSHI with scenes of hell, the *Gaki-zōshi* with scenes of hungry ghosts, and the *Yamai no sōshi* with scenes of illnesses, made their appearance. As can be seen from the titles, these scrolls treat rather grim subjects; nevertheless, the boldness of imagination and exaggerated depictions of figures found in the scrolls bring a sense of humor even to the ugly and grotesque. Other examples of comic art from the middle ages include the pictures found in the collections of popular short stories, OTOGI-ZŌSHI, from the Muromachi period (1333–1568).

Edo Period—— The growth of a popular culture in the Edo period (1600–1868) brought about a surge in comic pictures and FŪZOKUGA genre painting. These took on greater appeal in the form of woodblock-print books. The ŌTSU-E paintings, which made use of broad brush-strokes; the *toba-e* drawings with their exaggeration of human features; and the genre paintings of Kuwagata Keisai (also known as Kitao Masayoshi; 1764–1824) and Yamaguchi Soken (1759–1818) are examples of comic works from this period.

UKIYO-E artists also produced many comic works. SHARAKU, in particular, was skilled in bringing out the special qualities in the expressions of *kabuki* actors. The comic works of HOKUSAI are well known under the general title of *Hokusai manga*. Literati painters like BUSON and WATANABE KAZAN and the Zen monks SENGAI GIBON and HAKUIN also produced works in a humorous vein.

The Edo period saw the production of numerous comic works, but government restrictions limited the output of specifically satirical works to a small number that included the pictures of HANABUSA ITCHŌ and UTAGAWA KUNIYOSHI. However, news of the events leading to the collapse of the shogunate are said to have been transmitted to the people through cartoons and caricatures.

Modern Times—— Western artists who came to Japan in the days following the opening of the country, for example, Charles WIRGMAN of England (the founder of *Japan Punch* in 1862) and Georges BIGOT of France, exerted a large influence on comic artists; even KOBAYASHI KIYOCHIKA, the master of Meiji-period (1868–1912) *ukiyo-e*, produced *manga* incorporating Western elements. In 1905 Kitazawa Rakuten (1876–1955) founded the magazine *Tokyo Puck*, leading to the production of several such *manga*-related periodicals and the emergence of many *manga* artists in the years thereafter.

Newspaper comics and cartoons gained importance during the Taishō period (1912–26), and artists like Okamoto Ippei (1886–1948) attained fame in this field. In response to the depressed economic conditions of the early years of the Shōwa period (1926–), there was a trend toward the so-called *ero-guro-nansensu* (erotic, grotesque, nonsense) *manga* as well as proletarian themes in comics. In the period just before World War II there was an increasing militaristic slant in comic material. Following the defeat in World War II and the wide-scale introduction of American culture, there was a qualitative change in comic content to respond to the new mass society. See also COMIC MAGAZINES.   MIYAO Shigeo

Manjirō, John → Nakahama Manjirō

manners → etiquette

Mannō Pond

(Mannō Ike). Reservoir in Kagawa Prefecture, Shikoku, located on the northern slopes of the Sanuki Mountains. Its water is used to irrigate the Marugame Plain. It was first constructed in the beginning of the 8th century and repaired by the priest Kūkai in 821. It underwent extended repairs in 1959. When filled with water the area is 1.4 sq km (0.5 sq mi), and the volume of water is 15.4 million cu m (5,436.2 million cu ft).

Mansai (1378–1435)

Also pronounced Manzei. Buddhist priest of the Shingon sect and influential statesman of the middle years of the Muromachi period (1333–1568). Son of the aristocrat Imakōji (Fujiwara) Morofuyu, he entered the temple DAIGOJI near Kyōto and became its abbot in 1395. Mansai was a trusted confidant of the shōgun ASHIKAGA YO-

SHIMITSU (r 1369–95), who had earlier made him his *yūshi* (adopted son without right of inheritance). He also served two later shōguns: Ashikaga Yoshimochi (1386–1428; r 1395–1423) and ASHIKAGA YOSHINORI (r 1429–41). Mansai's power in political affairs earned him the sobriquet "Black-Robed Prime Minister." In 1428 he was granted the honorary title *jugō*, normally reserved for empresses and imperial princes. Mansai's diary for the years 1411–35, *Mansai jugō nikki*, is an important source for the religious and political history of the period.

mansaku → witch hazel

Manshū Jihen → Manchurian Incident

Manshūkoku → Manchukuo

Mantetsu → South Manchuria Railway

mantra

(J: *shingon*; literally, "truthful utterance"; also known in Japanese as *ju, mitsuju, mitsugon*). Sanskrit term that originally referred to words as the instrument of thinking, then to sacred verses and words transmitted by holy men under divine inspiration. Furthermore, mantras themselves are considered to have sacred, mystical, or magical power and are transmitted in secret from master to disciple. In Buddhism, mantra refers to sacred utterances considered to contain the substance of the enlightenment of the Buddhas and bodhisattvas, and their vows. The mantra has a special importance in Japanese esoteric Buddhism, as indicated by the name of the SHINGON SECT (Mantrayāna). Mantras, especially longer verses, are also called *darani* (Skt: *dhāraṇī*), and have been kept untranslated. These are written in Chinese transliteration of the Sanskrit and recited in a Japanese pronunciation.   MATSUNAMI Yoshihiro

Man'yōshū

The earliest extant collection of Japanese poetry. Divided into 20 books, it contains 4,516 numbered WAKA poems, the last and most recent of which is dated New Year's Day of the Japanese year corresponding to AD 759. The earliest ascriptions are a set of four assigned to Empress Iwanohime, who lived in the 4th century—though all attributions earlier than the first quarter of the 7th century are best regarded with skepticism. For several reasons the content of the *Man'yōshū* somewhat exceeds the total of numbered poems. Unnumbered variants raise the total slightly; there are also extended headnotes, footnotes, prose settings, letters, and other compositions—all in Chinese—and a few Chinese poems, to which no numbers have been assigned. Of the three Japanese poetic forms represented in the anthology there are approximately 4,200 TANKA ("short poems"), 260 CHŌKA ("long poems"), and 60 *sedōka* ("head-repeated poems"); exact totals will differ in accordance with which variants are counted. The figure for *tanka* includes the *hanka* or envoys which occur at the end of many *chōka*. However reckoned, the content of the *Man'yōshū* bulks large and occupies an important place in Japanese literature. It contains the overwhelming majority of poems preserved from before the end of the 8th century, which is to say almost all of what the Japanese of those days regarded as literature in their own language. Prose genres had yet to evolve; their first foreshadowings can be seen in the *Man'yōshū* as well as in the chronicles and other collections of a not ostensibly literary nature. The *Man'yōshū* really stands alone as the monument of Japan's first literary flourishing, whose span can be defined as more or less the century preceding this anthology's terminus of 759.

During this century Japan was in a ferment of growth and change, importing Chinese culture and institutions in a deliberate attempt to catch up with the most advanced country in the world. Although 8th-century Japan was rapidly acquiring a modernism of which the *Man'yōshū* was one product, it was still close to its primeval preliterate roots. Partially because the poetry that interested the compilers was not as totally aristocratic in outlook as tended to be true of the later commissioned IMPERIAL ANTHOLOGIES and because the poetic voice of the aristocrats was not uniformly imbued with the Chinese ideals of elegant indirection that later became so influential, the total effect of Man'yō poetry is one of wholeheartedness, sincerity, and robust passion—precisely the qualities that admirers of the anthology have pointed to over the centuries and that still draw readers to it as one of the most revered treasures of the national literature. The Japanese people feel that they can hear their own voices in the collection and not merely those of a high-toned literary clique. A more careful and critical reading of the anthology will quickly reveal highly complex artistry and more than a little of the elegant outlook supposedly characteristic of later ages. Nevertheless, the popular conception is valid to this extent: in its variety the Man'yōshū comes as close as any Japanese work ever has to being the mirror of the whole nation.

Title and Compilation——The name Man'yōshū is written with Chinese characters meaning "Collection of Ten Thousand Leaves." This title has an obvious poetic appeal, whether "leaves" is taken as a metaphor for "poems" (not for "pages," since the original manuscripts were in scroll form), or a sinicization of the Japanese word kotonoha, meaning "word," but literally "leaf of word." It has been plausibly argued, however, that the character for "leaf" is used here in its anciently well-attested sense of "age" or "generation" and that the title therefore should be understood as "Collection for Ten Thousand Generations." As with many other questions surrounding the Man'yōshū, this obscurity may never be cleared up.

The circumstances of the Man'yōshū's compilation are also obscure. Unlike some of the imperial anthologies, it has no preface, nor is it mentioned in contemporary documents. All that can be known about it must come ultimately from internal evidence. This evidence indicates that the Man'yōshū is the culmination of a process of anthology-making dating back at least several decades and that the person most extensively involved in its compilation was the poet ŌTOMO NO YAKAMOCHI (718?–785). There are recurrent references in the detailed editorial apparatus of the Man'yōshū to such older anthologies as the Koshū (Ancient Collection), Kokashū (Collection of Ancient Poems), and Ruijū karin (Classified Forest of Poetry), as well as to the existence of a number of collections of the work of individual poets, namely, those of KASA NO KANAMURA, TAKAHASHI NO MUSHIMARO, and Tanabe no Sakimaro, all of whom lived in the early or mid 8th century. There is reference also to a "Kakinomoto no Asomi Hitomaro Collection," but its content can hardly be ascribed to KAKINOMOTO NO HITOMARO in its entirety, being largely made up of anonymous tanka. None of these works has survived outside the Man'yōshū. "A certain text," "an old book," and so forth, are also frequently mentioned, if vague, source materials.

The aforementioned Ruijū karin is stated to have been compiled by YAMANOUE NO OKURA (660–ca 733), a poet who was a close friend of ŌTOMO NO TABITO (665–731). Tabito, an important poet and sponsor of poetry in his own right, was the father of Yakamochi. Yakamochi, with over 400 extant poems, is the best preserved of Man'yō poets. The last 4 of the 20 books of the Man'yōshū are definitely his compilation, chronologically arranged by him, and with personal notes on the circumstances of composition of each poem. The large number of other Ōtomo poets included in the anthology supports the hypothesis that at least one member of this family was instrumental in assembling the collection. Yakamochi is the most obvious candidate for the culminating role in what must have been a long process.

Historical Context——Chinese books began to come into Japan in the 5th century, and Buddhist scriptures followed in the 6th. Knowledge of their contents was at first limited to a tiny elite, instructed by Korean and then by Chinese masters. Japan at the time was in what is known as the Kofun (tomb mound) period (ca 300–710), during which clans claiming divine ancestry drew wealth from ricelands and other productive areas and controlled the services of specialized corporations of workers. The major clans were wealthy and powerful enough to raise enormous earthen tumuli (KOFUN) over the stone burial chambers of their leaders, a process of conspicuous expenditure which involved withdrawing valuable cropland and workers from production. Around these tumuli, which include some of the largest in the world, were ranged red-clay pottery figures called HANIWA, representing men, women, animals, and houses—no doubt symbols of the wealth of the dead. Many of the figures are clad in armor and mounted on horses—evidence that the Japan of the time was dominated by a class of equestrian warriors. The central polity, known as the YAMATO COURT, from its homeland in the Yamato area south of what became the city of NARA, was ruled over by the most powerful of the clans, the one that built the largest tumuli and claimed descent from the most revered deity, the sun goddess AMA-

TERASU ŌMIKAMI. This clan gradually established itself as divine rulers, and is the ancestor of the imperial family of present-day Japan. During the Kofun period its rule was by no means absolute; the country was a confederation of clans over which it presided from a succession of rude courts, which usually moved to a new location with the accession of a new sovereign. The religious beliefs of the people, or what we would now call their mythology, constituted an interrelated set of cults differing somewhat from clan to clan but focused on the worship of myriad life deities and on the performance of ceremonies to ensure bountiful harvests and the avoidance of pollution (KEGARE). Ceremonial cleanliness was the highest ideal of this religion, now referred to as SHINTŌ.

Death was the greatest threat in these life-oriented cults, the ultimate pollution, and the gigantic tombs imply something of the seriousness with which the passage to another world was contemplated. Ideas on this subject seem to have been twofold. The mythology in the earliest historical sources speaks of an underworld, a land of shadows and corruption called Yomi no Kuni, to which people (even gods) went after death. It is depicted as a horrific and revolting place. The stone burial chamber deep within the tumulus seems an image of this afterworld. There is also evidence that at least the members of the ruling clan were thought to go after death to the "high plain of heaven" (TAKAMAGAHARA), the abode of the sun goddess. This unresolved contradiction doubtless has something to do with the imperfect amalgamation of the various cults that made up the religion. It is worth dwelling on these matters because the feeling for death, along with the reverence for the imperial family and the awe evinced toward nature, was an important component in the tone of much of the most typical and impressive poetry of the Man'yōshū. The world out of which the early poetry emerged was one infused with godhead, and the feeling of awe runs through the poetic utterances of the time like a deep ground note.

The earliest examples of Japanese verse are found not in the Man'yōshū, but in the KOJIKI (Records of Ancient Matters) and the NIHON SHOKI (Chronicle of Japan), the oldest Japanese books, histories of Japan dating respectively to 712 and 720. Both begin their accounts with the creation of the world, and their earlier portions are basically rehearsals of the mythology. They also contain much legend, folktale, and song, in addition to genuine (and some not-so-genuine) history. What apparently are the earliest songs are lacking in a set prosodic structure, that is, a sense of set line-lengths and poetic forms. They are usually exclamatory, declarative, or narrative in mode, or sometimes dramatic, as if they were acted out while being recited. The jo or JOKOTOBA (imagistic preface) is already a dominant technique. There seems to have been from earliest times a predilection for working into the song's subject by the roundabout path of word play, and elaborate structures leading up to a key word are found frequently in early verse.

This penchant for preposited imagery continued to be developed in Man'yō poetry. There is also an observable tendency to alternate shorter and longer lines, and the range of verse included in the chronicles includes examples of perfectly regular tanka ("short poems") in the syllabic pattern of 5-7-5-7-7. There are also several old-style chōka ("long poems") in more-or-less loose alternation of long and short lines, but lacking the final 7-7 couplet of the form as it eventually came to be defined. At this point the content of the Man'yōshū begins to overlap that of the chronicles. There is no completely irregular verse, but a number of old chōka are included. Most of the chōka follow the classical form and are followed by one or more tanka as envoys (hanka). Another form found in the Man'yōshū is the sedōka. The 62 examples in the Man'yōshū are the largest surviving corpus of this form. Its syllabic pattern of 5-7-7-5-7-7 seems to be based on a repetition of the ancient "half-poem" (katauta) in 5-7-7. The over 4,000 tanka, however, are clearly the numerically dominant form of Man'yō poetry. When the chōka and sedōka fell into desuetude after the 8th century, it was the tanka that continued as the classic Japanese poetic form for centuries to come.

From the time of Prince SHŌTOKU (574–622) early in the 7th century there was a quickening movement in Japanese ruling circles to learn from China and remodel their country along its lines. Official embassies began to be sent to the gigantic continental empire in 607 and continued at intervals over the next three centuries. Men of outstanding intelligence accompanied these expeditions and remained as students in China, often for extended periods, bringing back learning both secular and religious. Knowledge of the accomplishments of China in statecraft, architecture, city planning, fine arts, music, literature, philosophy, historiography, and other areas of intellectual life came back to Japan in increasing volume. The fertilizing effect was extraordinary. Whole new worlds opened up to the Japanese—at least to those directly associated with the court and the burgeoning Buddhist establishment. As the 7th century drew on into the 8th, extensive palaces and eventually whole capitals were built on Chinese models, a bureaucracy was organized and law codes drawn up, and temples filled with marvels of painting and of sculpture in wood, clay, bronze, and dry lacquer were erected. Art styles derived from India through Central Asia and China suddenly burst in full splendor on the island kingdom. Continental artists and craftsmen were both the first creators of this art and the teachers of the Japanese, but the latter eagerly mastered the new techniques. Books and teachers of reading and writing also came across the sea to meet the needs of the newly literate elites. With the foundation of HEIJŌKYŌ (the modern city of Nara) in 710 Japan had its first experience of urbanity. The rectilinear street pattern and the sparkling tile roofs of the red-pillared palaces stood for an adventure in change that must have been enormously exciting to those living at the time. It was one of Japan's rare moments when it opened its doors wide to knowledge from abroad. Customs, costumes, ceremonies—all were welcomed by the Nara court. Music and dance from the hinterlands of Asia became part of the decorum of aristocratic Japanese life. The building of huge temples took up energies formerly used in erecting tumuli: the Kofun period was over and what it stood for became part of an archaic past. The change that came over Japan is seen nowhere more vividly than in the erection of the Great Buddha at the temple TŌDAIJI in Heijōkyō. This gigantic bronze figure of Vairocana was the largest in all the Buddha-lands of Asia, Japan's assertion of the preeminence of its religious fervor. Gilded, thanks to newly discovered gold mines, it shone out over a great throng of courtiers, ritual dancers, and Buddhist clergy when it was dedicated in 752. The emperor SHŌMU (r 724–749) had already three years earlier declared himself the "Servant of the Three Treasures," that is, of the Buddha, the Doctrine, and the Community of believers. This was an astonishing statement for a ruler with a claim to divinity as a descendant of the sun goddess.

The influence of the highly writing-oriented civilization of China with its already ancient literary and historiographical traditions worked to make its Japanese pupil aware of the desirability of having writings of its own. The compilation of national histories was of the first order of importance, and two were completed shortly after the founding of Heijōkyō, the *Kojiki* and *Nihon shoki* referred to above. Both contain many poems in the native language, as has already been noted. Aside from the poems, the *Nihon shoki* is written in classical Chinese, modeled on the style of the Chinese dynastic histories. The *Kojiki* is in a unique and unstable amalgam of Chinese and Japanese, and of the two parallel accounts is distinctly the less sinified. The *Nihon shoki,* a much longer and more detailed narrative, illustrates how the medium will affect the message, as early Japanese rulers are made to sound like Chinese Confucian monarchs, with speeches inspired by Chinese sources attributed to them. The Japanese also quickly became aware of the high value placed in China on the composition of poetry, some skill at which was a virtual requirement for a position in the bureaucracy. As part of their own training in reading and writing Chinese (the international language of East Asia) they began in the late 7th century to experiment with writing *shi (shih),* the most common form of Chinese poetry. By the middle of the 8th century the Nara court had developed enough literati for a collection to be made of their poems in Chinese, the KAIFŪSŌ, whose date of 751 is eight years earlier than the last poem in the *Man'yōshū.*

Efforts to write in Chinese, however, did not satisfy the literary urges of the Japanese. They wished not only to learn and copy but to emulate. They wanted to record a literature of their own, and the *Man'yōshū* was their first product. The ancient songs of the oral tradition already existed and could now be put down on paper. Merely recording was not all, however; something much more creative was happening. At the same time that the Japanese gained literacy and the ability to record, their reading—and eventually writing—of Chinese poetry made them aware of poetry as an art, of literary form, mode, and point of view. It is probably from this time that the basic alternation of short and long lines in the native prosody began to regularize itself into five- and seven-syllable units, and that the set forms of the *tanka, chōka,* and so forth started to evolve. The basic preference for preposited forms of modification and figurative expansion remained and was further developed. Long imagistic "prefaces" *(jo)* or *jokotoba* and one-line "pillow-words" (MAKURA KOTOBA) continued to be standard techniques; their possi-

bilities were fully realized only around the end of the 7th century, when the age of written books was at hand. Increased use of parallelism, particularly of the pattern a-b-a'-b', where the structure of a couplet is echoed and its sense altered in a contiguous couplet (for example, "In spring the mountains / Deck themselves with blossoms // In autumn the river / Spreads itself with fallen leaves"), undoubtedly owes much to the influence of balanced contrastive structures in Chinese, both prose and poetry. This mannered style of writing had been particularly popular in China during the Six Dynasties (222–589), a period whose literary ideals are reflected in the *Wenxuan (Wen-hsüan;* J: *Monzen,* early 6th century), an anthology very influential in Japan. In any event, parallel quatrains and sometimes even octets are very common in Man'yō *chōka,* and serve to slow down, complicate, and strengthen the sinuous line of the onflowing, modifier-modified syntax.

Japanese poetry thus became conscious of itself as an art, developed its native techniques, and adapted foreign ones, under what can only be called a beneficent Chinese influence. Other aspects of this influence have sometimes been looked at askance as corrupting the purity of the native Japanese spirit. The *kotodama,* or wordsoul, of the Japanese language speaks most truly, it is held, in the accents of true love, loyalty, and honesty. Anything more devious or roundabout would be a regrettable foreign intrusion. This view is not to be countenanced without substantial modification. The admirable qualities mentioned are present in copious quantities in Man'yō verse. The artistry with which they are expressed—and even the simplest poem has its artistry—is indebted to both native and foreign sources. Beyond this, the great size and variety of the *Man'yōshū* represent a world of diversity and growth. Simple emotions straightforwardly expressed are certainly part of that world, but only part. The effect of a poem in which a country girl speaks of her hands chapped in hulling rice or a fisher boy likens his girl to a sea lentil is all the greater in a total context which includes the experiments of courtiers in writing Chinese-style plum-blossom poems, or even actual Chinese verse and prose. The sea lentil is humble and native, the plum blossoms elegant and foreign, but in both cases the poems exploit the technique of analogy. The sea lentil poem, which also employs irony, is actually very artistic, that is, as much based on fully poetic stratagems as the plum blossom poems, if not as self-consciously "literary."

Pretended or "elegant" confusion (in such phrases, for example, as "Are they plum blossoms, or is it snow?") makes its first appearance in Japanese poetry in the *Man'yōshū,* in the party poems of Ōtomo no Tabito and his circle, in 730. This kind of elegant artfulness was to be deeply influential on the poetry of the Heian period (794–1185), but it is important to realize that poets of the early 8th century were already indulging in it. A poet like Ōtomo no Tabito leaves a very different impression from his great predecessor Kakinomoto no Hitomaro. Hitomaro, who did most of his work in the last two decades of the 7th century, speaks with the voice of the ancient bard, perfecting the traditions of his native verse. He seems very "Japanese," very close to the rootstock of his country's archaic essence. Tabito, by contrast, resembles more a Chinese literatus. It comes as a suprise to realize that the two were contemporaries in the last decades of the 7th century; but Tabito lived on, and his surviving poetry is from his old age. A great hinge of time seems to turn on the decades before and after the foundation of Heijōkyō in 710. A new and self-consciously modern literary society grew up in the new capital. The courtiers of Nara were reminiscent of their Chinese counterparts who were sent off to govern distant provinces. The desire to return to the capital, the feeling that absence from it was exile, owes not a little to Chinese example. Tabito's plum-blossom party, at which all the guests were expected to compose poems, took place in Kyūshū, where he served as governor-general of the defense headquarters of DAZAIFU. He is also the most likely author of a set of 11 *tanka* with an elegant Chinese preface, which constitute a fictional account, combining prose and poetry, set on the Matsura River in northern Kyūshū (MYS 5:853–863; reference is to *Man'yōshū,* book number, and poem number). This sequence owes its inspiration to at least two Chinese sources, the *Youxianku (Yu-hsienk'u;* Journey to the Abode of Immortals), a risqué Tang (T'ang) novelette by Zhang Wencheng (Chang Wen-ch'eng; ca 657–730), and the "Luoshen fu" (Lo-shen fu; rhyme prose on the Goddess of the River Lo), a poem by Cao Zhi (Ts'ao Chih; 192–232). The former work, whose author was contemporary with Tabito, was apparently brought back to Japan by returning students and was much admired for its elegant combination of sentiment and sensuality. Tabito adapts its balanced phrases in his preface to the Matsura River sequence. He also experimented with the Chinese version of *in vino veritas*, echoing the sentiments of the bibulous Seven Sages of the Bamboo Grove. His set of 13 *tanka* on the virtues of *sake* or rice wine (MYS 3:338–350) remained unique, as the theme was not taken up by other Japanese poets. The work of Tabito's friend Yamanoue no Okura is also unique. Okura is an example of a man intellectually formed by Chinese studies. He was a member of the official embassy to Tang China in 702 (see SUI AND TANG [T'ANG] CHINA, EMBASSIES TO), returning a few years later, but in order to have been chosen to go, he must have already been known as a student of Chinese. In any event, his themes are those of the Confucian humanist—support for family virtues, sympathy for the poor, and a somewhat dogmatic moralism. Okura enjoyed the pose of a learned, crusty old Chinese-style gentleman and has left long compositions in classical Chinese.

The correspondence between Tabito's son Yakamochi and Yakamochi's cousin Ōtomo no Ikenushi provides the most extensive example of literary behavior in the Chinese mode. Book 12 of the *Man'yōshū* contains series of exchanges between the two, with letters written in Chinese accompanying both Chinese and Japanese poems. What is most notable about this correspondence is the evidence it provides of the appeal of friendship between men as the inspiration of poetry. This is a characteristically Chinese ethos, which never developed to a comparable degree in Japanese. As with Okura's moral outrage, the thing to be regretted here is not the strength of Chinese influence but its ultimate weakness.

One specifically Chinese theme did fully penetrate Japanese verse at this time, however, and that was the love-story myth of Tanabata (see TANABATA FESTIVAL). From the moment of its introduction around the beginning of the 8th century, hundreds of poems were turned out annually on the themes of the lover stars Altair (the Herdsman) and Vega (the Weaving Maiden). Separated by the Milky Way (the "River of Heaven" in both Chinese and Japanese), the lover stars could meet only once a year, on the seventh night of the seventh month. The appeal of this romantic myth was immediate and enduring, and almost a dozen of the surviving Man'yō poems on the subject were written by the otherwise antiromantic Okura. In all of this, Japanese poetry maintained its linguistic distinctiveness and its faithfulness to ancient themes and techniques, and was never in danger in the Man'yō period of being swallowed up by the flood of interest in things Chinese. Instead, the native verse was modified and diversified under the impetus of Chinese-style learning and became a truly literary art.

Content and Structure —— The first two of the 20 books of the *Man'yōshū* form a pair. Each is arranged chronologically, starting with poems attributed to figures of remote antiquity and coming down to the early 8th century after the foundation of the capital at Nara. Together these two books present three of the main typological categories employed in the *Man'yōshū*—*zōka*, *sōmon*, and *banka*. Book 1 is made up entirely of *zōka*, "miscellaneous poems," a term adopted from the *Wenxuan*. In the Man'yō context the term refers to poems which in the tripartite scheme employed by the compilers cannot be classified as either love poems or elegies. The 84 poems of Book 1 include *chōka* and *tanka* by courtiers and members of the ruling family, with many on progresses and other "imperial" themes.

Book 2, by contrast, is made up of *sōmon* and *banka*, each group constituting a separate chronological sequence. The term *sōmon* is also derived from the *Wenxuan* and other Chinese sources, but it was the *Man'yōshū* compilers who elevated it to a position of equality with *zōka* and *banka*. *Sōmon* are love poems. The word implies an exchange of inquiries or endearments; in practice the poetry is predominantly one of longing, true to what became the essence of the classical love tradition. There are to be sure a number of jocular exchanges between lovers, and such a cry of triumph as MYS 1:95, whose author exults in having got the girl, but love in separation is already the most common type. There are 65 poems in the *sōmon* group. *Banka* are poems occasioned by death. The term, which literally means "pulling poem," refers to dirges accompanying the pulling of a funeral hearse and also derives from a category found in the *Wenxuan*. It is thought that at least until Kakinomoto no Hitomaro's time at the end of the 7th century dirges were actually sung at court funerals in Japan. The poems labeled *banka* in Book 2 and elsewhere in the *Man'yōshū* are not all of this type; several are reflective meditations considerably removed in time from the death of the person involved. Of the ones which can plausibly be read as funeral songs, there are two main types—public elegies on the deaths of members of the court, and private laments over the loss of

someone close to the poet, usually a wife. Death is spoken of as an awesome mystery, and the power of grief is evoked as something which brings about a kind of temporary dementia in the mourners. The dead are sometimes said to be "hidden in the stone"; their spirits hover in the air or mount the sky to the high plain of heaven. Before burial the bodies of members of the imperial family were kept for a period of temporary enshrinement in a building called the *araki no miya*, and this enshrinement was the occasion for the public elegies. *Banka* also include laments for those who died without burial or funeral rites, the corpses of unknown travelers found in the mountains or on the shore. *Banka* declined after about 700, as Buddhist ceremonies and music came to replace old native rites. There are 93 examples in the *banka* section of Book 2. Both the *sōmon* and the *banka* sections build to climaxes with the major poems of Hitomaro, whose work contributes greatly to the high quality and elevated tone of Books 1 and 2. It has even been suggested that these two books constitute a separate collection compiled by imperial command.

Book 3 in a sense is like Books 1 and 2 combined. It begins with 153 *zōka*, and follows these with 24 *hiyuka* and 66 *banka*. *Hiyuka* are poems containing analogies, varying from metaphor to allegory. In practice most of them are love poems, so that the category here corresponds to *sōmon* in Book 2. Again, each category is arranged in a self-contained chronological sequence, *zōka* and *hiyuka* from the late 7th century to 730s and *banka* from the reign of Empress SUIKO early in the 7th century to 744. There are many dated poems by members of the Ōtomo family, especially by Yakamochi, and so it seems that Book 3 may have grown out of a basic collection augmented from Ōtomo sources. It also contains *zōka* by Hitomaro; private travel poems; the group of poems in praise of *sake* by Yakamochi's father, Tabito; and poems in praise of mountains, notably Mt. Fuji. These latter are by YAMABE NO AKAHITO and Takahashi no Mushimaro, important poets of the first half of the 8th century.

Book 4 is made up entirely of *sōmon*. It is arranged in a roughly chronological fashion with many poems in the new Nara style of the early 8th century. Overwhelmingly a collection of *tanka*, of which there are 301 (including envoys or *hanka*), it also contains seven *chōka* and one *sedōka*. The early period of Ōtomo no Yakamochi is represented here, as are poems by other Ōtomo poets. It is quite plausible that Yakamochi was the compiler, drawing on both Ōtomo and other sources for love poems.

Book 5 is unique in its content and very different from everything that comes before it. Its 108 poems are classified as *zōka*, but this is misleading, as *banka* and *sōmon* are also included. In fact, poems of any type make up only part of this unusual collection: book 5 is about half prose, with 10 extended prefaces, five letters, and an independent composition, all in Chinese. There are also two Chinese poems. None of this non-Japanese material is represented in the numbering of the text. The book is basically a collection of the writings of the circle of Ōtomo no Tabito and his friend Yamanoue no Okura, whose interest in a Chinese style in life and letters emerges strongly in the *Man'yōshū*. All the items in this volume are arranged chronologically and dated, and the whole span covered is only five years, from 728 to 733. This period represents the last years of Tabito, who died in 731, and Okura, who probably died in 733 or not long after. Among the unusual contents of Book 5 is Okura's long prose piece, "A Text Mourning His Illness." Most of Okura's major *chōka* are also found here, including his great "Dialogue on Poverty" (MYS 5:892–893). The Matsura River sequence combines *tanka* with a fictional prose setting and has been attributed to both Tabito and Okura. There are also the poetic products of Tabito's famous garden party of 730, a series of 32 *tanka* by various poets on the elegant Chinese theme of appreciation of the flowering plum. All in all, Book 5 represents new directions in poetic and intellectual life and bears a strongly personal stamp.

Book 6 too is classified in its entirety as *zōka*. Its 160 poems include 27 *chōka*, 132 *tanka*, and 1 *sedōka*. The arrangement is chronological, running from 723 to 744. Nara poets such as Kasa no Kanamura, Yamabe no Akahito, Tanabe no Sakimaro, and the early Yakamochi are represented. Poems by Ōtomo poets are clearly dated, and so it seems likely that Yakamochi was the editor here. Most of the poems are on public topics, imperial progresses, and the like.

Book 7 is again a departure from what has gone before. Totally lacking in *chōka*, it is made up of 324 *tanka* and 25 *sedōka*, almost all of which are anonymous. Since there are no informative head-notes, it is impossible to determine any dates. The overall scheme of *zōka*, *hiyuka*, *banka* echoes that of Book 3, but the subcategories employed appear here for the first time. These constitute an arrangement by encyclopedia-like set topics. The *zōka* section introduces *eibutsuka*, "poems on things," beginning with the sky and the clouds and passing on to such terrestrial phenomena as mountains, rivers, and flowers. The concept derives from Six-Dynasties Chinese poetry. Modally these poems range from allegory to simple description. There are also numerous travel poems, a group of 24 *sedōka*, and various other subcategories. The *hiyuka* section also has a categorical arrangement, here called *kibutsu*, "referring to things." The poems are love analogies, in which the "thing" referred to functions as a metaphor. These too may work out to a point-by-point allegory, where the sea stands for love, the boat for the lover, the oars for his driving passion, the offshore deeps for the deepening of emotion, and the drying tide for the shallow feelings imputed to the girl he loves. Book 7 concludes with a group of *banka* in *tanka* form, interesting for their treatment of the newly introduced custom of cremation. The "Hitomaro Collection," *Koshū*, and *Kokashū* are cited as sources for over a hundred of the poems in this book.

The poems in Book 8 are divided into the four seasons, with each season subdivided into *zōka* and *sōmon*. This arrangement is a recognition of what is obvious from a study of later Japanese poetic anthologies—that season and love are not mutually exclusive categories. There is a chronological arrangement within each subsection, with the bulk of the poems belonging to the early and mid 8th century. Among major poets, Akahito and Okura are represented, as well as Yakamochi and other members of the Ōtomo family. The book contains 236 *tanka*, six *chōka*, and four *sedōka*.

Book 9 is the only book in the *Man'yōshū* to be made up of all three major categories—*zōka*, *sōmon*, and *banka*—and no others. Its 148 poems include 125 *tanka*, 22 *chōka*, and one *sedōka*. Dating of many poems is uncertain, but there seems to be a roughly chronological scheme at work. This book draws on all named sources, and has many poems on travel and on legendary material. The collections of Takahashi no Mushimaro and Tanabe no Sakimaro supply much of the latter. Poems on the Maiden Unai, Mama no Tegona, and the fisherman Urashima (see URASHIMA TARŌ) contribute to the storytelling quality of this portion of the *Man'yōshū*. In this respect it resembles Book 16 but lacks the latter's extended headnotes. There are no poems by members of the Ōtomo family.

With 539 poems, Book 10 is the longest book in the *Man'yōshū*. Its content includes 532 *tanka*, four *sedōka*, and three *chōka*. Most of these poems are anonymous and undated. Their arrangement combines features of Books 7 and 8. As in Book 8, the basic layout is by the four seasons, each subdivided into *zōka* and *sōmon*. Following the example of Book 7, encyclopedic topics are used as the third level of organization. Here too, *eibutsu* ("compositions on things") is allied to *zōka*, and *kibutsu* ("reference to things") to *sōmon*. It is obvious that "reference," that is, metaphor, is more characteristic of love poetry. Of the four seasons, autumn is numerically the dominant one. Many of the poems exhibit qualities of elegance and refinement bespeaking Chinese influence (as does the categorical arrangement). There are, for instance, 98 poems on the Tanabata story of the lover stars Altair and Vega in the autumn *zōka* section. The placement of this group of poems under *zōka* rather than *sōmon* is curious. It is thought that Yakamochi probably had little to do with the compilation of this book.

Books 11 and 12 form a pair. Each is composed of poems arranged by category; all are anonymous except for attributions to the "Hitomaro Collection"; and all are *tanka* except for 17 *sedōka* in Book 11. These are the only two books to contain the contrastive modal designations *tada ni omoi o nobu* and *mono ni yosete omoi o nobu*, respectively, "poems which express one's thoughts directly" and "poems which express one's thoughts by reference to things." These bear some resemblance to the *eibutsu* and *kibutsu* categories found in Book 7 and elsewhere, except that here both are types of love poetry. The poems that "make reference to things" show the encyclopedic tendencies of *kibutsu* poems elsewhere. There are also poems on parting and travel, "analogical poems" (*hiyuka*), and dialogue poems. Duplications indicate that the two books were compiled separately. It is thought that they were in existence by 720 and that Yakamochi had little to do with them. Book 11 has 489 numbered poems, and Book 12 has 379; both contain unnumbered variants as well.

Book 13 is divided into *zōka*, *sōmon*, *mondō* (dialogue poems), *hiyuka*, and *banka*, but its distinguishing feature is that it is a collection of *chōka*. Its 60 *tanka* all function as envoys, as does the single *sedōka*. The latter provides the only instance of *sedōka* as envoy in the *Man'yōshū*. Most of the poems are anonymous and undated

and quite old in technique if not in actual time of composition. Included are many short *chōka*, irregular *chōka*, *chōka* with no envoys, and *chōka* whose envoys do not fit. There are some poems, however, which seem to have been influenced by the manner of Hitomaro, as well as an elegy for a prince who died in 708, and a poem which may be dated to 722. It is thought that this book was compiled in the 720s, perhaps not by Yakamochi, out of largely orally transmitted poems to which the unknown editor or editors tacked on envoys with mixed success. The book contains 126 poems.

Book 14 is the only book in the *Man'yōshū* organized on a geographical basis. It consists of 238 *tanka*, anonymous and undated, composed in eastern Japan, at the time a remote frontier area. The poems, called *Azuma uta* or "songs of the Eastland," are rich in local dialect and purport to be the compositions of the common people. They are divided into the categories of *zōka*, *sōmon*, *hiyuka*, SAKI-MORI UTA, and *banka*, and subdivided by province of origin. *Sakimori uta* are the poems of the *sakimori*, the "guardians of the headlands," eastern conscripts sent for military service in the defense forces of northern Kyūshū. Although the imagery of the poems in Book 14 is often robustly rural, the universe of love they depict is not foreign to that of the courtiers. The fact that the province of Musashi is here treated as belonging to the TŌKAIDŌ (Eastern Sea Circuit) rather than the Tōsandō (Eastern Mountain Circuit) has been used to argue that this section of the *Man'yōshū* was edited after 771, when the province was shifted administratively from one to the other. The fact has also been taken to imply subsequent revision, or as implying that Musashi (the area surrounding present-day Tōkyō) communicated with the capital over the Tōkaidō route before 771. It has been suggested that the compiler or reviser was Takahashi no Mushimaro, who traveled to the eastern provinces and wrote about them. Yakamochi is also a plausible candidate because of his interest in the *sakimori* (evinced in Book 20). Whoever did the compilation, it is interesting that he arranged what are apparently poems of the common folk according to the usual literary categories of the *Man'yōshū*.

Book 15 falls into two parts, each in a sense the record of a journey. The first 145 poems were composed by members of an embassy from the Japanese court to the Korean state of SILLA in 736–737. Including five *chōka* and three *sedōka*, but mostly *tanka*, they stretch like stepping-stones along the Inland Sea to northern Kyūshū and across to Tsushima and back. They are for the most part poems of longing for home, true to the tradition of Japanese travel literature, but they also record impressions of sights along the way and of at least one amorous encounter. Unfortunately there are no poems about Silla itself, the goal of the voyage. In fact, the embassy was rebuffed by the Koreans. The last 63 poems, all *tanka*, constitute a separate group. They are love poems exchanged between Sano no Otogami (also known as SANO NO CHIGAMI NO OTOME) and her husband Nakatomi no Yakamori. Yakamori was sent into exile to Echizen Province (now part of Fukui Prefecture) in about 738, ostensibly for marrying Otogami, a minor female functionary at court. The details are obscure, and it has even been suggested that the whole story of Yakamori is a fiction. Be that as it may, the love poems in this group are among the most intense in the *Man'yōshū*, with many sharp evocations of deprivation and longing. Book 15 is marked by a complete absence of arrangement by category; the organizational principles are basically narrative and chronological.

Book 16 is made up of *zōka* and "poems with a story" (*yuen aru uta*), or according to another reading, "*zōka* with a story." It contains 92 *tanka*, eight *chōka*, three *sedōka*, and one *bussokusekika* (a poem in the pattern 5-7-5-7-7-7). Many of these have long prose settings either as headnotes or footnotes. In its experimental amalgam of prose and poetry, this part of the *Man'yōshū* harks back to Book 5, as it does to Book 9 in its use of legendary materials. It contains both the shortest *chōka* (seven lines) and the second longest. Dating of the poems is difficult; they may range from the late 7th to mid-8th century. Authorship is anonymous or disputed in many cases, but Yamanoue no Okura seems to have had his hand in at least some. The compilation may have been carried out by Yakamochi. Book 16 is of great literary interest because it contains the forerunners of fictional forms combining prose and poetry and because it features highly informal and even comic aspects which contain much that relates to the later poetic genres of *haikai* (see RENGA AND HAIKAI) and KYŌKA. Some verses are examples of word games, rising to the challenge of naming extremely disparate objects in a single poem. A few verses show an easy and comical interest in scatology.

Books 17–20 form a group distinct from the rest of the *Man'yō-shū*. These final four books are definitely the compilation of Ōtomo no Yakamochi, his own compositions and poems he received and collected, arranged chronologically with precise dates and context supplied by the great poet-anthologizer himself. They abandon the various typological and modal schemes employed elsewhere in the anthology, forming a kind of poetic diary (albeit with large gaps), a personal poetry collection added at the end of the public one. Book 17 begins with a group of poems from the year 730, when the 12-year-old Yakamochi's father Tabito was leaving his post at Dazaifu for the capital, and goes down to the spring of 748, when Yakamochi was serving as governor of Etchū (now Toyama Prefecture). The bulk of the book is made up of poems from the period of Yakamochi's tenure in that post, which began in the seventh month of 746. Along with much banquet poetry, there are Yakamochi's lament on the death of his younger brother Fumimochi in the fall of 746, his exchanges of Chinese prose and poetry, as well as *chōka* and *tanka*, with his cousin Ikenushi in the spring of 747, and the long poem on the loss of his hawk. Poetry by other acquaintances and members of the Ōtomo family is also included. The book contains a total of 142 poems.

Book 18 covers a little less than two years, from the third month of 748 to the second month of 750. During all this period Yakamochi was serving as governor of Etchū. It seems likely that part of this book has been lost, as nearly a year (from the fourth month of 748 to the third month of 749) is blank. Notable poems include Yakamochi's *chōka* on the discovery of gold in Michinoku (northeastern Honshū), his exchanges with Tanabe no Sakimaro, his prayer and thanksgiving for rain, and his Okura-style reproof of the immorality of one of his subordinates. His cousin Ikenushi had been transferred to Echizen, and there are fewer exchanges with him. The book contains 107 poems; all 10 of its *chōka* are by Yakamochi.

Book 19 brings Yakamochi back from Etchū to the capital. The book covers three years, from the third month of 750 to the second month of 753. Yakamochi's transfer came in the 7th month of 751. Structurally, the book is balanced by superb groups of spring poems, beginning with a set on peach and damson blossoms in the garden of the governor's residence in Etchū, and ending with poems on the wind in the bamboo, the song of the warbler, and the flight of the skylark three years later in Nara. Yakamochi's political fortunes waned after his return to the capital, and the last three poems are pervaded by a finely expressed melancholy. These poems as well as the opening set are *tanka;* many of the best poems in this book are *tanka,* often reflective in tone. Among the 23 *chōka* the most impressive ones were written before Yakamochi's return to Etchū. They range over his activities in his last months in Etchū, with vivid impressions of the fresh scenery of that mountain region. The book contains 154 poems in all.

Book 20 begins with the 5th month of 753, and ends on New Year's Day 759 with a felicitous banquet poem by Yakamochi, who by that time had become governor of Inaba Province (now part of Tottori Prefecture). The book contains a great deal of banquet poetry, but of more interest are the *sakimori* poems, of which there are over 80. The poems, mostly in *tanka* form, that the *sakimori* composed in farewell as they left their homes were of interest to Yakamochi, who collected them and preserved the authors' names—the largest group of named commoner poets in the *Man'yōshū*. He also tried his hand at expressing the sorrows of the *sakimori* in his own poetry. Melancholy and delicate nostalgia inform the output of Yakamochi in this, his last preserved poetic period. The book contains 224 poems.

Major Poets——The *Man'yōshū* is famed for its social range. There are poems by members of the imperial family and by members of the peasantry. Most of the named poets, as in later ages, are middle or lower-ranking courtiers, and it is to them that one must turn for a list of major poets. Of the many accomplished poets of royal blood, only one is listed below.

Princess Nukata (NUKATA NO ŌKIMI), born about 638 or somewhat later, lived at least into the 680s or 690s. Probably a descendant of the early-6th-century emperor Senka, she was intimately involved with the two most powerful monarchs of the 7th century, the brother emperors TENJI and TEMMU. Temmu (d 686; r 672–686) fathered a daughter by her while still a prince, but later she became a minor consort of his elder brother Tenji (626–672; r 661–672). There is evidence (MYS 1:20–21) that she was still loved by the younger brother. Whether or not the change of marriage partners

was of her own volition, she dutifully composed laments (MYS 2:151, 155) on Emperor Tenji's death in 672, as well as a poem of remembrance (MYS 4:488), which seems more than merely proforma. The bad blood that seemingly existed between Tenji and Temmu, and which culminated in the JINSHIN DISTURBANCE in 672, is sometimes related to these marital complications. Princess Nukata's best-known poem is MYS 1:16, a *chōka* expressing a preference for autumn over spring, composed in response to imperial command in the years of Tenji's reign at Ōmi (in what is now Shiga Prefecture; 667–672). This formal literary occasion is a landmark of sorts in the progress of Chinese-style culture at the Japanese court. That Princess Nukata was so honored implies recognition of her poetic talent.

Kakinomoto no Asomi Hitomaro (KAKINOMOTO NO HITOMARO) is the poet whose creativity dominates the late 7th century and, in large measure, the entire tradition of Man'yō poetry after his time. He was a courtier-official probably of low to middling rank, about whose life very little is known. It is apparent that, as with others of his status, his time was divided between service in provincial and central bureaucracies. At one time he was resident in Iwami (now part of Shimane Prefecture), a province on the Sea of Japan remote from the capital, and it seems plausible that he was in the provincial administration. His poetry, which is the only source for his biography, also refers to his traveling by boat through the Inland Sea. He had a wife in Karu, a village near the capital at Asuka, whose death he memorialized in a pair of *chōka,* and who bore him a child. Other poems refer to a wife whom he left behind in Iwami and who apparently outlived him. A valedictory verse has him dying on Kamo Mountain in the same province, mourned by this other wife. He was known as an author of *banka,* or laments, four of which define the period in which he is known to have been active. They are for Prince Kusakabe (d 689), Prince Kawashima (d 691), Prince Takechi (d 696), and Princess Asuka (d 700). We have no way of knowing how far outside the span of 11 years represented by these four dates Hitomaro's career extended, but it seems likely that it ended before the foundation of the Nara capital in 710. Hitomaro is in any event the culminating poet of the period before the new urbanity of the 8th century. He perfected the techniques of the earlier poetry, the formulaic style derived from the oral tradition, the use of metaphorical, preposited, imagistic structures, the parallelism and the long prosodic units. He created and maintained a lofty and majestic style, flexible and varied, laced through with compassionate irony, that brought to the *chōka* form its best moments. His themes were the sadness of parting, whether in life or death, the awesomeness of the imperial institution, and the mystery of man's fate. He also wrote about travel and invoked the sacredness of the land. His surviving poems total 17 *chōka* and 62 *tanka* (including envoys), exclusive of the 387 poems, mostly *tanka,* in the controversial "Hitomaro Collection," a component of the *Man'yōshū* whose content on stylistic, thematic, and other grounds seems too alien to Hitamaro to be accepted as his work.

Kaso no Asomi Kanamura (KASA NO KANAMURA) is another poet whose name is linked to a personal collection by the *Man'yōshū* compilers. The poems noted as drawn from it are accepted as his equally with the ones not so labeled. He is known to have been active from 715 to 733, and has left a small body of poems (11 *chōka,* 34 *tanka*), largely dealing with his travels in the imperial train. His poetry has echoes of Hitomaro in its phraseology and its praises of the Yoshino palace but injects a personal note of longing and attraction for the sights seen on his journeys.

Yamabe (or Yamanobe) no Sukune Akahito (YAMABE NO AKAHITO; d ca 736), like Kanamura and Hitomaro, followed his sovereign's progresses and memorialized them in verse. Such public poetry bulks large among his 13 *chōka* and 37 *tanka,* and Akahito too owes a great debt to Hitomaro for the grand manner established for the *chōka* by the earlier poet. Though his efforts along this line lack Hitomaro's depth and majesty, Akahito is far from being a mere follower, a purely derivative versifier. He brought to poetry an aesthetic appreciation of nature and a descriptive lyricism in the *tanka,* new and recognizably his own, which were in the long run more influential than Hitomaro's grandeur. As with Kanamura, whose poetic output is superficially very similar, practically nothing is known about his life. He was a low-ranking courtier of Emperor Shōmu (r 724–749), in whose entourage he often found himself.

Takahashi no Muraji Mushimaro (TAKAHASHI NO MUSHIMARO; fl ca 730) was of all the Man'yō poets the most interested in local legends and in mountains. He was primarily a *chōka* poet, having left 13 examples of the form; most of his 18 *tanka* are envoys. His notable poems include celebrations of Mt. Fuji, described as a living god, and the cult of sexual license on Mt. Tsukuba, as well as the long narrative account of the legend of the fisherman Urashima (Urashima Tarō), who married the daughter of the sea god. Mushimaro is known to have been in service to Fujiwara no Umakai during the 720s and 730s and was in the latter's provincial administration in Hitachi in eastern Japan (present-day Ibaraki Prefecture). Most of Mushimaro's surviving work is labeled as from a collection bearing his name.

Ōtomo no Sukune Tabito (ŌTOMO NO TABITO; 665–731), as is perhaps implied by the fact that his dates are known, was more of a personage on the political scene than most other major Man'yō poets. He rose to junior second rank in the court bureaucracy and to the position of *dainagon*, or major counsellor. The last position but one that he held, governor general of the defense headquarters at Dazaifu in northern Kyūshū, was literally his most important, as he presided over a poetically active circle of subordinates and acquaintances during his years there from 728 to 730. Most of Tabito's surviving work is in fact from his old age. He was primarily a *tanka* poet, having left only one *chōka*. The number of his *tanka* is in dispute, as vexed problems of attribution surround him and his friend Yamanoue no Okura (see below). About 75 *tanka* are a reasonable number to ascribe to him. He also wrote a few brief compositions in Chinese prose, which have been preserved in the *Man'yōshū*. His work shows a mind attuned to the elegance of Chinese Six-Dynasties prose and poetry; he is one of the earliest Japanese poets to display a consistent and dominant interest in Chinese themes and attitudes. His garden party in 730 in which he and his staff at Dazaifu composed graceful poems on the blossoming plums is but one example of this. He also wrote a sequence of 13 poems in praise of *sake*, thus experimenting with a favorite Chinese (not Japanese) theme. He was familiar enough with Chinese writings both old and new to adapt some of their phraseology into his own prose.

Yamanoue no Omi Okura (YAMANOUE NO OKURA; 660–ca 733) can usefully be viewed in comparison with his friend Tabito. He too has left mostly the poetry of his old age. It shows him to be of a crochety, moralistic, but also humorous and loving, character, with a strong sense of social outrage. Okura reveals his personality in fact more fully in his poetry than any other Man'yō poet, with the exception of Yakamochi. At least some of these personality traits relate to what apparently is an intellectual formation through Chinese studies. In contrast to Tabito's mock-serious encomiums to drunkenness, Okura adopts the stance of a caustic old Confucian gentleman, someone with a strong word of advice for everyone, and at the same time a family man who loves children and who sympathizes with the plight of the poor. Okura is the only major Man'yō poet who we know visited China. He was a member of the official embassy of 702 and probably returned in 707. His Chinese training may have provided one of his qualifications for being appointed lecturer to the crown prince in 721. Late in life he became governor of Chikuzen Province (now part of Fukuoka Prefecture) in northern Kyūshū at the same time that Tabito was governor general at nearby Dazaifu. Because of the above-mentioned problems of attribution it is hard to state the exact number of his extant poems, perhaps 12 *chōka* and 69 *tanka*. He also wrote some extended pieces of Chinese prose which have been preserved in *Man'yōshū* Book 5. His poetic manner is angular, personal, sometimes angry, as in his "Dialogue on Poverty." He treats of man's fate with a bitter resignation. His imagery is often humble and earthy. At the same time, he experimented with the newly imported romantic Tanabata theme of the lover stars Altair and Vega, who can meet only once a year.

Tanabe no Fubito Sakimaro (Tanabe no Sakimaro), the author of 10 *chōka* and 34 *tanka* in the *Man'yōshū*, wrote like Akahito and others in the manner established by Hitomaro on such public themes as flourishing and fallen capitals. He also wrote on travel, and—again like Hitomaro—on the discovery of a dead man by the wayside. He exchanged poems with Ōtomo no Yakamochi in 748 when the latter was governor of Etchū. Sakimaro's name, like those of Hitomaro, Mushimaro, and Kanamura, is attached to a private collection drawn upon by the Man'yō compilers.

ŌTOMO NO SAKANOUE NO IRATSUME (Lady Ōtomo of Sakanoue; fl ca 728–746) was the younger half-sister of Tabito and mother-in-law of Yakamochi. Her life seems to have spanned the first half of the 8th century. She is the author of 6 *chōka* and 77 *tanka* in the *Man'yōshū*, many of them addressed to other members of her family. She married three times, and by her last husband, her half-brother Sukunamaro, had the daughter who married her nephew Yakamochi. Her poetry makes plain her fondness for these two young people. She seems to have been a central figure in the Ōtomo clan after Tabito's death in 731. Her poetic talent was probably influential on the young Yakamochi.

Ōtomo no Sukune Yakamochi (ŌTOMO NO YAKAMOCHI; 718?–785) was the eldest son of Tabito. With 46 *chōka*, 432 *tanka*, and one *sedōka*, he is by far the most extensively preserved poet of his age: one in every 10 Man'yō poems is by him. He is also the leading candidate for compiler of the *Man'yōshū*, or at least of large parts of it. Books 17–20 are definitely his compilation, arranged in dated chronological order, with his own annotation. Like his father Tabito, he rose through the ranks of the court bureaucracy, but attained nothing higher than the position of *chūnagon* (middle counsellor) of junior third rank. From 746 to 751, during his late 20s and early 30s, Yakamochi served as governor of Etchū Province, a mountainous back-country area far from the capital. These years are recorded in detail in Books 17–19 and seem to have been fertile ones for his poetry. Yakamochi is a poet of great variety and amplitude. As a young man he exchanged love poems with a number of different women and acquitted himself well in the mode of the amorous *tanka*. He also wrote *chōka* in the grand manner, elegies, poems in praise of mountain scenery, and exhortations to his clansmen. He often speaks about his personal concerns, incidents in his life such as the loss of a favorite hawk. A note of delicate sadness is evident in his late nature poetry, and he was, like his father, an early practitioner of "elegant confusion," the pretended bemusement of the senses as between snow and plum blossom, à la chinoise. Too, he strikes some of the first self-conscious notes of specifically Buddhist awareness of life's illusory character in Japanese poetry. With his cousin Ikenushi he conducted extensive exchanges involving Chinese prose and poetry as well as *waka*. It is clear that he regarded himself as a literary man, a member of a tradition. He refers back to Hitomaro and casts himself in the role of a later lesser figure. But his tastes were wide-ranging, and it is due to his labors more than those of any other person that we have the *Man'yōshū* today. Unfortunately, whatever poems he may have written after 759 have not been preserved. His later years were vexed with political setbacks, and his death in 785 was followed by posthumous disgrace because of implication in an assassination. His titles were restored in 806. One hypothesis maintains that the *Man'yōshū* was among papers seized during an official search of his premises in connection with the assassination incident and was not circulated publicly until his name was cleared.

Anonymous Poems and the Problem of Social Range —— It is surprising to find a large number of poems in the *Man'yōshū* by people outside the circle of the court, people one would hardly even suspect in some cases were literate. There are, for instance, the rustic poems from Azuma (the Eastland) in Book 14 and the poems by eastern conscripts in Book 20. The world of many of the anonymous poems in Book 7 and Books 10–13 also seems to be that of the fisherfolk or other country dwellers. There is in fact a far larger number of anonymous poems in the *Man'yōshū* than of poems by any known poet. It is extremely difficult to give reliable figures because of many uncertainties in attribution, but 1,851 anonymous poems (1770 *tanka*, 71 *chōka*, and 10 *sedōka*) would be the smallest possible total. This great mass of verse must have come from a variety of sources, written and—directly or indirectly—oral. The question of the courtly vis-à-vis the (loosely speaking) "folk" elements in this poetry is very difficult to resolve. Even the most plausible utterances of the lower classes are usually in *tanka* form and are by no means folksong in any strict sense; and the romanticization and imitation of the lives of supposedly simpler people by the court nobility is a phenomenon that must also be acknowledged. It is impossible to say to what extent, if at all, the apparently most folkish poems may have been revised. What is clear is that attempts at precise modal subcategories such as those in Books 7 and 10–12 are used to arrange large bodies of anonymous material. Internal evidence, such as it is, suggests that some of this material is by courtiers and some by commoners (with or without revision) or by courtiers writing in a commoner mode, with a very large proportion representing a kind of universal viewpoint that could be shared by both. All of the hundreds of poems in these sections of the *Man'yōshū* are treated with an undifferentiated and highly literary editorial technique. Book 14 (the Azuma *uta*), the *sakimori* poems in Book 20, and certain poems in Books 15 and 16 provide support for the hypothesis that rustic-seeming poems are indeed by rustics, and that it is permissible as well to read the contents of Books 7, 10–12, and 13 with this assumption in mind. Thus the traditional esteem in which the *Man'yōshū* has been held as embodying the poetry of the nation from monarch to peasant is not lacking in validity.

The *Man'yōshū* is an enormous literary monument, a structure whose complexity and richness combine with its position in the very earliest period of the literature to raise unanswerable questions. The most imponderable of these is the relation of a Chinese-inspired and nurtured self-conscious literary sophistication to what had been until recently a preliterate, oral, native, verse tradition. A complexity of motivation surely has to be imputed to the compilers of the 8th century. A desire to elucidate and preserve the very roots of native belief, feeling, and identity is strongly suggested by the compilation of the early histories and by the careful collection and dating of what were believed to be very early poems in the *Man'yōshū*. The great respect paid to Hitomaro by Yakamochi and whatever other compilers the *Man'yōshū* may have had bespeaks a continuing reverence for the archaic, primal, undefiled source of the Yamato mystique. At the same time, the Nara poets who assembled the collection show their eagerness for the new, the foreign, the polished and elegant pose of the Chinese-style gentleman. To what extent might they have altered the old or the less advanced to accord with their tastes? The evidence supplied by the early *chōka* in Book 13 is mixed. The preservation of irregular *chōka* suggests that the old was prized for its own sake, while the presence of envoys which read as if they had been tacked on later points toward editorial meddling. The assignment of modal categories to the great collections of anonymous *tanka* in Books 7 and 10–12 does not demand the conclusion that the poems were composed to illustrate these categories. The achieved *tanka* form implies literary evolution and stability—historically brought about at least contemporaneously with, if not because of, the influx of Chinese poetry—but the modal grouping of the poems is more likely a step beyond, an afterthought of the compilers, as it were. It is best to view the content of the *Man'yōshū* as a poetic continuum from very early materials to mid-8th-century creations, some of which begin to show internalization of Chinese aesthetics, a shift in the native sensibility. And over all rises a superstructure of Chinese-inspired categories which makes the book a Japanese *Wenxuan* as the *Nihon shoki* is in part a Japanese dynastic history.

Man'yōshū Scholarship —— The study of the *Man'yōshū* has probably been the longest ongoing scholarly enterprise in Japan. Interest in this earliest Japanese poetic landmark has not been uniform during the 1,200 years that have elapsed since its completion, however. In fact, the first two centuries of this period are almost a total blank. Knowledge of the *Man'yōshū* may be counted among the cultural casualties of the shift of the capital from Nara to HEIAN-KYŌ (now Kyōto) in the period 785–794. Not that a move of twenty or thirty miles would in itself have had any appreciable effect, but the reasons which lay behind the move favored an emphasis on Chinese learning and the composition of Chinese verse in the early decades of the 9th century, with a concomitant lowering of the prestige attached to native poetry. The day of the great public poems was over, and the art of the *chōka* was lost with astonishing suddenness in the decades after Yakamochi. An even more adverse factor from the viewpoint of appreciation of the *Man'yōshū*, although highly favorable to later developments in literature, was the evolution during the 9th century of a simplified phonetic script. The orthography of the *Man'yōshū* became so unlike what people were reading and writing by the beginning of the 10th century and was in itself so complex that the anthology became practically unreadable.

The Man'yō Writing System —— Like all languages, Japanese had no writing system to begin with, nor did its speakers belong to one of the handful of cultures which invented such a system from scratch. Instead, like most civilizations, the Japanese adapted a foreign product. The peculiar nature of that adaptation derives from the fact that it started from a highly specialized and elaborate arrangement evolved to write a very dissimilar language. China was the major civilization of East Asia and its script was the first one the Japanese encountered. Adapting it to their own language was a major feat of linguistic engineering, with results that have been deeply formative at all levels of literary culture. The Chinese writing system was not a phonetic script, such as an alphabet or syllabary, which would need only minor adjustments to fit a new language, but was composed of complex graphic units representing entire words. The system had started as pictograms but evolved in such a way as to include pictographic, ideographic, and phonetic elements in highly sophisticated functional relationships. It was designed to write Chinese and nothing else. Two of its features, however, enabled it to be adapted. Each graph or character, by virtue of representing a monosyllabic Chinese word, is associated with the pronunciation of that word. If meaning were disregarded, the character could be used for its sound alone, to stand for a similar-sounding syllable in Japanese.

The other way in which Chinese graphs could be used to write Japanese has to do with the fact that all languages have words for a vast array of common objects and qualities. Thus a character representing the Chinese word for "hand" could be read as if it were the Japanese word for the same thing. In short, the character could be employed either phonetically or semantically. A consistent use of the phonetic approach would have resulted in a bulky but functional syllabary—a writing system representing syllables, combining consonant and vowel in the same symbol. In fact many Man'yō poems are written in accordance with this method, and characters so used are called *man'yōgana* (from *Man'yō* + *kana*, or "borrowed names," that is, characters used phonetically). The orthography of other poems combines the phonetic and semantic approaches, necessitating close attention to ascertain in which way a given character is being used. The possibilities of going astray are vastly multiplied under these conditions, but the principle involved is nevertheless the same as that underlying modern Japanese orthography. The system works because the semantic function can be used to represent nouns and verb and adjective stems, while the phonetic represents the suffixes and particles in which the language abounds.

The system evolved by the scribes of the *Man'yōshū* did not stop at this level of complexity, however. Superfluous complications were introduced in at least three different ways. One was that the phonetic use of characters was not limited to sound values borrowed from the original Chinese word. Once a character had been used semantically to represent a given Japanese word, its phonetic value could be and was used to represent the same syllable in another Japanese word. To take a very simple example, the character for "hand," a word pronounced *te* in Japanese, could be used to write the syllable *te* in any other word. Even greater attention was thus necessary to be sure whether a character was being used for its Chinese or Japanese sound value. A second way in which the system developed in the direction of a redundant complexity was the appearance of a phenomenon which might be labeled associative transference. Certain place names, for instance, came to be written with characters which could not possibly yield the desired pronunciation either phonetically or semantically. ASUKA, an important place in 7th-century Japan, in addition to having "spellings" based on phonetic principles either Chinese- or Japanese-derived, was often written with the characters "flying bird." This probably came about by way of a conventional epithet *(makura kotoba)* for Asuka, namely *tobu tori no* ("of the flying bird"), being applied to the place itself. A few examples of this phenomenon have survived in modern Japanese. Finally, playful rebuses are also found, providing the most convincing evidence of a deliberate attempt to make orthography an aesthetic end in itself. The word meaning "go out" is in one instance written with a series of graphs meaning "On top of the mountain there is another mountain." The connection is through the form of the character "go out," which resembles two characters for "mountain," one on top of the other.

The *Man'yōshū* text represents the high water mark of this early graphomania. During the succeeding century the tide turned in the direction of a more sober exploitation of the phonetic option. The characters used to represent the sounds of Japanese were simplified into the systems known today as *hiragana* and *katakana* (see KANA). *Hiragana* ("smooth *kana*") simplify the entire character in cursive form, and *katakana* ("square *kana*") represent isolated graphic elements from the character. The two systems duplicate one another, but *hiragana* has always been the more widely used. In neither system does the resultant symbol bear an obvious similarity to its parent graph. The Japanese at this point had acquired an efficient tool for writing their own language. Actually, both *kana* systems remained more complex than necessary, with a choice of symbols for the same syllable, until their rationalization in modern times. Nevertheless, by the beginning of the 10th century the literate public was so accustomed to their use that the *Man'yōshū* had become almost unreadable. The generation of poets who compiled the KOKINSHŪ, the earliest of the imperially sponsored *waka* anthologies, in 905, can have had little familiarity with the great work that was the forerunner of their labors. KI NO TSURAYUKI (872?–945) mentions the *Man'yōshū* in his famous Kana Preface to that anthology, and honors the names of Akahito and Hitomaro but betrays little understanding of the nature of their poetry.

Decipherment and Exegesis —— The first work on decipherment of the *Man'yōshū* was undertaken at imperial command in 951 by a committee of five scholar-poets, the same "Five Gentlemen of the Pear Chamber" (Nashitsubo no Gonin) who concurrently were working on the compilation of the GOSEN WAKASHŪ, the second imperial waka anthology. The five were Kiyowara no Motosuke (908–990), Ki no Tokifumi (dates unknown), ŌNAKATOMI NO YOSHINOBU (921–991), MINAMOTO NO SHITAGAU (911–983), and Sakanoue no Mochiki (dates unknown). By this time Japanese poetry had long been back in fashion. Empress Hirohata, the consort of then-reigning Emperor Murakami, expressed a desire to read the Man'yōshū, and this led to the commission given to these five scholar-poets. The results of their labors are referred to as the koten, the "old marks," "marks" meaning a manuscript provided with phonetic readings, annotations, and other aids. No koten manuscripts survive, but it is thought that the five scholars provided readings for about four thousand poems, mostly tanka.

All the exegetical work done by various hands in the next three centuries is collectively known as the jiten, "the next (or secondary) marks." The first surviving manuscripts of the Man'yōshū, fragmentary though they are, are products of jiten scholarship. The earliest is the Katsura text, a part of Book 4 copied in handscroll form in the mid-Heian period. Other early manuscripts include the mid-Heian Indigo Paper text, a handscroll fragment of Book 9, and the Genryaku Collation, dated to 1184, a manuscript in booklet form containing fragments of several books. There also survives a late Heian copy of Ruijū koshū, a Man'yōshū text rearranged under topical and formal headings by Fujiwara no Atsutaka (d 1120), in which 16 of the original 20 books remain.

The earliest complete Man'yōshū manuscript, however, is the Nishi Honganji text in book form. Dating from the latter part of the Kamakura period (1185–1333), it incorporates the shinten or "new marks," the readings supplied for still undeciphered poems by the monk SENKAKU (or Sengaku), whose work is considered fundamental to all later study of the Man'yōshū. Sengaku, who was born in 1203 and was still living in 1272, was a native of eastern Japan, where the tradition of Man'yō studies and high regard for the anthology flourished more than in the imperial capital at Kyōto. (While interest in the Man'yōshū as a literary model and inspiration had been felt by FUJIWARA NO TOSHINARI [Fujiwara no Shunzei; 1114–1204], his son FUJIWARA NO SADAIE [Fujiwara no Teika; 1162–1241], and other court poets at the beginning of the 13th century, it was above all the ill-fated young shōgun MINAMOTO NO SANETOMO [1192–1219] in Kamakura in eastern Japan who identified himself with the heroic Man'yō image and sought to write in its style.) With Sengaku, whose training in Buddhist Sanskrit studies is said to have contributed to his scholarly expertise, assignment of readings reached all Man'yō poems by the year 1246. Sengaku was also the author of the earliest extant Man'yō commentary, the Man'yōshū chūshaku, or Man'yōshū shō, probably completed in 1269. A commentary on selected poems, its level is not comparable to the linguistic sophistication displayed in the author's work in the assignment of readings. Sengaku proffers the opinion that the title of the Man'yōshū means "10,000 leaves of words" and attributes its compilation to the dual compilers TACHIBANA NO MOROE (684–757) and Ōtomo no Yakamochi. Moroe, an important Nara statesman, was a political patron of Yakamochi.

Further work on the Man'yōshū was carried on by the priest Yua (b 1291?) in the 14th century, and by the renga master SŌGI (1421–1502) and others in the 15th century. Meanwhile texts descended from Sengaku's work continued to be dominant and underlay the widely circulated Kan'ei printed edition of 1643.

It was in the Edo period (1600–1868) that Man'yōshū studies came into their own. During this time a large number of commentaries and critical works appeared, and interest in the ancient anthology sometimes took on the nature of a semireligious cult, so central was it to the deep reverence for the Japanese past displayed by the nascent National Learning (KOKUGAKU) movement. The first important figure in Edo Man'yō studies was the samurai-turned-scholar SHIMOKŌBE CHŌRYŪ (1624–86). Chōryū devoted much of his life to Man'yō studies, and was sponsored in his work by the daimyō patron TOKUGAWA MITSUKUNI (1628–1700). He did not live to complete the planned magisterial annotated edition but did publish in about 1661 a work explaining difficult words and lines called Man'yōshū kanken that was influential on later Man'yōshū scholarship. Mitsukuni's commission was picked up and brought to completion by Chōryū's friend, the priest KEICHŪ (1640–1701). Keichū was one of the greatest of Japanese scholars. Man'yō daishō ki, the work he produced, marks a watershed in Japanese literary scholarship. A complete commentary on the Man'yōshū, it is the result of great erudition, but more important, of original, independent research by a mind unfettered by medieval tradition. Completed in 1690, it stands in contrast to another work finished in the same year, the Man'yō shūsuishō of KITAMURA KIGIN (1624–1705). Kigin's work is treated as the first complete Man'yōshū commentary, probably because only the first half of Keichū's Daishōki circulated during his lifetime, but unlike Daishōki, Shūsuishō is a traditional-style compilation of earlier opinions.

KADA NO AZUMAMARO (1669–1736), the official founder of the National Learning movement, was another scholar interested in the Man'yōshū. An advocate of "evidence and reason" in studying the classics, Azumamaro was also convinced of the superiority of the "Japanese Way" over the Chinese Confucian orthodoxy then dominant in Japan. The Man'yōshū was thought of by Azumamaro and his followers as a principal repository of this ancient Japanese "Way," and his school inspired a Man'yō revival that had literary and ideological as well as scholarly aspects. It was KAMO NO MABUCHI (1697–1769), one of Azumamaro's students, who became the central figure in this revival. Mabuchi was a poet, ideologue, and scholar. As a poet he wrote in the Man'yō manner and even revived the long-defunct chōka. Like Azumamaro, he elevated the Man'yōshū to a critical position above the Kokinshū and later anthologies. He devoted his life to the elucidation and dissemination of the true and uncorrupted Japanese spirit of manly simplicity (masurao-buri), which he found in the Man'yōshū and other ancient works. Mabuchi's commentary Man'yōkō (1760–68) ranks with Keichū's Daishōki in importance. It provides a commentary on Books 1, 2, 13, 11, 12, and 14 of the Man'yōshū, in that order. These were the parts that Mabuchi considered the original form of the anthology. Commentary on the other books was added later by Koma Nobunari (1722–1802) and others among Mabuchi's disciples. Mabuchi's commentary is direct, intuitive, and tends toward dogmatism, with less scruple about evidence than had characterized Keichū's. Nevertheless, it has been highly influential in forming the image of the Man'yōshū prevalent down to our own day. Mabuchi, like others after Sengaku, continued to adjust the readings of the text, and many of his preferences, perhaps too casually arrived at, have become standard.

The greatest of all the Kokugaku scholars, MOTOORI NORINAGA (1730–1801), was not much drawn to the Man'yōshū, despite his admiration for Mabuchi. Ironically, the scholar who singlehandedly brought the Kojiki out of unreadable obscurity preferred the Shin kokinshū when it came to poetry. Nevertheless, KATŌ CHIKAGE (also known as Tachibana Chikage; 1735–1808), a pupil of Mabuchi, is said to have incorporated ideas of Norinaga's in his Man'yōshū ryakuge (ca 1800), the easiest and most popular of Edo-period Man'yō commentaries. One of the most indefatigable of all Man'yō scholars lived and worked at the very end of the Edo period. This was KAMOCHI MASAZUMI (1791–1858), a lowly retainer of the Tosa feudal domain in Shikoku (present-day Kōchi Prefecture), who was practically self-taught in the Man'yōshū. His Man'yōshū kogi (1845), with 141 volumes, was the most voluminous Man'yō commentary up to its time. It is noted for original insights and full use of evidence but has some shortcomings in the understanding of the poems. The leading Man'yō scholar of the late 19th century was Kimura Masakoto (1827–1913), whose life and career spanned the end of the old regime and the beginning of modern Japan. An erudite scholar who studied in the traditional schools of National and Chinese learning and went on to serve in the Meiji government, he produced numerous publications stressing fidelity to ancient manuscripts and a meticulous approach to textual problems. In the 20th century, Man'yō studies have flourished as never before. A number of multivolume commentaries have appeared, making the Man'yōshū ever more accessible to the reading public. Complete translations of the Man'yōshū have been made into English by J. L. Pierson, and into Russian by A. Y. Gluskina. The selection of 1,000 poems published in English translation by the Nippon Gakujutsu Shinkōkai in 1940 is also highly regarded. The most informed treatment of the Man'yōshū in English is that in Robert H. Brower and Earl Miner, Japanese Court Poetry.

■——Annotated editions of the Man'yōshū: Takagi Ichinosuke, Gomi Tomohide, and Ōno Susumu, ed, Man'yōshū, 4 vols in Nihon koten bungaku taikei, vols 4–7 (Iwanami Shoten, 1957–62). Omodaka Hisakata, ed, Man'yōshū chūshaku, 20 vols (1957–68). Kojima Noriyuki, Kinoshita Masatoshi, and Satake Akihiro, ed, Man'yōshū, 4 vols in Nihon koten bungaku zenshū, vols 2–5 (Shōgakukan, 1971–75). Works about the Man'yōshū: Tsuchiya Bummei, Man'yōshū nempyō (1932). Saitō Mokichi, Kakinomoto no Hitomaro, 5 vols (1933–40). Takagi Ichinosuke, *Yoshino no ayu* (1941). Sasaki Nobutsune, ed, *Man'yōshū jiten* (Heibonsha, 1952). Shimonaka Yasaburō, ed, *Man'yōshū taisei*, 22 vols (Heibonsha, 1953–55). Kojima Noriyuki, *Jōdai Nihon bungaku to Chūgoku bungaku*, 3 vols, (1962–65). Satake Akihiro, Kinoshita Masatoshi, and Kojima Noriyuki, *Man'yōshū kakku sakuin* (1966). Nakanishi Susumu, *Man'yōshū no hikaku bungakuteki kenkyū* (1968). Nakanishi Susumu, *Yamanoue Okura* (1973). Nakanishi Susumu, *Kakinomoto no Hitomaro, Nihon shijin sen*, II (Chikuma Shobō, 1977). Gomi Tomohide and Kojima Noriyuki, ed, *Man'yōshū kenkyū*, 7 vols (Hanawa Shobō, 1972–78). Translations: Nippon Gakujutsu Shinkōkai, tr, *The Man'yōshū: One Thousand Poems* (1940; repr 1965). Robert H. Brower and Earl Miner, *Japanese Court Poetry* (1961). J. L. Pierson, tr, *The Manyôsû*, 20 vols (1929–69). Ian Levy, tr, *The Ten Thousand Leaves: A Translation of the Man'yōshū, Japan's Premier Anthology of Classical Poetry*, vol 1 (1981). Edwin A. CRANSTON

Manza Hot Spring

(Manza Onsen). Located on the western slope of Shiranesan at an altitude of 1,555 m (5,100 ft), northwestern Gumma Prefecture, central Honshū. There is a sulfur spring, water temperature 60–95°C (140–203°F), which is said to have been discovered in 1764. Surrounded by primeval forests, a ropeway and lift to the summit of Shiranesan originate here. It attracts numerous skiers in winter.

manzai

A performing art in which a comic dialogue is carried on by two comedians. *Manzai* is said to have its beginnings in the Nara period (710–794) with a ceremony transmitted from China called *tōka* (Ch: *tage* or *t'a-ke*), songs whose rhythms were tapped out with the feet. *Manzai* was supported by the belief that at the beginning of each year blessings for the succeeding 12 months descended on every house. During the Edo period (1600–1868) performers even visited the imperial court and the houses of the great *daimyō*. The popularity of these performances in which a wit *(tayū)* and a straight man *(saizō)* went from gate to gate engaging in congratulatory repartee accompanied by an ebullient use of body and hand gestures spread throughout Japan, and in each part of the country there persisted a tradition of *manzai* known by the particular name of that region. Among others there are Yamato *manzai*, Owari *manzai*, Iyo *manzai*, Mikawa *manzai*, and Akita *manzai*. Each has retained its own characteristics and local color down to the present day. Though its use of language and dance has greatly influenced other genres of Japanese FOLK PERFORMING ARTS, it is most significant in giving birth to modern *manzai*, an important part of the repertory of the YOSE (centers of popular vaudeville-style entertainment).

Toward the close of the Edo period, *manzai* had begun to flourish in makeshift theaters, and by the first decade of the 20th century its popularity increased rapidly. During the period before and after the Russo-Japanese War (1904–05), *manzai* established itself, chiefly in the Kansai (Kyōto-Ōsaka) area, as an outstanding genre among the performing arts. In Ōsaka, Kyōto, and Kōbe *manzai* came to possess its own theaters. Nevertheless, performances still differed little from those of the Edo period. A musical *manzai*, a dramatic *manzai*, and a *manzai* of the dance developed, but as an integral art it was yet immature. By 1930, however, fresh subject matter was introduced by such well-known performers as Yokoyama Entatsu and Hanabishi Achako, and *manzai* could be heard on nationwide radio broadcasts. The dialogues of Entatsu and Achako became the standard, and they were considered masters by their fellow practitioners. After World War II, passing from the age of radio to that of television, numerous *manzai* artists were idolized, sometimes appearing in trios or introducing song to their humorous repartee. The creative energy necessary to the development of ever-new teams of performers might be said to be the very life force of a performing art fostered by a history reaching more than a thousand years into the past.
■——Misumi Haruo, *Sasurainin no geinō shi* (1974). Ozawa Shōichi, *Nihon no hōrōgei* (1974). ORITA Kōji

Manzanar Relocation Center

A wartime relocation facility for Japanese Americans, located near Lone Pine, Inyo County, California; in operation from 21 March 1942 until 21 November 1945. It held a maximum of 10,046 inmates at any one time; 11,062 persons were confined there in all. Internees came from southern and central California and from Bainbridge Island, Washington. The first of the relocation centers to open, it also functioned as an assembly center. The first major disturbance of the relocation program, the so-called Manzanar Riot, occurred here on 7 December 1942. See also JAPANESE AMERICANS, WARTIME RELOCATION OF; WAR RELOCATION AUTHORITY.
■——Arthur A. Hansen and David A. Hacker, "The Manzanar Riot: An Ethnic Perspective," in Hansen and Mitson, ed, *Voices Long Silent: An Oral History of the Japanese American Evacuation* (1974). Jeanne Wakatsuki Houston and James D. Houston, *Farewell to Manzanar* (1973). Roger DANIELS

Mao Zedong (Mao Tse-tung) (1893–1976)

(J: Mō Takutō). Chinese communist leader. Born into a well-to-do peasant family in Hunan Province, Mao received a traditional primary education. He read widely on contemporary affairs, however, and in 1913 enrolled in the First Normal School in Changsha (Ch'ang-sha), where he was deeply influenced by the intellectual ferment of the period. In 1918 he went to Beijing (Peking), where he met Li Dazhao (Li Ta-Chao), later a founder of the Chinese Communist Party (CCP). During the MAY FOURTH MOVEMENT of 1919, Mao wrote and engaged in political activity in Hunan. By 1920 he was a Marxist, and in July 1921 he attended the founding meeting of the CCP. During the early 1920s he worked in the Hunan party branch.

In 1925 Mao organized peasant associations in Hunan. He then went to Guangzhou (Canton) and in 1926 became director of the Peasant Movement Training Institute. During the Northern Expedition of 1926–27, he promoted the peasants' role in revolution. After the split between the Guomindang (Kuomintang; KMT) and the CCP in 1927, Mao directed the unsuccessful Autumn Harvest Uprising in Hunan.

By 1931 a communist base area had been established in Jiangxi (Kiangsi) Province, with Mao heading its government. He was not in charge of the party apparatus, however, and the party suffered from factionalism. In late 1934 the KMT siege of the Jiangxi soviet forced the communists to abandon their base. During the 6,000-mile (9,661-kilometer) "Long March" to Yan'an (Yenan), Mao emerged as party leader. During the Yan'an period (1935–49), Mao developed his political and military theories while directing an extensive base area in North China. Throughout the war with Japan, the CCP was nominally in alliance with the KMT. Nevertheless, civil war, never far below the surface, broke out again in 1946. By 1949 the CCP had defeated the KMT. The People's Republic of China was established with Mao as chairman of the government.

The early 1950s were marked by economic rehabilitation, reconstruction, and social transformation along Soviet lines. In 1958, however, Mao broke with the Soviet model and attempted a rapid, radical transformation of Chinese society and economy, known as the Great Leap Forward. The campaign involved large-scale mobilization of labor, collectivization of agriculture, and the creation of rural people's communes. The failure of this effort caused Mao's temporary eclipse in the early 1960s. Conflicts between Mao and his opponents in the CCP leadership culminated in the Cultural Revolution of 1966–69, in which Mao reasserted his authority over the party. Soon after his death in 1976, however, many of his closest associates fell from power.
■——Howard L. Boorman and Richard C. Howard, ed, *Biographical Dictionary of Republican China*, vol 3 (1967). Jerome Ch'en, *Mao and the Chinese Revolution* (1965). Donald W. Klein and Anne B. Clark, *Biographical Dictionary of Chinese Communism*, vol 2 (1971). Stuart Schram, *Mao Tse-tung* (1967). Stuart Schram, *The Political Thought of Mao Tse-tung* (1969). Robert ENTENMANN

maples

(*kaede* or *momiji*). *Acer* spp. Deciduous trees of the family Aceraceae. The genus *Acer*, family Aceraceae, includes more than 100 species and is distributed mainly in the temperate zone of the northern hemisphere. More than 20 of these species, all of them deciduous, are indigenous to Japan, and the beauty of their autumn foliage has been a frequent subject in literature and art. The leaves of many trees in the genus *Acer* are palmate, but some varieties have leaves which are not lobed, including various oval, elliptical, and ternate compound types. In addition, maples are characterized by opposite leaves and compound, two-seeded long-winged fruits.

The *iroha kaede* (Japanese maple; *A. palmatum*), also called Takao *momiji*, is widely distributed in Japan's mountain areas and extensively planted around houses. The double-serrated leaves are small in size, have 5–7 palmate lobes and, in autumn, turn a beautiful red. Those in the Takao area of Kyōto are particularly noted for their beauty. The *yamamomiji* (mountain maple; *A. palmatum* var. *matsumurae*) grows wild in mountain areas; the leaves are larger than those of the *iroha kaede* and have 7–9 deeply indented lobes. The *hauchiwa kaede* (*A. Japonicum;* also called *meigetsu kaede*) is indigenous to Hokkaidō, northern Honshū, and the central Honshū mountain area; it has large double-serrated leaves with 9–11 relatively shallow lobes. In addition to these, other well-known types include the *itaya meigetsu (A. sieboldianum),* the *asanoha kaede (A. argutum),* also called *miyama momiji,* and the *ogarabana (A. ukurunduense),* also called *hozaki kaede.* Numerous horticultural varieties have been developed from each of the above species, with a wide range of leaf shape, color, branch structure, etc.

Foreign maple species are also grown in Japan. It is uncertain how the *hananoki (A. rubrum* var. *pyenanthum)* arrived in Japan, but it is closely related to the red maple *(A. rubrum)* of eastern North America and grows wild in the moist fields of the basin of the river Kisogawa. It is cultivated in some areas for its small, deep red flowers, which appear before the new leaves in the spring, and for its foliage in the fall. The *satō kaede* (sugar maple; *A. saccharum*) is planted in parks, and the *tōkaede (A. buergerianum),* of Chinese origin, is cultivated mainly for planting along city streets or for use in BONSAI (dwarf-tree culture).

■——Uehara Keiji, *Jumoku daizusetsu* (1961).

MATSUDA Osamu

mappō → eschatology

maps

The oldest existing maps in Japan are preserved in the SHŌSŌIN repository in Nara. Some 10 in number, they are india ink drawings of reclaimed land *(kondenzu)* on linen or rice paper and date from the latter part of the Nara period (710–794). In the Heian period (794–1185), with the proliferation of proprietary estates (SHŌEN), similar maps, known as *shōenzu,* were made, but few survive. It is said that a map, no longer extant, of the whole country was made by the priest GYŌGI (668–749) during the Nara period, and in the 16th and 17th centuries maps called *gyōgizu* (Gyōgi maps) were widely circulated. However, they possessed only a crude degree of accuracy. Mapmaking flourished in Japan in the early 17th century following the introduction of European maps and improvements in woodblock printing techniques. In the Shōhō (1644–48), Genroku (1688–1704), and Tempō (1830–44) eras of the Edo period (1600–1868), the shogunate ordered the domains *(han)* to make maps of their territories, which became the basis for comprehensive maps of the country.

In 1775 the first known Japanese latitudinal map—the *Nihon yochi rotei zenzu*—was completed by the geologist NAGAKUBO SEKISUI. Although this map had lines running perpendicular to the latitude lines, they were not true longitudinal lines, nor was the map based on surveys. Far superior to all previous maps was the *Dai Nihon enkai jissoku zenzu* completed in 1821. Its makers used European surveying techniques and it was the result of 16 years of surveying under the direction of INŌ TADATAKA. Inō's method for measuring latitude proved to be unusually accurate, but that for measuring longitude was not so. Nevertheless his map was used by the British navy when it surveyed the waters around Japan, and later as the basis for the 1:200,000-scale maps that were widely circulated until the publication of the official Meiji government maps, the predecessors of current Japanese topographical maps.

In the early part of the Meiji period (1868–1912), nonmilitary maps fell under the authority of the Geography Department of the Home Ministry, and military maps under the Land Survey Department of the Army General Staff Office. In 1889, however, the latter became the sole governmental body responsible for the making of standard maps, and until 1945 all official Japanese maps were military-oriented. The original plan for the official pre–World War II standard map specified a scale of 1:20,000, but the scale was soon changed to 1:50,000 due to cost and time factors.

After World War II, the GEOGRAPHIC SURVEY INSTITUTE of the Ministry of Construction was made responsible for surveying and mapmaking. Until 1955, all maps were monochrome. By 1978, the

Maps

Detail of a map of central Honshū from the *Dai Nihon enkai jissoku zenzu* (1821). The blank areas at the upper left and lower right represent Wakasa Bay and Ise Bay respectively, but the other large areas without relief shading were unsurveyed. Latitude and longitude markings are also visible. Tōkyō National Museum.

institute had completed 1:25,000-scale maps covering the entire country excluding some isolated islands. These replaced the 1:50,000 maps as the standard. Undulations are indicated with contour lines, but there is no shading as found on European and American maps. Whereas the 1:50,000 maps were drafted from plane table surveys, the 1:25,000 maps were based on aerial surveys.

The first cadastral maps *(chisekizu)* were made in the early Meiji period, but their accuracy was limited, because they were made before the introduction of modern surveying techniques. The production of modern cadastral maps began in 1951; the scales are 1:5,000 for residential areas, 1:1,000 for agricultural areas, and 1:2,500 or 1:5,000 for forest and pasture areas. They are available to the public at city and town halls.

Other maps published in Japan include land condition and land utilization maps, published by the Geographical Survey Institute; geological maps, published by the Geological Survey of Japan; land classification maps, published by the National Land Agency; urban geophysical foundation maps, published by the Ministry of Construction; soil maps, published by the Ministry of Agriculture, Forestry, and Fisheries; population maps, published by the Statistics Bureau of the Prime Minister's Office; marine and aviation maps, published by the Maritime Safety Agency; and botanical maps, published by the Agency of Cultural Affairs. SHIKI Masahide

marathons

The marathon race is one of the most popular sports events in Japan, with the number of participants ranking among the highest in the world.

Japan's first real marathon was held in 1911 in preparation for the 1912 Stockholm Olympic Games. At the Olympic trials Kanaguri Shizō set a new world record with a time of 2 hours 32 minutes 45 seconds. Since then, a number of new records have been made by Japanese runners. In the post–World War II period, Japanese athletes have competed with good results in the Boston Marathon and other foreign marathons, as well as in the Olympic Games. In the 1964 Tōkyō Olympic Games, Tsuburaya Kōkichi won the bronze medal, and Kimihara Kenji won the silver medal at the 1968 Olympic Games in Mexico. Domestic marathons also became popular, with the Beppu, Ōtsu, and Fukuoka races being the best-known. The Ōme Marathon, held in February at Ōme on the outskirts of Tōkyō, annually attracts more than 12,000 male and female participants of all ages. MAEDA Wakaki

March 15th Incident

(San'ichigo Jiken). Massive arrests throughout Japan on 15 March 1928, in which about 1,600 people suspected of being communists were apprehended. The incident was the government's response to the renewed activities of the JAPAN COMMUNIST PARTY, which, on Comintern orders, had reestablished itself in December 1926. During the spirited first national election under the new Universal Manhood Suffrage Law (see UNIVERSAL MANHOOD SUFFRAGE

MOVEMENT), held in February 1928, the hitherto clandestine party became highly visible, as it engaged in a flurry of propagandizing in support of legal leftist parties. Reacting strongly, the government carried out the arrests.

These arrests constituted the government's second invocation of the PEACE PRESERVATION LAW OF 1925. (The first had been against university students during the winter of 1925–26.) The government carefully prepared for the March 15th arrests. Ministry of Justice officials took a leading role, as they had in the passage of the 1925 peace law and its first use. A "Thought Section" was created in the ministry to gather information on ideological crimes and to plan a counteroffensive; its first report was published on 1 January 1927. A few months later Prosecutor Shiono Suehiko (1880–1949), a close follower of former Justice Minister HIRANUMA KIICHIRŌ, was assigned the task of preparing the Tōkyō District Court for ideological cases. Shiono's bureau acted as the nerve center for preparing and executing the mass arrest.

At dawn on March 15, several thousand government agents raided more than 120 places throughout the nation—leftist political party and labor union headquarters, newspaper and publishing firms, and the homes of selected individuals. Special teams had orders to seize all documents concerning the Japan Communist Party.

About 500 of those arrested were ultimately prosecuted. Thousands of important documents were seized, including a party name list. The conservative cabinet of TANAKA GIICHI used the exposed inner workings of the Communist Party as an excuse not only to ban the Labor-Farmer Party (RŌDŌ NŌMINTŌ), the All Japan Proletarian Youth League (Zen Nihon Musan Seinen Dōmei), and the Council of Japanese Labor Unions (Nihon Rōdō Kumiai Hyōgikai) but also to revise the Peace Preservation Law of 1925, adding a death penalty (Emergency Imperial Ordinance 129, 29 June 1928). Moreover, Tanaka supported conservative bureaucrats who tightened control of the educational system. It was decided that thereafter teachers, students, and social science research groups would be strictly regulated. Significant changes occurred in the home and justice ministries as well: the number of SPECIAL HIGHER POLICE was increased, and they were assigned to all parts of the nation while "thought prosecutors" (shisō kenji) were assigned to the courts.

This incident was the first of a number of mass arrests aimed at destroying communism. About 3,400 people had been arrested by the end of 1928, and there were more arrests in the years that followed. The incident is deeply etched in the Japanese consciousness. KOBAYASHI TAKIJI's story "Senkyūhyakunijūhachinen sangatsu jūgonichi" (The Fifteenth of March, 1928) is based on the incident. See also APRIL 16TH INCIDENT.

■——Richard H. Mitchell, *Thought Control in Prewar Japan* (1976). Odanaka Toshiki, "San'ichigo yon'ichiroku jiken: Chian iji hō saiban to hōtei tōsō," in Wagatsuma Sakae, ed, *Nihon seiji saiban shi roku* (1970).   Richard H. MITCHELL

March Incident

(Sangatsu Jiken). Attempted coup d'etat by rightist army officers and civilians in March 1931. Participants included HASHIMOTO KINGORŌ and other field-grade officers belonging to his SAKURAKAI (Cherry Blossom Society); members of the General Staff, such as KOISO KUNIAKI and TATEKAWA YOSHITSUGU; and the rightist civilians ŌKAWA SHŪMEI and Kamei Kan'ichirō (b 1892). Convinced of the need for national reform along totalitarian lines, they hoped to overthrow the cabinet and establish a military government headed by General UGAKI KAZUSHIGE. To this end, they planned to attack the prime minister's residence and the headquarters of the RIKKEN SEIYŪKAI and RIKKEN MINSEITŌ parties, mobilize 10,000 people to surround the Diet, and force the resignation of the HAMAGUCHI OSACHI cabinet. (SHIDEHARA KIJŪRŌ was serving as acting prime minister at the time, Hamaguchi having been severely wounded by a rightist fanatic.) Their plans were aborted because of logistic difficulties, opposition from military men more concerned with the Manchuria–Mongolia problem than with domestic reform, and Ugaki's own reluctance to accept the post. This incident, the first of many military interventions in politics (see also OCTOBER INCIDENT; FEBRUARY 26TH INCIDENT; MAY 15TH INCIDENT), was kept secret by the army and not made known to the public until the end of World War II. The participants were not even censured, although many were dispatched to the GUANDONG (KWANTUNG) ARMY in Manchuria, where later that year they directed the unauthorized takeover of that territory. See MANCHURIAN INCIDENT.

Marco Polo Bridge Incident

(Rokōkyō Jiken). Clash between Japanese and Chinese troops that led directly to the SINO-JAPANESE WAR OF 1937–1945. On the night of 7 July 1937, Japanese troops conducting maneuvers under the terms of the Boxer Protocol of 1901 near the Marco Polo Bridge (J: Rokōkyō), 19 kilometers (12 mi) southwest of Beiping (Peiping; now Beijing or Peking), heard some shots and engaged in a skirmish with Chinese forces under General SONG ZHEYUAN (Sung Che-yüan). On 11 July a cease-fire agreement was concluded locally. However, on the same day, the KONOE FUMIMARO cabinet announced its plan to mobilize five divisions for possible service in North China. The Japanese officers in North China advised Tōkyō that no reinforcement was needed, but Army Minister SUGIYAMA HAJIME decided to dispatch one division from Korea—then a Japanese colony—and two brigades from the Japanese GUANDONG (KWANTUNG) ARMY stationed in Manchuria. On 23 July the Chinese government at Nanjing (Nanking) reversed its policy of accommodation by having Song's troops reenter Beiping. General Katsuki Kiyoshi, the new Japanese commander, with Tōkyō's approval launched an attack, and on 29 July occupied Beiping and Tianjin (Tientsin). Thus began the second Sino-Japanese War, which did not end until the conclusion of World War II in 1945.   David J. LU

marebito

Also known as *marōdo*. Literally "guests"; divine visitors believed to bring blessings of luck and wealth from the other world (TOKOYO) through periodic visits. The folklorist ORIKUCHI SHINOBU (1887–1953) described *marebito* as deified ancestral spirits who appear in human guise as noblemen, an aged couple, or the like, equipped for a journey. He held that itinerant monks, ascetics, artists, or faith healers were welcomed by people, since they might be divine visitors in disguise. Orikuchi noted that the belief in supernatural beings who bring favors was closely linked to the idea that hospitality should be extended to a visitor from afar who might be the bearer of new technical knowledge. Such a notion would be especially strong in a remote self-enclosed community. He also postulated that when new deities were introduced and eventually replaced indigenous ones, the older deities were relegated to a subordinate position and transformed into deities who visited occasionally.   Kyōko Motomochi NAKAMURA

Maria Luz Incident

A diplomatic crisis that occurred early in the Meiji period (1868–1912). On 9 July 1872 the Peruvian ship *Maria Luz*, bound for Peru carrying 229 Chinese coolies, sailed into Yokohama for repairs. Two coolies escaped to a British warship anchored nearby, complaining of the inhuman conditions on board the *Maria Luz*. The acting British minister, R. G. Watson, had the ship inspected, and finding conditions to be as the coolies had described, he asked Foreign Minister SOEJIMA TANEOMI to look into the matter. Since Japan had no formal diplomatic relations with either China or Peru, it was decided to set up a special court representing the Ministry of Foreign Affairs at the Kanagawa prefectural office and to appoint ŌE TAKU as judge. Two American legal experts, E. P. Smith and G. W. Hill, had been chosen by United States Secretary of State Hamilton Fish to serve as advisers, and they largely determined Japan's position in the case.

After hearing the testimony of captain and coolies, the court declared the captain guilty of illegally confining the coolies. It commuted his sentence but ruled that he must file for permission with the same court to execute his contract to carry the coolies to Peru. On 25 August, Ōe ruled that the contract was invalid for four reasons. First, contracts that obliged Japanese citizens or those under the protection of Japanese law to live in places beyond the jurisdiction of Japanese law, without their consent or the permission of the Japanese government, were not recognized by the government of Japan. Second, under a migration contract in which coolies could be passed on to a third party at will, it was evident that the sale of slaves was taking place, in clear violation of morality. Third, the captain's copy of the contract lacked seals of approval from the Peruvian consulate in China and the Chinese bureau of emigration and was therefore invalid. Fourth, since the purpose of the contract was to send laborers to Peru, where Japan had no legal jurisdiction, it could not be enforced under Japanese law; this followed the precedent of similar decisions made in many other nations. Thus the coolies could not be forced to reboard the *Maria Luz*; moreover, because some of the Chinese sailors who manned the ship had deserted, the captain was forced to abandon his ship and return to Peru on another vessel.

International reaction to Ōe's decision was mixed; Britain supported it, the United States refused to take a stand, and Germany stood opposed. Because of Germany's opposition, the case became a dispute under international law, and in February 1873 the Peruvian government sent a special envoy to Japan demanding compensation for damages and a formal apology for the defamation of the Peruvian flag. Through the good offices of the British minister, Harry S. PARKES, on 25 June 1873 Japan and Peru agreed to submit to arbitration by Tsar Alexander II of Russia. On 29 May 1875 the tsar declared that Japan was without blame in the case and upheld the decisions of the Japanese court. The *Maria Luz* case was an important victory for the Japanese, for it compelled the Western powers to recognize Japan as an equal before international law.

marine accidents inquiry

(*kainan shimpan*). Investigation conducted by the Marine Accidents Inquiry Commission (Kainan Shimpan Chō) into the causes of accidents at sea. The commission is part of the MINISTRY OF TRANSPORT. The system attempts to prevent the recurrence of accidents. The inquiry commission establishes the cause of the accident and announces its conclusion by issuing a ruling. When the accident is caused intentionally or by the negligence of a pilot or a technician in the course of his duties, the agency will take disciplinary measures and, if needed, make recommendations to parties related to the cause of the accident.

Marine accidents are defined by law as the infliction of damage to a vessel or related facilities; death or injury in connection with a vessel's construction, facilities, or operations; and the impairment of the safety or operation of a vessel. Hearings are initiated when a member of the commission becomes aware that there was an incident calling for a hearing or is in receipt of reports to that effect. The commission then investigates the facts, gathers evidence, and requests one of seven regional commissions to initiate hearings. The parties subject to a hearing are the captain, technicians, harbor pilots, and other similar parties, who then become the subjects of disciplinary proceedings. Such parties are in a position similar to that of a defendant in a criminal trial and have the right to obtain marine counsel (*kaiji hosa*, corresponding to a legal representative). Additional designated parties, who are thought by the commissioner to have some connection with the cause of the accident also participate in the hearing.

As a general rule, the hearing is conducted in the form of a court tribunal by a chief judge and other judges, who make their decision after relevant questioning, examination of the evidence, oral arguments, and the holding of deliberations. Examination of the evidence is usually conducted by the chief judge, and the finding of facts must be based on the evidence introduced during the hearing. Hearing procedures are established in written form. When individuals are subject to discipline as a result of the hearings, the decision must be based on the oral arguments. In accord with the judgment of the tribunal, the examinee is disciplined and recommendations are made to the related parties. In principle, these decisions are not supposed to influence civil and criminal proceedings, but in reality they do. Decisions can be appealed to the High Marine Accidents Inquiry Commission in Tōkyō, and from there to the Tōkyō High Court and to the Supreme Court. Designated parties related to the marine disaster cannot appeal to a superior court.

TANIKAWA Hisashi

marine mammals

Japan's marine mammals, with the exception of WHALES, are found in two principal habitats: the shores of Hokkaidō and northern sections of the Tōhoku area of Honshū, where seals and sea lions are found, and the waters off Okinawa, where dugongs are seen. In other parts of the country, marine mammals are extremely rare. Mammals of the suborder Pinnipedia, the *todo* (Steller's sea lion), the *wamon azarashi* (ringed seal), the *kurakake azarashi* (ribbon seal), and the *gomafu azarashi* (harbor seal) are seen in relatively large numbers. Colonies of *ottosei* (fur seal), which breed on the Komandorski Islands off the Kamchatka Peninsula, appear from fall to winter in the waters of Hokkaidō and the Tōhoku area; by April and May they return northward. The dugong of Okinawa is sometimes seen; many are believed to exist, but their habits are as yet unknown.

IMAIZUMI Yoshiharu

marine parks

(*kaichū kōen*). Government-designated ocean areas featuring distinctive seabed topography and an abundance of marine life, along with recreational and educational facilities located on adjoining coastal areas.

In 1962 in Seattle, Washington, the first World National Parks Conference adopted a resolution urging participating countries to create marine parks off their shores. In 1964, the Japan Association for the Protection of Nature (Nihon Shizen Hogo Kyōkai) established a committee which studied plans for marine parks and looked for appropriate sites. In 1967, the commission was made independent of the association and renamed the Marine Parks Center of Japan. Subsequently, pursuant to the National Parks Law as amended in 1970 and acting on the recommendation of the center, the government designated 10 areas as marine parks, mostly in subtropical areas such as Sabiura in the town of Kushimoto, Wakayama Prefecture. Twelve additional areas were designated in 1971 and seven in 1972, including sites in the Ogasawara Islands and Hokkaidō, bringing the total to 57 at the end of 1979.

Submerged observation platforms, visitors' centers, and other sightseeing facilities have been constructed at these parks to help promote the general public's awareness of the marine environment. The parks also provide a staging point for exploration of the ocean floor. At Kushimoto, construction of both the Sabiura Reasearch Institute and an aquarium was completed in 1971. In 1975 another institute was built in Yaeyama, Okinawa, and in the same year an International Convention on Marine Parks was held in Tōkyō.

Japan's 57 marine parks may be loosely divided into three groups on the basis of the ocean currents which condition their environments. There are 27 marine parks located on the fringe of the warm KUROSHIO current in Okinawa, Ogasawara, Kyūshū, Shikoku, and the Kii Peninsula of central Honshū. These parks contain subtropical coral reefs and many varieties of soft coral. Twenty-nine marine parks along the coast of the Sea of Japan are washed by the warm TSUSHIMA CURRENT. They are noted for their vast beds of sargassum and other seaweeds. The parks along the east coasts of northern Honshū and Hokkaidō, which border on the cold OYASHIO current, are noted for huge laminaria kelp and for marine mammals such as seals.

HIROSAKI Yoshitsugu

markets

(*ichi* or *ichiba*). Markets of ancient Japan are thought to have developed at the sites of festivals or song and dance gatherings (UTAGAKI); in fact, the word *ichi* may have evolved from *itsuki*, meaning "ceremony." The Chinese history WEI ZHI (*Wei chih*) states that as early as the 3rd century there existed in each district of Japan a marketplace for trading goods. Both the chronicle NIHON SHOKI (720) and the 8th-century poetry anthology MAN'YŌSHŪ mention marketplaces such as the Karuichi, Tsubaichi, and Atokuwaichi of Yamato (now Nara Prefecture) and the Eganoichi in Kawachi (now part of Ōsaka Prefecture).

Following the TAIKA REFORM of 645, markets were established in the east and west districts of the successive capital cities, first FUJIWARAKYŌ, and later HEIJŌKYŌ (now the city of Nara) and HEIAN-KYŌ (now the city of Kyōto). The east and west markets operated for alternate periods of half a month each, opening each day at noon and closing with a signal of three beats on a drum at sundown. (In Heiankyō, only the east market survived.) Government-sponsored markets were also held near the administrative offices in the provincial capitals (KOKUFU). Toward the end of the Heian period (794–1185) shops opened in the settlements of tradesmen, forming MARKET TOWNS. With the rise of great landed estates (SHŌEN) around the same time, rent collection centers and entrepôts also developed, especially in port towns. Other markets grew up in front of major temples and shrines (see MONZEN MACHI). Most opened three times a month; some were held according to the sexagenary cycle, with names like *tatsu no ichi* (market on the day of the dragon) or *tori no ichi* (market on the day of the rooster) designating the day of business (see JIKKAN JŪNISHI).

With the growing use of money from about the middle of the Kamakura period (1185–1333), periodic one-day markets (*higiri ichi*) became an important means of converting the estates' grain tax (NENGU) into cash. The provincial military governors (SHUGO) of the Muromachi period (1333–1568) tried to control and expand commerce, and even local landholders (MYŌSHU) were gradually drawn into the more market-oriented economy that then began to emerge (see the section on social and economic developments in HISTORY

OF JAPAN: Muromachi history). Following the Ōnin War of 1467–77, it became common to hold markets in villages six times a month; these were called *rokusaiichi*. By the end of the 15th century, peddlers of specialized goods called *takani* or *renjaku shōnin* were making the rounds of market sites.

Officials called *ichimokudai* were appointed to oversee the running of the markets near estates, although a growing number of markets were run by the increasingly independent villagers and merchants themselves. The Muromachi shogunate also encouraged trade for its own profit, and many markets were opened by local *daimyō* to enrich their CASTLE TOWNS. The national unifiers ODA NOBUNAGA and TOYOTOMI HIDEYOSHI established "free markets" (*rakuichi*), which offered exemption from trade taxes, and abolished the monopolistic privileges of merchants in the ZA (guilds; see RAKUICHI AND RAKUZA). In large cities like Kyōto, permanent small shops and wholesalers (TOIYA) supplying the shops began to compete for business with the periodic markets. In addition, special rice markets appeared in Kyōto's Sanjō and Shichijō thoroughfares, and wholesale markets specializing in salt and fish made their appearance in Yodo (now in the southern part of Kyōto).

Although rural *rokusaiichi* still flourished in many areas during the first years of the Edo period (1600–1868), urban development and the building of permanent facilities caused a decline in such markets by the mid-18th century. In the larger cities, wholesale markets specializing in such items as rice, vegetables, and fish prospered as suppliers to tradesmen. The DŌJIMA RICE MARKET in Ōsaka and the fish market in the Nihombashi district of Edo (now Tōkyō) became well known. The Dōjima Rice Market, in particular, went on to become a speculative commodity exchange. In the provinces, markets for silk and silkworm cocoons appeared in Kiryū and Ashikaga, while horse-trading markets were held regularly in Sendai and Morioka. (These market towns were located in what are now Gumma, Tochigi, Iwate, and Miyagi prefectures, respectively.)

Traditional markets with many small booths still operate in a number of towns, especially during festivals. Markets held annually in major cities include the New Year's *hatsuichi*, the *bon'ichi* selling offerings for the BON FESTIVAL, and the *toshi no ichi* for New Year's decorations (see YEAR-END FAIR). In Tōkyō and elsewhere, markets such as the *asaichi* (morning-glory market), *uekiichi* (tree and shrub market), TORI NO ICHI, HŌZUKI ICHI, and DARUMA FAIRS are now enjoying a resurgence of popularity.   *Toyoda Takeshi*

market towns

(*ichiba machi*). Settlements authorized to hold public marketing of goods on specified days every month. Often providing some services as well as commercial opportunities, each marketing center established a link with urban life for residents of nearby villages and served as the basic, small-scale trading arena for itinerant merchants.

Urban markets existed as early as the Nara period (710–794), but only in the Kamakura period (1185–1333) did they proliferate outside of administrative centers. Over the next several centuries the number of *ichiba machi* expanded enormously, bringing periodic trade outlets within a few hours' journey of most Japanese by the 15th or 16th century. Settlements gained and lost commercial functions in rapid succession; at a time of few big cities and of intense local competition, prospects for survival and prosperity shifted repeatedly.

With the growth in the population of cities that occurred just before and during the early part of the Edo period (1600–1868), some local markets were closed to reduce local competition or protect the prosperity of CASTLE TOWNS (*jōka machi*, almost all of which doubled as marketing centers) and of their privileged merchants. For example, village markets in the vicinity of the city of Kanazawa were ordered to close. The majority of periodic markets became firmly subordinated as commercial outposts of the castle towns and of the three central cities—Edo (now Tōkyō), Ōsaka, and Kyōto (see RAKUICHI AND RAKUZA).

After a further spurt in new marketing places promoted by policies to boost local trade, the estimated number of market towns (inclusive of all settlements with markets except castle towns) stabilized in the 18th century at close to 1,500. This stability lasted for roughly a century.

By the late Edo period, merchants in well-situated or specialized marketing places posed a serious challenge to the supremacy of castle town interests. At the same time, periodic markets declined or even disappeared in the face of more efficient transportation and daily shopping in village stores. Replacement of periodic markets with daily commerce—a transformation typical of modernizing societies—accelerated after the Meiji Restoration (1868). In 1875 all market licenses were abolished, although in some outlying areas such as the Tōhoku and western Kantō regions, periodic markets persisted even into the contemporary period.

During the Edo period a market town could retain the administrative status of a village or could be elevated to local prominence as a *zaigōmachi* (a place apart from the castle town that was recognized as a town and granted corresponding rights and duties). In either case, payment of a monthly fee to the *daimyō* qualified local residents, or those to whom they rented space along the main street, to erect temporary stalls and booths for displaying wares in the open. In large markets activities were separated by specialty with areas assigned for grain, salt, local crafts, and perhaps cocoons or other products. Special livestock markets also existed. In relatively sizable cities, usually only two or three *chō* (city wards) were awarded the right to share a rotating periodic market. Policies protected the status quo, yet it was still necessary to arbitrate between competing petitions from neighboring settlements vying for a market or for a particular marketing day.

In comparison to other commercialized premodern societies, including England and China, periodic markets in Edo-period Japan were proportionately few and the smallest ones met infrequently. Heavy rates of land taxation, often in rice, meant that resources flowed directly into the castle towns. Correspondingly, the average hinterland population and number of villages per market in Edo Japan far exceeded the figures for these other countries. During each 10-day cycle numerous market towns held market only once, others twice, and a few others three times. A number of places were even named for the day in the cycle when the market originally convened, for example, Yokkaichi ("Fourth-Day Market") in present-day Mie Prefecture.

Japan boasted a high percentage of populous market towns that more than compensated for this shortfall of marketing places. Unlike the smaller places that everywhere remained predominantly agricultural with populations, as in other villages, numbering in the hundreds, these larger centers often supported diverse nonagricultural pursuits and thousands of residents. Sometimes, as in the case of Atsuta, Mishima, and other places along the main routes between Edo and Ōsaka, they doubled as ports or as post stations (see POST-STATION TOWNS).

Representing a bridge between urban and rural, market towns reflected the isolation of local areas or their national commercial integration, the preeminence of periodic marketing or its replacement by specialized markets and stores. Dramatic changes in the role of marketing places within the settlement hierarchy testify to the dynamism of Japanese urban-rural relations for over more than 700 years.

■——Itō Yoshiichi, *Kinsei zaikatashi no kōzō* (1967). Gilbert Rozman, *Urban Networks in Ch'ing China and Tokugawa Japan* (1973).   *Gilbert Rozman*

Marquat, William Frederic (1894–1960)

Army major general who from 1945 to 1952 was chief of the Economic and Scientific Section of SCAP (the headquarters of the Allied OCCUPATION of Japan) and who thus headed one of the most important and successful of the Occupation activities. Born in St. Louis, Missouri, he served in France as an artillery specialist during World War I and throughout World War II with General Douglas MACARTHUR in the Pacific. He was head of the Civil Affairs and Military Government Section of the US Army staff after his service in Japan.   *Richard B. Finn*

marriage

Over the past several centuries, the legal requirements and personal expectations of marriage in Japan have changed radically, around a strong and unchanging tradition. The changes that have taken place have been neither accidental nor random, but specific reactions to new social situations, ideas from other cultures, and the result of urbanization and a growing population within Japan.

Major features of Japanese marriages do not seem to have changed very much over time. For example, bride and groom must always be from households of equal social standing. This means that every person considered a member of the household (IE) of the bride and of the groom must be of roughly equal standing—an issue of crucial importance in selecting a partner in marriage. Inept selection of mates is a mistake attributed to all members of a household. As the social standing of others besides the bride and groom is at stake, the more a household is aware of its current, past, and future influence in society, the more carefully each marriage must be considered.

Marriages are not celebrated simply because two young people are attracted to one another, although this forms one element in modern Japanese marriages. A high-status marriage is contracted only after careful consideration, by other adult household members and by skilled outside go-betweens, of its future impact on the households concerned. The wedding ceremony requires a go-between (NAKŌDO) for critical ceremonial roles and in recognition of the continuing need for consultation and mediation.

Japanese marriage is often characterized as a system of arranged marriages, where the bride and groom are introduced to one another by a go-between and the marriage is celebrated while they are still comparative strangers. The more important the household of either the bride or groom, the more likely this is still the case, even in modern urban Japan. But it is more accurate to characterize Japanese marriage simply as a system of public statements, through marriage, of the status of households.

Marriage and the Ie—— The bulk of the population prior to industrialization was agricultural, settled in small permanent communities (MURA) of households. That portion of the population not involved in agriculture was similarly stable in occupation and status and usually restricted to certain localities in residence. In these communities, status mobility from one generation to another was minimal and the relative standing of households within the village and in nearby villages was well known.

It was far more difficult to cover up scandals, genetic disabilities, or mismanagement of a household estate within small communities than between them. Households had to rely on geographically and socially well-placed relatives or upon the services of go-betweens to guarantee household similarity whenever they contemplated marriages at any distance. Because there was mutual affirmation of the equality of households of bride and groom through marriage, marriages tended to be within restricted groups of households.

Marriage within the community solved many of the problems of mate selection resulting from the Japanese insistence on equality. Approximately one in five marriages in rural Japan prior to industrialization took place between households already related through adoption or marriage. No household was more equal than one that was already related.

Furthermore, equality in marriage resulted in connections between households with similar economic and political views. Traditional, status-conscious marriages have rarely taken place across group or factional boundaries. This has helped to maintain stability as well as the encapsulated or segregated groupings so characteristic of Japanese society (see GROUPS).

In present-day Japan, marriage is still a public statement about the relative standing of two households. It is still critical to the career plans of well-placed young men and women, and it still involves a search for similarities in background. Today, there is less emphasis on the continuation of occupational or trade networks and amity between in-laws. There is more emphasis on a young couple branching or breaking away from their initial social placement at marriage by virtue of their own abilities to attract and maintain a higher status—to be eventually confirmed by the marriages of their children.

In conjunction with Japanese traditions of equality of households in marriage, marriage has not been strictly separated from ADOPTION, as it is in the West. When a household has no son as a successor, a husband can be adopted into the household on behalf of a daughter of the house, or a couple can be adopted as successors in a household. Personal attraction to an ineligible spouse can always be legitimated through the adoption of that person into another, eligible, household. In this system, emphasis is not on biological parentage but on the equality of those who produce legitimate children.

Changes in Japanese Marriage—— Certain marriage patterns have changed considerably in Japan since the 8th century. During the Heian period (794–1185), marked by the flowering of Japanese court aristocracy, there was considerable emphasis on marriage between equals, but it was not accomplished in the same way it is today. Marriage itself was not the focus of attention as a ceremony of primary importance to society. It was the selection of mates to create children that was vital.

Men of importance could have more than one mate, because the attention of households was not on the automatic placement of all children at the rank of their father. As children matured, they might be confirmed to the rank of their father or to a lesser rank to which he was entitled, or they could rely on their mother's father or brother to make public gestures indicating the child was of the mother's rank. Adoption into other households to achieve rank was very common, as were the claims of a woman's family to set her children on a more successful path than their father could.

The husband often resided temporarily with his wife at her family's residence, while maintaining spartan bachelor's quarters elsewhere. His clothes were supplied by his wife's household and indicated the rank he held. This often meant a bride's brothers were entitled to similar clothing, since they were from a household equal to that of the groom.

A young man and woman of the Heian period could contract fairly permanent liaisons, with their parents or guardians serving as guarantors for their fidelity. Any children of this guaranteed union were automatically recognized during their mother's pregnancy by the formal presentation to her of a sash—a gift from the young man as recognition of their child.

On the other hand, there was no understanding between the young men and women concerning other potential mates. As a result, high-ranking men and women often had several mates in their lifetimes. A powerful man of aristocratic society was not bound at any time to a single mate in monogamous marriage. He could maintain one wife in her own residence, permit another wife's father to maintain her in his residence, and conduct further flirtations with other women. By building a separate residence in which he lived and to which he brought one wife, he gave considerable permanence to their relationship.

A woman usually conducted herself carefully, since her pregnancies needed recognition by a man from another household of equal status for her children to have any importance in society. One way for her own household's importance to grow was for her to attract and retain the constant attention of a man from a household of slightly higher status. Women from low-ranking households found this harder to manage than those from high-ranking households, since the latter could contribute lavish gifts for the man's maintenance and claim titles for their children through their own household's influence.

Because the rank of a child, through mutual household recognition, determined the offices and rights the child would exercise as an adult, a higher-ranking child brought luster to the woman's household as long as it lived and was not adopted elsewhere. For women, status was confirmed through the offices of her children. For men, marriage with several wives increased the resources available to them, providing these resulted in the birth of children.

Among members of the imperial household, residence of children at the household of their mother led to what was in fact governance by maternal relations. This system of marriage politics depended upon continued ties of adoption and marriage and often involved the marriage of cousins as a means of continuing a link between households.

Marriages were endogamous, that is, they took place within a group of households. It is likely that endogamous marriage characterized all levels of Heian society, that marriages to cousins or adoptive cousins were frequent, and that important men of each rank were permitted to have more than one wife.

Farmers, artisans, and low-ranking warriors or attendants had less chance of building their household name through recognized liaisons with higher-ranking women. They had an easier guarantee of firm status through permanent marriages with one wife, though they could change wives without difficulty from the authorities if their wife's family was not in a position to challenge their right to do so, and especially if the man had been going to his wife's residence (see MUKOIRIKON) rather than building a residence or maintaining a residence for her.

Change to Permanent Marriage—— Between the 11th and the 15th centuries in Japan, the agricultural base became sufficiently stable through wet rice cultivation for centers of power to diversify, and for new titles to be within the reach of lower-ranking households. This meant that marriages began regularly to be contracted between households at some geographical distance. The role of go-betweens shifted from that of guardian and guarantor of the parentage of a child to that of guarantor of equality between two households.

Political imbalances, warring factions, and reprisals were common in these centuries. Occasionally they involved households related through marriage. But marriage itself became an important means of ceremonially cementing alliances. The focus of societal attention shifted from parentage of children to a guarantee of equality and cooperation by households through the marriage of a young couple.

Military titles, unlike those of the aristocracy, were liable to change in a single battle. Ranking depended less on parentage than on ability in the field or ties of kinship among those who fought. With the establishment of fiefs which could be held against challenge, lower-status marriages across fief boundaries were actively discouraged, while high-status marriages were politically reviewed and channeled by fief officials in large part because of the loyalties built up through kinship in military alliances.

With the change to permanent fiefs, the military gradually changed into a bureaucracy, and titles became more hereditary. At the same time, polygynous marriage or marriage with many wives became less common. In the case of higher-status marriages wives were taken from households at some distance. Their residence was with their husband and the marriage ceremony increasingly tended to guarantee the legitimacy of children. Where the bride resided in the husband's residence (see YOMEIRIKON), the children of other women by her husband were guaranteed only the chance of adoption into the household.

Confucian ethics, imported throughout this time from China, supported many of the preferences of military and bureaucratic households in marriage. Among these were marrying at a distance rather than within a close group, and marrying with lavish WEDDINGS. The Chinese ranking of wives and concubines also accorded with the Japanese marriage-style of this era.

Marriage in the Edo Period (1600–1868) —— As military households in Japan finally achieved permanent recognition of their relative status, and the recognition of their fiefs as permanent units, the marriage system became subject to many rules and regulations to preserve the *status quo.*

These regulations concerning marriage reveal many of the common maneuvers which lent themselves to political volatility and were therefore inhibited. Central was the law requiring reporting throughout all fiefs of marriages that households were contemplating, in advance of any marriage ceremony. A central repository of all data on its populace was prepared by each fief for the central government as well as for its own.

The status of every household was fixed in these registries, by the titles to which it could aspire, as well as by the marriages it had managed to make. Later marriages had to be cleared through officials in each residential unit, and their appropriateness confirmed by go-betweens. Only the children born of registered, equal-rank, primary marriages seem to have inherited their father's titles.

All households, noble to commoner, were registered (see HOUSEHOLD REGISTERS). In this way, it was possible to trace how well the population followed the strict regulations. Although marriages between cousins were sometimes restricted, they appear to have occurred frequently in rural areas and among households of extremely high noble rank. Strict endogamy, or marriage among a very limited number of households, was an indication of both low, practically unranked status and of high and protected status.

Military leaders initiated an elaborate pattern of high-ranking marriages-at-a-distance by establishing a system of permanent ranks and titles after the end of the 16th century. These weddings required a go-between who had the paramount role of ensuring the equality of both households and the stability of the marriage. In cities, commoners such as artisans and shopkeepers seem to have followed the monogamous marriage pattern employing go-between and guarantor adopted by the military. In any event, their marriages were carefully scrutinized by officials, who acted in this way as go-betweens for ensuring appropriate marriages.

In rural areas, however, villagers continued the aristocratic patterns of multiple liaisons, including night-visiting (YOBAI), use of young people's huts (*wakamono yado;* see WAKAMONO-GUMI) and dormitories, and similar variations. Sometimes younger sons remained unmarried, unable to establish households of their own, and unable to inherit the households of their birth. The idea of marriage was clearly tied to the existence of an *ie.* Even when marriages were formally recognized, it was often after the birth of one or more children. This reflected not only the wider choice of mates from equal households available to villagers but their greater distance from official registry offices. In some areas, it was considered acceptable for the wife to remain for some years at the residence of her parents even after the formal registration of a marriage.

Changes in Marriage as a Result of Industrialization —— Industrialization resulted in major changes in Japanese marriage patterns. This was partly because of sudden shifts in population, as households lost part or all of their members to urban areas, and partly because of sudden shifts in status following the success of new occupations, or the lowering of old occupations in social esteem. Cities in effect were a collection of household members who were unrelated and who previously were located in different areas of Japan.

Modern marriages continue the principles of equality and marriage within a known group. Far larger sets of households are related through marriage than was the case in traditional rural communities. The households usually have a shared prior relationship through economic endeavors or through the occupational situation of the bride, the groom, or other members of their households. There is still a considerable encapsulation of households into those more or less likely to be considered potential relatives. In part this results from the use of existing networks of contact, and in part because of continuing use of the same rough approximations or guidelines to denote equal status. Households of higher status are careful to limit the contacts of their daughters. Despite coeducational schooling, a marriage partner is not likely to be found in the public sector, such as the school. Occupational equality through working in the same industry or the same company is a more common determinant of similar status.

In present-day Japan, the selection of a bride or groom during childhood is uncommon. Efforts to locate a compatible spouse include company contact networks or civic events designed to introduce young people to one another as parallel in status, either occupationally or socially. The go-between has had an increasingly significant role to play in marriages where the bride and groom have not known one another previously.

The modern system of marriage has adjusted to pressure from the Western custom of love marriages *(ren'ai kekkon)* to some extent. Thus, go-betweens are sought for advice on appropriate mates, and the young couple then makes some effort to make a decision through dating before arrangements are made for a marriage. The acceptance of the love-match has meant that households, and in particular the parents of a young couple, do not have as final a say in the marriage arrangements as they had even 50 years ago.

Western ideas of dating form only one part of the process of finding a mate, however. Dating merely confirms or disallows previous judgments concerning the suitability of a bride or groom while the two are comparative strangers. It is not a primary means of locating suitable partners, since any marriage will have the potential to affect the careers of at least some family members of both households even today, even if the young couple sets up a separate residence.

Fifty percent of all males marry by age 29 and 85 percent by age 34. Women tend to marry about five years before men, since 30 percent are married between the ages of 20 and 24, and 78 percent by age 29. By age 34 nearly 90 percent of all females are married. Less than 8 percent remain unmarried.

Some scholars attribute this high marriage percentage to Confucian ethics of fidelity to household continuity or the obligation of every person to marry. The social pressure to marry includes the fact, however, that few unmarried persons (excepting those in certain occupations) are considered responsible adults until they marry and establish their own households.

The high marriage percentage also results from the existence of go-betweens and their function in marriage. Very few people expect to find a spouse through casual meetings and dates. The majority of marriages today are made as love-matches, but this type of marriage usually involves trying the arranged meetings (MIAI) which are the specialty of the go-between. The go-between, in turn, guarantees the emotional well-being and suitability of a marriage. There is a very profound implication that any future difficulties in a marriage will be smoothed over by a go-between, acting as an intermediary. The couple is obliged to permit the go-between to function in this role before initiating divorce proceedings. The choice of an influential person, particularly from the husband's workplace, gives a couple access, in theory, to the patronage of this go-between during future crises.

Several go-betweens can be used before a marriage takes place, some in the role of those who search for an equal mate and some in the future-mediator role. Marriages in which there is only a go-between for the marriage ceremony are becoming quite usual, but young men and women still have limited opportunities to meet one another by chance.

There are numerous marriage bureaus in modern urban Japan, an outgrowth of massive migrations to urban environments. These include established marriage bureaus of several different types, such as offices that maintain banks of photographs and resumés as a business, personnel departments in large industrial enterprises, sophisticated matchmakers who deal only in certain neighborhoods or types of households, or civic-service bureaus.

Currently, there are legal pressures against marriage between related persons. In Japan, where civil registries are so easily checked, this is an enforceable code. Marriages continue in some instances between cousins, but it is usual for these marriages to involve rather distant cousins. More often, the definition of endogamy has shifted from the former emphasis on prior relationships to the cementing of new relationships and new groupings. The go-between provides an opportunity in modern Japan for advantages that were either unnecessary or taken for granted in earlier groupings of households. The present system relies heavily on traditional requirements of suitable mates, but the context for the new ties has a much wider potential for change, given new ideas of what makes a mate suitable.

Because of the new understanding of the role of go-betweens as patrons and the use of confidantes in the work arena and of marriage bureaus to locate suitable equal mates, the percentage of Japanese who marry is high, and young couples can establish nuclear families without the constant need to rely on their families or neighbors for support in their lives together.

▬▬▬Robert O. Blood, Jr, *Love Match and Arranged Marriage, A Tokyo-Detroit Comparison* (1967). George A. De Vos, "The Relation of Guilt toward Parents to Achievement and Arranged Marriage among the Japanese," *Psychiatry* (August 1960). Gamō Masao, *Nihon kon'in girei* (1967). Joy Hendry, *Marriage in Changing Japan* (1981). William H. McCullough, "Japanese Marriage Institutions in the Heian Period," *Harvard Journal of Asiatic Studies* (1967). Masuda Kōkichi, "Bride's Progress: How a *Yome* Becomes a *Shūtome*," *Journal of Asian and African Studies* (1975), includes further listings of sources in Japanese. Ōmachi Tokuzō, *Kon'in no minzokugaku* (1967). Sadao Sugiyama and William J. Schull, "Consanguineous Marriages in Feudal Japan," *Monumenta Nipponica* (1960). Barbara B. Swann, "Affines, Office and Factionalism in Three Rural Japanese Settlements," PhD dissertation, Brandeis University (1978). Hiroshi Wagatsuma and George A. De Vos, "Attitudes toward Arranged Marriage in Rural Japan," *Human Organization* (1962). Yanagita Kunio, *Kon'in no hanashi* (1948). Barbara Bowles SWANN

marriage law

(kon'in hō). The legal term for marriage in Japan, *kon'in*, refers to the socially sanctioned relationship for sexual union between men and women and the contract that legalizes such a union. Modern Japanese marriage law is based on monogamy and legally protects as "marriages" only those unions between a man and a woman which meet certain legally established requirements.

Under the CIVIL CODE of 1898, marriage in Japan was conducted largely within the *ie* (family system), which was controlled by the *koshu* (head of the family). Thus, marriage involved one of the parties leaving his or her *ie*, or family, as a *yome* (bride, daughter-in-law) or *muko* (groom, son-in-law), to become part of the other party's family, and in order to do this, agreement between the heads of both households was necessary. In this system, husband and wife were far from equal: through marriage, the wife lost her legal capacity to engage in property transactions; management of her own property came under her husband's control; and only the wife had the duty of chastity. Following the provisions set down in the 1947 constitution, which protected individual dignity and the essential equality of the sexes, the Civil Code of 1947 abolished the *ie* system and completely eliminated the inequality of husband and wife.

Japanese civil law recognizes only marriages based on the fulfillment of the legal requirements. For the establishment of a marriage, the following requirements, the first formal, the rest substantial, must be fulfilled. (1) In accordance with the Family Registration Law (Koseki Hō; see HOUSEHOLD REGISTERS), notification in writing, properly witnessed, or in person by the two parties, or their proxies, and two adult witnesses or guarantors is required (the guarantors need not actually accompany the two parties or their proxies). Even when the husband-wife relation has already been established by a formal ceremony or by living together, it is not recognized as a marriage without this notification. (2) The parties must have agreed upon marriage. A marriage is invalid if the intent to marry is lacking, as in cases of mistaken or false identity. Marriages involving

fraud or intimidation may be annulled. (3) Males must be at least 18 years old, females at least 16. (4) When a woman remarries, at least six months must have passed since the day of dissolution or cancellation of her previous marriage. This is to determine paternity in case of pregnancy. (5) A marriage must not be bigamous. (6) Marriage cannot be consanguineous. Marriages between lineal relatives by blood, between collateral natural relatives within the third degree of relationship by blood, and between lineal relatives by marriage (even after the relationship has ended through divorce or dissolution) are forbidden. (7) Minors (those under 20 years of age) must obtain the consent of their parents. If one parent objects or is incapable of expressing intent, the agreement of only one parent is sufficient. Marriages which violate any of conditions 3 through 6 may be cancelled *(torikeshi)*.

Establishment of the marriage relationship results in the following. Both husband and wife are called by one of their surnames. Each becomes a relative by marriage of the other's blood relatives. Each assumes the duties of cohabitation, cooperation, and support. Each assumes the duty of fidelity. Minors who marry are considered to have attained their majority. Contracts between husband and wife may be annulled while they are married. Mutual rights of inheritance are recognized. Children born are rebuttably presumed legitimate. Husband and wife may each hold property separately, but property whose ownership is unclear is rebuttably presumed to be held in common ownership.

Legal marriage is dissolved by the death or a declaration of disappearance of one of the parties or by divorce. When a marriage is dissolved, the above conditions are cancelled. The exception is that in the case of dissolution by death, the surviving spouse does not automatically revert to his or her former surname, nor do the family relationships created by marriage automatically terminate. Rather, these matters are decided according to the intent of the surviving spouse. See also DIVORCE; INHERITANCE LAW; MARRIAGE.

KANNO Kōki

marshal

(shikkōkan). Court officer in charge of, among other things, the service of judicial documents and execution in civil cases dealing with movables. The Marshal Law (Shikkōkan Hō) of 1966 sets forth the details of the office. Marshals belong to the district courts and are subject to supervision by the court. Although they are public officials they do not receive a salary from the state but collect fees from the party for whose benefit their work is performed. The state subsidizes the marshal's income when it falls below a certain minimum.

TANIGUCHI Yasuhei

martial arts

(bujutsu; also called *bugei;* now usually called *budō* or "the martial way"). A general term encompassing such martial sports as KENDŌ (swordplay), JŪDŌ, and *kyūdō* (archery). The old expression BUGEI JŪHAPPAN (the 18 martial arts) refers to the arts of archery, horsemanship, spearmanship (SŌJUTSU), swordplay, swimming, IAI (sword drawing), the short sword, the truncheon *(jitte)*, dagger-throwing (SHURIKEN), needle-spitting, the halberd (NAGINATA), gunnery, roping, *yawara* (present-day *jūdō*), NINJUTSU (spying), the staff, *mojiri* (a staff with numerous barbs on one end), and the chained sickle (KUSARIGAMA). In the Edo period (1600–1868), in addition to academic subjects, warriors were required to learn six martial arts: swordplay, spearmanship, archery, horseback riding, *jūjutsu* (now known as *jūdō*), and firearms. These six, together with military strategy, were called the seven martial arts. These were taught under the name BUSHIDŌ (the Way of the warrior).

After the Meiji Restoration (1868), the content of martial arts changed greatly, reflecting the fact that they were no longer meant to be used in combat and were no longer exclusive attainments of the warrior class. Reflecting this new circumstance, *bujutsu* was replaced by the term *budō*, implying that one would be trained in spiritual principles rather than for combat. *Jūdō* thus replaced *jūjutsu* after the founding of the KŌDŌKAN *jūdō* school in 1882. Similarly, *kenjutsu* (the art of the sword) or *gekken* (sword striking) became *kendō* (the Way of the sword) when the Ministry of Education included it in the regular middle school curriculum in 1911.

Modern *budō* seeks the development of skills through physical exercise, and by establishing objective standards of skills, provides opportunities for competition. In this sense, it can be considered a form of sport. Yet *budō* is more than just a game. In order to clarify this, we must consider *bujutsu*, the antecedent of *budō*, from a historical and technical viewpoint.

Characteristics of Japanese Martial Arts —— Japan's martial arts developed along with the rise of the *bushi* or SAMURAI (warrior) class, which flourished from the end of the Heian period (794–1185) until the Meiji Restoration. During the period from the late 12th century until 1600, the martial arts were developed for use in actual battle and men were clad in armor. In the Edo period, when Japan enjoyed uninterrupted peace, the emphasis shifted to techniques for self-defense.

The martial skills can be roughly divided into three categories: countering violence by killing, by injuring, and without killing or injuring. The main techniques of swordplay aimed at "splitting the enemy in two with one swing of the sword," and those of *jūjutsu* at tumbling and restraining an adversary. In other words, swordplay and *jūjutsu* were two extremes, between which lie the use of such weapons as the spear, dagger, stick, truncheon, and such unarmed skills as striking, thrusting, and kicking.

In order to counter violence, there were occasions when killing was ultimately unavoidable. However, some thoughtful masters, discerning the deeper meaning of *waza* (skills), rejected killing in favor of spiritual awareness and self-discipline. For example, the main precept of the Shinkage school of swordplay, founded in the 16th century, is "no sword," that of the Yōshin school of *jūjutsu*, founded in the early Edo period is "no killing," and the Daitō school of *aiki jūjutsu* (see AIKIDŌ) adjured students to "neither let hit, nor hit; neither let kick, nor kick; neither let slay, nor slay." Famous sword masters of the early Edo period such as Itō Ittōsai and MIYAMOTO MUSASHI lived to regret the violence of their youth when they had dared to kill and wound opponents. KATSU KAISHŪ and YAMAOKA TESSHŪ are examples of sword masters who, though active in the maelstrom of late-Edo civil war, never once killed.

It may appear inconsistent to negate killing as the ultimate end of swordplay, but this is the chief distinction between martial power and sheer violence.

In order for martial power to counter violence, it must possess superior skill. It has long been said "to fight and win a hundred times is not good; to quell the enemy without fighting is the highest good." The intention of martial power was to overcome violence through martial dignity; and the basis of martial power was "martial virtue," which abhors violence but not the individuals who resort to violence.

Martial Arts and Spiritual Training —— Behind the Japanese martial arts lie the philosophies of Confucianism, Buddhism, and Taoism. The most outstanding and highly cultured among practitioners of the martial arts not only mastered *waza* (skills) but studied *michi* (the Way; another pronunciation of the Chinese character for *dō* in such words as *budō*). *Kokoro* (or *shin*; heart) which seeks the Way is *bushin* (martial heart), which does not succumb to violence. Thus the martial arts and spiritual training were inseparable. Through study of the skills, one learned presence of mind. Ultimately, such training was pushed to the point that presence of mind in daily life was considered important, for one had to be constantly prepared if one desired to be calm when facing death on the battlefield. In battle, *kokoro* was considered even more important than military skill. Warriors found greater virtue in a heart that is calm facing death than in martial prowess.

The founder of the Shinkage school of swordplay, Kōizumi Nobutsuna (16th century) called it "the heart that does not perish even if one plunges into flames or lies under a boulder." Miyamoto Musashi spoke of "the heart of stone." Edo-period treatises on swordsmanship deal with similar concepts. The *Fudō chishin myōroku* expounds on the "immovable heart" and "the heart that does not fail." The *Tengu geijutsu ron* states that "swordplay is a skill employed at the moment of death." The *Neko no myōjutsu* declares that "swordplay is not concerned with victory, but with the illumination of life and death in the face of great emergency." The secret of the Yagyū school (founded by Kōizumi's disciple Yagyū Muneyoshi in the late 16th century) was "a log spanning a torrent"; and that of the Mutō school was said to lie in understanding the single word *mu* (nothingness). These were all means of conquering the agitation of the heart during combat.

Side by side with such Buddhist interpretations of *kokoro*, we also find Confucian ideas in old documents concerning *jūjutsu*, the art of *yawara* (pliancy). According to the teachings of the Oguri school, "the single element of primordial power was divided into the positive and the negative, interaction of which produced the five natural elements. When the dual forces harmonize and the five ele-

ments form, they give birth to the myriad things of the universe. The source of everything is one." Again, "man, too, functions when provided by this single element with the dual forces and the five elements. While in motion or at rest the one is with him." Further, "by *yawara* we mean concentration on this element of harmony and control of the hard and strong with the tender and weak. Here *yawara* is represented by the Chinese character for *wa* (harmony; peace) rather than the customary *jū* (soft; pliant). This teaching led to frequent uses of the words *ki* (spiritual essence) and *yawara* (harmony, peace; softness, pliancy) in later *jūjutsu*.

In short, Japanese martial arts started with *waza* (skills for killing and fighting), and through searches for *kokoro* (the heart that transcends victory and defeat) were led to the Buddhist view of life and death and the Confucian way of natural harmony.

The Essence of the Martial Arts —— The basis of the martial arts resides in posture and body movement. Unlike other physical skills, the fundamental postures of the martial arts are standing upright and sitting upright. These are expressed as "natural body" in *jūjutsu* and "no stance" in swordplay, and are related to an etiquette that forms a correct attitude toward life. YOSHIDA SHŌIN stated that "ceremony is defense," and Miyamoto Musashi added that it is important to "make your daily self your martial self, your martial self your daily self." These principles illustrate the essence of the martial arts.

When the enemy attacks with a hit, thrust, kick, or weapon, one must have the deftness and mastery to parry by mere body movement. Skills such as "expression of the eyes," "interval" (MA), "yawara," "kuzushi" (pulling off balance) are contingent on this. Although methods differ, this principle is uniformly shared by all the martial arts, and it is no exaggeration to say that its acquisition is the beginning and end of martial training.

The martial arts entail danger. As soon as one has dodged the enemy's attack through proper posture and body movement, one counters by attacking when he is off guard. The means and methods for this are the basis for classification of the various martial arts. They can be roughly divided into those that use weapons and those that use the hands. Skills employing weapons aim to "strike and kill." Even when attacking the enemy empty-handed, the purpose of blows, thrusts, and kicks is to "strike and kill." On the other hand, unarmed skills such as throwing, restraining squeezing, and immobilizing do not necessarily aim to kill and injure, but to "control violence yet not hurt life." However, these too, depending upon how they are employed, can be dangerous. It is undeniable that the skills of martial arts always carry an element of danger.

In the old martial arts, these skills were mingled without clear demarcation. Swordplay was not only concerned with the use of swords, but also with the skills of empty-handed fighting. Although outwardly devoted to empty-handed fighting, *jūjutsu* was from the beginning a comprehensive martial art and included training in sword, spear, and stick. This was a natural aspect of training when actual warfare was contemplated.

Methods of Practice in the Martial Arts —— In early times, warriors mastered techniques and the laws of heart and mind through long periods of actual warfare. They then taught their skills through a system of practice patterns called *kata*. In order to learn the skills correctly, one is required to place importance on the *kata* and think deeply about them in order to understand their inherent logic.

Practice of set patterns is effected by standardizing the activities of one or both participants: one applies a certain pattern of attack, while the other succumbs to or counterattacks according to another set pattern. However, rigid training in forms is not sufficient for mastering the techniques of the martial arts; both parties must compete freely using the forms they have practiced. Through competition one can train the heart and learn the principle of change between attack and defense. Thus, practice of the martial arts inevitably requires opportunities to apply skills in action.

During the Warring States period (Sengoku period; 1467–1568) the battlefield served as a place for application of skills, whether of swordplay or of *jūjutsu*. However, the peaceful Edo period provided neither wars nor battles. Thus, such violent acts as *tsujigiri* (random street cutting) and *tsujinage* (random street throwing) were frequently practiced by those seeking experience, until the practice was outlawed. Even Yagyū Mitsuyoshi (1607–50), grandson of the founder of the Yagyū school and tutor to the Tokugawa shogunate, is said to have been officially permitted to practice *tsujigiri* on unsuspecting passersby.

Having lost the arena of actual combat, practicants concentrated on the forms. In time, however, they became preoccupied with detail and began losing real effectiveness. This was held in contempt by purists who described such methods as *kahō kempō* ("flower school swordplay"). In order to remedy this trend, new training methods were developed. The most notable are the Yagyū school's *fukuro-jinai* (bagged bamboo sword), practice using covered bamboo swords in mock sword fights, and the bamboo swordplay of the Jikishinkage and Ittō schools. This was the beginning of swordsmanship as the competitive sport it is today.

In *jūjutsu*, since the contents of *waza* were complex, the method of practicing by *randori* (free fighting) evolved. The Kyūshin and Kitō schools practiced *midare-geiko* (free training), an early example of training involving contact. In the Meiji period (1868–1912), the *randori* practice methods for mastering *nagewaza* (throwing skills) and *katamewaza* (defensive skills involving pressing, squeezing, and the use of joints) were perfected by the Kōdōkan school.

However, even after these new methods were initiated, it was difficult to dislodge the idea that training on the actual battlefield was superior. Furthermore, the conversion of combat into a game still involved physical danger. Therefore the feeling persisted that martial training was something to engage in at the risk of one's life.

The martial arts required a trained attitude toward death before actual battle, and came to be considered religious achievements through which one could become absolutely invincible regardless of the result of combat. Moreover, they became secret methods guarded from outsiders.

The martial arts became the means for group rather than personal defense and were taught to those who shared the same ideology. They were transmitted as secrets from master to disciple, and it was strictly prohibited to teach them to others. Even those of high social rank, at the time of joining a school, had to submit a pledge of secrecy called *kishōmon*. The Shibukawa school *Jūjutsu kishōmon* (1712) reads as follows: "Now that I will receive your training, I swear that, without your permission, I will not show or teach the slightest detail to anybody, not even to my closest relatives. Should I act contrary, I am content to receive the punishments of great and small gods all over Japan, especially of the Great God Hachiman." We can gain insight into the practice of the traditional martial arts from such documents. The development of the martial arts for group protection gave birth to sects and the headmaster system, in turn resulting in a deepening of content and a perfecting of style.

In the development of the martial arts, the religious, secretive, and sectarian aspects made significant contributions, but they were accompanied by exclusiveness, self-importance, and blind faith, qualities which do not suit modern society. After World War II, there was a need to modify certain views of the martial arts, and the emphasis shifted from practical arts intended for national defense, to sports that stress harmony and universality.

📖——Donn F. Draeger, *Classical Bujutsu* (1973). Donn F. Draeger, *Classical Budō* (1974). Kodokan Institute, *Kodokan Judo: A Guide to Proficiency* (1963). Daisetz T. Suzuki, *Zen and Japanese Culture* (1960).　　　　　　　　　　　　TOMIKI Kenji

martial law

(*kaigenrei*). The present CONSTITUTION of Japan has no provision for martial law, although article 78 of the Self Defense Force Law (Jieitai Hō) of 1954 empowers the prime minister to mobilize the SELF DEFENSE FORCES for the preservation of public peace. There were, however, specific provisions for martial law before World War II. Regulations were issued in 1882 by the Grand Council of State (DAJŌKAN) providing for the assumption of civil and administrative functions by the military during times of war or internal dissension. Subsequently, the Meiji Constitution of 1889 (art. 14) reserved for the emperor the right to invoke martial law. Full martial law was declared in the port of Ujina in Hiroshima Prefecture following the onset of the SINO–JAPANESE WAR OF 1894–1895; it was invoked again in the ports of Nagasaki, Sasebo, and Hakodate, as well as in Taiwan (then a Japanese colony), during the RUSSO–JAPANESE WAR of 1904–05. Martial law regulations were partially applied in Tōkyō when opposition to the Treaty of Portsmouth (1905) resulted in the HIBIYA INCENDIARY INCIDENT, again at the time of the great TŌKYŌ EARTHQUAKE OF 1923, and following the attempted military coup known as the FEBRUARY 26TH INCIDENT (1936).

Marubashi Chūya (d 1651)

One of the principals in the *rōnin* cabal behind the KEIAN INCIDENT of 1651. A *rōnin* (masterless *samurai*) and an expert lancer who ran a school of this martial art, Chūya joined YUI SHŌSETSU in plotting a public disorder, if not the overthrow of the Tokugawa shogunate. Their plan allegedly included blowing up the shogunate's arsenal (whose assistant commander, Kawara Jūrōbei, joined the conspiracy), burning the city of Edo (now Tōkyō), killing the shogunate's chief ministers, and even seizing Edo Castle. The plot was exposed, apparently through Chūya's own boastfulness, and he was arrested and executed together with 33 other plotters and their relatives on 24 September (Keian 4.8.10).

An interesting sidelight on this incident is that on being questioned whether theirs was not in fact a Christian conspiracy, Chūya and Kawara Jūrōbei replied by professing allegiance to the teachings of the Wang Yangming scholar KUMAZAWA BANZAN; this gave the Zhu Xi (Chu Hsi) ideologue HAYASHI RAZAN the opportunity to slander his fellow Neo-Confucian Banzan as a crypto-Jesuit.

George ELISON

Marubeni Corporation

One of Japan's leading *sōgō shōsha* (GENERAL TRADING COMPANIES). While primarily engaged in international and domestic trade, the company's operations also include contracting and financing of construction work, underwriting of property insurance, and leasing of real and movable properties. Its transactions cover virtually all fields of industry, ranging from mining, machinery, and construction to energy, chemicals, textiles, and marine products. The company is a key member of the Fuyō group, one of the major industrial-financial groups in Japan.

The company originated in 1858 and was reorganized in its present form in 1949. It has 50 domestic and 128 overseas branches and subsidiaries, with 231 affiliates in Japan and 150 abroad. Its international activities draw upon this worldwide network and its expertise in information exchange, financing, and the organization of development projects.

The company's future plans emphasize the improvement of material and product distribution systems; promotion of plant exports; and development of sources of energy, food, and other basic materials. Its main offices are in Tōkyō and Ōsaka. Of its sales for the fiscal year ending March 1982 of ¥11.5 trillion (US $47.8 billion), imports and exports accounted for 45.2 percent, offshore trade 17.2 percent, and domestic trade 37.6 percent. The trading volume classified by commodity was well balanced. Capitalization in the same year was ¥43.1 billion (US $179 million). The head office is in Tōkyō.

Marudai Food Co, Ltd

(Marudai Shokuhin). Meat processor producing ham and sausages. Founded in 1958. Initially the firm produced fish sausages, but in the 1960s it turned to the production of meat sausages and the general processing of meats. In the 1970s the firm entered the field of prepared foods, enabling it to become a comprehensive food processor. Possessing distinctive management policies, the firm has set up a direct sales system of retail outlets which avoid the use of wholesalers and employ a large percentage of part-time workers. Sales for the fiscal year ending February 1982 totaled ¥139 billion (US $591 million) and capitalization was ¥6.4 billion (US $27 million). Corporate headquarters are located in Ōsaka.

Marugame

City in western Kagawa Prefecture, Shikoku; includes part of the Shiwaku Islands. Marugame developed as a castle town with the construction of Marugame Castle in 1597. In the Edo period (1600–1868) it prospered as the landing point for pilgrims visiting KOTOHIRA SHRINE. Industries include textiles and chemicals; *uchiwa* (fans) are also made here. Of interest are the ruins of Marugame Castle. Pop: 70,840.

Maruichi Steel Tube, Ltd

(Maruichi Kōkan). Manufacturer of steel pipe and tubing. Founded in 1913, it is a leading firm in the industry. It is well known overseas through its trade name MKK. The firm owns 11 plants located in parts of Japan where there is a large demand for its products. Since 1957, approximately 30 percent of its products have been exported, and it has established five overseas plants. In the future the firm plans to increase the value-added revenue of its products. Sales for

Maruyama Ōkyo

Old Pine Tree in Snow (1765). Seen here are the influence of Chinese painting on Ōkyo, his concern with the realistic depiction of nature, and a sense for abstract design. Signature and seals of artist. Ink and pale gold on silk. 123.0 × 71.6 cm. Tōkyō National Museum.

the fiscal year ending March 1982 totaled ¥101.2 billion (US $420.4 million) and capitalization was ¥3.7 billion (US $15.4 million). The head office is in Tōkyō.

Marui Co, Ltd

Firm operating a chain of retail department stores that employ a system of installment payment. Marui is a leading department store in the number of customers holding credit cards and revenue obtained from purchases made on the installment plan. Founded in 1937, it modernized its installment plan in 1960 and was the first domestic firm to issue credit cards; a credit card boom followed. Since then, rapid expansion has been carried out through enlargement of its network of department stores and further modernization of its credit card system. In 1982 the firm owned 34 retail outlets, with a total sales floorage of 216,452 square meters (2,329,946 sq ft), centered in the Tōkyō metropolitan area and with most stores near railroad or subway stations. Marui credit card holders number over 4.5 million. All stores are connected by an on-line computer system which has greatly facilitated the issuance of credit cards. The firm is especially active in the sale of brand-name goods produced by leading overseas manufacturers. Future plans call for continued expansion at the rate of one or two new stores a year, chiefly in the Tōkyō metropolitan area, as well as product diversification. Sales for the fiscal year ending January 1982 totaled ¥260.8 billion (US $1.2 billion), of which clothing accounted for 46 percent and household goods 28 percent. In the same year capitalization stood at ¥8.4 billion (US $37.4 million).

Maruoka Hideko (1903–)

Researcher on social problems, particularly the lives of rural women. Born in Nagano Prefecture and raised in the countryside; original name, Ishii Hide. She graduated from the Nara Girls' Normal School (now Nara Women's University) and began teaching there. Widowed after a brief marriage, she chose to work with the survey division of the Sangyō Kumiai Chūōkai (Central Organization of Production Unions; see AGRICULTURAL COOPERATIVE ASSOCIATIONS) so that she could pursue her studies of rural women. Her pioneering book was *Nihon nōson fujin mondai* (1937, The Problems of Women in Japanese Farming Villages). At about the same time, she became close friends with the novelist TAMURA TOSHIKO.

She later spent several years in China with her second husband. Returning to Japan after World War II, she continued her studies and her writing, becoming especially concerned with educational problems. She worked for the establishment of parent-teacher associations (PTAS), campaigned in the antinuclear movement, and helped start the Mothers' Conferences (Hahaoya Taikai) in Japan in 1955. Her more recent works include *Aru sengo seishin* (1969, A Postwar Consciousness).

Maruyama Kaoru (1899–1974)

Poet. Born in Ōita Prefecture. Often called the poet of the sea. At age 19 he was admitted to the Tōkyō Shōsen Gakkō (now Tōkyō Mercantile Marine University) but had to withdraw because of beriberi and poor coordination. This unrealized dream of becoming a sailor affected him for much of his life. His first book, *Ho, rampu, kamome* (1932, Sails, Lamps, Seagulls), had few poems about the sea, but the deep sense of yearning and loss conveyed in the opening sequence established his later reputation. *Tenshō naru tokoro* (1943, Where the Bell Rings) is entirely about the sea and sailing; it describes his experiences aboard a four-masted bark in 1941. Poems about his two-month cruise on board a freighter in 1955 are collected in his anthology of sea poems, *Tsuresarareta umi* (1962, The Sea that Was Taken Away). Some of his best poems on other subjects are found in his last books: *Tsuki wataru* (1972, The Moon Crosses) and *Ari no iru kao* (1973, Face With Ants on It). In 1934 Maruyama joined HORI TATSUO and MIYOSHI TATSUJI in publishing the poetry magazine *Shiki* (Four Seasons). "Watashi to shiyū" (1970, My Poet Friends and I) is an account of his associations with other poets through this influential magazine.

——— *Maruyama Kaoru zenshū* (Kadokawa Shoten, 1976–77).
Hiroaki SATŌ

Maruyama Kenji (1943–)

Author. Born in Nagano Prefecture. Graduated from a technical high school. After an unsuccessful attempt at professional boxing, he began to write, supporting himself by working as a telegraph operator. He became one of the youngest recipients of the Akutagawa Prize for his novel *Natsu no nagare* (1966), a dry, impersonal account of the execution of a convict as seen through the eyes of a veteran executioner. Influenced by Hemingway's style and perspectives, Maruyama depicts young working-class people trying to escape from their humdrum lives, sometimes using pointless violence. His other works include the novelette *Mahiru nari* (1968) and the novel *Asahi no ataru ie* (1970).

Maruyama Masao (1914–)

Political scientist; known for his study of the history of political thought in Japan. Born in Ōsaka Prefecture. After graduation from the law department of Tōkyō University in 1937, he joined the faculty there, becoming a full professor in 1950 and retiring in 1971. Not only has Maruyama contributed greatly to the development of political science in Japan since the end of World War II, but by undertaking a penetrating analysis of Japan's actual social and ideological situation as seen from the viewpoint of democracy, he has had a profound influence on intellectual thought in Japan. Particularly noteworthy is his *Chōkokka shugi no ronri to shinri* (1946, The Logic and Psychology behind Ultranationalism), an analysis of the spiritual structure underlying the premodern and antidemocratic nature of the Japanese EMPEROR system. Other critical works by Maruyama include: *Nihon seiji shisōshi kenkyū* (1952; tr *Studies in the Intellectual History of Tokugawa Japan,* 1974), which examines political thought during the Edo period (1600–1868) and sheds light on the processes behind the modernization of Japanese thought and society; *Gendai seiji no shisō to kōdō* (1956–57; tr *Thought and Behavior in Modern Japanese Politics,* 1963), a collection of essays on various facets of Japanese government; and *Senchū to sengo no aida* (1976, Between the War and Postwar Eras). *FURUTA Hikaru*

Maruyama Ōkyo (1733–1795)

Painter and founder of the Maruyama school. Real name Maruyama Mondo. Born to a poor farming family in Tamba Province (now part of Kyōto Prefecture). In his youth Ōkyo was sent to Kyōto, where he studied painting with the KANŌ SCHOOL master Ishida Yūtei (1721–86). Yūtei's style was eclectic, as was typical of

Kanō painters of his day. Through Yūtei and through independent study, especially of the works of the artist WATANABE SHIKŌ, which he particularly admired, Ōkyo was exposed to realistic Western-derived techniques as well as to native RIMPA and TOSA SCHOOL elements. Ōkyo was also influenced by the work of painters of the NAGASAKI SCHOOL (who learned from imported Chinese paintings as well as from Chinese and Western books, copperplate etchings, and the like), and he is known to have studied Chinese works, particularly Chinese BIRD-AND-FLOWER PAINTING. It is also apparent that early in his career he began working from direct sketches of life, a practice that he advocated among his students.

In the 1750s Ōkyo did a series of megane-e (literally, "eyeglass pictures") or painted stereographs for use in a popular optical device, showing "three-dimensional" views of Chinese and Japanese landscapes. His earliest extant sketchbooks date from the 1770s and abound with realistic depictions of people and places around Kyōto. He was extremely prolific and his combination of realistic perspective and chiaroscuro together with traditional Kanō-school compositional techniques and decorative elements, such as gold leaf backgrounds, was received enthusiastically. Though he was skilled in all categories of painting, he was perhaps most adept at painting flowers and trees. He did many large-scale screen-and-wall paintings, first for the Emman'in temple in Ōtsu, and in later years for such establishments as the temple Daijōji near the Sea of Japan and the temple Kongōji in Kameoka and even, in 1790, for the Imperial Palace in Kyōto.

Ōkyo attracted many followers, the most notable of whom were Nagasawa ROSETSU, Komai Genki, Yamaguchi Soken, Oku Bummei, Yoshimura Kōkei, Kinoshita Ōju, Mori Tetsuzan, Hatta Koshū, Yamaato Kakurei, and Kameoka Kirei (the "10 great disciples of Ōkyo"). Other important pupils or followers were his son Ōzui, WATANABE NANGAKU, and MATSUMURA GOSHUN (the founder of the Shijō school). Ōkyo's influence on later generations of painters was great, and practically all the developments of the MARUYAMA–SHIJŌ SCHOOL can be traced to sources in Ōkyo's vast oeuvre. The abundance of forgeries and copies of his works is a reflection of his popularity.

———Iijima Isamu, Ōkyo (1958). Suzuki Susumu, Ōkyo to Goshun, no. 39 of Nihon no bijutsu (July 1969). St. Louis Art Museum and Seattle Art Museum, Ōkyo and the Maruyama-Shijō School of Japanese Painting (1980). *C. H. MITCHELL*

Maruyama–Shijō school

A major movement in Japanese painting in the Kyōto area in the late 18th and 19th centuries. Derived in large part from the Maruyama school, which was founded in Kyōto by MARUYAMA ŌKYO (1733–95). Ōkyo's student MATSUMURA GOSHUN (1752–1811) founded the Shijō school, named after his studio on Shijō Street in Kyōto. The artists who followed in the tradition of Ōkyo and Goshun have become known collectively as the Maruyama–Shijō school, a designation that probably dates from the end of the Edo period (1600–1868).

The painters of the movement incorporated realistic aspects based on Western-influenced perspective and shading and on direct sketching from life, but they never broke completely with traditional techniques and themes. Ōkyo's emphasis lay in capturing the appearance of nature, but his carefully structured compositions and interest in decorative gold backgrounds and meticulous detail were well within the native KANŌ SCHOOL and TOSA SCHOOL traditions in which he had been trained. Goshun, on the other hand, had begun as a BUNJINGA (literati painting) artist, as is reflected in his softer, more spontaneous brushwork.

Ōkyo's genius, revealed in such successful paintings as his Old Pine Tree in Snow (Setchū rōshō zu or Sesshōzu, 1765), welded together the disparate elements of realistic depiction, Chinese influence, and the indigenous Japanese sense for abstract design (see RIMPA). In his own day, his work was seen as radically innovative. An energetic and magnetic teacher, he attracted many followers, but only Goshun equaled him in skill and originality.

Goshun had studied literati painting with Yosa BUSON before working with Ōkyo and then establishing his own studio. Goshun's freer, more idiosyncratic brushwork and softer colors, added to a realistic portrayal of traditional subject matter, made his work more personal and subjective than Ōkyo's. MATSUMURA KEIBUN, OKAMOTO TOYOHIKO, and other members of the Shijō school are generally thought to have produced more elegant and refined work than did the Maruyama artists. Differences between Ōkyo's and Go-

shun's followers and their descendants decreased with time. The work of many later followers of the Maruyama–Shijō style lapsed into increasing refinement and mannerism as Ōkyo's precepts about sketching directly from nature were forgotten.

Of the traditional schools of painting in 19th-century Kyōto, many were heavily influenced by the Maruyama–Shijō style, including the Kishi, Mori, and later Rimpa schools, as well as the FUKKO YAMATO-E SCHOOL; by the beginning of the Meiji period (1868–1912), the similarities among these schools far outweighed their differences. Even today, artists working in the tradition of Japanese-style painting (NIHONGA) recognize their debt to the Maruyama–Shijō legacy.

———J. Hillier, The Uninhibited Brush: Japanese Art in the Shijō Style (1974). Owen E. Holloway, Graphic Art of Japan: The Classical School (1957). C. H. Mitchell, The Illustrated Books of the Nanga, Maruyama, Shijō, and Other Related Schools of Japan: A Biobibliography (1972). Suzuki Susumu, Ōkyo to Goshun, no. 39 of Nihon no bijutsu (July 1969). *C. H. MITCHELL*

Maruzen Co, Ltd

One of Japan's leading companies engaged in the import, publishing, and sales of Western books and a well-known purveyor of stationery and office supplies. Founded in Yokohama as the Maruya Shōsha in 1869 by Hayashi Yūteki, a student of FUKUZAWA YUKICHI, the company began as an importer of Western books, magazines, stationery, and medical supplies. In 1893, it was moved to Tōkyō, and its name was changed to Maruzen Co, Ltd. Maruzen continues today to import and sell Western literature and maintains a high reputation in the publishing world. *KOBAYASHI Kazuhiro*

Maruzen Oil Co, Ltd

(Maruzen Sekiyu). Firm engaged in oil refining and the manufacture and sale of petrochemical products. Known as a major "nonforeign" (minzoku-kei) oil company in Japan, it held eight percent of the gasoline market and ranked fourth in the industry in 1982. Founded in 1933, it first produced lubricating oil and other oil products. Following World War II the firm embarked on the refining of oil and in 1957 entered the petrochemical field. In 1968, with DAIKYŌ OIL CO, LTD, and others, it established the Abu Dhabi Oil Co, Ltd, a drilling firm, to ensure oil supplies. Not having ties with major international oil producers, Maruzen has sought crude oil from China, Indonesia, and Mexico, and continued to expand joint development projects in the Middle East and Alaska. The firm has also made efforts to increase its production of liquefied petroleum gas (LPG), liquefied natural gas (LNG), and coal, and has launched a project for the development of new energy sources, including oil sand and oil shale. Sales for the fiscal year ending March 1982 totaled ¥1.8 trillion (US $7.5 billion) and capitalization was ¥20.5 billion (US $85.2 million). The corporate headquarters are in Tōkyō.

Masakadoki → Shōmonki

Masamune Hakuchō (1879–1962)

Pen name of Masamune Tadao, one of the prominent writers of the naturalist school (see NATURALISM), whose work extends over the late Meiji (1868–1912), Taishō (1912–26), and Shōwa (1926–) periods. His complete works include many short stories and full-length novels, plays, and critical essays. Because he survived the other major figures of the naturalist movement, he was able to look back upon it with mature critical judgment and became its historian. His early involvement with Christianity, his apparent abandonment of it in his middle years, together with his affirmation shortly before his death that he had always remained a Christian, have provoked much discussion in Japanese literary circles, and provide a fascinating example of the interaction of Protestant Christianity with modern Japanese literature.

Hakuchō was born the eldest son in a prosperous family of 10 children in Okayama Prefecture. Physically frail in childhood, he spent much time reading Edo romances and adventure stories, and nurtured the hope of becoming a novelist. In 1892 he entered a private academy where he studied the Chinese classics as well as English, but he left after less than two years. It was during this period that he developed an interest in Christianity, going to a neighboring village to receive religious instruction. Later, illness forced him to go to a hospital in the city of Okayama, and there he studied English at a school run by American Protestant missionaries. The Bible instruction he received there was a memorable event for him. This mission school closed about half a year after Hakuchō enrolled; thereafter he stayed at home reading widely in literary works. Because of anxiety and a fear of death engendered by his frail health, his religious interest deepened, and he derived much solace from the works of the prominent Japanese Christian UCHIMURA KANZŌ.

Move to Tōkyō——In February 1896 Hakuchō went to Tōkyō, enrolling in the English department of the Tōkyō Semmon Gakkō, which later became Waseda University. During this same period, he heard the sermons of the noted Protestant preacher UEMURA MASAHISA, and in the following year was baptized and became a church member. Although he continued to be greatly influenced by the aforementioned Uchimura, he rejected his conservative *samurai* morality and attempted to develop his own modern urban consciousness. After several shifts in his academic emphasis at the university, he graduated in 1901. Through his encounter with the prominent naturalist critic SHIMAMURA HŌGETSU, he became a writer of a literary column for the YOMIURI SHIMBUN, one of Japan's leading national daily newspapers, in 1903, serving in this capacity until 1910. During this time he developed a reputation as a forthright critic, fearlessly attacking authority and convention. Together with his critical works, he began his own career in creative writing with a short story entitled "Sekibaku" (1904, Loneliness), which, however, received little attention.

The first story truly proclaiming Hakuchō's emergence as a naturalist writer of note was "Jin'ai" (tr "Dust," 1970) in 1907. In this short story he skillfully captures the bleakness of the life of a proofreader in a newspaper office. This and the stories which followed, such as "Doko e" (Whither?) in 1908, "Bikō" (1910, Faint Light), and the largely autobiographical "Doro ningyō" (1911, The Clay Doll) were deeply pessimistic almost to the point of nihilism, apparently negating any earlier profession of his Christian faith. Indeed, Hakuchō's stories during the high point of naturalism in the late Meiji period represent an extreme view of human life as essentially meaningless. Some critics have interpreted Hakuchō's attitude as resulting from the disparity between the high ideals he espoused in his youth and the actual state of Meiji society, especially of the middle and lower-middle classes which he depicted.

Middle Years and Turn to Drama——Although the naturalist movement declined rapidly in the early Taishō period, ironically Hakuchō produced some of his best stories in the naturalist mode at this time. *Shisha seisha* (1916, The Dead and the Living) has been recognized as one of his masterpieces, treating the breakdown of the family system in the face of the selfishness and insensitivity of contemporary urban life. Toward the end of the Taishō period his interests shifted more to criticism and drama; from 1924 he produced a succession of plays on much the same nihilistic theme as his fiction. Indeed, the title of his best-known play, *Jinsei no kōfuku* (1924, The Joys of Life), is wholly ironic, portraying as it does deep dissension among two brothers and a sister. Hakuchō's activity continued unabated into the Shōwa period although he found time for extensive travel within Japan, on the continent of Asia, and even in Europe.

War and Postwar Years——He spent the worst part of the war, 1944–45, secluded at his country home in Karuizawa in Nagano Prefecture, but he reemerged in the literary world shortly after the end of the war, displaying remarkable energy for a 66–year-old man. His major postwar output, like that of the middle and late Taishō period, was in the area of criticism and drama. His many reflective and retrospective essays appeared at this time. Moreover, as the "grand old man" of Japanese naturalism, he was awarded a succession of honors. His death in the autumn of 1962 became a major event in the Japanese literary world because the woman minister who attended him on his deathbed, UEMURA TAMAKI, the daughter of the man who had baptized Hakuchō more than 60 years earlier, wrote an essay contending that Hakuchō had regained his faith in the face of death. Other writers confirmed Hakuchō's faith, further surprising the Japanese reading public, which had viewed him as a confirmed skeptic and pessimist. Since his death Hakuchō has been the subject of several important studies and biographies, and his work is beginning to be evaluated in the West as well.

■ Masamune Hakuchō, *Masamune Hakuchō zenshū*, 13 vols (Shinchōsha, 1975). Gotō Ryō, *Masamune Hakuchō: Bungaku to shōgai* (1966). Ōiwa Kō, *Masamune Hakuchō ron* (1971). Robert Rolf, *Masamune Hakuchō* (1979). Tanabe Akio, *Hyōden Masamune Hakuchō* (1977). Valdo H. VIGLIELMO

Masanobu → Kanō Masanobu

Masaoka Shiki (1867–1902)

Poet and critic; a major contributor to the development of modern Japanese literature. Through his successful advocacy of a new realism for HAIKU and TANKA, the traditional verse forms, he made them viable genres in the postfeudal culture of Meiji-period (1868–1912) Japan. Shiki, whose given name was Tsunenori, was born in the town of Matsuyama in what is now Ehime Prefecture, western Shikoku, on 14 October 1867 to a modest *samurai* family. The impoverishment of the samurai following the MEIJI RESTORATION of 1868 was compounded in Shiki's case by the early death of his father. He was an excellent student, receiving besides his public school education a sound grounding in classical Chinese, in part from his maternal grandfather, Ōhara Kanzan, a respected Confucian scholar of the Matsuyama domain, who was the embodiment of samurai integrity.

Born on the eve of the Meiji period, Shiki participated in the heady sense of a new order. As a young student, he was drawn to the FREEDOM AND PEOPLE'S RIGHTS MOVEMENT, attended political rallies, and joined his school's public speaking and debating clubs, speaking out against suppression of civil liberties and for freedom of thought. These radical ideas earned him warnings from school authorities.

In 1883, at age 16, Shiki went to Tōkyō for further schooling to prepare himself for a career in law or politics. However, during the seven years before his enrollment in the literature department of Tōkyō University in 1890, his exposure to such epochal works as *Shōsetsu shinzui* (1885–86, The Essence of the Novel) by TSUBOUCHI SHŌYŌ and *Ukigumo* (1887–89; tr *The Drifting Clouds*, 1967) by FUTABATEI SHIMEI and to many translations of Western writings changed his goals. Forfeiting a scholarship, he withdrew from the university after 2 years to devote the 10 remaining years of his life to literature.

Shiki spent much effort on the reform of haiku verse. The contemporary haiku, which Shiki attacked vigorously, beginning in 1892 with the first series of his many polemic articles in the newspaper *Nihon*, were sterile and imitative, employing limited diction and subject matter. The master poet BASHŌ, who by this time was honored by monuments and in quasi-religious shrines, was the supreme model. Haiku as a genre was supposedly above reproach. Moral didacticism and adherence to traditional standards were the principal criteria of criticism. Such fossilized attitudes, wrote Shiki, were inappropriate for the new political, social, and technical order that the introduction to Western civilization had established. In their place he advocated freedom of diction and subject matter; the scholarly study of haiku history; the treatment of haiku as a serious literary genre subject to general literary standards; and the importance of realism or immediacy, which he termed *shasei* ("sketch from life"). The journalistic, polemical nature of his writings explains much that is extreme in his position, such as his declaration that the bulk of Bashō's haiku are worthless, with the remainder honored for their sublime tone. From 1893 to 1897 his views were gradually expanded through succeeding series of newspaper articles on Bashō, on the elements of haiku, and on modern haiku, and by his influential writings on BUSON. He also compiled a classified collection of haiku in 12 volumes. Included among his protégés were such well-known figures as KAWAHIGASHI HEKIGOTŌ, Yanagihara Kyokudō (1867–1957), and above all TAKAHAMA KYOSHI, the most influential haiku figure of his day. The haiku magazine *Hototogisu*, founded under Shiki's auspices, was a leading publication well into the Shōwa period (1926–).

By 1898, when the preeminence of Shiki's Nihon school of haiku was established, he turned to discussion of the *tanka* in a series of newspaper articles. The enervating effects of tradition were even more marked for this courtly form than for the haiku, particularly the insistence on a flowing elegance of style. The KOKINSHŪ (ca 905), the first imperial anthology, with its many beautiful poems, set the genteel standard. Attacking the ingrown, conventional schools, Shiki dismissed the *Kokinshū* as worthless, and he granted the second most esteemed anthology, the SHIN KOKINSHŪ, only a few good poems. He urged a return to the standards of the MAN'YŌSHŪ, the 8th-century anthology, which he admired for its manly vigor, artlessness of tone, and directness of mode—views espoused by small groups of poets since the time of KAMO NO MABUCHI, the great classics scholar. Again, Shiki attracted a devoted group, known as the Negishi Tanka Society, notably ITŌ SACHIO, whose transmission of Shiki's thought to SAITŌ MOKICHI, the foremost modern *tanka* poet, established Shiki as the founder of the modern *tanka* tradition. The publication ARARAGI, associated with Itō's group of the same name, remains the most prestigious *tanka* publication to the present day.

In 1889, when Shiki spat blood for the second time, he adopted the pen name Shiki, the Chinese pronunciation of the characters used to write the word *hototogisu*, the cuckoo, which in legend sang until it coughed blood. His illness was gravely aggravated by his trip to China as a war correspondent in 1895, just as the Sino-Japanese war ended, and he soon realized he was terminally ill with tuberculosis. He continued to write vigorously. By 1898 he was bedridden. In three journals dated 1901–02 (*Bokujū itteki, Byōshō rokushaku,* and *Gyōga manroku*), the agonizing progress of his physical deterioration is given in realistic, clinical detail. Interspersed among the prose entries are series of haiku and *tanka,* including some of his most appreciated verse. He died on 19 September 1902.

However innovative Shiki's theory seemed to his contemporaries, he himself generally kept to the formal elements of both the haiku and *tanka* forms, unlike his more revolutionary followers. An important element of his concept of the "sketch from life" as the basis of poetry is the need for immediacy so lacking in the mannered schools of his time. As might be expected, much of his verse seems determinedly mundane and banal in its realism, as he jettisons the old imitative practices in favor of a direct, rigorous confrontation with the poet's world. As he finds his own voice, the best of his mature work is marked by an austerity with a unique freshness, which has established him as one of the four masters of haiku along with Bashō, Buson, and ISSA (1763–1827). The following much-translated haiku illustrates his gift: "I looked back to see/ but the man I passed was lost/ in mist already." While his position as a *tanka* poet is not so clearly established, the same bareness of statement, set in the context of deathbed journals, lends his *tanka* a force and poignance which enhance the sense of his experience.

🔖 ——Masaoka Shiki, *Masaoka Shiki zenshū,* 22 vols (Kaizōsha, 1929–31). Robert H. Brower, "Masaoka Shiki and Tanka Reform," in Donald H. Shively, ed, *Tradition and Modernization in Japanese Culture* (1971). Kubota Masafumi, *Masaoka Shiki* (1967). Matsui Toshihiko, *Masaoka Shiki* (1973). Earl Miner, *Japanese Poetic Diaries* (1969). Makoto Ueda, *Modern Japanese Haiku: An Anthology* (1976).   *Kenneth* YASUDA

masculine language

A variety of Japanese which is typically used by males as a reflection of their masculinity. Limited though such treatments are, there have been more references to FEMININE LANGUAGE than the masculine variety in linguistic studies of the JAPANESE LANGUAGE. The implication is that masculine Japanese is included as part of the language proper and that feminine Japanese is a deviant variety which departs from the norm. It is not at all unusual for studies of the Japanese language to include a section on feminine language without one on the masculine counterpart. Statements about linguistic usage peculiar to females obviously imply a contrast between male and female, but it is the latter that is regarded as a special, noteworthy variety. Significantly, the terms *joseigo* and *onnakotoba,* referring to female language, occur comparatively frequently, but parallel terms referring to male language are rarely used.

At an early age, Japanese children become aware of sex differentiation overtly reflected in language. For example, while there are a number of neutral terms and patterns which can be used by all children in referring to themselves, only a boy is expected to refer to himself as *boku* (I), and his membership in the *boku* fraternity is reinforced by the use of this male term of self-reference—which is its only use among adults—as a term of address (an equivalent of "you") by adults talking to young boys. Thus, *Boku iku* (I-male will go) but (in speaking to a male child only) *Boku iku?* (Will you [literally, I-male] go?)

There is evidence that Japanese mothers tend to treat their male offspring with greater linguistic deference than they show their daughters: from an early age, sons are addressed more politely and with more solicitude than their sisters. As they interact with an increasingly wider network of acquaintances at play and at school, the concept of sexually differentiated language is reinforced by their peers, their teachers, and their textbooks. The male child is socialized to take his position in a society where language overtly reflects the different societal roles and behavior expected of males.

Lake Mashū

Much of the language used by men—and by women—is void of sexual differentiation: it is sexually neutral. But depending on the role a male is filling at the moment, he alters his linguistic style appropriately and communicates his interpretation of the situation through the particular style that he uses. In a manner parallel to feminine language, masculine language includes both features that occur almost exclusively in the language of males, and features that are qualitatively or quantitatively more typical of males in a given context. Lower pitch, distinctive voice quality and articulation, and particular sentence-final intonations are assumed, but other typically masculine features include (1) *Special terms of self-reference and address.* Examples: *boku* (I), *ore* (I), *kimi* (you), *omae* (you), *kisama* (you). Note that while women tend to use only contracted equivalents of more polite terms as alternates (for example, *atashi* for *watakushi*), Japanese men have a wide range of special words in addition to contractions, which they also use. Each one of these alternates has particular connotations of familiarity, rank, etc. (2) *Sentence particles.* Examples: Particles *ze* and *zo,* occurring at the end of statements are signals of masculinity and assertiveness, and *na,* in parallel use, is a masculine particle implying agreement and confirmation. (3) *Interjections.* Examples: *oi* (hey!), *ā* (yes) (4) *Plain, nondeferential forms of the verb and copula*—notably the verbal imperative and tentative, and *da, datta,* and *darō*—in sentence-final position, or before nonfeminine, sentence-final particles. Examples: *Koi* (Come here!); *Ikō* (Let's go); *Sō da yo* (That's right).

Often the identification of language as masculine is based on the occurrence of certain features in a particular context with marked frequency. For example, plain, nondeferential verb, adjective, and copula forms are, in general, more commonly used by men, and their frequent occurrence, particularly at the ends of sentences or before sentence-final particles, is typical of masculine speech. Other generalized masculine features are the frequent use of contracted speech and the rare use of the deferential *o-/go-* prefix.

In many contexts, polite language is a signal of feminine language, but the same language style is interpreted as sexually neutral in a context where all Japanese would regularly use polite language.

Masculine language is a variety that communicates assertiveness, strength, toughness, and vigor. In its most marked form, it occurs among males in situations where these qualities are appropriate and important. In many all-male communication situations, however, sexually neutral language would be considered more fitting. In other words, the style is adjusted to the subject matter and mood. When communication involves both sexes, the language of males varies even more markedly, depending on the context: it may be obviously masculine style (when the user is signalling authority, toughness, and strength); or sexually neutral style (signaling the linguistic neutrality typical of conferences, lectures, round-table discussions, class instruction, general conversation with nonintimates and strangers, editorials, and business letters); or even what is usually identified as feminine style (when the male wishes to convey empathy, gentleness, kindliness, and consideration toward the addressee).

On the other hand, a Japanese woman in a situation marked by characteristics usually associated with masculinity may reflect her role or attitude of the moment by using linguistic features usually identified as masculine. The use of *boku* (I) among some schoolgirls is an example of this phenomenon, which is becoming increasingly common as women gradually become more assertive and participate

Masks——Gigaku mask

Representation of Karura (Skt: Garuda), a Hindu god incorporated into Buddhism as one of the class of deities known as *tembu*. Carved from camphor wood, primed with a coating of kaolin, and painted with vermilion, blue, and green pigments. Height 30.3 cm. 7th century. Originally at Hōryūji, Nara Prefecture. Tōkyō National Museum.

Masks——Bugaku mask

An example of a 12th-century *ryōō* mask with typically grotesque features. Carved from cypress wood and brightly painted, this mask was used for one of the most popular *bugaku* dances. The eyes and chin are movable, as is the characteristic dragon perched on top. Height 40.7 cm. Itsukushima Shrine, Hiroshima Prefecture.

in situations previously recognized as all-male domains.

Thus, sexually differentiated language in Japanese refers to varieties containing features which are associated specifically with members of one or the other sex as they fill traditional, sex-oriented roles or positions in Japanese society. But not all male language is marked as masculine; it may be sexually neutral or, in some situations, even marked by features usually identified as feminine. Parallel statements can be made about feminine language as distinguished from the language of females.

Eleanor H. JORDEN

Mashiko

Town in southeastern Tochigi Prefecture, central Honshū. It is known primarily for its local pottery, Mashiko ware, produced here since 1853 and made famous by HAMADA SHŌJI. The Mashiko Sankōkan has a permanent display of Hamada's collection of folk arts. More than 100 kilns are located here. The town is also known for its tobacco leaves. Food, machinery, and watch factories have been established recently. Of note are the temples Saimyōji and Entsūji and the Tsuma Shrine. Pop: 22,105.

Mashiko ware

(mashiko-yaki). Folk-style pottery made in the town of Mashiko, Tochigi Prefecture. Mashiko became famous as the home of potter HAMADA SHŌJI (1894–1978). Although its reputation as a ceramic center is recent, some very ancient shards have been found there. In the latter part of the Edo period (1600–1868), Mashiko produced teapots, *suribachi* (mortars), cooking pots, and other kitchenware for the Kantō area. The industry was protected by the local *daimyō*. In 1853 local potters began producing a Shimotsuke ware, similar to the SŌMA WARE of what is now Fukushima Prefecture. However, like other less established folk-art centers during the early part of the 20th century, Mashiko fell into a decline. It was only after Hamada Shōji settled there in 1924 that Mashiko recovered financially. It is now a prosperous town and a tourist attraction, and the home of a number of serious potters. Hamada's son carries on his father's tradition, and several of Hamada's former students, including Shimaoka Tatsuzō, still live and work there. As a result of Hamada's fame, many foreign potters have also been attracted to Mashiko for study. Both the handmade and mass-produced wares of Mashiko are utilitarian tablewares.

Ellen F. CARY

Mashū, Lake

(Mashūko). Caldera lake in eastern Hokkaidō. Located on the eastern fringe of Akan National Park, this lake is said to be the most transparent in the world. Created about 7,000 years ago when the summit of a volcano caved in and the caldera thus formed was filled with water. Surrounded by cliffs averaging 300 m (984 ft) in height. Kamuishu Island (height 35 m, 115 ft), a lava dome, lies in the center of the lake. Rainbow trout have been released into the lake. Fog occurs frequently in summer. Area: 19.6 sq km (7.6 sq mi); circumference: 20 km (12 mi); depth: 212 m (695 ft); transparency in 1979: 35.8 m (117.4 ft), altitude: 351 m (1,151 ft).

masks

Masks made of clay, dry lacquer, or wood have long been an integral part of Japanese dance, ritual, and religious ceremony. Ranging from hauntingly beautiful portrayals of people to grotesque animal representations, Japanese masks reflect traditions from the Asian continent as well as indigenous ones. Masks from as early as the 7th century are preserved in temples, shrines, and museums, and new ones are still being modeled on them for performances today. Although clay masks dating from the latter part of the Jōmon period (ca 10,000 BC–ca 300 BC) have been unearthed, the majority of Japanese masks are carved from wood and sometimes painted with a layer of lacquer. They are primed with kaolin or powdered chalk and finally coated with polychromed pigments. A few are made of dry lacquer, cloth, or paper.

Gigaku Masks——The oldest types of wooden masks still preserved are those used in GIGAKU. Introduced to Japan in 612, *gigaku* consisted of a procession followed by skits performed on temple grounds. Legend traces the origin of *gigaku* to the kingdom of Wu in South China, but the physiognomy of the masks suggests a source closer to Persia. *Gigaku* flourished during the Nara period (710–794), then declined in popularity during the Kamakura period (1185–1333), and eventually died out. The masks and bits of costume that have been preserved serve as valuable clues to the nature of *gigaku*.

The fleshy, large-nosed features of *gigaku* masks have their origins on the Asian continent. Massive and sculptural, they are oversized, measuring 20 to 30 centimeters (7.9 to 11.8 in) wide, 30 to 40

Masks——Gyōdō mask

Representation of the Buddhist guardian deity Katen (Skt: Agni), originally a Hindu fire god. This type of mask was used in outdoor temple processions. Cypress wood, primed and painted. Height 30.2 cm. Late 10th century; repaired and repainted in 1086 and 1334 according to an inscription on the mask's interior. Kyōto National Museum.

Masks——Nō mask

Example of a *koomote* mask, one of several types representing young women. Central to the mask's dramatic quality is a mutable expression that centers in its eyes. An inscription on the mask's interior identifies it as a work by Hōrai based on an original by Tatsuemon. Wood, painted. Height 21.2 cm. Early 16th century. Tōkyō National Museum.

centimeters (11.8 to 15.7 in) tall, and 18 to 35 centimeters (7.1 to 13.8 in) deep, and are constructed so as to cover the top of the head as well as the face. A wooden hat or topknot carved as a part of the mask at times increases the height, while the outer rim of the mask extends back to include ears, a feature unusual on other Japanese masks. Empathy can be seen in the expressions of many of these freely executed masks. For instance, the *suikojū*, masks of drunken barbarian retainers, each express differently the joy or sorrow of inebriation in youth or old age.

A *gigaku* program required 14 different types of masks, which made up one set. Often a single carver would be responsible for a whole set. Early masks such as the 7th century ones from the temple HŌRYŪJI (now in the Tōkyō National Museum) have naive, straightforward expressions. Masks made in 752 for the temple TŌDAIJI and now housed in the SHŌSŌIN show great sophistication of technique. Some by Shōri no Uonari are made of dry lacquer, but most are carved from paulownia wood *(kiri)*, painted with lacquer, and then polychromed on a base of kaolin; many have an oil finish. They have shaded areas, black outlines around the features, and hair pasted on and held down with bronze disks.

Bugaku Masks—— At the time of the introduction of *gigaku* into Japan, a variety of other foreign dances were arriving from Korea, China, and Southeast Asia. These were incorporated into the court ceremonies and in the 9th century consolidated and systematized into court dance *(bugaku)* and the accompanying court music (GAGAKU).

Although the *bugaku* masks, like their dances, have remote continental prototypes, the refinement of the Heian-period (794–1185) court shows in their stylization. Each face captures an attitude or emotion. The smiling *chikyū* and the clown-faced *shintoriso* radiate joy, while stern masculinity marks the masks used for military dances. Gimmicks, such as dangling chins attached in such a way that their movement rotates the eyeballs, intensify the grotesque features of the bestial masks like *ryōō*, and *nasori*. Although *bugaku* masks vary greatly in size, measuring 19 to 33 centimeters (7.5 to 13 in) tall, 16 to 24 centimeters (6.3 to 9.4 in) wide, and 10 to 18 centimeters (3.9 to 7.1 in) deep, they tend to be smaller than *gigaku* masks. They are typically made of cypress *(hinoki)* and, rather than covering the head entirely, are placed in front of the face. Many do not have ears.

Some *bugaku* masks show similarities to those of *gigaku*. In size and fleshiness, the *ninomai* masks reflect their *gigaku* predecessors.

Both the *gigaku karura* and the *bugaku korobase* masks represent birds. The *kotokuraku* masks, which portray drunken barbarians, are similar in character to those used in the *gigaku* pieces referred to as *suiko*. The faces of these *kotokuraku* masks, though clearly not Japanese, have been refined and smoothed, to a supple fullness expressing ebullient joy. A special feature of the *kotokuraku* masks, illustrating the abstract formalization of *bugaku* masks, is the dangling nose, which swings back and forth as the dancers mimic increasing drunkenness.

The oldest *bugaku* mask, the only dry lacquer example extant, is a *ryōō*, probably dating from the 8th century. Some early masks in Hōryūji date from the beginning of the 11th century. The oldest masks to bear inscription dates are a set of 16 from Tōdaiji made in 1042. They have no lacquer ground, are gentle in expression, with wide, almond-shaped eye openings and incised medallions in the center of their foreheads.

Very few of the *bugaku* masks bear the names of their carvers, and most of these date from the 12th century. Many of these carvers—Jōkei, Inshō, Inken—were also sculptors of Buddhist statues. Indeed, the techniques and styles used in *bugaku* mask carving parallel those of Buddhist sculpture.

The social and political instability concurrent with the rise to power of the KAMAKURA SHOGUNATE (1192–1333) forced many dancers to flee the capital to the provinces, taking their masks with them. Although early Kamakura masks were still made according to orthodox methods, the dispersion led to a gradual decline in quality. In the 17th century, *bugaku* was reinstated by the shogunate as an official function, the making of masks was revived, and old masterpieces were copied with exacting skill.

Gyōdō Masks—— Gyōdō masks represent Buddhist figures. Worn in outdoor temple processions, which enact such events as the descent of 25 bodhisattvas coming to escort a soul to heaven *(raigō)*, these masks of superhuman size and engulfing form make the parading brocaded figure appear like a statue come to life. The masks of bodhisattva aim at meditative stillness. Yet even the more active figures like Jigokuten, the god of hell, or the Shitennō (Skt: Deva Raja; the Four Heavenly Kings) lack the dynamism and expressive depth of *gigaku* or *bugaku* masks. Serving primarily as a visual reminder of the figure it represents, the *gyōdō* mask's role is symbolic rather than dramatic.

Masks for Festivals—— FESTIVALS *(matsuri)* often require masks for religious rituals. Exorcism and agricultural rites often use ONI,

Masks ── Nō mask

Mask used exclusively for the play *Okina*, oldest in the Nō repertoire and performed only on ceremonial occasions. Called *okina*, this type of mask represents a venerable old man. There are two categories of *okina* mask, white and dark; shown is a white *okina*. Wood, painted. Height 18.1 cm. 14th century. Private collection.

Masks ── Kyōgen mask

Example of the *kobuaku* type of *kyōgen* mask. Its distorted features and silly expression typify the comic masks used in *kyōgen*. An inscription on its interior identifies it as the work of the mask carver Hōrai. Wood, painted. Height 18.9 cm. Early 16th century. Tōkyō National Museum.

tsuina, or TENGU masks, and sometimes the *bugaku* masks of *ryōō* or *nasori*. The *gigaku* lion dance, which requires at least two people, one for the body, and one to manipulate the mask, can be found throughout the Japanese islands. *Sato kagura*, dance plays about Shintō myth (see KAGURA), also use masks. Rice-planting rites such as *taue* sometimes use masks of women (*jōrō*) or old men (*jōmen*). Early examples of these provide invaluable clues to the indigenous form of Japanese masks that helped to inspire the makers of NŌ masks.

Nō and Kyōgen Masks ── The uniquely Japanese masks used in Nō and KYŌGEN plays emerged in the 14th and 15th centuries. Just as the Nō grew out of folk performance and blossomed into a highly sophisticated dramatic art based on poetic understatement and implication, so the masks used in the Nō drew on existing folk types and developed them into works of subtle and mutable expression.

The names of Nō masks refer to individual faces, not to roles or pieces, as in *bugaku* or *gigaku*. About 80 different masks comprise the necessary stock of a theater, but well over 200 are commonly used. Shallow in construction, most Nō masks are smaller than the average adult Japanese face. With the broad, flat features, low nose bridges, and wide cheekbones typical of the Japanese physiognomy, the masks seem like real people, but are also representative of certain types of human beings. Central to their dramatic quality is a mutable expression that centers in the eyes, so carved that they seem to move, to sadden, to brighten with the play of shadows caused by slight shifts of the head. The shape of the mouth and the flowing contours of the mask give it a sense of living immediacy.

In contrast to the sublime Nō masks, those for the *kyōgen* comedies, performed between Nō plays, have a joyous extroversion marked by distorted features. The types of *kyōgen* masks are limited because they are used only when the dramatic action calls for masks, as when a man disguises himself to frighten his master, or when the character is an animal, demon, or god. *Kyōgen* masks were often made by the same men who carved Nō masks.

Ten great mask carvers of the 14th and 15th centuries are responsible for the major types of Nō masks. Shakuzuru specialized in devils and demons, Koushi and Fukurai worked on old men's masks, Tatsuemon became famous for his young women's and men's masks, Yasha for his ghosts and beasts. These early masks are carved freely with simple, open expressiveness. Along with the systemization of all aspects of Nō during the 17th century, the masks were standardized in form and use. The best of the old masks were

chosen as models, and carvers like Zekan, Yūkan, and Kawachi made their livings producing copies. They no longer specialized in one style of mask. Because of changing ideals of beauty as well as regimentation of form, Edo-period (1600–1868) masks, particularly the young women's masks, express an increasingly introspective, elegant sadness.

Today the carver continues to use the techniques developed 500 years ago. He carves from cypress and paints with chalk powder, india ink, and earth pigments. As he works he continually checks the expression, holding the mask at arm's length and rotating it. He knows that though he works within the restrictions of predetermined size and form, the resulting mask must be a fresh creation, for it is only then that it will come alive as the actor moves on stage. Modern fluorescent lighting has replaced the traditional daylight or candlelight and has brought a new challenge to both carver and actor. The one must seek to retain the vitality and evocative power of the old masks, the other to transcend modernization and to participate in the timeless spirit of the mask.

📖 ── Kameda Tsutomu, Nagai Shin'ichi, and Tanabe Saburōsuke, ed, *Men to shōzō*, vol 23 of *Genshoku Nihon no bijutsu* (Shōgakukan, 1971). Kaneko Ryōun, *Nō kyōgen men* (1975). Donald Keene, *Nō: The Classical Theater of Japan* (1966). Nishikawa Kyōtarō, *Bugakumen* (1971), tr Monica Bethe as *Bugaku Masks* (1978). Nogami Toyoichirō, *Nōmen ronkō* (1944). Noma Seiroku, *Nihon no kamenshi* (1943). Noma Seiroku, Kobayashi Takeshi, Mori Hisashi, and Hayashi Kenzō, *Shōsoin no gigakumen* (1942). Ōkōchi Sadao, *Tokugawa Collection of Nō Robes and Masks*, tr L. A. Cort and M. Bethe (1977). *Monica* BETHE

Mason, Luther Whiting (1818–1896)

American music educator who introduced Western music to Japanese schools as an adviser to the Ministry of Education from 1880 to 1882. Born in Turner, Maine, poor and largely self-educated, Mason dreamed of being a missionary but instead became a teacher. After working as supervisor of music for the public schools in Louisville, Kentucky (1853), he went to Cincinnati, where he invented his immediately successful and immensely popular teaching method employing charts, songbooks, and teachers' guides. Summoned to the Boston school system in 1865, he remained there until he accepted an invitation from the Japanese government to visit Japan, extended through his former pupil IZAWA SHŪJI, in 1879.

Mason advanced the popularity and technical understanding of Western music, particularly of simple melodies for voice, piano, and parlor organ, through the music education system that he and Izawa developed for Japan's new normal and elementary schools. From sight-reading charts and songbooks Japanese children learned the seven-note scale, the five-line staff, Western notation, and part singing. Although many of the songs were harmonically Western (Mason favored pentatonic Celtic tunes and German melodies), the words were Japanese; and in an effort to fuse the two musical traditions, new texts were set to native music as well.

Mason also laid the foundation for a national music school, later called the Tōkyō Ongaku Gakkō (now part of Tōkyō University of Fine Arts and Music); began systematic instruction in piano, strings, and woodwinds; organized some of the earliest concerts of Western music; and encouraged local manufacture of musical instruments.

After returning to the United States, Mason continued to publish texts, including the four-volume *National Music Course* (1887–97). The Order of the Sacred Treasure, Fourth Class, was bestowed upon him by the Japanese government shortly after his death in Buckfield, Maine.　　　　　　　　　　　　　　　　　　　　　　　*Dallas* FINN

mass communications

Japan has been a world leader in the development of mass communications, typically defined as the rapid and inexpensive transmission of large quantities of news, opinion, educational and cultural information, and entertainment to all groups of the population by large-scale, complex organizations using advanced modern technology.

Historical Development——The Edo period (1600–1868) left Japan with a superb social base for modern mass communications in its geographically compact, culturally homogeneous, politically centralized, education-oriented and increasingly urbanized population. It was a relatively simple task, assiduously pursued from the Meiji period (1868–1912) onward, to rapidly import, adapt and often improve on technological infrastructures and hardware originally developed at a slower pace in the West. Nationwide postal and telegraph networks, a modern national educational system, and the first telephones and public electrification were all introduced during the 1870s, and by 1905 Japan enjoyed rail service the length of its main island, 95 percent primary school attendance, and one of the highest literacy rates in the world.

Modern Japan's initial phase of politically oriented limited-circulation newspapers, roughly replicating the traits of 18th- and early-19th-century opinion journalism in the West, was telescoped into the first two decades of the Meiji period. By the 1890s, in phase with Hearst's empire in the United States and the great London dailies, Japan was set to pioneer the development of mass-market, general-interest, commercial journalism, with nationalistic coverage of the Sino-Japanese and Russo-Japanese wars (1894–95 and 1904–05) providing the same surges in circulation and sensationalistic reporting as did the Spanish-American and Boer wars.

The spread of democratic institutions, university education, and urban lifestyle in the 20th century created enormous markets for newspapers, magazines, and books, and for the electronic media introduced directly upon development in the West: radio broadcasting from 1925, television in 1953, FM radio in 1959 and regular color television service from 1960. As of 1978 Japan ranked first in per capita circulation of newspapers (558:1,000) and second among the major nations in diffusion of television sets (251:1,000), and second in number of computers (48,832). The newspaper industry has generally been ahead of the West in introducing phototypesetting and facsimile processes, and Japan's electronic technology has either bested or kept close to America's in transistors, cable television (CATV), data transmission, multiplex broadcasting and video cassette recorders.

Structures and Functions——In organization, scale, and allocation of functions, however, the Japanese mass media have developed uniquely out of the indigenous economic and social structure, and philosophical bent. Both newspapers and book publishing display the same intensive oligopolistic competition among gigantic, tightly knit, enterprise groups characteristic of modern Japanese business as a whole, while television broadcasting illustrates the Japanese preference for government initiative in nurturing a new industry and setting general standards before throwing it open to private enterprise, eventually maximizing social benefits through a dual public and commercial system, as with the railways.

Competitive pressures in a basically unitary national market have left no room in Japan for the individualistic regional-city newspaper of the United States, or the highbrow daily of continental Europe. Despite overall intellectual sophistication, vast technological and staff resources, morning circulations of four to eight million for the top three papers, and a home delivery system insuring a stable core of loyal subscribers, Japan's newspapers have herded themselves into a striking uniformity of format, content, editorial viewpoint and reportorial style. The limited local competition consisting of single prefectural and four regional "bloc" papers takes its cue from the five national dailies (the YOMIURI SHIMBUN, ASAHI SHIMBUN, MAINICHI SHIMBUN, SANKEI SHIMBUN, and NIHON KEIZAI SHIMBUN) in a top-heavy configuration dictated by geographical intimacy, the predominance of Tōkyō and Ōsaka, and the drastic wartime consolidation in 1942 which eliminated a more varied structure.

Radio broadcasting was begun in 1925 by the private Tōkyō Broadcasting Station, with strong government backing. In 1926, the Japan Broadcasting Corporation (NHK) was granted a broadcasting monopoly as a corporate juridical body under firm control of the Ministry of Communications. In 1950 the new BROADCASTING LAW made provision for a commercial sector, and reorganized NHK as a strictly public service organization answering to an independent, government-appointed board and supported by receiver fees collected on the honor system. Since television broadcasting started in 1953, competition between the public and private sectors of Japan's dual system has delivered more quality than the commercially dominated American model, and far more variety than state-run television in France. NHK is the most popular news source, and provides lavish cultural and informational programming on both its general and educational channels. The five commercial television chains have been strengthened by tie-ups with the five national newspapers, and their initial concentration on entertainment has gradually broadened in emulation of NHK. The five commercial chains are: Nippon Television Network Corporation (NTV), Tōkyō Broadcasting System, Inc (TBS), Television Tōkyō Channel 12, Ltd, Fuji Telecasting Co, Ltd, and Asahi National Broadcasting Co, Ltd.

The functions of wire services, weekly magazines, and monthly journals in Japan have all been affected by the character of the newspapers. With the national dailies relying mainly on their own domestic and foreign newsgathering staffs, Japan's two news agencies, KYŌDŌ NEWS SERVICE and JIJI PRESS, play a supplementary role except for the local press. Generous attention to news analysis and cultural developments in the staid, serious-minded dailies has preempted the field for general newsmagazines on the order of *Time* or *Newsweek*, leaving to Japan's racy, lowbrow weeklies the scandal, political rumor, and pungent individualistic prose typical of an Anglo-American tabloid. Editorial blandness in the dailies and lack of a serious weekly press has also helped to create a mass circulation market for the bulging, sophisticated opinion monthlies which provide a running intellectual history of Japan in this century.

Journalists and Their Audience——Drawn from the top universities through stiff competitive exams, the journalists in Japan's major media firms enjoy high professional status and reflect the *samurai* origin of Meiji journalism in their self-appointed role as molders of public opinion. As such, they are joined by a broad public forum *(rondan)* of intellectual critics *(hyōronka)* who inject a lively stream of cultural and ideological debate into the mass media through daily columns, television symposia, and the opinion monthlies. Japan's highly literate public, deferential toward intellectual authority and eager for information and guidance in the pursuit of personal and corporate uplift, sustains an extensive high-grade sector of "mass quality" newspapers and television programs, as well as a teeming world of specialized magazines, comics, and books for every conceivable taste and age level.

The therefore surprising homogeneity, especially in news coverage, derives not only from market rivalries but also from the unique organization of newsgathering in Japan. The typical reporter writes not so much independent stories as raw material for reprocessing at the departmental desk, and the correspondents themselves are organized into exclusive PRESS CLUBS *(kisha kurabu)* attached to all major government institutions and public figures, which monopolize access to sources and largely dictate the flow and play of the news. Closed for the most part to foreign and Japanese regional correspondents, these clubs were originally organized by the government in the 1930s as a control mechanism, but they have survived thanks to the cozy trade-offs they permit between sources and reporters, and the comfortably noncompetitive and collaborative ties that they foster among their members.

News, Opinion, and Politics—— The combination of didactic journalism and reader deference on top of massive physical scale and product conformity has given the Japanese press enormous influence as opinion leader, government critic, and go-between in the national decision- and consensus-making process. Castigated both as mouthpiece for the government and as a permanently irresponsible opposition, its ambivalent Fourth Estate role as both watchdog and participant in power resembles that of the press in other industrial democracies. In Japan's closely knit mass society, however, the pervasiveness of its influence and the ambivalence of its role are more pronounced. The ongoing controversy in the West over press responsibility, bias, and adversary journalism has been even sharper in Japan, where group values and a more instrumental approach to the news have spawned a less open or independent reporting tradition than in the West. Criticism has focused on the tendency of the major dailies to heavily insinuate opinion through the choice and presentation of news articles, headlines, and captions rather than directly in their editorial pages, which refrain from endorsing political parties and uphold the code of "impartiality and nonpartisanship" nominally enjoined on reporting as a whole. In television, the deliberate self-effacement of lackluster anchormen has helped to maintain the political impartiality decreed by the Broadcasting Law.

The adversary and collusive relationships between government and press in Japan are most apparent in the historical and functional dimensions, respectively. Regulation and periodic suppression stretching from the PRESS ORDINANCE OF 1875 to militarist, wartime, and US Occupation censorship left a completely liberated press from 1952 which was in reflex opposition to a much weaker, democratic government, and for many years rather anti-American in tone. While censoriously monitoring the postwar performance of the Japanese government and of the United States, the top three dailies in particular have indulged the opposition parties and brooked no criticism of China (or until recently, the Soviet Union), on the unspoken premise that news manipulation to effect domestic and foreign policy changes is justified by the impotence of the formal political opposition, and the intractability of the conservative establishment.

After the Security Treaty demonstrations in 1960 the press censured itself for having fanned the flames of public violence, and international journalism in 1972 was shocked by evidence that certain Japanese firms had accepted a Chinese ban on unfavorable comment in order to maintain correspondents in Beijing (Peking). Although Japanese coverage of foreign countries is far more extensive and detailed than that which the Western press devotes to Japan, domestic and foreign news stories and analyses which do not conform to a Japanese paper's policy line are rigidly excluded.

Japanese journalism today enjoys far greater freedom from statutory restraint in the areas of libel, slander, parliamentary privilege, and official secrets than prevails, say, in Great Britain. This freedom is occasionally abused, most typically in exploiting the lone citizen who happens to be an entertainment celebrity or criminal suspect. The press, however, has often failed to attack government and business promptly and head-on over major evils such as graft or pollution, and it took foreign coverage in 1974 to initiate the Japanese press exposure and eventual resignation of then Prime Minister Tanaka on corruption charges (see LOCKHEED SCANDAL). The collaborative ties between the press and its sources in the press clubs, among club members, and between media management and big business, have all joined with general group psychology and restraints to produce a more comfortable relation between journalism and established power than would be deduced from the formal adversary stance.

Education, Culture, and Society—— The schoolmasterly instincts of the Japanese mass media are more benign on the social plane, where a strong sense of social responsibility and public service builds on the old Meiji tradition of modernization and enlightenment. Japanese newspapers are greatly superior to most American dailies in intellectual content, physical appearance, and literary style. Articles start and finish on the same page, and advertising is confined to detachable inserts and the bottom quarter or so of each page. Newspaper companies have sponsored and provided vast funds for art exhibits, symphony orchestras, academic symposia, and research projects, as well as more lucrative public-relations investments such as amusement parks and baseball teams. In television, the Broadcasting Law requires all stations to carry balanced cultural and educational as well as news and entertainment programming, and NHK is specifically enjoined to promote the elevation of cultural standards, preservation of cultural heritage, and creation of new cultural tradition. In 1978 culture and education, liberally defined, accounted for over 40 percent of programming on NHK's general network, and for over 37 percent on commercial television.

Mass communications have also contributed to political and social stability in postwar Japan. Television has virtually eliminated the urban-rural cultural gap, a divisive factor in the prewar period. The mass media and educational system together have greatly reduced the potential for class cleavage by spreading a uniform middlebrow, middle-class culture throughout the land, avoiding both the sharper intellectual stratifications of Europe and America, and the Westernized–traditionalist cultural split common to the developing countries. Finally, the flow of both public and inside information through the mass media and the journalists' grapevine provides an indispensable link between vertically isolated agents in Japan's national consensus-making process.

Standards of ethics, decency, and taste are monitored by the Newspaper Content Evaluation Center, the JAPAN ADVERTISING REVIEW ORGANIZATION, several broadcasting program consultative committees for television, the MOTION PICTURE CODE COMMITTEE, and the National Mass Communications Ethics Council, in a continuing effort to reduce the depiction of sex and violence, the vulgarization of television programming, and the frequency of libelous stories and violations of personal privacy. Japanese controls on hard-core pornography are draconian, but the sexually brutalizing cartoons in the weekly magazines and "juvenile" comics, and the late evening television teasers, offer more direct access to generally prurient material than do the mass media in the West.

Recent social concerns have included information glut and data "pollution," technological threats to privacy and individual freedom, and the gradual loss of psychological space in a postindustrial society dominated by computers, telecommunications, and hyperproductive mass media. The Japanese, who already inhabit one, have done most to develop the concept of the "information society" (jōhōka shakai), both as a popular notion and as a new academic discipline. See also NEWSPAPERS; BROADCASTING.

📖——The Japanese Press (Nihon Shimbun Kyōkai; annual). Kōza gendai jānarizumu, 6 vols (Jiji Tsūshinsha, 1973). Kōza gendai no shakai to komyunikēshon, 5 vols (Tōkyō University Press, 1974). Masami Itō, Broadcasting in Japan (1978). Shimbun no shuzai, 2 vols (Nihon Shimbun Kyōkai, 1968). Susumu Ejiri, Characteristics of the Japanese Press (1972). *Ivan P. HALL*

masu → salmons

Masuchi Yōjirō (1896–1945)

Scholar of management economics. Born in Kyōto and graduated from Tōkyō Higher Commercial School (now Hitotsubashi University). After working at the Sumitomo Company for a time, Masuchi became a professor at his alma mater in 1921. He helped establish the Japan Management Studies Association in 1926 and in 1928 started publishing Keiei keizaigaku kenkyū (Management Economics Studies). He went to Germany and studied under H. Nicklisch. Masuchi advocated "management economics," which focuses on the two basic themes of management's internal structure and its external relations. His main works include Keiei keizaigaku (1929, Management Economics), Kabushiki kaisha (1937, Joint-Stock Company), and Chingin ron (1939, On Wages). *KATSURA Yoshio*

Masuda

City in western Shimane Prefecture, western Honshū, on the Sea of Japan. A castle town of the Masuda family from the 14th century, it flourished later as a commercial center. Principal industries are textiles and lumber processing. Kakinomoto Shrine, dedicated to the poet KAKINOMOTO NO HITOMARO, is located here. Pop: 52,753.

Masuda Takashi (1848–1938)

Businessman; leader of the MITSUI financial combine. Born in Sado Province (now part of Niigata Prefecture), the son of a minor official.

Masuda and his father accompanied the 1864 Tokugawa shogunate mission to France to request the closing of the port of Yokohama (see SHOGUNATE MISSIONS TO THE WEST). In 1872 he entered the Ministry of Finance at the invitation of Vice Minister of Finance INOUE KAORU but resigned with Inoue the following year. Under Inoue's direction, Masuda headed a trading company, the Senshū Kaisha, which in 1876 was taken over by Inoue's business allies, the Mitsui merchant house. The business was reorganized as the Mitsui Trading Company (Mitsui Bussan Kaisha), and as its managing director Masuda helped to build up the Mitsui financial empire. His business ventures included the purchase and development of the MIIKE COAL MINES and the acquisition of resources in China; he also promoted able employees rapidly and worked for the development of business education in Japan. He was a noted art collector and connoisseur of the tea ceremony.

Masukagami

Historical tale attributed to NIJŌ YOSHIMOTO; probably written between 1338 and 1376. Beginning with the birth of Emperor Go-Toba in 1180, it traces some 154 years of court history through the reigns of 15 emperors up to the return of Emperor Go-Daigo from exile in 1333, including the relationship of the imperial court with the ruling shogunate government in Kamakura. Through the narrator, an old woman reminiscing about the past (a device used in the ŌKAGAMI and the IMAKAGAMI, both earlier historical tales), the world of the Kyōto court nobility is painted in nostalgic tones. Its elegant classical prose style is apparently modeled on that of the TALE OF GENJI (Genji monogatari).

Masumoto Hakaru (1895–　　)

Physical metallurgist. Developed the stainless invar (1929), New KS Magnetic Steel (together with HONDA KŌTARŌ in 1934), and numerous other metal alloys. Born in Hiroshima Prefecture. After graduating from Tōhoku University in 1922, Masumoto carried out research at the Research Institute for Iron, Steel and Other Metals at the same university under the direction of Honda Kōtarō. He became a professor there in 1933 and director of the research institute in 1950. In 1955 he was awarded the Order of Culture.

Masutomi Hot Spring

(Masutomi Onsen). Located in the town of Sudama, northwestern Yamanashi Prefecture, central Honshū. A radioactive mineral spring noted worldwide for the volume of its radium emanation; water temperature 30°C (86°F). The waters are said to be effective for gastroenteric disorders and neuralgia. This group of hot springs has been designated as a National Health Resort Hot Spring. A starting point for visits to Chichibu–Tama National Park

Matabei → Iwasa Matabei

Matagi

A people inhabiting the highlands of the Tōhoku (northern Honshū) region who live mainly in mountain huts and subsist almost totally by collective hunting; formerly called Yamadachi. During the latter part of the Edo period (1600–1868) the Matagi were patronized by various lords of Tōhoku domains (han) in exchange for tribute in the form of bear liver (for medicinal purposes) and furs. Some Matagi still maintain their traditional lifestyle, strictly observing customs and taboos and speaking a unique "mountain dialect" (yama kotoba). ────── NOGUCHI Takenori

matchlocks → hinawajū

mathematics, modern

From the 17th century to the first half of the 19th century Japanese mathematics was dominated by WASAN, a system unique to Japan. Present-day Japanese mathematics came entirely from Europe, having been introduced soon after the Meiji Restoration (1868) by KIKUCHI DAIROKU and Fujisawa Rikitarō (1861–1933), who had both studied in Europe.

The Tōkyō Mathematical Society (Tōkyō Sūgakusha), originally founded in 1877 to promote modern mathematics in Japan, was reorganized as the Tōkyō Mathematical and Physical Society in 1884 to include physicists. The society's publication during the 1890s of Japanese translations of specialized papers marked the transition of Japanese mathematics from the study of basics to research in more advanced areas. Research institutions were also established: in 1877 Tōkyō University was opened, followed by Kyōto University in 1892, and Tōhoku University in 1910. In 1911 Hayashi Tsuruichi (1873–1935), a professor at Tōhoku University, founded the *Tōhoku sūgaku zasshi*, (Tōhoku Mathematics Journal), the first professional journal for mathematics in Japan. The first achievement by a modern Japanese mathematician to win international recognition was the work of TAKAGI TEIJI on class field theory, presented in 1920 and 1922.

The founding of Kyūshū University, Ōsaka University, Nagoya University, and other institutes of higher learning also stimulated mathematical research in Japan. Ōsaka University, in particular, was noted as a center for abstract mathematics in the 1930s. Membership in the Tōkyō Mathematical and Physical Society spread nationwide and resulted in its reorganization in 1918 as the Mathematical and Physical Society of Japan (Nihon Sūgaku Butsuri Gakkai). In 1947, however, the society split into the Mathematical Society of Japan (Nihon Sūgakkai) and the Physical Society of Japan (Nihon Butsuri Gakkai). Since then, the memberships of both societies have increased over fivefold. The present membership of the Mathematical Society of Japan exceeds 4,000.

The new educational system established after World War II greatly increased the number of researchers in mathematics. The 11th International Mathematics Conference, held at Harvard University in 1950, marked the return of Japanese mathematicians to the international scene. The work of OKA KIYOSHI on analytic functions of several variables and Iwasawa Kenkichi's paper on Lie groups were highly regarded. In 1954 KODAIRA KUNIHIKO received the prestigious Fields Medal, as did HIRONAKA HEISUKE in 1970.

Japan has two major research institutes in mathematics. The Institute of Statistical Mathematics (Tōkei Sūri Kenkyūjo), under the Ministry of Education, was established in Tōkyō in 1944. The Research Institute for Mathematical Science (Sūri Kaiseki Kenkyūjo), affiliated with Kyōto University, was established in 1963 to support research in applied mathematics.

The decision to eliminate *wasan* from the standard school curriculum was made in 1873, soon after the Restoration. The first arithmetic textbook, written by Kikuchi Dairoku in 1886, was unprecedented in two ways: the normal top-to-bottom right-to-left pattern of writing was replaced by a horizontal left-to-right pattern, and the *wakachi-gaki* method of writing (leaving spaces between words or phrases) was adopted for easier comprehension.

A notable feature of the curriculum, even in the early period, was the parallel use of algebra and geometry at the secondary school level; the basics of differential and integral calculus were introduced at the secondary school level in the 1940s. In recent years the concept of sets has been included in elementary textbooks, while geometry has gradually been deemphasized. This has led to criticism, and there has been a move to return to more traditional methods.

Mathematical research in Japan is of the highest standards. The number of mathematics majors at national universities rose from about 10 a year at the beginning of the century to about 100 in 1940; in 1980 it was over 1,500. The number of mathematics majors who enter graduate schools at national universities each year averages 100. In the 1930s the Mathematical and Physical Society met only once a year for one day, in which 30 to 40 papers were presented. At present, however, the biannual meetings last for four days with five concurrent presentations, but even this extended period is not sufficient for all the papers to be presented. In addition, researchers in each area of specialization hold separate conferences; over 30 such meetings are held each year at the Research Institute for Mathematical Science alone. At present members of the Mathematical Society of Japan belong to at least one of the following research divisions: foundations of mathematics, algebra, geometry, theory of functions, functional equations, theory of functions of real variables, functional analysis, theory of probability, applied mathematics, and topology.

Japanese mathematicians have also published abroad extensively. The *Encyclopedic Dictionary of Mathematics* (1977, *Sūgaku jiten*), edited by the Mathematical Society of Japan, has been translated and published in English. Exchanges of researchers with foreign countries have been actively conducted. Small-scale international conferences are held every year in Japan, and foreign students come to study from developed and developing countries.

Despite its many achievements, Japanese mathematics is not without its problem areas. The rapid increase in the number of researchers has not been matched by a corresponding expansion of job opportunities, and the flood of papers written by these researchers cannot be published in the existing magazines and journals. On the other hand, in some areas such as combinatorics and classical analysis more researchers are needed. Because of the tendency to consider pure mathematics as the ultimate pursuit and research as the highest priority, pure mathematics has become isolated from other fields, and applied mathematics and educational activities are not given enough attention. Finally, although research groups in specialized fields have been formed all over the country in recent years, the tendency toward centralization in the large national universities has not yet been reversed. *Hitotsumatsu Shin*

mathematics, premodern → wasan

matsu → pines

Matsubara

City in Ōsaka Prefecture, central Honshū. It developed early on as a junction of the roads connecting the ancient capitals of NANIWAKYŌ and ASUKA. In recent years, much of its farming has been replaced by light industries producing textiles, artificial pearls, wire nets, and brushes. There are several ancient mounded tombs (KOFUN) in the area. Pop: 135,852.

Matsudaira family → Tokugawa family

Matsudaira Ietada (1555–1600)

Also known as Matsudaira Tonomo no Suke Ietada. Warrior of the Azuchi-Momoyama period (1568–1600), vassal of TOKUGAWA IEYASU (1543–1616), the founder of the Tokugawa shogunate. On his father Koretada's battlefield death at NAGASHINO in 1575, Ietada became head of the Fukōzu branch of the Matsudaira family, one of the "18 Matsudaira" of Mikawa (now part of Aichi Prefecture), Ieyasu's collateral kinsmen. He distinguished himself in Ieyasu's campaigns against TAKEDA KATSUYORI (1546–82), notably at the seizure of Takatenjin Castle in 1581, and in the KOMAKI NAGAKUTE CAMPAIGN against TOYOTOMI HIDEYOSHI in 1584, a stalemate leading to Ieyasu's acceptance of Hideyoshi's hegemony. When Ieyasu was assigned the Kantō provinces after the destruction of the Hōjō of Odawara in 1590 (see ODAWARA CAMPAIGN), Ietada was given a fief assessed at 10,000 *koku* (see KOKUDAKA) at Oshi in Musashi (now the city of Gyōda, Saitama Prefecture), a key outpost in the line of fortresses protecting Edo (now Tōkyō), Ieyasu's headquarters, on the north. In 1592 he was transferred to a similar position at Kashiro in Shimōsa Province (now part of Chiba Prefecture), and again in 1594 to Omigawa in the same province. In 1599 Ietada was appointed a captain of the garrison of Fushimi Castle, Ieyasu's residence in the Kyōto area; next year he died in the castle's defense when it fell to forces mobilized by ISHIDA MITSUNARI in a prelude to the Battle of SEKIGAHARA, where Ieyasu routed Mitsunari's armies and won the hegemony over Japan. Ietada's diary, *Ietada nikki*, is a valuable historical source for the years 1577–94.

Matsudaira Tonomo no Suke Ietada should not be confused with two contemporaries who also bore the name Matsudaira Ietada: Matsudaira Kii no Kami Ietada (1548–82) of the Katanohara Matsudaira, who likewise was present at Nagashino and fought alongside his namesake's father Koretada at the capture of Tobigasu, a fort dominating the high ground; and Matsudaira Jintarō Ietada (d 1581) of the Tōjō Matsudaira, who died heirless and was succeeded in his holdings by Ieyasu's son Matsudaira Tadayoshi (1580–1607). *George Elison*

Matsudaira Katamori (1835–1893)

Daimyō of the Aizu domain (now part of Fukushima Prefecture) and military governor of Kyōto; one of the leaders of the MOVEMENT FOR UNION OF COURT AND SHOGUNATE. In 1860, following the assassination of Great Elder II NAOSUKE, Katamori was called to Edo (now Tōkyō) to mediate between the Tokugawa shogunate and Mito, the home base of Ii's assassins. He was appointed to the new office of military governor of Kyōto (KYŌTO SHUGOSHOKU) in 1862, when the city was under the control of antiforeign, antishogunate extremists. In order to quell the violent activities of these extremist *samurai* and to bolster the shogunate, Katamori, together with MATSUDAIRA YOSHINAGA, advocated a policy of closer cooperation between the court and the shogunate in national affairs. He also made use of special police units, such as the SHINSENGUMI, to patrol the streets of Kyōto. In the late summer of 1863 the combined forces of the Satsuma and Aizu domains succeeded in driving from Kyōto the extremists led by men of the Chōshū domain (see COUP D'ETAT OF 30 SEPTEMBER 1863). When the extremists attempted to retake Kyōto the following year, Katamori again led Aizu and Satsuma troops and repelled them outside the palace gates (see HAMAGURI GOMON INCIDENT). After the formal restoration of imperial rule in 1868 (see MEIJI RESTORATION), Katamori returned to Aizu and resisted imperial takeover. Supported by an alliance of like-minded northeastern domains (the ŌUETSU REPPAN DŌMEI) and reorganizing his army along Western lines, he made a last-ditch effort to defend Tokugawa interests. He surrendered when Wakamatsu Castle was taken by imperial troops (see BOSHIN CIVIL WAR). He was punished relatively lightly by the new government but was never allowed to regain political importance.

Matsudaira Keiei → Matsudaira Yoshinaga

Matsudaira Nobutsuna (1596–1662)

A leading administrator of the early Tokugawa shogunate; known also as Chie Izu (Clever Izu) from his title Izu no Kami. Of modest background, Nobutsuna was assigned to serve TOKUGAWA IEMITSU at the latter's birth and remained his intimate throughout Iemitsu's term (1623–51) as shōgun. Nobutsuna became a senior councillor (*rōjū*) in 1633 and continued in that post under the next shōgun, TOKUGAWA IETSUNA. He was one of the principal architects of the shogunate's administrative system. In 1637–38 he served as special commissioner in charge of suppressing the SHIMABARA UPRISING, a rebellion of peasants affected by millenarian Christian beliefs; subsequently he undertook an inspection tour of those parts of Kyūshū associated with Christianity and with foreign contacts, and his observations contributed substantially to the final formulation of the shogunate's NATIONAL SECLUSION policy in 1638–39. Nobutsuna played an important part in the discovery and suppression of the KEIAN INCIDENT of 1651 (Keian 4) and the Jōō Incident of the following year (Jōō 1), abortive plots to overthrow the government resulting from the discontent of *rōnin*, *samurai* who had lost their livelihood because of the extensive disenfeoffment of *daimyō* in the first half of the 17th century. Nobutsuna is remembered also for the innovative techniques he introduced to increase agricultural production in his 75,000-*koku* (see KOKUDAKA) domain at Kawagoe in Musashi Province (now Saitama Prefecture). *George Elison*

Matsudaira Sadanobu (1758–1829)

Daimyō of the Shirakawa domain (now part of Fukushima Prefecture) and a senior councillor (*rōjū*) of the TOKUGAWA SHOGUNATE; best known as the initiator of the KANSEI REFORMS (1787–93), the second of the three great reforms by which the shogunate attempted to bolster its deteriorating finances (the others being the KYŌHŌ REFORMS of the 1720s and the TEMPŌ REFORMS of the 1840s).

Born in Edo (now Tōkyō) Sadanobu was the third son of TAYASU MUNETAKE, founder of one of the three junior collateral houses of the Tokugawa family (GOSANKYŌ), and grandson of TOKUGAWA YOSHIMUNE, the eighth shōgun and author of the Kyōhō Reforms. He was thus in line for the shogunal position in the event of a succession problem. In 1774, however, he fell victim to a political scheme of the *rōjū* TANUMA OKITSUGU and was ordered to be adopted by Matsudaira Sadakuni, daimyō of Shirakawa. Another junior collateral house, the Hitotsubashi, provided the next shōgun, TOKUGAWA IENARI, but Sadanobu was to return to the center of power as chief senior councillor (*rōjū shuseki*; 1787–93) and shogunal regent (*hosa*; 1788–93). Sadanobu succeeded his adoptive father in 1783; although still young, he quickly proved himself an able administrator, successfully guiding his domain through four years of crop failures and famines.

In the 1780s the shogunate faced a steadily worsening financial crisis. The social order was also seriously threatened by the combined effect of nationwide natural disasters (see TEMMEI FAMINE), destructive riots in the countryside and cities, and the bureaucratic corruption of the preceding regime, which had been dominated by the ruthless and extravagant Tanuma. Moreover, political tensions had developed between the shogunate and the domains as a result of Tanuma's centralizing policies.

Thanks to his own political maneuvering and that of the Tokugawa collateral houses as well as to his reputation for competence, Sadanobu was appointed *rōjū* in 1787, 10 months after Tanuma's resignation. He immediately began a thorough purge of Tanuma's clique. Sadanobu's bureaucratic reform has often been described as a reactionary reversal of Tanuma's mercantilist policies and as consisting mainly of the moralistic enforcement of sumptuary laws. Yet Sadanobu was innovative in many ways: he gave Edo greater economic independence from Ōsaka; he canceled the debts of shogunal retainers while devising a new purveyor system that gave the shogunate greater control over moneylenders; and he built up Edo's cash and rice supplies against future emergencies (see SHICHIBUKIN TSUMITATE).

Sadanobu's most controversial measure was the "Ban on Heterodoxy" (Kansei Igaku no Kin) of 1790, which limited the curriculum of the shogunal academy, the SHŌHEIKŌ, to a narrow version of the Zhu Xi (Chu Hsi) school of Neo-Confucianism (SHUSHIGAKU). Subsequently, Sadanobu introduced a compulsory examination system for shogunal retainers, the first of its kind. Hence the ban was not, as is often argued, a suppression of academic freedom but rather an administrative measure restricted to shogunate personnel. In this respect, however, its effects were far-reaching. The measure not only contributed to a Neo-Confucian revival in the latter part of the Edo period (1600–1868) but, most important, gave Japan a consistent bureaucratic ideology that continued down to the MEIJI RESTORATION (1868) and beyond to infuse into Japan's elite functionaries an ethos of public-spiritedness and dedicated service.

Two other problems demanded Sadanobu's attention: foreign relations and pro-imperial activities. Fifty years later these issues would become crucial to the fate of the shogunate. In the Laxman Affair, the shogunate confronted for the first time the question of opening the country to foreigners. In 1792 Adam LAXMAN tried to establish official trade relations between Japan and Russia in the north. Sadanobu, however, was able to maintain the Tokugawa policy of NATIONAL SECLUSION and avoid a clash with Russia by promising token trade in Nagasaki. The Russians left appeased and did not return for another 10 years.

In the so-called Title Incident of 1789 (Songō Jiken), Sadanobu, despite growing pro-imperial sentiment among courtiers and *samurai* refused a request from Emperor Kōkaku (1771–1840; r 1779–1817) to grant a new title, that of *daijō tennō*, reserved for retired emperors, to the emperor's father, Prince Sukehito (1733–86). The discontent with Sadanobu's authoritarian handling of the incident, together with growing resentment of his stringent sumptuary laws and the shōgun Ienari's coming-of-age, contributed to his sudden and early dismissal from his shogunate posts in 1793. He retired to Shirakawa, where he spent the rest of his active years directing domainal affairs.

📖 —— Matsudaira Sadanobu, *Rakuō Kō isho* (1893). Matsudaira Sadanobu, *Uge no hitokoto, Shūgyōroku* (1942). Herman Ooms, *Charismatic Bureaucrat: A Political Biography of Matsudaira Sadanobu* (1975). Shibusawa Eiichi, *Rakuō Kō den* (1937).

Herman OOMS

Matsudaira Tadanao (1595–1650)

Daimyō of the early Edo period; grandson of the first Tokugawa shōgun, TOKUGAWA IEYASU. In 1607 Tadanao succeeded his father, Yūki Hideyasu (1574–1607), as daimyō of Echizen (now Fukui Prefecture). He fought in the Ōsaka compaigns of 1614–15 (see ŌSAKA CASTLE, SIEGES OF) but felt that he was not adequately rewarded and became increasingly unruly after Ieyasu's death in 1616. He tyrannized his retainers, executing people at whim, and defied the shogunate on many occasions, even feigning illness to avoid SANKIN KŌTAI attendance in Edo (now Tōkyō). In 1623 he was finally deprived of his domain and exiled to Bungo Province (now part of Ōita Prefecture). KIKUCHI KAN's short story "Tadanao Kyō gyōjō ki" (1918, On the Conduct of Lord Tadanao) is a fictionalized account of Tadanao's career.

Matsudaira Tadayoshi (1580–1607)

Fourth son of TOKUGAWA IEYASU, the founder of the Tokugawa shogunate (1603–1867). While still an infant, Tadayoshi was made the head of the Tōjō Matsudaira, one of the "18 branches" of the Matsudaira family of Mikawa (now part of Aichi Prefecture), Ieyasu's collateral kinsmen. In 1592 he was given a domain assessed at 120,000 *koku* (see KOKUDAKA) at Oshi in Musashi (now the city of Gyōda, Saitama Prefecture); his incumbency there is noted for the start of an ambitious channel stabilization project on the Tonegawa, the Kantō region's most important river. Tadayoshi distinguished himself in the Battle of SEKIGAHARA (1600), where his father won hegemony over Japan. In the ensuing massive reassignment of lands, he received the 520,000-*koku* fief of Kiyosu in Owari Province (now Kiyosu Chō, Aichi Prefecture). Tadayoshi's posting to this area, which controlled the approaches to western Japan, illustrates Ieyasu's policy of entrusting strategically vital positions only to absolutely reliable men; it prefigured the establishment of the Owari branch of the Tokugawa family, one of the Three Successor Houses (GOSANKE). The founding father of the Owari Tokugawa lineage was, however, Ieyasu's ninth son, Tokugawa Yoshinao (1601–1650), into whose hands the province passed after Tadayoshi's early and heirless death.

George ELISON

Matsudaira Yoshinaga (1828–1890)

Known also as Matsudaira Keiei and by his pen name Shungaku. *Daimyō* of the Fukui or Echizen domain (now part of Fukui Prefecture) and adviser to the Tokugawa shogunate during its final years; leader of the MOVEMENT FOR UNION OF COURT AND SHOGUNATE. Born into the Tayasu family, one of the three junior collateral houses (GOSANKYŌ) of the Tokugawa family, he was adopted by Matsudaira Nariyoshi, the daimyō of Echizen. In the 1840s he carried out a series of progressive reforms in his own domain. After Commodore Matthew PERRY arrived in 1853 demanding trade, Yoshinaga repeatedly urged the shogunate to open Japan to foreign trade and technology but at the same time to improve coastal defenses and modernize its military forces. As a member of the faction supporting TOKUGAWA YOSHINOBU in the 1858 shogunal succession dispute, he incurred the wrath of the great elder *(tairō)* II NAOSUKE and was placed under house arrest. Yoshinaga was pardoned after Ii's assassination in 1860, and in 1862 he was appointed to the new office of shogunal prime minister *(seiji sōsaishoku)*. Together with Yoshinobu, who had become shogunal regent *(kōkenshoku)* in 1862, he attempted to reform the shogunate; he abolished the costly SANKIN KŌTAI system, under which daimyō were obliged to spend alternate years in Edo (now Tōkyō), and hoped to shore up the prestige of the shogunate by bringing the imperial court closer to the workings of government. He was dismissed from office, however, for urging the resignation of the shōgun TOKUGAWA IEMOCHI and, apart from a short term as military governor of Kyōto (Kyōto *shugoshoku*) in 1864, withdrew from active participation in political affairs. Yoshinaga remained a loyal supporter of the shogunate, opposing to the end the plans by the Chōshū and Satsuma domains to overthrow the Tokugawa. At the time of the MEIJI RESTORATION (1868) he mediated on behalf of the Tokugawa family. He later served as the head of several ministries in the new government.

Matsudo

City in northwestern Chiba Prefecture, central Honshū, on the river Edogawa. During the Edo period (1600–1868) it was a prosperous river port and one of the POST-STATION TOWNS on the highway Mito Kaidō. Since World War II metal and machinery industries have become its principal occupations. The establishment of housing complexes has made it a residential suburb of Tōkyō. Pop: 400,870.

Matsue

Capital of Shimane Prefecture, western Honshū; straddles the river Ōhashigawa. A castle town during the Edo period (1600–1868), Matsue is a part of the so-called Nakaumi New Industrial City, with machinery and textile industries. Of interest are Fudoki no Oka Park, the site of several tumuli (KOFUN); an 8th-century temple (KOKUBUNJI); Matsue Castle; the temple Gesshōji; Kanden'an, a teahouse built in the 18th century; the Koizumi Yakumo Kinenkan, a museum in honor of Lafcadio HEARN, who lived in Matsue; and Lake Shinji (Shinjiko). Pop: 135,563.

Matsue Plain

(Matsue Heiya). Located in northeastern Shimane Prefecture, western Honshū. Situated between Lake Shinji in the west and the lake called Nakaumi in the east, this low-lying plain is formed by sediment from the river Ōhashigawa, which flows between the lakes, and is susceptible to flooding. The major city is Matsue, which covers much of the plain, where numerous industrial development projects are underway. Area: approximately 40 sq km (15 sq mi).

Matsue Shigeyori (1602–1680)

HAIKU poet of the early Edo period. A prosperous Kyōto merchant, he was a major figure in the establishment of haiku as a new, innovative poetic genre independent of the older *renga* (see RENGA AND HAIKAI), showing in this more initiative than his teacher MATSUNAGA TEITOKU, who was more cautious in his approach. He quarreled with his fellow disciple NONOGUCHI RYŪHO over the selection of verses for a proposed Teimon (Teitoku school) anthology, became in turn estranged from Teitoku, and finally published the pioneering haiku anthology *Enokoshū* (1633) on his own. In 1638 he wrote *Kefukigusa*, an extensive guide to the vocabulary, rules, and techniques of haiku which clarified its distinction from *renga* and became a popular sourcebook for practitioners of the art. Through his friendship with NISHIYAMA SŌIN, he even influenced the emergence of the most radical school of haiku, the DANRIN SCHOOL, and it is worth noting that BASHŌ's first verses appeared in an anthology that he compiled in 1664, the *Sayo no Nakayama shū*. A man of strong and independent character, he was the object of criticism from less progressive quarters, but his great role in the early history of haiku is beyond question.

Matsugaoka Bunko

(Matsugaoka Library). Library specializing in collections of ZEN Buddhist classical texts. It was formally established in 1946 by D. T. SUZUKI, the renowned lay Buddhist philosopher, scholar, and author. Matsugaoka is a hill in Kamakura, Kanagawa Prefecture, where the Zen temple Tōkeiji is situated. The library was named by the chief priest of the temple and Suzuki's master, Shaku Sōen (1859–1919), who provided funds for establishing it. In excess of 50,000 volumes, the collections are housed in two reinforced concrete storerooms. Holographic works dating from the time of Shōichi Kokushi (1202–80) and other works considered NATIONAL TREASURES are found here. Suzuki donated a complete set of his own works, which number over 100 titles, to the library, as well as all of his personal property, including his many prizes and medals. The collections of his late wife, Beatrice, are also housed in the library. There is a wealth of material on religion in foreign languages as well.

Theodore F. WELCH

Matsui Sumako (1886–1919)

Japan's first Western-style actress; original name, Kobayashi Masako. Born in Nagano Prefecture into a former *samurai* family. After a brief first marriage, she moved to Tōkyō and married a teacher, Maezawa Seisuke (d 1923). Bored and frustrated, in 1909 she joined the drama group Bungei Kyōkai, led by TSUBOUCHI SHŌYŌ, which was introducing Western theater into Japan. Her husband left her the next year, just around the time she appeared on stage in her first major role, as Ophelia in *Hamlet*. She is probably best remembered for her 1911 portrayal of Nora in Ibsen's *A Doll's House,* which helped fire controversy over the emerging feminist movement in Japan.

Her acting was directed and inspired by Shōyō's protégé SHIMAMURA HŌGETSU, who eventually left his wife and children for her. When their affair became known in 1913, they left the Bungei Kyōkai and started a new drama company, the Geijutsuza, which toured throughout Japan and Manchuria. A recording of Matsui singing "Katusha's Song," from a play based on Tolstoy's *Resurrection,* became extremely popular. She also performed such roles as Anna Karenina, Salome, and Carmen. But apparently she felt unable to continue her career without Hōgetsu: just two months after his death, she committed suicide.

Matsukata fiscal policy

(Matsukata *zaisei*). Policy of retrenchment, deflation, and currency and banking reform adopted by the Meiji government in 1880–81 in response to the severe inflation and paper currency depreciation after 1877. It was largely carried out under Finance Minister MATSUKATA MASAYOSHI from 1881 to 1885. The immediate objective of the policy was to restore the value of paper money and its long-range goal was to establish a unified convertible currency system. These goals were to be achieved by creating a budget surplus with which to redeem inconvertible paper notes and to build up specie reserves, and by founding a central bank, the BANK OF JAPAN. Although it gave rise to a serious depression in the agricultural sector of the economy, the Matsukata fiscal policy brought order to the nation's financial system and set the stage for the rapid growth of modern industry after 1886.

The Financial Crisis of 1878–1880 —— In the years immediately preceding Matsukata's appointment as finance minister in October 1881, the Japanese economy was in the throes of a serious inflation triggered by the huge issue of inconvertible paper currency in 1877 and 1878. The government defrayed the cost of putting down the SATSUMA REBELLION of 1877 by printing ¥27 million in government notes and borrowing ¥15 million from one of the NATIONAL BANKS. Mainly as a result of this, the total issue of government and national bank notes increased by 55 percent between 1876 and 1878. Under the impact of excessive note issue, the economy began to show all the signs of a violent inflation. Prices rose rapidly, with that of rice doubling between 1877 and 1880. Interest rates also climbed, while the market value of government bonds declined. Furthermore, inflation stimulated imports, heightening the foreign trade deficit and accelerating the outflow of specie. The loss of gold and silver coupled with enormous note issues meant a sharp drop in the rate of specie held in reserve. By 1880 the ratio of specie to government and national bank notes had plunged to 4.5 percent. In consequence, the value of paper money fell alarmingly. From 1878 to 1881 government notes depreciated 35 percent relative to silver.

These inflationary trends had a variety of economic repercussions. To rural areas the inflation brought an actual reduction in the tax burden and a corresponding rise in prosperity. Landlords, in particular, received huge windfall profits owing to the combination of an increasing price and a fixed land tax paid in paper money. In the industrial sector, the speculative boom accompanying inflation spawned a number of small-scale enterprises, but key modern industries shared little in this expansion. In fact, the inflationary movement tended to restrict the development of modern industry, as rising interest rates discouraged long-term investment. The Meiji government, however, was hardest hit by the inflation, primarily because of the fixed income from the land tax, which during the years 1878–80 averaged over 70 percent of its total tax revenues. While the real value of its income was falling drastically, the government was receiving an increasingly smaller share of the proceeds from the land. This loss was only aggravated by a reduction in the land tax rate from 3.0 to 2.5 percent in 1877, just before the inflation began.

The Matsukata Reform —— By 1880 government leaders were agreed that they would have to take drastic steps in order to regain control of the financial situation. In May 1880 ŌKUMA SHIGENOBU, who had been finance minister until February of that year, came forward with a radical plan for redeeming the outstanding paper notes by raising a loan of ¥50 million in London. His proposal was defeated for being too risky, and in September 1880 the government decided instead to embark on a program of currency reform through financial retrenchment and increased taxation. Ōkuma and Councillor ITŌ HIROBUMI then jointly hammered out the details of this program. With Ōkuma's ouster from the government in the POLITICAL CRISIS OF 1881, Matsukata replaced SANO TSUNETAMI, Ōkuma's hand-picked successor as finance minister, and proceeded to carry out and extend the new financial program.

The Matsukata fiscal policy was basically a continuation of the policies devised by Ōkuma and Itō. Nevertheless, Ōkuma and Matsukata differed markedly in their views on the proper method of currency reform. Ōkuma called for the immediate recovery of all inconvertible paper money through foreign borrowing or domestic bond issues so that the results of the industrial promotion policy (see SHOKUSAN KŌGYŌ) he had been pursuing since the early 1870s would not be jeopardized. By contrast, Matsukata advocated the gradual withdrawal of inconvertible notes, together with the accumulation of specie, until paper currency was restored to face value, followed by the gradual replacement of the outstanding notes with convertible notes issued by a central bank. Thus, under the Matsukata program, short-run growth was sacrificed for long-term stability, as Matsukata's orthodox policies brought on the economic slowdown that Ōkuma had sought to avoid.

Matsukata fiscal policy

The 1878–1881 Inflation and the Matsukata Deflation

	Inconvertible paper currency in circulation			Specie reserve (million yen)	Ratio of government paper money to silver	Tōkyō wholesale price of rice (yen/koku)	Wholesale price index (1877=100)	Interest rate (%)
	Government paper money (million yen)	National bank notes (million yen)	Total (million yen)					
1877	105.8	13.4	119.2	15.1	1.033	5.34	100	10.0
1878	139.4	26.3	165.7	17.8	1.099	6.39	108	10.4
1879	130.3	34.0	164.4	10.0	1.212	7.96	130	12.0
1880	124.9	34.4	159.4	7.2	1.477	10.57	148	13.1
1881	118.9	34.4	153.3	12.7	1.696	10.59	164	14.0
1882	109.4	34.4	143.8	16.7	1.571	8.81	155	10.1
1883	98.0	34.3	132.3	25.9	1.264	6.31	131	7.9
1884	93.4	31.0	124.4	33.6	1.089	5.29	123	10.1
1885	88.3	30.2	118.5	42.3	1.055	6.61	128	11.0

NOTE: The interest rate is the annual average for loans between ¥1,000 and ¥10,000 in Tōkyō.
SOURCE: For columns 1, 2, and 5: Andō Yoshio, ed, Kindai Nihon keizai shi yōran (1975). For column 4: Ōishi Kaichirō and Miyamoto Ken'ichi, ed, Nihon shihon shugi hattatsu shi no kiso chishiki (1975). For columns 6–8: Henry Rosovsky, "Japan's Transition to Modern Economic Growth, 1868–1885," in Henry Rosovsky, ed, Industrialization in Two Systems (1966).

Upon taking office, Matsukata set about restoring the value of paper money by contracting the volume of currency in circulation and building up specie reserves. He continued the program initiated under Sano of cutting administrative expenditures and increasing existing indirect taxes and instituting new ones and began implementing the policy announced in November 1880 of selling off government enterprises (see KAN'EI JIGYŌ HARAISAGE). He thereby generated a budget surplus between 1882 and 1884 of ¥40.1 million, of which a third was used to recover inconvertible paper notes and the rest added to a reserve fund for acquiring specie from abroad in preparation for the resumption of convertibility.

Matsukata's fiscal measures succeeded in reversing the inflationary trends of the 1878–81 period. The tight money policy reduced the quantity of paper money by 23 percent between 1881 and 1885. Aided by a favorable balance of trade and a net inflow of specie, the reserve ratio of notes in circulation rose from 8 to 36 percent during the same years. Through contraction of the money supply and the accumulation of specie, parity between paper and silver was restored by 1886. Matsukata's policies also produced a sharp drop in commodity prices, with the price of rice cut almost in half and the general price level falling by a quarter between 1881 and 1884. Because of the fixed land tax, the deflation resulted in a huge increase in the real value of government revenues.

By 1885 the Matsukata deflationary program had provided the necessary stability for the creation of a unified convertible currency system. The Bank of Japan, established in 1882 as the central bank and given a monopoly of note issue in 1883, began issuing convertible Bank of Japan notes in May 1885. In the meantime, the government had set up a program for the conversion of national banks into ordinary commercial banks and for the gradual liquidation of their inconvertible bank notes. Finally, on 1 January 1886 all government notes became redeemable in silver at the Bank of Japan, marking the culmination of Matsukata's currency and banking reform.

Impact of Matsukata's Policies —— Clearly, Matsukata's policies ended in placing the government on a sound financial basis. In so doing, however, they severely depressed the economy, causing a wave of bankruptcies and forced mergers among the small, speculative ventures that had sprung up during the years of inflation. For example, between 1882 and 1885 the number of joint-stock companies fell from 3,336 to 1,279. Nevertheless, Matsukata's program supplied the requisite financial stability for sustained industrial growth. After 1886 the Japanese economy entered an upswing, as stable prices and relatively low interest rates encouraged business investment and the central bank guaranteed the convertibility of paper currency.

By far the Matsukata deflation hit the agricultural sector the hardest. The combination of falling agricultural prices and increased taxation led to a serious depression in rural areas, although other factors such as the poor harvest of 1884 and the working out of the effects of the LAND TAX REFORM OF 1873–1881 also contributed to agrarian distress. According to one estimate, total land taxes as a proportion of agricultural and forestry income soared from 11.2 percent in 1880 to 15.5 percent in 1882, 20.2 percent in 1883, and 25.0 percent in 1884. Moreover, the price of rice fell more sharply than did the general price level. Increases in indirect taxes added to the growing tax burden, the sake excise being raised some 250 percent and the tobacco excise 740 percent between 1880 and 1883. Largely as a result of these trends, between 1883 and 1890 nearly 368,000 peasant proprietors, or something on the order of 10 percent of all independent holders, were dispossessed for failure to pay taxes. An even larger number of farmers lost their holdings through mortgage foreclosure, an estimated one-seventh of total arable land being foreclosed in the years 1884 and 1885 alone. The economic decline of small proprietors is also evidenced by the drop in the number of people eligible to vote in elections for prefectural assemblies. In 1881 roughly 1.8 million people met the voting qualification of paying a land tax of at least ¥5, the amount assessed on 0.79 hectares (1.96 acres) of land. This figure had fallen to about 1.5 million by 1887, a loss of 17 percent in 5 years.

In short, the Matsukata fiscal policy heightened the burden placed on agriculture by the modernization program of the Meiji government. Yet, in terms of its objectives of curbing inflation, of restoring the value of paper money and therefore the real income of the government, and of establishing a unified convertible currency, the policy proved highly successful.

■——Ōishi Kaichirō, " 'Shokusan kōgyō' to 'jiyū minken' no keizai shisō," in Chō Yukio and Sumiya Kazuhiko, ed, Kindai Nihon keizai shisō shi, vol 1 (1969). Ōuchi Hyōe and Tsuchiya Takao, ed, Meiji zenki zaisei keizai shiryō shūsei, vols 1 and 11 (1931, 1932). Henry Rosovsky, "Japan's Transition to Modern Economic Growth, 1868–1885," in Henry Rosovsky, ed, Industrialization in Two Systems (1966). Unno Fukuju, "Matsukata zaisei to jinushisei no keisei," in Iwanami kōza: Nihon rekishi, vol 15 (Iwanami Shoten, 1976).
Steven J. ERICSON

Matsukata Masayoshi (1835–1924)

Finance minister, prime minister, and GENRŌ (elder statesman) of the Meiji period (1868–1912). Born 23 March 1835 in Kagoshima, the castle town of the Shimazu domain of Satsuma (now Kagoshima

Prefecture). His father was Matsuda Masaki, the second son of a GŌSHI (farmer-*samurai*) of Taniyama, a village south of Kagoshima. Lacking an inheritance, Masaki entered into trade between Kagoshima and the Satsuma subfief of the Ryūkyū Islands. Ambitious to obtain a samurai education for his sons, Masaki managed to change both his residence and status by becoming the adopted heir of Matsukata Shichiemon, a low-ranking samurai in charge of the production of guns in Kagoshima. Shichiemon was the 29th-generation descendant of a follower of Shimazu Tadahisa, who came to Satsuma from the Kantō area as a Minamoto henchman in the 12th century.

Masayoshi was the ninth child of Matsukata Masaki and his wife Kesako. At the age of 6 he became a member of the Gōjū, a unique Satsuma educational fraternity for samurai boys and young men up to age 25 which was designed to preserve martial spirit and fighting skills even in times of peace. Members led frugal, spartan lives, learning endurance and courage through mountain climbing and war games; they disciplined themselves and each other, practiced the martial arts daily, memorized *kambun* (Chinese) texts, and practiced calligraphy. In the Gōjū, Masayoshi became closely associated with SAIGŌ TAKAMORI and ŌKUBO TOSHIMICHI, eight and five years his senior respectively, who were to become leaders of the MEIJI RESTORATION (1868).

At the age of 13 Matsukata entered the Zōshikan, the domain Confucian academy, where he studied the Chinese classics, the history of Japan and Satsuma, and the martial arts. Here, he was introduced by two progressive teachers to unorthodox ideas outside the Zhu Xi (Chu Hsi) interpretation of Confucianism (SHUSHIGAKU), an event that helped determine the course of his life. These ideas were based on the Wang Yangming interpretation of Confucianism (YŌMEIGAKU), which was banned by the shogunate for its subversive emphasis on loyalty to the emperor as the only true sovereign. At the age of 15 he also started working part-time as a clerk-accountant in the financial office of the domain.

Matsukata came to the attention of his *daimyō*, SHIMAZU NARIAKIRA and became a member of the elite military corps that Nariakira was training for an eventual attack against the Tokugawa shogunate. When Nariakira died suddenly in 1858 SHIMAZU HISAMITSU, his half brother, succeeded him to power (though not to the post of daimyō). Hisamitsu suppressed an attempt to carry out Nariakira's antishogunate plan, which was led by an activist group (the Seichūgumi, "Spirited and Loyal Band") of which Ōkubo was the leader and Matsukata a member.

In 1862 Hisamitsu led Satsuma forces to Kyōto to present his policy for *kōbu gattai* (see MOVEMENT FOR UNION OF COURT AND SHOGUNATE). It was accepted by the court. He then escorted an imperial messenger to Edo to summon the shōgun to Kyōto. Matsukata was in Hisamitsu's entourage, which, on the return journey, encountered a group of four Britishers and killed one of them for supposedly disrespectful behavior (see RICHARDSON AFFAIR). Matsukata was one of the four chief guards of Hisamitsu's palanquin, and in the fray distinguished himself as the only one to remain at his post. From this time he rose rapidly in the Satsuma bureaucracy; he was appointed chief steward (*okonando*), the highest post an ordinary samurai could occupy, and in 1864 was appointed *giseishogakari*, a member of the policy-making body of the domain.

In 1866, as assistant commissioner for ships in charge of naval vessels, he decided upon a naval career and went to Nagasaki to study Western science, mathematics, and surveying. He also obtained practical naval knowledge from British officers on board warships in the port. His studies were frequently interrupted by trips back to Kagoshima, since Ōkubo and Saigō, who were in Kyōto plotting the overthrow of the shogunate, used him as their liaison with the domain government. In Nagasaki Matsukata was also charged with purchasing ammunition and ships for the coming conflict with the shogunate. At one time he bought the fastest and most modern ship available at great cost, planning to convert it into a warship that he would then command. When the ship was put to other uses, he abandoned all thought of a naval career. Ironically, the ship was converted a few months later into the warship *Kasuga*, which played a major role in a naval engagement off Kōbe in January 1868. Furthermore, naval men from Satsuma went on to become the founders of the modern Japanese navy. At the time of the Restoration Matsukata was still in Nagasaki, and he and a representative from the Tosa domain (now Kōchi Prefecture) took charge of maintaining order in the city, which had been left in turmoil after the flight of the shogunate authorities.

In April 1868, on behalf of the new central government, Ōkubo appointed Matsukata governor of Hita Prefecture, formerly a *tenryō* (shogunal domain) in the western extremity of what is now Ōita Prefecture. His assignment was to collect funds from the rich merchants of this area for the operation of the new government. He raised the enormous sum of 100,000 RYŌ. He established a strong administration in Hita, initiating programs of reforestation, constructing roads and bridges, and increasing food production by the reclamation of wastelands. He also abolished the custom of giving gifts to officials, reduced the social barriers between commoners and officials, and attempted to cut down the high rate of abortion by offering incentives to women to bring their unwanted children to the Yōikukan, an orphanage he had built. While still governor, Matsukata was appointed assistant minister of civil affairs in charge of special assignments. In 1870 he successfully handled the problem arising from Western outrage over the government's harsh treatment of a community of secret Christians (KAKURE KIRISHITAN) newly discovered in the Nagasaki area. He also succeeded in destroying a large-scale counterfeiting operation within the castle premises of the powerful former daimyō of Fukuoka.

Matsukata moved to Tōkyō in 1871 and, with the establishment of the Ministry of Finance, became assistant to ITŌ HIROBUMI, who was in charge of the Land Tax Reform. When Itō went abroad with the IWAKURA MISSION in late 1871, Matsukata succeeded him and worked for the next few years drafting the laws for the Land Tax Reform and supervising their (very difficult) implementation. The reform was of fundamental importance, since it converted the basis of agricultural taxation from a percentage of the annual yield to a fixed tax based on the value of the land. One major purpose was to produce a stable tax yield, on the basis of which the government could develop annual budgets; a secondary purpose was to clarify that landownership rested with the person paying the tax. (See also LAND TAX REFORM OF 1873–1881.)

In 1878 Matsukata made his first trip to Europe as the official Japanese representative to the Paris International Exhibition. He was able to observe first-hand the industrialized countries that Japan was attempting to follow. The diligence with which he studied the financing and organization of the Tobacco Monopoly Bureau in Paris brought him to the attention of the finance minister, Léon Say. Much impressed with Matsukata, Say invited him to occupy a desk in his office during his stay in Paris and instructed him in matters of modern finance. This proved excellent preparation for Matsukata's subsequent service as finance minister, and he later credited Say with the success of his own famous deflationary policies and for the establishment of the BANK OF JAPAN in 1882.

Matsukata replaced ŌKUMA SHIGENOBU as minister of finance in 1881, at a time when the Japanese economy was in critical inflationary trouble. The deflationary measures he undertook during the next few years (see MATSUKATA FISCAL POLICY) were a daring and successful experiment. They established confidence in the currency and financial institutions, thus creating the conditions under which modern economic growth could begin. These achievements marked the apogee of Matsukata's career. When the cabinet system was created by Itō in 1885, Matsukata continued as the first finance minister and served in this post in 7 out of the first 10 cabinets, occupying this critically important position for a total of 18 out of 20 years between 1881 and 1901. In the drafting of the Meiji CONSTITUTION of 1889, his chief contributions were in the articles on finance (arts. 62–72); he was also responsible for the enactment of the Finance Law, which went into effect concurrently with the constitution and became the basis of financial administration. It was also at his insistence that the Chinese indemnity following the SINO-JAPANESE WAR OF 1894–1895 was paid in London and Berlin in British money, thus laying a sound basis for Japan's continued economic growth and permitting the nation to adopt the gold standard in 1897.

By his own admission, Matsukata was never a politician, and he was unable to understand why political parties should be allowed to interfere in government operations. However, as a member of the Satsuma–Chōshū oligarchy (see HAMBATSU), he felt compelled to take his turn as prime minister and contend with the political parties in the Diet. During the first seven cabinets, a pattern was set of alternating between Chōshū (now Yamaguchi Prefecture) and Satsuma men as prime ministers. Since Matsukata's two old associates, Saigō and Ōkubo, were long since dead and the other Satsuma men, including Saigō's younger brother, SAIGŌ TSUGUMICHI, were felt to be unqualified for the post, Matsukata was persuaded to take the position of prime minister. He followed YAMAGATA ARITOMO of Chōshū from 6 May 1891 to 8 August 1892 and succeeded Itō of Chōshū from 18 September 1896 until 12 January 1898.

Matsukata's first cabinet was initially called the *kuromaku* ("black curtain" or hidden manipulator) cabinet, because the other members of the cabinet were secondary figures and he had accepted only on the premise that the de facto leaders would help him from behind the scenes. But the cabinet soon became known as the "catastrophe cabinet," when an attempt was made on the life of the visiting crown prince of Russia (later Tsar Nicholas II)—almost causing a grave international crisis—and a devastating earthquake hit Aichi and Gifu prefectures in the autumn of 1891. Matsukata's first term of office is best remembered for his dissolution of the lower house of the Diet when it refused to pass his budget and the infamous second general election of 15 February 1892, in which Home Minister SHINAGAWA YAJIRŌ, a Chōshū henchman of the Yamagata clique over whom Matsukata had little control, carried out a campaign of bribery and harassment of opposition politicians in an unsuccessful effort to win a majority of government supporters in the Diet. During Matsukata's second cabinet, he proved somewhat more flexible in dealing with the Diet. Following Itō's lead in taking the party leader ITAGAKI TAISUKE into the preceding cabinet as home minister, Matsukata took the other party leader, Ōkuma, into his cabinet as minister of foreign affairs and thereby obtained enough support in the Diet to avoid dissolving it again.

Matsukata retired from active government service in 1901, but he continued to be widely consulted and to exert considerable influence. In 1898 he had been named an elder statesman *(genrō)*, and after Yamagata's death in 1922 he was briefly the only survivor of this group, playing the role of selector of the prime minister on the emperor's behalf. In 1883 he had been made a count, and in 1905 he was promoted to marquis in recognition of his financial services during the RUSSO-JAPANESE WAR (1904–05). Finally in 1922, when he retired from the largely honorary post of lord keeper of the privy seal *(naidaijin)*, which he had held since 1917, he was given the highest noble rank of prince. He served from 1903 to 1912 as president of the International Red Cross of Japan. Matsukata died on 2 July 1924, at the age of 89, after being injured in the great Tōkyō Earthquake of 1 September 1923.

Matsukata did not read English or any other Western language, but he was a great reader in translation of Western books, journals, and newspapers. He also invited many Westerners to his home in Mita in Tōkyō. From early in his career he was deeply concerned with foreign policy and, beginning in 1869, presented many memorials on diplomatic matters, treaty revision, and Japan's relations with China and the countries of the West. Matsukata was a man of few words and disliked competitive games, but he loved the outdoors, taking pleasure in horticulture, agricultural experiments, and raising sheep and horses. His wife Masako raised 19 children, 9 of them the offspring of concubines. Several of these children had important careers in industry, banking, and diplomacy.

◼ ——Matsukata Masayoshi, *Report of the Adoption of the Gold Standard in Japan* (1899). Matsukata Masayoshi, *Report of the Post Bellum Financial Administration in Japan* (1901). Fujimura Tōru, *Matsukata Masayoshi: Nihon zaisei no paioniya* (1929). Fukai Eigo, *Jimbutsu to shisō* (1939). Fukai Eigo, *Kaihō nanajūnen* (1941). George Marvin, "The Alexander Hamilton of Japan," *Asia* (January 1925). Tokutomi Iichirō, ed, *Kōshaku Matsukata Masayoshi den*, 2 vols (1935). Tsuchiya Takeo, *Nihon shihon shugi no shidōshatachi* (1940). Haru REISCHAUER

Matsukawa Incident

A controversial criminal incident of the OCCUPATION period. On 17 August 1949, while Japan was still under military occupation by the United States following World War II, a mixed passenger and freight train of the Japanese National Railways was sabotaged and overturned near the village of Matsukawa in Fukushima Prefecture. Three crew members were killed. The Japanese government subsequently arrested and charged with the crime 20 Japanese citizens, 19 men and 1 woman, all of them leaders or members of either the National Railway Workers' Union (NRWU) or the Tōshiba Electric Company's Matsukawa factory union, and all but one of them members of the Japan Communist Party. These defendants were subsequently tried in the courts five times—once before the Fukushima District Court, twice before the Sendai High Court, and twice before the Supreme Court of Japan. On 8 August 1961 the Sendai High Court found all of them not guilty, and on 12 September 1963 the Supreme Court upheld this verdict. On 1 August 1970 the Tōkyō

High Court awarded damages to the Matsukawa defendants and their families and ordered the government to pay them ¥76,259,833 (US $212,927), the largest settlement against the state ever awarded in modern Japan. The Matsukawa Incident and subsequent trials is the most famous and one of the most controversial criminal law cases of postwar Japan.

The train sabotage incident was the most important outbreak of violence in opposition to the American Occupation's so-called reverse course. Until 1948 Occupation policy emphasized the "democratization" of the defeated country, but with the onset of the cold war and the revolutionary successes of the Chinese communists, the Americans altered their basic goals. In place of political reform, they gave first priority to rehabilitating the Japanese economy. The Americans did not reverse their democratic innovations, but they moved to curtail the communist domination of the trade unions. These unions had been created by the Occupation authorities themselves in the immediate postwar period, but they and many Japanese now felt that the communists had taken them over and were using them for revolutionary rather than economic purposes. The largest union in the country was the NRWU. In 1949 the supreme commander of the Allied powers (SCAP) ordered some 97,000 national railway workers dismissed from their jobs in order to reduce featherbedding and to balance the national budget as part of a scheme to bring inflation under control. These measures were part of the DODGE LINE, named after Joseph M. Dodge, an American banker sent to Tōkyō in February 1949 to establish basic policies for the economic rehabilitation of Japan.

Communist-dominated sections of the NRWU as well as communist-dominated unions in private industry, such as that of the Tōshiba Electric Company, retaliated against the Dodge Line with strikes, demonstrations, petitions, and other legal measures. The government charged in court that communist unions had also resorted to terrorist acts, including the MITAKA INCIDENT, the SHIMOYAMA INCIDENT, and, most serious, the Matsukawa Incident. Charges of communist terrorism were never sustained by the courts.

The initial trial of the defendants indicted for the Matsukawa sabotage was the first important capital case brought under the new Occupation-inspired Code of Criminal Procedure. This law sought to introduce Anglo-American adversary procedures into Japan's essentially indigenous and continental European legal heritage. The trial and appeals turned into a muddle of challenged evidence, revolving above all around the use of confessions in Japanese criminal law. (Eight of the defendants had confessed to the crime.)

Advocates of judicial reform and of civil liberties like the prominent novelist HIROTSU KAZUO took up the cause of the Matsukawa defendants and argued in public that they were not receiving fair trials or, more serious, that they were victims of a police frame-up. The case became a major cause célèbre among Tōkyō's leftist intellectuals during the 1950s. Their extensive publishing activities gave to the Matsukawa case a significance for the democratization of Japan and for the postwar political education of the Japanese public that went beyond the fate of the defendants.

During the 1960s various writers sensationalized the case, suggesting that the sabotage was actually caused by the American Occupation authorities in order to discredit the communist trade union movement. The novelist MATSUMOTO SEICHŌ is the best-known advocate of the American conspiracy theory. Although the statute of limitations covering the Matsukawa case has precluded further prosecution, there are no untried suspects, and the case remains formally unsolved.

◼ ——Hirotsu Kazuo, *Matsukawa jiken to saiban* (1964). Chalmers Johnson, *Conspiracy at Matsukawa* (1972). Matsukawa Undō Shi Hensan Iinkai, ed, *Matsukawa undō zenshi* (1965). Matsumoto Seichō, *Nihon no kuroi kiri* (1962). Chalmers JOHNSON

Matsukura Shigemasa (d 1630)

Daimyō of the early part of the Edo period (1600–1868). A hereditary vassal of the Tsutsui family (see TSUTSUI JUNKEI) of Yamato and Iga provinces (now Nara Prefecture and part of Mie Prefecture respectively), Shigemasa distinguished himself on the Tokugawa side at the Battle of SEKIGAHARA, and upon the disgrace of his master, Tsutsui Sadatsugu (1562–1615), in 1608 was accordingly made lord of a 10,000-*koku* (see KOKUDAKA) domain at Futami Gojō (now the city of Gojō) in Yamato. In 1616 he was promoted to a 40,000-*koku* domain at Shimabara in Hizen Province (now Nagasaki Prefecture), a region Christianized under its previous lords, the Arima (see ARIMA HARUNOBU). Initially lenient toward the Christian popula-

Matsumoto Castle

The five-story main keep (six stories on the inside) and a smaller keep of the castle's donjon, one of the largest extant in Japan. With few windows and black wainscotting, the donjon has a more somber appearance than later castles. It was completed in the late 16th century. National Treasure.

tion, Shigemasa was later instructed by the Tokugawa shogunate to apply stringent measures, and by 1628 "all the domain's peasants had reformed." The persecution of Christianity and extortionate taxation by the Matsukura sowed the seeds of the SHIMABARA UPRISING of 1637–38. Shigemasa is known also for his proposal to seize Luzon from the Spaniards; in 1630 he sent a ship to Manila to gather intelligence toward this end. The Spanish authorities, however, were forewarned; and, since Shigemasa died on 19 December 1630 (Kan'ei 7.11.16), five days after his spies had sailed, the project was abandoned. His son Katsuie succeeded Shigemasa as daimyō, but he was held responsible for the Shimabara Uprising and sentenced to death by the shogunate in 1638.　　　　*George* ELISON

Matsumae

Formerly Fukuyama. Town in southwestern Hokkaidō. From 1606 it became the castle town of the MATSUMAE FAMILY and served as a base for colonizing EZO, as Hokkaidō was then called. The principal occupation is fishing. Of interest are the castle and several temples connected with the Matsumae. Pop: 17,524.

Matsumae family

Warrior family who, during most of the Edo period (1600–1868), ruled Hokkaidō, southern Sakhalin, and the southern Kuril Islands, a region then known by the general name EZO. From the middle of the 15th century until 1869 Matsumae referred to the part of Hokkaidō that the Japanese had first occupied and where Japanese immigrants were allowed to settle; it corresponded roughly with the Oshima Peninsula in the southwestern corner of the island. Access to the rest of Hokkaidō, inhabited by the AINU people, was restricted.

The Matsumae family were descended from the Kakizaki family, warriors who established control over the Oshima Peninsula in the 15th century. After pledging fealty to the future shōgun TOKUGAWA IEYASU in 1599, the Kakizaki took the surname Matsumae. Subsequently the lords of Matsumae were classed as *tozama* (outer) *daimyō* with landholdings assessed at 30,000 *koku* of rice (see KOKUDAKA). Their domain in fact produced no rice but derived a substantial income from gold, timber, and fisheries. With the appearance of Russian ships along the Kuril Islands in the second half of the 18th century, Matsumae and Ezo became sensitive frontier regions and were twice placed under direct shogunate administration, from 1799 to 1821 and from 1854 to 1867. During these intervals the Matsumae family were relocated in scattered domains in eastern Honshū. When imperial forces subdued pro-Tokugawa diehards in the Battle of GORYŌKAKU (1869) after the Meiji Restoration, the Matsumae resumed nominal control over their ancestral lands until the domains were abolished and a new prefectural system established in 1871.

——Hokkaidō Chō, ed, *Shin Hokkaidō shi*, vol 1 (1968).
　　　　John J. STEPHAN

Matsumoto

City in central Nagano Prefecture, central Honshū. A provincial capital from the 8th century, it was the base of the Ogasawara family during the 14th and 15th centuries and a prosperous castle town in the Edo period (1600–1868). Industries include traditional woodwork and silk reeling, electrical machinery, and dairy products. Shinshū University and a base of the Ground Self Defense Force are located here. Attractions include Matsumoto Castle, the Matsumoto Municipal Museum, the Matsumoto Folk Arts Museum, and Kaichi Gakkō, one of Japan's first modern elementary schools, built in 1876. With numerous hot spring resorts, including Asama and Utsukushigahara, Matsumoto is the base for trips to the Northern Alps and the highlands called UTSUKUSHIGAHARA. Pop: 192,086.

Matsumoto Basin

(Matsumoto Bonchi). In central Nagano Prefecture, central Honshū. Flanked by the Hida Mountains on the west and the Chikuma Mountains on the east, it consists of piedmont alluvial plains below the fault scarp and river terraces. The area is known for horseradish (*wasabi*) and mulberry trees. Light industries are also being developed here. The major city is Matsumoto. Area: approximately 300 sq km (116 sq mi).

Matsumoto Castle

A castle located in the city of Matsumoto, Nagano Prefecture. Formerly known as Fukashi Castle. Construction of the original castle began in 1504 by the Shimadate, a small Sengoku-period (1467–1568) *daimyō* family who were vassals of the powerful OGASAWARA FAMILY. Control of the castle passed into the hands of the TAKEDA FAMILY between 1555 and 1582, when the Ogasawara regained possession. Later it was occupied by the Ishikawa family, a loyal retainer family of Tokugawa Ieyasu. Under the Ishikawa, the presently surviving five-story main keep was built in 1594 when the castle was expanded and refurbished. The structure is a good example of Edo-style castle construction. The donjon, composed of a five-story main keep, a smaller keep, and a turret tower, is an impressive structure and has been designated a National Treasure.

Matsumoto Folk Arts Museum

(Matsumoto Mingeikan). Located in the city of Matsumoto, Nagano Prefecture. One of the most charming of the folk arts museums, it was opened in 1962 and contains Japanese, Ainu, Korean, Southeast Asian, and some European and Near Eastern material. Maruyama Tarō collected the items and has arranged their interesting display.
　　　　Laurance ROBERTS

Matsumoto Jōji (1877–1954)

Legal scholar and statesman. Born in Tōkyō, Matsumoto joined the Ministry of Agriculture and Commerce after graduation from Tōkyō University in 1900. In 1903 he became an associate professor at Tōkyō University, teaching courses in commercial law and the CIVIL CODE. From 1913 he served concurrently as an adviser (*sanjikan*) to the Cabinet Legislative Bureau (Naikaku Hōseikyoku). He left the university in 1919 to serve as vice-president of the SOUTH MANCHURIA RAILWAY. In 1923 he became director-general of the Cabinet Legislative Bureau and in 1934 minister of commerce and industry in the SAITŌ MAKOTO cabinet. He was also active as a lawyer. As minister of state in the SHIDEHARA KIJŪRŌ cabinet in 1945, he was charged with the problems of constitutional revision; his draft for a new constitution was essentially a rewording of the Meiji CONSTITUTION and was rejected by the American Occupation authorities. After 1950, as chairman of the Public Utilities Commission (Kōeki Jigyō Iinkai), he was responsible for reorganizing the electric power industry. Matsumoto's works include standard commercial law texts such as *Kaishōhō* (1914, Maritime Commercial Law) and *Nihon kaishahō ron* (1929, Japanese Company Law), as well as collections of monographs such as *Shihō rombunshū* (1926, Essays in Private Law) and *Shōhō kaishaku no shomondai* (1955, Problems in the Interpretation of Commercial Law). He is also remembered for his many legislative contributions, including the enactment of the BANKRUPTCY LAW (Hasan Hō, 1922), the Bills and Notes Law (Tegata Hō, 1932), and the 1938 revision of the COMMERCIAL CODE.
　　　　Takeuchi Akio

Matsumoto Seichō (1909-   )

Novelist. Real name Matsumoto Kiyoharu. Born in Fukuoka Prefecture. Self-supporting from an early age, he worked as a commercial artist for the newspaper *Asahi shimbun* from 1937 to 1957, after which he devoted himself full-time to the writing that he had begun in his early 40s. He won the Akutagawa Prize in 1952 for his "Aru Kokura nikki den" a short story about a man who searches all his life without success for the *Kokura nikki,* the diary of a famous Meiji-period (1868–1912) novelist. He soon shifted his energies to mystery writing and produced three best-sellers in two years—*Ten to sen* (1957–58; tr *Points and Lines,* 1970), *Me no kabe* (1957), and *Kuroi gashū* (1958)—becoming the most successful mystery writer in Japan. His trademark is an original plot, based on actual events, about an ordinary man who becomes entangled accidentally in a political or economic conspiracy where he must act an uncommon role. All of his works are imbued with a deep sense of social injustice and sympathy for victims of the Japanese meritocracy. More recently, he was written a number of articles about enigmatic political events in ancient Japanese history. Other works include *Nihon no kuroi kiri* (1960, Black Mist over Japan), a mystery; *Kodaishi gi* (1966–67), a work on ancient history; and *Shōwashi hakkutsu* (1956–71), a 13-volume series on the history of the Shōwa period (1926–).

Matsumura Goshun (1752–1811)

Painter in the BUNJINGA (literati painting) tradition who founded the Shijō school; also a HAIKU poet and a calligrapher. Goshun was born to an established Kyōto family, but he left his inherited position at a government mint to pursue in earnest the study of painting with the literati painter and haiku poet Yosa BUSON. Goshun soon became known as Buson's star pupil. In 1781 family tragedy and financial troubles seem to have led Goshun to move to Ikeda in Settsu Province (now part of Ōsaka Prefecture). In 1789 Goshun returned to Kyōto. Although Buson had died several years earlier, Goshun continued to work in his style, as can be seen in his painting *Willows and Egrets,* a masterpiece of this period of his life.

Goshun eventually joined the workshop of MARUYAMA ŌKYO, apparently as an equal rather than as a pupil, a demonstration of Ōkyo's respect for Goshun's talent. Goshun soon adopted Ōkyo's emphasis on naturalistic depiction, which included Western perspective, as well as his thoughtful compositional methods and choice of subjects. However, Goshun's later work nearly always retained the *bunjinga* trademarks of relaxed, refined brushwork, softer colors, and overall subjective approach. His finest work was in landscape and BIRD-AND-FLOWER PAINTING. After Ōkyo's death, Goshun established his atelier at Shijō in Kyōto. Goshun's students and later followers included his younger brother, MATSU-MURA KEIBUN, and OKAMOTO TOYOHIKO. See also MARUYAMA-SHIJŌ SCHOOL.   C. H. MITCHELL

Matsumura Jinzō (1856–1928)

Botanist. Born in Hitachi Province (now part of Ibaraki Prefecture). The son of the *karō* (family elder) of the Matsuoka domain in Hitachi. After leaving the Daigaku Nankō (now Tōkyō University) without completing his studies, he worked at the Tōkyō University botanical gardens (now KOISHIKAWA BOTANIC GARDEN) where he studied botany. Later he studied in Germany under Julius von Sachs (1832–97) and others. After his return to Japan, he taught at Tōkyō University. He contributed to the introduction into Japan of subjects such as plant taxonomy and plant anatomy. He wrote numerous books and articles, including *Nihon shokubutsu meii* (1884).   SUZUKI Zenji

Matsumura Keibun (1779–1843)

Painter of the Shijō school; a follower of his elder brother, MATSU-MURA GOSHUN, the school's founder. Keibun lived and worked in Kyōto. Along with Goshun and OKAMOTO TOYOHIKO, Keibun is generally considered one of the three most important artists of the Shijō school. He was a close associate of the Confucian scholar Koishi Genzui (1784–1849) and was well versed in the art theories of the Ming (1368–1644) and Qing (Ch'ing; 1644–1912) dynasties. He also studied with MARUYAMA ŌKYO, and, in fact, his style reveals more affinity to Ōkyo than to Goshun. His finest and best-known work is in BIRD-AND-FLOWER PAINTING (*kachōga*). In his best

paintings he employs bright, distinctive colors in his birds, which are seen against a background of equally brilliant foliage. See also MARUYAMA-SHIJŌ SCHOOL.   C. H. MITCHELL

Matsumura Kenzō (1883–1971)

Politician. Born in Toyama Prefecture; graduate of Waseda University. Matsumura entered politics after working for the newspaper *Yūbin hōchi shimbun* and served 13 consecutive terms (1928–69) in the House of Representatives, apart from a brief period (1946–49) when he was barred from public office by the OCCUPATION authorities (see OCCUPATION PURGE). Throughout his long career he was identified with conservative politics, serving as both minister of welfare and minister of education in the cabinet of Prince HIGASHIKUNI NARUHIKO (1945), as minister of agriculture and forestry in the SHI-DEHARA KIJŪRŌ cabinet (1945), and as minister of education in the second HATOYAMA ICHIRŌ cabinet (1955). He was a great admirer of Chinese culture and during the early 1960s actively promoted the normalization of relations with the People's Republic.   HARADA Katsumasa

matsumushisō

(Japanese scabiosa). *Scabiosa japonica,* biennial herb of the family Dipsacaceae (teasel), which grows wild in sunny mountain areas throughout Japan. It reaches a height of 90 centimeters (35 in). The leaves are opposite and pinnate. In the summer and fall, it produces purple flower heads with blossoms 4–5 centimeters (1.6–2 in) in diameter at the top of thin flower stalks. In high mountain areas, the *takane matsumushisō* (*Scabiosa japonica* var. *alpina*), a shorter variety with large flowers, is found. Western varieties of scabiosa are imported and cultivated as ornamentals or for flowers.   MATSUDA Osamu

Matsunaga Memorial Gallery

(Matsunaga Kinenkan). Former gallery located from 1959 to 1980 in Odawara, Kanagawa Prefecture. It housed a distinguished collection, assembled by MATSUNAGA YASUZAEMON, which has since been moved to the Fukuoka Art Museum in Fukuoka, Fukuoka Prefecture. The collection consists of Japanese painting, calligraphy, sculpture, metalwork, ceramics, lacquer, and armor; Chinese bronzes, jades, sculpture, painting, calligraphy, and porcelain; Korean ceramics; and a few objects from the West. Among the Japanese paintings is a fragment of the sutra scroll painting *Ingakyō* of the Nara period (710–794); other paintings, from the Heian period (794–1185) through the Edo period (1600–1868), include the often reproduced *Flower Baskets* by the RIMPA painter KENZAN. The most famous Japanese painting is the 11th-century *Kinkan shutsugen* (The Buddha Rising from His Golden Coffin). The Chinese bronzes range from the Shang dynasty (2nd millennium BC) through the Han dynasty (206 BC–220 AD). A painting of the Sixth Zen Patriarch, Huineng, is by the 13th-century Chinese artist of the Song dynasty (Sung; 960–1279), Muqi (Mu-ch'i; J: MOKKEI).   Laurance ROBERTS

Matsunaga Sekigo (1592–1657)

Neo-Confucian scholar of the early part of the Edo period (1600–1868); also known as Matsunaga Shōsan. Born in Kyōto, the son of the famous literary figure MATSUNAGA TEITOKU. Sekigo was a leading disciple of the Confucian scholar FUJIWARA SEIKA, to whom he was related. He opened his own school in 1648 and is said to have trained more than 5,000 students, including KINO-SHITA JUN'AN. In addition to his profound knowledge of Neo-Confucianism, his learning extended to Buddhism and classical Chinese literature.

Matsunaga Teitoku (1571–1653)

Classical scholar and poet. Teitoku was the founder of the pioneering nationwide Teimon school of *haikai* (the prototype of HAIKU), which he helped to establish as a poetic genre of importance equal to the older WAKA and *renga* (see RENGA AND HAIKAI). Born in Kyōto to an old family, he received an extensive and distinguished education, studying *waka* and poetics with HOSOKAWA YŪSAI, *renga* with SATOMURA JŌHA, and philosophy and classics with the scholars close to TOYOTOMI HIDEYOSHI, whom he served as secretary. The principal encyclopedist of his time, Teitoku compiled various lexicons on *waka* and *renga*, made an important contribution to the study of etymology and dialects, and widely distributed his commentaries on classics such as the *Tsurezuregusa* of YOSHIDA KENKŌ. He strove to liberate classical learning from the tradition of secret oral transmission in order to make it more accessible to the common people. In the field of *haikai* his most important work is *Gosan* (1651), in which he elaborated the rules of *haikai* composition, thus establishing *haikai* as a genre of poetry. This book became the standard text of the Teimon school. Among Teitoku's disciples are many important *waka* and *haikai* poets, including KITAMURA KIGIN and YASUHARA TEISHITSU.

Matsunaga Yasuzaemon (1875–1971)

Businessman. Leading figure of the electric power industry. Born in Nagasaki Prefecture; studied at Keiō Gijuku (now Keiō University). He established Fukuhaku Electric Railways Co (later Kyūshū Electric Railways Co) in 1909 and took control of a majority of the public utilities corporations in northern Kyūshū in about 1915. He served on the boards of directors of many electric power companies and was elected president of the Japan Electric Association in 1924. He strongly opposed the nationalization of power companies advocated by the bureaucracy and the military in 1936, but, unable to halt it, he retired when the power business was finally nationalized in 1938. After World War II he staged a comeback, championing private ownership of power companies, and brought about the present network of nine regional power companies. He established the Central Research Institute of Electric Power Industry in 1953 and became its director.   *TOGAI Yoshio*

Matsuo Bashō → Bashō

Matsuoka Eikyū (1881–1938)

Japanese-style painter known for his paintings of historical subjects in the classical Japanese YAMATO-E style. Given name Teruo. Born in Hyōgo Prefecture. A pupil of the KANŌ SCHOOL artist HASHIMOTO GAHŌ and the *yamato-e* artist Yamana Tsurayoshi (1836–1902), he graduated from and taught at the Tōkyō Bijutsu Gakkō (now Tōkyō University of Fine Arts and Music). His promotion of the revived *yamato-e* style led to his involvement in the establishment of three *yamato-e* artists' groups: the Kinreisha in 1916, the Shinkō Yamato-e Kai in 1921, and the Kokugain in 1935. He was a member of the Imperial Fine Arts Academy (Teikoku Bijutsuin). The folklorist YANAGITA KUNIO was his elder brother.

Matsuoka Joan (1669–1747)

Specialist in *honzōgaku* (traditional pharmacognosy) who continued studies begun by INŌ JAKUSUI. Born in Kyōto, he first studied Confucianism, guided by YAMAZAKI ANSAI and ITŌ JINSAI. Later he studied pharmacognosy under Inō Jakusui. Matsuoka taught ONO RANZAN and Toda Kyokuzan (1696–1769).   *SUZUKI Zenji*

Matsuoka Komakichi (1888–1958)

Prewar labor leader. Matsuoka worked as a mechanic in various parts of the country from the age of 15. In 1906 he was baptized a Christian. In about 1912, he became involved in the labor movement and joined YŪAIKAI, Japan's earliest labor group, founded by SUZUKI BUNJI. As one of Yūaikai's leaders, Matsuoka worked to reorganize the group into a labor union in 1921. When left-wing members criticized him for his conservative unionism, he excluded them from SŌDŌMEI, the union he helped organize.

In 1929 Matsuoka represented Japanese labor at a meeting of the International Labor Organization (ILO). He became chairman of Sōdōmei in 1932. When the Sino-Japanese War broke out in 1937, he became a supporter of the war. After World War II, he reorganized Sōdōmei in 1946 and again served as chairman. In the same year he was elected to the House of Representatives. In 1947 he became Speaker of the House. After 1950 he was the Japanese representative at many international labor conferences.   *KURITA Ken*

Matsuoka Yōsuke (1880–1946)

Diplomat and foreign minister. Born in Murozumi, Yamaguchi Prefecture. In 1893 he went to Oregon, seeking an opportunity to restore his family's fortune, and graduated from the University of Oregon School of Law in 1900. In 1904, two years after his return to Japan, Matsuoka passed the foreign service examination. His diplomatic assignments included Shanghai, Dalian (Talien; J: Dairen), Beijing (Peking), St. Petersburg, and Washington, DC. At the Paris Peace Conference ending World War I, Matsuoka was the officer in charge of information for the Japanese delegation.

Dissatisfied with the diplomatic service, Matsuoka joined the Japanese-owned SOUTH MANCHURIA RAILWAY Company (SMR) as a director from 1921 to 1926. In 1927, at the request of the RIKKEN SEIYŪKAI party president TANAKA GIICHI, he traveled to Central and North China with the Seiyūkai politicians YAMAMOTO JŌTARŌ and MORI KAKU and met CHIANG KAI-SHEK. That same year he was appointed vice-president of the SMR. In 1930 he was elected to the House of Representatives as a Seiyūkai candidate. Calling Manchuria and Inner Mongolia "Japan's lifeline," Matsuoka was a strong advocate of the creation of a satellite state in Manchuria (see MANCHUKUO). In 1932 he was sent to Shanghai as a personal representative of Foreign Minister YOSHIZAWA KENKICHI to negotiate a truce to end the SHANGHAI INCIDENT, a brief military clash between Chinese and Japanese troops that had taken place in January of that year. In the face of international censure of Japanese aggression in Manchuria (see MANCHURIAN INCIDENT), Matsuoka initially favored Japan's remaining in the League of Nations, and as chief delegate from 1932 he worked diligently toward that end. When the League proceedings went against Japan on the Manchurian question (see LYTTON COMMISSION), Foreign Minister UCHIDA KŌSAI suggested that the delegation might walk out. Matsuoka took the position that Japan should withdraw to preserve its honor and led his delegation out of the League in 1933.

In December 1933 Matsuoka resigned from the Diet and embarked on his "political party dissolution *(seitō kaishō)* movement." This movement was suspended when Matsuoka was named president of the SMR in 1935. The SMR under Matsuoka saw great expansion in railway mileage and in research activities, such as coal liquefaction. However, the power of the SMR was diminished as the Manchukuo government, dominated by the Japanese GUANDONG (KWANTUNG) ARMY, took over more and more of the functions previously assigned to the company, including management of heavy industries. He resigned from the SMR in 1939.

From 22 July 1940 to 18 July 1941 Matsuoka was foreign minister in KONOE FUMIMARO's second cabinet. He concluded the TRIPARTITE PACT with Germany and Italy (27 September 1940), through which he hoped to negotiate with the United States from a position of strength and to put pressure on Chiang Kai-shek's government in Chongqing (Chungking) to end the war in China that had broken out in July 1937. His grand strategy included alignment with the Soviet Union; this was implemented by the signing of a neutrality pact (13 April 1941). During his trip to Berlin, Rome, and Moscow (March–April 1941), however, informal talks in Washington that had been initiated by Bishop James E. Walsh and Father James Drought and subsequently joined by Secretary of State Cordell HULL and Ambassador NOMURA KICHISABURŌ resulted in a "proposal for understanding." Matsuoka rejected this document on his return to Japan, and for this he was dismissed from the Konoe cabinet.

In April 1946, following the end of World War II, Matsuoka was indicted as a class-A war criminal but died in June, before the trial was concluded. Matsuoka was exceptionally skillful in his use of radio, newsreels, and newspapers; he liked to follow secret negotiations with dramatic announcements of results attained. His often contradictory statements were not those of a man deranged—as some assumed—but of a calculating politician who wished to appeal to the masses for his own political ends.

■ ——David J. Lu, *Matsuoka Yōsuke to sono jidai* (1981). Matsuoka Yōsuke, *Ugoku Mammō* (1931). Ogiwara Kiwamu, *Matsuoka Yōsuke: Sono hito to shōgai* (1974).   *David J. LU*

Matsuratō

A league *(tō)* of warriors (see BUSHIDAN) who controlled the Matsura region (in what is now Nagasaki and Saga prefectures) from the 12th through the 15th century. These several dozen warrior families, bound by both real and fictitious kinship ties, apparently stemmed from pirate groups. They fought on the losing side in the Battle of DANNOURA in 1185 but submitted to the victorious MINAMOTO NO YORITOMO soon afterward and received appointments as officials in local private estates (SHŌEN). In the middle of the 14th century the league was reorganized into "upper" and "lower" groups (Kami Matsura and Shimo Matsura). During the Muromachi period (1333–1568) the league drew up a set of regulations to ensure group solidarity; four of these, touching on such matters as concerted action vis-à-vis the Muromachi shogunate, the settling of intraleague disputes, and the treatment of absconding peasants and bondsmen, still survive.

matsuri → festivals

Matsusaka

Also known as Matsuzaka. City in central Mie Prefecture, central Honshū. It developed as a castle town after a castle was built by GAMŌ UJISATO in 1588; it was also an important POST-STATION TOWN on the route to the Ise and Kumano Sanzan shrines. Long known for its hard-working merchants (the MITSUI originally came from Matsusaka) and cotton textiles. It has lumber and glass industries and the surrounding area is known for its beef. Of interest are Suzunoya, the home of the scholar MOTOORI NORINAGA; the remains of Matsusaka Castle; and the complex of mounded tombs (KOFUN) at Takarazuka. Pop: 113,481.

Matsushima

A group of scenic islands in Matsushima Bay, Miyagi Prefecture, northern Honshū; composed of more than 260 tiny islands. Known as one of the so-called Nihon Sankei (Japan's three most beautiful sights, the other two being AMANOHASHIDATE and ITSUKUSHIMA), Matsushima's scenic beauty has been celebrated by the 17th-century *haiku* poet Matsuo Bashō. The temple Zuiganji, said to have been built in 828, has been designated a National Treasure. Activities in addition to tourism include the production of oysters and seaweed (*nori*).

Matsushima Bay

(Matsushima Wan). Part of southern Sendai Bay, Miyagi Prefecture, northern Honshū. Dotted with more than 260 small islands, Matsushima Bay has been a noted scenic spot since ancient times. Marine products are *nori* (a kind of seaweed) and oysters; seed oysters are exported overseas. Area: approximately 40 sq km (15 sq mi).

Matsushiro

District in the southern part of the city of Nagano, northern Nagano Prefecture, central Honshū. During the Edo period (1600–1868), Matsushiro was a castle town of the Sanada family, and *samurai* residences remain today. During World War II, the Imperial Headquarters of the armed forces was constructed underground here; it is now being used as a seismological observatory.

Matsushita Communication Industrial Co, Ltd

(Matsushita Tsūshin Kōgyō). Manufacturer of data processing, audiovisual, telecommunication, and acoustic equipment; measuring and control devices; and car stereos and other automotive instruments. It was founded in 1958 when three departments of the parent MATSUSHITA ELECTRIC INDUSTRIAL CO, LTD, formed a separate company. Its products are sold by MATSUSHITA ELECTRIC TRADING CO, LTD, throughout the world under the Matsushita group's well-known Panasonic brand; its export ratio stands at about 30 percent. Sales for the fiscal year ending November 1981 totaled ¥198.6 billion (US $887.6 million) and capitalization was ¥6.8 billion (US $30.4 million). The head office is in Yokohama.

Matsushita Daisaburō (1878–1935)

Japanese-language scholar. Born in Shizuoka Prefecture, Matsushita graduated from and later taught at Kokugakuin University. He established a theory of Japanese grammar that bears his name, based on the three units *genji, shi,* and *danku,* which closely approximated morphemes, words, and sentences, respectively. He also wrote grammatical studies of spoken Japanese. His principle works are: *Nihon zokugo bunten* (1901, A Grammar of Japanese Colloquialisms); *Kaisen hyōjun Nihon bumpō* (1928, Revised Standard Japanese Grammar); and *Hyōjun Nihon kōgohō* (1930, A Standard

Matsushima

Some of the many pine-covered islands in Matsushima Bay.

Grammar of Spoken Japanese). He also helped edit the *Kokka taikan* (1901–03; 1925–26), a comprehensive four-volume index to the great canon of Japanese classical poetry. *Uwano Zendō*

Matsushita Electric Industrial Co, Ltd

(Matsushita Denki Sangyō). One of the world's largest manufacturers of consumer electronic products. The company's products are marketed under the Panasonic and Quasar brand names in the United States and Canada and under the National trademark in the rest of the world. Audio hi-fi products are also marketed under the Technics trademark. "To contribute to the betterment of society"— a goal established by founder MATSUSHITA KŌNOSUKE—has been the managerial principle of the company since its establishment as a small electric fixture plant in 1918. The company was reorganized in its present form in 1935.

Matsushita Electric features the integrated production of components and finished products, including home appliances, consumer electronic items, communication and measuring equipment, industrial equipment, business machines, lighting equipment, tubes, semiconductors, and batteries. It has an active research and development program with basic and applied research conducted in 23 laboratories as well as in the engineering department of every product manufacturing division, and in 1981 possessed over 50,000 industrial patents in Japan and over 10,000 abroad. The company operates 40 manufacturing and 32 sales organizations in 33 countries, employing 38,000 people. It exports a wide range of products to more than 130 countries around the world. Sales for the fiscal year ending November 1981 totaled ¥2.3 trillion (US $10.3 billion), of which radio equipment accounted for 42 percent, home appliances 22 percent, communication and industrial equipment 14 percent, electronic components 13 percent, and others 9 percent. The export ratio was 32 percent and the company was capitalized at ¥71 billion (US $317.3 million) in the same year. Corporate headquarters are located in Kadoma, Ōsaka Prefecture.

Matsushita Electric Trading Co, Ltd

(Matsushita Denki Bōeki). Trading firm handling export and import operations for the group of companies affiliated with MATSUSHITA ELECTRIC INDUSTRIAL CO, LTD. Founded in 1935 by MATSUSHITA KŌNOSUKE. It initiated the export of electrical products to the United States in 1959 when, jointly with its parent, Matsushita Electric, it established the Matsushita Electric Corporation of America in New York. The company has built a worldwide manufacturing and sales network by setting up 32 overseas sales companies, 40 production companies, and 21 foreign-based offices. Sales for the fiscal year ending September 1981 totaled ¥1.1 trillion (US $4.8 billion) and capitalization stood at ¥5.4 billion (US $23.5 million). The corporate headquarters are in Ōsaka.

Matsushita Electric Works, Ltd

(Matsushita Denkō). Manufacturer of a wide variety of electrical and building products. A member of the Matsushita group, the company was founded in 1935 by MATSUSHITA KŌNOSUKE. Prod-

Matsuyama —— Dōgo Hot Spring

Located in eastern Matsuyama, the Dōgo Hot Spring is one of the oldest hot springs in Japan. The three-story wooden structure in the foreground, the Shinrokaku bathhouse, dates from 1894.

ucts include precision controls, switches, relays, and various construction materials. The company has 22 subsidiaries in Japan, and two overseas, Aromat in the United States and MS Relais in West Germany. Sales for the fiscal year ending November 1981 totaled ¥485.9 billion (US $2.2 billion), of which lighting equipment accounted for 32 percent, electrical construction materials 25 percent, building and plastics materials 32 percent, and personal care products and timepieces 11 percent. In that same year the firm was capitalized at ¥23.9 billion (US $106.8 million). The head office is in Kadoma, Ōsaka Prefecture.

Matsushita Kōnosuke (1894–   )

Founder of the Matsushita electric companies. Born into a poor farming family in Wakayama Prefecture, Matsushita worked at various manual jobs from the age of 9. In 1918 he opened a small electric fixture shop in Ōsaka, where he had a huge success in developing small bicycle lamp batteries. He enlarged this into a home electric appliance plant in 1933, and reorganized it as MATSUSHITA ELECTRIC INDUSTRIAL CO, LTD, in 1935, becoming its president. Although purged for a time by the Allied Occupation authorities after World War II, Matsushita returned to public life in 1947 and, after strenuous efforts, reconstructed his company. He established contractual ties with N. V. Philips' Gloeilampenfabriken in 1952 and had the highest personal income in Japan for that year. Always seeking innovations, Matsushita developed a series of home electric appliances and pushed his company to the forefront of the industry through introduction of mass-production systems and original sales tactics. He also placed extra emphasis on exports and made National an internationally known brand name. Even when American-style management swept through Japan in the postwar years, Matsushita stuck to traditional Japanese management practices. Matsushita launched the PHP (Peace and Happiness through Prosperity) movement in 1946 and advocated a management philosophy aimed at attaining peace and prosperity for society through business activities. Matsushita has also been involved in a variety of cultural activities, including establishment of the Asuka Conservation Association, promotion of Shintō studies, and creation of the Matsushita School of Government and Business.　　　　　　　　　　　　*Yui Tsunehiko*

Matsushita–Kotobuki Electronics Industries, Ltd

(Matsushita–Kotobuki Denshi Kōgyō). Manufacturer of electronic, heating, and acoustic equipment. A member of the Matsushita group of companies, it was founded in 1969 when three Matsushita-affiliated companies in Shikoku were merged. Its three chief products are color television sets, tape recorders, and electrical versions of the traditional *kotatsu* (a small quilt-covered table with a heating device underneath that is used to warm the feet and legs). In recent years the company has expanded its production of home videotape recorders. MATSUSHITA ELECTRIC INDUSTRIAL CO, LTD, controls 60 percent of the firm's stock. Sales for the fiscal year ending November 1981 totaled ¥213.9 billion (US $956 million), of which exports accounted for 70 percent, and capitalization was ¥6 billion (US $26.8 million). The corporate headquarters are located in the city of Takamatsu, Kagawa Prefecture.

Matsushita Reiki Co, Ltd

Manufacturer chiefly of refrigerators, freezers, and air conditioners. Member of the Matsushita group of companies. Founded in 1939 as Nakagawa Kikai for the manufacture of industrial machinery. After World War II, the firm, while still independent, initiated the production of refrigerators. In 1952 it was absorbed by MATSUSHITA ELECTRIC INDUSTRIAL CO, LTD, and began producing washing machines sold under the domestic brand name National. In 1962 it expanded into the fields of commercial refrigeration, freezing cabinets, and household freezers. The firm took on its present name in 1972. Aiming at increased diversification in the latter half of the 1970s, the firm began producing air conditioners. It has a compressor plant in Singapore. Matsushita Electric Industrial Co, Ltd, holds 50.5 percent of Matsushita Reiki stock. Sales for the fiscal year ending September 1981 totaled ¥138.2 billion (US $600.8 million) and capitalization stood at ¥7.9 billion (US $34.3 million). The head office is in Higashi Ōsaka.

Matsuura

City in northern Nagasaki Prefecture, Kyūshū, on the Genkai Sea. What was once a flourishing coal-mining town has become, under government sponsorship, a farming and industrial area. The scenic coastline offers good fishing and swimming. Pop: 24,565.

Matsuura Takeshirō (1818–1888)

Explorer of EZO (now Hokkaidō). Born in Ise Province (now Mie Prefecture), he explored Ezo three times from 1845 and made several maps. It was at his suggestion that Ezo was renamed Hokkaidō. After the Meiji Restoration (1868), he served as an official in the Hokkaidō Colonization Office (1869).

Matsuyama

Capital of Ehime Prefecture, Shikoku. It developed as a castle town after the construction of a castle by Katō Yoshiakira in 1603. Petrochemical and soda factories are located in a coastal industrial zone and citrus fruits are grown on nearby mountain slopes. The city is served by several railway lines and an airport. Visitors are drawn to the DŌGO HOT SPRING and Matsuyama Castle. Matsuyama has several literary associations, being the birthplace of the poets MASAOKA SHIKI and TAKAHAMA KYOSHI, and providing the setting for NATSUME SŌSEKI's popular novel *Botchan*. A traditional product is *iyo-gasuri*, a cotton cloth. Pop: 401,682.

Matsuyama Plain

(Matsuyama Heiya). Located in central Ehime Prefecture, Shikoku. Bordering the Inland Sea and located along the Median Tectonic Line with fault scarps in the south, it consists of alluvial fans of the river Shigenobugawa. Mandarin oranges are cultivated in the hills surrounding the rice-producing lowlands. Oil refineries and petrochemical plants are found along the seacoast. The major city is Matsuyama, and a well-known resort is Dōgo Hot Spring. Area: approximately 100 sq km (39 sq mi).

Matsuyama Zenzō (1925–   )

Screen writer and film director. Married to actress TAKAMINE HIDEKO. He has written frequently for directors KINOSHITA KEISUKE and KOBAYASHI MASAKI, among others. He joined SHŌCHIKU CO, LTD, in 1948, starting as an assistant director and working in the script department. He assisted Kinoshita Keisuke for several years. One of his fellow assistants was Kobayashi Masaki, with whom he later collaborated on several important projects, writing the screenplays for *Anata kaimasu* (1956, I'll Buy You), about the bidding for high-school athletes by professional baseball teams; *Kuroi kawa* (1957, Black River), on the effects of the American military presence in Japan; and Kobayashi's acclaimed masterpiece, *Ningen no jōken* (1959–61, The Human Condition), a harsh chronicle of one man's experience in World War II.

Matsuyama's favorite themes deal with important social issues, often involving individuals who suffer injustice. His debut film as a director, *Na mo naku mazushiku utsukushiku* (1961, Nameless, Poor, Beautiful), about the struggles of a deaf-mute couple to lead normal, productive lives, was highly praised. David OWENS

Matsuzaka → Matsusaka

Matsuzakaya Co, Ltd

Leading department store with headquarters in Nagoya. Founded in 1611 as a dry goods store. Although the firm was incorporated in 1910, its control has remained for generations in the Itō family, the founders. The company has a national network of nine department stores led by its Tōkyō (Ueno and Ginza) and Ōsaka stores. It makes purchases jointly with the Daimaru chain of department stores and has invested in, and made commercial agreements with, a number of regional department stores. Through its subsidiary, Matsuzakaya Store, it has diversified into the supermarket business. It has also begun the production of furniture, interior furnishings, and recreation equipment. In Hong Kong it has a joint venture company, Hang Lung Matsuzakaya. Sales for the fiscal year ending February 1982 totaled ¥343.2 billion (US $1.5 billion) while capitalization was ¥7.3 billion (US $31.5 million).

Mattō

City in central Ishikawa Prefecture, central Honshū, on the river Tedorigawa. Mattō developed as a distribution center for rice. In addition to a Japanese National Railways factory, automobile, machinery, ceramics, and foodstuff plants are located here. The temple Shōkōji maintains a small museum and what is believed to be the grave of the poet KAGA NO CHIYO, who was born here. Pop: 43,766.

mawari-dōrō

(revolving shadow lantern). A lantern designed to create shadow pictures. Introduced from China, the *mawari-dōrō* was popular during the Edo period (1600–1868) for viewing on summer nights. The lantern consists of a cylinder pasted over with paper silhouettes and placed inside a circular frame covered with thin paper or cloth; heated air from a lighted candle in the center of the cylinder causes this to revolve and produce moving images on the translucent outer covering. SAITŌ Ryōsuke

Mayama Seika (1878–1948)

Playwright, essayist, novelist. Born in Sendai, Miyagi Prefecture. After an unsettled youth, he went to Tōkyō to pursue a literary career and served his literary apprenticeship with OGURI FŪYŌ. He attracted attention as a promising naturalist writer with *Minami Koizumi Mura* (1907), a novel about peasant life, and several other works including plays. He subsequently spent 11 years in obscurity as a SHIMPA playwright before reemerging onto the literary scene in 1924 with a short historical play, *Gemboku to Chōei*, which was highly acclaimed. Over the next 18 years there followed a continuous stream of historical plays which were distinguished for their combination of historical accuracy and interplay of personalities. His most famous play cycle, *Genroku chūshingura* (1934–41), is a realistic retelling of the celebrated FORTY-SEVEN RŌNIN INCIDENT of 1703. Many of his dramas (about 200 in all) are still performed today. Mayama was also noted for his scholarly studies of the writers SAIKAKU and Takizawa BAKIN. Brian POWELL

May Day Incident

(Mēdē Jiken). Confrontation between demonstrators and police in Tōkyō on 1 May 1952. May Day is traditionally observed in Japan by radical labor groups and students to commemorate labor. There had been growing antigovernment and anti-American sentiment following the signing of the SAN FRANCISCO PEACE TREATY and the United States–Japan Security Treaty in September 1951. The treaties had become effective three days earlier, on 28 April, and frustration and dissatisfaction turned to anger when permission to hold a May Day rally in front of the Imperial Palace grounds was denied. After the official dispersal of the rally in Hibiya Park, about 300 demonstrators (mainly students) clashed with police in front of the Imperial Palace grounds. The police were armed with pistols and tear gas; the students, who were joined by several thousand participants from the rally, retaliated with sticks, poles, and stones. They also set fire to parked cars outside Hibiya Park belonging to American military personnel. Peace was finally restored at six in the evening. Two civilians were dead and over 2,000 injured. Under the Riot Law, 1,232 people were arrested, and 259 were indicted. The hearings took place over 17 years and 9 months. On 28 January 1970 the Tōkyō District Court found 81 people guilty of breaking the Riot Law and 11 of other misdemeanors. An appeal was made, and on 21 November 1972 the Tōkyō High Court found 16 defendants guilty of charges other than violation of the Riot Law. The incident was seen by Americans as being partly instigated by the Japan Communist Party. See also UNITED STATES–JAPAN SECURITY TREATIES.

Mayet, Paul (1846–1920)

German economist and one of many FOREIGN EMPLOYEES OF THE MEIJI PERIOD (1868–1912) who advised the government. Invited to Japan in 1875, Mayet assisted various government departments in formulating financial and economic policies, including plans for a postal savings system, fire and farm insurance, public bond issues, and an independent Board of Audit. He also taught language and statistics courses at several universities and made an important study of contemporary Japanese agriculture, pointing out the hardships faced by small farmers and the possibility of relief through land-tax reform. Returning to Germany in 1893, he served in the German Bureau of Statistics.

May 15th Incident

(Goichigo Jiken). Attempted coup d'etat by young naval officers on 15 May 1932; their assassination of Prime Minister INUKAI TSUYOSHI led to the demise of the party cabinet system. As a result of the ratification of the 1930 London Naval Treaty (see LONDON NAVAL CONFERENCES), which was seen by some elements as compromising Japan's naval security, a movement grew among young military officers to reorganize the state. The Japanese economy was then in deep recession, the farming villages being particularly impoverished, and the influence of the JAPAN COMMUNIST PARTY was growing; at the same time, party politics was tainted by corruption, and the large financial-industrial combines (zaibatsu) such as Mitsui and Mitsubishi seemed bent on taking advantage of the economic unease to reap enormous profits. To some it seemed that nothing short of radical national reform could solve Japan's problems. In the OCTOBER INCIDENT of 1931 army staff officers failed in their attempt to form a military government and decided, temporarily, to abandon "direct action" and resort to legal means. Within the navy, officers led by sublieutenant Fujii Hitoshi established contacts with the ultranationalist INOUE NISSHŌ with the aim of effecting a "SHŌWA RESTORATION" by assassinating leading political and business figures. They planned to act on 11 February 1932, but Fujii was mobilized and killed in the SHANGHAI INCIDENT. Inoue and his terrorist group then took the initiative and carried out a series of murders (see LEAGUE OF BLOOD INCIDENT). Not to be outdone, naval officers, led by sublieutenants Koga Kiyoshi and Nakamura Yoshio, planned their own course of action. They were reinforced by TACHIBANA KŌZABURŌ and his students from the AIKYŌJUKU, army cadets, and remnants of the League of Blood. Provided with funds and weapons by ŌKAWA SHŪMEI and other ultrarightists, this group struck on 15 May. They divided themselves into four groups; one attacked the official residence of Prime Minister Inukai and killed him, while others attacked the residence of Lord Keeper of the Privy Seal MAKINO NOBUAKI, the headquarters of the RIKKEN SEIYŪKAI party, and the Mitsubishi Bank. The group led by Tachibana attacked several transformer substations, hoping that with Tōkyō plunged into darkness, martial law would be declared as the first step toward the reorganization of the state. Apart from the assassination of the prime minister, however, nothing was accomplished, and all the participants surrendered to military police.

The officers were extremely short-sighted, with no definite follow-up plan and only a vague anticipation that military leaders would take some action after the declaration of martial law. After the incident, army leaders requested that martial law be proclaimed, but it was not. However, after the fall of the Inukai cabinet, army leaders informed political leaders that they were immovably opposed to any party cabinet. The elder statesman SAIONJI KIMMOCHI gave up his hopes for the continuation of party government and chose Admiral SAITŌ MAKOTO to form the next cabinet. Saitō, a man known for his moderate ideas, tried to form a "national unity" cabinet based on an equal balance of power among the military, the bureaucracy, and the political parties; but the retention of Army Minister ARAKI SADAO (widely suspected of sympathy with the young officers) ensured the unchecked influence of the military (GUMBU) in political affairs.

Of the men involved in the incident, the officers were subjected to courts-martial, while civilians like Tachibana and Ōkawa were indicted by the Tōkyō District Court. The trials began in 1933. Particularly in the case of the courts-martial, the patriotism of the defendants was widely publicized by the mass media under military pressure, resulting in public sentiment to reduce their punishment. The severest sentence, life imprisonment, was passed on Tachibana, and the longest for a naval officer was 15 years. This lenient treatment was to abet further "direct action" by military officers. See also MILITARISM.

Awaya Kentarō

May Fourth Movement

One of the political and cultural landmarks of 20th-century China. In the narrow sense the term refers to the May Fourth Incident, the 4 May 1919 student demonstrations in Beijing (Peking)—supported by students, merchants, and workers in other cities—against the decision of the Paris Peace Conference to transfer German rights in Shandong (Shantung) Province to Japan and against China's own officials for collaborating with the Japanese. However, it is more often used in a broader sense to refer to an intellectual movement that had already been in progress for several years and of which the 4 May demonstrations became a symbol. This movement was associated with the growth of nationalism, the development of a new literature written in the vernacular language, and an accelerated political radicalism. In brief, the term is a shorthand expression that sums up China's search between the mid-1910s and mid-1920s for antitraditionalist political, cultural, and social alternatives; while at the same time it is a symbol of passionate nationalism, often with a strongly anti-Japanese tinge.

The May Fourth Incident —— During World War I, Japan had acquired German rights in Shandong. It obtained Chinese recognition of these rights as part of the TWENTY-ONE DEMANDS in 1915 and later secured international recognition by signing secret agreements with France, Great Britain, Italy, and Russia in 1917. This was followed by a subsequent agreement with China in connection with the NISHIHARA LOANS in 1918. However, since China had joined the Allies in August 1917, the Chinese public expected the peace negotiators to follow the Fourteen Points announced by the American president Woodrow Wilson and to restore Shandong to China. But the Paris Peace Conference upheld Japan's treaty rights. When this decision became known in China in early May 1919, Beijing students felt betrayed by the foreign powers and China's own officials. On May 4 about 5,000 students gathered at the Gate of Heavenly Peace and marched on to the Legation Quarter, but they were barred from entering. The students then burned the residence of CAO RULIN (Ts'ao Ju-lin), the official regarded as the mastermind of collaboration with Japan. A number of students were arrested. Indignation against the government mounted. Throughout May and June, students, including women, organized unions and staged demonstrations not only in Beijing but also in other major cities. Among the student organizers were future leaders like Mao Zedong (Mao Tse-tung), Zhou Enlai (Chou En-lai), and Luo Jialun (Lo Chia-lun; b 1895). The students were supported by workers, who went on strike, and merchants, who boycotted Japanese goods. The protest was so overwhelming that the Beijing government, though it relied on Japanese support, had to dismiss three high officials favored by warlord DUAN QIRUI (Tuan Ch'i-jui). Moreover, the Chinese delegates in Paris refused to sign the peace treaty. Chinese students viewed this outcome as the triumph of nationalism.

The May Fourth Movement —— The students' triumph added vitality to a nationalistic intellectual movement that had been underway since the middle of the decade. The intellectual ferment was begun by men who had studied abroad and returned to teach at modern universities. Beijing University took the lead. Chancellor Cai Yuanpei (Ts'ai Yüan-p'ei; 1867–1940) assembled a number of talented men, including Chen Duxiu (Ch'en Tu-hsiu; 1879–1942) and Hu Shi (Hu Shih; 1891–1962). The best known of the magazines

established by the new intellectuals was Chen's monthly *Xin qingnian* (Hsin-ch'ing-nien; New Youth), which was launched in 1915. In its pages Chen advocated democracy and science, Hu Shi promoted the use of the vernacular language in writing, and LU XUN (Lu Hsün) attacked Confucianism in his "Diary of a Madman." The new Chinese intellectuals vehemently condemned tradition and eagerly promoted Western ideas of romantic love, the nuclear family, democratic government, technological development, and Marxism.

Despite their penchant for Western values, they intensely opposed the foreign powers' policy of aggression toward China. Two important political consequences of the May Fourth Movement were increased antagonism toward Japan as the embodiment of foreign aggression, and growing discontent with China's warlord governments. Students and journalists exposed the warlords' lack of patriotism (some of them had close associations with the Japanese), thus hastening their demise at the hands of the Nationalists (Guomindang; Kuomintang) in 1927–28. The May Fourth slogan "Save the Country from Imperialists and Warlords" was taken up by the Nationalists. More significantly, the intellectual and political fermentation of the time gave birth to the Chinese Communist Party, which held its first national congress in 1921. It favored a radical approach to change and after the late 1920s competed for power with the Nationalists. The struggle between these two parties polarized intellectuals, but both groups justifiably claim to follow in the tradition of the May Fourth Movement.

🔖——Joseph T. Chen, *The May Fourth Movement in Shanghai: The Making of a Social Movement in Modern China* (1971). Chow Tse-tsung, *The May Fourth Movement: Intellectual Revolution in Modern China* (1960). Gaimushō, *Nihon gaikō bunsho, 1918, vol 2, part 1; 1919, vol 2 part 2* (1969–70). Zhongguo Kexue Yuan (Chung-kuo K'o-hsüeh Yüan), *Wusi aiguo yundong ziliao (Wu-ssu ai-kuo yün-tung tzu-liao),* 3 vols (1959). *Madeleine CHI*

mayoke

Talismans or rituals believed to dispel evil sprits and demons and the personal misfortunes and natural disasters presumably caused by these agents. The practice of hanging charms (e.g., mushrooms, boar's feet, fish tails, sea shells, ladles, and magical inscriptions) from gates and eaves to prevent evil spirits from entering one's home or placing a sword at the pillow of a corpse are examples of *mayoke.* Since children are believed to be particularly susceptible to the predations of evil spirits that cause illness, there are special forms of *mayoke* for their protection. These include the practice of embroidering brightly colored protective insignia on the back of a child's *kimono* or tracing an X or the Chinese character for "dog" (the natural enemy of malevolent spirits) on a child's forehead with ash. The charms and amulets (GOFU) issued at temples and shrines are also believed to ward off evil spirits, as are other special appurtenances, such as the HAMAYA AND HAMAYUMI (lucky bow and arrow) sold at shrines at the NEW YEAR. See also BAKEMONO; ONI; SETSUBUN.

INOKUCHI Shōji

May 30th Incident

(Gosanjū Jiken). On 30 May 1925 the police at the SHANGHAI INTERNATIONAL SETTLEMENT fired on Chinese workers and students who were demonstrating against the killing of a Chinese worker in a Japanese textile mill by a Japanese foreman. The death of 13 protestors prompted nationwide strikes, demonstrations, and boycotts that became collectively known as the May 30th Movement. The movement marked a new height in agitation against foreign privileges and exploitation in China, as many different social groups joined in the protest. A further incident occurred on 23 June 1925, when British and French troops killed 52 Chinese in Guangzhou (Canton). The ensuing 15-month boycott against British-ruled Hong Kong drastically reduced British trade in southern China. The May 30th Movement saw the growth of a vigorous labor movement in Shanghai and other treaty ports. It also prompted modification of the privileges of foreign powers in China that had been made possible by unequal treaties. The Chinese gained some influence in the Municipal Council in Shanghai, hitherto controlled by foreigners, and after 1927 they were no longer subject to foreign courts. In 1925–26 the foreign powers finally held the tariff conference originally called for at the WASHINGTON CONFERENCE of 1921–22. The Japanese government sent a delegation led by SHIDEHARA KIJŪRŌ. These negotiations and a 1926 extraterritoriality commission meeting in Beijing (Peking) were disrupted by the nationalist party's Northern Expedition (1926–28), and Chinese tariff autonomy was not regained until 1933.

Mayuzumi Toshirō (1929–)

Composer. Born in Yokohama. Mayuzumi completed postgraduate studies at the Tōkyō Ongaku Gakkō (now Tōkyō University of Fine Arts and Music) and studied at the Paris Conservatory. He is responsible for introducing electronic music to Japan, and his *XYZ* (1953) was the first Japanese work composed in the manner of *musique concrète*. Influenced by Buddhist music, in 1958 he composed the symphony *Nehan* (Nirvana) and in 1963 the cantata *Keka* (Repentance). In 1976 he also arranged MISHIMA YUKIO's novel *Kinkakuji* as an opera which was first performed by the Berlin Opera. He has earned additional renown as the host for the television program "Concert without a Name." *ABE Yasushi*

Mazaki Jinzaburō (1876–1956)

Army officer. Born in Saga Prefecture. He graduated from the Army Academy in 1897. He was made a general in 1933 and appointed inspector general of military education a year later. Together with General ARAKI SADAO, Mazaki was considered a leader of the KŌDŌHA, the army faction that called for spiritual training rather than mechanization. Suspected of complicity in a Kōdōha plot to assassinate political figures, he was dismissed in 1935. The following year, when Kōdōha officers attempted a coup d'etat (see FEBRUARY 26TH INCIDENT), he was indicted on suspicion that he had assisted them, but was exonerated for lack of evidence. At the WAR CRIMES TRIALS after World War II, Mazaki was sentenced to prison for two years. *HATA Ikuhiko*

Meakandake

An active volcanic group in the Chishima Volcanic Zone, eastern Hokkaidō. It consists of stratovolcanoes with complex features. The foothills are covered with primeval forests of Yeddo spruce (*ezomatsu*) and Sakhalin fir (*todomatsu*). Meakan Hot Spring is located in the southwestern foothills. Meakandake is part of Akan National Park. Height: 1,503 m (4,930 ft).

meakashi

(private investigators). Agents hired by city commissioners (MACHI BUGYŌ) during the Edo period (1600–1868) to help the *dōshin* or basic police force in tracking down criminals. Because many of them were former offenders, they were knowledgeable about the underworld; they were also notorious for their skill in extracting confessions, for accepting bribes, and for otherwise abusing their position. Although the Tokugawa shogunate repeatedly prohibited the use of *meakashi*, they were considered indispensable. A survey in 1867 showed that as many as 381 *meakashi* were in the regular employ of the Edo (now Tōkyō) city commissioners alone.

Meckel, Klemens Wilhelm Jakob (1842–1906)

German military officer and adviser to the Japanese army. Born in Cologne, Meckel graduated from the Prussian Army Staff College in 1869. After serving in the Franco-Prussian War, he became a member of the General Staff and an instructor at the Staff College. After the Japanese army decided to adopt the German model of military organization, Meckel, then a major, was invited by the Japanese government in 1885 to teach at the Army War College and to advise the General Staff. He assisted KATSURA TARŌ and KAWAKAMI SŌROKU in modernizing military structure and strategy. Meckel's contributions, which included revising the universal conscription system, establishing a divisional system and a supreme command, and strengthening logistic systems, helped lay the groundwork for Japan's victory in the SINO-JAPANESE WAR OF 1894–1895. His primary emphasis on the infantry in offensive campaigns, however, is said to have led to enormous casualties in the RUSSO-JAPANESE WAR (1904–05). Returning to Germany in 1888, he served as head instructor at the Army War College and vice-chief of the General Staff, eventually entering the reserves as a major general.

■——G. Kerst, *Jakob Meckel: Sein Leben, sein Werken in Deutschland und Japan* (1970).

medals of honor

(*hōshō*). One of two categories of official medal awarded by the emperor, on the nomination of the cabinet, to people who have made distinguished contributions to society in various fields.

The awarding of official medals in Japan began with three kinds—the Medal with Red Ribbon, the Medal with Green Ribbon, and the Medal with Blue Ribbon—established by the 63rd proclamation of the Grand Council of State (DAJŌKAN) in 1881. Today there are six decorations. The Medal with Red Ribbon is given for lifesaving. The Medal with Green Ribbon is given to those who have shown extraordinarily virtuous conduct. The Medal with Yellow Ribbon is given in the field of business and industry, the Medal with Purple Ribbon in the field of social welfare, and the Medal with Dark Navy Blue Ribbon in the field of philanthropy. These six are equally ranked, and the Yellow Ribbon, Purple Ribbon, and Blue Ribbon are awarded twice a year, in spring and fall. The Red Ribbon, Green Ribbon, and Dark Navy Blue Ribbon are given when appropriate. All the medals are awarded to living persons. See also DECORATIONS. *HASHIMOTO Nobuyuki*

medical and health insurance

Health insurance is the most important component of the medical care security system in contemporary Japan. Since 1961, all Japanese citizens have been entitled to coverage under one of six basic health insurance schemes, depending upon employment status or place of residence. By 1980, 99.3 percent of the total population was covered under one of the six health insurance schemes; the remaining 0.7 percent was covered by the medical assistance program provided under the Daily Life Security Law (1950) or by special public categorical programs for diseases such as tuberculosis and mental illness. Medical care providers are reimbursed on a fee-for-service basis according to a fee schedule determined by the minister of health and welfare. Since 1973, persons 70 years or older are entitled to free medical care. While the problem of access to medical care for all Japanese citizens has been alleviated with the development of the health insurance system, the problems of quality, costs, and control remain acute. Because proposed solutions generally require state intervention, the health insurance system has become highly politicized.

The Health Insurance Law of 1922 is regarded as the first such measure to be adopted by an Asian state, and it remains the cornerstone of the contemporary social insurance structure in Japan. The structure has been developed incrementally and unevenly. It includes: National Health Insurance (1938), Seamen's Insurance (1939), Employees' Pension Insurance (1941), Workmen's Compensation Insurance (1947), Unemployment Insurance (1947), National Public Service Mutual Aid Association Insurance (1948), Day Laborers' Health Insurance (1953), Private School Teachers and Employees Mutual Aid Association Insurance (1953), Staffs of Agriculture, Forestry and Fisheries Institutions Mutual Aid Association Insurance (1958), National Pension Insurance (1959), Local Public Service Mutual Aid Association Insurance (1962), Farmers' Pension Insurance (1970), Children's Allowance Law (1971), and Employment Insurance (1974). These basic statutes have been supplemented by hundreds of amendments and other official rules and regulations, as well as by various other social welfare and public health measures. All Japanese citizens are covered by social insurance. However, in terms of contributions made and benefits received, the system has not produced equity. The imbalances and disparities are obvious to even the most casual observer and recognized by those who otherwise point with pride to the fact that Japan was the first Asian nation to have introduced social insurance measures and to have instituted health insurance and pensions for all citizens. What is true of the social insurance system in general is true of the health insurance system in particular.

Of the health insurance schemes based on employment status, the bulk of the coverage is provided by the Health Insurance Law of 1922 as amended. Enforcement of the original law, which was based on German models, was postponed until 1927 because of the Tōkyō Earthquake of 1923. The purpose of the law is to "provide for the payment of benefits to insured persons and to persons supported by them in case of sickness, injury or death attributable to causes or sources outside of their employment, or maternity" (art. 1). Insured persons are of three types: (1) compulsory insured persons, i.e., all employees of factories, mines, companies, banks, and other types of workplaces listed in the law in which five or more persons are regularly employed (almost all fields of work are included, with the important exceptions of agriculture, forestry, fishing, restaurants, and entertainment); (2) voluntarily and inclusively insured persons, i.e., employees of workplaces that do not fall under the compulsory provisons in which the employer has obtained the approval of the prefectural governor and more than half of the employees (insurance then becomes compulsory for all employees); and (3) voluntarily and continuously insured persons, i.e., anyone who has been insured for not less than two months may continue to be insured for six months following disqualification as an insured person, for example, during a change of employment. The dependents of insured persons are also entitled to benefits as provided for in the law. Excluded from coverage under the Health Insurance Law are persons who are employed for less than two months on a daily basis, seasonal workers, temporary employees, persons employed in jobs which have no definite workplace, and persons eligible for any other employee-based insurance scheme. This includes national and local government employees.

The Health Insurance Law provides for two types of insurers or insurance carriers, i.e., the government or a health insurance society. The latter may be formed by an employer regularly having 300 or more employees, or 2 or more employers having a combined total of more than 300 employees, subject to consent of more than half of the employees and the approval of the welfare minister. When a health insurance society is formed, the employer and all employees eligible for insurance become members. Such societies are incorporated and are responsible for the management of the program. They may either provide medical facilities and medical benefits in kind, or pay the necessary costs of medical care. Supervision of the affairs of health insurance societies is assigned to the MINISTRY OF HEALTH AND WELFARE. In the absence of a society, health insurance is managed by the government through the prefectural governor. In terms of the kind and quality of medical care benefits as well as other fringe benefits, the health insurance societies comprise the elite of insurance carriers in Japan. In 1980, there were 1,670 societies covering over 11 million members and over 16 million dependents. The societies are components of the National Federation of Health Insurance Societies, which has functioned as one of the major organized interest groups in the political arena. The federation's activities have been frequently contested by the JAPAN MEDICAL ASSOCIATION.

Health insurance is financed by contributions from employers and employees as well as by subsidies from the national treasury. Under both government and society management, the employer is responsible for payment of the total contribution and is authorized to deduct the employee's share from wages. The employee's share is determined according to a special formula and may be less than that of the employer in society-managed schemes while it is equal under government management. To supplement contributions from employers and employees, the Health Insurance Law provides that administrative expenses be paid from the national treasury. In addition to the partial payment of medical fees by the insured person, insurance medical care providers are remunerated for treatment and services by the insurance carrier. This may be done directly or through the Social Insurance Payment Fund. The latter has become the standard route, and all insurance programs other than National Health Insurance work through it. The Social Insurance Payment Fund is a public corporation with branch offices throughout Japan and supervised at the national level by the welfare minister.

The National Health Insurance Law provides coverage on the basis of residence rather than employment status and is essentially a residual program for persons not otherwise covered. By 1980, this included over 15.7 million households and over 44.6 million individuals. Cities, towns, and villages are the main insurance carriers, although there are national health insurance societies in many areas. National Health Insurance is financed by means of a special tax, by partial payment of costs by insurees, and by national subsidies. From the standpoint of the average citizen covered under this program as compared to the average person covered by one of the employee-based schemes, more is paid for less. Nevertheless, public support for the present health insurance is widespread. The major organized critic of the system is the Japan Medical Association, which proposes unification of the various health insurance schemes into a single universal program.

■——Joel H. Broida and Nobuo Maeda, "Japan's High Cost Illness Insurance Program: A Study of its First Three Years," *Public Health Reports* (March/April 1978). Masami Hashimoto, "Japan: Health Service Prospects, An International Survey," *The Lancet* (October 1973). T. Higuchi, "Medical Care through Social Insurance in the Japanese Rural Sector," *International Labor Review* (March 1974). Kenkō Hoken Kumiai Rengōkai, ed, *Shakai hoshō nenkan* (annual). Michael R. Reich and John J. Kao, *A Comparative View of Health and Medicine in Japan and America* (1978). Saguchi Takashi, *Nihon shakai hoken shi* (1960). Social Insurance Agency, Japanese

Government, *Outline of Social Insurance in Japan* (annual). William E. Steslicke, "Doctors, Patients, and Government in Modern Japan," *Asian Survey* (November 1972). William E. Steslicke, *Doctors in Politics: The Political Life of the Japan Medical Association* (1973). Tarō Takemi, "The Expansion of Health Insurance Medical Care," *Asian Medical Journal* (February 1978).　　　*William E. STESLICKE*

medical research → medicine

medicine

history of medicine
diseases
public health
drugs
traditional medicine
medical research

Systematized medical care in Japan dates from the 6th century; at that time the trial-and-error use of primitive medical herbs was replaced by Chinese medicine, which was introduced into Japan along with Buddhism. Chinese medicine was at first exclusively for the imperial family, but treatment spread gradually among the people. This medical tradition produced many noted Japanese physicians throughout the country and continued up to the time of the Meiji Restoration (1868). Along with the political, social, and cultural reforms of the Meiji Restoration, Western medicine was promoted as a national policy, and thus the way was opened for Japan's present modern medical system.

Japan's medical education system was modeled after the German system; however, after World War II the American system was introduced on a broad scale. Education and research have reached international standards, and there is an active program of international exchange. The Japan Medical Association (JMA) has general responsibility for the medical care of the people; the Japanese Association of Medical Sciences, a section within the JMA, has 73 member academic societies, which are responsible for education and research. Since 1961 the people of Japan have been covered by a national health insurance system that provides medical care to anyone without private coverage.

An understanding of man as a whole, inherited from Chinese medicine, forms the basis of Japanese medical care and acts as a brake against excessive specialization. Another fundamental principle of Japanese medical care is a relationship of trust and confidence between the physician and the patient. Accomplishments of recent decades include a dramatic reduction of the incidence of tuberculosis, a decrease in mortality rates for infants and young children, and an increase in the average life expectancy. In response to social changes, the nation is aiming at the establishment of a welfare society with a new concept of medical care.

■——Fujikawa Yū, *Nihon igaku shi* (1904), tr, from a German translation, by John Ruhrah as *Japanese Medicine* (1934). Japan Medical Association, ed, *Statistics of Medical Security in Japan* (1978). Ogawa Teizō, *Igaku no rekishi* (1964).　　*KUMAGAI Hiroshi*

HISTORY OF MEDICINE

Whatever native medicine existed in Japan before the introduction of Chinese culture in the 6th and 7th centuries was virtually replaced by Chinese medicine at that time, and medicine in Japan remained under the strong influence of Chinese medicine for more than a thousand years. This does not mean that a peculiarly Japanese tradition did not develop within Chinese medicine. In the 16th and 17th centuries, for example, there arose two Japanese schools of medicine, the so-called latter-day school (*goseihō*, or *kōseihō*) and the classicist school (*koihō*), both based on traditional Chinese medicine (*kampō*), but both seeking to modify it to conform to native realities. Although both schools looked to Chinese medical books to support their claims to orthodoxy, each contributed something distinctly original. It was the classicist school which finally succeeded in Japanizing Chinese medicine, but by the time this happened Western medicine had been introduced to Japan by the Portuguese, the Spanish, and most notably the Dutch, and the native schools of Chinese medicine were eventually overshadowed by it. The supremacy of Western medicine was established with the Meiji Restoration (1868), when the new government adopted German medicine as a model. After World War II, however, German medicine was replaced by the American system.

Introduction of Chinese Medicine——The native medicine of Japan is only fragmentarily described in chronicles such as the KO-JIKI and the NIHON SHOKI, both compiled in the early 8th century. It is believed that treatment largely relied on prayer and exorcism. By the 6th and 7th centuries, Chinese medicine, brought back to Japan by Japanese who had studied in China, had replaced native medicine. The YŌRŌ CODE (effective 757) included Japan's first medical code, the Ishitsuryō. Modeled after the medical system of Tang (T'ang) dynasty (618–907) China, it provided for a government office called the Ten'yakuryō (Ministry of Health) that was responsible for medical administration. The code also specified a system of medical education.

The coming to Japan in 754 of the Chinese priest GANJIN (Ch: Jianzhen or Chien-chen), who was an authority on herbal medicine, greatly influenced Japanese medicine. Sixty kinds of medicinal substances were included in the offerings made to the great Buddha of the temple Tōdaiji for the repose of the emperor SHŌMU (d 756) on the 49th day after his death. These medicaments may be seen at the SHŌSŌIN repository in Nara. It is known that in 808 a work entitled *Daidō ruiju hō* was published in an effort to retain a record of disappearing native medical practices, but it is no longer extant. The oldest extant medical treatise is the *Ishimpō* (982), written by TAMBA YASUYORI. It consists largely of quotations from Chinese works on medicine. During the Kamakura period (1185–1333), when Buddhism was at the peak of its influence, Buddhist monks exerted a substantial influence upon medicine as they included healing as part of their religious activities. Medical books of this period include the *Kissa yōjō ki* by the monk EISAI, and the *Ton'ishō* and *Man'anhō*, both by KAJIWARA SHŌZEN, also a monk. The priest Ninshō (1217–1303) dedicated himself to helping the destitute, founding hospitals (see HIDEN'IN) and seeking aid for lepers. In the following Muromachi period (1333–1568), Yūrin (d 1410) wrote another treatise, the *Fukendenhō*.

Latter-Day School of Medicine (16th–19th Centuries)——In China during the Jin (Chin; 1125–1234) and Yuan (Yüan; 1279–1368) dynasties, there had been major efforts to unify the traditional theories of acupuncture and moxibustion with herbal therapy. The main canon of the theory of acupuncture and moxibustion was the *Huang di nei jing* (Huang ti nei ching; Canon of Medicine), said to have been written before the birth of Christ, and that of herbal therapy was the *Shang han lun* (Essay on Typhoid, ca 3rd century). It was under the influence of this movement that the latter-day school of medicine (*goseihō* or *kōseihō*) emerged in Japan in the 16th century. Its leader was TASHIRO SANKI, a physician who had studied medicine in China during the Ming dynasty (1368–1644) and settled in the Kantō region. His most prominent disciple, MANASE DŌSAN, added his own clinical experience and knowledge to the branch of Jin-Yuan medicine that is called the Li-Zhu [Li-Chu] school from the names of its two Chinese founders. This school had a tendency toward impractical idealism, and Manase stressed the importance of simplicity and practicality in medical treatment.

The Classicist School of Medicine (17th–19th Centuries)

Criticism of the latter-day school of medicine led to the development of the so-called classicist school (*koihō*). Although this school regarded highly the positivist approach of the ancient *Shang han lun* and adopted the motto "Return to the *Shang han lun*," it was actually reformative. The emergence of the school marks the complete Japanization of traditional Chinese medicine. Its founder is often said to be NAGOYA GEN'I (1628–96), but it is generally agreed that the real founder was GOTŌ KONZAN. Gotō said that all diseases were caused by the congestion of *ki* (Ch: qi or ch'i), the vital energy that was believed to permeate the universe. Although he supported the then predominant three-cause theory defined in the *San yin fang*, a treatise written by the Chinese Chen Yan (Ch'en Yen; fl 1174), he held that diseases developed only after these three causes had obstructed the flow of *ki* throughout the body. He believed that even with all three causes present one did not necessarily become sick, and that *ki* served as a protective mechanism.

Gotō's pupil, KAGAWA SHŪTOKU, went even further. He rejected all abstract concepts relating to the body, such as the doctrine of yin and yang and that of the Five Elements, and criticized all the medical classics, including the *Shang han lun*. He developed Gotō's theory of etiology and said "Every human disease affects not only the individual yin or yang but also the body as a whole."

Another distinguished pupil of Gotō was YAMAWAKI TŌYŌ, who regarded the *Shang han lun* as the greatest work on therapeutics. He was critical of the yin-yang and Five Elements doctrines pertaining to the body, considering them to be useful only as classifiers of pathologic states. He was the first Japanese to dissect the human body (1754) and wrote a work called *Zōshi* based on his observations.

YOSHIMASU TŌDŌ was the most creative and influential of the physicians belonging to the classicist school. He also opposed the yin-yang and Five Elements doctrines and advocated a theory that all diseases came from one and the same poison (*mambyō ichidoku*). His theory was based on a hypothesis of the localization of pathologic sites; in other words, he thought that although all diseases had one cause, differences between them and the necessity for different treatments resulted from differences in the sites affected; hence, in treating different diseases, one should first determine the site affected by the poison. His may be the only solid pathological idea among the theories of traditional Chinese medicine, which (including those of Gotō Konzan) were largely based on humoral pathology. However, his son and successor, Yoshimasu Nangai (1750–1813), revived the traditional pathology under the pretext of developing his father's theory. He feared that his father's *mambyō ichidoku* theory might lead to a weakening in the theoretical structure of traditional medicine and finally to its disintegration.

The basically positivist classicist school produced a number of physicians, including Nagatomi Dokushōan (1732–66), who were receptive to *rampō* (Western [literally, "Dutch"] medicine), which was becoming increasingly popular at the time. Based on Nagatomi's theories, HANAOKA SEISHŪ, a student of Yoshimasu Nangai, successfully performed an operation on breast cancer in 1805, using an anesthetic that he had invented. Another distinguished physician in the same period was KAGAWA GEN'ETSU. A specialist in obstetrics, he wrote a treatise called *Sanron* (1766), in which he included a description of the correct inverted position of the fetus in utero.

Chinese Medicine and Western Medicine (16th–19th Centuries)——Western medicine was first introduced to Japan by Spanish and Portuguese missionaries who arrived in the 16th century. Western medicine in those days was called *namban* (southern barbarian) medicine. In 1557 the first Western-style hospital was established in Funai (now the city of Ōita) by a Portuguese priest named Luis de Almeida (1525–83?). Among the notable surgeons of this period were Christovão Ferreira (1580–1652; also known as Sawano Chūan), a Portuguese naturalized in Japan, and Kurisaki Dōki (1566–1651), who studied Western medicine in the Philippines.

After the NATIONAL SECLUSION policy took effect in 1639, the Dutch were the only Westerners officially allowed to visit Japan, though a few other Europeans did manage to enter classified as Dutchmen. European doctors who came to Nagasaki during the 17th century included Caspar Schambergen, a Dutchman who arrived in 1649 and founded the so-called Caspar school of surgery; Willem ten Rhijne (1647–1700), who arrived in 1674, taught Dutch medicine, and introduced the Japanese version of traditional Chinese medicine to the West; and Engelbert KAEMPFER, who visited Japan in 1690, taught Western medicine, and introduced Japanese culture to Europe. Among the surgical schools founded by government interpreters at Nagasaki were the Narabayashi school, the Nishi school, and the Yoshio school. Motoki Ryōi (1628–97), an official interpreter who was influenced by Rhijne, pioneered the translation of Western medical books. He translated a Dutch version of an anatomical work by Johann Remmelin and published it as the *Oranda zenku naigai bungō zu* (Dutch Anatomical Atlas of the Whole Body).

An extremely important event in the history of the introduction of Western medicine was the publication of the *Kaitai shinsho* by SUGITA GEMPAKU and other scholars of Rangaku (Dutch Studies; also known as WESTERN LEARNING) in 1774. Three years earlier, Sugita and MAENO RYŌTAKU had observed the dissection of the body of an executed criminal. They were deeply impressed by the close correspondence between the internal structure of the body and the anatomical charts in the Dutch version of a German medical book written by Johann Adam Kulmus (1689–1745) and decided to translate the book, together with their colleagues. After three years of work, they completed the translation and published it as *Kaitai shinsho*. Another famous doctor of this period was ŌTSUKI GEN-TAKU. From around this time Western medicine came to be known as *rampō* and began to rival traditional *kampō* medicine in popularity.

In 1775, Carl Peter THUNBERG, a Swedish scholar and distinguished pupil of Carolus Linnaeus, came to Japan. He taught some

Medicine

International Comparison of Death Rates, 1978
(per 100,000 population)

	Japan	United States	United Kingdom[1]	West Germany	France
All causes	607.6	883.4	1,192.9	1,179.6	1,026.6
Enteritis and other diarrheal diseases	2.0	0.9	0.6	0.7	1.6
Tuberculosis	7.2	1.3	1.8	4.2	4.6
Malignant neoplasms	131.3	181.9	258.1	252.9	228.2
Diabetes mellitus	8.5	15.5	10.0	27.5	15.8
Hypertensive diseases	16.4	7.3	14.0	21.5	14.7
Heart diseases	93.3	327.5	388.7	335.2	195.5
Cerebrovascular diseases	146.2	80.5	149.7	166.1	129.1
Pneumonia and bronchitis	35.3	34.9	155.3	62.5	29.2
Liver cirrhosis	14.0	13.8	3.9	27.6	30.8
Motor vehicle accidents	10.5	24.0	13.7	23.1	20.5
All other accidents	15.7	24.4	17.3	25.9	48.5
Suicides	17.6	12.5	8.2	22.2	17.2

[1] England and Wales only.

SOURCE: Japan: Prime Minister's Office, Statistics Bureau, *Japan Statistical Yearbook* (annual): 1982.
Others: United Nations, *Demographic Yearbook* (annual): 1980.

of the translators of the *Kaitai shinsho,* including NAKAGAWA JUN'-AN and KATSURAGAWA HOSHŪ, and carried out studies of Japan's traditional medicine, plants, and animals.

Important contributors to the development of Rangaku were three generations of the Udagawa family, Udagawa Genzui (1755–97), Udagawa Genshin (1769–1834), and UDAGAWA YŌAN. In 1792 Genzui translated a book on internal medicine written by Johannes de Gorter and published it as the *Seisetsu naika sen'yō.*

The most influential of the foreign teachers who visited Japan during the period of National Seclusion was a German doctor, Philipp Franz von SIEBOLD. He opened a school and trained many physicians who later became eminent, including TAKANO CHŌEI. In 1848 a Dutch doctor named Otto Mohnike (1814–87) successfully introduced Jennerian vaccination into Japan. In the same year, OGATA KŌAN opened the Jotōkan, an antismallpox clinic in Ōsaka. In 1858, the Shutōjo, a vaccination dispensary, was established in Edo (now Tōkyō) with funds donated by Rangaku scholars. The dispensary is regarded as the forerunner of the medical faculty of Tōkyō University (see IGAKUJO). The introduction of Jennerian vaccination dealt a decisive blow to the declining dominance of *kampō* medicine; however, the tradition of the latter has continued to the present day.

Modernization —— In 1869 the newly established Meiji government decided that Japanese medicine was to be modeled after that of Germany, and from that time until 1945 German medicine was extremely influential. Japan's first law concerning medicine was issued in 1874. Its purpose was to establish a Westernized administrative and educational system for medical and pharmaceutical affairs.

In the Meiji period (1868–1912), many German doctors were engaged as professors at Japanese universities. Erwin von BÄLZ, a physician, and Julius Scriba (1848–1905), a surgeon, were particularly important in the development of medicine in Japan. Foreign professors were gradually replaced by Japanese who had studied abroad, mainly in Germany. The number of medical faculties and colleges also increased sharply. Among the students who were sent abroad were KITAZATO SHIBASABURŌ, the originator of serotherapy and discoverer of the plague bacillus; HATA SAHACHIRŌ, who discovered a specific drug against syphilis in cooperation with Paul Ehrlich; NOGUCHI HIDEYO, known for his work on *Spirochaeta pallida;* TAKAMINE JŌKICHI, the first to isolate adrenaline in crystalline form; and SUZUKI UMETARŌ, who extracted a substance having an antiberiberi effect. Chemical analysis of traditional drugs was also carried out. Another major achievement was the isolation of the alkaloid ephedrine from *Ephedra sinica,* an herb long used for asthma, by NAGAI NAGAYOSHI in 1887. After World War II, German influence on Japanese medicine decreased sharply, being replaced by that of the United States.

The number of medical doctors in Japan in 1977 was approximately 140,000. This, together with the number of medical facilities and research laboratories, places Japan on a rank with the United States and European countries. However, certain problems have arisen: the impairment of the traditional relationship between doctors and their patients as a result of excessive mechanization; the abuse or misuse of drugs caused by excessive competition within the drug industry; and inadequacies in the existing health insurance system. There has also been an increasing number of medical lawsuits.

■ ——Ogawa Teizō, *Igaku no rekishi* (1964). ŌTSUKA Yasuo

DISEASES

From an international point of view, the diseases observed in Japan can be classified into the following types. First, there are diseases found throughout the world, including Japan, that can be managed by standard treatments. Among these are common disorders such as essential hypertension, peptic ulcers, and common colds. Second are those diseases whose frequency is markedly different in Japan than in other countries. For instance, stomach cancer is the most common type of cancer among the Japanese and its incidence is much higher than in Europe or the United States. On the other hand, some disorders are extremely rare or totally unknown in Japan, such as certain infectious diseases commonly found in Africa. Finally, there are some diseases that are frequently found in Japan but are almost absent in Western countries. Among these are several diseases that are also found in other Asian countries.

Diseases Common in Japan —— The disease incidence rate of the Japanese was 109.9 per 1,000 inhabitants in 1975. Disorders of the respiratory tract accounted for 30.8 percent of the total; circulatory system, 23.3 percent; digestive tract, 15.4 percent; nervous and sensory systems, 10.4 percent; osteo-muscular disorders, 6.3 percent; dermatologic disorders, 3.5 percent; metabolic and nutritional disorders, 2.6 percent; and infectious and parasitic diseases, 2.5 percent. In 1960 digestive tract disorders ranked first, respiratory tract disorders second, infectious and parasitic diseases third, and circulatory system disorders fourth; the most distinctive change during this 15-year period was a marked reduction in the incidence of infectious and parasitic diseases.

The leading cause of death in the 1930s was tuberculosis, while cerebral apoplexy ranked fourth. By 1951 tuberculosis was the second most common cause of death and cerebral apoplexy had risen to the first rank. Since then, the most common cause of death among the Japanese has been cerebral apoplexy. Tuberculosis has continued to decrease, while cancer ranked second, and cardiac disorders third. Deaths due to cardiac disorders ranked first in most Western nations (see table). This fact leads to the controversial question of why cerebral apoplexy is more common among the Japanese than cardiac disorders. Cerebral apoplexy and cardiac diseases, both disorders of the circulatory system, together accounted for 39.4 percent of the total number of deaths in 1978. Cancer ranked first as a cause of death in the 30–69 age group and accounted for 21.6 percent of all deaths in 1978.

Characteristics of Diseases Common in Japan —— *Infectious diseases.* Contagious diseases have declined in Japan as a result of improvements in living conditions, progress in medical science, and the widespread dissemination of knowledge concerning sanitation. Cholera, smallpox, the plague, yellow fever, relapsing fever, and rabies are hardly ever found. Typhoid fever, diphtheria, and poliomyelitis have also markedly decreased, to the point that practical training of students and interns in the treatment of these diseases has become increasingly difficult to conduct. Only a few cases of malaria are encountered each year in association with vectors from abroad. However, there has been only a slight decline in the number of cases of dysentery, scarlet fever, Japanese encephalitis, measles, tetanus, and influenza.

Japanese encephalitis is due to a type-B encephalitis virus, which is slightly different from that of Economo's encephalitis. It is carried by mosquitoes and appears in the summer, but whether this virus remains dormant through the winter in Japan or is brought in from the south every year is not clear. Izumi fever is a viral infectious disease specific to Japan and is accompanied by eruptions, abdominal pains, and other symptoms in the digestive tract. *Tsutsugamushi* disease is a rickettsial disease commonly encountered in the river valleys of Niigata, Yamagata, and Akita prefectures, but it is also commonly described on the Asian continent and in northern Australia. The bite of the larva of a tick produces an infection accompanied by fever, swelling of lymph nodes, and rashes such as papulae. Its causative agent was discovered by Japanese researchers and by the 1970s its incidence had dwindled to only a few cases per year. Influenza has a high incidence, but the type of virus involved is different with each epidemic. Dysentery patients decreased from 84,437 in 1956 to 5,833 in 1971. Type D was more common than in neighboring areas such as Taiwan and Korea, where dysentery B is predominant. However, dysentery B had again increased in Japan in the late 1970s. Some 90–95 percent of the bacilli are resistant to sulfa drugs and are becoming more resistant to antibiotics.

Parasitic diseases. Schistosomiasis japonica, also called Katayama disease, is found in the river basins of Okayama, Yamanashi, Fukuoka, and other prefectures. The adult *Schistosoma japonicum* produces a specific disease in the portal system, the intermediate host being a water snail, *Oncomelania nosophora* (also called the Katayama snail or Miyairi snail). This disease is also common in Southeast Asia and China. Because of thorough preventive measures taken after World War II, very few new patients suffering from this disease are now found. Japan has long had a reputation of being a country with many parasitic diseases, and Westerners tend to be afraid of eating raw food in Japan. In fact, it is now quite unusual to find patients suffering from these diseases, and this ironically poses a problem in the training of young physicians.

Neoplasm. Malignant neoplasm (cancer) constitutes a particularly important problem in Japan and ranks as the second leading cause of death. The number of deaths due to cancer has risen steadily, but it appeared to have stabilized in the late 1970s. In 1971 the cancer death rate was 133.5 males and 102.5 females per 100,000 inhabitants. Stomach cancer ranked first in both males and females. Next came lung cancer and biliary tract cancer in males, followed by cancer of the esophagus, cancer of the pancreas, and leukemia. Cancer of the uterus ranked second in females, followed by lung and biliary tract cancers, then mammary cancer and leukemia. The number of deaths due to cancer was much higher in the United States than in Japan, with 180.8 males and 145.6 females per 100,000 inhabitants in 1968. Lung cancer ranked first among American males, followed by lymphoma and intestinal cancer. In American females, the most common cancers were mammary, intestinal, lymphatic, and uterine. Stomach cancer, which ranked first in Japan, was far less prevalent in all Western countries, though it was a serious problem in Chile and the Soviet Union. Japan had the highest rate of liver cancer of all the industrially developed countries, a rate that has tended to rise gradually. Liver cancer is also rather common in Africa, India, and Asia. In the Japanese, liver cancer often occurs in association with liver cirrhosis, a combination thought to be accountable for the poor record of success in surgical removal.

Disorders of the respiratory tract. Tuberculosis, once the nation's number one killer, began to decrease in the mid-1930s, and by 1977 had dropped to the 11th rank as a cause of death, with 7.7 deaths per 100,000 inhabitants. It was previously common among the young, but has recently become more prevalent in the upper age range, as in Western countries. There were once many hospitals and sanatoria specializing in tuberculosis in Japan, but these have gradually been converted into hospitals specializing in thoracic disorders (mainly lung cancer) or in geriatric diseases.

Disorders of the circulatory system. Cerebral apoplexy was the leading cause of death in the late 1970s. While cerebral hemorrhage remains more common than cerebral infarction, occurrences of the latter have been increasing since the late 1950s. This is probably due to an important rise in cerebral arteriosclerosis as one of the causative factors of infarction. Ischemic heart diseases increased fourfold as a cause of death during the years between 1955 and 1975. A study carried out in the late 1960s by an American physician, A. Keys, and others reveals that ischemic heart diseases accounted for 9 deaths in Japan, 35 in the Netherlands, and 47 in the United States per 10,000 male inhabitants between the ages of 40 and 59. Intake of salt is much greater among the Japanese than among Westerners, which may partly account for the high incidence of hypertension. Based on these facts, a strong emphasis has been placed on a feasible means of early detection of hypertension. In 1973 5.6 mil-

lion people underwent medical examinations for disorders of the circulatory system. Stress is also considered an important factor in the fluctuation of blood lipids. Blood lipid levels are much lower in the Japanese than in Americans. However, second-generation Japanese Americans residing in Hawaii show intermediate levels.

The aortitis syndrome is common among the Japanese. This is an inflammatory disease particular to the aorta and the main adjacent arteries. It is often called Takayasu disease, named after Takayasu Migito (1860–1938), an ophthalmologist who reported characteristic lesions of the blood vessels in the central retina in 1908. As it is accompanied by an inability to palpate the radial artery, it is also called the "pulseless" disease (proposed by Shimizu Kentarō and Sano Keiji in 1948). It is common among young Asians 15 to 25 years old, and is five to seven times more common in females than in males.

Disorders of the digestive tract. In Japan the most common cancer of the digestive tract is stomach cancer, whereas intestinal cancer is the most common in Western countries. Viral hepatitis, occurring after blood transfusion, was a social problem until Ōkōchi Kazuo (b 1928) clarified the connection between hepatitis and the Au-antigen, which was discovered by Baruch S. Blumberg in 1964. This led to the study of the Hb-antigen. Viral hepatitis (especially B-type) becomes chronic in many cases and progresses to liver cirrhosis or even to liver cancer.

Blood disorders. Aplastic anemia is a common blood disease in Japan, with about 30 to 40 cases per million in the population. Internationally, the death rate from aplastic anemia is high in Japan and Northern Ireland, but low in Great Britain and Denmark. Hemoglobinopathies are also commonly encountered in Japan. Tamura and others investigated family histories showing cyanosis and named this disorder "Hereditary Nigremia," but it was later found to be caused by Hb-Iwate. Other disorders due to unstable hemoglobin such as Hb-Ube-1 (also known as Hb-Köln), Hb-Chiba (also known as Hb-Hammersmith), Hb-Mie, Hb-Sendai, Hb-Hirosaki, and Hb-Hyōgo have also been discovered. The death rate from leukemia in Japan ranks 30th in the world. Acute myelogenous leukemia is the most common type in Japan.

Endocrine and metabolic disorders. Hashimoto disease is a chronic thyroiditis that was first reported by Hashimoto Hakaru in 1912; it resembles a hard inflammatory goiter and is most common among 40- to 50-year-old females. Many cases diagnosed as myxedema could be Hashimoto disease. It is a type of autoimmune disease.

Several cases of primary aldosteronism were identified in Japan after the publication of Conn's (American physician, b 1907) paper in 1955, and 300 cases—the world's highest morbidity—had been reported by 1970. Primary aldosteronism is common in females, and represents less than 0.5 percent of all cases of hypertension in Japan, compared to 0.5 to 2 percent in the United States.

Nervous disorders. SMON (subacute myelo-opticoneuropathy), began to appear sporadically in Japan around 1955, with the number of cases increasing rapidly in the late 1960s. This disease affects the spinal cord, the peripheral nerves, and the optical nerves, and is usually preceded by abdominal pain and diarrhea. The theory of a viral etiology was advanced, but SMON was later determined to be caused by the toxic effects of chinoform (Iodochlorhydroxyquin), a drug used for the treatment and prevention of amoebic dysentery. New outbreaks of SMON virtually ceased in 1970 when chinoform was banned. See also SMON DISEASE.

MS (multiple sclerosis) did not exist among the Japanese before World War II, but it has become fairly common in the postwar period. MS is common in high latitudes and rarer in tropical zones. There are 60–80 cases per 100,000 inhabitants in Northern Europe, 30–40 in North America, 10–20 in Southern Europe, and 1–4 in Japan.

Allergic disorders. Asthma is increasing in Japan. It is sometimes caused by allergic reaction to such foods as *konnyaku* (a paste food made from the root of the devil's tongue plant), but in many cases it is the result of air pollution, as in the so-called Yokohama, Kawasaki, and Yokkaichi asthma (see POLLUTION-RELATED DISEASES).

Collagen disease. Behçet disease is a systemic inflammatory disorder. Some 2,500 cases have been found in Japan, probably the highest incidence in the world. Viral etiology is suspected, but causative linkages have not yet been established.

Poisoning. "Minamata disease" became famous as the name for organic mercury poisoning after a large number of people, mostly fishermen and their families in the city of Minamata in Kumamoto

Prefecture, were poisoned by eating fish and shellfish contaminated by methyl mercury discharged into the sea by the Chisso Corporation in the late 1950s. Mercury poisoning causes numbness of hands and feet, an unstable walk, narrowing of the visual field, deafness, and paralysis. This type of poisoning has also appeared in other parts of Japan (see POLLUTION-RELATED DISEASES).

Agricultural chemical poisoning began to appear in the 1950s and the number of cases reached 1,564 in 1964; however, this problem has decreased as a result of the development of exotoxins and government control over agricultural chemicals.

Globefish *(fugu)* poisoning is caused by a neurotoxin contained in the liver and ovaries of the fish, which is eaten as a delicacy in Japan. The government strictly controls the preparation of globefish, but poisoning still occurs occasionally. It causes a severe paralysis of the respiratory muscles. —— YOSHITOSHI Yawara

PUBLIC HEALTH

(kōshū eisei). Rapid economic growth in recent years has brought about a marked improvement in Japan's standard of living, and as a concomitant to this, remarkable progress has been made in all aspects of public health.

Health Service System —— At the national level, the MINISTRY OF HEALTH AND WELFARE is responsible for the general administration of public health, social welfare, and social security programs. In addition to the Minister's Secretariat, the Ministry of Health and Welfare consists of nine bureaus, including those of public health, environmental sanitation, and medical affairs. Affiliated institutions include national research institutes and hospitals and QUARANTINE stations at certain ports of entry.

Locally, departments or bureaus of health are found in each of the 47 prefectures, and, as of 1 April 1980, 855 health centers were in existence throughout the country. Municipalities also have offices in charge of public health. Other administrative bodies concerned with public health include the ENVIRONMENT AGENCY, which is responsible for the regulation of pollutants; the MINISTRY OF LABOR, which is concerned with the health of workers; and the MINISTRY OF EDUCATION, which deals with matters concerning health in the school system. See also HEALTH CARE SYSTEM.

Aging of the Population —— The age structure of the population is probably the single most important element in the consideration of public health needs. Both the birth rate and the death rate decreased drastically in the decade after World War II, and they have since remained low, leading to a longer life expectancy and an increase in the number of the aged. The population reached 117 million in 1981, while the percentage aged 65 years or older was 8.9. A report by the National Institute of Population Problems predicts that this percentage will increase to 14.3 by the year 2000. There has been a steady increase in average life expectancy, a widely used indicator of the health level of a nation. The figure in 1960 for males was 65.32 years and for females 70.19 years; in 1970 the figures were 69.31 and 74.66 years, respectively; and in 1980 the figures reached 73.32 and 78.83 years. Among the advanced countries of the world, those with the highest life expectancies for men were: Iceland (73.4 years in 1977–78), Japan (73.32 years in 1980), Sweden (72.1 years in 1976), and the Netherlands (72.4 years in 1979). Those for women were: Iceland (79.3 years in 1977–78), the Netherlands (78.9 years in 1979), Japan (78.83 years in 1980), and Norway (78.73 years in 1979).

With the growing number of the aged, there has developed a concern for their welfare, particularly for the bedridden or those who have no one to care for them. By 1972, virtually all local governments in Japan had established free medical care systems for people over 70 years. The Ministry of Health and Welfare had also instituted a free medical care system for those above 70 whose incomes fall within certain limits. See also POPULATION.

Death Trends —— The total number of deaths in 1976 was approximately 703,000, a death rate of 6.3 per 1,000 population. The infant mortality rate (number of deaths within one year of birth) is considered an important indicator of health conditions and living standards. The infant mortality rate in Japan decreased from 30.7 per 1,000 live births in 1960 to 13.1 in 1970, 11.3 in 1973, and 8.4 in 1978, placing Japan among those countries with low infant mortality rates.

The 1978 mortality rates, ranked by cause, were as follows: cerebrovascular diseases (146.2 per 100,000 population); malignant neoplasms (131.3); heart disease (93.3); pneumonia and bronchitis (35.3); accidents (26.2); natural causes (24.4); suicides (17.6); hypertensive diseases (16.4); liver cirrhosis (14.0); and diabetes mellitus (8.5). See table in the above section on diseases.

In 1935, infectious diseases caused 43.5 percent of the total number of deaths, while adult diseases such as cancer, cerebral apoplexy, and heart disease caused only 24.7 percent. By 1978, however, the former accounted for 7.6 percent, and the latter, 68.6 percent of total deaths.

Until 1950 tuberculosis ranked first among the causes of death (mortality rate per 100,000 population: 146), but its incidence decreased steadily. In 1977 it ranked 11th in the list of the leading causes of death (mortality rate: 7.7).

Among malignant neoplasms, stomach cancer has a higher mortality rate in Japan than other countries; this is thought to be a consequence of the Japanese diet. On the other hand, the incidence and mortality rate of breast cancer are strikingly low when compared with other countries.

Traffic accidents are increasing in frequency, particularly those involving pedestrians, although the overall number of car accidents is still small in comparison, for example, to the United States.

Prevention of Infectious Diseases —— The discovery of effective antibiotics, and the development of new and better preventive and treatment methods have led to a marked decrease in the incidence of acute and chronic infections. For example, administration of the Sabin-type live polio vaccine, first introduced in 1971, has brought a drastic reduction in the incidence of poliomyelitis. In 1975 only four cases were reported in Japan; in 1976 and 1977 not one was reported.

Tuberculosis has similarly decreased, largely due to the preventive effect of the BCG vaccine. Lyphilized BCG was introduced in 1950. With transcutaneous inoculation, adopted about 1973, local side effects accompanying inoculation have been minimized. Some 151.5 million people received the BCG vaccine between 1950 and 1977. According to a tuberculosis prevention survey carried out by the Ministry of Health and Welfare in 1973, 58.5 percent of the population had been inoculated with the BCG vaccine at least once.

There have been some serious incidents of bad side effects from preventive vaccination, particularly the smallpox vaccine. To cope with this problem, a fundamental revision was made of the Preventive Vaccination Law of 1948. Under a new law promulgated in June 1976, inoculation of the smallpox vaccine is given to people in specific areas, and only when there is danger of an epidemic.

Public Health Service —— For many years, government agencies responsible for public health in Japan have mainly been concerned with the prevention and treatment of diseases. Recently, however, increasing importance has been given to the promotion and maintenance of general health. In 1977 the Ministry of Health and Welfare began a new health promotion campaign. As part of this campaign, the ministry has been working closely with local health centers on health promotion programs such as regular checkups and dietary guidance. Other activities include the establishment of community health centers, the assignment of health service nurses to communities, and the formation of organizations dedicated to health promotion and health maintenance.

Future Problems —— The development of medical science and techniques has led to higher quality and diversity in medical care, and the establishment of a nationwide health insurance scheme has made medical care more accessible (see MEDICAL AND HEALTH INSURANCE). However, the problem of providing adequate care for those in remote areas still remains. In 1976, the Ministry of Health and Welfare began a vigorous effort to establish a more comprehensive emergency care system to cover traffic accidents and provide medical service at night and on holidays.

Many serious health problems remain unsolved, however. These include chronic degenerative diseases such as cancers and heart diseases; mental disorders resulting from overcrowding and the stress of urban life; diseases from environmental pollution and from food and drug additives, agricultural insecticides and fungicides (see POLLUTION-RELATED DISEASES), various iatrogenic disorders, and so-called "intractable diseases with unidentifiable causes" (see DISEASES, INTRACTABLE).

To cope with these problems, planning is needed on the national as well as the local level. Health services have sometimes been hampered by the quality and number of health service personnel available. This is particularly true of personnel in the field of public health. Securing an adequate number of personnel and establishing a good system of training are of the first importance.

—— Hashimoto Masami, "Japan, Health Services Prospects: An International Survey" in *The Lancet and Nuffield Provincial Hospital Trust* (1973). Hashimoto Masami, "Health Care and Medical Systems in Japan," *Comparative Medicine East and West*, 6.3 (1978). Ministry of Health and Welfare, *Health and Welfare Services in*

Japan (1977). Someya Shirō, "Trends in Health Manpower Development and Problems of Postgraduate Education in Public Health in Japan," *Bulletin of the Institute of Public Health* 25.3 (1976).

SOMEYA Shirō

DRUGS

The traditional medicine of Chinese origin known as *kampō* was the predominant form of medicine practiced in Japan until the late 19th century. In *kampō* it was normal for the physician to dispense his own preparations of the traditional Chinese herbal medicines *(kampōyaku)* after examining the patient. Western-style medicine had been introduced to Japan in the 16th century, and by the late 18th and early 19th centuries had begun to seriously challenge *kampō;* however, it was not until the Meiji period (1868–1912) when the government actively promoted the adoption of Western medicine, that Western drugs came into wide use. This section deals with drugs in modern Japan; for information on the traditional medicine, see the section on it below.

Manufacture and Supply of Drugs —— After the Meiji Restoration of 1868, Western drugs were imported to Japan in increasing quantities. Quality standards and analytical techniques were also introduced, and the government issued the first PHARMACOPOEIA OF JAPAN in 1886. The profession of pharmacy also became established; however many Japanese physicians prepared their own medicines, and the division of responsibilities between the two professions was not as clear-cut as it is in some countries.

Before World War I almost all modern drugs used in Japan were imported from foreign countries, especially Germany. When this importing was interrupted by the war, the domestic drug industry advanced rapidly both in scale and quality. Shortages of materials and destruction of factories during World War II, however, dealt a crushing blow to the industry.

After World War II, the drug industry gradually resumed its activities. This revival owed much to technological importation and other assistance from the United States and other countries. By the 1960s Japan's pharmaceutical industry was as prosperous as it had been in prewar days. Drug production increased eightfold between 1961 and 1975.

In 1975 drug production amounted to approximately ¥1.8 trillion (US $6.1 billion), some 82 percent of which was prescribed (ethical) drugs and 18 percent over-the-counter drugs. The total number of pharmaceutical companies was about 2,200, the largest 20 companies accounting for about 50 percent of total production. Antibiotics ranked first, with 20.3 percent of the total production, followed by central nervous system drugs (12.6 percent), metabolism agents (11.8 percent), cardiovascular drugs (8.7 percent), and gastrointestinal drugs (8.2 percent).

Approval and Reevaluation of Drugs —— The standards of approval for drug manufacture were made more stringent in 1967. Under the new regulations, the manufacturer is required to present data showing substantial evidence of the efficacy of the drug, and in order to obtain approval of new chemical compounds, clinical data must be collected from 150 or more patients at five or more hospitals. This revision was modeled on the Kefauver-Harris Drug Amendment (1962) to the US Food and Drug Administration's standards. As a result, the number of drug manufacture approvals sharply decreased after 1968 (with the exception of 1970). In addition to the above requirements, pharmaceutical companies were prohibited from advertising prescription drugs in the mass media or in magazines other than professional ones.

The number of drugs currently on the Japanese market is about 40,000, half of which are prescription and the other half over-the-counter. The prescription drugs include about 13,000 pharmaceuticals approved for use in the health insurance medical system. A reevaluation of drugs that had been approved before 1967 was begun in 1972, and by March 1978 14 reports were published. Nearly 5 percent of the drugs were judged to be ineffective and removed from the market.

Drug Consumption and Related Problems —— There is some truth to the statement that the Japanese tend to depend excessively upon drugs for medical treatment. For example, if a doctor advises a patient with a common cold to stay in bed but prescribes no drugs, the patient is often dissatisfied and thinks the doctor is not doing his job properly. On the other hand, if the doctor prescribes not only symptomatolytic drugs, such as antipyretics, but also relatively expensive antibiotics and vitamins, the patient is satisfied. If he is given an injection in addition to the above prescription, he may be even more satisfied. Under the present medical system in Japan, a doctor's income increases in proportion to his willingness to please his patients with a plethora of prescriptions.

Routine use of health-aid drugs. The routine use of health-aid drugs such as vitamins and "stamina" pills is another example of the Japanese penchant for drugs. It is estimated that a large portion of the population takes a few tablets after every meal, even if they are not suffering from any particular disease. Almost all the health-aid drugs contain vitamin B_1 (thiamine) or its derivatives, a reflection of deficiencies of that vitamin in the traditional Japanese diet of polished rice. (It was a Japanese biochemist, SUZUKI UMETARŌ, who first succeeded in isolating the substance later known as vitamin B_1.)

Drug expenditures. The ratio of drug expenditures to total national medical expenditures can be seen by a comparison among a set of five variables over a period of 15 years from 1961, the year the national health insurance system came into being, until 1975. The five variables are: (1) the total national budget; (2) total recorded national medical expenditures (i.e., the total medical expenses paid by the national health insurance, private group insurance, and social security programs plus medical payments made as the individual's share under any of the above programs); (3) total medical insurance expenditures (the above minus the individual's share); (4) total drug production; and (5) wage levels. In 1961 drug production was equal to about 10 percent of the national budget; the figure dropped to 8 percent in 1975. The ratio of national medical expenditures to the budget was 26 percent in 1961 and 30 percent in 1975. In other words, there were no great changes over 15 years. The most noteworthy contrast is between increases in wage levels and medical insurance expenditures. Wage levels increased sevenfold between 1961 and 1975, while medical insurance only doubled. A breakdown of total national medical expenditures for 1975 shows that physicians' fees accounted for 44.1 percent of the total expenditures and payments for drugs 30 percent. However, if the drug-related portion of physicians' fees—i.e., for dispensing drugs (a normal practice for physicians in Japan) and administering injections—is added, drug expenditures amount to as much as 39.8 percent, a high percentage, of total national medical expenditures. Nevertheless, when one considers that the rate of increase in medical insurance expenditures is much smaller than that for wage increases, it cannot be simply concluded that Japan's ratio of drug expenditures to national medical expenditures is excessively high compared to that of other countries.

Drug abuse. In 1951, Japan established the world's first drug control law regulating the two powerful central nervous system stimulants, amphetamine and methamphetamine. In the 1970s there was a steady increase in the number of known violations of the law (1,618 cases in 1970 and 8,422 in 1975), and drug abuse is now seen as a serious social problem (see DRUG ABUSE). See also PHARMACEUTICAL INDUSTRY.

KUBO Fuminae

TRADITIONAL MEDICINE

(kampō; literally "Chinese medicine"). The Japanese term *kampō* refers to the traditional Chinese herbal medicine that was dominant in Japan until the 19th century. It was then largely supplanted by Western medicine, though it continues to be practiced even today. It was first brought back from China by Japanese students in the 6th and 7th centuries and like other aspects of Chinese culture was adopted with little modification. It was only after the 15th century, when the general public began to have access to the benefits of medicine, that efforts were made to adapt Chinese medicine to Japan's climate, environment, and people.

The Two Major Schools of Kampō —— There were two major schools of traditional Chinese medicine in Japan, the so-called latter-day school of medicine (*goseihō* or *kōseihō*) and the classicist school of medicine *(koihō).* Most of the *kampō* schools existing in Japan today are based on the *koihō* school with some elements from *goseihō.*

The founder of *goseihō* was TASHIRO SANKI. Tashiro went to China in 1487 and for 12 years studied the medical arts of the Li-Zhu (Li-Chu) school, a branch of the Chinese medicine that had evolved during the Jin (Chin; 1125–1234) and Yuan (Yüan; 1279–1368) dynasties (the so-called Jin-Yuan medicine). After returning to Japan, he applied his knowledge to the medical treatment of the ruling military class and the general public. It was MANASE DŌSAN, one of Tashiro's pupils, who first modified Chinese medicine. He constructed his own medical theory by combining Tashiro's teaching with his own experience. This he set down in the treatise called *Keitekishū* (1574), which marked the beginning of a really Japanese form of Chinese medicine.

Koihō medicine became increasingly popular from the 17th century onward. Its theory was simpler and its approach more positivist than that of the *goseihō* school; it was based on a Chinese medical classic, *Shang han za bing lun* (*Shang han tsa ping lun;* Essay on Typhoid and Miscellaneous Diseases), which dealt with observed symptoms and prescribed methods of treatment that had been established after long practical experience. The original version of this work was written by Zhang Ji (Chang Chi; 142?–210?) during the Later Han dynasty (25–220). When it was revised during the Song (Sung) dynasty (960–1279) it was divided into two parts, the *Shang han lun* (Essay on Typhoid) and the *Jin kui yao lüe* (*Chin k'uei yao lüeh;* Synopsis of the Golden Chamber). The first part dealt with the treatment of typhoid (the term "typhoid" in this context represented all acute diseases accompanied by fever) and the second part with the treatment of other diseases.

Characteristics of Kampō —— *Kampō* as practiced in Japan differs from the original Chinese medicine in the following respects: (1) fewer drugs are used (the Japanese use 100 to 200, while the Chinese pharmacopoeia includes as many as 500); (2) the drugs used are relatively easy to obtain; (3) smaller doses of drugs are administered; and (4) prescriptions specified in the *Shang han lun* are applied to nonfebrile chronic diseases as well as to acute diseases accompanied by fever.

Kampō drugs. The drugs used in *kampō* medicine are called *kampōyaku* or *kan'yaku*. These are all crude drugs and are mostly of vegetable origin, although some are of animal and mineral origin. The crude drugs are mixed according to a formula (there may be as many as 10 or more ingredients, and each formula is given a name), then prescribed either singly or in combination for a specific symptom. For example, there are as many as 20 different formulas for treating the common cold, depending on the symptoms.

Shō (syndrome or evidence). The pattern of symptoms known as *shō* is the object of diagnosis, and the investigation of it includes the following important points. The syndrome pattern is determined by observing various subjective and objective symptoms according to the doctrines of *kampō* medicine. The *shō* is then given a name according to the drug which will be prescribed for its treatment. For example, the *kakkontō shō* (*kuzu* root infusion syndrome) would indicate a febrile state. The *shō* functions as prior evidence that the prescription will improve the patient. Some practitioners use the term *shō* in classifying the patient's physical constitution, disease characteristics, and causes, employing terms such as *jitsushō, kyoshō, yōshō, inshō, kitaishō, ketsutaishō,* and *suitaishō.*

Diagnostic Factors or Criteria for the Determination of Shō

Kyo-jitsu (emptiness-fullness). 1. *Jitsushō* (the syndrome of fullness) is observed when the patient is replete with vital force and other energies and his body is fighting well against the disease. In this case, the doctor administers drugs that have substantial effects, such as sweating agents, e.g., ephedra, and cathartics such as rhubarb and Glauber's salt. 2. *Kyoshō* (the syndrome of emptiness) is observed when the vital force and natural healing power of the patient are weak or passive. For this syndrome, the doctor prescribes drugs that will enhance the absorption of nutrients and build up the strength of the body.

In-yō (Ch: yin-yang). 1. *Yōshō* (the syndrome of positiveness) is observed when the patient has a sensation of heat (*netsushō;* "heat evidence") and definite symptoms. In this case, sweating agents (ephedra) and cooling agents (gypsum) are employed. 2. *Inshō* (the syndrome of negativeness) is obtained when the patient is feeling chilly (*kanshō;* "chill evidence") and usually has few symptoms, e.g., nonfebrile hepatitis. For this syndrome, the doctor prescribes drugs that will warm the body and enhance metabolism, such as aconite root and Asiasarum.

Ki-ketsu-sui. 1. *Ki* (Ch: *qi* or *ch'i*) is the vital force that flows through the universe and enhances the function of the body and mind. Abnormal activity of the vital force causes depression, edema, congestion, and other physical disorders. In this case, the *kampō* practitioner prescribes a medicine that restores the condition of the vital force to normal. 2. *Ketsu* (blood) is a concept that involves blood fluid and its related functions. One of the common abnormalities in *ketsu* is *ketsutai* (stagnancy of *ketsu*). It causes not only congestion and hyperemia but also a wide variety of physical and mental symptoms. In female patients, the stagnancy of *ketsu* often results in menstrual disorders. For all these symptoms, the doctor prescribes *kampō* drugs that enhance blood circulation. 3. The concept *sui* (water) involves all the water in the human body. Health is supposed to be the state of the body in which *sui*, as well as *ki* and *ketsu*, circulates steadily. Congestion of *sui* results in the development of edemas, muscular and articular pains, and other physical and mental symptoms. In this case, the doctor administers an agent that accelerates water circulation.

States of Febrile Disease (The Theory of the Three In and Three Yō) —— According to the theory of *kampō*, stages of febrile diseases are classified as follows: The pyrogenic (or hot) stage of a febrile disease is classified as *yō* (Ch: *yang*) and divided into three categories: *taiyō, shōyō,* and *yōmei.* The succeeding stage, in which exhaustion, chill, and finally death occur is classified as *in* (Ch: *yin*) and also divided into three categories: *taiin, shōin,* and *ketchin.* The doctor prescribes sweating agents for *taiyō* diseases, bupleurum-root drugs for *shōyō* diseases, and rhubarb, Glauber's salt, or gypsum for *yōmei* diseases. Similarly, he prescribes peony-root drugs for *taiin* diseases and aconite-root drugs for both *shōin* and *ketchin* diseases.

Examination Methods Used in Kampō —— The *kampō* practitioner employs four methods for examining the patient. The four diagnostic methods (the *shishin* or four *shin*) are referred to as *bōshin, bunshin, monshin,* and *sesshin.* All these sensory examinations are made to evaluate the condition of the patient on the basis of diagnostic factors such as the above-mentioned three factors, *in-yō, kyo-jitsu,* and *ki-ketsu-sui,* and eventually to determine his *shō* (syndrome).

In *bōshin* (visual examination) the doctor looks at the patient's face, nails, and tongue for any abnormalities. In *bunshin* (auscultory and olfactory examination) the doctor uses his ears and nose to diagnose the patient. *Monshin* (interrogation) involves questioning the patient about his sensations, dreams, etc and examining some of the more pertinent information in detail. This requires a broad knowledge of *kampō* on the part of the practitioner. *Sesshin* (palpation) consists chiefly of pulse feeling and abdominal palpation. Abdominal palpation is a unique feature of Japanese *kampō* medicine and is made to evaluate the physical and mental condition of the patient, as well as such diagnostic factors as *kyo-jitsu* and *ki-ketsu-sui,* and finally to determine his *shō.* Yamada Terutane

MEDICAL RESEARCH

(*igaku kenkyū*). Medical research in Japan owes much to European, primarily German, medical techniques introduced in the late 19th century and to American techniques introduced after World War II. Today, medical research is largely oriented toward the biomedical sciences, and a multidisciplinary approach is being taken in most efforts on public health and welfare problems.

The best Japanese research in the fields of pathology, microbiology, anatomy, physiology, and biochemistry has reached international standards. In the postwar period, 10 scientists received the Japan Academy Prize for pathology and anatomy-related research, 18 for physiological, pharmacological and biochemical research, and 12 for microbiological and immunological research.

The immediate postwar period in Japan was marked by the prevalence of acute and chronic infectious diseases, in particular tuberculosis. Research done at this time resulted in rapid progress in the field of fermentation techniques, a remarkable advancement in prevention of various infectious diseases, marked decline in the infant mortality rate, and a notable improvement in the quality of the nation's nutrition. Successful research on various antibiotics led to an emphasis on the elucidation of cellular physiology and the biochemistry of infectious agents per se and thereby contributed to rapid progress in the field of cell biology in general.

In the course of the search for the mechanisms causing bacterial drug resistance, a new era was initiated in microbial genetics, and the R-factor, a bacterial plasmid assumed to be responsible for drug-resistance, was discovered in 1960 by Mitsuhashi Susumu. Likewise, molecular biological research methodologies gained firm ground, exerting a great influence on further developments in microbiological studies.

Building on work in medical entomology and zoology introduced from the United States after the war, medical microbiology made a strong recovery. Most notable were work on Japanese B encephalitis, the *tsutsugamushi* disease, and filariasis. Almost total eradication of filariasis was soon accomplished, while forms of endemic rickettsiosis were still extant.

Japanese cancer researchers pioneered in experimental chemical carcinogenesis: as early as 1915 Yamagiwa Katsusaburō and Ichikawa Kōichi (1888–1948) produced for the first time an artificial skin cancer by painting coal tar on the ears of rabbits, a crucial step in experimental tumor research. Then, in 1934, Sasaki Takaoki and Yoshida Tomizō were the first to induce liver cancer (hepatoma) in rats by oral administration of an azo dye. Another pioneering medical scientist, Kinoshita Ryōjun, was the first to induce liver cancers in rats by oral administration of p-N-dimethylaminoazo-benzol (butter yellow) in 1936.

Early in the postwar period, the use, in rats, of Yoshida ascites sarcoma cells, the only transplantable tumor cells at the time, enabled cancer researchers to discover synthetic antitumor chemotherapeutic agents, some of which are still in use, such as mitomycin C (Hata Tōju et al, 1956) and bleomycin (UMEZAWA HAMAO et al, 1959). Other synthetic antitumor drugs such as nitromin and tespamin, now widely used, were also developed in Japan.

In contrast to the strong tendency of prewar medical research to concentrate on basic medical science, the investigators of the postwar period had a tendency to concentrate on clinically applied medical science. One specialty was stomach cancer, the most prevalent type of malignancy in Japan. The latest, most remarkable success in this territory was the production of stomach cancer in rats and dogs using N-methyl-N'-nitrosoguanidine and N-ethyl-N'-nitrosoguanidine (Sugimura Takashi et al, 1967). This animal model has enabled many clinical cancer researchers to improve diagnostic and therapeutic techniques for patients with stomach cancer, particularly the newly developed endoscopy and radiographic techniques (double-contrast radiography). Other notable advances in early detection were made in angiography, ultrasonic scanning devices, the CT scanner, and a wide range of techniques in cytodiagnosis. Paralleling a widespread application of diagnostic devices and appropriate surgical devices, steady progress is being made in comprehensive cancer chemotherapy in combination with radiological, immunological, and endocrinological treatments.

Toxicological studies have been advanced by an unfortunate series of incidents of industrial mismanagement of chemical wastes, resulting in such POLLUTION RELATED DISEASES as Minamata disease (organic mercury poisoning), itai itai disease (sensory nerve disorders caused by cadmium poisoning), and Kanemi oil disease (poisoning by PCB-contaminated cooking oil; see KANEMI OIL POISONING INCIDENT). A genetic toxicity test system using microorganisms has become a potent tool for the detection of mutagenic substances in both synthetic and natural forms, including pyrolysates (extracted from overheated food proteins). Since many carcinogenic substances concurrently show mutagenicity, this system is also applicable to the screening of carcinogens in environmental health sciences.

A series of diseases brought about by the complex interaction between genetic and environmental factors is also being studied. The government provides assistance to researchers for work on intractable diseases (see DISEASES, INTRACTABLE). The search for the cause of intractable liver diseases is also becoming an important concern. Finally, the feasibility of using recombinant DNA techniques in medical research may exert a far-reaching influence on the currently predominant disease-oriented science, resulting in a move toward new concepts in health-oriented life science. These innovations, brought forth by highly flexible international cooperation, may influence the future of medical science in general.

Yamamoto Tadashi

medieval ceramics → ceramics

medieval literature → literature

Megijima

Island in the eastern Inland Sea, approximately 3 km (2 mi) north of the city of Takamatsu, Kagawa Prefecture, Shikoku. Known as the Onigashima (Island of Ogres) in the folktale of *Momotarō*, (The Peach-Boy). Principal activities on the island are coastal fishing and the cultivation of sweet potatoes and wheat. Area: 2.7 sq km (1 sq mi).

Meguro Ward

(Meguro Ku). One of the 23 wards of Tōkyō. On the Musashino Plateau. Meguro Ward developed rapidly as a residential area after the Tōkyō earthquake of 1923. Institutes of higher learning located here include the Faculty of General Education of Tōkyō University, Tōkyō Institute of Technology, and Tōkyō Metropolitan University. Pop: 273,751.

meibutsugire

("specialty cloth"). General name for various dyed fabrics imported mainly from China from the Kamakura period (1185–1333) to the early part of the Edo period (1600–1868); particularly popular among tea connoisseurs and upper-class warriors. These fabrics were used in various ways in the TEA CEREMONY, for example, as cloth coverings for tea utensils, for the mountings for hanging picture scrolls, and as garments for priests and monks. KOBORI ENSHŪ and Matsudaira Fumai (1751–1818) established a nomenclature for about 100 pieces, which was later classified according to the age when they were imported. The majority of these fabric pieces are Chinese fabrics of the Song (Sung; 960–1279), Yuan (Yüan; 1279–1368), and Ming (1368–1644) dynasties, including fabrics of the types known in Japan as DONSU (damask), NISHIKI (brocade), KINRAN AND GINRAN (gold and silver brocade), *kantō* (woven stripes), and *inkin* (gold leaf imprint). Others came to Japan via China from Persia, India and Southeast Asia. Names for these fabrics were taken from the type or design of the cloth, the names of tea-ceremony utensils used on a particular occasion, the temple or shrine that owned it, or the person who used it. *Meibutsugire*, regarded as exquisite items, were selected by the highly educated and aesthetically refined tea masters of the time. The preservation of *meibutsugire* has been very important. Their influence on Japanese dyeing techniques and design after the Azuchi-Momoyama period (1568–1600) is historically significant.

HIROI Nobuko

Meidensha Electric Mfg Co, Ltd

Manufacturer of heavy electric machinery such as generators, transformers, and motors; also engages in electrical work in construction projects. A member of the SUMITOMO group of companies since 1966. Founded in 1897 as a manufacturer of electric motors and generators, the firm played a pioneering role in the development of domestic technology. Today it is an integrated producer of electric machinery. In recent years it has developed new products, including water treatment equipment and instruments for detecting gas leakage. It has established a joint venture production company in Singapore. Sales for the fiscal year ending March 1982 totaled ¥115.6 billion (US $480.2 million) and capitalization was ¥8 billion (US $33.2 million). The corporate headquarters are located in Tōkyō.

meigen

(resounding bowstrings). A custom that originated in the Heian period (794–1185) whereby the chamberlains (*kurōdo*) plucked their bowstrings to make a sound that would ward off evil spirits when the emperor entered his bath. *Meigen* is still practiced today at the birth of an imperial prince. The common people had their own magical and symbolic variants of *meigen;* in southern Kyūshū, for example, they traditionally shot an arrow into the garden to expel harmful spirits upon an infant's first emergence from the house. See also HAMAYA AND HAMAYUMI; YABUSAME.

INAGAKI Shisei

Meigetsuki

Also known as *Shōkōki*. Diary of the courtier and noted poet FUJIWARA NO SADAIE. There are many extant manuscripts, and the number of chapters varies; it is written in Chinese (*kambun*) and covers the years 1180–1235, though with several lacunae. *Meigetsuki* is a valuable cultural source, for there is much discussion of the composition of poetry. Moreover, since Sadaie enjoyed the patronage of the retired emperor GO-TOBA, taught poetics to MINAMOTO NO SANETOMO, and served as an official of the KUJŌ FAMILY, which had close ties with the Kamakura shogunate, his diary also contains important information about courtier-warrior relations early in the Kamakura period (1185–1333). It is of further historical importance because parts of *Meigetsuki* were used as a source for the AZUMA KAGAMI, the history of the Kamakura shogunate.

G. Cameron HURST III

Meigō ōrai

(Akihira's Letter Writer). Earliest example of a genre called ŌRAIMONO; i.e., collections of models for letter writing. Compiled ca 1058 by FUJIWARA NO AKIHIRA (989–1066), an eminent Confucianist. Also called *Meigō shōsoku, Unshū ōrai,* or *Unshū shōsoku*. Model letters and their replies, written by males only, are arranged

Emperor Meiji

The emperor photographed toward the middle of his reign.

by season. These letters are written in HENTAI KAMBUN (a heavily Japanized form of classical Chinese) and contain abundant honorific expressions in the polite styles. These furnish valuable linguistic material for studying the epistolary language of men in the 11th century. *Gisaburō N. KIYOSE*

Meiji Canal

(Meiji Yōsui). Irrigation canal on the Okazaki Plain, central Aichi Prefecture, central Honshū. It extends from the river Yahagigawa to Mikawa Bay. Construction of this and supporting canals was completed in the 1880s, allowing agricultural development of the Okazaki Plain for the first time. The canal now services the city of Anjō, one of Japan's leading truck-gardening areas, and its vicinity, irrigating about 7,000 hectares (17,290 acres) of paddy fields. Length: 50 km (31 mi); total length of branch canals: 300 km (186 mi).

Meiji Constitution → constitution

Meiji, Emperor (1852–1912)

The 122nd sovereign *(tennō)* in the traditional count (which includes several nonhistorical emperors); reigned 1867–1912. Called Meiji posthumously from the name of the Meiji period (1868–1912). Son of Emperor KŌMEI and Yoshiko, daughter of the great counselor *(dainagon)* Nakayama Tadayasu (1809–88). He became crown prince in 1860 as Mutsuhito (his personal name) and succeeded to the throne at the age of 14. Because of his youth, Nijō Nariyuki (1816–78) served as regent *(sesshō)*. He took as his empress Ichijō Haruko (1850–1914; later Shōken Kōtaigō, or Empress Dowager Shōken). From an early age he studied calligraphy, poetry, and the principles of righteous government with his parents. After their deaths, he received his education from his father-in-law, Tadayasu. Although known as a strong-willed boy who loved wooden swords, hobby horses, and war games, he is said to have fainted at the sound of gunfire during the 1864 HAMAGURI GOMON INCIDENT, in which domainal troops exchanged shots at the palace gates.

In the movement leading to the overthrow of the TOKUGAWA SHOGUNATE, he, or rather the imperial institution, became the rallying point (see SONNŌ JŌI). With the MEIJI RESTORATION (1868), the dual system of government was destroyed, and the emperor was once more made the supreme authority. The CHARTER OATH outlining the philosophy of the new government was issued in the emperor's name, and the capital was moved from Kyōto to Tōkyō. Emperor Meiji's long reign was to be marked by momentous events (see HISTORY OF JAPAN: Meiji history). The IMPERIAL RESCRIPT TO SOLDIERS AND SAILORS, the Meiji Constitution, and the IMPERIAL RESCRIPT ON EDUCATION were promulgated. The DIET was founded. Japan's industrial revolution was carried out. Important developments also occurred in foreign affairs: the extension of diplomatic relationships, the revision of the Unequal Treaties (see UNEQUAL TREATIES, REVISION OF), the signing of the ANGLO-JAPANESE ALLIANCE, the SINO-JAPANESE WAR OF 1894–1895, the RUSSO-JAPANESE WAR, and the annexation of Korea (1910).

Throughout his reign, the supreme power of the state and command of military forces were increasingly concentrated in the emperor's hands. Indeed, the Meiji Constitution had declared that "the Empire of Japan shall be reigned over and governed by a line of Emperors," that "the Emperor is sacred and inviolable," and that the emperor combined "in himself the rights of sovereignty." In fact, however, it is difficult to clarify to what extent these state and foreign policies originated from the "direct imperial rule" of Emperor Meiji as an individual. To be sure, there were power struggles between the civil and the military, the army and navy, and various cliques (see HAMBATSU). There were also struggles on a personal level among those who had contributed to the restoration, such as ITŌ HIROBUMI, ŌKUBO TOSHIMICHI, SAIGŌ TAKAMORI, and KIDO TAKAYOSHI. Therefore it is likely that the emperor expressed his own political views from time to time. It is known that in the 1873 controversy over a proposed invasion of Korea (see SEIKANRON) the emperor supported the policy of giving priority to internal affairs and that he fully endorsed the 1875 edict promising the establishment of a constitutional government. He is said to have been unhappy with the decision to go to war with China in 1894 and to have sent a messenger to report the opening hostilities to the Ise Shrine and to his father's tomb. Again, he hesitated until the last moment before the Russo-Japanese War, expressing his feeling in a poem:

Yomo no umi	On all four seas
Mina harakara to	I thought all men were brothers,
Omou yo ni	Yet in this world
Nado namikaze no	Why do winds and waves
Tachisawaguran	Now rise and stir?

This poem was later read aloud by his grandson Hirohito (later Emperor Hirohito) at the imperial conference convoked on 6 September 1941 when relations between the United States and Japan had reached an impasse. Yet on the whole the emperor stood above politics, a benevolent father-figure rather than a stern monarch.

As befitting an "enlightened ruler," government leaders saw to it that the emperor heard lectures on Japanese and European history, Chinese classics, French and German law, and, for a brief while, German language. Among his tutors, MOTODA NAGAZANE, who lectured on the Confucian *Analects,* left a deep influence both as a scholar and as a human being. In 1871 and 1872 some outstanding former retainers of pre-Meiji *daimyō* were added to the imperial entourage, which had previously consisted only of aristocrats, in order to bring the *samurai* spirit and ethos *(bushidō)* into the palace. It is said that the emperor occasionally gathered favorite retainers for *sake* parties and discussed with them battles, the rise and fall of various countries, and the situation of the Franco-Prussian War then in progress. In literature he preferred old military chronicles such as the GEMPEI SEISUIKI, the TAIHEIKI, and the Chinese *Romance of the Three Kingdoms.*

Emperor Meiji was not generally fond of European-style innovations. He accepted changes that were unavoidable for diplomatic reasons, such as ceremonial uniforms, but as a rule he opposed unreasonable imitation of the West and forbade discarding traditional ceremonies and rites. On his frequent trips through the country, he showed an interest in maintaining historical sites and other famous places. At the same time he showed certain proclivities for change: he permitted the female attendants of the empress to attend, though in a corner, the ceremony promulgating the constitution. He enjoyed Western food, especially river fish and vegetables and was interested in Western music and sports. For a Japanese he was of robust build. It is said that he was eloquent and had a sense of humor.

In his role as supreme commander of the military forces, the emperor was conscientious and dedicated. When the Sino-Japanese War broke out, he went to the Hiroshima headquarters and, according to an attendant, stayed in a room without amenities, thinking of the place as the battlefield. He attended military meetings from early morning till midnight. When reports came in from the front at any time of night, he arose at once to discuss the progress of the Japanese forces with his officers. During the Russo-Japanese war too, he was austere in his personal habits. The hard work and anxiety of the war years left him looking markedly aged. His fatal illness a few years later is said to have resulted from his exhaustion at that time.

He died on 30 July 1912 and was buried in the Momoyama Mausoleum in Fushimi, Kyōto. His death symbolically brought to an end the era of Japan's successful transformation into a modern state.

The leading writer of the period, NATSUME SŌSEKI, had the protagonist in one of his novels (Kokoro) relate, "Emperor Meiji passed away in the prime of the summer's heat. I felt that the spirit of Meiji had started and ended with him." Erwin von BÄLZ, the German physician who had known him for years, included this tribute in his memoirs: "Later generations of Japan will probably paint a halo around his image, but in any case, this new era in which Japan entered modern world history is connected to the name of Emperor Meiji." See also EMPEROR.

——Marius B. Jansen, "Monarchy and Modernization in Japan," *Journal of Asian Studies* 36.4 (1977). Kunaishō Rinji Teishitsu Henshūkyoku, ed, *Meiji Tennō ki*, 13 vols (1968–75). Rikugunshō, ed, *Meiji Tennō ondenki shiryō*, 2 vols (1966). Watanabe Ikujirō, *Meiji Tennō*, 2 vols (1958).

Shumpei OKAMOTO

Meiji Enlightenment

(bummei kaika). Term applied to the movement of thought and belief during the early part of the Meiji period (1868–1912) when the Meiji government adopted a policy of modernization and began to introduce Western civilization into the country. With the restoration of direct imperial rule (see ŌSEI FUKKO), the new government implemented a series of policies to eliminate the old feudal political system and to establish the foundations of a modern centralized state. Under the slogan A Rich Country and a Strong Military (fukoku kyōhei) the Meiji government abolished the feudal socioeconomic system, adopted modern production methods, and established universal conscription. In parallel with this, under the slogan Civilization and Enlightenment (bummei kaika), the government also carried out a movement to educate the general populace.

Thus, the government took the initiative by issuing Western uniforms to the army and navy and encouraging government officials to wear Western clothes. It also encouraged people to eat Western foods, cut off their topknots, and stop wearing swords (HAITŌREI). It adopted the Gregorian calendar, implemented telegraph and postal services, and started constructing RAILWAYS. In education, it established a nationwide public school system aimed at educating responsible citizens of a modern state. People like FUKUZAWA YUKICHI and others associated with the MEIROKUSHA tried to introduce Western civilization through their writings. Increased intercourse with the West and with foreigners also stimulated the adoption of Western ideas and values such as political liberty and equality, as evidenced in the FREEDOM AND PEOPLE'S RIGHTS MOVEMENT.

During the early 1870s, when enthusiasm for Civilization and Enlightenment was particularly high, the adoption of Western civilization sometimes took extreme forms. Many Japanese regarded their own tradition as antiquated and useless and took Civilization and Enlightenment to mean the wholesale imitation of anything Western. A reaction set in around 1880, particularly in view of the rising people's rights movements, and the government attempted to revive conservative Confucian values and thought.

UMETANI Noboru

Meiji Gakuin University

(Meiji Gakuin Daigaku). A private, coeducational university located in Minato Ward, Tōkyō. The descendant of James Curtis Hepburn's Eigakujuku and the Brown's School of Samuel Robbins Brown, Meiji Gakuin was formed in 1886, and attained university status in 1949. It maintains faculties of letters, economics, sociology, and law, and offers night courses in all departments. It is known for the following institutes: Institute of Linguistic and Cultural Studies, Christian Research Institute, Foreign Language Institute, Institute of Sociology and Social Work, Institute of the Department of General Education, Institute of Science and Law, and Research Institute of Industry and Economy. Enrollment in 1980 was 7,383.

Meiji government, early → Dajōkan

Meiji history → history of Japan

Meiji Ishin → Meiji Restoration

Meiji Jūyonen no Seihen → Political Crisis of 1881

Meiji Mura

Originally built in 1885 in Kusakabe, Yamanashi Prefecture, to serve as a district office, this wooden structure was moved to Meiji Mura in 1965.

Meiji Milk Products Co, Ltd

(Meiji Nyūgyō). Manufacturer of products such as milk, ice cream, butter, cheese, margarine, powdered milk, and frozen foods. Products are sold under the Meiji brand name. The company was established in 1917. MEIJI SEIKA KAISHA, LTD, is a related firm. A tie-up with Borden, Inc, of the United States is Meiji Nyūgyō's chief international activity. Continued efforts are being made to develop the company into a general food enterprise. Sales for the fiscal year ending March 1982 totaled ¥326.8 billion (US $1.4 billion), of which fluid milk products accounted for 45 percent, manufactured dairy products 17 percent, ice cream 12 percent, and others 26 percent. Capitalization stood at ¥9.8 billion (US $40.7 million) in 1982. The corporate headquarters are in Tōkyō.

Meiji Mura

Outdoor museum in Inuyama, Aichi Prefecture. Opened in 1965 as a major project to preserve buildings and artifacts from the Meiji period (1868–1912). The buildings, which have been brought from all over Japan, include churches, banks, stores, hospitals, government buildings, private homes, and a prison. There are Western- and Japanese-style structures. The residences of the Meiji-period writers MORI ŌGAI and NATSUME SŌSEKI and parts of the original IMPERIAL HOTEL of Tōkyō designed by Frank Lloyd Wright are preserved here. There are also several running trains and trolley cars from the period. Area: 50 hectares (124 acres).

Meiji Mutual Life Insurance Co

(Meiji Seimei Hoken Sōgo Kaisha). Leading life insurance company; member of the Mitsubishi group. Meiji Mutual Life was established in 1881 as Japan's first modern life insurance company. It became a mutual life insurance company in 1947. It was active in exploring new fields, and after World War II initiated various new types of insurance, including life insurance on a monthly installment plan for workers, group term insurance, and old-age insurance that provides 10 to 30 times the amount insured at the time of maturity in the event of death. In 1976 it expanded overseas with the purchase of stock in the Pacific Guardian Life Insurance Co (Hawaii) and in 1981 established another US subsidiary, Meiji Realty Inc of America (New York). It has also strengthened its affiliation with the América Latina Companhia de Segaros (Brazil) and concluded group insurance agreements with major life insurance companies in the United States, Europe, and Southeast Asia. With the rapid growth of the elderly population in Japan, the company is currently facing the problem of how to satisfy the needs of older retired persons. In the fiscal year ending March 1982 revenue from insurance premiums totaled ¥787 billion (US $3.3 billion), of which ¥587.3 billion (US $2.4 billion) was generated by individual insurance premiums, ¥68.3 billion (US $284 million) by group premiums, and ¥96.9 billion (US $402.5 million) by group annuity premiums. As of 31 March 1982, its total assets amounted to ¥2.5 trillion (US $10.4 billion), while insurance contracts totaled ¥62 trillion (US $257.6 billion). Corporate headquarters are located in Tōkyō.

Meiji period

The reign of Emperor MEIJI; the beginning of the modern period (*kindai*) of Japanese history. It began on 23 October 1868 (Keiō 4.9.8), when the new sovereign, who had become emperor on 13 February 1867, selected the era name Meiji ("Enlightened Rule") for his reign, although the era was extended retroactively to 3 January (Keiō 3.12.9), when the restoration of direct imperial rule (ŌSEI FUKKO) had been proclaimed; it ended with the emperor's death on 30 July 1912. In contrast to previous reigns, when as many as five or six era names (NENGŌ) had been adopted in succession under a single ruler, it was decreed that thenceforth only one *nengō* would be assigned to each reign (*issei ichigen*). The Meiji period was a momentous epoch that saw the transformation of feudal Japan into a modern industrialized state with a parliamentary form of government and its emergence as a world power through military adventures abroad. See also HISTORY OF JAPAN: Meiji history.

Meiji Restoration

(Meiji Ishin). Narrowly defined, the coup d'etat of 3 January 1868 in which antishogunate forces led by the great southern domains Satsuma (now Kagoshima Prefecture) and Chōshū (now Yamaguchi Prefecture) seized the Imperial Palace in Kyōto and announced the formal return of political power from the TOKUGAWA SHOGUNATE to the emperor (see ŌSEI FUKKO). More broadly, the series of political, social, and economic changes in the third quarter of the 19th century that resulted in the dismemberment of the BAKUHAN SYSTEM of the Edo period (1600–1868) and Japan's development into a unified, modern state in the Meiji era (1868–1912). The era-name (*nengō*) Meiji was chosen to indicate that the young emperor, Mutsuhito (see Emperor MEIJI), would institute "enlightened rule." The term "restoration" was later chosen to indicate a return to ancient governmental institutions and imperial rule after eight centuries of warrior control over civil affairs. The early proclamations of the Restoration leaders related Japan's turn to Western forms to its appropriation of Chinese institutional models in the 7th and 8th centuries.

Background——The diplomatic and political crises of mid-19th-century Japan came at a time of institutional and intellectual disquiet. Three aspects of this context are particularly important.

First, the Tempō era (1830–44) was marked by economic dislocations brought about by a series of famines in the years 1833 to 1836 (see TEMPŌ FAMINE). Although these famines were particularly severe in northeastern Japan, their effects were felt nationwide. The shogunate's efforts to increase the flow of rice to the cities received only limited cooperation from the domainal governments. Agrarian insurrections were numerous and more nearly regional in scale than ever before (see HYAKUSHŌ IKKI). In Ōsaka, ŌSHIO HEIHACHIRŌ raised a revolt that laid waste large parts of that center of national commerce. The unsuccessful reforms of the shogunal minister MIZUNO TADAKUNI, in addition to implementing the usual restrictions and sumptuary controls, attempted to increase the centralization of the shogunate by expropriating vassal domains in the Kantō and Kansai areas (see AGECHIREI). These efforts aroused widespread resistance. The Tempō emergencies also gave rise to reform programs, with varying degrees of success, in many domains. For example, the reform effort in Mito (now part of Ibaraki Prefecture) achieved little, but in Satsuma and Chōshū financial consolidation of the domainal governments was more successful (see TEMPŌ REFORMS).

A second source of uneasiness was the approach of the West. Russian and British efforts to end Japan's policy of NATIONAL SECLUSION had had little effect, but they had sufficed to alert such writers as HAYASHI SHIHEI and HONDA TOSHIAKI to the possibility that Japan's seclusion was endangered. The early decades of the 19th century saw increased Japanese interest in the activities of the Western countries. In Mito, FUJITA TŌKO began as early as 1826 to suspect a general European plot against Japan. The news of China's defeat at the hands of the West in the Opium War (1839–42) came as chilling confirmation of such fears of the West, especially for conservative scholars steeped in Chinese Confucianism. Chinese books about the West, like Wei Yuan's *Haiguo tuzhi* (*Hai-kuo t'u-chih*, 1844; Illustrated Gazetteer of Maritime Countries), went through many editions in Japan and produced alarmed commentary from official Confucians like Shionoya Tōin (1809–67).

Third, the Japanese intellectual world was changing with the impact and diffusion of WESTERN LEARNING and the influence of nativist National Learning (KOKUGAKU). Interest in Dutch books had begun to increase in the last decades of the 18th century. In 1811 the shogunate attached officials for the translation of foreign books (*bansho wage goyōgakari*) to its Bureau of Astronomy, but they channeled only one stream of a translation movement so broad that SUGITA GEMPAKU, in his memoirs (1815), compared it to the translation of works from China a millennium earlier. On the whole, the works translated had only limited political content; but in a time of crisis, when a book seemed to touch upon matters of national policy, the translation movement could appear subversive. The Tempō era witnessed a direct confrontation between the shogunate and a group of Western Learning scholars who warned of possible dangers from the regime's refusal in 1837 to receive the English ship *Morrison* and the Japanese castaways it sought to return (see MORRISON INCIDENT). In 1839 this group of outstanding scholars were tried and convicted for criticizing shogunate policy (see BANSHA NO GOKU).

In the late Edo period there was also a rapid diffusion of the nationalistic school of Kokugaku. Concern with national identity was a natural product of these years of intellectual ferment and social crisis. In the Mito domain, Kokugaku nationalism was blended with Confucianism by scholars like Fujita Tōko and, outstandingly, AIZAWA SEISHISAI (see MITO SCHOOL). Aizawa's work SHINRON (1825) became steadily more influential as a call for loyalty to the imperial house with its divine origins and sacred mission for Japan's unique national polity (KOKUTAI). Mito scholars helped to shape the thinking of their lord, TOKUGAWA NARIAKI, an important figure in national politics after the advent of Commodore PERRY in 1853. An early and prominent center of loyalist thought and activity, Mito produced the assassins who in 1860 murdered the shogunal great elder (*tairō*) II NAOSUKE, who sought to accommodate Western demands for a commercial treaty. (The term "loyalist" is used here to refer to political activists who professed supreme allegiance to the emperor and became increasingly hostile to the shogunate for its allegedly immoral usurpation of imperial power.)

The Tempō years produced the political figures and the ideology that were to dominate the Restoration. That the problems of the time constituted a true "crisis," as modern historians usually claim, is not certain; that these problems later became critical with the coming of the West cannot be doubted.

The Opening and Its Consequences——The American flotilla led by Commodore Perry brought an end to Japan's seclusion (see OPENING OF JAPAN). Although Perry's arrival was not entirely unexpected, the shogunate was quite unprepared for the problems it raised.

Perry presented his demand for a treaty in July 1853. Between then and his return the following spring, the shogunate, conscious of its inability to repulse his demand by force, took the first of a number of steps that galvanized the ruling stratum of Japanese society. Copies of the American letter were circulated among the *daimyō* in the hope of building support for whatever response was to be made. It had the opposite effect. The daimyō responses, of which 59 survive, ranged from Tokugawa Nariaki's resolute call for defiance and preparation for conflict to Ii Naosuke's cautious advocacy of relaxation of the existing laws. The replies showed no clear pattern by category of domain size or location, but they made it clear that no response—short of successful resistance to the American proposal—would produce the consensus the shogunate sought. In December the shogunate announced that it would try to avoid a definite reply to Perry and make every effort to preserve peace, and that meanwhile preparations for possible conflict should be made.

On his return to Japan, Perry secured the KANAGAWA TREATY of 31 March 1854; this opened the ports of Shimoda and Hakodate to foreign ships for supplies and repairs but made no provision for trade. In 1856 Townsend HARRIS arrived at Shimoda to take up his duties as United States consul general, and he pointed to the second round of warfare between China and Britain and France (1856–60) as an indication of what Japan might expect if it failed to grant a new treaty that incorporated trade privileges. By the end of 1857 Harris had been received in the shogunal capital of Edo (now Tōkyō), where he began to work out the essentials of such a treaty. Late in February 1858 the HARRIS TREATY was drafted; it provided for trade at Nagasaki, Hakodate, and Kanagawa and for future arrangements at Niigata, Hyōgo, Edo, and Ōsaka, as well as for extraterritoriality and moderate customs rates.

With these additional concessions, the consensus among Japanese decision makers became more fragile. Shogunate officials had tried to include Tokugawa Nariaki in their confidence, but the passing of leadership of the Senior Council (RŌJŪ) from ABE MASAHIRO to HOTTA MASAYOSHI resulted in the exclusion of Nariaki as preparations for trade and diplomacy went forward. Hotta next turned to secure approval of the new treaty from the Kyōto court. Although he saw this as a formality, and Harris regarded the entire maneuver as a delaying tactic, Hotta encountered opposition that had been fostered there by Nariaki and like-minded daimyō. The Harris Treaty now became linked with the issue of shogunal succession.

The shōgun Tokugawa Iesada (1824–58) was childless. His adoptive successor would normally have come from the Kii line of the Tokugawa house, but its candidate was a mere child at the time. Calls for an able and mature shōgun to deal with the foreign crisis focused instead on the adoptive head of the Hitotsubashi line, TOKUGAWA YOSHINOBU, who was in fact Nariaki's son. A number of "reform" daimyō—YAMANOUCHI TOYOSHIGE of Tosa (now Kōchi Prefecture), Date Munenari (1818–92) of Uwajima (now part of Ehime Prefecture), SHIMAZU NARIAKIRA of Satsuma, and MATSUDAIRA YOSHINAGA of Echizen (now part of Fukui Prefecture)—combined to lobby, in Kyōto and Edo, for the selection of Yoshinobu, the succession issue being the first of several issues on which they would join efforts. Interference of this sort at the very core of Tokugawa house concerns produced counter-efforts by hereditary (FUDAI) vassals like Ii Naosuke of Hikone (now part of Shiga Prefecture) to separate the treaty and succession issues. Ii was successful in this, but because Emperor KŌMEI was hostile to the Harris Treaty, the Tokugawa cause failed to secure imperial approval; the shogunate had succeeded in separating the two issues, but at the cost of losing the treaty. Ii Naosuke was appointed great elder in the early summer of 1858. Shortly afterward he abandoned a second effort to obtain imperial approval out of fear that British and French forces, now victorious in China, would be brought to bear on Japan. Meanwhile, the succession issue was resolved in favor of the Kii line (the future TOKUGAWA IEMOCHI), and proimperial sentiment was further alienated by heavy-handed steps to secure the imperial princess KAZU as his consort. Shogunate efforts to build a consensus among the daimyō and at court had instead resulted in hardening divisions, and the ripples produced by the original request to the daimyō soon spread outward to their retainers and more lowly followers.

Once the ports were opened in 1859, a foreign presence gave concrete meaning to slogans like jōi (Expel the Barbarians!). Political disagreements widened, for several SHOGUNATE MISSIONS TO THE WEST (the first to Washington in 1860) confirmed in responsible leaders' minds the necessity of opening the country, while the presence of foreigners in Japan provided provocation for xenophobes. Foreign trade raised the price of staples like tea and silk by providing new market demand for them; it also threatened the soundness of Japanese currency because of differences between the relative value of gold and silver in Japan and abroad. All this helped to worsen a price spiral that struck particularly at those who, like samurai, were on fixed incomes. Furthermore, the treaties with the United States were quickly followed by agreements (known collectively with the Harris Treaty as the ANSEI COMMERCIAL TREATIES) with other Western powers. The same conditions of institutionalized inequality (most-favored-nation clauses, extraterritoriality, fixed tariffs) that the Western powers had fixed on the China coast they now imposed on Japan. Antiforeign incidents, more frequent than in China, led to Western demands for satisfaction and recompense that were served not on the perpetrators but on the shogunate. As a result the opening of Japan began a process of weakening for the shogunate. Forced to take unpopular steps, it was cast as proforeign and indifferent to the desires of the court. Inevitably, it became the target of cries of SONNŌ JŌI.

The Impact of Ii Naosuke —— With Ii Naosuke as tairō, shogunate mainliners tried to overcome their opponents by repression in what has come to be known as the ANSEI PURGE. Consultation had failed, and since unilateral actions were certain to arouse opposition, there seemed no alternative to force. Hotta was dismissed, and his bureaucratic associates were removed. Next, the opposition was silenced: Tokugawa Nariaki was placed under house arrest, Hitotsubashi (Tokugawa) Yoshinobu was banned from Edo Castle, and the daimyō of Echizen, Owari (now part of Aichi Prefecture), and Tosa were ordered to retire in favor of their successors. Shimazu Nariakira, the Satsuma daimyō, died before Ii's vengeance reached him, but some of his trusted retainers were retired. At Kyōto the nobles who had worked with the daimyō were also dismissed from their court offices. Next Ii pressed the emperor for approval of the diplomatic actions that had been taken. Approval was grudgingly granted in February 1859, though the decree characterized the Harris Treaty as "a blemish on our Empire and a stain on our divine land."

Such punishment of daimyō meant a reshuffling of administrative posts in the domains and dismissal or punishment of the advisers who had led the daimyō into trouble. Ii's victory meant exile for SAIGŌ TAKAMORI of Satsuma and execution for HASHIMOTO SANAI of Echizen, Rai Mikisaburō (1825–59), son of the historian RAI SAN'YŌ, and many other loyalists. Plot and counterplot, terror and repression, accounted for the lives of over 100 loyalists, including the Chōshū teacher YOSHIDA SHŌIN.

The impact of these events can be seen in the careers of many individuals. In Chōshū the advent of Commodore Perry had stirred a young Yoshida Shōin in 1854 to try to leave Japan aboard one of Perry's ships in the hope of studying the outer world at first hand. Thwarted in this wish and imprisoned by the shogunate for his offense, Shōin immersed himself in the study of the classics and began to write and teach. Released and able to devote himself fully to his studies, he collected in his private academy, Shōka Sonjuku in Hagi, a remarkable group of young students who absorbed his rage against the shogunate's apparent subservience to foreigners, disrespect to the court, and arrogance toward Japanese. Shōin's boldness grew with his anger, and he prepared plots for the assassination of shogunate officials. This resulted in his extradition to Edo and execution there in 1859. In this manner testaments, martyrs, and slogans accumulated for the future struggle.

Ii Naosuke's victory seemed total, but its cost was high. The dream of a new unity under Tokugawa leadership that had led Mito and Echizen (Tokugawa Nariaki and Matsudaira Yoshinaga) to propose Yoshinobu as shōgun in a reform administration was gone. Shogunal repression fanned the discontent that the treaty and succession issues had stirred. A response was not long in coming. As Ii Naosuke proceeded to Edo Castle on 24 March 1860, his escorts' swords under cover to protect them from a late spring snow, his entourage was ambushed by a party of 1 Satsuma and 17 Mito loyalists. They made off with Ii's head and left a document denouncing him for his affronts to the court and to the sacred land of the sun goddess. See SAKURADAMONGAI INCIDENT.

These events ushered in years of individual and collective violence. The ripples begun by the shogunate's request for daimyō opinion in 1853 had now reached the attention of lower samurai at the outermost circumference of the ruling class. There they found individuals in whom frustration with the limitations of hereditary rank and ritualized humility combined with a keen sense of their calling as men of the sword. The crisis of the times and their expectation of a confrontation with the West had led them to place renewed emphasis on their warrior training. Poorly informed about their country's predicament and inclined to be critical of their highborn superiors, they were also intent upon preserving the prestige and standing of their domains—which they saw as warrior peer groups—over rival domains. Consequently they grew indignant at the punishment of their daimyō by Ii Naosuke. Educated in their country's traditions and schooled in a combination of Confucian loyalism and Shintō nativism, they professed a "pure" and "selfless" loyalty to their daimyō and emperor. Given a conflict, however, the emperor came first; they were quick to dismiss the caution or doubts of their immediate superiors, the domain officials, while professing a "higher loyalty." This profession of supreme loyalty to the emperor was to become their great virtue (taigi), even if it meant technical disobedience to their superiors and abandonment of family and domain to become RŌNIN (masterless samurai).

History knows these men as shishi, "men of high purpose." Their intensity and reckless courage made them a potent force for disruption. Some entered national politics as members of close-knit groups formed around a charismatic leader-teacher like Yoshida Shōin or TAKECHI ZUIZAN of Tosa. Others attached themselves as individuals to the entourages of court nobles, received protection from officials of other domains, or found shelter in the support of like-minded rural samurai (GŌSHI) or even merchants. The grounds of Kyōto temples contain the graves of hundreds who died there, and many others met their end in other areas. They were a small fraction of the samurai class, but in a day of limited participation in politics, this large a group of men, with so little stake in the existing structure of rank and privilege of their class, was enough to affect national politics by pushing responsible officials to actions—or caution—they might otherwise have avoided. Shogunate officials were able to convince the Western envoys of the real dangers they faced. Court representatives became more credible negotiators on the stage of politics, and officials of Chōshū, Satsuma, and Tosa, which produced so many such activists, had to take them into account in making their plans. The domain of Mito in fact disappeared altogether as a serious factor in national politics because of a civil war forced by its *shishi* in 1864 (see MITO CIVIL WAR).

"Union of Court and Shogunate" —— The daimyō who had lobbied for the selection of Yoshinobu as shōgun in 1858 wanted an adjustment of the balance of power between themselves and the shogunate. The selection of the "able, mature" Yoshinobu as heir would, they thought, have brought this to pass. A reformed shogunate would have relaxed its controls over its vassal domains so that they could turn to programs of self-strengthening. The imperial court's frequent injunctions to the shogunate to consult the daimyō during the negotiations over the treaties carried the same message. Shogunate regulars correctly saw the entire movement as a threat to their hegemony, and Ii Naosuke's resolute repression had been designed to nip it in the bud.

Ii's murder brought the movement to the fore again. The phrase now used to describe it was "union of court and shogunate" *(kōbu gattai)*. The years 1861 to 1864 saw a succession of proposals designed to implement such a program (see MOVEMENT FOR UNION OF COURT AND SHOGUNATE). The attempts failed, however, partly because they had to contend with increasing violence as extremist activists created selective disorder to force their superiors into more intransigent positions. More important still, there was no single program. The successive proposals were springboards in a competition for influence among the three great southwestern domains of Chōshū, Satsuma, and Tosa. Their failure left a shogunate that had weakened itself by its concessions in the face of a critical political struggle.

The *kōbu gattai* movement was revived by Chōshū, whose official NAGAI UTA devised a resolution designed to moderate the differences between shogunate and court considerably to the court's advantage. He proposed to make it clear that the shogunate exercised its administration and hegemony "in accordance with the orders of the court"; in short, the court would set policy and the shogunate would execute it. Court circles having agreed to this, Nagai went on to Edo to try to negotiate its acceptance there. Events overtook him in the form of a more insistent proposal sponsored by Satsuma. This called for pardons for all punished in 1858, the appointment of Tokugawa Yoshinobu and Matsudaira Yoshinaga to high shogunate office, dismissal of incumbent Tokugawa leaders, and designation by the court of important daimyō to act as its representatives in keeping the shogunate to its word. SHIMAZU HISAMITSU, father of the young Satsuma daimyō, was sent with a large military force to escort the court noble dispatched with these plans to Edo. But even before the Satsuma leader reached Edo, these proposals resulted in important changes, not all of them expected.

Yoshinaga and Yoshinobu were appointed to high shogunate office, the former as shogunal prime minister *(seiji sōsaishoku)* and the latter as shogunal regent *(kōkenshoku)*. In addition, the Aizu daimyō MATSUDAIRA KATAMORI became protector of Kyōto (KYŌTO SHUGOSHOKU). All this added a "great daimyō" element to the shogunate's regular bureaucratic machinery. The posts filled by Yoshinaga and Yoshinobu created a buffer between the Edo bureaucracy and the great lords of the southwest; in negotiations that followed, Yoshinaga and Yoshinobu exasperated Edo officials—who had an entirely realistic view of diplomacy—as frequently as they did the court. Since their loyalties were ultimately to the Tokugawa cause, however, they shared with Edo suspicions of Satsuma's ambitions to dominate the country.

Further, it was announced that the young shōgun Iemochi would make a visit to Kyōto. No shōgun had done this since the time of TOKUGAWA IEMITSU in 1634. He too had been given as consort an imperial princess, and the designation now of Princess Kazu as Iemochi's consort constituted a new effort by the shogunate to gain legitimacy and strength from the court. But there the comparison ended: Iemitsu's trip had been made when the shogunate was at the height of its strength, while Iemochi found himself seeking support for power that was beginning to wane.

Iemitsu's trip had also been preliminary to the full institutionalization of SANKIN KŌTAI controls over the daimyō, under which they were required to reside in Edo in alternate years. In 1862 this situation too was reversed. In October the period of daimyō residence at Edo was reduced to 100 days in three years, ostensibly to permit the daimyō to practice the economies needed for military preparation. When the shogunate subsequently attempted to return to the old system of alternate-year residence, the daimyō simply refused to comply.

While these shogunal accommodations were still in progress, a more sweeping set of *kōbu gattai* proposals was put forth, indicating a desire to subordinate the shogunate more fully to Kyōto direction

and purpose. This time the military escort for the court noble dispatched to Edo, SANJŌ SANETOMI, was provided by the young Tosa daimyō Yamanouchi Toyonori. Tosa's participation resulted from an upheaval in that domain. YOSHIDA TŌYŌ, a "moderate" reformer close to the former daimyō Yamanouchi Toyoshige, had been murdered by Tosa loyalists who wanted their domain to join in national politics. Their leader, Takechi Zuizan, was an advocate of full imperial authority and of exclusion and had helped to arrange Tosa's appointment as escort for the Sanjō mission. Reaching Edo at the end of 1862, the mission presented the shogunate with a demand for the immediate expulsion of the foreigners from Japan. Thus each of the latter two missions in the *kōbu gattai* movement upstaged its predecessor to reveal the inherent fragility of any scheme that tried to redress the balance of court and shogunal authority in a setting of competitive distrust.

The net result of these moves can be summarized as follows. Shogunate reforms of 1862 had established new posts that added a "great daimyō" element to the shogunate bureaucratic machinery. Relaxation of the *sankin kōtai* system limited Tokugawa ability to restrain the movements of its feudatories. The granting of permission to the daimyō to build and purchase large ships laid another element of the seclusion system to rest and increased the military capability of domains that, like Satsuma, Chōshū, and Tosa, could afford such luxuries. The shogunate itself, it should be noted, had been vigorous in the pursuit of Western-style training and technology for the development of its naval capability. Bureaucratic accommodation for this new program had been provided in the person of KATSU KAISHŪ, newly appointed as a naval commissioner *(gunkan bugyō)*. After his dismissal in 1865 he was replaced by OGURI TADAMASA.

All these moves took place amid a rising tide of antiforeign rhetoric that drove leaders to adopt a posture of seeking to revoke or restrict concessions to the treaty powers at the same time that they were implementing them and utilizing them for the purchase of modern armaments. The shogunate's first mission to the West reached Washington, DC, in 1860 to exchange formal ratification of the Harris Treaty (see UNITED STATES, MISSION OF 1860 TO). Two years later a second mission left for Europe to seek extensions of the schedules that had been agreed upon for the opening of additional ports. The mission was partly successful, since loyalist attacks on the British legation in Shinagawa in 1861 and on the shogunate's commissioner for foreign affairs *(gaikoku bugyō)* in 1862 had convinced the treaty powers that shogunate warnings about political pressures were based on fact. These concessions in no way satisfied the demands of loyalists during the discussion of *kōbu gattai* proposals, however, for they saw foreign affairs as the shogunate's most vulnerable point.

Actually, neither side in these negotiations was united. Satsuma leaders warned the court against insisting on things that could not possibly be accomplished, while opinion in Tosa and, after dismissal of its first proposal, Chōshū was strongly antiforeign. Edo bureaucrats knew that expulsion was impossible, but Yoshinobu and Yoshinaga played for time by seeming to accept the court's xenophobic position. The arrival of the Tosa loyalists in Kyōto in 1862 added another large group of extremists to that scene. Now the court instructed the shogunate to revoke the treaties and expel the foreigners. As disagreements widened in the spring of 1863, the lords of Satsuma, Tosa, and Uwajima returned to their domains. Yoshinobu, operating in a setting dominated by loyalist extremism, accepted 25 June 1863 as the date for "expulsion." His intent, historians suggest, was to buy time by beginning what he knew would be a hopeless negotiation. Chōshū, however, anticipated him by ordering its batteries to fire on foreign shipping in the Shimonoseki Strait on that day.

The order for expulsion drew quick Western reaction. British representatives, already aroused by the murder of an Englishman by Satsuma samurai in Hisamitsu's entourage in 1862 (see RICHARDSON AFFAIR), had been pressing for shogunate payment of damages and Satsuma punishment of the offending samurai. When they failed to obtain satisfaction, a British flotilla bombarded and burned much of the castle town of Kagoshima in August 1863, soon after the Chōshū closing of the strait. Shortly afterward shogunate and Satsuma forces combined to expel Chōshū from Kyōto in order to relieve the court of loyalist and antiforeign intimidation (see COUP D'ETAT OF 30 SEPTEMBER 1863). A year later (September 1864) a combined Western force shelled and silenced the Chōshū batteries at Shimonoseki (see SHIMONOSEKI BOMBARDMENT).

Jōi (Expel the Barbarians!), samurai-style, had been proven impracticable. The Satsuma and Chōshū military establishments had seen first-hand the superiority of Western gunnery. The expulsion of Chōshū forces from Kyōto deprived individual swordsmen of their sanctuary there. Shogunate hardliners began to dream of reasserting their control. For others *jōi* remained an incendiary slogan and long-range goal, but only as yoked to *sonnō* (Revere the Emperor), and ultimately subordinated to *tōbaku* (Overthrow the Shogunate).

Regional Reform —— With the failure of exclusion and of *kōbu gattai*, various domains as well as the shogunate directed their energy to regional programs that combined political control with military preparations for future crises. *Jōi* had now to be translated into larger programs for increasing the nation's wealth and military power (FUKOKU KYŌHEI) so that it might gain equality with the West. For the great southwestern domains in particular, individual heroism took second place to preparation for domain-wide participation. This reorientation resulted from the events of 1864.

Chōshū's closing of the Shimonoseki Strait, the expulsion of its forces from Kyōto by shogunate-Satsuma combined action, and the flight of loyalist court nobles to Chōshū (SHICHIKYŌ OCHI) had left Chōshū isolated among the domains. Incidents in Yamato (TENCHŪGUMI REBELLION) and Tajima in the Kansai area, where small groups of loyalist zealots tried to revolt in presumed obedience to the now defunct imperial edict calling for expulsion, increased the number of loyalist casualties as well as loyalist survivors who sought refuge in Chōshū. In 1864 the Mito Civil War broke out, and the defeat of the Mito loyalists added hundreds more loyalist casualties. Within Chōshū, radicalism became more pronounced as the domain's isolation increased. Irregular militia groups (KIHEITAI) formed predominantly from lower-rank samurai and nonsamurai village leaders proved easier to organize than to control. In August, loyalists prevailed upon Chōshū leaders to authorize an expedition to Kyōto. Having fought its way almost to the palace gates, the Chōshū force was driven back with heavy losses (see HAMAGURI GOMON INCIDENT). Chōshū loyalists next had to face the humiliation of the four-nation naval bombardment that reopened the Shimonoseki Strait to Western shipping. There followed a political overturn in Chōshū as radicals and conservatives struggled for control of the domain. Since the leaders who survived this struggle went on to become pivotal figures in the Meiji state, these events have engrossed the attention of historians seeking social signficance in Restoration politics.

In the fall of 1864, after Chōshū's unsuccessful raid on Kyōto and the four-nation bombardment of Shimonoseki, the imperial court declared Chōshū in rebellion and authorized a punitive expedition (see CHŌSHŪ EXPEDITIONS). A heterogeneous shogunate force under the command of the daimyō of Owari set out for Chōshū. High on its staff was Saigō Takamori of Satsuma, who preferred negotiation to destruction of Chōshū lest that destruction provide a precedent for a resurgent shogunate. Agreements were worked out for a formal apology from Chōshū, the suicides of three Chōshū house elders, its suppression of the irregular militia companies, and its surrender to the Fukuoka domain (now Fukuoka Prefecture) of the loyalist court nobles Chōshū had sheltered. When these terms were agreed to and the heads delivered, the expedition was declared a success and disbanded.

In Chōshū, however, the leaders of the irregular militia units refused to comply. In January 1865 they began to attack regular domainal forces, thus changing the political balance once more; by March 1865 important Chōshū loyalist leaders had been restored to office. In these events the Restoration leaders TAKASUGI SHINSAKU, YAMAGATA ARITOMO, ITŌ HIROBUMI, INOUE KAORU, and KIDO TAKAYOSHI figured prominently. By the late spring of 1865 the shogunate had announced the need for a second punitive expedition against Chōshū; but before imperial authorization had been gained and the striking force was put together, another year would pass.

Chōshū leaders used this period for intensive military preparation. This took the form of importation of Western rifles via Nagasaki, purchase of Western steamships, and integration of the irregular militia forces with the domain's samurai units. The certainty of conflict lent urgency to intensive drill, and "Chōshū patriotism," strengthened by moral conviction of upholding the "true" imperial and national interest, lent fervor to the cause. Middle-ranking loyalists like Kido Takayoshi held high domainal office and set domain policy. The bloodletting of the previous years had thinned the ranks of extremists and obscurantist conservatives alike, and the domain was assuming the nature of a "nation in arms"—the goal of much later Meiji rhetoric—with commoners serving alongside samurai in mixed militia units.

Similar steps, though without comparable intra-class feuding, characterized developments in Satsuma. Shimazu Hisamitsu had never lost control of his domain's affairs in the way that his counterpart, Mōri Takachika (1819–71), had in Chōshū; Satsuma had never seriously advocated the exclusion of the foreigners and Hisamitsu had left Kyōto for Kagoshima when in 1863 Kyōto opinion turned in favor of that impossible policy. Hisamitsu had earlier appointed a leader of the Satsuma loyalist faction, ŌKUBO TOSHIMICHI, to office on the understanding that Ōkubo would work to restrain loyalist extremists until Hisamitsu deemed it appropriate to intervene in national affairs. In 1864 Hisamitsu recalled from exile Saigō Takamori, who had been exiled to a southern island during Ii Naosuke's purge several years earlier. Satsuma's willingness to cooperate with shogunate forces in restraining Chōshū loyalists was enhanced by the awareness of Ōkubo and Saigō that a full Chōshū victory would leave Satsuma in second place behind a rival domain. Once Chōshū was at a disadvantage, however, a full shogunate victory would have been equally undesirable; hence Saigō's efforts to mediate the settlement with Chōshū during the first punitive expedition.

Meanwhile Satsuma began to improve relations with the more reasonable wing of the loyalist movement. When Katsu Kaishū was dismissed as shogunate naval commissioner in 1864, he arranged for Satsuma to protect a young Tosa loyalist, SAKAMOTO RYŌMA, whom he had taken under his wing. Nakaoka Shintarō, another Tosa loyalist, who had fought in one of the Chōshū militia corps, also received Saigō's help in protecting Kyōto loyalist nobles. Saigō's intervention raised Satsuma in the esteem of the Chōshū loyalists. When Takasugi Shinsaku and his militia units returned to power in Chōshū, the way was open for an agreement with Satsuma. The Tosa loyalists Sakamoto and Nakaoka served as middlemen in the negotiations, and Saigō for Satsuma and Kido for Chōshū sealed a mutual defense agreement in March 1866 (see SATSUMA–CHŌSHŪ ALLIANCE). The shogunate could no longer count on the help of Satsuma to settle scores with recalcitrant Chōshū leaders. Satsuma's help made it possible for Sakamoto Ryōma to set up a commercial company that utilized a small steamer to transport Western guns from Nagasaki to Chōshū and Chōshū grain to Satsuma. *Rōnin* from Tosa also served to mediate between the refugee Kyōto nobles (now in Dazaifu in the Fukuoka domain) and Satsuma, the domain whose cooperation with the shogunate had resulted in their flight from Kyōto in the first place. Satsuma thus prepared to change directions. Henceforth its efforts in diplomacy and self-strengthening would help its own cause and not the shogunate's.

The domain of Tosa also swung into line. Because its daimyō had been "promoted" by Tokugawa Ieyasu, the founder of the shogunate, Tosa, unlike Chōshū and Satsuma, was not obsessed by a traditional antipathy to Tokugawa rule. Nonetheless, Tosa was anxious to be a part of whatever settlement might result and particularly eager to prevent a full military confrontation from which it could only expect to emerge in second place. The former daimyō, Yamanouchi Toyoshige, first solidified his support and subdued dissent. When loyalism fell on evil days in the summer of 1863, he returned to Tosa and summoned his loyalist retainers to him. Takechi Zuizan's group was gradually deprived of power, interrogated about its recent presumption in setting domain policy, and punished. Takechi himself was imprisoned and ordered to commit suicide in 1865. Loyalists in eastern Tosa who tried to rise in revolt were wiped out. With the domain under control again, its administration came back into the hands of disciples of the assassinated Yoshida Tōyō. Policy turned to expanding domainal income and military strength: a trading company was set up to market Tosa products in Nagasaki and Ōsaka; foreign ships and foreign guns were bought; and military reforms brought Western-style troop formations and equipment, the units so formed being controlled by ITAGAKI TAISUKE and GOTŌ SHŌJIRŌ.

Tosa officials next showed interest in using their exiled loyalists, who were becoming prominent in national politics. After proper conciliatory moves, Sakamoto Ryōma and Nakaoka Shintarō were reinstated as Tosa vassals. Sakamoto's shipping company became a sort of domainal enterprise (the KAIENTAI), and Nakaoka headed a land unit (RIKUENTAI).

The same pattern characterized the policies of the shogunate itself. After the foreign chastisement of Chōshū the shogunate tried to reinstate the *sankin kōtai* system, but the important daimyō paid it no heed. It was suddenly clear that the shogunate was now in fact just another regional polity, although a very large one, and no longer a real national hegemon. All the powerful domains now had secondary headquarters at Kyōto as well as Edo, and the shogunate could no longer control their channels of communications. Even the foreign representatives gathered near Ōsaka in 1865 to be closer to the court. Shogunal authority had in the last analysis always rested upon force, and in 1866 it was clear that the shogunate could no longer impose its will upon its strongest vassals. When a Tokugawa-led army finally attacked Chōshū a second time in the summer of 1866, this ungainly collection of forces from 32 domains met disaster at every point at the hands of the better trained and motivated Chōshū troops. The timely death of the shōgun Iemochi provided a face-saving pretext to call a halt to the fighting. Satsuma leaders had worked to slow compliance with shogunate demands for cooperation. They also worked to limit the shogunate's success in dominating the imperial court.

From this point on shogunate leadership passed securely into the hands of its own "self-strengthening" faction. Tokugawa Yoshinobu became shōgun at last, and reformist bureaucrats, many of whom, like Oguri Tadamasa, had had direct experience of the West, replaced the traditionalist counselors of the past. The shogunate began speeding military reforms. It now relied principally on its own territory, its own house vassals, and its own forces. *Fudai* autonomy took second place to centralization, and a tax reform promised to produce a shogunate army capable of doing its own work without calling on the motley collection of forces that had been humiliated by Chōshū. French technical assistance was utilized to establish a naval yard at Yokosuka (see YOKOSUKA SHIPYARDS), and modern warships were ordered from the United States and Europe. Students were sent to Europe to study, and further diplomatic missions, one led by the shōgun's younger brother, toured the Western world. The shogunate could now compete effectively for national leadership as the strongest among equals, and it had great advantages with its central position, superior resources, and foreign recognition.

Restoration —— These developments led to a confrontation of two forces, the one a somewhat wobbly Satsuma–Chōshū alliance, and the other an increasingly centralized shogunate gaining in military capability and political confidence. Satsuma and Chōshū had good access to able courtiers in Kyōto, including the astute IWAKURA TOMOMI, who began to suggest the desirability of an "imperial restoration" as the most probable way of reasserting national prestige and controlling the foreigners. The shogunate retained the authority to deal with the foreign powers, who were themselves now a substantial political force. Their insistence on access to additional ports and treaty rectification induced the shogunate to secure imperial approval of the treaties in November 1865 and a uniform 5-percent tariff limitation, as in China, in June 1866.

As the crisis deepened, the death of Emperor Kōmei and the succession of his 15-year-old son increased the possibilities of maneuver at the court. Yoshinobu's evident success in shogunate reforms and his acceptability to the foreigners alarmed leaders in Satsuma and Chōshū. The year 1866 brought a French military mission, a Franco-Japanese trading company to organize and channel international trade as a source of income, and an intensified program of import of ships and weapons. It seemed that rapid reform might strengthen the shogunate to the point where it could no longer be overthrown.

Plans now developed in Satsuma and Chōshū to forestall successful completion of the shogunate reforms. In the summer of 1867 the foreign powers helped provide the occasion. It had been agreed that Hyōgo (now Kōbe) should be opened as a treaty port, and Yoshinobu now requested that the court withdraw its opposition to this step. Satsuma (and Iwakura) countered by proposing a prior shogunal pardon of Chōshū in order to bring it back into decision-making councils; in turn the opening of Hyōgo would be accomplished in such a way as to make it clear that foreign relations were under the authority of the court. The shōgun was to suffer a reduction of territory and join the ranks of the daimyō. Neither Satsuma nor the shogunate was able to have its way, but Yoshinobu forced his solution through the court councils; Hyōgo was to be opened, while to Chōshū an unspecified "lenient" policy would be applied. The shogunate won a temporary victory, but at the cost of convincing its rivals that strong steps would be required to unhorse it.

Tosa adopted a moderate position. Yamanouchi Toyoshige remained reluctant to oppose the shogunate. A compromise policy for Tosa was devised by Sakamoto Ryōma, who pieced together ideas he had first heard from shogunate officials in the days of his employment by Katsu Kaishū. He proposed to Gotō Shōjirō that Yoshinobu be persuaded to resign as shōgun and recognize the authority of the emperor; a bicameral legislature (filled, presumably, with daimyō and vassals respectively) would be established to ensure a broad consensus for decisions, while offices would be open to "men of talent," and an imperial army and navy would be set up. Implicit in this plan was the assumption that Yoshinobu, while resigning his powers, would remain the first among equals in the new conciliar structure (see KŌGI SEITAI RON).

On this basis a Tosa–Satsuma agreement was reached, Tosa agreeing to add its forces to a military campaign if Yoshinobu should refuse to agree. It was late in October 1867 before Gotō Shōjirō could present the Tosa proposal to high shogunate officials in the form of a letter from Yamanouchi Toyoshige to Tokugawa Yoshinobu. By then Satsuma and Chōshū leaders had prepared their plans for the use of force. Yoshinobu found the Tosa proposal acceptable, and a number of his counselors had already suggested comparable plans to him. On 8 November (Keiō 3.10.13) Yoshinobu announced his acceptance to representatives of Satsuma, Tosa, Aki (now Hiroshima Prefecture), Bizen (now part of Okayama Prefecture), and Uwajima. On the 9th he formally submitted his resignation to the court (TAISEI HŌKAN), and on the following day it was accepted. On 19 November Yoshinobu added a resignation of his title as shōgun.

Satsuma leaders, however, had retained their doubts about the adequacy of a voluntary resignation that left Yoshinobu still powerful, surrounded by hereditary vassals and a strong military and naval establishment. His recent ability to overwhelm court objections to the opening of Hyōgo suggested that not much more than a change of titles might be involved. Ōkubo and Iwakura had managed to get a court edict (one whose authenticity has never been fully established) in which the boy emperor authorized the dismissal of Yoshinobu and punishment of his Kyōto guardians. Timid courtiers withdrew this once the shōgun had resigned, forcing Ōkubo and Iwakura to begin all over again. Violence still seemed likely, as their plans for a military confrontation were far advanced and strong forces were already mobilized.

On 3 January the Satsuma-loyalist conspirators acted. They surrounded the Kyōto palace to secure custody of the emperor, after which an imperial edict was issued abolishing all existing offices in favor of an emergency council of imperial princes. In the first meeting of the council—unattended by Yoshinobu—it was decided that the former shōgun would have to surrender his lands as well as his offices. He failed to do so and instead let his vassals persuade him to move troops toward Kyōto to remonstrate with the court. These troops were defeated in a sharp engagement that began a series of conflicts known as the BOSHIN CIVIL WAR.

The civil war ended with the surrender of the last Tokugawa naval units in Hokkaidō in June of 1869. Tokugawa power had been crushed. It found remarkably few supporters in the end. In northeastern Japan a league of daimyō (ŌUETSU REPPAN DŌMEI) resisted the new "Imperial Army," made up of Satsuma, Chōshū, and Tosa troops, but more out of fear of losing their autonomy to southerners they distrusted than out of loyalty to the Tokugawa. The vast majority of domains, uncertain which way to turn, chose not to act, leaving the field clear for the determined assaults of the imperial army against a demoralized, disunited, and confused Tokugawa cause whose leader chose not to resist. Casualties were heavy, particularly in the siege of Wakamatsu Castle in Aizu, but once Edo Castle was surrendered after a conference between Saigō, representing the new regime, and Katsu, the old, the issue was never in doubt. In 1868 the reign name was changed to "Meiji," and the emperor declared "restored."

The early years of the Meiji period saw the new government proceed cautiously to achieve unity and centralization. The confiscated Tokugawa lands were not returned to daimyō rule but used as the base for the new centralization. Edo, renamed Tōkyō, became the national capital. An imperial oath issued in the spring of 1868, the CHARTER OATH, promised participation through councils, reform, fairness, and a search for wisdom throughout the world. In 1869 domain administration was made uniform, and samurai ranks were reduced and simplified. In 1871 the domains were rationalized in size and changed to prefectures, and the daimyō were replaced by appointed governors (see PREFECTURAL SYSTEM, ESTABLISHMENT OF). Farmers were permitted the dignity of family names, given title to their lands and freedom of movement and occupation, and assigned a tax payable in money (see LAND TAX REFORM OF 1873–1881). Universal schooling was proclaimed (see EDUCATION ORDER OF 1872), and conscription replaced the hereditary samurai with a commoner army (see CONSCRIPTION ORDINANCE OF 1873). Samurai stipends were reduced, then changed to pensions, and in 1876 converted to bonds (see CHITSUROKU SHOBUN). Samurai revolts broke out, especially in the southwest, where samurai expectations had been highest, culminating in the great SATSUMA REBELLION led by Saigō Takamori in 1877. With the defeat of the rebels the Meiji government, headed by a coalition of Satsuma and Chōshū bureaucrats, was free to begin work on the final institutionalization of centralized power under the aegis of a newly restored imperial house.

Interpretations —— Because the Meiji Restoration constitutes the pivotal point in Japan's emergence as a modern nation-state, and because its leaders established a pattern of institutions that endured virtually without change until 1945, attempts to characterize the Restoration as a historical process have occasioned a great deal of scholarly debate. Prior to the Japanese defeat in World War II official orthodoxy stressed the disinterested role of patriotic loyalists who brought about the return of legitimate imperial rule after centuries of military usurpation. Critical scholarship, recognizing the importance of the role of the sonnō jōi activists, has tried to analyze them by rank and area. The samurai activists were predominantly of less than middle rank, a status they shared with the majority of their peers. They expressed in particularly bitter terms the widespread discontent with and disrespect for high-born vassals who monopolized positions of formal authority for the perpetuation of existing patterns of privilege. Loyalism provided these samurai with a legitimate pretext to disregard authority immediately superior to them in the interest of a "higher" loyalty, but their willingness to abandon home and family and to risk their lives left little doubt of their sincerity. Political participation of this sort was also invigorating and intensely rewarding after the torpor of ritualized subordination. Nevertheless, these frustrations were universal throughout Japan, and the concentration of loyalist enthusiasm and activism in certain areas showed the importance of charismatic individuals in locations that permitted domain ambitions and participation. The final Restoration of 1868 was, in a narrow sense, the product of great-domain maneuvers.

Historical scholarship has tended to adopt periodizations that vary with the emphasis desired. The actual transfer of government in 1868 can legitimately be described as a coup d'etat by Satsuma and Chōshū leaders, acting in concert with the court noble Iwakura Tomomi to utilize the legitimacy of the court against a shōgun who had already resigned his offices and titles and anticipated taking part in a new political structure as the most important of the feudal lords.

When the quarter-century between the coming of Perry (1853) and the collapse of the Satsuma Rebellion (1877) is taken as the unit of study, focus is placed on the need for central direction in response to the common Japanese perception of a Western imperialist threat to their nation's independence. The Satsuma Rebellion is accordingly portrayed as the last feudal or samurai reaction against national consolidation, the Restoration described as a nationalist revolution, and its measures as defensive modernization in the face of foreign danger.

Marxist historians have preferred to extend the period under investigation to begin with the Tempō reforms of the 1840s and to continue through the consolidation of the Meiji state, culminating in the promulgation of the CONSTITUTION of 1889, stressing the increase in bureaucratic control over aspects of economic life in the late Edo period and the efforts of the early Meiji state to stimulate industrial development. The era so described is frequently labeled "absolutist" to indicate its transitional role between Tokugawa feudalism and 20th-century capitalism.

From a longer 19th-century perspective that contrasts the structured though disintegrating order of the early decades of the century with the dynamic effect of Meiji reforms—political unification, the abolition of social and hereditary status, the free market in land, and freedom of occupation and residence—culminating in the limited but real representative system of the Meiji constitutional order, the Meiji Restoration can be seen as permitting and in fact constituting a capitalist revolution whose samurai leadership and nationalist goals place it in a class by itself; one whose characteristics indicate a "reactive" and "defensive" response that sets it off from the larger social explosions of Western revolutions, but one whose increase of freedom and choice nevertheless prepared the way for the dynamism of contemporary Japan.

■ ——W. G. Beasley, *The Meiji Restoration* (1972). Albert M. Craig, *Chōshū in the Meiji Restoration* (1961). Harry D. Harootunian, *Toward Restoration: The Growth of Political Consciousness in Tokugawa Japan* (1970). Marius B. Jansen, *Sakamoto Ryōma and the Meiji Restoration* (1961). E. H. Norman, *Japan's Emergence as a Modern State* (1940). Rekishigaku Kenkyūkai, ed, *Meiji ishin shi*

kenkyū kōza, 6 vols (1958–59), supplementary vol (1969). Sakata Yoshio, *Meiji ishin shi* (1960). Shigakukai, ed, *Meiji ishin kenkyū* (1929). Conrad Totman, *The Collapse of the Tokugawa Bakufu* (1980). Tōyama Shigeki, *Meiji ishin* (1951).   Marius B. JANSEN

Meiji Seika Kaisha, Ltd

Confectioner producing principally food and pharmaceutical products. The largest company in the confectionery industry in Japan. It was established in 1916 for the domestic production and export of Western-style confections. With the completion of a new plant in 1925, it began mass production of caramels, candies, chocolate, and canned fruits. It also entered the dairy product field, expanding through the absorption of a large number of dairy companies throughout the country. The dairy division became independent of the parent firm in 1940, assuming the name MEIJI MILK PRODUCTS CO, LTD.

After World War II, production was temporarily curtailed because of damaged equipment and facilities and a dearth of raw materials. However, mass production was resumed in 1952, and since the 1960s, the firm has succeeded in expanding production through emphasis on chocolate and cookies. It also started production and sales of such new products as snack foods, instant foods, and health foods. In 1946 it succeeded in producing penicillin. Since then it has solidified the foundation of its pharmaceutical division with the commercial production of numerous antibiotics, including streptomycin and kanamycin. Future plans call for research on and development of new pharmaceuticals and agricultural chemicals in the life-sciences field. It has joint venture manufacturing companies in South Korea, Singapore, Indonesia, Thailand, and Brazil, as well as a sales company in the United States. Sales for the fiscal year ending March 1982 totaled ¥189.5 billion (US $787.2 million), of which sales of confections and food products constituted 59 percent and pharmaceuticals 41 percent. In the same year the firm was capitalized at ¥14.2 billion (US $59 million). The head office is in Tōkyō.

Meiji Shrine

(Meiji Jingū). A Shintō shrine at Yoyogi, Shibuya Ward, Tōkyō, dedicated to the spirits of Emperor MEIJI (1852–1912) and his consort, Empress Shōken (1850–1914). In recognition of the great contribution made by Emperor Meiji to the modernization of Japan, the Imperial Diet passed a resolution in 1913 to build a shrine in his honor. More than 100,000 young people volunteered their labor for the enterprise. Similarly, trees were contributed from all regions of Japan for planting in the spacious park surrounding the shrine, which was finally completed in 1920. Virtually the entire shrine was destroyed in the air raid of 14 April 1945. The reconstruction of the shrine was finished in 1958 at a cost of ¥600 million (US $2.78 million) raised through a nationwide subscription. The annual festival is held on 3 November, Emperor Meiji's birthday, which is a national holiday (Culture Day).   Stanley WEINSTEIN

Meiji Sugar Mfg Co, Ltd

(Meiji Seitō). Major sugar refiner. Established in Taiwan in 1906. It was one of the four largest Japanese sugar companies before World War II. In 1940 MEIJI SEIKA KAISHA, LTD, and MEIJI MILK PRODUCTS CO, LTD, were made independent of the parent firm, and Meiji Sugar concentrated on sugar refining. However, since the 1960s, because of surplus production facilities and the decline in sugar demand, it has received financial assistance from the MITSUBISHI CORPORATION. Sales for the fiscal year ending March 1982 totaled ¥38.9 billion (US $161.6 million) and capitalization was ¥2 billion (US $8.3 million). Corporate headquarters are in Tōkyō.

Meiji University

(Meiji Daigaku). A private, coeducational university whose main campus is located in Chiyoda Ward, Tōkyō. Its predecessor was the Meiji Hōritsu Gakkō (Meiji Law School) founded in 1881. The school was renamed Meiji University in 1903. In 1929, the women's division for the study of law and commerce was opened, the first school in Japan to offer higher education to women in these fields. The university has maintained a liberal atmosphere based on its motto "rights and freedom." Other campuses are located in Suginami Ward, Tōkyō, and the city of Kawasaki, Kanagawa Prefecture. It maintains faculties of law, commerce, politics and economics, letters, business management, agriculture, and engineering. Night courses are offered in law, commerce, politics and economics, and letters. It is noted for its museum of archaeology and also for its institutes of sciences and technology, social sciences, and cultural sciences. Enrollment was 25,231 in 1980.

Meireki Fire

(Meireki no Taika). A fire in March 1657 (Meireki 3.1). It broke out at the temple Hommyōji in the Hongō section of Edo (now Tōkyō) and raged for two days, sweeping through most of the city. The central tower of Edo Castle burned, as did *daimyō* residences, townsmen's houses, temples, and bridges. More than 100,000 people were said to have died either in the conflagration itself or from exposure to the snowstorm that struck the city the following day. The Tokugawa shogunate established first-aid stations and distributed food and money to the homeless. When the city was rebuilt, the breadth of roads and spacing of houses were standardized, and fire lanes were installed at various intersections. The expense of these measures depleted the shogunal treasury and was one reason for the currency debasement carried out by OGIWARA SHIGEHIDE. The fire is also known as the "Furisode (young girl's *kimono*) Fire," for it was thought to have been caused by sparks from a *kimono* being burned in an exorcism ceremony.

Meirokusha

(Meiji 6 Society). Intellectual society proposed by the statesman MORI ARINORI in 1873, the sixth year of the Meiji period (1868–1912), and founded on 1 February 1874 for the purpose of "promoting civilization and enlightenment" (see MEIJI ENLIGHTENMENT). Through its journal, the *Meiroku zasshi*, and the series of public lectures delivered at its meetings, the society played a leading role in introducing and popularizing Western ideas during the early years of the Meiji period. Its 33 members included some of the most eminent educators, bureaucrats, and thinkers of 19th-century Japan.

Founding——Mori undoubtedly conceived the idea of forming a society of leading Japanese intellectuals devoted to popular enlightenment while serving as Japan's first envoy to the United States from 1871 to 1873. During that time he became impressed by the activities of American academic societies and the views on universal education of Horace Mann (1796–1859) and other American educators. Upon returning to Japan in the summer of 1873, Mori recruited NISHIMURA SHIGEKI and eight others to organize a group of intellectuals to promote Western learning and establish models of ethical behavior for the Japanese. The resulting Meirokusha was formally set up in February 1874, its by-laws stressing the society's role in "furthering education in Japan" and establishing biweekly meetings for the purpose of exchanging views "to broaden knowledge and illuminate understanding."

Goals and Methods——Though holding in common the goal of making Japan strong and prosperous, the members of the Meirokusha advocated three different approaches to that end. Confucian humanists such as NAKAMURA MASANAO, Nishimura, and Sakatani Shiroshi (1822–91) reasoned that Western strength and prosperity resulted from the moral strength of its people and exhorted the Japanese to study this secret of the West's success and tread the same path. In *Meiroku zasshi*, they wrote such articles as "How to Change the Character of the Japanese People," "Theory on Nourishing the Spirit," and "Two Items That Are Necessary for Moral Government."

Thinkers such as KATŌ HIROYUKI, TSUDA MAMICHI, NISHI AMANE, and KANDA TAKAHIRA emphasized the organic nature of society and held that the West's strength was derived from rationally constructed and operated institutions and societies. They stressed the unique national polity (KOKUTAI) of Japan, constitutional government, and universal education in such articles in the *Meiroku zasshi* as "Treatise on the Balance of Trade," and "The American System of Government." Nishi's long series "Jinsei sampōsetsu" (Life's Three Treasures) emphasized the importance of social welfare from a utilitarian point of view.

The pragmatists, led by FUKUZAWA YUKICHI, were often as interested in what worked as in why it was successful. They felt that by joining the special strengths of the Japanese with successful Western values and institutions they could make their nation the Britain of the East.

These three approaches to nation building were not mutually exclusive. Mori, for example, could be placed in all three of the above groups. Although the society's members disagreed as to whether priority should be given to creating new people or new institutions, the two were ultimately inseparable. Most agreed that good education was the foundation of both.

Membership——The charter members of the Meirokusha were Mori Arinori, Nishimura Shigeki, Fukuzawa Yukichi, Katō Hiroyuki, MITSUKURI RINSHŌ, Mitsukuri Shūhei (1826–86), Nakamura Masanao, Nishi Amane, Sugi Kōji (1828–1917), and Tsuda Mamichi. Others who joined either as regular or corresponding members during the next two years were, in order of their election, Hatakeyama Yoshinari (1843–76), Shimizu Usaburō (1829–1910), Sera Taichi (1838–1919), Sakatani Shiroshi, Shibata Shōkichi (1841–1901), Sugita Gentan (1818–89), Koyasu Takashi (1836–98), MAEJIMA HISOKA, Kanda Takahira, William Elliot GRIFFIS, Kashiwabara Takaaki (1835–1910), NAGAYO SENSAI, Takagi Saburō (1841–1909), Tomita Tetsunosuke (1835–1916), Akiyama Tsunetarō (1843–1911), Kuki Ryūichi (1852–1931), Furukawa Masao, TANAKA FUJIMARO, TSUDA SEN, Asai Harubumi, ŌTSUKI FUMIHIKO, Hida Shōsaku (1842–1921), and Tsuji Shinji (1842–1915). Varying in age from 27 (Mori) to 56 (Sugita), all of the members, except Griffis, Sakatani, and possibly Sera, had studied both Jugaku (Confucian Studies) and Yōgaku (WESTERN LEARNING) by 1874; 20 had studied Dutch, 22 English, 3 French, 1 German, and 2 Russian. The members included physicians, Confucian scholars, merchants, and quite a few bureaucrats. Fifteen had traveled abroad, and 25 had at one time been teachers before joining the society. Although most of the members came from the Tokugawa domains, Mori and Hatakeyama were from Satsuma (now Kagoshima Prefecture). In all, the Meirokusha was an extremely diverse group of individuals with one important thing in common: they had been educated in feudal Japan but looked forward to the day when the Japanese would take their place among the most advanced peoples of the world. Furthermore, they were convinced that scholars like themselves had a key role to play in that transformation.

The End of the Meiroku Zasshi——From the beginning, however, the members of the Meirokusha were divided over the nature of that role: should scholars willingly work with and through the government, as did Mori and most of the society's members, or, following Fukuzawa's example, should they stand outside the government in order to push it in the proper direction? This issue clearly influenced the decision to suspend publication of the *Meiroku zasshi*. With the promulgation of the PRESS ORDINANCE OF 1875 and LIBEL LAW OF 1875, Fukuzawa maintained that the constraints were too great to continue publishing the journal in good conscience. His argument proved persuasive, and on 1 September 1875 the society voted to cease publication. Although members of the Meirokusha continued to meet on a fairly regular basis until as late as 1900, the influence of the society diminished sharply after the last issue of the *Meiroku zasshi* appeared in November 1875.

📖——Carmen Blacker, *The Japanese Enlightenment: A Study of the Writings of Fukuzawa Yukichi* (1964). William R. Braisted, tr, *Meiroku Zasshi: Journal of the Japanese Enlightenment* (1976). Ivan Parker Hall, *Mori Arinori* (1973). Thomas R. H. Havens, *Nishi Amane and Modern Japanese Thought* (1970). Ōkubo Toshiaki, ed, *Meiji keimō shisō shū*, vol 3 of *Meiji bungaku zenshū* (Chikuma Shobō, 1967). Donald H. Shively, "Nishimura Shigeki: A Confucian View of Modernization," in Marius B. Jansen, ed, *Changing Japanese Attitudes toward Modernization* (1965). Jerry K. FISHER

Meiryō kōhan

(Illustrious Examples). A collection of anecdotes about the first five Tokugawa shōguns and retainers in their service during the period 1600–ca 1680; written by Sanada Zōyo, a shogunal retainer, in 40 volumes. Basing his account on hearsay, the author intersperses personal observations throughout his narrative. Anecdotes about scholars and women and references to social customs of the period are also included.

meishi → name cards

meisho zue

Illustrated guidebooks published during the Edo period (1600–1868). As a result of peace and improvements in traveling conditions, increasingly larger numbers of people were able to go on pilgrimages to temples and shrines and to visit famous sites. The guidebooks published during this period were well illustrated and filled with detailed information on the history, legends, and special products of each place. Among the most famous were the *Miyako meisho zue* (6 vols, published in 1780) edited by Akizato Ritō and illustrated by Takehara Shunchōsai; and the *Edo meisho zue* (7 vols, published between 1830 and 1840), completed by three generations of the Saitō family from Chōshin to his grandson Gesshin and illustrated by Hasegawa Settan (1778–1843). Other books were the *Tōkaidō meisho zue* and the *Kisoji meisho zue*, guidebooks to stops on the major highways. Guidebooks on pilgrimages to temples and shrines included the *Zenkōji meisho zue*, the *Ise sangū meisho zue*, and the *Kompira sankei meisho zue*. Guidebooks on individual provinces, such as Yamato (now Nara Prefecture) and Kawachi (now Ōsaka Prefecture), were also published. NISHIKAWA Osamu

Meitoku Rebellion

(Meitoku no Ran). Attempt in 1391 (Meitoku 2) by Yamana Ujikiyo (1344–91) and his nephew Mitsuyuki (d 1395) to overthrow the government of the shōgun ASHIKAGA YOSHIMITSU (1358–1408). Descendants of a cadet branch of the Ashikaga family, Ujikiyo and Mitsuyuki, as lords of 11 of the 66 provinces of Japan, wielded power rivaling that of the shōgun. Provoked by Yoshimitsu, they marched on Kyōto but were defeated by shogunate forces and their lands divided among the triumphant generals. By means of his victories in this and the ŌEI REBELLION, and by establishing his ascendancy over Toki Yoriyasu (1318–87), Yoshimitsu was able to consolidate shogunal dominance over the nation. A detailed record of the Meitoku Rebellion is contained in *Meitokuki* (ca 1392–93).

Meiwa Incident

Incident in 1767 (Meiwa 4) in which two scholars, YAMAGATA DAINI and Fujii Umon (1720–67), were executed by the Tokugawa shogunate for alleged subversive activities. Closely following the HŌREKI INCIDENT, in which court nobles were punished for criticizing the shogunate, this incident was another example of the shogunate's effort to suppress the growing proimperial *(sonnō)* movement. Yamagata was a teacher of Confucianism and military science in Edo (now Tōkyō) and in 1759 had written *Ryūshi shinron*, in which he criticized the shogunate for usurping the emperor's power. Fujii, also a scholar, had fled Kyōto in the wake of the Hōreki Incident and lectured at Yamagata's school on military tactics, using as an illustration an attack on Edo Castle, the shogunal headquarters. Their activities were reported to the Edo city magistrate, and in 1766 the two men, with some 30 other suspects, were arrested for plotting rebellion. No conclusive evidence was found, but Yamagata and Fujii were executed the following year. The shogunate took advantage of the incident to send TAKENOUCHI SHIKIBU, a noble implicated in the Hōreki Incident, into permanent exile. KAWAUCHI Hachirō

Mendenhall, Thomas Corwin (1841–1924)

Distinguished American physicist, contributor to scientific knowledge about electricity, gravity, seismology, and meteorology; popular speaker on science and able education administrator. Noted in Japan, where he served as a government-employed teacher (1878–81), for introducing the professional study of physics.

Recommended to the Japanese government by Edward S. MORSE, Mendenhall taught the first systematic course in physics at Tōkyō University, where he built the first physics laboratory; conducted studies of the earth's mass by measuring gravity at sea level and at the top of Mt. Fuji (Fujisan); began regular meteorological observation, later taken up by the government; and promoted the study of earthquakes. He also helped found the Japan Seismological Society.

In his spare time Mendenhall gave translated public lectures on scientific developments. These events were well attended as much for his considerable skill as a speaker as for the enthusiasm of the Japanese of the early years of the Meiji period (1868–1912) for Western science and technology, which had been introduced to them just a decade before. Mendenhall's usefulness to the first generation of Japanese scientists was enhanced by his later prominence in the United States as a government official and president of Worcester Polytechnic Institute. Dallas FINN

menko

Children's game and toy, made of circular or square pieces of clay, board, lead, paper, and so forth, originating in the Kamakura period (1185–1333). From the 18th century on the game pieces were made of unglazed earthenware about 3 centimeters (1 in) in diameter. Later they were made of clay, and since the beginning of this century they have been made of paper. To play, one player's *menko* is placed on the ground; his opponent then attempts to flip it over by throwing his own *menko* at the first player's piece. During the Edo period (1600–1868), the pieces were decorated with pictures of *sumō* wrestling champions. Today, pieces are often painted with pictures of children's favorite cartoon or comic characters. SAITŌ Ryōsuke

mental illness

Major diagnostic categories for behavioral and mental disorders affecting one's normal functioning in society are the same in Japan as they are in the West. Symptom patterns among adult Japanese patients clearly indicate the presence of schizophrenia, affective psychoses, depression, neuroses, and character disorders. Troubled children in Japan, like their Western counterparts, exhibit fears of heights, water, and animals and suffer from headaches, loss of appetite, and stomachaches. Even the rates of occurrence of major types of mental illness such as schizophrenia and depression appear quite similar to those of the United States and Western Europe. However, within these broad diagnostic categories Japanese patients have characteristic symptom patterns.

Introduction —— From at least the Heian period (794–1185) the belief existed that insanity was the result of possession by animals or other creatures. From region to region the particular invading spirit varied but included were the fox, dog, weasel, hedgehog, rabbit, cat, monkey, and the goblinlike KAPPA. The possessed person acted strangely, with violence or withdrawal. Treatment was by nonmedical practitioners such as shamans or, more recently, religious cult healers. Belief in possession continues in some rural areas.

In a study of 56 shamans during the summers of 1958–60, Sasaki Yūji found that about a third of the curers themselves showed psychiatric symptoms, a fact suggesting that for some of them shamanism is a way of redirecting pathological traits into socially acceptable, constructive ends.

Comparative studies of hospitalized psychiatric patients in Japan and the United States are often conflicting, with results that depict Japanese patients as more violent, less violent, displaying more generalized and diffuse symptoms, displaying specific patterns of dependency, and so forth. These investigations of very disturbed, psychotic hospitalized patients have not been particularly fruitful because of the noncomparability of the hospitals and populations studied, discrepancies in the way information was obtained in the two cultures, and faulty interpretations of findings.

In content alone, the delusions of a few psychotic Japanese patients, such as the delusion that one is the emperor or the emperor's child, may be unique to Japan, but the culture-specific content of delusions is gradually declining, conforming to that of the West.

The most characteristically Japanese symptom patterns are found in the neuroses. Not as severe as psychoses, which usually require some period of hospitalization and tranquilizing medication, the neuroses are milder disabilities that cause misery without loss of contact with reality. Japanese neurotic patients often show a syndrome of phobias, self-deprecation, tension (particularly in social relationships), withdrawal, and various somatic complaints. Social phobias such as discomfort around social superiors and persons of the opposite sex; concern that one's facial expression will reveal inner thoughts; worries about blushing, body odor, and staring; and feelings of inferiority and failure are common, particularly among young people in their teens, twenties, and even early thirties.

Social Causes of Mental Illness —— The phobias involving interpersonal contact seem strongly rooted in Japanese society and culture. In a society in which family overprotection and defensiveness against outsiders is common, social sensitivity and self-control are valued, and dependency is charactertistically dealt with more comfortably than aggression, neurotic overconcern in the social sphere can be expected. In extreme cases, worries about thoughts "leaking" out to others or about talking in one's sleep indicate a general fear that one's inner self is being publicly exposed under conditions outside one's own control. Feeling stripped of the capacity to censor appropriately the expression of his thoughts, the Japanese neurotic considers himself alienated from society and unable to generate the civilized social relationships available to those who have self-control. Extreme self-consciousness exacerbates this condition, as does a focusing of attention on these perceived faults. Doi Takeo, a noted Japanese psychoanalyst, has emphasized the desire to be loved passively as the foundation for Japanese neuroses (see AMAE). David Reynolds, an American psychological anthropologist, has focused on the social sensitivity. Kim Jhong Hae, a Korean psychiatrist, and others have stressed the element of suppressed anger.

A number of factors have been put forward as causes of mental illness in modern Japan. Since the rates of serious disorders such as schizophrenia seem relatively constant from culture to culture and across time, these factors probably exert their strongest influence on neuroses. Pressure for achievement in the educational arena begins early and continues unrelentingly well into the protracted adolescence of Japanese students. In fact, most of the patients treated for social phobias are upwardly mobile students, white-collar workers, and, secondarily, skilled tradespeople. Those are the members of society most strongly caught up in the drive for education-based success.

Rapid social change has moved many people from a rural to a fast-paced urban life. Migration to cities with the accompanying stress of overpopulation and noise, pollution of various sorts, transportation problems, increased rates of crime and broken homes has undoubtedly contributed to the occurrence of mental illness. "Western" values of independence and individualism have made an appearance, but they do not on the whole fit well in the Japanese social structure, though recently there is some pressure to promote and value such traits. Value conflicts are a resultant source of stress. During the ongoing transitional period in which Japan seeks some harmonious blend of Eastern and Western values, problems of anomie and interpersonal stress are to be expected.

Changes in Symptoms over Time—— If modernization has contributed to the occurrence and form of mental illness, one would expect differences in the frequency of mental disorders and in the content of symptom patterns in recent years. Indeed, such changes, at least in symptom patterns, are to be found.

Rates of mental illness in the general population are difficult to determine. Katō Masaaki, director of Japan's National Institute of Mental Health, reviewing national epidemiological surveys conducted in 1954 and 1963, found an overall decrease in mental disorders (from 1.5 percent to 1.3 percent) and slight increases in psychoses (from 0.5 percent to 0.6 percent), particularly in the elderly (from 1.0 percent to 1.42 percent). On the other hand, measures of persons seeking and receiving treatment show a steady increase since World War II. Mental hospital beds have increased tenfold, from fewer than 20,000 in 1950 to over 275,000 in 1975. In 1975 the rate of 247 beds per 100,000 persons in Japan was slightly higher than the comparable rate of 238 beds in the United States. The length of stay in hospitals has also increased, despite the advent of tranquilizing medication, which in the West has sharply cut inpatient treatment periods. Of course, increases in beds and increases in numbers of patients treated do not necessarily reflect an increase in mental illness within the population, only that facilities are utilized as they become available.

Changes in the content of mental illness symptoms are also revealing. Among neurotic patients there seems to be a decline in hysterics and neurasthenics, that is, in those who rigidly deny their psychosocial problems and express their disturbances in primitive somatic forms such as overall bodily weakness or psychologically based paralysis or numbness. A concomitant increase in anxiety neuroses and depression since World War II reflects the public's recognition and acceptance of the psychological nature of the patients' problems. Psychosomatic complaints such as headaches, heart palpitations, and gastrointestinal disorders are increasingly interspersed with complaints of tension, apathy, isolation, and sadness. As patients have become more sophisticated about the nature of minor forms of mental disturbance, their perceptions and interpretations of symptoms have moved away from the exclusively somatic toward the psychological.

Particularly among young urban Japanese, symptom complexes increasingly resemble those of the West. This is true for both neurotic and psychotic cases, but the trend is somewhat more clearly discernible among males.

A study of the delusions of schizophrenic patients from 1901 to 1965 at the large public Matsuzawa Hospital in Tōkyō showed an increase in delusions of being followed and of physical injury and a decrease in delusions of grandeur and of being possessed. These

changes appear to parallel those of Western schizophrenic patients over the same time period.

Recent studies of hospitalized patients in Japan indicate that, like those in the United States, middle- and upper-class patients tend to express their disorders in intellectualizing and self-punishing ways. In contrast, lower-class patients tend to be more action-oriented and somewhat more ready to express aggression outwardly.

Attitudes toward Mental Illness—— To some extent mental illness is culturally defined. For example, compared with that of the United States, the general population in Japan is less likely to consider alcoholism as mental illness. (Recently, however, the permissiveness surrounding social drinking in Japan is being countered with medical and educational efforts aimed at redefining normal behavior in this area.) Similarly, a quiet, withdrawn young girl is not likely to be considered mentally ill in Japan, because such behavior is within the range of normal behavior for young women. Also, Japanese traditionally expect neurasthenic oversensitivity in scholars, poets, and novelists, which would be viewed as destructive and neurotic in other occupational groups.

Still, the general attitude toward psychiatric hospitalization, outpatient treatment, and those who receive psychiatric care is strongly negative. Opinion surveys indicate that the Japanese prefer to believe that mental hospitals are treatment-oriented rather than custodial institutions, yet they wish to keep the hospitals segregated from the community. Moreover, they resist placing a family member in a psychiatric facility. Partly, this reluctance is due to lack of acquaintance with the types of mental health facilities that have recently become commonly available. More important is the tradition of keeping mental illness secret within the family. Until recently, the pattern has been to hide disturbed members. Particularly among the older and less educated, there is a strong belief in the hereditary nature of mental illness. Thus, public exposure of severe mental illness could result in shame to the family and difficulty in finding acceptable marriage partners for other family members. Often only the threat of violence from the disturbed member, accompanied by disruption and exposure of the illness to the public eye, will prompt hospitalization. Patients whose psychosis has progressed for years within the sheltered family circle are likely to be extremely difficult to treat effectively when finally hospitalized.

Attitudes concerning severe disorders are slowly becoming more tolerant. As for mild neurotic complaints, the Japanese have customarily used minor illnesses and expressions of distress as ways of communicating indirectly about strain in interpersonal relations and problems at home, in the neighborhood, and at work. Until alternative and more open and direct ways of communication become available, one can expect little change in the area of symptomatic expression. See PSYCHOTHERAPY; SUICIDE; SHAMANISM.

■■——William Caudill, "The Cultural and Interpersonal Context of Everyday Health and Illness in Japan and America," in *Asian Medical Systems* (1976). William Caudill and Carmi Schooler, "Symptom Patterns and Background Characteristics of Japanese Psychiatric Patients," in *Mental Health Research in Asia and the Pacific* (1969). Juris G. Draguns et al, "Symptomatology of Hospitalized Psychiatric Patients in Japan and the United States," *Journal of Nervous and Mental Disease* 152 (1971). Katō Masaaki, "Psychiatric Epidemiological Surveys in Japan," in *Mental Health Research in Asia and the Pacific* (1966). Hsien Rin, Carmi Schooler, and William Caudill, "Symptomatology and Hospitalization," *Journal of Nervous and Mental Disease* 157 (1973). Terashima Shōgo, "The Structure of Rejecting Attitudes toward the Mentally Ill in Japan," in *Mental Health Research in Asia and the Pacific* (1966). Yamamoto Kazuo, "A Comparative Study of Patienthood in Japanese and American Mental Hospitals," in *Transcultural Research in Mental Health* (1972).   David K. REYNOLDS

meoto-jawan

(husband-and-wife cups). A pair of teacups or rice bowls, one large and one small, of the same shape and design. Two pine trees of differing size, lined up like a husband and wife, are called *meoto-matsu* (husband-and-wife pine trees); there was an old custom of praying to such trees for a good marriage match, as the pine is a symbol of permanence. *Meoto-jawan* can be regarded as symbolic of the steadfastness of the husband-wife relationship. Couples also use *meoto-bashi* (husband-and-wife chopsticks).

                                                   TSUCHIDA Mitsufumi

Meranoshō

District in west central Miyazaki Prefecture, Kyūshū, in the Kyūshū Mountains, on the upper reaches of the river Hitotsusegawa. According to legend, there was once a village here made up of the defeated warriors of the TAIRA FAMILY. Today the district is greatly changed by the dams and hydroelectric plants built in recent years. The special local products are tea, lumber, and *shiitake* (a species of mushroom).

merger, corporate

(*kigyō gappei*). The joining together of two or more companies by contract to form one company. Mergers occur for various economic reasons, such as business expansion, rationalization of business operations, avoidance of competition, and market monopolization. There are two types of merger: merger by absorption in which one company survives, absorbing the other company or companies, and merger by consolidation, in which all the companies involved are dissolved and a new company is established. The great majority of mergers in Japan are mergers by absorption.

Any company organized under Japan's COMMERCIAL CODE, whether a LIMITED PARTNERSHIP COMPANY (*gōshi kaisha*), an UNLIMITED PARTNERSHIP COMPANY (*gōmei kaisha*), a LIMITED LIABILITY COMPANY (*yūgen kaisha*), or a JOINT-STOCK COMPANY (*kabushiki kaisha*), may be a party to a merger. However, there are various restrictions. For example, when a joint-stock company is a party to a merger, the surviving or newly established company must also be a joint-stock company; the merger of a limited partnership company or an unlimited partnership company requires the approval of all the partners; and the merger of a limited liability corporation or a joint-stock company requires the approval of the merger contract by special resolution of members' or STOCKHOLDERS' GENERAL MEETING.

A merger becomes effective upon the registration of the absorption by the surviving company or of the consolidation by the newly established company at the Legal Affairs Bureau (Hōmukyoku) in the place where the company's head office is located. The surviving company or the newly established company absorbs the personnel of the dissolved company and generally succeeds to the rights, duties, and obligations of each of the dissolved companies simultaneously with their dissolution. Further, the ANTIMONOPOLY LAW prohibits the merger of domestic companies if the merger substantially limits competition or constitutes an unfair trade practice.

KITAZAWA Masahiro

meshi

Boiled grains, generally rice; in polite language, *gohan*. Since rice is the staple food of the Japanese, the word *meshi* has come to mean "meal." White rice is ordinarily accompanied by side dishes (*okazu*), but there are also various other ways of serving it: with seasonal vegetables, pieces of chicken, and so on, cooked or mixed in; as SUSHI lightly flavored with vinegar; or as *kayu* (rice gruel). The Japanese like to eat boiled rice in the form of *onigiri*, small rice balls formed in the hands and flavored with salt and sometimes sesame seeds. A pickled plum (UMEBOSHI) is often put inside each rice ball. *Chazuke* (*ochazuke* in polite language), a bowl of rice over which one pours green tea, often accompanied by *tsukemono* (pickles), is also a favorite. TSUJI Shizuo

metalwork

Artifacts made of metal have been widely used in Japan for utilitarian as well as artistic purposes. Metal objects made of bronze and of iron were first introduced into Japan from Han China during the Yayoi period (ca 300 BC–ca AD 300), probably in the 3rd century BC (see BRONZE AGE; IRON AGE). By about 100 BC native craftsmen used these metals to produce arrowheads, swords, daggers, halberd blades, coins, mirrors, bells, and ornaments. Bronze tended to be controlled by the ruling class and to be associated with ceremonial and official uses, while iron was largely restricted to more humble, utilitarian purposes. Japan had a plentiful supply of copper, which was usually employed in the form of alloys, mainly bronze. Gold was found in the sand of riverbeds and extracted through a series of washings. The first gold mine in Japan was discovered in 749 in northern Honshū. However, gold was not used very widely in Japan except for the gilding of Buddhist images and vessels (see KIRIKANE).

Metalwork

An 8th-century silver vessel engraved with scenes of hunting. One of the Shōsōin treasures, this vessel is thought to have been made in Japan but shows significant Chinese and West Asian influence. Height 49.35 cm. Shōsōin, Nara.

Metalwork

A Muromachi-period iron teakettle of the type used in the tea ceremony. Cast in Ashiya, a region in Chikuzen Province (now part of Fukuoka Prefecture) famed for its iron kettles, it bears an autumnal motif of deer and maple trees against a pebbled ground. Height 19.5 cm. 14th century. Private collection.

A gold alloy known as *shakudō*, consisting of copper with a 3–6 percent admixture of gold, was a Japanese invention and was used as a gold ground for inlay designs of gold, silver, and copper. Although a considerable portion is found in certain leads, silver is rather rare in Japan and is not widely used in Japanese art. Iron was used widely, especially for swords and tools of all types. The most common process in making metal objects was casting, but various metalworking techniques such as forging, embossing, beating, chasing, engraving, damascening, and plating were employed by Japanese craftsmen.

The most remarkable metal objects of the early period are the large bronze bells known as DŌTAKU, which are decorated with relief designs representing scenes from contemporary Japanese life. With the introduction of Buddhism during the 6th century AD, gilded bronze images of the Buddhist deities began to play an important role in religious observances. The most famous was the DAIBUTSU (Great Buddha) in Nara, which was dedicated in 752. Historical sources differ as to the amounts of various metals used in the image. According to one source about 441 metric tons (485 short tons) of copper, 7.6 metric tons (8.4 short tons) of tin, 390 kilograms (858 lbs) of gold, and 2 metric tons (2.2 short tons) of mercury were used in its construction. Outstanding objects of decorative art from the same period may be found in the SHŌSŌIN repository in Nara; notable are beautiful silver vessels engraved with hunting scenes, BRONZE MIRRORS in the Tang (T'ang) China style, swords, daggers, and all kinds of metal utensils. During the Heian (794–1185) and

Kamakura (1185–1333) periods, swords and armor were the outstanding products of metal workers, and their masterpieces are regarded as artistic treasures to the present day. Beginning with the Muromachi period (1333–1568), the iron teakettles used in the TEA CEREMONY began to play an important role, and the best of them are rightly admired as masterpieces of Japanese craftsmanship. In the Azuchi-Momoyama (1568–1600) and Edo (1600–1868) periods, all kinds of new and important uses were found for metal. Under European influence, firearms as well as clocks were made. The great castles and palaces employed metal decorations for their ornamental door handles called *hikite* and ornamental metal coverings called *kugikakushi* were employed to hide the nails used in these structures. However, the most significant works of art produced in metal were the swords and sword guards (TSUBA) which were fashioned with lavish care. Craftsmen working in metal, such as the members of the Gotō family, were considered among the leading artists of the time. There was also a widespread use of ornamental metalwork during the later Edo and the Meiji (1868–1912) periods, with bronze jars, vases, and sculptural figures enjoying great popularity. Several of the so-called LIVING NATIONAL TREASURES of Japan are swordsmiths and metal workers, reflecting the high esteem skilled craftsmen working in metal continue to enjoy.

—— Katori Hotsuma, *Nihon kinkō shi* (1932). Okada Yuzuru, *Japanese Metalwork in the Pageant of Japanese Art*, vol 4, tr S. Kaneko (1952).   *Hugo* MÜNSTERBERG

Meteorological Agency

(Kishōchō). Government office established in 1956 as an extraministerial bureau of the Ministry of Transport. Its chief function is the careful charting of the weather, but it also conducts research on such related phenomena as earthquakes, volcanoes, geomagnetism, and ocean currents. The data compiled from this observation and research are used to implement programs aimed at protecting the people from natural disasters and hazardous traffic conditions, as well as promoting the development of agriculture, marine industries, construction, and other related industries. Branch institutes include the Meteorological Research Institute, Aerological Observatory, College of Meteorology, and the Kakioka Observatory for Magnetic Phenomena.

Metropolitan Expressway Public Corporation

(Shuto Kōsoku Dōro Kōdan). A public corporation whose purpose is to construct new automobile toll roads connecting Tōkyō with adjacent districts. It was established in 1959, with half of its capital provided by the government. It aims to alleviate traffic congestion and improve the functioning of the urban transportation system. When the corporation was established, its principal task was the construction of roads in preparation for the 1964 TŌKYŌ OLYMPIC GAMES. In 1982 the corporation had 19 routes extending for a total of 152.5 kilometers (94.8 mi) and was used by an average of 700,000 automobiles daily. In 1982 the corporation was constructing 7 more routes; with their completion, the total network will be extended to 248.1 kilometers (154.2 mi). See also EXPRESSWAYS.

Hirata Masami

metsuke

Also known as *yokome*. Inspectors or censors. The title existed from the 15th century, when certain retainers acted as high-level spies for military rulers. The position was regularized under the Tokugawa shogunate (1603–1867). Just as inspectors general (ŌMETSUKE) reported to the senior councillors (RŌJŪ) on the *daimyō*, *metsuke* acted as the "eyes and ears" of the junior councillors (WAKADOSHIYORI) in supervising the conduct of the shōgun's direct vassals (HATAMOTO and GOKENIN). Furthermore, they evaluated the performance of other shogunate officials and staff. They had the unusual privilege of deciding among themselves on any new appointments whenever a vacancy occurred; all 10 were drawn from among the *hatamoto*. They carried out their work through lesser officials known as *kachi metsuke* and *kobito metsuke*. In addition, each *daimyō* domain had its own autonomous system of inspectors for internal control.

Mexico and Japan

During the late 16th and early 17th centuries, Mexico, together with the Philippines, served as a colonial base from which the Spanish conducted relations with Japan. In 1614, however, following an edict of expulsion directed at Catholic priests, relations via Mexico ceased, and by 1624 relations between Spain and Japan had been terminated completely (see SPAIN AND JAPAN).

In 1821 Mexico gained its independence from Spain. At the time, however, Japan was still enforcing a policy of NATIONAL SECLUSION, and it was not until 1873 that direct contacts with Japan were resumed. In 1888 Mexico signed with Japan the latter's first treaty with a Western nation that was not "unequal," a milestone in the Japanese drive for a revision of the Unequal Treaties (see UNEQUAL TREATIES, REVISION OF).

The 1890s and the first decade of the new century saw an aborted Japanese immigration scheme in the Mexican state of Chiapas, the importation of Japanese miners, and a project to lease a fishing base in Baja California. Furthermore, an esoteric fascination with Japanese *haiku* poetry on the Mexican side coincided with attempts at serious historic inquiry into past relations in both countries.

The Mexican revolutionary process, which began in 1910, involved individually various members of the Japanese diplomatic community as well as immigrants. Among the sympathizers, the Marxist KATAYAMA SEN played an important role in the organization of the Mexican Communist Party between 1919 and 1921.

During World War II the Mexican government declared war on Japan and sent a combat fighter squadron to the Pacific. In the late 1950s, following the termination of the state of war, major Japanese trading companies established offices in Mexico City, and until 1974 considerable cotton exports to Japan, largely through US channels, helped maintain the trade balance in Mexico's favor. Though protectionist policies kept the importation of Japanese goods to a minimum, direct Japanese investment in Mexico began on a large scale in 1960, when Nissan established an automobile assembly plant.

In a show of interest in more active relations, Adolfo Lopez Mateos in 1962 became the first Mexican president to visit Japan. Under the administration of President Luis Echeverria (1970–76), relations became quite extensive. Both countries undertook massive exchanges of students and trainees, and Mexico expanded its imports of Japanese capital and technology.

The subsequent discovery of major Mexican petroleum reserves has had a considerable impact on Japanese energy planning and should provide a base for ever-increasing and more balanced commercial activities in the public and private sectors. The future promises expanded scientific, technological, and cultural ties between the two countries that can boast of the most prolonged transpacific relationship.

—— Ishida Takeshi, *Mehiko to nihonjin* (1973). Lothar Knauth, *Confrontación Transpacífica* (1972). Maruya Yoshio, *Mekishiko—sono kokudo to shijō* (1975). Raten Amerika Kyōkai, ed, *Raten Amerika jiten* (1978).   *Lothar G.* KNAUTH

meyasubako

Box for "appeals" *(meyasu)* posted by the shogunate during the Edo period (1600–1868). In carrying out the KYŌHŌ REFORMS, the shōgun TOKUGAWA YOSHIMUNE decided in 1721 to post a suggestion box outside one of the gates of Edo Castle for the use of townspeople and peasants. Under lock and key the box was carried to the shōgun, who personally read the contents for ideas in formulating his policies. It was at the suggestion of a physician, for example, that a hospital, the KOISHIKAWA YŌJŌSHO, was established. Again, the fire-prevention program of the city was based on suggestions made by the commoners of Edo. Even after Yoshimune's retirement, *meyasubako* continued in use.

mi

A shallow basket shaped like the body of a coal shovel, high in back and flat in front; woven of bamboo strips with wisteria vine or strips of cherry bark woven in to give it strength. Originally used by peasants as a winnowing basket, it is now more commonly used in gardening. There are many folk beliefs associated with the *mi*; in some parts of Japan it is used for offerings at the "Little New Year's" (Koshōgatsu) on 15 January (see NEW YEAR) or at MOON VIEWING time in early fall.

miai

The formal meeting, via the introduction of a go-between (NA-KŌDO), of a man and woman seeking marriage partners. The parents of the prospective partners and the go-between attend the *miai*, which often takes the form of a dinner at a restaurant or attendance at a theatrical or musical event. After the formal meeting, the couple may continue to see each other depending on their initial feelings for one another. A marriage formed from such a meeting is called a *miai kekkon*, or "arranged marriage," in contrast to a *ren'ai kekkon*, or "love marriage," where two people fall in love and marry without the intercession of a go-between. The *miai kekkon* is seen as a continuation of the wedding practices of the premodern warrior class, where marriage was seen not as a union of individuals but of families. Since World War II, relations between young men and women have become more liberalized and "love marriages" are more common, but "arranged marriages" are still carried out on a wide scale. See also MARRIAGE. — NOGUCHI Takenori

Mibuchi Tadahiko (1880–1950)

First chief justice of the post–World War II Supreme Court. Born in Okayama Prefecture. Graduated from Kyōto University in 1905, he became judge of the Tōkyō District Court in 1907 and of the Great Court of Cassation (Daishin'in) in 1923. He concurrently taught civil law at Keiō University. He resigned from his judgeship in 1925 and worked as legal counsel to the Mitsui Trust and Banking Company. Mibuchi became the first chief justice of the Supreme Court in 1947 when the court was created under the postwar CONSTITUTION. Until his retirement in 1950, he strove to build a firm basis for the court's new role as the guardian of the constitution and of human rights, emphasizing in particular its power of judicial review. Mibuchi is also remembered for his trenchant judicial opinions. His writings included *Mimpō gaisetsu* (1924, Outlines of the Civil Code), *Shintakuhō tsūshaku* (1926, Interpretation of the Law of Trusts), and *Seken to ningen* (1950, The Public and the People). — SATŌ Kōji

Mibudera

A ranking temple of the RITSU SECT of Buddhism, located in Nakagyō Ward, Kyōto. According to the tradition of the temple, Mibudera was established on the initiative of Emperor SHŌMU (r 724–749) by the monk GANJIN (688–763; Chinese name: Jianzhen or Chienchen), who introduced the Ritsu sect into Japan from China. In fact, however, the founder was Kaiken, a monk from the temple MIIDERA, who in 991 erected at the site of Ganjin's former residence a chapel dedicated to the bodhisattva Jizō. This subsequently became the nucleus of the temple, which was finally completed in 1005. Emperor Shirakawa (r 1073–87) in 1077 accorded Mibudera the status of *chokuganji*, i.e., a temple at which prayers were regularly offered for the well-being of the imperial family and the tranquillity of the nation. In 1299 the Shingon monk Shukō (1223–1311) took up residence here and introduced the *dai nembutsue*, i.e., huge gatherings at which thousands of people chanted the name of Amida Buddha in a state of ecstasy. Mibudera suffered extensive damage from fires over the centuries, but was restored after each disaster. Most of the present buildings date from the last major reconstruction, which took place in 1825. The main hall (*hondō*), however, is a recent structure built in 1967 to replace the earlier one destroyed by a fire in 1962, which also claimed many of its treasures. Mibudera is known for a type of masked, wordless comic play known as the *Mibu kyōgen*, performed annually between 21–29 April, which has its origin in the *dai nembutsue*. The object of worship in the temple is an image of Jizō made by the master sculptor JŌCHŌ (d 1057). — Stanley WEINSTEIN

Mibu no Tadamine (fl ca 910)

Poet, courtier, one of four compilers of the first imperial anthology of classical (WAKA) poetry, the KOKINSHŪ (ca 905, Collection of Ancient and Modern Times). One of the so-called Thirty-Six Poetic Geniuses (SANJŪROKKASEN). Son of a minor official, Tadamine held various relatively obscure court posts and never rose above the sixth court rank. As a poet, however, Tadamine was considerably more prominent. In 905 he was appointed compiler of the *Kokinshū* along with KI NO TSURAYUKI, KI NO TOMONORI, and ŌSHIKŌCHI NO MITSUNE. His poetic style is typical of the *Kokinshū*, with its pose of elegant confusion, wit, and subjectivity, but he also retains traditional features of early poetry, showing a fondness for the *jokotoba*, or semimetaphorical "preface," and the MAKURA KOTOBA or "pillow word." Some 35 of his poems are included in the *Kokinshū*. Later imperial anthologies contain a total of 40-odd more of his poems. His personal collection, *Tadamineshū*, exists in two main versions of which one contains 60 poems and the other 122.

Tadamine is also the author of a very brief but important poetic document dated 945 and called by later poets *Wakatei jisshu* (Ten Styles of Japanese Poetry) or *"Tadamine juttei"* (Tadamine's Ten Styles). In it he names 10 poetic styles: archaic, ethereal, direct, suggestive, declarative of feelings, of heightened emotion, of captivating charm, metaphorical, of elegant beauty, and bilateral. Under each heading are five exemplary poems followed by a few phrases of comment, but the categories overlap in some cases and make little sense in others, and it is evident that Tadamine himself had difficulty differentiating them. Nevertheless, the document was extremely influential, establishing a precedent for distinguishing 10 styles of classical poetry. In its preference for illustration rather than explanation, it is also the prototype of the most important genre of Japanese poetic treatise. It was widely quoted and inspired numerous similar works (often with altered categories) by later poets.
🕮——Robert H. Brower and Earl Miner, *Japanese Court Poetry* (1961). — Robert H. BROWER

mice → rats and mice

michi

(literally, "the Path," "the Way"). Written with a Chinese character (Ch: *dao* or *tao*) that is also pronounced *dō* in many Japanese compound words. A term used in the Far East, i.e., the Chinese cultural sphere, to denote the fundamental principle underlying a system of thought or belief, an art, or a skill. Also used by extension to refer to a system of thought or belief in its entirety or to the entire body of principles and skills that constitute an art. In this later sense it is used in Japan, in the pronunciation *dō*, as part of name of a number of traditional skills or codes of behavior, as in *chadō* or *sadō* (the Way of tea, i.e., the tea ceremony), *shodō* (the Way of writing, i.e., calligraphy), *kendō* (the Way of the sword), *bushidō* (the Way of the warrior), and so forth.

In ancient China *dao*, in the sense of an ethical norm for human action, was an important concept in CONFUCIANISM, and in a more mystical sense it gave its name to the philosophy known as Taoism. Later, in Neo-Confucianism (see SHUSHIGAKU), it took on a metaphysical signficance, expressing the idea of the one and only absolute principle.

In Edo-period (1600–1868) Japan the term, pronounced *michi*, became one of the central concepts of the school of Japanese Confucianism known as KOGAKU (the Ancient Learning), with a meaning close to the present-day word *shinri* (truth). Such thinkers of the school as YAMAGA SOKŌ (1622–85) and ITŌ JINSAI (1627–1705), in criticizing the metaphysical interpretation of the term in Neo-Confucianism, asserted that *michi* was a road or ethical standard that human beings must follow. For OGYŪ SORAI (1666–1728), another thinker associated with the school, *michi* had a much more concrete and objective significance, referring to the institutions established by the emperors of ancient China.

Michiko, Princess (1934–)

Wife of Crown Prince AKIHITO. Eldest daughter of Shōda Eizaburō, former chairman of the Nisshin Flour Milling Co, Ltd. Graduate of the English Literature Department of Sacred Heart University in Tōkyō. Princess Michiko, the first commoner to become the bride of a crown prince in Japan, married Crown Prince Akihito in 1959. Princess Michiko has three children: Hiro no Miya Naruhito (Prince HIRO), Aya no Miya Fumihito (Prince Aya), and Nori no Miya Sayako (Princess Nori). She serves as honorary vice-president of the Japanese Red Cross Society.

Midagahara

Highland on the western slope of TATEYAMA, eastern Toyama Prefecture, central Honshū. Said to have been created by an eruption of Tateyama. Noted for its alpine flora. Popular for skiing, hiking, and climbing, it has inns and a bus route. Elevation: 1,000–2,000 m (3,280–6,560 ft); area: about 7 sq km (2.7 sq mi).

Middle East and Japan

Japan's first contact with the Middle East was in the early 20th century when Japanese scholars of Asia first traveled to the area. At that time, Japanese capitalism was in the early stages of development, and the possibilities of trade and economic relations spurred interest in the Middle East.

By the mid-1920s, the volume of trade between Japan and the Middle East, excepting oil, was a mere 3 percent of total Japanese foreign trade, a percentage that remained unchanged in the early 1980s. Nonetheless, Japan was considered a strong competitor to Western European powers in the region. Japan concluded a treaty of commerce and navigation with Turkey in October 1930, a treaty of amity with Afghanistan in November of the same year, and a treaty of amity with Iran in October 1939. A legation in Egypt was established in January 1936.

Formal relations between Japan and these countries were suspended during World War II but resumed relatively soon after the war, in part because the Arab-Islamic countries did not regard Japan as a nation bent on colonialism. Japan thus steadily expanded its trade with the Middle East, whose markets partially replaced those it had lost in continental China and North Korea. During the 1960s, in step with the expansion of its energy industries, imports from the Middle East reached 20 percent of the total volume of Japanese trade, while exports comprised 10 percent of the total, making the Middle Eastern countries vital trade partners, next in importance only to North America and Asia. Japan's industrial structure became increasingly dependent on imported Middle Eastern oil. In 1958 the ARABIAN OIL CO, LTD, of Japan signed a concession for the production of oil in the Saudi Arabia–Kuwait neutral zone. Beginning in the 1970s, Japan has increased its economic cooperation with Saudi Arabia, Iran, and other Persian Gulf nations.

In the course of deepening its ties with the Middle Eastern countries, Japan has concluded the following agreements: a trade agreement with Turkey in February 1955; cultural agreements with Egypt in March 1957 and Iran in April 1957; a trade agreement with Egypt in November 1958; an agreement on economic and technical cooperation with Iran in December 1958; trade agreements with Iraq in June 1964 and Iran in June 1968; a tax treaty with Egypt in September 1968; a cultural agreement with Afghanistan in April 1969; an agreement with Syria for the dispatch of Japanese overseas cooperation volunteers in October 1969; economic and technical cooperation agreements with Iraq in August 1974 and Saudi Arabia in March 1975; an agreement on reciprocal protection of investment with Egypt in January 1977; and a cultural agreement with Iraq in March 1978.

Japan's Middle East policy underwent a change in 1973. The Arab oil strategy, adopted during the fourth Middle East war, came as a blow to Japan because of its dependence on the region's oil. In response Japan announced a new pro-Arab Middle East policy on 22 November 1973. The gist of the announcement was a pledge to support United Nations Security Council Resolution 242 (1967), which called for Israeli withdrawal from the occupied territories. The new policy was reiterated in a December 1974 interview given by a high official in the Ministry of Foreign Affairs, who criticized the Israeli occupation of Arab territory, and again in a January 1976 speech to the UN Security Council on the issue by Japanese Ambassador Saitō Shizuo.

In August 1979, Foreign Minister Sonoda Sunao delivered a policy statement stressing the interdependence of Japan and the Middle Eastern nations. He also made the following points: "First, it is essential that peace in the Middle East be just, lasting, and comprehensive. Second, such a peace should be achieved through the early and complete implementation of the UN Resolution 242 [1967] and 338 [1973] and through respect for the legitimate rights of the Palestinians under the UN Charter. Third, all possible avenues to peace should be explored, taking into account the aspirations of all the peoples concerned in the Middle East and the legitimate security requirements of the countries of the region."

Japan has also increased its diplomatic efforts in the Middle East in the years since 1973. Special envoys visited 16 countries, including the oil-producing countries, between December 1973 and January 1974. High government officials from Arab countries have also visited Japan, and the Japanese foreign minister visited Egypt in 1974 and Iran, Kuwait, the United Arab Emirates, and Saudi Arabia in 1978. Also in September 1978, Prime Minister Fukuda Takeo visited Iran, Qatar, the United Arab Emirates, and Saudi Arabia. Fukuda's trip, which followed his visit to the nations of the Association of Southeast Asian Nations (ASEAN), was an element of Japan's so-called all-directional diplomacy and took place while the peace talks between Israel and Egypt were beginning to bear fruit. The visit deepened mutual understanding and served to confirm the interdependence of the oil-producing nations and Japan as a major oil consumer.

The amount of the Japanese government's overseas development assistance (ODA) funds supplied to the countries of the Middle East totaled $347.78 million in 1978, which amounted to 22.7 percent of Japan's total ODA. Japan has also been supplying assistance funds to the United Nations Relief and Works Agency for Palestinian Refugees in the Near East (UNRWA) since 1953.

■——Chūtō Chōsakai, *Chūtō–Kita Afurika nenkan, 1981–82* (1981). Japan Foundation, *Dialogue: Middle East and Japan, Symposium on Cultural Exchange* (1978). Matsumoto Shigeharu, Itagaki Yūzō, ed, *Chūtō handobukku* (1978).   URANO Tatsuo

middle schools → elementary and secondary education

Midō Kampaku → Fujiwara no Michinaga

Midō Kampaku ki

Also called *Hōjōji Nyūdō Sadaijin ki*. Diary of the court official FUJIWARA NO MICHINAGA (966–1028; also known as Midō Kampaku), who was perhaps the preeminent political figure of the entire Heian period (794–1185). The diary covers the years from 998 through 1021. Fourteen chapters in Michinaga's own hand and 12 more copied later in the Heian period are preserved in the library Yōmei Bunko in Kyōto. It is an important historical source for the period when the Fujiwara family reached the height of their political power. See REGENCY GOVERNMENT.   G. Cameron HURST III

Midorikawa

River in Kumamoto Prefecture, Kyūshū, originating in the mountains on the border between Kumamoto and Miyazaki prefectures and flowing west through the Kumamoto Plain to Shimabara Bay. Several dams, including the Midorikawa Dam, and electric power plants are located on the river. Forestry and power development projects are in progress. Length: 75 km (47 mi).

Midway, Battle of

(Middouē Kaisen). The decisive battle fought between the Japanese and United States fleets in the area of the island of Midway in the central Pacific, 4–6 June 1942 during WORLD WAR II. On the morning of 4 June the Japanese *kidō butai* (mobile striking force), with a nucleus of four aircraft carriers, attacked Midway Island. The Japanese forces were surprised by attacks from American carriers and, eventually suffering the loss of all four of the aircraft carriers, one heavy cruiser, and a large number of aircraft and personnel, were forced to withdraw. This battle became the turning point of the Pacific War, for after Midway, the initiative passed to the United States, and Japan had to stand on the defensive.   ICHIKI Toshio

Mie Prefecture

(Mie Ken). Located on the eastern side of the Kii Peninsula in central Honshū and bordered by Ise Bay to the east, Kumano Sea to the south, and Wakayama, Nara, Kyōto, Shiga, Gifu and Aichi prefectures to the west and north. The northern part of the prefecture is composed of two level areas, and the ISE PLAIN along the coast, as well as the UENO BASIN further inland, are separated by low mountains. The climate is temperate along the coast but runs to extremes in the basin area. The southern part of the prefecture is mountainous and heavily forested, with a mild climate and heavy precipitation.

Numerous remains from prehistoric settlements and tumuli (see KOFUN) attest to early habitation. Proximity to the Kyōto-Nara region and the preeminence of the ISE SHRINE led to the area's rapid development in the early historical period. Divided into the provinces of Ise, Shima, and Iga after the Taika Reform of 645, it came under the domination of a succession of feudal lords and developed a flourishing agriculture and commerce. Its present name and boundaries were established in 1876.

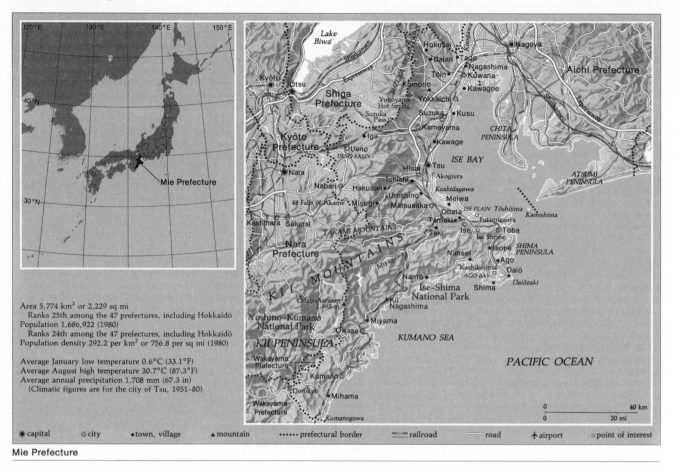

Mie Prefecture

Rice, fruit, and vegetables are produced on the Ise Plain, while the city of MATSUSAKA is famous for its beef. Forestry is a major activity in the southern area. Heavy and chemical industries, along with the older textile and ceramics industries, center on YOKKAICHI and SUZUKA in the north. The cultured-pearl industry was first developed in TOBA.

The Ise Shrine, the principal shrine of the native cult of Shintō, brings numerous pilgrims and tourists to the prefecture annually. Other attractions include the cultured-pearl beds at Toba, the coastal scenery of ISE–SHIMA NATIONAL PARK, and the mountains of YOSHINO-KUMANO NATIONAL PARK. The cities of Matsusaka and UENO still retain vestiges of castle towns. Area: 5,774 sq km (2,229 sq mi); pop: 1,686,922; capital: Tsu. Other major cities include Yokkaichi, ISE, Matsusaka, Suzuka, and KUWANA.

Mifune Kyūzō (1883–1965)

Jūdō master. Born in Iwate Prefecture. Mifune left Keiō University without earning a degree and entered the KŌDŌKAN in 1903. A man of short stature, he worked out the strategy called *kūkinage,* which enables a short man to throw a big man. He devoted himself to the spread and the development of *jūdō,* teaching younger generations at Kōdōkan. In 1945 he reached the 10th or highest rank in *jūdō.* His memoirs have been published as *Jūdō kaikoroku* (1953).

TAKEDA Fumio

Mifune Toshirō (1920–   )

The first Japanese movie actor since HAYAKAWA SESSHŪ to achieve international star status, Mifune Toshirō was born in China. Repatriated after World War II with his family, he arrived in Japan with a high-school certificate and no particular skills. Thinking he might become an actor, Mifune entered one of the "new face" contests of the TŌHŌ CO, LTD, in 1947 and failed. He had, however, been noticed by a senior Tōhō director, YAMAMOTO KAJIRŌ, who recommended him to a former pupil, Taniguchi Senkichi.

Taniguchi used him in his own debut film, *Shin baka jidai* (1947, The New Age of Fools), and in his second picture as well. This was

Ginrei no hate (1947, To the End of the Silver-capped Mountains), where Mifune, playing a postwar gangster, made a personal hit.

Another Yamamoto pupil who had seen these Taniguchi films (and helped write the scenario for the second), decided to cast Mifune in the important gangster role in his new film, *Yoidore tenshi* (1948, Drunken Angel). This was KUROSAWA AKIRA, a director with whose name and career Mifune has since been firmly linked. He has appeared in 16 of the director's 26 pictures, from *Yoidore tenshi* through *Akahige* (1965, Red Beard).

It was in his fifth Kurosawa picture, RASHŌMON (1950), that Mifune, playing the role of the bandit Tajōmaru, achieved worldwide fame. Within Japan his popularity (never extreme and not to be compared to that of such postwar idols as Ishihara Yūjirō) was based mainly upon his recreation of a familiar role—the nihilistic *samurai* hero, brought up to date in such films as *Yōjimbō* (1961) and *Tsubaki Sanjūrō* (1962, Sanjūrō). In the West, however, his apparently uninhibited performance in *Rashōmon* impressed an audience not used to the grand style in film acting. Also, his rapist role exuded a sexuality long found readily acceptable in "foreign" actors (Hayakawa, Valentino, Novarro) and now rendered newly respectable by its appearance in a "difficult" and important "art" film.

Mifune himself has always credited Kurosawa for his successes, saying that only under that director has he ever done anything of which he can be proud as an actor. Observation would seem to uphold that opinion. With Kurosawa he is an actor of enormous variety and subtlety, as in his single best performance, that of Sutekichi, the thief in *Donzoko* (1957, The Lower Depths). Without Kurosawa, including the film he himself directed, *Gojūman no isan* (1963, The Legacy of the Five Hundred Thousand), Mifune's performances have been undistinguished.

After breaking with Kurosawa, Mifune turned increasingly to television work and to roles in foreign films. In none of these vehicles (including a lengthy reprise of the *Sanjūrō* character on television), however, did he again reach a full display of his talents.

Donald RICHIE

Mihara

City in southeastern Hiroshima Prefecture, western Honshū, on the Inland Sea. Served by the Japanese National Railways and national highways, it is the center of textile, cement, and brewing industries. Ferries and passenger ships connect it with Imabari in Shikoku. Pop: 84,450.

Miharayama

Volcano in the Fuji Volcanic Zone; located on the island of ŌSHIMA, one of the Izu Islands, south of Tōkyō. A volcano composed of basalt, it spews out smoke continuously. It erupted in 1777–78 and in 1950–51. It attracts many tourists. The entire island is part of Fuji–Hakone–Izu National Park. Height: 758 m (2,486 ft).

Miho no Matsubara

Grove of pine trees in the southeastern part of the city of Shimizu, Shizuoka Prefecture, central Honshū. Located on the coast of the Miho Peninsula, it offers a magnificent view of Mt. Fuji (Fujisan). An ancient pine tree associated with the HAGOROMO LEGEND, concerning a celestial maiden who danced for a fisherman, is in Miho Shrine (see photo at SHIMIZU).

Mihonoseki

Town in northeastern Shimane Prefecture, western Honshū, on the eastern Shimane Peninsula. An important port town until the early part of the Meiji period (1868–1912), it has many sites of historic interest, including the Miho Shrine and the temple Bukkokuji. Fishing and marine products industries are active. It is part of the Daisen–Oki National Park, with a scenic coast and good fishing and swimming. Pop: 8,485.

Mihoro Dam

Located on the upper reaches of the river SHŌGAWA, northwestern Gifu Prefecture, central Honshū. Completed in 1961, it was Japan's first rock-filled dam. Mihoro Number 1 Electric Power Plant, located below the dam, has a maximum output of 215,000 kilowatts. Height of embankment: 131 m (430 ft); storage capacity: 329.7 million cu m (11.6 billion cu ft).

Miidera

Formally known as Onjōji. Head temple of the Jimon branch of the TENDAI SECT of Buddhism, located in the city of Ōtsu, Shiga Prefecture. Miidera was founded in 774 by Prince Ōtomo no Yota. After falling into disrepair, it was restored in 859 by the eminent Tendai monk ENCHIN (814–891), who became its abbot. Well known through descriptions in literature, the temple had traditionally been the center of both Tendai esoteric Buddhism and SHUGENDŌ, an indigenous religious tradition based on ascetic practices in the mountains.

Although Miidera began as a branch temple of ENRYAKUJI, the head temple of the Tendai sect on nearby Mt. Hiei (HIEIZAN), the two fell into conflict as Miidera became the center of a powerful faction that nearly overshadowed its head. All followers of the Enchin line were expelled from Hieizan in 993 and Miidera buildings themselves were razed several times by militant monks (see WARRIOR-MONKS) of Enryakuji from then through the 15th century. The temple was restored each time through the successive patronage of the court, the aristocracy, the Minamoto family, and the Ashikaga shogunate.

After the ex-emperor Shirakawa appointed the monk Zōyo (1032–1116) overseer (kengyō) of the KUMANO SANZAN SHRINES, an important Shugendō center and Zōyo founded the Shugendō temple SHŌGOIN in Kyōto, Miidera became the head temple of the Honzan branch of Shugendō. It is also one of the 33 temples (Saikoku Sanjūsansho) along the route of the pilgrimage to images of the bodhisattva KANNON, a practice that grew in popularity during the 15th century.

During the Edo period (1600–1868), Miidera became a center of itinerant minstrels who both entertained and edified the masses with popularized portrayals of Buddhist teachings. The temple abounds in artistic treasures as well, including the main hall, built in 1599, and the shrine dedicated to Shiragi Myōjin, the famed guardian deity of warriors and poets.

Miike Coal Mines

(Miike Tankō). Coal mines located on Ariake Bay in Kyūshū, extending over parts of Fukuoka and Kumamoto prefectures. Coal was discovered at the site of the first mine in the latter half of the 15th century, and by the end of the Edo period (1600–1868) two more mines had been opened by the Yanagawa and Miike domains (now Fukuoka Prefecture). In 1873 the mines were taken over by the Meiji government, which raised production through technical improvements as well as the use of convict labor. From 1876 Mitsui Bussan, the trading arm of the MITSUI business group, was the sole exporter of Miike coal, and in 1889 the government sold the mines to Mitsui under its program of transferring state enterprises to private interests (see KAN'EI JIGYŌ HARAISAGE). MITSUI MINING CO, LTD, established in 1892, introduced further innovations to increase the productivity of the mines, which formed the basis of the nascent Mitsui combine's wealth. Mitsui invested heavily in railways and built up the port of Miike to facilitate transportation of coal. After World War I it branched out into coal-related industries, contributing to the expansion of the city of Ōmuta, Fukuoka Prefecture, as an industrial center. After World War II the Miike mines were the scene of several large-scale labor strikes, which culminated in the MIIKE STRIKE of 1960. In 1963 an explosion at the mines took the lives of 458 persons and led to popular demands for improved mine safety legislation. At present the annual output is about 5 million metric tons (5.5 million short tons).

Miike strike

(Miike sōgi). Japan's most protracted large-scale labor dispute; it took place in 1960 at the MIIKE COAL MINES, a major component of the MITSUI MINING CO, LTD, located near Ōmuta in Kyūshū. A strike and lockout beginning in January continued for 282 days. A settlement between union and employer was reached after a series of conciliation efforts by the CENTRAL LABOR RELATIONS COMMISSION and a split-off from the union of a sizable group of miners who formed a competing organization. The significance of the strike was that, although it was centered in the Miike mines, it involved an almost total confrontation between the labor movement and big business backed by the government. The basic issue was employment security for the miners, who were resisting loss of their jobs under a national policy to convert from domestically mined coal to other, relatively cheaper sources of energy, notably petroleum imports. At stake was whether Japan could compete successfully in world markets and become a leading industrial power.

The Miike dispute first emerged in the spring of 1959, when the union made its annual demand for a general wage increase. Almost all of the 48,000 Miike workers were organized in a single "enterprise-wide" union that was part of the federation of Mitsui Mining unions and, in turn, a member of Tanrō (Japan Coal Miners' Union), at that time one of the largest industrial union affiliates (membership 200,000) of Japan's major labor organization, the left-wing General Council of Trade Unions of Japan (SŌHYŌ).

Instead of offering a wage increase, the company called for the discharge of 6,000 miners at Miike, on the grounds that the mines were running at a loss and required "rationalizing" in line with government policy to cut the mining work force, concentrate its efforts on high-productivity mines, and reduce the price of coal to compete with oil. The company therefore called for workers to retire "voluntarily" with special separation pay. The Miike union flatly rejected the proposal, believing that Mitsui actually wanted to eliminate the most active union members and thus weaken the union's solidarity. Several intermittent work stoppages ensued in the next few months. In December 1959 the company issued a list of workers it wished to dismiss, including many of the union activists. When the union continued in its refusal to compromise and insisted that all members retain employment in the mines, management declared a lockout on 25 January 1960, which was followed by the union's call for a full strike. Almost immediately, however, some 4,000 miners formed a new union, allegedly with company assistance, and returned to work; the striking union set up picket lines to prevent this return. A pitched battle ensued, leaving one person dead and more than 1,750 injured.

Big business and organized labor as a whole drew up battle lines over the Miike conflict. Banks and other major companies provided Mitsui Mining with financial backing. Sōhyō and Tanrō raised funds, mobilized nationwide worker support for the strikers, and dispatched as many as 300,000 unionists to join the picketing and demonstrations at Miike during the course of the strike. Police forces accumulated a total of 740,000 man-days on assignment to the mine, according to some estimates. At one point the company obtained a court injunction to halt the picketing, which the strikers ignored.

In August the Central Labor Relations Commission finally got both sides to agree informally to a conciliation offer, which included reduction of the dismissals to 1,200 workers, a grace period for "voluntary" retirement with extra compensation, and government and employer programs to retrain dismissed miners for new jobs inside and outside the company. Although Mitsui Mining immediately agreed, it was not until 1 November that the union signed the new compact. By that time, about half its members had quit to join the second union, while nationwide support for the strikers had begun to wane.

In the wake of the Miike strike, the government adopted a series of new laws to ease the transition from mining to other occupations. From 1958 to 1962, employment in the coal mines fell from almost 300,000 to about 180,000. By 1967 it was reduced to 120,000 and has since declined further. While output per miner rose dramatically and coal production stabilized during that time, coal as a source of energy dropped from more than 50 percent to less than 40 percent of the total supply. Although the strike failed to prevent the ENERGY REVOLUTION in Japan, it demonstrated organized labor's tenacious insistence on job security at the enterprise level, even at the risk of dividing its own ranks.

◾——Iwao Ayusawa, *A History of Labor in Modern Japan* (1966). Kazuo Ōkōchi, Bernard Karsh, and Solomon B. Levine, ed, *Workers and Employers in Japan: The Japanese Employment Relations System* (1973).   Solomon B. LEVINE

Mikage

District in the city of Kōbe, Hyōgo Prefecture, western Honshū, in the ward of Higashi Nada, facing Ōsaka Bay. It is a wealthy residential district in the Ōsaka–Kōbe area. Its good quality water contributes to the excellence of the *sake* produced in the area. In the nearby Rokkō Mountains (Rokkōzan) a superior-quality granite known as *mikageishi* is quarried.

Mikami Akira (1903–1971)

Japanese linguist. Born in Hiroshima Prefecture; graduated from the department of engineering, Tōkyō University, in 1927. Mikami studied Japanese grammar while teaching mathematics at a high school in Ōsaka and eventually formulated a new, creative approach to Japanese grammar. His insistence that Japanese has no true grammatical subject *(shugo)* and that the term should therefore be dropped in descriptions of the language particularly attracted attention within the field of linguistics. He later became a professor of mathematics at Ōtani Women's College in Kyōto. His works include *Gendai gohō josetsu* (1953), *Zō wa hana ga nagai* (1960), *Nihongo no ronri* (1963), *Nihongo no kōbun* (1963), and *Bumpō shōron shū* (1970).

Mikami Sanji (1865–1939)

Historian. Born in Harima Province (now part of Hyōgo Prefecture). Graduate of Tōkyō University, where he later taught Japanese history. He became chief editor of the DAI NIHON SHIRYŌ, the monumental compilation of historical sources, and also served as an advisor to the Imperial Household Ministry. A specialist in the Edo period (1600–1868), he wrote several works, including *Shirakawa Rakuō Kō to Tokugawa jidai* (1891, Matsudaira Sadanobu and the Tokugawa Period) and *Edo jidai shi* (1943–44, History of the Edo Period).

mikan

Tangerine-like citrus fruits grown in great quantities in Japan and the most important Japanese citrus fruit; often called Satsuma orange or, less accurately, mandarin orange. A member of the family Rutaceae. Since the late 19th century the most important variety of *mikan* has been the *unshū mikan (Citrus unshiu)*, which is among the most cold-resistant of all citrus trees, bears fruit abundantly, and suffers comparatively little from blight despite Japan's heavy rainfall. This variety is thought to have been discovered about 400–500 years ago as a chance seedling from a seed of Chinese origin washed

ashore by an ocean current to what is now Kagoshima Prefecture in southern Kyūshū. The fruit was not esteemed highly for many years, the traditional Kishū *mikan (C. deliciosa)* being preferred. However, during the Meiji period (1868–1912), new varieties of the *unshū* mikan were developed, with a wide range of ripening seasons and other characteristics, and, as a result, strains specific to various localities were developed. The *unshū mikan* then replaced the Kishū *mikan* in popularity. *Mikan* fruits average about 100 grams (3.5 oz) in weight. Great numbers of trees have been planted since the end of World War II, and the *mikan* now boasts the largest area under cultivation and production volume among fruit trees in Japan. In recent years growers have suffered from sluggish prices due to overproduction, and it is estimated that they will have to cut production by 20 percent in the future. The fruit is also used for canning and for making juice. Some 25–30 percent of the total crop is processed; the weak flavor of the juice is fortified by blending with orange juice. The *mikan* is exported to Canada and other countries; it is also grown in Florida and Alabama in the United States, the Caucasus region, the Black Sea coast of the Soviet Union, and Spain.
                                                        NAGASAWA Katsuo

Mikasa

City in west central Hokkaidō, on the river Ikushumbetsugawa. With the opening of the Horonai Coal Mine in 1880 and a railway line—the first in Hokkaidō—to Otaru, coal mining was for many years its principal industry. The closure of many mines has resulted in a decline in the population. Onions, watermelons, and melons are grown here. Pop: 23,319.

Mikasa, Prince (1915–   )

(Mikasa no Miya Takahito). Fourth son of Emperor TAISHŌ and brother of Emperor HIROHITO. A graduate of the Army War College, he served in China and later at Imperial Headquarters during World War II. Critical of his own involvement in the war as a member of the imperial family, he turned to the study of European and Middle Eastern history at Tōkyō University in 1947 and has directed the Society for Middle Eastern Studies in Japan since 1954.

Mikata Five Lakes

(Mikata Goko). In western Fukui Prefecture, central Honshū. Located west of the city of Tsuruga along Wakasa Bay, this group is composed of lakes Mikata, Suigetsu, Suga, Hiruga, and Kugushi. Mikata and Suigetsu are lagoons while the others are tectonic lakes. Saltwater fish inhabit Lake Hiruga, while freshwater fish such as carp, crucian carp, and pond smelt inhabit Lake Mikata. The lakes form part of Wakasa Bay Quasi-National Park.

Mikatahara

Also called Mikatagahara. Diluvial upland on the eastern side of Lake Hamana, northwestern part of the city of Hamamatsu, Shizuoka Prefecture, central Honshū. An old alluvial fan of the river Tenryūgawa. The forces of Takeda Shingen and Tokugawa Ieyasu fought here in 1572. Principal agricultural products are mandarin oranges and tea leaves. Many housing projects are being built here. A Japanese Self Defense Forces airfield and a motorcycle racetrack are located here. Elevation: 30–110 m (98–361 ft).

Mikawa Bay

(Mikawa Wan). Inlet of the Pacific Ocean between the Atsumi and Chita peninsulas, southern Aichi Prefecture, central Honshū. Divided into Atsumi Bay in the east and Chita Bay in the west. Well known for its *nori* (a seaweed) cultivation. There is an industrial zone in the Chita Bay area. Mikawa Bay forms the Mikawa Bay Quasi-National Park. Area: approximately 540 sq km (208 sq mi).

Mikawa monogatari

Three-volume autobiographical work by ŌKUBO HIKOZAEMON, a direct vassal (bannerman; *hatamoto*) of the Mikawa domain (now part of Aichi Prefecture); written in 1622. The first two volumes deal with the history of the TOKUGAWA FAMILY before TOKUGAWA IEYASU's unification of the country in 1600, emphasizing the achievements of Hikozaemon's ancestors, who had served Ieyasu's forebears before his rise to supreme power. The last volume is a memoir of the author's own life in the service of Ieyasu and his successors TOKUGAWA HIDETADA and TOKUGAWA IEMITSU. The author, who wrote the book to express his dissatisfaction with the reduced circumstances of the Ōkubo family, who he thought had been inadequately rewarded for their loyal service, nevertheless admonished his descendants to continue to serve the Tokugawa faithfully. Copies of the book were widely circulated. The *Mikawa monogatari* is interesting for its examination of the lord-vassal relationship and for the light it sheds on the *samurai* ethic during the Sengoku period (1467–1568).

Miki

City in southern Hyōgo Prefecture, western Honshū. A castle town during the 14th and 15th centuries, it later became known for its carpentry tools, knives, and *sake*. It is now a residential suburb of Kōbe. Pop: 70,201.

Miki Bukichi (1884–1956)

Politician. Born in Kagawa Prefecture. Graduated from Waseda University. He practiced law for several years before being elected to the House of Representatives in 1917 as a candidate of the political party KENSEIKAI and to the Tōkyō Municipal Assembly in 1922. After World War II he participated in the founding of the Japan Liberal Party (Nihon Jiyūtō). In 1946 he was elected to the House of Representatives but was barred from office (1946–51) during the OCCUPATION PURGE. He became secretary general of the LIBERAL PARTY in 1953, and in 1954 formed the NIHON MINSHUTŌ (Japan Democratic Party) with HATOYAMA ICHIRŌ, whom he supported in his successful bid for the premiership against YOSHIDA SHIGERU. Throughout his career Miki exercised significant political power behind the scenes.

Miki Kiyoshi (1897–1945)

Philosopher. Born in Hyōgo Prefecture. After studying at Kyōto University with NISHIDA KITARŌ and HATANO SEIICHI, Miki continued his studies in Europe under Martin Heidegger and Heinrich Rickert, returning to Japan and becoming a professor at Hōsei University in 1927. He opened a new phase in Japanese philosophy by analyzing the philosophical foundation of Marxism from a humanitarian point of view. His theory had great impact on Japanese intellectuals at the time. In 1930 he was arrested for violating the PEACE PRESERVATION LAW OF 1925 and was barred from all public offices. Nevertheless, he became active in journalism and sought to give concrete form to his philosophical ideas. Miki was particularly interested in the relationship between the structure of the historical world and its operative logic. He tried to explain the historical world as developing out of the process of dialectic resolution of subject and object and of logos and pathos. Seeking a new humanism that transcended nihilism, he developed what he called "the logic of creativity" (*kōsōryoku no ronri*) to encompass not only abstract logic but that of concrete human action as well. He was imprisoned in March 1945 for harboring a communist sympathizer and died in prison a month after the end of World War II.   *TANIKAWA Atsushi*

Mikimoto Kōkichi (1858–1954)

Developer of the cultured pearl. Born in what is now Mie Prefecture. In 1883 he started production of pearls by raising pearl oysters (*akoyagai; Pinctada martensii*) in Ago Bay on Shima Peninsula in Mie Prefecture. In 1893 he succeeded in producing a spheroid pearl and in 1898 harvested pearls from oysters which had been seeded in 1895. His cultured pearls were first introduced overseas in 1897, when he displayed spheroid specimens at an international exposition of marine products in Norway and received a silver medal. In 1905 he finally succeeded in producing perfectly round cultured pearls, and from about 1913 he began to have appreciable harvests.

In 1899 he opened a store in Tōkyō in order to sell both cultured and natural pearls. In 1911 he established stores and appointed agents in London and New York and set up branches in Chicago, Los Angeles, San Francisco, Bombay, Beijing (Peking), and Nanjing (Nanking). In 1919 he sent perfectly round cultured pearls to his London shop and offered them for sale at a price 25 percent cheaper than natural pearls, creating chaos on the market. Accusations that his cultured pearls were only imitations of real pearls gained considerable publicity, but eventually it was scientifically proven that they were no different from natural pearls. Gradually the value of Mikimoto pearls was accepted throughout the world and Mikimoto became known as the "pearl king." Until late in life he devoted himself to the pearl business and provided leadership in the industry. The farm he founded at Ago Bay is to this day the center of Mikimoto pearl operations. See also PEARLS.   *ARUGA Yūshō*

Miki Rofū (1889–1964)

Poet. Real name Miki Masao. Born in Hyōgo Prefecture. A precocious poet, while still a student at Waseda University he published his first collection of poems, *Haien* (1909, The Desolate Garden). First active in the movement for colloquial free verse, he soon turned to symbolist poetry. From 1920 to 1924 he was an instructor at a Trappist monastery in Hokkaidō, eventually being baptized in 1922; his life there is reflected in many of his essays and also poetry collections which include *Shinkō no akebono* (1922, The Dawn of Faith) and *Kami to hito* (1926, God and Man). He also participated in the nursery song movement of the 1920s that was led by *Akai tori* (Red Bird), the children's magazine founded by SUZUKI MIEKICHI. "Akatombo" (Red Dragonfly) and other songs have been collected in *Shinjujima* (1921, Pearl Island). Other works are *Shiroki te no karyūdo* (1913, The Hunter with the White Hand), a collection of poems noted for their sheer rhythmic virtuosity, and *Nihon katorikkukyō shi* (1929), a history of Catholicism in Japan. In 1927 the Vatican bestowed on him the title of the Knight of the Holy Sepulcher at Jerusalem for his writings on Catholicism.

Miki Takeo (1907–   )

Politician and prime minister (1974–76). Born in Tokushima Prefecture. A graduate of Meiji University, he also studied for several years at the University of California at Berkeley. A member of the House of Representatives since 1937, Miki belonged to several conservative parties (as a founding member of the KOKUMIN KYŌDŌTŌ, he served as minister of communications in KATAYAMA TETSU's coalition cabinet in 1947) before joining the LIBERAL DEMOCRATIC PARTY (LDP) in 1955. He served as director-general of the Economic Planning Agency (1958) and as minister of international trade and industry (1965–66) and of foreign affairs (1966–67) in the SATŌ EISAKU cabinets. Miki headed a small faction outside the main stream of LDP politics, and in a compromise between the FUKUDA TAKEO and ŌHIRA MASAYOSHI factions, he was elected president of the LDP and prime minister in 1974 after the resignation of TANAKA KAKUEI. Miki resigned in 1976 following LDP setbacks in the general election. As prime minister, he was confronted by a variety of problems, including the LOCKHEED SCANDAL and the recession following the OIL CRISIS OF 1973.

Miki Tokuchika (1900–1983)

Religious leader and the founder of the PL KYŌDAN. Born in Ehime Prefecture, son of Miki Tokuharu (1871–1938), who had been a Buddhist priest of the ŌBAKU SECT. He and his father were active members of a forerunner religion called Tokumitsukyō, founded in 1912 by Kaneda Tokumitsu (1863–1919). The Miki family continued Kaneda's work after his death, changing the name of the sect in 1931 to Hito no Michi Kyōdan (the Way-of-Man Organization). Under the militarist regime during World War II they were accused of subversive heterodox teachings; Tokuharu was imprisoned in 1936, Tokuchika in 1937, and the group was disbanded. After the war, Tokuchika was released and in 1946 he reestablished the group under the name Perfect Liberty Kyōdan, modifying the organization and style, as well as the doctrinal teachings and general spirit to take on a Western aspect. Twenty-one mottoes of life beginning with "Life Is Art" were drawn up. He was a leading figure in the establishment of the Union of New Religious Organizations in 1951 and became involved in the peace movement led by religious groups.   *Kenneth J. DALE*

Mikkabi

Town in western Shizuoka Prefecture, central Honshū, on the northern shore of Lake Hamana. It is known for the paleolithic human remains discovered here, the so-called Mikkabi Man. An important transportation center since ancient times, it is served by the Tōmei

Expressway interchange. Local products include tiles, rush for making *tatami* mats, mandarin oranges, and eels. Pop: 16,144.

mikkyō → esoteric Buddhism

miko

In ancient times a female shaman who played a prominent part in the early Shintō cult by acting as medium for the KAMI during his descent at the time of a ritual *(matsuri)*. The term now has two meanings: (1) a woman capable of transmitting through trance the utterance of a supernatural being; (2) a female officiant at a Shintō shrine, often a young girl, who does not necessarily have psychic or shamanistic power.

In the early cult the *miko* is thought to have come to her office through election by a spiritual being, usually a *kami*. The gift was bestowed either through a dream or through sudden involuntary possession, *kamigakari*. Thereafter she probably had to consolidate the power given to her by a regime of *gyō* or ascesis (see ASCETICISM). Evidence about the early *miko* is fragmentary, but examples may be discerned in the NIHON SHOKI (720, Chronicle of Japan) in the shape of Yamato Totohi Momoso Hime and the Empress Jingū. Clay HANIWA thought to represent *miko* wear a necklace of *magatama* beads (see BEADS, ANCIENT) and a peculiar flat board-like hat. She is believed to have attained the necessary condition of trance in which the god could speak through her mouth by violent dancing and singing of magical invocatory songs. In some cases, as with the Empress Jingū, a second person, known as *saniwa*, was required to bring her to the required trance, to summon the god and send him away.

With the TAIKA REFORM of the mid-7th century the *miko* was banished from the ceremonies of the court and relegated to cults practiced outside the capital. With the advent of Buddhism her status was still further reduced. The role of active summoner came to be carried out by a Buddhist priest or YAMABUSHI, so that the *miko* became a mere passive mouthpiece for the god's utterance. Insight into her ancient role may be gained from study of the comparable women in the religion of the Ryūkyū Islands, the *nuru* or *noro* and the *yuta*, and of the Ainu *tsusu*.

Modern counterparts of the ancient *miko* may be found among the founders of certain *shinkō shūkyō* (NEW RELIGIONS), such as NAKAYAMA MIKI, DEGUCHI NAO, and KITAMURA SAYO. Women acting as mouthpieces for gods or *hotoke* (ancestral spirits) may also still be found in many rural districts, particularly the Tōhoku (northern Honshū) area. The blind *itako* of Aomori Prefecture, though now much debilitated, are rightly regarded as the remnant of a true shamanic medium tradition. See also SHAMANISM.

📖 ——Nakayama Tarō, *Nihon fujo shi* (repr 1969). Sakurai Tokutarō, *Nihon no shamanizumu* (1974). Carmen Blacker, *The Catalpa Bow* (1975). *Carmen* BLACKER

mikoshi

A portable Shintō shrine, sometimes referred to as a sacred palanquin. A *mikoshi*, also called *shin'yo*, is basically a highly ornate miniature replica of a shrine that rests on two long horizontal poles. Its roof is often decorated with an elaborate gilded phoenix.

Before the introduction of the *mikoshi*, a mirror with a branch of the *sakaki* tree or some other object symbolic of a divine presence was carried around, sometimes on horseback. The use of a palanquin-like structure, i.e., a *mikoshi*, began in the 8th century, the first recorded occurrence being the transfer of the deity of the USA HACHIMAN SHRINE in Kyūshū by palanquin to Nara where the deity was to safeguard the construction of the Great Buddha image (749) at the temple Tōdaiji. By the 10th century it had become a common practice in Kyōto to carry the deity from a shrine through the community in a *mikoshi* on the occasion of the *ekijinsai*, a festival aimed at pacifying malevolent spirits that were believed to cause epidemics. In the 12th and 13th centuries the *mikoshi* from the Hie and Kasuga shrines were often brought into Kyōto by unruly monks (WARRIOR-MONKS) of the nearby Enryakuji and Kōfukuji, two powerful Buddhist temples, in an effort to intimidate the secular authorities into accepting the demands of the clergy.

Nowadays the *mikoshi* is carried on shrine festival days through the parish, i.e., the village or ward, on the shoulders of some 20 or 30 people. While the procession in some cases is a solemn affair, it often tends to be raucous, with the participants pushing the *mikoshi*

Mikoshi

A *mikoshi* being carried during the Sanja Festival of the Asakusa Shrine in Tōkyō.

in zigzag fashion, first in one direction and then in another. This tempestuous movement of the *mikoshi*, known as *mikoshi furi* (shaking of the *mikoshi*) is commonly thought to reflect the turbulent character of the deity enshrined in the *mikoshi*, often in the form of a sacred mirror *(shinkyō)*. The progression of the *mikoshi* through the community is taken to signify a visit of the deity to his parishioners *(ujiko)* so that his protection can be extended to them for the coming year. Often the *mikoshi* is placed in temporary resting places known as *otabisho*, where offerings of *sake* (rice wine) and food are made by the residents of the area. The *otabisho* are considered to be original sites of the performance of ritual.

Stanley WEINSTEIN

mikotonori → imperial edict

mikudarihan

(literally, "three and a half lines"). Popular term for a letter of divorce used by commoners during the Edo period (1600–1868). At that time, only the husband could legally initiate a divorce. In contrast to divorce proceedings among the *samurai* class, in which both the husband's family and the wife's family were required to submit notices to the shogunate, all that was required for a commoner was a letter of divorce, handed by him to his wife or to his wife's father or brother. *Mikudarihan* followed a format—three and a half lines confirming the divorce and giving the wife permission to remarry. A discontented wife could ask her husband to write a *mikudarihan* or, as a last resort, seek refuge in a temple (see KAKEKOMIDERA).

Mikuni Mountains

(Mikuni Sammyaku). Mountain range running east to west forming the boundary of Gumma, Nagano, and Niigata prefectures, central Honshū. The major peaks are Shirasunayama (2,140 m; 7,019 ft), TANIGAWADAKE (1,963 m; 6,439 ft), and Mikuniyama (1,636 m; 5,366 ft). The range divides the region into the Sea of Japan and Pacific climatic zones. Most of the peaks are part of Jōshin'etsu Kōgen National Park.

Mikuni Pass

(Mikuni Tōge). Extends through the MIKUNI MOUNTAINS, southern Niigata Prefecture and northern Gumma Prefecture, central Honshū. It is a major artery of communication. The highway Mikuni Kaidō was important both before and during the Edo period (1600–1868), providing the area's only access to Edo (now Tōkyō). The Shimizu Tunnel of the Japanese National Railways was opened in 1931, and the Mikuni Tunnel of National Route No. 17 was opened in 1959. Altitude: 1,300 m (4,264 ft).

Mikuni Rentarō (1923–   )

Film actor. Real name Satō Masao. Born in Gumma Prefecture. Mikuni joined Shōchiku Motion Picture Company (see SHŌCHIKU

CO, LTD) and made his debut in the role of a morally concerned reporter in KINOSHITA KEISUKE's *Zemma* (1951, The Good Fairy). In 1952 he was forced to leave Shōchiku after he was attacked by the media for falsifying his academic background. He continued working as a freelance actor, appearing in such memorable roles as a mentally unbalanced youth in Shibuya Minoru's *Honjitsu kyūshin* (1952, Doctor's Day Off); a man with a criminal record in UCHIDA TOMU's *Kiga kaikyō* (1965, The Straits of Hunger), and a rapist in IMAI TADASHI's *Echigo tsutsuishi oyashirazu* (1964, A Story from Echigo). Mikuni's stage presence is powerful, although his performance as the nihilistic revolutionary KITA IKKI in Yoshida Yoshishige's *Kaigenrei* (1973, Martial Law) revealed another aspect of this highly versatile actor. *Itasaka Tsuyoshi*

militarism

(gunkoku shugi). An ideology and a course of political action aimed at the domination of politics, culture, and all other aspects of social life by military values. War and preparation for war become so important that all else is subordinated to them. Many Japanese scholars believe that Japan was to some extent a militaristic society throughout its pre-World War II modern history. It became pervasively militaristic, they think, after the London Naval Conference crisis of 1930 and the MANCHURIAN INCIDENT of 1931 placed Japan on the road to war in 1937 and 1941 and to disastrous defeat in 1945 (see SINO-JAPANESE WAR OF 1937–1945). While the seeds of militarism were sown in the 19th century and grew even in the "democratic" 1920s, the fruit did not mature until the years 1930–45, when the imperial Japanese armed forces played an increasingly central role in the country's life and administration (see GUMBATSU).

The military was able to influence Japanese society for a number of reasons. To begin with, almost all of Japan's leaders during the Meiji period (1868–1912) were former *samurai*. Whether they served in business, the military, or the civil bureaucracy, their background and outlook were those of the martial elite. Moreover, many of their successors in the Taishō (1912–26) and Shōwa (1926–) periods were either descended from samurai or influenced by samurai values and so continued to view Japan's domestic and international requirements from a military point of view. Second, many of Japan's problems from the 1860s until the 1940s necessitated, or seemed to necessitate, military solutions. In fact, some scholars argue that the basic motivation for industrialization and modernization was martial and that this impetus laid the foundation for the military's power and prestige. The Meiji leaders came to power by subduing the armed resistance of the Tokugawa shogunate and faced uprisings of discontented samurai and peasants throughout the 1870s. At the same time, the militarily expansionist policies of the Western powers threatened Japan; moreover, the perception of this threat continued during most of the modern period, intensifying in the 1930s. Since Japanese leaders did not wish their country to suffer the fate of China and become a semi-colony of the Western powers, they tended to support policies that gave the development of national wealth and power (FUKOKU KYŌHEI) priority over the fostering of democracy. Third, after the SINO-JAPANESE WAR OF 1894–1895, Japan too joined the colonizers, and both the creation and the defense of its empire, which almost all leaders supported, called for a strong military.

Although most leaders thus professed belief in the need for a strong military, some worked for its fulfillment more diligently than others. Those most committed to enhancing the power of the armed forces and to introducing martial values into civilian life were army leaders affiliated with the faction of Field Marshal YAMAGATA ARITOMO. Yamagata had a profound influence on both the military and the civilian government during the Meiji and Taishō periods. As a civil bureaucrat, he helped to create a centralized system of LOCAL GOVERNMENT, to write the patriotically focused IMPERIAL RESCRIPT ON EDUCATION, and to make the Meiji CONSTITUTION of 1889 as illiberal as possible. As a military bureaucrat, he founded the modern conscription system and with his protégés created many of the other institutions that underlay the militarism of the 1930s. In January 1873 Yamagata instituted the CONSCRIPTION ORDINANCE, which, by elevating commoners, broke the samurai class's centuries-old monopoly in military matters. The ordinance provided the army with enough conscripts to enable it to suppress the SATSUMA REBELLION of 1877 but not enough to enable it to function well as an organ of militaristic indoctrination because of peasant resistance to the law's onerous requirement of three years' active duty, the numerous exemptions allowed, and the army's limited need for soldiers in the

1870s. Only after the 1889 and 1927 revisions of the law by Yamagata's protégés, KATSURA TARŌ, TERAUCHI MASATAKE, and TANAKA GIICHI could the army begin to turn a fighting machine into an organ to educate the public.

These revisions reduced the number of exemptions from service and lengthened the term of reservist obligation. The purpose of these changes, carried out under German influence, was twofold, one logistic and the other ideological. On the one hand, the army could increase the pool of soldiers available for war by drafting and training more men for a shorter period of time and then keeping them in the reserves for a longer period. On the other hand, the army could indoctrinate thousands of men with the military-patriotic values of the emperor cult, for the IMPERIAL RESCRIPT TO SOLDIERS AND SAILORS, which Yamagata had the emperor promulgate in 1882, had made unquestioning loyalty to the emperor the basis of military training.

Also providing a basis for the growth of military power in the 1930s were the various freedoms from civilian restraint that the government, under the influence of Yamagata and other officers, gave the army and navy. In 1878 the army set up the ARMY GENERAL STAFF OFFICE equal in authority to, and independent of, the ARMY MINISTRY; the navy later followed suit. The chiefs of the army and Naval General Staff Offices, which were responsible for military planning and operations, reported directly to the emperor and so could act free of civilian control. Unlike the army and navy ministers, they were not cabinet members and had no responsibility to the prime minister. Thus, in military matters, the general staffs constituted a separate government. See also NAVAL GENERAL STAFF OFFICE.

The independence of the general staffs was legally confirmed by the Meiji Constitution. Article 11 of this document stated that the emperor "has the supreme command" (TŌSUIKEN) of the army and navy, and article 12 that he alone "determines the organization and peace standing" of the armed forces. What these provisions meant was that the chief of staff of each service, and to a lesser extent the army and navy ministers, *could* under certain circumstances report directly to the emperor rather than to the prime minister. In other words, they were legally free of civilian authority. Although neither the army nor the navy ever used this constitutional prerogative to circumvent the prime minister, it was still a powerful weapon; the government often trimmed its sails to military winds because of its fear that the armed forces would take independent action.

The army and navy also had decisive leverage over any civilian government through their unique power to designate or withdraw their ministers from the cabinet. Between 1898 and 1945, only officers on active duty, and therefore subject to military discipline, served as army and navy ministers (see GUMBU DAIJIN GEN'EKI BUKAN SEI). Since the law required that the prime minister resign if he could not fill all cabinet posts (and he could not appoint army and navy ministers without the services' cooperation), the military could bring down or block the formation of a cabinet at any time. This power was invoked only once, in January 1937, when the army ironically prevented General UGAKI KAZUSHIGE from forming a cabinet by refusing to provide an officer for its ministerial post, but as with the "right of supreme command," the military was able to influence the government simply by threatening to exercise this authority, especially in the late 1930s.

As important to the rise of militarism in the 1930s as these constitutional and legal powers were the weapons that enabled the military to build a secure foundation of popular support for itself. The military created this social basis for militarism through the formation of a patriotic ideology and the creation or manipulation of a number of organizations to spread its values. The men who molded this ideology in the Meiji period did so not to militarize the country but to unify what they saw as a dangerously divided and weak nation. Nevertheless, the code that they formed, based on the feudal warrior ethic (BUSHIDŌ), the pre-Meiji cult of the emperor, and their vision of the traditional family, played a crucial role in the patriotism that underlay the militarism of the 1930s. Soldiers and citizens, like the samurai of old, were exhorted in the name of the emperor to show loyalty, obedience, courage, frugality, simplicity, diligence, and cooperation in their daily lives. The emperor was not seen merely as the sovereign: he was a man-god *(arahitogami)* descended from the sun goddess AMATERASU ŌMIKAMI. Thus the emperor, whose dynasty the ideologists claimed had reigned in an unbroken line for over 2,500 years, became the focus of modern Japanese nationalism. Moreover, this emperor was seen as the national father in a hierarchically ordered family, with people in positions of authority, both military and civilian, acting as his representatives. When a soldier obeyed his commanding officer and a civilian served government officials, they also obeyed and served their emperor. The government then introduced these ideals into the military and civilian educational curricula, and, by the end of the Meiji period, millions of soldiers, sailors, and civilians alike had learned the basic patriotic-military-filial values of what many Japanese scholars call the "emperor system" *(tennō seii;* see EMPEROR).

Army and navy leaders believed that only they could provide the "ultimate national schooling"; although public elementary schools taught patriotic values, they could not do so as correctly as the military, which was led by the most courageous, patriotic, and filial of Japan's citizens, its officer corps. The problem with the army and navy as schools, however, was that at most only one of every five eligible males 20 years of age served in the armed forces at any time before 1937. Thus, at the beginning of the 20th century, military leaders sought ways to supplement the indoctrinating work of the school and conscription systems and found them in a series of civilian organizations controlled or influenced by the military.

In 1910 Terauchi and Tanaka founded the first of these, the IMPERIAL MILITARY RESERVISTS' ASSOCIATION, a centralized paramilitary organization with village branches and hamlet subunits. All men who passed the conscription physical examination were eligible to join. By the 1930s, 3 million men between the ages of 20 and 40 had served in the organization, over half of them never having been in the regular military. The association not only enlisted a large percentage of eligible men, especially in rural areas, but also carried out a wide range of functions that helped to build grassroots support for the armed forces. Members fought fires, repaired roads and irrigation canals, policed the hamlet, helped families with members on active duty, marched in close-order drill on the shrine or school grounds, and participated in patriotic ceremonies. Often a landlord or his son led these activities.

By the outbreak of World War I, thousands of Japanese men had received the military's message through the schools and veterans' association, but the system missed a large age group, those who had graduated from elementary school at age 14 but were still too young for entry into the army or reservist group. To fill this gap, in 1914–15 Tanaka and several civilian followers of Yamagata in the home and education ministries established a national youth association headquarters to unify local youth organizations throughout the country. Although the national association came under the jurisdiction of the home and education ministries, its local branches, which performed a combination of community, military, and patriotic duties, were usually led by reservists. By the 1930s this federation, then known as the DAI NIPPON RENGŌ SEINENDAN, had 2.5 million members, mainly in rural areas.

Tanaka and his successor as army minister, Ugaki Kazushige, added the final touch to the military training of Japan's youth when in 1925 they formed youth training centers with a four-year curriculum of vocational, physical, and military training. Run by a community's elementary school principal with the aid of his teaching staff and local reservists, these centers gave 100 hours of military drill and 100 hours of other instruction per year to the 85 percent of Japanese men who did not matriculate in middle schools. Initially, 800,000 youths were enrolled. In 1935, when these centers merged with similar local vocational schools, some 2 million students were attached to them.

By the 1930s the armed forces had built powerful, independent positions from which they could exert a strong influence on Japanese society. Long-standing civilian support for military values, an unfettered legal position, and an elaborate network of paramilitary organizations—all of these factors converged in the 1930s with the sense of crisis that began to permeate Japanese society, enabling the military and its civilian supporters to push through policies that increasingly militarized Japan and led it to war. This sense of crisis was heightened by the world depression that began in 1929 and by the imposition of trade barriers by Western powers; this led more and more Japanese leaders to believe that Japan must solve its problems by itself and that its military offered the best solutions. Those who after 1930 continued to advocate internationalism and to resist military "solutions," like Foreign Minister SHIDEHARA KIJŪRŌ in 1930–31, were routed from government; by the mid-1930s, even some of those with impeccable patriotic credentials like the generals WATANABE JŌTARŌ and NAGATA TETSUZAN fell before the accelerating patriotic-militaristic juggernaut.

The crucial turning point in the rise of militarism was the London Naval Conference crisis of 1930. The Minseitō government of Prime Minister HAMAGUCHI OSACHI, which was committed to cooperation with the United States and Great Britain, negotiated a naval limitation treaty that many Japanese, including Naval Chief of Staff KATŌ HIROHARU, the army's leadership, members of the opposition Rikken Seiyūkai party and of the radical right, and much of the public, believed was forced on Japan by the two Western naval powers and endangered Japan's national defense. Although Hamaguchi managed to have the treaty ratified, the tumultuous debate that occurred between its signing and ratification, including an unsuccessful attempt by Katō to invoke the right of supreme command, created the public mood for antiforeign militarism. By the end of 1931 Hamaguchi had been shot, his government felled, and Manchuria seized by insubordinate army officers, and more and more people had become opposed to cooperation with the United States and Great Britain and committed to Japan's going it alone militarily in the international arena.

From 1930 on, army and navy officers involved themselves in a series of incidents that, although lacking an overall blueprint or a consistent pattern of participation, indicated the degree to which the military was able to act freely. On 18 September 1931, two middle-level staff officers in the GUANDONG (KWANTUNG) ARMY engineered an incident in Mukden that led to their army's seizure of Manchuria. On 15 May 1932, naval cadets murdered Prime Minister INUKAI TSUYOSHI; at their trial, encouraged by petitions of support from thousands of rightists and reservists, the assassins flaunted their radical, militaristic patriotism. In 1935 the army, the radical right, and thousands of reservists, led by the president of the Imperial Veterans' Association, former Chief of the Army General Staff Suzuki Sōroku (1865–1940), persecuted the respected constitutional scholar MINOBE TATSUKICHI for what they thought was the flagrant lese majesty of his "emperor-as-organ" theory (TENNŌ KIKAN SETSU). On 26 February 1936, elements of the army's First Division, led by their young platoon and company commanders, seized central Tōkyō and assassinated a number of ranking government officials (see FEBRUARY 26TH INCIDENT). In July 1937 a local clash between small units of Chinese and Japanese troops on the outskirts of Beiping (Peiping; now Beijing or Peking) grew bit by bit into a full-scale war (the Sino-Japanese War of 1937–45). It has often been written that these and other incidents between 1930 and 1937, and especially the February 26th Incident, enabled the army and navy to take control of Japan's government. Direct evidence proving this cause-and-effect relationship is difficult to find. But one thing is clear: the uprisings, assassinations, and other clashes of the 1930s demonstrated the military's freedom from outside influence. Even the general who served as prime minister at the time of the attack on Pearl Harbor in December 1941, TŌJŌ HIDEKI, had difficulty in controlling his own army.

Can we conclude that the armed forces' independent power, built on the twin foundations of popular support and legal freedom from government control, made Japan a militaristic society during World War II? According to our definition of militarism, the answer is yes and no: Japanese society had many elements of militarism, but military domination of politics, culture, education, and the economy was incomplete. After war with China broke out in 1937, military values came to permeate every aspect of society. Officers held many nonmilitary cabinet posts. The nation's resources were used increasingly for the army and navy; industrial raw materials, agricultural produce, farm horses, temple bells, and even jewelry were requisitioned for the war effort; sericulture, the second leading source of farm income before 1939, already hit hard by the world depression and by competition from rayon, largely disappeared because of the military's need for more essential crops; factories geared up to make uniforms, tanks, planes, ships, and shells. The content of the educational system became increasingly militaristic and patriotic. Small neighborhood associations (TONARIGUMI) were formed where they did not already exist to bring the populace under tighter government control. The army's military police became increasingly involved in the surveillance of civilians. And finally, free from civilian control, the army and navy made diplomatic and strategic decisions that had calamitous consequences, culminating in Japan's disastrous defeat in 1945.

Yet, in spite of the pervasiveness of military influence in Japan between 1937 and 1945, the army and navy were never able to dominate Japanese society totally. Army efforts, beginning in 1936, to create a state-controlled economy met with stiff resistance from civil bureaucrats, party politicians, and businessmen. Competition was rife in the wartime economy. At the height of World War II in 1942–45, the military, the civil bureaucracy, and private industry fought among themselves for scarce materiel. Companies even attempted to stockpile resources for postwar use.

Political competition was also widespread. The army in 1942 failed in an attempt to wrest control of the IMPERIAL RULE ASSISTANCE ASSOCIATION from the Home Ministry. In the 1942 general election for the lower house of the Diet, the army tried unsuccessfully to destroy the final vestiges of the power of the old party politicians; in spite of the army's vigorous campaign against candidates who had been members of political parties before their dissolution in 1940, the overwhelming majority of those elected were former party men who retained their seats in the Diet. In other words, although military values pervaded every aspect of Japanese society during World War II, the military did not have a free hand; Japan's militarism was limited inasmuch as the army and navy could not completely dominate the nation's economic and political life.

■ ———James B. Crowley, *Japan's Quest for Autonomy* (1966). Fujiwara Akira, *Gunjishi* (1961). Fukuchi Shigetaka, *Gunkoku Nihon no keisei* (1959). Roger F. Hackett, *Yamagata Aritomo in the Rise of Modern Japan, 1838–1922* (1971). Richard J. Smethurst, *A Social Basis for Prewar Japanese Militarism* (1974).

Richard SMETHURST

military factions → gumbatsu

military education in the schools

(*gunji kyōren*). Military training was included in the school curriculum in Japan from the Meiji period (1868–1912) up to the end of World War II. It was based on a government policy expressed in the slogan *fukoku kyōhei* (rich country, strong military).

During the 1880s "infantry exercises" (*hohei sōren*) were carried out in the middle schools. (Graduates of middle schools were either exempted from regular compulsory military service or entitled to a shortened term of such duty.) In response to demands from the education minister, MORI ARINORI, "military-style calisthenics" (*heishiki taisō*) was also introduced into the teacher-training schools. Following the Russo-Japanese War (1904–05) the trend grew stronger, and military training courses called *kyōren* became part of the curriculum for both boys and girls at the elementary and secondary school level. After World War I career officers were assigned to the faculty of middle schools, higher schools, and college-preparatory schools (*yoka*). "Youth training centers" (*seinen kunrenjo*) for working youth also made their appearance throughout the country. With the onset of World War II, emphasis on military training grew even stronger, and *kyōren* became mandatory even at the universities. The end of the war brought about the abolition of all military training in the school system.

KURAUCHI Shirō

Milne, John (1850–1913)

British seismologist. Born in Liverpool. A graduate of Kings College of London University, Milne later studied geology and minerology at the Royal School of Mines. Upon the invitation of the Japanese government, he went to Tōkyō in 1876 to teach geology and mining at Kōbu Daigakkō (later part of Tōkyō University). Following an earthquake on 22 February 1880, with other scientists, he founded the Seismological Society of Japan and its journal, *Transactions of the Seismological Society of Japan*. A seismograph that he devised was used in observation posts throughout Japan. Milne returned to England. In recognition of his services Milne was awarded the Order of the Rising Sun by the Japanese government in 1895.

mimai

Expression, material or intangible, of one's sympathy or wish to console or encourage on occasions such as death in a family, illness, or fire. Warriors on the battlefield in feudal times, people confined to hospital, or actors and musicians before or after a performance, typically receive *mimai* from their supporters. Specific types of *mimai* are distinguished by prefixing the name of the occasion, as in *byōki mimai* for an illness or *kaji mimai* after a fire.

Mimai is performed formally by visiting the person or the family in need of support. When visiting is not possible, a letter or a phone call is acceptable, though considered less proper. Such expressions of sympathy or encouragement are often accompanied by a gift, especially when visiting is involved. Food is the most common type of *mimai* gift. Such food gifts were believed in the past to possess magic power (see GIFT GIVING).

In Japan *mimai* is considered obligatory among close relatives and intimate friends; not to demonstrate one's concern when *mimai* is called for is deemed an outright breach of etiquette and can result in social sanction. If one has received *mimai*, it is necessary to reciprocate when the giver of *mimai* is in a similar situation. Thus *mimai* is an example of those reciprocal obligations that are such an important component of Japanese social relations. See also ON; GIRI AND NINJŌ.

Harumi BEFU

Mimana → Kaya

Mimasaka

Town in northeastern Okayama Prefecture, western Honshū. It is mainly an agricultural district, producing tea, vegetables, and fruit. There is also dairy farming. The Yunogō Hot Spring has been known since ancient times. An interchange on the Chūgoku Expressway makes it easily accessible. Pop: 14,171.

Mimikawa

River in Miyazaki Prefecture, Kyūshū, originating in the village of Shiiba in the northwestern part of the prefecture and flowing east to empty into the Hyūga Sea at the city of Hyūga. The upper reaches form V-shaped gorges, which have long been detached from the coastal areas. The river is used to generate electric power. Length: 102 km (63 mi); area of drainage basin: 883 sq km (341 sq mi).

mimpon shugi

(literally, "people-as-the-base-ism"). A philosophy espoused by the political scientist YOSHINO SAKUZŌ, it served as the major theoretical underpinning of the so-called TAISHŌ DEMOCRACY, the liberal political movement of the Taishō period (1912–26). Yoshino developed this concept (the term had already been used by scholars like UESUGI SHINKICHI) in a series of articles, published between 1914 and 1918 in the magazine CHŪŌ KŌRON, intended to criticize arbitrary bureaucratic rule. He chose to render "democracy" as *mimpon shugi*, rather than the more common translation *minshu shugi*, because the latter term suggested the notion of popular sovereignty, and its implicit rejection of imperial sovereignty would have caused official condemnation of his views. In Yoshino's mind *mimpon shugi* stood for government by and for the people, but in the name of the emperor; it was concerned less with the locus of sovereignty than with its practical application to representative democracy. His ideas had a profound influence on the UNIVERSAL MANHOOD SUFFRAGE MOVEMENT; but after 1925, though still supported by moderate socialists and liberal party politicians, *mimpon shugi* gradually lost influence as intellectuals and the labor movement gravitated toward more radical thought.

Mimpōten → Civil Code

Mimpōten ronsō → Civil Code controversy

Min → Sōmin (Buddhist priest); Min, Queen (Korean queen)

Minabuchi no Shōan (fl early 7th century)

Scholar-priest, reportedly of Chinese descent, also known as Minamibuchi no Shōan. He accompanied a mission led by ONO NO IMOKO to the Sui dynasty (589–618) of China in 608 and studied there for the next 32 years. After his return to Japan in 640, he taught Confucian texts to Prince Naka no Ōe (later Emperor TENJI) and FUJIWARA NO KAMATARI, the initiators of the TAIKA REFORM of 645. Although Shōan, with his extensive knowledge of Chinese political institutions, is thought to have influenced the shape of the new government that resulted from the reform, there is no record that he actually participated in state affairs.

Minakami

Town in northern Gumma Prefecture, central Honshū, on the river Tonegawa. The hot springs at Minakami, Tanigawa, and Yubiso, as well as skiing on Tenjindaira, draw many visitors. It is also the base camp for climbing TANIGAWADAKE. Pop: 8,747.

Minakami Takitarō (1887–1940)

Novelist; literary critic. Real name Abe Shōzō. Born in Tōkyō. Even as a student at Keiō University, he contributed poems and fiction to *Subaru* and *Mita bungaku*. He studied in the United States and traveled in Europe before becoming, in 1917, an executive at the insurance company founded by his father. Combining his business career and professional writing throughout his life, Minakami wrote many novels dealing with the lifestyle of white-collar workers during the 1920s and 1930s. Principal works include *Ōsaka no yado* (1925), a novel, and *Kaigara tsuihō* (1918–39), a collection of essays.

Minakami Tsutomu (1919–   )

Novelist. Born in Fukui Prefecture. Attended Ritsumeikan University but did not graduate. From a young age he engaged in various professions in order to support himself. He established his name as a mystery writer with *Kiri to kage* (1959) and *Umi no kiba* (1960), both based on political or social issues. With his autobiographical novel *Gan no tera* (1961), which received the Naoki Prize, he began to develop a new theme—the lyrical treatment of the sorrows of women, notably of those bound to a life of poverty in the remote Hokuriku region where he was raised. Such novels include *Goban-chō yūgirirō* (1962) and *Echizen takeningyō* (1963). Other works are the mystery *Kiga kaikyō* (1962), dealing with the TŌYA MARU DISASTER, and *Uno Kōji den* (1971), a biography of his mentor UNO KŌJI. In 1973 he received the Yoshikawa Eiji Prize and in 1975 the Tanizaki Prize.

Minakata Kumakusu (1867–1941)

Biologist, ethnologist, and folklorist. Born in Kii Province (now Wakayama Prefecture). After dropping out of the First Higher School (Daiichi Kōtō Gakkō) in 1886, he spent 15 years in Europe and the United States, studying and traveling widely. While serving on the research staff of the British Museum, he made the acquaintance of SUN YAT-SEN. Throughout his life he remained strongly independent, even eccentric. His studies encompassed both the humanities and the natural sciences: he was versed in several Western languages as well as in Japanese classics, folklore, and archaeology, and in the course of his scientific research he discovered many new types of fungus and slime mold. He wrote many articles for the British journal *Nature* and helped F. V. Dickens to translate the 13th-century essay collection *Hōjōki* into English. After 1910, as Japanese FOLKLORE STUDIES burgeoned through the efforts of the pioneering scholar YANAGITA KUNIO, Minakata had considerable influence. He contributed hundreds of articles to folklore journals and other magazines and propounded theories based on his extensive knowledge of world folklore. One of his best-known works is *Jūnishi kō* (serialized 1914–24, On the Twelve Horary Signs).

——Minakata Kumakusu, *Minakata Kumakusu zenshū*, 12 vols (Heibonsha, 1971–75). Kasai Kiyoshi, *Minakata Kumakusu* (1967).

HINOTANI Akihiko

Minakuchi

Town in southern Shiga Prefecture, central Honshū, on the river Yasugawa. In the Edo period (1600–1868) Minakuchi was a castle town and one of the POST-STATION TOWNS on the highway Tōkaidō. Electrical appliances and farm machinery are produced. Tea is cultivated on the riverbanks. Pop: 27,471.

Minamata

City in southern Kumamoto Prefecture, Kyūshū, on the Yatsushiro Sea. Minamata is primarily known as the site of Minamata disease, a disease of the central nervous system that was caused by industrial discharges from a local carbide plant owned by Nippon Chisso Hiryō (now Chisso Corporation; see POLLUTION-RELATED DISEASES). Yunoko and Yunotsuru hot springs are located nearby. Pop: 37,150.

Minamata disease → pollution-related diseases

Minami Ashigara

City in western Kanagawa Prefecture, central Honshū, on the river Sakawagawa. A temple town (MONZEN MACHI) of Saijōji, an important temple of the Sōtō Buddhist sect, it has become industrialized since the establishment of a plant by Fuji Photo Film Co, Ltd, in 1934. Pop: 39,919.

Minami Chita

Town in Aichi Prefecture, central Honshū. Situated on the Chita Peninsula, it is a base for ocean and coastal fishing. Farming is also active, utilizing water from the AICHI CANAL. Seaweed *(nori)* is cultivated in the coastal waters. A recreational area for Nagoya residents, Minami Chita is known for its good fishing, swimming, and mandarin orange groves, which are open to the public. Pop: 27,018.

Minami Daitōjima

Island approximately 350 km (217 mi) east of Okinawa. One of the Daitō Islands. It is a coral island with steep cliffs. The central lowlands are about 50 m (164 ft) lower than the surrounding land and form numerous sinks and hollows. The chief activity is the cultivation of sugarcane. Area: 26.6 sq km (10.3 sq mi).

Minami Jirō (1874–1955)

Army general. Born in Ōita Prefecture, he graduated from the Army War College in 1903. He served in a variety of army posts before becoming vice-chief of the General Staff in 1927 and earning the rank of general in 1930. In 1931 he was appointed army minister in the second WAKATSUKI REIJIRŌ cabinet and, following the MANCHURIAN INCIDENT that year, after some initial doubts supported the total military conquest of Manchuria. In 1934 Minami was named commander-in-chief of the GUANDONG (KWANTUNG) ARMY, the Japanese field army in Manchuria, and ambassador to the Japanese puppet state of MANCHUKUO. Implicated in the young officers' revolt of 1936 (see FEBRUARY 26TH INCIDENT), he was forced to resign his posts and was placed on the reserve list. He served for six years as governor-general of Korea (then under Japanese rule) before being appointed to the Privy Council in 1942. At the WAR CRIMES TRIALS after World War II, Minami was sentenced to life imprisonment as a class A war criminal.

Minami Kikan

Japanese military intelligence bureau concerned with Burma (1941–42); its official name was Nampō Kigyō Chōsakai (Committee for Research on Enterprises in the Southern Region). Under the command of Army Colonel Suzuki Keiji (b 1897; known in Burmese as Bo Mogyo), it gave military training to 30 Burmese nationalist youths, including AUNG SAN, and eventually helped to organize the Burma Independence Army. See also BURMA AND JAPAN.

ŌNO Tōru

Minami Torishima

Also known as Marcus Island or Week Island. A coral island approximately 1,200 km (745 mi) southeast of the island of Chichijima. One of the Ogasawara (Bonin) Islands located south of Tōkyō. At latitude 24° 17′ north and longitude 153° 58′ east, the easternmost point in Japan. It is the site of an observatory of the Meteorological Agency. Area: 2 sq km (0.8 sq mi); circumference: 5 km (3 mi).

Minamoto family

One of the four great families, including also the TAIRA FAMILY, FUJIWARA FAMILY, and TACHIBANA FAMILY, that dominated court politics during the Heian period (794–1185); its descendants remained central to Japanese government until the Meiji Restoration of 1868.

Origins——Like the Taira, the Minamoto family was an offshoot of the imperial family, created by a practice known to anthropologists as dynastic "shedding." In the Asuka (latter part of the 6th century to 710) and Nara (710–794) periods the proliferation of im-

Minamoto family —— Genealogy

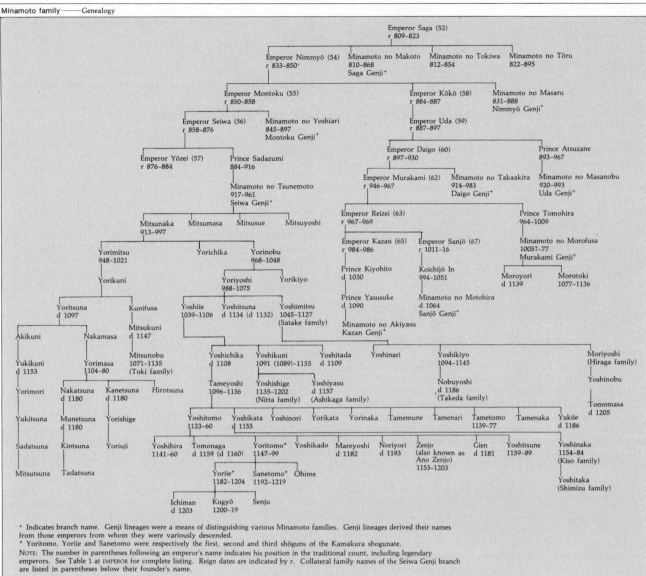

+ Indicates branch name. Genji lineages were a means of distinguishing various Minamoto families. Genji lineages derived their names from those emperors from whom they were variously descended.
* Yoritomo, Yoriie and Sanetomo were respectively the first, second and third shōguns of the Kamakura shogunate.
NOTE: The number in parentheses following an emperor's name indicates his position in the traditional count, including legendary emperors. See Table 1 at EMPEROR for complete listing. Reign dates are indicated by r. Collateral family names of the Seiwa Genji branch are listed in parentheses below their founder's name.

perial kinsmen led to succession disputes and was a great drain on the treasury. It became customary, therefore, to exclude from the dynastic lineage kinsmen five or more generations removed from the ruler and to give them surnames like ordinary nobles (the imperial house had no surname). In Heian times dynastic shedding was continued, with the additional purpose of creating strong noble lineages to offset the rising power of the Fujiwara family. Now, however, sons and daughters of emperors were also shed from the dynasty. In 814 Emperor SAGA (r 809–823) created the surname Minamoto for 33 of his 50 children, the most notable of them being the courtier-officials Minamoto no Makoto (810–868) and Minamoto no Tokiwa (812–854). Thereafter, all members cut off from the imperial line were surnamed either Minamoto or Taira. Relying on this group, a sort of "imperial faction," Saga was able to check the influence of the Fujiwara and other great noble families and keep political power in his own hands.

Structure —— The Minamoto family was commonly referred to as the Genji, using alternate pronunciations of the Chinese characters for Minamoto (gen) and uji, or family (ji), and the different Genji lineages were known by the names of the emperors from whom the recipients of the surname were variously descended: in addition to

the original "Saga Genji" there were Minamoto lineages tracing their origin to 10 of Saga's successors, most notably Seiwa (r 858–876), UDA (r 887–897), and Murakami (r 946–967).

Because its constituent lineages were all ultimately related, the Minamoto family is often called a clan; but despite its unity under the patriarchy of Saga, as new lines were created it retained little cohesion and no effective overall leadership. Although the head of the Murakami Genji claimed some sort of chieftainship from the 11th century onward, the individual lineages functioned as separate families.

As their numbers increased and their distance from imperial ancestors widened, the Minamoto gradually lost their quasi-imperial status and enjoyed no more power and privilege than other nonroyal nobles. Those of recent creation, however, retained ties with the imperial house; one prince who had been shed from the dynasty, had received the name Minamoto no Sadami, and had served in several government posts was reaccepted into the ruling line and enthroned as Emperor Uda in 887.

The Murakami Genji —— Most Minamoto lineages remained in the capital as civil officials, some of their members rising to high positions while others occupied middle-ranking bureaucratic posts.

Of these, the Murakami Genji became the most prominent. The founder of the lineage was Minamoto no Morofusa (1005?–77), a son of Prince Tomohira (964–1009) and grandson of Emperor Murakami, who gave him the Minamoto surname in 1020. Morofusa became minister of the right *(udaijin),* and his two sons became ministers of the left *(sadaijin)* and of the right. Between 1087 and 1093, the period when political power passed from the Fujiwara regents (see REGENCY GOVERNMENT) to the retired emperors (see INSEI), members of this lineage came to control many of the highest official posts, briefly eclipsing the dominance of the Fujiwara. In fact, under the emperors GO-SANJŌ (r 1068–73) and SHIRAKAWA (r 1073–87; d 1129), the Murakami Genji cooperated with the sovereigns and the ruling house to such a degree that scholars have recognized a revival of an "imperial faction" reminiscent of Saga's time. The Murakami Genji were, moreover, skillfully allied by marriage with the Fujiwara regents' house, so that Minamoto influence in Heian court politics was significant.

The Seiwa Genji —— Although the Murakami Genji established the Minamoto at court, it was the branch descended from Emperor Seiwa that was to gain greater fame in Japanese history. The first Seiwa Genji was Minamoto no Tsunemoto (917–961), a son of Prince Sadazumi (884–916) who was granted the surname by his grandfather Seiwa in 961. Tsunemoto first assumed a provincial post in Musashi (which includes what is now Saitama and Tōkyō prefectures and part of Kanagawa Prefecture) and later held jobs in other provinces, participating in military campaigns against the regional rebel chieftains TAIRA NO MASAKADO and FUJIWARA NO SUMITOMO in 940.

Tsunemoto's military prowess, however, was not highly regarded. The reputation of the Seiwa Genji as warrior chieftains really began with his son Mitsunaka (913–997), who served in many provinces and allied himself with the Fujiwara at the court. His son MINAMOTO NO YORIMITSU became a protégé of the powerful regent FUJIWARA NO MICHINAGA; another son, Yorinobu (968–1048), suppressed the rebellion of TAIRA NO TADATSUNE in 1031. It was under the leadership of the these two men that the Seiwa Genji came to be known as the "claws and teeth" of the Fujiwara.

During the 11th century the Seiwa Genji further developed their tradition of warrior leadership and built a provincial power base that extended throughout eastern Japan. Yorinobu's son Yoriyoshi (988–1075) pacified the northeast in the EARLIER NINE YEARS' WAR of 1051–62, and his son MINAMOTO NO YOSHIIE completed the job in the LATER THREE YEARS' WAR of 1083–87. The latter victory established Yoshiie as the most renowned warrior in the land, and because of this reputation he was both courted and feared by the civil aristocracy.

After Yoshiie's time, however, the fortunes of the Seiwa Genji waned. His son Yoshichika (d 1108) was killed in a rebellion in Izumo Province (now part of Shimane Prefecture). His grandson Tameyoshi (1096–1156) was executed after the HŌGEN DISTURBANCE of 1156. His great-grandson MINAMOTO NO YOSHITOMO was killed for his part in the HEIJI DISTURBANCE of 1160, and another great-grandson, MINAMOTO NO TAMETOMO, rebelled and committed suicide in 1177. Thereafter, the influence of the Genji in the capital reached a low ebb, only the elderly MINAMOTO NO YORIMASA (a distant cousin of the main line) representing the family as TAIRA NO KIYOMORI and his kinsmen seized absolute power.

After the Heiji Disturbance, however, Kiyomori had unwisely spared the youngest sons of Yoshitomo—MINAMOTO NO YORITOMO, MINAMOTO NO YOSHITSUNE, and Minamoto no Noriyori (d 1193). In 1180 Yoritomo mounted a full-scale rebellion against Taira rule (see TAIRA–MINAMOTO WAR); within five years he had destroyed the Taira, subjugated all of eastern Japan, and established a military government (the KAMAKURA SHOGUNATE; 1192–1333) that inaugurated nearly 700 years of warrior rule in Japan.

Yoritomo was succeeded as shōgun by his sons MINAMOTO NO YORIIE and MINAMOTO NO SANETOMO. With the death of the latter in 1219, the main line of the Seiwa Genji came to an end. Other lines, including the HOSOKAWA FAMILY, NITTA FAMILY, OGASAWARA FAMILY, TAKEDA FAMILY, and YAMANA FAMILY (named in the 12th and the 13th centuries for the districts or estates where they lived), survived and made up a large proportion of the great warrior families of medieval Japan. One of these collateral lines, the ASHIKAGA FAMILY, later founded the second national military government, the MUROMACHI SHOGUNATE (1338–1573); and TOKUGAWA IEYASU, founder of the TOKUGAWA SHOGUNATE (1603–1867), could also trace his descent from the Seiwa Genji. Thus, this lineage and its offshoots played an important role in Japan's political history during some 900 years.

📖 —— G. Cameron Hurst, *Insei: Abdicated Sovereigns in the Politics of Late Heian Japan* (1976). Jeffrey P. Mass, *Warrior Government in Early Medieval Japan* (1974). Minoru Shinoda, *The Founding of the Kamakura Shogunate* (1960).

G. Cameron HURST III

Minamoto no Raikō → Minamoto no Yorimitsu

Minamoto no Sanetomo (1192–1219)

Third shōgun of the Kamakura shogunate, classical (WAKA) poet; second son of the first shōgun MINAMOTO NO YORITOMO and his wife HŌJŌ MASAKO.

Sanetomo was born at Kamakura, the shogunal capital, in the same year in which his father was officially appointed shōgun by a reluctant Kyōto court. In 1199, Yoritomo died at the age of 52, and was succeeded as shōgun in 1202 by his eldest son MINAMOTO NO YORIIE (1182–1204), a sickly young man who was a puppet in the hands of his ruthless mother Masako and her father, HŌJŌ TOKIMASA. In 1203, however, Yoriie broke with Masako, and in league with his own allies plotted the overthrow of his mother's family. The plan leaked out, and Yoriie's chief supporter was murdered, while Yoriie himself was confined at Shuzenji on the Izu Peninsula southwest of Kamakura. In the same year, the Hōjō family falsely announced his death to the Kyōto court and succeeded in having Sanetomo designated shōgun, although it was actually not until 1204 that Yoriie was assassinated at the behest of his grandfather Tokimasa.

In this milieu of murder, intrigue, and struggles for power, Sanetomo became shōgun at the age of 11. Already attracted to the elegant life of the Kyōto nobility, which he continued to gaze upon from afar (he was never permitted to visit the imperial capital), he was married in 1204 to the daughter of a courtier of rank, the former major counselor Fujiwara no Nobukiyo. Thenceforth, by dint of insistent pressure upon the reluctant imperial government, especially the court of the retired emperor GO-TOBA, he was awarded various nominal court ranks and offices, finally attaining the post of minister of the right *(udaijin)* in 1218. Meanwhile, his very life was in danger at Kamakura, as the regent *(shikken)* Tokimasa plotted in 1205 to depose Sanetomo and replace him with his own son-in-law. The plot was foiled by Masako and her brother HŌJŌ YOSHITOKI, who placed their father under house arrest in Izu. However, Yoshitoki proved to be even more dangerous than his father, and in the background loomed the unscrupulous Masako, whose final approval was required for all important measures. Although Sanetomo resented their despotism, he was quite powerless. Miserable, frustrated, and frightened, he pressed the Kyōto court for honors and promotions at least in part to awe his mother and her family, and in part, it is said, because he felt such honors were the only way to add luster to the Minamoto line, which he knew would end with him. Ironically, it was on a ceremonial visit to the Tsurugaoka Hachiman Shrine at Kamakura to give thanks for his promotion to minister of the right that Sanetomo was assassinated by his nephew, the priest Kugyō, who blamed him and Yoshitoki for the murder of his father, Yoriie.

Character and Cultural Interests —— The portrait of Sanetomo that emerges from contemporary accounts is not entirely consistent. In one source he is described as weak, effeminate, and totally uninterested in swordsmanship, hunting, and other military pursuits that his father Yoritomo tried to encourage. In another account he is said to have been both sensitive and manly, gentle, attractive, and commanding even greater devotion from his vassals than Yoritomo himself. It is at least certain that as he sought even higher status at the Kyōto court he became increasingly fascinated by the traditional culture of the Heian nobility. His interests extended from the literary arts to the aristocratic game of KEMARI, or kickball, but it is for his poetry that he is famous today.

Poetry —— Sanetomo is said to have begun to write classical verse when he was 14 years old. In 1208, at the age of 16, he obtained a copy of the latest imperial anthology, the great SHIN KOKINSHŪ (ca 1205, New Collection from Ancient and Modern Times), and in 1209 he sent a selection of 30 of his poems for criticism to the foremost court poet, Fujiwara no Teika (FUJIWARA NO SADAIE; 1162–1241). Teika no doubt replied with a courteous praise of Sanetomo's verses, but at the same time it is clear that he disapproved of the very poems for which Sanetomo is admired today—his youthful, exuberant, and archaistic imitations of the 7th- and 8th-century poetry of the MAN'YŌSHŪ. It is thus evident that Sanetomo had become enamored of the *Man'yōshū* well before Teika himself sent him a copy in 1213, but just how is not quite so clear. At all events, although the *Man'-yōshū* was studied, revered, and to a limited extent alluded to by court poets, the critics and arbiters strictly forbade imitating its poetry or borrowing such of its diction and imagery as were considered crude, ugly, and inelegant. Oblivious of these caveats, and with all the enthusiasm of youth, Sanetomo composed poems in the Man'yō style. Though derivative, often sentimental, and sometimes more than faintly ludicrous, his Man'yō verses nonetheless have an undeniable novelty, freshness, and immediacy in the context of an overrefined and conventional court tradition. Favoring direct declaration and the noble forthrightness of the so-called "lofty style," Sanetomo combined this mode with primitivistic imagery of almost savage power in his best-known poems. Owing to the Man'yō revival among the "national scholars" of the 17th century and later, and particularly the enthusiasm of the influential Meiji poet MASAOKA SHIKI, both Sanetomo and his poetry have enjoyed a revival in modern times.

Under Teika's tutelage, he also learned to write poems of unexceptionable correctness, rehearsing the time-honored clichés and poses of traditional verse. That little originality shines through these more conventional poems suggests Sanetomo's essentially limited talent and potential. Of course, he was accorded the deference and attention due to his exalted rank and position, and it is for this reason, no doubt, that Teika included 25 of his more conventional poems in the ninth imperial anthology, the *Shin chokusenshū* (ca 1234, New Imperial Collection), and that an additional 66 are found in later imperial collections.

The *Kinkai wakashū*, Sanetomo's personal collection, commonly called the *Kinkaishū*, "The Collection of the Kamakura Minister of the Right," exists in three main versions. The most authoritative is a copy made by Teika in his own hand and bearing the date 1213, which contains 663 poems. These can be supplemented from other texts and sources to constitute a total corpus of 716 poems. To what extent these additional 53 poems postdate the Teika text is not certain, but it may be surmised that Sanetomo's output diminished greatly during the last years of his life.

■——Robert H. Brower and Earl Miner, *Japanese Court Poetry* (1961). Robert H. BROWER

Minamoto no Shitagau (911–983)

Often spelled Shitagō. One of the major literary figures of the mid-10th century and the most noteworthy of the so-called Five Men of the Pear Chamber (Nashitsubo no Gonin), who were chosen by Emperor Murakami in 951 to compile the second imperial anthology of Japanese poetry, the GOSEN WAKASHŪ, and also to study the MAN'-YŌSHŪ, a scholarly endeavor in which Shitagau was particularly outstanding. He was not only one of the best Japanese poets of his time but also a renowned poet and scholar in Chinese, and was a frequent participant at formal literary functions, both in Japanese and Chinese. His career as a literatus was one of great brilliance. His official career, however, was one of relative obscurity and failure: he graduated as a scholar of the court university (DAIGAKURYŌ), but held only minor posts, the highest of which was a provincial governorship, and was for many years without any official post at all. On the personal side, he lost his two daughters in 962, and this, added to his failure in public life, produced in him a strong strain of pessimism, discernible in much of his personal poetry. But by and large his compositions lack genuine lyrical feeling and are characterized rather by technical skill, wit, and a somewhat scholarly Chinese flavor. His works include the *Minamoto no Shitagau shū*, his personal poetry collection, and the WAMYŌ RUIJU SHŌ (Classified List of Japanese Readings), an early Japanese dictionary of Chinese characters. Several prose romances have also been attributed to him, but there is no conclusive evidence that he was in fact their author. As one of the outstanding poets of his time, he is included among the SANJŪROKKASEN (Thirty-Six Poetic Sages), and 51 of his poems are included in imperial anthologies from the *Gosen wakashū* onwards.

Phillip T. HARRIES

Minamoto no Tametomo (1139–1177)

Military leader of the latter part of the Heian period (794–1185); eighth son of Minamoto no Tameyoshi (1096–1156) and younger brother of MINAMOTO NO YOSHITOMO. A warrior of imposing physique and fierce character, he was especially skilled in archery. At age 13 Tametomo was sent to Kyūshū, where he became a powerful warlord and defied the court; in consequence his father lost his court post and his headship of the Minamoto family. Both father and son

supported the retired emperor Sutoku in the HŌGEN DISTURBANCE of 1156; Tameyoshi was put to death, but Tametomo was banished to the island of Ōshima in Izu Province (now part of Shizuoka Prefecture). There he attempted to seize local power but in 1177 was attacked by court forces and committed suicide. There is a legend that he escaped to the Ryūkyū Islands, where he founded a kingly line. G. Cameron HURST III

Minamoto no Tameyoshi → Hōgen Disturbance

Minamoto no Toshiyori (1055?–1129)

Also known as Minamoto no Shunrai. Classical (WAKA) poet, compiler of the fifth imperial anthology, KIN'YŌ WAKASHŪ (ca 1127, Collection of Golden Leaves). Son of the distinguished courtier and poet MINAMOTO NO TSUNENOBU, Toshiyori never gained high office, rising no higher than the post of director of the Bureau of Carpentry and Repairs for the imperial household *(moku no kami)*. This office he resigned about 1111, at which time he held the relatively low junior fourth court rank. According to one source, in his youth he was taken as an adopted son by Tachibana no Toshitsuna (1028–94), but when his own father Tsunenobu was sent away to be governor-general of the military headquarters at Dazaifu in Kyūshū, Toshiyori accompanied him and remained at Dazaifu until his father's death in 1097. For some time thereafter he appears to have lived an unhappy life in rather straitened circumstances. He is thought to have gone to Ise in 1122 in the retinue of the high priestess of the Ise Shrine, and to have returned to the capital the following year. In 1124, perhaps to atone for having passed over Toshiyori's father as compiler of the fourth imperial anthology, *Go shūishū* (1086, Later Collection of Gleanings), the retired emperor SHIRAKAWA honored Toshiyori with the command to compile the fifth anthology of native poetry. Toshiyori, who was a radically innovating and rather eccentric poet, was hard put to please his royal patron; Shirakawa rejected the first draft because it contained too many poems by older poets and the second because it contained too few, at last accepting the third draft. The first two drafts were copied and circulated, however, and it was the second draft that was most widely known until modern times. Toshiyori was criticized for his choice of title, *Kin'yōshū* (Collection of Golden Leaves), because of its inauspicious associations. (It was written in Buddhist scripture that a rain of golden leaves fell on the day of the Buddha's death.) Worse yet, the *Kin'yōshū* consisted of only 10 books instead of the 20 made standard by the first imperial anthology, the KOKINSHŪ. The final version of the anthology accepted by Shirakawa contained fewer than 650 poems. Toshiyori's contemporary, Fujiwara no Akinaka (1059–1129), compiled a work (no longer extant) entitled *Ryōgyokushū* (Collection of Genuine Jewels), in which he is said to have cast scorn upon Toshiyori's judgment.

Toshiyori was even more controversial as a poet than as an editor. A daring innovator and experimentalist, he stands out as a colorful figure in an otherwise rather unremarkable age. He was opposed by the arch-conservative of the day, FUJIWARA NO MOTOTOSHI, and the two clashed more than once as rival judges at important poetry contests. Toshiyori had three quite different and distinctive styles, although the first two were often combined. The first—and perhaps the style preferred by Toshiyori himself if not by posterity—was a convoluted, rhetorically complex manner, in which he seems to push the traditional "Fujiwara style" of witty ingenuity and farfetched conceits to the utmost limit. The second style, even more strikingly unconventional than the first, and often combined with it, is characterized by unusual diction rather than contorted rhetoric. Toshiyori was unique in the age for his bold experiments with vulgar and colloquial diction borrowed from the spoken language of the day, as well as for his use of archaic words and homely images borrowed from the first anthology of native poetry, the 8th-century MAN'YŌSHŪ. The conservative poets of the time admired the *Man'yōshū* as much as Toshiyori and perhaps studied it more diligently, but did not condone borrowing from it the inelegant, "low" language that had been banished from Japanese poetry since the age of KI NO TSURAYUKI and the *Kokinshū*. Toshiyori was probably given the courage to make such bold experiments by the example of the outstanding iconoclastic poet of the 10th century, SONE NO YOSHITADA (fl ca 985), whom he greatly admired, and ultimately by the example of Chinese poetry, particularly the poems in colloquial language of Bo Juyi (Po Chü-i; 772–846). Indeed, it was perhaps the Chinese example most of all that appeared to Toshiyori to offer canonical authority and a guarantee of the respectability of the innovating colloquial poetry that he flaunted in the faces of his shocked contemporaries. And although rejected by his age, as he surely knew they would be, many of his vulgar images and colloquialisms were accepted by the poets of several generations later, particularly the innovating Kyōgoku–Reizei poets of the late 13th and 14th centuries.

Toshiyori's third style, the style in which later poets generally considered his most memorable poems to have been written, is a quiet, reflective mode of natural description, a style that he may be said to have inherited from Tsunenobu and passed on to the following generations of FUJIWARA NO TOSHINARI (Shunzei) and FUJIWARA NO SADAIE (Teika). This style, too, did not have general acceptance in its day, although even conservative poets were beginning to acknowledge some merit in the mode of natural description and to suffer it under certain circumstances.

More than 200 of Toshiyori's poems are included in various imperial anthologies from the *Kin'yō wakashū* on. To his personal collection, which he compiled himself about 1128 after completing the *Kin'yō wakashū*, he gave the title *Samboku kikashū* (Collection of Eccentric Poems as Useless as Dead Wood). It contains more than 1,600 poems, including a great many in his unconventional style. It is indicative of Toshiyori's altered reputation in later ages that the conservative poet KENSHŌ (fl 1161–1207) considered *Samboku kikashū* important enough to write a commentary on 99 of its most difficult poems. Toshiyori was also the author of a poetic treatise known by various names, of which *Toshiyori zuinō* (Toshiyori's Essentials) is the most common. It is said to have been written around 1115 for the daughter of the regent Fujiwara no Tadazane, and consists chiefly of traditional poetic rules and lore: definitions of the various forms of poetry, the poetic "sicknesses" *(yamai),* superior poems, various styles, metaphor, proper and improper poetic diction, allusion and allusive variation, poetic place names, explications of difficult poems, anecdotes, and poetic traditions and practices. Though showing little sign of Toshiyori's eccentricity, the treatise was widely circulated and quoted and is the precursor of numerous similar works of the 12th century and later.

📖——Robert H. Brower and Earl Miner, *Japanese Court Poetry* (1961).
Robert H. BROWER

Minamoto no Tsunenobu (1016–1097)

Classical (WAKA) poet, musician, and courtier; poetic innovator credited with gaining social acceptance for vernacular descriptive poetry on nature. Like his older contemporary, FUJIWARA NO KINTŌ, Tsunenobu was unusually accomplished in poetry, music, and calligraphy—arts prized by the aristocratic court society of his day—and he is the subject of admiring anecdotes preserved in medieval tale collections. His political career was also very successful. He was admired for his firm judgment and open personality and, as a member of the warrior Minamoto family, provided a measure of relief from the complete dominance of the Fujiwara. Indeed, it is thought that Tsunenobu, who rose to the position of grand councillor *(dainagon)* and the second court rank, was favored by the determined and capable Emperor GO-SANJŌ (1034–73) and by his son, Emperor SHIRAKAWA (1053–1129), in part because their aim was to curb or, if possible, to break the power of the Fujiwara family by governing their own courts as ex-emperors. Such a policy did not prevent Tsunenobu from suffering the disappointment of being passed over as compiler of an imperial anthology of poetry, however, nor from being dispatched at the age of 79 as acting viceroy of the military headquarters at Dazaifu in Kyūshū—an assignment regarded as political exile by the Heian court. At any rate, he traveled to that provincial outpost and remained there until his death two years later.

As a musician, Tsunenobu was a master of the lute (BIWA) and was regarded as the founder of the Katsura school of lute playing. In poetry he was an acknowledged authority and was prominent as both participant and judge in a number of poetry contests during the 1080s and 90s. Adept in both traditional and new styles, he was regarded as an innovator for his experiments with a new mode of descriptive poetry, a mode of simple declaration and forthrightness which was characterized as lofty *(take takashi)* or grand *(tōjiroshi).* His high social and political standing gave a quasi-official sanction to his experiments, which were opposed by the conservatives, who adhered jealously to the traditional Fujiwara style of subjective wit and courtly elegance. The artistic opposition tended to take on political overtones, and a split between reactionaries and innovators developed in the competition between Tsunenobu and the younger but

poetically conservative FUJIWARA NO MICHITOSHI (1047–99) as poetic arbiters of the day and for the honor of compiling the fourth imperial anthology, the *Go shūishū* (1086, Later Collection of Gleanings). Although Tsunenobu's seniority and experience made him the logical candidate for honor, this time he was passed over by Emperor Shirakawa, who appointed Michitoshi, a personal favorite. Tsunenobu expressed his indignation in the first known critique of its kind, *Nan goshūi* (Errors in the *Go shūishū*), in which he attempted to discredit Michitoshi's judgment by showing that 84 of the poems chosen for the anthology were not qualified for inclusion.

Although Chinese descriptive poetry of the 9th and early 10th centuries was no doubt the ultimate inspiration for Tsunenobu's descriptive poetry in Japan, he legitimized, so to speak, a mode that had virtually disappeared from Japanese poetry since the MAN'YŌSHŪ (8th century). From his time on, more and more descriptive poetry begins to appear in the successive imperial anthologies, finding its most beautiful and complex expression in the descriptive symbolism of the late 12th and early 13th centuries.

📖——Robert H. Brower and Earl Miner, *Japanese Court Poetry* (1961).
Robert H. BROWER

Minamoto no Yoriie (1182–1204)

Eldest son of MINAMOTO NO YORITOMO and HŌJŌ MASAKO; second shōgun of the Kamakura shogunate. Yoriie became head of the Minamoto house at his father's death in 1199 and shōgun in 1202, but because of his unsteady character, his maternal relatives, the HŌJŌ FAMILY, established a council of senior officials at the head of the shogunal government, leaving Yoriie essentially powerless. When he became gravely ill in 1203, the council divided authority over shogunal land rights between his infant son Ichiman and his younger brother MINAMOTO NO SANETOMO. Angered, Yoriie joined with his father-in-law, HIKI YOSHIKAZU, in a plot against the Hōjō. The plot failed, and Yoshikazu was killed. Yoriie was forced to abdicate and was banished to a temple in Izu Province (now part of Shizuoka Prefecture), where he too was killed in the following year, allegedly at the order of HŌJŌ TOKIMASA.

G. Cameron HURST III

Minamoto no Yorimasa (1104–1180)

Also known as Genzammi Yorimasa. Military aristocrat and poet of the Heian period (794–1185). His poems are preserved in the private collection *Yorimasa kashū* and in the general anthologies SHIN KOKINSHŪ and SENZAI WAKASHŪ, but he is better known for his political and military role in three critical events of the 12th century. In the HŌGEN DISTURBANCE of 1156, Yorimasa allied himself with MINAMOTO NO YOSHITOMO and TAIRA NO KIYOMORI, and took the side of Emperor GO-SHIRAKAWA against the retired emperor SUTOKU's unsuccessful attempt to assert his authority. In a similar situation in the HEIJI DISTURBANCE of 1160, he initially backed the party of Go-Shirakawa (by then the retired emperor), which included Yoshitomo, against the supporters of Emperor Nijō (1143–65; r 1158–65); when the latter faction, led by Kiyomori, appeared to be gaining the upper hand, Yorimasa changed sides, contributing to Yoshitomo's defeat and Kiyomori's rise to preeminence in Kyōto. As the sole remaining Minamoto of stature in a capital dominated by the Taira, he was promoted rapidly; but he was jealous of Kiyomori. In 1180 Yorimasa associated himself with Go-Shirakawa's son Prince Mochihito (1151–80), who issued an edict calling for the overthrow of the Taira regime. When Kiyomori ordered their arrest, Yorimasa and Mochihito sought the support of the warlike priests of the Onjōji, a monastery of the Buddhist Tendai sect located to the east of Kyōto across the Higashiyama range of hills (now the city of Ōtsu). When Taira forces attacked that monastery, the two plotters attempted to flee to Nara but were overtaken in Uji and killed in the ensuing skirmish. Their actions, however, marked the beginning of the TAIRA–MINAMOTO WAR (1180–85), in which the Taira hegemony was indeed destroyed by the rival military house of Minamoto, led by Yoshitomo's son, the future shōgun MINAMOTO NO YORITOMO.

George ELISON

Minamoto no Yorimitsu (948–1021)

Military leader of the Heian period (794–1185), popularly known as Minamoto no Raikō; eldest son of Minamoto no Mitsunaka (913–997). He served as governor in several provinces of central Japan, as well as commander of guards in the capital, and formed a

Minamoto no Yoritomo

Detail of a portrait attributed to Fujiwara no Takanobu. Hanging scroll. Colors on silk. Late 12th century. Jingoji, Kyōto. National Treasure.

close alliance with the powerful regent FUJIWARA NO MICHINAGA. Under the leadership of Yorimitsu and his younger brother Yorinobu (968–1048), the Seiwa Genji branch of the MINAMOTO FAMILY became known as the "claws and teeth" of the Fujiwara and were generously rewarded for their services. Yorimitsu in 1018 contributed the furnishings for Michinaga's new Tsuchimikado mansion, astounding everyone with his opulence. Yorimitsu's prowess as a warrior and archer is celebrated in the KONJAKU MONOGATARI. He is the hero of a popular legend in which he kills the ogre Shuten Dōji. ———————————————————— *G. Cameron HURST III*

Minamoto no Yoritomo (1147–1199)

Founder of the KAMAKURA SHOGUNATE (1192–1333), the first warrior government in Japan. Yoritomo was the third son of MINAMOTO NO YOSHITOMO, the leader of the Seiwa Genji, the branch of the Minamoto family descended from the emperor Seiwa (850–880). Although largely responsible for the imperial victory in the HŌGEN DISTURBANCE of 1156, Yoshitomo was not rewarded as generously as TAIRA NO KIYOMORI. In January 1160 (Heiji 1.12) he took advantage of Kiyomori's absence from the capital and joined other disgruntled courtiers in a coup known as the HEIJI DISTURBANCE. The young Yoritomo participated alongside his father. Kiyomori returned to Kyōto and routed the rebels, who became separated in their flight eastward. Yoshitomo was killed, and Yoritomo wandered aimlessly in the snowy mountains of Mino Province (now part of Gifu Prefecture), where he was finally captured and returned to Taira headquarters. Kiyomori spared his life because of the intercession of the Taira lady IKE NO ZENNI. Yoritomo, then only 13, was exiled to eastern Japan.

In the province of Izu (now part of Shizuoka Prefecture), Yoritomo was placed under the watchful eyes of two Taira adherents, first ITŌ 'SUKECHIKA and later HŌJŌ TOKIMASA. Yoritomo became romantically attached to daughters of both his captors and eventually married HŌJŌ MASAKO, the strong-willed daughter of Tokimasa. Enjoying considerable freedom under Tokimasa's protection, Yoritomo had frequent news from the capital and time for hunting and other military-related activities; he also came into contact with local warrior leaders. Tokimasa became fond of Yoritomo, and when war broke out between Taira and Minamoto forces, he supported Yoritomo from the outset.

The Taira-Minamoto War ——— By the late 1170s Kiyomori's dominance of the court was so complete that even his erstwhile patron, the retired emperor GO-SHIRAKAWA, began to plot against him. In 1180 Prince Mochihito (1151–80), a disgruntled son of Go-

Shirakawa who had been passed over for succession, and MINAMOTO NO YORIMASA, the sole Seiwa Genji remaining at court, raised a revolt against Taira rule. Mochihito issued an edict calling for all Minamoto, loyal warrior bands, and temples to rise up and strike down the Taira. The two attempted to raise a force of warrior monks at the Onjōji monastery but were repulsed and fled south toward Nara. Their revolt ended in a battle at Uji, just south of the capital, where Mochihito was killed and Yorimasa took his own life.

The prince's edict reached Yoritomo in May of 1180 (Jishō 4.4), and he spent the next three months carefully calculating his response. By September (Jishō 4.8) he had raised enough support to risk an attack against the Taira. Yoritomo declared his intentions by attacking the local Taira deputy-governor *(mokudai)*. Although he used the prince's edict to justify his actions, Yoritomo was actually in rebellion.

Yoritomo gathered about him a larger force and moved into Sagami Province (now Kanagawa Prefecture) to confront the Taira army. In his first major encounter, the Battle of Ishibashiyama, Yoritomo was soundly defeated; he barely escaped with his life to the Hakone Mountains, finally making his way by boat to the peninsular province of Awa (now part of Chiba Prefecture) in mid-September (Jishō 4.8).

Soon, however, Yoritomo received pledges of support from local leaders, including former enemies, so that when he decided to establish his headquarters at Kamakura his troops were said to number some 27,000. He left Kamakura to meet a large Taira army, and by early November (Jishō 4.10) he was in command of an army of 200,000 encamped on the east bank of the river Fujikawa (or Fujigawa) in Suruga (now part of Shizuoka Prefecture). Even if these figures are exaggerated, since he had but 300 men initially, it was an impressive feat to muster so many supporters in so short a time.

Yoritomo won the Battle of FUJIGAWA through luck. Late at night, a startled flock of geese rose screeching in flight; and the Taira forces, believing that a surprise attack was under way, panicked and fled. Presented with the opportunity to pursue the Taira and avenge his father's defeat, Yoritomo instead heeded the advice of his generals first to consolidate his power in the east.

Yoritomo accordingly returned to Kamakura, where he spent most of the period from late 1180 to 1183 building a solid base of political and economic support. He conquered recalcitrant Minamoto bands like the SATAKE FAMILY of Hitachi (now Ibaraki Prefecture) and knit together a powerful vassalage structure of related and nonrelated warriors. Yoritomo created the SAMURAI-DOKORO (Board of Retainers) in late 1180 to regularize the procedures, duties, and responsibilities involving him and his expanding group of vassals. During this period there was little fighting between the Taira and the Minamoto, but it was a critical time for Yoritomo in establishing his own authority as a feudal lord.

The final destruction of the Taira was precipitated by a kinsman, MINAMOTO NO YOSHINAKA, who had early declared for Yoritomo but refused to commit forces. As he gathered more troops, both Yoritomo and the Taira eyed Yoshinaka suspiciously, and the Taira finally sent an army against him. Yoshinaka successfully countered, splitting their forces and driving them back toward and then out of Kyōto. By late 1183 the Taira, including the young emperor ANTOKU, had fled westward, leaving Yoshinaka in command of Kyōto.

Yoshinaka and his men created havoc and confusion, however, and did not pursue the Taira. In January 1184 (Juei 2.12), Yoritomo sent his brothers Noriyori (d 1193) and MINAMOTO NO YOSHITSUNE against him. Quickly defeating Yoshinaka, the two generals remained in the capital only eight days before proceeding against the Taira. They reduced the stronghold at Ichinotani in neighboring Settsu Province (now part of Ōsaka and Hyōgo prefectures) by March 1184 (Juei 3.2).

To pursue the Taira to their stronghold in the west, Yoritomo needed boats to negotiate the Inland Sea, more provisions and horses, and the assistance of Taira partisans in the area. This took him several months to organize. During the latter part of the year Yoritomo also established two more offices, the KUMONJO (Public Documents Office) and the MONCHŪJO (Board of Inquiry), to exercise the expanding jurisdiction of his far-flung government in the field.

Finally, in March of 1185 (Juei 4.2), Yoshitsune launched an attack against the Taira bastion at Yashima on the island of Shikoku, shattered the defenders and sent them fleeing south to Kyūshū. Yoshitsune gathered a fleet of 840 boats to pursue them, and on 25 April (Juei 4.3.24) the Taira and Minamoto fleets met at the Battle of

DANNOURA at the southern tip of Honshū. The Taira were decisively defeated, their generals captured or killed, and the seven-year-old emperor Antoku drowned. See also TAIRA-MINAMOTO WAR.

Consolidation of Power —— Yoritomo was now the most powerful figure in Japan, but a number of problems remained. His relationship with his brother Yoshitsune was fast deteriorating over the matter of vassalage; he had yet to receive imperial and hence legal recognition of the de facto powers he had seized during the war; and certain parts of Japan, notably northern Honshū, were still independent of his control.

Many of Yoritomo's problems were solved when Yoshitsune fled north to avoid being captured and killed by Yoritomo's troops. When Yoshitsune was branded a rebel, Yoritomo received court authorization to appoint his men as constables (SHUGO) in each province and as stewards (JITŌ) in each estate (SHŌEN) throughout the country to assist in apprehending Yoshitsune, who sought sanctuary in Hiraizumi, the stronghold of the ŌSHŪ FUJIWARA FAMILY leader Fujiwara no Hidehira. In 1189 the latter's son forced Yoshitsune to commit suicide, hoping to win Yoritomo's support, but Yoritomo personally led an army north to destroy the Ōshū Fujiwara, and he left his own officials in control of the area when he returned to Kamakura. Thus Yoshitsune was eliminated and the north subjugated.

Yoritomo succeeded in having KUJŌ KANEZANE made imperial regent (sesshō, later kampaku) and a number of sympathetic nobles appointed to the Noble Council (Gisō). Yoritomo also had his son-in-law Ichijō Yoshiyasu (1147–97) made constable of the capital. Thus, he quickly achieved a certain amount of legitimacy for his powers as well as a measure of influence in court circles. Kanezane became the major point of contact between Kamakura and the capital.

After subjugating the north, Yoritomo visited Kyōto in 1190, receiving certain court appointments that he soon resigned, having duly impressed the nobles with his power. Back in Kamakura he devoted himself to the task of organizing his warrior government, which now enjoyed jurisdiction over all of eastern Japan. In 1192 Yoritomo was granted the title of SHŌGUN, so that in name as well as fact he was supreme commander throughout Japan.

In 1195 Yoritomo again visited the capital for the dedication of the reconstructed temple Tōdaiji. Kanezane was ousted from power in 1196, and antishogunate elements came to dominate the court. Yoritomo planned to go to Kyōto once more, but he died before he could do so. The immediate cause of his death was a fall from his horse.

Assessment of Yoritomo —— Yoritomo established Japan's first national WARRIOR GOVERNMENT; its basic structure survived for nearly 700 years, displacing the civil administration in Kyōto as the real locus of political power. From defeat and exile at age 13, Yoritomo rose to mastery over much of Japan in the brief span of about 20 years; and he achieved his position outside the traditional channels of political advancement, by creating an entirely new regime. As a man possessed of a distinguished lineage, with an early background of court life and long experience as a provincial warrior, Yoritomo was perhaps uniquely suited for his role as the founder of warrior government.

Though his own personal charisma was strong enough to win over even fierce warrior opponents, this quality was not readily institutionalized. His sons MINAMOTO NO YORIIE and MINAMOTO NO SANETOMO succeeded Yoritomo as shōgun, but neither possessed his qualities of leadership. They were unable to keep control of the Kamakura shogunate in Minamoto hands, and it passed to the family of Yoritomo's father-in-law, Hōjō Tokimasa, ironically of alleged Taira origin.

It was the very success of Yoritomo and the qualities that brought him success that have made him an unloved figure in Japanese history. In military chronicles such as the HEIKE MONOGATARI, GIKEIKI, and GEMPEI SEISUIKI, he is portrayed as shrewd, calculating, and even ruthless in the pursuit of his goals, and as lacking in humanity, particularly with regard to the conflict with his brother Yoshitsune. In a society that valued blood over vassalage, Yoritomo insisted on obedience to him as a feudal lord, from kin and nonkin alike. In contrast Yoshitsune is seen as a more romantic and militarily more brilliant figure, and Yoritomo is pictured as jealous of his younger brother's successes. Yoshitsune's tragic death won for him a place in the hearts of the Japanese; but Yoritomo's role in the shaping of Japanese history was surely more significant.

📖 ——Endō Motoo, *Gempei shiryō sōran* (1966). Jeffrey P. Mass, *Warrior Government in Early Medieval Japan* (1974). Nagahara

Keiji, *Minamoto no Yoritomo* (1958). Minoru Shinoda, *The Founding of the Kamakura Shogunate* (1960). Watanabe Tamotsu, *Genji to Heishi* (1955). Yasuda Motohisa, *Minamoto no Yoritomo* (1958).

G. Cameron HURST III

Minamoto no Yoshiie (1039–1106)

Also known as Hachiman Tarō Yoshiie. Military leader of the late Heian period; one of the first great warriors produced by the Seiwa Genji branch of the MINAMOTO FAMILY. His military career began when he helped his father, Minamoto no Yoriyoshi (988–1075), to subdue the Abe family of Mutsu Province (now Aomori, Iwate, Miyagi, and Fukushima prefectures) in the EARLIER NINE YEARS' WAR (1051–62). Appointed governor of Mutsu in 1083, Yoshiie again pacified the north when the Kiyohara family rebelled in the LATER THREE YEARS' WAR (1083–87). Because the imperial court considered this conflict a private matter and failed to provide support, Yoshiie rewarded his men with his own resources, thus establishing a powerful Minamoto base in northeastern Honshū. Local landholders commended so much land to him that the court prohibited the practice.

G. Cameron HURST III

Minamoto no Yoshinaka (1154–1184)

Better known as Kiso Yoshinaka. Warrior of the Heian period (794–1185). Yoshinaka was raised in the Kiso area of Shinano Province (now Nagano Prefecture) by Nakahara Kanetō, the husband of his wet nurse, after his own father was killed by Minamoto no Yoshihira (1141–60). With MINAMOTO NO YORITOMO and other Minamoto warriors Yoshinaka rose in rebellion against the rule of the TAIRA FAMILY in 1180. In 1183 he seized the capital and turned the TAIRA–MINAMOTO WAR into a triangular conflict, holding Kyōto while the Taira were in the west and Yoritomo in the east. The unruliness of his troops and his high-handed actions against the court, particularly the retired emperor GO-SHIRAKAWA, finally forced Yoritomo to dispatch his brothers MINAMOTO NO YOSHITSUNE and Noriyori (d 1193) to Kyōto, where they engaged and defeated Yoshinaka's forces. Yoshinaka himself managed to escape with his mistress, TOMOE GOZEN, but was eventually killed in the nearby province of Ōmi (now Shiga Prefecture). His military exploits, as well as those of his mistress, have been popularized in numerous story books (OTOGI-ZŌSHI) and NŌ plays.

G. Cameron HURST III

Minamoto no Yoshitomo (1123–1160)

Warrior of the Heian period (794–1185). The eldest son of Minamoto no Tameyoshi (1096–1156), he built up a power base in eastern Japan but later came to odds with his father. In 1156 Yoshitomo, with TAIRA NO KIYOMORI, played a major role in Emperor GO-SHIRAKAWA's victory in the HŌGEN DISTURBANCE, which resulted in the death of many Minamoto warriors, including his father and younger brother, who fought on the losing side. Angered by Kiyomori's receipt of greater rewards, Yoshitomo launched a rebellion in 1160 (see HEIJI DISTURBANCE). He was betrayed and killed while fleeing to the east, but his sons MINAMOTO NO YORITOMO, Noriyori (d 1193), and MINAMOTO NO YOSHITSUNE lived to destroy Kiyomori's descendants in the TAIRA–MINAMOTO WAR (1180–85).

G. Cameron HURST III

Minamoto no Yoshitsune (1159–1189)

Warrior of the latter part of the Heian (794–1185) period and early part of the Kamakura (1185–1333) period; a principal figure in the TAIRA–MINAMOTO WAR, he has been immortalized in legend and history as Japan's foremost tragic hero. Yoshitsune was born the son of MINAMOTO NO YOSHITOMO and Tokiwa Gozen; he was a younger brother of MINAMOTO NO YORITOMO by a different mother. Known as Ushiwakamaru as a child, he later assumed the name Genkurō.

In 1160, during the HEIJI DISTURBANCE, Yoshitomo was killed by the TAIRA FAMILY; his wife and children were captured, but their lives were spared. Yoshitsune's mother later married Fujiwara no Naganari, and Yoshitsune was raised in his household. At the age of seven, Yoshitsune was sent to the Kurama temple on the outskirts of Kyōto to become a page to the abbot. Eager, however, to avenge the death of his father, he fled the temple and sought shelter with Fujiwara no Hidehira, leader of the ŌSHŪ FUJIWARA FAMILY in Hiraizumi.

In 1180, on receiving word that Yoritomo had raised an army in Izu, Yoshitsune hastened to join his campaign and was reunited with his brother at Kisegawa soon after Yoritomo's victory against the Taira in the Battle of FUJIGAWA. In early 1184, as Yoritomo's deputy, Yoshitsune led forces to attack MINAMOTO NO YOSHINAKA, who had been occupying Kyōto and defying the court. He defeated and killed Yoshinaka in Ōmi (now Shiga Prefecture). The same year he defeated the Taira at Ichinotani in Settsu Province (near modern Kōbe), having attacked them from the rear after leading his troops though the treacherous Hiyodorigoe pass. Upon his return to Kyōto, he strengthened the defenses of the city and put in order the administration of the surrounding area. In 1185 Yoshitsune again set out to subjugate the Taira and through his brilliant tactics destroyed them completely in the Battle of DANNOURA. He returned triumphant to Kyōto.

Since defeating Yoshinaka, Yoshitsune had acted as a liaison between Yoritomo, who remained in Kamakura, and the emperor in Kyōto. He was well thought of by the retired emperor GO-SHIRAKAWA, who held actual power, and by the court aristocracy. His good relations with Go-Shirakawa, particularly after his victory at Ichinotani, aroused Yoritomo's suspicions. Go-Shirakawa craftily exploited the situation by appointing Yoshitsune as hōgan or kebiishi no jō (head imperial police commissioner) without notifying Yoritomo. The two brothers were further estranged when Yoshitsune clashed with KAJIWARA KAGETOKI, Yoritomo's direct retainer, over questions of policy. Yoshitsune traveled to Kamakura with the hope of placating Yoritomo, but he was not allowed to enter the city.

Yoritomo's hostility eventually forced Yoshitsune to join with his uncle Minamoto no Yukiie (d 1186) in a rebellion. In late 1185 Yoshitsune requested and received a decree from Go-Shirakawa to attack Yoritomo. Not many, however, were willing to join him; moreover, hearing that Yoritomo had dispatched a large army to Kyōto and fearing that the capital would be turned into a battlefield, he quietly left Kyōto for the Settsu coast. En route, he and his followers met with a storm at sea, and with his five remaining followers he sought refuge in the mountains of Yoshino.

Yoshitsune remained in hiding for a year and a half and finally made his way to Hiraizumi, once more to receive the protection of Fujiwara no Hidehira. Hidehira died in 1187, and in 1189 his son Yasuhira yielded to Yoritomo's pressure and attacked Yoshitsune's fort in Koromogawa, forcing Yoshitsune to kill his wife, his daughter, and himself. Yoshitsune was 30 years old.

The poignant story of Yoshitsune's life has long appealed to the Japanese. The phrase hōgan-biiki (partiality for Yoshitsune, hōgan—his title as head of the imperial police—being an epithet for Yoshitsune) expresses both sympathy for an ill-fated person and partiality toward the underdog. This sentiment has given rise to numerous legends about Yoshitsune, such as the story that he did not die but fled to Hokkaidō, or that he escaped to the continent and reemerged as Genghis Khan. The GIKEIKI, a fictional biography of Yoshitsune compiled in the Muromachi period (1333–1568), has proved a rich source for later literary works about Yoshitsune and his faithful retainer BENKEI.

📖 ——Watanabe Tamotsu, Minamoto no Yoshitsune (1966).

YASUDA Motohisa

Minamoto-Taira War → Taira-Minamoto War

minasu

(to deem; literally, "to look upon as"). A device in Japanese law corresponding closely to the concept of legal fiction or constructive act, whereby the existence of fact A has the same legal effect as the existence of fact B (i.e., A is looked upon as B). For example, in Japanese law, upon the issuing of a declaration of disappearance with regard to a missing person, such person is deemed to be dead (Civil Code, art. 31). The legal consequences of such declarations are the same as if the person had died in fact. An existing marriage is considered dissolved and inheritance commences. Moreover, even if it is subsequently established that the declaration of disappearance was contrary to fact (that is, that the person declared missing is actually still alive), the legal effects of death are not void unless the declaration of disappearance is cancelled.

In this respect, the effect of a legal fiction differs from that of a rebuttable presumption (suitei). In the case of the latter, the existence of fact A is only tentatively considered to be proof of the existence of fact B. Therefore, if the parties establish that fact B does not actually exist, the legal effects which would normally flow from its existence will not result.   SASAKI Kinzō

Minatogawa, Battle of

(Minatogawa no Tatakai). Battle between the armies of ASHIKAGA TAKAUJI and forces led by NITTA YOSHISADA and KUSUNOKI MASASHIGE on 4 July 1336 (Engen 1.5.25) in the area of the river Minatogawa in Settsu Province (now part of Hyōgo Prefecture), near Kōbe. Emperor GO-DAIGO had succeeded in overthrowing the Kamakura shogunate (1192–1333) and establishing direct imperial rule in Kyōto (see KEMMU RESTORATION). However, one of his generals, Ashikaga Takauji, turned against him and retreated to Kyūshū. In the spring of 1336 Takauji returned with a new army, intent on capturing Kyōto. He was met on the banks of the Minatogawa by a detachment of loyalist warriors led by Kusunoki Masashige. Nitta Yoshisada, the commander-in-chief, deployed his men at Wada no Misaki. Takauji's superior forces overwhelmed Masashige, and he committed suicide. Takauji then defeated Yoshisada at Ikuta and triumphantly entered Kyōto. Installing Emperor Kōmyō (1322–80; r 1336–48), a member of a rival branch of the imperial house, on the throne, he established the Muromachi shogunate (1338–1573), thus effectively terminating the Kemmu Restoration. See NORTHERN AND SOUTHERN COURTS.

minato machi → port towns

Minato Ward

(Minato Ku). One of the 23 wards of Tōkyō. A bustling business area and site of numerous foreign embassies, legations, and luxurious residences. The port of Tōkyō is located in eastern Minato Ward, a district with many factories and warehouses. The Tōgū Palace and the Geihinkan (Imperial Guest House) are located in the northern part of the ward. Restaurants and nightclubs abound in the Akasaka and Roppongi districts. Tourist attractions include the Tōkyō Tower, the World Trade Center, and the Buddhist temples Sengakuji and Zōjōji. Pop: 201,045.

Minchō (1352–1431)

Also known as Kichizan Minchō. Zen monk-painter of the temple TŌFUKUJI in Kyōto. A native of the island of Awajishima (now in Hyōgo Prefecture). Early in his career he became a disciple of Daidō Ichii (d 1370), a priest of the temple Ankokuji on Awajishima, from whom he received the name Kichizan. When Daidō later moved to Tōfukuji, Minchō apparently followed and became the densu or superintendent in charge of the monastic buildings; thus he also became known as Chōdensu. He is considered one of the last major priest-painters to work in traditional Buddhist figure-painting styles. Although basically conservative, Minchō's works sometimes combine the traditional techniques of Buddhist painting with the new mode of landscape INK PAINTING (suibokuga).

The earliest recorded instance of his painting activities is his 1383 self-portrait (known through a later copy) painted for his ailing mother, whom he could not visit. At this time he was engaged in painting a monumental set of 50 paintings on the theme of the Gohyaku Rakan (Five Hundred Arhats), which he completed in 1386. The surviving 47 paintings are now in Tōfukuji and in the Nezu Art Museum in Tōkyō. These paintings reflect the influence of Chinese paintings that were produced by professional painters in Ningbo (Ningpo), Zhejiang (Chekiang), and exported to Japan during the Muromachi period (1333–1568).

Most of Minchō's extant works are in the Tōfukuji Collection. Among these are the Portrait of Shōichi Kokushi (who was also known as Enni Ben'en; d 1280), founder of Tōfukuji, and a nehanzu (1408; Sakyamuni Entering Nirvana), the largest painting of its kind, exhibited publicly each year in February to commemorate the Buddha's death. A Bodhidharma triptych depicting Bodhidharma flanked by the two Taoist characters Liu Haichan (Liu Hai-ch'an) and Li Tieguai (Li T'ieh-kuai) shows influences from the new Yuan-dynasty (Yüan; 1279–1368) style of Chinese painting and is close to the famous paintings of the same subject by Yan Hui (Yen Hui; fl late 13th to early 14th centuries) at the temple Chionji in Kyōto.

Evidence for Minchō's monochrome ink paintings begins with his Portrait of Daidō Ichii (1394; Nara National Museum). Among the landscapes attributed to him is the Kei'in shōchiku (1413; Cottage by a Stream; Nanzenji, Kyōto). Several *Byaku-e Kannon* (*White-robed Kannon*) paintings, including one in the MOA Museum of Art in Atami, are also attributed to him. Minchō's most important disciples were Reisai (fl 1453–63) and Sekkyakushi (fl ca 1452).

📖 ——Tanaka Ichimatsu, *Kaō, Mokuan, Minchō*, vol 5 of *Suiboku bijutsu taikei* (Kōdansha, 1974). Yoshiaki SHIMIZU

Mine

City in western Yamaguchi Prefecture, western Honshū. It has several large lime and cement plants; some 80 percent of the marble in Japan is produced here. Pop: 21,939.

mineral rights

(*kōgyōken*). The right to recover and use minerals, pursuant to the Mining Law (Kōgyō Hō) of 1950, under which the government has authority to grant such rights. The legal system of mining concessions had its origins in 1872 with the promulgation of the Kōzan Kokoroe (Mining Instructions). The following year, modern Japan's first mining law, Nihon Kōhō (Japan Well Law), established the system of mining rights for the recovery and use of underground resources. Consistent with this law, the Japanese Civil Code of 1888 recognized that ownership of land does not include ownership of the underlying minerals. Subsequently in 1939, the Mining Damage Compensation Regulation (Kōgai Baishō Kitei), Japan's first strict liability compensation law, was enacted. This law survives as part of today's Mining Law (1950) and was invoked in several landmark cases as one of the grounds for relief of the victims of post-World War II pollution.

Pursuant to this law there are two categories of mining right—prospecting rights and digging rights—both of which, as a general rule, may be granted only to Japanese citizens or Japanese juristic persons (HŌJIN). Prospecting rights are granted for a period of two years and can be extended twice (three times for oil prospecting rights). The holder of a mining concession has a duty to begin mining operations within six months of the granting of the concession. Japanese law also recognizes mineral leases. That is, the holder of a mining concession may contract with a third person to permit such a person to extract minerals from the area covered by the holder's concession. A mineral lease may be granted for an initial period of up to five years and may be extended. The law also contains a list of minerals subject to mining concessions, and new minerals are added from time to time. ISHIMURA Zensuke

mingei → folk crafts

mingu

Traditional types of tools and other daily or ceremonial utensils used by the common people. The word *mingu* was coined by the folklorist SHIBUSAWA KEIZŌ. The 1975 CULTURAL PROPERTIES LAW (Bunkazai Hogo Hō) categorizes *mingu* as *yūkei minzoku bunkazai*, or tangible folk culture properties. The 10 subcategories described in the law are (1) utensils and objects used in daily life, including clothing and bathing and cooking equipment; (2) objects used in work, such as looms or fishing equipment; (3) objects used in transportation and communications; (4) objects used in trade; (5) objects used in societal organizations such as WAKAMONO-GUMI; (6) objects used in connection with folk beliefs; (7) objects concerned with folk knowledge, such as calendars, fortune telling, and medicine; (8) objects used in the FOLK PERFORMING ARTS; (9) objects used in family ceremonies, such as births, weddings, and funerals; and (10) objects used in annual events, such as the decorations made for the NEW YEAR.

Up until the folk craft movement begun by YANAGI MUNEYOSHI, the great diversity of folk crafts and customs had been virtually ignored when cataloging the cultural properties of the country. In the early part of the 20th century the significance of folk objects in the daily life of the Japanese was discussed, and these fast-disappearing materials became the object of much research and collecting. With the enactment of the first Cultural Properties Law in 1950, especially important articles were identified and the protection and preservation of all folk objects and crafts was ordered by the government. See also FOLK CRAFTS. MIYAMOTO Mizuo

miniature gardens → hakoniwa

Minidoka Relocation Center

A wartime relocation facility for Japanese Americans located near Hunt, Jerome County, Idaho, in operation from 10 August 1942 until 28 October 1945. It held a maximum of 9,397 persons at any one time; a total of 13,078 persons were confined there. Internees came from the Pacific Northwest area. See also JAPANESE AMERICANS, WARTIME RELOCATION OF; WAR RELOCATION AUTHORITY.

📖 ——Robert C. Sims, "The Japanese American Experience in Idaho," *Idaho Yesterdays* 22 (1978). Monica Sone, *Nisei Daughter* (2nd ed, 1979). Roger DANIELS

Minimum Wage Law

(Saitei Chingin Hō). Before World War II Japan had no minimum wage law. There were minimum wage provisions in the postwar Labor Standards Law and the Labor Union Law. However, these were ineffectual, and in 1959 the Minimum Wage Law was enacted in order to ensure minimum standards for workers who receive wages below general levels. Under this law the minimum wage differs according to industry, profession or region. As the law was originally enacted, minimum wages could be based on agreements among representatives of management, on labor-management agreements, or on the recommendations of the Minimum Wage Deliberative Council, but the first of these methods was abolished by a 1968 amendment. The government agencies responsible for implementing the Minimum Wage Law are the Ministry of Labor and the directors of local government labor standards offices but with deference to the opinions of the Minimum Wage Deliberative Council, which is made up of representatives of labor, management, and the general public. See also LABOR LAWS; LABOR STANDARDS INSPECTION OFFICES.

mining

This article is concerned with the mining of inorganic materials; for a discussion of coal mining, see the article on COAL.

Mining in Japan has a long history, dating back to the 7th century. Metal and nonmetal inorganic deposits have been found throughout the country. However, despite Marco Polo's mention of Japan as a land of inexhaustible gold, these deposits have contained relatively small reserves, and in recent decades mines have been decreasing in number.

There have been three peak periods in the history of mining in Japan. The first extended from the 7th to the 9th centuries. It was during this period that the great image of Buddha was erected at the temple TŌDAIJI in Nara (completed 752). Historical sources differ as to the amounts of various metals used in the image. According to one source about 441 metric tons (485 short tons) of copper, 7.6 metric tons (8.4 short tons) of tin, 390 kilograms (858 lbs) of gold, and 2 metric tons (2.2 short tons) of mercury, all thought to have been mined domestically, were used in its construction. The next peak came in the 16th to 18th centuries, an age of gold and silver crowned by the erection of the lavishly decorated Azuchi Castle (1576) and Fushimi Castle (1594; see the section on culture in HISTORY: Azuchi-Momoyama history). Warlords of this period also encouraged gold and silver mining as a source of funds, leading to the discovery and development of many mines such as those on the island of Sado (from the 16th century; see SADO MINES), Ashio in what is now Tochigi Prefecture (1601), Innai in what is now Akita Prefecture (1607), and Besshi in what is now Ehime Prefecture (1690). A third peak came in the period after the Meiji Restoration of 1868. New technology was introduced from the West under the guidance of Francois J. Coignet (1835–1902) and Curt Netto (b 1847) and great increases in production were achieved.

In terms of mining methods, the gathering of placer gold was the only kind of gold mining in the 7th to 9th centuries. Silver mining was carried out by lode mining from the beginning. Gold mines were found mainly in eastern Japan and silver mines in western Japan. Although some was mined in Satsuma, the westernmost province of Japan (now Kagoshima Prefecture), after the 17th century, more of it was mined in the east. Consequently, during the Edo period (1600–1868) gold coins tended to be used for business transactions in eastern Japan, including Edo (now Tōkyō), while silver, valued by weight, tended to be used in western Japan, including Kyōto and Ōsaka. Small-scale mines are thought to have existed in the 7th and 8th centuries in various places in western Japan, including Nagato and Suō provinces (both now part of Yamaguchi Prefecture). These produced high-grade copper which was used to cast the great Buddha at Nara and to strike coins.

Gold mines can be divided into those where the ores contain roughly equal amounts of gold and silver and those where the ores contain 10 times as much silver as gold. Many of the famous Japanese gold mines fall into the latter category; these include the mines at Sado, KUSHIKINO in Kagoshima Prefecture, Toi in Shizuoka Prefecture, Seikoshi in Shizuoka Prefecture, and Konomai in Hokkaidō Prefecture.

Silver mines can be divided into those where the ores also contain gold; those where silver coexists with lead and zinc ore deposits; those with the black ore known as *kurukō*, which has a mixture of silver, copper, lead, and zinc; and those with silver ores alone.

The Taishū Mine on the island of Tsushima, Nagasaki Prefecture, in operation since the 7th or 8th century, and the Nakatatsu Mine in Fukui Prefecture, the Hosokura Mine in Miyagi Prefecture, and the Kamioka Mine in Gifu Prefecture, are silver mines where lead and zinc are also found. The Kosaka Silver Mine in Akita Prefecture has black ore deposits, and the IKUNO SILVER MINE in Hyōgo Prefecture contains only silver ores.

Copper mines include those containing chalcopyrite, those containing cupriferous pyrites with chalcopyrite and iron pyrites, and those containing black ore. The Yoshioka Mine in Okayama Prefecture, the Ashio Mine, the Akenobe Mine in Hyōgo Prefecture, and the Osarizawa Mine in Akita Prefecture contain chalcopyrite deposits, while the Besshi Mine and the Hitachi Mine in Ibaraki Prefecture contain bedded cupriferous pyrite deposits. Black ore deposits are being worked at the Kosaka, Hanaoka, Matsumine, Fukasawa, and Ezuri mines, all of which are located in northern Akita Prefecture.

Some copper mines, such as those at Sado, Besshi, Ashio, and Ikuno, have been in operation for more than 300 years. However, the land strata in Japan are flexed and cut by faults, so that few large-scale deposits are found.

Almost all Japanese sulfur mines have stopped operating since sulfur is produced in the process of refining oil. Some 170 million metric tons (187 million short tons) of limestone are produced annually, chiefly responding to the needs of the cement industry.

See also ASHIO COPPER MINE INCIDENT; ASHIO COPPER MINE LABOR DISPUTE; BESSHI COPPER MINE LABOR DISPUTES; NATURAL RESOURCES.

——Chishitsu Chōsajo, ed, *Nihon kōsanshi* (1961). Shigen Enerugī Chō, ed, *Kōgyō binran* (annual). HAGA NAMIO

mining industry

Metal mining in Japan, as represented by the copper, lead, and zinc industries, is tied directly to the refining industry, and has played an important role in the domestic supply of raw materials. The national supply of nonferrous metal ore is largely imported and prices are therefore greatly affected by international supply and demand. Increased domestic labor costs, depletion of high-yield ore deposits, and the difficulties of mining exploration have led to a decline in the industry. The number of actively mined deposits decreased rapidly from 635 mines with 72,028 workers in 1955 to 89 mines with 14,766 workers in 1978. The 1977 ratios of domestic supply of metal ores were 12 percent of copper, 38 percent of lead, and 40 percent of zinc, figures which represented significant declines from 1955 figures of 64 percent of copper, 65 percent of lead, and 90 percent of zinc. In 1977 the nation's consumption of copper and zinc (1,130,000 metric tons or about 1,246,000 short tons of copper and 670,000 metric tons or about 739,000 short tons of zinc) ranked third in the world, and consumption of lead (250,000 metric tons or about 276,000 short tons) ranked sixth. The Japanese government has endeavored to promote development of overseas resources through such organizations as the Metal Mining Agency of Japan. Through a system of reserves for stabilizing imports on nonferrous metals, the government has sought to strengthen friendly and cooperative relations with resource-exporting countries. See also COAL; IRON AND STEEL INDUSTRY; MINING.   NAKAGAWA MASAYUKI

mining pollution

(*kōgai*). Mining pollution in Japan is classified by cause as follows: (1) land excavation; (2) the discharge of mine pit water or waste water; (3) the dumping of waste rock, tailings, or slag; and (4) the discharge of metallic smoke into the atmosphere. As a result of a series of mining pollution damage cases, dating back to the 1890s, preventive measures against mining pollution have been instituted over the years, though surface ground cave-ins, surface subsidence, and ground fissures pose a continuing problem. It is feared that the dumping of waste water and tailings may cause injury to life and property in the event of future earthquakes or floods, both of which occur frequently in Japan.

History——One of the earliest and best-known examples of mining pollution in Japan was the copper poisoning case at the Ashio Mine in Ibaraki Prefecture, which was caused by the discharge of mine pit water and waste water into a nearby river, the Watarasegawa, during a flood in 1878. The greatest resultant damage was to crops on surrounding farmland in the 1890s. Some 33,000 hectares (80,850 acres) of cultivated land suffered damage, leading to serious political and social problems (see ASHIO COPPER MINE INCIDENT). Another famous case resulted from smoke pollution at the Besshi Mine. The smelting furnace of the mine was located at Motoyama (the mine site) in the city of NIIHAMA, Ehime Prefecture, until about the middle of the Meiji period (1868–1912). However, because of the great damage by noxious smoke inflicted on farm crops in the vicinity of the smeltery, it was removed to SHISAKAJIMA, an isolated island in the sea 20 kilometers (12 mi) to the north of Niihama, in 1905. The smoke, which had hitherto been confined to the area around Motoyama, unexpectedly spread to an area 40 kilometers (25 mi) from the coast and caused a great amount of damage. An agreement was concluded between the owner of the mining concession and the injured parties in 1910. Since that time, limitations have been placed on the operational period of the smeltery and the amount of ore to be treated. Indemnities have been paid every year.

Smoke damage from the Kosaka Mine in Akita Prefecture and the Hitachi Mine in Ibaraki Prefecture was also the cause of great controversy. The two mining companies carried out experiments to vary the height of their smeltery smokestacks, but they remained a source of smoke pollution. A disastrous accident occurred in 1936 at the Osarizawa Mine in Akita Prefecture in which a tailing dam collapsed, resulting in heavy loss of life. This accident was a turning point, and laws setting forth indemnities for injury and loss were passed.

Progress in science and technology helped prevent damage caused by mine water, waste water, and smoke in later years. With the enactment of stronger pollution laws and technological advancements in pollution control, problems of this kind have largely disappeared. Improvements have also been made in the methods of damage investigation. However, mining injuries are a continuing problem and have occurred in the coal fields of Kyūshū. A record preserved at the MIIKE COAL MINES shows that in the middle part of the Meiji period indemnity had already been paid for damage caused by the drying up of a nearby water well and the leakage of an irrigation pond. After World War I, injuries from coal mining began to attract public attention. With the expansion of mining, injuries increased, provoking a call for more rehabilitation programs and larger indemnities. See also COAL.

Recent Problems——The *itai itai* ("ouch-ouch") disease, which had been afflicting people in the basin of the river Jinzūgawa, Toyama Prefecture, was first thought to be an endemic disease. In 1957, however, a new theory was set forth, namely that it was caused by cadmium contained in mine waste water flowing from the Kamioka Mine. This caused a controversy in medical circles. The Ministry of Health and Welfare embarked upon an investigation and concluded in 1968 that the disease was caused by cadmium discharged from the Kamioka Mine and the company had to pay reparations. See also POLLUTION-RELATED DISEASES.

As the result of a massive coastal earthquake which hit the region of Izu–Ōshima in 1978, a part of the confining levee of the tailing dam Hōzukizawa (14 meters or 46 feet in height) of the Mochikoshi Mine in Shizuoka Prefecture collapsed. About 60,000 cubic meters (2 million cubic feet) of tailings, and about 20,000 cubic meters (700,000 cubic feet) of embankment earth flowed out into the surrounding rivers. The rivers Mochikoshigawa and KANOGAWA were both polluted.

In recent years a number of injuries have occurred from coal mining, mainly in Kyūshū. Because of a lack of information concerning the original mine owners and the difficulties involved in suing for compensation in many cases, the Temporary Measure Act for injury from coal mining was enacted in 1963. The Coal Mine Damage Corporation was established to ensure the smooth payment of indemnities and well-organized rehabilitation.

Countermeasures and Problems in the Future——It is not likely that mining pollution caused by mine water, waste water, and smoke from smelting will occur in the future. However, it is quite possible that damage from mining caused by the dumping of waste and tailings will occur, since Japan has frequent earthquakes and localized flooding arising from torrential downpours. Countermeasures against future environmental pollution resulting from the open-pit mining of limestone and the need for comprehensive rehabilitation programs for coal-mining related injuries are particularly important.

📖——Kamioka Namiko, ed, *Shiryō kindai Nippon no kōgai* (1971). NOHARA Hiroshi

ministerial deliberative council

(shingikai). A collegial or advisory body attached to a central government administrative organ which investigates and deliberates matters upon inquiry from the head of the administrative agency or, when so authorized by legislation, upon its own initiative. Deliberative councils are established under provisions of law; in 1975 there were in existence 246 such advisory bodies, such as the University Chartering Council (Daigaku Setchi Shingikai) of the Ministry of Education. These councils serve various roles in government: some act to gather information through hearings, while others act as deliberative organs. Deliberative councils, however, are not empowered to independently determine public policy or to act as enforcement agencies. Deliberative councils are also established at the local government level, in which case they act in response to inquiry of the governor of the local government unit. KOTANI Kōzō

Ministry of Agriculture, Forestry, and Fisheries

(Nōrin Suisan Shō). Ministry of the national government responsible for the administration and regulation of the agricultural, forestry, and fishing industries. Separated from the Ministry of Agriculture and Commerce (Nōshōmushō) in 1925, it became the Ministry of Agriculture and Forestry (Nōrinshō). The name was changed again in 1978 to the present one. Headed by a cabinet minister appointed by the prime minister, its primary concern lies with the protection of the Japanese farmer and with the promotion of Japanese agriculture. Since 1945 the PRIMARY INDUSTRIES have declined drastically, and the farming industry, once dominant in Japan, has suffered accordingly. In an effort to halt this erosion, the ministry has consistently sought to improve farmers' incomes by encouraging the expansion of agricultural production, restricting imports of food products, and seeking higher prices for farm products. The ministry drafts legislation for the agricultural sector and has sought to maintain agricultural subsidies and price support schemes.

Other important functions of the ministry include the setting of standards and grades for farm products; inspection of exports of food products; supervision of food markets and commodity exchanges; conducting research and providing information, extension, and statistical services; registering brands of commercial fertilizers and farm chemicals; and undertaking various land reclamation and improvement projects.

The ministry has jurisdiction over the Food Agency, Forestry Agency, and Fisheries Agency (Shokuryōchō, Rin'yachō, Suisanchō). The Food Agency is in charge of the inspection of agricultural products and sets the prices of many food items. It also administers the import and export of many food products. The Forestry Agency is responsible for the administration and management of Japan's forest land, forestry development, and inspection of lumber products. The Fisheries Agency handles all aspects of fishery administration, including the protection and improvement of fishery resources, repair and maintenance of fishing ports, research on fishery resources and fishery culture, and the licensing of all inland and coastal fishing.

In addition to these agencies, the ministry consists of the Minister's Secretariat and the economic affairs, agricultural structural improvement, agricultural production, animal industry, and food and marketing bureaus. Daniel A. METRAUX

Ministry of Construction

(Kensetsushō). Ministry of the national government responsible for administration related to civil engineering and construction; established in 1948. The ministry has five bureaus. The Planning Bureau formulates national, regional, and local land-use and building development plans and adopts measures to stimulate and improve the CONSTRUCTION INDUSTRY. The City Bureau formulates policies concerning the construction, improvement, development, and conservation of cities, and is active in all phases of urban planning and urban renewal. The River Bureau administers programs concerning rivers and seacoasts and oversees the construction and maintenance of dams. The Road Bureau is responsible for the supervision of road improvement, construction, and maintenance projects. The Housing Bureau is in charge of housing programs. The ministry also supervises several important public corporations, including the HOUSING AND URBAN DEVELOPMENT CORPORATION, the JAPAN HIGHWAY PUBLIC CORPORATION, and the WATER RESOURCES DEVELOPMENT PUBLIC CORPORATION.

Ministry of Education

(Mombushō). Ministry of the national government responsible for the administration of Japan's public educational system and for the setting of national educational standards as well as for the promotion of cultural activities. It provides guidance, advice, and certain fiscal assistance to prefectural and local boards of education. It also has substantial control over the curricula, the production and content of textbooks, the training of teachers, and the standards of equipment used in schools. The ministry exercises direct jurisdiction over the national universities as well as over nationally established junior and technical colleges, museums, and education research institutes.

The ministry is also involved in numerous international educational exchange programs and is concerned with all matters pertaining to foreign students in Japan and Japanese students abroad. It provides a number of scholarships for foreign students and scholars for study and research in Japan.

Before 1945 the ministry had considerable power and influence over the nation's centralized educational system based on the principles of the IMPERIAL RESCRIPT ON EDUCATION (1890). American planners during the Allied Occupation (1945–52) felt that Japan's educational system had to be decentralized as an essential step toward the development of a democratic society. Locally elected boards of education were given full authority over schools in their districts, and the ministry became primarily an advisory body.

By the mid-1950s, however, many of the former powers and responsibilities were returned to the ministry. With the passage of the Board of Education Law of 1956, members of prefectural and local boards of education were appointed by governors or mayors with the approval of the respective local assemblies, and superintendents of prefectural boards had to be approved by the ministry. The law also gave the ministry limited veto power over the acts of prefectural and local boards.

The Agency for Cultural Affairs, which is attached to the ministry, is responsible for a wide range of cultural activities, including the promotion of culture and the preservation and utilization of cultural properties, the sponsorship of numerous cultural events in Japan and abroad, matters concerning copyrights, improvement and diffusion of the Japanese language, and designation, custody, and restoration of Important Cultural Properties (see NATIONAL TREASURES).

The ministry is headed by a cabinet minister appointed by the prime minister. Daniel A. METRAUX

Ministry of Finance

(Ōkurashō). The government agency responsible for financial matters, including budgeting, taxes, banking, stocks and bonds, and international monetary affairs. The ministry was founded in 1869. In early years its officials included many leading figures of the Meiji period—ŌKUBO TOSHIMICHI, INOUE KAORU, ITŌ HIROBUMI, SHIBUSAWA EIICHI, MATSUKATA MASAYOSHI—and was assigned broad responsibilities, including not only finance but industry, trade, agriculture, transportation, communications, and supervision of local government. However, by 1898 the basis of its present duties and organization had been established: the ministry comprised the Secretariat; three main bureaus—budget, tax (including tariffs), and financial (including banking)—the mint; the tobacco monopoly; and local tax and customs offices. At about the same time, to preclude influence from political parties, the principle was established that all high posts, excluding only the minister and parliamentary vice-minister, must be occupied by career civil servants, a system still in force today.

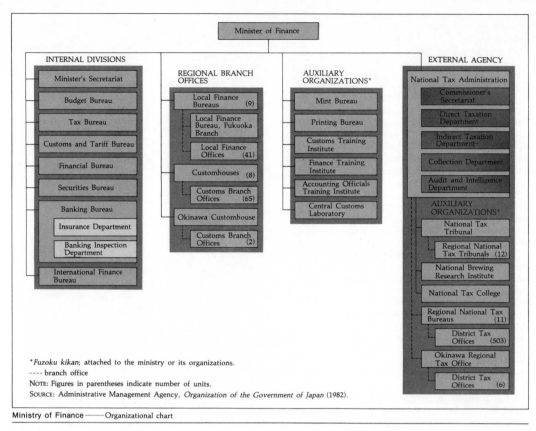

Ministry of Finance ——— Organizational chart

Fuzoku kikan; attached to the ministry or its organizations.

---- branch office

NOTE: Figures in parentheses indicate number of units.

SOURCE: Administrative Management Agency, *Organization of the Government of Japan* (1982).

History ——— The history of the Ministry of Finance is usually told in terms of alternating inflationary and deflationary periods. During the years when ŌKUMA SHIGENOBU was finance minister (1873–80), available revenues were very restricted, and the ministry had no alternative but printing money to cover the enormous costs of dismantling feudalism and building a modern state. The economy was rescued from the resulting severe inflation of 1878–81 by Matsukata Masayoshi, minister from 1881 until (with interruptions) 1900, who applied such classically stringent remedies as putting the yen on the silver (and later gold) standard, raising taxes and cutting expenditures enough to insure budget surpluses, and establishing a European-style central bank (the BANK OF JAPAN, 1882). These reforms brought price stability and laid the foundation for modern economic growth, which was quite rapid in the three decades (encompassing three wars) until 1920. The next 10 years saw shifting economic conditions and ended in a return to orthodox fiscal principles and the gold standard, which had been suspended in 1917, under conservative Finance Minister INOUE JUNNOSUKE in 1929. However, this policy turned out to be ill-timed, since it magnified the effects of the world depression and brought on severe deflation, particularly damaging to the rural economy. A change in government in December 1931 brought the experienced TAKAHASHI KOREKIYO back as minister of finance, and he implemented a policy of "pump-priming" the economy by borrowing to increase government expenditures, especially for the military; as a result, industry boomed until the start of the war in 1937.

During wartime and the early OCCUPATION period, chronic shortages meant that control over materials tended to outweigh financial controls, and Finance Ministry influence correspondingly declined. However, concern about inflation led to the mission of Detroit banker Joseph M. Dodge, who enforced severe austerity: tight credit, a fixed exchange rate, and enough cuts in expenditure to allow a "super-balanced" budget for 1949 (see DODGE LINE). As with Matsukata's policies in 1881, the ensuing deflation had some difficult social consequences but did become the basis for the "economic miracle" of postwar Japan.

Role in Economic Growth ——— The impact of the Ministry of Finance in the contemporary period may be seen from two angles. Within Japan, it has usually been a restrictive, conservative force opposing the more expansionist MINISTRY OF INTERNATIONAL TRADE AND INDUSTRY, ECONOMIC PLANNING AGENCY, and ruling LIBERAL DEMOCRATIC PARTY. Viewed from outside, however, the

ministry appears central to the government's dynamic growth-first policy. Compared with the West, a high proportion of Japanese public expenditure has gone into capital accumulation, and more generally, government spending has been minimized to keep taxes and deficit financing down (the total tax plus social insurance burden rarely exceeded 25 percent of the national income, compared with 35–50 percent elsewhere). More funds are therefore available for private investment. Partly because the securities market was undeveloped, it was the banks which both received savings from the public and supplied investment funds to industry. Artificially low interest rates, made possible by tight foreign exchange controls, created a high demand for funds and allowed the channeling of investment into capital-intensive industries with high growth potential. Tariff policies and management of the enormous postal savings and social insurance trust funds were also directed toward growth objectives. Finally, short-term economic regulation has most often been stimulative, except for brief cooling-off periods following an inflationary surge or balance-of-payments crisis. Nearly all the institutions and processes mentioned here fall within the bailiwick of the Finance Ministry.

Status ——— The Ministry of Finance is usually considered the most powerful and prestigious organization in the government, indeed in all Japan. Each year it enrolls 20 to 25 of the nation's brightest graduates (a majority from the law faculty of Tōkyō University); each year its retired bureaucrats move on to top jobs in business and politics—in 1974, 25 Finance Ministry alumni were in the Diet, several in leadership positions in government or the ruling party. Finance Ministry officials are often resented as an "elite within the elite," but they are usually also respected for their competence, willingness to work hard, and well-developed sense of national purpose; journalists call them "the samurai of the Japanese government."

Budgeting ——— The Finance Ministry's power partly stems from its control of the budget, since other agencies must come to it for funds; accordingly, the Budget Bureau (Shukeikyoku) has highest status within the ministry. Japan's modern budget system has a long history: as early as 1917, the American historian and reformer Charles BEARD could remark that the Japanese budget "contains nearly all the elements of a modern plan . . . at a time when the balance sheet is almost unknown to American legislators" (*Municipal Research*, March 1917). In the prewar period, despite constitutional limitations, the Diet's right of budgetary approval was an important source of influence for the political parties. The 1947 CONSTITUTION strengthened the formal parliamentary power of the purse, and though since the beginning of majority party government in 1955 the budget has rarely been amended in the Diet, the Liberal Democrats have had considerable influence over spending. Japanese budgeting is rather complicated: in addition to the general account *(ippan kaikei)*, the Finance Ministry compiles 41 special accounts *(tokubetsu kaikei)*, accounts for several public corporations, and the Fiscal Investment and Loan Program (ZAISEI TŌYŪSHI). The process begins with the preparation of ministry requests; these are submitted by 31 August, reviewed and cut by the Budget Bureau, and reported as the "Finance Ministry draft" in December or January. There follows a week of "revival negotiations" *(fukkatsu sesshō)* when the Finance Ministry responds to appeals from the ministries and the majority party. The resulting "Government draft" is passed by the cabinet and sent to the Diet, where it provides the occasion for opposition party attacks on the full range of governmental policy before passage around 1 April, the beginning of the fiscal year. Until 1965, the Japanese budget was "balanced" in the sense that General Account expenditures were completely covered by tax revenues, but since then a portion of the budget has been financed by national bonds (see BONDS, GOVERNMENT). Compared with other industrialized nations, the Japanese budget has grown very rapidly, reflecting GNP growth. On the other hand, expenditure patterns, expressed as shares of total spending, have been relatively stable, at least from about 1960 until the mid-1970s.

Other Functions —— Briefly glancing at the rest of the Finance Ministry organization, the Minister's Secretariat (Daijin Kambō), as well as its normal staff functions, engages in economic forecasting and other research and supervises the government tobacco monopoly. The Tax Bureau (Shuzeikyoku) is responsible for tax policy, revenue forecasting, and supervision of tax administration; it also oversees the liquor industry. Actual tax collections are handled by the semiautonomous National Tax Administration Agency (Kokuzeichō) through its over 500 district tax offices. The Financial Bureau (Rizaikyoku) is in charge of managing the national debt, trust funds, and government-owned property, and making loans to local governments. The Banking Bureau (Ginkōkyoku) controls interest rates, licenses banks, supervises the Bank of Japan and other government financial institutions, and regulates the insurance industry. The International Finance Bureau (Kokusai Kin'yūkyoku) is in charge of foreign exchange, the balance of payments, and both incoming and outgoing foreign investment. The functions of the securities (Shōkenkyoku) and customs and tariff (Kanzeikyoku) bureaus, and the external mint and printing bureaus, are as indicated by their names. In no small measure, the central role in economic policy making played by the Ministry of Finance is a consequence of this unusually broad scope of important responsibilities.

▄ ——John Creighton Campbell, *Contemporary Japanese Budget Politics* (1977). Kōichi Emi, *Government Fiscal Activity and Economic Growth in Japan, 1868–1960* (1963). William W. Lockwood, ed, *The State and Economic Enterprise in Japan* (1965). Ōkurashō Hyakunen Shi Henshūshitsu, ed, *Ōkurashō hyakunen shi* (3 vols, 1969). Sakakibara Eisuke and Noguchi Yukio, "Ōkurashō-Nichigin ōchō no bunseki," *Chūō kōron* (August 1977; tr as "Dissecting the Finance Ministry–Bank of Japan Dynasty," *Japan Echo*, Winter 1977). Suzuki Yukio, *Keizai kanryō* (1969). Yasuhara Kazuo, *Ōkurashō* (1974).
                                                                                      John Creighton CAMPBELL

Ministry of Foreign Affairs

(Gaimushō). Ministry of the national government primarily responsible for Japan's political relations with the outside world. Established in 1869 by the newly instituted Meiji government, the ministry quickly assumed a preeminent position in Japan's bureaucratic leadership due to the sense of urgency created by a hostile international environment and the need to establish a formalized working relationship with the Western powers. Among the prominent political figures who served as foreign minister during the Meiji period (1868–1912) were INOUE KAORU, ŌKUMA SHIGENOBU, SAIONJI KIMMOCHI, KATŌ TAKAAKI, and KOMURA JUTARŌ. With the exception of the 1930s and the first half of the 1940s, when the military gained ascendancy, the ministry provided the organizational structure, channels of communication, and informed leadership necessary to plan and implement Japan's foreign policy.

Origin and Development —— Upon its establishment in 1868, the Meiji government created an agency to deal with diplomatic relations under the leadership of a governor for foreign affairs *(gaikoku jimu sōsai)*. After undergoing several structural transformations, the

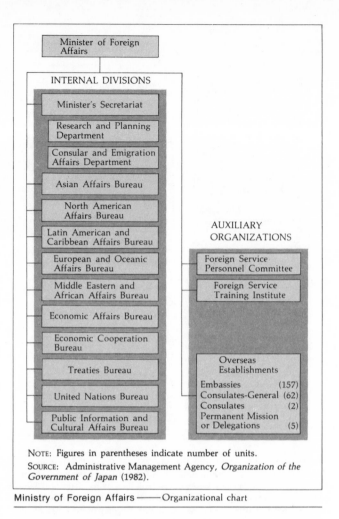

NOTE: Figures in parentheses indicate number of units.
SOURCE: Administrative Management Agency, *Organization of the Government of Japan* (1982).

Ministry of Foreign Affairs —— Organizational chart

agency formally adopted the name Gaimushō on 15 August 1869. In December 1885 the government instituted the cabinet system of national administration, and in February 1886 the ministry was reorganized into one secretariat and six bureaus—i.e., general affairs, commerce, investigation, translation, records, and statistics—under the direction of the foreign minister.

The influence wielded by the ministry has varied considerably during its existence. In its early years the ministry stood at the summit of the bureaucratic hierarchy, reflecting in part the prominence accorded foreign relations by a nation newly opened to the outside world. Revision of the Unequal Treaties concluded with Western nations was the most pressing international issue of the day, and Japan's self-imposed isolation of nearly 300 years during the Edo period (1600–1868) meant that only the Foreign Ministry had the linguistic expertise and administrative resources to gather intelligence on foreign countries, analyze alien legal and political systems, and negotiate Japan out of second-class status onto an equal footing with the major powers of the West (see UNEQUAL TREATIES, REVISION OF). By the late 19th and early 20th centuries, however, the ministry's monopoly on foreign policy decision making was increasingly challenged. Although the ministry maintained leadership in such purely diplomatic activities as the conclusion of the Anglo-Japanese Alliance in 1902, the military gained ascendancy as Japan's involvement in armed conflict grew—first in the SINO-JAPANESE WAR OF 1894–1895, then in the RUSSO-JAPANESE WAR of 1904–05, and finally in World War I.

By the MANCHURIAN INCIDENT of 1931, the military had clearly usurped much of the ministry's control over foreign policy decision making. In 1933 a committee, comprising the prime minister and ministers of foreign affairs, finance, the army, and the navy, was formed to coordinate foreign policy, and immediately after the outbreak of war with the United States in 1941, a military-dominated wartime council further eroded the ministry's diplomatic functions. The creation of the Greater East Asia Ministry in September 1942 led the foreign minister, TŌGŌ SHIGENORI, to resign in protest. With the abolition of the military and Privy Council in the postwar period, the ministry regained some of its former power. Intraorganizational and environmental factors, however, have worked to constrain it from assuming the preeminent position it enjoyed during the Meiji period.

Functions—— The reasons for the diminishing role of the ministry in foreign policy decision making can be understood by examining the foreign policy issues at stake, the Foreign Ministry's major competitors, and the internal organization and goals of the ministry itself.

Reflecting Japan's rapid growth in the postwar period, economic issues have comprised an important element of foreign relations. This has brought to the fore those government bureaucracies primarily responsible for Japan's economic well-being. Thus negotiations concerning the export of products (for example, textiles, color television sets, and steel) have been handled by the MINISTRY OF INTERNATIONAL TRADE AND INDUSTRY, while international monetary and financial agreements (for example, relating to the reversion of Okinawa or, more generally, to the International Monetary Fund or World Bank) are the special preserve of the MINISTRY OF FINANCE. Preparations for the Tōkyō Round of trade talks involved not only the Foreign Ministry but also the ministries of finance, international trade and industry, agriculture, forestry, and fisheries, and the Economic Planning Agency. The negotiations surrounding the Nuclear Nonproliferation Treaty, involving technical and strategic issues, were similar, as many other agencies in addition to the Foreign Ministry participated. Because training in foreign languages and international studies is no longer limited to officers of the Foreign Ministry, these agencies are often able to form direct lines of communication with their counterparts abroad without using the Foreign Ministry as an intermediary. In addition, the politicized nature of many of the economic issues in particular means that domestic pressure groups will demand that their interests be directly represented abroad.

The Foreign Ministry finds itself unable to assume a central role in economic or technical negotiations in part because its explicit policy of training generalists has not produced functional specialists. Furthermore, not unlike the British Foreign Office or the US State Department, the ministry's "internationalist" philosophy often clashes with the expressed desires of domestic interest groups. The ministry's mission of maintaining Japan's good standing in the international community, even at the expense of domestic interests, has made it particularly vulnerable to criticism at home. Having minimal ties with the political and business community—as evidenced by the small number of retirees who participate in AMAKUDARI (the practice of taking a job with private industry after retiring from government service)—the ministry can expect little by way of a domestic constituency or clientele to rally support for its policies. Finally, while its consular and diplomatic functions (for example, passports, visas, cables) increase geometrically, the ministry's financial and personnel resources are among the smallest of any comparable agency of any major industrialized nation.

Organization and Personnel—— The ministry comprises 10 bureaus, 2 departments, and the Minister's Secretariat. Each bureau or department is headed by a director general and contains several divisions, each led by a director. There are 63 divisions in all. Under the foreign minister, who is usually a politician with a Diet seat and who is appointed by the prime minister, are one administrative vice-minister, the senior career official of the ministry; one parliamentary vice-minister; two deputy vice-ministers; and several dozen counselors, who rank between directors-general and directors, attached to the bureaus and departments.

Although there is considerable exchanging of personnel with other ministries and agencies on a short-term basis, lateral entry for permanent positions is extremely rare, whether from other ministries, public agencies, or nongovernmental institutions. Entry is usually made on one of three levels, determined by the results of the entrance examination. Between 20 and 30 new recruits enter each year on the basis of their score on the Higher Foreign Service Examination and intensive personal interviews. The middle-level personnel must pass the Foreign Service Specialist Examination. The supporting staff enter the ministry based on their performance on the National Personnel Authority's Principal Junior Entrance Examination.

Of the over 3,500 employees in the ministry, slightly over 300 hold the top-ranking positions above deputy division head and its equivalent either at the Tōkyō headquarters or at overseas diplomatic and consular missions. A high proportion of these senior officials are graduates of the Law Faculty of Tōkyō University. Among

the 403 higher-level Foreign Ministry entrants between 1965 and 1980, roughly half were graduates of Tōkyō University, and 5 universities—only 1 a private institution—accounted for 90 percent of the total.

Future Prospects—— An interesting experiment, generally considered successful, took place between November 1977 and December 1978 when Ushiba Nobuhiko, a career foreign ministry official, served as minister for external economic affairs. Drawing on the staff support of the Foreign Ministry's Bureau of Economic Affairs, Ushiba headed a task force comprising representatives from the ministries of finance, international trade and industry, agriculture, forestry, and fisheries, foreign affairs, the Economic Planning Agency, and the Prime Minister's Office in order to coordinate Japan's trade policy with the United States and Europe. Similar efforts may be necessary in the future to transcend bureaucratic rivalries and to formulate a coherent set of policies in an increasingly complex world of multilateral relations.

——Banno Masataka, *Gendai gaikō no bunseki* (1971). Fukui Haruhiro, "Policy-making in the Japanese Foreign Ministry" in Robert Scalapino, ed, *The Foreign Policy of Modern Japan* (1977). Gaimushō Hyakunen Shi Hensan Iinkai, ed, *Gaimushō no hyakunen,* 2 vols (1969). Igarashi Yasuji, *Gaimushō* (1974). Kawamura Kinji, *Gaimushō* (1956). Kusayanagi Taizō, *Kanryō ōkoku ron* (1975). Nagano Nobutoshi, *Gaimushō kenkyū* (1975). Ushiba Nobuhiko and Hara Yasushi, *Nihon keizai gaikō no keifu* (1979).

Glen S. FUKUSHIMA

Ministry of Health and Welfare

(Kōseishō). Government ministry responsible for the administration of public health, SOCIAL WELFARE, and SOCIAL SECURITY PROGRAMS. It plays a leading role in public health, paying particular attention to the health and welfare of mothers and children, and regulates drugs and medicines. Its Social Insurance Agency (Shakai Hoken Chō), an extraministerial office established in 1962, manages the NATIONAL HEALTH INSURANCE and government PENSIONS programs.

The ministry was formed in 1938 from a bureau of the HOME MINISTRY and reorganized in 1948. Headed by a cabinet minister, it has nine bureaus and operates over 90 national hospitals, over 150 national sanatoriums, the National Cancer Center, and other institutes including the Institute of Population Problems and the National Institute of Health. See also GOVERNMENT, EXECUTIVE BRANCH.

Ministry of Home Affairs

(Jichishō). Cabinet ministry in charge of coordination and communication between the central and local governments. The ministry is also responsible for the administration of Japan's election system.

Established in 1960, the ministry has assumed only a few of the functions of the powerful pre-World War II HOME MINISTRY (Naimushō). It is in fact the smallest of all cabinet ministries, with a staff of slightly more than 500 employees. Insofar as it administers government grants-in-aid programs and oversees local finance, however, the ministry still exerts considerable influence over LOCAL GOVERNMENT. The ministry consists of three main bureaus (Local Administration Bureau, Local Finance Bureau, and Local Tax Bureau) and one agency (Fire Defense Agency).

Ministry of International Trade and Industry

(MITI; Tsūshō Sangyō Shō or Tsūsanshō). Ministry of the national government responsible for the formulation and implementation of trade and industrial policy for the nation. Together with the ministries of finance, construction, transportation, and agriculture, forestry and fisheries, as well as the ECONOMIC PLANNING AGENCY, MITI occupies a central position in what the Japanese call the "economic bureaucracy." Since the end of the Allied Occupation (1952), MITI has been regarded as one of the three most powerful and prestigious ministries of the central government (together with the ministries of finance and foreign affairs), and prior service as minister of one or preferably all three of these ministries has been an indispensable qualification for a politician who aspires to the prime ministership.

MITI's primary function until the early 1970s was to lead the private sector of the economy toward rapid economic growth; it was responsible for the introduction of new technology into Japan, the heavy industrialization of the economy, the rapid expansion of ex-

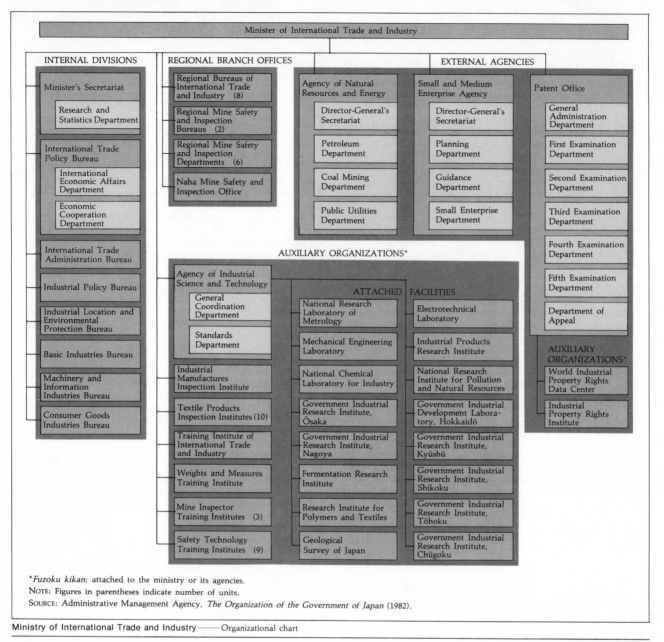

Ministry of International Trade and Industry——Organizational chart

Inside the chart:

Minister of International Trade and Industry

INTERNAL DIVISIONS

Minister's Secretariat
- Research and Statistics Department

International Trade Policy Bureau
- International Economic Affairs Department
- Economic Cooperation Department

International Trade Administration Bureau

Industrial Policy Bureau

Industrial Location and Environmental Protection Bureau

Basic Industries Bureau

Machinery and Information Industries Bureau

Consumer Goods Industries Bureau

REGIONAL BRANCH OFFICES

Regional Bureaus of International Trade and Industry (8)

Regional Mine Safety and Inspection Bureaus (2)

Regional Mine Safety and Inspection Departments (6)

Naha Mine Safety and Inspection Office

EXTERNAL AGENCIES

Agency of Natural Resources and Energy
- Director-General's Secretariat
- Petroleum Department
- Coal Mining Department
- Public Utilities Department

Small and Medium Enterprise Agency
- Director-General's Secretariat
- Planning Department
- Guidance Department
- Small Enterprise Department

Patent Office
- General Administration Department
- First Examination Department
- Second Examination Department
- Third Examination Department
- Fourth Examination Department
- Fifth Examination Department
- Department of Appeal

AUXILIARY ORGANIZATIONS*
- World Industrial Property Rights Data Center
- Industrial Property Rights Institute

AUXILIARY ORGANIZATIONS*

Agency of Industrial Science and Technology
- General Coordination Department
- Standards Department

Industrial Manufactures Inspection Institute

Textile Products Inspection Institutes (10)

Training Institute of International Trade and Industry

Weights and Measures Training Institute

Mine Inspector Training Institutes (3)

Safety Technology Training Institutes (9)

ATTACHED FACILITIES

National Research Laboratory of Metrology

Mechanical Engineering Laboratory

National Chemical Laboratory for Industry

Government Industrial Research Institute, Ōsaka

Government Industrial Research Institute, Nagoya

Fermentation Research Institute

Research Institute for Polymers and Textiles

Geological Survey of Japan

Electrotechnical Laboratory

Industrial Products Research Institute

National Research Institute for Pollution and Natural Resources

Government Industrial Development Laboratory, Hokkaidō

Government Industrial Research Institute, Kyūshū

Government Industrial Research Institute, Shikoku

Government Industrial Research Institute, Tōhoku

Government Industrial Research Institute, Chūgoku

*Fuzoku kikan; attached to the ministry or its agencies.
NOTE: Figures in parentheses indicate number of units.
SOURCE: Administrative Management Agency, *The Organization of the Government of Japan* (1982).

ports, and the import of adequate supplies of energy and industrial raw materials.

Given its powers and pervasive influence throughout the economy and society, MITI acquired a controversial reputation. Admirers hailed it as the leader of the Japanese "economic miracle"—the rapid postwar transformation of Japan in approximately 20 years from smoldering ruins to the world's third most productive economy. On the other hand, foreign rivals of Japan charged MITI with being the corporate headquarters of "JAPAN INCORPORATED," meaning that the ministry fostered extremely close relations between government and business in Japan and worked to exclude foreign competition from the Japanese market. Domestic critics blamed MITI for many of the pollution and international economic problems that became increasingly evident during the early 1970s. MITI has no exact parallel with any ministry of economic affairs in other advanced capitalist nations, and its role as a planning and guidance organ of the Japanese government in the context of one of the world's most vigorous open market economies has elicited much analysis and commentary within Japan and abroad.

Origins and Development—— Since the Meiji Restoration of 1868, the Japanese government has taken an active role in private economic affairs to maintain national independence and to foster economic development. MITI is the direct bureaucratic descendant

of the Ministry of Agriculture and Commerce (NŌSHŌMUSHŌ; 1881–1925), the Ministry of Commerce and Industry (Shōkōshō; 1925–43; 1945–49), and the Ministry of Munitions (Gunjushō; 1943–45). It was created in 1949 through the union of the Trade Agency and the Ministry of Commerce and Industry, and direct continuity exists between the personnel and many of the policies of these earlier agencies and MITI. The creation of MITI came about as part of the DODGE LINE—the basic change in American policy during the Occupation from attempts to "democratize" the Japanese economy to attempts to rehabilitate it. By uniting all controls over industrial recovery and international trade into one governmental agency, Japanese and American leaders hoped to end Japan's reliance on American aid, stop the postwar inflation, and provide governmental leadership and assistance for the restoration of industrial productivity and employment. Throughout its first decade and a half, MITI exercised virtually total control over all imports and exports in Japan; no transaction of any importance could be completed without its approval. MITI used its powers to direct imported technology, funds, and natural resources to those sectors of the economy—at first, coal, steel, shipbuilding, and electric power—that, in conjunction with business leaders, it designated as critical to Japan's rapid economic growth. MITI's overall policy was to transform Japan from a light-industry, Asia-oriented economy to a heavy-industry, globally oriented economy. It also erected formidable barriers to protect the Japanese economy from international competition (see also INDUSTRIAL POLICY).

These policies succeeded spectacularly, so much so that by the mid-1960s Japan's foreign economic partners demanded that Japan dismantle its structure of economic controls and liberalize foreign trade and international transfers of capital to and from Japan. After much resistance and domestic political controversy, MITI gradually complied with these demands, but it also continued through informal ADMINISTRATIVE GUIDANCE to enhance Japan's international competitive ability and to develop an industrial structure in terms of size and number of firms in important industries that compared favorably with Japan's main reference economies, those of the United States and West Germany.

Around the time of the reorganization of the ministry in July 1973 and the development of the OIL CRISIS OF 1973, MITI decisively abandoned its older policies of industrial protection and guidance. It reoriented its work toward developing nonpolluting, high-technology industries in Japan, and toward promoting close ties of cooperation and mutual benefit with Japan's foreign customers and suppliers of raw materials.

MITI's Powers and Influence——Of the five economic ministries or agencies, MITI is the smallest in terms of personnel and budget. It has always preferred to perform its functions through the use of its extensive legislation-based licensing and approval authority and through its powers to recommend appropriate loans and investments to institutions such as the JAPAN DEVELOPMENT BANK. MITI is more akin to a highly influential "think tank" than it is to ministries with extensive powers of subsidization (e.g., construction or health and welfare) or budgetary control (e.g., finance). The ministry is known for its internal democracy, and it attracts more creative and outspoken officials than most other branches of the central government. Much of MITI's influence derives from its extremely close ties with big business and from the fact that most of its high officials, upon "retirement" at about age 50, are offered and accept positions as executives of Japan's leading private corporations (see AMAKU-DARI).

Many (often the most influential) of Japan's postwar politicians have come to office from prior careers as high bureaucrats in the ministries. Of the 15 postwar prime ministers through SUZUKI ZENKŌ, 7 were former officials. However, only one of them, KISHI NOBUSUKE, was a former trade and industry career bureaucrat. Kishi was vice-minister of commerce and industry from October 1939 to January 1941, minister of commerce and industry from October 1941 to October 1943, and vice-minister of munitions from October 1943 to July 1944. MITI's only other major representative in the postwar political world was Shiina Etsusaburō (1898–1979), vice-minister of commerce and industry from October 1941 to October 1943 and from August 1945 to October 1945, and vice-minister of munitions from April 1945 to August 1945.

Another aspect of MITI's power is the influence that its officials exercise over other ministries and agencies of the government. MITI sends more officials abroad to serve in missions and legations than any other governmental agency except the Ministry of Foreign Affairs. It also controls and staffs the Japan External Trade Organization (JETRO), a worldwide trade promotion and commercial information service. MITI has authority over the largest number (27) of the numerous public corporations and mixed public-private enterprises of the Japanese government, including the Japan Petroleum Development Corporation, the ELECTRIC POWER DEVELOPMENT CO, LTD, and the SMALL BUSINESS FINANCE CORPORATION. It sends many of its senior officials on temporary duty to the DEFENSE AGENCY, SCIENCE AND TECHNOLOGY AGENCY, and Economic Planning Agency; and it totally controls the Natural Resources and Energy Agency, the Small and Medium Enterprise Agency, and the Patent Office as semidetached organs of its home office. MITI also sponsors and controls over 20 civilian advisory commissions (shingikai), including the prestigious INDUSTRIAL STRUCTURE COUNCIL. These advisory commissions are an important organizational channel through which MITI communicates its plans and policies to the private sector and receives in turn the views of industrial leaders.

MITI exemplifies Japan's unusual capability for providing governmental assistance and leadership to a market economy while also maintaining a high degree of competition and a strong private enterprise system, and avoiding the worst excesses of bureaucratism. Given Japan's dearth of natural resources, its dependence on foreign trade, and its highly industrialized economy, MITI performs func-

tions of importance to Japan closer to those of a ministry of national defense than to those of a purely commercial agency.

MITI consists of the Natural Resources and Energy Agency, the Patent Office, the Small and Medium Enterprise Agency, and the following bureaus: the minister's secretariat, international trade policy, international trade administration, industrial policy, industrial location and environmental protection, basic industries, machine and information industries, and consumer goods industries.

■——Chalmers Johnson, "MITI and Japanese International Economic Policy," in Robert Scalapino, ed, *The Foreign Policy of Modern Japan* (1977). Sangyō Seisaku Kenkyūjo, ed, *Tsūsanshō nijūnen gaishi* (1970). Seisaku Jihō Sha, ed, *Tsūsanshō* (1968). US Department of Commerce, *Japan: The Government-Business Relationship* (1972). *Chalmers JOHNSON*

Ministry of Justice

(Hōmushō). Government ministry in charge of administering Japan's legal system and of handling legal matters of the state. Its major responsibilities include the drafting of laws and ordinances relating to the judicial system, administration of the penal system, and the rehabilitation of criminals. It administers civil matters like the registration of families, aliens, corporations, and real estate. It represents the Japanese government in litigation, and it is charged with the protection of civil liberties.

Public prosecutor's offices (kensatsuchō) administratively belong to the Ministry of Justice. The public prosecutor, however, acts independently of the minister of justice. Only in very rare cases does the minister give orders to the public prosecutor general.

Also under the jurisdiction of the ministry are the Admission Commission of the National Bar Examination, the Public Security Examination Commission, and the PUBLIC SECURITY INVESTIGATION AGENCY.

Ministry of Labor

(Rōdōshō). Ministry of the national government responsible for the administration and implementation of the government's labor policy on national and local levels. One of its major functions is the dispersal of unemployment compensation and workmen's accident compensation. It is also involved in numerous employment and vocational training programs and is responsible for the formation and supervision of labor standards and wage guidelines and for the improvement of working conditions for women and minorities. Two important commissions are attached to the Ministry of Labor; the CENTRAL LABOR RELATIONS COMMISSION (Chūō Rōdō Iinkai; Chūrōi) mediates or arbitrates labor disputes in private industry, and the Public Corporation and National Enterprise Labor Relations Commission (Kōkyō Kigyōtai Tō Rōdō Iinkai; Kōrōi) mediates or arbitrates disputes in public corporations.

Established in 1947, the ministry is headed by a cabinet minister appointed by the prime minister.

Ministry of Posts and Telecommunications

(Yūseishō). Ministry of the national government which supervises Japan's approximately 20,000 post offices and its entire mail service system. It also administers the postal savings, life insurance, and pension programs offered by the post offices. The ministry controls licensing of radio and television broadcasting and exerts some limited, indirect control over the NIPPON TELEGRAPH AND TELEPHONE PUBLIC CORPORATION (NTT) and the International Telegram and Telephone Company (KOKUSAI DENSHIN DENWA CO, LTD; KDD).

Ministry of Transport

(Un'yushō). Ministry of the national government responsible for administering and supervising all forms of transportation in Japan and formulating national land, sea, and aviation policies (see TRANSPORTATION). Among its many functions, the ministry is responsible for the regulation and supervision of the shipping and motor transportation industries, the administration of all ports and harbors, inspection and registration of ships, road vehicles, and aircraft, the formulation of contracts for road construction, and the supervision of the JAPANESE NATIONAL RAILWAYS and JAPAN AIR LINES CO, LTD, both public corporations. As part of its supervision of the Ship Bureau, the ministry grants licenses for ship construction and subsi-

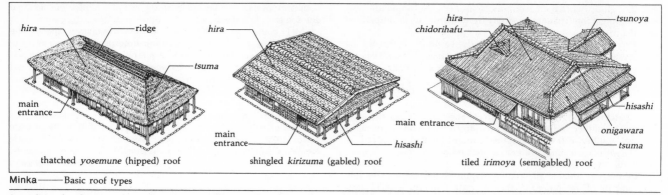

hira——ridge
hira
tsuma
main entrance

thatched *yosemune* (hipped) roof

hira
main entrance
hisashi

shingled *kirizuma* (gabled) roof

hira
chidorihafu
tsunoya
hisashi
onigawara
tsuma
main entrance

tiled *irimoya* (semigabled) roof

Minka——Basic roof types

In traditional architecture the term *hira* ("flat and broad") denotes the roof plane that runs parallel to the ridgepole, and *tsuma* ("end") denotes a sloping end roof. The term *kirizuma* ("without *tsuma*") refers to a gabled roof. *Minka* are usually constructed with a *hisashi,* a pent roof which forms a porchlike area along one or more sides of the building.

dizes the construction of ships. Its Maritime Safety Agency (Kaijō Hoan Chō) has police powers to deal with criminal activities in coastal waters and is responsible for the maintenance of facilities for safeguarding navigation and assisting ships in distress. The ministry's marine accidents inquiry agencies *(kainan shimpan chō)* investigate and judge sea casualty cases. The ministry also supervises the METEOROLOGICAL AGENCY of Japan, which is responsible for the collection and dissemination of information about and the observation and forecasting of all meteorological, terrestrial, and hydrological phenomena.

Initially established in 1920, the ministry is headed by a cabinet minister appointed by the prime minister.   *Daniel A.* METRAUX

minka

General name for traditional-style houses of the nonruling classes, usually dwellings of rather simple construction, that were built before Japanese architecture came under Western influence in the late 1800s.

Types and Construction Materials——*Minka* in farming villages differ from those in cities in both plan and method of construction. The former are called *nōka* (farmhouses) and the latter *machiya* (townhouses). A further distinction is made for the houses of fishing villages, *gyoka.* The houses of lower ranking members of the *samurai* or warrior class are also sometimes included in the *minka* category.

Minka were traditionally made of readily available materials, wood being the most easily obtainable and widely used. Wood was used in the thick columns and beams of the framework, as well as for the walls, floor and ceiling, and for the roof. Bamboo, grass, and clay were also traditionally important building materials. Bamboo was layered between columns as laths and plastered over with clay to form walls. Grass was used to make thatch for roofing, and straw for the coarse, thin *mushiro* matting and TATAMI mats to be used on the floor. Clay was also baked into ROOF TILES. Rock was used to lay stone foundations for support but was not employed for walls.

Design Characteristics——*Minka* differed considerably in style depending on the period or region in which they were built. There are, however, certain general design features which transcend the differences of period and region. Basic among these are the following. The skeletal framework of the typical *minka* was composed of a number of interconnecting frames, consisting of joined columns and beams. The walls were merely fitted between the columns and were not load bearing. Since these intervals between columns did not need to be load bearing, wide openings could be created. On the outdoor or exterior side of the house, these openings were closed by a set of sliding inner lattice doors known as *shōji* and an outer set of heavy wooden doors. Inside, the interval between columns was partitioned by paneled doors or lattice doors covered with heavy paper *(fusuma).* Such doors used to close off the openings are collectively called *tategu.* The interior of the house was divided into an area called the *doma,* which had a compacted earthen floor, and an area with the floor raised about 50 centimeters (20 in) off the ground. People sat directly on the raised floor, which was usually covered with *tatami* or *mushiro* mats. For cooking, a furnace-like oven (KA-MADO) built of clay was installed in the *doma.* In the floored area

Minka

A farmhouse in Shirakawa, Gifu Prefecture. The steeply pitched roof and multistoried construction are typical of the style called *gasshō-zukuri.*

was located an open hearth *(irori)* for burning firewood for heat but no chimney was provided.

Roof Forms——Since most of Japan lies within the temperate zone and has heavy rainfall, the roofs of the *minka* are steeply pitched. These roofs are classified as thatched roof *(kayabuki yane),* shingle roof *(itabuki yane)* or tile roof *(kawarabuki yane).* Because stones are sometimes used to keep the shingles from being blown away, this type of shingle roof is also called *ishioki yane* (stone-laid roof). Roofs also differ in their shape, of which there are three basic types. The first is the simplest in which planes slant down on two sides from a central ridge *(mune),* and is called a *kirizuma* (gabled) roof. The second type in which planes slant down to the four sides of a rectangular building is called a *yosemune* (hipped) roof. The third is an intermediate form between the *kirizuma* and *yosemune*— gables are attached to a roof with four slanting planes—and is called the *irimoya* (semigabled) roof. The roof of a farmhouse is usually thatched and in either *irimoya* or *yosemune* style, while many townhouses have tile roofs in a *kirizuma* style. Some *minka* have more ornate roofs that are composites of the three basic styles.

A special treatment is required where the slanting planes of the roof come together; in the *minka* such places are used for decorations. In a tile roof, tiles are also placed on the ridge, but the ends are decorated with *onigawara* (ridge end tile with a gargoyle-like design). With thatched roofs, care must be taken to prevent the ridge cover from blowing away, and here too ridge decorations *(munekazari)* are provided. In tile-roofed buildings or in *minka* built where there is heavy snowfall, a hole is made and a smoke vent is built into the roof. The smoke vent may have either a small monitor roof *(koshi yane)* over the ridge or a dormer gable *(chidorihafu);* in either case, it serves to ornament the otherwise simple roof surface.

Farmhouses——The arrangement of rooms in Japanese houses is called *madori.* In the standard layout of early-19th-century farmhouses, four rooms were next to the *doma;* this was called a *yoma-dori* (four-room arrangement). There was a large sliding plank door

Minka

Interior of a 17th-century lumber dealer's house in the town of Imai, Nara Prefecture. A shop with living quarters, this house has a work area with an earthen floor (the *doma*) and raised *tatami*-floored rooms beyond. The *kamado* in the foreground contains a rice kettle with a wooden cover.

Minka

An example of a *magariya*, an L-shaped farmhouse in which one of the wings (the left one here) is a stable. Tōno, Iwate Prefecture.

called the *ōdo* giving access to the *doma* and serving as the front entrance for the building. The *doma*, which took up a third of the total floor area, was used for farming tasks and cooking. For these purposes, an earthen oven and a sink made of wood were located to the rear of the *doma*. Water was carried in from a well outside and was kept in a jar. A corner of the *doma* was also used to store foodstuffs kept in barrels. There were four rooms next to the *doma* but there was no corridor; one went through one room to get to another. This was facilitated by the intermediate partitions which were either sliding plank doors or *fusuma*.

Of the four rooms, the two closest to the *doma* were used for daily activities by the family. The room to the rear had a hearth made of hardened clay in the floor about 1 square meter (11 sq ft) in size. Here firewood was burned for warmth and light. A lamp wick in a dish of oil was also used for light, but because oil was expensive this was not generally used in *minka*. The entire family gathered around the hearth, particularly at mealtimes, and the seating arrangement was socially determined. The side furthest from the *doma*, called the *yokoza*, was where the head of the household sat. Of the two sides adjacent to the *yokoza*, the side to the rear of the house was occupied by the housewife, as this was close to the sink and convenient for performing housework duties. Other female members of the family also sat here. The other side adjacent to the *yokoza*, close to the entrance, was given to an intimate visitor or, when there was no visitor, to the male family members. The fourth side, next to the *doma*, was used for piling firewood.

The room behind the *yokoza* was called the *nando* or *nema*, and in the past the family slept in this narrow, dark space; when quilts (*futon*) came to be used for BEDDING, the room to the front was also

used for sleeping. A decorative alcove (*tokonoma*) for displaying a picture or flowers was built in this front room, which was used for receiving guests on more formal occasions; this room was called the *zashiki* or *dei*. Outside this front room was a long narrow veranda (*engawa*) which was used for enjoying the breeze in summer and the sun in winter. The latrine and bath were often built as separate buildings or as lean-tos under the eaves.

Townhouses——Because the width of an urban site was limited, townhouses tended to have deep, rectangular plans. Behind the main building (*omoya*) stood the storehouse (*kura* or *dozō*; see STOREHOUSES, TRADITIONAL) or a detached *zashiki*, and to provide direct access to these the *doma* penetrated to the backyard. Along this *doma* was a row of three rooms. The one closest to the road was called *mise*, and here goods were displayed or business talks held. The middle room was used by the head of the household as an office and also as a place where the family could receive visitors. The rear room faced an enclosed garden; this was built like a *zashiki*, complete with *tokonoma*, but was actually used for the daily activities of the family. In a large house on a wide site, there were sometimes two rows of rooms.

In many cases there was a second floor. The second-floor portion, generally called *zushi*, had a low ceiling on the road side and this area was used as storage; the side facing the backyard was used as a room. The entrance to the *doma* was a plank door called *ōdo* which could be slid open or suspended from above. A smaller door (*nakakuguri*) which was used when the shop was closed was often built into the *ōdo*. The front of the first floor had panels called *shitomido*, a fixed grill which could also be turned up. There were many types of grill—varied in the thickness of members and in their spacing—and an interesting composition could be created from different types. In western Japan, the columns in the second-floor wall were often completely covered by the wall surface in a style called *ōkabe-zukuri*; often there was a grill window provided in the wall. East of Kyōto, the columns often showed on the second floor wall in a style called *shinkabe-zukuri*. A small side wall (*sodekabe*) built between the first floor eaves and the second floor roof is commonly found in townhouses throughout Japan.

Differences in Design——At first *minka* were of a style called *tate-ana jūkyo*, a rude structure of thatched roof over an oval depression of some 50 centimeters (20 in) dug in the ground. The Japanese *minka* as we know it developed from the end of the 16th century to the beginning of the 17th century. About half of the farmhouse in this period was occupied by the *doma*, and the floored area was composed of three rooms; this is called the *sammadori* (three-room arrangement) or *hiromagata* style. Nearly all activities from daily chores to receiving formal guests took place in a broad space with a hearth next to the *doma*. At night, the family slept without any special bedding in the narrow *nando* located behind the *yokoza*. The *nando* had only a small entrance on the *yokoza* side and was very much closed off. The other room had few openings to the outside, and overall the building was a very closed structure. The *minka* eventually changed from this three-room arrangement to the four-room arrangement.

In southern Kyūshū and in some places in Honshū along the Pacific coast, there is a type of *minka* called the divided-roof type (*buntō-gata*); although the entire house has a rectangular plan, the *doma* and the floored area have separate roofs. The ridges are perpendicular to each other; where the *doma* and the floored area meet, there is a large gutter above to catch the rain and lead it outside. In the Amami Islands, south of Kyūshū, the house is made up of a collection of separate buildings, each with a different function, such as *omoya* (main building), kitchen, storage, and livestock pen.

In certain areas in Ehime Prefecture, Hyōgo Prefecture, and the Kantō region, there are many houses with floors made of bamboo, over which are spread thick mats. Before the longitudinal saw came to be commonly used, the only way to produce boards was by splitting wood, a difficult and time-consuming process. Thus floors of bamboo were often used as a substitute.

In the villages of Shirakawa in Gifu Prefecture and Gokayama in Toyama Prefecture are found many *minka* with steeply pitched but commodious roofs in the style called *gasshō-zukuri*. The space under the roof was used to accommodate several levels of shelves for silkworms.

In areas such as Akita and Iwate prefectures with heavy snowfall, an overhang called *tsunoya* is built in front of the *doma* to facilitate getting in and out of the house and to shelter a cow or horse. In Akita Prefecture, the ridge of this projection meets the slanting plane of the main roof, and in Iwate Prefecture it is continuous with the ridge of the main roof; the former is called *chūmon-zukuri* and the latter *magariya*. The *tsunoya* is used for storage and as a stable.

The style of townhouses also differs in eastern and western Japan. In western Japan the roof is tiled, and the second floor and both ends are covered with clay and finished with plaster. This is called an *ōkabe* style wall. Old townhouses built in this style may be seen in the town of Imaichō in Nara Prefecture. In eastern Japan, the roof is shingled, and the wall is often a *shinkabe*, i.e., the columns are left exposed. In large cities like Edo (now Tōkyō), however, fires were frequent, so the outside of the building came to be covered with a heavy coating of clay, just as in storehouses (*dozō*). The townhouses that survive in Kawagoe in Saitama Prefecture are of this type, which in this case is specially called *dozō-zukuri*.

Preservation —— Old *minka* are greatly diminished in number. Representative buildings have been classified by the government as Important Cultural Properties (see NATIONAL TREASURES) and are given special care. There are also places throughout Japan where old *minka* have been collected and are on display, among them Nihon Minkaen in the city of Kawasaki, Kanagawa Prefecture; Hida Minzoku Mura in the city of Takayama, Gifu Prefecture; Hyakumangoku Bunkaen Edo Mura in the city of Kanazawa, Ishikawa Prefecture; Nihon Minka Shūraku Hakubutsukan in the city of Toyonaka, Ōsaka; and Shikoku Minka Hakubutsukan in the city of Takamatsu, Kagawa Prefecture.

■ ——Futagawa Yukio and Itō Teiji, *Nihon no minka* (1957–59). Itō Teiji, *Minka* (1970). Kawashima Chūji, *Horobiyuku minka* (1973). Kon Wajirō, *Minka* (1959). Nihon Kenchiku Kyōkai, ed, *Furusato no sumai* (1962). Ōta Hirotarō, *Minka no mikata shirabekata* (1967). Sugimoto Shōji, *Nihon minka no kenkyū* (1969). Suzuki Mitsuru, *Minka* (1975). *Suzuki Mitsuru*

Minkan denshō

(Oral Folklore). Journal for the study of folklore and ethnology. At a conference of Japanese ethnologists held in 1935 to commemorate the 60th birthday of the noted scholar and folklorist YANAGITA KUNIO, it was decided to found a society that would act as a national coordinating organ for the field. In September of the same year, the society, called Minkan Denshō no Kai, put out the first issue of its organ, *Minkan denshō*. Small in format, it published reports on materials and sources relating to folklore studies, correspondence from various groups, and reviews. The format was later enlarged to include papers. The journal ceased publication in 1952, but was immediately followed by *Nihon minzokugaku* (Bulletin of the Folklore Society of Japan), the journal of the Nihon Minzoku Gakkai. Another publication by the same name, *Minkan denshō*, has been put out by the Minkan Denshō Shiyūkai. *Ōtō Tokihiko*

Mino

City in southern Gifu Prefecture, central Honshū, on the river Nagaragawa. In 1606 Mino became a castle town of the Kanamori family. It has long been known for its Mino *washi* paper, the production techniques of which have been designated a National Treasure by the government. Mino is also a center for machine-made paper. Pop: 26,825.

mino → straw raincoats

Minobe Ryōkichi (1904–   )

Economist and politician. Born in Tōkyō, the son of the jurist MINOBE TATSUKICHI. After graduating from Tōkyō University, where he became interested in Marxian economics under ŌUCHI HYŌE, he taught at Hōsei University. He was arrested in 1938, along with other suspected leftists in the so-called POPULAR FRONT INCIDENT, and was removed from the university by the government. After World War II he became a professor at the Tōkyō University of Education. He was elected governor of Tōkyō Prefecture in 1967 with the support of the socialist and communist parties. He was elected again in 1971 and 1975. As governor, Minobe stressed social welfare and opposed the government's emphasis on rapid economic growth. After retiring from the governorship, he was elected to the House of Councillors in 1980.

Minobe Tatsukichi (1873–1948)

Scholar of constitutional and administrative law. Born in Hyōgo Prefecture, he graduated from Tōkyō University in 1897 and entered the Home Ministry. From 1899 to 1902 he studied abroad, principally in Germany, and on his return became a professor at his alma mater, first in administrative law and the history of the Japanese legal system and later in constitutional law. Minobe opposed the ultraconservative constitutional theories of HOZUMI YATSUKA and the latter's follower UESUGI SHINKICHI; he became known as a champion of democratic constitutionalism, advocating the "emperor-as-organ-of-the-state" theory (TENNŌ KIKAN SETSU), party cabinets, and the expansion of civil liberties. His views were influential in academic and official circles, for he was a member of the committee for the higher civil service examination. Minobe was appointed to the House of Peers in 1932, but his opposition to the repressive PEACE PRESERVATION LAW OF 1925 and his support of the ratification of the 1930 arms reduction treaty resulting from the LONDON NAVAL CONFERENCES incurred hostile criticism from right-wing forces. In 1935 he was charged with lese majesty for expounding the emperor-as-organ theory, which was considered subversive of the national polity (KOKUTAI); he was forced to resign from the House of Peers, and some of his works were withdrawn from publication. His many writings include KEMPŌ SATSUYŌ (1923, Outline of the Constitution) and *Nihonkoku kempō genron* (1946, Principles of the Japanese Constitution). He was the father of MINOBE RYŌKICHI. *Nagao Ryūichi*

Minobu

Town in southwestern Yamanashi Prefecture, central Honshū, on the river Fujikawa. Minobu developed as a temple town around Kuonji (see MINOBUSAN), the head temple of the Nichiren sect. The town is visited year-round by pilgrims and tourists. Its principal industry is lumber. Pop: 9,807.

Minobusan

The head temple of the NICHIREN SECT of Buddhism, located in Minami Koma District, Yamanashi Prefecture. Minobusan, the official name of which is Kuonji, was built in 1281 by Hakii Sanenaga, a lay follower of NICHIREN (1222–82), on the site of a small hermitage that Nichiren occupied after he returned from exile in 1274. After Nichiren's death in Ikegami in Edo (now Tōkyō), his remains were brought here for burial. The temple was supported by the Takeda family, who as *daimyō* controlled the region until the end of the 16th century, and subsequently by the Tokugawa family. In 1706 it was designated a *chokuganji*, i.e., a temple commissioned by the imperial family to offer prayers regularly for their well-being as well as for the prosperity of the empire. Much of Kuonji was destroyed in a fire in 1875, but it has since been rebuilt. *Stanley Weinstein*

Mino Kamo

City in southern Gifu Prefecture, central Honshū, on the river Kisogawa. In the Edo period (1600–1868) it flourished as a river port and POST-STATION TOWN on the highway Nakasendō. Electrical appliances and textile plants are located here. Local produce includes persimmons and pears. It is the starting point for shooting the rapids of the Kisogawa, popularly known as the "Japan Rhine." Pop: 39,532.

Minolta Camera Co, Ltd

Manufacturer and distributor of optical products and business machines, primarily cameras and copying machines. Its Minolta brand name is well known internationally. It is one of the few optical goods manufacturers in the world to produce lenses from raw materials to the finished product. Founded in 1937, it assumed the present company name in 1962. The company expanded into overseas markets with photographic products soon after World War II. Overseas subsidiaries include two in the United States, five in Europe, and three in Southeast Asia. The company is engaged in international cooperation with E. Leitz Wetzlar GmbH of West Germany. Important goals include new product development and further expansion in the field of business machines. Sales for the fiscal year ending March 1982 totaled ¥132.3 billion (US $549.6 million), of which photographic goods accounted for 52 percent and business machines 48 percent. For the same year the export ratio was 83 percent and the company was capitalized at ¥5.9 billion (US $24.5 million). The head office is in Ōsaka.

Minomura Rizaemon (1821–1877)

Businessman. Builder of the MITSUI financial empire. Born in Shinano Province (now Nagano Prefecture), he worked for a cooking and lamp oil wholesaler in Edo (now Tōkyō), where he came to the attention of OGURI TADAMASA, commissioner of finance ·(kanjō bugyō) in the Tokugawa shogunate. Through Oguri's good offices, Rizaemon was adopted as heir by the Minomura family, chief clerks of the Mitsui family business. During the BOSHIN CIVIL WAR, at the time of the Meiji Restoration (1868), Minomura persuaded the Mitsui family to contribute funds to the imperial forces and, after the Restoration, sought preferential treatment for Mitsui by the new government in the form of lucrative commissions and other advantages (see SEISHŌ). As Mitsui's top manager, he helped to establish the Mitsui Bank and Mitsui Trading Company, two enterprises that eventually formed the core of the Mitsui ZAIBATSU.

Minoo

City in northwestern Ōsaka Prefecture; 16 km (10 mi) north of Ōsaka, of which it is fast becoming a residential suburb. Its northern section is part of the Meiji no Mori Minoo Quasi-National Park, which contains the TŌKAI SHIZEN HODŌ (a hiking trail), Minoo Park, the temple Ryōanji, and Minoo Falls. Pop: 104,113.

Mino Province

Also called Nōshū. One of the eight provinces (kuni) of the Tōsandō region in central Honshū. With the establishment of the prefectural system in 1871 it became part of GIFU PREFECTURE. In the middle years of the Heian period (794–1185), members of the MINAMOTO FAMILY settled here; their descendants, the TOKI FAMILY, ruled Mino as military governors (SHUGO) for 11 generations in the late part of the Muromachi period (1333–1568). In 1567 ODA NOBUNAGA seized Gifu Castle and took control of the area. Intersected by major highways and strategically situated close to the capital of Kyōto, Mino Province was repeatedly a battleground in civil wars. The Battle of SEKIGAHARA in 1600, which made way for the TOKUGAWA FAMILY to rule Japan for 250 years, was the most famous of these. The area was known for its production of pottery (MINO WARE) and rice paper (Mino paper), both of which are still among the main industries of Gifu Prefecture.

minorities

Although racially, culturally, and ethnically, the Japanese are one of the most homogeneous peoples of the world, there are minority groups such as the BURAKUMIN, AINU, Koreans, Okinawans, and Chinese.

The largest minority group in Japan today consists of the approximately 2 to 3 million burakumin (descendants of outcasts), who live in some 5,000 ghettos (dōwa chiku, literally, "integration districts") located throughout the nation, not including Hokkaidō. Countless thousands of "passing" burakumin live in large urban areas, although there is always the possibility that their background will be revealed when personal investigations are conducted prior to marriage or employment. Such organizations as Buraku Kaihō Dōmei (Buraku Liberation League) and the Zenkoku Dōwa Kyōiku Kenkyū Kyōgikai (National Research Council for Integration Education) are actively engaged in eradicating discrimination.

The ancestors of another minority group, the Ainu, a proto-Caucasoid group who possessed a Neolithic culture, migrated to Japan during prehistoric times. Over the centuries many Ainu intermingled with and married newer immigrants from the Asian continent, but they remained an ethnic group. In the more recent past, the Ainu were confined to the islands of Hokkaidō, southern Sakhalin, and the Kurils. The most numerous of these three groups were the Hokkaidō Ainu, who were primarily hunters and fishermen. They were eventually encouraged by the Japanese government to take up farming, but many who were not accustomed to agricultural management failed, and they lost much of their land. Today (1979), the Ainu, who number 24,160, are economically among the poorest groups in Japan, and unemployment remains high. While blatant discrimination against the Ainu has waned and many of the younger generation are being assimilated into the general population, the Ainu tradition is continued in some villages through the use of the Ainu language, food and clothing, and the observance of traditional festivals. The Ainu Society established in 1931, has been renamed the Utari Association, and it continues to bolster morale among its members.

The Korean minority, according to 1981 alien registration statistics, has a population of 667,325, or 84.2 percent of the resident foreigners who are required to register with the government every three years. A large proportion of the Koreans live in the Kinki (Kyōto–Ōsaka) region, especially in Ōsaka. Koreans are subject to discrimination in housing, employment, marriage, and education. While most Korean students attend public schools, in many prefectures there are special schools for Koreans ranging from nursery through high school, and there is one college in Tōkyō with some 1,200 students. See KOREANS IN JAPAN.

The people of OKINAWA first came into contact with the Japanese when the Ryūkyū Islands were invaded in the early 17th century by the Shimazu, rulers of the Satsuma domain (now Kagoshima Prefecture) in Kyūshū. A number of Okinawans were brought to the shogunal capital of Edo (now Tōkyō) and were made to parade in Chinese dress, in part because the Ryūkyū Islands had been a tributary of China. Because of the distance from the mainland, and because the people spoke a variant form of Japanese, Okinawans were considered second-class citizens. Following World War II, Okinawa was occupied by the United States. The continued occupation, even after the signing of the peace treaty, and the huge military bases were not well received by the people. Most Okinawans were glad when the Ryūkyū Islands reverted to Japan's jurisdiction in 1972. Okinawa became a prefecture in 1979. The minority status of the Okinawans continues, as attested to by their lower educational level, lower income, and higher unemployment rate as compared with the national average.

More than 55,000 Chinese live in Japan, according to 1981 statistics. In contrast to other minorities, a substantial proportion of the Chinese are wealthy merchants and owners of restaurants. There are few predominantly Chinese residential areas, the thriving Chinatown in Yokohama being the exception.

MURAKOSHI Sueo and I. Roger YOSHINO

minority rights

The 1947 CONSTITUTION of Japan provides for equality under the law and prohibits discrimination in political, economic, or social relations because of race, creed, sex, social status, or family origin (art. 14). Despite these provisions, minority groups in Japan (which comprise about 4 percent of the population) continue to face varying degrees of discrimination in employment, housing, marriage, and education. These minority groups include children of interracial ancestry, the handicapped, the BURAKUMIN, Okinawans, AINU, Koreans, Chinese, and other foreign residents.

Japan's system of HOUSEHOLD REGISTERS (koseki) has been one contributing factor in the continued de facto discrimination against Burakumin and other minorities. Employers and others have had the right to obtain a copy of a person's family register; the family register will indicate where the person's family is originally from, and with that information one can usually determine the social or racial origins of the person. Efforts have been made in recent years to eliminate this practice. In 1969 the Special Measures for Assimilation Law (Dōwa Taisaku Jigyō Tokubetsu Sochi Hō) was passed; and in 1976 the Family Register Law (Koseki Hō) was amended to allow the mayor of a city or the head of a town or village to refuse a request for a copy of the family register when "it was clearly made on unjustifiable grounds."

Efforts have also been made to eliminate discrimination against the handicapped. In 1960 the Promotion of the Employment of the Handicapped Law (Shintai Shōgaisha Koyō Sokushin Hō) was passed. This law set standards for private industry (1.3 percent of its workforce) and the government (1.7 percent of its workforce) pertaining to the employment of the handicapped. Incentives, monetary and otherwise, were provided for companies meeting the standard. The law lacks bite, however, since no penalties are set for those not meeting the standard; such penalties are now under consideration.

Foreigners face some legal discrimination as well as de facto social discrimination. Immigration laws, for example, are highly restrictive. There are also certain professions, besides the national civil service, which are not open to foreigners.

Japanese women, although not a minority, face discrimination as well. As of 1977, the average female worker earned ¥141,664 (US $528) per month, and the average male worker earned ¥253,698 (US $945). Many companies have also set an earlier mandatory retirement age for women or forced them to retire when they had children; however, recent court rulings have declared such practices void (see EQUALITY OF THE SEXES UNDER THE LAW). Furthermore, since Japanese citizenship is patrilinear, women married to foreigners are unable to pass on their Japanese citizenship to their children. This issue and many others concerning discrimination are now being contested in the courts. See also MINORITIES.

Inger-Johanne HOLMBOE

Minor Offenses Law

(Keihanzai Hō). This law, enacted in 1947, specifies 34 minor crimes that are subject to the comparatively light punishment of detention (1–30 days) or a petty fine (¥20–4,000). Types of crime include: (1) Crimes nearly identical to those already specified in the Police Offenses Penal Regulations (Keisatsukan Shobatsu Rei) and the Law of Summary Procedures for Police Offenses (Ikeizai Sokketsu Rei). For example, the law specifies such crimes as the following: concealing oneself in a vacant house without good cause; carrying a dangerous instrument in a concealed fashion; vagrancy; begging or causing another to beg; and mischievously interfering with another person's business. (2) Offenses newly created by the Minor Offenses Law include: peering into places such as public baths; playing music at an inordinately loud volume so as to disturb others; and causing a disturbance in places of public entertainment or on public transportation facilities.

The Police Offenses Penal Regulations were occasionally abused in their use as a method of suppressing mass movements, such as the farm and labor movements, and as an expedient in the investigation of crimes. The Law of Summary Procedures for Police Offenses, which existed as a law of procedure for dealing with these offenses, had created a set of simplified procedures that did not give sufficient consideration to the human rights of suspects and defendants. In light of these facts, the Police Offenses Penal Regulations and the Law of Summary Procedures for Police Offenses were both abolished, and the Minor Offenses Law was established, providing for disposition of these cases following the procedures specified in the Code of CRIMINAL PROCEDURE. Article 4 of this law provides that "in applications of this law, consideration must be given to avoiding improper encroachments upon the rights of the people, and there must not be abuses of this law which deviate from the original purpose of this law and use it for another purpose."

Sawanobori TOSHIO

minoue sōdan

Personal advice columns in newspapers and women's magazines in the form of requests from readers and responses by specialists, scholars, and others. The first such column in Japan appeared in the magazine *Jogaku zasshi* in 1886. The first column permanently established in a daily newspaper was in the *Yomiuri shimbun* in 1914. Those requesting advice through such columns have been predominantly female. During World War II personal advice columns disappeared, but in the postwar period they have become popular again. Since the end of the war, there has been a tendency for requests for advice to be selected for their interest as reading matter, with correspondingly entertaining replies. In recent years, personal advice programs have become a prominent part of Japanese television.

Tsuchida MITSUFUMI

Mino ware

(mino-yaki). Ceramics produced in Mino Province (now Gifu Prefecture). Although the Mino area has had a long ceramic tradition that may be traced from SUE WARE, it was during the Azuchi–Momoyama period (1568–1600) that the famous ceramic styles preferred for the TEA CEREMONY, such as Shino, *kiseto, setoguro,* Oribe, and *temmoku,* came into prominence there.

Mino Province shared a border with Owari Province (now Aichi Prefecture), which included the city of SETO, the site of the most famous ceramics center in eastern Japan. The development of ceramics in the two provinces showed a similar pattern until the mid-

dle of the 16th century. The early Sue ware was followed by ash-glazed wares in the Heian period (794–1185), a similar but somewhat inferior quality utilitarian ware (YAMACHAWAN) in the medieval period, and Chinese Song (Sung; 960–1279) style glazed pottery in the late 14th and 15th centuries. The distribution of Mino ceramics, however, was controlled by the neighboring Owari Province, whose local authorities banned the use of the term Mino. Consequently, prior to the Meiji Restoration (1868), no distinction was made between the wares of the two provinces, which were all known as SETO WARE.

Tradition has it that the national unifier ODA NOBUNAGA, then lord of Owari, annexed Mino Province in 1567 and began patronizing Mino-ware production for the tea ceremony. Recent excavations, however, have yielded Mino ware of an earlier date that resembles the later tea wares.

It was in the early 16th century, when fine tea-ceremony ware was being made, that the rather inefficient single-chamber subterranean kiln known as the *anagama* was replaced by the larger semisubterranean *ōgama* kiln.

An opaque, white ash glaze, used to produce white *temmoku* teabowls, was the forerunner of the nearly pure feldspathic Shino glaze, the first white glaze in Japan. Under its irregular application on such vessels as teabowls and water jars are simple iron-oxide painted decorations ranging from a reddish brown to a very dark brown. Gray and red Shino glazes were also developed, depending on the coloration of the iron slip. *Kiseto* (Yellow Seto) is either plain or decorated with incisions and copper green underglaze designs. *Setoguro* (Black Seto) is produced by removing the fired pieces from the kiln and cooling them immediately. Production of these types reached its height in the closing decades of the 16th century in the kilns located in the hills of Ōhira and Ōgaya.

Near the end of the 16th century, production was revolutionized by the multichambered climbing kiln (*noborigama*), which was introduced into Mino from Karatsu, Kyūshū. In the next decades, intensive activity at the Motoyashiki kiln saw the peak production of so-called Oribe ware (see FURUTA ORIBE), although this type had actually appeared earlier, in small quantities, at the semisubterranean kilns. Oribe ware is characterized by unconstrained application of green glaze along with feldspathic glaze and by a wide variety of shapes and painted decoration. Many Oribe and *kiseto* pieces consisted of dishes made for use in the *chakaiseki* meal, a part of the tea ceremony, or were teabowls and other utensils for the tea ceremony.

A few potters revived the production of Oribe ware late in the Edo period (1600–1868). In 1930 ARAKAWA TOYOZŌ discovered the Mino kiln sites and was later instrumental in launching the 20th-century revival of Shino ware. For this work he was designated one of Japan's LIVING NATIONAL TREASURES in 1955.

Yoshiko KAKUDŌ

Min, Queen (1851–1895)

Consort of the Korean king KOJONG (1852–1919; r 1864–1907), 26th ruler of the YI DYNASTY, whom she married in May 1866. "Min," though it is often so used in English, was not actually her personal name, but that of her clan; hence she was "the Min Queen" (Kor: Min Bi; J: Bin Hi). Although a member of the same lineage as the king's mother, Min was a political rival of his father, the prince regent (TAEWŎN'GUN) and is thought to have been responsible for appointing many of her relatives to government office between 1875 and 1894. She also competed with the Taewŏn'gun to manipulate the king. The Japanese officials who directed the modernizing KABO REFORM concluded that her removal was essential to secure control of the king and the success of the reforms. The minister to Korea, MIURA GORŌ, took matters into his own hands; on 8 October 1895 he sent a Japanese military party to enter the palace and murder the queen, which they did.

Miura and his henchmen were tried before a military court in Tōkyō and punished, but Japan's influence in Korea swiftly evaporated. Enraged Koreans formed "Righteous Army" units that assaulted pro-Japanese Korean officials and attacked Japanese military units. Russia led other nations in protesting the assassination and provided protection for Kojong when he fled to its legation in Seoul in February 1896. In order to defuse the crisis, the new Japanese minister to Korea, KOMURA JUTARŌ, met with his Russian counterpart, Karl I. Vaeber. The Komura–Vaeber Memorandum, signed in Seoul on 14 May 1896, committed both countries to ensuring the safety of the king and permitted the stationing of Japanese troops in Korea to protect Japanese property. The memorandum formed the basis for the YAMAGATA–LOBANOV AGREEMENT signed in Moscow the following month and marked the Russian ascent to a dominance of Korean affairs that lasted until the RUSSO-JAPANESE WAR of 1904–05.

——Kikuchi Kenjō, *Chōsen saikin gaikō shi: Taiinkun den* (1910). James Palais, *Politics and Policy in Traditional Korea* (1975).
C. Kenneth QUINONES

Minsei

Abbreviation of Nihon Minshu Seinen Dōmei (Democratic Youth League of Japan), an organization sponsored by the JAPAN COMMUNIST PARTY (JCP) to increase membership and train future leaders. The league claims to have 200,000 members, mostly young workers and students. Established in 1923 as Nihon Kyōsan Seinen Dōmei (Japan Communist Youth League), it was suppressed by the government in 1933. It was reorganized as Nihon Seinen Kyōsan Dōmei (Japan Youth Communist League) in 1946 and given its present name in 1956. The Minsei became the core of the so-called Yoyogi faction (named after the location of the JCP headquarters in Tōkyō) of the ZENGAKUREN (the All-Japan Federation of Student Self-Governing Associations), and for a while it dominated the postwar student movement.

Minshatō → Democratic Socialist Party

minshingaku

Urban popular songs of Chinese origin that flourished in Japan in the 18th and 19th centuries. They were of two kinds. The first date from the end of the Ming (J: Min) dynasty (1368–1644), when a certain Wei Hou emigrated from China to Nagasaki and brought the musical tradition with him. In the 18th century, his descendant Wei Hao taught and promoted these songs in Kyōto, where they gained great popularity among the court nobility. After Wei's death at the end of the 18th century, interest in this art waned. The second wave of importation of Chinese songs came during the 19th century, toward the latter part of the Qing (Ch'ing; J: Shin) dynasty (1644–1911). At that time, a handful of the earlier Ming songs were also incorporated into the Qing repertory, hence the name *minshin* (Ming-Qing) *gaku*. The name continued to be used even when the repertory no longer contained the Ming pieces; it was also applied to works composed in Japan after the style of the Chinese importations.

Wei was said to have had over 200 songs in his repertory. The texts of 50 of these are preserved in a collection printed in 1768, and over a dozen more songs are found in other 19th-century works. The collection of 50 songs was printed with space between the columns of text, so that students could fill in the musical notation themselves. At least one copy of such a text with musical notation completely filled in still survives.

The Qing-dynasty songs were brought to Japan by another Chinese immigrant, Jin Qinjiang (Chin Ch'in-chiang), at the beginning of the 19th century. He taught in Nagasaki and Kyōto, where the songs became extremely popular, especially among the literati. Soon after Jin, another man, Lin Dejian (Lin Te-chien), also came to Nagasaki to teach this kind of Chinese song. Lin's disciples spread the art to various large cities in Japan, including Ōsaka, Edo (now Tōkyō), and Nagoya. Different schools of performance styles arose. Among the prominent Japanese artists who continued and developed the tradition were the sisters Hirai Renzan and Nagahara Baien. Renzan was said to have several hundreds of followers. The numerous schools centered mainly in two areas; the so-called Keian group was active in the Kantō area, and the Nagasaki group was concentrated in the Kyōto–Ōsaka region. The former was known for a more simple and austere style, emphasizing the ritual aspects of performance, while the latter stressed virtuosity in performing technique.

Because of the Sino-Japanese War of 1894–95, the art quickly went out of fashion. Today only a few artists still perform it, notably Nakamura Kira of Nagasaki. The influence of these Chinese songs upon the Japanese musical scene can be seen in the development of two kinds of Japanese popular music called *kankan-bushi* and *hōkai-bushi,* both of which derived from passages in the Chinese songs.

Like the Ming-dynasty songs, most of the Qing-dynasty works are short and lyrical in nature. The Ming texts preserved today are mostly from well-known literary works, such as "On the First Full

Moon" by Xin Qiji (Hsin Ch'i-chi), "Drinking Alone Under the Moon" by Li Bo (Li Po), or "Guanju" ("Kuan-chu") from *The Book of Poetry*. The Qing texts have many more songs in the vernacular, which seem to come from a more popular genre, for example, "The Water-Vat Man" and "Red Embroidered Shoes." The most famous pieces are "The Jasmine Flower" and "The Nine Ring Puzzle." There are among the Qing works also a few longer narrative songs based upon episodes from *The Romance of the Three Kingdoms* and *The Water Margin*. Occasionally words in spoken dialogue are found interspersed among the stanzas, resembling a dramatic presentation. The Qing repertory totals about 150 songs. In addition there exist also about 50 pieces composed by Japanese artists with texts in Japanese.

Formerly both the Ming- and Qing-dynasty songs were accompanied by many instruments, including flutes, double-reed pipes, plucked string instruments, drums, a set of small gongs, and wooden clappers. The Ming orchestra had in addition a small zither and a mouth organ. The Qing orchestra added a xylophone, several kinds of bowed fiddles , and the three-stringed *sanxian (san-hsien),* a long-necked fretless lute similar to the Japanese SHAMISEN. In modern performances the chief accompanying instrument is the moonharp; a fiddle is added only occasionally. Some of the Chinese songs can be sung either in Chinese or in Japanese translation. The singing style is simple with little ornamentation. The instruments play in unison, very close to the voice line.

Most of the over 50 existing collections of Qing-dynasty songs were printed in the 18th century and can be found in private and public libraries in Japan. Practically all the music is written in the Chinese *gongche (kung-ch'e)* system (a kind of pitch notation). One work, dated 1716, contains tablature for the flute. The Chinese texts mostly have notations in the indigenous Japanese KANA syllabary written on the side to help readers to pronounce the words in the Chinese fashion.

——Hatano Tarō, *Outline History of Moonharp Music,* no. 7, *Journal of the Yokohama City University* (1976), annotated list in Japanese of 53 collections, plus facsimile of 3 works. Hayashi Kenzō, "Mingaku hatchō ni tsuite," in *Tanabe sensei kanreki kinen Tōa ongaku ronshū* (1943). Hayashi Kenzō, "Minshingaku," *Ongaku jiten* (Heibonsha 1957). William P. Malm, "Chinese Music in 19th Century Japan," *Asian Music* (1975), illustrations and extensive bibliography.
Rulan Chao PIAN

minshuku

Private homes that provide lodging and meals to tourists. They are officially registered with the local authorities and listed in a brochure *(Minshuku gaido: Zenkoku)* put out by the Japan Travel Bureau. Some *minshuku* in Tōkyō and other cities are equipped to cater to foreigners. In 1979 there were about 27,000 *minshuku* nationwide.
NAITŌ Kinju

Minshutō

(Democratic Party). Political party formed in March 1947 under the leadership of ASHIDA HITOSHI. Not to be confused with the NIHON MINSHUTŌ (Japan Democratic Party). The Minshutō joined with the JAPAN SOCIALIST PARTY and the People's Cooperative Party (KOKUMIN KYŌDŌTŌ) to form a coalition cabinet under KATAYAMA TETSU in May 1947; seven ministers in this cabinet were from the Minshutō. After the fall of the Katayama cabinet in February 1948, Ashida became prime minister, supported by the same three parties. Ashida resigned eight months later when he was implicated in the SHŌWA DENKŌ SCANDAL, and the party eventually dissolved in 1950. Some of its members joined the LIBERAL PARTY (Jiyūtō), and some merged with the Kokumin Kyōdōtō (People's Cooperative Party) to form the People's Democratic Party (Kokumin Minshutō), which was reorganized as the Japan Reform Party (Nihon Kaishintō) in 1952. See also POLITICAL PARTIES.

mintō

(popular parties). A term loosely applied to the liberal parties of the early 1890s, such as the JIYŪTŌ and the RIKKEN KAISHINTŌ, that opposed the government led by the clique (HAMBATSU) from the former domains of Satsuma (now Kagoshima Prefecture) and Chōshū (now Yamaguchi Prefecture). The designation was used in contrast to the derogatory term *ritō* (bureaucrats' parties) by which the liberals referred to progovernment associations such as the KOKUMIN KYŌKAI and the Taiseikai (an association founded by TSUDA

MAMICHI and other scholar-bureaucrats). Some scholars attribute both terms to NAKAE CHŌMIN, the intellectual spokesman of the FREEDOM AND PEOPLE'S RIGHTS MOVEMENT. The *mintō* coalition, led by the Jiyūtō and the Rikken Kaishintō, gained a majority in the first and second general elections (1890 and 1892) held under the Constitution of the Empire of Japan. Despite the government's efforts to undermine the coalition, the *mintō* parties persistently challenged the government's budget proposals, which included large military appropriations. In 1891 and 1892 they succeeded in reducing the military budget. See also POLITICAL PARTIES.

Minumadai Canal

(Minumadai Yōsui). Irrigation canal in eastern Saitama Prefecture, central Honshū. It draws water from the river Tonegawa to irrigate approximately 15,000 hectares (37,050 acres) of farmland. Construction was completed in 1728 by Izawa Tamenaga on the orders of the eighth shōgun, Tokugawa Yoshimune. Length: 84 km (52 mi).

Miroku

(Skt: Maitreya; literally, "The Benevolent One"). A bodhisattva now in the Tuṣita (J: Tosotsu) heaven who will, millions of years hence, descend to this world to attain Buddhahood and lead its inhabitants to enlightenment. According to the Maitreya scriptures, those who declare their faith in Maitreya through worship, meditation, and invocation of his name will, after their death in this world, be reborn in the Tuṣita heaven where they can behold Maitreya, hear him preach the Buddhist law (dharma), and enjoy the pleasures of his heavenly realm; and, when the time finally comes for Maitreya to make his earthly descent, they will accompany him and participate in his meritorious work, thus contributing toward their own realization of Buddhahood.

Maitreya was among the first Buddhist divinities known to and worshiped by the Japanese, a stone image of Maitreya having been brought to Japan from the Korean kingdom of Paekche in 584. By the 7th century Maitreya had become one of the most important figures in the Japanese Buddhist pantheon (see also KANNON and JIZŌ), as is attested by the many superb images dating from that period found in the temples CHŪGŪJI, KŌRYŪJI, Yachūji (in Ōsaka), and HŌRYŪJI. The Maitreya cult was overshadowed in the 12th century by the Pure Land faith centering on the Buddha AMIDA (Skt: Amitābha) which was then sweeping Japan. Nevertheless, Maitreya has continued to be venerated until today, sometimes merged with traditional religious views of high mountains (see MOUNTAINS, WORSHIP OF), within certain voluntary religious associations (KŌ), which regarded him as a type of messiah. His worship has been adopted and actively promoted by such "new religion" organizations as the REIYŪKAI and the ŌMOTO.　　　　　Stanley WEINSTEIN

Miruna no zashiki

(The Forbidden Room). Folktale; also known as *Uguisu no ichimon sen* (The Nightingale's Penny). A man takes lodgings in an isolated house in a mountain pass. The beautiful mistress of the house leaves it in his charge but forbids him to look into the back room. He keeps his word and after a year is given a roll of cloth and a coin that turns out to be a treasure. His neighbor, hearing of the fortune, goes to stay at the house, but he breaks the taboo and meets disaster. The motif of taboos against seeing certain things is found throughout Japan.　　　　　SUCHI Tokuhei

Misasa

Town in central Tottori Prefecture, western Honshū. Surrounded by mountains, Misasa chiefly produces lumber and *shiitake* (a species of mushroom). The Misasa Hot Spring is known for its high radium content. The Institute for Thermal Spring Research of Okayama University is located here. Other attractions include NINGYŌ PASS and Oshikakei, a gorge. Pop: 8,770.

Misato

City in southeastern Saitama Prefecture, central Honshū. Formerly a farming district noted for its early harvest rice and vegetables, within the last decade it has become an industrial and residential town. Pop: 98,222.

Misawa

City in eastern Aomori Prefecture, northern Honshū, on the Pacific coast. Misawa developed after World War II as an American Air Force base; it is now a base for the Japan Air Self Defense Forces. Efforts are being made to develop new industries. Apart from services related to the military, its principal activity is farming. Pop: 39,976.

Misawa Homes Co, Ltd

(Misawa Hōmu). Manufacturer of wooden prefabricated houses. The company is engaged in every aspect of the industry from basic materials research to production, sales, and service. It was founded in 1951; its forerunner, Misawa Lumber Co, was established in 1906. The company is known for its emphasis on research and development and for its integrated housing supply system. The Misawa Homes Institute of Research and Development, capitalized at ¥1 billion (US $4.7 million) in 1979, is one of the largest private housing research institutes in the world. Production and distribution are handled by 23 factories, 135 dealers, and over 1,200 licensed contractors. The company has conducted operations in the Antarctic and 12 foreign countries, including the United States, Iceland, Indonesia, Australia, Saudi Arabia, the Soviet Union, Vietnam, and Madagascar. A wholly owned subsidiary, Misawa Homes of Canada, Ltd, was set up in 1972 and is engaged in the supply of single-family homes and townhouses.

Sales for the fiscal year ending March 1982 totaled ¥109.6 billion (US $455.3 million), more than 90 percent of which was generated by wooden prefabricated houses; capitalization in that year stood at ¥2.6 billion (US $10.8 million). The head office is in Tōkyō.

miscellaneous schools

(kakushu gakkō). A category of schools in the classification established by the Ministry of Education. It includes schools outside the regular school system, most of them vocational and technical training schools. These schools have assumed an increasing importance in post–World War II Japan, as a result of the decline of vocational education in the public school system and the increase in demand for trained workers. The various schools fall into the following categories: clothing and home economics (cooking, Japanese and Western clothing, home economics); medicine, hygiene, and social welfare services (medical and dental technology, acupuncture, moxa treatment, midwifery, cosmetology, hairdressing, child care); technical (construction, engineering, electronics, television repair, automobile repair); business (typing, bookkeeping, real estate, secretarial skills); arts (design, photography, music, dance, tea ceremony, calligraphy, flower arranging); and cultural and other (foreign language, college preparation, agriculture, religion). These schools offer a certificate upon completion of the course of study, and an increasing number of employers regularly hire graduates of such training programs.

Kakushu gakkō numbered over 5,300 in 1980, most of them privately operated. Over 724,000 students attended these schools in 1980; more than 50 percent of the students were women. In order to qualify for certification by the local municipality, the course requirements must include more than one year of study and more than 680 hours of classroom instruction. In addition, the Ministry of Education in 1976 established a higher category of school with special requirements for certification; there were 2,520 such special training schools (senshū gakkō) in 1980. Many of the medical and engineering institutes are comparable to junior colleges in the level of training offered.　　　　　SAITŌ Kenjirō

Mishihase

Also read Shukushin. Aborigines described in the ancient chronicle *Nihon shoki* (720) as having lived in northern Japan; possibly a tribe of the EZO. In 658 the general ABE NO HIRAFU was sent by the YAMATO COURT to subdue them. The name Mishihase (Ch: Sushen) was earlier applied by the Chinese to a Tungusic people who lived in the Amur, Sungari, and Ussuri river basins of Manchuria from about the 8th to the 3rd centuries BC, but it is believed that there was no connection between the two peoples and that the Japanese arbitrarily borrowed the name from ancient Chinese records to refer to unassimilated tribal groups in the north.

Mishima

City in western Shizuoka Prefecture, central Honshū, on the Izu Peninsula. In the Edo period (1600–1868) it prospered as a post-station town on the highway Tōkaidō and as a shrine town centering on Mishima Taisha, a shrine revered by warriors. Now it is the site of foodstuff, chemical, and textile industries. The National Institute of Genetics is located here. It is the base for trips to Mt. Fuji (Fujisan), Hakone, and Izu. Pop: 94,613.

Mishima

Island in the Sea of Japan, approximately 45 km (28 mi) northwest of Yamaguchi Prefecture, off western Honshū; under the jurisdiction of the city of Hagi. Warmed by the Tsushima Current, the island is largely agricultural and is famous for Mishima cattle. A place of exile for the Hagi domain and a former coastal lookout, the island is now the site of a Self Defense Forces radar base. A group of more than 200 ancient tombs on the island has aroused much interest in recent years. Area: 7.8 sq km (3 sq mi).

Mishima Michitsune (1835–1888)

Also known as Mishima Tsūyō. Bureaucrat of the Meiji period (1868–1912). Born in the Satsuma domain (now Kagoshima Prefecture), Mishima was active in the movement to overthrow the Tokugawa shogunate. Entering the government soon after the MEIJI RESTORATION in 1868, he served as governor of several prefectures. In 1882, while governor of Fukushima Prefecture, his high-handed methods in levying taxes and labor for the construction of roads and bridges incurred concerted opposition from local residents. His ruthless suppression of an uprising (FUKUSHIMA INCIDENT) led to the KABASAN INCIDENT two years later. In 1885 he was appointed superintendent-general of the Tōkyō Metropolitan Police; in enforcing the PEACE PRESERVATION LAW OF 1887 (Hoan Jōrei) he banished 570 members of the FREEDOM AND PEOPLE'S RIGHTS MOVEMENT from Tōkyō.

Mishima Tokushichi (1893–1975)

Physical metallurgist. Discoverer of the MK alloys, a series of powerful magnetic materials that led to the development of the Alnico V magnet used in over 90 percent of today's high-fidelity loudspeakers. Born in Hyōgo Prefecture, Mishima graduated from Tōkyō University and taught there from 1921 to 1953. He is also noted for his research on stainless steel and other metals used in vacuum tube electrodes. He received the Order of Culture in 1950.

Mishima Tsūyō → Mishima Michitsune

Mishima Yukio (1925–1970)

An important writer of fiction, drama, and essays whose sensational death on 25 November 1970 brought his name to the attention of people all over the world. The actions of the last hours of Mishima's life created widespread concern over a possible revival of Japanese militarism, but his appeal for a revision of the constitution which would permit rearmament had no perceptible effect on the government.

Interpretations of the meaning of Mishima's suicide intrigued not only his biographers but also students of Japanese culture. Even critics who professed to be concerned exclusively with Mishima's literary works found it difficult to ignore this extraordinary climax to the life of a man who had seemed to be consecrated to a search for beauty, and they found clues to Mishima's final acts in schoolboy compositions or in what they could learn about his early childhood. There is hardly a figure in Japanese literary history who offers such a richness of material for the amateur psychoanalyst.

Mishima (whose real name was Hiraoka Kimitake) was born in Tōkyō on 14 January 1925. His father, a government official, was the son of a former governor of Karafuto (Southern Sakhalin). Mishima, though proud of this grandfather, never discussed his grandfather's peasant ancestry, but he commonly referred to the family of his paternal grandmother, who belonged to the upper samurai class.

As a boy Mishima was sent to the Peers' School (Gakushūin). Boys who attended this school did not necessarily belong to the nobility, but nonaristocrats like Mishima were often made to feel like outsiders. Mishima's literary inclinations also made him an outsider in a school where the Spartan education advocated by General NOGI MARESUKE, the school president at the time of his suicide in 1912, prepared young men to be soldiers and not poets. Mishima's early story "Tabako" (1946, The Cigarette) relates with what scorn he was treated by members of the rugby club when he confessed that he belonged to the school literary society. His experiences at that time are so faithfully depicted in this story and in "Shi o kaku shōnen" (1954; tr "The Boy Who Wrote Poetry," 1977) as to suggest autobiography or the I-NOVEL. But Mishima's purpose in writing these stories had little in common with the obsession for truth of the I-novelists; for Mishima, the facts served mainly as points of departure for observations and analyses.

"The Boy who Wrote Poetry" describes, for example, the boy's fascination with words, a trait that remained with Mishima throughout his life. His vocabulary was unusually rich, and he could effortlessly compose pastiches of the literary styles of the past. His elaborate use of metaphor was a conspicuous feature of his style as far back as the poetry he composed as a boy. Mishima's metaphors were not always effective, but he never forsook the use of ornate expression. Although he was capable of writing realistic dialogue that perfectly captured the inflections of daily speech, the works that meant the most to him were written in a deliberately artificial language. He mocked those who insisted on natural, banal dialogue. Another constant feature of Mishima's writings was the prominence he gave to sudden discoveries of the meanings of experiences. Every sight, every gesture, tended to arouse in him a flash of understanding, however implausible it might seem at times.

First Writings —— As a boy Mishima was especially impressed with the poetry of TACHIHARA MICHIZŌ, whose influence also molded Mishima's appreciation of classical WAKA poetry. Mishima's own poems, his first publications, appeared in the literary magazine of the Peers' School. While still publishing these poems Mishima began to write his first prose work of consequence, "Hanazakari no mori" (1941, The Forest in Full Flower). The story abounds in the metaphors and aphorisms that are typical of Mishima's later works, and the themes would also recur. The narrator describes ancestors who in some sense still live within him. They share with him various tastes, notably a love for the sea and for the sun of the south. The sea, a recurrent motif in Mishima's writings, became a metaphor for all of life in his tetralogy Hōjō no umi (1965–70, The Sea of Fertility), and Mishima's worship of the sun and the south would be associated with his cult of the body.

The expression in "Hanazakari no mori" suggests the influence of Mishima's mentors at the Peers' School, who not only encouraged his study of the Japanese classics but brought him into contact with the NIHON RŌMANHA (Japanese Romanticists), a group of intellectuals who insisted on the uniqueness of the Japanese people and their history. Mishima's devotion to Japanese tradition, both in this work and much later, was combined, however, with a strong attachment to the West. The ancestral "memories" included such exotic objects as a Bible encased in lacquer and mother-of-pearl, a combination of Western content and Japanese surfaces that typified many of his works.

Mishima was much taken as a student with the essays of Oscar Wilde. Even after the outbreak of the war with Britain and America, he continued to read, generally in Japanese translations, the works of Wilde and other writers who had been denounced as decadents. It is not difficult to imagine the effect that Wilde's paradoxes, especially those contained in Intentions, one of Mishima's favorite books, had on the young and inexperienced student. But his love for Western literature, which he retained throughout his life, did not lure him away from Japanese traditions. Unlike most postwar writers, who insisted on the break between themselves and pre-Meiji literature, Mishima read the classics for pleasure and inspiration. His love of the NŌ plays especially influenced his writings, as we know not only from his modern Nō plays but from episodes in various novels that were modeled on situations in the old plays.

"Hanazakari no mori" was intended for the literary magazine of the Peers' School, but Mishima's adviser was so impressed by the manuscript that he proposed publishing it in Bungei bunka (Literary Culture), the little magazine that he and other Peers' School teachers edited. Bungei bunka was a slim magazine of limited circulation, but it had high standards and was read all over the country. The other editors hesitated to publish the work of a middle-school student, and they were concerned about what the boy's parents might say. They decided to protect young Hiraoka Kimitake by persuading him to use a pen name of their invention, Mishima Yukio.

In October 1944, even as defeat in the war became increasingly certain, "Hanazakari no mori" was published in book form. It was a time of an acute paper shortage, and there could hardly have been a less propitious moment for publishing some rather precious stories, but the 4,000 copies of the original printing sold out within a week, no doubt because people were starved for literature that would take their minds off the war.

Although Mishima would one day gain notoriety for his advocacy of the way of the sword in a Japan that was committed to peace, he was unenthusiastic about the war while it was taking place, and was at pains to avoid being conscripted. He seems to have been more concerned about his writing even than about the defeat: he began the story "Misaki nite no monogatari" (1945, A Story at the Cape) in July 1945, and continued it during the chaotic months that followed. In January 1946 he visited KAWABATA YASUNARI with the manuscripts of two stories, "Chūsei" (1945, The Middle Ages) and "Tabako," and in June at Kawabata's recommendation, "Tabako" was published in *Ningen* (Humanity), a new and important literary magazine. At the time Mishima was still a student of the Law Department of Tōkyō University.

Kawabata's high opinion of the young author was not shared by most members of literary circles. Indeed, if Mishima's career had terminated at this point his writing would surely have been forgotten. But in terms of Mishima's oeuvre, "Tabako" was a first, poignant expression of real feelings, as opposed to the carefully contrived situations he had borrowed from other works of literature. Mishima may not have been pleased by this development, which ran counter to the literary wisdom he had garnered from Wilde's aphorisms on the relative importance of art and life. His continued resistance to reality was revealed in his first full-length novel, *Tōzoku* (1946–48, The Thieves), an implausible and unsuccessful portrayal of two young members of the aristocracy who are irresistibly drawn toward suicide.

The central characters in *Tōzoku*, as in others of Mishima's early works, belong to the aristocracy. This was natural, in view of his education at the Peers' School, but the attention he gave to a tiny segment of Japanese society, which had officially ceased to exist after the war, discredited him in the eyes of some critics, who complained even after his death that Mishima had never written about the common people. This charge was untrue, as the most cursory examination of the characters in Mishima's works reveals. As a matter of fact, few modern writers have treated as wide a spectrum of Japanese society as Mishima. Presumably what the critics object to is not Mishima's narrowness of vision but his failure to indict capitalist society for its contradictions. However, it is also true that Mishima was one of the rare 20th-century writers who described the aristocracy. This did not necessarily demonstrate special admiration for the class; indeed, his experiences with young aristocrats at the Peers' School were disillusioning. But Mishima found it congenial to write about a class he knew well when expressing his own views on the nature of the human condition.

Tōzoku appeared in 1948. This was one of the most productive years of Mishima's career, though he had become an official in the Ministry of Finance. Exhausted by the strain of writing at night after a day spent at the office, he resigned his post in September.

In July 1948 Mishima was invited to join the group that published the magazine *Kindai bungaku* (Modern Literature). Most members of the group were left wing in their sympathies, and Mishima from the first was an outsider. Even toward the end of his life, when he overtly expressed rightist views, he remained essentially apolitical, and he treated professional rightists harshly in several novels. He was caustic also in his criticism of the businessmen and politicians who ran the country, though his grounds were unlike those of the *Kindai bungaku* writers; Mishima was indignant because the postwar leaders of Japan in their search for profits had forgotten Japanese tradition.

As a boy Mishima had shown no special interest in the young officers who had staged coups in the 1930s against the ruling class, but he gradually came to admire their beautiful, undiscriminating patriotism because it transcended personal ambitions and even the instinct of self-preservation. He eventually would even advocate emperor worship, but for Mishima the emperor was the abstract essence of Japan itself, not a reigning monarch. Indeed, in *Eirei no koe* (1966, The Voices of the Heroic Dead), the spirits of the kamikaze pilots denounce the present emperor for having denied his divinity: if the emperor was not a god, their deaths had been meaningless. Mishima's politics grew increasingly abstract until they became an extension of his aesthetics.

In January 1949 Mishima published in *Kindai bungaku* the first of several essays on the art of Kawabata. He always professed great admiration for the older writer, but although both men were devoted to Japanese tradition, the term had different meanings for each. Even when their preferences coincided, as in their admiration for the *waka*, it was for dissimilar reasons: Kawabata was moved by the economically phrased evocations of natural beauty, Mishima by the baroque passion he detected underneath the lovely surfaces. For Kawabata the past meant *tawayameburi*, the feminine aspects of Japanese culture; for Mishima the past was typified by *masuraoburi*, the masculine traditions of the warrior.

Confessions of a Mask —— In July 1949 Mishima published his most self-revelatory work, the novel *Kamen no kokuhaku* (tr *Confessions of a Mask*, 1958). This novel was respectfully reviewed and sold well. It established his reputation and continued to be rated at or near the top of his entire oeuvre, even after he had published 30 or more books.

Confessions of a Mask was not fully understood even by readers who greatly admired it. The homosexual proclivities of the hero, which prevent him from feeling desire for the girl he loves, were so baffling to the critics that some supposed that the intent must be parody. The curious fact is that neither at this time nor later was the work read as an avowal of a guilty passion. The American publishers who were first offered the translation of the novel rejected it, fearing it would "brand" Mishima, but Japanese readers have interpreted it instead as an exceptionally sensitive account of a boy's gradual self-awakening. The homosexual elements are attributed to sexual immaturity or else are explained as symbolic of the aridity of the postwar world. Mishima himself at times denied the truth of his confessions, but it is impossible to escape the impression that he was faithfully conveying his experiences and emotions. There is no question but that he altered his materials, and he presented only aspects of his life that contributed to the overall plan of the book, but this does not make of it a parody.

In *Confessions of a Mask* Mishima boldly used materials that ran counter to everything that literature had taught him. Unlike the young men in the novels he had read, he failed to win the hand of the girl he loved not because she was betrothed to another, but because he could no longer endure the mask of the normal young man which society and literature had pressed against his face. His reaction was not self-pity, an emotion he despised, nor dismay over the terrible fate that had been imposed on him; instead, he recounted the process that had led him to recognize his identity.

Confessions of a Mask is stylistically uneven, the first half being more imaginative and poetic than the second. Little attempt was made to impart individuality to any character other than the narrator, who is portrayed almost entirely from within. His emotional life is presented in a series of revelatory insights that occur independently of other persons and without a trace of humor. Yet the intensity and truth of the vision justifies the high reputation of the novel. The combination of truth and beauty, after a series of stories that had contained only beauty, made *Confessions of a Mask* the crucial work in Mishima's development as an artist.

The 1950s —— Mishima's writings were much sought by editors after the success of *Confessions of a Mask*, and before long he was publishing works of popular fiction that he would disown in later years as necessary evils. The inducement to write such works was largely financial, but possibly Mishima enjoyed thinking of himself as an author who could satisfy any literary taste. He continued until the year of his death to devote about a third of his time each month to writing popular fiction and essays in order to be able to live comfortably and to spend his remaining time on serious fiction and plays.

Mishima's next important work was *Ai no kawaki* (1950; tr *Thirst for Love*, 1969). The success of *Confessions of a Mask* might well have tempted him to continue in the same vein, despite his professed aversion for the I-novel, but he deliberately chose to write a work of fiction which, on the surface at least, was unrelated to his own life. The setting is a part of Japan that Mishima hardly knew, and the central figure is a widow, Etsuko, who has become the mistress of her late husband's father. The minor characters are well drawn, but the main theme is Etsuko's intense but unavowed love for a young farmer named Saburō. During the climactic scene of the novel Etsuko, watching as Saburō cavorts at a festival, gashes his back with her nails, an echo of the sexual fantasies at the end of *Confessions of a Mask*. When Saburō, at last becoming aware of Etsuko's love, responds, she is terrified, calls for help, and kills him with her father-in-law's scythe. The condition of her love was that it be unreciprocated, another echo of the earlier novel.

Mishima reportedly told friends that Etsuko was actually a man. Although there is nothing unfeminine about her, it is not difficult to imagine what he meant. Etsuko's craving for the strong, sunburned, unintellectual Saburō recalls the love of the narrator of *Confessions of a Mask* for healthy young males, and the compulsion to wound the object is much the same.

But whatever personal factors went into the character of Etsuko, *Thirst for Love* marked Mishima's break with confessional writing. The choice of the path of fiction, as opposed to increasingly refined or penetrating analyses of his own psyche, was undoubtedly the right decision, but it may have cost Mishima his masterpiece, the novel that would have described how this first internationally recognized Japanese writer had experienced the conflicting attractions of Japanese and Western traditions. Mishima had removed his mask to make his confession, but he later seems to have convinced himself that the mask was his real face, and once he put it back on, it only rarely slipped, revealing someone quite unlike the Mishima of the powerful body and heroic laugh.

In 1952 Mishima went abroad. The high point of his journey was Greece, which had fascinated him from childhood. It proved more wonderful in reality than he had anticipated, and made him realize that the dark pictures of life he had hitherto painted had been incomplete. The first product of this insight was the novel *Shiosai* (1954; tr *The Sound of Waves*, 1956). He drew inspiration from the ancient Greek romance *Daphnis and Chloë*, following the plot, but importing a Japanese atmosphere by transforming the shepherd and shepherdess of the original into a fisherboy and fishergirl who live on a small island off the Ise coast. He manipulated the old tale brilliantly, giving it new life by impeccably chosen details. Probably Mishima thought of *The Sound of Waves* as essentially an exercise in style. Apart from a general desire to depict the brighter side of human life, he wanted to prove that he could make the most hackneyed of tales seem new by his skill as a writer. The enormous popularity of the book was a surprise and even a disappointment. Perhaps the most important contribution to Mishima's artistic development made by *The Sound of Waves* was to show that classical literature, whether of Japan or the West, could serve as an effective substitute for personal experience.

Mishima liked to think of himself as a classical writer. The term is appropriate especially in the case of works that can fully be appreciated only if their prototypes are recognized. This was true of Mishima's modern Nō plays; though they retain the main themes of the original works, they twist the materials in a manner that intrigues or even shocks contemporary audiences. His use of recent events was similar. Most critics believe that his finest work was the novel *Kinkakuji* (1956; tr *The Temple of the Golden Pavilion*, 1959), which describes the events leading up to the burning of the famous Kyōto temple. The conclusion of the novel—the conflagration—is known from the outset, and the reader's interest is held not by curiosity as to what will take place but by the desire to discover *why* the monk feels he must destroy a national treasure. Mishima attributed to the monk subtle but compelling reasons for his action, without worrying over the likelihood that an indifferently educated youth with a paralyzing stutter could formulate such complex ideas. It is a measure of Mishima's success that he persuades readers that a wholly deplorable act was justifiable in terms of the liberation of one man.

No other work by Mishima, excepting possibly the final tetralogy, can be compared to *The Temple of the Golden Pavilion* in its combination of insight and brilliant execution, but Mishima produced in between these two major works half a dozen other novels which, even when not wholly successful, deserve attention. Mishima poured his full efforts and talent into *Kyōko no ie* (1959, Kyōko's House) but failed in his attempt to recapture in this novel the decade of the 1950s, as filtered through his own experiences. The comparative failure of this novel, the first serious setback Mishima had known in his literary career, naturally disappointed him, but his depression did not last long.

The 1960s—— *Utage no ato* (1960; tr *After the Banquet*, 1963), though on a smaller scale, was far more successful. However, this novel was based so closely on the events surrounding the campaign of the veteran politician ARITA HACHIRŌ for the governorship of Tōkyō that Arita sued Mishima for invasion of privacy (see AFTER THE BANQUET CASE). Mishima eventually lost the case, but the literary importance of this novel does not depend on its being a roman à clef; it is a work of the imagination that employs factual materials

freely to create in Kazu, the wife of the politician, one of Mishima's most perfectly realized characters.

In 1962 Mishima published his most unusual novel, *Utsukushii hoshi* (The Beautiful Star), a combination of science fiction and a long dialogue on whether or not man is worthy of preservation. This was the closest Mishima ever came to writing an avant-garde novel, and its failure to attract wide attention came as another blow. It may also have discouraged him from being more adventurous in future works. Mishima seemed to have passed the peak of his literary career, but he became more of a public figure than ever. He startled people when in 1967 he secretly spent a month training with the Self Defense Forces, and in 1968 he formed a private army of 100 men, the Tate no Kai (Shield Society), which was sworn to defend the emperor. These activities brought him more attention than this writings, but they did not usurp his energies. His best full-length plays, *Sado kōshaku fujin* (1965, tr *Madame de Sade*, 1967) and *Waga tomo Hittorā* (1968, tr *My Friend Hitler*, 1978) date from this period, as does the long essay *Taiyō to tetsu* (1968; tr *Sun and Steel*, 1970) in which he deplored the emphasis given by intellectuals to the mind and insisted on the importance of the body.

Hojō no umi (The Sea of Fertility) the final tetralogy, began to appear serially in September 1965. Mishima continued to produce monthly installments until the day of his death, finding the pressure of deadlines a necessary stimulus. As early as 1950 he had stated his interest in writing a work on the theme of reincarnation, and he read works of both Buddhist and European philosophy when preparing this work. He became especially interested in the *yuishiki*, or "consciousness only" doctrine that runs through the entire work. When the first volume appeared he acknowledged that inspiration had also been provided by the Heian romance HAMAMATSU CHŪNAGON MONOGATARI (The Tale of the Hamamatsu Middle Counselor). The four volumes each bear a separate title: *Haru no yuki* (1965–67; tr *Spring Snow*, 1971), *Homba* (1967–68; tr *Runaway Horses*, 1973), *Akatsuki no tera* (1968–70; tr *The Temple of Dawn*, 1973), and *Tennin gosui* (1970–71; tr *The Decay of the Angel*, 1974). However, the title of the whole (derived from the Latin name of a sea of the moon) gave the best clue to Mishima's purpose in writing the tetralogy: although its name suggests fertility, the lunar sea is in fact arid. But even if it was Mishima's conclusion that life is meaningless, he acted otherwise. His fascination with death always implied another self observing the self that was dead, and a belief in reincarnation may have been not only congenial but necessary to a man who lacked other religious convictions.

Mishima believed that *The Sea of Fertility* was the product of all he had learned as a writer, and wryly remarked to friends that when he finished the work there would be nothing left for him to do but kill himself. It is natural to suppose that with greater age and experience of the world Mishima could in fact have written even finer works, but he did not think so. He applied to himself his theory that the longer people live, the less admirable they become.

Mishima was the most gifted and achieved the most of the writers of his generation. The international literary prizes that he came close to winning ultimately eluded him, but his reputation, both in Japan and in the West, seems secure.

■——Works by Mishima: *Mishima Yukio zenshū* (Shinchōsha, 1973–76). *Ai no kawaki* (1950), tr Alfred H. Marks as *Thirst for Love* (1969). *Kinjiki* (1951–53), tr Alfred H. Marks as *Forbidden Colors* (1968). *Manatsu no shi* (1952), tr Edward G. Seidensticker as "Death in Midsummer," in Yukio Mishima, *Death in Midsummer and Other Stories* (1966). *Shiosai* (1954), tr Meredith Weatherby as *The Sound of Waves* (1956). *Kinkakuji* (1956), tr Ivan Morris as *The Temple of the Golden Pavilion* (1959). *Kindai nōgaku shū* (1956), tr Donald Keene as *Five Modern Nō Plays* (1957). *Kamen no kokuhaku* (1958), tr Meredith Weatherby as *Confessions of a Mask* (1958). *Utage no ato* (1960), tr Donald Keene as *After the Banquet* (1963). *Gogo no eikō* (1963), tr John Nathan as *The Sailor who Fell from Grace with the Sea* (1965). *Haru no yuki* (1965–67), tr Michael Gallagher as *Spring Snow* (1969). *Sado kōshaku fujin* (1965), tr Donald Keene as *Madame de Sade* (1967). *Taiyō to tetsu* (1965), tr John Bester as *Sun and Steel* (1970). *Homba* (1967–68), tr Michael Gallagher as *Runaway Horses* (1973). *Hagakure nyūmon* (1968), tr Kathryn Sparling as *Yukio Mishima On Hagakure* (1977). *Waga tomo Hittorā* (1968), tr Hiroaki Sato as "My Friend Hitler," *St. Andrews Review* 4.3 and 4.4 (1977, 1978). *Akatsuki no tera*, tr E. Dale Saunders and Cecilia Segawa Seigle as *The Temple of Dawn* (1973). *Tennin gosui*, tr Edward G. Seidensticker as *The Decay of the Angel* (1974).

Works about Mishima: Hiraoka Azusa, *Segare Mishima Yukio* (1972). Donald Keene, *Landscapes and Portraits* (1971). Matsumoto Tōru, *Mishima Yukio ron* (1973). Masao Miyoshi, *Accomplices of Silence* (1974). John Nathan, *Mishima* (1974). Noguchi Takehiko, *Mishima Yukio no sekai* (1968). Saeki Shōichi, *Hyōden Mishima Yukio* (1978). Henry Scott-Stokes, *The Life and Death of Yukio Mishima* (1974). Kinya Tsuruta and Thomas E. Swann, *Approaches to the Modern Japanese Novel* (1976). Makoto Ueda, *Modern Japanese Writers* (1976). Hisaaki Yamanouchi, *The Search for Authenticity in Modern Japanese Literature* (1978). Donald KEENE

mishōtai

In Shintō, a sacred metal or wooden disk that has at its center a Buddhist or Shintō image, either painted or represented in relief. Originally referring to the object of worship (*goshintai*) in the main sanctuary (*honden*) of a shrine, the *mishōtai* ("the divine true body") is derived from the sacred mirror (*shinkyō*) used in Shintō rituals. As notions of religious syncretism took hold in the 9th century on and shrines came increasingly under the influence of Buddhism, sacred mirrors were decorated with depictions of Buddhas, who were believed to represent the original Indian forms (HONJIBUTSU) of the Shintō deities (see HONJI SUIJAKU). These Buddhist images (or the mystical syllables written in an Indic script that symbolized the Buddhist divinities) were either painted directly on the surface of the mirrors or depicted in relief. Gradually mirrors were replaced by wooden or metal disks decorated with Buddhist images and symbols. These embossed disks, known popularly as *kakebotoke* (hanging Buddhas), were produced in large numbers between the 13th and 16th centuries. Often inscribed on the reverse with the name and vows of the donor, they were presented as votive offerings at both Shintō shrines and Buddhist temples (see EMA) or sometimes buried in the ground in sutra mounds (*kyōzuka*). Stanley WEINSTEIN

miso

Bean paste. Made by mixing steamed soybeans with salt and a fermenting agent (*kōji*) made of rice, wheat and soybeans fermented with an *Aspergillus* fungus; together with soy sauce (*shōyu*), it is the basic flavoring of Japanese cuisine. *Miso* is a good source of protein, especially the amino acids lysine and threonine, but it also contains a large amount of salt, as much as 8 to 15 percent. Introduced from China in the 7th century, it became popular during the Muromachi period (1333–1568). It was formerly made in each household, but is now mass-produced commercially. Many smaller-sized businesses, however, sell their own *miso* specialties.

The color, aroma, and taste of *miso* differ according to the combination of ingredients, which vary from place to place. *Shiromiso*, made in the Kyōto area, contains less salt and is sweeter, more delicate in flavor. The most widely used, Shinshū *miso*, made chiefly in Nagano Prefecture, is reddish and saltier. Hatchō *miso*, made in Aichi, Gifu, and Mie prefectures, is darker in color and has a slightly tart taste.

Miso is most commonly used for making soup (*misoshiru*), being blended bit by bit into a soup base made with *kombu* (genus *Laminarea*), bonito flakes or *niboshi* (dried sardines). Bean curd and vegetables or dried seaweed are usually added. *Misoshiru* and rice are an indispensable part of a Japanese-style breakfast. Because of its strong flavor, *miso* is often used for marinating or cooking fish. It is also used as a preservative. *Miso* can be used as a dressing mixed with rice vinegar (*sumiso*), yuzu (citron) peel (*yuzumiso*), roasted and ground sesame seeds (*gomamiso*), or bits of bream (*taimiso*). ŌTSUKA Shigeru

misogi

The Shintō rite of ablution. The word *misogi*, derived from *misosogi* (pouring water on the body), refers to the ritual cleansing of the body with water to remove both physical and spiritual defilements. Since Shintō lays great stress on purity and cleanliness, the act of cleansing the body assumes enormous importance and must be performed before any ceremony begins.

According to the *Kojiki* (712, Records of Ancient Matters), the rite of *misogi* originated with Izanagi no Mikoto (see IZANAGI AND IZANAMI), the divine progenitor of the Japanese islands. After the death of his spouse (Izanami no Mikoto), the distraught Izanagi descended to Yomotsukuni (or Yomi no Kuni, the Land of Night) in search of her. There he became contaminated by the impurities

associated with decay and death. After his return to this world through a cave that led up from Yomotsukuni, he traveled to Tachibana in northern Kyūshū, where he washed away his impurities (see KEGARE) in a river. It was during this ritual bathing that he gave birth to three of the most important Shintō deities: AMATERASU ŌMIKAMI (the divine imperial ancestress), SUSANOO NO MIKOTO, and Tsukiyomi no Mikoto (the moon god).

Various types of purification rituals using water are still performed. The one most frequently observed is the rinsing of the hands and mouth before worshiping at a shrine. Between the *torii* (gateway) and oratory (*haiden*) of a shrine there is a large stone basin usually standing in an open wooden structure known as a *temizuya* (or *chōzuya*) at which the visitor is expected to cleanse himself. Similarly, before all festivals the priest is required to bathe thoroughly, a practice commonly known as *kessai*. Although originally done in a river, the purification of the priest now takes place in a public bath.

Mizugori (washing away impurities by water) involves still another type of purification. Literally meaning "removing impurities by water," *mizugori* is performed by standing virtually nude under a waterfall or by pouring buckets of cold water over oneself. It differs from *misogi* in that it is basically an ascetic practice undertaken for a specified period to demonstrate one's sincerity and conviction to the deities. In many parts of Japan the ritual of *misogi* still survives in festivals, as, for example, when scantily clad young men carrying a portable shrine (*mikoshi*) plunge into the sea or river, a practice called *hama-ori* (going down to the beach). See also HARAE. Stanley WEINSTEIN

Misogikyō

One of the SECT SHINTŌ groups. Based on ideas developed during the latter part of the Edo period (1600–1868) by the Shintō priest Inoue Masakane (1790–1849) who, after studying PURE LAND BUDDHISM and other religious practices, began teaching that unity between deity and man can be attained through purification from defilement. The group advocates a purification ritual (MISOGI) and deep controlled breathing. Its doctrines emphasize faith in AMATERASU ŌMIKAMI and other Shintō deities. The sect was formally organized in 1875 and claimed some 120,000 followers in 1977. Kenneth J. DALE

Misora Hibari (1937–)

Singer of popular songs. Real name Katō Kazue. Born in Yokohama, the daughter of a fishmonger. By the age of 12, she established herself as a professional, appearing on the stage of major theaters in Tōkyō and Yokohama and making her first record. Her hit songs include "Kanashiki kuchibue" (1949, Sad Whistling), "Ringo oiwake" (1952, Apple Flower Song), and "Yawara" (1965), all sentimental lyrics following the tradition of modern popular songs. She starred in numerous films—often portraying the spirited tomboy or the heroine of the back alleys.

mission schools

Schools run by Christian missionaries for general and religious education. Since the arrival of the first Protestant missionaries in 1859, mission schools have served as an effective means for their religious activities. At first many offered tutoring and home instruction, principally in English. After 1871 when the ban on Christianity was lifted, theological colleges and other Christian schools were established. Through the 1880s many progressive Japanese welcomed mission schools as centers for Western-style education.

In the first half of the 20th century, mission schools grew steadily in quality and number. They often pioneered advances in educational content and method, assuming an important role in women's education. Most of the top-ranked professional schools accredited by the government when it issued the Professional Schools Ordinance (Semmon Gakkō Rei) in 1903 were mission schools. After private universities were first authorized by the government in 1918, the Christian-sponsored DŌSHISHA UNIVERSITY, RIKKYŌ UNIVERSITY, and KANSEI GAKUIN UNIVERSITY were among the few private schools to receive full accreditation (in 1920, 1922, and 1932, respectively).

Mission schools suffered a temporary setback during the 1930s and World War II with the rise of militarism and nationalism but since then have flourished. As of 1978 the Christian-influenced institutions include 33 universities or colleges, 52 junior colleges, 104 senior high schools, 78 junior high schools, and 31 elementary schools. Of these institutions 13 were founded in the 1870s and 23 in the 1880s.   *Hiratsuka Masunori*

mission to Europe of 1582

(Tenshō Ken'ō Shisetsu). The mission of four young Japanese boys to the courts of Philip II of Spain and Pope Gregory XIII. It was conceived by the Jesuit Alessandro VALIGNANO and organized under the auspices of three CHRISTIAN DAIMYŌ in Kyūshū, ŌTOMO SŌRIN (Francisco), ARIMA HARUNOBU (Protasio), and ŌMURA SUMITADA (Bartolomeu). The mission left Japan in February 1582 and returned in July 1590.

Aims of the Mission —— The arrival in Japan of Francis XAVIER in 1549 marked the beginning of the missionary work of the JESUITS in that country and particularly in Kyūshū. The Jesuits quickly formed the opinion that the exclusion of other religious orders from Japan was necessary for the proper growth of Christianity there. Father Valignano, on his first visit to Japan in 1579, realized that it would be extremely advantageous to the mission there to send a group of Japanese Christians to Rome. First of all, it would demonstrate to the Pope how the Jesuit work in East Asia could make up for the losses suffered by the Catholic Church in Europe as a result of the Reformation and thus secure the Pope's support for the Jesuit monopoly in Japan. In addition, Valignano hoped to get financial subsidies from the Pope. Another aim was to introduce Europe to the Japanese. Though known as "the mission of the lords of Kyūshū," it was entirely Valignano's idea. In fact, recent studies have revealed that Ōtomo Sōrin, supposedly the mission's most eminent sponsor, was told of the project only at the very last minute, if then.

The Members —— After considerable discussion it was decided to send four young boys who would be able to withstand the long and arduous trip: ITŌ MANCIO, who would act as leader and represent the Ōtomo daimyō family, CHIJIWA MIGUEL, who would represent the Arima and Ōmura daimyō families, and NAKAURA JULIÃO and HARA MARTINHO. They were all 12 to 13 years old and students at the Jesuit seminary in Arima. Valignano, who at the beginning thought he would accompany them all the way, chose another 16 people to complete the party. Of these, Father Diego Mesquita, who later replaced Valignano, was to act as interpreter; Father Nuño Rodrigues was to precede the party to Rome to request the Pope's support; and Brother Jorge de Loyola was to stay on in Spain to study printing and then return with the equipment necessary to set up a press in Japan.

The Journey —— The journey was long because of the monsoons and enforced waits for connecting boats. Leaving Nagasaki on 20 February 1582 (Tenshō 10.1.28), the envoys stayed in Macao from 9 March to 31 December. They were forced to make another long stay in southern India, in Goa and Cochin (27 March 1583–20 February 1584). While they were at Goa, Valignano received orders from the general of the Society of Jesus to stay in India as provincial. The mission rounded the Cape of Good Hope on 10 May 1584 and finally reached Lisbon on 10 August. After visiting Lisbon, Evora, and Villa Viçousa in Portugal, they entered Spain, and on 14 November 1584 they were warmly received by Philip II. On 1 March 1585 they proceeded to Livorno (Leghorn) in Italy, and thence to Pisa, where they were received by Francesco I dei Medici, grand duke of Tuscany. This was the beginning of a triumphant progress through the various Italian states; in accordance with papal wishes, their hosts vied with one another in hospitality. In Rome, Pope Gregory XIII took the young envoys to his heart and granted all of Valignano's requests. Even before the mission reached Rome, he had issued a papal bull confirming that Japan was the prerogative of the Jesuits. Having already showered the envoys with gifts, on 23 March 1585 he convoked in their honor a consistory to emphasize yet again that he considered the boys ambassadors in every sense. Pope Gregory died on 10 April, but his successor, Sixtus V, proved to be equally well disposed toward the mission. Leaving Rome, the party crossed to the Adriatic coast, visiting Ancona, Bologna, and Ferrara, and finally arrived at Venice, where they were given a spectacular reception. Particularly memorable was the procession in St. Mark's Square and the cavalcade of boats that accompanied them through the canals of the city. From Venice they visited Padua, Vicenza, Mantova, and Milan on their way to Genoa, where they reembarked for Spain on 8 August 1585. They finally left Lisbon on 12 April 1586 and arrived back in Nagasaki four years later (July 1590).

Achievements —— Valignano had achieved his first aim—that of a Jesuit monopoly in Japan—even though it was to be lost when Span-

ish Franciscans were allowed entry into Japan in 1593. But nothing came of his hopes of introducing Europe to the Japanese, for Japan had changed significantly during the mission's eight-years' absence. In 1587 the military hegemon TOYOTOMI HIDEYOSHI had presented the Jesuits with his Expulsion Edict, which, though not implemented in full, had been a warning note (see ANTI-CHRISTIAN EDICTS). Nevertheless, Hideyoshi agreed to receive Valignano and the four young men at his palatial castle in Kyōto, the Juraku no Tei, on 3 March 1591 (Tenshō 19; 1st month, 8th day intercalary) but only because Valignano came in his official capacity as envoy of Dom Duarte de Menezes, viceroy of Portuguese India. The four young men were able to publicize what they had learned only in their small circle in Kyūshū. Nevertheless, the mission made an enormous impression in Europe. Though they were not absolutely the first Japanese to set foot in Europe—a certain Bernardo, for instance, a follower of Xavier, had visited Lisbon and Rome during the years of 1553–55—this was the first time that popular interest in Japan was aroused, and there appeared numerous published accounts of the aspect and demeanor of these exotic people from the other side of the world.

◼ —— Adriana Boscaro, *The First Japanese Ambassadors to Europe: Political Background to a Religious Journey* (1970). Adriana Boscaro, *Sixteenth-Century European Printed Works on the First Japanese Mission to Europe* (1973). Matsuda Kiichi, *Tenshō ken'ō shisetsu* (1977). Tōkyō Daigaku Shiryō Hensanjo, ed, *Tenshō ken'ō shisetsu kankei shiryō*, in *Dai Nippon shiryō*, part 11, *bekkan* 1–2 (1959–61).   *Adriana BOSCARO*

Misumi

Town in west central Kumamoto Prefecture, Kyūshū. With the completion of the Yamanami Highway, Misumi has become an important port for goods to Shimabara and a convenient stop on the Beppu–Aso–Unzen tourist route. It is also a base for sightseeing in the islands of Amakusa. Mandarin oranges are grown. Pop: 13,271.

Mita bungaku

(Mita Literature). Literary journal founded by Keiō University's Department of Letters to compete with the rival Waseda University's WASEDA BUNGAKU; published from May 1910 to the present with numerous intervals when publication lapsed because of financial or operational difficulties. Under first editor NAGAI KAFŪ, newly installed professor of literature at Keiō and a leader of the antinaturalist camp, *Mita bungaku* joined forces against the so-called Japanese naturalism with SHINSHICHŌ and SUBARU. Its contributors were a diverse lot, including such writers and poets as MORI ŌGAI, IZUMI KYŌKA, NOGUCHI YONEJIRŌ, YOSANO AKIKO, KITAHARA HAKUSHŪ, TANIZAKI JUN'ICHIRŌ, and ABE JIRŌ. It also carried works by former Keiō affiliates and produced a group of so-called pure *Mita bungaku* writers that included KUBOTA MANTARŌ, MINAKAMI TAKITARŌ, SATŌ HARUO, KINOSHITA MOKUTARŌ, and HORIGUCHI DAIGAKU. Publication was stopped by Keiō officials in 1925, however, when controversy arose over the allotment of financial resources to various university magazines. At this time, angry *Mita bungaku* staff members, led by Minakami and Kubota, took over and ran it as an independent journal.

The second series of *Mita bungaku* appeared from April 1926 to November 1944 and introduced a large number of new writers, among whom were HARA TAMIKI, ISHIZAKA YŌJIRŌ, SHIBATA RENZABURŌ, OKAMOTO KANOKO, and IBUSE MASUJI. Minakami died in 1940 but *Mita bungaku* continued to appear until late 1944 when it was finally forced to suspend publication. Revived in 1946, during the postwar era it has survived frequent interruptions to publish a number of prizewinning works by writers like ENDŌ SHŪSAKU, ETŌ JUN, YASUOKA SHŌTARŌ, MATSUMOTO SEICHŌ, and YOSHIYUKI JUNNOSUKE.   *Theodore W. GOOSSEN*

Mitaka

City in east central Tōkyō Prefecture, central Honshū. The area served as a hunting ground for the Tokugawa shōguns during the Edo period (1600–1868). Farming was the principal activity up to the early part of the Shōwa period (1926–). However, with the establishment of munitions plants during World War II, the population of the city increased rapidly. It is now primarily a residential and commercial city. Attractions include Inokashira Park and the temple Zenrinji, where the graves of the writers MORI ŌGAI and DAZAI OSAMU are located. Also located in the city are the Tōkyō Astronomical Observatory and International Christian University. Pop: 164,449.

Mitaka Incident

Controversial criminal incident of the OCCUPATION period. On 15 July 1949 an unmanned electric train with its operating handle tied down drove out of control into the suburban Mitaka station, west of Tōkyō, derailed, and killed six people standing on the platform. The Japanese government subsequently indicted 10 persons on a charge of train sabotage resulting in death, an offense that carries the death penalty in Japan. All 10 were members of the National Railroad Workers' Union (NRWU), and 9 were prominent members of the Japan Communist Party. The government treated the incident as an instance of terrorism perpetrated by the communist-dominated NRWU in opposition to the efforts of the government and of the American Occupation authorities to rehabilitate Japan economically and to end the Japan Communist Party's domination of the railroad workers' union. The Mitaka Incident was one of three major instances of violence that occurred during 1949, when the Supreme Commander for the Allied Powers (SCAP) sought to implement the so-called reverse course in Occupation policy: the shift from an emphasis on the democratization of Japan to an emphasis on economic recovery and alliance with the United States. The other two incidents were the MATSUKAWA INCIDENT and the SHIMOYAMA INCIDENT.

The government's indictments of the communist leaders were based on a confession the police obtained from Takeuchi Keisuke, a railroad employee who had been discharged in the massive layoffs of personnel from the Japanese National Railways during 1949. After a trial that was continuously disrupted by communist demonstrators and observed in the courtroom by members of SCAP's counterintelligence services, the Tōkyō District Court in August 1950 released all of the defendants except Takeuchi, who had confessed. When the case was reviewed on appeal, the Tōkyō High Court sustained the verdicts of innocent for the nine communists but increased Takeuchi's sentence to death. His appeal to the Supreme Court against the death penalty was denied in June 1955. Takeuchi and his supporters initiated new appeals, based on allegedly new evidence. However, on 18 January 1967, Takeuchi died of natural causes in Sugamo Prison, protesting to the end that his confession had been extracted from him by force and that he was innocent.

The importance of the Mitaka Incident (together with the Matsukawa and Shimoyama incidents) lay in the public anger it aroused against the Communist Party and against the radical trade unions that had come into being during the early years of the Occupation. The press and public concluded that the communists were willing to employ terrorist tactics against innocent people to further their policies. Although these charges were never proved in court against the Communist Party—the courts held that Takeuchi alone was responsible for the Mitaka crime—the climate of political opinion in Japan during 1949 and 1950 turned hostile to communism. This helped the government of Prime Minister YOSHIDA SHIGERU to move Japan toward economic recovery, the SAN FRANCISCO PEACE TREATY of 1952, and the security alliance with the United States.

■ ——Chalmers Johnson, *Conspiracy at Matsukawa* (1972).

Chalmers JOHNSON

Mitamura Engyo (1870–1952)

Scholar and essayist. Born Mitamura Genryū in the city of Hachiōji, Tōkyō Prefecture. He worked as a local newspaper reporter before becoming a regular contributor to the influential conservative magazine *Nihon oyobi nihonjin* (1907–30, Japan and the Japanese), edited by MIYAKE SETSUREI. Although largely self-taught, he possessed a broad knowledge of the history and culture of the Edo period (1600–1868) and wrote many biographical sketches as well as essays on the manners and customs of Edo (now Tōkyō). His works are collected in *Mitamura Engyo zenshū* (Chūō Kōron Sha, 1975–).

Mitford, Algernon (1837–1915)

In full, Algernon Bertram Freeman-Mitford, first Baron Redesdale (of second creation). English author, linguist, and diplomat; attaché in the British legation at Edo (later Tōkyō) from 1866 to 1870. Member of a distinguished family noted for public service and literary talent, he is best known for his *Tales of Old Japan* (1871), one of the first popular books in English on Japanese customs and folktales.

Born in London, Mitford began his travels at the age of three, when his parents moved to France. He attended Eton and Christ Church College, Oxford, leaving without a degree in 1858. Entering the diplomatic service at St. Petersburg (now Leningrad) in 1863, he was torn between his linguistic and cultural interests and his professional career. Posted in Beijing (Peking) in 1865, Mitford, already fluent in French and German and with a reading knowledge of Arabic, began to study Chinese. The next year he was transferred to Japan, where he studied Japanese under Sir Ernest SATOW. Arriving at a time of turmoil, Mitford witnessed (and later described in his *Memories,* 1915) the events surrounding the MEIJI RESTORATION of 1868.

Mitford retired from the Foreign Office in 1873 and settled into the life of a literary gentleman in the intellectual and artistic Chelsea district of London, home of the writer Thomas Carlyle and the painter James A. M. Whistler. His major works include *Bamboo Garden* (1896), *Attaché at Peking* (1900), and *Further Memories* (1917). A short work of special interest is his *Garter Mission to Japan* (1906), an account of the visit to Japan of King Edward VII's nephew, Prince Arthur of Connaught, to present the Order of the Garter to Emperor Meiji. The trip was a sentimental return for Mitford, who had known Japan's elder statemen in 1868, and an event that symbolized the emergence of Japan as a major world power following the ANGLO-JAPANESE ALLIANCE of 1902 and Japan's victory over Russia in 1905.   *Dallas FINN*

MITI → Ministry of International Trade and Industry

Mito

Capital of Ibaraki Prefecture, central Honshū. Situated on the river Nakagawa, the city developed with the construction of a castle by the Daijō family in the Kamakura period (1185–1333). Later, under the rule of the Edo and Satake families, after the Battle of Sekigahara (1600), it became the castle town of Tokugawa Yorifusa, the 11th son of the victorious hegemon TOKUGAWA IEYASU. The Mito domain flourished throughout the Edo period (1600–1868) as the base of one of the three senior collateral families (GOSANKE) of the Tokugawa and was noted for its capable *daimyō,* such as TOKUGAWA MITSUKUNI and TOKUGAWA NARIAKI. It was also, paradoxically, the center of an emperor-oriented school of learning (MITO SCHOOL). Local products include flour, tobacco, and *nattō* (fermented soybeans). Of historic interest are the site of the former Mito Castle, KAIRAKUEN Park, and Kōdōkan, a school established by Nariaki in 1841. Pop: 215,563.

Mito Civil War

(Tengutō no Ran). Uprising by the proimperial, antishogunate (SONNŌ JŌI) Tengutō faction in the Mito domain (now part of Ibaraki Prefecture) in 1864. The culmination of a long and bitter factional rivalry within the domain, it resulted in the deaths of some 1,300 Mito people and hundreds from other domains. It devastated Mito, ruining its finances, ravaging its territory, and decimating its manpower. With the CHŌSHŪ EXPEDITIONS of 1864 and 1866 and the BOSHIN CIVIL WAR of 1868–69, it was one of the three major wars accompanying the disintegration of the Tokugawa shogunate.

Throughout the Edo period (1600–1868) factional rivalries and outbursts of unrest (OIE SŌDŌ) had been quite common in the *daimyō* domains. In Mito the rivalries were inflamed by ideological tensions and broader political issues, and it was these that turned factional rivalry into historic tragedy. The ideological element stemmed from the scholarly tradition of the DAI NIHON SHI, the monumental history of Japan undertaken by TOKUGAWA MITSUKUNI, and the proimperial consciousness fostered by the MITO SCHOOL of learning. During the 19th century, as foreign vessels increasingly intruded into Japanese waters, Mito scholars such as AIZAWA SEISHISAI advocated basic reforms to enable Japan to cope with both the foreign interlopers and growing domestic problems. In 1829 TOKUGAWA NARIAKI became daimyō of Mito and undertook a vigorous program designed to achieve those purposes. Nariaki's forceful policies generated intense political conflict in Mito. A conservative faction impeded many of his plans, while a radical faction (the Tengutō) bitterly resented their resistance.

The quarrels within Mito became entangled with shogunate politics during the TEMPŌ REFORMS and led to Nariaki's enforced retirement in 1844. But during the diplomatic crisis following the arrival of Commodore PERRY in 1853, ABE MASAHIRO, the shogunate leader, solicited Nariaki's cooperation. The return of Nariaki to vigorous participation in national affairs, and especially his pursuit of imperial connections, renewed the tensions in Mito. The shogunate leader II NAOSUKE's subsequent repression of Mito (see ANSEI PURGE) brought those tensions to the snapping point. Factional agitation threatened to become military conflict as hundreds of Mito warriors surged about the countryside.

The tumult was calmed temporarily when Ii was murdered by *samurai* from Mito and the Satsuma domain in 1860 (see SAKURADAMONGAI INCIDENT), but it was revived three years later when the shogunate failed to comply with imperial court orders to expel all foreigners. The Tengutō faction strongly criticized the shogunate and advocated forceful explusion. In early 1864 they resolved to support the court and expel the foreigners. Their subsequent actions pitted them against more cautious groups in the domain, led to months of confused maneuvering and deployments, and finally precipitated civil war in Mito.

FUJITA TŌKO's son Fujita Koshirō (1842–65) and others at Mito led Tengutō forces southwest to Mt. Tsukuba (Tsukubasan). Repeatedly defying orders from both their daimyō, Tokugawa Yoshiatsu, and the shogunate to return to their homes, they began foraging operations that led shogunate officials and Mito conservatives under Ichikawa Hirosane to deploy forces of suppression.

By mid-1864 Fujita's group had acquired hundreds of supporters, including large numbers under the proimperial activist TAKEDA KŌUNSAI. The shogunate mobilized all its available forces, and what had begun as an intradomain quarrel assumed the proportions of a major insurrection against the Tokugawa regime. For a few weeks it was not clear whether daimyō forces in the Kantō region would support the shogunate as ordered or give at least moral support to the insurgents. In the autumn of 1864, however, the daimyō finally obeyed their orders to mobilize, and the insurrection was crushed in three months. The effort required the full might of the shogunate, Ichikawa's Mito forces, and the troops of about a dozen Kantō domains—more than 12,000 troops deployed against some 2,000 insurgents.

In the resulting settlement the shogunate punished the insurgents ruthlessly, and during the next three years conservatives ruled Mito with a heavy hand. At the time of the Meiji Restoration (1868) surviving members of the Tengutō again took to the field; now on the winning side, they wreaked a savage vengeance on their erstwhile oppressors. The bitterness of the internal quarrels of Mito lasted for decades afterward, and the tragedy has colored the interpretation of Mito history even to the present.

🔲——Ernest W. Clement and C. Tani, "The Mito Civil War," *Transactions of the Asiatic Society of Japan* 19 (1891). *Mito Han shiryō* (1915, repr 1970). Takagi Shunsuke, "Mito Han sonnō jōi undō no sonraku shusshin giseisha," *Ibaraki Ken shi kenkyū* 13 (1969).

Conrad TOTMAN

Mito Kōmon → Tokugawa Mitsukuni

Mito school

(Mitogaku). A school of thought deriving from Shintō and Confucianism, its development is usually divided into two stages. The origins of the Mito school can be traced to the early part of the Edo period (1600–1868), when TOKUGAWA MITSUKUNI, the lord of the Mito domain (now part of Ibaraki Prefecture), founded the Historical Research Institute, SHŌKŌKAN, for the purpose of compiling the DAI NIHON SHI (History of Great Japan, completed in 1906). The members of the early Mito school had remarkably heterogeneous philosophical backgrounds. Among the members of the Shōkōkan were followers of Taoism, Buddhism, and Shintō, as well as Confucianists of various schools. This open-mindedness of Mitsukuni is reflected in the epitaph he wrote for himself: "He honored Shintō and Confucianism, and he stood against Shintō and Confucianism. He revered Buddhism and Taoism, and he opposed Buddhism and Taoism." The most outstanding representatives of this early period included Mitsukuni and his teacher SHU SHUNSUI, a Chinese scholar who had fled China after the fall of the Ming dynasty and settled in Japan, as well as KURIYAMA SEMPŌ, MIYAKE KANRAN, and ASAKA TAMPAKU. The early stage of the Mito school ended around 1720 when the major part of the *Dai Nihon shi*, consisting of the main annals *(hongi)* and the biographies *(retsuden)*, was presented to the shogunate.

The late Mito school began around 1790 when Tachihara Suiken (1744–1823) was director of the Shōkōkan. Most outstanding among

his students was FUJITA YŪKOKU, whose *Seimeiron* (1791, On the Rectification of Names) is, in its advocacy of the proper moral order in society, almost a guideline for late Mito scholarship. Together with his student AIZAWA SEISHISAI, the author of *Shinron* (1825, New Discourse), and his son FUJITA TŌKO, who wrote KŌDŌKAN KI JUTSUGI (1845–49, Commentary on the Manifesto of Kōdōkan Academy), Yūkoku became a propagator of Mito *samurai* nationalism, exemplified in the famous slogan SONNŌ JŌI (Revere the Emperor, Expel the Barbarians). In contrast to the early phase, the studies of the late Mito school had a more distinct character and can be more properly called a school. Its main orientation derived from the ethics of the Zhu Xi (Chu Hsi) school of Confucianism (SHUSHIGAKU), the "oneness of theory and action" of the Wang Yangming school of Confucianism (YŌMEIGAKU), the institutional approach of OGYŪ SORAI's school of Ancient Learning (KOGAKU), and the mythohistorical thinking of the Neo-Shintoist KOKUGAKU (National Learning). Even the technically oriented WESTERN LEARNING left its imprint on late Mito thought. The institutional center was the Kōdōkan Academy of Mito founded by TOKUGAWA NARIAKI, a student of Aizawa Seishisai.

The late Mito school attempted to find solutions for the internal crisis within the feudal system and the external threat of the Western world. Mito scholars felt the West would destroy not only Japan's social and political systems but also the true character of the Japanese nation, the "body of the nation" (KOKUTAI), and its identity as the "country of the gods" (*shinkoku*). Accordingly, they focused on the clarification of the concept of *kokutai*, with the emperor at the pinnacle of the nation's hierarchical structure, and urged people to find their proper place within this structure and to fulfill their moral obligations. Attacking what they saw as the moral degeneration of the age, they also campaigned for political and military reforms.

In this regard, it may be said that the school tended to political conservatism. Yet their works were read widely throughout the country and constituted the ideological thrust of the proimperial antishogunate movement during the last critical years of the Edo period. Furthermore, even after the MEIJI RESTORATION (1868), the Mito school exerted a formative influence on the nationalist ideology of the new imperial regime, an ideology that stressed the Japanese spiritual tradition and developed further the concept of the *kokutai*. Although the influence of this school has been slight since World War II, there remains a handful of scholars who feel responsible for the preservation of the school's ideals. These are mainly associated with the Historical Society of Mito and other traditionalist groups such as the Shintō-oriented Kōgakukan University at Ise.

🔲——D. M. Earl, *Emperor and Nation in Japan: Political Thinkers of the Tokugawa Period* (1964). H. D. Harootunian, *Toward Restoration* (1970). Hashikawa Bunzō, "Mitogaku no genryū to seiritsu," *Nihon no meicho*, vol 29 (Chūō Kōron Sha, 1974). K. Kracht, *Das Kōdōkanki-jutsugi des Fujita Tōko (1806–1855)* (1975). K. Kracht, " 'Name' (mei) und 'Anteil' (bun)," *Oriens Extremus* 23 (1976). K. Kracht, "Antimodernismus als Wegbereiter der Moderne," *Bochumer Jahrbuch zur Ostasienforschung* 1 (1978). K. Kracht, "Seiyō nihongaku no Mito Han mitogaku kenkyū," *Mito shigaku* 9 (1978). K. Kracht, "Philosophische Reflexionen am Abend der Feudalgesellschaft," *Bochumer Jahrbuch zur Ostasienforschung* 2 (1979). Matsumoto Sumio, *Mitogaku no genryū* (1940). Nagoya Tokimasa, *Mitogaku no kenkyū* (1975). Takasu Yoshijirō, *Mitogaku jiten* (1942).

Klaus KRACHT

Mitsubishi

Business enterprise begun by IWASAKI YATARŌ in the early 1870s; major financial and industrial combine (ZAIBATSU) of the pre–World War II era, second in size only to MITSUI; and enterprise grouping (KEIRETSU) of the postwar period. Mitsubishi was founded on Iwasaki's acquisition of the commercial enterprises of the Tosa domain (now Kōchi Prefecture), substantial aid from the Meiji government, and the great entrepreneurial skill of Iwasaki and his successors.

In 1870, when the new government ordered the discontinuance of domain-operated enterprises, the trading and shipping firm of the Tosa domain was reorganized as a semipublic company under the management of Iwasaki Yatarō, who had gained a reputation for business skill by revitalizing the firm's Nagasaki branch. When the government abolished the domains in 1871 (see PREFECTURAL SYSTEM, ESTABLISHMENT OF), the company received 11 ships and other facilities of the Tosa domain; it was expected to contribute to the new prefecture's revenues and provide employment for its former *samurai*. Through political connections, however, the aggressive

Iwasaki managed to turn this semipublic firm into a private enterprise, and in 1873 he named it the Mitsubishi Commercial Company (Mitsubishi Shōkai). The name Mitsubishi (literally, "three diamond shapes") was taken from a crest *(mon)* of that description, widely used in Shikoku, that Yatarō adopted as his trademark. According to family tradition, he chose this name rather than Iwasaki for his business in order to disassociate the family name from the quest for profit.

Iwasaki profited greatly from the TAIWAN EXPEDITION OF 1874. Because the Mitsubishi fleet of 11 ships was insufficient to transport the government forces, the state purchased 13 additional ships and entrusted them to Mitsubishi. Subsequently the government gave the ships to Iwasaki outright with an annual subsidy for their operation. Strengthened by this largesse, in 1875 the company was renamed Mitsubishi Steamship Company (Mitsubishi Kisen Kaisha) and in the same year received a navigation charter from the government. In 1877 the company gained from another military venture, the suppression of the SATSUMA REBELLION in Kyūshū. The government again gave Iwasaki ships and a subsidy in return for marine transport during the campaign.

Mitsubishi now owned virtually the entire Japanese commercial fleet. The rival Mitsui group found this situation unacceptable, and in 1882 it persuaded the government to assist it and some other firms in founding a second steamship company, the Kyōdō Transport Company (Kyōdō Un'yu Kaisha). Competition between the two shipping firms became so intense that it drove both of them to the verge of bankruptcy, and in 1885 they were merged to form the NIPPON YŪSEN company, which came under the de facto control of Mitsubishi.

Established only in the Meiji period (1868–1912) and involving only two family lines, Mitsubishi did not have the highly formal structure that characterized the older and more ramified Mitsui house. The leadership of the company came to alternate every generation between the family of Yatarō, the founder, and that of his younger brother Iwasaki Yanosuke (1851–1908). Yanosuke assumed control of business operations on Yatarō's death in 1885, he was succeeded in 1896 by Yatarō's son Hisaya, who was in turn succeeded in 1916 by Yanosuke's son IWASAKI KOYATA, president of Mitsubishi until his death in 1945.

Although he began in shipping, Iwasaki Yatarō quickly diversified his enterprise and laid the foundation of a financial and industrial empire. He acquired the first of the Mitsubishi metal mines, the Yoshioka Copper Mine, in 1873 and the first of its coal mines, the TAKASHIMA COAL MINE, in 1881. In 1880 he established a money-lending, exchange, and warehousing operation.

Iwasaki Yanosuke added banking to the firm's activities when in 1885 he took over management of the 119th National Bank, which was in financial difficulty; in 1895 the bank became the financial arm of Mitsubishi, Ltd. Enormously important to Mitsubishi's future development was the government's decision in 1884 to lease to Mitsubishi the NAGASAKI SHIPYARDS, which it had inherited from the Tokugawa shogunate. When the government decided in 1887 to sell its leased properties to the lessees (see KAN'EI JIGYŌ HARAISAGE), Mitsubishi came into possession of an industrial facility that is still an important part of the enterprise. In 1887 the company added real estate to its range of activities. In order to raise money, the government sold to Mitsubishi a large tract of land in front of the Imperial Palace in Tōkyō that the company developed into the Marunouchi business district.

In 1893, when the company-law provisions of the COMMERCIAL CODE went into effect, Yanosuke organized Mitsubishi, Ltd (Mitsubishi Gōshi Kaisha). The various Mitsubishi enterprises were made divisions of this limited partnership. They began to be separately incorporated again during the period of broad economic growth during and immediately following World War I. Because the key Mitsubishi enterprises had experienced a quarter-century of shared growth as divisions of the partnership, the economic activities of the Mitsubishi complex were well integrated. By contrast, the top holding company of Mitsui did little more than coordinate the activities of its key subsidiaries, which for the most part grew up outside of the holding company.

Under Iwasaki Koyata, Mitsubishi proceeded to establish independent joint-stock companies, which it controlled through majority shareholding. Between 1917 and 1919, seven subsidiaries were spun off from Mitsubishi, Ltd—shipbuilding and engineering, iron and steel, mining, trading, banking, marine and fire insurance, and warehousing. In the years 1919–21 two subsidiaries—Mitsubishi Internal Combustion Engine (later Mitsubishi Aircraft) and MI-

TSUBISHI ELECTRIC CORPORATION—were set up as spinoffs of the shipbuilding and engineering concern. Beginnings were made in other fields as well—the trust business, oil refining, and the aircraft and chemical industries. Reversing the "spinoff" process, MITSUBISHI HEAVY INDUSTRIES, LTD, was formed in 1934, the product of a merger of Mitsubishi Shipbuilding and Engineering with Mitsubishi Aircraft. Two Mitsubishi enterprises had arrangements with American companies whereby the latter provided technology in return for equity participation; they were Mitsubishi Electric, in which Westinghouse acquired a 9.8-percent interest, and MITSUBISHI OIL CO, LTD, in which Tidewater Oil acquired a 50-percent interest.

As a result of expansion and diversification, Mitsubishi had developed by 1928 into a giant *zaibatsu;* its holding company, Mitsubishi, Ltd, was capitalized at ¥120 million and controlled 10 first-line designated subsidiaries, 11 second-line designated subsidiaries, and numerous subaffiliates with a total paid-up capital of ¥590 million.

In preparation for and during World War II, the Mitsubishi companies expanded greatly, both within the domestic economy and in Japans' empire, the GREATER EAST ASIA COPROSPERITY SPHERE. By the end of the war, Mitsubishi, Ltd, which had been reorganized as a joint-stock company in 1937, controlled 209 companies, including 11 first-line designated subsidiaries and 8 second-line designated subsidiaries. The holding company had a total paid-up capital of ¥240 million. The total paid-up capital of the subsidiaries was ¥3.1 billion (¥2.7 billion domestic and ¥413 million abroad).

Between 1946 and 1950, the Mitsubishi combine was broken up by the ZAIBATSU DISSOLUTION measures of the Allied Occupation. Since the 1950s, the former Mitsubishi subsidiaries have been loosely affiliated as an enterprise grouping *(keiretsu)*. The holding company has been replaced by a presidents' club (Kin'yōkai; "Friday Club"), which meets regularly and provides some coordination of policy. Different writers on the Mitsubishi *keiretsu* put the count of member companies differently, but it is generally thought that the 1971 size of the grouping was some 85. See also CORPORATE HISTORY.

📖——*Business History Review* 44 (Spring 1970), Special Issue: Japanese Entrepreneurship. Eleanor M. Hadley, *Antitrust in Japan* (1970). Johannes Hirschmeier and Tsunehiko Yui, *The Development of Japanese Business, 1600–1973* (1975). Iwasaki Yatarō Iwasaki Yanosuke Denki Hensankai, ed, *Iwasaki Yatarō den,* 2 vols (1967). Mochikabu Kaisha Seiri Iinkai, *Nihon zaibatsu to sono kaitai, shiryō* (1950), contains comprehensive bibliography of Japanese and Western works on Mitsubishi to 1950. Mitsubishi Economic Research Institute, ed, *Mitsui, Mitsubishi, Sumitomo* (1955). State-War Mission on Japanese Combines, *Report to the Department of State and the War Department,* pt 1 (1946). Hidemasa Morikawa, "The Organizational Structure of the Mitsubishi and Mitsui Zaibatsu, 1868–1922: A Comparative Study," *Business History Review* (Spring 1970). Kozo Yamamura, "The Founding of Mitsubishi: A Case Study in Japanese Business History," *Business History Review* 41 (Summer 1967). *Eleanor M.* HADLEY

Mitsubishi Bank, Ltd

(Mitsubishi Ginkō). Major city bank based in Tōkyō with branches in Ōsaka and other large cities. Fourth largest city bank in Japan in deposits behind DAI-ICHI KANGYŌ BANK, LTD; FUJI BANK, LTD; and SUMITOMO BANK, LTD. Mitsubishi Bank's predecessor was the Mitsubishi Exchange Office, established in 1880 by IWASAKI YATARŌ, founder of MITSUBISHI. The Mitsubishi Exchange Office later became the banking division of Mitsubishi Company, but in 1919 it became independent of its parent firm as Mitsubishi Bank, Ltd. After World War II it changed its name to the Chiyoda Bank but reverted to its original name in 1953. It has played a leading role in industrial financing; since the 1960s it has also expanded transactions with consumer and small business loans.

It is also active in international operations, engaging in trade financing and providing assistance to Japanese enterprises for flotation of Euro-bonds, American depositary receipts (ADRs), and European depositary receipts (EDRs). It also provides loans to developing nations as well as to various international institutions, and underwrites yen-based foreign bonds. It entered the overseas financial market in 1920 with the establishment of branches in New York and London. It reopened its New York branch in 1952 and, with successive additions, in 1982 had eight overseas branches. In the same year the bank had operational bases in a total of 21 foreign cities and 5 overseas subsidiaries, including the Mitsubishi Bank of California. It has also set up a worldwide operational network through the formation of joint venture banks. It has a total of 205 domestic branch banks. At the end of March 1982 its total assets were ¥20.4 trillion (US $84.7 billion); deposits ¥14.9 trillion (US $61.9 billion); annual ordinary profit ¥87.3 billion (US $362.7 million); and its capitalization stood at ¥111.3 billion (US $462.4 million).

Mitsubishi Chemical Industries, Ltd

(Mitsubishi Kasei Kōgyō). Comprehensive chemical maker. One of the chief firms in the Mitsubishi group of companies, it has the largest share of the domestic market for chemical products. Founded in 1934 under the name Nihon Tāru Kōgyō, it was capitalized on an equal basis by MITSUBISHI MINING & CEMENT CO, LTD, and ASAHI GLASS CO, LTD. Originally a manufacturer of coal chemical products, it was solidly established before World War II as a chemical company manufacturing coke, tar products, dyestuffs, and fertilizers. In the mid-1960s it moved into the petrochemical field, becoming a comprehensive chemical firm. It has a total of five plants, including the main Kurosaki plant in the city of Kita Kyūshū. In Yokohama it has established a major research center, as well as the Mitsubishi Kasei Institute of Life Sciences, one of the largest organizations of its kind in the world. In recent years, utilizing technology it previously developed, it has diversified into the fields of pharmaceuticals, medical-care equipment, analytical instruments, and information-processing equipment. In 1982 it had overseas liaison offices in five countries, including the United States and West Germany, and was engaged in joint ventures in Brazil, Malaysia, Norway and the United States. Sales for the fiscal year ending January 1982 totaled ¥756.1 billion (US $3.4 billion), of which sales of petrochemical products amounted to 43.4 percent; carbon products 30.1 percent; chemicals 12.7 percent; agricultural chemicals 11.1 percent; and other products 2.7 percent. In the same year the export ratio was 11.2 percent and the firm was capitalized at ¥53 billion (US $236 million). Corporate headquarters are located in Tōkyō.

Mitsubishi Corporation

(Mitsubishi Shōji). As Japan's largest *sōgō shōsha* (see GENERAL TRADING COMPANIES), Mitsubishi Corporation's activities extend to all corners of the world. Its trade transactions in the fiscal year ending March 1982 totaled ¥14.7 trillion (US $61 billion), a figure equal to about one-quarter of Japan's national budget for the same year. The company handles some 25,000 categories of products. With over 60 domestic and 130 overseas offices and subsidiaries, its telecommunications network extends more than 455,000 kilometers (282,732 mi). The company utilizes this network to gather and distribute the latest information to its customers worldwide.

Approximately 41.7 percent of the company's business is in domestic transactions, 32.9 percent in import, 17.6 percent in export, and 7.8 percent in transactions outside Japan. It is organized into nine business divisions: project development and construction, fuel, ferrous metals, nonferrous metals, machinery, food, textiles, chemicals, and general merchandise. Mitsubishi Corporation functions as a business organizer in such projects as oil exploration, mineral resources development, airport construction, and heavy chemical plant construction. The company engages in all facets of the undertakings from initial surveys, planning, funding, and materials procurement to construction and operation.

The company originated in a shipping business founded in 1870 by IWASAKI YATARŌ and took the name Mitsubishi Gōshi Kaisha in 1911. The trading division of this company was organized as an independent entity under the name Mitsubishi Shōji Kaisha in 1918. In 1947 Mitsubishi Shōji was ordered to dissolve by the Allied Occupation authorities and its business was partitioned into 139 small firms. It made a dramatic comeback and started to regain its prewar position by regrouping the dissolved companies in 1954. The corporate name in English was changed from Mitsubishi Trading Company to Mitsubishi Corporation in 1971. Capitalization stood at ¥63.5 billion (US $263.8 million) in 1982. The head office is in Tōkyō.

Mitsubishi Electric Corporation

(Mitsubishi Denki). Manufacturer of heavy electrical machinery, household electrical products, electronic equipment, and industrial machinery. Affiliated with the Mitsubishi group of companies. Its transformers for electrical power transmission have a worldwide reputation. It was founded in 1921 when the electric equipment division of the Mitsubishi Engineering & Shipbuilding Co (currently MITSUBISHI HEAVY INDUSTRIES, LTD) was set up as an independent firm. Initially engaged in the manufacture and repair of electrical equipment for ships and mining operations, it has since commenced production of equipment for electric power generation and transmission, as well as household appliances. With the increase in demand for large-scale generators after World War II and the swift growth of the market for household appliances since the 1950s, sales have mushroomed. The company became a well-established manufacturer of television sets, refrigerators, air-conditioners, and other household appliances. At the same time it expanded production facilities for semiconductors, communication equipment, and other electronic products, thereby becoming an integrated manufacturer of electrical products. Since the mid-1970s, it has placed major emphasis on the export of production plants and the development of high-efficiency solar batteries. It established joint venture manufacturing companies in India, Taiwan, Thailand, and South Korea in the 1960s. In 1981 its manufacturing and sales subsidiaries, which numbered more than 60, were located in Asia, Australia, Europe, the United States, and Latin America. Sales for the fiscal year ending March 1982 totaled ¥1.3 trillion (US $5.4 billion), third in the industry after HITACHI, LTD, and TŌSHIBA CORPORATION. Of the total revenue of fiscal 1981, household appliances accounted for 25 percent, electronic equipment and industrial machinery 33 percent, heavy electrical machinery 26 percent, and others 16 percent. In the same year the export rate was 22 percent and capitalization stood at ¥75.2 billion (US $312.4 million). The head office is in Tōkyō.

Mitsubishi Estate Co, Ltd

(Mitsubishi Jisho). Major real estate company engaged chiefly in the leasing of land and buildings, but also in the sale of real estate. It is the largest owner of buildings located in the Tōkyō business office district, Marunouchi. Together with the MITSUI REAL ESTATE DEVELOPMENT CO, LTD, and the TŌKYŪ LAND CORPORATION, it is one of the three major real estate companies in Japan. Although it was founded in 1937, the firm traces its origins back to the purchase of land in the Marunouchi district from the government in 1887 by Iwasaki Yanosuke of the MITSUBISHI group.

Today Mitsubishi Estate is highly diversified. In addition to managing office buildings, it engages in the design, supervision, and subcontracting of construction and public works projects; the construction and sale of houses; the dredging of ports and rivers; land reclamation; management of leisure facilities; and the purchase and sale of real estate. Its building management division owns 75 buildings throughout Japan with a total floor space of 2,260,000 square meters (24,328,000 sq ft), which it leases to major domestic and foreign companies. It has handled the construction of Izumi Park Town (in Miyagi Prefecture), the largest housing tract built in Japan by a private firm, as well as other land and housing development projects. Its design and project supervision division, employing 400 architects and engineers, is the largest private architectural design office in Japan. Its subsidiary, Mitsubishi Estate New York, Inc, operates jointly with other major American real estate companies to develop housing projects. Future plans call for strengthening of its building management division and expansion of its housing projects division. In the fiscal year ending in March 1982 total sales were ¥147.4 billion (US $612.3 million), of which building leases accounted for 68 percent, sale of houses and condominiums 20 percent, architectural design and project supervision 11 percent, and others 1 percent. In the same year capitalization stood at ¥49 billion (US $203.5 million). Corporate headquarters are located in Tōkyō.

Mitsubishi Gas Chemical Co, Inc

(Mitsubishi Gasu Kagaku). Manufacturer of chemicals. Founded in 1951, it was the first company in Japan to succeed in using natural gas as a raw material for chemicals. It is a member of the MITSUBISHI group. Principal products include methanol, formalin, polyols, ammonia, urea, compound fertilizer, xylenes, plasticizers, hydrogen peroxide, sodium hydrosulfite, and synthetic resins. The company is known for its integrated production system. It has also acted as a general consultant to the chemical industry in concert with leading construction firms and machinery and equipment manufacturers. Sales for the fiscal year ending March 1982 totaled ¥207.2 billion (US $860.8 million), distributed as follows: xylenes 33.0 percent, industrial chemicals 18.4 percent, methanol 16.8 percent, synthetic resins 13.8 percent, ammonia 12.3 percent, petroleum products 5.4 percent, and licensing fees 0.3 percent. In the same year the export ratio was 12.8 percent and the company was capitalized at ¥18.1 billion (US $75.2 million). The head office is in Tōkyō.

Mitsubishi Heavy Industries, Ltd

(Mitsubishi Jūkōgyō). Japan's largest heavy machinery manufacturer. It is engaged in shipbuilding, plant construction, and production of engines, construction machinery, air conditioning equipment, machine tools, pollution control equipment, and airplanes. It is also Japan's largest defense contractor and one of the central firms of MITSUBISHI, which dates back to the 1875 establishment of the Mitsubishi Mail Steamship Co. In 1887 the government-owned NAGASAKI SHIPYARDS was transferred to the Mitsubishi Company, providing it with a firm business foundation. In 1917 the Mitsubishi Shipbuilding Co, Ltd, separated from the Mitsubishi Company, and in 1934 it took the name Mitsubishi Heavy Industries, Ltd. In the same year the company absorbed the Mitsubishi Aircraft Co, Ltd; it took over the Yokohama Dock Co, Ltd, the following year. In 1945 Mitsubishi Machine Tool Manufacturing Co, Ltd, was also absorbed. The company served as the core of the heavy industry division of the Mitsubishi ZAIBATSU. It was also a leading Japanese munitions maker, producing a wide range of military equipment, including the battleship MUSASHI and the famous ZERO FIGHTER. By the end of World War II, the company employed 430,000 workers. It was divided into three regional companies as part of the Allied Occupation's ZAIBATSU DISSOLUTION program in 1950, but it regrouped in its present form in 1964. In 1970 the automobile division became the independent MITSUBISHI MOTORS CORPORATION.

The company maintains its technological headquarters at its main office in Tōkyō; elsewhere in Japan, it has 6 branch offices and 12 production plants. It has 4 liaison offices and 10 representatives operating overseas, as well as 7 overseas subsidiary companies and joint ventures. Mitsubishi Heavy Industries receives orders for the construction of large-size plants in foreign countries through the international trade networks of the MITSUBISHI CORPORATION. Sales for the fiscal year ending March 1982 totaled ¥1.68 trillion (US $6.98 billion), of which power systems generated 32 percent; construction machinery, precision machinery, engines, refrigerating and air-conditioning machinery 15 percent; machinery 15 percent; chemical plants and engineering 7 percent; shipbuilding and steel structures 21 percent; and aircraft, special vehicles, and other products 10 percent. The export ratio was 36 percent and the company was capitalized at ¥125.6 billion (US $521.8 million) in the same year.

Mitsubishi Metal Corporation

(Mitsubishi Kinzoku). Company engaged in the smelting and processing of copper, zinc, lead, gold, and silver. The second largest smelter of copper in Japan, it possesses superior technologies for precision molding and stamping. The company was founded in 1873 when IWASAKI YATARŌ, the founder of the Mitsubishi ZAIBATSU, started operating the Yoshioka Copper Mine in Okayama Prefecture. It later purchased copper and tin mines in various parts of the country to expand its mining and smelting operations. In 1918 the company was separated from the parent firm under the name Mitsubishi Metal Mining Co, Ltd. After World War II it began to place more emphasis on smelting and metal processing than on mining, but it has invested in mines in the Philippines, Australia, Peru, and Venezuela, and is importing ore from them. It is also engaged in aluminum processing through its subsidiary, Mitsubishi Aluminum Co, Ltd, and in the processing of nuclear fuel for reactors through another subsidiary, Mitsubishi Nuclear Fuel Co, Ltd. Sales for the fiscal year ending March 1982 totaled ¥301.7 billion (US $1.3 billion), and capitalization stood at ¥24.2 billion (US $100.5 million) in the same year. Corporate headquarters are located in Tōkyō.

Mitsubishi Mining & Cement Co, Ltd

(Mitsubishi Kōgyō Semento). Company engaged in the manufacture of cement, the sale of oil and coal, and other projects, including the production and sale of construction materials. It is a member of the MITSUBISHI group. Mitsubishi Mining & Cement's forerunner was Mitsubishi Mining Co, which began as the mining division of the Mitsubishi company but became independent of the parent firm in

1918. It took its current name in 1973. For many years its principal line of business was coal mining, but in 1954 it expanded into the field of cement production. Despite the fact that it was a latecomer in this field, Mitsubishi Mining & Cement is currently one of the largest cement producers in Japan. The company is also engaged in overseas exploration for oil, coal, and iron ore. Sales for the fiscal year ending March 1982 totaled ¥245.2 billion (US $1 billion), with 53 percent generated by cement, 33 percent by oil, 9 percent by construction materials, and 5 percent by other products. In the same year the company was capitalized at ¥18.9 billion (US $79 million). The head office is in Tōkyō.

Mitsubishi Motors Corporation

(Mitsubishi Jidōsha Kōgyō). Manufacturer of automobiles, trucks, and buses and their components and spare parts. A member of the MITSUBISHI group, it was founded in 1970 when the motor vehicle department of MITSUBISHI HEAVY INDUSTRIES, LTD (MHI) became an independent firm. A joint venture company, with MHI owning 85 percent of the shares and Chrysler Corporation 15 percent, was begun in 1971. Mitsubishi Motors has achieved high technical development in such products as the MCA–Jet system, which meets the most stringent emission control standards of Japan, and the silent shaft system, which reduces vehicle vibrations and noise. It has overseas subsidiaries in the United States, Europe, Australia, and Southeast Asia, with distribution channels worldwide. Sales for the fiscal year ending March 1982 totaled ¥1.1 trillion (US $4.6 billion); of this, 53 percent came from the overseas market, and 47 percent from the domestic market. Car sales generated 67 percent of the revenue, with trucks and buses accounting for the remaining 33 percent. The company was capitalized at ¥35 billion (US $145.4 million) in 1982. Corporate headquarters are located in Tōkyō.

Mitsubishi Oil Co, Ltd

(Mitsubishi Sekiyu). The oil refining and sales company of the MITSUBISHI group. It was established in 1931, with 50 percent of its capital provided by the Getty Oil Co of the United States. After World War II the company continued its association with Getty Oil while spearheading the efforts of the Mitsubishi group to develop overseas oil resources. It has established a subsidiary in Abu Dhabi, and is currently exploring for oil in the Persian Gulf region. In cooperation with MARUZEN OIL CO, LTD, the company has constructed a huge crude oil transport and storage base on Okinawa. Sales for the fiscal year ending March 1982 totaled ¥1.3 trillion (US $5.4 billion); capitalization stood at ¥15 billion (US $62.3 million) in the same year. Corporate headquarters are located in Tōkyō.

Mitsubishi Paper Mills, Ltd

(Mitsubishi Seishi). Manufacturer of pulp, paper, and photographic papers. A member of the MITSUBISHI group, the company traces its origins back to 1898 when Iwasaki Hisaya bought a paper mill operated by James and John Walsh, forming the Kōbe Paper Mill Company. It assumed its present name in 1917. Its main products include high-grade papers (coated and thin paper) and photographic papers. Major advances have been recorded in sales of color-photo and noncarbon copy papers in overseas markets. The company had stationed engineers in New York and Düsseldorf. Further development is anticipated in the areas of information processing and graphic arts materials. Important goals of the company include strengthening its position in the photographic paper market at home and abroad, and increasing its share of the business systems' market (information processing, noncarbon copy and thermo papers). Sales for the fiscal year ending March 1982 totaled ¥143.7 billion (US $597 million), distributed as follows: papers 64 percent, photographic papers 26 percent, pulp 9 percent, and others 1 percent. Capitalization stood at ¥7.3 billion (US $30.3 million) in the same year. The head office is in Tōkyō.

Mitsubishi Petrochemical Co, Ltd

(Mitsubishi Yuka). The largest producer of ethylene in Japan. Mitsubishi Petrochemical was founded in 1956 with funds invested jointly by the MITSUBISHI group and Shell Petroleum. The company constructed a petrochemical complex in Yokkaichi, Mie Prefecture, and in 1959 it began production of ethylene with an annual capacity of 22,000 metric tons (24,250 short tons). In 1971 it opened another complex in Kashima, Ibaraki Prefecture, raising its annual production capacity for ethylene further by 300,000 metric tons (330,000 short tons), and making the company the largest petrochemical producer in Japan. It is currently planning to diversify its operations by expanding its fine chemicals department. It has established joint enterprises in Taiwan and the Philippines where production is being carried out, and set up a joint sales company in Hong Kong. In 1981 the ratio of exports was 5 percent. In the same year annual sales were ¥370.8 billion (US \$1.7 billion), of which ethylene-related products accounted for 45 percent, propylene-related products 24 percent, aromatic compounds 4 percent, and others 27 percent. It was capitalized at ¥16 billion (US \$66.5 million) in 1982. Corporate headquarters are located in Tōkyō.

Mitsubishi Rayon Co, Ltd

Company engaged in the manufacture of chemical and synthetic fibers, especially acrylic fiber, and synthetic resins. The brand names Vonnel (acrylic) and Soluna (polyester) are well known abroad. A member of the MITSUBISHI group, it was established in 1933. The post–World War II history of the company has been marked by the introduction of foreign technology: in 1955 it concluded a technical cooperation agreement with the world's largest acetate maker, the Celanese Corp of the United States, and a similar tie-up with the Chemstrand Co of the United States in 1957 opened up the field of acrylic fiber production. Also in 1957 an agreement was reached with an Italian firm, Montecatini, for the production of polypropylene resins and fibers. Since then, the company has acquired technology from the Pittsburgh Plate Glass Co of the United States, in order to diversify its resin division, and from the Akzo N.V. of the Netherlands, for the production of polyester fibers. Mitsubishi Rayon also exports its own technology; in 1973, for example, it exported its continuous cast process technology for the production of metacrylic resins to E. I. DuPont de Nemours & Co. Sales for the fiscal year ending March 1982 totaled ¥198.8 billion (US \$825.9 million), of which exports accounted for 15 percent. It was capitalized at ¥16.9 billion (US \$70.2 million) in the same year. Corporate headquarters are located in Tōkyō.

Mitsubishi Steel Mfg Co, Ltd

(Mitsubishi Seikō). A company engaged in the manufacture and sale of special steels, springs, forged and cast steel, and machinery parts, Mitsubishi Steel Manufacturing was established in 1949. The company produces hot-worked springs through an integrated process. It is closely affiliated with MITSUBISHI HEAVY INDUSTRIES, LTD, and MITSUBISHI MOTORS CORPORATION. It has offices in New York, Chicago, and Düsseldorf and its head office in Tōkyō. Sales totaled ¥75.9 billion (US \$315.3 million) and capitalization stood at ¥7.2 billion (US \$29.9 million) in the fiscal year ending in March 1982.

Mitsubishi Trust & Banking Corporation

(Mitsubishi Shintaku Ginkō). Established in 1927 as one of the MITSUBISHI zaibatsu's financial organs, the Mitsubishi Trust & Banking Corporation was begun under the name Mitsubishi Trust Co. In 1948 the bank took the name Asahi Trust Bank and engaged in both trust and ordinary banking operations; the current name was adopted in 1952. The bank increased its volume of funds through loans in trust and also expanded early into the enterprise annuity trust field. Operations were diversified by the underwriting of securities investment trusts and the purchase and sale of real estate. The bank also makes long-term funds available to enterprises for capital investment and provides housing loans to private individuals. Together with the MITSUBISHI BANK, LTD, and MEIJI MUTUAL LIFE INSURANCE CO and the TOKIO MARINE & FIRE INSURANCE CO, LTD, Mitsubishi Trust & Banking Corporation provides financial services to the Mitsubishi group. The bank has established joint financial institutions in Hong Kong and Brussels. At the end of March 1982 the volume of the bank's funds was ¥9.7 trillion (US \$40.3 billion), of which 46 percent was loan trust; capitalization stood at ¥37.5 billion (US \$155.8 million) in the same year. The head office is located in Tōkyō.

Mitsubishi Warehouse & Transportation Co, Ltd

(Mitsubishi Sōko). The largest warehousing company in Japan, the Mitsubishi Warehouse & Transportation Co was established in 1887. A member of the MITSUBISHI group, it is engaged in harbor transport, the handling of export and import cargoes, land transport, and real estate, in addition to warehousing. It has subsidiary firms in the United States. Sales for the fiscal year ending March 1982 totaled ¥58.5 billion (US \$243 million); capitalization stood at ¥6.7 billion (US \$27.8 million) in the same year. Corporate headquarters are located in Tōkyō.

Mitsuchi Chūzō (1871–1948)

Politician. Born in Kagawa Prefecture, Mitsuchi graduated from Tōkyō Higher Normal School (later Tōkyō University of Education) in 1897 and, after studying in Europe, became a teacher at his alma mater. He then worked for the newspaper Tōkyō nichinichi shimbun (now Mainichi shimbun) before joining the political party RIKKEN SEIYŪKAI and winning election in 1908 to the first of 11 consecutive terms in the lower house of the Diet. His abilities were recognized by TAKAHASHI KOREKIYO, who appointed him chief secretary in the Takahashi cabinet (1921–22). Mitsuchi subsequently served as education and finance minister in the TANAKA GIICHI cabinet (1927–29), communications minister in the INUKAI TSUYOSHI cabinet (1931–32), and railway minister in the SAITŌ MAKOTO cabinet (1932–34), becoming leader and financial expert of the Seiyūkai. In 1934 he was indicted for perjury in connection with the TEIJIN INCIDENT but was acquitted in 1937. In 1940 he was appointed to the Privy Council. After World War II, Mitsuchi returned to politics as home minister and transportation minister in the SHIDEHARA KIJŪRŌ cabinet (1945–46).

mitsuda-e

An ancient painting technique employing oil-based pigments; often used in combination with lacquer. The medium consists of powdered pigments added to a base of perilla oil and a small amount of lead-oxide (mitsudasō) that have been heated together.

The technique, which may have originated in Persia, was in common use in China from the Tang (T'ang; 618–907) through the Ming (1368–1644) dynasties, and it reached Japan in the 7th century. The earliest extant Japanese example of its use is the 7th-century Tamamushi Shrine in the temple HŌRYŪJI in Nara. During the Azuchi-Momoyama period (1568–1600) and early part of the Edo period (1600–1868), mitsuda-e was used extensively in the decoration of lacquer serving trays.

Mitsuda Kensuke (1876–1964)

Specialist in leprosy known for his leper-relief work. Born in Yamaguchi Prefecture, Mitsuda graduated from the medical school Saisei Gakusha. He decided to study leprosy after performing autopsies on lepers as a nonregular student of pathology at Tōkyō University, and worked at the Tōkyō Shi Yōikuin, a social welfare institution supported by the city of Tōkyō. He believed that leprous patients should be isolated, and succeeded in having a leprosy ward established in the institution. In 1909 Mitsuda began work at the first public leprosarium in Japan, Zensei Hospital (now the Tama Zenshōen) in Tōkyō. In 1931 he became the first president of the National Leprosarium, Nagashima Aiseien, in Okayama Prefecture. He is also known for discovering the Mitsuda reaction, a test for determining the type of leprosy. Mitsuda received the Order of Culture in 1951. NAGATOYA Yōji

Mitsui

Wealthiest merchant house of the Edo period (1600–1868), the largest business combine (ZAIBATSU) of the pre–World War II era, and a major enterprise grouping (KEIRETSU) of the postwar period. The House of Mitsui was founded in 1673, when MITSUI TAKATOSHI established dry-goods stores in Kyōto and Edo (now Tōkyō). It moved into its second line of activity when Takatoshi opened money lending and exchange shops in Edo in 1683, in Kyōto in 1686, and in Ōsaka in 1691. In 1691 the Tokugawa shogunate appointed two members of the Mitsui family as chartered merchants (GOYŌ SHŌNIN) to transmit receipts from the sale and exchange of tax goods in

Ōsaka, the commercial center of the country, to Edo, the administrative center.

To oversee its diverse enterprises and shops in several cities, Mitsui in 1709 established in Kyōto a coordinating body, the Ōmotokata, which held monthly meetings and was the precursor of the much later holding company. House rules and procedures were codified in 1722, when Takatoshi's son expanded upon certain provisions of his father's will. A distinctive feature of the House of Mitsui was that it was composed of several houses: the senior main family, five junior branches of the main family, and three (later five) associate families.

Mitsui maintained close ties to the Tokugawa shogunate until the end of the Edo period. However, in the 1860s, perceiving that the shogunate's days were numbered, Mitsui's general manager, MINOMURA RIZAEMON, also established relations with antishogunate leaders, especially with INOUE KAORU; this made possible the company's continued enjoyment of government favor after the Meiji Restoration of 1868 (see SEISHŌ).

The Mitsui combine was built on three principal subsidiaries: Mitsui Banking, Mitsui Trading, and Mitsui Mining.

Banking. Having overthrown the shogunate, the Restoration leaders found themselves with a host of financial responsibilities. In February 1868 the new government decided to delegate operational aspects of the collection, storage, and expenditure of tax revenues to the three largest merchant houses: Mitsui, Ono, and Shimada. Initially the government required no security for these funds from the merchant houses. Later, when the amounts increased, it required a bond of from 25 to 33 percent. In 1874 the government suddenly increased its bonding requirement to "the equivalent of the amount on deposit." The Ono and Shimada houses soon went bankrupt, but Mitsui avoided that fate, reportedly through advance warning from Inoue Kaoru, who had only recently stepped down as finance minister. Thus Mitsui came to enjoy exclusive use of national tax revenues until the establishment of the BANK OF JAPAN in 1882.

Mitsui was eager to convert its moneylending and exchange business into a Western-type bank and so petitioned the government in 1871. In 1872 the government enacted the National Bank Ordinance, modeled on the United States National Bank Act (see NATIONAL BANKS). Mitsui was obliged at first to join with the ONOGUMI in forming in 1872 a bank that became the First National Bank in 1873, but three years later it was allowed to establish independently the MITSUI BANK, LTD, which opened in 1876 with 31 branches and subbranches and a capitalization of ¥2 million. The bank was used to finance Mitsui commercial and industrial undertakings, and its resources were available to others only when they were not needed for Mitsui purposes.

Trading. The Mitsui Trading Company (Mitsui Bussan Kaisha) was formed in 1876 through the merger of a Mitsui trading firm founded in 1797 with another established by Inoue Kaoru during a brief absence from the government in 1873–75. MASUDA TAKASHI, the vice-president of Inoue's company, became managing director. Even before the new company was formally established, Masuda obtained for it exclusive rights to the sale of coal from the MIIKE COAL MINES, which the government had inherited from the shogunate. This arrangement, which lasted until 1888 when Mitsui bought the mines outright, led the company into close contact with British merchants, who considered Miike coal the best in East Asia to fuel their steamships. Before long, Mitsui Trading had established offices in Shanghai, Hong Kong, and Singapore, as well as India and even London. In 1893, when the company-law provisions of the COMMERCIAL CODE went into effect, Mitsui Trading was reorganized as an unlimited-liability partnership.

Mining. Mitsui Mining, Ltd, grew out of the Miike mines. When the government put them up for competitive bid in 1888 (see KAN'EI JIGYŌ HARAISAGE), Mitsui won out over the MITSUBISHI group. In 1892 Mitsui Mining was established to manage the Miike operation, and it subsequently acquired other coal and metal mines. Through its own mines and its subsidiaries, Mitsui Mining came to control one-third of the nation's coal output and a substantial portion of its metal production.

Family constitution and holding company. The ōmotokata, or coordinating body, founded in 1709, combined family-council and business functions until 1892, when the business operation was separated from family affairs and reorganized as a limited partnership. The separation was formalized in the 1900 family constitution, which also specified family relationships more clearly. This step was taken because of the realization that, with the great expansion of Mitsui business interests since the Meiji Restoration, overall policy

decisions could not be left solely to the head of the house, as prescribed in the 1722 will. Prepared by Inoue Kaoru, who had been chief adviser to Mitsui since 1891, the new constitution gave policy-making functions to the heads of the 11 houses that made up the Household Council and simplified the distribution of property among them.

Under NAKAMIGAWA HIKOJIRŌ, general manager of the combine from 1891 to 1900, Mitsui began to invest heavily in industrial enterprises, including the Shibaura Engineering Works, the ŌJI PAPER CO, LTD, and the Kanegafuchi Spinning Company. To provide better coordination for Mitsui's diverse activities, a holding company, Mitsui Gōmei Kaisha, was established in 1909 as an unlimited partnership capitalized at ¥50 million. All Mitsui enterprises were soon reorganized as joint-stock companies, which the Mitsui families controlled through the partnership. In 1914 the holding company and its 12 key subsidiaries had a combined capitalization of ¥237 million. By 1931 Mitsui Gōmei's capital had increased to ¥300 million and the number of key subsidiaries to 40, with a total nominal capital of over ¥1 billion.

From zaibatsu to keiretsu. Mitsui was now a full-fledged *zaibatsu*, a huge financial, industrial, and commercial combine. In the early 1930s the company increasingly came under attack by militarists and ultranationalists for its alleged manipulation of political parties and its selfish pursuit of profit. After the assassination of DAN TAKUMA, managing director of Mitsui Gōmei, by a rightist in 1932, his successor, IKEDA SHIGEAKI, sought to end such criticism by effecting a "conversion" *(tenkō)* of Mitsui into a patriotic and socially conscious enterprise. The company made donations to charities and community organizations; Mitsui family members withdrew from active roles in management; the leadership was gradually changed through a mandatory retirement system; and Mitsui opened some shares to public subscription.

Cooperating with the military, Mitsui continued to expand during the war years and increased its ability to raise capital by first merging Mitsui Gōmei with Mitsui Trading in 1940 and then reorganizing them as independent joint-stock companies in 1944. By the end of World War II Mitsui had become a mammoth combine, consisting of a holding company with paid-up capital of ¥400.076 million and 273 related companies, including 10 first-line designated subsidiaries and 12 second-line designated subsidiaries, with a total paid-up capital of nearly ¥3.5 billion (¥3.1 billion domestic; ¥0.4 billion abroad). Between 1946 and 1950, however, Mitsui was broken up into its constitutent parts through the ZAIBATSU DISSOLUTION measures undertaken by the Allied Occupation.

In the 1950s the now independent Mitsui companies began to associate loosely in an enterprise grouping *(keiretsu)*. In the Mitsui *keiretsu*, as in those of Mitsubishi and SUMITOMO, the powerful holding company has been replaced by two loosely organized presidents' clubs, the Monday Club and the Second Thursday Club, composed mainly of the presidents of the former key subsidiaries of the *zaibatsu*, which meet regularly and provide some coordination of policy. The latter is the more exclusive and hence prestigious. Although different writers put the number of companies differently, some take the Mitsui group in 1971 to have consisted of some 70 companies, 19 of which were represented in the presidents' club. See also CORPORATE HISTORY.

■——Eleanor H. Hadley, *Antitrust in Japan* (1970). Johannes Hirschmeier and Tsunehiko Yui, *The Development of Japanese Business, 1600–1973* (1975). State-War Mission on Japanese Combines, *Report to the Department of State and the War Department*, pt. 1 (1946). Mitsubishi Economic Research Institute, ed, *Mitsui, Mitsubishi, Sumitomo* (1955). Mochikabu Kaisha Seiri Iinkai, *Nihon zaibatsu to sono kaitai, shiryō* (1950), has bibliography of Japanese and Western works on Mitsui. Hidemasa Morikawa, "The Organizational Structure of the Mitsubishi and Mitsui Zaibatsu, 1868–1922: A Comparative Study," *Business History Review* 44 (Spring 1970). Tsuchiya Takeo, "Mitsui zaibatsu no hatten," *Chūō kōron* (August–September–October 1946). Tsunehiko Yui, "The Personality and Career of Hikojiro Nakamigawa, 1887–1901," *Business History Review* 44 (Spring 1970). Eleanor M. HADLEY

Mitsui & Co, Ltd

(Mitsui Bussan). A general trading company *(sōgō shōsha)*, second in scale only to the MITSUBISHI CORPORATION. Its balance of overseas investments is the largest in Japan. It was established in 1876 as an enterprise of the MITSUI family. The company's operations expanded with the industrialization of Japan, and by the end of World

War II it had become the largest trading firm in the nation. In 1947 it was broken into 223 companies by order of the Allied Occupation authorities, as part of the ZAIBATSU DISSOLUTION program. The present Mitsui & Co was established in 1959 through the amalgamation of several companies, centered on Daiichi Bussan. With the liberalization and rapid growth of the Japanese economy in the 1960s, Mitsui & Co began to expand its information network, solidify its business activities, develop new markets, expand its financial capacity, and accelerate its investments.

The company·handles a wide range of products, but the proportion of metals (31 percent), machinery (15 percent), and chemicals (13 percent) is increasing. Mitsui's handling of intangible products such as information, knowledge, technology, and service is also on the increase. The company is playing a key role in the development and import of overseas resources and the modernization of distribution systems. Domestic transactions and foreign trade occupy equal parts of the firm's business, and it handles about 10 percent of Japan's entire foreign trade volume. The companies established by Mitsui before World War II include TAISHŌ MARINE & FIRE INSURANCE CO, LTD, TŌYŌ MENKA KAISHA, LTD, TŌRAY INDUSTRIES, INC, MITSUI ENGINEERING & SHIPBUILDING CO, LTD, and MITSUI O.S.K. LINES, LTD. Companies established after the war include MITSUI PETROCHEMICAL INDUSTRIES, LTD, NIPPON UNIVAC KAISHA, LTD, Nippon Atomic Industry Group Co, Mitsui Ocean Development & Engineering Co, and Mitsui Oil Exploration Co. Mitsui & Co serves as organizer for the entire Mitsui group and attempts to establish and foster new industries and expand the scope of the enterprise group. It has a total of 149 overseas offices, branches, and companies incorporated abroad. Sales for the fiscal year ending March 1982 totaled ¥13.2 trillion (US $54.8 billion), and capitalization stood at ¥48.8 billion (US $202.7 million). The head office is in Tōkyō. See also GENERAL TRADING COMPANIES.

Mitsui Bank, Ltd

(Mitsui Ginkō). One of Japan's major banks, Mitsui Bank ranked sixth in deposits among the 13 "city banks" (toshi ginkō) in the country in 1982 and is one of the major enterprises of the MITSUI group. Established in 1876 by the Mitsui family, it was the first private bank in Japan and grew into one of the major components of the Mitsui ZAIBATSU. It became a joint-stock company in 1909; in 1943 it merged with the Dai-Ichi Bank (now DAI-ICHI KANGYŌ BANK, LTD), but the merger was dissolved in 1948. The bank specializes in securities and foreign exchange. Mitsui's overseas network includes 10 branches (in New York, Los Angeles, San Francisco, and elsewhere), 1 agency, 13 representative offices, 4 Mitsui-owned ventures, 18 joint ventures, and 878 correspondence banks (1982). In 1965 Mitsui became the first Japanese bank to establish an on-line computer system. Future plans call for upgrading managerial efficiency to cope with the predicted low growth of the national economy, expanding its network of branches, and strengthening its international division. As of the end of March 1982 the bank's balance of deposits totaled ¥12.5 trillion (US $52 billion), of which 45 percent were time deposits, 9 percent ordinary deposits, 10 percent current deposits, and 36 percent deposits-at-call and others. It was capitalized the same year at ¥76 billion (US $315.7 million). The head office is located in Tōkyō.

Mitsui Bunko → Mitsui Research Institute for Social and Economic History

Mitsui Construction Co, Ltd

(Mitsui Kensetsu). A company engaged in public works and real estate development. One of the larger construction companies in Japan, it is a member of the MITSUI group. In 1941 MITSUI REAL ESTATE DEVELOPMENT CO, LTD, purchased the forerunner of Mitsui Construction (established in 1890) in order to expand into construction and to provide management for the buildings in its possession. The company became independent and took its current name in 1952. The MCS (Mitsui Checkered System) construction method, a unique structural construction system developed by the company in 1968, is utilized widely in the building of medium- and high-rise buildings. The company adopted computers early and introduced automatic drawing instruments and numerical control equipment to lead other construction companies in the development of new technologies such as designing and drawing systems for land devel-

ment and building construction. Sales for the fiscal year ending May 1982 totaled approximately ¥290.3 billion (US $1.2 billion); capitalization stood at ¥7.5 billion (US $31.7 million). The company's head office is in Tōkyō.

Mitsui Engineering & Shipbuilding Co, Ltd

(Mitsui Zōsen). A comprehensive heavy industry company engaged in the manufacture and repair of ships, ocean development equipment, steel structures, chemical plants, and industrial machinery, Mitsui Engineering & Shipbuilding Co was established in 1917 as the shipbuilding division of MITSUI & CO, LTD, and became independent in 1937. It took its current name in 1976. It is a member of the MITSUI group. The company was the first in the world to produce fully automated ships and triple-engine, triple-screw, high-speed, diesel container ships. It is currently placing emphasis on the manufacture of new and high-quality products through technical tie-ups with major overseas companies. Subsidiaries have been incorporated in Hong Kong and Brazil. Future plans call for the reinforcement of its land division by exporting desalinization and electric power plants. Sales for the fiscal year ending March 1982 totaled ¥364.4 billion (US $1.5 billion), of which ships generated 35 percent; chemical plants 19 percent; power units for land use 11 percent; ship machinery 20 percent; marine projects 6 percent; steel structures and civil engineering 6 percent; and others 3 percent. The export ratio was 62 percent and capitalization stood at ¥30.3 billion (US $125.9 million). Corporate headquarters are located in Tōkyō.

Mitsui Mining & Smelting Co, Ltd

(Mitsui Kinzoku Kōgyō). Producer of nonferrous metals, especially zinc, of which it is the world's largest. Its four principal lines of business are mining, smelting, processing, and the manufacture of construction materials. In recent years the company has emphasized the development of new metals and electronic items. Formerly the metals division of the MITSUI MINING CO, LTD, the company became independent of its parent firm in 1950 under the name Kamioka Mine Co. The current name was adopted in 1952. The company was initially engaged in the mining and smelting of nonferrous metals and later expanded into metal processing and the production of construction material. Domestic zinc and lead mining is centered on the Kamioka Mine in Gifu Prefecture; mines are also being developed in Fukui, Kagoshima, and Shimane prefectures. The company also operates mines in Peru and is exploring for copper deposits in that country and in Panama. It has seven smelting and four processing plants in Japan and five affiliated firms in Ireland, Taiwan, and the United States. Sales for the fiscal year ending March 1982 totaled ¥257.1 billion (US $1.1 billion), of which ingots and precious metal generated 58 percent, processed products 24 percent, chemicals 12 percent, and others 6 percent. The company was capitalized at ¥24.3 billion (US $100.9 million) in the same year. Corporate headquarters are located in Tōkyō.

Mitsui Mining Co, Ltd

(Mitsui Kōzan). Company engaged in the operation of domestic coal mines; the import of foreign coal; and the sale of oil, coke, cement, and construction materials. A member of the MITSUI group, the company dates back to 1874 when the Mitsui combine purchased part of the Kamioka Mine. In 1888 the government transferred its MIIKE COAL MINES to the combine, and in 1892 a mining company was established with the Kamioka and Miike mines as its main holdings. The present company was organized in 1911. It developed numerous mines in Hokkaidō, Kyūshū, and Sakhalin and absorbed many related companies, becoming one of the largest enterprises in Japan as well as a key member of the Mitsui ZAIBATSU. However, under the ZAIBATSU DISSOLUTION program following World War II, it returned exclusively to coal production. In order to cope with the switch from coal to oil as Japan's primary source of energy, Mitsui Mining attempted to rationalize its coal operations while diversifying through the sale of oil, construction materials, and coke. It established Mitsui Mining Overseas Co, Ltd, in 1977 in an effort to step up overseas activities, and is currently engaged in the exploration of overseas coal fields, utilizing such advanced techniques as water-powered coal mining. The company also provides consulting services. It produces 7 million metric tons (7.7 million short tons) of coal annually at its mines in Miike (Fukuoka and Kumamoto prefectures), Sunagawa, and Ashibetsu (both in Hokkaidō), satisfying approximately 40 percent of Japan's total demand. Sales for the fiscal year ending March 1982 totaled ¥379.1 billion (US $1.6 billion), of which coal generated 38 percent, construction material 16 percent, coke 23 percent, oil 6 percent, and others 17 percent. Capitalization stood at ¥6 billion (US $24.9 million) in the same year. Corporate headquarters are located in Tōkyō. See also MITSUI MINING & SMELTING CO, LTD.

Mitsui O.S.K. Lines, Ltd

(Ōsaka Shōsen Mitsui Sempaku). The second largest liner operator in Japan, Mitsui O.S.K. Lines was established in 1964 through the merger of the Ōsaka Shōsen and the Mitsui Steamship companies. Ōsaka Shōsen was founded in 1884 and operated regular routes to North America, Africa, and the Indian Ocean before World War II. A member of the SUMITOMO group, it was one of the largest operators of high-speed cargo ships in the world. Mitsui Steamship was formed in 1876 to transport goods handled by the MITSUI & CO, LTD, trading firm. Later it completed a network of regular routes to Southeast Asia. With the merger of the two companies, Mitsui O.S.K. Lines became a comprehensive shipping company with regular routes, tramp routes, tankers, and special transport ships. In the mid-1960s the company began containerization of its transport ships, and in 1968 it started using full container ships on its California route. Since then, the northern Pacific, Europe, New York, Mediterranean, and other trunk routes have also undergone containerization. In 1965 the company constructed Japan's first ship for the exclusive transport of automobiles; in 1971 it introduced the first computerized automatic tanker. Joint ventures are under way with local shipping concerns in various cities in Southeast Asia and Saudi Arabia; the firm also shares the management of container terminals in Oakland, Los Angeles, Sydney, and other ports. The company's fleet included 337 ships with a total of 11.1 million deadweight tons in 1980. Sales for the fiscal year ending March 1982 totaled ¥537.5 billion (US $2.2 billion), of which regular routes generated 41 percent, special ships 37 percent, tramps 8 percent, tankers 2 percent, and ships loaned out and others 12 percent; capitalization stood at ¥37.8 billion (US $157 million). Corporate headquarters are located in Ōsaka.

Mitsui Petrochemical Industries, Ltd

(Mitsui Sekiyu Kagaku). An integrated petrochemical company and leading Japanese producer of high-density polyethylene, Mitsui Petrochemical was established in 1955 by seven MITSUI-affiliated firms and KŌA OIL CO, LTD. The company has constructed a petrochemical complex at Iwakuni in Yamaguchi Prefecture and also produces ethylene, polyethylene, and aromatics at a complex in Chiba Prefecture. Jointly with the Nippon Petrochemical Company, Mitsui Petrochemical established the Ukishima Petrochemical Company to create a third ethylene center. Subsidiaries operate in South Korea and Belgium. In the fiscal year ending in March 1982 sales totaled ¥280.3 billion (US $1.2 billion), of which the share of ethylene derivatives was 40 percent, propylene derivatives 32 percent, aromatics 14 percent, and others 14 percent; exports constituted 12 percent of those sales. Capitalization stood at ¥11.0 billion (US $45.7 million) the same year. Corporate headquarters are located in Tōkyō.

Mitsui Real Estate Development Co, Ltd

(Mitsui Fudōsan). A real estate company engaged primarily in lot sales of land and houses; it ranks first in Japan in sales of real estate. Originating as the real estate division of the MITSUI combine, the company was established as an independent enterprise in 1941. At that time, it began to diversify from a specialization in the leasing of land and buildings. The company started to develop land through dredging and reclamation projects in 1957; the development and sales of residential and villa land was begun in 1961. In 1968 Mitsui Real Estate completed Japan's first high-rise building, the Kasumigaseki Building in Tōkyō, which inaugurated an age of high-rise construction. In 1969 it started the construction and sale of individual homes and established the Mitsui Real Estate Sales Co. Mitsui Homes Co, Ltd, was a 1974 spin-off, through which Mitsui began selling houses constructed by a wood-framing method. It thus became a leading comprehensive land and housing developer. The company invested in Trade & Industrial Development, Ltd, of Singapore in 1972. Other overseas projects included the construction and sales of distribution warehouses in the suburbs of Los Angeles and

Seattle and the development of townhouses in Saudi Arabia and Singapore. Recent projects included the construction of a Tōkyō Disneyland, in conjunction with Walt Disney Co of the United States, and of Japan's largest shopping center in Chiba Prefecture. Sales for the fiscal year ending March 1982 totaled ¥197.9 billion (US $822.1 million), of which sales of houses and residential land comprised 68 percent, leasing of land and buildings 24 percent, and appraisals and others 8 percent. Capitalization stood at ¥16 billion (US $66.5 million) in the same year. The head office is in Tōkyō.

Mitsui Research Institute for Social and Economic History

(Mitsui Bunko). Library and museum of records and documents belonging to the founding family of the MITSUI financial empire. Located in Tōkyō, its ranks with the YŌMEI BUNKO of the Konoe family and the SEIKADŌ BUNKO of the Iwasaki family as one of the most outstanding private collections of books and family records that have survived to the present. The Mitsui library houses important documents, including more than 20 versions of Mitsui Takafusa's CHŌNIN KŌKEN ROKU, the oldest extant Mitsui literary piece, the "house constitution," and other meticulously kept records of a financial and genealogical nature dating from the end of the Genroku era (1688–1704).   Theodore F. WELCH

Mitsui Sugar Co, Ltd

(Mitsui Seitō). Japan's largest sugar refining company, with a domestic market share of approximately 13 percent. The company produces refined, liquefied, and cube sugar. It was established in 1970 through the merger of the Mitsui-affiliated Ōsaka Sugar Refining Co, the Shibaura Sugar Co, and the Yokohama Sugar Refining Co in order to reduce excess production capacity. Pressed by the high price of raw sugar and a stagnant market, the company has relied on financial assistance from MITSUI & CO, LTD. It has joint venture firms in Thailand and Singapore. Sales for the fiscal year ending September 1981 totaled ¥73.3 billion (US $318.7 million). It was capitalized at ¥4.2 billion (US $18.3 million) in the same year. Corporate headquarters are located in Tōkyō.

Mitsui Takatoshi (1622–1694)

Wealthy merchant of the Edo period (1600–1868) and founder of what later became the MITSUI financial and industrial conglomerate. Born in Matsusaka, Ise Province (now Mie Prefecture); fourth son of a *sake* brewer and pawnbroker. Takatoshi initially made his fortunes as a rice broker and moneylender. In 1673 he opened the Echigoya *kimono* shops in Kyōto and Edo (now Tōkyō). These stores, accepting only cash and no credit, flourished because they sold goods at a low profit in large quantities. Takatoshi also successfully instituted a system for the division of labor *(bungyō)* in his stores and encouraged workers' productivity by granting bonuses. He later opened a money exchange in Edo and Ōsaka and became official money exchanger to the shogunate. Takatoshi accumulated vast sums of money in his lifetime and reputedly left 81,000 gold pieces *(ryō)* to his heirs.

Mitsui Tōatsu Chemicals, Inc

(Mitsui Tōatsu Kagaku). A comprehensive chemical company, Mitsui Tōatsu was established in 1968 through the merger of Mitsui Chemical Industries and Tōyō Kōatsu Industries, both members of the MITSUI group. The former's chief product was coal-based dyestuffs, while the latter primarily produced urea fertilizer. Mitsui Tōatsu produces a wide range of products, including petrochemicals, fine chemicals, industrial chemicals, plastics, fertilizers, and pharmaceuticals. The urea production technology of the former Tōyō Kōatsu has been exported to more than 20 foreign countries. Sales for the fiscal year ending March 1982 totaled ¥433.3 billion (US $1.8 billion), of which industrial chemicals accounted for 41 percent, synthetic resins 26 percent, fine chemicals 13 percent, fertilizers 12 percent, and others 8 percent; exports provided 11 percent of the total sales. Capitalization stood at ¥32.9 billion (US $136.7 million) in the same year. Corporate headquarters are located in Tōkyō.

Mitsui Trust & Banking Co, Ltd

(Mitsui Shintaku Ginkō). The oldest trust and banking institution in Japan. A member of the MITSUI group, it was established in 1924 and in 1981 was Japan's third largest trust company in deposits. Its major services are long-term finance and asset management; other financial activities include banking, international business, securities, and real estate. The company maintains 47 domestic offices as well as offices in New York, London, and Singapore, and overseas representative's offices in Los Angeles, São Paulo and Sydney. Two subsidiaries, Mitsui Trust Finance (Hong Kong) Ltd and Mitsui Trust (Europe) S.A., operate in Hong Kong and Brussels respectively. Total funds as of 31 March 1981 were ¥7.1 trillion (US $29.5 billion), distributed as follows: loan trusts 53 percent, deposits 25 percent, money trusts 12 percent, and others 10 percent. Capitalization stood at ¥37.5 billion (US $155.8 million) in the same year. The bank's head office is located in Tōkyō.

Mitsui Warehouse Co, Ltd

(Mitsui Sōko). A company engaged in warehousing and port and land transportation, Mitsui Warehouse was established in 1909 and took its present name in 1942. A member of the MITSUI group, it is the second largest company in the field and the leading container terminal operator in Japan. The company has expanded into the international distribution business in recent years, with joint venture firms in Hong Kong, the Netherlands, and Singapore, as well as offices in New York, Singapore, and Taipei. Future plans envision the establishment of an integrated international transportation system through tie-ups with major distributors in the West. Sales for the fiscal year ending March 1982 totaled ¥50.7 billion (US $210.6 million), and capitalization stood at ¥6.5 billion (US $27 million). Corporate headquarters are located in Tōkyō.

Mitsukaidō

City in southwestern Ibaraki Prefecture, central Honshū. During the Edo period (1600–1868) it flourished as a port town on the river Kinugawa. Principal agricultural products are rice and vegetables; electrical appliance, machinery, and transport machinery plants are located here. Only 43 km (27 mi) from Tōkyō, in recent years it has become a residential area for commuters to Tōkyō. Pop: 40,434.

Mitsuke

City in central Niigata Prefecture, central Honshū. Its silk weaving industry, developed in the first half of the 19th century, has been replaced by knitted goods and synthetic fabrics industries. Rice and tobacco are grown. There are carp hatcheries. The Mitsuke Oil Field has one of Japan's most productive oil wells. A kite-flying festival is held in June. Pop: 41,830.

Mitsukoshi, Ltd

The largest department store company in Japan, Mitsukoshi, Ltd, traces its origins back to 1673 when MITSUI TAKATOSHI opened the Echigoya dry goods store in Nihombashi, Edo (now Tōkyō). This enterprise became the foundation of the MITSUI family fortune, which later launched the Mitsui ZAIBATSU, a powerful financial-industrial combine. After the Meiji Restoration of 1868, the Mitsui family expanded into banking, trade, and mining; the dry goods store became independent in 1904. With the Westernization of the Japanese lifestyle in the 20th century, the company began to handle a wide range of merchandise in addition to dry goods, thus becoming a full-fledged department store. In 1908 Echigoya completed a three-story, Western-style store in Tōkyō and stocked it with high-quality, expensive goods. The store took pride in its interior decorations, and its regular art exhibitions attracted a middle- and upper-class clientele, strategies which improved the store's financial footing.

The name Mitsukoshi, Ltd, was adopted in 1928. In the 1930s the company opened a number of branch stores, making it the largest department store in East Asia. After World War II Mitsukoshi fell into financial difficulties, but it managed to recover and has since surpassed its prewar peak. To counter competition from chain stores, which began the mass-merchandising of inexpensive goods in the 1960s, Mitsukoshi has placed increased emphasis on the marketing of fashionable goods and products of high artistic and cultural value. The firm opened a branch in Paris in 1971 and later opened subsidiary sales companies in Rome, Düsseldorf, and Singapore. Mitsukoshi subsidiaries operate throughout Europe and the United States to purchase goods for import. In 1982 the company had a total of 14 department stores in Japan. Sales for the fiscal year ending February 1982 totaled ¥586.4 billion (US $2.5 billion), of which 41 percent was generated by clothing, 21 percent foodstuffs, 15 percent sundries, 11 percent household goods, and 12 percent others. Capitalization stood at ¥21.7 billion (US $92.3 million) in the same year. Corporate headquarters are located in Tōkyō.

Mitsukuri Gempachi (1862–1919)

Historian; pioneer in the study of Western history in Japan; grandson of MITSUKURI GEMPO and son of Mitsukuri Shūhei (1826–86), both scholars of WESTERN LEARNING. Born in Edo (now Tōkyō). Mitsukuri studied English and zoology at Tōkyō University before going to Germany in 1886 to continue his zoological studies. He later changed specialties and undertook the study of European history under Heinrich von Treitschke (1834–96) and Leopold von Ranke (1795–1886). In 1892 he returned to Japan to teach at the Tōkyō Higher Normal School (Tōkyō Kōtō Shihan Gakkō) and the First Higher School (Daiichi Kōtō Gakkō). He went to France in 1900 to do research on the French Revolution and on his return in 1902 became a professor of Western history at Tōkyō University. Mitsukuri also taught military history at the Army War College and Naval War College. Among his works are Seiyōshi kōwa (1910, Lectures on Western History), Furansu dai kakumei shi (1919–20, History of the French Revolution), and Naporeon jidai shi (1923, History of the Napoleonic Period).

Mitsukuri Gempo (1799–1863)

Physician and scholar of WESTERN LEARNING. Born in the Tsuyama domain (now part of Okayama Prefecture), Gempo studied traditional Chinese medicine in Kyōto before succeeding his father as physician to the daimyō of Tsuyama in 1822. He accompanied his lord to Edo (now Tōkyō), where he studied Western medicine with Udagawa Shinsai (1769–1834), a fellow native of Tsuyama. In 1839 Gempo was appointed an official interpreter in the Tokugawa shogunate's Office of Astronomy (Temmonkata). He was a member of the mission led by KAWAJI TOSHIAKIRA that negotiated with the Russian envoy Evfimii Vasil'evich PUTIATIN at Nagasaki in 1853. The following year he participated in the talks that led to the signing of the KANAGAWA TREATY with the United States. In 1856 Gempo was named an instructor in the BANSHO SHIRABESHO, the newly established shogunate center for Western studies. Gempo wrote many books on Western medicine and translated Western books on various kinds of technology. His translation Suijōsen setsuryaku (Concise Explanation of Steamships) was used by the Satsuma domain (now Kagoshima Prefecture) to build Japan's first steamboat.

Mitsukuri Kakichi (1858–1909)

Zoologist. Born in Edo (now Tōkyō). Studied at Keio Gijuku (now Keio University), at Daigaku Nankō (now Tōkyō University) and, afterwards, in the United States and England. After returning to Japan, he was the first Japanese professor of zoology at Tōkyō University. He carried out research mainly in the fields of taxonomy and embryology; he was a pioneer in these fields in Japan. He helped found the Misaki Marine Biological Station of Tōkyō University at Misaki in Kanagawa Prefecture. He also contributed to the development of biological education in general. *Suzuki Zenji*

Mitsukuri Rinshō (1846–1897)

Legal scholar and bureaucrat. Born in Edo (now Tōkyō), Mitsukuri pursued WESTERN LEARNING under his grandfather, MITSUKURI GEMPO, and served in the BANSHO SHIRABESHO, the translation bureau of the Tokugawa shogunate. He succeeded Gempo as a shogunate retainer in 1864. In 1867 he accompanied a shogunate mission to the Paris Exposition and after his return became an official translator in the new Meiji government, undertaking the translation and compilation of Western law codes. Together with the French jurist and government adviser Gustave Emile BOISSONADE DE FONTARABIE, Mitsukuri helped to draft new civil and commercial codes. As a member of the MEIROKUSHA, he was active in the Westernization movement of the 1870s. Mitsukuri later became vice-minister of justice in the KURODA KIYOTAKA cabinet (1888–89), a member of the House of Peers, and chief justice of the Administrative Court. He also served as president of Wafutsu Hōritsu Gakkō, the predecessor of Hōsei University.

Mitsuminesan

Mountain in western Saitama Prefecture, central Honshū. Mitsumine Shrine on the summit attracted many pilgrims during the Edo period (1600–1868). Part of Chichibu–Tama National Park. Height: 1,100 m (3,608 ft).

Mitsumine Shrine

(Mitsumine Jinja). Shintō shrine at the foot of the group of high mountains known as Mitsumine in the Chichibu district, Saitama Prefecture, dedicated to Izanagi no Mikoto and Izanami no Mikoto, the two divine progenitors (see IZANAGI AND IZANAMI). According to tradition, the shrine was founded in AD 111 by the hero Yamatotakeru no Mikoto (see YAMATOTAKERU, PRINCE) during a campaign to bring eastern Japan under imperial sway. During the Kamakura period (1185–1333) the shrine became a center for the practice of the Honzan branch of SHUGENDŌ, a Buddhist-Shintō syncretic cult. The amulets issued by the shrine are believed to be particularly efficacious in preventing misfortunes stemming from wild animals, fire, and burglars and have attracted pilgrims, especially during the Edo period (1600–1868). The annual festival is observed on 8 April.

Stanley WEINSTEIN

Mitsunaga Hoshio (1866–1945)

The founder of DENTSŪ, INC, an advertising agency. Born in Kumamoto Prefecture, he was at first a journalist. After switching jobs, Mitsunaga started an advertising and communications company, named Nihon Kōkoku Kabushiki Kaisha in 1901. This was followed by the establishment of Dempō Tsūshinsha, which contracted with foreign news agencies such as Reuters to supply newspapers with domestic and foreign news. The two companies were united in 1907 on equal terms and formed Nihon Dempō Tsūshinsha, Ltd, which is the predecessor of the present Dentsū. Mitsunaga endeavored to establish the advertising business in Japan on a firm basis and was highly original in his approach. *KAWAKAMI Hiroshi*

Mitsutani Kunishirō (1874–1936)

Western-style painter. Born in Okayama Prefecture, he went to Tōkyō in 1891 and studied painting at the Fudōsha, the art school of Koyama Shōtarō (1857–1916). In 1900 and 1901 he traveled and exhibited in France, where he studied briefly with Jean-Paul Laurens (1838–1921); returning to Japan in 1902, he was one of the founders of the Pacific Painting Society (Taiheiyō Gakai). He later served as a judge at the BUNTEN, the Ministry of Education's annual exhibition. He was influenced by the French avant-garde, particularly Henri Matisse, during a second Paris sojourn (1911–14), and this resulted in a radical change in his painting style. In 1925 he was appointed to the Imperial Fine Arts Academy (Teikoku Bijutsuin). In his late years he traveled frequently to China and his paintings became increasingly decorative and stylized.

Mitsuya plan

(Mitsuya Kenkyū; "Three Arrows Studies"). A series of studies concerning the deployment of the Self Defense Forces; carried out by the JOINT STAFF COUNCIL of the Self Defense Forces in 1963 and officially known as the Shōwa 38 United Defense Map Studies. The contingency plan was based on a possible military conflict on the Korean peninsula and covered various details on the mobilization of the Self Defense Forces, the cooperative strategy to be used between the United States and Japan, and requests to be made to the Diet and administrative offices. The studies were criticized from many quarters as an infringement of the principle of CIVILIAN CONTROL OF THE MILITARY, the command prerogatives of the United States Forces in Japan, and the constitutional limitations on the Self Defense Forces. The affair was taken up in the Diet in 1965, and those responsible were eventually dismissed. Thereafter, contingency studies of this nature were considered taboo in the Self Defense Forces, but more recently there has been a tendency to see such studies as a legitimate activity of the Self Defense Forces.

IWASHIMA Hisao

Miura

City in southeastern Kanagawa Prefecture, central Honshū. Its port of Misaki is a base for deep-sea fishing, with one of the largest tuna catches in Japan. Agricultural products include *daikon* (Japanese radish) and watermelon. Attractions include the island of JŌGA-SHIMA and ABURATSUBO Bay. Pop: 48,685.

Miura Anjin → Adams, William

Miura Baien (1723–1789)

Philosopher and educator of the mid-Edo period. Skeptical of conventional explanations of nature and society, he independently formulated his own epistemology and ontology. This system of thought contained a process of logical development, called *jōrigaku,* which was remarkably similar to the dialectical method proposed by Hegel.

Born in 1723 in Bungo Province (now part of Ōita Prefecture) and educated to continue in his family's tradition of practicing medicine, Baien early developed a deep interest in philosophy and absorbed himself in Chinese, Indian, and Japanese philosophies, Neo-Confucianism, natural science, ethics, economics, and Dutch. He set up a private school in the home where he was born and seldom left it throughout his lifetime. Although his school drew students from throughout the country, until the Meiji period (1868–1912) his philosophic formulations attracted few followers and little interest beyond his local area.

Main Works —— Baien's three main works, *Gengo* (1775), *Zeigo* (ca 1786), and *Kango* (ca 1763), constitute one of the most thoughtful and original philosophical systems created in the Edo period. In *Gengo* he undertook to explain all phenomena in terms of a universal principle, which he called *jōri.* He saw the universe grounded in the principle of oppositions, with all beings and other phenomena arising out of the interaction of sets of "dialectical" opposites. This introduction to philosophy combined what we now call epistemology and ontology.

Zeigo supplements *Gengo* by criticizing and synthesizing various teachings of ancient and contemporary writers in the light of his theory of *jōri. Kango,* an introduction to ethics, applied *jōri* to an analysis of the ethics of human relationships and the proper display of human feelings and will. In a fourth book, *Kagen* (1773), he applied his abstract speculation to actual problems, tracing the history of currency circulation in Japan and analyzing wage and price fluctuations.

Many of the individual points of his thesis remain incompletely understood, primarily because of their originality. Summarized below are the central points of his theory.

Rejection of preconceptions. Learning, Baien believed, begins with the rejection of perceptual habits *(naraiki).* Such preconceptions lead to self-deception, e.g., the results of judgments made about the world solely from the viewpoint of an animal that walks upright and has an opposable thumb. Once the individual becomes free from his habits of thinking, everything in the universe—including human beings—is seen as "one thing." So long as phenomena are viewed subjectively or anthropomorphically, Baien asserted, man cannot attain the truth of any of them—an argument that immediately recalls Francis Bacon's rejection of preconceptions in his description of the four *idola.*

The skeptical mind. Baien further pointed out that people tend to limit their curiosity and skepticism to things when they are in an unusual state, e.g., the earth quaking. Humans never ask why earthquakes are not the usual state of affairs. Instead, they rest secure in stereotyped thinking shaped by words, concepts, habits—in short, preconceptions. In what was tantamount to a destructive critique of the rectification of names theory in contemporary Neo-Confucianism, Baien lambasted man's tendency to think in terms of "eyes are supposed to see, ears to hear, heavy things to fall, and light things to float."

The anticoncept and unification. To uncover truth, Baien advocated that one take no book or man, even a sage or Buddha, as a teacher. Instead, one should make the universe one's teacher and friend and the object of study and argument. Thereby one could pursue truth and attain a detached philosophical understanding with a mind unfettered by the preconceptions of any academic school or faction.

Baien described his original method of thought as *hankan-gōitsu* (anticoncept and unification). By "anticoncept" he meant the ability to see a problem or object from its opposite side and to posit a question on the basis of such understanding. In other words, by creating an "anticoncept" one followed a matter's logical sequence, *jōri*. Such progress still left the next stage of unifying these opposing concepts as part of an ongoing intellectual development. This exposition of logical criticism strikingly resembles the Hegelian triad of thesis, antithesis, and synthesis.

Jōri is manifested as opposites such as mind and body, fine and coarse (*sei* and *so*), hidden and revealed (*botsu* and *ho*), spirit and matter (*ki* and *butsu*), yin and yang (J: *in* and *yō*). By viewing *jōri* with a detachment based on unification through "anticoncepts," one can, argued Baien, grasp the essence of things.

In *Kagen*, Baien applied his method of "tracing back to the essence (*gen; moto*) and reaching the branches" to discover on his own "Gresham's Law," the principle that "bad money drives out good."

Social and Educational Activity——While engaged in philosophical speculation and writing, Baien taught many students at his own school according to his developing philosophy. He took the most un-Confucian step of opening his school to all people regardless of class, age, sex, or legal status. Calling his students "brothers," "friends," or "gentlemen," he made no distinction between teacher and student in their common pursuit of truth. To a degree unheard of in his day, he stressed free discussion and study so that even his own thought was open to his students' criticism. Also, he provided poor students with food and clothing to encourage them to continue their studies.

Baien's concern with local issues led him to apply his ideas, though in more conventional Confucian proposals. He led a frugal life and gave away his savings. He and his sympathizers set up a charity (*jihi mujin*) which stored up money and grain for disaster relief. In concerning himself with such matters, he sought to apply his learning to the welfare of others.

■——Miura Baien, *Baien zenshū*, 2 vols (Meicho Kankōkai, 1912). Saigusa Hiroto, *Miura Baien no tetsugaku*, in *Saigusa Hiroto chosakushū*, vol 5 (1972–73). Taguchi Masaharu, *Miura Baien no kenkyū* (1979).   Imai Jun

Miura Chora (1729–1780)

HAIKU poet of the late 18th century. Born in Shima Province (now part of Mie Prefecture), he spent long years traveling throughout the country, composing verses with local poets, before settling down in Yamada in Ise Province (also now part of Mie Prefecture). A friend of Yosa BUSON, he was a member of the group of poets who led the haiku revival movement of the period. His verses have a persistent quality of simplicity and plainness and occasionally a suggestion of *aware* (pathos; see MONO NO AWARE) that is characteristic of traditional WAKA poetry. Main haiku collections: *Chora bunshū* (1786) and *Chora hokkushū* (1784).

Miura family

Powerful warrior family of Sagami Province (now Kanagawa Prefecture) who claimed descent from the Kammu Heishi branch of the TAIRA FAMILY. Miura Yoshiaki (1092–1180), assistant governor of Sagami, led his entire family in supporting the rebellion of MINAMOTO NO YORITOMO in 1180. His son Yoshizumi (1127–1200) was rewarded with appointment as military governor (*shugo*) of Sagami and was admitted to the inner councils of Yoritomo's shogunate; his grandson Yoshimura (d 1239) was also given the military governorships of Kawachi (now part of Ōsaka Prefecture) and Kii (now Wakayama Prefecture) for aiding the shogunal regent (*shikken*) HŌJŌ YASUTOKI in the JŌKYŪ DISTURBANCE of 1221 and was appointed a member of the Council of State (HYŌJŌSHŪ). The Miura thus became a major vassal family of the Kamakura shogunate, second only to the HŌJŌ FAMILY in influence. Yoshimura's son Miura Yasumura (d 1247) married a daughter of Hōjō Yasutoki and was appointed to the Hyōjōshū; but he was later forced into rebellion by HŌJŌ TOKIYORI and ADACHI KAGEMORI, who both resented his power, and the entire family was destroyed and their lands confiscated in the HŌJI CONFLICT of 1247.   G. Cameron Hurst III

Miura Gorō (1846–1926)

Army officer and politician. Born in the Chōshū domain (now Yamaguchi Prefecture), he joined the KIHEITAI, the most famous of the peasant-*samurai* military units formed in Chōshū, and participated in the movement to overthrow the Tokugawa shogunate (1603–1867). After the Meiji Restoration of 1868, he entered the Army Ministry and distinguished himself in the suppression of the HAGI and SATSUMA REBELLIONS. Although a native of Chōshū, Mi-

ura was throughout his life a sharp critic of the Chōshū–Satsuma monopoly of government power (HAMBATSU). In 1881 he was demoted for opposing the proposed sale of government property in Hokkaidō (see HOKKAIDŌ COLONIZATION OFFICE SCANDAL OF 1881). In 1884 he accompanied General ŌYAMA IWAO on an investigative tour of European military organizations, but soon after his return he was placed on the army reserve list for his insistence on radical military reform. In 1889 Miura joined others in successfully opposing Foreign Minister ŌKUMA SHIGENOBU's plan for the revision of the so-called Unequal Treaties (see UNEQUAL TREATIES, REVISION OF). Appointed minister to Korea in 1895, he was arrested and imprisoned for his part in the assassination of Queen MIN, but was later released. Miura entered politics as a member of the KENSEI HONTŌ party and in 1897 campaigned against the proposed increase in the land tax. Named to the Privy Council in 1910, he was active in his later years as a behind-the-scenes manipulator. While Miura was active in the MOVEMENT TO PROTECT CONSTITUTIONAL GOVERNMENT and in other attempts to promote party government, his political philosophy was essentially nationalistic rather than liberal.

Miura Hiroyuki (1871–1931)

Historian. Also known as Miura Kaneyuki. Born in Shimane Prefecture. After graduating from Tōkyō University, he joined the Shūshikyoku (now the HISTORIOGRAPHICAL INSTITUTE, TŌKYŌ UNIVERSITY) to edit the section of the DAI NIHON SHIRYŌ covering the Kamakura period (1185–1333). He also lectured at Tōkyō University. In 1909 he was appointed to a professorship at Kyōto University, where he lectured on medieval and legal history and paleography. Miura's work on the medieval commercial city of SAKAI (*Sakai Shi shi*, 1924) set a standard for the compilation of local history. He was awarded the Imperial Academy Prize (Teikoku Gakushiin Shō) for his *Hōseishi no kenkyū* (1918, Studies on Legal History).

Miura Ken'ya (1821–1889)

Ceramist. Born in Edo (now Tōkyō), he was adopted at age five into a family that specialized in making earthenware dolls. Ken'ya continued this trade until he was discovered by the potter Nishimura Bakuan (1784–1853), sometimes called the fourth master in the line of Ogata KENZAN. Ken'ya studied painting under TANI BUNCHŌ and also studied MAKI-E lacquer techniques. Although he lived in Edo, his varied interests took him to many parts of Japan. He studied shipbuilding with the Dutch at Nagasaki after his curiosity was aroused by the arrival of Commodore Matthew C. PERRY's ships in 1853. Later Ken'ya was hired by the Sendai domain to build its first modern ship. His other interests included geology, but his business ventures, such as his attempt to corner the market in silver coins and to produce porcelain insulators for the new electrical industry, were generally unsuccessful. He is best known for his pottery, mostly made in Edo, and low-temperature work with bold designs in underglaze oxides or overglaze enamels. He also made pieces in the Oribe style (see FURUTA ORIBE), but his most characteristic work was in the style of Kenzan.   David Hale

Miura Kinnosuke (1864–1950)

Internist; founder of neurointernal medicine in Japan. Born in Mutsu (now Fukushima Prefecture).· A graduate of Tōkyō University, Miura studied with Erwin von BÄLZ. He went to Europe in 1889 to pursue further studies, and upon returning home, became a professor at his alma mater. He carried out research on Gerlier's disease, which had broken out in northwestern Honshū, and also studied *Ascaris ovis*, an intestinal nematode parasite. Miura played an important role in founding the Japanese Society of Internal Medicine and the Japanese Society of Neurology. He also rendered valuable service to the cause of Franco-Japanese medical exchange. In 1929 he became the first director of the Tōkyō Fraternity Memorial Hospital (Dōai Kinen Byōin). He received the Order of Culture in 1949.   Nagatoya Yōji

Miura Peninsula

(Miura Hantō). Located in Kanagawa Prefecture, central Honshū. Extending south into the Sagami Sea, it is bounded to the east by Tōkyō Bay and the Uraga Channel, and to the west by Sagami Bay. This hilly, densely populated region is the location of numerous cities, including Kamakura, Yokosuka, Zushi, and Miura, and is a major residential and recreational area for Tōkyō. The region is one of historic importance; it has numerous temples and shrines, especially around Kamakura. There are some industrial areas, especially around Yokosuka, which is a large naval base. The beaches remain popular despite the pollution of Tōkyō Bay.

Miura Saku (1881–1945)

Also known as Sack Miura. Japanese journalist in Brazil. Born in Ehime Prefecture, Miura emigrated to Brazil in 1908. As publisher of the newspaper *Nippaku shimbun* from 1919, he led public opinion among Japanese immigrants. He was a strong supporter of the cooperative movement. Miura was exiled to Japan as a result of a conspiracy by political enemies, and was jailed there during World War II. He was discharged, and died shortly after the war ended. In his outspokenness and courage Miura was a unique figure among the Japanese immigrants in Brazil. *SAITŌ Hiroshi*

Miura Shumon (1926–)

Author. Born in Tōkyō. Graduate of Tōkyō University. Professor of Japanese literature at Nihon University. In the early 1950s he started writing short stories, mostly based on ancient Chinese history, but in the late 1950s he turned to stories about the emptiness and ennui in the lives of middle-aged white-collar workers who came of age during World War II. His wife, SONO AYAKO, is also a writer. Miura's major works include *Meifu sansuizu* (1951) and *Hakoniwa* (1967).

Miura Tetsuo (1931–)

Novelist. Also called Miura Tetsurō. Born in Aomori Prefecture. Graduate of Waseda University. Affected in his youth by the suicides of two of his three sisters and the disappearances of his two brothers, he was tortured by shame and despair. He began to write as a student. His works, which are largely autobiographical, reflect his painful awareness of what he called his "cursed blood" and his wish for a fresh life. He won the Akutagawa Prize for his short story "Shinobugawa" (1960), an account of the love between a poor student and a maid. His principal works include *Umi no michi* (1967–69), a novel.

Miwa Kyūwa (1895–1981)

Potter in Hagi, Yamaguchi Prefecture. Original name, Miwa Kunihiro. The 10th generation of his family to become a potter in the HAGI WARE tradition, he took the name Kyūsetsu when his father retired in 1927. Following his own retirement in 1967, he was called Kyūwa and his brother Setsuo (b 1910), also a potter, inherited the name Kyūsetsu. Recognized by the government as a LIVING NATIONAL TREASURE in 1970, Kyūwa was a conscientious technician renowned for his TEA CEREMONY bowls, fresh-water jars, and sculptured figures. The thick, milky-white, Korean-style glaze he formulated is much admired and imitated. *Jeanne CARREAU*

Miwa Shissai (1669–1744)

Confucian scholar of the Edo period (1600–1868). Born in Kyōto. He studied with SATŌ NAOKATA, a leading disciple of the Neo-Confucian scholar YAMAZAKI ANSAI. Shissai later returned to the Wang Yangming school (see YŌMEIGAKU), however, and was expelled by his teacher. After a period of lecturing in various domains, he eventually settled in Edo (now Tōkyō) to open his own school, the Meirindō. Shissai is chiefly remembered for popularizing the Wang Yangming school, which emphasized meditation and the unity of knowledge and action.

Miwata Masako (1843–1927)

Educator. Maiden name, Uda. The daughter of a scholar, she was herself well-educated in the Japanese and Chinese classics and taught at her father's private school in Kyōto; in 1866 she was appointed as a tutor in the household of the court noble IWAKURA TOMOMI. In 1869 she married Miwata (or Miwada) Mototsuna (also known as Tsunaichirō; 1829–79), an activist for the cause of the MEIJI RESTORATION up to 1868 and later a Meiji government official. After his death she again began teaching; in 1887 she opened her own private school in Tōkyō and also taught in government-sponsored schools. In 1901 she helped to organize and joined the staff of Nihon Joshi Daigakkō (now JAPAN WOMEN'S UNIVERSITY). The next year she opened her own girls' school, Miwata Jogakkō (from 1903, Miwata Kōtō Jogakkō; now Miwata Gakuen). She was aided by her adopted son, Miwata Gendō (1870–1965), who took over the school's leadership after her death. She published a number of works on women's education, emphasizing her conservative views. She was also active in the AIKOKU FUJINKAI (Patriotic Women's Society).

Miwayama

Hill north of the city of Sakurai, Nara Prefecture, central Honshū. A beautiful conical mountain composed of gabbro. On the western slope is Japan's most ancient road, known as the Yamanobe no Michi. Also on the western slope is Ōmiwa Shrine. The forests are protected as part of a sacred precinct. Height: 467 m (1,532 ft).

Miyabe Kingo (1860–1951)

Botanist specializing in plant taxonomy and plant pathology. Born in Edo (now Tōkyō). After graduating from Sapporo Nōgakkō (now Hokkaidō University), he became a commissioner in the Hokkaidō Colonization Office and also carried on studies in plant taxonomy under the guidance of YATABE RYŌKICHI of Tōkyō University. Later he went to the United States and studied fungology at Harvard University. He did research in the geographical distribution of plants in the northern region of Japan, discovered the distribution boundary in the Kuril Islands (called Miyabe's line), and made other important contributions in this field of study. He is also regarded as a pioneer in plant pathology. *SUZUKI Zenji*

Miyagawa

River in central Mie Prefecture, central Honshū, originating in the Kii Mountains and flowing northeast to enter Ise Bay at the city of Ise. The Miyagawa Dam and the gorge called Ōsugi are located on the upper reaches. The river is part of Yoshino–Kumano National Park. Length: 90 km (56 mi).

Miyagawa Chōshun (1683–1753)

UKIYO-E artist. Also known as Miyagawa Nagaharu or Chōzaemon. He worked exclusively as a painter and not as a designer of prints. The name Miyagawa is said to have derived from his birthplace in Owari Province (now Aichi Prefecture). He came to Edo (now Tōkyō) to learn the techniques of the two main schools of Japanese painting, the TOSA SCHOOL and the KANŌ SCHOOL, but was also attracted by the work of the *ukiyo-e* artists Hishikawa MORONOBU and Kaigetsudō Ando (see KAIGETSUDŌ SCHOOL). In 1750 he was invited by Kanō artists to assist in restoring paintings at the TŌSHŌGŪ, the Tokugawa shrine at Nikkō. A quarrel arose regarding his fees, however, and in the ensuing melee, his son and disciples mortally wounded several of the Kanō painters. For his part in this, Chōshun was banished to Izu for two years. His work is mainly in the *bijin* (beautiful women) genre, and all of them display excellent brushwork and a superb sense of color. Foremost among them are the *Yūjo monkō zu* (Courtesans Sniffing Incense) and the *Ryūka bijin zu* (Beauties under the Willows). There is also a scroll by Chōshun depicting scenes from the theater (the *Engeki zukan),* and a scroll of genre scenes *(Fūzoku zukan).* Chōshun is the founder of the Miyagawa school of *ukiyo-e,* whose members worked primarily with paintings and not with prints. His disciple, Katsukawa Shunsui, who is said to have changed his name from Miyagawa to Katsukawa after his teacher's disgrace, was in turn a teacher of the great artist of the theatrical print, KATSUKAWA SHUNSHŌ.

Miyagawa Kazuo (1908–)

Cinematographer; born in Kyōto. In 1926, after graduation from Kyōto Commercial School, Miyagawa joined the Kyōto Nikkatsu studios and became a cameraman. His photography is characterized by balanced composition and unobtrusive camera handling, giving his work a certain solidity. His long takes, completely devoid of wasted space, greatly influenced France's so-called New Wave of young filmmakers. Though not as well known among the general public as many of the directors he worked with, Miyagawa's shots,

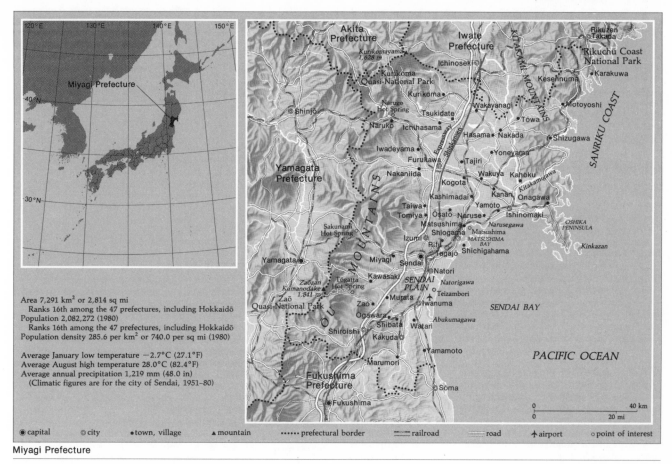

Area 7,291 km² or 2,814 sq mi
  Ranks 16th among the 47 prefectures, including Hokkaidō
Population 2,082,272 (1980)
  Ranks 16th among the 47 prefectures, including Hokkaidō
Population density 285.6 per km² or 740.0 per sq mi (1980)

Average January low temperature −2.7°C (27.1°F)
Average August high temperature 28.0°C (82.4°F)
Average annual precipitation 1,219 mm (48.0 in)
  (Climatic figures are for the city of Sendai, 1951–80)

⊙ capital   ○ city   ● town, village   ▲ mountain   ····· prefectural border   ⌗ railroad   ═══ road   ✈ airport   ○ point of interest

Miyagi Prefecture

including that in which he captures the sharp play of sunlight spilling through the trees in RASHŌMON (1950, directed by KUROSAWA AKIRA), are memorable. His hand-held camera work in *Tōkyō orimpikku* (1964, directed by ICHIKAWA KON; American release, *Tokyo Olympiad*) established new methods for the documentary film.   *ITASAKA Tsuyoshi*

miyage

Souvenir gift that one brings back from a trip. Every locale in Japan has its specialities in food, folk art, crafts, and so forth. Japanese travelers feel a strong obligation to bring back such items as gifts to be given not only to family members but also to relatives, neighbors, and friends. If one has received a *miyage* in the recent past, one has an obligation to reciprocate. Also, when leaving for an extended trip, one often receives a farewell gift *(sembetsu)* from friends and relatives and one is expected to present *miyage* in return. This custom explains why many Japanese tourists abroad seem to be busy buying gifts, even to the extent of sacrificing sight-seeing. Because of its obligatory nature, *miyage*-buying is often perceived as a burden; however, it is partly by fulfillment of such mutual obligations that the Japanese maintain social solidarity and cooperation.

Miyage should be distinguished from *temiyage*, a gift that one takes when visiting a friend or relative. *Temiyage* are usually sweets, fruits, or other nonstaple foods. Whereas one makes a call specifically for the purpose of delivering *miyage*, *temiyage* are given incidentally at most social calls. See also GIFT GIVING.
      Harumi BEFU

Miyagi Michio (1894–1956)

Composer and performer of SŌKYOKU (music for KOTO). Born in Kōbe to the supervisor of an American-owned tea warehouse, the young Miyagi was early exposed to Western music. He was mainly brought up by his divorced mother. By the age of seven he was completely blind; at eight he began his studies with the Ikuta school *koto* master Nakajima Kengyō II. After many struggles (his father failed in business and could no longer support him), he met the SHAKUHACHI master Yoshida Seifū and embarked on a long and highly successful career as composer and as concert and recording

artist. His many compositions, which were adventurous for their day, are in a hybrid style showing Western influence; they are mostly for Japanese instruments, but occasionally use Western instruments too, as in the famous piece *Haru no umi* (1929). He also invented new Japanese instruments, notably the *jūshichigen* (17-stringed *koto*). Aesthetically, Miyagi's music is sweet, but sometimes sentimental.

——Miyagi Michio Zenshū Kankō Kai, ed, *Miyagi Michio zenshū*, 3 vols (1957–58, repr 1972).   *David B. WATERHOUSE*

Miyagi Prefecture

(Miyagi Ken). Located in northern Honshū and bordered by Iwate Prefecture to the north, the Pacific Ocean to the east, Fukushima Prefecture to the south, and Akita and Yamagata prefectures to the west. The western section of the prefecture is part of the ŌU MOUNTAINS, which descend to a line of foothills and then to a coastal plain in the east. Major rivers, which include the ABUKUMAGAWA and KITAKAMIGAWA, generally flow eastward from the mountains to the Pacific. The northern coastal area is heavily indented, and the southern coast is composed of the sandy beaches of SENDAI BAY. The climate is cool with dry, clear winters. Winters in the coastal area are mild.

Archaeological discoveries suggest that the Miyagi area was fairly well developed at an early period of Japanese history. After the TAIKA REFORM of 645, it became part of the Mutsu Province. In the Heian period (794–1185) it came under the dominance of the ŌSHŪ FUJIWARA FAMILY, but later was ruled by a succession of feudal warlords. It flourished under the rule of the DATE FAMILY in the Edo period (1600–1868), becoming the principal cultural and economic center of northeastern Honshū. Its present name was acquired in 1872, and its boundaries were established in 1876.

Agriculture and fishing remain the principal activities, with rice as the major crop. It is one of Japan's principal fishing areas, producing large quantities of tuna and halibut. Industrial development has increased in recent years and further development is anticipated with the completion of the Tōhoku Expressway and the Tōhoku Shinkansen (a high-speed railway). Present industries include metal, machine, paper, and pulp production.

The city of SENDAI continues to be the cultural and educational center of the six prefectures of the Tōhoku region (northeastern Honshū). The TANABATA FESTIVAL held there each summer is one of the most famous in Japan and attracts numerous visitors. The coastal view of MATSUSHIMA has traditionally been counted as one of Japan's most scenic areas, and other parts of the coast are included in RIKUCHŪ COAST NATIONAL PARK. There are also many hot spring resorts, among which Narugo, Tōgatta, and Sakunami are representative. Area: 7,291 sq km (2,814 sq mi); pop: 2,082,272; capital: Sendai. Other major cities include Kesennuma, Ishinomaki, Furukawa, Shiogama, and Izumi.

Miyagi Tamayo (1892–1960)

Public official and politician who worked especially on problems of women and children. Born in Yamaguchi Prefecture; maiden name, Ueda. She graduated from Nara Women's Higher Normal School (now Nara Women's University) in 1914 and joined the staff of the ŌHARA INSTITUTE FOR SOCIAL RESEARCH. She studied in the United States under Japanese government sponsorship from 1922 to 1924, and in 1927 she became the first women juvenile probation officer in Japan. That same year she left her post to marry Miyagi Chōgorō (1878–1942), who became minister of justice in 1939. Beginning in 1947, she served 12 years in the House of Councillors, where she was a member of the RYOKUFŪKAI group. She campaigned vigorously for the PROSTITUTION PREVENTION LAW of 1956, and she was known as an authority on social and labor problems, especially those concerning juveniles.

Miyagi Yotoku (1903–1945)

Marxist artist implicated in the Richard Sorge espionage ring. Born in Okinawa, he went to California at age 16 to help on his father's farm. He graduated from the San Diego Art School in 1925 and held a one-man exhibit in Los Angeles, which was favorably reviewed. He became very active in a Japanese socialist group and joined the Workers Party of America (later the Communist Party). At the same time, Kitabayashi Tomo, in whose home he was living, also joined the Workers Party. In 1933 he went to Japan as a Comintern agent and began to work with Sorge; Kitabayashi followed shortly thereafter. He was arrested along with Sorge, Kitabayashi, and other group members in 1941 and died of tuberculosis in Sugamo Prison, Tōkyō, before the completion of his trial. See also SORGE INCIDENT; OZAKI HOTSUMI. *Karl G.* YONEDA

Miyajima → Itsukushima

Miyajima Seijirō (1879–1963)

Businessman. Born in Tochigi Prefecture. After graduating from Tōkyō University, Miyajima joined the Sumitomo company. In 1914 he rebuilt NISSHIN SPINNING CO, LTD, into one of Japan's six most important spinning ventures. Miyajima became the company's president in 1919, serving in that capacity and as chairman until 1945, when SAKURADA TAKESHI took over. He helped to establish the Industrial Club of Japan in 1917 and played an important role in the nation's business and industrial community. *KOBAYAKAWA* Yōichi

Miyake Issei (1938–)

Fashion designer. Born in Hiroshima Prefecture. Graduate of Tama University of Arts (Tōkyō). His fashion creations are noted for their originality and unconventional designs. In 1976 he was invited as a participating artist to the Festival d'Automne in Paris. He was the recipient of the 1976 Mainichi Design Award. *HAYASHI* Kunio

Miyakejima

Volcanic island approximately 70 km (43 mi) south of the island of Ōshima, south of the Izu Peninsula, central Honshū. Administratively under the Tōkyō prefectural government, it is one of the IZU ISLANDS. The highest peak on the island, Oyama (814 m; 2,670 ft), is a central cone, which has erupted as recently as 1962. Miyakejima is part of the Fuji–Hakone–Izu National Park; air and sea routes between the island and Tōkyō have facilitated tourism. Cattle are raised; a special product of the island is butter. Area: 55.1 sq km (21.3 sq mi).

Miyake Kaho (1868–1943)

Novelist, essayist, and poet; one of Japan's first modern women writers. Born in Edo (now Tōkyō), oldest daughter of the government official TANABE TAICHI. Original name: Tanabe Tatsuko. She graduated from Tōkyō Women's Higher School (now Ochanomizu University) and also studied writing at the private school of the woman poet Nakajima Utako (1841–1903), where one of her younger classmates was the novelist HIGUCHI ICHIYŌ.

Her first novel, *Yabu no uguisu* (1888, The Warbler in the Grove) depicts the effects of modernization on women at various social levels, and she followed this with a number of similar stories. In 1892, she married the philosopher and journalist MIYAKE SETSUREI; from 1920, she often edited and contributed articles on women's issues to one of her husband's magazines, *Josei nihonjin* (Japanese Women). Her books also include the poetry collection *Hana no shumi* (1909, In Praise of Flowers). Although her works are not widely read today, she provided an example of success to inspire later women writers.

Miyake Kanran (1674–1718)

Confucian scholar of the Edo period (1600–1868); younger brother of MIYAKE SEKIAN. Born in Kyōto, he studied first with ASAMI KEISAI, and later with KINOSHITA JUN'AN, both associated with the Zhu Xi (Chu Hsi) school of Neo-Confucianism (see SHUSHIGAKU). In 1699 Kanran entered the service of TOKUGAWA MITSUKUNI, *daimyō* of the Mitō domain (now Ibaraki Prefecture), and participated in the compilation of the monumental history of Japan, DAI NIHON SHI. On the recommendation of the scholar-statesman ARAI HAKUSEKI, he was named a Confucian adviser to the shogunate in 1711.

Miyake Sekian (1665–1730)

Confucian scholar of the Edo period (1600–1868). Born in Kyōto. With his younger brother MIYAKE KANRAN, he studied under ASAMI KEISAI, a scholar of the Zhu Xi (Chu Hsi) school of Neo-Confucianism (see SHUSHIGAKU). After teaching for several years in Edo (now Tōkyō), he went to Ōsaka, where he opened a private school. In 1724 a disciple, Nakai Shūan (1693–1758), built a school, the KAITOKUDŌ, with funds donated by local merchants and invited Sekian to be its head. Sekian devoted the remainder of his life to teaching Ōsaka merchants his own brand of Confucianism, a blend of the Wang Yangming (YŌMEIGAKU) and Zhu Xi schools of Neo-Confucianism.

Miyake Setsurei (1860–1945)

Critic, philosopher, and historian. Real name Miyake Yūjirō. As one of the leading publicists of modern Japan, he called for the development of a new national consciousness, self-reliance, and self-affirmation on the part of the Japanese at a time when the nation was sedulously imitating the West.

Miyake was born in what is now the city of Kanazawa, Ishikawa Prefecture, the son of a physician. In 1883 he graduated from Tōkyō University, where he studied philosophy. After teaching briefly at several schools, Miyake decided, together with SHIGA SHIGETAKA, Sugiura Jūgō (also known as SUGIURA SHIGETAKE), and others, to found an organization that would counter what they saw as excessive adulation of the West. In 1888 they established the SEIKYŌSHA (Society for Political Education) and its magazine NIHONJIN (The Japanese). The magazine (renamed *Nihon oyobi nihonjin* in 1907) served also as a platform for criticizing the cliques (HAMBATSU) that dominated politics of the time and for awakening the public conscience on issues such as the ASHIO COPPER MINE INCIDENT. Miyake wrote for CHŪŌ KŌRON, *Jitsugyō no Nihon*, and other leading publications and became a mentor to several journalists, including HASEGAWA NYOZEKAN and TAOKA REIUN. Major writings are *Uchū* (1908, The Universe), in which he attempted to formulate a comprehensive system of philosophy synthesizing Eastern and Western thought, and the six-volume *Dōjidai shi*, a detailed chronicle of the people and events of his time. With his wife, the writer MIYAKE KAHO, he launched in 1920 the magazine *Josei nihonjin* (Japanese Women).

■——Miyake Setsurei, *Miyake Setsurei shū*, vol 33 of *Meiji bungaku zenshū* (Chikuma Shobō, 1967). Miyake Setsurei, *Dōjidaishi*, 6 vols (1949–54). Margaret Neuss, "Zur Rolle der Heldenbiographien im Geschichtsbild Miyake Setsureis und Yamaji Aizans," *Oriens Ex-*

tremus, 25.1 (1978). Kenneth Pyle, *The New Generation in Meiji Japan* (1969). Yanagida Izumi, *Tetsujin Miyake Setsurei sensei* (1956).　　　　　　　　　　　　　　　　*Margret* NEUSS

Miyake Shōsai (1662–1741)

Confucian scholar of the Edo period (1600–1868). Born in Harima (now part of Hyōgo Prefecture), he studied with YAMAZAKI ANSAI, a scholar of the Zhu Xi (Chu Hsi) school of Neo-Confucianism (see SHUSHIGAKU). In 1690 Shōsai entered the service of the Oshi domain (now part of the city of Gyōda in Saitama Prefecture). He incurred the *daimyō's* anger for his outspoken views, especially his criticisms of the shōgun TOKUGAWA TSUNAYOSHI, and was confined to Oshi Castle for three years. After his release he went to Kyōto, where he opened a school. Together with SATŌ NAOKATA and ASAMI KEISAI, Shōsai was considered one of the three outstanding disciples (Sanketsu) of Ansai, although he never supported Ansai's SUIKA SHINTŌ theories.

Miyake Yonekichi (1860–1929)

Historian and educator. Born in the Wakayama domain (now Wakayama Prefecture), Miyake studied at Keiō Gijuku (now Keiō University) but withdrew without graduating. His later erudition was largely self-acquired. From 1881 he taught at Tōkyō Higher Normal School, and in 1886–88 he traveled to the United States and England to acquaint himself with modern methods of scholarship. In 1890 Miyake joined the staff of the Tōkyō Imperial Household Museum (now Tōkyō National Museum) and served as its director from 1922 to 1923. In 1929 he was appointed the first president of the new Tōkyō Bunrika University (successor of Tōkyō Higher Normal School and later Tōkyō University of Education).

Miyake's research interests included the history of the SILK ROAD and the study of ancient INSCRIPTIONS such as the KWANGGAET'O MONUMENT and the gold seal supposedly given to a Japanese ruler by the Chinese emperor in AD 57 (see KAN NO WA NO NA NO KOKUŌ NO IN). He encouraged the incorporation of anthropological and archaeological findings into the study of history. He founded the Archaeological Society (now Archaeological Society of Nippon). His major works are collected in *Bungaku hakase Miyake Yonekichi chojutsushū* (1929, Collected Works of Dr Miyake Yonekichi).　　　　　　　　　　　　　　　*ABE Gihei*

Miyake Yoshinobu (1939–　　)

Featherweight-class weight lifter. Born in Miyagi Prefecture. Graduate of Hōsei University. Schoolmaster at the Physical Training School of the Self Defense Forces. He contributed much to Japan's reputation in weight lifting, winning gold medals in the TŌKYŌ OLYMPIC GAMES in 1964 and in the Mexico Olympics in 1968. He held 48 world records in the 12 years before his retirement in 1972.　　　　　　　　　　　　　　　　　　*TAKEDA Fumio*

Miyako

City in eastern Iwate Prefecture, northern Honshū, on the Pacific Ocean. Miyako has been a fishing port since the Edo period (1600–1868); principal catches are salmon and *samma* (saury). After World War II Miyako developed into an industrial city with numerous fertilizer, plywood, lumber, foodstuff, and electric appliance plants. It is part of the Rikuchū Coast National Park. Pop: 62,478.

miyakogusa

Lotus corniculatus var. *japonicus*. A Japanese variety of the bird's-foot trefoil. A perennial herb of the pea family (Leguminosae) which grows wild along grassy roadsides or on river banks. The thin fasciculate stem may grow either vertically or horizontally and reaches a length of about 15–30 centimeters (6–12 in). The ternate compound leaves are alternate and the leaflets obovate. In the spring and summer, the plant produces flower stalks from its leaf axils with 1–3 butterfly-shaped bright yellow flowers. The flowers of the subvariety *nishiki miyakogusa* (*Lotus corniculatus* var. *japonicus* subvar. *versicolor*) change their color from yellow to red.　　　　　　　　　　　　　　　　　　*MATSUDA Osamu*

Miyako Islands

(Miyako Shotō). Group of islands southwest of the main island of Okinawa forming the eastern part of the Sakishima Islands. Administratively a part of Okinawa Prefecture, they consist of the island of MIYAKOJIMA and seven others. These islands are low, composed of limestone, and frequently ravaged by typhoons and drought. Principal activities are sugarcane cultivation and bonito fishing. Area: 227 sq km (87.6 sq mi).

Miyakojima

Island approximately 300 km (186 mi) southwest of the main island of Okinawa. The main island of the Miyako Islands. A level island in the shape of a triangle, Miyakojima is composed of Ryūkyū limestone; it is frequently struck by typhoons and drought. The principal activities are sugarcane cultivation and bonito fishing. Area: 158 sq km (61.0 sq mi).

Miyakonojō

City in southwestern Miyazaki Prefecture, Kyūshū. A castle town during the Edo period (1600–1868), it is now a commercial city. Agricultural products are tea, tobacco, rape seed, and rice. Sericulture and dairy farming also flourish. Other local items are furniture, bamboo bows (80 percent of the nation's entire production), and bamboo swords for the traditional sport KENDŌ (fencing). Pop: 129,006.

Miyakonojō Basin

(Miyakonojō Bonchi). In the southern Kyūshū Mountains, in southwestern Miyazaki Prefecture, Kyūshū. Along the upper reaches of the river Ōyodogawa, the basin consists of alluvial fans and uplands composed of volcanic ashes. Rice is cultivated on the fans, while sweet potatoes, tobacco, and mulberry trees are grown on the uplands. Dairy farming also flourishes here. The major city is Miyakonojō. Area: approximately 760 sq km (293 sq mi).

Miyako no Nishiki (1675–?)

Writer of UKIYO–ZŌSHI (popular fiction) of the mid-Edo period. Born in Settsu (now part of Ōsaka Prefecture). He set off for Kyōto to study but was disinherited when his family discovered he had spent his school fees and stipends in the city's bordellos. Moving to Ōsaka, he became a disciple of NISHIZAWA IPPŪ and started to write popular fiction. His best-known work, *Genroku taiheiki* (1702), is highly original, if somewhat self-promotional and filled with gossip about writers and their works, among them Ihara saikaku. He departed for Edo (now Tōkyō) in 1703, where he was apprehended for vagrancy and sent to Satsuma (now Kagoshima Prefecture) to labor in a gold mine. Pardoned in 1710, he returned to the Ōsaka-Kyōto area, but nothing is known of his subsequent life.

Miyako no Yoshika (834–879)

Courtier, scholar and poet of Chinese; cocompiler of the *Montoku jitsuroku* (879, Chronicle of Emperor Montoku), fifth of the so-called Six National Histories (RIKKOKUSHI). Born into a family of scholars of Chinese learning, he was trained at the court unversity (Daigakuryō) and quickly gained a reputation for wit, learning, and talent for composition in Chinese, eventually becoming one of the most distinguished Chinese scholars and poets of the early Heian period. He was appointed ambassador to the kingdom of BOHAI (Po-hai) in 872 and later held various other official posts. Examples of his compositions in Chinese are included in most of the old anthologies of Chinese writings by Japanese. Of his personal collection, *Toshi bunshū* (Collected Works of Master Miyako), three books (no. 3–5) are still extant.　　　　　　　　　　　　　*Robert H.* BROWER

Miyako shimbun

Japan's first evening newspaper launched in 1884 under the banner *Konnichi shimbun*. The name was changed to *Miyako shimbun* in 1888 and it became a theater trade paper published mornings. Fukuda Eisuke took over as company president in 1919 and turned it into a highly successful enterprise. The enormously popular work *Daibosatsu Tōge* (Daibosatsu Pass), written by NAKAZATO KAIZAN and said to be the founding work of POPULAR FICTION (taishū bungaku), was serialized in the Miyako. The paper had a distinctly literary flavor compared to other newspapers. Because of wartime pressures, in 1942 it merged with the KOKUMIN SHIMBUN to form the TŌKYŌ SHIMBUN which continues to be an influential Tōkyō daily.

miyamairi

(visiting the shrine). The custom, still observed today, of taking a newborn infant to the local Shintō shrine. It is observed on the 20th, 30th, 50th, or even 100th day after birth, depending on the locality. If the infant is taken on the 20th day, the midwife or paternal grandmother takes the mother's place, for the latter is still considered ritually impure. The purpose of the visit is to have the infant recognized by the local tutelary deity (UJIGAMI) as a member (ujiko) of the Shintō community, and the infant is often made to cry in order to ensure that the god has heard. Today the baby is usually carried by its paternal grandmother and accompanied by both parents.

INOKUCHI Shōji

Miyamoto Kenji (1908–)

Politician and JAPAN COMMUNIST PARTY (JCP) leader. Born in Yamaguchi Prefecture; graduate of Tōkyō University. While still a student, he established a reputation when his essay on the writer AKUTAGAWA RYŪNOSUKE, "Haiboku no bungaku" (1929, The Literature of the Defeated), won first prize in a competition sponsored by Kaizō magazine. Miyamoto joined the JCP in 1931 and continued his literary activities as a member of the Puroretariya Sakka Dōmei (Proletarian Writers' Union). He married the writer MIYAMOTO YURIKO in 1932. In 1933 he became a member of the central committee of the outlawed JCP; that same year he was arrested and remained in prison until the end of World War II. He joined the newly reorganized JCP immediately after his release but was purged in 1950 by Occupation authorities (see RED PURGE). Since 1958 Miyamoto has been a central figure in the JCP; in 1977 he was elected to the House of Councillors.

Miyamoto Musashi (1584–1645)

Master swordsman and painter of the Edo period (1600–1868); known also by his artistic sobriquet Niten. Born in either Mimasaka (now part of Okayama Prefecture) or Harima (now Hyōgo Prefecture). Like many other *samurai* whose lords had fought on the losing side in the Battle of SEKIGAHARA in 1600, Musashi was a *rōnin* (masterless samurai). He developed the *nitōryū* or two-sword style of fencing, and, according to his own account, he was victorious in more than 60 sword fights during his extensive travels throughout Japan. In 1637 he fought for the Tokugawa shogunate in suppressing the SHIMABARA UPRISING, and in 1640 he became an instructor in swordsmanship for the Hosokawa *daimyō* family in Kumamoto. His book on swordsmanship, *Gorin no sho* (tr *The Book of Five Rings*, 1974) is considered a classic. Said to have been written in a mountain cave in 1643 and transmitted to a disciple on his deathbed, the book is divided into five sections—earth, water, fire, wind, and void—corresponding to the five elements that make up the Buddhist universe. Each section treats one aspect of the art; the "water" section, for example, deals with dress, posture, footwork, and other technical details, while the "fire" section presents Musashi's views on the spirit of swordsmanship.

Musashi was also a highly accomplished *suiboku* painter (see INK PAINTING) and calligrapher. His paintings of eagles, shrikes, Hotei (see SEVEN DEITIES OF GOOD FORTUNE) and Bodhidharma, the Zen Buddhist patriarch, are characterized by bold yet incisive brushwork, reflecting his training in Zen Buddhism. His most famous work, *The Shrike (Koboku meigeki zu)*, may be seen at the Nagao Museum in Kanagawa. Musashi's exploits have been celebrated in popular literature, including a *kabuki* play by TSURUYA NAMBOKU. More recently he was the subject of YOSHIKAWA EIJI's best-selling novel *Miyamoto Musashi* (1935–39; tr *Musashi*, 1981).

Miyamoto Yuriko (1899–1951)

Novelist. Born in Tōkyō as the first child of Chūjō Seiichirō (1868–1936), a noted architect trained at Cambridge University, and Chūjō Ashie, the daughter of NISHIMURA SHIGEKI, a scholar of eth-

ics and cofounder of the magazine *Meiroku zasshi*. At the age of 12, the precocious Yuriko started writing short stories. While attending Ochanomizu Women's High School she read classical Japanese and Russian literature, particularly the works of Dostoevsky and Tolstoy. Her first novel, *Mazushiki hitobito no mure* (A Flock of Poor People), written when she was 17 years old and a freshman at Japan Women's University, was published in the magazine *Chūō kōron* in January 1916 with the endorsement of TSUBOUCHI SHŌYŌ, who was an acquaintance of her father. The novel, which is based on her own experiences at her grandfather's estate in Fukushima Prefecture, depicts the misery of the poor peasants and reveals her strong faith in humanity and commitment to the betterment of the poor. It also launched her as a promising young novelist.

In 1918, Yuriko accompanied her father to New York, where she met and, despite her mother's strong objections, married Araki Shigeru, a scholar of the ancient Persian language fifteen years older than herself. The marriage soon proved to be disastrous; it brought five years of what Yuriko called her "swamp period," a period of psychological struggle and creative stagnation which lasted until her divorce in 1924. Her experience during this period provided the material for her first major work, *Nobuko* (1924–26), an autobiographical novel in which Yuriko, tracing her growth as an intellectual woman up to the time of her divorce, examines the institution of marriage, traditional ideas about relations between the sexes, and her own struggle to attain fulfillment in life.

In 1927, Yuriko left for Soviet Russia accompanied by Yuasa Yoshiko (b 1896), a woman translator of Russian literature with whom she had been living since her divorce. After a three-year stay abroad, mainly in Russia, where she was particularly impressed with the working women, she joined the All-Japan Proletarian Artists' Association (NAPF) in 1930 (see PROLETARIAN LITERATURE MOVEMENT). In the same year, she became the coordinator of NAPF's Women's Committee and the editor of the journal *Hataraku fujin* (Working Women). Her life after the divorce, her complex relationship with her translator friend, and her final decision to go to Soviet Russia in search of a new life are dealt with in *Futatsu no niwa* (1947, The Two Gardens), a sequel to *Nobuko*, while her experiences in Soviet Russia and Europe form the basis for *Dōhyō* (1947–50, Road Signs).

In 1931 she joined the Japan Communist Party (JCP) and met MIYAMOTO KENJI (b 1908), a young communist literary critic whom she married in 1932. From 1932 on, leftist activities were suppressed by the government with increasing severity, the publication of journals became difficult, and Yuriko's works became the target of strict censorship. She was arrested repeatedly between 1932 and 1942, spending a total of more than two years in prison; Kenji was arrested in December 1933 and remained imprisoned until 1945. Despite these hardships and the torture she experienced in prison, Yuriko refused to give up her ideological beliefs, and continued to write.

Although she produced little creative work during the war period, she was prolific in essay writing. She devoted herself to literary criticisms and essays on women and women writers; the latter were collected in 1948 under the title of *Fujin to bungaku* (Women and Literature). The voluminous letters Yuriko and Kenji exchanged during these years, collected in *Jūninen no tegami* (1950–52, The Letters of Twelve Years), are an impressive record of their love and their commitment to communism.

In 1942, she was again arrested, but four months later was sent home unconscious after suffering a heat stroke; her eyesight was impaired for an entire year and her heart was damaged. The experiences of these years and of the confusion at the end of the war were the basic materials for *Banshū Heiya* (1946–47; tr *Banshū Plain*, 1963), while *Fūchisō* (1946) depicts her reunion with Kenji.

The years between 1945 and her sudden death in 1951 were the most active and productive of her life. Finally united with her husband, who became a leading member of the JCP, she too resumed full-fledged political activities, helping to establish the Shin Nihon Bungaku Kai (New Japanese Literature Association), a group of writers committed to an "antiimperialist" and "democratic" movement. She was also founder of Fujin Minshu Kurabu (Women's Democratic Club) and the editor-in-chief of *Hataraku fujin*. Most of her major novels, including *Futatsu no niwa, Banshū Heiya, Fūchisō* and *Dōhyō*, were written during this period. In 1947 she received the Mainichi Book Award for *Fūchisō* and *Banshū Heiya*.

Yuriko's short stories, most of which are collected in *Sangatsu no daiyon nichiyō* (1940, The Fourth Sunday in March), depict working-class men and women and the growth of class consciousness.

Yet her major literary achievements are clearly in her autobiographical novels, throughout which the protagonist tries to liberate herself from her own upper middle-class background and to contribute to human welfare by fighting against war and the exploitation of the working class and women. Her novels, which mirror life in the early part of the Shōwa period (1926–) in Japan, are widely regarded as significant achievements in modern Japanese literature.

Yuriko's critical essays range from literary criticism and analyses of women writers to theoretical arguments on proletarian literature and socialist realism. Deeply concerned with the question of literature and politics, and particularly critical of the dogmatic position of the party on literature, she began writing a lengthy work entitled "1950," in which she planned to address herself to the question of literature and politics. She was, however, able to finish only a preliminary essay before her death; this appeared under the title "Ningensei, seiji, bungaku: ikani ikiru ka no mondai" (1950, Human Nature, Politics and Literature: The Question of How to Live).

■ ——Works by Miyamoto Yuriko: *Miyamoto Yuriko zenshū*, 15 vols (Kawade Shobō, 1953). *Miyamoto Yuriko hyōron senshū*, 4 vols (Shin Nihon Shuppan Sha, 1964). *Miyamoto Yuriko senshū*, 12 vols (Shin Nihon Shuppan Sha, 1969). *Miyamoto Yuriko zenshū*, 29 vols (Shin Nihon Shuppan Sha, 1979–81). With Miyamoto Kenji: *Jūninen no tegami*, 2 vols (1950–52). Works about Miyamoto Yuriko: Hirabayashi Taiko, *Miyamoto Yuriko* (1972). Nakamura Tomoko, *Miyamoto Yuriko* (1973). Nakano Shigeharu, *Kobayashi Takiji to Miyamoto Yuriko* (1972).   Noriko Mizuta LIPPIT

Miyanouradake

Mountain on the island of YAKUSHIMA, Kagoshima Prefecture, Kyūshū. It has beautiful forests of the huge cedars known as *yakusugi* from an elevation of 1,000 to 1,500 m (3,280–4,920 ft). A belt of the bamboo grass known as *yakuzasa* grows near the summit, and wild deer and monkeys are numerous. It is the highest mountain in the Kyūshū region. Part of the Kirishima–Yaku National Park. Height: 1,935 m (6,347 ft).

Miyatake Gaikotsu (1867–1955)

Also called Miyatake Tobone. Journalist and cultural historian. Born in Sanuki Province (now Kagawa Prefecture). Miyatake wrote contemporary satire for a series of magazines and newspapers that he himself published. His writings, which bordered on the pornographic, gained a large readership but also incurred the displeasure of government authorities, who imprisoned him in 1889 on a charge of LÈSE MAJESTY after he published a parody of the promulgation of the Meiji Constitution. Altogether, Miyatake spent over four years in prison for repeated literary indiscretions. From the Taishō period (1912–26) he devoted himself to the history of the demimonde and the history of journalism in Japan. Miyatake was appointed curator of the Meiji Newspaper and Periodical Library (Meiji Shimbun Zasshi Bunko) when it was established at Tōkyō University in 1926; the library included Miyatake's own private collection of materials pertaining to popular culture. He served as curator until his resignation in 1949. He is the author of more than 100 books, including *Meiji enzetsu shi* (History of Public Speaking in the Meiji Period), *Waisetsu fūzoku shi* (History of Salacious Manners), and *Tobakushi* (History of Gambling).

miyaza

Council of lay elders representing a limited number of distinguished families which claimed a close association with a local ancestral shrine (*miya*; see UJIGAMI). The *miyaza* presided over religious practices of the community. Along with the closed and privileged trade association ZA, it developed through the medieval period, especially after the 15th century, as an autonomous institution within each community. One of its members was chosen yearly to serve as the shrine official called *tōya* and to run annual village festivals, until the Edo period, when the priestly position began to be assumed by permanent clergy (KANNUSHI) and the *miyaza*'s privileges were gradually diffused to the organization of parishioners (*ujiko*).   Stuart D. B. PICKEN

Miyazaki

Capital of Miyazaki Prefecture, Kyūshū, on the Hyūga Sea. Formerly a farming area, it developed rapidly after it was designated the prefectural capital in 1873. The outlying farming areas are noted for their rice, cucumbers, tomatoes, and pumpkins. The city is served by the Japanese National Railways, national highways, and an airport. Visitors are drawn to the semitropical island of AOSHIMA, Heiwadai Park, and the Miyazaki Shrine. Miyazaki University and various cultural halls and museums are located here. Pop: 264,858.

Miyazaki Ichisada (1901–)

The leading historian of China in 20th-century Japan. Born in Nagano Prefecture; received his doctorate in 1944 from Kyōto University. Professor emeritus of Chinese history at Kyōto University, where he taught from 1934 to 1965. Miyazaki's most important work is his research on the Song (Sung) dynasty (960–1279) and on the development of absolute monarchy from the Song through the Qing (Ch'ing) dynasty (1644–1911), but he has covered many aspects of Chinese culture in all periods. A consistent theme in his work is the development by despotic monarchs of mechanisms of control over the vast empire. He believes that Chinese history must be viewed as a part of world history, and he is known for his periodization of Chinese history on the analogy of European history as a framework for understanding it in relation to the latter, an elaboration of the periodization theory of NAITŌ KONAN. Miyazaki's major works include *Kakyo* (1946, The Civil Service Examination System); *Kyūhin kanjin hō no kenkyū: Kakyo zenshi* (1956, Studies on Bureaucratic Advancement before the Examination System); *Kakyo: Chūgoku no shiken jigoku* (1963; tr *China's Examination Hell*, 1963); *Rongo no shin kenkyū* (1974, New Study of the Confucian Analects); and *Chūgokushi*, 2 vols (1977–78, A History of China). Collections of his articles and essays are *Ajiashi kenkyū*, 5 vols (1957–78, Studies in Asian History) and *Ajiashi ronkō*, 3 vols (1976, Studies in Asian History).   KAMACHI Noriko

Miyazaki Plain

(Miyazaki Heiya). Coastal plain. Central Miyazaki Prefecture, Kyūshū. Mostly uplands with river terraces formed by the river Ōyodogawa. Its Pacific Ocean coast is about 60 km (37 mi) long and has long sand dunes. Vegetables, sweet potatoes, and mandarin oranges are cultivated on the uplands and rice on the lowlands. The major city is Miyazaki. Length: approximately 60 km (37 mi); width: approximately 20 km (12 mi).

Miyazaki Prefecture

(Miyazaki Ken). Located in southeastern Kyūshū and bordered by Ōita Prefecture to the north, the Pacific Ocean to the east, Kagoshima Prefecture to the southwest, and Kumamoto Prefecture to the west. The terrain is largely mountainous, and principal mountain ranges include the KYŪSHŪ MOUNTAINS in the north and the Wanitsuka Mountains in the south. The main level areas are located around the city of MIYAZAKI on the coast, along the numerous rivers which flow eastward into the Pacific and several inland basins in the southern part. The climate is warm with heavy precipitation, especially in the form of frequent typhoons and spring gales, which are sometimes highly destructive.

Numerous archaeological excavations testify to Miyazaki's early cultural and political development. Known after the TAIKA REFORM of 645 as Hyūga Province, it was ruled by a succession of military families during the early feudal period and came under the control of the Tokugawa shogunate in the Edo period (1600–1868). The present name and boundaries originated in 1873 but were not established permanently until 1883, after a period of union with the neighboring prefecture of Kagoshima.

Miyazaki has long suffered from its remoteness from Japan's major economic, political, and cultural centers, and remains somewhat underdeveloped to this day. Agriculture is the major occupation, the principal crops being rice and sweet potatoes, although poor soil conditions and damage caused by frequent typhoons hinder productivity. Some fruit, vegetable, and dairy items are produced for large urban markets. Industry is minimal, but the mountains in the western part of the prefecture are a rich source of hydroelectric power for the industrial areas of northern Kyūshū.

The unspoiled mountain scenery of KIRISHIMA–YAKU NATIONAL PARK, the Nichinan seacoast in the south, and places like Takachiho that are associated with early Japanese legends attract many tourists. Area: 7,734 sq km (2,985 sq mi); pop: 1,151,575; capital: Miyazaki. Other major cities are MIYAKONOJŌ, NOBEOKA, and HYŪGA. See map on following page.

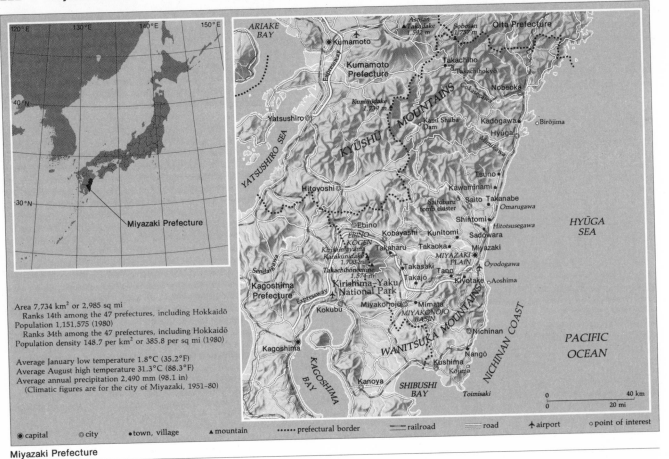

Area 7,734 km² or 2,985 sq mi
  Ranks 14th among the 47 prefectures, including Hokkaidō
Population 1,151,575 (1980)
  Ranks 34th among the 47 prefectures, including Hokkaidō
Population density 148.7 per km² or 385.8 per sq mi (1980)

Average January low temperature 1.8°C (35.2°F)
Average August high temperature 31.3°C (88.3°F)
Average annual precipitation 2,490 mm (98.1 in)
  (Climatic figures are for the city of Miyazaki, 1951–80)

◉ capital　　◎ city　　• town, village　　▲ mountain　　•••••• prefectural border　　══ railroad　　══ road　　✈ airport　　○ point of interest

Miyazaki Prefecture

Miyazaki Shrine

(Miyazaki Jingū). Shintō shrine in the city of Miyazaki, Miyazaki Prefecture, Kyūshū; dedicated to the legendary first emperor, JIMMU, and his father, Ugayafukiaezu no Mikoto, and mother, Tamayorihime no Mikoto. According to tradition, the shrine is situated on the original site of the Takachiho no Miya, Jimmu's palace. Jimmu's spirit was first worshiped here by his grandson, Takeiwatatsu no Mikoto. The shrine sanctuary is popularly believed to have been erected at the time of the legendary emperor Keikō. Despite its national significance, the shrine was maintained mainly through efforts of local *daimyō* patrons. After the Meiji Restoration the shrine was accorded imperial patronage. The annual festival is observed on 26 October.

Stanley WEINSTEIN

Miyazaki Tōten (1871–1922)

Political activist and close friend and associate of the Chinese republican revolutionary SUN YAT-SEN. Born in Kumamoto Prefecture; real name Miyazaki Torazō. He attended the Ōe Gijuku, a school run by TOKUTOMI SOHŌ, where he first encountered the ideas of the FREEDOM AND PEOPLE'S RIGHTS MOVEMENT. He later attended Tōkyō Semmon Gakkō (now Waseda University). Tōten was attracted to Christianity early on but later became disenchanted. As a young man he became interested in China and was soon an ardent supporter of East Asian unity. In 1899 he was commissioned by the Foreign Ministry to gather information about revolutionary activities against the ruling Manchu dynasty in China. After his return to Japan he met Sun Yat-sen, who was in exile there, and the two became friends. Tōten worked to secure Japanese support for Sun's cause and to raise money for the revolutionaries. Tōten and Sun also attempted, unsuccessfully, to send arms to Emilio AGUINALDO (1869–1964), the leader of the Philippine independence movement. In 1900 Tōten joined Sun in the abortive uprising at Huizhou (Waichow), north of Hong Kong. He described the uprising in the concluding chapter of his autobiography, *Sanjūsannen no yume* (The Thirty-Three Years' Dream), published in 1902. It was soon translated into Chinese and contributed to Sun's growing fame. When Sun returned to Japan in 1905, Tōten introduced him to HUANG XING (Huang Hsing), the Hunanese revolutionary, and helped the two form the Tongmeng Hui (T'ung-meng Hui; Revolutionary United League). Tōten went to China immediately after the overthrow of the Manchu dynasty in 1911 and devoted the rest of his life to the service of the revolution in China. See also TAIRIKU RŌNIN.

Miyazaki Yasuji (1916–)

Olympic swimmer. Born in Shizuoka Prefecture. At the 1931 All-Japan Championship meet, Miyazaki set a new Japanese record in the 100-meter freestyle with a time of 59.2 seconds. In 1932 he won the 100-meter freestyle (58.2 seconds) at the Los Angeles Olympics. As a member of the 800-meter relay team he won another gold medal, with a time of 8 minutes, 58.4 seconds.

TAKEDA Fumio

Miyazaki Yasusada (1623–1697)

Agronomist of the early part of the Edo period (1600–1868). Born in the Aki domain (now part of Hiroshima Prefecture). In 1647 he entered the service of the domain of Fukuoka (now part of Fukuoka Prefecture), but resigned at the age of 30 to take up the life of a farmer on land enfeoffed to him in the village of Myōbaru in Fukuoka. At the same time Miyazaki read Chinese works on agriculture and botany and traveled extensively in western Japan, studying various farming techniques and talking to experienced farmers. He wrote up his findings in 1696 as the *Nōgyō zensho* (Agricultural Encyclopedia), which was published the following year with an introduction and appendix by KAIBARA EKIKEN, the Confucian scholar.

Miyazawa Kenji (1896–1933)

Poet and author of children's stories. A devout Buddhist, he spent much of his life laboring to improve the material and spiritual lives of peasants in the impoverished farming communities of Iwate Prefecture in northern Japan. Miyazawa received little notice during his lifetime, but since World War II the sincerity of his work, reflecting a life of spiritual struggle, has attracted growing attention.

Miyazawa was born on 27 August 1896, the eldest of five children, in the rural village of Hanamaki, Iwate Prefecture, to a prosperous and pious Buddhist family of pawnbrokers. Except for brief periods in Tōkyō, he lived out his life in this bleak, snowbound region sometimes called the "Tibet of Japan." A good student, he graduated in 1918 from the Morioka Higher Agricultural and Forestry School, where he remained for two postgraduate years conducting a soil survey.

Differences with his father, centering on disagreements between them over religion and his repugnance for the pawnshop business and its profiting from dealings with poor farmer-clients, were a major source of dissatisfaction in his life. He early yielded his primogenital rights of inheritance to his younger brother, who eventually replaced the pawnshop with a hardware store. Failing to convert his father from the JŌDO SHIN SECT of Buddhism to the more activist NICHIREN SECT, Miyazawa left home for Tōkyō in 1921. He insisted that the Jōdo Shin doctrine was weak and scorned its preoccupation with money and social status.

After a nine-month stay in Tōkyō, during which he faithfully attended a Nichiren study group and wrote many children's stories, Miyazawa returned home to Iwate because of the illness of his sister Toshiko. In December 1921 he became a teacher at a local agricultural high school. Three years later, in 1924, he financed at considerable expense the publication of a collection of children's stories titled *Chūmon no ōi ryōriten* (The Restaurant of Many Orders) and the first section of his most famous work of poetry, *Haru to shura*. Both books failed, but brought him to the attention of the poets TAKAMURA KŌTARŌ and KUSANO SHIMPEI, who admired him greatly and introduced his work to the literary world. For a short time he also taught adult education courses geared primarily for farmers on methods of improving the quality of their communities.

Resigning his teaching post in 1926, Miyazawa began three years of intense effort to improve the plight of poor farmers. He himself attempted to farm on family-owned land, organized farmers' groups for lectures on soil management, and began the study of Esperanto. He also tried to establish an agrarian art movement and traveled about the countryside lecturing on the science of rice cultivation. Only this last venture was successful. Soon, however, the rigors of overwork brought on an attack of pleurisy which incapacitated him for three years.

His last employment was in 1931 with a rock-crushing firm whose products were intended to improve the soil. His father advanced funds to help the company to expand, and Miyazawa worked with his customary zeal. But the pleurisy returned, and he was again bedridden with only intermittent periods of light activity until his death on 21 September 1933. The country folk of Iwate fondly remember him as "Kenji *bosatsu*," or "Kenji the bodhisattva," for his efforts to help poor farmers.

Miyazawa was a gifted, prolific writer; manifest in his work is a particularly acute sensitivity to the land and the people who make their living from it. Working rapidly, he wrote a large number of children's stories—many gay and humorous—which he intended as an aid in moral education. Among other works of prose are a few plays written for his students, but it is his poems, evoking a simple yet strong passion for the Japanese countryside, which have attracted an international readership.

Although he wrote traditional 31-syllable verse (TANKA) and longer poems in conventional rhythms, it is *Haru to shura*, a collection of some 400 poems in free verse, dated from 1922 to his death, that represents Miyazawa's mature work. His poems are marked by great freedom in diction, liberally employing scientific terms, foreign words, Chinese compounds, Sanskrit phrases, and even some Esperanto; by the use of spoken rather than literary language; by nontraditional subject matter and imagery, such as rice planting or manure gathering; and by bold rhythm patterns and cadences shaped by head rhymes and repetitive vowel sounds. He was familiar with the work of the early modern poets who preceded him, and his abiding concern for the plight of the farmers and his sometimes perversely private imagery demonstrate his debt to the proletarian and romantic schools (see PROLETARIAN LITERATURE MOVEMENT).

His particular poetic tone derives from two sources. The first is a synesthesia, as when music becomes color, apparent after his introduction during the period 1921 to 1926 to the music of Debussy, Wagner, and Strauss. Closely related are his mystic visions, in some of which he saw the bodhisattva Kannon, the Buddha himself, or fighting, crying demons.

The second and more public source of his poetry rises from his lifelong struggle to submit himself to the karmic laws of his Buddhistic heritage, through absolute celibacy, renunciation of material values, and a life of such severe self-denial and service that it seems

an act of discipline just short of overt flagellation. His poetry records with irony, pain, and passion the defeats and triumphs of his spiritual progress. Repeatedly he celebrates the renewal and joy of sky, clouds, snow, mountains, and all growing things. Or he stands mute in the thunder and rain in ruined rice fields. Takamura Kōtarō saw him not as a poet but as a man who wrote poetry. Miyazawa struggled throughout his life to help those around him overcome poverty and misery and was more a compassionate human being than a self-conscious poet. In this vein, his works still speak forcefully to the modern sensibility.

📖——Works by Miyazawa: *Miyazawa Kenji zenshū*, 12 vols (Chikuma Shobō, 1968). John Bester, tr, *Winds from Afar* (1972), translations of short stories by Miyazawa. Hiroaki Sato, tr, *Spring and Asura* (1973), translations of selected poems by Miyazawa. Gary Snyder, *The Back Country* (1968), contains Snyder's translations of some of Miyazawa's poems. Works about Miyazawa: Nakamura Minoru, *Miyazawa Kenji* (1958). Sakai Tadaichi, *Hyōden Miyazawa Kenji* (1975).   Kenneth YASUDA

Miyazawa Toshiyoshi (1899–1976)

Scholar of constitutional law. Born in Nagano Prefecture, he was graduated from Tōkyō Unversity in 1923 and taught in its law faculty from 1925 to 1959. He was a student of MINOBE TATSUKICHI, to whose chair he succeeded in 1934, and carried on his mentor's politically liberal interpretation of the Meiji Constitution of 1889. After World War II, as a member of what was then the House of Peers, Miyazawa was appointed to a commission to discuss the draft of the new CONSTITUTION that was approved by the Diet in 1946. Thereafter he was a leading defender of the constitution, organizing the CONSTITUTIONAL PROBLEMS STUDY GROUP in 1958 and writing many books, including the authoritative *Nihonkoku kempō* (1955, The Constitution of Japan).   John M. MAKI

Miyazu

City in northern Kyōto Prefecture, central Honshū, on Miyazu Bay. The city developed as a castle town and as a port during the Edo period (1600–1868). It is now a fishing base and a trading port as well as the administrative and political center of the region. Industries include metals, processed seafood, and textiles. A chief attraction of the city is the scenic AMANOHASHIDATE on the coast. Pop: 28,880.

Miyoshi

City in northern Hiroshima Prefecture, western Honshū, on the river Gōnokawa; the most important city of the northern part of the prefecture. The city thrived as a river port and castle town in the early part of the Edo period (1600–1868). Served by the Japanese National Railways and highways, it is principally known for its farming, cattle, woodworking, and food processing. Its cormorant fishing *(ukai)* is also well known. Pop: 37,875.

Miyoshi Basin

(Miyoshi Bonchi). In northern Hiroshima Prefecture, western Honshū. Situated between the Chūgoku Mountains and the highland called the Kibi Kōgen, it is at the confluence of several tributaries of the river Gōnokawa. Rice, grown in the low-lying regions, and tobacco are the principal crops and cattle are also raised. The major city is Miyoshi. Area: approximately 50 sq km (19 sq mi).

Miyoshi Jūrō (1902–1958)

Playwright, poet. Born in Saga Prefecture. Graduate of Waseda University. Although he launched his literary career in the early 1920s as an anarchist poet, he soon shifted his sympathies to Marxism. He participated actively in the so-called PROLETARIAN LITERATURE MOVEMENT, writing plays filled with left-wing sentiment such as *Kubi o kiru no wa dare da* (1928) and *Tanjin* (staged in 1930). Disillusioned, however, with what he saw as the sterile formalism and political monomania of the proletarian literature movement, he underwent ideological conversion (see TENKŌ) in the mid-1930s. Many of his plays thereafter focused on the lives and thoughts of ordinary people, whose goodwill and sincerity he admired. His major works are the plays *Kirare no senta* (1934), *Bui* (1940), and *Ho-*

noo no hito (1951), and a collection of critical essays, *Nihon oyobi nihonjin* (1954).

Miyoshi Kiyoyuki (847–918)

Scholar-official of the Heian period (794–1185). In the AKŌ INCIDENT OF 887, a power struggle centering on Fujiwara no Mototsune's appointment as imperial regent *(kampaku),* Kiyoyuki opposed SUGAWARA NO MICHIZANE and was said to have been partly responsible for Michizane's downfall in 901. Kiyoyuki excelled in Chinese poetry and prose and was fond of collecting tales of the supernatural. His "Iken fūji jūnikajō," a memorial in 12 sections presented in 914 to Emperor DAIGO, has historical value for its detailed analysis of the deteriorating condition of the country, especially its finances, the moral decay of its ruling class, and the breakdown of the RITSURYŌ SYSTEM of administration.

Douglas E. MILLS

Miyoshi Manabu (1861–1939)

Botanist. Born in Edo (now Tōkyō); graduated from Tōkyō University. He studied plant physiology and plant ecology in Germany under Wilhelm Pfeffer (1845–1920). After returning to Japan, he taught at Tōkyō University, and contributed to the introduction of these studies into Japan. He coined the Japanese word for ecology, *seitaigaku.* He was also concerned about the preservation of natural monuments and campaigned for laws providing for such preservation. These were enacted in 1919 (see CONSERVATION). He played a major role in teaching the Japanese about botany through his many publications, such as *Shokubutsugaku kōgi* (1889, Lectures on Botany).

SUZUKI Zenji

Miyoshi Sanninshū

(Miyoshi Triumvirs). Iwanari Tomomichi, Miyoshi Nagayuki, and Miyoshi Masayasu; principal captains of Miyoshi Nagayoshi (also known as Miyoshi Chōkei; 1522–64), the regional warlord and usurper of the Muromachi shogunate's powers. After Nagayoshi's death, the triumvirs attempted to continue the Miyoshi party's domination of the shogunate, of Kyōto, and of the capital region. The origins of the Miyoshi were in Awa Province (now Tokushima Prefecture) on Shikoku, but the triumvirs based themselves in SAKAI, drawing on the resources of that city's rich merchants. In league with the notorious *daimyō* of Yamato Province (now Nara Prefecture), Matsunaga Hisahide (1510–77), they killed the shōgun Ashikaga Yoshiteru in 1565; for three years thereafter, their influence was such that contemporary Jesuit missionary reports call them "the rulers of the realm." In 1568 they installed Ashikaga Yoshihide (1540–68) as shōgun, but later that year they were checkmated by the hegemon ODA NOBUNAGA, who occupied Kyōto and emplaced ASHIKAGA YOSHIAKI in the shogunate. In 1569 they attacked Yoshiaki's Kyōto residence by surprise but were defeated; their action impelled Nobunaga to take measures of intimidation against the city of Sakai, their supporter. Nobunaga's campaign against their forts at Noda and Fukushima (now parts of the city of Ōsaka) in 1570 was the immediate cause of the outbreak of hostilities between him and the Ōsaka HONGANJI, the headquarters of the Jōdo Shin sect (see IKKŌ IKKI). The end of the Miyoshi Triumvirs came in 1573, when Iwanari Tomomichi took Yoshiaki's side in the shōgun's conflict with Nobunaga and was defeated and killed.

George ELISON

Miyoshi Tatsuji (1900–1964)

A poet of great range and subtlety, usually considered in the first rank of modern Japanese writers, Miyoshi is noted primarily for a large body of free verse of generally moderate length. Miyoshi's interest in technique led him to write in a variety of forms, from the modernist style prose poem to the four-line lyric in the manner of the French poet Francis Jammes. His more involved poems portray isolation and loneliness as conditions basic to contemporary life; yet, in their highly literary diction, complex manipulation of language, and presentation of the poet as eternal traveler, these same poems hark back to certain early modern and classic periods of Japanese verse. Miyoshi has also written light verses—one of them a veritable lullaby known and recited by untold numbers of Japanese, which runs as follows:

> The snow falls on Tarō's roof, putting Tarō to sleep.
> The snow falls on Jirō's roof, putting Jirō to sleep.

Born in Ōsaka, Miyoshi was the eldest son in a large family of modest means. During his childhood and early youth he suffered a number of misfortunes. Five of his nine brothers and sisters died early in life, and Miyoshi himself was sent for a time to a family in Kyōto for adoption. After a brief stay in Kyōto he went to his grandparents' home in Hyōgo Prefecture and for several years thereafter stayed alternately with the grandparents and with his own parents in Ōsaka. Miyoshi's early life was further disturbed by severe bouts of neurasthenia, which necessitated long absences from elementary school.

In 1915 Miyoshi withdrew from middle school and, at the behest of his father, enrolled in the Ōsaka Army Cadet School. For the next six years he pursued a military life, including a brief tour of duty in Korea in 1919. Defying his father, Miyoshi withdrew from the Tōkyō Military Academy in 1921 and in the following year enrolled in the Third Higher School of Kyōto, where he studied literature. For several years he had been reading Marx and the Bible and, as early as 1914, had begun following literary trends in Japan and composing his own HAIKU.

After leaving the military, Miyoshi spent the rest of his life involved with poetry in various ways. It was 1930 before he published his first major volume of free verse, *Sokuryōsen* (The Surveying Ship), but thereafter his production was steady and highly varied. Miyoshi studied French literature at Tōkyō University from 1925 to 1928, and his noted translations of Baudelaire as well as several prose writers were undertaken so that he could make a living within the field of literature. Miyoshi was also active as an editor and critic. With Itō Shinkichi (b 1906) he arranged the definitive edition of the poet HAGIWARA SAKUTARŌ's works; with YOSHIKAWA KŌJIRŌ, the scholar of Chinese literature, he wrote a best-selling commentary on Tang poetry. He also wrote an extremely popular book on the various kinds of Japanese poetry and what is commonly regarded as the best study of Hagiwara Sakutarō. In 1952 he received the Japan Art Academy Award; he became a member of the academy in 1962.

On the personal level, the adult life of Miyoshi Tatsuji remained as unsettled as in the days of his youth. His marriage in 1934 to Satō Chieko—the niece of the poet SATŌ HARUO—ended in divorce 10 years later; his subsequent marriage to Hagiwara Ai—the younger sister of Hagiwara Sakutarō—lasted only six months. During the years of his first marriage, Miyoshi, despite the birth of two children, was constantly changing his residence. He built a home for his family in Tōkyō in 1936 only to move to Kamakura in 1938 and on to Odawara in 1939.

A considerable number of Miyoshi's poems seem to be primarily a play of images. Even when such images predominate, the presence of a lone observer of the scene is implied or in some cases stated explicitly. The images usually suggest a mood of forlornness—a crow settles on a water conduit running above a country lane and sways back and forth, or seagulls fly off, leaving the ocean behind. Often, as in a celebrated prose poem describing a trek through an Izu mountain pass, the poet describes a moment of pleasurable pause in his travels and then moves on. The generally bleak mood of Miyoshi's poetry is occasionally broken by humorous lyrics or by cheerful works evoking memories of his supposedly unhappy childhood. Finally, there are poems like the following, where the humor and forlornness come together, and the image of the cat is inseparable from the poet's relation to the animal.

> My cat is growing old.
> She rests in dingy fur upon a window sill,
> Mourns the unreal evening light disappearing.
> A thread drawn across her clam-face,
> The two eyes ever asleep;
> My cat is growing old.
> Silver tears slide from her eyes;
> She wakes in the evening chill
> Startled at darkness closing in.
> She mistakes tears for milk, and licks.
> My cat is growing old.

📖——Works by Miyoshi Tatsuji: *Miyoshi Tatsuji zenshū*, 12 vols (Chikuma Shobō, 1964–66). *Miyoshi Tatsuji shishū* (Kadokawa Shoten, 1968). *Miyoshi Tatsuji shishū* (Iwanami Shoten, 1971).

James A. O'BRIEN

Miyoshi Yasunobu (1140–1221)

Official in the early years of the Kamakura shogunate (1192–1333). Born into a middle-ranking courtier family who served as hereditary

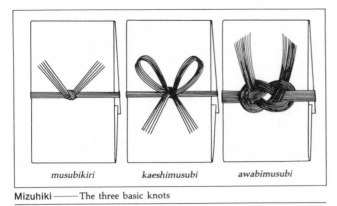

| musubikiri | kaeshimusubi | awabimusubi |

Mizuhiki———The three basic knots

The *musubikiri* is a single knot that cannot easily be untied and symbolizes an event that it is hoped will occur only once, whether congratulatory (a wedding) or unfortunate (a funeral or illness). The *kaeshimusubi*, a knot that can easily be untied and retied, and the elaborate knot called *awabimusubi* are used for such congratulatory occasions as birthdays and graduation ceremonies.

clerks in the Grand Council of State (DAJŌKAN), he held a post in the Empress's Office (Chūgūshiki). His mother was a sister of MINAMOTO NO YORITOMO's wet nurse, and through this connection Yasunobu became identified with the cause of the exiled Yoritomo, supplying him with news from Kyōto. One of the first courtiers to join Yoritomo when he rebelled in 1180, Yasunobu was appointed head of the Board of Inquiry (MONCHŪJO) when Yoritomo established that body in 1184. Together with ŌE NO HIROMOTO, he made a major contribution to the organization of the shogunate government. ———*G. Cameron HURST III*

Mizoguchi Kenji (1898–1956)

World-renowned film director whose more than 80 feature films, beginning in 1922, made him the dean of Japanese film directors at his death. He was diverted to filmmaking from painting, and the use of diagonal lines in the composition of his shots reflects the traditional Japanese painter's horror of symmetry. His films from the late 1930s are characterized by long takes, fluid camerawork, and beautiful mise-en-scene. Several of his films won international prizes after World War II.

Mizoguchi made his first films at a studio that was partial to stories dealing with the problems of the poor and class conflict. This tendency reflected the relatively liberal climate in Japan of the 1920s. His work in these films probably provided him with the theme he was to employ in all his major films beginning with *Nihombashi* (1929): the sacrifice (voluntary or involuntary) of a woman for a man's success or for the sake of the family. In *Nihombashi*, a woman becomes the mistress of a wealthy man in order to give her brother a college education. When he graduates, she disappears from his life. He rejects the opportunities open to him and goes in search of his sister. Other films in the same vein were *Tōjin Okichi* (1930, Okichi, the Foreigner's Mistress), *Taki no Shiraito* (1933, Taki no Shiraito, the Water Magician), and *Orizuru Osen* (1934, Osen's Downfall).

In 1936 he directed two films which are among the best Japanese films ever made: *Naniwa erejii* (Ōsaka Elegy) and *Gion no shimai* (Sisters of the Gion). Both are set in modern Japan. *Naniwa erejii* dealt with the predicament of a telephone operator who is the sole support of her family. She is eventually forced to become the mistress of a banker, and things go very well for her family until she is arrested for immoral behavior. When a lenient judge lets her off and she goes home, not sympathy but hostility for having jeopardized the family's well-being awaits her. Stung by the rejection, the woman flees her home for an uncertain future. In *Gion no shimai* Mizoguchi contrasts the moral codes of two sisters who are GEISHA. The older clings to the traditional ways, while the younger is critical of the old order. When the former's patron declares bankruptcy, she takes him in and supports him, much to the disgust of her sister, who proceeds to dupe a wealthy man into believing that her sister is anxious to have him as her patron. But the older woman rejects the man outright. The scheming younger woman beguiles a *kimono* shop clerk, who is smitten with her, and manages to obtain a kimono from him. The clerk, who has juggled the figures in the ledger, is

discovered and fired. When he realizes that the woman has no intention of honoring her pledge to marry him, he pushes her out of a moving car. She is severely injured. Her sister visits her in the hospital to tell her that the man for whom she has sacrificed everything has left her. The two sisters cry out against fate which has offered them the same bitter pill.

In 1939 Mizoguchi directed *Zangiku monogatari* (The Story of the Last Chrysanthemum), a fine film about the life of a young KABUKI actor who is inspired by his infant brother's nursemaid to mature from a callow actor to a skilled thespian. The focus is on the woman who gives up her life to see the actor triumph. When he is disowned by his family, she goes to live with him, and together they suffer all the miseries of the life of touring actors; but she sees this as invaluable training for him. At last the chance comes to prove himself, and he is invited to rejoin the main company in Tōkyō, but on the proviso that he divorce his wife. Aware of the condition, the woman vanishes. He locates her on the night of his debut in Ōsaka, but discovers that she is dying. She sends him away, telling him that his participation in the ceremonies is more important than her death. He leaves, and while he is receiving the wild adulation of the crowds, she dies.

In 1941, under pressure from the military government calling for national-policy films, Mizoguchi made *Genroku chūshingura* (1941–42, The Loyal Forty-Seven Rōnin of the Genroku Era), a two-part version of the story of the 47 RŌNIN (masterless *samurai*) who avenge the death of their lord, but did not turn it into the usual spectacle, and omitted the climactic raid of the men on the enemy stronghold (see FORTY-SEVEN RŌNIN INCIDENT).

Mizoguchi made some of his most famous films after the war: *Yoru no onnatachi* (1948, Women of the Night); *Saikaku ichidai onna* (1952, The Life of Oharu), which won a directorial prize at the Venice Film Festival; *Ugetsu monogatari* (1953, Ugetsu); *Sanshō-Dayū* (1954, Sanshō the Bailiff or The Bailiff); *Chikamatsu monogatari* (1954, A Story from Chikamatsu or Crucified Lovers); and *Akasen chitai* (1956, Street of Shame). In these films there are prostitutes, a peasant woman who is killed in the civil wars of 16th-century Japan, a governor's wife who is sold into prostitution while her daughter is sold into slavery, a wealthy merchant's wife who commits adultery and is sentenced to death, and in *Saikaku ichidai onna*, a court lady who, for loving not wisely but too well, falls from the highest stratum of society to the lowest, and ends up a streetwalker. It is the best among Mizoguchi's films, and is arguably one of the best films made anywhere.

📖———Audie Bock, *Japanese Film Directors* (1978). Michel Mesuil, ed, *Kenji Mizoguchi*, Cinéma d'aujourd'hui 31 (Editions Seghers, 1965). Tsumura Hideo, *Mizoguchi Kenji to iu onoko* (1958). Ve-Ho, *Mizoguchi Kenji* (Editions Universitaires, 1963). Yoda Yoshikata, *Mizoguchi Kenji no hito to geijutsu* (1964). ———*Frank T. MOTOFUJI*

Mizuhara Shūōshi (1892–1981)

HAIKU poet. Real name Mizuhara Yutaka. Born in Tōkyō. Graduate of the Faculty of Medicine, Tōkyō University. Mizuhara practiced at his own private hospital and also taught at Shōwa Medical College. He studied poetry under TAKAHAMA KYOSHI, the leader of the influential modern haiku coterie that produced the magazine HOTOTOGISU. He soon became an important figure within the group, helping to bring it to its "golden age" in the 1920s. Later, however, he turned from Kyoshi's objective realism to a more subjective expressionism, and founded the haiku magazine *Ashibi* in 1928. In 1966, he became a member of the Japan Art Academy (Nihon Geijutsuin). Principal haiku collections are *Katsushika* (1930) and *Shūen* (1935).

mizuhiki

Decorative string used primarily to tie gift-wrapped articles but also to make ornaments. A narrow strip of good quality paper made from mulberry pulp is twisted into a string, soaked in starchy water left after rinsing uncooked rice, and allowed to dry until hard. A single strand of this string may be used for tying a lock of hair or a bundle of paper. To make a *mizuhiki* for gift-wrapping, several strands are laid flat side by side and glued together at the middle. Normally each half of the length is dyed a different color. For congratulatory occasions such as weddings, string dyed half in gold and half in silver is used. For other happy or neutral occasions, a red and white string is commonly used. A black and white, gray and white, or yellow and white combination is used to tie the condolence gift (*kōden*) and other gifts given in connection with funerals. The string is wrapped once horizontally around the wrapped article and tied in front. Occasions of celebration (SHŪGI) require certain types of knots, while mourning or inauspicious occasions (*bushūgi*) require others. For celebrative occasions, a small piece of folded paper (NO-SHI) is placed on the upper right-hand corner of the wrapping paper. For less formal occasions, wrapping paper imprinted with *mizuhiki* and *noshi* may be used.

Mizuhiki are also used to construct decorative ornaments, such as cranes, turtles, and pines, traditional symbols of good fortune. These constitute part of a customary set of gifts to be exchanged between the families of the bride and the groom prior to a wedding.

Harumi BEFU

Mizuki

(literally, "Water Fort"). A fortification—consisting of a large earthwork with a moat—built across a valley near what is now the town of Dazaifu in Fukuoka Prefecture. The fortification was completed in about 664 and served to protect DAZAIFU (the government headquarters in Kyūshū) from attack. The earthwork, approximately 14 meters (45 ft) high and 35 meters (114 ft) thick at the base in its original form, survives today in two sections whose combined length is about 1.2 kilometers (0.75 mi).

Mizuki Yōko (1913–   )

Screenwriter who showed a sharp social consciousness in her dramatic creations. Real name Takagi Tomiko. Born in Tōkyō, she studied screenwriting under YASUMI TOSHIO and collaborated with him on many projects. Her first screenplay to be made into a motion picture was *Onna no isshō* (1949, A Woman's Life), directed by Kamei Fumio. Other screenplays include *Mata au hi made* (1950, Until the Day We Meet Again), directed by IMAI TADASHI, which depicts the love between a girl and her boyfriend who has been conscripted just before the war's end and is on his way to the front; *Ukigumo* (1955, Floating Clouds), directed by NARUSE MIKIO, which is about the heartache of a woman in love with another woman's husband; *Kiku to Isamu* (1959, Kiku and Isamu), directed by Imai Tadashi, about a brother-sister pair who are half Japanese, half black and live in a mountain village. Each of these three pictures won best film award for its respective year; together they represent the best of Mizuki's writing in the 1950s. From the 1960s, however, the deemphasis of quality that accompanied the general decline in movies had a detrimental effect on her work. She made a brief comeback with *Kaidan* (1964, Kwaidan) directed by KOBAYASHI MASAKI and based on the original story by Lafcadio HEARN. In recent years she has drawn attention with her screenplays for television.

ITASAKA Tsuyoshi

Mizunami

City in southeastern Gifu Prefecture, central Honshū, on the river Tokigawa. It was the base of the Toki family, military governors (*shugo*) of this district during the Muromachi period (1333–1568). An abundance of good-quality clay has made Mizunami a center in the production of china and pottery, especially Western-style tableware for export. Pop: 40,066.

Mizuno Corporation

A company engaged in the manufacture and sale of sporting goods and sportswear, Mizuno Corporation was established in 1906 and is the largest company in its field in Japan. It has sales companies in the United States and England and a manufacturing plant in Taiwan. Mizuno has tie-ups with six overseas sporting goods firms. Future plans call for the expansion of overseas sales, particularly of baseball shoes and golf equipment; the company has plans to establish manufacturing plants for these products in the United States. Sales for the fiscal year ending February 1982 totaled ¥106.2 billion (US $451.6 million); capitalization stood at ¥4 billion (US $17 million). Corporate headquarters are located in Ōsaka.

mizunomi-byakushō

Landless peasants of the Edo period (1600–1868); literally, "water-drinking peasants," a reference to the thin, watery gruel on which they subsisted. In some regions very small landholders were also classified as *mizunomi-byakushō*.

The lowest stratum of the peasantry, they earned their livelihood as tenant farmers or day laborers. Although most held no land at all, some enjoyed the right to collect fertilizer and firewood from village-owned fields and mountains (see IRIAI). Unless specified by their tenancy contracts, they did not pay the annual land tax (NENGU), but they were sometimes liable for village or other taxes such as BU-YAKU and MUNABETSUSEN.

Although *daimyō* attempted to limit the growth of the *mizunomi* class by restricting land sales, they were usually unsuccessful because they failed to deal with the causes of tenancy. In the first half of the Edo period, many large landholders found it profitable to turn their hereditary servants (GENIN) into rent-paying tenants. Later, as the practice of primogeniture became widespread, younger sons of landed peasants were forced to seek employment as tenants or laborers, often outside their own villages. Finally, many landed peasants became *mizunomi-byakushō* when high taxes and heavy debts forced them to sell their land. Some industrious and fortunate *mizunomi-byakushō*, however, were able to acquire land either by purchase or by reclamation (SHINDEN KAIHATSU), thereby becoming landed, taxpaying peasants (HOMBYAKUSHŌ).

Philip BROWN

Mizuno Rentarō (1868–1949)

Bureaucrat of the pre-World War II Home Ministry. Politician of the RIKKEN SEIYŪKAI, an important political party of the first half of the 20th century. Born in Tōkyō. Mizuno graduated from Tōkyō University in 1892 and entered the Home Ministry that same year. He rose to vice-minister by 1912 and served subsequently as home minister in the cabinets of TERAUCHI MASATAKE (1918), KATŌ TO-MOSABURŌ (1922–23), and KIYOURA KEIGO (1924). By the mid-1920s he had become a protégé of the Seiyūkai leader HARA TAKA-SHI. Mizuno is often considered the quintessential bureaucrat-politician.

Mizuno was appointed education minister in the Seiyūkai cabinet of TANAKA GIICHI in 1927. However, when Tanaka proposed to replace Home Minister SUZUKI KISABURŌ (who had resigned under Diet pressure because of interference in the 1928 general elections) by reorganizing assignments in the cabinet and adding Mizuno's political rival KUHARA FUSANOSUKE as minister of communications, Mizuno tendered his own resignation in protest. Tanaka obtained an imperial decree ordering Mizuno to remain in office. Tanaka's use of the throne in party politics caused a political uproar, and Mizuno resubmitted his resignation. This time it was promptly accepted. Mizuno left the Seiyūkai in 1935.

Richard YASKO

Mizuno Shigeo (1899–1972)

Businessman. Born in Shizuoka Prefecture. Graduate of Tōkyō University. Mizuno joined the Japan Communist Party in 1925 and was arrested in 1928. Following his release from prison in 1929, he left the party. Drawing on his experiences as a former communist, he played a key labor relations role for the business-industrial community after World War II. Mizuno served as president of Bunka Hōsō (a broadcasting corporation), Fuji Television Network, and Sankei Shimbun (a newspaper company); laid the cornerstone for the Sankei group; and acted as an adviser to Prime Minister Ikeda Hayato. Along with SAKURADA TAKESHI, KOBAYASHI ATARU, and NAGANO SHIGEO, he was regarded as one of the most influential leaders of the business-industrial community of his day.

ITŌ Hajime

Mizuno Tadakuni (1794–1851)

Daimyō of the Hamamatsu domain (now part of Shizuoka Prefecture) who as leader of the Tokugawa shogunate pursued a largely unsuccessful program of reform, the so-called TEMPŌ REFORMS during the early 1840s.

Tadakuni was born in Edo (now Tōkyō), the son of Mizuno Tadamitsu, daimyō of the Karatsu domain (now part of Saga Prefecture; assessed at 60,000 *koku*; see KOKUDAKA) in Kyūshū. He appears to have been raised in a frugal and disciplined household, studying Confucianism, developing his poetic skills, and preparing to succeed his father as daimyō. In later years, when he was assigned by the shogunate to Kyōto, he studied National Learning (KOKUGAKU) and the ancient music (GAGAKU) of the Heian court.

In 1812, at the age of 18, Tadakuni became the 11th head of his branch of the Mizuno family. From the outset he expressed an interest in solving the fiscal problems of the Karatsu domain and took steps to reduce expenditures. Three years later, however, he was

Mizushima

The Mizushima industrial area. Dredging of the harbor has made possible the handling of 100,000-ton tankers.

named *sōshaban* (master of shogunal ceremony). In 1817 he was promoted to JISHA BUGYŌ (commissioner of temples and shrines) and transferred from Karatsu, which his family had held since 1762, to a comparable domain headquartered at Hamamatsu. His vassals opposed the transfer because of its costs, but it was said that Tadakuni had requested it to enhance his prospects for promotion within the shogunate and to avoid the traditional duty of Karatsu daimyō to defend the port of Nagasaki.

With Tadakuni's assistance most of his 275 vassals made the move with their families to Hamamatsu, and for several years he attempted to deal with his new domain's debts and domestic difficulties. In 1825, however, he was appointed Ōsaka JŌDAI (keeper of Ōsaka Castle). He took up residence in Ōsaka later in the year but was soon promoted to KYŌTO SHOSHIDAI (Kyōto deputy) and had to move again early in 1827. With the new promotion he also received the rank-title of *Echizen no kami*, by which he was later known. By then, too, he had acquired a reputation as an upright but somewhat inflexible man; he also made it known that he intended eventually to occupy a seat in the senior council (RŌJŪ). The following year his ambition was realized: he returned to Edo to serve in the western enceinte of Edo Castle as *nishinomaru rōjū* (senior councillor to the heir apparent) and guardian to the four-year-old son (Iesada) of the shogunal heir, Tokugawa Ieyoshi (1793–1853).

In 1834 Tadakuni was reassigned to the central enceinte *(hommaru)* as a regular *rōjū*, and during the next three years he distinguished himself as an administrator. Even as his shogunate responsibilities were growing, however, he found Hamamatsu's affairs intruding more and more on his time. Starting in 1830 poor harvests began to generate discontent and local disturbances in the domain, and matters were worsened by domainal tax increases that more than offset Tadakuni's relief measures. An exceptionally serious crop failure in 1836 prompted him to cashier some incompetent domain officials, make extensive changes in administration, reduce tax levies sharply, and carry out substantial relief measures. He also adopted a general policy of domainal autarchy and anticommercialism in the belief that it would help to conserve Hamamatsu's food supplies. Fearing that unrest in adjacent domains might spread into Hamamatsu, he increased his military preparedness. In succeeding years, however, one natural disaster followed another, slashing his tax receipts, prompting him to set up granaries, and forcing him to undertake more relief measures and to cut governmental expenditures.

The troubles that faced Tadakuni the daimyō were only a portion of more widespread natural disasters and public unrest that faced Tadakuni the *rōjū*. As the 1830s drew to a close he and others within the shogunate became convinced that some sort of major political reform was necessary. Furthermore, incidents involving foreign vessels suggested the likelihood of a serious diplomatic crisis in the near future.

Early in 1837 the venerable senior councillor Ōkubo Tadazane (b 1778) died, and in his place Tadakuni took the all-important financial portfolio *(kattekata)* and assumed a preeminent role in the council of *rōjū*. A fortnight later the shōgun TOKUGAWA IENARI retired and was succeeded by Ieyoshi. The new shōgun shared Tadakuni's belief that reform was imperative, but despite some didactic pro-

nouncements and relief efforts the change in shogunate leadership produced no basic policy changes as long as Ienari remained alive and in control.

In February 1841 Ienari died. Four months later Tadakuni had Ieyoshi formally announce his intention of instituting sweeping reforms that would revitalize the shogunate, modeled on the KYŌHŌ REFORMS and KANSEI REFORMS. Tadakuni's Tempō Reforms, which echoed his earlier efforts at Hamamatsu, were carried out with great diligence for two years. However, several of his measures gained him enemies and undermined his support within the shogunate, and in the fall of 1843 he resigned from office.

In the following months Tadakuni's successors encountered a series of awkward political problems, and in the summer of 1844 they agreed to his reappointment as chief senior councillor *(rōjū shuseki)*. Tadakuni found, however, that he lacked real power, and his attempts to revive the reforms bore no fruit. That situation prompted him to turn his attention to Hamamatsu instead, and he concentrated on realizing there the military reform that he had tried without success to initiate nationally. At the end of 1844 he promulgated extensive orders designed to field effective coastal defense forces and to keep the peace within Hamamatsu by organizing peasant constabulary units under domainal control and by promoting the use of firearms.

After seven frustrating months as *rōjū* Tadakuni resigned a second time. His political rivals, most notably ABE MASAHIRO, moved decisively to destroy his influence. Tadakuni was held responsible for his subordinates' corruption and mistakes and was forced to retire as daimyō. He was ordered into domiciliary confinement near Edo, and his family was deprived of part of its lands. His son succeeded to the family headship and was transferred to an impoverished 50,000-*koku* domain at Yamagata in northern Japan.

Tadakuni remained under house arrest and in disgrace for five years until his death. He busied himself studying, inquiring about his son's affairs at Yamagata, discussing principles of governance with visitors, and finding such solace as he could in composing poems. Only as he lay dying, a lonely and disappointed old man, did the shogunate formally pardon him for his failings.

——Kitajima Masamoto, *Mizuno Tadakuni* (1969). Conrad Totman, "Political Succession in the Tokugawa Bakufu: Abe Masahiro's Rise to Power, 1843–1845," *Harvard Journal of Asiatic Studies* 26 (1965–66). *Conrad* TOTMAN

Mizusawa

City in southern Iwate Prefecture, northern Honshū, on the river Kitakamigawa. Mizusawa developed early on as the military outpost for subduing the EZO when SAKANOUE NO TAMURAMARO built a palisade (Isawajō) here in 802. It was a castle town of the DATE FAMILY during the Edo period (1600–1868). Local products are rice, fruits, and Nambu cast iron goods. The Latitude Observatory of Mizusawa is located here. Pop: 55,226.

Mizusawa, Latitude Observatory of

(Mizusawa Ido Kansokujo). Government-operated astronomical observatory in the city of Mizusawa, Iwate Prefecture. Founded in 1899 to cooperate with other nations in the observation of polar motion. The first head of the observatory was the astronomer KIMURA HISASHI, who discovered the Z-term. It serves as the central station of a network of six observatories located at different points on the same latitude throughout the world.

Mizushima

An area on the outskirts of the city of Kurashiki, Okayama Prefecture, western Honshū, facing the Inland Sea. Once a small fishing and farming village, in 1941 it became an industrial area almost overnight with the establishment of an aircraft manufacturing industry. After World War II, new industries were set up including steel production, oil refining, and the manufacture of other chemical and heavy industrial products. As a result the area faces a serious water pollution problem today. One of the country's largest heavy industrial complexes is located here.

Mizushima San'ichirō (1899–   )

Chemist who contributed to the understanding of the molecular structure of matter through his studies of dipole moments, infrared absorption, and the Raman effect. Born in Tōkyō, he graduated from Tōkyō University, where he later became a professor. He also served as director of the laboratories of the Nippon Steel Corporation. In 1961 he received the Order of Culture. His publications include *Structure of Molecules and Internal Rotation* (1954).

Mizutani Yaeko (1905–1979)

Actress. Real name Matsuno Yaeko. Born in Tōkyō. With the aid of her brother-in-law Mizutani Chikushi, a trustee of the Geijutsuza theatrical troupe, she made her stage debut in 1916 as Mizutani Yaeko in the role of Sergia in *Anna Karenina*. Her first film performance was in Hatanaka Ryōha's *Kantsubaki* (1921, Winter Camellia). For this movie she used a stage name, Fukumen Reijō (Masked Maiden), for fear that she would be discovered and expelled from the girls' school she was attending. Although she appeared in films such as Tanaka Eizō's *Hototogisu* (1927) and SHIMAZU YASUJIRŌ's *Jōriku daiippo* (1932, First Steps Abroad), she acted primarily on stage, reviving the nearly defunct Geijutsuza and becoming Japan's leading stage actress in such roles as Nora in Ibsen's *A Doll's House* in 1924. In 1956 she was awarded the Japan Art Academy Prize. She became a member of the Japan Art Academy in 1967, and in 1971 was designated a Person of Cultural Merits (Bunka Kōrō Sha). In 1937 she and the *kabuki* actor Morita Kan'ya XIV were married, but were divorced in 1950. Her daughter Mizutani Yoshie is also an actress.　　　*ITASAKA Tsuyoshi*

MOA Museum of Art

(MOA Bijutsukan). Located at Atami, Shizuoka Prefecture; formerly known as the Kyūsei Atami Art Museum. This museum, originally opened in 1957, and its sister museum, the HAKONE MUSEUM OF ART in Hakone, belong to the SEKAI KYŪSEI KYŌ (Religion for the Salvation of the World). The collections were assembled by the late founder of the church, OKADA MOKICHI. In January 1982 a new four-story complex was completed, and the museum was renamed in honor of Okada (MOA is an abbreviation for Mokichi Okada International Association). It is in a large garden and includes a tea ceremony room *(chashitsu)* and a Nō theater. It houses a collection of Chinese and Japanese painting, calligraphy, ceramics, and sculpture; Chinese bronzes; Japanese lacquer, metalwork, and prints. It also has a number of European art holdings. One Chinese painting is of the Tang (T'ang; 618–907) dynasty and comes from the Turfan region of Central Asia; other Chinese paintings are of the Song (Sung; 960–1279) and Yuan (Yüan; 1279–1368) dynasties. Among the Japanese paintings are a section of the sutra scroll painting *E inga kyō* (Nara period; 710–794), a portrait of the priest IKKYŪ, *namban* screens (see NAMBAN ART), a fragment of HON'AMI KŌETSU's "deer scroll," and a large group of UKIYO-E prints. Chinese bronzes date from the Shang (2nd millenium BC) to the Tang dynasty. Japanese ceramics include pieces by CHŌJIRŌ, Hon'ami Kōetsu, and NONOMURA NINSEI. Among the European pieces are works by Monet, Renoir, Maillol, and Henry Moore.　　　*Laurance ROBERTS*

Mobara

City in central Chiba Prefecture, central Honshū. A distribution center for agricultural and marine products since the Edo period (1600–1868). With the discovery of natural gas in 1931, Mobara developed into an industrial city with chemical and electrical appliance plants. It is also a commercial center. Pop: 71,521.

Mobil Sekiyu

A Japanese subsidiary of the Mobil Corporation of the United States, Mobil Sekiyu's chief lines of business are the sale, export, and import of oil and petrochemical products. It was established in 1933 as a branch of the Standard Vacuum Oil Company, which was divided into the Mobil Corporation and the Esso Standard Oil Company in 1961. The company obtains crude oil from the Mobil Corporation and supplies it to TŌA NENRYŌ KŌGYŌ and Kyokutō Sekiyu Industry for refining. It sells various types of oil products on the Japanese market, along with petrochemical products supplied by the Mobil Chemical Co and Tōnen Sekiyu Kagaku. The company has 12 branches and 42 storage installations in Japan. Annual sales were ¥1.1 trillion (US $5.02 billion) in 1981; capitalization stood at ¥11 billion (US $50.2 million) in the same year. Corporate headquarters are located in Tōkyō.

Mochizuki Yūko (1917–1977)

Film actress. Real name Suzuki Mieko. Born in Tōkyō. Leaving high school, she became a dancer at various night clubs in the Asakusa and Shinjuku sections of Tōkyō. After working for the theatrical group Mingei, she joined the studios of Shōchiku Motion Pictures. Appearing in Shibuya Minoru's *Yonimme no shukujo* (1948, The Fourth Lady), she won acclaim for her lively down-to-earth style. She performed in several other films directed by Shibuya, among them, *Ten'ya wan'ya* (1950, Crazy Uproar) and *Honjitsu kyūshin* (1952, Doctor's Day Off). She also appeared in KINOSHITA KEISUKE's *Nihon no higeki* (1953, A Japanese Tragedy), *Narayama-bushi kō* (1958, The Ballad of Narayama); NARUSE MIKIO's *Bangiku* (1954, Late Chrysanthemums); and YAMAMOTO SATSUO's *Niguruma no uta* (1959, The Song of the Cart). Mochizuki's performances as the ideal Japanese mother, strong yet self-effacing, appealed particularly to female audiences, and on the strength of this she ran successfully for the House of Councillors in 1971.

ITASAKA Tsuyoshi

modernization

Modernization is the process of economic, political, and social change by which a developed society is transformed into a society with characteristics shared by more developed societies. The theory of modernization, which resulted from the effort by Western social scientists to develop a universal view of the process of modern transformation that would comprehend the varied experiences of postwar developing nations, is an attempt to conceptualize the modernization process, identifying the components of that process and building a general model of modernization.

One of the first steps taken by scholars in developing a unified theory of modernization has been to describe the result of the modernization process, namely, the condition of modernity. Through this effort at description, social scientists have reached general agreement on the criteria of modernity—the shared characteristics of modern societies. These characteristics include a measure of self-sustaining economic growth, a degree of mass political participation, an increase in social mobility, a diffusion of secular-rational values, and a transformation in personality enabling individuals to function effectively in a society that operates according to the above conditions.

The next step has been to analyze the process of modernization itself. Some consensus has been achieved on the identification of the components of modernization, which are seen to include such subprocesses as industrialization, urbanization, bureaucratization, and secularization. Scholars have come to recognize, however, that there is no single model of modernization but rather a variety of models, principally because the subprocesses of modernization begin at different times, move at different rates, and follow different sequences.

The Conference on Modern Japan ——— The application of modernization theory to Japan, an approach that has profoundly influenced Western scholarship on Japan since the 1950s, represented partly an attempt to inject into Japanese studies the latest ideas and methods developed by Western social scientists, and partly an attempt to counter the predominantly Marxist thrust of scholarship in Japan with a powerful alternative approach. This effort reached its high-water mark following the establishment of the Conference on Modern Japan under the auspices of the Association for Asian Studies in 1959. During the 10 years of its existence, the conference sought to pool the results of current research and to promote the modernization approach to the study of modern Japan by organizing a battery of six seminars on various aspects of Japan's modern development and publishing the proceedings in the series *Studies in the Modernization of Japan* (1965–71).

In addition, the conference sponsored a preliminary meeting of Japanese and American scholars, held in Hakone, Kanagawa Prefecture, in 1960, to deal with problems involved in defining modernization as a concept and in applying it to the Japanese case. The Western participants at the Hakone meeting, led by John W. Hall, Edwin O. REISCHAUER, and Marius B. Jansen, advocated an approach to the study of modern Japan based on the universal theory of modernization then being developed in the Western social sciences, a method that would facilitate dialogue with scholars in other fields and provide an objective ground for cross-national comparison. Within this broad conceptual framework, they called for a rigorous empiricism, in contrast to the prevailing Marxist approach in Japan, which tended to rely heavily on theory at the expense of empirical observation.

The Japanese participants at the Hakone conference, including MARUYAMA MASAO, KAWASHIMA TAKEYOSHI, Furushima Toshio, and Tōyama Shigeki, were generally critical of the proposed approach, in part because its Western proponents disavowed the making of value judgments in scholarly work, a practice characteristic of the approach taken by most Japanese scholars. For the most part, the Japanese participants, deeply influenced by their own nation's presurrender experience of militarism and war, believed that scholarship on Japan should be harnessed to political ends, specifically the effort to democratize Japanese society, by identifying factors that had hindered the establishment of democracy in the course of Japan's modern development. They therefore argued that democratization should be included as one of the subprocesses of modernization. In addition, they emphasized the necessity of taking into consideration the level of capitalist development in discussing a given country's modernization. The preoccupation of the Japanese participants with the concepts of democracy and capitalism, both considered too parochial and value-laden by their Western counterparts, served to highlight the difference between Japanese and Western scholars in their choice and handling of historical issues.

Japanese Views in Historical Perspective —— This conference was by no means the first time that Japanese scholars had confronted the issue of modernization. In fact, the Japanese since the Meiji period (1868–1912) had often reflected critically on the rapid development of modern technology and industry that was transforming their country into a modern industrialized nation.

In July 1911, for example, NATSUME SŌSEKI delivered a lecture in Wakayama entitled "The Development of Modern Japan" in which he examined the problems brought on by the so-called MEIJI ENLIGHTENMENT. Sōseki maintained that Japan's "external enlightenment," its outward progress in industry and technology, had not been matched by an "internal enlightenment"—a modernization of personal values and attitudes. However, Sōseki's arguments did not receive wide acceptance or undergo further development. The Japanese have always had a pronounced tendency to view modernization not as a continuing organic process but as an ultimate value or goal to be realized.

Even in the 1920s, during the heyday of TAISHŌ DEMOCRACY, the stance taken by YOSHINO SAKUZŌ and other liberal thinkers was based not on the ideas set forth by Sōseki—on the internalization of democratic values by the Japanese—but rather on the importation of full-fledged democracy from the West.

In the 1920s and 1930s, Japanese Marxist scholars, in viewing modernization as a basically progressive movement whose advance was hampered by restrictive feudal elements, also failed to examine fully the broad range of issues encompassed by the concept and process of modernization. The biased and narrow views characteristic of ULTRANATIONALISM, on the other hand, tended to negate modernization altogether and to see it as something to be overcome. Such ideas spearheaded the rise of militarism in the 1930s, as the traditionalists' call for a nativist movement—"a return to that which is Japanese" (Nihon kaiki)—gained wide acceptance. As a result, the task of singling out modernization as a specific problem and of examining its effects was left to the postwar period, when the taboos against analyzing the impact of the emperor system on Japan's modernization had been eliminated.

Thus it was only after World War II that Japanese scholars as a whole began seriously to examine the issue of Japan's modernization. Intensely aware of the disasters wrought by Japan's modernization at home and abroad, they sought through their research to promote the realization of "postwar democracy." The special concerns of the Japanese participants at the Hakone conference derived from their involvement in this intellectual and political activity.

During the 1960s and 1970s, however, a significant number of Japanese intellectuals began to view modernization not as an ultimate goal but as a potentially negative process with undesirable side-effects. This change had its impetus in the myriad problems brought about by the high economic growth during that period. Realizing that Japan's "economic invasion" of other Asian countries had aroused vehement opposition in these countries, they intensified their examination of the relationship between Japan's modernization and imperialism before World War II.

Intellectuals also pointed out various internal problems accompanying modernization, including the increase in pollution and occupational diseases, the concentration of population in the cities and the accompanying desertion of farms, the depletion of natural resources, and the many social problems that prosperity has brought with it. Thus, in the past decade, the predominant Japanese approach of

viewing modernization as an ultimate value to be achieved has changed noticeably. It remains to be seen what course the study of Japan's modernization will take in Japan, but in the West scholars have begun to view Japan as a valid model of modernization in itself and not as a case study of a single universal process of development.

📖 —— Ronald P. Dore, *British Factory-Japanese Factory* (1973). John Dower, ed, *Origins of the Modern Japanese State* (1975). Kawashima Takeyoshi, *Nihon shakai no kazokuteki kōsei* (1950). Maruyama Masao, *Nihon no shisō* (1961). James Morley, ed, *Dilemmas of Growth in Prewar Japan* (1971). Tetsuo Najita, *Japan* (1974). Herbert E. Norman, *Japan's Emergence as a Modern State* (1940). Edwin O. Reischauer, *The Japanese* (1977). Tōyama Shigeki, *Meiji ishin* (1951). Tōyama Shigeki, *Nihon kindai shi*, vol 1 (1975). HARADA Katsumasa

modern philosophy

Introduction of Western Philosophy —— Philosophy in the strict sense of the academic discipline practiced in the West did not make its appearance in the history of Japanese thought until after the Meiji Restoration in 1868, although in the broader sense "philosophical" thinking existed from ancient times. Buddhism and Confucianism, for example, both contain lofty philosophical thought. However, philosophy *(tetsugaku)* in a strict academic sense entered Japan only after the Meiji Restoration. In 1862, even before the Meiji Restoration, NISHI AMANE and TSUDA MAMICHI, both employed in the shogunate BANSHO SHIRABESHO (Institute for Investigation of Barbarian Books), had been sent to Holland to study Western philosophy and social science. They did research in these various disciplines and labored to introduce and establish them upon their return to Japan. This was the start of the first real importation of Western philosophy into Japan, as well as the starting point for modern Japanese philosophical thinking.

What Nishi and Tsuda brought back to Japan was mainly the utilitarianism of John Stuart Mill and the positivism of Auguste Comte, which at the time were exerting a great influence on the Dutch philosophical world. Although trained in traditional Confucian thought, they were able to take in Western philosophy and to use it to criticize existing academic disciplines, hoping thus to promote the modernization of their country.

Following the Meiji Restoration, these two men joined forces with such figures as FUKUZAWA YUKICHI, KATŌ HIROYUKI, NISHIMURA SHIGEKI, and NAKAMURA MASANAO to form the group known as MEIROKUSHA. The organization played a decisive role in the "civilization and enlightenment" (*bummei kaika;* see MEIJI ENLIGHTENMENT) movement of the early Meiji years. In 1871 NAKAE CHŌMIN, upon his return to Japan after studies in France, introduced French theories of democratic revolution, beginning with the social philosophy of Jean Jacques Rousseau. This served as the theoretical basis for the FREEDOM AND PEOPLE'S RIGHTS MOVEMENT. Just before his death, Nakae produced his *Zoku ichinen yūhan* (1901), in which he attempted to articulate his own materialistic, atheistic view of the universe. In 1877 the Japanese government established Tōkyō University, which was until the early 1880s a center for the introduction of the evolutionary theories of Darwin and Spencer. Katō Hiroyuki, a former advocate of natural human rights, used this evolutionist thinking as a rational basis for his conversion to social Darwinism, a position from which he began attacks on the Freedom and People's Rights Movement.

Traditional Thought and Modern Philosophy —— The third decade of the Meiji period (1868–1912) saw a decline in the influence of the Freedom and People's Rights Movement. In promulgating the Meiji CONSTITUTION in 1889 and the IMPERIAL RESCRIPT ON EDUCATION in 1890, the government moved quickly to pave the way for a system based on the ideology of an emperor-centered state. As is clear from the rescript, by giving a contemporary, nationalistic guise to traditional thought, it hoped to propagate a new system of morals for the people. In response to these official guidelines, a number of movements that employed Western philosophy to produce modern expressions of traditional Confucian and Buddhist thought developed in Japanese intellectual circles. First attempts included the remodeling of Confucian thinking by Nishimura Shigeki and the reexamination of Buddhist philosophy by INOUE ENRYŌ.

Along with these movements appeared a tendency at state-supported academies to supplant British and French Enlightenment philosophy with German idealism. Among those who played a decisive role in leading and promoting this movement was INOUE TETSUJIRŌ. In 1884 Inoue traveled to Germany as the first student sent by the Ministry of Education to study the humanities. Upon his return to Japan, he became a professor in Tōkyō University's philosophy department. During his long tenure, he applied himself to introducing the idealist philosophy of Hartmann and Hegel, using it to criticize the Enlightenment moral philosophy taught by the previous generation of Japanese thinkers. This idealist philosophy was to serve as the foundation for the new state-centered morality, in which ethics was to be understood as consisting of loyalty and filial piety. In this Inoue was attempting a philosophical fusion of Eastern and Western thinking through a reexamination of traditional Japanese thought. The fusion did not, however, go beyond a mixture—a compromise between Western philosophy and Buddhist concepts.

ŌNISHI HAJIME, while belonging to the same line of academism as Inoue, made use of the idealist methods of criticism found in the philosophy of Kant to attack the tendencies toward anti-Enlightenment and state-centered thought that he found in Inoue. His thought was characterized by a critical Enlightenment ideology and an opposition to ideas of state supremacy. Opposing Inoue's speculative metaphysics, he sought to establish a critical metaphysics based on epistemology and to develop his own fusion of Eastern and Western thought. Although an untimely death cut it off, his work opened a road to the development of modern Japanese philosophy.

The Formation of Academic Philosophy —— The years following the third decade of the Meiji period saw the introduction and study of German philosophy vigorously carried out in state-supported academic circles. In particular, during the fourth decade of the Meiji period there was a movement to introduce idealist and personalist ethics as found in Kant, Fichte, Friedrich Paulsen, and Thomas Hill Green. This trend corresponded to the emergence of ethical idealism in the intellectual world in general, as shown, for example, in the formation of the Teiyū Ethics Society or in the development of religious spiritualism (see UCHIMURA KANZŌ; KIYO-ZAWA MANSHI; TSUNASHIMA RYŌSEN). Underlying this was the growth in Japan of a modern self-awareness and a search for new ways to view human existence.

During the same time, again influenced by German thought, there appeared several general introductions to philosophy as well as histories of philosophy, indicating a progression in the understanding of Western philosophical systems and of their history. The study of Western philosophy in Japan now entered the stage of deeper understanding and original research, and was established as an academic discipline.

In the latter part of the Meiji period and in the early part of the Taishō period (1912–26), state-supported academic circles concentrated on the introduction of Neo-Kantianism, the main current in German academic philosophy at the time. Philosophy departments were established at Kyōto University in 1906 and at Tōhoku University in 1922. During this period the people most influential in introducing and developing Western philosophy as represented in Neo-Kantian idealism were KUWAKI GEN'YOKU, Tomonaga Sanjūrō, NI-SHIDA KITARŌ, and HATANO SEIICHI. Philosophical research at universities became increasingly technical and specialized as scholars carried out detailed studies of original texts. This in turn produced a tendency to import philosophic problems themselves. In the midst of these developments Nishida Kitarō, while absorbing Western systems and methods, grappled with his own set of philosophical problems in an attempt to create an original system.

The Philosophies of Nishida and Tanabe —— As mentioned above, the fourth decade of the Meiji period was characterized by the introduction and study of Western idealist ethics and the emergence of a modern consciousness of the self. The publication in 1911 of Nishida's first treatise, *Zen no kenkyū* (tr *A Study of Good*, 1960), was a response to this particular trend. In searching for a philosophical foundation for the modern Japanese consciousness of the self, Nishida produced his own system of thought, with roots in personal experience and in the traditional thought of the East. In this sense, his book was the first truly original treatise in philosophy produced in modern Japan.

Nishida's originality is seen primarily in his concept of "pure experience," which underlies the subsequent development of his philosophy. Although the expression "pure experience" can be found in the writings of such philosophers as Ernst Mach, William James, and Wilhelm Wundt, Nishida drew upon his experience in Zen meditation to give new meaning to the word. According to Nishida, pure experience was a state transcending the dichotomy of subject and object; it was the state of union of subject and object, a state which in turn was reality itself. He took all dualities, such as mind and things or subject and object, as expressive of the differen-

tiation and development of pure experience. Nishida attempted to find herein the principles underlying morality, the arts, and religion.

He failed, however, to develop his theory fully and logically in *A Study of Good*. It was in later works that, in coming to grips with the various schools of Western philosophy, he deepened his own thought and gave it a logical form. The result was a philosophical system known as the "Nishida philosophy." Although many criticisms from various positions have been made of Nishida's thought and insights, his achievements nevertheless remain significant in the history of modern Japanese philosophy, in that they mark the first attempt by a Japanese to approach Western philosophy from a personal standpoint and to produce a universal philosophical system by giving a logical and ontological form to traditional Japanese thought.

Among the individuals who were strongly influenced by the Nishida philosophy but who later created their own philosophical systems were Tanabe Hajime and Takahashi Satomi. Nishida lectured for several years at Kyōto University in a post at which Tanabe succeeded him. Between them they formed the nucleus of what is usually called the Kyōto school. Takahashi Satomi was the central figure in Tōhoku University's philosophy department.

In his earlier academic career Tanabe was primarily influenced by the Neo-Kantian school (in particular, the Marburg school) and did pioneering work in the philosophy of science and of mathematics. He moved from inquiry into the origins of science toward ontology and, with the advent of the Shōwa period (1926–), embraced the Nishida philosophy. Taking a critical position toward Hegel and Marx, he propounded an "absolute dialectic," which united both ideological dialectics and materialism in a higher synthesis after negating them separately. Tanabe went on to criticize the "logic of place" (*basho no ronri*) propounded in the Nishida philosophy, which he found insufficiently related to such factors as people, state, and society. Where Nishida had posited only two categories, genus (*rui*) and individual (*ko*), Tanabe gave special considerations to an additional category of species (*shu*) existing between the other two. This was the basis of Tanabe's "logic of species" (*shu no ronri*), a concept which subsequently led to his formulation of an independent philosophy. The logic of species made an ideological absolute out of the state as a political reality; it thus contained elements of a doctrine of state supremacy.

Following World War II, Tanabe went through a period of intense self-examination on this point and arrived at a belief in an absolute other power as found in the teachings of PURE LAND BUD-DHISM. We can see this in writings such as the 1946 work *Zangedō to shite no tetsugaku* (Philosophy as the Way of Atonement).

While inheriting the ideas of the Nishida philosophy, Takahashi Satomi, like Tanabe, took a critical stance toward the principal schools of Western philosophy. He eventually arrived at a personal philosophic position characterized by the term "dialectical totality," in which he attempted to embrace and yet transcend dialectical thought through love, which he called "absolute nothingness." This also had its roots in the Pure Land Buddhist belief in an absolute other power. The thought systems of Nishida, Tanabe, and Takahaski, while attempting to give logical and ontological forms to traditional thought, tried to supply original answers to the problems of modern philosophy.

Taishō Democracy and Philosophy —— Just as individuals like Nishida and Tanabe were central in the formation of the Kyōto school, Kuwaki Gen'yoku, who succeeded Inoue Tetsujirō at Tōkyō University as head of the philosophy department, became the nucleus of what came to be called the Tōkyō school. Kuwaki started out as an adherent of the Neo-Kantian school (particularly the Southwest German school). He staunchly supported that school's position of intellectualist rationalism and contributed to the development of academic philosophy in Japan. During the high tide of liberal party politics (see TAISHŌ DEMOCRACY) following World War I, Kuwaki took part in the Reimeikai movement, in which YOSHINO SAKUZŌ played a central role. He also collaborated with SŌDA KIICHIRŌ as an exponent of culturalism (*bunka shugi*), which was based on the cultural and value philosophy of the Southwest German school. Kuwaki continued to defend his position of "liberalistic culturalism." During the years before World War II he maintained an opposition to fascism, albeit in the negative form of noncooperation.

The culturalism proposed by Kuwaki and Sōda became one of the main currents of thought during the Taishō period, along with such trends as self-culturalism (*kyōyō shugi*), personalism (*jinkaku shugi*), and humanism (*jindō shugi*). These various schools of thought all had internal connections with the democratic tendencies of the Taishō period and were based on similar social and philosophical foundations: they also had their start in the emergence of a new Japanese middle class and were influenced by the trend toward individualism found in the newly born middle-class consciousness. These all, in one form or another, expressed a desire to break with the current ideas of state supremacy and to move toward the development of new values and approaches to life. Culturalism was an attempt to bring culture in general into daily life. Self-culturalism attributed the highest value to the spiritual development of the self based on the introduction of various cultural and human values into one's own life. Both of these positions developed out of contact with idealistic philosophies from modern Germany based on personalism.

With the emergence of self-culturalism and personalism appeared works like ABE JIRŌ's *Santarō no nikki* (1914–18, Santarō's Diary) and Kurata Momozō's *Ai to ninshiki to no shuppatsu* (1921, The Beginnings of Love and Knowledge), philosophical essays which revealed the interior lives of the authors. Both works found a wide readership among young intellectuals. Although these writings at times descended to mere word-painting and simple sentimentalism, they succeeded in freeing philosophy from academic strictures and thus brought it closer to everyday life.

About this time WATSUJI TETSURŌ, from a position based on culturalism and personalism, reexamined the cultural and philosophical traditions of East Asia in general and of Japan in particular. With the beginning of the Shōwa period, he began a critical assessment of Heidegger and other Western philosophers, and went on to establish his own anthropological stance. Known as "Watsuji ethics," it consisted of a reorganization of traditional thought in the area of ethics. Among other examples of attempts of philosophical examination of Japanese culture was KUKI SHŪZŌ's *Iki no kōzō* (1930, The Structure of *Iki*).

Marxist Philosophy——After World War I the philosophical aspects of Marxism began to receive attention and became the object of conscious adoption and research. The ideas of socialism, including Marxist ideology, had already been introduced to Japan during the early years of the Meiji period. But it was not until the Sino-Japanese War of 1894–95, the ensuing rapid development of capitalistic industry, and the profusion of social and labor problems that these ideas began to have a real connection with social realities in Japan. Interest in socialism grew, and 1898 saw the birth of the Society for the Study of Socialism (SHAKAI SHUGI KENKYŪKAI), which examined the principles of socialism and their possible adoption in Japan. With the exception of KŌTOKU SHŪSUI, the key figures in this group were all members of the Unitarian Church, which had earlier introduced American liberal theology. Their members included Murai Chishi, ABE ISOO, and KATAYAMA SEN. Starting from a rational, Christian humanism, they sought to realize those ideals through socialism. Kōtoku Shūsui had been influenced earlier by the Freedom and People's Rights Movement, but after studying with Nakae Chōmin, he too attempted to realize such ideas as freedom, equality, and world brotherhood through socialism. Kōtokū's thought, however, still had strong traces of idealism and humanism derived from traditional Confucian learning.

In 1901 Japan's first socialist-based political group, the SHAKAI MINSHUTŌ, was formed with Nakae and Kōtoku as central figures. Party objectives included total abolition of the military, direct vote by the people, and abolition of the aristocracy. The party was immediately banned by the government. In 1903, on the eve of the Russo-Japanese War (1904–05), Kōtoku and SAKAI TOSHIHIKO formed the HEIMINSHA and launched a spirited antiwar campaign in their newspaper, the *Heimin shimbun* (Commoners' News).

Following the war, Kōtoku traveled to the United States, where he came under the influence of anarcho-syndicalist thought. He abandoned parliamentarianism and legalism, stressing the need for direct action by the workers. This brought to the surface many of the philosophical and emotional conflicts submerged in the socialist movement, such as opposition between Christian and materialist, parliamentarianism and direct action. Amid these disputes Kōtoku was executed for involvement in the so-called HIGH TREASON INCIDENT OF 1910, and the socialist movement in Japan entered what is known as its "winter season."

The socialist movement revived in the generally freer political climate following World War I. The first principle to hold sway was anarcho-syndicalism, descended from the direct-action movement of the Meiji years. Its leader, ŌSUGI SAKAE, took a position which strongly emphasized individual freedom and opposed power and authority. Differing on this stance were Sakai Toshihiko and YAMA-

KAWA HITOSHI, who, influenced by the Russian Revolution, had adopted bolshevism (Marxist-Leninism). A dispute broke out between the anarchist and bolshevist factions—the so-called Anaboru Ronsō. The bolshevist cause gradually gained ascendancy, and in 1922 the JAPAN COMMUNIST PARTY was formed illegally as a branch of international communism. With the emergence of Marxist ideological movements in Japan the philosophical aspects of Marxism began to attract attention.

Individuals had been laboring since the early Meiji years to introduce the study of Marxism in Japan. Up to then, such research had concentrated mainly on the socialist and economic aspects of Marxism. It was not until the late Taishō and early Shōwa periods that the philosophical aspects of Marxism received any serious attention. KAWAKAMI HAJIME, a pioneer in the study of Marxian economics in Japan, initially embraced Marxism as a form of idealistic humanism. After criticism from KUSHIDA TAMIZŌ, FUKUMOTO KAZUO, and Sakai Toshihiko, Kawakami reflected on the weak points in his understanding of Marxism and undertook a reassessment of its philosophic foundations, arriving eventually at a more truly Marxist stance.

Fukumoto went to Europe to study Marxist philosophy under Lukacs and others and returned to Japan in 1924. Upon his return, he wrote criticisms of Kawakami Hajime and Yamakawa Hitoshi, which exerted considerable influence for a time on the socialist movement in Japan. The influence of Fukumoto's thinking diminished sharply when its emphasis on ideological debate and sectionalism was criticized by the Comintern in 1927. Fukumoto's suggestions nevertheless served to encourage discussion of the philosophical aspects of Marxism.

With these events of the early Shōwa years, interest in Marxism grew quickly among the academic philosophers. MIKI KIYOSHI attempted to construct a new philosophical basis for Marxism. A student of Nishida Kitarō, he had studied in post–World War I Germany and received instruction in hermeneutics under Heidegger. His friendship with Karl Mannheim had led to a strong interest in Marxism.

Following his return to Japan, Miki became professor of philosophy at Hōsei University in 1927. His first treatise, *Ningengaku no marukusuteki keitai* (A Marxist Form of Anthropology), was followed by several other papers. These studies drew upon the hermeneutics of Heidegger to interpret Marxist philosophy as a modern form of anthropology and represented an attempt to establish Marxism in the field of philosophy as "the modern consciousness." This anthropological approach to Marxism drew fire from more traditional Marxist circles. Miki's work, however, approached Marxism philosophically and led the departure from the educationalist-culturalist humanism of the late Taishō period.

Miki was arrested in 1930 for violating the PEACE PRESERVATION LAW OF 1925. He gradually drew away from Marxism, and coming closer to the Nishida philosophy, attempted to establish a new theory of action for the intellectual in *Kōsōryoku no ronri* (1939, A Logic of Intellectual Creativity). Toward the end of World War II he was arrested a second time, for violating the Security Enforcement Law, and died in prison shortly after Japan's surrender.

With the outbreak of the SINO-JAPANESE WAR OF 1937–1945, the domestic establishment increasingly took on fascistic characteristics. In the intellectual world totalitarianism and Japanism (Nihon shugi) appeared. During this period the Materialism Study Society (Yuibutsuron Kenkyūkai) continued to·make known in Japan the development and application of Marxist philosophy in the Soviet Union, using this as a weapon to oppose various right-wing ideologies in Japan. Tosaka Jun was a central figure in the society. He had begun from a Neo-Kantian position in his studies concerning the concept of space and of science, but under the influence of Miki Kiyoshi, he moved toward a Marxist stance and became the founder of dialectical materialism in Japan. As may be seen in his essays, *Nippon ideorogii ron* (1935, A Treatise on Japanese Ideologies), Tosaka took an uncompromising stand against fascism, and his writings are characterized by a spirit of scientific criticism. Other philosophers who took action as members of that organization were Oka Kunio, SAIGUSA HIROTO, Nagata Hiroshi, and Kozai Yoshishige. Because of their efforts, Marxist philosophy in Japan finally moved out of its rudimentary stage into independent development. Increasingly harsh repression forced the society to disband in 1936, and Tosaka, like Miki, died in prison the year the war came to a close.

Concomitant with the emergence of Marxist thought and movements was a growing interest in philosophic circles in historical and social problems, particularly dialectics and Hegelian philosophy. Philosophers like Nishida and Tanabe began to turn their attention to these questions. At the same time, the rapid inroads of war and MILITARISM led to the increased influence of such totalitarian philosophies as Japanism and imperial supremacism *(kōdō shugi)* under the guidance of people like KIHIRA TADAYOSHI and Kanokogi Kazunobu. These ideologies used government backing to suppress free speech. This type of thought-control gradually forced itself not only on Marxism but other philosophical schools as well, and, as World War II drew to a close, the intellectual climate was completely arid.

The Post–World War II Situation —— Japan's defeat in World War II was a severe blow to the emperor-centered ideology fostered since the Meiji Restoration. It also marked the start of a movement toward political and social democracy. In the philosophical realm Japanism and imperial supremacism were thoroughly discredited. Many philosophical schools—Marxism, existentialism, pragmatism, the philosophies of Nishida and Tanabe, all the thought systems that had been suppressed immediately before or during the war—reappeared. Marxism and existentialism received particular attention, and spirited discussion took place on the concept of autonomy, the meeting point of these two philosophical approaches. In the 1950s, following social and intellectual changes both at home and abroad, internal divisions occurred within Japanese Marxist circles. Japan's economic resurgence brought about many new philosophical developments, including the introduction of analytic philosophy and pragmatism. The country's success in achieving industrialization brought an awareness of the many contradictions contained in this accomplishment. In philosophical circles there were also reassessments of the modern Western civilization on which Japan had modeled itself and of traditional Japanese thought and culture. Japanese philosophy entered another stage of development, embracing the rich heritage both of its own culture and of the West.

📖 —— Koyasu Norikuni and Furuta Hikaru, *Nihon shisōshi tokuhon* (1979). Miyakawa Tōru and Arakawa Shigeo, ed, *Nihon kindai tetsugaku shi* (1976). Shimomura Toratarō and Furuta Hikaru, ed, *Nihon tetsugaku,* vol 4 in *Tetsugakushi taikei* (1977).

Furuta Hikaru

modern prints

Many Japanese artists in the 20th century have worked in the print mediums with notable success. Their debt to the traditional art of woodblock printing (UKIYO-E) is undeniable, but as with other arts, the legacy of the past was both a boon and a burden. With *ukiyo-e* prints the woodblock had been raised to dazzling heights and had become a truly Japanese medium. At the same time, there was in Japan a lingering disdain for *ukiyo-e* as a plebeian art, an attitude which transferred to all prints, no matter how far removed from *ukiyo-e* in subject and style. Thus the modern Japanese print artist faced the challenge of discovering new and relevant possibilities in a traditional format and of creating a place for himself in the modern art world.

Japan's modern print artists divided into two schools. In general terms, one school tried to revive the *ukiyo-e* tradition, continuing its themes and working within its framework—that is, designing for publishers whose artisans did the carving and printing. The other school seized on the woodblock as a native medium but used it to express a new vision born of exposure to Western art; these artists took over the whole artistic process themselves.

In the first school, KOBAYASHI KIYOCHIKA (1847–1915) was a forerunner, although he worked mainly in the 19th century; his use of light and shade in landscape reflects his study of Western painting. HASHIGUCHI GOYŌ (1880–1921) produced only about 15 prints but his portraits of women rival the *ukiyo-e* masters in virtuosity. Kawase Hasui (1883–1957) designed hundreds of effective landscapes. Yamamura Toyonari (1885–1942) and Natori Shunsen (1886–1960) did portraits of KABUKI actors. ITŌ SHINSUI (1898–1972), although primarily a painter, designed both landscapes and portraits of women. YOSHIDA HIROSHI (1876–1950), though he is better known for his watercolors, also produced prints, which he published himself using his own carvers and printers. His sons Toshi (b 1911) and Hodaka (b 1926) are print artists today. Paul Jacoulet (1902–60), who was French but was a lifelong resident of Japan, like Yoshida published his own prints, pushing woodblock to new limits in virtuoso carving and printing. But it was the second school that proved to be more significant, for it brought the Japanese print into the arena of contemporary international art.

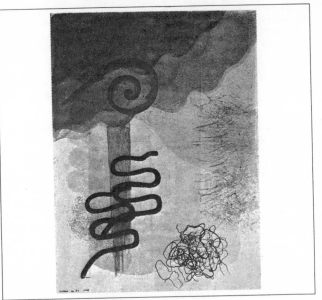

Modern prints —— Onchi Kōshirō

Solitude: Lyric #11. Woodblock print. 82 × 58 cm. 1949. National Museum of Modern Art, Tōkyō.

Sōsaku Hanga —— Yamamoto Kanae (1882–1946), his friends, and his followers created a movement that they called *sōsaku hanga* ("creative prints") because they believed that in prints, as in painting and sculpture, the artist should perform the entire creative process, carving and printing as well as designing. Yamamoto's print *Fisherman* (1904) marked the beginning of this movememt.

The *sōsaku hanga* movement gathered strength in the 1920s and 1930s, despite the general indifference of Japan's art establishment. It flowered after World War II when foreigners resident in Japan became enthusiastic, began serious collections, and introduced the prints to appreciative audiences abroad.

Two artists were dominant in this period, ONCHI KŌSHIRŌ (1891–1955) and HIRATSUKA UN'ICHI (b 1895), men quite opposite in work and personality. Onchi, although he produced strong portraits and studies from nature, was more interested in abstract design, and he restlessly modified the woodblock print through his use of paper, cloth, and found objects like leaves. Hiratsuka stayed with traditional techniques and worked most characteristically in forceful black and white, producing landscapes and portraits of great power. MUNAKATA SHIKŌ (1903–75) also worked primarily in black and white but his blacks were calligraphic, of infinite gradation. He drew on folkloric Buddhist themes, and because the powerful FOLK CRAFTS *(mingei)* movement found kinship with his work, he was the first of these artists whose work was widely admired and collected in Japan as well as abroad.

Many notable artists worked in the woodblock; the following list of artists and their subjects is merely a representative selection. Kōsaka Gajin (1877–1953): powerful forms of softly edged black on white. Maekawa Sempan (1888–1960): humanistic and very Japanese in style and subject matter, in the tradition of the purely Japanese style called YAMATO-E. Kawanishi Hide (1894–1965): scenes of Kōbe in vivid primary colors. Kawakami Sumio (1895–1972): records of the early impact of the West on Japan and the bowler-hat-with-*kimono* kind of cultural hybrid it produced. Hatsuyama Shigeru (1897–1973): sophisticated fairytale fantasies in delicate colors. Hashimoto Okiie (b 1899): a loving record of Japan's castles, with a flair for architectural detail and a feeling for old stone walls. Azechi Umetarō (b 1902): mountains and mountaineers, boldly simplified. Yamaguchi Gen (1903–76): poetic abstracts, frequently incorporating natural objects. Sasajima Kihei (b 1906): landscapes and Buddhist deities in sinewy, calligraphic black and white, often heavily embossed. Saitō Kiyoshi (b 1907): snowy landscapes of his native Aizu, studies of Buddhist sculpture and of Kyōto's temples and gardens evoked in rich earth tones. Ono Tadashige (b 1909): mostly urban landscapes in deeply dyed colors. Mizufune Rokushū (b 1912): designs inspired by worn and weathered objects, tinged with Buddhist sensibility. Hagiwara Hideo (b 1913): strong abstract designs and imaginative techniques. Sekino Jun'ichirō (b

Modern prints —— Munakata Shikō

A print from the *Nyonin Kanzeon,* a series of 12 representations of the bodhisattva Kannon as a voluptuous woman. At the right appear lines from "Nyonin bosatsu," the poem by Okamoto Kanoko that inspired the series. Woodblock print. 29.5 × 45.0 cm. Munakata Print Gallery, Kanagawa Prefecture.

1914): a contemporary look at subject matter in the *ukiyo-e* tradition. Yoshida Masaji (1917–71): arrangements of parallel lines, black on white or pale rose. Kitaoka Fumio (b 1918): technical assurance in far-ranging styles and subjects. Kinoshita Tomio (b 1923): masks and faces in jagged, close lines of high tension. Maki Haku (b 1924): inventive calligraphic variations. Iwami Reika (b 1927): textures of driftwood in abstract arrangements.

While the woodblock predominated, it was by no means the only medium in use. Oda Kazuma (1882–1956) pioneered in color lithography and demonstrated complete mastery of that technique. Hasegawa Kiyoshi (1891–1980), Hamaguchi Yōzō (b 1909), and Komai Tetsurō (1920–76) were etchers of distinction. Mori Yoshitoshi (b 1898) turned the traditional stencil-dyeing technique into a medium of fine art with his vigorous, bold prints; Watanabe Sadao (b 1913) continued on that path using Christian themes.

By the close of the 1950s Japanese prints and Japanese artists had won international prizes, were in the collections of major museums abroad, and finally achieved recognition at home. They had made the print mediums respectable for later artists.

Oliver STATLER

Prints of the 1960s and 1970s —— Those Japanese printmakers who were born after 1930 and reached their prime in the 1960s and 1970s experimented with print techniques that were currently being employed by their Western counterparts, and largely neglected the traditional Japanese favorite, the woodblock print. Of particular interest to those Japanese artists has been the silkscreen. Since the mid-1970s, Japanese silkscreens have been gaining the attention of Western artists eager to learn from the Japanese who have acquired great technical skill in this medium. Aiō (known abroad as Ay-O; b 1931), with the assistance of printer Okabe Tokuzō, creates rainbow color silkscreens. His masterpiece *Rainbow Hokusai* (1970) required 33 different color screens for its execution. Funai Yutaka (b 1932), Yayanagi Tsuyoshi (b 1933), YOKOO TADANORI (b 1936), Funasaka Yoshisuke (b 1939), Takeda Hideo (b 1948), and Oda Mayumi (b 1941) are only a few of the dozens of exceptional contemporary silkscreen print artists, each with his or her own individual vision. Oda's silkscreen prints of goddesses, for example, recreate Japanese deities from a feminist point of view. Noda Tetsuya (b 1940) and Yoshida Katsurō (b 1943) have been particularly successful in combining silkscreen with photography. Noda further combines his silkscreens with woodblock printing and uses the finest handmade Japanese papers.

Lithography is a second imported print medium in which the Japanese now excel. Many young Japanese artists have been impressed by the potential of color lithography. Under the auspices of the Rockefeller Foundation and the Japan Society of New York, the American artist Arthur Flory established a lithography workshop in Tōkyō from July 1960 to July 1961, where he introduced lithography to many of Japan's professional artists. Although not students of Flory, Yoshihara Hideo (b 1931), Arakawa Shūsaku (b 1936), and Ida Shōichi (b 1940) have become leaders of lithography today. Ara-

kawa, who has lived in New York since 1962, often combines lithography with silkscreen and embossing; he executes prints as a practical way to popularize the idea expressed in his philosophical work *Mechanism of Meaning* (1963).

Etching is a third medium which has come into prominence in Japan. Ikeda Masuo (b 1934) is the prolific etcher laureate, internationally acclaimed, whose best work has been created on metal plates with color roulette, drypoint, etching, engraving, or mezzotint. Other etchers of note include Shirai Akiko (b 1935), Kimura Kōsuke (b 1936), Tanaka Ryōhei (b 1933), and Miyashita Tokio (b 1930).

Matsubara Naoko (b 1937) continues Munakata Shikō's passion for the woodblock in a style that reveals its source in the master. She finds particular strength in nature's creations—trees, for example, and human hands. Kidokoro Shō's (b 1934) color woodblock prints are also a worthy return to the more traditional approach to printmaking.

Mary W. BASKETT

—— Frances Blakemore, *Who's Who in Modern Japanese Prints* (1975). Fujikake Shizuya, *Japanese Woodblock Prints,* vol 10 of *Tourist Library* (Japan Travel Bureau, 1957). Kawakita Michiaki, *Gendai hanga II,* vol 8 of *Nihon hanga bijutsu zenshū* (Kōdansha, 1960). James A. Michener, *The Modern Japanese Print, An Appreciation* (1962). Gaston Petit, *Forty-four Modern Japanese Print Artists* (1973). Oliver Statler, *Modern Japanese Prints: An Art Reborn* (1956).

Mogamigawa

River in central and northern Yamagata Prefecture, northern Honshū, originating in the mountain Azumasan on the border between Yamagata and Fukushima prefectures and flowing north through the Yonezawa and Yamagata basins; thereafter it changes course to flow northwest through the Shinjō Basin and Shōnai Plain and enters the Sea of Japan at the city of Sakata. It is known for its swift currents. It was used for transportation until railway lines were opened. Numerous electric power plants are located along the river. The water is used for irrigation, industry, and drinking. The volume of water is abundant because of melting snow. Length: 229 km (142 mi); area of drainage basin: 7,040 sq km (2,717 sq mi).

Mogami Tokunai (1755–1836)

Explorer of Hokkaidō, Sakhalin, and the Kuril Islands during the late 18th and early 19th centuries. Born in Dewa (now Yamagata Prefecture) into a peasant family, he joined a group of fishermen and visited EZO (now Hokkaidō), where he conceived a deep concern for the yet uncharted northern frontier which was then beginning to feel the effects of Russian approaches. In 1781 he went to Edo, became a servant in the household of a minor shogunal official, and studied surveying and navigation under the renowned mathematician HONDA TOSHIAKI. In 1785 he took Honda's place on a shogunal expedition to Ezo. The following year, he surveyed southern Sakhalin and the southern Kurils, making the earliest recorded visits by a Japanese to Etorofu (Iturup) and Uruppu (Urup) Islands. An encounter with a Russian on Etorofu led Mogami to anticipate a number of "northern activists" of the 1790s (HAYASHI SHIHEI, Honda Toshiaki) by calling attention to Ezo's importance for national defense. During the next two decades, he conducted several surveys of Sakhalin and the Kuril Islands, sharing with MAMIYA RINZŌ the reputation of a great solitary explorer of northern latitudes. An astute observer of the AINU and the Russians (he learned both their languages), Mogami illuminated through several works the ethnography as well as the geography of insular northeast Asia.

—— Mogami Tokunai, *Ezo zōshi,* ed Yoshida Tsunekichi (1965).

John J. STEPHAN

Mogi Keizaburō (1899–)

Businessman. Born Iida Katsuji in Chiba Prefecture. Graduate of Tōkyō University of Commerce (now Hitotsubashi University). He joined Noda Shōyu (presently KIKKŌMAN SHŌYU CO, LTD), and was adopted by the Mogi family, the owners of the company, because of his excellent performance in labor relations. He ascended to the company's presidency in 1962 and chairmanship in 1974. He revolutionized the production processes and management set-ups of soy sauce manufacturing, one of the most traditional of all Japanese industries. Active in overseas expansion, Mogi started soy sauce production in the United States in 1973.

YAMADA *Makiko*

Mōka

City in southeastern Tochigi Prefecture, central Honshū, on the river Kinugawa. As shogunate territory during the Edo period (1600–1868), it was the location of an intendant's office (*daikansho*). Known early for its production of Mōka cotton cloth, it later developed as a farming and commercial city. More recently, the establishment of several industries, notably, machinery and metal goods, and the construction of a housing complex have led to a rise in the population. Farm produce includes rice and vegetables. Pop: 52,764.

mokkan

(wooden tablets). Thin, irregular strips of wood used for writing, mainly during the 7th and 8th centuries. They were probably adopted from China, where bamboo and wood strips had been in use since before the Han dynasty (206 BC–AD 220). The Chinese examples, however, were cut into uniform lengths of 30 or 45 centimeters (12 or 18 in), and several of them had to be tied together for a message of any length. In Japan the length of the message, which was written on both sides of the *mokkan*, generally determined the size, which averaged 10–25 centimeters (4–10 in) long and 2–3 centimeters (0.8–1.2 in) wide.

It is only since 1961 that *mokkan* have been excavated in quantity. The first such excavations were at the Heijō Palace near the present-day city of Nara (see HEIJŌKYŌ). As of the early 1980s 32,000 tablets were known from some 40 different sites, including the palaces at HEIANKYŌ, ASUKA KIYOMIHARA NO MIYA, NANIWAKYŌ, FUJIWARAKYŌ, and NAGAOKAKYŌ, as well as the military outposts of DAZAIFU and TAGAJŌ, regional administrative centers, post stations (see EKISEI), and temples established by both the state and influential lineages (UJI). The oldest *mokkan* date from the mid-7th century, although most date from the late 7th through the 8th centuries. *Mokkan* have also been excavated from medieval sites such as Ichijōdani, the stronghold of the ASAKURA FAMILY, influential in northwestern Japan during the 15th century.

Mokkan were used as labels, to issue directives, for record keeping, for practicing calligraphy or jotting notes; some were specifically used as talismans or scroll title tags. Those used as directives mainly deal with the movement of goods and people within the palace precincts, such as requests for certain commodities, summonses, permits to enter the palace compound, and so forth. Records generally deal with the receipt and disbursement of goods and the work performance of government officials. Medical prescriptions and lists of Chinese characters have also been found.

Mokkan used to label tax goods sent in from the provinces (SO, YŌ, AND CHŌ) are of particular interest for information on the tax system of the time. They tell specifically what products besides rice were accepted for tribute, what products were substituted for corvée labor, and so forth. It is important to note, however, that labels written before the promulgation of the TAIHŌ CODE (701) do not record *chō* and *yō* taxes, indicating that these were post-Taihō innovations. Again, the format and style of writing on the salt-tax labels from Wakasa Province (now part of Fukui Prefecture) show that the collection of tax goods took place at the district (*gun*) level rather than at the provincial (*kuni*) level (see KOKUGUN SYSTEM).

📖 ——Nara Kokuritsu Bunkazai Kenkyūjo, ed, *Nara kokuritsu bunkazai kenkyūjo shiryō*, vols 5 (1969), 8 (1975), 12 (1978), 17 (1980), 18 (1980).　　　　　　　　　KANŌ Hisashi

Mokkei (fl 13th century)

(Ch: Muqi or Mu-ch'i). A 13th-century Chinese Zen monk-painter. A native of Sichuan (Szechwan) Province in western China, he was a man of letters who became a Zen monk in middle age, under the master Wuzhun Shifan (Wu-Chun Shih-fan; d 1249), and established the temple Liutongsi (Liu-t'ung ssu) on the outskirts of Hangzhou (Hangchow) in Zhejiang (Chekiang) Province. During his long stay there, he became associated with many eminent monks. Accomplished in monochrome ink paintings of landscapes, figures, birds and flowers, and animals, he achieved considerable fame among his Chinese contemporaries. With the rise of literati painting (Ch: wenrenhua or wen-jen-hua; J: BUNJINGA) in 14th-century China, his reputation declined. His works were treasured in Japan, however, and only there have any of his paintings survived. His ability to capture the atmosphere of a particular moment and to combine telling detail with a sense of space has profoundly influenced Japanese INK PAINTING since the 14th century.

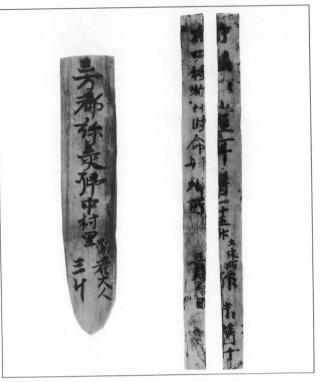

Mokkan

Two *mokkan* excavated from the Heijō Palace site. Left: A salt-tax label from Wakasa Province. 201 × 41 × 4 mm. Right: Front and back views of a *mokkan* recording the requisition of foodstuffs for the imperial kitchen. 259 × 19 × 4 mm. 8th century. Nara National Research Institute of Cultural Properties.

Mokuami (1816–1893)

Full name, Kawatake Mokuami. Also called Kawatake Shinshichi II. A KABUKI dramatist of Edo (now Tōkyō) whose career spanned over half a century from the late Edo to the early Meiji periods.

Noted for his *sewa-mono* (domestic plays), which pictured the lives of the ordinary townspeople of the Edo period (1600–1868), he first established his reputation as the creator of *shiranami-mono* (plays depicting the activities of thieves). They depicted thieves, murderers, swindlers, and similar underworld figures as main characters and were regarded at the time as a daring departure from the typical *sewa-mono* whose characters were usually ordinary commoners. *Tsutamomiji Utsunoya Tōge* (1856, Bun'ya's Murder), *Sannin Kichiza kuruwa no hatsugai* (1860, Three Men Called Kichisa—written for the actor, Ichikawa Kodanji IV (1812–66)—and *Aotozōshi hana no nishiki-e* (1862, Benten, the Thief)—composed expressly for the young Onoe Kikugorō V (1844–1903), a leading performer of the Meiji period (1868–1912)—are ranked among the finest works in this category.

Soon after the Meiji Restoration (1868), Mokuami began writing *katsureki-mono* ("living history" plays), which stressed factual accuracy, literary excellence, and moral teachings. These modified versions of the traditional *jidai-mono* (historical plays) were presented largely at the insistence of Ichikawa Danjūrō IX (1838–1903), the most influential actor of this era. The audience, however, consistently rejected these efforts to change the familiar style and content of the *jidai-mono*, despite the latter's glaring factual errors and extravagant embellishments. *Takatoki* (1884, Takatoki and the Goblins), originally part of a longer three-act play, is a rare example of a *katsureki-mono*, which is still performed today.

In the early Meiji period, the influx of Western ideas, technology, and material culture led to a profound transformation of Japanese society, described by Mokuami in *zangiri-mono* ("cropped hair" plays). Recasting the setting of the *sewa-mono* in the modern period, he presented kabuki actors in Western clothes with their hair in *zangiri*, or cropped, style—instead of the usual topknot and middle part. Those who adopted the *zangiri* haircut were openly declaring their rejection of an outmoded past.

The *zangiri-mono* offered countless examples of Western exoticisms, including military uniforms, European dresses, newspapers, telegraphs, steamboats, trains, hot air balloons, cameras, pocket watches, and gaslights. At the same time, they often presented topical themes, such as the plight of the ex-*samurai*, compulsory education, military conscription, and the schoolgirl—then, a novel phenomenon. However, as a rule, *zangiri-mono* failed to provide more than a superficial view of early Meiji society; the basic beliefs and attitudes expressed by the characters often merely echoed those of the bygone Edo period.

Mokuami also wrote a number of *matsubame-mono,* adaptations of well-known plays from the NŌ theater, long identified as the exclusive entertainment of the samurai class. The kabuki versions of *Tsuchigumo* (1881, Ground Spider), *Ibaraki* (1883, Demon Ibaraki), and the like are frequently included in the current kabuki program.

Mokuami has long been recognized for his powerful lyrical passages recited by chanters to *shamisen* accompaniment, an effective device for supporting the vital action on the stage or for intensifying the mood of the dramatic situation. His *sewa-mono* are particularly popular for their brilliant display of this masterful technique.

In November 1881, he announced his official retirement as an active kabuki playwright by relinquishing his title of Kawatake Shinshichi to one of his disciples and assuming the familiar name of Kawatake Mokuami. Nevertheless, he continued to write until his death in 1893.

Mokuami wrote some 360 plays during his lifetime, a singular achievement for any dramatist. Nearly half of the plays in the present kabuki repertory are his. See also ICHIKAWA DANJŪRŌ; ONOE KIKUGORŌ.

📖 ——S. Aubrey and Giovanna M. Halford, *The Kabuki Handbook* (1956), contains summaries of plays by Mokuami. Kawatake Mokuami, *Kosode Soga azami no ironui* (1859), tr Frank T. Motofuji as *The Love of Izayoi and Seishin* (1966). Kawatake Shigetoshi, *Kawatake Mokuami* (1940). Donald Keene, *World Within Walls: Japanese Literature of the Pre-Modern Era 1600–1867* (1976).

Ted T. TAKAYA

Mokuan Reien (?–ca 1345)

Painter-monk; the first Japanese practitioner of INK PAINTING (*suibokuga*) whose full name is known. He was a Zen monk active in the Kamakura region before he went to China as a pilgrim. The little biographical information that is known comes from one of his contemporaries who, after returning to Japan from his own trip to China, told it to the scholar-monk GIDŌ SHŪSHIN (1325–88).

The diary of Gidō, *Kūge nichiyō kufūshū,* reports that Mokuan's earlier name was Zeichi and that he was a disciple of Kenzan Sūki (1286?–1323). Like many other Japanese monks, Mokuan was probably in Yuan (Yüan) dynasty (1279–1368) China as early as 1329 on a pilgrimage to such monasteries as Baoningsi (Pao-ning-ssu) at Jinling (Chin-ling; now Nanjing), Jincisi (Chin-tz'u-ssu) at Hanzhou (Han-chou), and Benjuesi (Pen-chüeh-ssu) in Jiaxing (Chia-hsing). Mokuan remained in China well over 10 years, attaining a high clerical position. At Benjuesi under the abbacy of Liaoan Qingyu (Liao-an Ch'ing-yü; 1283–1363), Mokuan was the Tripitaka-keeper. Around 1341–42, the compilation and publication of the *Collected Sayings* (J: *Goroku*) of Gulin Qingmou (Ku-lin Ch'ing-mou; d 1329), the teacher of Liaoan, was undertaken by his Chinese and Japanese disciples. Mokuan helped to raise money for this project by making and selling straw sandals. In the autumn of 1344, while waiting for a ship to take him back to Japan, Mokuan visited the Chengtiansi (Ch'eng-t'ien-ssu) monastery of Pingjiang (P'ing-chiang) in Suzhou (Su-chou), presumably meeting with its learned abbot, Nanchu Shishuo (Nan-ch'u Shih-shuo). Mokuan never returned to Japan, however, for he is reported to have died shortly after his Suzhou sojourn.

That he had intended to return to Japan is recorded by the erudite monk Chushi Fanqi (Ch'u-shih Fan-ch'i; 1296–1370) in his *Collected Sayings,* which mentions Mokuan as a painter and records a farewell poem Chushi gave him. Chushi's *Collected Sayings* is the sole Chinese account of Mokuan.

Gidō's diary mentions that during Mokuan's stay in China, he visited the Liutongsi (Liu-t'ung-ssu) temple on West Lake, a temple adjacent to the temple where the Chinese painter-monk Muqi (Much'i; J: MOKKEI; fl ca 13th century) had once resided. The visit undoubtedly gave rise to a legend that Mokuan was the "reincarnation of Muqi." This legend later appeared in various other sources, including the painting manual *Kundaikan sō chōki,* which confused Mokuan with an earlier Chinese painter named Moan (Mo-an). However, HASEGAWA TŌHAKU (1539–1610) is reported in the *Tō-*

haku gasetsu (Discourse on Painting by Tōhaku) to have rightly recognized Mokuan as Japanese. The confusion about Mokuan's nationality was probably also a result of the fact that Mokuan's paintings closely resembled contemporary Chinese paintings, especially those traditionally attributed to Muqi.

Six works that are generally considered to be by Mokuan are extant today. These include the *White-Robed Kannon* in ink on silk in the Agata Collection; the paintings of the wandering monk Hotei (Ch: Budai or Pu-tai) in the Atami, Sumitomo, and Masaki collections, respectively; and the *Four Sleepers* in the Maeda Ikutokukai Foundation. Each of these contains either Mokuan's seals or inscriptions by contemporary Chinese monks. The sixth painting, another *White-Robed Kannon* in ink on silk, is in the Freer Gallery of Art, Washington, DC. This painting carries an inscription by the monk Liaoan Qingyu, and although it does not bear the seals of Mokuan, the style is unmistakably his.

📖 ——Tanaka Ichimatsu, *Kaō, Mokuan, Minchō,* vol 5 of *Suiboku bijutsu taikei* (Kōdansha, 1974).   Yoshiaki SHIMIZU

Mokubei → Aoki Mokubei

Mokujiki

(literally, "one who eats wood"). A discipline of extreme asceticism, probably originating in Taoist ideas of sagehood, that was practiced by some Buddhist monks in Japan. The term also refers to the monks themselves, who subsisted on a diet of uncooked wild fruits and vegetables. In addition, it was used as a part of the names of these monks, two of whom are especially famous.

Mokujiki Ōgo (1536–1608). Monk of the SHINGON SECT. He was born into a warrior family in Ōmi Province (now Shiga Prefecture), but became a priest at Mt. Kōya (Kōyasan), the center of the Shingon sect, in 1573. When the warlord TOYOTOMI HIDEYOSHI was about to attack Mt. Kōya in 1585, Ōgo persuaded Hideyoshi not to destroy the temples. Later, under Hideyoshi's patronage, he built or restored many temples on Mt. Kōya and elsewhere. After the Toyotomi forces were defeated in the Battle of SEKIGAHARA in 1600, he retired to a small temple on Ōmi and studied *renga* (linked verse) under SATOMURA JŌHA. Ōgo's collection of rules for *renga* composition, entitled *Mugonshō,* is a classic in this field.

Mokujiki Gogyō (1718–1810). Monk of the Shingon sect. Also known as Mokujiki Myōman. Born in a peasant family in Kai Province (now Yamanashi Prefecture), he became a monk in 1739 and took the vows of a *mokujiki* in 1762. From the time he was 55 until he was 90 he traveled throughout Japan, carving more than 1,000 Buddhist figures, which he gave to local temples or families. His sculptures are neither stylistically refined nor technically skilled but are unaffectedly original in their humor, warmth, and piety.

moles

(*mogura*). In Japanese, *mogura* is the general name for animals of the family Talpidae, order Insectivora; five species inhabit Honshū, Shikoku, and Kyūshū. Three of these are members of the subfamily Talpinae, the typical moles of the Old World. The Azuma mogura (Mogera wogura) has a body length of 12 centimeters (4.7 in), weighs about 70 grams (2.5 oz), and inhabits plains and mountainous areas of Honshū northward from the Kantō Plain; the Kōbe *mogura* (M. kobeae) has a body length of about 16 centimeters (6.3 in), weighs 110 grams (3.9 oz), and is found south of the Kantō Plain. The *mizuramogura* (Euroscaptor mizura), with a body length of about 8 centimeters (3.1 in) and a weight of about 35 grams (1.2 oz), is a relict species that inhabits subalpine and alpine zones. All three species are extremely common within their own habitat areas and create conspicuous mole hills.

The shrew moles *himizu* (Urotrichus talpoides) and *himehimizu* (Dymecodon pilirostris), both of the subfamily Uropsilinae, are native to Japan but closely resemble the shrew moles (genus Neurotrichus) of the Pacific coast of North America. Both species inhabit wooded districts but in distinct vertical distribution, with *himizu* below, and *himehimizu* above, elevations of 1,600 meters (5,200 ft). Both species dig tunnels under layers of fallen leaves but do not make mole hills. Japanese moles live on earthworms, centipedes, and other soil-dwelling animals. They bear annual litters of three to five young in spring through summer.

According to a Japanese legend the mole, dazzled by the glaring sun, contemplated shooting it down with a bow and arrow but was punished and burrowed under the ground. The folk belief that moles die when exposed to the sun persists to this day.

IMAIZUMI Yoshiharu and SANEYOSHI Tatsuo

mollusks → shellfish

Mombetsu

City in northeastern Hokkaidō, on the Sea of Okhotsk. Mombetsu was developed by the Matsumae domain in the 1680s. A base for fishing in the northern seas, with the principal catch being codfish, saury, crab, and scallops. Seafood processing is the main occupation. It also has sugar beet and dairy farming. Pop: 33,863.

Mombushō → Ministry of Education

momijigari

The traditional pastime of viewing autumn foliage. Like cherry-blossom viewing (HANAMI) in the spring, it was popular among the court aristocracy of the Heian period (794–1185). The nobles went boating on ponds in the gardens around their mansions, playing music and composing poetry while viewing the fall colors, or went on excursions into the mountains to gather brightly colored leaves. From the 12th to the 16th centuries the Tatsutagawa area near Nara, and the OGURAYAMA and ARASHIYAMA areas near Kyōto, famed for their autumn leaves, were described in numerous poems and paintings. In the Edo period (1600–1868), the custom spread among the common people. With the improvement of public transportation after the Meiji period (1868–1912), people began to visit distant places noted for their beautiful foliage, as well as nearby places, and the tradition continues to be popular today.

Mommu, Emperor (683–707)

The 42nd sovereign (tennō) in the traditional count (which includes several nonhistorical emperors); reigned 697–707. His father, Prince Kusakabe, was the eldest son of Emperor TEMMU; his mother, who succeeded him as Empress Gemmei (661–722; r 707–715), was the fourth daughter of Emperor TENJI. Mommu ascended the throne on the abdication of his grandmother Empress JITŌ. He married FUJI-WARA NO FUHITO's daughter Kyūshi, who, although she was not granted the title of empress (KŌGŌ), enjoyed considerable prestige because of the great political influence of her father. Indeed, Mommu acquiesced in all of Fuhito's policies, most notably the enactment of the TAIHŌ CODE in 702.   *KITAMURA Bunji*

Momotarō

(Peach Boy). Popular folktale recounting the adventures of the boy Momotarō. Born from a peach found by an elderly woman washing clothes on a riverbank, Momotarō is adopted by the woman and her husband. Maturing quickly, he goes off with a dog, a pheasant, and a monkey to conquer Ogre Island and returns home with treasures for his foster parents. The tale exists in many versions; in its present form it became widely popular late in the Edo period (1600–1868) through the genre of literature known as KUSAZŌSHI.

Similar tales of how a child of unusual birth performs remarkable deeds against considerable odds are found throughout Japan. These tales, including the tale of Kaguyahime (see TAKETORI MONO-GATARI), Oyayubitarō (The Boy as Small as a Thumb), and ISSUM-BŌSHI (One-Inch Boy), fall into the folktale genre *chiisako monogatari* (tales of a tiny child). *Momotarō* also falls into the category *hyōchakutan* (tales of being washed ashore), in which a child endowed with supernatural powers by gods beyond the sea or far upstream comes to confer good fortune on the human world; this genre of folktale is commonly found among people living close to the water.   *SUCHI Tokuhei*

Momoyama period → Azuchi-Momoyama period

mon → crests

monasticism

Japanese monasticism has been predominantly Buddhist. Shintō, though influenced by Buddhism and closely intertwined with it through much of Japanese history, developed neither regulated cenobitic communities nor a strong eremitic tradition. Taoist mon-

asteries and hermitages existed in China, and Taoist ideas percolated into Japan, but there were no institutional expressions of Taoist monastic life. Iberian missionaries were active in 16th-century Japan. They built colleges and seminaries to train missionary priests. The European monastic orders were not, however, strongly represented in the Christian mission effort which was spearheaded by the Society of Jesus. It is only since the reopening of Japan to Western Christian influence in the 19th century that a Trappist monastery and several Trappist convents have been established.

The dominant expression of monastic life in Japan has therefore been the Buddhist cenobitic tradition in the form of the religious community, or Saṃgha (J: Sōgya), living in monasteries and nunneries (J: tera) or hermitages (J: in or an), and operating under the rules of the Vinaya, supplemented by sectarian and secular regulations. Japan has produced plenty of mountain ascetics and hermits but throughout earlier Japanese history the political authorities favored stable, closely regulated community organizations under state sponsorship and control. From the moment of its introduction to Japan the Buddhist Saṃgha was closely integrated with the Japanese state and the ruling elite, generously patronized as a source of spiritual welfare and protection for its patrons and the state, and tightly regulated. And, as in other parts of the world, Japanese monasteries have served as sources of learning and culture and have been major landholders and centers of urban development and commercial activity.

When Buddhism was introduced into Japan in the 6th century, as in other Asian countries where the religion had already taken root, the monastic order, or Saṃgha, was venerated together with the Buddha and the Dharma (J: Hō), the Buddha's teachings, as one of the "Three Treasures" of Buddhism.

Among the first patrons of Buddhism in Japan were members of the powerful SOGA FAMILY led by SOGA NO UMAKO, his niece Empress SUIKO (554–628), and her regent, Prince SHŌTOKU (574–622). The earliest record of enrollment of Japanese in the Saṃgha is to be found in the 8th-century chronicle, the NIHON SHOKI, where it is recorded that in 584 Soga no Umako had three young women enroll as nuns under the direction of a former Buddhist monk from Korea. The Nihon shoki gives the impression of a surge of monastic foundation in the late 6th and early 7th centuries under the patronage of the Soga family and Prince Shōtoku. In 593 relics of the Buddha were placed in the foundation stone of the pagoda of the monastery Hōkōji built by Umako. The monastery was completed in 596 and two Korean monks were installed to head it. In 606 a 16-foot (52-meter) high copper image of the Buddha was set in the main hall. Empress Suiko, in 594, instructed Prince Shōtoku and the clan chieftains to promote the prosperity of the Three Treasures. The chieftains, Omi and Muraji, competed with one another in erecting Buddhist shrines for the blessing of their sovereign and parents. These were known as tera, temples or monasteries. Prince Shōtoku, for his part, is credited with the foundation of SHITENNŌJI (593), Ikarugadera (HŌRYŪJI, 607), and other monastic complexes, with the writing of commentaries on the Lotus Sutra and other texts, and with the promotion and protection of the Three Treasures in his Seventeen-Article Constitution.

The Saṃgha grew rapidly. By 623 there were in Japan 46 monasteries, 816 monks, and 569 nuns. Archaeological evidence indicates that by the end of the 7th century there were several hundred monastic foundations in Japan. Some of these held large communities. An entry in the Nihon shoki for the autumn of 690 states: "On this day alms of silk cloth, silk thread, cotton, and cotton cloth were bestowed on 3,363 monks of seven monasteries who had completed the summer retreat." Moreover, by the end of the century, Buddhist communities were being established in more remote parts of Japan, sometimes by forcibly settling groups of Korean immigrants: "The monks, nuns, and lay people who immigrated from Paekche, in total 23 men and women, were all settled in the province of Musashi" (Nihon shoki, 684).

The proliferating Buddhist monastic institution naturally presented the ruling authorities with problems of regulation and control. Disciplinary problems were evident even in Prince Shōtoku's day. In 623, for instance, a Buddhist monk killed his grandfather with an axe. Empress Suiko ordered the punishment of the offender and went on to declare: "When those who have chosen the Buddhist Way break their Law how can lay people be admonished? From this time on, Registrars—sōjō and sōzu—shall be appointed and charged with the supervision of monks and nuns." In establishing the first administrative framework for the new monastic order in Japan it was natural that Suiko and Prince Shōtoku should look to continental examples. The *sōjō* and *sōzu* were modeled on secular offices used to regulate the Saṃgha in Southern China and Paekche (J: Kudara).

Secular control over monastic life and the alignment of monasteries with the state bureaucracy were more thoroughly enforced by the promulgation of "Regulations for Monks and Nuns" (Sōniryō) within the Taihō and Yōrō *ritsuryō* codes of the early 8th century. Based on Tang (T'ang) Chinese models, these regulations reinforced the ecclesiastical law, or Vinaya, and defined the place of the burgeoning monastic institution and its inhabitants in ancient Japanese society. Some articles in the Sōniryō—such as those punishing improper registration, drinking liquor, eating proscribed foods, or consorting with members of the opposite sex—were intended to stiffen traditional Buddhist monastic practice. Other items—including those forbidding monks and nuns to build private retreats, plead civil suits in clerical dress, lend their names to lay people to avoid taxes, accumulate private fortunes, engage in fortune telling and proselytizing among the masses—clearly deal with local problems or were aimed at asserting state control over the Saṃgha and excluding monks and nuns from political meddling.

The inclusion of the Sōniryō within the *ritsuryō* administrative codes was an explicit assertion of the fact that the Japanese Saṃgha, like its counterparts in Korea and China, was not to be permitted autonomy under its own rule. The doctrinal studies, sutra readings, and prayer ceremonies conducted by monks and nuns were not directed at the succour or salvation of the mass of population but at the welfare and protection of elite patrons and the secular state. Those sutras were favored which, like the Lotus Sutra, the Sutra of the Golden Light or the *Vimalakīrti-nirdeśa-sūtra*, not only held out the promise of salvation but offered magical protection to the state and moral guidance and example for the ruler and his ministers. Monks and nuns were viewed not as independent spiritual agents but as clerical adjuncts of the state bureaucracy. The Buddhist monastic establishment was placed under the supervision of the Ministry of Civil Affairs (Jibushō) by whom the registrar general of monks (sōgō) was appointed. Those wishing to enter the religious life had to secure official permission, take a state-sponsored examination, and undergo the official ordination procedures at a recognized ordination platform. Private ordination was forbidden. This was partly to prevent laymen securing tax exemption by claiming monk's status but it was also aimed at maintaining secular control over the monastic order.

Government control over tonsuring (tokudo) and ordination (jukai) of monks and nuns gave the secular authorities the means, nominally at least, to regulate the growth and behavior of the Saṃgha. State control was undercut, however, by the lavish official patronage of Buddhism. By building great monasteries and conducting elaborate prayer ceremonies at every natural disaster, imperial sickness and death, or auspicious occasion, the rulers found it necessary to ordain monks and nuns en masse, with a consequent dilution of standards. Nor were the secular officials able to eliminate private ordinations and the activities of unordained priests and nuns. These unofficial monks (shidosō) lived a semisecular life in the countryside, healing the sick, preaching the rewards of heaven and the pains of hell, and practicing asceticism and divination. Their world found expression in an early collection of Buddhist tales and fables, the NIHON RYŌIKI compiled by Keikai, a married priest attached to Yakushiji in Nara.

Most officially registered monks conformed to official expectations and devoted their energies to abstruse Buddhist textual studies and prayer ceremonies. A few, however, like the monk GYŌGI (668–749) were dissatisfied with the remoteness, pomp, and ease of life in the official monasteries and tried to take the message of Buddhist salvation to the common people. Gyōgi organized the building of preaching halls, bridges, and irrigation ditches in villages. He quickly became a popular cult hero. At first his irregular practice was proscribed as infringing the Sōniryō. He was later pardoned and his support sought in securing mass donations for the building of the great Buddha image for TŌDAIJI. Other monks who were dissatisfied with the ceremonious atmosphere of the official monasteries in the capital of Heijōkyō (now Nara) built mountain retreats where they devoted themselves to private study and contemplation.

The promulgation of the Sōniryō and the establishment of an ordination platform at Tōdaiji and later at TŌSHŌDAIJI by the Chinese monk GANJIN, who came to Japan in 754 to establish the Vinaya teaching (see RITSU SECT), provided a solid foundation for the proper conduct of the officially regulated Buddhist monastic life. In spite of the efforts at regulation, however, abuses were again becoming evident by the late 8th century. The Saṃgha had been greatly expanded and enriched by Emperor SHŌMU (701–756), an ardent Buddhist. Shōmu had ordered the building in every province of a monastery and nunnery in which prayers would constantly be offered for the welfare of the country and its ruler. The hub of this network, and a symbol of imperial authority, was the colossal bronze and gilt statue of the Vairocana Buddha in Tōdaiji. He had also sponsored the building of several large monasteries in the capital and ordered the tonsuring of thousands of monks and nuns. The wave of temple building provided a massive stimulus to architecture, sculpture, painting, and the importation of Chinese culture.

The cost was high, however. Shōmu exhausted the state treasury by his grandiose temple and statue building and in declaring himself a "slave of the Three Treasures" he came closer than any Japanese ruler before or since to setting the Saṃgha above the state. Monasteries and monks attained new heights of influence in the society of Heijō. Using the privileges and tax exemptions permitted them under the *ritsuryō* codes, monasteries amassed tax-free lands, depriving the state of much needed income and land for redistribution. Swelling monastic populations further deprived the court of labor, tax yield, and military service. Wealth and power fed arrogance on the part of monks and monasteries. Vinaya regulations were flouted. Some monks engaged in usury. Others began to vie with nobles for political power within the court. The HOSSŌ SECT monk Gembō (d 746) was ousted from the capital in 745 and exiled to Kyūshū by FUJIWARA NO NAKAMARO for his support of an attempted coup by the Tachibana and other anti-Fujiwara nobles. A more serious case of ecclesiastical involvement in politics was provided by DŌKYŌ (d 772), who secured considerable political power and whom an infatuated empress wished to set on the imperial throne.

Emperor KAMMU's decision in 784 to move the capital from Heijō was dictated, in part at least, by his desire to remove the court and government from clerical influence and to allow himself leeway in which to institute monastic reform as well as overhaul of the *ritsuryō* administrative and land systems. The great monasteries of Heijō were expressly forbidden to follow the court to the new capital, Heiankyō (now Kyōto), where provision was made for the building of only two monasteries well to the south of the Imperial Palace. As part of his reform effort Kammu sought to reemphasize the Sōniryō, to reassert secular scrutiny over monastic administration, and to check monastic acquisition of public lands. He introduced changes in ordination procedures to encourage selection of monks on the basis of their understanding of Buddhist doctrine rather than for their skill in ceremonial functions. Limits were again placed on the number of monks and nuns that could be ordained each year and the ordination examinations were recast to place more emphasis on scholarly understanding of sutras and less on rote memorization of selected passages.

Kammu is sometimes described as a Confucian emperor who had little sympathy for Buddhism. His aim, however, was reform of the Saṃgha, not its destruction. That he was not hostile to Buddhism is evident from his patronage of the young monks SAICHŌ and KŪKAI, both of whom introduced fresh currents of Chinese Buddhism into Japan. In addition to the new TENDAI SECT and SHINGON SECT doctrines and practices which they brought back from China, Saichō and Kūkai were both advocates of strict monastic discipline and service to the nation. In his "Regulations for the Two Students Annually Appointed by the Court" Saichō insisted that Tendai novices on Mt. Hiei (HIEIZAN) should support themselves, remain on the mountain for 12 years of intense study and meditation, and afterwards serve the nation according to their abilities as religious leaders, teachers, or functionaries. ENRYAKUJI, the monastic center of Tendai Buddhism, was located outside the capital. The monastery was designated a center for the protection of the nation (chingo kokka) and, shortly after Saichō's death, was given the right to conduct ordinations. It grew rapidly to become the major religious establishment in Japan and a source of learning and culture.

In appealing to Emperor Saga to be allowed to build a Shingon monastery on Mt. Kōya (KŌYASAN), Kūkai argued that it would be for the sake of the nation as well as all religious-minded individuals: "I should like to clear the wilderness in order to build a monastery there for the practice of meditation, for the benefit of the nation and of those who desire to discipline themselves." In addition to esoteric and exoteric observances Kūkai, like Saichō, stressed monastic discipline: "If we wish to walk in the Way of Buddha, unless we observe the precepts, we cannot reach the goal. Never violate either Exoteric or Esoteric Buddhist precepts; firmly observe them and maintain yourselves clean and pure." Saichō himself had shown interest in

Kūkai's Shingon teachings. After Saichō's death esoteric practices rapidly infiltrated Enryakuji and other Tendai centers. Moreover, the strong aesthetic emphasis in Shingon won great favor among members of the imperial court. The great monasteries of Heijō survived, but by the early 9th century they had been eclipsed by the powerful wave of Tendai and Shingon Buddhism.

Enryakuji, Onjōji (MIIDERA), Kōyasan, TŌJI, and other Tendai and Shingon monasteries exerted a profound impact on the religious life of the Heian period (794–1185). They attracted large numbers of monks, including some of the best minds of the age. They held out to lay people, as well as monks and nuns, the promise of salvation to all who were sincere in their religious practice and performance of good works. They offered prayers for the well-being of the sick and dying and the welfare and protection of the nation.

By the 12th century, however, dissatisfaction with the prevailing forms of exclusive monastic life was becoming increasingly evident. This time, however, the impetus was not merely to reform monastic life but rather to reject it and look for salvation within society and among ordinary, everyday experience. Much of the dissatisfaction and demand for reform found expression in the great Tendai center of Enryakuji. Behind the reform movement lay powerful feelings of pessimism about the age, the quality of monastic practice, the very possibility of attaining salvation through one's own striving. Young monks who looked about them could see that monastic regulations were flouted, that monasteries and monks were waxing rich and comfortable. They could see that society was afflicted by natural disasters, epidemics, and warfare in which armed monks played their part. They could see that the capital was falling into ruin, the court and nobility divided and helpless to impose political order or resist the emergence of provincial warrior bands. Many felt that these social evils were simply manifestations of a deeper spiritual deterioration. Japan, it was commonly believed, had entered the Later Age of the Buddhist Law (mappō; see ESCHATOLOGY) when the attainment of salvation by self-effort in study, prayer, good works, or even diligent monastic practice had become all but impossible. In such circumstances, some argued, a person's best recourse was to rely on the saving merits of the Buddha.

From the 10th century devotion to AMIDA—belief that salvation in Amida's Pure Land of the Western Paradise could be attained by contemplation of Amida or the invocation of his sacred title, the NEMBUTSU—had become a powerful current in Tendai monasteries. The Pure Land teaching (see PURE LAND BUDDHISM) was expressed most graphically by GENSHIN (942–1017) and taken out of the monastic context and carried to the common people by KŪYA (903–972), HŌNEN (1133–1212), SHINRAN (1173–1263), and IPPEN (1239–89), all of whom shared the conviction that Amida's vows to save all sentient beings applied to men and women, high and low, whether they were able to perform meritorious works, offer prayers or merely feel the stirrings of faith and trust.

As the tide of popular Buddhism swept through Japan in the 12th and 13th centuries, the distinction between monks and lay people was blurred. The Pure Land leaders, in varying degrees, questioned or rejected the exclusive, celibate monastic life. They chose to live in society where they could offer their message of salvation to all, to warriors and farmers, women and outcasts. Hōnen, and some of his more conservative Pure Land disciples, continued to uphold the validity of the traditional monastic discipline, including the vows of celibacy and sobriety. Shinran, Hōnen's most radical follower, however, not only lived as a fugitive among poor farmers; he also believed that the most base people, through the very sense of their own sinfulness, might have the greatest chance of triggering the operation of Amida's compassion. Breaking his vow of celibacy he took a wife, thus asserting that monastic discipline was not essential to salvation and that the family, or small group of lay devotees, could be the center of religious life. These attitudes of Shinran were perpetuated among his followers in the True Pure Land school (JŌDO SHIN SECT) which grew to become the most populous branch of Japanese Buddhism. Ippen rejected the sedentary monastic life for one of constant pilgrimage and mendicancy. He offered the message of the nembutsu to samurai, nobles, outcasts, and peasants throughout Japan. Women as well as men followed him on his pilgrimages and joined in the dancing nembutsu.

The Pure Land movement was only one manifestation of the popular upsurge of Buddhism in the late 12th and 13th centuries. ZEN was another powerful current. In their emphasis on seated meditation, zazen, as a single practice accessible to all and in their assertion that enlightenment was attainable by all, Zen pioneers shared some of the ideals of the popular movement. But Zen mas-

ters also reemphasized the monastic ideal. Together with new meditation techniques and Zen-related texts, they also brought from China Zen monastic rules (shingi), the characteristic Zen monastery centered on the communal meditation hall (sōdō), and all the forms of Chinese Zen monastic life. In his Kōzen gokoku ron (Promotion of Zen for the Protection of the Country) EISAI stressed that "the practice of Zen begins with the precepts." DŌGEN, too, in his writings and his training of monks at EIHEIJI emphasized a stern monastic discipline. Chinese emigré monks like Lanqi Daolong (Lan-ch'i Tao-lung; J: RANKEI DŌRYŪ) who came to Japan from the mid-13th century, enforced the strictest standards of Song (Sung) Zen monastic practice. The Zen monastic institution grew rapidly. In the process Zen monasteries became centers for the diffusion in Japan of Chinese learning and culture.

The challenge presented by Pure Land, Zen, and NICHIREN's Lotus teaching provoked reform in the older monastic schools of Buddhism during the 13th century. This was most evident in the case of the Vinaya (Ritsu) school revival. Ritsu school monks like EIZON (1201–90) and his disciple Ninshō (1217–1303) criticized the leaders of the popular movement for their denial of traditional monastic discipline. But they also recognized the need for a revitalization of Japanese monastic practice through strict adherence to the precepts of the Vinaya and through greater concern for social problems. Both Eizon and Ninshō spent long periods traveling in rural areas of eastern Japan preaching on the Vinaya and organizing local welfare projects.

The centuries between the 12th and 16th are often presented as a time of dissolution for monastic Buddhism: religiously, because of the growth of rival Pure Land, True Pure Land, and Nichiren schools; politically and economically, because warrior governments and local warrior chieftains were less subject to monastic pressure than the court had been and less cooperative in protecting monastic estate holdings from warrior depredations; culturally, as the new groups of warriors and merchants developed their own cultural style and cultural centers.

It would be misleading to think, however, that traditional monastic Buddhism was moribund or reduced to social insignificance in medieval Japan. The older monasteries of the capital region continued to draw recruits, to draw income from their scattered estates (SHŌEN), to maintain monastic armies, to engage in commerce and moneylending, to sponsor guilds of merchants and entertainers, and to serve as centers of learning and artistic patronage. There was, too, as we have seen, a reemphasis of the monastic ideal in the medieval Zen and Ritsu movements. Even those new schools of Buddhism whose founders had rejected aspects of the monastic life, assumed quasi-monastic forms. The successors of Shinran, Nichiren, and Ippen, in giving sectarian character to their teachings, adopted more settled, regulated community lives. Politically and militarily the True Pure Land followers of HONGANJI were as much a factor in the power struggles of the 16th century as the soldier monks of Enryakuji or Kōfukuji had been in the 11th and 12th centuries.

It was not until the mid-16th and 17th centuries that monastic Buddhism was brought firmly under warrior control or that monasteries fully lost their spiritual, intellectual, and cultural vitality. In their military struggles to unify the country ODA NOBUNAGA and TOYOTOMI HIDEYOSHI razed Enryakuji, reduced Honganji and Negoroji, and confiscated lands from many monasteries. Where Nobunaga had used Christianity as a counter to Buddhism, Hideyoshi was wary of both, and TOKUGAWA IEYASU, the third unifier and founder of the Tokugawa shogunate, used Buddhist monasteries and temples in his efforts to eradicate Christianity. But Ieyasu and his Tokugawa successors turned increasingly to secular Confucian scholars for advice on statecraft and diplomacy and used Neo-Confucianism as a bulwark for their system of rule. Buddhist leadership in the intellectual domain was ended and monastic involvement in the shaping of the national political configuration was eliminated.

Between the 17th and 19th centuries Buddhist monasteries and temples enjoyed a generally comfortable, if reduced, position within the Tokugawa political order. They were used by the Tokugawa as centers for the registration of the local population. Villagers and townspeople were obliged to support their local temple irrespective of their personal religious interests. Buddhist institutions enjoyed the patronage of the Tokugawa and many of the daimyō. But they were also subjected to close political control. Under the "Regulations for Temples" (Jiin Hatto) entry to the monastic life was carefully regulated, monastic hierarchy precisely elaborated, and detailed prohibitions enforced. Monks and nuns were encouraged to devote themselves to study rather than to proselytization or welfare activity. The Tokugawa reform of the monastic order was external and administrative; it did little to promote spiritual revival. What vitality was evident in the Tokugawa period was provided by the introduction from China of ŌBAKU SECT Zen monasticism in the 17th century, the efforts of Zen monks like HAKUIN to revitalize RINZAI SECT monastic practice and promote Zen among the common people, or the spread in urban areas of the Confucianized ethical teachings of ISHIDA BAIGAN and the SHINGAKU movement.

Even during the Tokugawa period the Buddhist establishment was subjected to criticism from Confucian and Shintō scholars that it was corrupt and out of tune with Japanese society and values. In some domains, especially those like Mito where the Shintō-inspired National Learning (KOKUGAKU) was strong, Buddhist monasteries were disestablished, Buddhist monks and nuns defrocked, and monastic lands confiscated.

The Meiji Restoration (1868), however, brought all branches of Buddhism face to face with a crisis of survival. The new Meiji government was less accommodating toward Buddhism than the Tokugawa regime had been. Looking for an appropriate national creed, the Meiji leaders severed the long-standing connection between Shintō and Buddhism and sought to elevate Shintō into a national ideology. This policy was interpreted by some ideologues as a license to eradicate Buddhism. In many parts of the country monasteries and temples were vandalized, monks and nuns laicized. The vandalism was quickly suppressed, but the violence of the anti-Buddhist movement, coupled with the reappearance in Japan of Christian missionaries, served as a salutary warning to Buddhists that reform and modernization of the Saṃgha were called for if Buddhism was to establish a place for itself in Meiji society and the modern world.

Monks like FUKUDA GYŌKAI (1806–88) and Shaku Unshō (1827–1909) were among the first Buddhists to recognize the need for a drastic regeneration of sectarian Buddhism. They led a movement to wipe out monastic abuses and to restore strict observance of the Vinaya among religious and laypeople. In succeeding decades the various branches of Buddhism, monastic and nonmonastic, strove to institute reforms, to train their monks and priests more thoroughly in critical textual analysis, to introduce Western methods in Buddhology, to counter the Christian missionary drive, and to bring Buddhism into alignment with national sentiment and objectives.

Strengthened by these reform efforts all branches of monastic Buddhism were at least partially successful in making the transition to contemporary society. Some monasteries were closed, most have much smaller communities than they had in earlier times, but a substantial number are still active.

🔲 —— Nihon shoki (720), tr W. G. Aston as Nihongi: Chronicles of Japan from the Earliest Times to A.D. 697 (1896, repr 1956). Martin Collcutt, Five Mountains: The Rinzai Zen Monastic Institution in Medieval Japan (1981). Yoshito S. Hakeda, Kūkai: Major Works (1972). Ienaga Saburō et al, ed, Nihon bukkyō shi (1967). Hideo Kishimoto, ed, Japanese Religion in the Meiji Era (1956). Joseph Kitagawa, Religion in Japanese History (1966). Tsuji Zennosuke, Nihon bukkyō shi, 10 vols (1953). W. P. Woodard, "Study on Religious Juridical Persons Law," Contemporary Japan, 25 and 26 (1958, 1959).
Martin C. COLLCUTT

Monchūjo

(Board of Inquiry). A judicial body of the Kamakura (1192–1333) and Muromachi (1338–1573) shogunates that adjudicated disputes between vassals (GOKENIN) over land rights, as well as other property cases. It was established in 1184 by MINAMOTO NO YORITOMO, with MIYOSHI YASUNOBU as its first head (shitsuji); the post became a prerogative of the Miyoshi family. Staff members were called YORYŪDO. The office gradually expanded its role in settling legal questions until it became the shogunate's chief judicial arm outside Kamakura (the MANDOKORO, or Administrative Board, settled cases within the city). After 1249, however, cases concerning shogunal vassals were put under the jurisdiction of the newly created High Court (HIKITSUKE), and the Monchūjo dealt mainly with litigation concerning commercial transactions, loans, indentured servants, and goods (see ZATSUMU SATA). Under the Muromachi shogunate, most of the Monchūjo's duties were taken over by the Kyōto Mandokoro, and the office was reduced to archival work.

monetary policy

The use of official powers of control over money and credit to advance national economic goals.

Monetary policy has been an important contributor to Japan's post–World War II success in achieving high overall growth while maintaining reasonably satisfactory price stability. Through much of this period, the monetary authorities' role has been one of ensuring adequate liquidity growth to fuel naturally buoyant private demand during economic expansion, and of applying restraint by holding down credit growth whenever excessive aggregate demand began to reveal itself in a foreign trade deficit, thereby threatening stability. During the 1950s and 1960s the Japanese authorities achieved an impressive record of success in handling the policy requirements of this cyclical growth pattern. Starting in the latter part of the 1960s, changes in the economic and financial structure—themselves a natural result of the very success of Japan's postwar growth policy—began to alter both the demands made of monetary policy and the effectiveness of traditional tools used to carry it out. The most important of these changes was the disappearance of the external balance-of-payments constraint—the fear of running out of foreign exchange reserves, which had been the immediate signal for every postwar episode of monetary restraint before 1969. The process of adapting monetary policy to these new conditions—as well as to important changes in the world economic order—was a major challenge of the 1970s, and continues to be one in the 1980s.

The Mechanics of Monetary Policy —— The BANK OF JAPAN, the country's central bank, is entrusted with the necessary powers for executing monetary policy. The bank participates in the formulation of policy in close collaboration with the MINISTRY OF FINANCE, but, as in most countries, important decisions affecting overall policy are made by the ministry or the government as a whole. The methods available to the Bank of Japan are similar to those used by central banks in other countries, but the relative importance attached to particular instruments reflects characteristics of the Japanese economy and its financial system.

In the background of all postwar anticyclical policy has been a consistent underlying policy of fostering low interest rates—rates below those at which all willing borrowers would find credit available in the amounts desired. Interest rates on bank deposits and short-term loans are subject to infrequently charged legal maxima, and other rates—including many bond yields—are kept low by official "guidance" of varying degrees of formality. The Bank of Japan's own discount rates (including penalty rates when these become relevant) are consistently below the cost of alternative funds at times when credit is being tightened, and commercial banks are always ready to borrow more from the central bank at the official discount rate than it is willing to lend. Changes in the Bank of Japan's rate thus do not exert an important influence through cost effects. This is generally true also of the administrated bank lending rates that are tied to the bank's rate. Discount rate changes do have an important announcement effect, however, as they have usually been among the first public steps following an official decision to put on the monetary brakes.

Although it has deprived the authorities of one instrument of short-term stabilization policy, the low-interest-rate policy is thought by many to have supported the government's growth objectives by encouraging investment. On the other hand, low interest rates have evidently not discouraged either personal or corporate savings at rates that are extraordinarily high by international standards. And there is little question that the low-interest-rate policy, by retarding the development of securities markets, contributed to the effectiveness of the central bank's non-price-control instruments, since it made the corporate sector exceptionally dependent on the banking system as its source of finance. This policy lies at the heart of the postwar approaches. However, their applicability began to decline in the 1970s, and the management of an orderly movement toward more flexible interest rates has become a primary objective of official policy.

Adjusting the quantity of its own lending to commercial banks has long been the most important control tool used by the Bank of Japan. Sustained rapid growth of the economy led to immense requirements for monetary growth, and such growth in turn necessitated rapid increases in "high-powered" or "reserve" money (currency and commercial bank deposits with the Bank of Japan). Central banks can supply reserve money to the economy by financing the government's deficit, buying foreign exchange from the private sector when the economy is in an overall balance-of-payments

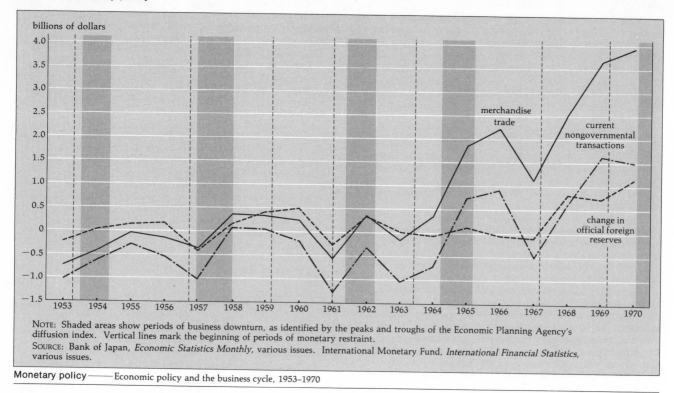

NOTE: Shaded areas show periods of business downturn, as identified by the peaks and troughs of the Economic Planning Agency's diffusion index. Vertical lines mark the beginning of periods of monetary restraint.

SOURCE: Bank of Japan, *Economic Statistics Monthly*, various issues. International Monetary Fund, *International Financial Statistics*, various issues.

Monetary policy——Economic policy and the business cycle, 1953–1970

surplus, and extending credit to the private sector. Since Japan did not have large government deficits or foreign exchange surpluses before the 1970s, central bank lending necessarily contributed most of the increase in reserve money. This large quantitative role made it relatively easy for the central bank to curtail monetary growth at appropriate points simply by changing its own discount policy.

Additionally, Japan's financial structure developed, with official encouragement, in such a way that "indirect" financing dominated more than in many other countries: i.e., needed funds were overwhelmingly channeled through financial intermediaries that are more or less directly under the thumb of the monetary authorities. The enormous investment requirements of rapid growth kept Japanese corporations relatively dependent on outside, as opposed to internal, sources of finance, and underdevelopment of the securities markets meant that external finance was predominantly borrowed from banks during most of the postwar period. Private savers, offered few attractive choices in the assets they could hold, placed most of their savings in bank deposits (as opposed to securities or insurance, which are more popular in both the United States and the United Kingdom, for instance). These characteristics greatly enhanced the importance of flows through the banking system and thus the direct leverage of the banking authorities over the economy.

Bank of Japan credit through loans and discounts has been mainly confined to the 15 or fewer large banks classified as "city banks" (see BANKING SYSTEM). For all their importance, those banks typically account for less than one-half of total lending by private financial institutions; the strong effect of changes in central bank discounting policy therefore depends heavily on their quick and smooth transmission from city banks to others. An important linkage has been provided by the call money market, which for many years was the sole money market in which interest rates were usually allowed to rise to market-clearing levels. As in the federal funds market of the United States, the main participants are financial institutions, with the large city banks typically acting as net borrowers while local banks and other financial institutions are net providers of funds. A move by the central bank to restrict lending at its discount window immediately pushes the city banks into the call market for increased borrowing, raising interest rates, and making placement of funds there more attractive to other financial institutions as an alternative to lending to their own customers. Monetary ease or restraint thus affects the flow of credit throughout the banking system, and not just through city banks themselves.

The Bank of Japan engages in sales and purchases of securities (primarily government bonds, after these began to be floated in 1965). Generally these are not open market operations, given the underdeveloped state of such markets, but negotiated transactions

with individual financial institutions. They are more appropriately regarded as a substitute for changes in central bank lending to adjust reserve positions of individual city banks than as a market-oriented instrument to be compared with securities operations of the US Federal Reserve. This situation began to change in the 1970s as the size of the government debt and its annual financing requirements grew, and as the idea of allowing more flexible interest rates began to receive official acceptance. Bank of Japan market operations in government securities thus began to grow more important by the early 1980s.

Since 1959 most deposit money banks have been required to hold reserves, in the form of deposits with the Bank of Japan, in fixed ratio to their own deposit liabilities. The banks do not hold excess reserves voluntarily, so that changes in these required ratios do have a significant effect on liquidity. The ratios have always been low, and the volume of deposits involved is small relative to banks' outstanding borrowing from the central bank, which therefore has found it easier to adjust liquidity through the control of borrowing than through adjustment of the reserve requirements. However, reserve requirements have sometimes been changed to help effect the central bank's anticyclical policy.

In times of restraint, the Bank of Japan has frequently issued guidelines (*madoguchi shidō*, "window guidance") to limit the volume of lending by individual city banks and, since the late 1960s, by some other large financial institutions. These supplement the restraint methods described above, although they affect only part of the banking system.

An important contributor to monetary control has been the authorities' close control of flows of capital between Japan and other countries. Although Japanese banks have been encouraged since the early 1960s to borrow in the United States and Eurodollar markets in order to finance Japan's international trade and foreign investments, this activity has been carefully guided so as not to interfere with domestic monetary policies. It is true that even Japan's comparatively tight controls on international capital movements were not able to prevent huge inflows from occurring during the worldwide currency upheavals of the 1970s. But relative to the large size of the Japanese economy and its liquidity needs, even these exceptional flows were not of sufficient magnitude to disrupt domestic monetary control seriously for any period of time. This insulation from international capital flows began to change by the late 1970s, however, as the result of liberalization measures including the new Foreign Exchange Control Law of 1979.

Monetary Policy before the Late 1960s——During the first 15 years after the Allied OCCUPATION ended in 1952 (i.e., 1953–68), periodic breaches of the external balance-of-payments constraint were almost always the first signal prompting official moves toward monetary restraint. Rapid domestic expansion inevitably led imports to soar, causing the external trade balance—and, even more, the overall balance on private current transactions—to dip into deficit and foreign exchange reserves to decline. This led to a quick succession of monetary tightening measures, usually involving a combination of the policy instruments described in the preceding section. All four of the brief business downturns of this period (see figure) were initiated by such policy turns.

In each of the four contractions, several quarters of lowered growth in money and credit led rather quickly to a slowdown of gross national product (GNP) expansion. A large part of the growth fluctuation was accounted for by changes in business investment, which represents a larger proportion of GNP in Japan than in most industrial countries. The reversal of balance-of-payments deficits came mainly through sharp deceleration or decline in imports, although export growth also accelerated in two of the four contractions. That Japan's imports are predominantly of raw materials and other goods used in production makes them extremely responsive to short-run changes in domestic activity.

Decelerating monetary growth was usually reflected within a few quarters in sharply reduced inflation rates, as the result of which Japan was able to maintain virtually unchanged average prices for the manufactures that it exported over the 1950s and 1960s as a whole. This meant a gradual improvement in Japan's competitiveness in international markets, which is the main reason that the foreign trade gap was eventually eliminated. Private domestic demand also picked up quickly and strongly each time the monetary authorities switched from restraint to ease, and the growth rates achieved in the 15-year period as a whole were little short of miraculous. Monetary policy can thus be judged to have been highly successful with respect to both its growth and stability goals during those years.

Monetary Policy in a Changing Setting: The 1970s and Beyond

In retrospect, one of the most striking features of the balance-of-payments pattern, shown in the figure, is the steady upward trend running through all the cycles. This trend was a simple and inevitable result of the fact that export growth consistently exceeded import growth when measured over the entire business cycle. Figures like these provided a basis for concluding by the late 1960s (as the Organization for Economic Cooperation and Development, OECD, did in its official annual *Economic Survey of Japan,* published in 1969) that Japan's chronic problem of periodic balance-of-payments deficit was gone, and might indeed have given way to a tendency toward imbalance in the surplus direction. At about this time, some economists also began predicting a turning point in Japan's growth rate, pointing to the disappearance of special conditions which had made possible the "miracle" growth of the 1950s and 1960s. This downward shift in growth rates did not actually materialize until after 1973, although its reasons were closely interrelated with the earlier turning point of the external balance.

These changes, and attendant shifts in financial structure, have drastically altered the context in which monetary policy operates. Business investment, no longer dominant as it once was, is also not as automatically buoyant a force of cyclical recovery as it was when continuously high growth was taken for granted by private expectations. Without the pressure of enormous capital requirements for high growth, the chronic financial deficit of the business sector has declined, reducing the corporate dependence on bank credit that has been one of the Bank of Japan's main levers on the economy. The reduced net borrowing of the business sector has as its counterpart growing financial deficits in the foreign sector (the flow of funds' reflection of external current-account surplus) and the public sector. A corollary of the latter has been the increased importance of fiscal management in anticyclical policy. The size of the government's debt and annual financing requirements also make the traditional approach to financing the debt—essentially forcing government securities on the commercial banks at unattractive interest rates—less manageable, placing pressure on the authorities to allow development of genuine securities markets. Additional pressure toward interest rate flexibility is created by the growing international involvement of Japanese banks and corporations, which makes it increasingly difficult to insulate domestic financial markets from developments in foreign markets. As noted already, serious liberalization steps were begun in the 1970s although the process inevitably has been slow. As happens in many countries with sizable government deficits, unwillingness to permit high interest rates on the government's own securities has at times outweighed the desire to foster free financial markets, and this has in fact hampered the Bank of

Japan's efforts to tighten money on several occasions since the mid-1960s.

At the same time that monetary policy had to adapt to these changes generated by the maturing process of the Japanese economy itself, there were drastic changes in the world economy as well. First, the yen was involved in the major exchange-rate realignment of 1971—the first change in the yen-dollar parity since it was fixed by the Occupation authorities in 1949—and then the industrial countries abandoned fixed exchange rates altogether in 1973. While in an immediate sense these were externally imposed changes, in a more fundamental sense they were not, since the failure of Japanese economic policy to avoid huge surplus imbalances in external trade was one of the reasons that the Bretton Woods system of pegged exchange rates was no longer able to function in the 1970s. This change was followed by two major escalations of world petroleum prices, in 1974 and 1979, which necessitated massive adjustments for the heavily oil-based Japanese industrial structure. Accommodating these huge and totally unfamiliar changes posed severe tests for Japanese monetary policies, and it is hardly surprising that the record is not one of unmixed success.

Monetary policy passed an important milestone in the last quarter of 1969, when the Bank of Japan moved to tighten money because of domestic considerations alone at a time when there was no deficit in the external sector to worry about. Inflation was stabilized within a few months, but the recession that began in mid-1970 proved more difficult to get out of than earlier ones; activity remained sluggish throughout 1971, and one of the most serious consequences of this was the movement of Japan's external balance into a huge and internationally disruptive surplus. As would be true through most of the 1970s, the authorities recognized that easy monetary policy alone was no longer capable of initiating quick recovery of the Japanese economy, but were not completely successful in replacing it with a sufficient, well-timed fiscal stimulus.

The drastic revaluation of the yen exchange rate occurred in late 1971, when the economy was still in recession. The further depressive impact of this action was overestimated by the authorities, and its effect on the trade surplus perhaps underestimated, so that the next two years witnessed large errors in the opposite direction of excessive monetary (and also fiscal) expansion. Even before the increase in world oil price of 1973, inflation had reached the neighborhood of 20 percent. When the price hike was announced, the authorities—fearing both additional inflation and a massive external deficit resulting from the higher cost of oil imports—embarked on a severely restrictive policy. Once again they were successful in stabilizing the price level, but the economy's ability to adjust to higher oil prices had been underestimated, and the twin problems of stubborn domestic recession and intolerable external surplus reemerged. The same set of problems had to be dealt with after the second "oil shock" in the late 1970s, and the unpredictable swings of Japan's current account balance of payments, between huge deficits and surpluses, continued to be a disruptive influence. However, the lesson of the 1973-74 experience was well remembered, and the brief outburst of excessive monetary growth followed by extremely rapid inflation was not repeated in subsequent cycles.

The experience with monetary policy in the post-1965 period clearly has not been as uniformly satisfactory as in earlier years. But the difficult events of the 1970s did show that the traditional tools of monetary control can still be effectively used in Japan for stabilization. Japan in fact did better than most other countries during that decade, in sustaining growth as well as containing inflation. With the improved use of fiscal policy and the continuing effort by monetary authorities to develop financial institutions that will allow effective use of open market operations to execute future policy, there is reason to expect that Japanese policy will continue to be successful in both its growth and stability goals, thereby contributing to world economic stability as well.

■——Gardner Ackley and Hiromitsu Ishi, "Fiscal, Monetary and Related Policies," in Hugh Patrick and Henry Rosovsky, ed, *Asia's New Giant* (1976). The Bank of Japan, *Economic Statistics Monthly.* The Bank of Japan, *Economic Statistics Annual.* The Bank of Japan, Economic Research Department, *The Japanese Financial System* (annual). Michael W. Keran "Monetary Policy and the Business Cycle in Postwar Japan," in David Meiselman, ed, *Varieties of Monetary Experience* (1970). Ryutaro Komiya and Yoshio Suzuki, "Inflation in Japan," in Lawrence B. Krause and Walter S. Salant, ed, *World Inflation* (1977). Organization for Economic Cooperation and Development (OECD), *Monetary Policy in Japan* (1972). Hugh T. Patrick, *Monetary Control and Central Banking in Contemporary Japan*

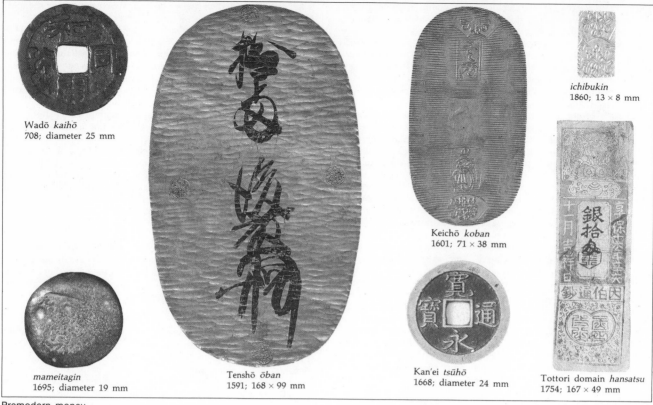

Wadō *kaihō*
708; diameter 25 mm

mameitagin
1695; diameter 19 mm

Tenshō *ōban*
1591; 168 × 99 mm

Keichō *koban*
1601; 71 × 38 mm

Kan'ei *tsūhō*
1668; diameter 24 mm

ichibukin
1860; 13 × 8 mm

Tottori domain *hansatsu*
1754; 167 × 49 mm

Premodern money

Japanese coins issued from the 8th to the 19th centuries and a bill issued in the 18th century. The type of Tenshō *ōban* shown is called the *naga ōban* ("long" *ōban*); struck in 1591, it is one of the largest gold coins in the world.

(1962). Yoshio Suzuki, *Gendai Nihon kin'yūron* (1974) tr John Greenwood as *Money and Banking in Contemporary Japan* (1980).
Patricia Hagan Kuwayama

money → yen; money, premodern

money offerings

(saisen). Money offered at a Shintō shrine or Buddhist temple in repayment for the fulfillment of a petition or prayer (GANKAKE) or simply on the occasion of a visit for worship. At shrines and temples it is not at all unusual for offering boxes to be positioned directly in front of the main hall. This feature is thought to date only from the Edo period (1600–1868), although the custom of offering newly minted coins to Shintō or Buddhist deities and gods has existed since ancient times. Prior to the spread of the custom of giving money, it was common to offer *ohineri,* a handful of rice wrapped in paper; this custom is seen even today. Although some people wrap their money offerings in paper, it is customary simply to throw in loose bills or coins.
Ōtō Tokihiko

money, premodern

Old Chinese coins have been unearthed from ancient remains of the Yayoi period (ca 300 BC–ca AD 300) and tombs of the Kofun period (ca 300–710), and coins are mentioned in the NIHON SHOKI (720). However, it is not thought that they were widely employed as currency, a function long fulfilled by rice, cloth, and other items. The first coins minted in Japan were the silver and copper WADŌ KAIHŌ (Wadō-era coins). Issued in 708, they were patterned after coins of the Chinese Tang (T'ang; 618–907) dynasty. Between 760 and 958 there were at least 11 more coinages (see KŌCHŌ JŪNISEN), but barter trade continued to be the rule. In order to encourage their circulation the government granted stipends to officials in coin, and an ordinance in effect from 711 to 800, the Chikusen Joi Rei (Law Granting Rank to Coin Savers), raised the rank of persons who had accumulated coins. Although their circulation was established to a limited extent in the areas surrounding Heijōkyō (now Nara) and

Heiankyō (now Kyōto), the capital cities during the Nara (710–794) and Heian (794–1185) periods, in the 9th century the quality and quantity of coins fell off due to a shortage of copper. In the 10th century the Bureau of the Mint (Chūsenshi) was abolished, and in 987 the use of government-minted coins was prohibited.

For nearly five centuries, until late in the Muromachi period (1333–1568), the government did not mint any coins but used those imported from China, Korea, Annam, and other countries. During the Kamakura period (1185–1333) a great number of Song (Sung) coins (SŌSEN) from China flowed into Japan, and during the Muromachi period a large number of Ming coins (see KŌBUSEN; EIRAKUSEN) were imported. The increasing circulation of coinage led to the development of a system of cropland valuation for tax purposes called KANDAKA and based on *kammon,* a unit of copper cash. As privately minted coins of poor quality came into circulation, there arose the practice known as ERIZENI (coin selection), in which coins were evaluated and the poorer ones discriminated against. Refusal to accept coins at face value was detrimental to the economy because it decreased the value of circulated coins and tended to raise prices. Around the end of the Muromachi period the economy became stablized and many copper mines were opened, creating conditions favorable to the minting of a national currency. TOYOTOMI HIDEYOSHI, a unifier of the country, minted in the last quarter of the 16th century various large gold coins known as Tenshō ōban (Tenshō-era ŌBAN). These were oval coins approximately 15 centimeters (5.9 in) long and 10 centimeters (3.9 in) wide. He also struck copper coins called Tenshō *tsūhō* and Bunroku *tsūhō* (coins of the Tenshō and Bunroku eras).

The policy of minting coins was continued by the Tokugawa shogunate (1603–1867). It established a firm economic foundation by monopolizing the minting of coins, fixing a standard exchange rate for debased coinages (BITASEN), and in 1609 proscribing the use of the Chinese coins known as *eirakusen*. In the early part of the Edo period (1600–1868) the shogunate established a *kinza* or gold mint (see KINZA, GINZA, AND ZENIZA) and minted *ōban* (equivalent to 10 RYŌ), KOBAN (1 *ryō*), and *ichibukin* (one-fourth of 1 *ryō*). The *ōban* and the *koban* were oval-shaped and, though initially not of uniform size, were gradually standardized. *Chōgin* (silver bars) and *mameitagin* (round or rectangular pieces of silver) were minted at

Mongol invasions of Japan

A section of the *Mongol Invasions Picture Scroll* (*Mōko shūrai ekotoba*) showing warriors from a small Japanese attack vessel boarding a large Mongol ship. One of two scrolls. Colors on paper. Completed around 1293. Imperial Household Agency.

ginza (silver mints); the exchange rate of silver was determined by weight. The *momme*, 3.75 grams (0.132 oz), was the standard unit of measure. A thousand *momme* was one *kan*, one-tenth of a *momme* was a *bu*, and one-hundredth of a *momme* was a *rin*. *Zeni*, coins with square holes at their centers, made of copper, iron, or brass were minted at the various *zeniza* (*zeni* mints). In 1636 the mintage called Kan'ei *tsūhō* (Kan'ei-era coins) was officially designated the national currency, and thereafter *zeni* were all called Kan'ei *tsūhō* regardless of the era in which they were struck. In 1670, with the amount of Kan'ei *tsūhō* sufficing to meet demand, the use of older coinages was proscribed. With this, the premodern-period system of gold, silver, and *zeni* was fully established.

The financial situation of the Tokugawa shogunate subsequently deteriorated and beginning under the rule of TOKUGAWA TSUNAYO-SHI (r 1680–1709) coins of poorer quality were minted, plunging the economy into confusion. The Keichō (era) *koban*, struck from 1601 to 1695, weighed 17.85 grams (0.63 oz) and were 84.29 percent gold, but the Man'en (era) *koban*, minted from 1860 to 1867, weighed only 3.3 grams (0.12 oz) and were only 56.78 percent gold. The issuance of paper currency (HANSATSU) by various domains *(han)* wrought further confusion. In 1661 the Fukui domain (now part of Fukui Prefecture) was the first domain to print its own currency, and by the early part of the Meiji period (1868–1912) a total of 244 domains had issued paper money. A survey conducted in 1870 reported that a total of 1,600 types of paper currency with a face value of 30 million *ryō* had been printed. The opening of Japan to the West in 1854 led to the massive introduction of *yōgin* (Mexican silver dollars), causing additional complications. In 1871 the Shinka Jōrei (New Currency Regulation) was issued, making the YEN (equivalent to 1 *ryō*) the basic unit of currency, and by 1879 the exchange of pre-Meiji currency had been completed.

Mongaku (fl late 12th century)
Priest of the SHINGON SECT in the latter part of the Heian (794–1185) and early part of the Kamakura (1185–1333) periods; secular name, Endō Moritō. He was once a warrior (HOKUMEN NO BUSHI) in the service of Jōsai Mon'in, a daughter of Emperor TOBA; but he mistakenly killed a lady (Kesa, the wife of Minamoto no Wataru) whom he loved and renounced the world, first wandering in the mountains of Kumano (now part of Wakayama Prefecture) and then going to the temple JINGOJI (which he later helped to restore) on Mt. Takao (Takaosan), northwest of Kyōto. From 1173 to 1178, for importuning the retired emperor GO-SHIRAKAWA for funds for Jingoji, he was exiled to Izu Province (now part of Shizuoka Prefecture), where he became a close associate of MINAMOTO NO YORITOMO, who had lived there in exile since 1160. The funds were eventually supplied by Go-Shirakawa, and the rebuilding completed in 1182. Following Yoritomo's founding of the KAMAKURA SHOGUNATE, Mongaku traveled far and wide gathering intelligence for him. In 1199 he was implicated in a plot led by Minamoto no Michichika (1149–1202) against the shogunate and was exiled to the island of Sado (now part

of Niigata Prefecture) and then to Kyūshū, where, according to legend, he died at the age of 80. The story of Mongaku has been recounted in numerous *kabuki* plays and dances; his ill-fated love for Lady Kesa has been fictionalized in AKUTAGAWA RYŪNOSUKE's short story "Kesa to Moritō" (1918, Kesa and Moritō), which in turn served as the basis for the film *Jigokumon* (1953, Gate of Hell).

G. Cameron HURST III

Mongol invasions of Japan
Khubilai Khan (1215–94), the first Mongol emperor of China, twice sent naval expeditions against Japan in the late 13th century when the Kamakura shogunate (1192–1333) refused to acknowledge his suzerainty and send tribute to his court. On both occasions, in 1274 (Bun'ei II) and 1281 (Kōan 4), the Mongols landed in western Japan, but each time a fortuitous storm forced them to withdraw after a brief engagement with the Japanese defenders. (The two assaults are known in Japan as the Bun'ei no Eki or Bun'ei War and the Kōan no Eki or Kōan War, respectively.) Although the invasions themselves were brief, they were preceded and followed by protracted diplomatic contacts and defense preparations, and they created a state of emergency in Japan that lasted for more than 30 years. This was the only time before the mid-19th century that Japan was seriously threatened from abroad.

Mongol challenge and Japanese response. When Khubilai came to power in 1260, the Mongol empire, which spanned most of the Eurasian continent, was nearly complete. Southern Song (Sung; 1127–1279) China was encircled except to the sea; Korea was devastated and helpless (see MONGOL INVASIONS OF KOREA). After consolidating his position as Great Khan, Khubilai turned his attention to Japan at the same time that he undertook the final conquest of the Southern Song dynasty. He may have been attracted by the fabled gold and pearls of Japan, but it is more likely that he hoped to complete the economic and military isolation of South China by bringing Japan under his sway.

A state letter, transmitted by Korean envoys, reached Japan early in 1268. Sent by the "Emperor of Great Mongolia" to the "King of Japan," it demanded that Japan submit to a tributary relationship or face invasion. The Japanese ignored this letter and several others that arrived during the next few years. The court at Kyōto, which had rejected the suzerainty of China since the time of Prince SHŌTOKU (see SUI AND TANG [T'ANG] CHINA, EMBASSIES TO), was insulted by the terms of the letter and unwilling to contract such a relationship. The leaders of the Kamakura shogunate, landowners in the eastern provinces, had no interest in foreign relations. Whatever foreign goods they required came from South China; moreover, they relied heavily on the advice of Zen monks from the Southern Song, which the Mongols were trying to destroy.

Nonetheless, all concerned knew the fate of Korea and realized the gravity of the threat of invasion. The court nobles were terrified and offered up urgent prayers at temples and shrines. The military leaders of the shogunate, sworn to defend the country, were more confident but hastened to strengthen their defenses. The shogunate alerted its vassals (GOKENIN) in the western provinces and ordered vassals who held fiefs in Kyūshū but had remained in the east to hurry to their posts and join local vassals in guarding the northwestern coast of Kyūshū in monthly rotation.

Mongol invasions and Japanese defense. Early in November 1274 an armada of nearly 900 vessels carrying more than 40,000 troops—Mongols, Chinese, Jurchen Tatars, and Koreans—set out from the southern tip of Korea. After devastating the islands of Tsushima and Iki, the fleet appeared at Hakata Bay on 18 November, and the following day landed troops at several points, and attacked the town of Hakata. Confounded by the Mongols' cavalry tactics and superior weaponry, the Japanese defenders were forced to retreat to an ancient fortress near Dazaifu, several miles inland. The invaders did not pursue but retired to their ships at nightfall. During the night a fierce gale blew and wrecked much of the Mongol fleet, forcing it to withdraw with the loss of perhaps one-third of its men. (Some claim, however, that their withdrawal was intentional and the storm occurred on their way back to Korea.)

Although a timely storm had saved the Japanese from defeat, they had proved no match for the invaders on land or sea. Moreover, Khubilai renewed his demands in 1275, and, after beheading his envoys, the Japanese authorities fully expected another attack. The Kamakura shogunate reorganized the coastal defense system, extended it to the western coast of Honshū, where the latest Mongol embassy had landed, and required warriors who were not its vassals *(hi gokenin)* to share guard duty with the *gokenin*. Two other measures, which later proved effective, were the formation of a navy of small attack vessels and the construction by Kyūshū warriors of an earth-and-stone wall around Hakata Bay.

Meanwhile, with the fall of the Southern Song dynasty in 1279, Khubilai turned his attention once more to Japan. His final embassy to Japan (1279) having been beheaded like the previous one, he prepared in earnest for a new expedition.

Early in June 1281 two Mongol fleets, comprising a total of 4,400 warships bearing 140,000 men, set out simultaneously from Korea and from South China. The Eastern Route Army from Korea, after again laying waste Tsushima and Iki, arrived first at Hakata on 23 June and landed troops at several places in northwest Kyūshū; but the Japanese defenders, with the help of the wall at Hakata, prevented it from gaining a secure foothold during weeks of fighting, while the small Japanese attack vessels harassed its cumbersome transports. When the Southern Route Army from China belatedly arrived, and the combined Mongol forces were preparing an overwhelming assault on Hakata, a typhoon arose suddenly on 16 August and destroyed most of the Mongol fleet, forcing the remainder to withdraw; more than half of its men were killed or drowned.

The principal reasons for the Mongols' failure to conquer Japan were Khubilai's reliance on recently subjugated Korean and Chinese conscripts for the bulk of his forces and the determined resistance led by the Kamakura shogunate. However, to the Japanese, who believed that their land was protected by the gods and whose faith had been deepened by the "divine wind" (KAMIKAZE) of a few years before, this second storm was a confirmation of divine favor.

The divine wind did not, however, immediately dispel the Mongol threat. Khubilai never lost his determination to punish Japan. On several occasions before his death in 1294 he began serious preparations for another campaign, but each time he was diverted by instability within the Mongol empire. Although Khubilai's successors showed little interest in Japan, the shogunate not only maintained but also strengthened its defenses on the western coast, which remained on military alert for nearly 20 years.

Effects of the Mongol invasions. Western Japan was remote from the base of the military regime at Kamakura and was the region where its authority had been weakest. The Mongol invasions forced the shogunate to extend its control to the western provinces and to take over even more of the functions of the imperial government. To improve military control, Kamakura appointed shogunal deputies (TANDAI) in Kyūshū and in western Honshū; and, to coordinate the war effort more efficiently, the regent HŌJŌ FAMILY concentrated the most important posts in their own hands. This extension of authority and assumption of responsibility caused serious political and economic problems for the shogunate.

The fact that the defense of Japan was conducted largely by local military governors (SHUGO) helped to strengthen local ties and weaken the blood ties on which the Kamakura military society had been founded; and the necessary concentration of power by the Hōjō caused deep resentment among leading vassals who were

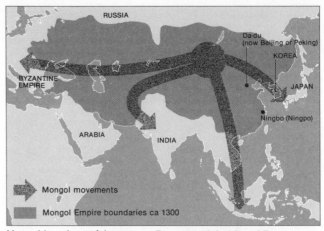

Mongol invasions of Japan———Expansion of the Mongol Empire

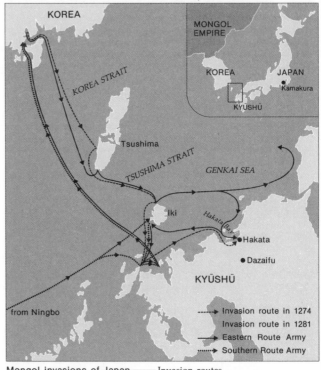

Mongol invasions of Japan———Invasion routes

eliminated from positions of influence. Moreover, the cost of the 30-year mobilization was enormous. Victory over the Mongols yielded no booty or confiscated lands, and there was no tax system through which the expense of the war could be shared by the country as a whole. The entire burden, therefore, fell on the shogunate and its vassals, who suffered great economic distress. The vassals needed reimbursement for their expenditures and expected rewards for their loyalty and valor. Since the shogunate had nothing to give them, widespread bitterness and disaffection arose among the warrior class, on which the power of the shogunate rested. Thus the Mongol invasions contributed to the downfall of the Kamakura shogunate, despite the fact that its authority and effectiveness reached a peak during the crisis.

———Aida Nirō, *Mōko shūrai no kenkyū* (1958). Hatada Takashi, *Genkō: Mōko teikoku no naibu jijō* (1965). Kyotsu Hori, "The Economic and Political Effects of the Mongol Wars," in John W. Hall and Jeffrey P. Mass, ed, *Medieval Japan: Essays in Institutional History* (1974). Ikeuchi Hiroshi, *Genkō no shin kenkyū* (1931). Ishii Susumu, "Mōko shūrai ekotoba no rekishiteki haikei," in *Nihon emakimono zenshū* (Kadokawa Shoten, 1964). Kuroda Toshio, *Mōko shūrai, Nihon no rekishi*, vol 8 (Chūō Kōron Sha, 1965). Nakamura Hidetaka, "13–14 seiki no Tōa jōsei to Mongōru no shūrai," in *Iwanami kōza: Nihon rekishi*, vol 6 (Iwanami Shoten, 1936). Ryō Susumu, *Mōko shūrai* (1959). George Sansom, *A History of*

Monkeys

scamp in folktales is based upon the actual experience of the Japanese, whose crops and fruit trees were ravaged and whose houses were invaded by monkeys. As a result, legends were created in which monkeys imitated humans, made wine, and displayed deep affection.

There was a superstition that monkeys had the power to keep diseases away from horses, which gave rise to the custom of keeping a monkey tied to a post in stables. This superstition survived until modern times in such forms as a picture of a monkey pasted on stable walls, the belief that the touch of a dried monkey's hand would heal horses' diseases, and the practice of burying a monkey's skull under stables. Faith healers whose prayers and dancing monkeys were thought to cure ailing horses, are said to be the origin of monkey shows *(sarumawashi)*, once a common STREET ENTERTAINMENT in Japan. From the Edo period (1600–1868) such showmen put on a variety of performances other than mere dancing and until recent times made house-to-house visits.   SANEYOSHI *Tatsuo*

━━━Itani Jun'ichirō, *Takasakiyama no saru* (1973). Saneyoshi Tatsuo, *Dōbutsu no nihonshi* (1973).

Monnō (1700–1763)

Philologist and Buddhist priest of the Edo period (1600–1868). Born in the Kuwada district of Tamba (now Kyōto Prefecture), he learned Chinese and studied the phonetics of Chinese characters (KANJI). In particular, his study of the *yunjing (yün-ching;* J: *inkyō)*, the tables of Chinese syllables, was an epoch-making achievement. He also wrote on KANA and was well versed in astronomy. His works include *Makō inkyō,* 2 vols (1744), *San'on seika,* 2 vols (1752), and *Waji taikan shō,* 2 vols (1754).   UWANO *Zendō*

monogatari bungaku

(narrative literature). The term *monogatari bungaku* is used, in its widest sense, to cover a variety of prose works of the 9th through the 15th centuries, often in contrast to WAKA *bungaku* (poetry), NIKKI BUNGAKU (journals or diaries), and ZUIHITSU *bungaku* (essays or random notes).

Individual works, or *monogatari,* range from long romances through historical accounts to short anecdotes, and although they are written primarily in prose and in a narrative mode, they usually contain a significant number of poems. This is a result partly of the wide use of poetry on social occasions, partly of a pervasive concentration on the lyrical moment in even the longest of narratives, and partly of the origin of much prose writing in the creation of stories around poems, a practice that gave rise to and is exemplified in the *uta monogatari* (stories about poems or poem tales). Because of the social and occasional nature of most poems, such stories tended toward realism. But the other major source of early prose writing, the retelling of folktales and fantasies, often derived from or influenced by Chinese examples, tended toward the unreal, although the resulting tales were closer to true narrative. It was the gradual mingling of these two streams during the 10th century that led to the emergence of mature prose narrative.

Monogatari literally means "talk of things," and it was in the popular pastime of storytelling among court ladies that prose narrative developed. Even after they had become a written form, *monogatari* retained their oral character, for they were often read aloud to a large or small audience, depending on the type of *monogatari.* Of the varieties that eventually developed, some scholars allow only *uta monogatari* and *tsukuri monogatari* (courtly romances) under the term *monogatari bungaku,* which they restrict to Heian court romances and their later imitations. Here, however, the term is taken to include a variety of *monogatari* which compose the corpus of classical narrative prose, as outlined below.

Uta Monogatari (Stories About Poems or Poem Tales)

These consist of a number of tales or chapters formed around poems with prose parts ranging in length from one line to several pages. They constitute an in-between stage in the development of prose narrative, since they have progressed beyond mere collections of poems with simple elaborative headnotes, but have not yet reached a mature narrative form. Of the three extant accepted members of the genre, ISE MONOGATARI (Tales of Ise), early 10th century, is of greatest literary and poetic value, and its 125 tales achieve a certain unity through the implication that they form the biography of a single hero.

Japan to 1334 (1958). Yamada An'ei, *Fukutekihen* (1891). Yamaguchi Osamu, *Mōko shūrai: Genkō no shinjitsu no kiroku* (1964). Yomiuri Shimbun Sha, ed, *Kamakura bushi,* vol 4 of *Nihon no rekishi,* (Yomiuri Shimbun Sha, 1965).   Kyotsu HORI

Mongol invasions of Korea

Mongol armies first invaded Korea in 1231. The KORYŎ dynasty (918–1392) quickly submitted, but once the Mongols had withdrawn, the court moved to Kanghwa Island off Korea's west coast and was able to defy the Mongols for some 25 years, while the latter continually invaded and devastated the peninsula. By 1259, however, Korean resistance was crushed and its kings became puppets who had no choice but to cooperate fully in the MONGOL INVASIONS OF JAPAN. Despite its exhaustion from war, Korea was forced to supply a fleet of 900 ships and provisions for 30,000 troops (7,000 of them Korean) for the invasion of 1274, and another 900 ships and provisions for 40,000 men (10,000 Korean) in 1281. Although the Koreans collaborated in the invasions of Japan, they kept the Japanese informed of Mongol intentions throughout this period. Mongol rule in Korea was weakened in 1356 by revolts that coincided with uprisings in China; it ended with the fall of the Mongols' Yuan (Yüan) dynasty in China in 1368. The Koryŏ dynasty fell with the Yuan, and Korea remained in chaos until the founding of the YI DYNASTY in 1392.   *C. Kenneth* QUINONES

monkeys

(saru). Macaca fuscata. The Japanese macaque is a medium-sized monkey with a short tail. The head and body measure about 60 centimeters (24 in) in length and the tail about 7 centimeters (2.8 in). It weighs about 12 kilograms (26 lb). The fur color is burnt amber. The exposed skin of the face and the callous buttock pads (ischial callosities) are red. It is distributed in Honshū, Shikoku, and Kyūshū. About 100 monkeys in six troops inhabit the Shimokita Peninsula of Aomori Prefecture at the northern end of Honshū, which is the northernmost habitat of any primate in the world. Monkeys are relatively common wild mammals in Japan, with 29,194 individuals in 425 troops confirmed (1962). Living in woods, they feed on fruit, young foliage, seeds, insects, and shellfish. They move rapidly, both in trees and on the ground and range over an area of from 3 to 15 square kilometers (1.2–5.8 sq mi). A troop is usually composed of 20 to 150 individuals but in one case has reached a total of 660. Each troop consists of a group of male leaders and females at the center surrounded by many inferior young males; order is maintained by means of a strict hierarchical system. The mating season is autumn through winter and a single offspring is born during spring or summer.   IMAIZUMI *Yoshiharu*

To the Japanese the monkey is a clever and friendly buffoon. Japanese myth contains mention of a monkey deity, Sarutahiko, and some Shintō shrines treat the monkey as a divine messenger.

In folktales the monkey often plays the role of an adversary but invariably blunders and ends the fool. The monkey's reputation as a

YAMATO MONOGATARI (ca 951, Tales of Yamato) is less successful as a work, since its 173 unconnected tales give little sense of unity, and its second half consists of anecdotes in which poetry plays a very insignificant role, for which reason the work is sometimes classified as *setsuwa* (see section on *setsuwa* below).

HEICHŪ MONOGATARI (ca 960, Tales of Heichū) is the most unified of the three, for its separate tales all recount the love affairs of one historical figure and are ordered into a seasonal sequence, a technique borrowed from poetry collections and revealing the origins of *uta monogatari.*

Tsukuri Monogatari (Courtly Romances or Prose Fiction)

Earliest of these true narratives is TAKETORI MONOGATARI (Tale of the Bamboo Cutter) from the early 10th century. Its plot clearly shows its dependence on earlier fairy tales and fantasies, but the society depicted is that of the Heian court, and there is some sophistication of narrative technique together with the beginnings of satisfying character portrayal. Its successor, UTSUBO MONOGATARI (Tale of the Hollow Tree), late 10th century, is also dependent on fantastic themes, but shows advances in realism in its descriptions of court intrigues and love affairs. Characterization, however, is disappointingly flat. An advance both in characterization and realism is achieved in OCHIKUBO MONOGATARI (Tale of the Lower Room), late 10th century, in which elements of the fantastic have completely disappeared, although fairy-tale elements remain in the form of a wicked stepmother, or Cinderella theme. The development of *tsukuri monogatari* reaches its climax in the unrivaled masterpiece TALE OF GENJI *(Genji monogatari)* of the early 11th century.

Later romances, all strongly influenced by *Genji monogatari,* are generally of poor quality, and tend to have complicated plots involving hopeless love, with thin characterization. The most important romances of the late Heian period are HAMAMATSU CHŪNAGON MONOGATARI (11th century, Tale of Middle Counselor Hamamatsu), SAGOROMO MONOGATARI (ca 1070, Tale of Sagoromo), and *Yowa no nezame* (late 12th century, Midnight Awakening). An important collection of short stories is TSUTSUMI CHŪNAGON MONOGATARI (significance of the title is unknown), 12th to early 13th century, consisting of 10 stories and a fragment, notable for their humor and grotesqueness.

Considerable numbers of romances, called GIKO MONOGATARI (pseudoclassical tales), were written up to the 15th century. Most are of little merit, but worthy of note are SUMIYOSHI MONOGATARI (Tale of Sumiyoshi), a Kamakura-period (1185–1333) reworking of an earlier story; *Koke no koromo* (ca 1250, Robe of Moss); and *Iwashimizu monogatari* (ca 1270, Tale of Iwashimizu), which is somewhat unusual in recounting the love affair of a provincial warrior and the daughter of a court noble. The authorship of most of these romances is unknown or hotly disputed, but the three earliest are generally thought to be by men, while many of the later ones are attributed to women.

Rekishi Monogatari (Historical Tales) ——

In the late 11th century, under the influence of mature prose romances, the EIGA MONOGATARI (Tales of Glory) appeared, first of a line of eight historical narratives, successors to the RIKKOKUSHI (Six National Histories). Although their historical content is generally accurate, they tend to concentrate on unofficial, personal aspects of courtiers' lives, emphasizing emotional and aesthetic values. ŌKAGAMI (Great Mirror), late 11th or early 12th century, is the most satisfying as literature and uses the device of a 150-year-old narrator who has lived through the events described, a technique copied in subsequent works. These two tales, of unknown authorship, cover 887–1092 and 850–1025 respectively. Most important among later tales are: IMAKAGAMI (ca 1170, Mirror of the Present), *Mizukagami* (12th century, Water Mirror); and MASUKAGAMI (1338–76, Clear Mirror).

Gunki Monogatari (Military Tales) ——

These appeared in response to the emergence of a dominant warrior class following the wars of the late 12th century, wars that are the subjects of the first three tales: HŌGEN MONOGATARI (Tale of Hōgen), HEIJI MONOGATARI (Tale of Heiji), both early 13th century, covering respectively the wars of 1156 and 1160, and HEIKE MONOGATARI (Tale of the Heike), early 13th century to late 14th century, covering the war of 1180–1185. The change from earlier, courtly *monogatari* is not only one of subject matter and interest but also of language, which constitutes a major change in the development of narrative prose style. Other noteworthy examples are: GEMPEI SEISUIKI (The Rise and Fall of the Genji and the Heike), mid-13th to the 14th century; and TAIHEIKI (Chronicle of Great Peace), mid-14th century. Usually, passages of these tales were chanted aloud to an audience, and their authorship is unknown. See also GUNKI MONOGATARI.

Setsuwa ——

Often treated as a separate genre under the heading SETSUWA BUNGAKU (tale literature), these *monogatari* developed parallel to, rather than from, other types of *monogatari,* and they differ greatly in style and language from the courtly romances. They consist of collections of brief anecdotes almost entirely devoid of characterization or literary embellishment. While the origins of the form lie in Buddhist miracle tales, secular tales quickly adopted this form and became an important and often more satisfying ingredient of many collections. Their chief value lies in their humor and their depiction of the practical, even earthy, side of life as a complement to the idealized and aesthetic courtly romances. The best of these collections are: KONJAKU MONOGATARI (ca 1120, Tales of a Time That is Now Past); UJI SHŪI MONOGATARI (13th century, Collection of Tales from Uji); and KOKON CHOMONJŪ (1254, Collection of Things Heard Past and Present).

■ ——Donald Keene, tr, "The Tale of the Bamboo Cutter," *Monumenta Nipponica* 11.4 (1956). Hiroshi Kitagawa, Bruce T. Tsuchida, tr, *The Tale of the Heike* (1975). Helen Craig McCullough, tr, *The Taiheiki* (1959). Helen Craig McCullough, tr, *Tales of Ise* (1968). Helen Craig McCullough, *The Okagami* (1980). William H. and Helen Craig McCullough, tr, *A Tale of Flowering Fortunes* (1980), a translation of *Eiga Monogatari.* D. E. Mills, tr, *A Collection of Tales from Uji* (1970). Edwin O. Reischauer, tr, *Heiji Monogatari,* in *Translations from Early Japanese Literature.* Edward G. Seidensticker, tr, *The Tale of Genji* (1976). Wilfred Whitehouse, tr, *Ochikubo Monogatari* (1934). William R. Wilson, tr, *Hōgen Monogatari* (1971). Joseph K. Yamagiwa, Edwin O. Reischauer, tr, *Tsutsumi chūnagon monogatari* in Edwin O. Reischauer, Joseph K. Yamagiwa, *Translations from Early Japanese Literature* (1951). Marian Ury, tr, *Tales of Times Now Past* (1979). *Phillip T. HARRIES*

mono no aware

A literary and aesthetic ideal cultivated during the Heian period (794–1185). At its core is a deep, empathetic appreciation of the ephemeral beauty manifest in nature and human life, and it is therefore usually tinged with a hint of sadness; under certain circumstances it can be accompanied by admiration, awe, or even joy. The word was revived as part of the vocabulary of Japanese literary criticism through the writings of MOTOORI NORINAGA (1730–1801).

According to Norinaga, the word *aware* (or *ahare* in traditional orthography) is etymologically a combination of two interjections, *a* and *hare,* each of which was uttered spontaneously when one's heart was profoundly moved. In its earliest usage, *aware* seems to have been an exclamation indicating the presence of any intense emotion, whether joyous or sad, painful or loving, and that breadth of meaning was retained when the interjection came to be employed as an abstract noun. The Heian court nobility toned down the emotional intensity and limited the semantic comprehensiveness of the term, modifying the meaning of *aware* so as to stress elegant beauty, gentle melancholy, and the Buddhist sense of ephemerality. Altered to suit the taste of the time, the word also came to be used extensively in the Heian period, not only in its noun form but also as a verb *(awarebu)* and as an adjectival *(aware naru)* or adverbial *(aware to)* phrase. It occurs as many as 1,044 times in the TALE OF GENJI *(Genji monogatari),* Murasaki Shikibu's early-11th-century masterpiece, an enormous increase from the total of only nine occurrences in the MAN'YŌSHŪ, the oldest anthology of Japanese classical poetry of three centuries earlier. Its usage, however, became less frequent after the 11th century: the HEIKE MONOGATARI (mid-13th century) includes only 170 instances of *aware;* the TAIHEIKI (ca 1370), 253. Pessimistic overtones are even more pronounced in these later occurrences, as the word lost all its happier connotations to the derivative term *appare.* By Norinaga's time *aware* referred almost exclusively to "pathos," "sorrow," or "grief," and this remains true of today's usage as well.

Norinaga was the first scholar to notice the frequent occurrence of *aware* in the *Genji monogatari* and to attempt a serious study of its implications. From his studies, he concluded that *aware* as it appeared in that court romance was an important aesthetic ideal pervading all Heian literature, prose and poetry alike. In order to distinguish this ideal from the ordinary *aware* used in his own time, he called it *mono no aware,* a phrase that occurs only 14 times in the *Genji monogatari. Mono* implies "things," and *no* is a possessive particle; thus *mono no aware* means, literally, "a deep feeling over things." But, explaining the connotations of "things," Norinaga pointed out that the word *mono* was used when one spoke in broad general terms. *Mono,* in other words, universalizes the meaning of *aware.* Accordingly, the "deep feeling" of *mono no aware* is not an emotion deriving from someone's idiosyncrasy, but rather a feeling which emerges from the hearts of all sensitive men under given circumstances. A sad thing is sad to any man of cultivation and breeding; if there is anyone who fails to feel sad, he is heartless or, in Norinaga's idiom, he does not know *mono no aware.*

In Norinaga's view, then, *mono no aware* is a purified and exalted feeling, a feeling close to the innermost heart of man and nature. A person who understands *mono no aware* is a more complete individual because he is more perceptive, empathetic, and capable of understanding true human reality. In this sense, *mono no aware* as conceived by Norinaga can be said to be a humanistic value. Yet, insofar as the concept of *mono no aware* has been derived from Heian culture, it inevitably points toward a perception of human reality imbued with elegant beauty and Buddhistic pessimism, even though Norinaga, as a Shintō scholar, made some attempt to argue otherwise. Theoretically the meaning of *mono no aware* is as comprehensive as the whole range of human emotions, but in its actual usage it tends to focus on the beauty of impermanence and on the sensitive heart capable of appreciating that beauty.

📖——Shigeru Matsumoto, *Motoori Norinaga* (1970). Motoori Norinaga, *Genji monogatari tama no ogushi* (1796). Nishida Masayoshi, *Nihon no bi* (1970). Ōnishi Yoshinori, *Yūgen to aware* (1939). Watsuji Tetsurō, *Nihon seishinshi kenkyū* (1926).   *Makoto* UEDA

Mononobe family

Powerful family of the YAMATO COURT (ca 4th century–ca mid-7th century). According to the chronicles *Kojiki* (712) and *Nihon shoki* (720), their ancestors served under the legendary emperor JIMMU in his conquest of central Honshū and in Emperor Chūai's expedition against the KUMASO people of Kyūshū. Together with the ŌTOMO FAMILY, the Mononobe had hereditary charge of military affairs, and during the 5th century the heads of both families shared the important hereditary post of *ōmuraji* (great *muraji*; see UJI–KABANE SYSTEM). In the 6th century, however, with Mononobe no Arakabi's (d 535) suppression of the Rebellion of IWAI and then ŌTOMO NO KANAMURA's failure to protect the Japanese enclave of KAYA from Korean encroachment, the office of *ōmuraji* became the prerogative of the Mononobe. Through their numerous branch families, the Mononobe also held considerable power in the provinces. They later joined with the Nakatomi in opposing the pro-Buddhist policies of the newly ascendant SOGA FAMILY. The conflict came to a head over the question of imperial succession; in 587 MONONOBE NO MORIYA was killed in a battle mounted by the Soga, and the family was all but annihilated.   KITAMURA *Bunji*

Mononobe no Moriya (?–587)

Official of the YAMATO COURT; son of Mononobe no Okoshi, who as *ōmuraji* (chief minister) competed with members of the ŌTOMO FAMILY for power in the court. Succeeding his father, Moriya served as *ōmuraji* under the emperors Bidatsu (r 572–585) and Yōmei (r 585–587). During the reign of the former, the Mononobe family opposed the spread of Buddhism under the sponsorship of SOGA NO UMAKO; Moriya is said to have ordered all temples and monasteries built by the Soga to be burned and religious images thrown into a canal in Naniwa (now Ōsaka). After the death of Emperor Yōmei, Moriya conspired to raise Prince Anahobe, a son of Emperor KIMMEI, to the throne. He and his family were killed by an army led by Umako, and power fell into the hands of the Soga.   KITAMURA *Bunji*

mononoke

Vagrant spirits of the living or the dead believed to possess a person and cause death or illness. *Mononoke* are associated mainly with the Heian period (794–1185), appearing for example in the early-11th-century novel the TALE OF GENJI (*Genji monogatari*). A person's spirit was believed to detach itself from the body permanently at death, or temporarily during times of emotional stress. Such a spirit was termed *mononoke* when it possessed another person either from anger, jealousy, or vengeful resentment. See also GORYŌ; EXORCISM.   INOKUCHI *Shōji*

monopoly and oligopoly

(*dokusen; kasen*). The degree of oligopolistic control of the Japanese economy did not increase during the post–World War II period of high growth when markets were expanding rapidly, but such control has been on the rise now that growth has slowed. A Fair Trade Commission survey, measuring concentration as the combined market share of the top three companies in each industry, found that concentration had risen on the index from 100 in 1967 to 104 in 1976. The aggregate index, however, masks contradictory trends. In already highly oligopolistic industries (i.e., where the market share of the top three companies exceeds 70 percent, such as the beer, photographic film, and passenger car industries), concentration on the index fell from 100 to 95.7 over the same decade. On the other hand, concentration rose in industries where the three leaders' market share ranged from 30 to 70 percent. Moreover, there were changes in rank among the top three companies in many industries. Fiscal 1977 saw the top-ranked firm change in the foods, textiles, paper, chemicals, petroleum products, iron and steel, machinery, electrical machinery, and transportation equipment industries. In other industries, the first-ranked firm stayed on top but lost some share of the market, reflecting intensified competition. See also ANTIMONOPOLY LAW; INDUSTRIAL ORGANIZATION.

MASUDA *Yūji*

Montblanc, Charles, Comte des Cantons de (1832–1893)

Belgian aristocrat and adventurer; European agent for the Satsuma domain (now Kagoshima Prefecture). Montblanc first visited Japan in 1861–62. Returning to Paris, he offered his services as adviser and guide to the shogunate missions of 1864 and 1865 but was rebuffed by Tokugawa officials. He gained the confidence of some Satsuma students in London, however, and signed an agreement with them in Brussels to serve as Satsuma's agent in the formation of a joint French-Satsuma trading company and the development of Satsuma's natural resources in return for European arms and manufactured goods. He also arranged for Satsuma's independent participation in the Paris Exposition of 1867. In late 1867 and in early 1868 he accompanied Satsuma's leaders to Kyōto, where he provided valuable diplomatic advice during the early weeks of the new Meiji government. As reward for his service, Montblanc was named Japan's minister and consul-general in Paris, a post he held until an embassy was established late in 1870.

📖——Mark D. Ericson, "The Tokugawa Bakufu and Léon Roches," PhD dissertation, University of Hawaii (1978). Inuzuka Takaaki, *Satsuma Han Eikoku ryūgakusei* (1975).

Mark D. ERICSON

monzen machi

(temple town). Literally, "a town in front of the gate," referring to a built-up area located near the entryway to a Buddhist temple or a Shintō shrine. The commercial district which developed along the road to a popular temple or shrine sold religious objects, offered food and lodging to visitors, and in noteworthy instances, formed the nucleus for a substantial urban community.

During the 13th to 16th centuries religious organizations often provided the security and the concentration of resources essential for the formation of marketing centers (see MARKET TOWNS) or cities. Along with secular contenders for local power and wealth, they competed as sponsors of commercial enterprise and urban growth. Special factors also combined to link religious organizations with trading activities. The heritage of SHŌEN (landed estate) property rights and revenues had given major temples and shrines long experience in financial management and in business patronage; in an era of *shōen* decline, religious organizations were forced to search for alternative sources of income through commercial gains and taxes. Moreover, the religious awakening evident in the increased popularity of pilgrimages to temples and shrines required the services of an embryonic tourist industry.

In the long run, however, community vitality rarely rested on these factors. Prosperity frequently depended on the popularity of the recently established periodic market or on the acquisition of a post station (see POST-STATION TOWNS). Even when the tradition of the religious origins of the commercial district persisted, the character of the settlement might differ very little from places without a *monzen machi* legacy.

Monzen machi during the Edo period (1600–1868) made up only an insignificant portion of the overall urban network. The consolidation of urban functions in a reduced number of CASTLE TOWNS involved religious organizations as well as military, administrative, and commercial groups. Rather than being at the center of the city, temples and shrines were often reestablished near the periphery. Unlike in the previous period, they exerted little impact on the principal city-building forces.

In two respects, however, even castle towns and other large cities preserved some of the character of *monzen machi*. First, authorities did take special cognizance of urban areas in which temples and shrines were concentrated. In some large cities such as EDO (now Tōkyō), a separate administrative apparatus (JISHA BUGYŌ) governed these areas. Second, the wards (*chō*) near the entryways to religious structures not only were in some instances placed under this separate administration, they were also able to perpetuate the blend of religiously oriented shops and other commerce that represented the *monzen machi* heritage.

Genuine *monzen machi* persisted as outlying settlements with small-scale commerce. With the boom in modern tourism, such *monzen machi* as Uji-Yamada, near the ISE SHRINE, have attracted sightseers and vacationers. As during all but their early history as a settlement type, *monzen machi* are valued primarily as historic and religious sites. See also PILGRIMAGES. *Gilbert* ROZMAN

moon viewing

(*tsukimi*). Moon viewing has long been a popular pastime in Japan, especially on Jūgoya, the night of the full moon of the eighth month, which was the 15th night (*jūgoya*) of the month in the old lunar calendar. The Japanese adopted the Chinese custom of setting out melons, green soybeans, and fruits in the garden as offerings to the moon on this day. Jūgoya is considered to be the "harvest moon" and is an occasion for thanksgiving and partying. Sprays of *susuki* (eulalia) are displayed on the veranda and tiny skewered dumplings (*dango*) and vegetables are offered to the moon. It is said that displaying *susuki*, which resembles the rice plant, will ensure a good harvest. Because new sweet potatoes (*satsumaimo*) are offered, the full moon on Jūgoya is also known as the "sweet potato moon" (*imo meigetsu*). A repeat viewing of the "harvest moon" is held on the 13th day of the ninth lunar month.

The significance of the full moon is reflected in the celebrations of Koshōgatsu ("Little New Year") on the 15th day of the first month, and in the BON FESTIVAL, the Buddhist festival of the dead, on the 15th day of the seventh month.

Moon viewing is a common theme in Japanese poetry, particularly in WAKA and HAIKU. It ranks with SNOW VIEWING and HANAMI (cherry-blossom viewing) as the three most favored settings for declarations of love and poetic outpourings of the soul. When a poet uses simply the word *tsukimi*, it refers to the harvest full moon. INOKUCHI *Shōji*

Moraes, Wenceslau de (1854–1929)

Portuguese naval officer, diplomat, and writer. As a naval officer stationed in the Portuguese colony of Mozambique and later Macao, Moraes wrote essays and short stories on Asia, many of which appeared in Lisbon newspapers. In 1889 he made the first of several visits to Japan. He was deeply attracted by Japan and its people and left the navy in 1898 to seek a permanent home there. He was able to secure a temporary post with the Portuguese diplomatic service, and with the formal establishment of the Portuguese consulate in Ōsaka the following year, he was appointed vice consul. In 1912, following the death of his Japanese wife Fukumoto Yone, and the political upheaval in Portugal, he retired from public service. He then lived with Yone's niece Saitō Koharu until her death three years later, passing his remaining days in Tokushima on the island of Shikoku. His writings on Japan have been translated into Japanese and collected in *Teihon Moraesu zenshū*, 5 vols (Shūeisha, 1969).

moral education

(*dōtoku kyōiku*). Moral education in Japanese schools, especially at public schools, is not based on religion but is secular in nature. In the period before World War II, so-called moral training had an excessively nationalistic and authoritarian bias (see SHŪSHIN), but after the war this was done away with. The present moral education encourages students to be morally self-directing and stresses preparation for life in a democratic society. Moral education is not confined to social studies classes but is included in all school activities. Since 1958 one hour a week has been set aside for moral education

in elementary and middle schools. Moral values in everyday life, one's obligations in personal relationships, the family, society, and so forth are discussed in the classroom. NISHIMURA *Makoto*

morality

In the West the concept of morality is based on custom and tradition, as can be seen in the derivation of the word morality from the Latin *mores*. This is not the case in China and Japan, where the corresponding word, pronounced *dōtoku* in Japanese, is written with two Chinese characters, the first of which means "the Way." Confucius expounded the Way thus: "In the morning hear the Way; in the evening die without regrets" (*Analects* 4:8). The idea of *logos* and the way of sainthood are both represented in this idea of the Way. As is implied in Lao Tzu's saying that "the Way which can be named is not the true Way," morality is a universal principle hidden in the inner part of man that governs his thinking and acting.

Morality in the East is thus not merely a system of ethics, that is, an act of human society, a model for living. It consists of the attitude of man towards absolute being (religion), other human beings (ethics) and towards other creatures and things (technology).

In discussions of morality, one important problem is the relation between morality and law. Human beings require rules of law in order to live harmoniously, especially to effect the smooth running of mainly public activities. Such an objectified system controls human actions externally. Morality, on the other hand, acts as the support for ethics and becomes man's internalized index for conduct. Within this broader sphere there is the Aristotelian approach, in which law stands over ethics but is also complementary in that ethics serves as its foundation. In the Confucian view, on the other hand, *li* (J: *ri*; decorum, rites) is the essence of morality, which implies that morality transcends laws.

Japanese morality at present is going through a process of transition similar to what is taking place elsewhere as it seeks to come to terms with problems occasioned by the impact of technology on human life, e.g., problems of the environment, sexuality, and euthanasia. See also ETHICS, EAST AND WEST. IMAMICHI *Tomonobu*

Morgan, Yuki (1881–1963)

Maiden name, Katō; born in Kyōto. A *geisha* in the Gion section of Kyōto from the age of 14, in 1904 she accepted an offer of marriage from an American, George Dennison Morgan, a nephew of the financier J. P. Morgan. Their marriage created a journalistic sensation in both Japan and the United States, and they chose eventually to settle in France. After her husband's death in 1915, Yuki remained in France; she lived in the home of the linguist S. Tandart (1877–1931) and helped with the posthumous publication of his *Dictionnaire cambodgien–français* (1935). She was drawn to the Catholic faith and supported church activities with her wealth. Returning to Japan in 1938, she lived modestly in Kyōto and continued her association with the Catholic Church, into which she was baptized in 1953. Her life has been the subject of a musical play and several novels and biographies.

Mori Arimasa (1911–1976)

Philosopher. Born in Tōkyō, Mori graduated from Tōkyō University in 1938. After teaching at Tōkyō Unversity, he taught Japanese language and literature at the University of Paris and the Institute of Oriental Languages in France from 1950 until his death. Mori's central concern was the investigation into the essence of Japanese and European cultures. His interest can be traced to his formative years when urban Japanese were strongly influenced by Western culture and to his need to explore a new direction for Japan in the aftermath of World War II. Central to his philosophy is the concept of "experience" (*keiken*), through which abstract words and concepts come alive in a truly meaningful way. His writings include *Pasukaru no hōhō* (1938, Pascal's Way), *Babiron no nagare no hotori nite* (1957, By the Waters of Babylon). TAKAHASHI *Ken'ichi*

Mori Arinori (1847–1889)

Viscount. Prominent educational statesman, diplomat, and outspoken proponent of Western thought and social practices early in the Meiji period (1868–1912). As the first minister of education (1885–89) he imposed much of the elitist, statist, and utilitarian structure and tone of prewar Japanese education.

Arinori (also pronounced Yūrei) was born into a *samurai* family in the Satsuma domain (now Kagoshima Prefecture), on 23 August 1847 (Kōka 4.7.13). Educated in the Chinese classics at the Zōshikan (a samurai school) and in English at the Kaiseijo (School for Western Learning) in Kagoshima, he was secretly dispatched by the domain under the alias of Sawai Tetsuma to Britain in 1865, where he studied naval surveying, mathematics, and physics for two years. Crossing to America in 1867 at the invitation of his close British mentor, the author-diplomat Laurence OLIPHANT, Mori spent a year with the Brotherhood of the New Life, a spartan religious colony at Brocton, New York, run by the ex-Swedenborgian spiritualist and sexual mystic, Thomas Lake HARRIS. He returned to Japan in 1868 to join the new Meiji government, taking a variety of administrative posts.

Forced to resign in 1869 after prematurely proposing the abolition of sword-wearing, he opened a school for English in Kagoshima (1869–70) before returning to a lifelong government career in the Foreign Office (1870–84) and the Ministry of Education (1885–89).

As Japan's first envoy to Washington (1871–73), Mori cultivated American political and intellectual leaders, surveyed US educational and social institutions, and read the works of John Stuart Mill and Herbert Spencer. Returning to Tōkyō as deputy vice foreign minister (1873–75) and vice foreign minister (1878–79), with a year as ambassador (1876–77) to Beijing (Peking), Mori organized Japan's first modern intellectual society and magazine (the MEIROKUSHA and *Meiroku zasshi*, respectively), in 1873. In 1875 he founded the first commercial college, the Shōhō Kōshūjo (now Hitotsubashi University), in order to promote the economic, social, educational, and moral uplift he considered the key to Japan's national survival.

As a member of the MEIJI ENLIGHTENMENT movement of the 1870s, Mori advocated religious freedom and secular education in *Religious Freedom in Japan* (1872); adoption of a modern school system in *Education in Japan* (1873); abandoning the Japanese language in favor of English (*kokugo haishiron* in his personal correspondence of 1873); the social, but not political, emancipation of women in "Saishōron" (1874–75, On Wives and Mistresses); and the adherence of all nations to *jōri* (reason) and the principles of international law.

Although neither a convert nor a churchgoer, Mori retained a strong ethical appreciation of Protestant Christianity and drew heavily on Spencer for his advocacy of military-style physical fitness drills in "Shintai no nōryoku" (1879, On Physical Fitness) and for his ethic of "cooperation of self and other" (*jita heiritsu*) in the *Rinrisho* (Ethics Textbook) of 1888.

Consistently a political gradualist, Mori had disavowed American-style democracy in *Life and Resources in America* in 1871. He stressed the historical importance of the emperor in *Education in Japan* in 1873 and in 1883 prepared a bilingual draft constitution, *On a Representative System of Government for Japan/Daigi seitairon*, featuring functional representation, indirect elections, and a pivotal political role for the emperor.

Continuing frustrations with the revision of the Unequal Treaties (see UNEQUAL TREATIES, REVISION OF) while ambassador to London (1880–84) and conservative constitutional advice from close Western mentors, including Ulysses S. Grant and Herbert Spencer, only deepened Mori's concern for a strong, stable state and for an educational system which would support it. Although Mori's ideas probably owed much to the praise of French and German models by English reformers like A. J. Mundella and Matthew Arnold, his suggestions toward a more centralized, state-oriented system fit the constitutional plans of ITŌ HIROBUMI (1841–1909), who took Mori into his first cabinet in 1886.

As education minister, Mori, in response to economic stringencies and political challenges to the government, brought all schools under firmer ministry control and imposed a severe regimentation on the normal schools through his quasi-military drills. Practical education and service to the state were emphasized, and the training of an elite class was assured by the multiple tracking of primary and secondary schools, the creation of the privileged HIGHER SCHOOLS (*kōtō gakkō*), and the redesignation of Tōkyō University as "Imperial." See IMPERIAL UNIVERSITIES.

Viewing world conflict with Spencer as more commercial than military, Mori was in many ways a Victorian-style nationalist seeking to operate in a lingering traditional context. Although denounced by postwar progressives as a reactionary, he grated on his own generation of Japanese as an outspoken, heavily Anglicized harbinger of change and was assassinated by a Shintoist fanatic on 11 February 1889.

━━━━Mori Arinori, *Mori Arinori zenshū* (Sembundō, 1972). Ivan Parker Hall, *Mori Arinori* (1973). Kimura Kyō, *Mori sensei den* (1899). Ōkubo Toshiaki, *Mori Arinori* (1942).   *Ivan P. HALL*

Mōri family

Warrior family active as provincial leaders and later as *daimyō* at the southwestern tip of Honshū from the Kamakura period (1185–1333) until 1868. Particularly proud of their ties with the imperial court since the Heian period (794–1185), the Mōri encouraged a high level of culture in their domain, even inviting court nobles to visit from the capital in Kyōto. Their direct ancestor was ŌE NO HIROMOTO, political adviser to the first three shōguns of the Kamakura shogunate. His son Suemitsu adopted the surname Mōri when he was given an estate in Mōri, Sagami Province (now Kanagawa Prefecture). The family's power base shifted to Aki Province (now part of Hiroshima Prefecture) when Mōri Tokichika was appointed estate steward (JITŌ) there in 1336. MŌRI MOTONARI greatly expanded the family domain, beginning with his victory over the AMAKO FAMILY in 1540; he came to control as many as 10 provinces in southwestern Honshū. His grandson Mōri Terumoto (1553–1625), a trusted ally of TOYOTOMI HIDEYOSHI, was defeated by TOKUGAWA IEYASU at the Battle of SEKIGAHARA in 1600. The family was punished by having its domain reduced to the two provinces of Suō and Nagato, the latter more commonly known as Chōshū (now Yamaguchi Prefecture). The fact that all their retainers were crowded into these provinces gave Chōshū an unusually high percentage of *samurai*. Yet Chōshū's rice production and wealth increased, and the Mōri were still counted among the most powerful *tozama* (outside) daimyō. Their castle was at Hagi until 1863, when they moved to Yamaguchi. Chōshū's last daimyō, Mōri Yoshichika, although not as politically active as the SHIMAZU FAMILY of Satsuma (now Kagoshima Prefecture), carried out successful economic reforms and allowed his domain to become a center for the movement that overthrew the Tokugawa shogunate in 1867–68 (see MEIJI RESTORATION).

Moriguchi

City in central Ōsaka Prefecture; borders the city of Ōsaka to the southwest. Moriguchi thrived as a post-station town during the Edo period (1600–1868). It is the site of numerous electric machinery and appliance, textile, and machine tool factories, most notably those of the Matsushita Electric Industrial Co, Ltd, and the San'yō Electric Co, Ltd. It is a satellite city of Ōsaka. Pop: 165,635.

Mori Hanae (1926–   )

Fashion designer. Born in Shimane Prefecture. Graduate of Tōkyō Women's Christian University. Her striking designs with their oriental flavor have won her international fame. Recently her fashion activities have become global in scope. A member of the Paris world of high fashion, she has also designed uniforms for public officials in the People's Republic of China. She is a recipient of the Nieman Marcus Award.   *HAYASHI Kunio*

Mori Kaku (1882–1932)

Also known as Mori Tsutomu. Entrepreneur and politician. A native of Ōsaka, upon graduation from the Tōkyō Middle School of Commerce and Industry (Tōkyō Shōkō Chūgakko) in 1901, he was sent by the MITSUI company to its Shanghai branch as a trainee and formally entered its employ in 1905. During assignments to various Mitsui branches in China he established the China Enterprise Company (Chūgoku Kōgyō Kaisha), later renamed China–Japan Enterprise Company (Chūnichi Jitsugyō Kaisha), to facilitate Japanese investments and development of resources in China. Retiring from Mitsui in 1920, Mori joined the RIKKEN SEIYŪKAI party and was elected to the Imperial Diet five times. Attaining a position of leadership in the Seiyūkai, he and his fellow party members KUHARA FUSANOSUKE and SUZUKI KISABURŌ established close ties with rightists and military leaders such as HIRANUMA KIICHIRŌ and TANAKA GIICHI and advocated an expansionist policy on the Asian continent. See also TŌHŌ KAIGI.

Mori Kansai (1814–1894)

MARUYAMA–SHIJŌ SCHOOL painter and the last Mōri family artist of note. Born in the castle town of Hagi, Chōshū domain (now Yamaguchi Prefecture), he was the son of a hereditary retainer to the

Mōri *daimyō*. As a boy he studied with Ōta Denryū. He went to Ōsaka in 1835 and received his most important training from Mori Tetsuzan (1775–1841), whose daughter he married and whose name he took upon adoption into the family. Because of his proimperial activities before the Meiji Restoration (1868), he traveled much and finally settled in Kyōto. There he succeeded Shiokawa Bunrin (1808–77) as head of the Jounsha, the successor to the Maruyama–Shijō exhibitions, which had been held in Kyōto from 1792 until 1864. He first established his reputation with his painting on the theme *Red Cliff,* which won a silver medal at the first Domestic Painting Competitive Exhibition (Naikoku Kaiga Kyōshinkai) in 1882. He was appointed imperial household artist *(teishitsu gigeiin)* in 1890, but aside from this he repeatedly declined official honors and prizes. Active as a teacher, he taught at the Kyōto Prefectural Painting School (Kyōto Fu Gagakkō) from its beginning in 1880, and he also opened his own painting school. His most notable pupils were Yamamoto Shunkyo (1871–1933) and Nomura Bunkyo (1854–1911). He painted directly without preliminary sketches and rarely repeated subject matter. His style, like that of MARUYAMA ŌKYO, relies more on wash, shading, and color than on line. His later work, much like that of KŌNO BAIREI, often included outlines and modeling brush strokes reminiscent of literati painting (BUN-JINGA). *Frederick* BAEKELAND

Morikawa Kyoroku (1656–1715)

Also known as Morikawa Kyoriku. *Haiku* poet of the Edo period; one of the ten principal disciples of BASHŌ and a systematic interpreter of his poetics. As a *samurai* in the service of the Hikone domain in Ōmi Province (now Shiga Prefecture), Kyoroku was well versed in the cultural pursuits of his class, such as painting in the Kanō style and composing Chinese poems, but it was only after a series of deaths in his family that he was seriously drawn to haiku. He taught himself from works of Bashō, apparently with such success that when he finally met Bashō in Edo (now Tōkyō) in 1692, the master immediately felt a spiritual kinship with him. Kyoroku had to return to Hikone the following year, 1693, and Bashō recorded their parting in the fine HAIBUN piece called *Saimon no ji* (Parting at the Brushwood Gate). Ultimately, however, Kyoroku is less memorable as a poet than as an interpreter of the poetic principles and practices of Bashō-style haiku. Among his notable publications are *Hentsuki* (1698), an anthology interspersed with instructive commentaries, and *Uda no hōshi* (1702?), a study of the various usages and philosophy of the Bashō school. *Haikai mondō* (1697–98), a record of his debates with MUKAI KYORAI in 1697–98, further illustrates his critical acumen with regard to the central issues of Bashō's poetics. He is probably best remembered as the compiler of the influential *Fūzoku monzen* (1706, also known as the *Honchō monzen*) the first extensive collection of the *haibun* prose writings of the Bashō school.

Mori Masayuki (1911–1973)

Actor. Real name Arishima Ikumitsu. Born in Tōkyō, the eldest son of novelist ARISHIMA TAKEO. He enrolled in the philosophy department at Kyōto University but left to become a stage actor. He subsequently joined the theater group Gekidan Theater Comèdie, performing at the Tsukiji Little Theater (Tsukiji Shōgekijō) in Tōkyō. Later his appearances on stage at the Bungakuza, Tōkyō Geijutsu Gekijō, and Gekidan Mingei brought him tremendous popularity. Invited to join Tōhō (see TŌHŌ CO, LTD) productions, he made his film debut in SHIMAZU YASUJIRŌ's *Haha no chizu* (1942, Mother's Map). Although he continued to act on stage, he became increasingly in demand as a film actor, appearing in such masterpieces as YOSHIMURA KŌZABURŌ's *Anjōke no butōkai* (1947, A Ball at the Anjō House) and *Waga shōgai no kagayakeru hibi* (1948, Bright Days of My Life); KUROSAWA AKIRA's *Rashōmon* (1950) and *Hakuchi* (1951, The Idiot); and NARUSE MIKIO's *Ukigumo* (1955, Floating Clouds). Mori was known for his sensitive interpretations of inner torment. His performance in *Hakuchi,* in particular, won him an enthusiastic following among women. *ITASAKA Tsuyoshi*

Morimoto Kaoru (1912–1946)

Playwright. Born in Ōsaka; graduated from Kyōto University majoring in English literature. He began writing plays while still in college and attracted attention with psychological plays in which the characters engage in high-sounding intellectual dialogue. His early

representative plays include *Hanabanashiki ichizoku* (1935) and *Taikutsu na jikan* (1937). In 1941 he joined the Bungakuza (Literary Theater), a theater company organized by KISHIDA KUNIO. His *Tomishima Matsugorō den* (1942), a historical drama based on a novel by Iwashita Shunsaku, scored a hit in 1942 and was made into a movie titled *Muhōmatsu no isshō* (1958, shown abroad as Rickshaw Man). In 1945 he wrote *Onna no isshō* (1945; tr *A Woman's Life,* 1961–62) for actress Sugimura Haruko (b 1909), which became another Bungakuza hit. In 1960 Sugimura performed this play in China, and it was later staged in Russia in the translated version. Morimoto wrote radio dramas and other scenarios, and translated Thornton Wilder's play *Our Town* into Japanese.

Mōri Motonari (1497–1571)

Daimyō and military leader in western Honshū during the late part of the Muromachi period (1333–1568). The second son of Mōri Hiromoto, Motonari became head of the MŌRI FAMILY of Aki Province (now part of Hiroshima Prefecture) in 1523. To maintain their independence during the chaos of the Sengoku period (1467–1568), the Mōri had allied themselves first with the neighboring AMAKO FAMILY and later with the ŌUCHI FAMILY.

With the help of the Ōuchi, Motonari seized extensive domains in Aki and Bingo provinces (now Hiroshima Prefecture) and in 1540 defeated the Amako family. When his ally ŌUCHI YOSHITAKA was attacked and murdered by a vassal, Sue Harukata (1521–55), in 1551, Motonari made war on Sue, defeating him in 1555 in a celebrated battle on the island of Itsukushima. After this victory Motonari destroyed the remains of the Amako, occupied the lands of the Ōuchi, and challenged the ŌTOMO FAMILY in Kyūshū. By the time of his death he had become master of the provinces of Aki and Bingo; Suō and Nagato (now Yamaguchi Prefecture); Bitchū (now part of Okayama Prefecture); Inaba and Hōki (now Tottori Prefecture); and Izumo, Oki, and Iwami (now Shimane Prefecture)—all in western Honshū—as well as parts of Kyūshū and Shikoku. Thus he was strong enough to present a serious challenge even to ODA NOBUNAGA. Yet he was known not only as a successful military leader but also as a superb diplomatic strategist and an accomplished poet. A well-known anecdote concerns his use of three arrows to show to his three sons the strength of alliance: each arrow could be broken separately, but the three arrows when held tightly together could not be broken. Two of these sons, Kobayakawa Takakage (1533–97) and Kikkawa Motoharu (1530–86), were adopted as the heirs of nearby daimyō and thus added their strength to the Mōri domain.

Morimoto Rokuji (1903–1936)

Archaeologist. Born in Nara Prefecture. A graduate of Unebi Middle School in Nara, Morimoto was interested in archaeology from an early age. He studied archaeology with MIYAKE YONEKICHI from 1924 and became a teaching assistant at Tōkyō Higher Normal School (later Tōkyō University of Education). In 1929 he founded the Tōkyō Archaeological Society (Tōkyō Kōko Gakkai) and became editor of its journal, *Kōkogaku* (Archaelogy). From 1931 to 1932 he studied in France. Morimoto's interests centered on the wet-rice agricultural technology of the Yayoi period (ca 300 BC–ca AD 300) and on the mounded tombs (KOFUN) of ancient Japan. His works include *Nihon kōkogaku kenkyū* (1943, Studies on Japanese Archaeology) and *Nihon nōkō bunka no kigen* (1941, The Origins of Agriculture in Japan). *ABE Gihei*

Morinaga & Co, Ltd

(Morinaga Seika). The largest confectioner in Japan, Morinaga was established in 1899 in Tōkyō. It began as a small but pioneering producer of Western-style confections, and took its current name in 1912. Utilizing modern advertising and promotion, and mechanized production, Morinaga expanded its market and became one of the leading confectionery and packaged grocery companies in the nation. In order to become self-sufficient in raw material, the company created the predecessor of MORINAGA MILK INDUSTRY CO, LTD, in 1917. Morinaga began organizing a chain of retail outlets before World War I and today has a nationwide distribution network. The company is affiliated with the Sunkist Co of the United States, whose canned soft drinks it sells on the domestic market. Sales for the fiscal year ending March 1982 totaled ¥108.6 billion (US $451.1 million), and capitalization stood at ¥8.7 billion (US $36.1 million). Corporate headquarters are located in Tōkyō.

Mori Ōgai

Photographed in 1911, the year he began serial publication of the novel *Gan* (Wild Goose).

Morinaga Milk Industry Co, Ltd

(Morinaga Nyūgyō). Company engaged in the manufacture and sale of milk, dairy products, soft drinks, and foodstuffs. Morinaga Milk Industry's predecessor was the milk division of MORINAGA & CO, LTD, which in 1921 began the first commercial production of powdered milk in Japan. Becoming independent in 1949, it expanded operations to produce butter, cheese, and casein, and is now a prominent member of the dairy industry in Japan. It was a pioneer in exporting technology abroad and currently has three joint venture firms incorporated overseas, as well as offices in the United States, Europe, and Taiwan. Sales for the fiscal year ending March 1982 totaled ¥275.7 billion (US $1.1 billion); the company was capitalized at ¥6 billion (US $24.9 million). Corporate headquarters are located in Tōkyō.

Morinaga Powdered Milk Incident

A major case of food poisoning in 1955 which affected about 12,000 infants, with more than 130 deaths. Throughout western Japan newborn children suffered from loss of appetite, fever, rashes, diarrhea, dark spotting of the skin, and convulsions that sometimes ended in death. The first victims began appearing in June 1955. In August a professor at the Okayama University School of Medicine identified the causative agent as arsenic in powdered milk produced by the MORINAGA MILK INDUSTRY CO, LTD.

The immediate source of the arsenic was disodium phosphate, used by Morinaga as a stabilizer to make the powdered milk more soluble in water. Morinaga had purchased an inferior grade of disodium phosphate, suitable for industrial use but not intended for human consumption. It contained about 21 to 35 parts per million of arsenic. The company carried out no safety test of either the stabilizer or the final product.

The Morinaga poisoning case was initially resolved in December 1955 by a five-man committee of medical specialists appointed by the minister of health and welfare. The committee announced that the poisoning had no aftereffects and recommended deaths to be compensated by payments of ¥250,000 and all other injuries by ¥10,000. Fourteen years later, Maruyama Hiroshi of Ōsaka University undertook the first follow-up study and demonstrated that there were serious aftereffects, including a high incidence of cerebral palsy and brain damage.

The Morinaga case had a long legal history. In 1955 in the Tokushima District Court, the local prosecutor's office filed criminal charges against a Morinaga production manager and factory superintendent for professional negligence in failing to test the purity of the disodium phosphate. They were acquitted after an eight-year trial, but the Takamatsu High Court ordered a retrial and was supported by the Supreme Court. On 28 November 1973 the Tokushima District Court sentenced the production manager to three years in prison and acquitted the factory superintendent. Based on this decision, in December 1973, 18 years after the incident, Morinaga, the Ministry of Health and Welfare, and a patients' association signed an agreement providing the poisoning victims with assistance for the duration of their lives.

——Iijima Nobuko, *Kōgai rōsai shokugyōbyō nempyō* (1977). Morinaga Miruku Chūdoku Higaisha Bengo Dan, ed, "Morinaga miruku chūdoku jiken no keii to genjō," *Jurisuto* (15 January 1974).
Michael R. REICH

Morinaga, Prince (1308–1335)

(Morinaga Shinnō). Also known as Prince Moriyoshi, Daitō no Miya, and Ōtō no Miya. The eldest son of Emperor GO-DAIGO, he entered the Buddhist priesthood at an early age and was made chief priest of the Tendai sect in 1327. When Go-Daigo attempted to overthrow the Kamakura shogunate in 1331 (see GENKŌ INCIDENT), Morinaga fought on his father's side at the head of a group of warrior-monks. When the emperor's army suffered a setback, the prince went on to raise forces in support of the imperial cause, eventually leaving the priesthood. When his father succeeded in restoring direct imperial rule in 1333 (see KEMMU RESTORATION), Morinaga was appointed supreme military commander but soon fell afoul of the powerful warlord ASHIKAGA TAKAUJI, who was to overthrow Go-Daigo's government in 1336. Prince Morinaga, exiled to Kamakura by Takauji, was killed there by Takauji's brother ASHIKAGA TADAYOSHI.

Mori Nobuteru (1884–1941)

Businessman and politician. Founder of the Mori Kontserun (from the German *Konzern*), a financial and industrial combine. Born in Chiba Prefecture. After operating a family iodine production venture, he became a prominent businessman as a result of the strong support of the Suzuki family of AJINOMOTO CO, INC fame. Mori expanded his business rapidly after successful ventures in the production of ammonia and refining of aluminum. By 1937 Mori had formed his own industrial combine, centered on electrochemical and metallurgical manufacturing. The holding company Mori Kōgyō controlled 14 direct subsidiaries, including SHŌWA DENKŌ, and six affiliates. Mori also served as a member of the House of Representatives.
UDAGAWA Masaru

Mori Ōgai (1862–1922)

One of the greatest men of letters in Japan's modern period. Novelist, critic, and medical scientist. Real name Mori Rintarō. Born in Tsuwano, Iwami Province (now part of Shimane Prefecture). The Mori family, founded in the mid-17th century, were hereditary domain physicians in the service of the *daimyō* of Tsuwano, the Kamei family. The early education of Ōgai, the eldest son, was predicated on the assumption that he would succeed his father as domain doctor. Starting at the age of seven, he attended classes in the Confucian classics at the domain school and took private lessons in Dutch, the language of Western medical studies in the Edo period (1600–1868).

In 1872, following the abolition of the daimyō domains the previous year, the Mori family moved to Tōkyō. Ōgai temporarily boarded at the house of the eminent scholar-official from Tsuwano, NISHI AMANE, and attended a private school to receive instruction in German, which had replaced Dutch as the language for medical studies in the Meiji period (1868–1912). Eventually the Mori family settled in the village of Koume in Mukōjima on the eastern bank of the Sumida River (Sumidagawa). In January 1874 Ōgai was admitted to the government medical school, which developed into the Tōkyō University Medical School after the foundation of the university in 1877. During his eight years of medical school, he received a comprehensive education in Western medicine from his German teachers. He graduated from the school in 1881 at the age of 19.

During his early years at medical school, Ōgai developed a taste for literature, reading extensively the late-Edo-period vernacular novels (see GESAKU) of BAKIN, TAMENAGA SHUNSUI, and SANTŌ KYŌDEN and taking lessons in classical Chinese composition from the writer Yoda Gakkai (1833–1909). Later, after his family moved in 1879 to Senju in the northeastern suburbs of Tōkyō, he studied Chinese poetry and Chinese medicine with Satō Genchō (1818–1897), a former professor of the shogunate's School of Oriental Medicine, who, left behind by the modernization of medicine, lived in a back alley of that town. By the time he graduated from medical school, Ōgai was a proficient writer of both prose and poetry in Chinese.

After graduation, he entered the army and began his career as a medical officer. He chose for his special fields military medical administration and hygiene. In 1884, at the age of 22, he was sent by the army to Germany, where he studied for four years with the leading experts of his fields: Franz Hofmann of Leipzig University, Wilhelm Roth of the Saxon Army in Dresden, Max von Pettenkofer of Munich University, and Robert Koch of Berlin University. His research focused on the nutritional value of the army diet and the hygienic conditions of army barracks. Rejecting the idea that adequate nutrition for soldiers required a Western diet, he concluded that the traditional Japanese diet based on rice was nutritionally sufficient and that rice should continue to serve as the staple of the diet served Japanese soldiers. He also argued that the traditional Japanese house was hygienically superior to the multistoried Western buildings.

During his years in Germany, Ōgai read extensively in European literature. He paid particular attention to the major German authors Lessing, Schiller, Goethe, Hoffman, and Wagner, but read as well the works of non-German authors such as Shakespeare, Calderon, Rousseau, and Turgenev.

Returning to Japan in 1888, he continued his service in the medical corps of the army. He campaigned for the development of scientific medical research in Japan, publishing a medical journal on his own and introducing among other subjects Richard Krafft-Ebing's writings on sexual psychology. Outside his career in the army, he waged a campaign for the creation of a modern Japanese literature, publishing his own literary journal, the *Shigarami sōshi* (The Weir Magazine). He was a staunch "antirealist" in literature. Leaving the study of reality to medicine and history, he assigned literature to the spiritual and emotional domain of life. He opposed the modern materialism that leads to the reckless pursuit of the gratification of desires. In his first literary article, published in January 1889, Ōgai rejected Emile Zola's idea of an "experimental novel," which he understood as an application in literature of Claude Bernard's theory of "experimental medicine." Opposing TSUBOUCHI SHŌYŌ's theory of realism, he insisted on the necessity of ideals in literary works. Materializing his theory in his work, Ōgai published three original short stories: "Maihime" (1890, The Dancing Girl), "Utakata no ki" (1890, The Mirage), and "Fumizukai" (1891, The Letter Carrier). Criticizing in them contemporary European literature, he parodied the works of Richard Wagner ("Utakata no ki") and Ivan Turgenev ("Maihime"), rejecting Wagner's fascination with devastating "Death in Love" and Turgenev's sympathy with Bakunin's anarchism. In the last piece of the trilogy, "Fumizukai," he advocated Goethe's spirit of "labor and renunciation," which he regarded as akin to the traditional East Asian faith in the way of heaven.

After 1892 Ōgai withdrew from the literary scene, although he continued to be involved in literature in his private life. In 1889 he married Akamatsu Toshiko, the daughter of Vice Admiral Akamatsu Noriyoshi (1841–1920), an old friend of Nishi Amane, but divorced her the following year. The divorce irreparably damaged his relationship with Nishi Amane. For the following 12 years he remained a bachelor, not marrying again until 1902 when, at the age of 40, he married Araki Shigeko, 18 years his junior, at the express wish of his mother. In 1892 he bought a house in Shiomizaka (popularly known as Dangozaka) in the Sendagi area of Tōkyō, into which he moved with his aging parents and two younger brothers. He christened his newly built study the Kanchōrō (The Tide-Viewing Tower). The house remained his home for the rest of his life. At the outbreak of the Sino-Japanese War of 1894–95, he was sent to Manchuria and, after Japan's victory the following year, to Taiwan. In 1899 he was appointed head of the medical corps in Kokura in Kyūshū and, as he put it, was in "exile" for 3 years. In 1902 he returned to Tōkyō, having been appointed head of the medical corps there. During the Russo-Japanese War of 1904–05, he was again sent to Manchuria. In 1907 he was promoted to surgeon general and was appointed head of the medical divison of the Army Ministry, the highest post within the medical corps. He held these posts for 9 years until his retirement in 1916.

During the 17 years between 1892 and 1909, Ōgai did not publish much. The only significant works from this period are *Sokkyō shijin* (1892–94; 1897–1901), a masterful translation of Hans Christian Andersen's novel *Improvisatoren,* and *Doitsu nikki* (German Diary; written during the years 1884–1888), which he rewrote from the original Chinese diary kept during his years in Germany into the present classical Japanese text during his years of "exile" in Kokura. In 1909 Ōgai, at the age of 47, resumed activity as a novelist. For the remaining 13 years of his life, he wrote and published energetically. His works in these years may be divided into three groups. From 1909 to 1912 he wrote fiction based on his own experiences, such as the short stories "Hannichi" (1909, A Half Day), "Shokudō" (1910, Office Restaurant), "Mōsō" (1911, Fantasy), "Hyaku monogatari" (1911, One Hundred Tales), "Kano yō ni" (1912, As if . . .), and the novels *Wita Sekusuarisu* (1909, Vita Sexualis), *Seinen* (1910–11, A Youth), *Gan* (1911–13, Wild Goose), and *Kaijin* (1911–12, Ruins), the last incomplete.

Deeply impressed by the suicide of General NOGI MARESUKE following the death of Emperor Meiji in 1912, Ōgai wrote "Okitsu Yagoemon no isho" (The Death Note of Okitsu Yagoemon), in which he described the joy of a *samurai* who commits ceremonial suicide following his master's death. In the following four years, he wrote a series of historical stories, such as "Abe ichizoku" (1913, The Abe Family), "Gojin ga hara no katakiuchi" (1913, The Vendetta at Gojiin ga hara), "Ōshio Heihachirō" (1914), "Sakai jiken" (1914, The Sakai Incident), "Sanshō dayū" (1915), and "Takasebune" (1916, The Takase Boat). In these stories he dealt with the problem of the anarchic impulse for destruction and self-annihilation and presented various examples of the conversion of that impulse into constructive emotions such as patriotic sentiment and readiness for self-sacrifice.

In 1916 he turned to biographies of doctors of Chinese medicine in the late Edo period: *Shibue Chūsai* (1916), *Izawa Ranken* (1916–17), and *Hōjō Katei* (1918–21). The literary value of these massive and meticulous biographies of obscure Tokugawa doctors has been controversial. However, Ōgai himself regarded them, particularly *Izawa Ranken,* as his major work. One of his reasons for writing these biographies of forgotten Chinese doctors was to pay tribute to Satō Genchō, with whom he had studied Chinese medicine in his youth. Shibue Chūsai occupied the post at the School of Oriental Medicine to which Satō Genchō succeeded, and Isawa Ranken was Chūsai's teacher.

After his retirement from the army, Ōgai was appointed in 1917 the head of the ZUSHORYŌ and the Tōkyō Imperial Household Museum. He remained in both posts until his death on 9 July 1922 from kidney failure caused by chronic tuberculosis. See also the section on Natsume Sōseki and Mori Ōgai in LITERATURE: modern fiction. 📖——Mori Ōgai, *Mori Ōgai zenshū,* 53 vols (Iwanami Shoten, 1951). *Yoshiyuki* NAKAI

Morioka

City in central Iwate Prefecture, northern Honshū, on the river Kitakamigawa. Morioka developed as a castle town of the Nambu domain after the construction of a castle by Nambu Nobunao in 1599. It has long been known for its traditional Nambu ironware. Iwate University is located here. The "Chagu chagu umakko," a parade of colorfully caparisoned horses in June, is a popular tourist attraction. Also of interest are the remains of Morioka Castle in Iwate Park, the Morioka City Local History Hall, and the home of the politician HARA TAKASHI. Pop: 229,123.

Mori Rammaru (1565?–1582)

A page of the presence *(koshō)* at the court of the hegemon ODA NOBUNAGA. Personal name Naritoshi; son of Mori Yoshinari (1523–1570) and brother of Mori Katsuzō (1558–1584), distinguished captains of Nobunaga's forces. Historical sources, such as SHINCHŌ KŌ KI and Nobunaga's extant epistolary corpus, make it clear that Rammaru from about 1579 occupied a fairly important position as Nobunaga's intermediary with other notables and as a member of his secretariat. In the main, however, Rammaru's notoriety derives from works of fiction, which portray him as Nobunaga's minion. Rammaru and his two younger brothers, Bōmaru and Rikimaru, also Nobunaga's pages, died alongside their lord in the HONNŌJI INCIDENT of 1582. *George* ELISON

Morisada mankō

A book on customs of the Edo period (1600–1868) written by Kitagawa Morisada (b 1810). Although completed 1853, the manuscript was unpublished until 1908, when it appeared as the *Ruijū kinsei fūzoku shi.* Two fascicles are believed to be missing from the original 35. A native of the Ōsaka area, Morisada is believed to have later moved to Edo (now Tōkyō). In the book, begun in 1837, the author set down what he had heard and observed about local mores and customs, adding new information from time to time. For facts predating the Bunka–Bunsei eras (1804–30), he relied on written sources. The information is divided into sections on housing, trades and occupations, currency, food and drink, clothing, houses of prostitution, theaters, and other categories. Of special interest are his comparisons of the different customs of Kyōto, Ōsaka, and Edo. Copiously illustrated, the book is an invaluable source for information on late Edo customs and folkways, particularly about the artisans of that period. *Ōtō Tokihiko*

Morishige Hisaya (1913–   )

Actor known for his comic roles. Born in Ōsaka Prefecture, he attended Waseda University. In 1936 he joined the Tōhō Theater Group (Tōhō Gekidan); he also performed on stage at the Nichigeki Theater, the Tōgeki Theater, and with the Roppa Troupe. Toward the end of World War II he worked as a radio announcer in Manchuria. Returning to Japan after the war, he was active in several vaudeville theater groups including the Teitoza, Kūkiza, and Moulin Rouge. His first motion picture was *Koshinuke nitōryū* (1950, Chicken Swordsman) directed by Namiki Kyōtarō. This was followed by Haruhara Masahisa's big hit *Santō jūyaku* (1952, Third-class Executive). He appeared in the entire *Santo jūyaku* movie series, playing an undependable gadabout ladykiller, a role that became his trademark. In TOYODA SHIRŌ's *Meoto zenzai* (1955, Marital Relations or Love is Shared Like Sweets) and *Neko to Shōzō to futari no onna* (1956, A Cat, Shōzō, and Two Women), he was perfectly cast in the part of the good-for-nothing man. His natural flair for this kind of role carried over into Toyoda's *Ekimae ryokan* (1958, Station Hotel) which developed into an *Ekimae* series. Morishige is also popular as a singer known for his own special "*morishige-bushi*" style of singing which especially appeals to the older generation. *ITASAKA Tsuyoshi*

Morishima Michio (1923–   )

Economist. Born in Ōsaka Prefecture. After graduating from Kyōto University in 1946, he became a professor at Kyōto and Ōsaka universities. Later he was appointed a professor at the London School of Economics. Morishima helped to elevate Japan's scholastic standards in modern economics, especially in the field of mathematical processes. His work in mathematical approaches to Marxist economics achieved international distinction. Morishima won the Order of Culture in 1976. His works, written in both Japanese and English, include *Dōgakuteki keizai riron* (1950), an attempt to synthesize John R. Hicks's and Paul Samuelson's theories of stabilization conditions; *Kindai shakai no keizai riron* (1973, Economic Theories of Modern Society); *Theory of Economic Growth* (1973); and *Marx's Economics* (1973). *YAMADA Katsumi*

Mori Sosen (1747–1821)

Painter. Real name Mori Shushō. Lived in Ōsaka from his youth. He was trained in the KANŌ SCHOOL of painting. Sosen became famous for his paintings of monkeys. His first paintings were of tame monkeys, but later he went to the mountains and spent three years observing and sketching wild animals, developing a remarkable skill based on direct observation and detailed sketches from life. Sosen shared this approach with the artists of the MARUYAMA-SHIJŌ SCHOOL and is sometimes considered an unofficial adherent of the school. He was also adept at painting deer and other animals. His paintings of other subjects were not much appreciated and his landscapes and figure paintings were judged extremely poor. Sosen's older brothers, Mori Yōshin (1730–1822) and Mori Shūhō (1738–1823), were also competent painters. Later generations of the family produced a succession of artists, the last being MORI KANSAI (1814–94). *C. H. MITCHELL*

Morita Akio (1921–   )

Businessman. Cofounder of SONY CORPORATION. Born in Aichi Prefecture, he graduated from Ōsaka University. Morita established Tōkyō Tsūshin Kōgyō (later Sony Corporation) in 1946 together with IBUKA MASARU, becoming president in 1971 and chairman in 1976. Morita handled the financial and business matters of the company, marketing Sony products all over the world. He led Sony to great success by "Americanizing" it through the establishment of a plant in San Diego, California, as well as by starting an important business through Sony Trading Corporation. Morita had Sony's stocks listed on the New York Stock Exchange (the first time for a Japanese company), and has contributed to the company's internationalization in many other ways. *YAMADA Makiko*

Morita Kan'ya

A well-known family line of KABUKI actors which began with Morita Kan'ya I (d 1679), an actor who was also the owner (*zamoto*) of the Moritaza, founded in 1661, one of the three principal kabuki theaters in the city of Edo (now Tōkyō). He was followed by Kan'ya II (1676–1734), Kan'ya III (d 1722), and Kan'ya IV (d 1743), all notable performers. Other outstanding artists of this family acting tradition were: Kan'ya VI (1724–80), who was both *tachiyaku* (performer of leading male roles) and ONNAGATA (female impersonator); Kan'ya VIII (1759–1814), a superb dancer; and Kan'ya XI (1800–63), a gifted *tachiyaku* and dancer.

During the Meiji period (1868–1912), Kan'ya XII (1846–97) distinguished himself as the manager of the Moritaza and, later, the Shintomiza, a theater built in 1875. In 1872, he moved the Moritaza from the outskirts of Edo where the kabuki theater district was then located to the center of the town. Breaking with the past, he initiated Western-style developments such as seats, gaslights, fireproofing, and lavatory facilities (traditionally everyone went to the nearby teahouses). Like Ichikawa Danjūrō IX (see ICHIKAWA DANJŪRŌ), Kan'ya XII worked to improve the social status of kabuki theater. By aggressively cultivating friendships among members of the Meiji elite, he persuaded aristocrats, politicians, and foreign dignitaries, like former US President Ulysses S. Grant and his wife in 1879, to attend his theater. Finally, in 1887, the imperial family was present at a series of special performances held at the residence of a high official. Although Kan'ya XII successfully raised kabuki to previously unrealized social respectability, his ambitious plans led to desperate financial difficulties; by 1894, he lost ownership of his theater. He wrote under the pen name Furukawa Shinsui and was a pupil of the great kabuki playwright Kawatake MOKUAMI. Kan'ya XII's son, Kan'ya XIII (1885–1932), was never a theater owner but an actor throughout his life. In traditional kabuki plays, he performed best in *wagoto* (male romantic leads); he also worked actively through his own theater troupe to promote newly written kabuki plays and Western dramas in translation. Kan'ya XIV (1907–75), the nephew of Kan'ya XIII, excelled in male romantic roles such as Yosaburō in *Yo wa nasake ukina no yokogushi* (1853) by Segawa Jokō III (1806–81).

——Kimura Kinka, *Morita Kan'ya* (1943).   *Ted T. TAKAYA*

Morita Sōhei (1881–1949)

Novelist and translator of Western literature. Original name Morita Yonematsu. Born in Gifu Prefecture, he graduated from the English literature department of Tōkyō University. A follower of novelist NATSUME SŌSEKI, he won acclaim as a writer when his novel *Baien* (1909, Smoke) was serialized in the newspaper *Tōkyō asahi shimbun* (now *Asahi shimbun*) on Sōseki's recommendation. Highly autobiographical, the novel is based on Sōhei's unsatisfying marriage and his subsequent meeting with Haruko, later known as the major feminist leader HIRATSUKA RAICHŌ, and their unsuccessful attempt to commit double suicide, an incident which created a great public stir. Shortly afterwards he joined the literary department of the *Asahi shimbun*. In 1920 he accepted a teaching position at Hōsei University, where he remained for 10 years. Most of his later works are either historical novels or translations of Western authors such as Gogol and Dostoevsky. Following World War II, he joined the Japan Communist Party but was not politically active. Besides a two-volume biography of Natsume Sōseki, his other works include the novels *Rinne* (1923–25, Reincarnation) and *Hosokawa Garashiya fujin* (1949–50) based on the life of the 16th-century Christian HOSOKAWA GRACIA.

Morita therapy

(Morita *ryōhō*). A form of psychotherapy named after its originator, Morita Masatake (also known as Morita Shōma; 1874–1938), to treat a cluster of neuroses which are termed *shinkeishitsu* (nervosity). A graduate of Tōkyō University Medical School and a contemporary of Freud, Morita was familiar with European medicine, psychiatry, and psychotherapy, as well as with Buddhist philosophy and with ZEN in particular. His disciples, many of whom were former patients, have continued to develop and expand Morita's method in their teaching, writing, and hospital administration and practice. Jikei University School of Medicine in Tōkyō, where Morita taught, is the academic center of Morita therapy.

According to Morita therapists, *shinkeishitsu* stems from a hypochondriacal temperament characterized by excessive introversion, self-consciousness, and hypersensitivity to one's mental or physical condition. Interlocked with this tendency is the inner dilemma of the perfectionist who, overly concerned with the discrepancy between the desirable and the actual state of self, compulsively struggles to overcome that deficiency, only to end up in a state of self-repulsion. The perfectionist is further driven into a vicious circle of psychic interaction (*seishin kōgo sayō*) whereby sensation and awareness become intensified and finally crystallize into a syndrome. *Shinkeishitsu* is differentiated symptomatically into three types: (1) the ordinary type, primarily involving bodily disturbances such as insomnia, headache, and fatigue; (2) the obsessive or phobic type, including anthropophobia; and (3) the paroxysmal or anxiety type, exemplified by palpitation seizures.

As Morita suggested, the *shinkeishitsu* personality may be biologically determined, but Japanese culture probably reinforces the tendency. The term *shinkeishitsu* is commonly used to describe, without derogatory connotation, a normal but sensitive individual and indeed the symptoms of neurasthenia, anthropophobia (*taijin kyōfushō*) in particular, provide a key to the understanding of normal Japanese personality types. The morbid fear of looking straight into another person's eyes or of blushing, for instance, seems to reflect, to an extreme degree, the cultural concern for maintaining decorum in front of others as well as sensitivity to approval and disapproval by others.

The central tenet of Morita therapy is "accept things as they are" (*aru ga mama ni*). Patients are directed to abandon their "unnatural" compulsion to control mind and body and, instead, to live with their problems, and to reenact their suffering, for example, erythrophobic patients are encouraged to blush as much as possible. The patient is advised to forget the past, concentrate on self-realization through bodily experience rather than verbal exchange, and attend to the world of facts, rejecting speculation and conjecture.

Actual practice varies among therapists, but some patterns are observable. Although treatment on an outpatient basis is practiced, hospitalization for about a 40-day period is preferred. Two major stages of therapy are clearly distinguished: bed rest and work. Bed rest, roughly for a week, in seclusion and without diversion, encourages the patient to suffer and eventually endure. The subsequent work stage is subdivided into three phases: light, moderate, and heavy. The assigned work is not contrived; it generally takes the form of contributing to the hospital's maintenance, e.g., laundry and meal preparation. This points to the familial or communal nature of the hospital, often involving the director-therapist and his or her family residing therein. The bonds between staff members and patients often last long after release from the hospital. See also PSYCHOLOGY IN JAPAN; PSYCHOTHERAPY.

🔖 ——Kondō Kyōichi, "The Origin of Morita Therapy," in William P. Lebra, ed, *Culture-Bound Syndromes, Ethnopsychiatry, and Alternate Therapies* (1976). Kōra Takehisa, "Morita Therapy," *International Journal of Psychiatry* (1965). Takie Sugiyama Lebra, "Shinkeishitsu and Morita Therapy," in *Japanese Patterns of Behavior* (1976). Morita Masatake, *Shinkeishitsu no hontai to ryōhō* (1960). David K. Reynolds, *Morita Psychotherapy* (1976).

Takie Sugiyama LEBRA

Morito Incident

The prosecution of MORITO TATSUO for publishing in January 1920 a scholarly article on the Russian radical Peter Alekseevich Kropotkin (1842–1921). His trial, which stretched from 30 January to 22 October 1920, was politically significant because it involved the issues of academic freedom and free speech, because it set justice officials to thinking about measures to suppress what they saw as dangerous ideologies flowing into Japan, and because it prompted Prosecutor-General HIRANUMA KIICHIRŌ and other bureaucrats to create semiofficial groups to stamp out subversive thought.

Morito, an assistant professor of economics at Tōkyō University, published an article entitled "Study on the Social Thought of Kropotkin" ("Kuropotokin no shakai shisō no kenkyū") in the first issue of *Keizaigaku kenkyū*, a journal of economics. The article summarized the anarchistic communism of Kropotkin and defined the ideal society. While Morito repudiated violent means of changing society and criticized flaws in Kropotkin's theories, he accepted the idea of eventually putting Kropotkin's thought into practice by legal means.

Criticism by campus rightists brought the article to the attention of the authorities. Unfortunately for Morito, Prime Minister HARA

TAKASHI and other officials were eager for a chance to express their displeasure with radical university professors and anxious to reinforce the national moral tone. They decided on 13 January to prosecute Professor Morito and Professor ŌUCHI HYŌE, the journal's editor.

At the closed trial Morito and Ōuchi were charged with violating article 42 of the PRESS LAW OF 1909, one clause of which made it treasonable to act in defiance of the constitution. Among the distinguished group of lawyers and intellectuals who supported the defendants was SASAKI SŌICHI. Sasaki argued that Morito had presented only a value judgment about an ideal social system and had intended neither to destroy the social structure nor to defy the constitution and that therefore the essay did not contain any illegal material. Sasaki warned the court that to punish a person for writing something that might precipitate an antistate action was to enter a hazy area where the law can never be exact.

In spite of a spirited defense, the court ruled on 3 March that while Morito had not violated article 42, he had violated article 41, which covered crimes disturbing the public peace. The prosecution appealed the case, and the new court, which interpreted the term "sedition" broadly, held that Morito had violated article 42 and imposed a sentence of three months in jail and fined him ¥70; Ōuchi was sentenced to one month and a fine of ¥20. In the review by the Great Court of Cassation, the judges concentrated on the meaning of the term "high treason." The defense pointed out that Morito had not only illustrated the flaws in Kropotkin's arguments but had also emphasized legal change in society. The court agreed that he seemed to advocate peaceful change, but the judges felt that they must uphold the decision of the Appeals Court because throughout the entire article Morito was propagandizing a harmful ideology that endangered the existence of the nation. Morito entered prison on 4 November.

In one sense, this case was a preview of the political trials of the following decade, in some of which the Meiji CONSTITUTION and various political problems became the issues instead of the facts of criminal law involved in the particular case. This court decision proclaimed new boundaries for publication and speech, and at the same time the trial informed the general public that steps were being taken to promote traditional ideologies.

🔖 ——Richard H. Mitchell, *Thought Control in Prewar Japan* (1976). Miyachi Masato, "Morito Tatsuo jiken: Gakumon no jiyū no hatsu no shiren," in Wagatsuma Sakae, ed, *Nihon seiji saiban shi roku: Taishō* (1969).

Richard H. MITCHELL

Morito Tatsuo (1888–)

Economist, educator, and politician. Born in Hiroshima Prefecture. After graduation from Tōkyō University, Morito became an assistant professor in its department of economics. In 1920 he was dismissed from the university and briefly jailed for publishing a sympathetic study of the Russian anarchist P. A. Kropotkin (see MORITO INCIDENT). On his release from prison he joined the ŌHARA INSTITUTE FOR SOCIAL RESEARCH, where he continued to study labor and educational issues; he also studied in Germany. After World War II Morito was elected three times to the House of Representatives as a member of the Japan Socialist Party and worked for important educational reforms as minister of education in the cabinets of KATAYAMA TETSU and ASHIDA HITOSHI from May 1947 to October 1948. He later served as president of Hiroshima University, chairman of the Japan Scholarship Foundation, and chairman of the CENTRAL COUNCIL FOR EDUCATION.

Moriyama

City in southwestern Shiga Prefecture, central Honshū, on the eastern shore of Lake Biwa. In the Edo period (1600–1868) Moriyama developed as one of the post-station towns on the highway Nakasendō. Long a center of rice production, fishing, and pearl cultivation, it has also developed textile and chemical industries. Pop: 46,763.

Moriyama Takichirō (1820–1871)

Interpreter who participated in important diplomatic negotiations at the end of the Edo period (1600–1868). Born to a family of hereditary interpreters of Dutch (ORANDA TSŪJI) in Nagasaki, he studied English with Ranald MACDONALD, an American who had jumped ship in Japan. When the Russian admiral E. V. PUTIATIN came to

Nagasaki in 1853 seeking trade, and again when Commodore Matthew PERRY visited in 1854, Moriyama acted as chief interpreter. He also helped in the compilation of an English–Japanese dictionary, *Egeresugo jisho wage*. In 1862 Moriyama accompanied the overseas mission led by TAKENOUCHI YASUNORI to seek postponement of the opening of ports and cities as stipulated by various treaties (see SHOGUNATE MISSIONS TO THE WEST). After the Meiji Restoration (1868), instead of seeking a government post, he opened a school in Tōkyō; his students included NUMA MORIKAZU, FUKUCHI GEN'ICHIRŌ, and TSUDA SEN.

morning glories

(asagao). *Pharbitis nil* or *Ipomoea nil*. One of the commonest garden plants in Japan, the morning glory has been grown since ancient times on fences or in pots with a pole or other support. This annual twining herb of the family Convolvulaceae has alternate, usually three-lobed pointed leaves with long leafstalks. In summer large funnel-shaped flowers open in early morning and close by midmorning. They are usually bluish purple, but are sometimes white, red, purple, or variegated.

The 1,000-year-old book ENGI SHIKI records that morning glories were brought to Japan for medicinal use, the seeds serving as a laxative and diuretic as they do still. Another Japanese species of morning glory is the wild species *noasagao* (*P. indica*) with heart-shaped leaves and blue flowers, which is found in southern coastal areas of Honshū and points south. It is thus clear that the *asagao* mentioned in early poems of the 8th century anthology *Man'yōshū* is not the morning glory but some other native plant such as the KIKYŌ (balloonflower). Once imported, morning glories soon won a place as garden plants because of their beautiful flowers, and Heian-period (794–1185) literature records that they were cultivated in the gardens of the court and nobles. It is thought that these early morning glories were closer to the wild variety, which is closer to the ivy-leaved morning glory (*I. hederacea*) found in America than those cultivated now. Cultivation techniques advanced during the Edo period (1600–1868), when many new varieties were developed, and illustrated catalogs of these were published one after another. At the beginning of the Meiji period (1868–1912), their popularity waned, but in the late 19th century the cultivation of mutant varieties with unusual shapes gradually became popular. Cultivation of large-blossomed varieties flourished during the Taishō period (1912–26), and seeds were exported overseas.

In Japan morning glories are now broadly divided into those prized for the size of their blossoms, with some over 20 centimeters (8 in) in diameter, and those prized for their form. There is much variety in color, pattern, shape, and leaf shape. The large-flowered types are the most commonly cultivated. See also MORNING GLORY FAIR.　　　　　　　　　　　　　　　　　　　*Matsuda Osamu*

morning glory fair

(asagaoichi). Annual event held around the Kishibojin temple in the Iriya district of Tōkyō. Until the end of the 1920s, morning glory vendors were a common sight in the streets of Tōkyō, and the morning glories sold in the compound of the Kishibojin became especially famous. Since the blossoms closed by 9 o'clock, customers often arrived before daybreak. The fair is held in early July; similar fairs are held in other areas. See also MORNING GLORIES.

Inokuchi Shōji

Morohashi Tetsuji (1883–1982)

Sinological historian, philosopher, literary scholar and lexicographer, best known for his compilation of the 13-volume *Dai kanwa jiten* (1955–60, Great Chinese-Japanese Character Dictionary), which is universally accepted as the most authoritative and exhaustive dictionary of the Chinese language and which contains all the Chinese characters used in China and Japan throughout written history. Born in Niigata Prefecture, he attended the department of Chinese and Japanese in Tōkyō Higher Normal College (1904–08) and, later, the graduate department of the same school (1909–10). He later taught at Tōkyō Higher Normal College (1910–45) and Tōkyō University of Arts and Sciences (1929–45).

He also served as director of the Seikadō Library of the Iwasaki family, known for its collections of classical Chinese documents. After his retirement from Tōkyō University of Arts and Sciences, he

taught at Kokugakuin University and Aoyama Gakuin University. From 1957 to 1964, he served as president of Tsuru University.

Before the completion of the *Dai kanwa jiten*, Morohashi was known for his works on the Confucianists of the Song (Sung) dynasty (960–1279), on the Four Books and Five Classics, and on the Chinese family system, including *Jugaku no mokuteki to sōju no katsudō* (1929, Goals of Confucianists and the Activities of Song Confucianists); *Rongo shūchū* (1939, Annotations to the Confucian Analects); *Keigaku kenkyū josetsu* (1936, Introduction of the Study of the Five Classics); and *Shina no kazokusei* (1940, The Chinese Family System).

The compilation of the *Dai kanwa jiten* had been conceived a few years before the official contract for its publication was signed in 1928. The first of the 13 volumes was published in 1943, but all Morohashi's data—the product of an effort of more than a decade and a half—was destroyed in an air raid in February 1945. However, he reconstructed his data from three copies of the 15,000-page proof which survived the air raid and completed the project. All Morohashi's publications, excluding dictionaries, are contained in the 10-volume collected works, *Morohashi Tetsuji zenshū* (1975–77, Taishūkan Shoten). See also DICTIONARIES.　　　　　*Susumu NAGARA*

Moromoriki

Diary of the 14th-century courtier Nakahara Moromori, who served as senior secretary (daigeki). His diary, in some 50 chapters, covers the years 1339–68, as well as parts of 1371 and 1374 in some copies. Because of Moromori's position at court, this work, which deals mainly with court administration and ceremonies, is valuable for understanding the various problems attendant on the division of the imperial house into the NORTHERN AND SOUTHERN COURTS after Emperor GO-DAIGO's unsuccessful KEMMU RESTORATION of 1333–36. This diary is also known as *Moroshigeki*, having at one time been mistakenly attributed to Moromori's brother. There is another *Moromoriki* by Oshikōji Moromori (1714–44), who also served as senior secretary at the court. His 15-chapter diary covers the years 1729–37 and 1740.　　　　　*G. Cameron HURST III*

Moronobu (?-1694)

The most prominent of the early UKIYO-E artists. Full name Hishikawa Moronobu. Born at Hoda (now in Chiba Prefecture), son of the noted brocade artisan Hishikawa Kichizaemon. Moronobu presumably studied the family craft under his father, but several years after the latter's death in 1662 he went to nearby Edo (now Tōkyō) and became an *ukiyo-e* artist, possibly under the tutelage of the KAMBUN MASTER. Moronobu's first signed and dated works are the illustrated book *Buke hyakunin isshu* (One Hundred Verses by Warriors) and sections of a painted handscroll depicting YOSHIWARA pleasure-quarter scenes (in the collection of the Tōkyō National Museum), both from the spring of 1672. These early works already reveal a mastery of genre depiction and group composition, indicating considerable prior study and practice—including training in the classical KANŌ SCHOOL and TOSA SCHOOL styles—as well as showing the influence of the Tosa-style genre pioneer IWASA MATABEI.

With the death, or retirement, around 1673 of his mentor the Kambun Master, Moronobu became the preeminent *ukiyo-e* artist of Edo, a position he was to maintain until his death two decades later. In addition to his numerous paintings (widely copied but only rarely extant in the originals), Moronobu's illustrated books and albums number at least 150. These include novels, verse anthologies, guidebooks, JŌRURI plays, courtesan and actor critiques, *kimono* pattern books, SHUNGA (erotica) texts and albums, and *ukiyo-e* picture books. In the last two categories Moronobu produced some of the classic masterpieces of *ukiyo-e* illustration, and several of the major early *ukiyo-e* prints are to be found among the frontispiece plates to Moronobu's *shunga* albums.

Moronobu's importance lay in his effective consolidation of the ephemeral styles of early genre painting and illustration. His style is one of controlled, powerful brush strokes and solid, dynamic figures, a manner eminently suited to the woodblock medium and a style that provided the necessary groundwork for the *ukiyo-e* masters of the following two centuries.

Moronobu's principal pupils or followers were Furuyama Moroshige, Ishikawa Tomonobu, and SUGIMURA JIHEI, but lesser work—mainly in the field of *ukiyo-e* painting—is also known by his son Morofusa and his pupils Moronaga, Masanobu, Tomofusa, and

Morohira, all using the Hishikawa name. Although Moronobu was not favored directly with pupils of genius, his style was revived, modified, and transmitted to the next generation within a decade of his death by TORII KIYONOBU I, TORII KIYOMASU I, OKUMURA MASANOBU, and the KAIGETSUDŌ SCHOOL.

■———Richard Lane, *Masters of the Japanese Print* (1962). Richard Lane, *Images from the Floating World* (1978). Richard Lane, *Shunga Books of the Ukiyo-e School: I—Moronobu: Series One through Series Four* (1973, 1974, 1976, 1978).   Richard LANE

Morrison Incident

(*Morrison gō* Jiken). An incident in 1837 in which an American merchant ship, the *Morrison,* was fired upon when it attempted to approach the Japanese coast. The repulse of the ship was in accordance with the Tokugawa shogunate's order forbidding foreign vessels to enter Japanese waters (see GAIKOKUSEN UCHIHARAI REI).

The *Morrison's* ostensible purpose in coming to Japan was to repatriate seven shipwrecked Japanese sailors. The American trading firm of Olyphant and Co, owners of the ship, and the American Board of Foreign Missions, which had given aid to the castaways in Macao, saw the situation as an opportunity to break Japan's long tradition of NATIONAL SECLUSION and to initiate trade and Christian proselytizing. The firm dispatched the *Morrison* from Macao in 1837 bearing the castaways, missionaries, and gifts and a Chinese letter of greeting to the shōgun. The ship attempted to enter Uraga Bay near Edo (now Tōkyō) but was immediately driven off. A month later it reappeared at Kagoshima Bay only to be fired on again, whereupon it returned to Macao with the castaways.

The shogunate authorities had never communicated with the *Morrison* and remained completely unaware of its mission until informed a year later in a report from the Dutch trade commissioner at Nagasaki. It was the shogunate's decision to repel the *Morrison* that inspired the WESTERN LEARNING scholars WATANABE KAZAN and TAKANO CHŌEI to write tracts critical of the seclusion policy. Their action incurred severe repression of Western Learning and its proponents (see BANSHA NO GOKU).

Morse, Edward Sylvester (1838–1925)

American zoologist and director of the Peabody Museum in Salem, Massachusetts; an outstanding early collector of Japanese artifacts; and author of works on a wide variety of subjects concerning Japan, from archaeology to architecture and folklore. Born in Portland, Maine, he studied conchology at Harvard University and taught at Bowdoin College, Maine, from 1871 to 1874. In 1877 he traveled to Japan at his own expense to study Pacific Ocean brachiopods. He established a marine biology laboratory at Enoshima in Kanagawa Prefecture and shortly thereafter was invited to teach zoology at the new Tōkyō University. From 1877 until he returned to the United States in 1879, Morse organized the university's zoology department and was instrumental in establishing the Japanese Imperial Museum. Morse helped introduce modern scientific methods to the study of zoology and biology in Japan, introduced and popularized Darwinian theories, and discovered the important ŌMORI SHELL MOUNDS (Ōmori *kaizuka*) in what is now the southwestern part of Tōkyō. Through his work at Ōmori, Morse became interested in Japanese pottery and returned to Japan in 1882–83 to assemble the outstanding collection of ancient to contemporary Japanese ceramics now housed at the Boston Museum of Fine Arts. Morse was awarded the Order of the Rising Sun (Kyokujitsushō) in 1898 and the Order of the Sacred Treasure (Zuihōshō) in 1922.

■———Edward S. Morse, *Japan Day by Day* (1917). Dorothy Wayman, *Edward Sylvester Morse: A Biography* (1942).
                    Edward R. BEAUCHAMP

mortars → usu

Mosse, Albert (1846–1925)

German legal adviser to the Japanese government in the late 1880s. Born in Grätz (now Poznan), Mosse studied law under Rudolph von GNEIST at the University of Berlin. In 1882, at the request of the German government, he and Gneist gave lectures on constitutional law to ITŌ HIROBUMI and his group, who were then touring Europe to study various constitutional systems. Like his teacher, Mosse advised that a Prussian-style monarchical constitutionalism was best

suited to Japan. In 1886 he was invited to Japan as a legal adviser. He assisted Itō and INOUE KOWASHI in drafting the 1889 Meiji CONSTITUTION; as an adviser to the Home Ministry, he also helped YAMAGATA ARITOMO draft laws for local government. Returning to Germany in 1890, Mosse became a judge in Königsberg and taught law at its university. In 1907 he became an administrative adviser to the city government of Berlin.   NAGAO Ryūichi

mosses

(*koke* or *kokerui*). Small plants of the division Bryophyta. The Japanese archipelago, whose climate ranges from subarctic to subtropical, is home for about 2,000 of the approximately 25,000 species of Bryophyta identified worldwide. The same species that inhabit the subarctic zones of North America and Europe are found in Hokkaidō and in the high mountains of the northern part of Honshū, while those inhabiting the tropical zone of East Asia are also found in southwestern Japan. Mosses growing in deciduous broad-leaved forest areas of Japan resemble those of the Himalayas and the Appalachian Mountains of North America. Taking advantage of the wealth of native species, the Japanese have developed distinctive styles of moss horticulture. The best known of these is the moss garden (*kokeniwa*), in which the ground is covered by mosses of the genus *Polytrichum*, genus *Leucobryum*, genus *Rhizogonium*, and others, and deciduous trees and rocks are arranged among them. Many examples of these gardens are found in temple precincts in Kyōto, and in recent years they have come to be cultivated in private homes as well. The other horticultural style is moss tray gardening (*koke bonkei*), in which a miniature landscape is created in a shallow wooden box with mosses as its base component.   INOUE Hiroshi

mother-of-pearl inlay

(*raden*). Decorative technique used in Japan mainly with wood and lacquer ware. The technique originated in the Near East and was introduced to Japan via Tang-dynasty (T'ang; 618–907) China around the 8th century; preserved in the SHŌSŌIN art repository in Nara are Tang Chinese mirrors and musical instruments decorated with mother-of-pearl inlay. In the 11th century, mother-of-pearl inlay was used with the MAKI-E lacquer technique, a uniquely Japanese innovation. Among the finest examples of Japanese *raden* are the interior of the Konjikidō (Golden Hall) of the CHŪSONJI temple in Iwate Prefecture and a lacquered cosmetics box with a design of wheels floating in water (Tōkyō National Museum). From about the 13th century, technical improvements were made that resulted in a better openwork method, which was used particularly for saddle decoration. In the 17th century the inlay technique was used by craftsman Ogawa Haritsu (1663–1747) and in many works of the RIMPA school. The method using abalone, or sea-ear shells, sometimes referred to as *aogai*, became popular from the Muromachi period (1333–1568).   NAKASATO Toshikatsu

Motion Picture Code Committee

(Eirin Kanri Iinkai). A voluntary control organ of the Japanese motion picture industry formed to oversee and impose censorship standards on the depiction of sex and violence on the screen. The committee was established under an order issued by the American Occupation forces in 1949. It implements and supervises application of the Motion Picture Code of Ethics (Eiga Rinri Kitei) established by Eiren (abbreviation of Nihon Eiga Rengōkai), a united federation of Japan's major motion picture companies. First known as Eiga Rinri Kitei Kanri Iinkai, it changed its name to the present Eirin Kanri Iinkai in 1957. Although the committee is not vested with any legal power, it confers with movie producers and recommends alterations of scenes that are too graphic or unsavory in films. Movies that have not obtained the approval of the Motion Picture Code Committee cannot be screened for public viewing.   SHIRAI Yoshio

motion pictures → film, Japanese

Motobu

Town on the island of Okinawa, Okinawa Prefecture. Motobu was the site of the Okinawa International Ocean Exposition in 1975. Principal products are pineapples, sugarcane, bonito, and tuna. There is regular ferry service to the islands of Iejima, Iheyajima, and Izenashima. Pop: 15,311.

Motoori Norinaga

Self-portrait, 1790. Detail of hanging scroll. Colors on paper.
115.1 × 53.4 cm. Motoori Norinaga Kinenkan, Matsuzaka, Mie Prefecture.

Motoda Nagazane (1818–1891)

Confucian scholar and educational theorist of the Meiji period; also known as Motoda Eifu. Born to a *samurai* family of the Kumamoto domain (now Kumamoto Prefecture), he studied at the domainal school under YOKOI SHŌNAN, who introduced him to the pragmatic or realist *(jitsugaku)* school of Neo-Confucianism. In 1871, on the recommendation of ŌKUBO TOSHIMICHI and others, Motoda entered the Imperial Household Agency as tutor *(jidoku)* to Emperor Meiji, through whose trust and favor he became a court adviser in 1886 and a member of the Privy Council (Sūmitsuin) in 1888. As a leader of the conservative faction in the court he helped to establish an educational ideology for the Meiji government centered on patriotism and reverence for the emperor. Motoda's principal writings include Kyōgaku Taishi (1879, Outline of Learning), in which he set forth his theories of education, and *Yōgaku kōyō* (1882, Essentials for the Education of Youth), an imperially sponsored textbook for moral training. He also took part in the drafting of the IMPERIAL RESCRIPT ON EDUCATION, promulgated in 1890.   *TANAKA Akira*

Motonobu → Kanō Motonobu

Motoori Haruniwa (1763–1828)

Scholar of Japanese language and literature; born in Ise (now Mie Prefecture), the eldest son of MOTOORI NORINAGA. He lost his sight in his late twenties. Supporting himself as an acupuncturist, he trained students and wrote two books on Japanese grammar. In his Kotoba no yachimata, 2 vols (1806–08), and Kotoba no kayoiji, 3 vols (1828), he classified Japanese verbs into seven conjugations, and studied transitive and intransitive verbs by dividing them into six types. He also dealt with phonological mutations and other aspects of language, further developing the Motoori school's studies of inflected words.   *SHIMADA Masahiko*

Motoori Norinaga (1730–1801)

Classical scholar of the Edo period who was largely responsible for bringing the KOKUGAKU (National Learning) movement to its culmination. Literary name Suzunoya. His works, totaling more than 90 titles and 260 volumes, are characterized by a rigorous philological approach, a recognition of the emotional nature of man, and a profound sense of reverence for Shintō mythology. His ultimate aim as a scholar was to discern the identity of Japanese culture through an intensive study of the ancient classics, especially the KOJIKI (712,

Records of Ancient Matters). Norinaga was also the only literary theorist of his period who clearly recognized the intrinsic value of literature and defended it against the prevailing moralistic views.

Childhood and Youth——Norinaga was born in 1730 at Matsusaka in the province of Ise (now part of Mie Prefecture), near the ISE SHRINE. According to his own account, his mother conceived him shortly after her husband, Ozu Sadatoshi, prayed to a Shintō deity for a child. Sadatoshi, a prosperous wholesaler of cotton goods, died when Norinaga was 10 years old. Under his mother's care young Norinaga received a broad education ranging from study of the Chinese classics and Japanese classical poetry (he composed WAKA from an early age) to archery and the TEA CEREMONY. In 1748 he was adopted by another merchant family and began working in the paper business, but the adoption was dissolved two years later. Sensing his aversion to a business career, Norinaga's mother decided to have him become a physician and in 1752 sent him to Kyōto for medical studies.

During his six-year stay in Kyōto, Norinaga studied much more than medicine. As a student of Chinese medicine he read many Chinese classics under the tutelage of Hori Keizan (1688–1757), a scholar of great erudition whose interests extended from Confucianism to Kokugaku and Japanese poetry. Living in Keizan's house, Norinaga became familiar with the works of KEICHŪ, a founder of the Kokugaku movement, and of OGYŪ SORAI, an influential Confucian scholar. The writings of the former introduced him to the philological study of literature, while those of the latter awakened him to the significance of antiquity, albeit in the Chinese context. Norinaga's interest in poetic composition grew more serious, too, as he became a student of well-known *waka* masters and often attended poetic gatherings. He took his medical training first under Hori Genkō (1686–1754) and then under the noted pediatrician Takekawa Kōjun (1725–80). Norinaga seems to have had no great enthusiasm for the subject of medicine, but he wanted to fulfill his mother's wishes, and he also knew he would require a secure means of livelihood in order to continue his classical studies. All in all, his life in Kyōto was a rewarding one which gave him both a vocational training and a broad humanistic education.

Norinaga drafted his first major work, *Ashiwake obune,* toward the end of his sojourn in Kyōto. Written largely in dialogue form, it expounded his concept of *waka* and touched on various issues relating to the nature, history, and art of poetry. Central to his argument was the contention that "the 31-syllable poem emerges when the poet gives proper expression to his emotions." Norinaga saw verse writing as the instinctive act of a person moved by intense emotion, an act totally independent of political and moral purposes. He ranked the composition of *waka* higher than that of Chinese verse on the grounds that a Japanese, when touched by a strong sentiment, would vent it spontaneously in his native language. Nevertheless, Norinaga refused to place *waka* at the root of Japanese civilization, according that honor to Shintō instead. These ideas, though not yet fully developed, clearly show the direction of the young author's thoughts.

Early Works in Literary Criticism——Norinaga returned to Matsusaka in 1757 and immediately began practicing medicine. By this time he had changed his family name from Ozu to Motoori, apparently out of his desire to mark the beginning of a new life. Three years later he married Murata Mika, a merchant's daughter, but the marriage broke up in three months. In 1762 he married again, this time a physician's daughter named Kusabuka Tami. The second marriage was a lasting one, which produced two sons and three daughters in the next 14 years.

As his life became settled, Norinaga began to offer informal lectures on the Japanese classics at his residence. He held classes on the TALE OF GENJI *(Genji monogatari)* nine times each month, continuing the course for some 8 years until he covered the entire tale. His lectures on the MAN'YŌSHŪ, the oldest extant anthology of classical Japanese poetry, which dates from the 8th century, were given three times per month over a period of more than 10 years. Similar sessions were conducted on other classics of Japanese literature such as the KOKINSHŪ (ca 905, Collection from Ancient and Modern Times), ISE MONOGATARI (mid-10th century, Tales of Ise), Makura no sōshi (ca 1000, The Pillow Book; see SEI SHŌNAGON), and his favorite poetry anthology, the *Shin kokinshū* (1205, New Collection from Ancient and Modern Times). He continued this practice to the end of his life, giving the complete lecture series on the *Genji monogatari* three times, and the one on the *Man'yōshū* twice. These facts indicated his indefatigable energy as well as his total devotion to literary studies.

Working as a physician in the daytime and a lecturer in the evening, Norinaga still managed to find time to engage in writing. By 1763 he had completed two works on Japanese literature. The first, *Shibun yōryō,* was a general study of the *Genji monogatari* that discussed its theme, authorship, age, textual history, and so forth. Among a number of new insights presented therein, the most original was Norinaga's proposal to interpret the tale in light of a literary ideal he termed MONO NO AWARE. Defining this as an empathetic appreciation of human feeling, he argued that the *Genji monogatari* benefited its readers because by transmitting *mono no aware* it made them more perceptive of the inner workings of the human psyche. Norinaga recognized the same ideal in other forms of literature as well. In his *Isonokami sasamegoto,* a dialogue on poetry completed around 1763, he made *mono no aware* the focus of his discussion of *waka* theory and practice. Although the work was basically a revision of *Ashiwake obune,* his argument had become more systematic now that he had a central concept to unify his ideas. "Poetry emerges when a person is touched by *mono no aware,*" he declared. To Norinaga, *mono no aware* had come to seem a grand principle that functioned both as the fount of inspiration for the literary artist and as the source of emotional impact on the reader.

From Literary Scholar to Classicist —— The year 1763 witnessed another event that had a profound effect on Norinaga's life: his meeting with KAMO NO MABUCHI. Though they met for only one evening, Norinaga came to revere the aging Kokugaku scholar as his mentor and continued to forward him numerous questions thereafter. What Norinaga learned from Mabuchi was, above all, the paramount significance of the pre-Heian period in studying Japanese civilization. He was made to realize the urgent need for going beyond the *Genji monogatari* to the earliest of all Japanese classics, the *Kojiki.* The following year he began writing *Kojiki den,* a detailed study of that Shintō classic that was to become his lifework.

During the next 25 years, Norinaga curtailed his travels and devoted himself wholeheartedly to the study of antiquity. Besides working on *Kojiki den,* he authored a number of shorter studies in this productive period of his career. By 1771 Norinaga had written *Naobi no mitama,* an outline of his interpretation of ancient Japanese mythology. According to this treatise, Shintō deities are powerful but irrational beings who rule the world in a way often incomprehensible to human intelligence. Norinaga attacked Confucian and Buddhist scholars for attempting to know the unknowable and for misleading their contemporaries through an overly optimistic estimation of man's intellect. He saw the image of ideal society in Japanese antiquity where, in his opinion, the land was in perfect order under the reign of emperors, descendants of the Shintō deities. The same nationalistic belief prompted Norinaga to write *Gyojū gaigen* (or *Karaosame no uretamigoto*) six years later, this time focusing on the history of Japan's foreign relations. The main targets of Norinaga's criticism were Confucian-minded political leaders who in his opinion had taken a subservient attitude toward China. He also wrote *Kuzubana* in 1780 and *Kenkyōjin* in 1785, both polemic works counterattacking Neo-Confucian scholars who had criticized his own Kokugaku stand.

In order to read the *Kojiki* and other ancient classics intensively, Norinaga had to make an analytical study of the language of antiquity, and his efforts along this line resulted in several philological works. *Himokagami,* written in 1771, and *Kotoba no tama no o,* completed eight years later, represent his attempts to examine the use of grammatical particles in the classics. *Kanji san'on kō,* completed in the early 1770s, was a study in Sino-Japanese phonology. In his *Jion kana zukai* of 1775, Norinaga tried to establish a proper correlation between Chinese ideograms and Japanese phonetic symbols. All these philological works are distinguished by Norinaga's careful inductive method and his unfailing passion to seek a linguistic model in the early classics. His contentions, however, were sometimes tainted by his bias against foreign civilizations.

Achievements of Later Years —— As the number of his writings increased, Norinaga's reputation as a scholar and teacher rose. By the early 1780s he had more than 140 students, some of whom came from other provinces, studying with him at one time. In 1787 the *daimyō* of Kii Province (now Wakayama Prefecture), solicited his advice on government, and Norinaga responded with *Hihon tamakushige.* Five years later the daimyō of Kaga Province (now part of Ishikawa Prefecture) invited him to serve as the chief Kokugaku instructor there, but Norinaga declined the offer, as he did not wish to leave Matsusaka. Shortly afterwards he accepted a position offered by the daimyō of Kii, whose castle was closer to his home. To propagate his teachings, Norinaga began to travel frequently over a

10-year period beginning in 1789; he took at least seven trips out of his home province.

Although these activities inevitably curtailed his time for writing, Norinaga was still able to produce some important works. By 1787 he had written *Tamakushige* in an effort to relate his Shintō ideas more closely to political philosophy. About the same time he produced *Kakaika* in reply to UEDA AKINARI, who had attacked some of his contentions in philology and classical studies. In 1789 he wrote *Kamiyo no masagoto,* retelling ancient myths in a language easier for contemporary readers to understand. During the 1790s he completed several exegetical studies of the Japanese classics. The most notable was *Genji monogatari tama no ogushi* of 1796, an exhaustive study of the massive tale. At the work's outset Norinaga provided a general introduction explaining, among other things, his concept of *mono no aware,* then went on to present detailed annotations on specific words and phrases.

His lifework, *Kojiki den,* was finally completed in 1798, 34 years after it was begun. The 44-volume work was the first comprehensive study of the *Kojiki* ever attempted. It began with a long introduction incorporating his earlier treatise, *Naobi no mitama,* then went on to annotate the text in minute detail. In this work, Norinaga avowed, "I have attempted to present everything there is about the study of antiquity." Indeed, *Kojiki den* was as much an encyclopedia of ancient history as an exegetical study of the text. Norinaga drew upon his vast knowledge of antiquity, always maintaining a scholarly attitude and including nothing that could not be proven by evidence. However, his objective methodology as a classical scholar never seemed to affect his subjective beliefs as a Shintoist. Norinaga was highly rational in unraveling linguistic problems in the text, yet highly irrational in his literal belief of the myths described therein.

In addition to *Kojiki den,* two works stand out among Norinaga's later writings. *Tamakatsuma* is a collection of over 1,000 essays on miscellaneous topics which Norinaga wrote in his spare time from around 1793 on. The essays touch on many lifelong concerns, sketching the outline of his philosophy in an informal manner. *Uiyamabumi,* written immediately after the completion of *Kojiki den* and intended as a guide for young students, lucidly expounds the aim and method of classical students. Norinaga's definition of Kokugaku appears therein: "Classical learning is a study independent of all the latter-day theories; it attempts to seek out the ultimate origin of things by directly examining the classical texts and learning about antiquity in detail." Characteristically, Norinaga urged the young scholars to write *waka* as a means of understanding the ancient world intuitively; in his view, an ideal classicist was not only a philologist but also a poet. Norinaga himself had written poetry throughout his life, and by 1798 he had compiled *Suzunoyashū,* an anthology of his own literary writings which includes over 2,500 *waka.*

The last three years of Norinaga's life were devoted primarily to lecturing. He now taught some 500 students, still following the same rigorous schedule he had maintained for the past 40 years. He also went on lecture tours from time to time. Especially successful was a series of lectures given in Kyōto in the summer of 1801; these attracted a large audience, including members of the court aristocracy. His exertions, however, seem to have had an adverse effect on the aging scholar's health, and Norinaga died in the autumn of that year after only a few days' illness.

Norinaga's writings had a considerable impact on later ages. His approach to the study of language, further refined by his son Haruniwa (1763–1828), contributed to the evolution of Japanese philology by its insistence on objective methodology. His meticulous inductive method in exegetical studies provided a model for many later scholars, including the noted historical and textual researcher BAN NOBUTOMO. Norinaga's interpretation of Shintō was further elaborated by HIRATA ATSUTANE and became part of an ideology that eventually brought about the Meiji Restoration of 1868; this same ideology was later utilized by Japan's militarist government to help promote nationalism in the years leading to World War II. Interest in Norinaga has not waned despite the vastly changed cultural climate in the second half of the 20th century, and his life and thought have been the subject of study by such eminent intellectuals as KOBAYASHI HIDEO and YOSHIKAWA KŌJIRŌ. His principal works remain mandatory reading for the study of the identity of Japanese civilization.

📖 ——*Motoori Norinaga zenshū,* 22 vols (Chikuma Shobō, 1968–77). Kobayashi Hideo, *Motoori Norinaga* (1977). Shigeru Matsumoto, *Motoori Norinaga* (1970). Muraoka Tsunetsugu, *Motoori Norinaga* (rev ed 1928). Sagara Tōru, *Motoori Norinaga* (1978). Yoshikawa Kōjirō, *Motoori Norinaga* (1977). *Makoto* UEDA

Motoori Ōhira (1756–1833)

Edo-period KOKUGAKU (National Learning) scholar and disciple of MOTOORI NORINAGA. Born in Ise (now part of Mie Prefecture). He was adopted by Norinaga, whose own son (MOTOORI HARUNIWA) had become blind, and thus Ōhira considered himself the guardian of his father's poetic and scholarly traditions and transmitted them to over a thousand students. His works include *Kagurauta shinshaku* (1827) and *Kogakuyō* (1809). See also JAPANESE LANGUAGE STUDIES, HISTORY OF.

Motoyakushiji remains

Site of a late-7th-century temple, located in Kidono, the city of Kashiwara, Nara Prefecture. The temple was begun in 680 to fulfill a pledge by Emperor TEMMU, who had prayed to the Yakushi Buddha (see NYORAI) for the recovery of his consort (later Empress JITŌ), and was completed in 698. With the removal of the capital from FUJIWARAKYŌ to HEIJŌKYŌ in 710, the temple too was relocated (see YAKUSHIJI); but the original temple survived until the middle of the 11th century.

According to the Heian-period (794–1185) *Yakushiji engi,* a document on the origins of the Yakushiji, the building plans for both temples were the same—the so-called Yakushiji style, consisting of a square compound occupied by two pagodas (one at each of the south corners), with the main hall in the center and a lecture hall to the north. The arrangement of the surviving foundation stones confirms this. Excavations in 1937 uncovered a fragment of a clay Buddha image believed to date from the time of the temple's construction, several kinds of old coins, and fragments of roof tiles. See also BUDDHIST ARCHITECTURE.　　　　*KITAMURA Bunji*

Motoyama Hikoichi (1853–1923)

President of the national newspaper MAINICHI SHIMBUN. Born in what is now Kumamoto Prefecture, he worked as a government employee, chief copy editor of a newspaper, and manager of a construction company before he became an adviser to the *Ōsaka mainichi shimbun* in 1889 and its president in 1903. He adopted a policy of rationalization of management, and under his leadership the paper became a rival of the *Ōsaka asahi shimbun* (see ASAHI SHIMBUN). In 1911 Motoyama bought out the *Tōkyō nichinichi shimbun* and continued to publish the *Mainichi shimbun* in Tōkyō. He is credited with transforming the Japanese newspaper industry into a modern enterprise.　　　　*ARIYAMA Teruo*

Mōtsuji

Temple of the TENDAI SECT of Buddhism. Located in Hiraizumi, Iwate Prefecture. Said to have been founded in 850 by the priest ENNIN. Its central hall used to house a statue of the Buddha Yakushi (Skt: Bhaiṣajyaguru). During the early days of its existence, services were conducted here for the protection of the country. Destroyed during the conflict between warring factions of the nobility, the temple was reconstructed by Fujiwara no Kiyohira and his son Fujiwara no Motohira beginning in 1105. During the lifetime of Fujiwara no Hidehira, Motohira's son, Mōtsuji consisted of over 40 subsidiary temples *(tatchū)* and over 500 separate living quarters for priests, which exceeded the number for CHŪSONJI at that time. Along with Chūsonji, Mōtsuji reflected the prosperity of what is called Hiraizumi culture. After a series of disastrous conflagrations that left only cornerstones and a large landscape garden, a new main hall was built at the present site in 1899. Every year a festival is held from the 14th to the 20th day of the 1st month of the lunar calendar; a ritual dance (ENNEN) performed at the end of the festival has acquired fame and has been designated an intangible cultural asset. The temple houses many important art objects. See also MŌTSUJI REMAINS.　　　　*Michiko Y. AOKI*

Mōtsuji remains

Site of the temple MŌTSUJI in Hiraizumi Chō, Iwate Prefecture; founded by ENNIN in 850, it was destroyed by fire and rebuilt in 1105 by Fujiwara no Motohira (see ŌSHŪ FUJIWARA FAMILY). Archaeological excavations since 1930 have revealed the basic outlines of the temple compound. The main hall faced south, and corridors on either side connected it to the drum and bell towers. South of the main hall was a large pond with a central island positioned on the axis formed by the main hall and the south gate, a plan that was adopted by many Jōdo sect temples late in the Heian period (794–1185). East of the main temple compound was the Kanjizaiōin, a chapel built by Motohira's wife. Excavations in 1972 revealed that this complex too centered on the garden and pond, and in the late 1970s plans were being made for reconstructing the site. See also BUDDHIST ARCHITECTURE.　　　　*KITAMURA Bunji*

mountaineering

(tozan). Since 85 percent of Japan's land mass is composed of mountainous terrain, mountain climbing, be it for pilgrimage, pleasure, or research, has always been popular. Participants range in skill from hikers who enjoy easy trail climbing on small mountains to the most skilled and well-equipped alpinists who engage in rock and ice climbing of extremely high mountains. In recent years Japanese mountaineers have ventured overseas in search of new conquests and have successfully scaled many of the world's highest peaks.

From ancient times the Japanese people have regarded mountains with considerable awe, looking upon them as dwelling places of the gods (KAMI) and in some cases as deities in their own right (see MOUNTAINS, WORSHIP OF). Mountain locations were often chosen as sites for both Shintō shrines and Buddhist temples, as in the case of SENGEN SHRINE on Mt. Fuji (FUJISAN) and ENRYAKUJI temple on HIEIZAN, and pilgrimages were made to these holy sites. Among the earliest recorded ascents of a sacred mountain in Japan are those of TATEYAMA (Toyama Prefecture), said to have first been climbed in 701, and of HAKUSAN (Ishikawa Prefecture) in 717. A religious sect known as SHUGENDŌ, which advocated mountain climbing as a form of asceticism, sprang up in the Heian period (794–1185) and grew in popularity during the Kamakura (1185–1333) and Muromachi (1333–1568) periods. During the Edo period (1600–1868) many pilgrimages to sacred mountains were organized, and people eagerly climbed such peaks as Mt. Fuji and ONTAKESAN in the Kiso Mountains.

With the Meiji period (1868–1912) came the first significant achievements in modern mountain climbing by native and foreign botanists, geologists, topographers, and others. Particularly notable contributions were made to modern mountain climbing in Japan by the English missionary Walter WESTON, who bestowed the name JAPANESE ALPS on the country's largest mountain range, and by the geologist SHIGA SHIGETAKA. The popularity of mountain climbing grew tremendously, and in 1905 the Japan Alpine Club was founded with the assistance of Weston. Members of the club successfully ascended the various peaks of the Japanese Alps. MAKI YŪKŌ's ascent of the east face of Mt. Eiger in the Bernese Alps in 1921 sparked interest in rock and ice climbing among Japanese climbing enthusiasts.

After World War II, mountain climbing became popular again, with the Japan Alpine Club leading the way. In 1953 members of the Waseda University Mountaineering Club climbed Mt. Aconcagua in the northern Andes, and in 1956 the Japan Alpine Club succeeded in scaling Mt. Manaslu in the central Himalayas. Their achievements brought a "mountaineering boom" to Japan, and great advancement was made in mountain climbing techniques. In 1960 the Japan Mountaineering Association was created under the auspices of the Japan Amateur Sports Association. Among other feats by Japanese alpinists were the first successful ascent of Mt. Everest during the postmonsoon period in 1973, the 1975 conquest of Mt. Everest by TABEI JUNKO, the first woman to climb Everest, and the conquest of Karakoram's K-2 in 1977. As of 1978, seven of the sixteen 8,000 meter (26,250 feet) class peaks in the world had been climbed by Japanese. In the Alps, Hasegawa Tsuneo made successful solo climbs of the north walls of Mt. Eiger, the Matterhorn, and the Grandes Jorasses, clearly demonstrating the level of competence of Japanese mountain climbers. The Japanese have also successfully scaled peaks in South America, Alaska, Africa, Antarctica, and other parts of the world.　　　　*YUASA Michio*

mountains, worship of

(sangaku shinkō). Mountains in Japan were regarded as holy places from ancient times. *Sangaku shinkō* (literally, "mountain beliefs") began as a form of nature worship centered upon beautiful mountains, smoking volcanoes, or heavily forested mountain ranges. The belief that mountains were the dwelling places of spirits and gods (KAMI) developed gradually. Hunters in the mountains made offerings to mountain *kami* (YAMA NO KAMI) and revered them as the masters of the animals. Farmers in villages lived under the protection of the mountain *kami,* who were believed to be the suppliers of

water for rice growing. Farmers climbed mountains in early spring to welcome the *kami* to the village and pray for a good harvest.

Traditionally, Japanese also thought of mountains as the dwelling place of ancestral spirits (see AFTERLIFE). The spirit of a deceased person remained in the cemetery near the mountain, but after the memorial service marking the 33rd anniversary of death, the spirit, now purified, went to the mountain as an ancestral spirit (see ANCESTOR WORSHIP). The ancestral spirit was called a mountain *kami* and was thought to remain there. Folk belief held that in winter, the *kami* remained in the mountain, but in spring, came down to become a *kami* of the rice paddy and protect farming endeavors (see TA NO KAMI). After the harvest, the *kami* returned to the mountain.

For the *kami* of the mountain and the paddy (simultaneously the deified ancestral spirit) shrines were built in villages, and the spring and autumn festivals were dedicated to these *kami* (see FESTIVALS: matsuri). As early as the Nara period (710–794), such holy mountains also served as training places for priests practicing austerities. During the early part of the Heian period (794–1185) the Buddhist monks SAICHŌ and KŪKAI advocated a religious life in the mountains, and mountains consequently became the chief centers for ascetic and spiritual exercises of priests.

During the Heian period, a form of religion called SHUGENDŌ developed, the goal of which was to develop supernatural powers through mountain asceticism. During the Kamakura (1185–1333) and Muromachi (1333–1568) periods, Shugendō became a driving force behind the worship of mountains. The head temple of one Shugendō sect was located in Kumano (TENDAI SECT related) and the other was centered in Yoshino (SHINGON SECT).

During the Edo period (1600–1868), Shugendō tended toward magico-religious practices. By the end of the Edo period, the cult of mountain climbing was practiced enthusiastically on Mt. Fuji (Fujisan; see SENGEN SHRINE) and at Mt. Ontake (Ontakesan) in the region of the river Kisogawa. Shugendō was abolished in the Meiji period (1868–1912), but revived after World War II. In modern times, the worship of mountains has continued to be practiced along with Shugendō in certain shrines and temples on sacred mountains.

MIYAKE Hitoshi

mourning

(*mo*). The observance of mourning in Japan was originally connected to the belief that exposure to death constituted a form of ritual impurity (KEGARE), which called for taboos surrounding relatives of the deceased. The period of mourning thus varied according to the closeness of one's relation to the deceased: in some regions there were set periods of mourning of 100 days for a parent or child, 49 days for a sibling, and 7 days for a cousin. Mourning consisted of remaining at home in seclusion, abstaining from animal food and the performance of one's usual occupation, and, above all, avoiding contact with Shintō deities while in the state of contamination by death.

There were also distinctions between two periods of heavy and light mourning, *ki* and *fuku*, respectively. *Ki* referred to the heavy mourning observed during the first 7 days following a death, while *fuku* was inclusive of the mourning observed for 49 days after a death.

The practice of not sending New Year's greetings on the year following the death of a parent or sibling is still observed.

INOKUCHI Shōji

Movement for Union of Court and Shogunate

(Kōbu Gattai Undō). A political movement of the 1860s that attempted to strengthen Japan in the face of foreign pressures by forging a more unified leadership embracing the imperial court in Kyōto, the Tokugawa shogunate in Edo (now Tōkyō), and the leaders of the major domains.

From the 17th century political theorists had discussed the nature of the court-shogunate relationship. The official Tokugawa position was that the court had charged the shōgun with managing the affairs of state so as to secure the well-being of court and people. In this view the court's proper role was strictly passive. By the 19th century, however, scholars of the MITO SCHOOL of historical studies and those associated with the school of National Learning (KOKUGAKU) were asserting that the court should take a more active part in national affairs. It was not clear how that was to be done, and in any case until the late 1850s this view did not lead to any effective political activity on the national level.

During 1857 the issue of a diplomatic treaty with the United States (see HARRIS TREATY) created great tension among shogunal

leaders and advisers. TOKUGAWA NARIAKI, the powerful leader of the Mito domain (now part of Ibaraki Prefecture) and an active adviser in Edo, solicited imperial support for a rejection of American demands. Thereafter members of the court began to participate actively in state affairs, meeting in Kyōto with officials of the shogunate and several domains and corresponding with sympathizers throughout the country.

During the following year the shogunate leader II NAOSUKE tried to terminate this court-daimyō association by a policy of harsh repression (see ANSEI PURGE), and in 1859 he tried to neutralize the daimyō by forging closer ties between the court and the shogunate. To this end he planned to arrange a marriage between the new shōgun, TOKUGAWA IEMOCHI, and the emperor's sister Princess KAZU (the marriage took place in March 1862). This enterprise was explained as part of an overall policy of *Kōbu gattai* or court-shogunate unity. After Ii's assassination in 1860 his successors, ANDŌ NOBUMASA and KUZE HIROCHIKA, continued this policy of court-shogunate unity, but in 1862 Andō himself was badly wounded by assassins and forced to retire from office. During the confusion following Andō's withdrawal SHIMAZU HISAMITSU, the dynamic leader of the Satsuma domain (now Kagoshima Prefecture), became actively involved in national affairs, sending troops to Kyōto and Edo and cooperating with the court to exert pressure on the shogunate. He succeeded in replacing court-shogunate unity with court-daimyō unity.

Thus by 1863 the concept of *kōbu gattai* had developed into two fundamentally opposed policies. During the next four years leaders of the shogunate and the great domains waged a seesaw battle for control of the court, both employing the rhetoric of *kōbu gattai*.

While leaders of the court, the shogunate, and the great domains were thus attempting to realign the central relationships of the political elite, other men were developing more ambitious plans that in the end rendered *kōbu gattai* obsolete. One such development was the SONNŌ JŌI (Revere the Emperor, Expel the Barbarians) movement. Proponents of *sonnō jōi* wished to restore political authority to the emperor and have the court rule Japan in place of the shogunate and the daimyō domains. This movement made its appearance early in the 1860s and in 1863 resulted in an early attempt at imperial restoration (see COUP D'ETAT OF 30 SEPTEMBER 1863). The "restoration" aborted, but in following years *sonnō* ideology was manifest in several attempted coups d'etat and eventually found realization in the MEIJI RESTORATION of 1868.

The other development, which began to be evident from about 1864, was a spreading conviction among influential officials within the shogunate and great domains that the limited reforms envisaged by the *kōbu gattai* movement were inadequate for the times. People such as ŌKUBO TOSHIMICHI of Satsuma, KIDO TAKAYOSHI of Chōshū (now Yamaguchi Prefecture), IWAKURA TOMOMI of the court, and OGURI TADAMASA of the shogunate became convinced that nothing short of forceful unification of the country would enable Japan to survive as an independent nation.

During 1867 these two strands of thought, imperial restorationism and unification by force, coalesced into a powerful political movement that pitted leaders of the shogunate against leaders of Satsuma and Chōshū. In this context the *kōbu gattai* movement was reduced to a conservative compromise strategy by which people such as MATSUDAIRA YOSHINAGA of the Fukui or Echizen domain (now part of Fukui Prefecture) and YAMANOUCHI TOYOSHIGE of the Tosa domain (now part of Kōchi Prefecture) tried to avoid civil war. The compromise, which was most fully articulated by Tosa in late 1867 (see KŌGI SEITAI RON), would have left intact both the decentralized feudal structure and the class hierarchy of the Tokugawa system. But that, too, failed, and the *kōbu gattai* movement, which a few years earlier had seemed the vanguard of political action, became an anachronism that was swept aside in the BOSHIN CIVIL WAR of the Restoration.

——W. G. Beasley, *The Meiji Restoration* (1973). Konishi Shirō, *Kaikoku to jōi*, in *Nihon no rekishi*, vol 19 (Chūō Kōron Sha, 1966). Tanaka Akira, "Bakumatsu no seiji jōsei," in *Iwanami kōza: Nihon rekishi*, vol 14 (Iwanami Shoten, 1962). Conrad TOTMAN

Movement to Protect Constitutional Government

(Kensei Yōgo Undō). Name adopted by two separate political movements, the first during the TAISHŌ POLITICAL CRISIS of 1912–13 and the second in 1924, both of which aimed to secure party control of the cabinet.

1. When the second SAIONJI KIMMOCHI cabinet fell because of army resistance to his attempts at financial retrenchment, the retired elder statesman (GENRŌ) in December 1912 designated KATSURA TARŌ, a former general from Chōshū (now Yamaguchi Prefecture), to serve a third term as prime minister. Members of the political parties RIKKEN SEIYŪKAI and RIKKEN KOKUMINTŌ, together with certain liberal intellectuals, journalists, and businessmen, decided to challenge the political dominance of cliques from the former Satsuma (now Kagoshima Prefecture) and Chōshū domains (known as HAMBATSU) and the military's power to interfere in government. To that end they organized a popular protest movement "to protect constitutional government," which drew tens of thousands to rallies throughout Japan. In January 1913 Katsura tried to strengthen his position by forming his own political party, the RIKKEN DŌSHIKAI, which half of the members of the Kokumintō quickly joined; but the Seiyūkai and the remaining members of the Kokumintō refused to cooperate and submitted a no-confidence resolution against Katsura's cabinet. Struggling to stay in power, Katsura induced the emperor to issue a rescript ordering that the no-confidence resolution be withdrawn. Although Saionji was inclined to obey the emperor, the members of the Seiyūkai adamantly refused. With the Diet building often surrounded by jeering crowds, Katsura saw that he could not hope to win an election, and so he resigned in February. The Seiyūkai did not immediately gain control of the government; instead it chose to cooperate with the newly designated cabinet of the moderate former admiral YAMAMOTO GONNOHYŌE. Yet the parties had greatly increased their influence, and the way was opened for the Seiyūkai leader HARA TAKASHI to form Japan's first truly party-dominated cabinet in 1918.

2. In 1924 liberal factions of the political parties Seiyūkai, KENSEIKAI, and KAKUSHIN KURABU joined forces in a second movement to protest the resurgence of "transcendental" (i.e., non-party) cabinets. Non-party cabinets had been formed in June 1922 by Admiral KATŌ TOMOSABURŌ and in September 1923 by Admiral Yamamoto. The appointment in January 1924 of still another non-party prime minister, KIYOURA KEIGO, president of the Privy Council, aroused the ire of party politicians. The Seiyūkai split in two, the short-lived SEIYŪ HONTŌ faction supporting the new cabinet and the rest of the Seiyūkai joining the Kenseikai and Kakushin Kurabu in opposition. Kiyoura dissolved the Diet and called a new election in May 1924. The three opposition parties, calling for reform of the House of Peers, universal manhood suffrage, and financial retrenchment, won a major victory that allowed them to form a coalition cabinet headed by the Kenseikai leader KATŌ TAKAAKI (see GOKEN SAMPA NAIKAKU). This second movement, however, was less successful in gaining popular support, and internal dissension forced the resignation of the coalition cabinet in July 1925. See also TAISHŌ DEMOCRACY.   *Matsuo Takayoshi*

moxa treatment

(kyū). Moxibustion. Traditional East Asian medical treatment in which cones of moxa or a similar substance, each half the size of a rice grain, are applied on the skin at specific points *(keiketsu)* and then ignited. It is believed that the resulting heat makes the body react and adjust any physical irregularities. As recently as 100 years ago, moxa treatment was regarded in Japan as an effective means of health maintenance. Even today, it is occasionally employed as a treatment.

Moxa is a combustible substance made of the fine hairs densely matted on the undersurface of the leaves of *yomogi* (mugwort; *Artemisia vulgaris* var. *indica*). It is yellow and has an odor. As moxa cones burn on the skin for two or more minutes, a sensation of intense but bearable heat is felt. This sensation, however, turns into a pleasant feeling as the body adapts to the heat. In some illnesses the warm sensation is produced only after the combustion is repeated 10 to 30 times at the same point.

The points to be stimulated by heat are chosen according to disease or symptom. According to the traditional Asian idea of medicine, there is a certain reciprocal relationship between therapeutic points and diseases or symptoms. This was described in the oldest Chinese medical classic *Huang di nei jing* (*Huang ti nei ching*; The Yellow Emperor's Classic or the Canon of Medicine), which is said to have been written 2,000 years ago. According to this account, there are about 360 therapeutic points or *keiketsu* distributed over the human body, all of which fall into some 20 systems according to definite rules. Of these systems, called *keiraku*, 12 are regarded as fundamental. Each system is associated with a certain internal organ

and named after it, e.g., *haikei* (lung system), *daichōkei* (colon system), *ikei* (stomach system), and so forth. These 12 *keiraku* systems form a circle through which *kiketsu*, the energy essential for human life, circulates. It is when the smooth circulation of this energy is obstructed at crucial points *(keiketsu)*, that disease occurs, and hence the need to detect which points are affected and to apply moxa accordingly. See also MEDICINE: traditional medicine.

Shirota Fumihiko

Moyoro shell mound

Archaeological site located on a sand dune at the mouth of the Abashiri River near the city of Abashiri, Hokkaidō; composed of deposits from the Final (ca 1000 BC–ca 300 BC) and Continuing (ca 300 BC–ca AD 700) JŌMON CULTURE and the OKHOTSK CULTURE (8th–12th centuries), with some AINU burials in the upper strata. *Moyoro* is an Ainu word for "bay." Near the shell mound are Jōmon and Okhotsk dwellings, the latter including some 27 PIT HOUSES with interior hearths and niches for the ritual deposit of bear and other animal skulls. Several hundred flexed burials have been found in the Okhotsk stratum, some with pots covering the heads. Ainu burials are in straight position. Funerary goods include iron halberds and swords.

This site has been jointly excavated several times since 1947 by a joint Tōkyō University and Hokkaidō University team; the investigations and collections of Yonemura Kioe are also well known.

Abe Gihei

Mozume Takami (1847–1928)

Japanese-language scholar. Born in Bungo Province (now Ōita Prefecture). Trained in KOKUGAKU (National Learning), Chinese classics, and Western studies, he worked for the Imperial Household Ministry and taught at Tōkyō University. He is noted chiefly as a lexicographer, having compiled the dictionaries *Kotoba no hayashi* (1888) and *Nihon daijirin* (1894) as well as *Kōbunko* (1916–18), a 20-volume compendium of writings from Japanese and Chinese classics and from Buddhist scriptures.   *Shimada Masahiko*

mube

Stauntonia hexaphylla. A climbing evergreen shrub of the family Lardizabalaceae which grows wild in mountain areas of Kyūshū, Shikoku, and Honshū west from the Kantō region. It is also planted in gardens. Although similar to the deciduous AKEBI, the *mube* is an evergreen, hence its alternate name *tokiwa akebi* (evergreen *akebi*). It has a long stalk and palmate compound leaves with 5 to 7 leathery oval leaflets. Around May, it produces 3 to 7 flowers, white outside and pale reddish purple inside, on each long stem growing out of the leaf axils. There are six sepals, the three outer lanceolate and the three inner linear, and there are no petals. In autumn, it bears purple egg-shaped fruits 5 centimeters (2 in) in length. Since its pulp is white and sweet, it was formerly used as a flavoring before sugar became common. The *mube* is considered an auspicious plant in Japan because its palmate leaves grow to three, then five, and finally seven leaflets from a single original leaf, thus corresponding to a traditionally auspicious numerical series. Like the *akebi*, the *mube* was exported to Western countries as an ornamental in the 19th century and is grown in southern regions of the United States.

Matsuda Osamu

Mu-ch'i → Mokkei

Muika

Town in southern Niigata Prefecture, central Honshū. Also known as Muikamachi. Situated on the river Uonogawa, during the Edo period (1600–1868) Muika developed as a castle town and one of the post-station towns on the highway Mikuni Kaidō. It is still served by the Japanese National Railways Jōetsu Line and National Route No. 17. A hot spring and several ski resorts are located here. Pop: 27,547.

mujin

(literally, "inexhaustible"). Traditional associations (KŌ) formed for the purpose of pooling their members' funds. The members (usually 10 to 20) were required to pay in specific sums of money on a regular basis. After a certain reserve had accumulated, they were entitled to take turns drawing cash to pay for livestock, farming implements, and other major expenses. An association was dissolved when the funds were used up.

Mujin are also called *tanomoshi*. *Tanomoshi* first appeared during the Kamakura period (1185–1333) as mutual financial aid societies for poor farmers. During the Muromachi period (1333–1568), organizations with the same function, but called *mujin*, achieved popularity, and the terms *mujin* and *tanomoshi* became synonymous. (Now the two are sometimes distinguished on the grounds that the word *tanomoshi* is used more in the Kansai region, and *mujin* in the Kantō region.) *Mujin* became even more popular during the Edo period (1600–1868), in cities as well as rural communities. After the Meiji Restoration (1868), *mujin*, along with pawnshops, were the financial centers of the common people. Gradually *mujin* with the structure of companies began to appear, and a law regulating them was established in 1915. *Mujin* remained in operation even after the modern banking system became firmly established in the 1930s. In 1951, *mujin* companies became mutual financing banks (*sōgo ginkō*). Even now, informal *mujin* of the traditional type can still be found.

mujō

(impermanence; transience; mutability; Skt: *anitya*). Originally a Buddhist term expressing the doctrine that everything that is born must die and that nothing remains unchanged. The Chinese characters for *mujō* are also pronounced *tsunenashi*. The phrase *shogyō mujō* (all the various realms of being are transient) is the first of the Three Laws of Buddhism. Japanese have traditionally been keenly aware of the impermanence of things, and the sense of *mujō* has been a major theme in literature. Works of the medieval period (13th to 16th centuries) such as the *Hōjōki* (The Ten-Foot-Square Hut) of KAMO NO CHŌMEI, the *Tsurezuregusa* (Essays in Idleness) of YOSHIDA KENKŌ, and the *Heike monogatari* (Tale of the Heike) are especially noted for this essentially Buddhist view of life.

📖 ——Karaki Junzō, *Mujō* (1965). Kobayashi Chishō, *Mujōkan no bungaku* (1959). *FUKUDA Hideichi*

Mujū Ichien → Shasekishū

Mukai Kyorai (1651-1704)

HAIKU poet of the Edo period; one of the 10 principal disciples of BASHŌ. Real name Mukai Kanetoki. Son of a Confucian physician in Nagasaki. He excelled in the martial arts but at age 23 decided to go to Kyōto to study poetry. In 1686 he went to visit Bashō, who was living in Ise; his unpretentious sincerity immediately won him the master's trust and affection, and whenever Bashō visited Kyōto, he stayed at Rakushisha, Kyorai's country cottage in Saga. Bashō's book, *Saga nikki*, is about his stay there in 1691. With NOZAWA BONCHŌ, Kyorai edited the *Sarumino* (1691), the finest among the seven representative anthologies of the Bashō school. His lasting reputation, however, is based on his authorship of the *Kyoraishō* (1702–04); along with HATTORI TOHŌ's *Sanzōshi*, it is one of the most authentic sources on Bashō-school aesthetics. Principally a record of the conversations of Bashō and his disciples on haiku, it includes discussion of the important concepts of *fueki ryūkō* ("permanence and change"), SABI (lonely, austere beauty), and *shiori* (an indefinable quality of pathos).

Mukai Tadaharu (1885-1982)

Businessman. Important figure in the MITSUI *zaibatsu* (financial and industrial combine) in the early 1940s. Born in Tōkyō. Immediately after graduating from Tōkyō Higher Commercial School (now Hitotsubashi University) in 1904, Mukai joined MITSUI & CO, LTD. He later became chairman of the trading company and managing director of Mitsui Gōmei Kaisha, a holding company of the Mitsui *zaibatsu*, in 1939. He reorganized this *zaibatsu* in the following year. After a dispute with the military, Mukai retired from active participation in business in 1943. He was finance minister in 1952.
TOGAI Yoshio

Mukawa

River in southern Hokkaidō, originating in the northern part of the Hidaka Mountains and flowing southwest to enter the Pacific Ocean

at the town of Mukawa. Regions along the river are covered with coniferous forests, and there is a lumber industry. The water is used for irrigation. Length: 138 km (86 mi); area of drainage basin: 1,250 sq km (483 sq mi).

Mukden, Battle of

(Hōten Kaisen). Last and fiercest land battle of the RUSSO-JAPANESE WAR; fought in March 1905. The Russians had gathered a huge force of 320,000 near the strategic city of Mukden (now Shenyang) in Manchuria, in northeast China. Moving from the west were Japanese forces, totaling 250,000, which hoped to destroy the main Russian army. Because of insufficient men and ammunition and the difficulties of terrain and weather, this objective was not achieved; the Japanese forces captured Mukden on 10 March 1905, after 10 days, but the Russian army was able to escape. Until 1945, 10 March was celebrated as Army Day (Rikugun Kinembi).
KONDŌ Shinji

Mukō

City in southern Kyōto Prefecture, central Honshū. With convenient access to Kyōto and Ōsaka, Mukō is rapidly becoming a residential suburb of the two cities. It has machine, textile, and foodstuff industries. The hilly western section is noted for its bamboo shoots. Strawberries are also grown. Pop: 50,604.

Mukōgaoka shell mound

A shell mound, dating mainly from the Latest Jōmon period (ca 1000 BC–ca 300 BC), in which the first YAYOI POTTERY was discovered in 1884 by Arisaka Shōzō, TSUBOI SHŌGORŌ, and others; located in Yayoi Chō in the Mukōgaoka district of Tōkyō. Several shell mounds are located in this area, and the site where the first Yayoi pottery was discovered is not exactly known. Originally regarded as merely transitional ware from the earlier JŌMON POTTERY, Yayoi pottery was not given its name until later, and the YAYOI CULTURE was not formally introduced to the academic world until 1923. See also SHELL MOUNDS.

📖 ——Sugihara Sōsuke, "Musashi Yayoi Chō shutsudo no yayoi-shiki doki ni tsuite," *Kōkogaku* 11.7 (1940). *J. Edward KIDDER, Jr.*

Mukogawa

River in eastern Hyōgo Prefecture, western Honshū, originating in the Tamba Mountains and flowing through the western part of the Ōsaka Plain to enter Ōsaka Bay between the cities of Amagasaki and Nishinomiya. The middle reaches are noted for scenic gorges and numerous hot springs. The water is used by the cities of Kōbe, Nishinomiya, and Amagasaki for drinking and for industrial purposes. Length: 66 km (41 mi); area of drainage basin: 273 sq km (105 sq mi).

mukoirikon

Also called *shōseikon*. Matrilocal marriage. The couple often come from the same locale and meet at the house of the wife's parents during courtship. Wedding ceremonies are sponsored by the wife's family and are less elaborate than in the case of patrilocal marriages (YOMEIRIKON). The practice of *mukoirikon* begins with a preliminary stage of courtship initiated at the discretion of the couple involved and with little interference from the family heads. The future bridegroom then makes a formal visit to his bride and her family, which is called *hatsumukoiri* (bridegroom's first visit). He exchanges wine cups and drinks with his future in-laws. The groom continues to visit the bride at her home for a specified interval, after which the couple chooses to remain or move to a separate residence.

Mukoirikon developed in the Nara (710–794) and Heian (794–1185) periods and was common among the court aristocracy as well as among lower classes of society. The practice of *mukoirikon* diminished with the rise of the warrior class but has continued to the present among a few communities of traditional laborers such as fishermen.
NOGUCHI Takenori

Mukyōkai

(Nonchurch Christianity). An indigenous Japanese Christian movement that developed out of a Bible study group around the turn of the 20th century and was led by UCHIMURA KANZŌ (1861–1930). The Mukyōkai Christians reject church denominations as materialistic, formalistic, sectarian, exclusivist, intolerant, Western in nature, and not appropriate to the Japanese people. Consequently, they reject dogma, liturgy, and church institutions. Numbering some 35,000 believers, the movement consists of independent Bible study groups, each led by a teacher, and informally integrated through the mutual exchange of published literature and occasional common activities. Each group is reorganized upon the death or retirement of its leader. Spiritually, the movement emphasizes personal religious experience and an ethic of hard work, duty, and honesty. It thus attempts to synthesize the spiritual tradition of Japan with the Christian gospel as interpreted in the puritan manner.

Appealing particularly to members of the intelligentsia who were critical of Japan's modernization process, the movement has actively participated in the debate of social issues since its inception. Early leaders included NAMBARA SHIGERU and YANAIHARA TADAO. Before and during World War II, the Mukyōkai strongly opposed Shintō nationalism and Japanese imperialism. Today, nonchurch Christians are critical of the government's conservative policies, and tend to support progressive parties. The movement is seen by many Japanese as an indigenous Christianity free of foreign elements. Following the Mukyōkai example, several new independent Christian movements have developed in Japan. All affirm independence from foreign churches, indigenous leadership, limited organization, Bible meetings, and evangelical charisma. One of the most popular among these movements is the Makuya or "Tabernacle of Christ," which has about 60,000 members and was founded by Teshima Ikurō (1910–73).

■——Carlo Caldarola, "Non-Church Christianity in Japan: Western Christianity and Japan's Cultural Identity," *International Journal of Contemporary Sociology* (October 1973). Carlo Caldarola, *Christianity: The Japanese Way* (1978). Carlo Caldarola, *Uchimura Kanzō to Mukyōkai: Shūkyō shakaigakuteki kenkyū* (1978). John F. Howes, "The Non-Church Christian Movement in Japan," *Transactions of the Asiatic Society of Japan* (1957). Iwakuma Naoshi, *Mukyōkai to wa nani ka* (1967). William H. H. Norman, "Non-Church Christianity in Japan," *International Review of Missions* (1957).

Carlo CALDAROLA

multinational enterprises

Firms that operate direct subsidiaries or engage in joint ventures outside of their home country. The number of such firms has expanded greatly since the liberalization of international trade and investment brought about in the mid-1950s by the International Monetary Fund (IMF) and the General Agreement on Tariffs and Trade (GATT). Corporations commence multinational operations in order to gain direct access to raw materials, cheap sources of labor, and international markets. In recent years, host countries have become increasingly concerned about potential foreign domination of their economies, and certain political and legal restrictions have been imposed on the operation of multinationals.

Japanese Multinational Enterprises——Prior to World War II, Japanese enterprises operated overseas in China, Manchuria, Korea, Taiwan, and southeast Asia. These enterprises conducted limited manufacturing operations and provided transportation and other services in Japanese colonies and other areas where Japanese political influence was strong, but they cannot be called multinational enterprises in the present sense of the term.

In the postwar period, the first Japanese enterprises to engage in multinational activities were mineral resource companies, which began foreign investment after 1951. Because of Japan's relative poverty in natural resources, raw materials extraction and import has continued to be a primary field of multinational operation. Also appearing early on the multinational scene were the GENERAL TRADING COMPANIES, which established branches in key world markets. Overseas manufacturing activities began after 1955, first in Latin America and then in Southeast Asia. Since the late 1960s, much of Japanese foreign investment has been concentrated in offshore production facilities, primarily in Southeast Asia, Taiwan, and South Korea. In recent years, investment in production facilities in the industrialized nations of the West has shown a notable increase.

By mid-1978, the overseas assets of Japanese multinational corporations had a total book value of about US $20 billion, a sum approximately one-seventh that of American multinationals. This total was divided into three roughly equal areas: natural resource development, manufacturing, and marketing and other service-

related activities. These investments were distributed geographically as follows: East and Southeast Asia 30 percent, North America 24 percent, Latin America 16 percent, the Middle East 13 percent, Europe 9 percent, Oceania 4 percent, and Africa 4 percent. During the 1980s, it is expected that Japanese investments in Europe and the United States will increase sharply. See JAPANESE BUSINESS IN AMERICA.

In the past decade, the overseas investments of Japanese banks, manufacturers, and trading firms have grown rapidly, reaching a level of US $2–3 billion annually, compared with US $700–900 million annually in the late 1960s. The OIL CRISIS OF 1973 and the subsequent economic recession dampened investment activity, but the pace quickened once more after 1976. Even before the sharp appreciation of the yen vis-à-vis the dollar in 1977 and 1978, the new thrust of Japanese investment was clearly different from that of the 1960s.

The Character of Japanese Investment——The unusual character of Japanese overseas investments reflects the unique path of the nation's economic growth since industrialization began in the 1870s. First, multinational activities have been spearheaded by SMALL AND MEDIUM ENTERPRISES that tend to be more export-oriented than large Japanese firms. These smaller-scale businesses continue to make up a significant portion of the Japanese economy. They initiated overseas activity early in the post–World War II era, largely in response to the threat that Asian export markets would disappear as local economies developed. The ready supply of low-wage labor in less-developed countries was also a lure to overseas investment, especially after Japanese economic growth resulted in a steady increase in labor costs at home.

A second characteristic has been the important role played by the general trading companies (*sōgō shōsha*) and specialty trading companies (*semmon shōsha*). These firms have frequently taken the initiative in organizing manufacturing and service activities abroad, especially through the arrangement of appropriate business partners in host countries. The trading firms, manufacturers, and business partners from the host countries form unique three-way JOINT VENTURES. In recent years, however, a tendency has been seen among large Japanese corporations to act independently of the trading firms, in part because they have developed their own body of knowledge of international business.

A third feature is the unusual practice of joint investment by two or three Japanese firms in an overseas operation, such as a synthetic fiber weaving plant or an electric products factory. These firms are often competitors at home, but they pool technical and managerial resources for the success of their business abroad. In other cases, competitors will make informal agreements to respect each other's sphere of operation overseas. Fourth, although Japanese investors have shown their preference for majority ownership and control of their subsidiaries overseas, they have demonstrated a greater propensity to form joint ventures with foreign partners than have their American and European counterparts.

Problems of Japanese Multinationals in the 1980s——As more and more Japanese corporations shift the emphasis of their foreign operations from export to direct investment, they increasingly encounter the difficulty of adapting Japanese management methods to foreign environments. Many corporations have been accused of excluding foreign managers from executive positions and from the decision-making processes of their subsidiaries. Foreign nationals also claim to have been discriminated against in salary and other benefits. A close examination of these allegations, however, often reveals a paradoxical dichotomy. On the one hand, foreign employees of Japanese subsidiaries enjoy the de facto job security accorded the employees of major enterprises in Japan. On the other hand, foreign managers are unable to participate in the informal networks of personal communication and decision making that tend to characterize Japanese CORPORATE CULTURE.

A problem on a different front has been the emergence of significant anti-Japanese sentiment in Southeast Asia. The high concentration of Japanese multinational activity in this region, especially in labor-intensive, low-technology industries, has made Japanese business the target of considerable political opposition. The tendency of Japanese businessmen to deal primarily with other Japanese when operating overseas reinforces the belief that the multinationals have little concern for the economic health of the host countries (see SOUTHEAST ASIA, THE PACIFIC ISLANDS, AND JAPAN). If Japanese multinational activity is to continue the expansion of recent decades, it will be necessary to find ways to dispel these suspicions and resentments.

■ ——Yoshi Tsurumi, *The Japanese Are Coming: A Multinational Interaction of Firms and Politics* (1976). Raymond Vernon, *Storms over Multinationals: The Real Issue* (1977). Michael Y. Yoshino, *Japanese Multinational Enterprise* (1976). Yoshihiro TSURUMI

Mumyō-zōshi

(The Nameless Booklet). Also pronounced *Mumyō sōshi*. Early-Kamakura-period (1185–1333) work devoted primarily to criticism of Heian-period (794–1185) fiction (see MONOGATARI BUNGAKU). In addition to serving as a valuable source for understanding the critical standards of its day, the *Mumyō-zōshi* provides a tantalizing overview of a rich literary tradition only partially extant today.

The author adopts the KANA orthography and narrative framework of the historical work ŌKAGAMI, positing a fictional setting in which the narrator, an 83-year-old nun out gathering flowers as offerings to the Buddha, is invited into a dilapidated mansion occupied by several aristocratic ladies. They pass the entire night in desultory conversation on various subjects, beginning with an enumeration of "things cherished in this world": the moon, letter writing, dreams, tears, the NEMBUTSU, and the LOTUS SUTRA.

Much of the literary criticism that follows is devoted to an evaluation of outstanding chapters, characters, and scenes in the early 11th-century classic, the TALE OF GENJI, with earlier works dismissed as lacking in sophistication. *Mumyō-zōshi's* appraisal of post-*Genji* fiction includes relatively detailed treatment of extant works such as SAGOROMO MONOGATARI, YORU NO NEZAME, and HAMAMATSU CHŪNAGON MONOGATARI, as well as discussion of many works now lost (*Kakuremino, Asakure, Iwa utsu nami,* and *Hatsuyuki,* to mention only a few), providing an intimation of the broad scale of late Heian fiction which the literary historian would otherwise be denied. The criterion established for judging *monogatari* is simple: works that evoke a sense of *aware* (deeply felt emotion; see MONO NO AWARE) are praised while others are faulted for being unrealistic, prosaic, or poorly constructed.

The *monogatari* section is followed by a perfunctory analysis of imperial and private poetry anthologies (see IMPERIAL ANTHOLOGIES; SHIKASHŪ), and finally by brief selections on the poetic gifts and accomplishments of famous literary ladies such as ONO NO KOMACHI, SEI SHŌNAGON, IZUMI SHIKIBU, and MURASAKI SHIKIBU, as well as several empresses. For an appraisal of the characters of famous men, the reader is referred to the *Ōkagami*.

Internal evidence suggests that the *Mumyō-zōshi* was composed sometime between 1196 and 1202 by the woman known to us only as the adopted daughter (and biological granddaughter) of FUJIWARA NO TOSHINARI, to whom the work is traditionally attributed; or by a female contemporary close to the literary circles of FUJIWARA NO SADAIE and FUJIWARA NO TAKANOBU.

■ ——Yamagishi Tokuhei, *Mumyō sōshi* (1973). Thomas ROHLICH

munabetsusen

(house tax). A tax imposed on each household during the Kamakura (1185–1333) and Muromachi (1333–1568) periods. Also called *munabechisen, munebetsusen,* and *muneyaku.* At first *munabetsusen* was levied only occasionally to pay for extraordinary court or temple and shrine expenses. In the Muromachi period, however, when the shogunate and estate *(shōen)* proprietors lost the ability to collect land taxes effectively from the military governors *(shugo)* and land stewards *(jitō)*, *munabetsusen* became a permanent tax and an important source of revenue. Some warlords of the 16th century resorted to similar forms of taxation, but the practice seems to have died out by the early 17th century, when the HONTO MONONARI and other taxes were established. Philip BROWN

Munakata Shikō (1903–1975)

Woodcut artist. Born in the city of Aomori, the son of a poor blacksmith and the third of 15 children. Munakata became the best-known artist of his day, and through his work brought about the general acceptance in Japan of printmaking as one of the fine arts. Though he had only an elementary school education, he had a passion for art and from early childhood spent all his spare time drawing and studying Western painting and organized a local art group that put on exhibitions. In 1924 he decided to become a full-time painter in oils, and moved to Tōkyō. Supporting himself by odd jobs, he submitted his work without success to the annual imperial art exhibition (Teiten), until in 1928 one of his oil paintings was finally accepted. The same year he turned to woodcuts and became a pupil of HIRATSUKA UN'ICHI, who at this time was a leader in the creative printmaking *(sōsaku hanga)* movement. Many doors now opened to him, and in the 1930s he exhibited his woodcut prints widely. In 1936 he also came to know YANAGI MUNEYOSHI, the art critic and founder of the Japan Folkcraft Museum (Nihon Mingeikan), the potters KAWAI KANJIRŌ and HAMADA SHŌJI, and other figures active in the FOLK CRAFTS *(mingei)* movement. His house and most of his woodblocks were destroyed in the Tōkyō air raids of May 1945. After the war his reputation spread rapidly both at home and abroad, and he produced countless woodcuts, paintings in watercolor and oil, calligraphic scrolls, and illustrated books. His work is in many institutional and private collections in Japan, the United States, and Europe, and three Japanese museums are named after him. He received many Japanese and international awards, including the First Prize, Print Division, São Paulo Bienal (1955); the Grand Prix, Venice Biennale (1956); and the Order of Culture (1970).

Munakata's huge output shows a variety of influences, Japanese and Western, but at all times overflows with the driving vigor of his dynamic personality. Nearsighted from his youth onwards, he worked with incredible speed and intensity, responding to urges whose release might be prompted by the briefest verbal or visual cues. Nevertheless, the apparent artlessness of his work in some cases was the result of profound immersion in a subject. In his unconventional way, he was a deeply religious man: the Shintō rituals and festivals with which he was brought up fascinated him throughout his life; later, through his friend Kawai, he came under the strong influence of Buddhism; he also imbibed the aesthetic theories of Yanagi, whose *mingei* ideals suited both his temperament and his style. In Western art, he admired Van Gogh above all, but he also admired Toulouse-Lautrec, Matisse, and the German expressionists. In Japanese art, he loved Azuchi-Momoyama period (1568–1600) screen painting, the Zen sculpture of ENKŪ, the ink painting of IKE NO TAIGA, and the works of certain of his own contemporaries, such as the works of TOMIOKA TESSAI and Yorozu Tetsugorō, and, of course, those of his fellow artists in the *mingei* movement. Often, however, his inspiration came from poetry, religion, or music. His subjects were extremely diverse. His prints, black-and-white or hand-colored from the back of the print, range from postcard size to 14 meters (46 ft) in width. He worked with the simplest of tools but achieved spectacular compositional effects, notably in some of his earlier prints, in which the dense black or white shapes of the figures appear to be bursting out of the rectangular frame. Among his finest works in woodcut are: *Utou* (1938; 31 woodcuts based on the Nō play of the same name); *Shaka jū dai deshi* (1939; Ten Disciples of the Buddha); *Nyonin Kanzeon* (1949; 12 woodcuts of Avalokiteśvara based on poems by OKAMOTO KANOKO); *Yūzen suru nyosha tachi tachi* (1953; large woodcut of six female figures); *Hanakari shō* (1954; large woodcut inspired by an ancient mural at Tonggou [T'ung-kou], Manchuria); *Ryūryoku kakō shō* (1955; 12 woodcuts of trees, flowers, etc); *Seiten shō hangakan* (1956; 35 woodcuts based on poems by Hara Sekitei).

■ ——*Munakata Shikō zenshū*, 12 vols (Kōdansha; 1977–79); Unagami Masaomi, *Munakata Shikō: Bijutsu to jinsei* (1976). Naoko MATSUBARA

Munakata Shrines

One of the principal Shintō shrine complexes of northern Kyūshū, consisting of three separate shrines, located in the coastal town of Genkai, approximately 30 kilometers (19 mi) north of the city of Fukuoka, and on two islands of the Genkai Sea. Although remains of Jōmon (ca 10,000 BC–ca 300 BC) ritual sites indicate great antiquity, the Munakata Shrines attained national political significance during the three or four centuries (5th to 9th centuries AD) when official diplomatic missions were exchanged between Japan and the Chinese and Korean kingdoms on the Asian mainland. Dedicated to three female sea-deities, the Munakata Shrines were located near the ports of embarkation for these missions and were the sites of religious observances to pray for safe passage on the dangerous voyages to the continent. Mention of the Munakata Shrines in the KOJIKI (712) and NIHON SHOKI (720), early chronicles of Japanese history in which the three female deities are listed as daughters of AMATERASU ŌMIKAMI, account for the particular attention accorded the shrines by the rulers of the YAMATO COURT.

The Munakata Shrine complex consists of three separate shrines: the Hetsumiya, the main or first shrine, located on the mainland of

Kyūshū and dedicated to the deity Ichikishimahime; the Nakatsumiya, dedicated to Takitsuhime (Tagitsuhime) and located on the island of Ōshima about 12 kilometers (7 mi) off the Kyūshū coast; and Okitsumiya, dedicated to Tagorihime and located on the island of OKINOSHIMA, approximately 50 kilometers (31 mi) off the Kyūshū coast. The two island shrines have always been simple structures, but the buildings of the Hetsumiya Shrine on the mainland are major architectural constructions; repeatedly restored, the present buildings were constructed in 1578–90 by Kobayakawa Takakage and are designated as Important Cultural Properties.

The cult of the Okitsumiya Shrine on Okinoshima is of particular interest because of the large quantity of ritual relics excavated there in recent years. Objects, including bronze mirrors, musical instruments, jewels, and ceramic ware, were apparently deposited at the island shrine by Japanese embassies and other seafarers offering their final prayers there before setting off for Korea or China. A series of archaeological expeditions, beginning in 1954, have uncovered thousands of such objects, many of which have been designated national treasures and are preserved in a specially established museum within the precincts of the Munakata Hetsumiya Shrine. The earliest ritual objects have been attributed to the 1st century AD (Early Yayoi period), and the latest to the 9th century. The variety and vast quantity of these ancient objects have given the island of Okinoshima the popular name "SHŌSŌIN of the Sea," after the treasure house of the temple Tōdaiji in Nara. The annual festival is held on 15 November; other important festival rituals are held in early October. Subordinate and branch shrines number about 9,000 all over Japan.   Peter M. GRILLI

munebetsusen → munabetsusen

Munenaga, Prince (1311–1385)

(Munenaga Shinnō). Second son of Emperor GO-DAIGO. In 1330 he succeeded his half-brother Prince MORINAGA as chief priest of the Tendai sect of Buddhism. With Morinaga he supported his father's attempts to recover political authority from the faltering Kamakura shogunate (see GENKŌ INCIDENT), attempts that resulted in the KEMMU RESTORATION of 1333. Go-Daigo's restoration was short-lived, however, and, leaving the priesthood in 1337, Munenaga took part in numerous battles against the turncoat general ASHIKAGA TAKAUJI. In 1374 he retired to the Southern Court at Yoshino (see NORTHERN AND SOUTHERN COURTS), where he compiled a poetic anthology, the Shin'yō wakashū (1381, Collection of New Leaves).

Munetaka, Prince (1242–1274)

(Munetaka Shinnō). Second son of Emperor GO-SAGA and sixth shōgun of the KAMAKURA SHOGUNATE (1192–1333). The first imperial prince to serve as shōgun, he was selected for the post in 1252 by the shogunal regent (shikken) HŌJŌ TOKIYORI, who retained all political power. In 1266 Munetaka was accused of plotting against Hōjō rule; he was deposed and returned to Kyōto, where he later entered the Buddhist priesthood. A waka poet of distinction, he left several collections, including Keigyoku wakashū (Collection of Precious Gems) and Ryūyō wakashū (Collection of Willow Leaves).

Muqi (Mu-ch'i) → Mokkei

mura

(village). The smallest unit of LOCAL GOVERNMENT; also, the "natural" village, specifically the self-contained agricultural community. The word mura is believed to be derived from mure (group) and muragaru (to cluster) and to be closely related to Korean mul (district) and mail (village).

Before the TAIKA REFORM of 645, the mura is thought to have been a subdivision of the agata (see AGATANUSHI), a unit of the kuni (province). With the establishment of the RITSURYŌ SYSTEM of government in the late 7th and early 8th centuries, a new village unit, the RI (renamed GŌ in 715), consisting of 50 households (ko), replaced the mura as the basic administrative unit (see GŌRI SYSTEM). Sixteen to 20 ri formed a gun (district), the principal subdivision of the kuni (see KOKUGUN SYSTEM). The mura, however, remained as a geographical, social, and economic entity. With the disintegration of the ritsuryō system and the growth of private estates (SHŌEN) in the middle of the Heian period (794–1185), the old system was abandoned, and the mura emerged once more as the basic administrative unit, functioning as the farthest extension of the governing network under the shōen proprietor. Physically, a mura consisted of as many as 20 houses enclosed by a fence (kaito or kakiuchi) and inhabited largely by extended families or groups of related families. The houses were situated usually at the mouths of valleys or along rivers, and the inhabitants acted collectively to manage woods and fields (see IRIAI), control the water supply, and maintain roads and shrines. By the mid-1300s, many of these mura gathered together to form their own organs of self-government, with wealthier peasants (HYAKUSHŌ) serving as headmen. See GŌSON SYSTEM.

In the 1580s the territorial boundaries of the mura were clearly demarcated in the great cadastral survey (KENCHI) carried out by the military hegemon TOYOTOMI HIDEYOSHI. The average annual yield of the land (KOKUDAKA) of each mura was determined and the tax assessed accordingly. During the Edo period (1600–1868) the mura remained the primary unit of administration and tax collection. After the Meiji Restoration (1868) the government combined the villages into new and larger mura and machi (towns), placing in each a government office (yakuba) and primary and secondary schools. The original, "natural" mura within the larger units were renamed ōaza. These ōaza survive to this day as the basic neighborhood communities in rural areas.   MINEGISHI Sumio

Muragaki Norimasa (1813–1880)

Official of the Tokugawa shogunate who in the 1850s and 1860s held numerous posts connected with foreign affairs. Born in Edo (now Tōkyō), the son of a high-ranking Tokugawa retainer. In 1854 he was appointed a shogunate comptroller (KANJŌ GIMMIYAKU) and given the additional duty of inspecting coastal defenses in EZO (now Hokkaidō). Later that year he was sent to Shimoda, on the Izu Peninsula, to assist in treaty negotiations with the Russian envoy E. V. PUTIATIN, who had come seeking trade. Thereafter, as commissioner of Hakodate (HAKODATE BUGYŌ), commissioner of foreign affairs (GAIKOKU BUGYŌ), and commissioner of Kanagawa, he exerted himself in the construction of coastal fortifications and the development of Ezo. In 1860 he was named vice ambassador of the shogunal mission to the United States to ratify the HARRIS TREATY (see UNITED STATES, MISSION OF 1860 TO). He remained an important foreign-affairs adviser until his retirement from politics after the Meiji Restoration in 1868.

━━ ——Muragaki Norimasa, Kōkai nikki (1861), tr Helen M. Uno as Kōkai Nikki: The Diary of the First Japanese Embassy to the United States of America (1958). Masao Miyoshi, As We Saw Them: The First Japanese Embassy to the United States (1979).

murahachibu

Loosely, village (mura) ostracism. The practice of barring a household from full participation in the social and economic life of the rural community. The ostracized household is itself also called murahachibu.

Until the recent past the Japanese hamlet of 15 to 20 households acted as a corporate entity whose member households regularly performed communal religious rites and exchanged mutual aid and labor, particularly for the purpose of rice production and irrigation. Conduct such as cutting firewood in the communal forests without permission or revealing illegal or shameful village actions to the police or outsiders, was cause for a charge of wrongdoing to be brought against the household at a hamlet council meeting. If it was unanimously agreed that the charges were valid, an official notification of ostracism was delivered to the household. Such notices routinely contained the phrase, "having disturbed the harmony of this otherwise peaceful community." For the most part, murahachibu was defined as an indefinite status, but upon occasion a term of years was specified.

The sentence was imposed upon the entire household. Its members were shunned, mutual aid relations abrogated, and participation in communal rites forbidden. Yet relations were rarely severed completely. In some districts the hamlet assisted even murahachibu in the event of a fire or death, and in others hamlet members attended weddings at such households. Because the break was partial, hachibu (eight parts) is said to refer to the parts of normal relationships that were suspended. Another possible origin of hachibu is a corruption of hajiku (to reject or repel).

The presence within its boundaries of an ostracized household was evidence both of the sanctioning power of the hamlet and of a breakdown in its ability to maintain harmony. Consequently, unless the offense was too heinous, efforts to reinstate the household were eventually undertaken with the aid of a go-between. A successful effort resulted in the hamlet's acceptance of an abject admission of guilt and a promise never again to disturb the harmony of the hamlet. Where reconciliation was impossible, however, the psychological and economic pressures were so great that the *murahachibu* often simply moved away. As the vast majority of families has shifted to wage-work and salaried employment, the power of the hamlet and incidence of ostracism have steadily diminished.

The practice of *murahachibu* is one example of a wide range of social sanctions imposed on their members by Japanese social groups, in an effort to maintain power and autonomy and to resolve conflict within the group. It is purely extralegal in character since no recourse is made to the authorities, the courts, or the relevant legal codes. However, in the unlikely event that a case of *murahachibu* went to court, the ostracism would be considered intimidation under the Criminal Code, and slander under the Civil Code.

■——Arai Kōjirō, *Seisai*, in *Nihon minzokugaku taikei*, vol 4, (Heibonsha, 1959). Robert J. Smith, "The Japanese Rural Community: Norms, Sanctions, and Ostracism," *American Anthropologist* (June 1961). Takeuchi Toshimi, "Mura no seisai," *Shakai keizai shi gaku* (1938).   Robert J. SMITH

muraji → kabane

Murakami

City in northern Niigata Prefecture, central Honshū. A castle town from the 16th century, it has long been known for its tea, salmon, and *tsuishu*, a kind of red lacquer ware. The site of IWAFUNE NO KI, a 7th-century military outpost for subduing the EZO tribesmen, and the Senami Hot Spring are located nearby. Pop: 33,540.

Murakami Genzō (1910-   )

Novelist. Born in Korea, the son of a Japanese government official. After completing middle school in Tōkyō, he worked for some time as a playwright for a small theater. Receiving the Naoki Prize in 1940 for *Kazusa fudoki*, he became established as a writer of popular historical novels. After the war, he wrote a best-seller, *Sasaki Kojirō* (1949–50), which dealt with the famous rivalry between the swordsmen Sasaki Kojirō and MIYAMOTO MUSASHI from the loser Kojirō's perspective, the reverse of the commonly told story. Other major works include *Minamoto no Yoshitsune* (1951–55) and *Hiraga Gennai* (1957).

Murakami Kagaku (1888–1939)

Japanese-style painter. Real name Murakami Shin'ichi. Born in Ōsaka. He studied art at the Kyōto Bijutsu Kōgei Gakkō and later studied painting at the Kyōto Shiritsu Kaiga Semmon Gakkō (now Kyōto City University of Arts), from which he graduated in 1911. With TSUCHIDA BAKUSEN, Ono Chikkyō (1889–1979), and others, he helped establish the Kokuga Sōsaku Kyōkai, an association of artists dedicated to the budding national interest in modern Japanese-style painting (see NIHONGA). He exhibited annually at the Ministry of Education Bunten exhibitions, but after 1925 poor health forced his withdrawal. His extant oeuvre is large. His earlier works are predominantly paintings of mountains, and his later ones are of Buddhist subjects, executed in an introspective lyrical style.

Murakami Kijō (1865–1930)

HAIKU poet. Real name Murakami Shōtarō. Born in Edo (now Tōkyō). The son of a *samurai* of the Tottori domain (now Tottori Prefecture). Worsening deafness, which afflicted him from his late teens, made impossible the military and judicial career that he at first aspired to, and he ended up working as a scribe in the city of Takasaki, where he lived in poverty with his large family. Under the tutelage of MASAOKA SHIKI and later TAKAHAMA KYOSHI, he came to be considered one of the major poets of the HOTOTOGISU school, which emphasized photographic description *(shasei)* in haiku. Because of his life of poverty and his touching verses about animals and insects, he has been compared with the Edo-period haiku poet

Kobayashi ISSA. His main collections are *Kijō kushū* (1917), *Teihon Kijō kushū* (1940), and *Kijō haiku hairon shū* (1947).

Murakami Namiroku (1865–1944)

Novelist. Real name Murakami Makoto. Born in Sakai in what is now Osaka Prefecture. Drifting from job to job, he began to work for the newspaper *Hōchi shimbun* in 1890. The next year he published *Mikazuki*, a novel about a swordsman, in which he reaffirmed traditional virtues. It was an immediate success. Murakami continued to write popular historical novels and essays until about 1920, after which he devoted his energies to business ventures.

Murakami Naojirō (1868–1966)

Historian. Born in what is now Ōita Prefecture. A graduate of Tōkyō University, he traveled to Europe in 1899 to do research on Japan's relations with European countries during its period of NATIONAL SECLUSION (1639–1853). Murakami taught at various schools, including the Tōkyō School of Foreign Studies and Taihoku (Ch: Taibei or Taipei) University in Taiwan, before accepting a professorship at Jōchi (Sophia) University. He was named president of the university in 1945. Murakami is best known for his translations of correspondence and reports by Jesuits in Japan during the 16th century and of the records kept by Dutch merchants in Nagasaki. They include *Deshima rankan nisshi (Daghregister des Comptoirs Nagasacque)*, 3 vols (1938–39) and *Nagasaki: Oranda shōkan no nikki (Dagregister des Comptoirs Nangasaqui)*, 3 vols (1956–58).

Murakami Takejirō (1882–1969)

Metallurgist who contributed to the advancement of Japanese metallurgy with his research on special metal alloys and arc welding. Born in Kyōto Prefecture, he graduated from Kyōto University. In 1922 he became a professor at Tōhoku University and later served as director of its Research Institute for Iron, Steel, and Other Metals. He received the Order of Culture in 1956.

mural painting → screen and wall painting

Muramatsu Shōfū (1889–1961)

Novelist. Real name Muramatsu Giichi. Born in Shizuoka Prefecture; he attended Keiō University but left before graduating. He achieved recognition with the 1917 story, "Kotohime monogatari," based on his youthful experiences in the Yoshiwara brothel district of Tōkyō. Although he produced numerous popular romantic novels, he is better known for his biographical novels. Works include *Shōden Shimizu Jirochō* (1926–28), a popular treatment of a well-known 19th-century gambler, *Honchō gajin den* (1940–43), and *Kinsei meishōbu monogatari* (1952–61).

Murano Shirō (1901–1975)

Usually regarded as a poet in the modernist tradition, Murano Shirō was active as both a poet and critic throughout his life. Almost all of his poetry is free verse in the modern colloquial language, and much of it has a prose-like stylistic quality. However, a startling use of imagery and an uncompromising existentialism give a unique cast to most of his poems. During his twenties Murano was part of the group behind the modernist journal *Shi to shiron* (Poetry and Poetics) and later in life he performed important editorial work for the poetry journal *Mugen* (Infinity). Murano also wrote a number of critical and analytical books on modern Japanese poetry, including the Showa-period volume of the Chikuma Shobō Publishing Company's three-volume set *Kanshō gendaishi* (The Appreciation of Modern Poetry).

Murano was born in Tōkyō. Like a number of other poets who wrote free verse, Murano underwent an apprenticeship in the composition of *haiku* when he was a schoolboy. By the time he entered Keiō University in 1921, Murano had published some of his haiku. However, the poet chose to major in economics and to master German at the university as a means of countering the sentimentality to which, in his judgment, the composition of Japanese verse so readily led. After graduating from Keiō, Murano began a lifelong and successful career in business.

The poet himself attributed the hard, realistic features of his verse to the nature of his professional studies and career. The influence of early 20th-century German poetry, especially the movement known as the *Neue Sachlichkeit* (New Objectivity), is also apparent. His first volume of verse, *Wana* (1926, The Snare), consists mainly of witty, satiric exercises, but in his second volume, entitled *Taisō shishū* (1939, Poems on Exercise), Murano clearly reveals his concern for objectivity by portraying athletes in the midst of certain gymnastic exercises or engaged in such sports as boxing or hurdling. Describing these activities afforded Murano the opportunity to construct hard, mechanistic images almost totally resistant to the moods and emotions of previous Japanese poetry. After the war, Murano continued to write poetry with a hard, objectively rendered surface. But, in volumes like *Jitsuzai no kishibe* (1952, The Shore of Reality), *Bōyōki* (1959, A Record of Lost Sheep), and *Sōhaku na kikō* (1963, Pale Journey), critics such as Ayukawa Nobuo see an attempt to starkly render the condition of a psyche beset by existentialistic anxieties.

In a startling declaration during the mid-1920s, the poet KITAGAWA FUYUHIKO claimed the Japanese language did not naturally possess the mellifluous qualities often attributed to it. Murano, eschewing the musicality and impressionism of a HAGIWARA SAKUTARŌ in favor of the generally realistic images of a BASHŌ, followed the suggestions of Kitagawa for the development of a new, modern kind of Japanese verse. Murano consistently favored a poetic line more elastic than that of most of his contemporaries—a line that would expand or contract considerably in accord with the particular thought or image. With him each line advances the poem a discernible measure and functions so clearly in the resolution as to occasionally prompt the stricture that a Murano poem is no more than the sum of its parts.

📖 ——*Murano Shirō zen shishū* (Chikuma Shobō, 1968).

James A. O'Brien

Murano Tōgo (1891–)

Architect. Born in Saga Prefecture. In 1918 he graduated from Waseda University and went to work in the office of Watanabe Setsu, establishing himself as a major architect within the next decade. Murano opened his own firm in 1929. He is noted for his thorough professionalism and for his mastery of a wide range of styles. His half-century-long career has produced the starkly modern Sogō Department Store in Ōsaka (1936), the Nippon Life Insurance Company Hibiya Building with its art nouveau theater interior (1963), as well as numerous *sukiya*-style houses (see SUKIYA-ZUKURI). Other impressive structures include the Ube Civic Hall (1937), the World Peace Memorial Cathedral (1953), and the Japan Lutheran Theological Seminary (1970). *Watanabe Hiroshi*

Muraoka Hanako (1893–1968)

Writer and translator of children's literature; social commentator. Original name, Yasunaka Hana. Born in Yamanashi Prefecture, she graduated in 1913 from Tōyō Eiwa School for Women and taught for three years. Even before her marriage in 1919 and the births of her son and daughter, she began writing and translating stories for children. From 1932 to 1941 she was widely known as the producer and announcer of the children's news hour on the radio station JOAK, the predecessor of NHK (Japan Broadcasting Corporation). After World War II she continued to write and translate children's literature and at the same time was active as a social commentator, a director of NHK, and a member of various advisory committees for the government. She was also a managing director of the Fusen Kaikan (Women's Suffrage Center), vice-president of the Japanese National Commission for UNESCO (see UNESCO ACTIVITIES IN JAPAN), and editor of the Christian magazine *New Age*. Her postwar works include translations of Pearl Buck, Emily Dickinson, and L. M. Montgomery's series beginning with *Anne of Green Gables* (1908; tr *Akage no An*, 1950).

Muraoka Iheiji (1867–1942)

A notorious procurer of KARAYUKI SAN, Japanese prostitutes who were sent overseas from the Meiji period (1868–1912) to the end of World War II. His autobiography is one of the few informative records concerning illegal Japanese migration to the Asian continent and Pacific Islands, although its reliability has been questioned in recent studies. Born in the Shimabara domain (now part of Nagasaki Prefecture), the son of a poor fish vendor, Muraoka left school at age 12 to support his family after his father's death. He went to Hong Kong at age 18 and thereafter engaged in a wide variety of occupations, many of them disreputable, throughout China and Southeast Asia. Among the few good deeds he claimed to have done were rescuing kidnapped Japanese women in Xiamen (Amoy) and inland China, collecting donations from Japanese in Southeast Asia for Japan during the Russo-Japanese War (1904–05), and founding a school for Japanese children in the Philippines. His life was full of illegal activities, but his rather simple, energetic patriotism earned him a reputation that provoked both admiration and hatred, and distinguished him from other Japanese adventurers of the period.

📖 ——Muraoka Iheiji, *Muraoka Iheiji jiden* (1960).

Chiyoko Ishibashi

murasaki

Lithospermum erythrorhizon. A perennial herb of the family Boraginaceae which grows in sunny mountain areas throughout Japan and is also found in Korea and China. The stem stands 30–60 centimeters (12–24 in) in height and branches out at the upper part. The alternate leaves are narrow and tapered and, like the stem, densely covered with small hairs. During summer, it produces white flowers on the branch tips which are followed by hard, glossy fruits. The dark purple root grows thick and straight and reaches 5–10 centimeters (2–4 in) in length. This root was formerly important as a source of purple dye, especially in the Nara period (710–794), when the plant was cultivated in gardens called *murasakien*. This purple (*murasaki*) was regarded as the noblest color during the Heian period (794–1185). *Murasaki* roots produced in the Iwate district were known as *Iwate shikon* and were particularly prized in the Kamakura period (1185–1333). There were also many *murasaki* plantations throughout Japan during the Edo period (1600–1868), when the production of *murasaki* roots became a monopoly of the *daimyō* domains. Since the Meiji period (1868–1912), synthetic dyes have replaced the *murasaki* root. However, its elegant color has recently been rediscovered and favored by some connoisseurs. *Murasaki* root is also used in traditional remedies for burns, skin disease, and frostbite. *Matsuda Osamu*

Murasaki Shikibu (fl ca 1000)

Celebrated court lady and author who lived from the late 10th century into the early 11th and wrote a large part, if not all, of the *Genji monogatari* (TALE OF GENJI), the all-time classic of Japanese literature. The work known as the *Murasaki Shikibu nikki* (Diary of Murasaki Shikibu) is also attributed to her, as is *Murasaki Shikibu shū*, a collection of poems. She is generally held to be the greatest master of narrative prose in the history of Japanese literature.

Name, Family, and Early Life —— Of her life, almost nothing can be said with certainty. No holograph manuscript survives of any of the works attributed to her, and for her authorship of the *Genji monogatari* the chief support is a tradition running back to the Heian period (794–1185) and, somewhat more tenuously, to her own lifetime. If the *Murasaki Shikibu nikki* is authentically the work of Murasaki, then there can be no doubt that she wrote a least a part of the *Genji monogatari*. Problems of *Genji* authorship are complex, but almost no one in the near millennium since its composition has challenged her authorship of a major part of that work. Few would put her share at less than two-thirds.

She seems to have been known during her lifetime as Tō no Shikibu, but the sobriquet by which she is known today has prevailed since the late Heian period. Tō, the Sino-Japanese reading for the character *fuji* or "wisteria," clearly designates the FUJIWARA FAMILY, to a cadet branch of which she was born. Shikibu refers to the Shikibushō or Ministry of Rites, in which both her father and her brother held office.

Two theories have been advanced to explain the Murasaki element: that because it means "purple" it refers to the wisteria of her family name; and that it derives from the name of Genji's great love in the *Genji monogatari*. That the name of so important a literary figure has not survived need not cause surprise, since the names of few ladies other than princesses and mothers of crown princes are recorded in the surviving genealogies of the day.

The SOMPI BUMMYAKU of the Muromachi period (1333–1568) gives her a common ancestor in the male line with FUJIWARA NO MICHINAGA, the most powerful statesman of her time, and makes them fifth cousins. By perhaps the generation of her grandfather, Murasaki's branch of the family had slipped to the second level of the clan hierarchy, that of provincial governors, treated with disdain in much Heian narrative literature. Her father, Tametoki, served as a provincial governor during her youth, and at that level his career ended.

Murasaki Shikibu's family had for some generations displayed considerable literary talents. Her great-grandfather, Fujiwara no Kanesuke, was of sufficient renown to be numbered among the Thirty-Six Poetic Geniuses (SANJŪROKKASEN). The poem most frequently alluded to in the *Genji monogatari* (there is an allusion in the first chapter) is by Kanesuke. Her father acquired a certain eminence for his writings in Chinese, and near relatives are represented in the IMPERIAL ANTHOLOGIES of verse (*chokusenshū*). Her mother was also from a cadet branch of the Fujiwara.

Though the year of her birth is not known, scholarly conjecture centers with near unanimity upon the eighth decade of the 10th century and ranges over most of that decade. Of her childhood little is known save what she has told us in her diary, and it does not go beyond informing us that she had a good head and was better at Chinese studies than her brother. Her quickness at mastering a lesson in Chinese history, a famous passage in her diary tells us, caused her father to remark upon the pity of her not having been born a man.

It may be assumed from what is known of her father's career that she spent her early years in the imperial capital of Heiankyō (now Kyōto). In 996 he was posted as governor to Echizen (now part of Fukui Prefecture), which bordered the Sea of Japan almost exactly north of the capital. The fact that he petitioned the emperor for a provincial assignment suggests that the family had been living in straitened circumstances. It is generally believed that Murasaki Shikibu accompanied her father to Echizen, for what may have been her only period of residence outside the capital. Her descriptions of the sea in the *Genji monogatari*, for example, suggest the wild shores of the Sea of Japan far more than they do the shores of the Inland Sea which are supposedly being chiefly described therein.

She would by 996 have been well past the nubile age for Heian women, and it is most unlikely that a father would have taken a married daughter on a provincial assignment. The possibility that she had already been married and widowed has been suggested. If there was an earlier marriage no record of it survives, nor do there seem to have been children.

Middle Years —— Very late in the 10th century—the exact date is in doubt—she was married to a distant kinsman, a fourth cousin, also a Fujiwara. Her husband was probably more than 20 years her senior and a man with grown children at the time of the marriage. A comparison of their careers, indeed, suggests that her father and her husband may have been about the same age.

She had one daughter, and was widowed in 1001. To the daughter, known as Daini no Sammi, have been attributed the last chapters of the *Genji monogatari*, but there is no concrete evidence to support the claim.

Some time in the first decade of the 11th century she was summoned to court as a lady-in-waiting to the empress Akiko or Fujiwara no Shōshi (see JŌTŌ MON'IN), daughter of Fujiwara no Michinaga. The *Murasaki Shikibu nikki* gives a date very late in 1008 by the lunar calendar (which would convert to early the following year by the solar) as the anniversary of her entry into court service, but does not say which anniversary. It is not unlikely that she had by 1008 been at court for two or three years.

Nor does the *nikki* say when the *Genji monogatari* was begun or finished. The implication that she had already attracted notice for her writing is strong, however, and quite probably the literary name she had acquired for herself was the reason for her being summoned to court. She does not seem to have been very eager for the honor or very happy with it when it came, but that it was an honor is undeniable. A late marriage to an unlikely bridegroom may be accounted for by the theory of an earlier marriage, but it suggests, in the absence of such extenuation, that her stores of charm and beauty were not adequate reason for the invitation to court. A famous passage in the *nikki* in which she comments upon the inclinations and endowments of other court ladies suggests, further, that she may have been a somewhat tart and cross-grained sort of lady. The literary salon was already by her time an established institution, and she was the great woman pioneer in the art of prose fiction, which in the preceding century had been dominated by men. The likelihood, therefore, is that she began writing the *Genji monogatari* in the early years of her widowhood, and that because of it she attracted Michinaga's

Murasaki Shikibu

Detail of an imaginary representation of Murasaki Shikibu at work on the *Tale of Genji* painted by Tosa Mitsuoki several centuries after her death. Colors on silk. 160 × 53 cm. 17th century. Ishiyamadera, Shiga Prefecture.

notice and was invited into the service of his most important daughter.

The economics of literary and artistic activity argue a similar conclusion. Large supplies of paper were at the command of only the rich and powerful. There is reason to believe that several copies of the *Genji monogatari* were very soon in circulation among the court aristocracy. Even if they were on paper of inferior quality, and the inferior quality of the paper may account for the disappearance of the holograph copy or copies, the resources of a provincial governor would not have provided adequate supplies. The material resources for the completion of her great work thus became available to Murasaki Shikibu only after she had attracted the attention of Michinaga and been invited to court.

Probably no more than four or five years elapsed between her debut at court and the conclusion of the *nikki*; and although there is occasional carelessness and confusion in the *Genji monogatari*, it bears far more the signs of deliberation and meditation than of haste. It is therefore probable that she continued to write through the remainder of her court service, however long that may have been, and after.

The most elementary facts support the likelihood. It is a very long work and, as a court lady, she had other things to do. She was known as "the chronicle woman" (*Nihongi no tsubone*), the *nikki* tells us, and she gave the empress instruction in the poetry of Bo Juyi (Po Chü-i). Remarks in the *Genji monogatari* about painting, calligraphy, and the polite arts establish that her learning was not only bookish, and from her collected poems we learn that she was adept at one of the varieties of Chinese *koto* or zither. She was not merely left alone to write her book.

Late Years and Achievement —— Information about her late years is also meager. The empress was widowed in 1011. It is known that Murasaki Shikibu remained in her service for a time thereafter, but the dates of her departures from court and of her death are a matter for speculation. She is mentioned in the *Shōyūki*, the diary of Fujiwara no Sanesuke (957–1046), in an entry for the early summer of 1013. She was then still in Akiko's service. It is the last piece of specific information about her life.

Her father returned from his post as governor of Echizen in 1014, and in 1016 entered the Buddhist priesthood at the temple MIIDERA. The theory has been advanced that Murasaki Shikibu's death was the occasion for his taking holy orders, but in that regard nothing can be proved.

The implicit evidence in the *Genji monogatari* itself perhaps tells us as much about her life as does any explicit evidence. It argues for single authorship, with the possibility of later additions and revisions. The need to find a place in its development at which a second author took over from the first poses an exercise in the impossible. The *Genji monogatari* grows and develops just as an author might be expected to grow, and at the end suggests a serene rejection of the world such as comes with age and experience. The reasonable conclusion is that an aging Murasaki Shikibu wrote the last chapters. If hers were approximately the years of Genji, then she lived about a half-century, and died in the third decade of the 11th century. There is in the northern part of Kyōto a bit of land, to all appearances a grave, which is said to be the grave of Murasaki Shikibu. Scholars who wish it in fact to be her grave have put together a reasonably persuasive argument.

Murasaki Shikibu would have a place in the literary histories had the *Genji monogatari* been lost and her other works survived. The *nikki* would doubtless be found in the canon of Heian literature, if only because not many diaries, or works which go by that name, survive from the Heian period. In the small company of works that do survive, it is not the most interesting. It has a scattered and fragmentary look, and the character of the lady herself seems small and narrow. One looks in vain for the charity and tolerance that are at the heart of the *Genji monogatari* and account in large measure for its greatness. In her *nikki*, Murasaki Shikibu only has kind words for ladies not of sufficient substance to be likely rivals. Of ladies whom she must have recognized as genuine literary rivals, her remarks are somewhat ill-tempered. The magnanimity and wide humanity of the *Genji monogatari* are wanting.

There are 123 poems, not all of them attributed to Murasaki Shikibu herself, in the *Murasaki Shikibu shū*, her "collected poems." Most of the poems in the *nikki* are also in the collection, and most of Murasaki Shikibu's poems in the imperial anthologies are from the *shū*. She was not considered a major poet in her own day, and she does not seem so in ours. There is a certain blandness in her poetry, very representative of her day, if not of the most interesting which that day had to offer. The first poem in the *shū* is her most famous, honored with a place in the HYAKUNIN ISSHU (Single Poems by 100 Poets):

> It comes again, this midnight moon, and now
> Is lost among the clouds. And did I see it?

Without the *Genji monogatari*, her achievements might seem worthy and estimable, but they would not seem splendid. It is the *Genji* that makes them unique in the history of Japanese literature. There was nothing like it in Japan through all the later centuries until our own. That uniqueness was recognized by early leaders of the modern literary movement, and the example of the *Genji monogatari* was urged upon those who would be modern.

In the late Heian period and after there were imitations of the *Genji*, but the imitation did not go beyond outward forms, and did not seem to take note of the quality which more than any other accounts for Murasaki Shikibu's excellence, her interest in the complexities of the human spirit and her ability to create the illusion of individual life upon the written page. In most premodern Japanese narrative prose literature the characters are caricatures and stereotypes. She was a dramatic writer in the sense of achieving her effects and conveying her messages through the mediation of character rather than through the lyrical devices of simile and metaphor. The main tradition of Japanese literature has been lyrical.

She is generally placed beside SEI SHŌNAGON at the very pinnacle of premodern prose literature. Sei Shōnagon, however, seems much less boldly original and much nearer the main lyrical tradition. Murasaki Shikibu may well have been the finest writer of her time the world over, and she belongs on any list of the superior novelists of all time.

The name she quickly made for herself has not diminished in the centuries since. In the middle ages she became an almost mythological figure. In the Nō play *Genji kuyō*, for instance, she is revealed to be an incarnation of KANNON, patron deity of ISHIYAMADERA, a temple not far from Kyōto, at which an old tradition has it that she commenced writing the *Genji monogatari*.

Since the late 19th century the cult of the "modern" has had the effect of enhancing her reputation, or of making it possible to see what is most important in her writing. It may be that no one knows her real name, but every Japanese knows and admires "Murasaki Shikibu."

🔖——Imae Gen'e, *Murasaki Shikibu* (1966). Kanda Hideo and Ishikawa Harue, *Murasaki Shikibu: Sono seikatsu to shinri* (1956). Oka Kazuo, *Murasaki Shikibu no kenkyū* (1947). Annie Shepley Omori and Kōchi Doi, tr, *Diaries of Court Ladies of Old Japan* (1935), including the *Murasaki Shikibu nikki*. Shimazu Hisamoto, *Murasaki Shikibu: Hito to sono sakuhin* (1948). Shimizu Yoshiko, *Murasaki Shikibu* (1973). Tsunoda Bun'e, *Murasaki Shikibu no shimpen* (1965). Tsunoda Bun'e, *Murasaki Shikibu to sono jidai* (1966). Tsunoda Bun'e, *Wakamurasaki shō: Wakaki hi no Murasaki Shikibu* (1968). Edward G. SEIDENSTICKER

murasaki shikibu

(Japanese beauty-berry). *Callicarpa japonica*. A deciduous shrub of the family Verbenaceae which grows wild in mountain areas and on hills in Honshū, Shikoku, Kyūshū, and the southern part of Hokkaidō. It reaches a height of around 2–3 meters (7–10 ft) and has toothed oval leaves pointed at both ends. In June and July, it produces clusters of small pale purplish flowers which ripen into small round purple fruits. The plant was named after MURASAKI SHIKIBU, the author of the TALE OF GENJI. Similar species native to Japan include the *yabumurasaki (Callicarpa mollis)* and the *komurasaki (Callicarpa dichotoma)*. MATSUDA Osamu

Murata Harumi (1746–1811)

KOKUGAKU (National Learning) scholar and WAKA (31-syllable classical poem) poet of the late Edo period. Born in Edo (now Tōkyō). He studied under noted classicist KAMO NO MABUCHI and succeeded him as a mainstay of the Kokugaku school. He believed the flowing elegance of the early 10th century KOKINSHŪ, the first imperial collection of Japanese classical poetry, embodied the ideal poetic style. Together with KATŌ CHIKAGE, Harumi was a leading figure of the Edo school of *waka*. Disagreeing with the anti-Confucian views of the eminent Kokugaku scholar MOTOORI NORINAGA, he infused his work with a broad appreciation of both the Japanese and the Chinese literary traditions. He is noted for his rediscovery of the long-lost SHINSEN JIKYŌ (late 9th or early 10th), the oldest extant Chinese-Japanese dictionary.

Murata Minoru (1894–1937)

Film director. A pioneer of early Japanese cinema, he is remembered for making one of the first true Japanese masterpieces, *Rojō no reikon* (1921, Souls on the Road). Murata came to cinema from a career in SHINGEKI theater, where he had led his own troupe. The financial difficulties of his troupe and several others led to the formation of a repertory cinema troupe with Kaeriyama Norimasa (1893–1964) and in turn led Murata to join the newly formed Shōchiku Kinema in 1920. There he teamed with OSANAI KAORU to make *Rojō no reikon*, a film composed of two interwoven stories: a wealthy young man leaves home and later returns destitute with wife and child; two men just released from prison are treated kindly by people they meet on the road as they travel. Murata went on to make numerous other successful pictures, all of which expressed an interest in the sanctity of the individual and humane social conventions. Many of his films were drawn from European dramas and carefully adapted to fit Japanese situations. Murata's contributions to early Japanese cinema were in his promotion of dramas about contemporary life at a time when period films held sway, and in his concern for character and atmosphere over story. His films laid the foundation of Japanese realism. David OWENS

Murata Seifū (1783–1855)

Also called Murata Kiyokaze. Leading official of the Chōshū domain (now Yamaguchi Prefecture) and architect of its reform program of 1838–45. Educated at the Meirinkan, the domainal academy, he rose quickly in the Chōshū administrative hierarchy. In 1838 he was appointed director of a temporary reform ministry to meet the domain's enormous debt and to solve other problems caused by drought, famine, and peasant uprisings earlier in the decade.

To improve Chōshū's financial situation Murata devised a system of repayment of *samurai* debts to merchant creditors at low interest rates over extended periods. Besides enforcing the usual sumptuary regulations, Murata in 1840 took the unprecedented step of publishing the domain's budget and soliciting suggestions. He sold domainal monopolies to merchant guilds at a profit and increased the amount of gold and silver in the domain's coffers by taking these metals in payment for Chōshū products while forbidding their use in payment to other domains. During his administration, the Meirinkan opened its doors to low-ranking samurai who had previously been excluded, and other schools for the domain's samurai were opened in Chōshū and in the capital, Edo (now Tōkyō). Expert swordsmen were invited to teach in Chōshū, and Chōshū samurai were sent to other domains to study.

In 1845 Murata was forced to resign, largely because his plans conflicted with the interests of merchants and their samurai supporters. He was reinstated in 1855 but died shortly afterward. Although Murata's financial reforms did not succeed in rebuilding Chōshū's finances, they did result in the creation of special reserve funds and an alleviation of the samurai's financial burdens. He, like YOSHIDA SHŌIN, TAKASUGI SHINSAKU, and other Chōshū leaders in the mid-19th century, sought a revival of traditional samurai morality untainted by selfish commercial concerns.

Murata Shōzō (1878–1957)

Businessman. Born in Tōkyō. Graduate of Tōkyō Higher Commercial School (now Hitotsubashi University). Murata joined Ōsaka Shōsen Kaisha Co (now MITSUI O.S.K. LINES, LTD) and built it into a major shipping company by introducing high-speed regular freight service between Yokohama and New York in 1930. He served as company president from 1934 to 1940. He also served as postal and communications minister in 1940 and 1941, and as ambassador plenipotentiary to the Philippines in 1943. Murata became president of the Japan Association for the Promotion of International Trade (Nihon Kokusai Bōeki Sokushin Kyōkai) in 1954, working for the normalization of Japan–China relations and promotion of trade between the two countries.   KATSURA Yoshio

mura yakunin

Village officials in general during the Edo period (1600–1868). Villages were under the authority of samurai administrators known as DAIKAN or GUNDAI (intendants), but their affairs were mostly handled by village officials (mura yakunin) of rural commoner status (nōmin) who were chosen locally by election, appointment, or heredity.

There were four general types of mura yakunin. Ōjōya (also called ōkimoiri, ōsōdai, etc) were the highest-ranking, representing the interests of several villages, overseeing affairs in the area, and in some instances acquiring quasi-samurai status (MYŌJI TAITŌ) and exercising great influence over intendants. Ōjōya were sufficiently powerful that in 1713 the Tokugawa shogunate abolished the post in its own domains (tenryō), although ōjōya continued to function in daimyō lands.

The other three village offices, known collectively as jikata san'yaku (or murakata san'yaku), were titled SHŌYA (nanushi in the Kantō region), kumigashira (known in some places as TOSHIYORI or OSABYAKUSHŌ), and hyakushōdai. Shōya, chosen from among notable families of the village, were the senior officials in charge of a village and directly answerable to the intendant for matters such as the collection of land taxes (nengu). Kumigashira, subordinate to shōya, were spokesmen for the neighborhood mutual-responsibility groups called GONINGUMI. Hyakushōdai were selected from among wealthy villagers to represent village interests against outsiders, check on the behavior of shōya and kumigashira, and help assure fair allocation of tax and other obligations and equitable resolution of disputes.

Together these officials constituted the link between rulers and rural populace. Whether, when, and under what conditions the pressure from above or below was greater and whether mura yakunin functioned more to benefit rulers or ruled or a segment of one of the groups is a subject of lively disagreement among historians.

■■——Harumi Befu, "Duty, Reward, Sanction, and Power: Four-Cornered Office of the Tokugawa Village Headman," in Bernard S. Silberman and H. D. Harootunian, ed, Modern Japanese Leadership (1966). Harumi Befu, "Village Autonomy and Articulation with the State," Journal of Asian Studies 25.1 (1965).   Conrad TOTMAN

Murayama

City in central Yamagata Prefecture, central Honshū. A castle town of the Mogami family until the Edo period (1600–1868), Murayama developed as a market and post-station town on the highway Ushū Kaidō. Today it is an administrative and commercial center. Its principal occupation is the processing of dairy products, meat, and lumber; rice and sericulture also figure prominently. It is the birthplace of MOGAMI TOKUNAI, an early explorer of Ezo (now Hokkaidō). Pop: 32,325.

Murayama Ryōhei (1850–1933)

Newspaperman; longtime president and owner of the newspaper ASAHI SHIMBUN. Born in Ise Province (now Mie Prefecture). He opened a Western-style variety store in Ōsaka in 1871, and in 1879 became titular owner of the the Ōsaka shimbun, which his friend

Kimura Heihachi and Kimura's son Noboru had founded. Murayama subsequently bought the Asahi in 1881, and in two years his astute management secured for it the largest circulation in the country. He began publication of the Tōkyō asahi shimbun in 1888. He continued to expand the newspaper firm and set a precedent that other large newspapers followed by broadening its activities to include sponsorship of various events such as middle-school baseball tournaments and cultural exhibits.   ARIYAMA Teruo

Murayama Tomoyoshi (1901–1977)

Playwright, producer. Born in Tōkyō, he enrolled at Tōkyō University but withdrew to go to Germany, where he studied German expressionist painting. After his return home he joined several avant-garde drama groups and became a leading figure in the proletarian theater movement of the 1920s (see PROLETARIAN LITERATURE MOVEMENT). After World War II, Murayama became head of the Tōkyō Geijutsuza (Tōkyō Art Troupe), and in 1960 he led the troupe on a visit to China, the first such trip made by a Japanese "new theater" (SHINGEKI) company. His works include "Byakuya"(1934), a short story, and a two-volume collection of plays, Murayama Tomoyoshi gikyokushū (1971).

Murdoch, James (1856–1921)

Educator, journalist, and author of the first major English-language history of Japan. Born in 1856 to a farmer-merchant family near Aberdeen, Scotland, through prodigious application he won a fellowship to Aberdeen University and subsequent study at Oxford, Göttingen, and the University of Paris. His brilliance in foreign languages earned him an assistant professorship at the age of 24, which he soon resigned to emigrate to Australia. There he taught and worked as a journalist until he moved to Japan in 1889. With the exception of a short stay in a socialist community in Paraguay during 1893, he taught in various Japanese-government higher schools until 1917. He then returned to Australia to found a Japanese studies program at the University of Sydney. Among the students Murdoch taught in Japan were the writer NATSUME SŌSEKI and the scholar of English Yamagata Isoo (1869–1959). Yamagata later became Murdoch's research associate for his great three-volume History of Japan, which, though begun in 1903 and completed in 1917, was not published as a unit until 1926. Murdoch, whom Yamagata described as "the most studious person" he had ever seen, started to learn written Japanese when almost 50 but later read both contemporary and classical texts with ease. Lonely and diffident, he shunned social contacts and hated administrative detail.   John F. HOWES

Murōji

A temple affiliated with the Buzan branch of the SHINGON SECT of Buddhism (see HASEDERA). Built in a mountain forest across the river from the village of Murō, Nara Prefecture. Located about 25 kilometers (15.5 mi) southeast of the city of Nara, Murōji was founded in the late 8th century. Unlike other Nara temples whose halls are laid out according to a preconceived plan, Murōji buildings, modest in size, are erected on a few small plots of flat land along the mountain slope. Stone steps lead from one building to the other. The kondō (main hall), pagoda, mirokudō (hall of Maitreya), and kanjōdō (initiation hall), give the impression of being tucked away among old cryptomeria cedar trees. The temple houses a number of excellent sculptures carved during the Heian period (794–1185). The approach to this idyllic spot is marked by a colossal stone image of the Buddha MIROKU engraved in elegant lines in the living rock between 1207 and 1208.

Although the precise origin of Murōji is unknown, its site was regarded as sacred since ancient times. It has long been associated with monks who left worldly city temples to devote themselves to ascetic and magical practices in the mountains. There are many legends related to Murōji. One tells of the wandering ascetic and miracle worker EN NO GYŌJA who founded a temple there in 681 on behalf of Emperor Temmu. According to another tradition Murōji was founded by the monk Kenkei (d 793) of the temple KŌFUKUJI as an expression of gratitude to the local deities who restored the crown prince, the future emperor Kammu, to health in response to prayers that were offered in the year 778.

From that time onward Murōji was associated with the Kōfukuji, family temple of the powerful FUJIWARA FAMILY, which led to the prosperity Murōji enjoyed during the Heian period. Even though it

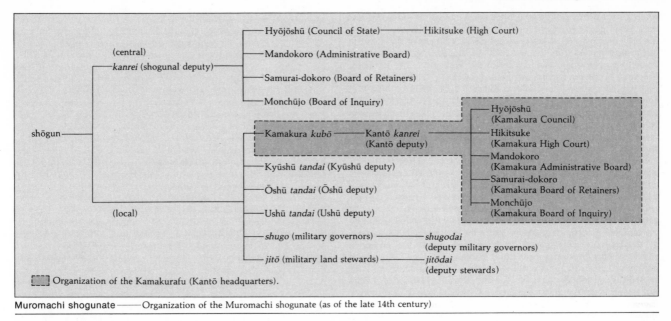

Muromachi shogunate ——Organization of the Muromachi shogunate (as of the late 14th century)

was primarily an esoteric temple, the close relationship Murōji had with Kōfukuji, a temple noted for traditional Nara learning, continued until 1694 when Murōji became formally affiliated with the Shingon sect. Because Murōji admitted women as visitors and participants in esoteric rituals, which Mt. Kōya (Kōyasan), the center of the Shingon sect, did not, Murōji was popularly called "the women's Mt. Kōya (nyonin Kōya)"; a stela bearing this inscription was placed by its entrance gate in the Edo period (1600–1868).

The oldest building of Murōji, constructed either late in the 8th or early in the 9th century, is the five-storied pagoda, designated a National Treasure. Because of the narrow plots of land available, this pagoda, 16.2 meters (53.2 ft) high, is the smallest in Japan. Its roofs, covered with cedar bark, are slightly curved and diminish almost imperceptibly in size as they rise, lending the building a slender, graceful appearance.

The kondō was also built on a narrow strip of land during the 9th century. In 1672, when an extra bay was added as a hall of worship, it was propped up by wooden pillars raised on stone terraces. Small in scale the structure is unobtrusively fitted into the mountain side. Its roof is covered with cedar shingles in keeping with the trees surrounding it. The inner sanctuary is dominated by large wooden images of the early Heian period centering around the historical Buddha, Śākyamuni, made during the 9th century. Behind him, on five wooden panels is painted a MANDALA of Taishakuten (Indra). Much smaller in size than the main images are the lively statues of the Jūni Shinshō (the Twelve Divine Generals) in the front row of the altar. They were carved during the Kamakura period (1185–1333).

The mirokudō contains an outstanding image of a seated Śākyamuni carved during the 9th century out of a single block of cedar wood. Its drapery is rhythmically arranged in the rolling-wave manner (hompashiki) characteristic of the Jōgan sculptural style. See also BUDDHIST SCULPTURE.

📖 ——Roy Andrew Miller, Murōji, An Eighth Century Japanese Temple: Its Art and History (1954).　　　Lucie R. WEINSTEIN

Muro Kyūsō (1658–1734)

Neo-Confucian scholar of the Edo period (1600–1868); given name Naokiyo. The son of a doctor, Muro Gemboku, who practiced in Edo (now Tōkyō), in 1672 he entered the service of MAEDA TSUNANORI, the enlightened daimyō of the Kanazawa domain (now Ishikawa Prefecture). He was subsequently sent by the domain to study with KINOSHITA JUN'AN, the Neo-Confucian scholar, in Kyōto. At the recommendation of scholar-statesman ARAI HAKUSEKI, he was appointed Confucian scholar to the shogunate in 1711. When the eighth shōgun TOKUGAWA YOSHIMUNE, dissatisfied with the formalistic teaching of Confucian doctrine at the shogunal academy (SHŌHEIKŌ), set up a separate school (Takakura Yashiki) in 1719, Kyūsō was named to its staff. From 1722 until his death he was private tutor to the shōgun. Although Kyūsō was a fellow student of Haku-

seki under Jun'an and in communication with Confucianists of the YAMAZAKI ANSAI school, he neither adopted Hakuseki's positivist approach nor Ansai's views on the essential unity of Shintō and Confucianism. Unlike many other Confucianists of his time, he refused the Japanization of Neo-Confucianism and maintained the strict orthodoxy of the Zhu Xi (Chu Hsi) doctrine (see SHUSHIGAKU). His works include Daigaku shōku shinso (1702), a statement of his philosophical position, Akō gijin roku (1703, rev 1709), a defense of the vendetta by the forty-seven rōnin (see FORTY-SEVEN RŌNIN INCIDENT), and Sundai zatsuwa, a collection of essays.

MIYAKE Masahiko

Muromachi bakufu → Muromachi shogunate

Muromachi history → history of Japan

Muromachi period

A period of great cultural achievement and persistent social disorder that lasted from the fall of the Kamakura shogunate in 1333 until 1568, when the warlord and emergent hegemon ODA NOBUNAGA entered Kyōto. The period is named for the location in Kyōto of the shogunal residence. It is also commonly known as the Ashikaga period, after the family who held the post of SHŌGUN in Kyōto from 1338 to 1573. The choice of dates must depend on one's judgment of when the government gained and lost its legitimacy or effectiveness, and scholars are not in agreement. Some political historians would considerably shorten the Muromachi period, arguing that the years 1336–92 (NORTHERN AND SOUTHERN COURTS) or the years 1467–1568 (SENGOKU or late Muromachi) should be counted as separate periods. Others have proposed only minor changes in the dates accepted here, choosing for example to begin the period with the promulgation of the KEMMU SHIKIMOKU, the shogunate's fundamental legal code, in 1336, or to end it in 1573, when Nobunaga expelled the last Ashikaga shōgun, ASHIKAGA YOSHIAKI, from his capital city. The SHOKUHŌ SEIKEN, a new regime created by Nobunaga and his successor TOYOTOMI HIDEYOSHI, reunified Japan, ushering in the AZUCHI–MOMOYAMA PERIOD (1568–1600) of Japanese history. See also HISTORY OF JAPAN: Muromachi history.

Muromachi shogunate

The Muromachi shogunate, or bakufu (1338–1573), was the second of Japan's three military regimes (see WARRIOR GOVERNMENT), falling between the KAMAKURA SHOGUNATE (1192–1333) and the TOKUGAWA SHOGUNATE (1603–1867). Established by ASHIKAGA TAKAUJI, its name derives from the Muromachi district of Kyōto, where the shogunal palace and administrative headquarters were located after 1378. It is also known as the Ashikaga shogunate in reference to its ruling house. Under the Ashikaga, the shōguns and their government greatly expanded the scope of military rule, asserting authority over most political and military affairs of the country, including the conduct of foreign relations, and leaving to the emperors little more than a ritualized residual sovereignty. The Ashikaga shōguns, however, lacked the great advantage in the balance of power between shōgun and local military lords (daimyō) that was enjoyed by the third shogunal house, the Tokugawa. Hence, the MUROMACHI PERIOD (in this encyclopedia dated 1333–1568; see also PERIODIZATION), though it lasted for more than 200 years, rarely saw the assertion of a strong centralizing command by the shōgun.

Shōgun and Shugo—— In extending its influence beyond its headquarters at Kamakura, the first shogunate had relied on its network of military land stewards (JITŌ) and provincial commanders (SHUGO) chosen from among its own vassals (GOKENIN). The Kamakura shogunate's authority, though limited, had been exercised effectively within the still viable structure of imperial provincial government. Under the Muromachi shogunate, the shugo added to the military powers they already had most of those previously held by the civil provincial governors (KOKUSHI), thereby becoming in effect military governors. The combination of shōgun, shugo, and jitō now carried much more of the total burden of government both nationally and locally. But although the Muromachi system of warrior government handled a greater volume and variety of administrative, legal, and military transactions than its predecessor, neither shōguns nor shugo acquired the independent enforcement power to exercise fully the authority they claimed. The balance of political-military power on which the Ashikaga house rested its rule was weakened by the fact that many shugo were as powerful as the Ashikaga house itself. The Ashikaga hegemony depended critically upon the support of vassal shugo houses, and much less on its own capacity to maintain a private force recruited from its numerous but individually weak jitō-grade vassals. The shōguns never commanded a private army that could hold its own against the strongest of their major vassals, let alone against a combination of shugo.

During the last years of the Kamakura shogunate, the ASHIKAGA FAMILY had emerged as one of the most powerful of the Kamakura vassals. It held the shugoships of Mikawa and Kazusa and estates in the provinces of Shimotsuke (now Tochigi Prefecture), Kazusa (now part of Chiba Prefecture), Sagami (now part of Kanagawa Prefecture), Mikawa (now part of Aichi Prefecture), and Tamba (now part of Kyōto and Hyōgo prefectures). For its military forces it could count upon a large number of branch families (collectively known as ichimon) that had taken root in those provinces. In Takauji's generation the ichimon included such names as the HATAKEYAMA, Niki, HOSOKAWA, Kira, IMAGAWA, TOGASHI, Isshiki, Shibukawa, and SHIBA. In the course of the fighting that brought the Ashikaga hegemony into being, numerous other warrior families allied themselves with the Ashikaga as TOZAMA (nonkin) vassals. Upon becoming shōgun, Takauji naturally tried to place heads of the more reliable branch families as shugo in as many provinces as possible. By the end of the 14th century, of the 67 provincial appointments recorded, 42 were held by Ashikaga kinsmen. But family connection was never an absolutely reliable bond, as the many defections that occurred during the civil wars of the period of NORTHERN AND SOUTHERN COURTS (1336–92) were to prove. Moreover, shugo themselves were not all-powerful in the provinces to which they were assigned.

Shugo were appointed to one or more whole provinces (kuni) in which they were given responsibility to maintain order, administer justice, and ensure the delivery of taxes. Shugo were in their own right military lords with considerable landholdings and personal following, but their lands were not necessarily located in their provinces of assignment. Most of the area of any given province was occupied by the estates of court nobles, religious organizations, and local military proprietors (KOKUJIN), some of whom might be direct vassals (gokenin) of the shōgun. Shugo, especially those brought in from outside by the Ashikaga shōguns, had to compete with these absentee and local proprietors for land and manpower. In this contest the shugo possessed certain advantages by virtue of their association with the shogunate. Shugo, for instance, could retain lands vacated as a result of judicial or military action for themselves or other warrior houses, thereby enlarging their own holdings or bands of retainers. Shugo had the authority to levy certain provincewide imposts (TANSEN AND TANMAI) for special purposes, and they could award half-tax (HANZEI) rights to local warrior families—a practice that permitted the local use of half the estate taxes due absentee proprietors for wartime commissariat expenses. Using techniques of

Muromachi shogunate

The Ashikaga Shōguns

	Shōgun	Term of office[1]
1.	Takauji (1305–1358)	1338–1358
2.	Yoshiakira (1330–1368)	1359–1368
3.	Yoshimitsu (1358–1408)	1369–1395
4.	Yoshimochi (1386–1428)	1395–1423
5.	Yoshikazu (1407–1425)	1423–1425
6.	Yoshinori (1394–1441)	1429–1441
7.	Yoshikatsu (1434–1443)	1442–1443
8.	Yoshimasa (1436–1490)	1449–1474
9.	Yoshihisa (1465–1489)	1474–1489
10.	Yoshitane (1466–1523)	1490–1493[2]
11.	Yoshizumi (1480–1511)	1495–1508
	Yoshitane	1508–1521[2]
12.	Yoshiharu (1511–1550)	1522–1547
13.	Yoshiteru (1536–1565)	1547–1565
14.	Yoshihide (1540–1568)	1568
15.	Yoshiaki (1537–1597)	1568–1573[3]

[1] In some instances a successor was not named until several years after the death or resignation of the former shōgun.
[2] Yoshitane was forced to resign in 1493 but was restored in 1508.
[3] Legal resignation in 1588.

this sort, as well as direct military action, to acquire more lands and followers, shugo managed to expand their strength locally, but increasingly at the expense of the shōgun's central interests.

During the 15th century, as some shugo and kokujin became more powerful and locally entrenched, they were able to assemble unitary domains which, though at first not as large as whole provinces, were more compact and militarily viable. In Japanese parlance they became SHUGO DAIMYŌ. As this happened, the shogunal connection became increasingly less useful in the local power struggle. The shogunate, for its part, tried to keep the shugo dependent on the shōgun by juggling shugo appointments, by using its provincial gokenin to protect its local interests, and by interfering in the household affairs of its shugo houses. Such maneuvers were the essence of Muromachi politics.

Distribution of Power—— The first (Kamakura) and third (Tokugawa) shogunates were based in the Kantō region, far removed from Kyōto. The Kamakura shōgun had been able to rely on existing organs of provincial government to maintain the basic structure of the country while it exerted its influence through certain limited administrative channels. The Tokugawa shōguns had the power in hand to control Kyōto and the western provinces from the Kantō. Ashikaga Takauji, despite the fact that his family's base of power was in the Kantō, was obliged to settle in Kyōto for the obvious reason that his hold over the capital area was too precarious for it to be left unattended. This created for the Muromachi shogunate a "Kantō problem."

To maintain a presence in the Kantō region, Takauji created at Kamakura a branch shogunate, known as the Kamakurafu, to which he posted his second son with the title KANTŌ KANREI (Kantō deputy). The Kantō headquarters, though subject to oversight from Kyōto, was given considerable freedom in local affairs. Its jurisdiction extended to the eight Kantō provinces plus Izu (now part of Shizuoka Prefecture) and Kai (now Yamanashi Prefecture), and later to Mutsu (now Aomori, Iwate, Miyagi, and Fukushima prefectures) and Dewa (now Akita and Yamagata prefectures). Before long the head of the Kantō Ashikaga house adopted the style of KUBŌ (a title reserved for the shōgun), and passed the office of kanrei to the UESUGI FAMILY, who had served as the chief managers of the Kamakurafu. The tendency toward separatism became so strong that ultimately the Kyōto government was obliged to take military action. In 1439 the Ashikaga Kantō line was extinguished by an army assembled by the sixth shōgun, ASHIKAGA YOSHINORI. Thereafter the Uesugi family, serving as kanrei, became the highest officials at Kamakura.

Kyūshū presented the Ashikaga in Kyōto with similar problems of control. In the southern island most of the provinces had long been subordinated to entrenched military houses like the SHIMAZU, ŌTOMO, SHŌNI, and ŌUCHI. Takauji had little choice but to leave these houses in place as *shugo*. As a regional representative of the shogunate in Kyōto, however, the Ashikaga shōguns kept in northern Kyūshū, usually at Hakata, the head of an influential branch family with the title of Kyūshū TANDAI (Kyūshū deputy). Of these IMAGAWA SADAYO, who served in the post from 1371 to 1395, was outstanding for his ability to bring the Kyūshū *shugo* to the support of the Muromachi shogunate. But Kyōto's ability to control the western end of the Inland Sea and the northern coast of Kyūshū, so critical to the then-flourishing TALLY TRADE with Korea and China, was never direct or complete, even under the strongest of *tandai*.

Powers of the Shogunate—— As is apparent from the above, the power of the Muromachi shogunate extended directly only to the central region of Japan, some 45 out of a total of 68 provincial units (66 *kuni* and 2 *shima*, or islands). It was within this sphere that the Ashikaga position was secure. In these provinces, there were at any one time some 20 active *shugo* houses, since many held more than one province concurrently. As of the end of the 14th century, roughly 10 Ashikaga branch families held 31 of the 45 shugoships in the central region. All *shugo* in this area were required to build residences in Kyōto to be available for shogunate service.

Although government under the Ashikaga shōguns took shape as a balance of forces between the shōgun and his *shugo*, it is natural that the shōgun should have sought to occupy a status well above that of the coalition that supported him. From its own estates (*goryō*), the Ashikaga house derived some income and military service. The extent of these lands is not clear. One important source of income and military support came from placing the entire province of Yamashiro (now part of Kyōto Prefecture) under shogunate control by having the head of the Board of Retainers (SAMURAI-DOKORO) serve as *shugo*. Aside from this, the shōgun's lands were scattered over many provinces. These holdings were used as sources of income but more importantly as fiefs to support the household retainers who served as shogunate administrators and guardsmen. The shōgun's palace guards, the *hōkōshū*, were recruited both from shogunal estates and from lesser branches of *shugo* houses. But these units, while sufficient to maintain order in the capital city, never numbered more than a few hundred mounted men. Military action on behalf of the shogunate was always undertaken by troops under shogunal order from loyal *shugo* houses. The ability of a shōgun to exert force therefore depended greatly on his capacity to motivate a sufficient number of *shugo* to follow his direction. The one who managed this best was the third shōgun, ASHIKAGA YOSHIMITSU, who had great success in sending out coalition armies against threats to the shogunate posed by aggressive *shugo* houses. The eighth shōgun, ASHIKAGA YOSHIMASA, however, proved unable to maintain the balance of power. The result was the ŌNIN WAR (1467–77), which put all *shugo* houses on one side or the other of a military struggle that lasted 11 years and brought to an end the shogunate's ability to influence affairs beyond the capital city.

Of course, the shōgun's powers were not limited to the use of military force alone. Vested in the office of shōgun were certain legal and customary prerogatives and a charisma derived from the possession of high court rank and an aristocratic style of life. The post of shōgun was itself an imperial appointment, and with it went the expectation of high court status. Takauji achieved the second rank, senior grade. Yoshimitsu moved a step higher to first rank, junior grade; his successors up through Yoshimasa did likewise. Such ranks assimilated the Ashikaga house into the high court nobility, far above other military lords in prestige and proximity to the emperor, who was still venerated as the ritual sovereign. A further dimension was added to the shōgun's public image when Yoshimitsu in 1403 accepted the designation "king of Japan" from the emperor of Ming China; but this did not become regular practice.

Part of the Ashikaga shōguns' demonstration of their achievement of aristocratic status was their conspicuous patronage of the arts. Beginning with the shogunal residences, the so-called Hana no Gosho (Palace of Flowers), the KINKAKUJI (Golden Pavilion), and the GINKAKUJI (Silver Pavilion), the Ashikaga house gave expression to the values of a new elite culture, which fused the traditional style of the civil nobility with the dynamism of the warrior aristocracy (see KITAYAMA CULTURE; HIGASHIYAMA CULTURE). It is significant that this style of life was basically urban and cosmopolitan and that the Ashikaga were able to continue it, even after their loss of effective power in the provinces, through control of Kyōto and its commercial wealth and by participation in the China trade.

Machinery of Government—— Two men are credited with giving shape to the machinery of Muromachi government. Ashikaga Takauji, the military organizer and strategist, was concerned primarily

with the balance of power (the "feudal" dimension), while his younger brother ASHIKAGA TADAYOSHI devoted himself to establishing the administrative organs of government (the "bureaucratic" dimension). The promulgation of the KEMMU SHIKIMOKU (Kemmu Code) in 1336 demonstrated the Ashikaga's intent to follow the Kamakura model for military rule. But they also recognized the need to bring peace to Kyōto and to protect their commercial interests. The early Ashikaga shōguns took over a great deal, in both administrative organization and personnel, from the Kamakura shogunate. Unlike the Minamoto line in Kamakura, the Ashikaga house was able to retain its hold on the office of shōgun from beginning to end, and the first eight shōguns, at least, played significant roles in the functioning of Muromachi government.

For the first few years after its founding the Muromachi shogunate was run by the shōgun with the aid of a general manager (*shitsuji*), a post held by a succession of kin and quasi-kin vassals. In 1362 the office was renamed KANREI and upgraded to what can be translated as "deputy shōgun." In 1367, just as Hosokawa Yoriyuki (1329–92) was named *kanrei*, Yoshimitsu succeeded as head of the Ashikaga house. He was then a minor, and so the office of *kanrei* was briefly something of a regency. But the post was not permitted to become the possession of any one family; rather it was passed around in succession between three *ichimon* families, the Shiba, Hosokawa, and Hatakeyama. These three houses, rather than compete with the Ashikaga house, served as a sort of inner bloc of powerful *shugo* committed to its support. Under the mature Yoshimitsu, the office of *kanrei* became a bridge between the shōgun and the provincial *shugo*. Evidence of this is seen in the establishment of a council of *shugo* (*yoriai*) consisting of the heads of the three *kanrei* houses and other powerful *shugo* houses like the YAMANA, Isshiki, and Imagawa.

The *kanrei-yoriai* system worked well up to the time of the sixth shōgun, Yoshinori, who tried to bypass the *kanrei* and *yoriai* and to engage in direct personal rule through his inner staff of hereditary administrators (*bugyōnin*). This action put the *shugo* at odds with the shōgun. Yoshinori's assassination in 1441 by a disgruntled *shugo* put an end to strong shogunal rule. In course of time the office of *kanrei* became a vehicle through which a succession of provincial military lords sought to use the shōgun for their own ends.

The functional organs of the Muromachi shogunate were at first closely patterned on the Kamakura model. Assisting in this process were a number of specialists in legal and administrative matters who had had previous experience in Kamakura. In the Kamakura shogunate the HYŌJŌSHŪ (Council of State) established in 1226 had developed into the primary deliberative council under the HŌJŌ FAMILY regency. Ashikaga Takauji set up a Hyōjōshū in Kyōto, staffing it with professional administrators like the Nakahara, Miyoshi, and NIKAIDŌ and the heads of several Ashikaga branch families like the Kira, Yamana, Ishibashi, and Isshiki. The development of the *kanrei* system inevitably affected this arrangement, and ultimately the *kanrei*'s *yoriai* took over the functions of the Hyōjōshū.

Another important office adopted from Kamakura was the Samurai-dokoro (Board of Retainers), used by Takauji as his war council. Its head, known as the *shoshi*, was selected from among a group of four important *shugo* houses, the Yamana, AKAMATSU, Isshiki, and KYŌGOKU. These families, two kin and two not, served as a secondary bloc of support for the Ashikaga house. The head of the Samurai-dokoro came to have two principal functions: to serve as *shugo* of Yamashiro, the "home province," on behalf of the shogunate; and to maintain law and order in the capital district. The second function was taken over from the imperial police (the KEBIISHI) and was carried out quite effectively until after the Ōnin War, when the Samurai-dokoro disappeared as a functioning organ of shogunal government.

The body that proved most influential and durable in the Muromachi shogunate was the MANDOKORO or Administrative Board. Established first as the main office for managing the shōgun's household administration and finances, including the collection of taxes, its heads were at first drawn from the Nikaidō, one of the families of administrative specialists that had served the previous shogunate. Later it was headed by the Ise, a family that had long served as Ashikaga household administrators. The rise in importance of the Mandokoro came in two stages. First, under the sixth shōgun, Yoshinori, it was used as a means of circumventing the *kanrei-yoriai* system and of concentrating power in his hands. Yoshinori's assassination put an end to this effort. Thereafter, and second, as the shōgun lost power and withdrew from participation in government affairs, the shōgun became increasingly the puppet of hereditarily entrenched civil officers *(bugyōnin)* of the Mandokoro and military service families (the *hōkōshū*) who made up the palace guard. It was these groups of lower-level service officers that managed to carry the by now powerless Ashikaga house into the 16th century.

Decline and Demise —— By the start of the 16th century the provinces were in the hands not of centrally appointed *shugo* but of self-made SENGOKU DAIMYŌ—powerful military lords of *shugo* and *kokujin* origin who were rapidly extending both their territorial grasp and their autonomy from central authority. In response to this development the Ashikaga house could have moved in either of two directions, toward military self-strengthening that would make it competitive with the daimyō or toward retreat into merely ceremonial suzerainty. It chose the latter. As already noted, the eighth shōgun, Yoshimasa, unable to control his *shugo,* sat by helplessly as the Ōnin War devastated his capital. Thereafter the shogunate as a government declined rapidly, and only the status of shōgun remained. But it was kept alive, as much by the interests that depended on that status as by any sign of vigor in the Ashikaga house. Support came from three sources: the above-mentioned hereditary shogunate staff, various religious institutions that had been patronized by the Ashikaga house, and military houses that sought to legitimize their de facto local power by gaining recognition from the symbolic head of the warrior class. For instance, the occupation of Kyōto by ODA NOBUNAGA in 1568 was justified as an effort to support ASHIKAGA YOSHIAKI, who was destined to be the last of the Ashikaga shōguns. When Nobunaga ousted Yoshiaki from Kyōto in 1573, the Muromachi shogunate was finished as a functioning institution. The exiled Yoshiaki, however, continued to behave as shōgun, and his pretensions were supported by powerful daimyō; so that, strictly speaking, the Muromachi shogunate retained a shadowy legal existence until Yoshiaki's resignation in 1588. See also HISTORY OF JAPAN: Muromachi history.

📖 ——John W. Hall and Jeffrey P. Mass, ed, *Medieval Japan: Essays in Institutional History* (1974). John W. Hall and Toyoda Takeshi, ed, *Japan in the Muromachi Age* (1977). Jeffrey P. Mass, *Warrior Government in Early Medieval Japan* (1974). Nagahara Keiji, *Sengoku no dōran,* vol 14 of *Nihon no rekishi* (Shōgakukan, 1975). George Sansom, *A History of Japan, 1334–1615* (1961). Sasaki Gin'ya, *Muromachi bakufu,* vol 13 of *Nihon no rekishi* (Shōgakukan, 1974). Satō Shin'ichi, "Muromachi bakufu ron," in *Iwanami kōza: Nihon rekishi,* vol 7 (Iwanami Shoten, 1963). H. Paul Varley, *The Ōnin War* (1967). H. Paul Varley, *Imperial Restoration in Medieval Japan* (1971).   *John W.* HALL

Muroo Saisei (1889–1962)

Poet, novelist, and essayist. From around World War I through World War II, Muroo was a prolific writer. In poetry he was quickly recognized as a born lyricist who, in free style and slightly unorthodox classical language, wrote amiable short poems on humanistic subjects, such as youthful loneliness and longing for love and homeland. He also composed HAIKU (17-syllable poems) of which he published several collections. In prose he wrote autobiographical novels with lyrical qualities equal to his verse, many short stories, some studies of classical and modern Japanese poets, and numerous essays.

Muroo's first book, *Ai no shishū* (1918, Poems of Love), contained the following, entitled "Springtime":

> As I write poetry
> Permanence comes
> Touches my forehead
> So swiftly
> It leaves no trace
> Trying to catch it
> I've not been successful
> And time passed
> With stains on my heart
> Sensations on my forehead
> I still write poetry
> Roaming town to town
> Stepping in puddles

Throughout more than 20 books of verse which contain about 1,300 poems in all, Muroo maintained basically the same style and mode, affected little by the times.

Muroo was an illegitimate child, born Obata Terumichi in Kanazawa, Ishikawa Prefecture. He was adopted, and worked as a page at a district court after quitting school in the seventh grade. His superior, who happened to teach *haiku* on the side, introduced him to literature. In 1910 he left Kanazawa for Tōkyō and, through his contributions to the journal *Zamboa* (Shaddock), came to know KITAHARA HAKUSHŪ (1885–1942) and HAGIWARA SAKUTARŌ (1886–1942). Hagiwara praised Muroo's "unprecedented, liberal rhythm which was like a genius's and unrestricted, fresh emotions which were like a baby's." In 1916 Muroo and Hagiwara started the journal *Kanjō* (Feeling), which became a major medium for those poets who were dissatisfied with the naturalist and decadent poetry of the time. Their relationship paralleled somewhat that of Goethe and Schiller. However, compared with Hagiwara, who relied on his instinct to create a unique world of beauty, Muroo often dealt with the harshness of reality, rendering almost moralistic interpretations. Muroo the poet was honest about what he saw and naive enough to express it in a forthright manner. As a result, some of his works apparently lack depth.

After he married in 1918, Muroo associated with novelist AKUTAGAWA RYŪNOSUKE (1892–1927) and began writing novels. His first work in prose was *Yōnen jidai* (My Childhood), which was followed by *Sei ni mezameru koro* (As I Was Awakened to Sex) and *Aru shōjo no shi made* (The Death of a Certain Girl), all in 1919. However, as Japanese writers cultivated new ideas and techniques in their literature and expanded their vision and sought to deepen their introspection, he was somewhat isolated from the main current.

His longest novel, *Anzukko* (1956–57, Apricot Child), was to show, according to him, "how a writer should summarize his works in his lifetime or how he has lived." It was autobiographical, resembling the works of the older naturalist school. He was awarded the Yomiuri Literary Prize for this novel in 1958, and the following year he won the Mainichi Book Award for the critical biography *Waga aisuru shijin no denki* (1958, The Lives of the Poets I Love) and the Noma Literary Prize for *Kagerō no nikki ibun* (1958–59, A Supplement to the *Gossamer Years*), a long novel based on the famous Heian-period (794–1185) diary KAGERŌ NIKKI. In 1960 he established the Muroo Saisei Poetry Prize and continued to be active in all literary genres until he succumbed to lung cancer.

📖 ——Muroo Saisei, *Muroo Saisei zenshū,* 14 vols (Shinchōsha, 1964–68). Muroo Saisei, "Ani imōto" (1934), tr Edward Seidensticker as "Brother and Sister," in Ivan Morris, ed, *Modern Japanese Stories* (1961). Atsumi Ikuko and Graeme Wilson, "The Poetry of Muroo Saisei," *Japan Quarterly* 18.3 (1971). Nakano Shigeharu, *Muroo Saisei* (1968). Shimpo Chieko, *Muroo Saisei* (1962).   *James R.* MORITA

Muroran

City in southwestern Hokkaidō, on Uchiura Bay. Muroran was at times directly administered by the Matsumae and Nambu domains as well as by the shogunate during the Edo period (1600–1868). Its port, opened in 1872, developed as a shipping center for coal from the Ishikari Coalfield. A steel plant constructed at the end of the Meiji period (1868–1912) led to its industrialization; today there are large cement factories, steel mills, oil refineries, and shipyards clustered around the port. Pop: 150,200.

Muroto

City in southeastern Kōchi Prefecture, Shikoku. It is a base for fishing fleets that operate as far away as the Indian and Atlantic oceans; the principal catch is bonito and tuna. The processing of marine products is consequently the major industry. Vegetables and fruits are grown in the coastal areas. The cape of MUROTOZAKI, the most scenic feature of the Muroto–Anan Coast Quasi-National Park, is located here. Pop: 26,085.

Murotozaki

Cape in Kōchi Prefecture, southeastern Shikoku. Famous for its rocky coast, lush subtropical trees, and lighthouse. Located in the path of frequent typhoons, the cape suffers much damage every year. Hotsumisakiji, one of the 88 pilgrimage temples of Shikoku, is located here. Murotozaki is part of the Muroto–Anan Coast Quasi-National Park.

Murray, David (1830–1905)

American educator. One of the FOREIGN EMPLOYEES OF THE MEIJI PERIOD who served as an adviser to the Ministry of Education, he is noted for his important contribution in inaugurating a modern education system in Japan.

Murray graduated from Union College, New York, in 1852 and later taught at Rutgers College. In 1872, when MORI ARINORI, the Japanese chargé d'affaires and acting minister to the United States at the time, sought the opinions of five prominent American educators about what Japanese education should be like, Murray submitted a written opinion. As a result, he was invited to Japan in 1873. As top-ranking foreign adviser to the Ministry of Education, he directed the implementation of the EDUCATION ORDER OF 1872. He surveyed the state of education throughout the country in order to extend the primary education system and reported to the ministry those areas where improvements seemed necessary. Murray also argued the importance of education for women and urged the establishment of a girl's normal school. On his advice, the government founded the Tōkyō Women's Normal School (now OCHANOMIZU WOMEN'S UNIVERSITY); Murray set up Japan's first kindergarten there. He took particular interest in the establishment of Tōkyō University, drawing up plans and seeing to the adoption of a system of university degrees and graduation modeled on that of American and British universities. In addition, institutions like the Japan Academy and National Museum were established upon his recommendation. He returned to the United States in January 1879.

TERASAKI Masao

musasabi → flying squirrels

Musashi

Battleship of the Imperial Japanese Navy of the YAMATO class. With a displacement of 64,000 tons, the *Musashi* was 250 meters (820 ft) long, 39 meters (128 ft) wide, and mounted with a main battery of nine 46-centimeter (18-in) guns. Construction at the Mitsubishi Heavy Industries' Nagasaki Shipyards was begun in 1938 and completed in August 1942. The *Musashi,* which became the flagship of the Combined Fleet in February 1943, was sunk on 24 October 1944 at the Battle of LEYTE GULF. *ICHIKI Toshio*

Musashi Murayama

City in north central Tōkyō Prefecture. Until recently a farming village, the city has undergone rapid urbanization with the establishment of several automobile plants in 1961 and the construction of an enormous housing complex in 1966. There are also factories producing electric machinery and precision instruments. Local products are Sayama tea and Murayama–Ōshima *tsumugi* (pongee). Pop: 57,194.

Musashino

City in east central Tōkyō Prefecture. Formerly an agricultural district, it became a residential suburb after the Tōkyō Earthquake of 1923. It was temporarily the site of several factories during World War II. The central shopping area of Kichijōji and Inokashira Park are popular. Seikei University is located here. Pop: 136,895.

Musashino Plateau

(Musashino Daichi). Diluvial upland; extends from Tōkyō to Saitama Prefecture, southwestern Kantō Plain, central Honshū. Surrounded by the three rivers Tamagawa, Irumagawa, and Arakawa and by Tōkyō Bay. Elevated from the Tamagawa's diluvial fan. From the Meiji period (1868–1912), urbanization and road building proceeded rapidly. The woodland and cultivated land typical of the Musashino Plateau are now replaced by housing projects, factories, and other urban facilities. Elevation: 20–180 m (66–590 ft).

Musashi Province

(Musashi no Kuni; also called Bushū). One of the 15 PROVINCES *(kuni)* of the Tōkaidō region of central Japan established in 646 at the time of the TAIKA REFORM; now Tōkyō, Saitama, and eastern Kanagawa prefectures. The YAMATO COURT (ca 4th century–ca mid-7th century) settled naturalized Koreans (KIKAJIN) in the region to develop the land. The central government, through its provincial officials *(kokushi),* gradually took over much of this land, making it into pasturage (MAKI); but it was later absorbed by private estates *(shōen)* during the Heian period (794–1185). In the late Heian period powerful local families in Musashi formed warrior bands (see MUSASHI SHICHITŌ), and the lord–vassal structure of these groups laid the basis for the feudalism of the medieval period (13th–16th centuries). After the establishment of the Kamakura shogunate (1192–1333), Musashi came under the direct rule of the MINAMOTO FAMILY and HŌJŌ FAMILY. For most of the Muromachi period (1333–1568) the UESUGI FAMILY governed the province as the shogunal deputies for the Kantō region (KANTŌ KANREI). Early in the 16th century the "Later Hōjō" family (see HŌJŌ SŌUN) gained control of most of the Kantō region but were destroyed by TOYOTOMI HIDEYOSHI in the ODAWARA CAMPAIGN of 1590. After TOKUGAWA IEYASU established his shogunate in 1603, Edo (now Tōkyō) became the political center of Japan, and most of Musashi was administered directly by the shōguns until the Meiji Restoration of 1868.

Musashi Shichitō

(Seven Bands of Musashi). Major warrior bands (BUSHIDAN) that were active from about the 10th century in the Musashi area, north, west, and south of present Tōkyō. The exact origin of these bands is unclear, but they are apparently descended from court nobles who had been sent out as provincial governors in the past. Each band was held together by real and fictive ties of kinship as well as by shared military ambitions. Their centers of power tended to shift as they fought with one another or opened up new agricultural lands. Although it is not clear which families constituted the seven bands at any given time, the best known are the Yokoyama, Kodama, and Inomata. All of them became vassals of the MINAMOTO FAMILY, but they retained their identity down through the 14th century. They figure in such military chronicles as the GEMPEI SEISUIKI (mid-12th century) and the TAIHEIKI (14th century).

Museum of Modern Japanese Literature

(Nihon Kindai Bungakukan). A facility that combines the features of library, museum, and literary center for the purposes of display, research, bibliographic control, and reprinting of modern Japanese literature. Through the efforts of writers like TAKAMI JUN (later the first director of the museum) and ITŌ SEI and scholars like Inagaki Tatsurō (b 1901) and Odagiri Susumu (b 1924), support from literary groups, scholastic societies, corporations, mass media, and the government was received in the spring of 1962 for the realization of a collection of modern literature begun at Ueno Library in 1964. In April 1967 the collection was moved to permanent quarters in Komaba Park in Tōkyō's Meguro Ward. Holdings include the works and papers of novelists Takami Jun and AKUTAGAWA RYŪNOSUKE and of the socialist politician SUZUKI MOSABURŌ. The noncirculating collection now totals over 200,000 volumes, including several thousand periodicals. The museum also presents exhibits. Because this facility emphasizes preservation of literary, sociological, and historical materials, many publishers contribute two copies of each new literary work to the museum. In addition to gifts in kind, funds are received from a variety of sources, including dues from membership associations, entrance fees, the Ministry of Education, and revenue from sales of publications. *Theodore F. WELCH*

museums

Japan probably has more museums in relation to its population than any other country in the world: the *Zenkoku hakubutsukan sōran* (1978), a catalog recording all the museums in Japan, lists about 1,500. The systematic collection and public presentation of art objects, however, only began in the early years of the Meiji period (1868–1912). These endeavors grew slowly until 1940; since 1945 the development has been phenomenal. Several factors have contributed to this growth: (1) many private collections have become public museums within the last few years; (2) Buddhist temples and Shintō shrines have received encouragement from the government to build adequate treasure houses in which to store and display their possessions; (3) increasing interest in Japanese archaeology has led to the building of museums at many archaeological sites; and (4) the recent desire to preserve the artifacts of an older and vanishing agricultural life has resulted in an abundance of museums containing folk art and ethnographical collections as well as reconstructions of typical premodern agrarian villages.

The history of art collecting in Japan, however, dates from the 8th century, when the world's oldest existing collection of art objects was founded: that in the SHŌSŌIN, the treasure house connected with the Nara temple TŌDAIJI. This collection consists of the ritual objects used in 752 in the consecration ceremony for the central image of the Tōdaiji and many possessions of the emperor SHŌMU (d 756), dedicated to the temple by his widow. It has remained largely intact to the present. In addition, almost all temples and shrines built up their own collections of documents and precious objects, preserving them with varying degrees of care over the centuries. In later years various shōgun and *daimyō* families collected art; a number of their holdings have come down to the present time. The holdings of the shōgun ASHIKAGA YOSHIMASA (1436–90), consisting largely of art objects from China, are, although long since dispersed, recorded in a catalog compiled by the painter and connoisseur NŌAMI (1397–1471).

National Museums——The history of Japanese museums opens with the establishment of the TŌKYŌ NATIONAL MUSEUM in 1871. It began as an exhibition gallery housed at the Yushima Seidō, a building in the precincts of the Confucian shrine in the Kanda district of Tōkyō, and contained artistic, historic, scientific, and natural history exhibits. Its creation was, in part, an attempt to redress the destruction and neglect that traditional Japanese art had suffered in the wave of fashion for all things Western that had accompanied the opening of the Meiji period.

The space at the shrine became so crowded that the collections were moved to the former residence of the Shimazu family at Kōjimachi in 1873, where they remained until 1882. Additional purchases were made, for example, of objects shown at the international expositions in Vienna in 1873 and in Paris in 1878. These included a Heian-period (794–1185) painting of Fugen Bosatsu (the bodhisattva Samantabhadra), lacquer writing boxes by Ogata KŌRIN and HON'AMI KŌETSU, and a vase by NONOMURA NINSEI.

In 1882 the collection was moved to its present site in Ueno Park and housed in a large two-story brick building, the Second National Exhibition Art Pavilion. Designed by the English architect Josiah CONDER, it was considered his masterpiece. Four years later the museum, which had been under the jurisdiction of the Ministry of Agriculture and Commerce, was assigned to the Ministry of the Imperial Household. By 1887 the museum was being used less as a center for international exhibitions and was beginning to assume more of its present character as a showplace for Japan's artistic heritage. In 1900 it was renamed the Tōkyō Imperial Household Museum.

The early activities of the museum were spurred by a report on the Vienna Exposition of 1873, written in 1875 by Gottfried WAGENER, who was employed by the Japanese emissary to the exposition, SANO TSUNETAMI. In the report Wagener wrote at length on the need for Japan to preserve, study, and practice its native art. Sano also urged the Japanese government to establish an art museum. In addition, the influence of the Japanese critic, connoisseur, and art teacher OKAKURA KAKUZŌ (1862–1913) and of the American scholar Ernest FENOLLOSA (1853–1908) was of great importance in the preservation and collection of Japan's traditional arts.

In 1908 a second building, the Hyōkeikan, was added; a Beaux-Arts-style edifice, it now contains the Japanese archaeological collections. Conder's building, the Second National Exhibition Art Pavilion, was damaged in the Tōkyō Earthquake of 1923 and was replaced in 1938 by the present Western-style building crowned with a somewhat oriental-style roof; it houses the collections of Japanese art objects from historical times.

In 1947 the museum was placed under the control of the Ministry of Education and was renamed the National Museum; three years later it became the Tōkyō National Museum. Another building was erected in 1954 to show the objects, mostly of the Asuka period (late 6th century–710) presented by the authorities of the Nara temple HŌRYŪJI in 1878 to the imperial household and now on loan to the museum. The arts of China, Korea, and India and East Asian ethnographical material may be seen in still another building, the Tōyōkan, opened in 1968; prominent international and local loan exhibitions are held in special galleries in this building.

The other two national art museums, in Kyōto and Nara, have a far less involved history. The one in Kyōto was established by the imperial household and was opened to the public in 1897. It was given to the city in 1924 and became a national museum in 1951. Its original building, designed by Katayama Otokuma (1853–1917), still stands but is used only occasionally for temporary exhibitions—its place taken by a more suitable contemporary building. This museum not only preserves and houses paintings, sculpture, and other treasures belonging to temples in the vicinity (its original purpose), but also houses objects from private collections and owns a considerable collection of Japanese art of all periods.

The Nara National Museum was established in 1895, also with an original building by Katayama Otokuma, which was supplemented in 1973 by a handsome edifice in traditional *kura* (storehouse) style designed by YOSHIMURA JUNZŌ. It was intended to house and display works of art belonging to temples and shrines in the Nara area; it now has, in addition, a collection of its own. It is noted for its Buddhist sculpture and its annual showing of objects from the Shōsōin.

Far smaller than the three national museums, the Kamakura National Treasure House yet serves a similar purpose. Built in 1928, it is a storage house and exhibiting center for the sculpture, paintings, and other important objects, largely of the Kamakura (1185–1333) and Muromachi (1333–1568) periods, owned by temples, shrines, and private collectors in the Kamakura region.

Private Museums——Apart from the national museums, the finest traditional Japanese and Chinese art objects on public view are found in the treasure houses of the temples and shrines and in the private collections that have become public. Among the latter are a number that were formed by daimyō families, of which the most important is that of Tokugawa Yoshichika (1886–1976), who was the 19th lord of Owari Province (now Aichi Prefecture) and a descendant of the first lord of Owari, Tokugawa Yoshinao (1600–1650), the 9th son of the first Tokugawa shōgun, TOKUGAWA IEYASU. The collection is displayed, a few objects at a time, in the Tokugawa Art Museum, Nagoya, which was opened in 1935 and is under the auspices of the Tokugawa Reimeikai Foundation of Tōkyō. Swords, armor, Nō costumes and masks, lacquer furniture, Chinese and Japanese ceramics, calligraphy, paintings from the Chinese Song (Sung) and Yuan (Yüan) dynasties (960–1368), and Heian-period (794–1185) scrolls of the TALE OF GENJI (see GENJI MONOGATARI EMAKI) and the *Hatsuki no monogatari emaki* are among the more than 12,000 pieces in this collection.

Objects from another daimyō collection, that of the Hosokawa family, vassals of the Ashikaga shōguns and lords of Higo Province (now Kumamoto Prefecture) under the Tokugawa, are shown at the Eisei Bunko Foundation in Tōkyō. Tea-ceremony items, Nō robes and masks, swords, armor, Chinese antiquities, and Japanese paintings from the Kamakura period to the present are among the major pieces.

The Seisonkaku, a large Japanese-style villa built in the city of Kanazawa in 1863 by Maeda Nariyasu (1811–1884), daimyō of the region, is one of the few buildings in Japan to display the possessions of a daimyō family in their original surroundings. Another is the Matsuura Historical Museum (opened in 1955) at Hirado, Nagasaki Prefecture, with household objects, paintings, calligraphy, and documents relating to the early foreign trade in the area, all once the property of the Matsuura family, daimyō of Hirado, and now on display in part of the family's former residence. A third is the Mōri Museum at Hōfu, Yamaguchi Prefecture, where the paintings (including SESSHŪ TŌYŌ's famous landscape scroll of the four seasons), calligraphy, armor, and costumes of the MŌRI FAMILY, daimyō of Suō Province (now part of Yamaguchi Prefecture), may be seen in a former Mōri residence set in a large garden.

Other private collections also are on display in Japanese-style houses. The collection of the Hoppō Bunka Museum (established in 1945), near the city of Niigata, featuring Chinese sculpture and ceramics and a broad range of Japanese art, is on view in a rambling house and a storehouse, surrounded by an attractive garden, the property of the Itō family; that of the Homma family at Sakata, Yamagata Prefecture, now in the Homma Art Museum (opened in 1947), is shown in part in the former residence of the family. But the use of such houses for museum purposes is fairly limited: Western-style buildings are the general rule.

The amount and variety of traditional Japanese art that may now be seen in Tōkyō in private collections formed since the Meiji Restoration (1868) and made accessible to the public is extraordinary. One of the finest is that of Gotō Keita (1882–1959), on view at the GOTŌ ART MUSEUM, a handsome building designed by YOSHIDA ISOYA and opened in 1960. Of equal importance is the NEZU ART MUSEUM, housing the collection of the late Nezu Kaichirō (1860–1940), which opened in 1940. Other specially housed collections include the Chinese and Japanese objects gathered by Hatakeyama Issei (1881–1971) and shown in the quiet and pleasant atmosphere of the HATAKEYAMA MUSEUM, which opened in 1964.

The Japanese and Chinese paintings, sculpture, ceramics, lacquer, and books which formed the private collection of ŌKURA KIHA-CHIRŌ are shown in the two-story Chinese-style building of the Ōkura Museum. First exhibited publicly in 1917, then damaged by the 1923 earthquake, the museum was rebuilt and opened again in 1928. The collection of Chinese and Japanese art made by members of the Iwasaki family has been on view at the SEIKADŌ BUNKO, a few objects at a time, since 1977.

Several important museums are housed in office buildings: the IDEMITSU ART GALLERY, founded by IDEMITSU SAZŌ (1885–1981) of the Idemitsu Kōsan Company, in the International Building; the RIC-CAR ART MUSEUM, containing prints from Hiraki Shinji's collection, which opened in 1972 in the Riccar Building; the Suntory Art Gallery, since 1975 in the Suntory Building; and the YAMATANE MU-SEUM OF ART installed in the Yamatane Building in 1966. In 1980 the Idemitsu Museum opened a separate facility for Near Eastern art (especially ceramics) in the suburbs of Tōkyō.

Near Tōkyō there are three other museums to be mentioned: the Tokiwayama Collection at Kamakura, put together by Sugawara Tsūsai, which consists of Chinese and Japanese paintings and calligraphy with emphasis on ink paintings of the Muromachi period; the Tōyama Art Museum (1970), deep in the countryside of Saitama Prefecture, which houses the collection of the Tōyama Gen'ichi; (1890–1972); and the collection of the KANAZAWA BUNKO (Kamakura portraits, calligraphy, Chinese and Japanese classics, Buddhist sutras, and Zen writings), which is housed in a building in the precincts of the temple Shōmyōji in Yokohama and owes its early origin (ca 1275) to the HŌJŌ FAMILY. The former MATSUNAGA MEMORIAL GALLERY at Odawara possessed a particularly fine collection of Japanese and Chinese art, which is now housed in the Fukuoka Art Museum in the city of Fukuoka.

The Ōsaka–Kōbe area is not far behind Tōkyō in its wealth of private collections on public display. The largest is the FUJITA ART MUSEUM; the collection was made by FUJITA DENZABURŌ and his descendants and was installed in a storehouse on the family property in Ōsaka and opened to the public in 1954. An earlier foundation, dating from 1934, is the Hakutsuru Art Museum in Kōbe which, among other important items, houses the fine Chinese bronzes from the collection of the *sake* brewer Kanō Jihei. The collection made by KOBAYASHI ICHIZŌ is in the ITSUŌ ART MUSEUM, a Western-style house (opened in 1957) and an adjoining gallery (added in 1973) at Ikeda, Ōsaka Prefecture. Muromachi paintings form the main part of the collection of Masaki Takayuki in the Masaki Art Museum at Tadaoka, Ōsaka Prefecture, opened in 1968. Chinese and Japanese paintings, calligraphy, and ceramics are featured in both the Egawa Museum of Art at Nishinomiya, Hyōgo Prefecture (the collection of Egawa Tokusuke), which was opened in 1973, and the Kōsetsu Art Museum (the collection of MURAYAMA RYŌHEI), which opened the same year in Kōbe. Chinese and Japanese paintings and ceramics from the collections of members of the Yamaguchi family form the basis of the exhibits at the Tekisui Art Museum (1961) at Ashiya, Hyōgo Prefecture.

In Kyōto is the remarkable group of Chinese bronzes brought together by Sumitomo Kichizaemon VII before his death in 1926. The bronzes can now be seen in a handsome building, the SEN'OKU HAKKOKAN, that replaces an older one on the family property. A building opened in 1970 houses the Chinese bronzes and the Chinese, Japanese, and Korean ceramics that form the collection of the Neiraku Art Museum at Nara. The collection was assembled by Nakamura Junsuke.

Throughout Japan there are other, equally elegant and rewarding, museums: the large Adachi Art Museum set in gardens in the countryside of Shimane Prefecture, with the 20th-century Japanese paintings brought together by Adachi Zenkō and first shown in 1970; the Ehime Cultural Hall (1955) at Imabari, Ehime Prefecture, housing the ceramics and lacquer collection formed by Ninomiya Kaneichi; the Kumaya Art Museum (1965) at Hagi, Yamaguchi Prefecture, with a collection of Japanese paintings, calligraphy, pottery, and lacquer, all the property of the Kumaya family; the Nakamura Memorial Art Museum at Kanazawa, Ishikawa Prefecture, which contains the collection given in 1966 to the city by Nakamura Eishun; the Sano Art Museum (1966) at Mishima, Shizuoka Prefecture, the collection of Sano Ryūichi, with its interesting Japanese and Chinese art and its remarkable group of swords; and the Shōgetsu Art Museum (1974) at Wakakusa, Yamanashi Prefecture, which has an excellent collection of Edo (1600–1868) and Meiji (1868–1912) paintings formed by Kasai Toshio and his father.

There is one museum in a class by itself: the YAMATO BUNKA-KAN near Nara. It is unique in Japan in having a collection built up since 1945 under the direction of trained art historians—Yashiro Yukio (1890–1975) and Ishizawa Masao (b 1903). Set on a site of great natural beauty in a handsome building designed by Yoshida Isoya, it opened to the public in 1960. Its collections of East Asian art, its displays, and its publications are among the finest in Japan.

Treasure Houses——Equally rich and even more varied collections of Japanese art are located in the treasure houses of the older and more important Buddhist temples and Shintō shrines. They range in location from Kyūshū to northern Honshū; the greatest number, however, are in the Kyōto–Nara–Ōsaka area, as this region was for centuries the seat of government and the cultural center of Japan.

The importance of the Shōsōin as an ancient collection has been mentioned previously; it is never open to the public, but selections from it are shown once a year, in the autumn, at the Nara National Museum. Second in importance for its contents is the HŌRYŪJI GREAT TREASURE HOUSE, opened in 1939. The KŌFUKUJI TREASURE HOUSE and the TŌSHŌDAIJI Treasure House in Nara, opened in 1959 and 1970 respectively, have important collections of sculpture, while the Kasuga Taisha Treasure House, also in Nara, houses objects from the shrine's ancient regalia in a building opened in 1973. The KŌYASAN TREASURE HOUSE, built in 1921, preserves and displays objects belonging to the temples on Mt. Kōya (Kōyasan) in Waka-yama Prefecture.

Among the treasure houses in Kyōto, that of the temple DAIGOJI, opened in 1935, has the most varied collection; the treasure house of the temple TŌJI was opened in 1965 with an important group of Buddhist objects. The KŌRYŪJI Treasure House (1922) is known for its appealing wooden figure of Miroku Bosatsu (the bodhisattva Maitreya) from the Asuka period. The Chion'in, the temple Dai-hōonji, and the temple Rokuhara Mitsuji established treasure houses in the 1970s; the last two are noted for their Heian and Kamakura sculpture.

Relics of Prince SHŌTOKU (574–622), the founder of the temple SHITENNŌJI in Ōsaka, and sculpture from the 6th to the 14th century are preserved in the Shitennōji Treasure House, opened in 1970. The ITSUKUSHIMA SHRINE on Miyajima in the Inland Sea had a treasure house as early as 1896 to house Heian and Kamakura armor and Nō masks and the sutras offered to the shrine between 1164 and 1167 by the TAIRA FAMILY. Another shrine in the Inland Sea, Ōya-mazumi, has in its treasure house one of the greatest collections of early arms and armor in Japan.

The Munakata Taisha Treasure House, Genkai, Fukuoka Prefecture, contains such extraordinary objects as a miniature gilt-bronze loom and KOTO (Japanese zither), plus *magatama* (see BEADS, AN-CIENT), flat stone rings, and gilt-bronze horse trappings excavated between 1954 and 1971 at the shrine at Okitsunomiya on the island of Okinashima in the Sea of Genkai (Genkai Nada). The fine wooden Buddhist sculptures, largely of the Heian period, that belong to the temple Kanzeonji at Dazaifu, Fukuoka Prefecture, are well shown in this temple's treasure house, opened in 1959. The Ku-mano Hayatama Taisha Treasure House, Shingū, Wakayama Prefecture (1907), exhibits the fans, hair ornaments, and household objects listed in a 1390 inventory. The Chūsonji Treasure House (1955) at Hiraizumi, Iwate Prefecture, preserves gilt-wood coffers and their contents, all of the late Heian period when the ŌSHŪ FUJIWARA FAMILY controlled northern Honshū.

Archaeological Museums——There are two key dates in the history of Japanese archaeology. In 1879 the American scholar and collector of Japanese pottery Edward Sylvester MORSE published his work on the Jōmon-period (ca 10,000 BC–ca 300 BC) ŌMORI SHELL MOUNDS. In 1884 specimens of Yayoi (ca 300 BC–ca AD 300) ware were first discovered in the Yayoi district of Tōkyō. Although notable collections of pre-Buddhist objects were built up before 1940, especially by the Tōkyō National Museum, Tōkyō University, and Kyōto University, prewar ultranationalism with its insistence on a literal interpretation of the myths relating to the origin of the Japanese people prevented the carrying out of proper archaeological studies. Since 1945, however, scientific excavations have been conducted all over Japan, and many of the finds are now shown in a host of new museums frequently located at or near the excavation sites.

One of the most attractive of these museums is the Saitobaru Burial Mounds Museum in Saito, Miyazaki Prefecture, noted for its architecture and its setting in the SAITOBARU TOMB CLUSTER area, now made into a park. The IDOJIRI ARCHAEOLOGICAL HALL, opened in 1974 at Sakai, Nagano Prefecture, has excellent Jōmon potteries. Objects from the Yayoi-period TORO SITE at Shizuoka are collected in the SHIZUOKA MUNICIPAL TORO SITE MUSEUM opened in 1972.

In Hokkaidō, the Moyoro Shell Mound Branch (1966) of the Abashiri Municipal Local Museum shows a cross section of the nearby MOYORO SHELL MOUND. At Hachinohe, Aomori Prefecture, the Hachinohe Municipal History and Ethnography Hall (1975) has a group of late-Jōmon objects from the adjacent Korekawa site. The International Christian University at Mitaka, Tōkyō Prefecture, exhibits the middle-Jōmon pieces excavated on the university grounds.

Other site museums are: the Togariishi Archaeological Hall (1955), northeast of Chino, Nagano Prefecture, with stone and pottery objects from the Jōmon site of Togariishi; the Shiojiri Municipal Hiraide Site Archaeological Museum (1954) with finds from the HIRAIDE SITE in Shiojiri, Nagano Prefecture; and the Shibayama Haniwa Museum (1957) with fine HANIWA pottery from the two adjoining tumuli at Shibayama, Chiba Prefecture. Kofun-period (300–710) swords in their gilt-bronze scabbards and gilt-bronze horse trappings, all from a large burial mound in the immediate vicinity, may be seen in the Kinreizuka Archaeological Collection (1956) at Kisarazu, Chiba Prefecture. The 14 DŌTAKU (bronze bells) and the short sword-blades excavated at Sakuragaoka, Kōbe, form the chief exhibit at the Kōbe Municipal Archaeological Hall (1969). Archaeological material from a number of sites, all in the neighborhood, make up the collection at the Nara Prefectural Archaeological Museum (1940) at Kashihara and at the Machida Municipal Museum (1973), Tōkyō Prefecture.

A complete survey of Japanese archaeology is offered by the collections of Kokugakuin University and Meiji University, both in Tōkyō. The archaeological collection of the Kyōto University Faculty of Letters is equally extensive, but is arranged more for study than display. The Beppu University Ancient Culture Museum (1978) at Beppu, Ōita Prefecture, has an excellent collection of Jōmon pottery vessels. The greatest archaeological collection on display, however, remains that of the Tōkyō National Museum.

Ethnographical Museums —— Japan's efforts to preserve its native heritage can be seen in the ever-increasing number of museums devoted to its folk arts and ethnography.

The traditional Japanese folk arts, and the work of those contemporary potters, textile designers, and other artists influenced by them, were first given a permanent public display center in the Japan Folk-Craft Museum which, with the financial help of ŌHARA MAGOSABURŌ, opened in Tōkyō in 1936. These collections were assembled by the original director, YANAGI MUNEYOSHI, who first perceived the artistic value of this branch of Japanese art and encouraged contemporary artists and craftsmen. He also collected AINU material as well as folk arts from Europe and America. The interior of the museum, reminiscent of that of a Japanese farmhouse, and the choice of objects with the emphasis on aesthetic quality, influenced the design and display of the many folk museums that have opened since 1945. Of these, the folk-art section of the Chidō Museum (1950) at Tsuruoka, Yamagata Prefecture; the Kurashiki Folk Art Museum (1948) at Kurashiki, Okayama Prefecture; the MATSUMOTO FOLK ARTS MUSEUM at Matsumoto, Nagano Prefecture; the Ōsaka Japan Folk Art Museum (1971) at Suita, Ōsaka Prefecture; the SANUKI FOLK ARTS MUSEUM at Takamatsu, Kagawa Prefecture; the Tottori Folk Art Museum (1949) and the collection of Yoshida Shōya at Tottori, Tottori Prefecture; and the Toyama City Folk Art Museum (1965) outside Toyama, Toyama Prefecture, are among the best of their kind.

The great interest in folk arts has also led to the preservation of regional types of farmhouses assembled in groups to form outdoor museums. Now fast disappearing in the country, such buildings, often with high-pitched roofs and half-timbering, are peculiar to Japan, and their preservation has been recently undertaken by both private and municipal interests. There is Edo Village (at Yuwaku Machi, near the city of Kanazawa), where farmhouses and several more sophisticated buildings have been assembled. Residences from Takayama and the surrounding countryside may be seen at the HIDA FOLKLORE VILLAGE just outside Takayama, Gifu Prefecture, while in Takayama itself a number of houses, such as that of the Kusakabe family, have been converted to museums. A wide range of farmhouses can be seen at the Japanese Village Farmhouse Museum (1960) at Toyonaka, Ōsaka, and the Kawasaki Municipal Park of Japanese Houses (1967) at Kawasaki, Kanagawa Prefecture. The warehouses that lined the canal at Kurashiki have been preserved by being converted to museums and shops and have made that section of Kurashiki one of the most attractive urban quarters in Japan.

A delightful and rewarding collection of buildings is that at the Sankeien at Yokohama, a large park first opened to the public in 1906. It was originally the property of Hara Tomitarō, who brought together most of the buildings—villas, teahouses, a temple, a pagoda, a rich farmer's house—which are of various dates and among the finest of their kind.

In an effort to preserve something of Japan's urban architecture of the recent past, more than 50 buildings of the Meiji and Taishō (1912–26) periods, most of them in the Western style, have been reerected in another large park, the Meiji Village Museum (see MEIJI MURA), at Inuyama, near Nagoya. Opened in 1965, this museum-park offers a nostalgic and historically interesting view of the foreign styles prevalent in the late 19th and early 20th centuries.

The agricultural tools and fishing gear of the old unmechanized farming and fishing life of Japan, now rapidly disappearing, are shown in many places. They are displayed in the farm buildings of the "village" museums and in such fine ethnographical museums as the Seto Naikai Historical and Folklore Hall (1973) at Takamatsu, Kagawa Prefecture, the Tōhoku Historical Museum (1974) at Tagajō, Miyagi Prefecture, the AOMORI PREFECTURAL MUSEUM (1973) at Aomori, and the Nara Prefectural Ethnographical Museum (1974), at Kōriyama, as well as in a plethora of small local museums. Such collections have generally little or no aesthetic value, but their historical and educational importance is considerable.

Many of the white-walled medieval castles that once dotted Japan have been destroyed; most of the few that exist—original, rebuilt, or new—now serve as museums and generally include local historical material. Those at Hikone, Hirado, Hiroshima, Kōchi, Kumamoto, Nagaoka, Odawara, and Ōsaka have such collections, while the one at Nagoya also exhibits the screens and painted wooden doors saved from the palace in the castle precincts that was destroyed in World War II.

A special group of museums, with collections of Ainu material, is located in Hokkaidō. The most important is the Hokkaidō University Ainu Museum in memory of John BATCHELOR at Sapporo; others include the Abashiri Municipal Local Museum (1937), the Hakodate Municipal Museum, and the Kushiro City Center for the Study of Buried Cultures. Also of interest is the Hokkaidō Historical Museum (1971) at Sapporo, which has a large display on Ainu life and customs as well as a section on the Japanese pioneer settlers in Hokkaidō.

Particular mention should be made of the National Museum of Ethnology at Suita, Ōsaka Prefecture; a large, impressive building opened in 1977, it is equipped with every conceivable audio-visual aid to supplement its collections of artifacts from East Asia, Oceania, Africa, Europe, and America.

Prefectural Museums —— Another notable phenomenon in post–World War II Japan is the development of prefectural museums. As of 1978, there were few prefectures that did not have one in existence, under construction, or being planned. Most of these museums are large, and several are architecturally distinguished. Among such buildings are the KUMAMOTO PREFECTURAL ART MUSEUM at Kumamoto (1976) and the Saitama Prefectural Museum at Ōmiya (1971), both designed by MAEKAWA KUNIO; the Kagawa Prefectural Cultural Center (1966) in Takamatsu, designed by Ōe Hiroshi; the Gumma Prefectural Museum of Modern Art (1974) at Takasaki by ISOZAKI ARATA; and the Ibaraki Prefecture History Hall (1966) at Mito by Mori Kyōsuke.

Little of the older arts of Japan can be seen in most of these museums: they are generally of too recent origin to have built up systematic collections. However, they usually have extensive collections of Meiji and 20th-century Japanese art, often of a local nature, and many also have considerable local archaeological and ethnographical material. In addition, they are hosts to a constant series of loan exhibitions organized locally or sent out from Tōkyō, largely of contemporary material. Typical of such prefectural museums and indicative of their location all over Japan are the Aomori Prefectural Museum, the Kōchi Prefectural Cultural Hall at Kōchi, the Okayama Prefectural Museum at Okayama, the Okinawa Prefectural Museum at Naha, the Saga Prefectural Museum at Saga, the Tōhoku Historical Museum at Tagajō, and the Wakayama Prefectural Museum at Wakayama.

There are also prefectural museums specializing in one aspect of the local culture, such as the Nagasaki Prefectural Art Museum (1965) at Nagasaki with its collection of NAGASAKI SCHOOL paintings, and the Wakayama Prefectural Modern Art Museum (1970) at Wakayama showing the works of local artists.

Municipal Museums —— The larger municipal museums are as varied in scope as the prefectural ones. One of the largest, the Kita Kyūshū Municipal Art Museum at Kita Kyūshū, Fukuoka Prefecture, a vast construction designed by Isozaki Arata and dramatically crowning a hill, opened in 1974; it has a collection of Japanese paintings—primarily in oil and frequently by Kyūshū artists—from the Meiji period to the present, shown a few at a time, together with a constant series of loan exhibitions.

In Ōsaka there are two municipal museums: the Ōsaka Municipal Museum (1960) with its interesting display illustrating the history and culture of Ōsaka, and the ŌSAKA MUNICIPAL MUSEUM OF FINE ARTS. The Kurayoshi Municipal Museum at Kurayoshi, Tottori Prefecture, designed by Kosumi Tōru and opened in 1972, houses a small but growing collection of contemporary art and local archaeology in a building thoroughly contemporary in style yet retaining a feeling of traditional Japanese architecture. The Sendai City Museum (1961) at Sendai, Miyagi Prefecture, preserves many of the possessions of the DATE FAMILY, daimyō of Sendai, as well as mementos of local history. The ones at Kumamoto and Nagoya, opened in 1978, offered every indication when seen in 1977 of being important additions to the local museum scene.

Modern-Art Museums —— The foremost collecting and exhibiting museum of contemporary Japanese art is the Tōkyō National Museum of Modern Art. It was established in 1952 in the Kyōbashi section of Tōkyō and now occupies a large building, designed by TANIGUCHI YOSHIRŌ, in Kitanomaru Park; it opened in 1969. (The original building is now the National Film Center.) Its collection contains works by every Japanese artist of note since the Meiji period, plus a selection of contemporary Western prints. In 1977 the museum restored a nearby Meiji building in Kitanomaru Park and opened an annex, the Crafts Gallery, that is devoted to modern textiles, ceramics, lacquer, and other Japanese crafts.

The Tōkyō Metropolitan Art Museum in Ueno Park was established in 1926 as a center for government and privately sponsored temporary exhibitions. Now housed in a large new building that replaced the old one in 1975, it is still the most active exhibition center in Tōkyō; it also has a collection of some 900 pieces of Japanese art covering the last 50 years.

Several of the new prefectural and municipal museums have large collections of Japanese art from the Meiji period to the present. Among these are the Hiroshima Prefectural Art Museum (1968) at Hiroshima, the Hokkaidō Modern Art Museum (1977) at Sapporo, and the Hyōgo Prefectural Museum of Modern Art (1970) at Kōbe. The Kyōto City Art Museum (1933) and its neighbor, the Kyōto National Museum of Modern Art (1963), have permanent collections of 19th-century and contemporary Japanese art; the former, however, is primarily an exhibiting center and the latter is best known for its contemporary Japanese ceramics.

Western-Art Museums —— Painting and sculpture in the Western manner became fashionable in the 1870s; during the end of the 19th century and the early years of the 20th century many Japanese painters and sculptors went abroad to study, mainly to Paris. Western art was occasionally brought to Japan for temporary exhibitions, but the first collection of Western art to be permanently exhibited in Japan was that of the Ōhara Art Museum at Kurashiki, opened in 1930. The basis of this collection was formed by ŌHARA MAGOSABURŌ on the advice of the Japanese painter Kojima Torajirō (1881–1929) and the French artist Edmond-François Aman-Jean (1860–1935); it consisted almost entirely of French painting and sculpture of the 19th and early-20th centuries. The museum has now broadened its scope, and there are paintings of the Italian Renaissance and of the Dutch and Flemish 17th century as well as works by well-known American and Italian artists of the 20th century.

The government's own collection of Western art is housed in the NATIONAL MUSEUM OF WESTERN ART in Ueno Park, Tōkyō, in a building designed by Le Corbusier that opened in 1959 and was renovated and expanded in 1979.

The two museums just mentioned are the only important ones devoted solely to Western art; however, contemporary Western and Japanese works are shown together in several other institutions. The Bridgestone Museum of Art (1952) in Tōkyō and its affiliate, the Ishibashi Art Museum in Kurume, Fukuoka Prefecture, house the collection of ISHIBASHI SHŌJIRŌ (1889–1976), president of the Bridgestone Tire Company, a collection consisting largely of Japanese paintings in the Western style and Western paintings, mainly 19th-century French.

Western 19th-century art—chiefly prints—and Japanese contemporary paintings, sculpture, and prints make up most of the collec-

tion of the KANAGAWA PREFECTURAL MUSEUM OF MODERN ART at Kamakura. The Nagaoka Contemporary Art Museum (1964) at Nagaoka, Niigata Prefecture, is known for its fairly large collection of contemporary Japanese and Western paintings and prints, the Western section a rarity for a smaller Japanese city.

The HAKONE OPEN-AIR MUSEUM is the creation of the Fuji–Sankei group of companies in the media industry. Set in a garden area on the slope of a hill overlooking a wooded valley, it provides a striking setting for a collection of 19th- and 20th-century sculpture.

A 1975 addition to the ranks of institutions showing the art of both East and West is the Ikeda Museum of Twentieth-Century Art at Itō, Shizuoka Prefecture. It houses, in a handsome glass building, the collection of the industrialist Ikeda Eiichi, which consists of many European paintings and prints and the works of contemporary Japanese artists.

Ceramics Museums —— With ceramics holding such a high place in Japanese aesthetics, it is natural that a number of museums should be devoted to the display of ceramics alone. The kiln-site museums are the most numerous. Bizen, in Okayama Prefecture, the site of BIZEN WARE, boasts two such museums: the Bizen Ceramics Hall (1977), displaying Bizen ware by contemporary potters and a small collection of Old Bizen, and the Bizen Old Ceramics Art Museum, with a collection of some 500 fine pieces of Old Bizen. The Arita Ceramic Museum (1954) at Arita, Saga Prefecture, is known for its shards excavated at the kiln-sites of ARITA WARE, NABESHIMA WARE, and KARATSU WARE. The tools and instruments used in making the preindustrial SETO WARE are collected in the Seto City History and Folklore Gallery in Aichi Prefecture (1978). The Aichi Prefectural Ceramic Museum, a large research and exhibit facility for old ceramics of the area (including Seto ware, MINO WARE, and Oribe ware) also opened in 1978. Early TOKONAME WARE is on view at the Tokoname Ceramic Research Center (1961), and good pieces of KUTANI WARE may be seen at the Ishikawa Prefecture Art Museum (1959) at Kanazawa (the Kutani kilns are nearby). TAMBA WARE predominates at the Hyōgo Prefecture Ceramic Museum (1966) at Kōbe. Shards from kiln-sites producing Oribe, Shino, Kodai, and other wares make up the larger part of the collections at the Gifu Prefecture Pottery Exhibition Hall (1971) at Tajimi, while ECHIZEN WARE is the specialty of the Fukui Prefecture Ceramic Hall (1971) in the village of Miyazaki.

Imari and Nabeshima porcelains of the finest quality can be seen at the Kurita Art Museum (1975) at Ashikaga, Tochigi Prefecture, and its branch in Tōkyō. Pottery by the "old masters" of the contemporary folk-art movement—HAMADA SHŌJI, KAWAI KANJIRŌ, TOMIMOTO KENKICHI, and the Englishman Bernard H. LEACH—are displayed at the Ōhara Pottery Hall in Kurashiki. A broad survey of Japanese, Chinese, and Korean ceramics is offered by two sister museums, the MOA MUSEUM OF ART and the HAKONE MUSEUM OF ART (the Hakone collection contains only Japanese items). The Kikusui Handicraft Museum (1932) at Kawanishi Machi, Yamagata Prefecture, covers the same field but to a lesser extent. The Idemitsu Museum in Tōkyō, mentioned previously, has an outstanding ceramics collection as well as a permanent study display of Japanese wares.

Museums of Individual Artists —— Museums devoted to the work of one artist are more prevalent in Japan than in the West. All these institutions date after 1945 and cover a variety of fields; many of them have been established by the family of the artist. Among the recent artists represented this way are: the sculptor ASAKURA FUMIO (1883–1964) at the Asakura Sculpture Gallery; the Japanese-style painter KAWABATA RYŪSHI (1885–1966) at the Ryūshi Memorial Gallery; KAWAI GYOKUDŌ (1873–1957) at the GYOKUDŌ ART MUSEUM at Ōme; and the Japanese-style painter YOKOYAMA TAIKAN (1868–1958) at the Yokoyama Taikan Memorial Gallery. All of these are in Tōkyō. Others include the potter KAWAI KANJIRŌ (1890–1966) at the Kawai Kanjirō Memorial Gallery in Kyōto; the potter TOMIMOTO KENKICHI (1886–1963) at the Tomimoto Kenkichi Memorial Gallery in Higashi Ando, Nara Prefecture; the printmaker MUNAKATA SHIKŌ (1903–75) at the Munakata Shikō Memorial Museum of Art at Aomori; the sculptor OGIWARA MORIE (1879–1910) at the Rokuzan Art Museum at Hotaka, Nagano Prefecture; the BUNJINGA painter TAZAKI SŌUN (1815–98) at the Sōun Art Museum in Ashikaga; and the last great bunjinga painter, TOMIOKA TESSAI (1837–1924), at the TESSAI ART MUSEUM, Takarazuka, Hyōgo Prefecture.

Among the earlier artists with museums devoted to displaying their work are: the itinerant priest ENKŪ (ca 1632–95), whose rough-hewn carved wooden figures are shown in the Enkū Exhibition Hall at the temple Senkōji, not far from Takayama, Gifu Prefecture; IKE

NO TAIGA (1723–76), with calligraphy and paintings in the Ike no Taiga Art Museum, Kyōto; MARUYAMA ŌKYO (1733–95) and Nagasawa ROSETSU (1754–99), with screens and scrolls at the Kushimoto Ōkyo–Rosetsu Gallery, Kushimoto, Wakayama Prefecture; and the Zen priest RYŌKAN (1758–1831), with a large selection of calligraphy and other material in the Ryōkan Memorial Gallery at his birthplace, Izumozaki, Niigata Prefecture.

Religious Foundation Museums —— A special feature of the Japanese museum world is the category of museums founded and maintained by religious sects. Despite the sectarian connection, these collections are of wide-ranging artistic interest and are not confined to illustrating specific religious tenets.

The oldest of these foundations, the TENRIKYŌ's Tenri Sankōkan at Tenri, Nara Prefecture, was founded in 1937; it contains a large collection of Japanese and Chinese pre-Buddhist antiquities and ethnographical material from the Middle East, the classical world, North and South America, Africa, the Asiatic mainland, and the South Pacific. These were the first foreign ethnographical collections to be seen publicly in Japan.

The Moa Museum of Art at Atami, Shizuoka Prefecture, and its sister museum, the Hakone Museum of Art, opened in 1957 and 1952 respectively, belong to the SEKAI KYŪSEI KYŌ church. These collections were assembled by the founder of the church, OKADA MOKICHI (1882–1955).

The Fuji Art Museum, containing a miscellaneous collection of European, Middle Eastern, and East Asian art, is housed in a large and elaborate building opened in 1973 on the grounds of the Sōka Gakkai's temple Taisekiji at Fujinomiya, Shizuoka Prefecture.

Special Museums —— Certain aspects of Japanese and Chinese culture have given rise to museums specializing in collections that have no Western counterparts. Among such are those with collections of CALLIGRAPHY: the Museum of Calligraphy (1936) and the Japan Calligraphy Museum (1973), both in Tōkyō; and the Imabari City Kōno Shin'ichi Memorial Cultural Hall (1968) at Imabari, Ehime Prefecture. The Sword Museum (1967) in Tōkyō has the only public collection in Japan devoted wholly to SWORDS. Japanese ARMS AND ARMOR are the specialties of the Kyōto–Arashiyama Art Museum (1976) in Kyōto and of the Nichimura Museum (1963) at Iwakuni, Yamaguchi Prefecture. LACQUER WARE is the specialty of the Hida Takayama Shunkei Lacquer Institute at Takayama, Gifu Prefecture, and of the Kaisendō Museum (1953) at Kaminoyama, Yamagata Prefecture. NAMBAN ART—screens, lacquer items, paintings, and prints by Japanese artists from the late 16th to the 18th century depicting foreigners and foreign objects in Japanese surroundings—are shown in the Kōbe Municipal Museum of Namban Art (1951). The clothes, swords, ladders, and other paraphernalia used by the *ninja*—the men who served as spies for the Tokugawa shogunate or local daimyō—are to be found in the Igaryū Ninja Yashiki at Ueno, Mie Prefecture.

Masks used in the lion dance (SHISHI-MAI) in Shintō festivals are on view at the Lion-Mask Gallery (1977) in Takayama; the *yatai* (festival floats; see DASHI) used in the Sakurayama Hachiman Shrine's twice-yearly festivals are exhibited at the Takayama Festival Cart Hall (1968).

Funding, Educational Activities —— The operating funds for the national museums are supplied by the Agency for Cultural Affairs, the cultural division of the Ministry of Education. Construction costs, maintenance, salaries, and purchase funds for the prefectural museums are supplied by the prefectural governments; expenses for the municipal museums are provided by the municipal governments. Foundations established by the donors or the companies with which the donors are connected pay for the running expenses of the private museums, while admissions and occasional contributions from religious groups and parishioners defray the expenses of the temple and shrine treasure houses. The national government in some cases pays for part of the construction costs of new treasure houses. Generally the director of a national museum is appointed for a term of two years by the Ministry of Education; this officer is usually an administrator with little or no knowledge of the arts. The vice-director is usually a specialist in some field of art.

Many of the museums have libraries and other study facilities. Almost all have pamphlets or booklets about their collections, and a large number have illustrated catalogs while a few have splendid definitive catalogs of their collections. The Tōkyō National Museum sponsors the art historical monthly publication *Museum* and the Yamato Bunkakan publishes *Yamato bunka,* a biannual journal of Eastern art. Every national, prefectural, and municipal museum mounts loan exhibitions, with illustrated catalogs accompanying those of special importance. Lectures and guided tours are offered by nearly all institutions.

Exhibition Principles —— Because Japanese and Chinese hanging scroll paintings can fade from too long exposure to light and can become misshapen from being hung up too long, they are generally shown for only a month at a time. The same time limitation usually applies to the showing of handscrolls *(makimono),* textiles, and prints. Ceramics and lacquer are usually changed three to four times a year, archaeological material less frequently, and sculpture almost never.

The holdings of such museums as the Tōkyō National, Kyōto National, Fujita, Gotō, Nezu, Idemitsu, and MOA—to name but a few—are so large that only a small percentage of the permanent collection is on view at any one time. Some of the prefectural museums have only small permanent collections and serve chiefly as exhibiting centers for loan shows. Many other museums also have an active loan exhibition program, and since they do not usually have a special gallery for such displays, the entire permanent collection may be removed to make room for them. There is, as a rule, no way of predicting what may be on view in any museum at any given time, but the quality of the objects and the manner of installation are generally of remarkably high quality.

Foreign Museums —— Japanese art was known to the West in the 18th century only through the export of lacquer and Imari and Kakiemon porcelains. Prints made their appearance in Europe shortly after the middle of the 19th century and were eagerly sought out after they became popular in France. It was not, however, until the late 19th century that Western scholars were able to begin systematically studying and collecting Japanese art.

Outside of Japan, the United States has by far the greatest number of museums with holdings of Japanese art. The most important is the Museum of Fine Arts in Boston. Others with significant collections (listed alphabetically) are: the Art Institute of Chicago; Brooklyn Museum, New York; Center of Asian Art and Culture: Avery Brundage Collection, San Francisco; Cleveland Museum of Art; Detroit Institute of Arts; Fogg Art Museum, Cambridge; Freer Gallery of Art, Washington; Honolulu Academy of Arts; Kimbell Art Museum, Fort Worth; Metropolitan Museum of Art, New York; Nelson Gallery–Atkins Museum, Kansas City; Philadelphia Museum of Art; Seattle Art Museum; Worcester Art Museum; and Yale University Art Gallery, New Haven.

In England, the outstanding collections of Japanese art are at the Ashmolean Museum, Oxford; the British Museum, London; the Fitzwilliam Museum, Cambridge; and the Victoria and Albert Museum, London.

On the continent there are collections at the Museum of Arts and Crafts, Hamburg; the Museum of Oriental Art, Cologne; and the Museum of Far Eastern Art, West Berlin. Others are in the Guimet Museum, Paris; the Baur Collection, Geneva; the Museum Rietberg, Zurich; the Royal Museum of Art and History, Brussels; the National Museum of Ethnology, Leiden; the Austrian Museum of Applied Arts, Vienna; and the Museum of Far Eastern Antiquities, Stockholm.

◾ ——Bijutsu Shuppansha, *Guide to Art Museums in Japan* (1977). Kaneko Shigetaka, *Guide to Japanese Art* (1963). Mayuyama Junkichi, *Guide to Art in Japan* (1970). Muramatsu Kan, *Bijutsukan sampo* (1960). Nihon Hakubutsukan Kyōkai, *Zenkoku hakubutsukan sōran* (1978). Laurance P. Roberts, *Roberts' Guide to Japanese Museums* (1978). Tōkyō To Hakubutsukan Kyōgikai, ed, *Tōkyō no hakubutsukan* (1977). Laurance ROBERTS

Musha Incident

(Musha Jiken). An insurrection in October–November 1930 against the Japanese colonial governor-general by members of the aboriginal Takasago tribe in the village of Wushe (J: Musha), Taiwan. As a special administrative district under direct police control, the Musha region suffered from police repression, delayed payment of wages and abuse of native women. On 27 October some 300 tribesmen stormed the local police office, seized weapons and ammunition, and killed 134 Japanese who were attending a school sports event. Fearing that the incident would spark a full-scale rebellion, the colonial administration retaliated with a military force of 2,000 men, tear gas, and planes, leaving more than 500 (some estimates say 1,000) Taiwanese dead. The governor-general, Ishizuka Eizō (1866–1942), resigned, and the colonial government tightened its control of aborigines.

Mushanokōji Saneatsu (1885–1976)

Novelist, playwright, poet, and painter. Born in Tōkyō; attended Tōkyō University. Although Mushanokōji's writing has frequently been criticized as pompous and naive, critics agree that he played a pivotal role in the literary coterie Shirakaba (White Birch; see SHIRAKABA SCHOOL).

While nearly all members of the Shirakaba were of aristocratic background, Mushanokōji's family was one of the most illustrious. For many generations members of the family had been court poets. His father, Saneyo, was a viscount who had gone to Europe with the IWAKURA MISSION and spent several years studying the classics in Germany. Saneatsu was the eighth and youngest child of his parents. None of the first five children had lived past the age of one, and all he knew as siblings were his brother Kimitomo and his sister Ikako. He was particularly close to Ikako, who he believed had saved him from drowning. When Saneatsu was 15 she died, causing him great shock and grief. Saneatsu's father had died before Saneatsu was three, and after his father's death the family did not have much money. During his early years at the Peers' School (see GAKUSHŪIN UNIVERSITY) Mushanokōji was not a good student. Although he was bright and had great perseverance, he apparently did not like to study and spent most of his time reading. By the time he reached his late teens he had become an avid reader of UCHIMURA KANZŌ, KŌTOKU SHŪSUI, and SAKAI TOSHIHIKO. He was rather weak and sickly and could not compete successfully in physical activities at school, and to compensate for this he became a skilled debater. He also began to do some writing on his own and was encouraged in this decision by his uncle Kadenokōji Sukekoto, who introduced him to the Bible and to the works of Tolstoy.

In August 1907 he left the University to form a literary group called the Jūyokkakai with SHIGA NAOYA, KINOSHITA RIGEN, and Ōgimachi Kinkazu (1881–1960). This became the nucleus of the Shirakaba school. The group circulated a handwritten magazine called Bōya (Perspective) and met every week to discuss literature and to comment on each other's writings. Bōya was the first of many magazines that Mushanokōji was to inspire and organize throughout his long career. This magazine also served as a model for several similar groups. In 1910 Mushanokōji helped organize these groups, including the Jūyokkakai, into the literary coterie Shirakaba. ARISHIMA TAKEO, who was at the time a student at Sapporo Agricultural School in Hokkaidō, also joined the group, which published the first issue of its magazine, Shirakaba, in April 1910. In the same year Mushanokōji published one of his most important works, Omedetaki hito (Good-Natured Person), a largely autobiographical account and an extremely naive expression of optimism and self-confidence in the face of reality. This early work presages some of the characteristics of his later writings—a straightforward declarative style and a confidence in his own views, even when they depart from social norms. Another characteristic is the reaffirmation of the meaning of life as opposed to the despair of the Japanese naturalists or the decadence of other Japanese writers. Mushanokōji was proposing a philosophical and artistic alternative to NATURALISM, and yet he preserved some of the elements that were central to the naturalist philosophy. In particular, he retained the ultraindividualism of the earlier writers, but instead of seeing man as subject to his own instincts he saw man as controlling his own destiny by the assertion of his will. Again, in contrast to the naturalists, who placed great emphasis on individuality but who saw the individual as alienated and desperate, Mushanokōji believed that he could find a happier and more satisfactory way of life. He believed that asserting the individual ego did not necessarily bring people into conflict with one another. Although he became more socially involved later, in his early years he believed that the artist should be aloof from society. In 1913 he wrote, "Literature must be concerned with human life, but it is not necessary for it to be concerned with society. Indeed, it would be closer to the truth to say that there should not be any interference with it."

Toward the end of World War I, the Shirakaba group came under increasingly heavy criticism from the naturalists on the grounds that their humanistic optimism cut them off from social and historical concerns. Mushanokōji responded to this criticism by trying to make his works more socially relevant. For example, he wrote a play, Aru seinen no yume (1916, One Youth's Dream), which was a polemic opposing the war. In 1918 he went to Hyūga in Kyūshū to establish a utopian commune called Atarashiki Mura (New Village). He still occasionally contributed to Shirakaba and serialized one important piece called "Detarame," but most of his energy went into his utopian community, his new magazine, Atarashiki mura, and a long work called Aru otoko (1921–22, A Certain Man), which was serialized in the magazine KAIZŌ. Nevertheless, by the time he drifted away from the Shirakaba school he had done what he had set out to do, namely, to provide a viable alternative to the philosophy of the naturalist writers.

The aim of the members of Atarashiki Mura was to be self-sufficient through farming. Although Mushanokōji has often been called the leader of the group, the idea was for each person to do his own work and find his own enjoyment; no one was to coerce anyone to work. The decision-making process of the group was unique: whenever financial issues arose, a vote was taken, but the decisions were never made on the basis of a simple majority; for example, if 70 percent favored doing something, then 70 percent of the money would be spent for it. Thus the majority decision was not binding on the minority. Mushanokōji left the community in 1926 but remained its spiritual leader. The significance of this experiment was that it was one of the few cases in which members of the Shirakaba school tried to realize their ideals in social, rather than purely individual, terms. In 1939 a proposed hydroelectric dam threatened to flood the communal village and it was moved to Saitama Prefecture. The village continues today with a small group of people.

By the time Mushanokōji left the village, Shirakaba had ceased publication, and in 1927 he founded another magazine, Daichōwa (Great Harmony). He edited the magazine and did the illustrations for some of the cover designs. The contents of the magazine showed his developing interest in the culture of Asia, a trend that had begun earlier and was characteristic of other Shirakaba school members. The magazine discussed and reproduced works of such traditional Japanese artists as HOKUSAI and had a special issue devoted to the study of Asian culture, as well as articles introducing Western art.

By the end of the 1920s, Mushanokōji had developed another interest. In 1929 he exhibited several paintings at the fourth Kokugakaiten (National Art Exhibit). Also in December of that same year he established an art gallery called the Hyūgadō in the Kanda district of Tōkyō. He thereafter held exhibits of his works and contributed to other art exhibits from time to time.

In 1936 Mushanokōji traveled to Europe and the United States, but in spite of his appreciation of Western art he was apparently not very enthusiastic about America. In 1942 he published a book of essays called Daitōa sensō shikan (My Feelings on the Greater East Asian War). As a result of his uncritical acceptance of the war, he was removed from public office under the OCCUPATION PURGE (he had been a member of the House of Peers). Mushanokōji received the Order of Culture in 1951, and became a member of the Japan Art Academy the following year.

Although many of his works can be criticized for their naiveté and simplicity, Mushanokōji was faithful to his beliefs, and his achievements were summarized by AKUTAGAWA RYŪNOSUKE, who said that "Mushanokōji opened the literary windows and let in some fresh air."

◼ ——Mushankōji Saneatsu, Mushanokōji Saneatsu zenshū, 25 vols (Shinchōsha, 1954–57).   Dennis M. SPACKMAN

mushi

An important concept in Japanese traditional popular psychology and in interpersonal relationships. The word mushi, which means literally "worm" or "bug," is used in a number of idioms to describe certain emotions or feelings. When one is depressed, one is said to be "possessed by the worm of depression" (fusagi no mushi). When a person is in a bad temper, "the worm is in the wrong place" (mushi no idokoro ga warui). When a person persists in anger, it is because "the worm in his abdomen has not calmed down" (hara no mushi ga osamaranai). When a man is suddenly tempted to have an extramarital affair, it may be explained as the result of "the worm of fickleness" (uwaki no mushi). If a person has an unreasonable dislike for another, it is because his "worm does not like the person" (mushi ga sukanai). If a child has violent temper tantrums, the mother may take the child to a shrine to have "the worm of tantrum (kan no mushi) sealed off." A selfish person who expects much out of others, without ever reciprocating is described as a person "with too good a worm" (mushi ga yosugiru). When one has a premonition, it is called "a message from the worm" (mushi no shirase). It might be that the Japanese in their traditional reluctance to hold an individual responsible for impulsive behavior, attribute such behavior to an external agent, which has made its way into his body, i.e., the "worm." If the person were acting on his own impulses, he would have to be condemned as a disruptive member of the community, whereas if he is the victim of a *mushi*, the *mushi* can always be "sealed off," and he can return to the community without too much guilt.

📖 ——Hiroshi Wagatsuma, "Study of Personality and Behavior in Japanese Society and Culture," in Edward Norbeck and Susan Parman, ed, *The Study of Japan in the Behavioral Sciences* (1970). Wagatsuma Hiroshi, *Korekara no ikuji to shitsuke o kangaeru* (1971).

Hiroshi WAGATSUMA

mushifūji

(literally, "sealing up of a worm or insect"). A kind of exorcism formerly used on sick children, usually employing spells, prayers, and talismans. When a child had convulsions, fever, or indigestion for no apparent reason, the disorder was sometimes attributed to a MUSHI, or worm, that was believed to inhabit the child's body. To exorcise the *mushi*, one could give the child doses of such nostrums of traditional Chinese medicine as roasted, powdered frog or reptile. One alternative was to take the child to a shrine or temple, have special prayers recited, and have the name of a Shintō deity written on the palms of his hands or the characters for the fifth day of the fifth month (the Boys' Festival) written on the soles of his feet. Another was to affix a paper talisman to the front doorway or to the SHINTŌ FAMILY ALTAR. See also EXORCISM.

INOKUCHI Shōji

mushin

(literally, "lacking heart or depth of feeling"). Also pronounced *kokoronashi*. A term used in both literary aesthetics and Buddhism with somewhat different meanings. Used in opposition to USHIN ("having heart, feeling"). As an aesthetic term *mushin* refers to the absence of elegance and refinement in concept or literary expression; on occasion it may even mean a positive attempt to be amusing or even vulgar—exemplified in *mushin renga*, or comic linked verse (see RENGA AND HAIKU) as opposed to serious elegant WAKA or linked verse; the latter was termed *ushin*. In Buddhism the term *mushin* denotes one who is free from mundane desires or attachments, i.e., one who is enlightened. In the same sense an innocent or guileless child is also described as *mushin*. In everyday parlance *mushin* may also mean begging.

The term was originally used, in the native pronunciation *kokoronashi*, to mean without discretion and good judgement or lacking sensitivity; it was used in this sense in the Heian period (794–1185) classics UTSUBO MONOGATARI and *Makura no sōshi* (see SEI SHŌNAGON). It could also mean lacking an understanding of artistry or human sentiment or being devoid of good taste, a sense in which it is used in the TALE OF GENJI (*Genji monogatari*). The famous line by the poet-priest SAIGYŌ, "*kokoronaki mi ni mo aware wa shirarekeri*," if interpreted in this sense would mean "Even an insensitive man can feel sadness." However, when Saigyō and others like him who had taken the tonsure described themselves as *kokoronaki mi* ("a person without a heart"), they were using the phrase in the Buddhist sense of detachment from the ordinary passions and attractions: "Even a person without a heart can know deep feeling."

📖 ——Araki Yoshio, *Chūsei Kamakura Muromachi bungaku jiten* (1961, 1966). Sen'ichi Hisamatsu, *The Vocabulary of Japanese Literary Aesthetics* (1963).

FUKUDA Hideichi

mushrooms

(*kinoko*). Approximately 4,000 species of mushroom grow in Japan, a number equal to or exceeding that for all of Europe. This is a result of Japan's wide variety of climatic regions. Japan is a forest country, and the Japanese have been familiar with forest mushrooms since ancient times, but field mushrooms of the type common in Europe are relatively rare. Mushroom gathering is one of the pleasures of fall for the Japanese, with the *matsutake* (*Tricholoma matsutake*) and *honshimeji* (*Lyophyllum shimeji*) the most highly valued species. However, the *matsutake*, which grows mainly in forests of Japanese red pine (*akamatsu*), has become increasingly rare in recent years and is now a costly delicacy. The *matsutake* and *honshimeji* are both mycorrhizal fungi which cannot be cultivated, but other types of mushroom are cultivated on a large scale. The *shiitake* (*Lentinus edodes*), which is one of the wood rot fungi, is the most popular of these. Together with the white mushrooms of Europe and padi straw mushrooms (*Volvariella volvacea*) of East Asia, the *shiitake* is one of the world's three most commonly cultivated mushrooms.

Shiitake is planted by inoculating pure cultured spawn of *shiitake* mycelia in logs of oak and other fagaceous trees. These logs are called bed logs. When a bed log is placed in the forest, it produces fruit bodies every spring and sometimes also in the fall. In addition, a technique for producing *shiitake* at any time of year by keeping bed logs indoors has been developed. *Shiitake* is sold in both raw and dried form. Its cultivation is generally a secondary occupation for farm households, but some specialize in mass production. *Shiitake* is planted all over Japan, and annual production is worth approximately ¥120 billion (US $600 million). Its taste and fragrance make it an important ingredient in Japanese and Chinese cooking. Recently it has also started to gain recognition as a health food, and large quantities are being exported. Other edible Japanese mushrooms include the *enokitake* (winter mushroom; *Flammulina velutipes*), the *hiratake* (oyster mushroom; *Pleurotus ostreatus*), and the *nameko* (slimy mushroom; *Pholiota nameko*), all of which are cultivated in sawdust mixed with sterilized rice bran.

📖 ——Imazeki Rokuya and Hongō Tsuguo, *Colored Illustrations of Fungi of Japan*, 2 vols (1957, 1965).

IMAZEKI Rokuya

musical instruments

Although many different musical instruments have been used in the various kinds of traditional Japanese music, the most characteristic and most favored sounds are those produced by plucked strings, flutes, and percussion. Within each of these categories, fine discriminations are made according to the type of sound considered appropriate for each genre. Bowed strings and reed instruments are comparatively rare in Japanese music history, and trumpets, whether metal or shell, are even rarer. For convenience, Japanese musical instruments are here considered in terms of the standard Sachs-Hornbostel classification.

Idiophones —— This group includes a large number of bells, gongs, metallophones, percussion sticks, plaques and tubes, and vessel rattles. Among bronze bells (*kane*) are the following: prehistoric bell-shaped objects (*dōtaku*), not all of which were of functional design; large Buddhist bells (*bonshō, kane*), suspended and struck from the outside; the large Buddhist resting bell (*kin*); and small Buddhist hand-bells (*rin*). Gongs include the small gong (*shōko*) of court music; metallophones include the Buddhist *dora* and *kei*, and the *hōkyō* of ancient court music; percussion sticks include the wooden clappers (*shakubyōshi*) of court music; percussion plaques include the Buddhist "fish board" (*gyoban*); percussion tubes include the Buddhist "wooden fish" (*mokugyo*); vessel rattles include bronze pellet bells (*suzu*), usually multiple. Many of these and other idiophones are used in KABUKI MUSIC.

Membranophones —— Most Japanese drums usually have two membranes, which may be nailed or laced, and are usually struck with sticks. For nailed drums, the body is usually barrel-shaped; for laced drums, it is hourglass-shaped or occasionally cylindrical. Nailed drums include the large drum (TAIKO) of court and festival music; and a miniature drum carried by dancers (*keirōko*). Hourglass drums include the small drums (*kakko, san no tsuzumi*) of court music and the three drums (*kotsuzumi, ōtsuzumi, taiko*) of Nō drama. Again, these and other drums make their appearance in kabuki music. There are also rattle drums (*furitsuzumi*) of various kinds. It is worth noting that the most general Japanese word for drum, TSUZUMI, derives from the Sanskrit *dundubhi*.

Chordophones —— Japanese stringed instruments include zithers, long and short lutes, and an angular harp now obsolete. The zithers, belonging to the Far Eastern zither family, include the ancient six-stringed zither (*wagon*), the classical thirteen-stringed zither (KOTO), the modern seventeen-stringed zither (*jūshichigen*), and the rare one-stringed zither (*ichigenkin*) and two-stringed zither (*yakumogoto*). All these are plucked, usually with a plectra. Long lutes include various kinds of SHAMISEN and the bowed KOKYŪ. Short lutes comprise various kinds of BIWA, and the "moon lute" (*gekkin*) of popular Sino-Japanese music. The angular harp was the *kugo* of 8th-century court music.

Aerophones —— Most Japanese aerophones are end- or side-blown flutes, but there is also the free-reed mouth organ (SHŌ), a cylindrical oboe (HICHIRIKI), and some other rare types. End-blown flutes (*tatebue*) include the bamboo SHAKUHACHI and the obsolete *hitoyogiri*. Side-blown flutes (*yokobue*) include those of court music (*ryūteki, komabue, kagurabue*), the Nō flute (*nōkan*), and the flute of festival and other popular music (*shinobue*).

📖 ——Tanabe Hisao, *Nihon no gakki* (1964).

David B. WATERHOUSE

music, religious

Japanese religious music may be taken to comprise not only liturgical chant and its instrumental accompaniment, but also various kinds of secular music which are performed in the context of a religious ceremony or which are imbued with the spirit or teachings of organized religion, especially of Shintō or Buddhism. The tendency to syncretism which is characteristic of the Japanese approach to religious belief and practice makes it hard sometimes to draw a sharp distinction between the sacred and the profane. Thus, Japanese court music and dance are closely associated both with State Shintō and with the old Nara Buddhism; the music of Nō drama and the solo shakuhachi repertoire are governed by medieval Buddhist ideals; and the attitude of some traditional musicians toward their art is at times reminiscent of a religious cult. Apart from this, moreover, the structure of medieval Buddhist chant has had a profound influence on all later Japanese vocal music, whether for the Nō, puppet, or kabuki theatres, or for private entertainment.

The two most important kinds of purely religious music are Shintō and Buddhist. Christian music has a history which goes back to the 16th century; and since the Meiji period many new sects, such as Tenrikyō, have developed their own musical conventions, often borrowing from the music of other religious traditions. There are also in folk music (see FOLK SONG) a few traces of the shamanistic practices of ancient Japan.

Shintō Music——The oldest description of Japanese music and dance is preserved in the legend that the goddess Ame no Uzume no Mikoto performed an obscene dance before the Rock-Cave of Heaven, and so enticed the sun goddess from hiding. This dance is the first known KAGURA, "music of the gods", or Shintō music. In a kagura the gods are invited down to enjoy the performance; and the "siege for the gods" (shinza or kamu-kura; whence the word kagura) is ritually purified in various ways, above all through ritual dance.

Mikagura, as a branch of court music (gagaku), has existed in organized form for some 1,500 years, and at present consists of a long ritual song cycle (apparently formalized in the 11th century), which is performed once a year on the night of 15 December. It is accompanied by wooden clappers (shakubyōshi, played by the lead singer); the regular court music oboe (HICHIRIKI); a transverse flute (kagura-bue); and a six-stringed zither (wagon) of antique pattern. The musicians sing in a clear, bold but leisurely style; and the music has some of the simplicity and purity of Shintō itself.

Distinct from this is the so-called sato kagura, "village kagura," comprising a great variety of local musics, usually associated with particular shrines, towns, or regions. This music is most often heard on the occasion of festivals; and the typical ensemble (hayashi) consists of transverse flutes and drums of various kinds. A number of large shrines, especially, have old traditions of kagura performed by miko (priestesses or shrine maidens): these include the miko dances at Kasuga Shrine in Nara, and at various shrines in Tōkyō. In western and southern Japan the most widely distributed type is Izumo kagura, associated originally with the great shrine at Izumo (Izumo Taisha; see IZUMO SHRINE); there is a related type at the Atsuta Shrine, Nagoya; and this in turn has affinities with the Edo kagura of old Tōkyō, elements of which can be seen even in the far north of Honshū. Izumo kagura uses miko, but also had close connections with the old sarugaku-Nō drama; and Edo kagura too has theatrical connections, having been influenced by the Mibu kyōgen farces from Mibudera, Kyōto. Another important type of kagura is that of the great shrines at Ise (Ise Jingū; see ISE SHRINE), which was commonly performed in return for donations—a custom found elsewhere at Shintō shrines. In northern Japan there are other distinct types, notably yamabushi kagura (mountain ascetics' kagura); bangaku (guards' dances); and shishi-mai (lion dances).

Buddhist Music——The earliest documented Buddhist music to reach Japan was the masked dance-drama known as gigaku, which was introduced from Korea in 612 but probably derived from Kučā in Central Asia. Its 10 dances, which had no words, were accompanied by an ensemble of transverse flute, narrow cylindrical drum, and small bronze gong.

Buddhism itself reached Japan in 538 or even earlier; and it may be assumed that some form of liturgical chant (shōmyō) came with it. However, the oldest document referring to chant is a decree of 720. The Eye-Opening Ceremony for the Great Buddha of Tōdaiji in 752 included performances of shōmyō as well as various kinds of court music and dance. The chanting on this occasion was performed not only by Japanese monks but also by the Indian monk Bodhisena, who taught Sanskrit at Daianji from 736 until his death

in 760. Today the only remnant of Nara Buddhist chant is the omizutori ceremony performed annually at the Nigatsudō of Tōdaiji.

Another kind of early Buddhist music was mōsō biwa, "blind monks' lute," which has Indian roots and may have existed in Japan by the Nara period or earlier, especially in Kyūshū.

The earliest kind of Japanese shōmyō is known as wasan, hymns of praise in Japanese, as opposed to bonsan and kansan, which were in Sanskrit and Chinese respectively. Two wasan texts by Gyōki (668–749) have been preserved. In the 9th century, however, Japanese Buddhism received a new stimulus from the Tantric teachings introduced by Saichō (767–822) and Kūkai (764–835). New types of chant were developed to accompany the complicated ritual of the Tendai and Shingon schools; and wasan was further elaborated by the famous Tendai monks Ennin (794–864; also called Jikaku Daishi) and Eshin (942–1017; also called Genshin). Eshin also invented the kōshiki, a chanted exposition of Buddhist teaching, in prose. Other varieties of Heian Buddhist chant include kada (Skt: gāthā: hymns describing Buddhist doctrines and virtues, in Chinese or in Japanese); rongi (catechism); saimon (prayers); goeika (pilgrims' hymns); zukyō (recitation of sutras); nembutsu (formula of invocation to a Buddha, usually repeated indefinitely); and kyōke (similar in content to kōshiki, but with a different structure). The last of these influenced sōga, the feast songs of the Kamakura period.

In general, Japanese Buddhist chant since the Heian period divides into two great streams, Tendai and Shingon. The three schools of Zen Buddhism (Rinzai, Sōtō, and Ōbaku) introduced some new elements from Song (Sung) and Ming liturgical music, but their influence can be seen rather more in secular music, notably in the shakuhachi music transmitted by the Fukeshū, a sect of mendicant friars. The evangelical schools (Jōdoshū, Nichirenshū, Jishū, etc.) have on the whole followed Tendai models, but have been less conservative, so that modern music of Jōdo Shinshū, for example, includes harmonized hymns in the style of Methodist Christianity.

Japanese Buddhist chant is the richest surviving tradition of Buddhist cantillation, surpassing even those of Korea and Tibet; and its history is quite fully documented. Its structure depends on the use of fixed melodic patterns (senritsukei), which are identified by name, practiced individually, and then strung together in sequences. The resulting chant may be narrative in character, with one note per syllable, or more melismatic, with long decorative flourishes, especially in kōshiki and rongi. Some pieces (jokyoku) are in free rhythm, while others (teikyoku) are more metrical; but various permutations of these types are possible.

The tonal system of shōmyō has traditionally been considered as an adaptation of that of court music; and in Tendai particularly the chant might actually be accompanied by a gagaku ensemble, playing one of the regular court music pieces. Court music is based on a series of Chinese heptatonic scales; but it is more natural to analyze shōmyō functionally in terms of a more limited series of nuclear tones and passing notes. The ordinary service is accompanied only by bronze or wooden idiophones of various kinds.

Since the middle of the 12th century the leading school of Tendai shōmyō has been Ōhararyū, though it is now apparently dying out. In Shingon the leading school is Nanzan Shinryū, though subschools such as Buzanha remain strong. Both Tendai and Shingon use systems of neumes placed on the left-hand side of the text characters, and indicating the rise and fall of the melody, vocal ornaments, and accents. The Tendai notation is called meyasu hakase; that of Shingon is goin hakase.

Christian Music——Gregorian chant was introduced to Japan by the first Jesuit missionaries, and by 1563 they could boast that a thousand converts performed a Laudate Dominum. A Japanese Mass had been compiled in 1553; and as early as 1559 mission schools had been set up where music was taught to young children. This system was greatly extended later in the century, and included the teaching of secular Western music and musical instruments as well as choral singing. By the early 17th century pipe organs were being made in Kyūshū; and the Jesuit press in Nagasaki produced a manual of church liturgy in 1605, containing pages with musical notation. All this activity was brought to an abrupt halt by the persecutions of the 1620s and later, though some hymns were preserved down to the Meiji period among crypto-Christian groups. During the past hundred years much Christian music of a newer type has been introduced, especially by American missionaries.

——Ebisawa Arimichi, Yōgaku engeki kotohajime (1947). Robert Garfias, "The Sacred Mi-Kagura of the Japanese Imperial Court," Selected Reports (Institute of Ethnomusicology), 1.2 (1968). Honda Yasuji, Kagura: kenkyū to shiryō (1966). Iwahara Taishin, Nanzan

Shinryū shōmyō no kenkyū (1932, repr 1971). Iwahara Taishin, ed, *Chūin shido kegyō shidai (Rishubō tebiki),* 6 vols (repr 1965). Kataoka Gidō, ed, *Tendai shōmyō: kaisetsu sho* (book accompanying set of 4 LP recordings, Polydor SMN-9001; Tōkyō Nihon Guramofon Kabushiki Kaisha, 1964). Kindaichi Haruhiko, ed, *Shingon shōmyō: kaisetsu sho* (book accompanying set of 4 LP recordings, Polydor SMN-9002; Tōkyō Nihon Guramofon Kabushiki Kaisha, 1964). Nishitsunoi Masayoshi, *Kagura kenkyū* (1934). Ōyama Kōjun, *Bukkyō ongaku to shōmyō.* (1959; corrected repr 1962). Shiba Sukehiro, ed, *Kagura: kaisetsu sho* (book accompanying set of 6 LP recordings, Polydor SMN-9003; Tōkyō Nihon Guramofon Kabushiki Kaisha, 1966). Suzuki Chiben, *Nanzan Shinryū shōmyō shū (karifu),* 2 vols (1957). Tateishi Akio, *Bukkyō kayō no kenkyū* (1969). Taya Raishun, *Wasanshi gaisetsu* (1933).

David B. WATERHOUSE

music, traditional

A term applied to the variety of music performed in Japan from ancient times to 1868 and to forms of such music that are played today. Though archaeological materials and Chinese documents provide evidence of music in Japan as far back as the 3rd century BC, the traditional history of Japanese music normally starts with the Nara period (710–794). Thus the history of Japanese music is about as long as the history of Western music. Both histories contain a great variety of musical styles and both began from analogous bases: the nomenclature, music theory, and performance practice of a new religion and of a high culture overseas. In the West these were Christianity and the remnants of Greek culture, while in Japan they were Buddhism and the vibrant traditions of Tang (T'ang) dynasty (618–907) China.

Early History (400–1200) —— Traditionally, documented Japanese music history begins in 453 when 80 musicians from a Korean kingdom (SILLA) were said to have been imported for use in an imperial funeral. Buddhism was established as an official court religion by the 6th century, and its sounds and music theories became influential in Japan. In the 7th century the importation of additional Korean musicians and dancers and the return of Japanese from secular or religious training in mainland East Asia further enriched the sources of music in the courts and temples. By the 8th century, it was necessary for the court to establish a music bureau (Gagakuryō) to handle the variety of music required, generically known as GAGAKU.

Chinese and Korean courts or monasteries were the sources and models of most of this music but, because of the international dynamism of continental Asia from the 7th through the 10th centuries, one can find influences from South and Southeast Asia as well. The fact that Japan seemed to be "at the end of the line" in this cultural diffusion is of particular interest, for many traditions remained in Japan long after they had disappeared in the lands of their origins. The instrumental and dance repertoires of *gagaku* reflect such origins in their classification into two categories: *tōgaku,* pieces derived from Chinese or Indian sources, and *komagaku,* music from Korea and Manchuria. Historical sources tell us about yet other ensembles and pieces from Southeast Asia, and indigenous compositions are also part of the scene. As performed today, court music is played either as dance music *(bugaku)* or instrumental music *(kangen).* The standard full *kangen* ensemble consists of approximately 16 musicians performing on a variety of percussion, string, and reed instruments. In pieces accompanying dance, the stringed instruments are left out, and smaller combinations are used for vocal music accompaniment. The basic *gagaku* tone systems are derived from Chinese theoretical models but have acquired Japanese characteristics, particularly in their approach to modes. The titles of *gagaku* pieces are evocative of scenes, stories, or persons that are usually reflected in their dance versions. As in all Japanese music, improvisation hardly exists in *gagaku,* though the interpretations of pieces vary.

Perhaps the most impressive symbols of the glory and variety that were part of early court music in Japan are the musical instruments and dance masks preserved in the SHŌSŌIN, a storehouse of imperial houshold goods and temple accessories built in Nara in the mid-8th century. Among the 45 musical instruments that have survived there in some 1,200 years of silence are beautiful lutes whose decorations include such exotic items as parrots, oases, bactrian camels, and Central Asian horsemen. The harp *(kugo)* in this collection can be traced back through Chinese and Central Asian paintings of Buddhist heavens to bas reliefs found in ancient Babylon.

We cannot trace as easily the sounds of these rare musical resources. Only one scrap of lute (BIWA) notation is found in the Shōsōin, but a few part books for other instruments have survived from the 10th through the 13th centuries and are relatively abundant after that time. These documents are primarily memory aids rather than detailed notation, so that present-day performances from them may be very different from their original intent. Nevertheless, the continuation of the *gagaku* tradition today, along with similar musical traditions in Korea and Vietnam, give us sonically rewarding and historically tantalizing insights into one of the most brilliant periods of East Asian musical history.

Another rich source of early musical information in Japan is the literature of the 10th and 11th centuries. Diaries and novels are filled with courtiers who seem to be involved constantly with performing instrumental music, dancing in festivals or ceremonies, or singing classical or popular songs. The titles of some of the pieces listed in such books are still found in *gagaku* sources, but the solo instrumental and vocal literature was particularly evanescent. Today the slow chants that survive in the vocal repertory of *gagaku* seem but a very pale shadow of what must have been a colorful tradition.

Another constant concern of this period which had musical implications was religion. Buddhism flourished along with the indigenous Shintō tradition in its ritual demands and resultant musical necessities. For example, hundreds of musicians and dancers were assembled for the dedication of a giant Buddhist statue at the Tōdaiji temple in Nara in 752, while Shintō ritual songs and dances have remained as required parts of imperial annual cycles for centuries. As in the music history of most civilizations, the scholarly writings of religious orders are major sources of knowledge on varying early musical theories and notations in Japan, and these sources contributed most strongly to the development of new musical arts in the centuries that followed.

The Period 1200–1500 —— As implied above, the ancient musical traditions of Japan have carried on to modern times, but each period produced other styles of music that better suited its own needs and tastes. During the turbulent change from a court-dominated to a military-dominated culture, more theatrical genres of music became popular. The *biwa* of the court became the accompaniment not only of itinerant priests and evangelists but also of chanters who recited long historical tales, particularly the HEIKE MONOGATARI. Pantomime theatricals at Buddhist temples and Shintō shrines gradually combined in the 14th century with the rich heritage of folk theatricals to produce a new form known as NŌ drama. The writings of one of its founders, Zeami Motokiyo (1363–1443), contain a viable blend of earlier Buddhist and courtly music theory with "modern" theater. Declaiming, singing, and dancing actors join with a chorus singing in unison and three drums and a flute to perform a style of drama that has survived to this day. Its rules of melodic structure and of rhythmic patterns, along with the overall formal design of the plays, have had profound effects on all the music and theater that followed in Japan, as well as on several schools of 20th-century Western drama.

The Period 1500–1868 —— The 13-stringed *koto* (zither) tradition is one of the few types of ancient courtly solo and chamber music that continued to develop in the 16th century, primarily in the mansions of the rich or in temples. At first one finds remnants of older traditions, but by the 17th century quite different *koto* pieces appeared, particularly in the new Ikuta school. The founding of the Yamada school in the 18th century further enriched the repertoire. Both these schools have continued to the present day, and their solo and chamber music form the basis of what most Japanese would consider to be their "classical" music. The end-blown SHAKUHACHI (bamboo flute) also developed new schools of performance and repertory during this period, but it is the three-stringed plucked lute (SHAMISEN) that best represents the new musical styles and new audiences of the 16th through the 19th centuries. Plebeians and the peasantry had always had music in Japan (as elsewhere in the world), but the growth of a mercantile, urban society during this period called for music suitable to its patrons. Popular, dance, and theatrical music were much in demand, and the newly introduced *shamisen* provided an excellent accompaniment for such genres.

Screen paintings of the 16th century show cities like Kyōto seemingly filled with street dances and parades which used batteries of percussion plus flutes to support highly energetic dancing. The ancient traditions can be spotted in a few imperial compounds, but the populace is more often seen crowding into the licensed quarters and theater districts. In the latter one sees the melodramatic puppet theater (later called BUNRAKU) and the delightfully flamboyant and sensual KABUKI theater. By the 18th century, the narrative tradition of the puppet theater (known generically as JŌRURI) had become a major source of literature which was performed by skilled chanters *(tayū)* with *shamisen* accompaniment. The kabuki theater adopted some of this material for its own plays, but it also developed a combination of other genres of *shamisen* music plus the percussion and flute ensemble *(hayashi)* of the Nō along with an eclectic assortment of folk and religious instruments. All these made for a theater music that truly reflected the colorful style of a new era.

A logical outgrowth of an economically and socially supported theater music was the creation in the 19th century of compositions using theatrical genres and instruments but intended for dance recital or purely concert performances. The *shamisen* genre called NAGAUTA was particularly active in this new field. Such concerts were originally held in private mansions but, by the end of the century, actual concert halls for such music were common. All in all, the 19th-century music of Japan became analogous to the 19th-century "standard repertory" of Western music in Europe, though the composers and sounds were very different indeed. New *biwa* (lute) narrative traditions also appeared at this time. Thus, on the eve of the "modernization" of Japan, there was a large reservoir of viable traditional music.

The Modern Period——The two major problems of traditional music in Japan after the Meiji Restoration of 1868 were official censure of the monopolistic guild system controlling performance and teaching, and the fierce interest in and competition from Western models. Most traditional music was able to adapt its guild systems to the requirements of modern society, and the acquisition of a professional name *(natori)* is still an important artistic and financial goal for much of the Japanese music and dance world. In a subtle way, it also retains an influence on Western music activities in Japan. The social and economic recovery of Japan since 1945 has allowed it the luxury of supporting its traditional music as well as keeping up with the latest Western developments. The music education system of Japan was designed rather rigidly on Western models and materials, and the Japanese music industry has been most aggressive in promoting Suzuki violins and Yamaha pianos; however, there are a sufficient number of young Japanese who have turned to traditional musical forms to assure that, in a modern electronic and plastic world, there will continue to be in Japan an appreciation of and support for musical sounds derived from native traditions and played on instruments made of natural materials.

Since the historical length and variety of the tradition have been shown to be equal to those of Western music, it is obviously difficult to come up with many valid statements about its general characteristics. Nevertheless, there are a few comments which may prove useful. First, most Japanese music shares with its East Asian counterparts a general tendency to be word-oriented. Except for the variation *(dammono)* pieces for the *koto,* Japanese traditional music either has a vocal part with text or a title that evokes some image. Another aspect of word orientation is that the actual music of a specific vocal piece may react to the meaning of the text with a subtlety and effectiveness equal to that of Schubert songs in the West. It is not obvious to a Western listener, because the text is not fully understood and the significant musical signals are in idioms quite different from Western experiences. These conventionalized signals can be recognized just as one learns to "appreciate" Western music through lecture courses. Such knowledge can be used for deeper enjoyment and even for evaluations of the performance of Japanese classical vocal music.

Since court orchestral music is so very different from kabuki theater music, it might seem unreasonable to make any general comments about instrumental genres. However, the general concept of the chamber music sound ideal seems to apply to almost all Japanese traditional ensembles over the past 1,200 years. Thus, no matter how large or small an ensemble may be, the tone color of the instruments combined is such that the sounds do not "melt" into a single experience as they do in some Western orchestral music.

Another important feature is the general lack of interest in the type of vertical sound units known in the West as chords or harmony. The basic orientation of Japanese music is linear, without those vertical supports so precious to Western classical traditions. They are not needed in Japan because other, equally effective, musical means are used to give the music a sense of tension and release and of movement through time toward a logical close. In Japanese traditional music two factors supersede any need for chords. One is the careful use of "pillar tones," central pitches in changing tone systems which are used as points of resolution from pitches just above or below them. The experienced listener waits with anticipation for a seemingly static pitch to resolve down or up to one of these pillar tones. The other major factor is rhythm. If only a single vocalist and one accompanying instrument are performing, one will note that they seldom coincide in entrances unless the tempo is quite fast or cadence occurs. This serves two functions; it allows one to hear the text "between" the sounds of the accompaniment, and it creates some sonic tension which will be resolved at the cadence.

An extension of this concept is the "slide rule" effect in which various melodic or rhythmic lines in a piece do not seem to start on the same first beat. Internally they are quite rigid, but vertically they create a sense of disjunction, like two lines on a slide rule. In Japanese music the lines always get back together at the cadence, but in the previous section they provide a most valid sense of tension, quite unlike though analogous to the tension-release needs of Western music. If a percussion ensemble is used, as in Nō and kabuki, another important Japanese concept is evident: the use of named stereotyped rhythmic patterns. These patterns tend to appear in progressions and thus, like Western traditional harmony, they play a very vital role in giving music a sense of progression in time.

Perhaps the most difficult aspect of traditional music for non-Japanese listeners is that it is generally through-composed. It does not state a theme and then develop it as in the standard western classical tradition. Instead, it moves on to new musical ideas. What gives it a sense of logical progression are its conventions of form, which are stated most generally by the terms *jo, ha,* and *kyū* (introduction, scattering, rushing toward the finale).

Some of these concepts are difficult to comprehend without actually hearing the music. However, perhaps two final generalizations may serve as convenient starting points for an understanding of the rest. In much of Japanese traditional music, there is a general goal of establishing a maximum effect with minimum material. There are, of course, many flamboyant styles of music in Japan but, when one is dealing with so-called classical music, one is often struck by the seemingly inactive nature of the music: nothing seems to happen. However, once one has "become used to the reduced volume and activity, it is possible to become deeply involved in the artistry of "less action—more meaning." By the same token, the static artistry of Japanese music can be appreciated as much as Brahms or Stravinsky. The challenge is to the flexibility of the listener, not the composer or performer. Our final generalization is that originality, so favored by musicians in the romantic and early modern periods in the West, was seldom the concern of Japanese composers. Their goals were more like those of Bach or Mozart, i.e. to use the established conventions with total artisan-like skill. The goal of modern listeners, perhaps, should be to be able to appreciate such varieties of sameness in both the Western and Japanese music worlds.

——Eta Harich-Schneider, *A History of Japanese Music* (1973). William P. Malm, *Japanese Music and Musical Instruments* (1959).
William P. MALM

music, Western

The story of Western music in Japan (i.e., of music in the West European tradition) begins with the arrival of the Portuguese missionaries in the 16th century. The first pipe organs were brought to Japan in 1579 by the Italian Jesuit, Alessandro VALIGNANO, and Western stringed instruments, namely viols and rebecs, were known even earlier and were widely used for both religious and secular music. A Portuguese musician, Ayres Sanchez, set up a music school at about the same time, and, in 1582, 15 of its pupils traveled to Maçao, Goa, and Europe, returning in 1590. In 1591 a Portuguese ensemble played before the hegemon TOYOTOMI HIDEYOSHI on clavier, harp, lute, and rebec. From 1606 to 1613 pipe organs were manufactured in Nagasaki and Arima. (Jesuit letters contain other scattered information about the progress of Western music in Japan.)

There is little doubt that European music and musical instruments appealed to the Japanese, and one Japanese instrument, the KOKYŪ, was partly inspired by the rebec. However, the expulsion of the missionaries in 1613 put an end to this activity, and it does not appear that the Dutch trading colony on DEJIMA had much musical influence until the 1830s, when TAKASHIMA SHŪHAN, a student of Western military science, formed in Nagasaki a Dutch-style fife-and-drum band. This was widely imitated in other domains during the years preceding the Meiji Restoration (1868).

Meiji Period (1868–1912)——The profound social upheavals of this period had great effects on music, not least because Japanese official attitudes were still strongly influenced by Confucianism, which maintained that correct ritual and music were important for good government. Thus, the old imperial court music was revived, and NŌ drama, which had been the official entertainment of the old regime, was discouraged. The old system of state protection for blind musicians and its associated guilds were abolished, and the mendicant Fuke sect of SHAKUHACHI players was proscribed. On the other hand, Western music was actively encouraged.

In conformity with Confucianism, vulgar music had to be excluded, and, since Japanese acquaintance with Western music was still limited, only two genres, military music and children's educational music, could be regarded as wholesome. In 1869 an Englishman, John William Fenton, began teaching in Yokohama 30 bandsmen from the Satsuma domain (now Kagoshima Prefecture). This was the first brass band in Japan, and Fenton was the first of many foreign music teachers. He was followed by the German Franz Eckert (1852–1916), who taught music to the navy, and a Frenchman, Dacron, who taught the army. Eventually Japanese brass bands began to make public appearances, in the new public parks, for example, and their novel music, often in three time, earned the nickname *jinta* (because its rhythm went *jintatta, jintatta*).

Meanwhile, a series of educational reforms was passed, making provision for the teaching of Western music. In 1875 IZAWA SHŪJI was sent to study in Massachusetts for four years; on his return he organized the Music Study Committee (Ongaku Torishirabe-Gakari), Japan's first official school of Western music. He invited his old teacher from Boston, Luther Whiting MASON, to be its director. Mason arrived in 1880. The new school, which taught some Japanese music as well, was primarily intended to train teachers.

Mason stayed three years and was succeeded by Eckert. Other early instructors who arrived between 1886 and 1909 were: Guillaume Sauvlet (Dutch pianist), Rudolf Dittrich (1861–1919; Austrian composition teacher), Raphael von Koeber (1848–1923; composition teacher), August Junker (1870–1944; German conductor, violinist), Hermann Heidrich (b 1855; German pianist), Heinrich Werkmeister (1883–1936; German violinist, composer), Rudolph Ernest Reuter (b 1888; American pianist), and Hanka Petzoldt (d 1937; Norwegian pianist, singer). Their best Japanese pupils went abroad to study, above all to Germany: for example, Kōda Nobu (1870–1946; pianist, sister of the writer KŌDA ROHAN); her sister Andō Kō (1878–1963; violinist); TAKI RENTARŌ (1879–1903; composer); Miura Tamaki (1884–1946; singer); and Kuno Hisa (1886–1925; pianist).

The relationship between the new Western music and traditional Japanese music was still problematic, though Izawa himself advocated a new music which would be a blend between the two. In 1881 a Western music group within the court music department gave its first concert (of Western and Japanese songs), and when the Music Study Committee was renamed the Tōkyō Music School (Tōkyō Ongaku Gakkō; now Tōkyō University of Fine Arts and Music) in 1898, *koto* music was played at the opening ceremony. Three collections of children's and choral songs (*shōka*) edited by the school in the 1880s, and others published later in the period, contain a mixture of Japanese and European (especially Scottish) pieces. In general, it proved easier to maintain the two systems side by side than to reconcile them. Attempts were made, for example, to harmonize SHAMISEN music, and the songs of Taki Rentarō showed that Japanese could compose successfully in a Western idiom, but the immensely popular GUNKA (military songs) came closest to satisfying Izawa's prescription. In music education, the official emphasis was increasingly laid on Western music. Another institution of the period was the ROKUMEIKAN, an Italianate structure where polite society gathered weekly to practice ballroom dancing.

At the turn of the century other organizations for Western music came into being: the Meiji Music Society (Meiji Ongaku Kai) in 1898, which gave spring and autumn concerts, at which one-third was Western music (*yōgaku*) and two-thirds was Japanese music (*hōgaku; see* MUSIC, TRADITIONAL); the Imperial Music Society (Teikoku Ongaku Kai) in 1907, under the composer Komatsu Kōsuke (1884–1966), who had studied in Paris with Widor and d'Indy; and the Tōkyō Philharmonic Society, organized by Werkmeister and the music pedagogue Suzuki Yonejirō (1868–1940) and devoted entirely to Western music. At the same time, several other Western music schools were started, all in Tōkyō.

Taishō and Prewar Shōwa Periods (1912–1940) —— As a result of World War I and also of the Russian Revolution, numerous refugees, performing musicians among them, passed through Japan on their way to the United States. Until this time Japanese audiences had not been exposed to performances by Western musicians of the first rank: the concerts in the Meiji period, with few exceptions, were given by Western or Japanese music teachers, their pupils, and other amateurs. There were no full-time groups performing symphonic or chamber music and no outstanding soloists.

From 1917 onward a series of recitals and concert tours was given by foreign artists, mainly White Russian or Italian, and in the 1920s various Western artists were invited to perform in Japan. Among them were Mischa Elman (Russian violinist), in 1921; Efrem Zimbalist (Russian violinist) and Leopold Godowski (Polish pianist), in 1922; Fritz Kreisler (Austrian violinist) and Jascha Heifetz (Russian violinist), in 1923; Mischa Levitski (Russian pianist), Jacques Thibaud (French violinist), Jan Kubelik (Czech violinist), Andrès Segovia (Spanish guitarist), Miguel Fleta (Spanish tenor), and John McCormack (Irish tenor), in 1929.

The only regular symphony orchestra then was that of the Tōkyō Music School. In 1914 the Tōkyō Philharmonic Society had given its first orchestra concert, under YAMADA KŌSAKU, but it faded from the scene two years later. Otherwise, ensemble music was chiefly provided by the army and navy bands, which now performed also at Hibiya Music Hall, Tōkyō, and in the new Japanese cinemas. In 1922, however, the Tōkyō Symphony Orchestra was formed, and it gave its first concert the following year at the IMPERIAL HOTEL, under the Russian emigré conductor Jacques Gershkovich. It gave many other concerts during the summer of 1923, but the Tōkyō Earthquake in September of that year put an end to its activities. In 1925 Yamada Kōsaku formed the Japan Symphony Association, which gave concerts the same year in western Japan and in Tōkyō, where they combined forces with 33 Russian musicians from Harbin.

Notwithstanding the injunctions of the Meiji government that moral tone must be preserved in music, much of the foreign music hitherto cultivated was rather bad. But 1920 saw the first Japanese performance of Beethoven's Fifth Symphony, and the Ninth followed in 1924. Japanese broadcasting started the following year, and the first broadcast subscription concert took place in 1926. The program, conducted by Konoe Hidemaro (1898–1973), included Beethoven's Third Symphony. At the second concert Yamada Kōsaku conducted Dvořak's New World Symphony. There were several more such concerts the same year. Then Konoe and a partner formed a separate symphony orchestra, whose explicit aim was high-quality performances of European symphonic works. In 1927, sponsored by the newspaper *Asahi shimbun*, he staged a Beethoven festival, which included most of the symphonies and piano concerti. The final concert used an augmented orchestra of 150 musicians.

Meanwhile the procession of foreign guest artists and music teachers continued, and standards of Japanese performance gradually went up. Audiences too were becoming more appreciative, not least because of the gramophone. By 1937, Japan had become the largest market in the world for classical records, which were usually re-pressed from foreign matrices by Japanese subsidiaries of European and American companies. Record subscription clubs were a popular means of distribution and some sumptuous record sets were issued. Japanese interest in Western opera also developed strongly in the late 1920s and 1930s: the tenor Fujiwara Yoshie (1898–1976) had a successful stage career in Europe and America, as well as in Japan, where he formed his own opera company in 1934 (Fujiwara Kagekidan); and the coloratura soprano Sekiya Toshiko (1904–41) became well known in Italy as well as at home.

Despite all this activity, it is fair to say that composition lagged behind. After Taki Rentarō the most prominent names are Yamada Kōsaku and NAKAYAMA SHIMPEI. Other Western-style composers of the early 20th century were: Kitamura Sueharu (1872–1931); Mitsukuri Shūkichi (1895–1971); Sugawara Meirō (b 1897); Hashimoto Kunihiko (1904–49); Hirao Kishio (1907–54); Odaka Hisatada (1911–51); and Nobutoki Kiyoshi (1887–1965); but their works are little heard today. One of the influences on prewar composition was the Russian composer and pianist Aleksandr Cherepnin (b 1900), who lived in Shanghai in the 1930s and visited Japan several times. He performed works by Japanese composers, arranged for their publication, and instituted the Cherepnin Composition Award (1934–36). Another strong influence was that of the German composer and conductor Klaus Pringsheim (1883–1972), who lived and taught in Japan from 1931 to 1937. Cherepnin introduced the style of Prokofiev to Japan; and Pringsheim that of Bruckner and Mahler; Japanese were also influenced by Debussy and other French composers.

On the other hand, the Taishō period saw the flowering of a new genre called RYŪKŌKA, in which there was a strong Western element: some of the most lively and memorable music of the prewar period is of this light-hearted kind and a new instrument, the *taishō-goto,* modeled on the Autoharp, was well-suited to playing *ryūkōka.* Western influence also appears in the music of the *koto* performer MIYAGI MICHIO and of some other composers for traditional instruments.

World War II and After (1940–)—— After 1941 the Japan Symphony Orchestra, which had a broadcasting contract, was mainly responsible for keeping Western music alive for the Japanese, and even in 1945 it continued to give concerts at Hibiya Public Hall.

During the American OCCUPATION foreign influence on music was naturally very strong, and is seen above all in *ryūkōka.* However, interest in serious Western music was quickly revived. The old Tōkyō Symphony Orchestra was dissolved in 1945, but its name was adopted in 1951 by the Tōhō Symphony (formed 1945). The Japan Symphony (originally founded in 1927 as the New Symphony Orchestra) became the NHK (Japan Broadcasting Corporation) Symphony, and several other symphony orchestras were founded between 1947 and 1956. Opera was continued by Fujiwara Yoshie's company, by a short-lived rival company, and by the Nikikai organization, formed in 1952 for the study and performance of Western opera. Another influence was the so-called Rōon movement initiated by a workers' association, the Rōdōsha Ongaku Kyōgikai, in 1949 to enhance workers' appreciation of music. Both popular broadcasting and the first Japanese long-playing record made their appearance in 1951.

Composition was fostered by a number of groups, notably the Japan Contemporary Music Association (Nihon Gendai Ongaku Kyōkai), which under other names had existed before the war and which from 1950 promoted an annual festival. Other composers' societies were Shin Sakkyokuka Kyōkai (formed in 1946); Shinseikai (1946); Chijinkai (1948); and the experimental arts workshop Jikken Kōbō (1949). In addition to the composers who had been active earlier, the following may be mentioned: Matsudaira Yoritsune (b 1907); Ōsawa Hisato (1907–53); DAN IKUMA; Akutagawa Yasushi (b 1925, son of the writer AKUTAGAWA RYŪNOSUKE); MAYUZUMI TO-SHIRŌ; Yuasa Jōji (b 1929); Moroi Makoto (b 1930); FUKUSHIMA KAZUO; TAKEMITSU TŌRU; Miyoshi Akira (b 1933); Ichiyanagi Toshi (b 1933); and Takahashi Yūji (b 1938). Dan deserves mention for his charming opera *Yūzuru* (1952), based on a Japanese folk tale, and Mayuzumi for his symphonic poems inspired by esoteric Buddhism. Ichiyanagi is a pupil of John Cage; Takahashi of Iannis Xenakis.

Much postwar Japanese composition draws on the theories of Arnold Schoenberg, the first to use serialism being Shibata Minao (b 1916). The NHK electronic music studio was established in 1951, and many composers have now used such devices as *musique concrète,* synthesizers and so on. At least two composers' groups were interested in improvisation and "happenings": Group Ongaku (founded in 1960 and active till the mid-1960s) and New Direction (1962). A more nationalist group, Yagi no Kai (1953), was influenced by the ideas of Béla Bartók; and several composers have written for the Ensemble Nipponia (Nippon Ongaku Shūdan), an orchestra of traditional instruments formed in 1964 by Miki Minoru (b 1930), himself also a composer.

Foreign performers began to visit Japan again from 1950 and foreign orchestras from 1955. Meanwhile, Japanese musicians were again going abroad to study and perform; and since the 1960s some of them, such as the conductor OZAWA SEIJI, have established permanent reputations overseas. The most significant interchange, however, has been due to the pedagogue SUZUKI SHIN'ICHI. Before the war he was first violin in the Suzuki String Quartet, made up of four children of the violin maker Suzuki Seikichi; and the SUZUKI VIOLIN METHOD, which can be applied to other instruments, draws on the strong familial basis of traditional Japanese instruction in the arts.

Today, Western music flourishes in Japan as never before. Composition, performance, music education, instrument making, musicology, and music journalism are on levels which in quantity and quality bear comparison with those of Europe and North America. Thus, Tōkyō alone has six symphony orchestras; the music played on radio and television is mostly Western; Yamaha (founded 1887) is the largest piano manufacturer in the world, and so on. All types of Western music are heard and enjoyed: renaissance, baroque, romantic, modern, jazz, folk, and the multifarious kinds of popular music. Most Japanese are strangely ignorant of Japanese traditional music, but somehow it too has managed to survive and flourish amid so many foreign sounds and to influence modern Japanese composers of varying musical sympathies. The old opposition between national and Western music persists, but it is becoming more and more

blurred, so that record companies now distinguish between *junhō-gaku,* (pure national music), and Westernized kinds (especially *ryū-kōka*). A further kind is *shinhōgaku,* (new national music), serious music which draws on Western styles of composition. Thus it is apparent that music embodying the synthesis proposed by Izawa Shūji will coexist for a long time with many other kinds of music, Japanese as well as Western.

■——Endō Hiroshi, *Meiji ongaku shi kō* (1948). Horiuchi Keizō, *(Teihon) Nihon no shōka* (1970). Inoue Takeshi and Akiyama Tatsuo, ed, *Nihon no yōgaku hyakunen shi* (1966). Komiya Toyotaka, ed, *Japanese Music and Drama in the Meiji Era,* tr and adapted by Donald Keene and Edward Seidensticker (1956), English version of a 1954 book in Japanese by Komiya. William P. Malm, "The Modern Music of Meiji Japan," in Donald H. Shively, ed, *Tradition and Modernization in Japanese Culture* (1971). Elizabeth May, *The Influence of the Meiji Period on Japanese Children's Music* (1963). Miura Shunzaburō, *Hompō yōgaku hensen shi* (1931). Tanabe Hisao, *Meiji ongaku monogatari* (1965). Ushiyama Mitsuru et al, "Nihon no ongaku, II: Yōgaku," in *Ongaku jiten* (1959–60).

David B. WATERHOUSE

Musō Soseki (1275–1351)

The most prominent and influential Zen master of the GOZAN (Five Temples) system of Zen monasteries, and spiritual mentor to a number of emperors and military rulers of the Muromachi period (1333–1568). Born a descendant of Emperor UDA (r 887–897), in Ise province (now part of Mie Prefecture) and raised in Kai province (now Yamanashi Prefecture), Soseki studied Shingon Esoteric Buddhism and was ordained in 1292 at Tōdaiji in Nara. He grew critical of the established Buddhist sects and soon turned to the study of Zen. In 1299, at KENCHŌJI, one of the chief RINZAI SECT temples in Kamakura, he began receiving instruction from the Chinese master Yishan Yining (I-shan I-Ning; 1244–1317; J: ISSAN ICHINEI). Although he distinguished himself as one of the most promising disciples of the eminent Chinese monk, he left Kamakura to seek a life of seclusion in northern Japan. He later returned to Kamakura to study at Manjuji with the renowned Rinzai master Kōhō Kennichi (1241–1316) and in 1305 attained enlightenment. Rejecting the shogunal regent HŌJŌ TAKATOKI's summons to remain in Kamakura as a leader of the Kenchōji faction of Rinzai Zen, he lived in seclusion for the next 20 years. In 1325, at the request of Emperor GO-DAIGO, Soseki became the abbot of NANZENJI, one of Kyōto's Gozan temples. He retained this position for one year, returning to Kamakura in 1326 at the invitation of Takatoki. In 1333 Go-Daigo invited him back to Kyōto; he became abbot of Nanzenji again in 1334. (That year Nanzenji was named first in the Gozan hierarchy in Kyōto.) Soseki's move from the seat of the Hōjō regency to the capital coincided with Go-Daigo's successful rebellion, directed against the Hōjō family in Kamakura (see KEMMU RESTORATION). However, after Go-Daigo's flight from Kyōto to Yoshino in 1336 and the ascendance of ASHIKAGA TAKAUJI, Musō remained in the capital to serve Takauji and his influential brother ASHIKAGA TADAYOSHI.

In 1339, Soseki converted the Pure Land temple SAIHŌJI into a Zen monastery. His landscape gardening later provided models for other famous Zen-inspired gardens, including those at KINKAKUJI (1397) and GINKAKUJI (1483) in Kyōto. He is also known to have persuaded the Ashikaga to send a trading vessel to China (see TEN-RYŪJI-BUNE), the profits from which were used to build TENRYŪJI, a temple in memory of Emperor Go-Daigo. Go-Daigo, who died in exile in 1339, had bestowed upon Soseki the imperial title of Musō Kokushi (National Master Musō).

Soseki, more than any other individual, may be credited with the establishment of the Gozan system. At the time of his death, he had an enormous number of disciples; most of the monks were associated with the Gozan temples in Kyōto and Kamakura, and many of them later became very influential. Through his synthesis of Zen and Esotericism, his encouragement of Zen culture, and his political associations with the most influential members of Japanese society, Zen became firmly rooted in Japan.

■——Tamamura Takeji, *Musō kokushi* (1958).

T. James KODERA

Mutai Risaku (1890–1974)

Philosopher. Born in Nagano Prefecture. After graduating from Kyōto University in 1918, Mutai served as NISHIDA KITARŌ's assistant and later traveled to Germany and France in 1926. He studied

phenomenology with Husserl. Subsequently he taught at the University of Taipei, Tōkyō University of Education (where he served as president, 1945–48), and Keiō University. In his search to grasp man as a socio-existential entity, Mutai attempted to synthesize the methodology of phenomenology, Hegel's philosophy of history, and Nishida's philosophy with the concept of "spatial, contradictory self-identity" (*bashoteki mujunteki jiko dōitsu*). He later attempted to provide a basis from which this contemplative attitude could be transcended. His *Daisan hyūmanizumu to heiwa* (Third Humanism and Peace, 1951) was an attempt to set forth a socialist humanism based on Marxism and existentialism. See also MODERN PHILOSOPHY.
TAKAHASHI Ken'ichi

Mutō Akira (1892–1948)

Army officer. Born in Kumamoto Prefecture; graduated from the Army War College in 1920. As a staff officer in the GUANDONG (KWANTUNG) ARMY in 1936 and chief of operations on the General Staff in 1937, he helped to formulate the army's Manchurian policy. At the time of the MARCO POLO BRIDGE INCIDENT in July 1937, Mutō advocated Japanese occupation of China north of the Yellow River. In 1939 he was appointed chief of the Military Affairs Bureau. A central figure within the wartime army leadership, Mutō became head of the Imperial Guard Division in 1942 and chief of staff for Japanese forces in the Philippines in 1944. He was executed in 1948 as a class A war criminal.

Mutō Sanji (1867–1934)

Businessman and politician. Born in Gifu Prefecture. Studied at Keiō Gijuku (now Keiō University). After a stay in the United States, Mutō joined Mitsui Bank in 1893. Appointed manager of a Mitsui subsididary, Kanegafuchi Spinning Company (now KANEBŌ, LTD), in 1894, he held the post until 1930, and developed the company into one of the leading spinning ventures in Japan. Mutō was widely known for his practice of family-style corporate management. He formed the JITSUGYŌ DŌSHIKAI, a political party, in 1923 and was elected to the House of Representatives the following year. He strongly criticized the collusion between politicians and business executives. After retiring from politics in 1932, Mutō became president of Jiji Shimpō Sha, a newspaper company.
KOBAYAKAWA Yōichi

Mutsu

City in northeastern Aomori Prefecture, northern Honshū, on Ōminato Bay. Facilities of the Japanese Maritime Self Defense Force are located here. It was formerly the home port of Japan's first nuclear-powered ship, the *Mutsu*. Principal industries are farming and fishing. OSOREZAN, a mountain considered sacred by many Japanese, is located nearby. Pop: 47,609.

Mutsu

Battleship of the Imperial Japanese Navy. A sister ship of the NAGATO, it was built as part of the so-called HACHIHACHI KANTAI (Eight Eight Fleet) building program. The *Mutsu* was constructed at the Yokosuka Naval Dockyard. Completed in 1921, it had a displacement of 43,000 tons, a top speed of 25 knots, and a main battery of eight 40-centimeter (15.8-in) guns. The *Mutsu*, which participated in the Battle of MIDWAY during World War II, sank on 8 June 1943 in Hiroshima Bay after an accidental explosion in its magazine.
ICHIKI Toshio

Mutsu

Japan's first nuclear-powered ship. Built for the Japan Nuclear Ship Development Agency by ISHIKAWAJIMA–HARIMA HEAVY INDUSTRIES CO, LTD. Launched in Tōkyō, June 1969; 130 meters (426 ft) long, speed 16.5 knots, cargo capacity 8,300 tons. The nuclear reactor produces 36,000 kilowatts. Following its completion, the ship was moved to the port of Mutsu, Aomori Prefecture, which had been designated as its base. On 26 August 1974, after remaining in the harbor for 22 months, the *Mutsu* sailed out on a test run, despite the concerted opposition of local fishermen who feared nuclear pollution. On 1 September, a leak was discovered in the nuclear reactor and tests were stopped; however, the local government refused to allow the ship to reenter port. In October the ruling Liberal Demo-

cratic Party sent a representative to the city of Mutsu to negotiate, and, after it had been agreed to move the ship to another base within two years, the *Mutsu* was allowed to enter the harbor. The ship was eventually moved to the port of Sasebo in Kyūshū.

Mutsu Bay

(Mutsu Wan). Large bay on the northern coast of Aomori Prefecture, northern Honshū. Extends from the Shimokita Peninsula on the east to the Tsugaru Peninsula on the west. Opens into the Tsugaru Strait on the northwest. Principal activities are the cultivation of scallops and *nori* (a kind of seaweed).

Mutsu Munemitsu (1844–1897)

Japan's foreign minister from 1892 to 1896, Mutsu is best known for his accomplishments in ridding Japan of the "unequal treaties," which had been imposed upon Japan by the Western powers, and for his successful diplomacy during the SINO-JAPANESE WAR OF 1894–1895. As a youth Mutsu was a political activist; as an adult he was a politician and bureaucrat. His career, replete with failure as well as success, is comparable to those of many other early and middle Meiji-period (1868–1912) politicians who were on the winning side of the Meiji Restoration, but who were frustrated and sometimes pushed into opposition because of the new government's domination almost from the beginning by men of the Satsuma and Chōshū domains (now Kagoshima and Yamaguchi prefectures).

The sixth son of a retainer of Wakayama domain (now Wakayama Prefecture), in 1858 Mutsu deserted his domain for Edo (now Tōkyō), where he drifted and studied. Drawn to the proimperial (*sonnō jōi*) movement, he moved to Kyōto in 1862 and became a follower of the loyalist SAKAMOTO RYŌMA. After studying at KATSU KAISHŪ's naval school, Mutsu accompanied Sakamoto to Satsuma and eventually to Nagasaki, where he was part of the KAIENTAI, Sakamoto's trading company, which dealt in Western goods, arms, and knowledge.

Upon the restoration of imperial rule in early 1868, Mutsu received his first official appointment as a junior bureaucrat in the fledgling Foreign Office (Gaikoku Jimukyoku) of the new Meiji government. Mutsu then held a series of posts in the Kansai area, where he became involved in local politics. Dismissed from government employ, he went to Europe in 1870 on business for the Wakayama domain. A month after Mutsu returned in the summer of 1871, the domains were abolished and the new prefectural system established. He was appointed governor of Kanagawa Prefecture, a sensitive post because it included the foreign settlement at Yokohama. He soon resigned the governorship in order to concentrate on tax reform work at the Finance Ministry, where he headed the office in charge of the LAND TAX REFORM OF 1873–1881. Angered by the emerging Satsuma–Chōshū political monopoly, Mutsu resigned in 1874.

Mutsu rejoined the government in 1875 as a member of the GENRŌIN, a protolegislative "senate" which debated some governmental proposals. He was active in the Genrōin until June 1878, when he was implicated in an antigovernment plot that was based in the former Tosa domain (now Kōchi Prefecture). He was stripped of his governmental rank and position and sentenced to prison. Imprisoned in northern Japan, he devoted his time to reading and writing, including a translation of some of Jeremy Bentham's works.

Mutsu was freed by special pardon in 1883 and welcomed back to Tōkyō by both the government and the opposition parties and swiftly rehabilitated. An old acquaintance, ITŌ HIROBUMI, who was to become Japan's first prime minister two years later, led the effort to bring Mutsu back into the government. Itō, fresh from his constitutional studies in Europe, urged Mutsu to go abroad for study, offering financial support and a possible government post upon Mutsu's return. Mutsu went to Europe via the United States in 1884. After studying in London and Vienna, he returned to Japan in 1886 and received a post in the Foreign Ministry (Gaimushō). This appointment considerably worsened Mutsu's relations with the opposition parties, and he put all his energy into ministry work, particularly the problem of revising the "unequal treaties", as the ANSEI COMMERCIAL TREATIES of 1858 were called.

In 1888 Mutsu was appointed ambassador to the United States. Not long after arriving in Washington, he successfully concluded Japan's first equal treaty, the Treaty of Amity and Commerce with Mexico. In February 1889 he concluded a revised treaty of commerce with the United States. Mutsu returned to Japan in 1890 and

Myōe

Detail of a painting of Myōe in meditation. Hanging scroll. Colors on paper. Early 13th century. Kōzanji, Kyōto. National Treasure.

became the minister of agriculture and commerce in YAMAGATA ARITOMO's first cabinet. Mutsu was one of the first cabinet members not from a Satsuma–Chōshū background. Mutsu was elected to the first Diet from his home area of Wakayama, and used his contacts with the opposition parties to help effect the first Diet compromises.

In 1892 Mutsu became foreign minister in Itō Hirobumi's second cabinet. His major task was to push on with treaty revision. Mutsu's tenure as foreign minister was the zenith of his career and achievement. Resurgent antiforeign sentiment in Japan threatened to undermine treaty negotiations. Mutsu overcame this problem with adroit politics and successfully concluded the new equal treaty, the ANGLO-JAPANESE COMMERCIAL TREATY OF 1894 with Britain. The situation in Korea worsened in the early 1890s and Japan's rivalry with China for influence in that strategic peninsula exploded into the Sino-Japanese War of 1894–95 after Japan intervened in the TONGHAK REBELLION in 1894. Mutsu deftly guided Japan's wartime diplomacy and, as plenipotentiary with Prime Minister Itō, represented Japan at the Shimonoseki peace negotiations. The conclusion of the Treaty of SHIMONOSEKI with China on 17 April 1895 was the pinnacle of Mutsu's public life. Only six days later Russia, Germany, and France, in the so-called TRIPARTITE INTERVENTION, shattered Mutsu's triumph, forcing Japan to return the Liaodong (Liaotung) Peninsula, which it had gained as part of the peace settlement. Outraged over the humiliation, the Japanese public vented its wrath on Mutsu. Chronically ill from 1895, Mutsu resigned his portfolio in 1896 and died the following year. *Kenkenroku* (A Record of Suffering), Mutsu's personal account of the diplomacy of the Sino-Japanese War, is his best-known work (see also UNEQUAL TREATIES, REVISION OF).

📖 ——George Akita, *Foundations of Constitutional Government in Modern Japan, 1868–1900* (1967). Roger F. Hackett, *Yamagata Aritomo in the Rise of Modern Japan, 1838–1922* (1971).

Karl MOSKOWITZ

Mutsu Province

(Mutsu no Kuni). Originally called Michinoku no Kuni (Province of the Farthest Region); also known as Ōshū or Rikushū. One of the eight PROVINCES of the Tōsandō (Eastern Mountain Circuit) in northeastern Japan; established under the KOKUGUN SYSTEM in the early part of the 8th century, it comprised what is now Fukushima, Miyagi, Iwate, Aomori and a small part of Akita prefectures. As implied by its original name, Mutsu was an undeveloped frontier region, inhabited by the aboriginal EZO people. The provincial gov-

ernor's headquarters (KOKUFU) was established at TAGAJŌ. In 801 the government dispatched SAKANOUE NO TAMURAMARO to subdue the Ezo, and he succeeded in moving the frontier outpost farther north to IZAWAJŌ. In the middle of the Heian period (794–1185) a local warrior family, the ŌSHŪ FUJIWARA FAMILY, secured control over all of Mutsu; during the four generations of Ōshū Fujiwara rule, the family stronghold of HIRAIZUMI flourished as the military, political, and cultural center of northern Japan. Late in the Muromachi period (1333–1568) the province came under the control of the DATE FAMILY in the south and the Nambu family in the north. Under the Tokugawa shogunate (1603–1867) the territory of the province was divided among some 20 *daimyō* domains (HAN), of which Aizu and Sendai were the most powerful. The main products included gold, lacquer ware, TSUMUGI cloth, and horses. The landscape of this province and some of its historical sites have been immortalized in BASHŌ's poem-diary, *Oku no hosomichi* (ca 1694; tr *Narrow Road to the Deep North,* 1966). After the Meiji Restoration of 1868, the province's boundaries were redrawn to include only what is now Aomori Prefecture and a small part of Iwate Prefecture. The remainder of the former province was divided into the provinces of Rikuchū (most of what is now Iwate Prefecture and a small part of Akita Prefecture), Rikuzen (now part of Miyagi Prefecture and a small part of Iwate Prefecture), Iwaki (parts of what are now Miyagi and Fukushima prefectures), and Iwashiro (now part of Fukushima Prefecture). With the establishment of the prefectural system in 1871, all of these provinces were done away with along with the daimyō domains that they contained (see PREFECTURAL SYSTEM, ESTABLISHMENT OF).

mutual company

(*sōgo kaisha*). Also called a mutual insurance company (*sōgo hoken kaisha*); an incorporated juristic person organized for the purpose of providing mutual insurance. Mutual companies are not companies under the Commercial Code but under the Insurance Business Law (Hokengyō Hō). Mutual insurance refers to insurance offered by an association whose members insure each other. In order to establish a mutual company, the association must have at least 100 members and at least ¥30 million in funds. An association must receive the license of the competent minister in order to conduct a mutual insurance business. A mutual company must also indicate in its business name both the principal type of insurance it offers and the fact that it is a "mutual company." In 1979 there were 16 mutual companies in the life insurance field and 2 in other insurance. In contrast, the number of profit-making insurance companies, which are JOINT-STOCK COMPANIES, was 4 in life insurance and 20 in other insurance.

KITAZAWA Masahiro

Mutual Security Agreement

Also referred to as Mutual Security Assistance (both abbreviated MSA). In either case, a general term used to describe US military and economic assistance to friendly nations after World War II. The United States enacted the Mutual Defense Assistance Act in 1949 and the Mutual Security Act in 1951, and this legislation has been amended and revised since then. On the basis of these acts, the United States has provided large amounts of military equipment and other forms of military assistance to cooperating nations, including Japan (see UNITED STATES–JAPAN MUTUAL DEFENSE ASSISTANCE AGREEMENT).

Richard B. FINN

Myōe (1173–1232)

Also known as Kōben. Buddhist monk of the KEGON SECT who criticized the PURE LAND BUDDHISM of HŌNEN and advocated a revival of Nara and Heian Buddhism in the early part of the Kamakura period (1185–1333). Although his early studies and lifelong concerns centered on Kegon and SHINGON SECT Buddhism, Myōe borrowed freely from all schools, with more attention to practical effectiveness than doctrinal purity. His career is notable for remarkable meditative experiences and rigorous defense of traditional methods for attaining such altered states of consciousness.

Born in Kii Province (now Wakayama Prefecture) in 1173, Myōe lost his parents by the age of eight and was placed in the care of his uncle, a Shingon priest at the temple JINGOJI on the outskirts of Kyōto. After completing his training under the famous monk MONGAKU, Myōe left Jingoji and thereafter lived alternately in seclusion in the mountains of Kii, where he enjoyed the support of local officials who were his maternal relatives, and at Kōzanji (in Kyōto), which the retired emperor GO-TOBA granted him in 1206 for the purpose of reviving the Kegon sect. In translating Kegon philosophy into religious experience, Myōe relied primarily on Shingon methods and on the ideas of Li Tongxuan (Li T'ung-hsüan; 635–730), a Chinese lay advocate of the Huayan (Hua-yen; J: Kegon) school who was noted for his penchant for practicality. Accordingly, Myōe devised several Kegon–Shingon religious practices to suit a variety of clerical and lay temperaments.

This willingness to accommodate diversity led Myōe to criticize Hōnen's extremely exclusive Pure Land approach to salvation. Upon reading Hōnen's *Senchaku hongan nembutsu shū* (Selection of the *Nembutsu* of the Original Vow; see SENCHAKUSHŪ), Myōe was infuriated at what he regarded as Hōnen's betrayal of Pure Land teachings. Myōe's often bombastic *Zaijarin* (Smashing the Cart of Error) concluded that Hōnen was no longer a Buddhist by virtue of his rejection of all other practices, including the fundamental aspiration for enlightenment, in favor of the recitation of Amida's name (NEMBUTSU) alone. To support his accusations, Myōe relied heavily on Chinese and Korean Pure Land masters and presented himself as a proponent and defender of the Pure Land tradition.

Myōe's sense of tradition extended all the way back to the figure of Śākyamuni, the historical Buddha. At Kōzanji, Myōe tried to recreate in meditation places significant in the life and legends of Śākyamuni. Twice he made detailed plans to travel to India, but was deterred by illness and by an oracle of the deity of the Kasuga Shrine delivered through his aunt. Unable to go to India, Myōe attempted to transport Śākyamuni to Japan through a meditative exercise, by which he transformed Buddhist statutes into living Buddhas with whom he then conversed. While his writings are filled with regret for having been born centuries after Śākyamuni in the age of the degenerate law (*mappō;* see ESCHATOLOGY), when the Buddhist teaching was thought to be at its end, he compensated for this misfortune by imagining himself to be in the Buddha's constant presence. To Myōe, the sutras were bridges to the person of Śākyamuni himself and not just to his teachings.

Myōe's writings include Buddhist technical treatises and commentaries, meditation manuals, poetry, rituals, criticism, aphorisms, and a journal of his dreams recorded over a 40-year period. Other significant works are *Sanji sambōrai shaku* (On Worshiping the Three Treasures Thrice Daily), *Kegon shuzen kanshō nyū gedatsumon gi* (The Meaning of the Kegon Practice of Meditation and Illumination to Enter the Gate of Liberation), and *Kegon bukkō zammai kan hihōzō* (The Secret Treasury of the Meditation on the Buddha's Radiance in Kegon).

■——Shōjun Bandō, "Myōe's Criticism of Hōnen's Doctrine," *Eastern Buddhist,* new series (May 1974). Ishii Kyōdō, "Gommitsu no shiso Kōben," *Taishō Daigaku gakuhō* (1928). Kamata Shigeo, "Nihon kegon ni okeru seitō to itan," *Shisō* (November 1973). Sakamoto Yukio, *Kegon kyōgaku no kenkyū* (1973). Tanaka Hisao, *Myōe* (1971). Yamada Shōzen, "Myōe no yume to *Yume no ki,*" *Kanazawa Bunko kenkyū* (1970). George J. TANABE, Jr.

Myōen (?–1199)

Buddhist sculptor active in Kyōto during the latter part of the Heian period (794–1185) and early part of the Kamakura period (1185–1333). Myōen is known primarily as an important member of the EN SCHOOL of sculpture, which flourished through the 13th century. Among his known masterpieces are the Five Wisdom Kings of Buddhism (1176; Go Dai Myōō) in the temple Daikakuji in Kyōto.

myōgakin

(literally, "offertory money"). Tax imposed during the Edo period (1600–1868) by the Tokugawa shogunate and domain administrations on merchants, artisans, fishermen, and other tradesmen who, unlike farmers, did not pay regular land taxes. Initially requisitioned as a one-time payment for the privilege of operating a trade or business, in time *myōgakin* became a fixed annual tax, much like the UNJŌ tax. Payment was usually in cash, although goods or labor could be substituted. *Myōgakin* were of two kinds, those assessed on individuals, such as *sake* or soy sauce brewers and owners of inns or pawnshops, and those levied on KABUNAKAMA, or merchant monopoly associations. *Myōgakin* collected from the *kabunakama* of Edo (now Tōkyō) and Ōsaka became an important source of shogunate revenue.

Myōgisan

Mountain in western Gumma Prefecture, central Honshū. It has three peaks, Kondōzan, Hakuunzan, and Kinkeizan. Weathering and erosion have created odd-shaped rock formations and cliffs. The beautiful autumn foliage is a tourist attraction. Myōgi Shrine, dedicated to the legendary hero, Prince YAMATOTAKERU, is located here. It is part of the Myōgi–Arafune–Saku Kōgen Quasi-National Park. The highest peak is Kondōzan (1,104 m; 3,621 ft).

Myōjinshō

Underwater volcano about 130 km (80.7 mi) south of the island of HACHIJŌJIMA in the Izu Islands south of the Izu Peninsula off central Honshū. Active from 1928 with periodic eruptions. In September 1952 an observation boat was caught in an eruption and sank; there were no survivors.

myōji taitō

(literally, "surname and girded sword"). The official practice in the Edo period (1600–1868) of restricting the use of a surname (*myōji*) and sword-bearing (*taitō*) to families of *samurai (bushi)* and noble *(kuge)* status. During the Heian period (794–1185) surnames had gradually spread beyond the aristocracy, and they were widely adopted by warriors from the 12th to 16th centuries. After 1603 the TOKUGAWA SHOGUNATE sought to halt further diffusion of sword carrying and surname usage, although it did grant the privilege to a few commoners (for one generation, or in perpetuity) as a reward for meritorious service, most commonly as local administrators or official merchants. This privilege was not accompanied by a change in official status. Some samurai surrendered their *bushi* status, giving up the right to surname and sword, and the shogunate and *daimyō* occasionally stripped persons of *bushi* status and emoluments by official decree (KAIEKI). See also SWORD HUNT. Conrad TOTMAN

Myōjō

(Bright Star; also translated as Morning Star; Evening Star). Innovative and influential literary journal launched in 1900 by YOSANO TEKKAN as the organ of the Shinshisha (New Poetry Society), the society he founded in November 1899. It appeared in three separate series with long lapses in between. The first series was published from April 1900 to November 1908 and is regarded as the most important. Known for its sensual romanticism, epitomized by the poetry of Tekkan's wife YOSANO AKIKO, *Myōjō* became one of the most widely influential poetry magazines of the period and cultivated the talent of numerous young poets who firmly established modern poetry (see LITERATURE: modern poetry) in the Taishō period (1912–26). Members included Akiko, HAGIWARA SAKUTARŌ, ISHIKAWA TAKUBOKU, IWANO HŌMEI, KITAHARA HAKUSHŪ, KINOSHITA MOKUTARŌ, and SATŌ HARUO. Advisers were MORI ŌGAI, UEDA BIN, and BABA KOCHŌ. Though the first five numbers were printed newspaper-style, *Myōjō* quickly evolved into a sophisticated, sumptuously laid-out journal stressing the visual arts, TANKA, and Western-style poetry. Together with ARARAGI, the organ of the Negishi Tanka Society founded by MASAOKA SHIKI, it was a prime force in the *tanka* revival movement. The *Myōjō* poets were criticized for excessively "modernizing" traditional poetic forms, but their innovative brilliance was of formative influence in the development of modern Japanese poetry. After internal dissension caused *Myōjō* to cease publication, its members helped found SUBARU, a poetry journal which carried on the romantic tradition. *Myōjō* was later revived from 1921 to 1927 and again from 1947 to 1949, but no literary significance is attached to the latter two series. Theodore W. GOOSSEN

Myōkensan

Hill in northern Ōsaka Prefecture, central Honshū; a monadnock on the heaved-up peneplain. On the summit is Myōkendō, a temple of the NICHIREN SECT of Buddhism. Height: 662 m (2,171 ft).

myōkōnin

(Ch: *miaohaoren* or *miao-hao-jen*). One of the terms used by the Chinese Pure Land monk Shandao (Shan-tao; J: Zendō; 613–681) in the work known in Japanese as *Kangyōsho* (a commentary on the

Amitāyurdhyāna-sūtra) to praise those who are known for their devotional practice of recitation of AMIDA's name (J: NEMBUTSU). In the JŌDO SHIN SECT it has come to indicate the lay *nembutsu* practitioner, usually an illiterate, who has attained faith in Amida Buddha and lives his life manifesting deep gratitude for his birth in the Pure Land. Biographies of such people have been published in the *Myōkōninden*, the first collection of which was published in 1842. The profound experiential understanding of the workings of Amida displayed by a number of these *myōkōnin* has led such modern thinkers as Daisetz T. SUZUKI to emphasize the importance of their position in Japanese religious history. *Robert RHODES*

Myōkōsan

Volcano in the Fuji Volcanic Zone, southwestern Niigata Prefecture, central Honshū; the highest peak in the Myōkō Volcanic Group. It is the central cone of a double volcano, in the form of a lava dome. The foot of the mountain forms a wide plain and provides excellent skiing grounds; in the summer it is a resort area. Hot springs such as Akakura, Tsubame, and Myōkō are nearby. It is part of Jōshin'etsu Kōgen National Park. Height: 2,446 m (8,023 ft).

myōō

(Skt: *vidyārāja;* kings of light or wisdom). The third-ranking category in Japanese Buddhist iconography, the first two being NYORAI (Buddhas) and *bosatsu* (BODHISATTVAS) and the fourth, TEMBU (devas). *Myōō* were originally non-Buddhist Hindu deities who were adopted into the pantheon of ESOTERIC BUDDHISM. They are considered to be incarnations of the cosmic Buddha who proselytize and save obdurate nonbelievers with the power of sacred words (*vidyā,* which in this context means MANTRA or *dhāraṇī*). Most of them are represented with fierce visages: hair aflame, face contorted, and weapons in hand, they trample evil figures. The deities have been especially popular in Japan, chiefly since the introduction of esoteric Buddhist traditions in the 9th century, and numerous artistic representations are extant. The best known of the *myōō* are: Fudō Myōō (Skt: Acalanātha), Gōzanze Myōō (Trailokyaviṇaya), Gundari Myōō (Kuṇḍalī), Daiitoku Myōō (Yamāntaka), Kongōyasha Myōō (Vajrayakṣa), Aizen Myōō (Rāgarāja), and Kujaku Myōō (Mayūrāsana). The last, represented sitting on a golden peacock, expresses compassion, unlike the other fearful *myōō.* The first five are usually grouped together as the Go Dai Myōō (Five Wisdom Kings), as exemplified in the statuary at the temple TŌJI in Kyōto. The most popular of the *myōō* is Fudō; the temple Shinshōji (Naritasan) in Chiba Prefecture is the center of the Fudō cult. The Fudō images at the temples Onjōji (MIIDERA), Shōren'in in Kyōto, and Myōōin at KŌYASAN are respectively known as the Ki (Yellow), Ao (Blue), and Aka (Red) Fudō. *TSUCHIDA Tomoaki*

Myōshinji

Head temple of the Myōshinji branch of the RINZAI SECT of Buddhism, located in Ukyō Ward, Kyōto. Myōshinji was founded in 1337 by the retired emperor Hanazono (r 1308–18), who practiced Zen under the distinguished master Shūhō Myōchō (see SŌHŌ MYŌCHŌ), popularly known as Daitō Kokushi. Hanazono converted one of his private residences into a temple, subsequently designated Myōshinji, and invited Myōchō's eminent disciple Kanzan Egen (1277–1360) to serve as its first abbot. Hanazono retired to a newly constructed subtemple within the Myōshinji precincts. Although the temple prospered for a while, it eventually came under the control of the powerful NANZENJI and as a result entered a period of decline. Myōshinji regained its independence through the efforts of its seventh abbot, Nippō Sōshun (1368–1448), who refurbished its buildings and made it a center for Zen practice. Myōshinji was completely destroyed in the course of the Ōnin War (1467–77), but was restored through the heroic efforts of its ninth abbot, Sekkō Sōjin (1408–86), who enlisted the support of Emperor Go-Tsuchimikado (r 1464–1500). The foundation for the subsequent emergence of the temple as the major branch of Rinzai Zen was laid by the four major disciples of Sōjin. Myōshinji contains 57 subtemples and chapels, many of which are attached to tombs of *daimyō* patrons, and has 3,444 affiliated temples. The Myōshinji complex is noted for its many art objects, its superb gardens, and its temple bell, the oldest in Japan. *Stanley WEINSTEIN*

myōshu

Local landholders from about the 10th century through the 16th century, generally under the private estate system (see SHŌEN). Like the "rice-field masters" *(tato)* of the preceding centuries, they were designated by the local estate proprietors or managers (RYŌSHU) to control the parcels of land that made up the estates. By the 10th century, these land parcels had become the equivalent of private holdings and were called name fields *(myōden).* The system of name fields held by *myōshu* eventually appeared in the remaining public lands *(kokugaryō)* as well. From around the 12th to the 13th century, many less powerful cultivators also came to gain land privileges and increased independence and were known as new *myōshu* (shimmyō), in contrast to the original *myōshu* (hommyō). From the 14th century on, the term *myōshu* came to be broadly applied to any person or even religious institution that held *myōshu shiki,* i.e., the right to receive income from *myōden.*

The *myōshu* living on their lands were classed as commoners *(shomin)* but they often held considerable power, although of course their status varied with the times and the locale. Especially in regions further from central government control, they were responsible for the taxes and labor services of all those on their lands, including not only their own families but also tenants and subordinate families (see GENIN). They were often armed and responsible for military defense as well. Some with "*samurai* equivalent status" *(samuraibun)* eventually came to be called JIZAMURAI, i.e., local landholding warriors. As the estate system eroded, powerful landholders tended to become either armed vassals of provincial barons (KOKUJIN) and of emerging DAIMYŌ, or headmen (OTONA) of autonomous groups of cultivators (SŌ). It should be mentioned that the characters used to write *myōshu* are read *nanushi* when referring to village headmen of the Edo period (1600–1868; see SHŌYA).

mystery stories

Although the popular literature and drama of the Edo period (1600–1868) featured both outlaws and the supernatural, the true mystery or detective story *(suiri shōsetsu)* appeared in Japan only in the Meiji period (1868–1912), when the tradition started by Edgar Allen Poe was imported from abroad.

Early in the Meiji period, court trial novels and accounts of criminal investigations were already being introduced from the West to Japan, where they appeared alongside such Edo-style pieces as Kawatake MOKUAMI's outlaw plays and KANAGAKI ROBUN's tales of evil women. In 1887 translations were published of Anna Katherine Green's *XYZ* and Poe's "The Murders in the Rue Morgue." In the following year, KUROIWA RUIKŌ (1862–1920) became active as a translator and went on to publish over 30 works, which received phenomenal acclaim as newspaper serials. Of these translations, the works of Fortuné Castille du Boisgobey were the most numerous, followed by those of Emile Gaboriau, Wilkie Collins, and Anna Katherine Green. Kuroiwa Ruikō and other translators of that day adapted their works quite freely to make them more acceptable to their Japanese readers. Arthur Conan Doyle's *Adventures of Sherlock Holmes* (1891) was introduced to Japan in 1899. In addition, the works of William Tufnell de Queux, Richard Austin Freeman, Maurice Leblanc, Gaston Leroux, and others were well received. As for original writing, Ruikō's "Muzan" (1889) became a model for later short stories of the riddle-solving type. The writers of the KEN'YŪSHA group produced a number of imitative works aimed at a popular audience, but these were soon overtaken in popularity by a new genre that purported to be true accounts of criminal investigations. From about 1918, writers like TANIZAKI JUN'ICHIRŌ and SATŌ HARUO were publishing mysteries and bizarre stories; however, they were exploring the world of romanticism and aestheticism out of dissatisfaction with the "realistic" fiction of the day, and were not necessarily mystery writers per se.

The mystery magazine *Shin seinen,* which was first published in 1920, made a special effort to promote mystery stories from abroad. Inspired by these imported works, EDOGAWA RAMPO published his own "Nisen dōka" in 1923. Thereafter, time and time again, he demonstrated his originality and ingenuity in the categories of both orthodox mystery story and bizarre fantasy, becoming one of Japan's most celebrated writers in the genre. After his success, the number of Japanese writers willing to attempt original works increased, and mystery writing became an established profession, with its own literary circles and with *Shin seinen* as the most important medium of publication. Soon mystery writers separated into two groups: an orthodox group, which emphasized logic, and an innovative group, which encompassed the bizarre, fantasy, crime, mental perversion, adventure, and science fiction. Among the members of the former group were Edogawa Rampo, Kōga Saburō, Tsunoda Kikuo, HIRABAYASHI HATSUNOSUKE, and Hamao Shirō; among the latter were Kozakai Fuboku, Ōshita Udaru, Mizutani Jun, YOKOMIZO SEISHI, Jō Masayuki, Yumeno Kyūsaku, and Unno Jūza. When mystery novels began to be carried in magazines for the general public, they took on more and more the character of thrillers, and they could not get rid of an aura of eroticism. Writers such as OGURI MUSHITARŌ, Kigi Takatarō, and HISAO JŪRAN, who made their debut around 1933, tried to raise literary standards. As World War II approached, mystery stories were suppressed, and writers could produce only spy and adventure stories and science fiction.

With the end of World War II, released from restraints placed on their writing and still reflecting on wartime experiences, Japanese mystery writers were seized with an intense desire to write long stories built around logic. Yokomizo Seishi's *Honjin satsujin jiken* (1946), SAKAGUCHI ANGO's *Furenzoku satsujin jiken* (1947–48), Tsunoda Kikuo's *Takagike no sangeki* (1947), and Takagi Akimitsu's *Shisei satsujin jiken* (1948) competed with each other in an attempt to reach the level of works from abroad. Once again, works from other countries were allowed in, and an influx of new literary styles, led by the "hard-boiled" school, began to add variety to the Japanese mystery story. In addition to the above-mentioned writers, Kayama Shigeru, Yamada Fūtarō, Ōtsubo Sunao, Shimada Kazuo, Hikage Jōkichi, and Asuka Takashi made their appeaance.

Writers of the orthodox school who rejected sensationalism and emphasized logic continued to vie with each other in contriving new tricks. As a result, they came to neglect the human side, and readers eventually grew tired of the so-called great detectives who solved mysteries only for the sake of the mystery. With his *Ten to sen* (1957–58; tr *Points and Lines,* 1970) and *Me no kabe* (1957), MATSUMOTO SEICHŌ established a style that had both social and human interest, and he was followed by others like Arima Yorichika, MINAKAMI TSUTOMU, KUROIWA JŪGO, and KAJIYAMA TOSHIYUKI. These writers enlarged the mystery-reading audience, but the novels themselves departed from the intrigue of mystery solving and veered toward social criticism. The number of orthodox mystery novels rapidly declined. A reaction set in when the works of Yokomizo Seishi, which combined logical structure with romantic coloration, were once again welcomed and caused a boom by selling more than four million copies in paperback. Other popular writers include Ayukawa Tetsuya, Niki Etsuko, Tsuchiya Takao, Sasazawa Saho, and Sano Yō of the orthodox school; among those who write in a variety of styles are Takigawa Kyō, YŪKI SHŌJI, Chin Shunshin (Ch: Chen Shunchen or Ch'en Shun-ch'en), and Miyoshi Tōru. Morimura Seiichi and other newer writers have attempted to combine orthodox detective fiction with social consciousness.

Science fiction, which had once been included in the mystery genre, became a genre itself, while the mystery genre has had a tendency to diversify into such special types as spy stories, industry and corporation stories, court trials, the bizarre, and the fantastic. ■——Edogawa Rampo, *Tantei shōsetsu yonjūnen* (1961). Nakajima Kawatarō, *Nihon suiri shōsetsu shi* (1964).

NAKAJIMA Kawatarō

mythology

Japanese mythology is a composite of native themes committed to writing in the early 8th century and continental imports mainly under the aegis of Buddhism and Taoism. Generally speaking, Japanese myths are of a rather gentle nature. There is a trickster deity, but no divinity embodies evil, nor is there much confrontation, compromise being the touchstone of Japanese mythology.

THE MYTHS OF THE KOJIKI AND NIHON SHOKI

The main extant sources for early Japanese myths are the KOJIKI, or "Records of Ancient Matters," and the NIHON SHOKI (also known as *Nihongi*), or "Chronicle of Japan," both appearing in the first quarter of the 8th century. They represent the *terminus ad quem* of what was apparently a long oral tradition. Other sources are the KOGO SHŪI (Gleanings from Ancient Stories), which represents a protest written by Imbe no Hironari against a rival family and includes legends preserved in the IMBE FAMILY; the FUDOKI (provincial gazetteers), of which the most important, and the only complete one, is the *Izumo fudoki;* the *Shoku nihongi* (Chronicles of Japan, Continued); the 8th-century collection of poetry, MAN'YŌSHŪ (Col-

lection for Ten Thousand Generations or Collection of Ten Thousand Leaves); and the *norito,* religious liturgies, collected at the beginning of the 10th century in the ENGI SHIKI (Procedures of the Engi Era).

The Cycles——A number of hermeneutical problems face the student of Japanese mythology. Who compiled the myths and to what end? How does one correlate the analyses of the myths with, for example, historical and archaeological evidence? It also seems quite impossible to establish a single, coherent story of the origin of the cosmos, of which there are several versions.

There are two major cycles, or recurring successions of events, to consider when reading the myths that are treated in the *Kojiki* and the *Nihongi.* The first is the YAMATO cycle, tracing the divine origin of Japan and its rulers to AMATERASU ŌMIKAMI, the sun goddess, the Heavenly Illuminating One. The Izumo cycle, on the other hand, holds SUSANOO NO MIKOTO, the brother of Amaterasu, as its principal character. There is a third cycle, if we are to consider the later chapters of the chronicles, in which the two earlier cycles are unified by succeeding generations.

The Yamato Cycle——In Takamagahara, the High Plain of Heaven, there came into existence three independent deities: Ame no Minakanushi no Kami (Heavenly Center Lord), Takamimusubi no Kami (High Generative Force Deity), and Kamimusubi no Kami (Divine Generative Force Deity). Divine Generative Force is the feminine counterpart of High Generative Force, and they have children.

The land is young and resembles floating oil, or an egg, as it drifts about. Two divinities in the form of reed shoots sprout up and with the above deities form the so-called Separate Heavenly Deities, who are then followed by six generations of divinities. The account of the divinities listed up to this point is probably not based on the popular tradition but is doubtless the product of literati, who wished to lend a certain elegance to the native chronicle.

Izanagi and Izanami——The Japanese account actually begins with the birth of the seventh generation of deities in the form of Izanagi (the Male Who Invites) and Izanami (the Female Who Invites). They are bidden by the Heavenly Deities to solidify the drifting land and are given a Heavenly Jeweled Spear. Standing on the Heavenly Floating Bridge (Ama no ukihashi), they plunge the spear into the brine below them and stir it with a churning sound; as they lift it out, the drops falling from its tip coagulate to form the Self-Curdling Island (Onogoro).

Descending to the island, they erect a pillar and a great palace. Izanagi inquires about his sister's body, and she replies that, though formed, in one place it is insufficiently so. He replies that his own is in one place formed in excess and proposes to insert that part into the counterpart of his sister in order to produce land. Izanami agrees, and her brother proposes that they walk around the pillar and, on meeting, have sexual intercourse. This they do, but Izanami cries out in delight on meeting her brother.

Izanagi, on reflection, observes that it is not fitting in such circumstances for the woman to speak first. Nevertheless, they have intercourse, and the result is a deformed leech-child, which they discard by sending it off in a boat of reeds. (One version notes that the couple are uninstructed in the art of intercourse until they see a pair of wagtails in action.) The pillar in this sequence is often considered a phallus, perhaps also a symbol of fecundity not unlike the European maypole expressing the vital powers of a tree. The leech-child is a monstrosity, the result of improper marital procedure. After the leech-child the deities give birth to the Island of Awa, also considered a failure, and neither of the two are considered the deities' rightful descendants.

Izanagi and Izanami go back up to heaven and seek the counsel of the Heavenly Deities, who perform a divination. The deities point out the impropriety of the female's speaking first after the circumambulation of the pillar. The two deities walk around it again, this time with the male speaking first. They then produce a number of islands and other deities—35 in all, including the fire deity. In giving birth to the fire deity, Izanami is badly burned and lies down in pain. (This episode may be a mythological reference to the practice of burning the parturition hut after birth.) From her vomit, feces, and urine come other deities, until at last she dies. Izanagi is disconsolate, weeping as he crawls about her feet and her head; from his tears another deity comes into existence. He buries his wife on Mt. Hiba in Izumo Province or in Arima in Kumano Province.

Izanagi unsheathes the sword 10 spans long worn at his side and beheads the fire god who has caused his wife's death. From the blood on the sword three deities come into existence and from the sword guard, three more. From the head, chest, belly, genitals, left and right hands and feet other divinities are born.

The Land of Yomi——Desiring to see his wife, Izanagi goes off to find her in Yomi, the land of the dead. Izanagi reproaches her for their uncompleted work in creating land and implores her to return with him. She promises to request permission of the gods of Yomi, although she is dubious, for she has been polluted by eating impure food there. She is gone so long that the impatient Izanagi, unable to wait for her return, enters the palace where she lives. Lighting a fire with a tooth of his comb, he sees his wife's corpse teeming with maggots.

Horrified, Izanagi flees. His wife, furious at being seen in her present disgusting state, sends the hags of hell (shikome) after him. To distract them Izanagi undoes the vine holding up one side of his hair and flings it down. Immediately it bears grapes that the hags stop to devour. But they set out again in pursuit, and he then tosses down the comb he wears in his right hair knot. From it bamboo sprouts spring up. Again the hags stop to eat them. Then his wife sends a horde of Yomi braves after him, but he evades them too, brandishing his 10-span sword. At length he arrives at the Yomo Pass, where he finds three peaches; and when he flings them at his pursuers, they turn and flee.

Finally, as his wife joins the pursuit, he closes the pass with a great boulder, and the two, standing facing each other on either side, divorce. Izanami warns her husband that if he carries out the separation, each day she will strangle 1,000 persons in his land. Izanagi replies that under such circumstances he will cause 1,500 children to be born each day.

Birth of Amaterasu and Susanoo——Polluted by his contact with the land of Yomi, Izanagi purifies himself in a river. From his belongings and clothes 12 deities come into existence. The upper stream being too fast and the lower too slow, he bathes in the middle course. He washes out his left eye, and Amaterasu Ōmikami is born. From his right eye comes the moon deity, Tsukuyomi no Mikoto, and from his nose, Susanoo no Mikoto, or the Valiant, Intrepid Raging Male (Takehaya Susanoo). (The account recalls the Chinese Pangu [P'an-ku], who in dying produced the sun and moon from his left and right eyes.) Susanoo is to become the principal character in much of what follows, and he is surely the most clearly delineated of the often shadowy gods. His personality is complex; he has been variously identified as the trickster, a storm god, and a cultural hero, among others. He is considered a god of Izumo; and if he is here sired by the Yamato god Izanagi, the event, doubtless of later origin, permits the deity to fit into the official Yamato account. (A storm god, he is naturally born from his father's windy nose.)

Izanagi considers the three last-born deities as noble children. Giving Amaterasu his necklace, he bestows on her the mission of ruling the High Plain of Heaven. Tsukuyomi governs the realm of night. Susanoo is to rule the oceans, but does not obey his father's exhortations. He weeps and wails so much that the mountains wither and the rivers and seas dry up, causing malevolent deities to spring forth. Izanagi inquires as to the reasons for such behavior, and his son tells him that he wishes to visit his mother in the netherworld. Enraged, Izanagi expels him.

The Feuding of Amaterasu and Susanoo——Before departing, Susanoo goes up to heaven to take leave of his sister, making the rivers roar and the mountains tremble. Amaterasu is startled and skeptical about her brother's intentions, fearful he may usurp her lands. Doing up her hair like a man, with two knots on either side of her head, putting on two great quivers and a great arm-guard, and stamping her feet so that her legs sink into the earth up to her thighs, she awaits him. Susanoo reassures her, telling of his banishment by Izanagi; but his sister asks how she can be sure of his intentions. He proposes that they produce children together and judge his design by their nature. Amaterasu agrees, and breaking Susanoo's 10-span sword into three pieces, she chews them, spits them out, and produces three female deities. Susanoo chews the long string of jewels Amaterasu wears in her hair, and spitting them out, produces five male children. Amaterasu insists they are hers, since they come from her possessions.

Nevertheless, Susanoo claims victory, for lovely maidens are produced from his possessions, and he has thus demonstrated the purity of his intentions. Raging with victory, he runs amok, breaking the ridges between the rice paddies, filling in the water conduits, and smearing excrement in his sister's palace. Tolerant Amaterasu excuses him on grounds of drunkenness. But he goes too far when he flings a dappled pony he has skinned ("backward," perhaps a

kind of black magic) into the sacred weaving hall, and a weaver whose genitals are struck by a shuttle is killed.

Disappearance of the Sun——Amaterasu retires to the heavenly rock cave, and in the High Plain of Heaven all is dark. In consternation the gods assemble. They cause cocks to be gathered and make them crow. (Cocks summon the dawn, and in various cultures their crowing is associated with resurrection of the dead.) They commission the creation of a mirror, which they hang in a tree, and make various offerings.

At this point the goddess Uzume (Amenouzume no Mikoto) binds up her sleeves, dons a headband, and holding sasa (dwarf bamboo) leaves in her hands, overturns a bucket before the heavenly cave and stamps on it. Becoming divinely possessed, she exposes her breasts and lowers her skirt to reveal her genitals. (The exposure of the genitals to drive away evil spirits is not uncommon in several cultures.) The deities are delighted with the display, and their laughter rocks the High Plain of Heaven. Amaterasu, considering it strange that the gods are laughing when all is dark, inquires about the reason. Uzume tells her that the deities are so merry because there is among them a divinity superior to her, and at this point the mirror is exposed to her. Amaterasu, leaving the cave, approaches the mirror, and as she does so, two hidden divinities grasp her hands and prevent her return. Light is again restored to the High Plain of Heaven, and the gods decide to fine Susanoo 1,000 tables of gifts. They exorcise him by cutting off his beard, fingernails, and toenails, and he is again expelled.

The Izumo Cycle——Banished, Susanoo descends to Izumo on the west coast of the main island and sees a chopstick floating down a stream. Assuming there are people living upstream, he goes in search of them and finds an old couple weeping on either side of their daughter. The old man tells Susanoo that an eight-tailed dragon has yearly devoured his eight daughters and is due again. The terrifying creature has moss and cypress and cryptomeria trees growing on its back and a belly gory with blood. The old couple agree to give their daughter to Susanoo, who transforms her into a comb he inserts into his hair. He orders that a special wine be brewed and a fence with eight apertures be constructed. A barrel filled with the liquor is placed on a platform at each of the openings. The dragon appears and with his eight heads drinks from the eight barrels and falls into a drunken sleep. Susanoo draws his 10-span sword and slays the beast; but when his blade sinks into the middle tail it breaks, and he discovers a great sword, which he removes. Considering the weapon extraordinary, he presents it to his sister Amaterasu. This is the famous sword later known as Kusanagi (Grass Mower). It was afterwards given by Amaterasu to her grandson Emperor Ninigi, who was sent down to rule the land, and it eventually became one of the three IMPERIAL REGALIA.

Ōkuninushi no Mikoto and the Hare of Inaba——Susanoo builds a palace in Izumo and begins procreation. His sixth-generation descendant is Ōkuninushi no Mikoto (Master of the Great Land), hero of a number of legends. Ōkuninushi has many brothers, all of whom wish to marry Princess Yakami of Inaba, to whose land they proceed, taking Ōkuninushi along to carry their luggage. On the way they come across a rabbit stripped of its fur and lying by the roadside. They maliciously advise the poor creature to bathe in salt water and then to lie on a mountaintop and let the wind dry him off. This the rabbit does. The skin of his whole body cracks as it dries, and the animal is reduced to tears of pain. In response to Ōkuninushi's questions, it reveals the cause of its present predicament. Stranded on the isle of Oki, the rabbit had wished to cross to land, but there was no way. He persuaded a crocodile to prove its family's numerical superiority by placing its members head to tail from the island to the mainland. The rabbit offered to take the count by running over their backs. As he skipped over the last crocodile he revealed his deceit, and the duped reptile, seizing him, stripped off his fur. He then tells Ōkuninushi what the latter's brothers had advised. Ōkuninushi instructs the rabbit to wash himself in fresh water and then to roll in the pollen of gama (cattail) grass. He does so and is cured. The rabbit foresees that Ōkuninushi's brothers will never win the Princess Yakami. She, indeed, breaks with them and announces her decision to marry Ōkuninushi.

The Trials of Ōkuninushi——Infuriated and determined to kill Ōkuninushi, the brothers propose a boar hunt on Mt. Tema. They will drive the boar down the mountain into his waiting arms. If he does not catch it, they warn, it will kill him. They heat a great rock resembling a boar and roll it down the mountainside, and in seizing it Ōkuninushi is burned to death. But his mother goes up to heaven and intercedes with Kamimusubi, who dispatches Ark-shell Princess and Clam Princess to restore him to life. The former pulverizes her shell, and the latter mixes the triturate with water and rubs it on him.

Ōkuninushi changes into a beautiful young man, but his deceitful brothers lead him into the mountains, where they cut down a tree, insert a wedge into it, and force him inside the slit. The wedge is removed and Ōkuninushi is crushed to death. He is revived by his mother, who warns him to flee. His brothers catch him, but as they are adjusting their arrows, he slips through the fork of a tree and escapes.

Ōkuninushi goes to visit Susanoo in the netherworld; when he arrives at the palace the latter's daughter Suseri Hime comes out to greet him. It is love at first sight. Suseri Hime announces to her father the arrival of a beautiful deity. Susanoo with paternal prejudice calls him the Ugly Male of the Reed Plains, invites him in, and makes him sleep in a roomful of snakes. Suseri Hime gives Ōkuninushi a snake-repelling scarf, which he is to wave three times should the serpents attack him. He waves the scarf, the snakes flee, and the night passes peacefully.

The next night Susanoo installs Ōkuninushi in a room with centipedes and bees. Again Suseri Hime gives him an appropriate scarf and he emerges unscathed. Then Susanoo shoots an arrow that makes a humming sound as it flies and bids Ōkuninushi to fetch it. When the latter goes out into the field to do so, Susanoo lights a fire around the perimeter. But Ōkuninushi is saved by a mouse who indicates to him an underground cavern where he can take refuge. Ōkuninushi stamps his foot on the ground, which gives way, and he falls into a hole, where he waits in safety until the fire passes over. The mouse comes out and presents Ōkuninushi with the humming arrow.

Going out into the plain, Susanoo is surprised when Ōkuninushi appears and presents him with the arrow. Susanoo invites him into the palace and sets him to picking the lice from his head, on which there are also many centipedes. Suseri Hime gives him some *muku* nuts and red clay, which he chews and spits out. Susanoo, assuming that Ōkuninushi is biting and expectorating centipedes, is calmed and falls asleep.

Ōkuninushi ties Susanoo's hair to the rafters and blocks the door with a boulder. He flees with Suseri Hime on his back, taking with him Susanoo's sword, bow and arrow, and heavenly-speaking cither. In his flight the instrument brushes against a tree, and the sound awakens Susanoo, who, rising with a start, brings his palace down around him. Susanoo pursues them as far as the Pass of Yomo, where he shouts after them to use the weapons they have taken to subdue Ōkuninushi's rambunctious brothers. Ōkuninushi makes Suseri Hime his principal wife, an arrangement scarcely to the liking of Yakami, who returns to her home, leaving the child she has borne in the fork of a tree.

The Tiny Deity —— Ōkuninushi next goes to Cape Miho, in Izumo, where he sees sailing over the waves a small deity dressed in the skin of a wagtail. The deity will not reply when asked his name, nor does anyone know it. The wise divinity of rice paddies is called, and he identifies the god as Sukunahikona no Mikoto (also called Sukunabikona no Kami), who is perhaps another aspect of Ōkuninushi himself and a child of Kamimusubi. (The latter identifies him as one of his children who had previously slipped away.) Together the small deity and Ōkuninushi create land. Then Sukunahikona climbs a millet stalk, which, rebounding, flips him off into the Eternal Land (Toko Yo). Ōkuninushi despairs of creating land by himself, but then another deity arrives and offers his help.

Amaterasu's Messengers —— Amaterasu orders one of the sons she bore in her contest with Susanoo to descend and rule the land, which from the Floating Bridge of Heaven seems in an uproar. Soon another son is also dispatched to help, and this one descends but does not return for three years. Then Takamimusubi and Amaterasu, after consultation with the other Heavenly Deities, send Ame no Waka Hiko, with the deer-slaying bow and feathered arrows, but he plots to obtain land for himself and does not return for eight years. The gods then entrust to the pheasant Nakime the mission of finding out why the third messenger has been gone for eight whole years. It perches in a tree outside the messenger's door and transmits the message. The messenger finds all this ominous and shoots the pheasant, but the arrow passes through its breast and flies up backwards to Amaterasu and Takamimusubi. The latter observes that there is blood on the arrow's feathers. He throws it back down, and the arrow hits the messenger and kills him. At the messenger's funeral a curious event occurs: his friend and look-alike arrives, and the dead god's parents, mistaking him for their son, cling to him,

crying out that their child is still alive. The enraged friend cuts down the funeral house and kicks it away.

Next, two deities are dispatched to inquire of Ōkuninushi what he intends to do with the land. After various incidents, his sons agree to yield the land to the offspring of the Heavenly Dieties.

Ninigi no Mikoto —— Amaterasu and Takamimusubi bid their heir descend to the Central Land of the Reed Plains (Japan) and rule, but from his union with the daughter of Takakimimusuki a child is born who takes on his mission. This child is Ninigi no Mikoto. Just as he is about to descend, a radiance fills the High Plain of Heaven; it turns out to be the earthly deity Sarudahiko no Mikoto, who will serve as Ninigi's guide. Ninigi descends to earth bearing the three imperial regalia: curved beads *(magatama),* the mirror used to lure his grandmother from the rock cave, and the sword Kusanagi. He descends to the peak of Mt. Takachiho of Himuka in Tsukushi, (Kyūshū), where he builds a palace. His guide, Sarudahiko, is caught by a shellfish during a fishing expedition. Uzume (Amenouzume no Mikoto), after accompanying him back to heaven, returns to earth, gathers together all the fish, and asks if they are willing to serve the Heavenly Deities. Only the sea slug demurs, and Uzume slits his mouth with a dagger. The gash remains to this day.

Marriage of Ninigi —— Ninigi requests the hand of Konohanasakuya Hime (Blossoms-of-the-trees Blooming Princess), and her father in his joy also accords him the hand of her elder sister. The latter is ugly, and Ninigi sends her back, keeping only the Blooming Princess, with whom he has intercourse for one night. The father, shamed at having his elder daughter returned, explains that the life of the heavenly progeny would have been eternal, but now their life will henceforth be as brief as the blossoming of the trees. It so happens that the Blooming Princess is with child, but, as the couple had intercourse for only one night, Ninigi cannot believe it is his. The princess swears that its survival of an ordeal by fire will be proof. When she is about to deliver, she sets fire to the parturition hut, but the three children born are untouched by the flames.

The Luck of the Sea and the Luck of the Mountains —— Hoderi no Mikoto (a son of Ninigi) possessed the luck of the sea; his younger brother, Hoori no Mikoto (also known as Hikohohodemi no Mikoto), that of the mountain. The latter proposes that they exchange their luck, a request he repeats three times. At first his brother refuses, but at last he reluctantly consents. When Hoori fishes, however, not only does he catch no fish, he even loses his fishhook in the sea. His elder brother asks for it back, but Hoori, having lost it, is unable to comply. He breaks up his sword and makes 500 hooks, then 1,000, but his brother refuses to accept them, steadfastly demanding the original.

As Hoori laments by the seashore, a deity comes to counsel him. He puts Hoori in a boat and pushes him out to sea. After a time Hoori arrives at the sea deity Watatsumi's palace, which ostensibly is made of fish scales. By the gate stands a tree, which he climbs. A serving maid who comes to draw water sees the young man. He requests water, which she pours into a cup. Instead of drinking, however, he puts a jewel in his mouth and spits it into the goblet. It adheres to the vessel, which the maid presents to her mistress. The latter goes out to the gate to see the young man for herself and at once falls in love. The two young people are married. The father throws a great feast, and Hoori lives happily in the watery realm for three years.

Questioned about the reasons for his sighing one day, Hoori tells the sea deity about the fishhook. Watatsumi gathers the fishes of the sea together and asks who has taken the hook. They all answer that the sea bream has complained of not being able to eat because of a bone in its throat. Sure enough, the fishhook is there. Watatsumi returns it to Hoori after putting a curse on it. He advises Hoori to make a rice paddy on low ground if his brother makes one on high ground, and vice versa. Since the sea deity controls water, he promises that the elder brother will be destitute within three years. If his brother attacks him, Hoori is to use the tide-raising jewel that he is given by the sea deity to drown him, and if the brother in anguish pleads for his life, Hoori is to save him with the tide-ebbing jewel. A crocodile escorts Hoori home, giving him a dagger as it returns to the sea. Hoori does as he was instructed and causes such anguish to his elder brother that the latter gives in.

At this time the sea deity's daughter arrives on land, for she is about to give birth, and considers it unfitting for the child of Heavenly Deities to be born in the ocean. She warns her husband not to look at her, because she must revert to her original form at delivery. But, his curiosity piqued, he looks in secret and sees her turning into a great crocodile. His wife is ashamed when she learns that she was observed. Leaving her child behind, she returns to the sea, but despite her bitterness, sends a younger sister to nurse her offspring. The child, when he grows up, takes his aunt as wife and they have four children, one of whom returns to the ocean, the realm of his mother.

OTHER LEGENDS AND MYTHS

Among local legends one of the most important is that of the so-called land-pulling (kunibiki). The ruler of Izumo (this legend does not occur in the Yamato cycle), Ōmitsunu, a grandson of Susanoo, wishing to enlarge his narrow country, loops a long rope about the easternmost coast of Korea. Fastening the end to Mt. Sahime, he lets his people draw the land to Izumo, to which it is joined. The rope is left on the beach, which becomes known as the Long Hempen Beach (So no Nagahama). Similarly he takes land from islands in the Sea of Japan and attaches them to Izumo, adding the peninsula forming the northern part of the province. This type of land-building legend is not uncommon in island mythologies.

Fountains —— There are a number of legends about fountains, frequently connected with Kōbō Daishi (KŪKAI), the famous 9th-century Shingon master, although in northeastern Japan they are often associated with Minamoto no Yoshiie, the famous general who led expeditions against the Ainu in the 11th century. Kōbō Daishi, endowed with miraculous powers, digs into the ground, from which a fountain springs. In one instance he comes to a land devoid of water, where he receives the hospitality of an old woman. In order to repay her kindness he creates a fountain by thrusting his pilgrim's staff into the ground. Similarly, Yoshiie, one day to relieve his soldiers from thirst, lets fly an arrow, which pierces a rock and releases a fountain that is never to run dry. Hot springs are said to owe their existence to the little god Sukunahikona.

Fairies and Celestial Beings —— Spirits in general play an important part in Japanese folk beliefs, though, surprisingly, the SHINTŌ tradition is poorly endowed with such beings, who frequently remain ill defined and shadowy. For the most part, stories dealing with such creatures come from Chinese and Indian sources, which the Japanese have adapted to local conditions. Buddhist literature provides the vehicle through which Hindu legends come from Sanskrit literature, while Chinese stories spring from the Taoist tradition.

One of the more famous of a group of stories recounting the union of a celestial being with a human is that of Hagoromo (the robe of feathers), which has been incorporated into the famous NŌ play Hagoromo. In the basic story a number of heavenly maidens descend from heaven and bathe in a fountain (lake). They have their feathery garments (wings) on nearby bushes while they engage in their ablutions. A passerby, noticing the beautiful robes, takes one of them, and the maidens flee in alarm into the sky. But the one whose robe has been taken, now unable to escape, must remain behind and marry the man. She gives birth to a child and ultimately, is able to return to heaven by stratagem. The story, doubtless of Buddhist origin, is a version of the moon maiden who descends to earth but who later returns to heaven. Hagoromo tells of a heavenly maiden who descends to a sandy beach, where she can see the overwhelming beauty of Mt. Fuji. Overcome by the sight she forgets her heavenly home. A passing fisherman espies her feathered robe and so admires it that he refuses to return it. She persuades him to do so in return for a heavenly dance that she performs for him. The Nō play is a "dance piece," and her performance is central to it.

Another story of the same type is that of the Shining Princess (Kaguya Hime), commonly entitled The Tale of the Bamboo Cutter (Taketori monogatari). An old bamboo cutter discovers a tiny infant in a bamboo stalk, takes it home, and with his wife cares for it. As is typical of this kind of story, the child quickly reaches maturity, and the old bamboo cutter must marry her off. Of the many suitors five alone remain unshaken in their diligent pursuit of her, and in order to decide who is the most worthy, the Shining Princess assigns each one a task, promising to marry whoever is successful. For one reason or another all five fail, and the princess seems at last free of human attachment.

Meanwhile, the emperor, hearing of the girl's beauty, presses his suit with letters and poems. The princess is adamant in her refusal, although she takes care to say so in the most polite language. She must return to the moon, she says. To prevent this flight the emperor sends an army of warriors to guard her. But at nightfall, when the moon shines, the men are paralyzed and unable to keep the heavenly maiden from returning to her lunar home. She leaves a parting letter for the emperor and a box of medicines which the ruler

with his men take to the summit of Mt. Fuji and burn. This is why smoke issues from the volcano.

The Dragon Palace —— One of the oldest stories of this kind is Urashima Tarō. Early versions of it appear in the Nihon shoki and the Man'yōshū, and indicate a strong Buddhist and Taoist influence in attesting to a world beyond. Later the story was related to the Buddhist tradition of the Dragon Palace (Ryūgū) and the Dragon King's Daughter (Ryūgū no Otohime).

One day, Urashima is in his boat at sea when he sees heading toward him a comely young lady. She takes him deep into the sea to her home, a splendid palace, for she is the daughter of the sea deity. Urashima marries her, but after three years of happiness, he desires ardently to see his parents again. His understanding wife grants him his wish, but in order that he may return to her, she gives him a magic box, stipulating that it never be opened. Urashima returns home, but to his dismay everything has changed, for without knowing it he has been absent several hundreds of years. Hoping to return to the Dragon Palace, he opens the box his wife has given him, and from it rise wisps of smoke that drift toward the sea. Instantly his hair turns white and he dies an old man. The story of Hoderi and the luck of the sea cited above belongs to this general type.

Japanese folklore owes much to Buddhism and to Indian lore, most particularly in the form of the Dragon King, who is modeled on the Hindu nāga, whose habitat is the sea and whose body is serpentine in form. In Japan the Dragon King is early associated with the Japanese sea god, who wears a serpent in his crown and rules his watery kingdom from a splendid palace in the sea. The daughter of the Dragon King is Benten (Skt: Sarasvatī), guardian of music, bestower of wealth. She is associated with the BIWA, a sort of lute, and has been the object of a popular cult since the 12th century. She shares some characteristics with the heavenly maidens already mentioned and sometimes assumes the shape of a comely woman, thus attracting human beings.

Sennin —— From Taoism come the sennin, immortal men of the mountains, endowed with magic powers. Above worldly change and commotion, they can fly through the air and walk on the waves. Their home is variously in the sky, amid distant mountains, on certain happy islands. In the Japan of the 14th and 15th centuries a life of seclusion and withdrawal was admired, and stories of sennin became popular at this time.

Perhaps best known of the sennin type are Tōbōsaku, the Eastern Worthy, and Seiōbo, the Queen Mother of the West. Tōbōsaku is an old man, an immortal, who lives in the east and is regularly depicted holding a peach that he has stolen from the Queen Mother of the West. As a consequence of this act he cannot die. The peach symbolizes the rejuvenating aspect of spring, the old man, long life. The Queen Mother lives in the west, a woman of surpassing beauty who symbolizes youth. She is surrounded by supernatural youths and maidens, who consider her their sovereign.

Many sennin are associated with animals or plants and represent one or another of their qualities: Rafusen stands for the plum blossom, symbol of spring and bravery, for the plum tree blooms while the snow is still on the ground; Kiku Jidō (Chrysanthemum Child) stands for the flower of that name, dear to the Japanese. He is forever young and lives in the mountains by a spring surrounded by chrysanthemums that sends forth a stream with wonderful curative powers.

These and other sennin were imported to Japan from China, but Japan produced its own immortals, the most important of which is En no Ozunu, known as the Ascetic Master (Gyōja). He is said to have constructed a bridge from one mountain to another assisted by gods and spirits. One of the spirits of the mountain, being so ugly that he feared to appear with the other gods, held back and was punished by the Master by being confined to a cave, where he remains to this day. The image of the Ascetic Master is frequently seen in caves, seated on a chair and holding a staff in his hand.

But sennin can lose their supernatural powers if they yield to human passions. Thus the One-Horned sennin (Ikkaku), feuding with the Dragons who control rain, shuts them up in a cave so that no precipitation falls and the whole country is in the grip of a calamitous drought. The king of the land, hearing of the situation, sends a beautiful court lady, whose offering of wine the sennin accepts. He becomes intoxicated and his powers leave him. Though he tries to combat them, the Dragons escape, bringing rain to the countryside. Another ascetic, Kume no Sennin, who lives in the mountains near the Kume temple, possesses the miraculous power of flying through the air. One day as he is doing so, he glimpses the beautiful white feet of a woman washing clothes in a stream far below him. Losing his supernatural powers through his attraction to her, he falls to earth, unhurt, and marries the woman.

The Seven Gods of Good Fortune—— The 14th and 15th centuries were a period of eclecticism in Japan, and Taoist, Buddhist, and Shintō sources were not clearly distinguished. An example of this eclecticism is the establishment of the popular group of the Seven Deities of Good Fortune (Shichifukujin). (1) Ebisu, whose origin can be traced back to the miscarried first child of Izanagi and Izanami, brings the good fortune of the sea in the form of the sea bream, a symbol of good luck which he carries along with a fishing rod. (2) Daikoku, the "Great Black One," is a representation of the Hindu Mahākāla. (He was combined with the Japanese Master of the "Great Land," Ōkuninushi, his name being a homophone of an alternate name of the latter.) He is represented as a dark deity, carrying in his hand a mallet and over his shoulder a bag and standing on two bales of rice—the four items symbolic of inexhaustible wealth—and with a rat by his side. The mallet is a kind of magic wand, which produces whatever his worshipers may desire. The rat is associated with Daikoku. (3) Bishamonten (Skt: Vaiśravaṇa), originally a Buddhist deity, guardian of the north, is a giver of wealth, and the stupa he holds in his right hand supposedly contains money. The centipede is associated with him. (4) Benzaiten is the sole female deity of the group. She stands for womanly beauty and wealth, and her messenger is the white snake. (5) Fukurokuju, or the deity of good fortune, wealth, and long life, is said to symbolize the southern polar stars. He has an elongated head and is accompanied by the white crane, indicating longevity. (6) Jurōjin, the "Old Man of Long Life," is a *sennin* who is accompanied by a deer as he wanders among trees and grasses that stand for longevity. (7) Hotei cares especially for children. The bag he carries with him contains the treasures he bestows.

Nefarious Spirits—— The Japanese have a number of nefarious beings, which, influenced by Buddhism, take the form of hungry ghosts. Some are simply tormented by hunger, but others are of a vengeful nature, out to do evil against those toward whom they bear malice or even against innocent persons. There are angry spirits *(asura)*, too, usually ghosts of those who die in battle at the height of their anger. They fight among themselves or attack their former human enemies.

Devils *(oni)* range all the way from ogres to goblins. They are frequently featured with horns and a third eye on the forehead and have three-toed feet and pointed nails. Despite their forbidding aspect, *oni* have something of a comic aspect, and they are easily deceived. Their characteristics are evident in the well-known 12th-century story about the Wen Removal (Kobutori). An old man with a wen on his right cheek finds himself obliged to spend the night in the forest. He hears noises and, peering out from the hollow tree where he has sought shelter, sees a group of *oni* of all shapes. They are dancing, and the old man joins in, to the amazement of the devils, who are nonetheless delighted to have a human among them. They make him promise to return another night, and exact as a pledge of his earnestness the wen on his cheek, though, had they been more maliciously inclined, they might have taken his nose or his ears. Back home, the villagers are amazed to see that the lump on his cheek has vanished.

Another old man, this time with a wen on his left cheek, wishing it removed, joins the dancing *oni* on the advice of the first old man. But the devils realize by his awkwardness that it is not the same dancer. To punish him they affix to his right cheek the wen they had previously removed from the first man. He returns to the village in great distress, aware that one should never envy another's good luck.

Some *oni* bear a mallet not unlike Daikoku's. Such is the case with the One-Inch Boy (Issumbōshi). An old childless couple pray to the god of Sumiyoshi for a child, however small. Their request is granted, and a boy one inch tall is born to them. When he matures, although he does not gain in height, he makes his way to the capital, traveling down a river by means of a wooden bowl and chopstick provided by his parents. In the capital he enters the service of a nobleman. One day, as he escorts the daughter of the family to a temple, the couple are waylaid by an *oni* who threatens to eat them alive, but Issumbōshi leaps into the ogre's mouth, which he pricks with his sword, a needle, so that the devil spits him out in pain. Then the *oni* vanishes and the girl finds the mallet he has left behind. By its magical powers Issumbōshi is transformed into a full-grown man, and the two are married.

Heroic Tales—— Another young hero story is that of the Peach Boy (Momotarō). An old woman washing clothes in a stream sees a peach floating in the water. She fishes it out and takes it to her husband, who on opening it up finds a small boy. The couple care for him and raise him until he grows into a stalwart lad. Momotarō decides to visit the Island of Devils and sets out with a supply of dumplings provided by his mother. En route he meets a dog, who begs for a dumpling, which the Peach Boy gives him. Then a monkey and a pheasant join the company. They attack and overcome the devils and return to the old couple with much treasure.

Another heroic tale is that of Tawara Tōda, "Tōda of the Rice Bale." One night, crossing the famous bridge of Seta at the outlet of Lake Biwa, Tōda sees a great serpent, but passes by it with composure. He is later visited that night by a young woman who claims to be the daughter of the Dragon King and to admire the great courage Tōda exhibited at the Seta bridge. She requests him to slay the great centipede that is wreaking havoc among her relatives. Tōda takes his stand on the bridge, and when he sees two great lights like burning mirrors he fires arrows between them, but the missiles bounce back as if from an iron plate. Tōda, then realizing that the monster cannot stand saliva, wets a third arrow, kills the centipede, and saves the dragon race.

The next night Tōda is again visited by the lady, who expresses her thanks and invites him to visit her in the Dragon Palace. He follows her into the water, and later as he leaves the palace, the Dragon King gives him a bale of rice that proves to be inexhaustible, a roll of silk that supplies him with clothes forever, and a bell of Indian provenance, that he dedicates to a temple by the lake. He prudently keeps the first two gifts for himself.

Foxes, Cats, and Badgers—— A number of animals have played important roles in Japanese folk beliefs. The serpent has already been mentioned in relation to the dragon people; but the fox, the badger, and the cat are regularly accorded magical powers, the latter two certainly since the 14th century. The uncanny fox was particularly to be feared, because he could turn himself into a beguiling and seductive woman. This is exemplified by the 12th-century court lady Tamamo no Mae, really an old fox who had turned himself into a beautiful woman in order to tempt the ruler. Already successful in such black art in China and India, the fox's machinations were discovered by a nobleman in Japan, who broke the spell with a divine mirror, before which the beautiful woman revealed her true identity.

The badger is guileful like the fox but not so malicious. Both deceive men by turning themselves temporarily into humans. The cat, however, is particularly dreaded, for he frequently assumes human form permanently and does long-term evil. Most to be feared is a cat with a reddish coat, less is one with black, white, or brown coloring. Totally black cats were believed to be able to forecast weather and sailors thus considered them desirable.

The Sparrow—— Not all animals are malicious; some, like the sparrow, are known for their gratitude. Once an old woman, finding an injured sparrow, took it home and cared for it until it was well. She released it, and the grateful bird flew away, only to return some days later bearing a grain, which it gave to the old woman. She planted the seed, and from it grew an inexhaustible supply of gourds that she sold. The ones she dried furnished a limitless supply of rice. She was able to feed herself as well as her neighbors.

Next door lived a woman envious of her neighbor's good fortune. Hoping to reap similar benefits, she struck down another sparrow, nursed it back to health, and then released it. Later this sparrow too returned with a seed, which the woman planted and which indeed bore some gourds. But they were inedibly bitter, and though promisingly heavy, contained centipedes and scorpions and other disagreeable insects that stung the old woman to death.

The tongue-cut sparrow is even better known. Once a woman cut out a sparrow's tongue for eating her starch. A kind-hearted neighbor cared for the poor bird until it grew well. She and her husband visited the sparrow's house, which was made of bamboo, and were entertained by the sparrow and its comrades, who performed the famous sparrow dance for them. The couple was given two boxes, one large and the other small, but since they were not strong enough to carry the large box, they took the small one home and found it full of treasure.

The malicious neighbor, hearing of their good fortune, went to the sparrow's house with her husband and chose the large box to take home. It was filled with demons, who upon release devoured the greedy couple.

📖—— Works in Western Languages: Masaharu Anesaki, "Japanese Mythology," in *The Mythology of All Races*, vol 8 (1928). Michiko Y. Aoki, *Izumo Fudoki* (1971). W. G. Aston, tr, *Nihongi: Chronicles of Japan from the Earliest Times to A.D. 697* (1896, repr

1956). Basil Hall Chamberlain, tr, *Kojiki, "Records of Ancient Matters"* (1883). Serge Elisséeff, "The Mythology of Japan," in *Asiatic Mythology: A Detailed Description and Explanation of the Mythologies of All the Great Nations of Asia* (1932). Karl Florenz, *Japanische Mythologie: Nihongi, "Zeitalter der Götter": Nebst Ergänzungen aus andern alten Quellenwerken* (1901). Katō Genchi and Hoshino Hikoshirō, *Kogoshūi: Gleanings from Ancient Stories* (1937). Joseph M. Kitagawa, "Prehistoric Background of Japanese Religion," *History of Religion,* 2.2 (Winter 1963). Matsumoto Nobuhiro, *Essai sur la mythologie japonaise* (1928). Nelly Neumann, *Das Umwandeln des Himmelspfeilers: Ein japanischer Mythos und seine kulturhistorische Einordnung, Asian Folklore Studies—Monograph No. 5* (1971). Numazawa Kiichi, "Der Weltanfang in der japanischen Mythologie," *Internationale Schriftenreihe für soziale und politische Wissenschaften, Ethnologische Reihe,* vol 2 (1946). Ōbayashi Taryō, "Die Amaterasu-Mythe im alten Japan und die Sonnenfinsternismythe in Südostasien," *Ethnos,* 25 (1960). Ōbayashi Taryō, "Origins of Japanese Mythology, Especially of the Myths of the Origin of Death," *Monumenta Nipponica Monograph no. 25, Folk Cultures of Japan and East Asia* (1976). Ōbayashi Taryō, "The Origins of Japanese Mythology," *Acta Asiatica,* 31 (1977). Donald L. Philippi, *Kojiki* (1969). E. Dale Saunders, "Japanese Mythology," in Samuel Noah Kramer, ed, *Mythologies of the Ancient World,* (1961). E. Dale Saunders, "Mythologies du Japon," in *Mythologies des montagnes, des forêts et des îles* (1963). Yoshida Atsuhiko, "La Mythologie japonaise: essai d'interprétation structurale," *Revue de l'Histoire des Religions,* 160, 161, 163, (1961–63).

Works in Japanese: Higo Kazuo, *Nihon shinwa no rekishi-teki keisei* (1958). Kanda Hideo, *Kojiki no kōsō* (1959). Matsumae Takeshi, *Nihon shinwa no shinkenkyū* (1960). Matsumoto Nobuhiro, *Nihon no shinwa* (1956). Matsumura Takeo, *Nihon shinwa no kenkyū* (1955–58). Fujisawa Morihiko, *Shinwa densetsu denshōsetsuwa hen* (vol 1 of *Nihon minzokugaku zenshū;* Takahashi Shoten, 1971). Numazawa Kiichi, "Tenchi wakaruru shinwa no bunkashi-teki haikei," *Academia,* 1 (1952). Ōbayashi Taryō, *Nihon shinwa no kigen* (1961). Oka Masao, "Nihon bunka no kiso kōzō," *Nihon minzokugaku taikei,* 2 (1958). Takeda Yūkichi, *Kojiki setsuwa-gun no kenkyū* (1954).   E. Dale SAUNDERS

N

Nabari

City in western Mie Prefecture, central Honshū. During the Edo period (1600–1868) it developed as a castle town and POST-STATION TOWN on the route to the Ise Shrine. Both farming and industry are active, but many of Nabari's residents commute to Ōsaka. Located within the Murō–Akame–Aoyama Quasi-National Park, it offers such attractions as the gorge called Kōchidani and the 48 Waterfalls of Akame. Pop: 44,488.

Nabeshima family

Warrior family and *daimyō* of Saga in Hizen Province (now Saga and Nagasaki prefectures) from the Azuchi-Momoyama period (1568–1600) through the Edo period (1600–1868). A branch of the SHŌNI FAMILY, they rose to be household stewards for the RYŪZŌJI FAMILY, lords of Saga and deputy governors *(shugodai)* of Hizen. In 1590 Nabeshima Naoshige (1538–1618) forced the ineffectual family head, Ryūzōji Masaie (1566–1607), to retire and was recognized by TOYOTOMI HIDEYOSHI as daimyō of Saga in his own name, with an income of 357,000 *koku* (see KOKUDAKA). Naoshige fought in Hideyoshi's Korean expeditions (see INVASIONS OF KOREA IN 1592 AND 1597), at which time he brought back Korean potters as captives (see NABESHIMA WARE). Naoshige's son Katsushige (1580–1657) fought for the Toyotomi faction in the Battle of SEKIGAHARA (1600), but the Nabeshima soon afterward swore fealty to TOKUGAWA IEYASU, who confirmed them in their position and domains. Three collateral branches of the Nabeshima were enfeoffed as lesser daimyō in Hizen under the Tokugawa shogunate; in 1648 members of the main branch were granted the shogunal family name, Matsudaira. Toward the end of the Edo period (1600–1868), the family, notably NABESHIMA KANSŌ, set up modern industries.

Nabeshima Kansō (1814–1871)

Daimyō of the Saga domain (now Saga Prefecture); also called Nabeshima Naomasa. His capable and progressive leadership made Saga one of the most powerful domains at the end of the Edo period (1600–1868). Kansō succeeded his father in 1830 and undertook drastic reforms to strengthen Saga financially and militarily. He instituted land reforms to step up agricultural production, allowed capable lower *samurai* to fill positions of leadership, and took steps to stimulate commercial trade with other domains. He also encouraged the growth of such marketable commodities as ceramics and coal and created monopolies to maximize profits. The accumulated capital was used to modernize the domain's military and associated industries. Thus, in 1850 Saga became the first domain to possess an operable reverberatory furnace with which to manufacture heavy artillery. Kansō was a supporter of the MOVEMENT FOR UNION OF COURT AND SHOGUNATE, an attempt to shore up the failing Tokugawa shogunate by strengthening its ties with the imperial court in Kyōto. After the MEIJI RESTORATION of 1868, he served the new government briefly as a councillor *(gijō)* and as head of the Hokkaidō Colonization Office (KAITAKUSHI).

Nabeshima Naomasa → Nabeshima Kansō

Nabeshima ware

(nabeshima-yaki). Porcelain ware. Blue and white, celadon, and polychrome porcelains, mainly for table use, made in or near Arita, Hizen Province (now Saga Prefecture), Kyūshū, from 1628 to 1871. The Iwayagawachi kiln (1628–61) produced underglaze blue and white ware that was not of the highest quality. The Nangawara kiln (1661–75) made excellent blue and white and polychrome pieces. Both kilns were patronized by the local *daimyō*. On a larger scale,

Nachi Falls

View of the falls. The *torii* (gate) and other structures in the foreground form Hiryū Shrine, of which the falls are the sacred object.

the Nabeshima daimyō, lords of the Hizen domain, operated a kiln for their own exclusive needs at Ōkawachi from 1675 to 1871; the finest work, of a technical perfection unrivaled by other Edo-period (1600–1868) porcelain, was done in the late 17th and early 18th centuries, with a subsequent decline in quality most marked after 1804.

Nabeshima ware production was closely supervised, technical secrets were carefully guarded, and defective pieces were destroyed. At Ōkawachi, bodies were made and fired and transfer technique designs executed; overglaze polychrome pigments were applied and fired by a small number of artisan families in Arita. Among the carefully and uniformly potted pieces, dishes were most common, in four standard sizes with a characteristic high foot with a comb design. Less common were *sake* and food cups and least frequent were jars, flower vases, water containers, and incense burners.

Nabeshima designs—the most inventive, varied, striking, and asymmetrical among Japanese porcelains—were outlined in soft, pale, dull underglaze blue or, if polychrome, finished in strong, transparent, thinly applied red, yellow, and bluish green overglaze enamels. They mainly comprised flowers, shrubs, leaves, fruits, and vegetables, at times treated with considerable abstraction or else in overall textile patterns. After 1696, designs with a central white area as derived from Imari porcelains (see ARITA WARE) became characteristic, with the backs of dishes having underglaze blue decoration, usually peonies, chrysanthemums, scrolls, or jewels bound with ribbons.

Starting with Soeda Kizaemon (d 1654), the kilns were managed for many generations by the Soeda family and pigments were prepared by the Imaizumi family in Arita. Imaemon XII (1897–1975) and his son Imaemon XIII (b 1926) have carried on the family traditions at a high technical level.

Frederick BAEKELAND

Nachi Falls

(Nachi no Taki). Located on the upper reaches of the river Nachigawa, southeastern Wakayama Prefecture, central Honshū. It is the largest of the 48 waterfalls found along the river. A sacred falls of the Kumano Nachi Shrine, it attracts numerous ascetics. Located within Yoshino–Kumano National Park. Head: 133 m (436 ft).

Nachi–Fujikoshi Corporation

(known in Japan as Fujikoshi). Machine tool manufacturer engaged mainly in the production of bearings. It also produces cutting tools, hydraulic equipment, specialty steel, and environmental control systems. Nachi-Fujikoshi was established in 1928. It is the largest producer of cutting tools in Japan and one of the major manufacturers of bearings. It commenced foreign operations soon after being established; at present it has four overseas manufacturing companies and 11 sales firms, and its products are well known abroad under the brand name Nachi. It is currently striving to diversify production and become an integrated machine tool manufacturer. Sales for the fiscal year ending November 1981 totaled ¥98.3 billion (US $439.3 million) and the company was capitalized at ¥9.1 billion (US $40.7 million). Corporate headquarters are located in Toyama, Toyama Prefecture.

Nachi-Katsuura

Town in southeastern Wakayama Prefecture, central Honshū, on the Kumano Sea. Nachi-Katsuura was formed in 1951 by the merger of the towns of Nachi and Katsuura. Katsuura has the prefecture's largest fishing port. Katsuura and Yukawa hot springs on the coast, Nachi Shrine, one of the KUMANO SANZAN SHRINES, and NACHI FALLS attract visitors. Pop: 23,002.

Nachisan

Mountain group in southeastern Wakayama Prefecture, central Honshū. It includes Ōkumodorisan (966 m; 3,168 ft), Eboshiyama (909 m; 2,982 ft), and Myōhōsan (749 m; 2,457 ft). The area has many shrines and temples, including Nachi Shrine. The NACHI FALLS, in the headwaters of the river Nachigawa, is one of Japan's highest falls (133 m; 436 ft).

Nada

District in southeastern Hyōgo Prefecture, western Honshū, along the northern part of Ōsaka Bay extending from Nishinomiya to Kōbe. It developed as a *sake*-brewing center in the middle of the 19th century and the name Nada is associated with fine-quality *sake*. The coastal part of the district is industrializing rapidly, and its interior is an affluent residential area.

Naebasan

Also called Naebayama. Shield volcano in the Nasu Volcanic Zone, on the border between Niigata and Nagano prefectures, central Honshū. On the summit is Ime Shrine. It is a well-known ski area. Naeba International Skiing Ground is on the eastern slopes of Takenokoyama (1,790 m; 5,871 ft). Height: 2,145 m (7,036 ft).

Nagahama

City in northeastern Shiga Prefecture, central Honshū, situated on Lake Biwa. Nagahama had its origins in 1573 when TOYOTOMI HIDEYOSHI built a castle there. From the Edo period (1600–1868) it prospered as the temple town of Daitsūji and as a port and was known for its *hamachirimen*, a crepe silk, and mosquito nets. After World War II machine and resin industries were introduced. Daitsūji, also known as Nagahama Ombō, has many important buildings and a well-known garden. The remains of Nagahama Castle and the site of the Battle of ANEGAWA are also of interest. Pop: 54,934.

Nagai

City in southwestern Yamagata Prefecture, northern Honshū. Nagai was a castle town of the Katakura family in the early 17th century. It produces condensers, knitted goods, and Nagai *tsumugi* (pongee). Rice is the main agricultural product. There are several parks noted for their flowers; the autumn foliage along the gorge of the river Nogawa also attracts visitors. Pop: 33,287.

Nagai Kafū (1879–1959)

Novelist and essayist, noted for his lyrical portrayals of the rapidly vanishing remnants of late Edo- and Meiji-period urban culture. Born in Tōkyō as Nagai Sōkichi, the eldest son of a high-ranking bureaucrat. He was taught classical Chinese as a child but soon felt drawn to the world of Edo-period literature and arts under the influence of his mother. His interest in literature increased in proportion to his dislike of school, and although he entered the Chinese Lan-

guage Department of the Tōkyō School of Foreign Languages (now Tōkyō School of Foreign Studies) he rarely attended classes and eventually left school altogether. By then he had become immersed in the lifestyle of a typical urban dilettante, frequenting the pleasure quarters, the KABUKI theater, and other popular entertainments, taking SHAKUHACHI and SHAMISEN lessons, briefly becoming the pupil of a RAKUGO performer, and working equally briefly as an apprentice kabuki playwright.

In September 1898 he took a short story to the then popular writer HIROTSU RYŪRŌ and was accepted as a protégé. Like many aspiring writers at that time, he had exposed himself to Western literature, both in Japanese and English translation, and was strongly attracted to French literature. He became one of the leading advocates of Zola and "naturalism," a phase in his life that he later renounced, but that nonetheless left a deep imprint on his entire career.

All these activities led Kafū's father to send him on a face-saving journey to the United States in 1903. He spent four years there, first in Tacoma, Washington, and then at Kalamazoo College in Michigan. Later he became a clerk in a Japanese bank in New York City until, in July 1907, he was transferred to the bank's branch in Lyons, France. He left this job after eight months and proceeded to Paris, where he stayed for two months before returning to Japan. He was never to go overseas again. His collection of short stories and essays written in the United States was published under the title *Amerika monogatari* (1908, American Stories). Its highly lyrical and vivid style caught the imagination of the Japanese reading public, and he became a popular writer, producing short novels, stories, and essays in quick succession. Some of them, most notably *Furansu monogatari* (1909, French Stories) and *Kanraku* (1909; tr *Pleasure*, 1961), were banned by the government, allegedly because they contained highly critical and irreverent comments on Japanese society and its moral codes.

In 1910, he was appointed professor of literature at Keiō Gijuku (later Keiō University), where he founded and edited a noted literary journal, *Mita bungaku*. Two years later he married Saitō Yone, primarily to please his parents, but divorced her in less than five months, shortly after his father's death. He then married his mistress, Uchida Yai, a former *geisha*, who, however, soon left him on account of his frequent affairs with other women. In 1916, the restrictions of life as a college professor led him to quit both his teaching and editing positions.

Subsequently, he published several novels, stories, and essays, including *Udekurabe* (1916–17; tr *Geisha in Rivalry*, 1963), *Okamezasa* (1918–20, Dwarf Bamboo), and *Ame shōshō* (1917–21; tr *Quiet Rain*, 1964), all of which dealt with various aspects of life in the Tōkyō demimonde. After a decade of unproductivity, his *Tsuyu no atosaki* (1931, During the Rainy Season) heralded Kafū's return to the literary scene. This work was followed by *Bokutō kidan* (1937; tr *A Strange Tale from East of the River*, 1958), which is widely regarded as his masterpiece. In this novel, the brief affair of the protagonist with a prostitute is deftly intertwined with seasonal changes along the east bank of the river Sumida (Sumidagawa) in Tōkyō. During the war years (1937–45), pressures from the military authorities made it harder for Kafū to get his works published. Although he became quite popular after the war, partly because of his refusal to engage in wartime propaganda, he never regained his previous level of creativity.

Kafū was one of the first modern Japanese writers who, upon direct contact with the Western world, managed to create a literature that was rooted in tradition, in his case primarily that of the late Edo period, and at the same time marked by universalism. His grasp of Western literature was limited but this was compensated for by an unusual sensibility. His principal theme was the ever-changing city of Tōkyō and its pleasure quarters, and while he is frequently condemned as a writer of nostalgia for a past that he misrepresented, he managed to preserve in his works many aspects of Tōkyō life which disappeared after the Tōkyō Earthquake of 1923, the wartime destruction, and the postwar rebuilding. If his creative works, especially novels, seem to be limited in number as well as in scope, it is because he could create a fictional work only when his sensitivity was aroused and he had established a resonance with the French works which he deeply appreciated, especially those of Flaubert, Maupassant, and Henri de Régnier. The most successful works from his early career, such as *Yume no onna* (1903, Woman of the Dream) and *Sumidagawa* (1909; tr *The River Sumida*, 1956), to say nothing of his later ones, including *Okamezasa*, *Ame shōshō*, and *Bokutō kidan*, amply attest to this fact. His sensitivity is also appar-

ent in his collection of translations of French poetry *Sangoshū* (1913, Coral Anthology), despite numerous instances of misreading and mistranslation. Critics who confuse the artist's life with his works tend to label Kafū's writings and attitude toward life as dilettantish if not downright insincere, but there have been few modern Japanese writers who tried harder, with occasional success, to create a world of fiction that was neither provincial nor superficially Westernized.
■——*Kafū zenshū*, 29 vols, 2nd ed (Iwanami Shoten, 1971–74). Akiba Tarō, *Nagai Kafū den* (1976). Isoda Kōichi, *Nagai Kafū* (1979). Edward Seidensticker, *Kafū the Scribbler* (1965).

Mitsuko IRIYE

Nagai Nagayoshi (1845–1929)

Organic chemist and pharmacologist. Born in Awa Province (now Tokushima Prefecture); graduate of the Daigaku Nankō (now Tōkyō University). Nagai went to Europe as a government scholar and served as an assistant to Professor August Wilhelm von Hofmann of the University of Berlin. As one of the first doctors of pharmacy in Japan, he became chief engineer of the Dainippon Pharmaceutical Company. He studied the chemical compositions of various Japanese and Chinese herbal remedies, and, most notably, isolated the alkaloid ephedrine from *maō (Ephedra sinica)*. He served as a professor at Tōkyō University and the director of the Tōkyō laboratory of the Bureau of Public Health of the Home Ministry. Nagai was also the first president of the Pharmaceutical Society of Japan.

Sōda Hajime

Nagai Ryūtarō (1881–1944)

Politician, educator, and journalist who rose to prominence as an orator in the Diet during the Taishō period (1912–26). One of the most conspicuous "democrats" of the era of the so-called TAISHŌ DEMOCRACY, he became more conservative during the early 1930s, when national and international problems began to press in on the Japanese.

The son of a former *samurai* family of the Kaga domain (now Ishikawa and Toyama prefectures), Nagai grew up in the city of Kanazawa. He entered Dōshisha Middle School in Kyōto in 1897 but left after being involved in a student strike. In 1898 he entered Kansei Gakuin in Kōbe, where he completed his secondary education and became a Christian. From 1901 to 1905 he attended Tōkyō Semmon Gakkō (now Waseda University), gaining support from the school's founder, ŌKUMA SHIGENOBU. He graduated from the faculty of politics and economics after having studied under ABE ISOO, UKITA KAZUTAMI, and others. From 1906 to 1909 he studied at Manchester College, Oxford University. His major work there was a study of the English statesman Gladstone, and despite the anti-Oriental prejudice he encountered at the time, Nagai remained an admirer of the British parliamentary system throughout his life.

After returning to Japan, he received an appointment to teach social policy and colonial policy at Waseda, where because of the brilliance of his lectures he soon became one of the most popular instructors. At the same time, he worked as editor of *Shin Nippon* (New Japan), a leading liberal journal of the day and an organ for the views of his mentor Ōkuma. In 1917 Nagai left Waseda for a career in politics, running unsuccessfully for the Diet as an independent from the city of Kanazawa. From 1918 to 1919 he traveled abroad once more, studying world trends and attending the Versailles peace negotiations as an unofficial observer. Upon his return to Japan, he continued to write for leading liberal journals and also joined with a group of like-minded Japanese to form the Kaizō Dōmei (Reconstruction League), the purpose of which was to change Japan in line with post–World War I democratic trends. In 1920 he ran again for the lower house, this time successfully, and served in the Diet until his death.

With his progressive stance and eloquence, Nagai quickly rose to fame in the 1920s as a "champion of the masses" and later as a leader of the RIKKEN MINSEITŌ party. In the late 1920s and early 1930s, however, he became disillusioned with the tactics of the established parties, as well as with cooperative diplomacy with the Anglo-American bloc, and he began to seek out alternatives to solve Japan's problems.

From 1932 to 1934 he served as colonial minister in the "national unity cabinet" of SAITŌ MAKOTO and later accepted appointments in other nonparty cabinets—as minister of communications in the first KONOE FUMIMARO cabinet (where he sponsored a plan for the nationalization of the electric power industry) and later as communica-

tions minister and railroad minister in the ABE NOBUYUKI cabinet. He also served on the organization committee for Konoe's NEW ORDER MOVEMENT, participated actively in the IMPERIAL RULE ASSISTANCE ASSOCIATION, championed the cause of "Asia for the Asiatics," and served as an official in the Greater East Asia Ministry (Dai Tōa Shō). He died shortly before Japan's defeat. His son is Nagai Michio (b 1923), editorial writer for the newspaper *Tōkyō asahi shimbun* and former minister of education.
■——Nagai Ryūtarō, *Nagai Ryūtarō shi dai enzetsu shū*, 2 vols (1924 and 1930). Nagai Ryūtarō, *Watakushi no shinnen to taiken* (1938). Peter Duus, "Nagai Ryūtarō: The Tactical Dilemmas of Reform," in Albert M. Craig and Donald H. Shively, ed, *Personality in Japanese History* (1970). Peter Duus, "Nagai Ryūtarō and the 'White Peril,' 1905–1944," *Journal of Asian Studies* 31.1 (1971). Matsumura Kenzō, ed, *Nagai Ryūtarō* (1959). Sharon A. Minichiello, "New Patterns of Political Leadership in Taishō Japan: Nagai Ryūtarō, A Case Study," PhD dissertation, University of Hawaii (1975).

Sharon A. MINICHIELLO

Nagai Tatsuo (1904–)

Author. Born in Tōkyō. His first literary success came when his short story "Kappan'ya no hanashi" (1920) was praised by the well-known author KIKUCHI KAN. After 1927 he served as an editor of Kikuchi's literary magazine *Bungei shunjū*, going to Manchuria in 1942 to open a branch office and returning in 1944 to the Tōkyō home office as executive director. His most active period as a writer came after his release in 1947 from restrictions imposed under the US OCCUPATION PURGE for his role as a journalist during World War II. "Asagiri" (1949; tr "Morning Mist," 1962) and other short stories exhibit a *haiku*-like clarity and lightness. His 1965 story collection *Ikko sono ta* received both the Noma Prize and the Japan Art Academy Literary Prize that year. He was elected to the Japan Academy in 1969 and was awarded the Order of Culture in 1981. Other major works include the story "Kuroi gohan" (1923) and the novel *Kage futatabi* (1951).

Nagai Uta (1819–1863)

Official of the Chōshū domain (now Yamaguchi Prefecture). Recognized for his ability, Nagai rose swiftly in the domain administration and in 1858 became *jikimetsuke* (a *metsuke*, or inspector, who reported directly to the *daimyō* on all domain officials). In 1861 he submitted a memorial in which he recommended that Chōshū act boldly to resolve differences between the court and the shogunate and that it accept the ANSEI COMMERCIAL TREATIES, however humiliating, and pursue a policy of "expansion across the seas" to raise its own and Japan's prestige. With domainal permission, he spent much of that year traveling between Kyōto and Edo (now Tōkyō) putting forward his plan. He succeeded in obtaining imperial approval, but early in 1862, Chōshū, under the influence of KUSAKA GENZUI and TAKASUGI SHINSAKU, adopted an antiforeign imperial-loyalist position, and the court accepted an alternative plan from the Satsuma domain (now Kagoshima Prefecture) that was more favorable to the court. That summer Nagai abandoned his efforts and returned to Chōshū; early the next year he was ordered to accept responsibility for Chōshū's loss of national influence and commit suicide.

Nagako, Empress (1903–)

Nonreigning empress (*kōgō*). Consort of Emperor HIROHITO. Eldest daughter of Kuni no Miya Kunihiko (Prince Kuni). Graduated from the girls' middle school department of Gakushūin (the Peers' School; see GAKUSHŪIN UNIVERSITY). She married the then crown prince Hirohito in 1924 and became empress with his ascension to the throne two years later. Serving as honorary president of the Japanese Red Cross Society, Empress Nagako is also known for her Japanese-style paintings, done under the name Tōen. Two collections of her works have been published as *Tōen gashū* (1967) and *Kimpōshū* (1969).

Nagakubo Sekisui (1717–1801)

Geographer and cartographer whose *Nihon yochi rotei zenzu* (completed 1775, revised 1779) was the first Japanese-published map of Japan to incorporate the Western system of longitudinal and latitudinal notation. Nagakubo was born in Hitachi Province (now Ibaraki

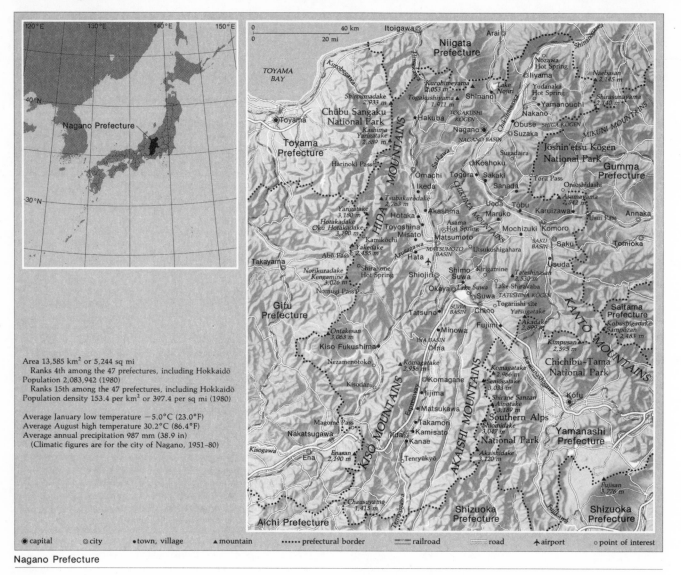

| ● capital | ○ city | ● town, village | ▲ mountain | •••••• prefectural border | ══ railroad | ═══ road | ✈ airport | ○ point of interest |

Nagano Prefecture

Prefecture). He was a Confucian scholar and geographer for the Mito domain (now Ibaraki Prefecture) and helped in the compilation of the DAI NIHON SHI.

nagamochi

An oblong, legless wooden chest that was used for storing clothing and household utensils. Until the early 20th century, the *nagamochi* was an indispensable part of a bride's dowry; it was slung from a long pole resting on the shoulders of two bearers and carried in the bridal procession. The number of *nagamochi* a bride brought with her reflected the wealth of her family. Bearers traditionally sang a wedding song known as *nagamochi uta*. Because they are bulky and difficult to transport, *nagamochi* have largely fallen from common use since the early 1900s. MIYAMOTO Mizuo

Nagano

Capital of Nagano Prefecture, central Honshū. Nagano was established in the Kamakura period (1185–1333) as the temple town (MONZEN MACHI) of ZENKŌJI, a temple dating from the early 7th century. During the Edo period (1600–1868), it developed as a market and POST-STATION TOWN on the highway Hokkoku Kaidō. Today it is a commercial center with thriving foodstuff and electrical machinery industries; its publishing and printing industries are among Japan's largest. Nagano is known for its apples and is Japan's largest producer of Chinese yams. Numerous cultural and educational facilities include Shinshū University and broadcasting stations. Apart from Zenkōji, which attracts more than 4 million visitors yearly, other attractions are the site of the Battles of KAWANAKAJIMA and the former castle town of MATSUSHIRO. Pop: 324,360.

Nagano Basin

(Nagano Bonchi). In northern Nagano Prefecture, central Honshū. Consisting mainly of alluvial fans below the fault scarp and the flood plain of the river Chikumagawa, this long, narrow basin is known for the cultivation of rice, apples, and apricots. It is the political and commercial center of Nagano Prefecture and has been undergoing industrialization. The major city is Nagano. Area: approximately 270 sq km (104 sq mi).

Nagano Osami (1880–1947)

Fleet admiral. Born in Kōchi Prefecture. Nagano graduated from the Naval Academy in 1900 and from the Naval War College in 1910. He served as naval attaché at the Japanese Embassy in the United States before becoming vice-chief of the Naval General Staff Office in 1930. Promoted to admiral in 1934, the next year he represented his country at the second of the LONDON NAVAL CONFERENCES. He was named navy minister in the HIROTA KŌKI cabinet in 1936, commander in chief of the Combined Fleet in 1937, and chief of the Naval General Staff Office in 1941. At the onset of World War II he was head of the Supreme Command of the Imperial Japanese Navy. He became a fleet admiral in 1943 and resigned his post as chief of the Naval General Staff Office in 1944. Nagano was charged as a class A war criminal at the WAR CRIMES TRIALS and died of illness in prison in 1947. ICHIKI Toshio

Nagano Prefecture

(Nagano Ken). Located in central Honshū and bordered by the prefectures of Niigata, Gumma, Saitama, Yamanashi, Shizuoka, Aichi,

Gifu, and Toyama. The terrain is largely mountainous, and major ranges include the Hida, Kiso, and Akaishi (see JAPANESE ALPS), as well as the Mikuni Mountains. Numerous rivers, including the SHINANOGAWA, Himekawa, KISOGAWA, and TENRYŪGAWA, flow between the mountains. Because of its mountainous terrain and distance from the sea, the climate is generally cooler and drier than that of surrounding prefectures. The extreme northern and southern areas, however, receive more precipitation.

Known after the TAIKA REFORM of 645 as Shinano Province, the Nagano area was crossed by several major highways linking eastern and western Japan, including the NAKASENDŌ, which was then called the Tōsandō. The area came under the rule of contending warlords such as the Uesugi and Takeda during the ascendancy of warrior rule and was divided into small domains during the Edo period (1600–1868). The present name dates from 1871, and the present boundaries were established in 1876.

Agriculture is a major occupation, with rice the main crop. Dairy cattle are also bred. The silk industry flourished before World War II, but more recently the precision machinery industry has become highly developed. Other industries include machinery, metals, food-processing, and woodworking.

Nagano's mountains, lakes, and hot springs make it a favorite tourist area. Parts of the four national parks of Jōshin'etsu Kōgen, Chichibu–Tama, Chūbu Sangaku, and the Southern Alps are located in the prefecture, and it also has three quasi-national parks. Area: 13,585 sq km (5,244 sq mi); pop: 2,083,942; capital: Nagano. Other major cities include MATSUMOTO, UEDA, and IIDA.

Nagano Shigeo (1900–)

Businessman. Born in Shimane Prefecture, he graduated from Tōkyō University. In 1925 he became manager of a bankrupt firm, Fuji Iron, which he proceeded to revitalize. He became director of the purchasing department in 1934 when Fuji Iron merged with Nippon Steel Co (now NIPPON STEEL CORPORATION). In 1941 he was a member of the Iron and Steel Control Council, but after World War II he returned to Nippon Steel as managing director while serving as vice-director of the ECONOMIC STABILIZATION BOARD. In 1950 Nippon Steel split into Fuji Iron and Steel and YAWATA IRON AND STEEL WORKS in accordance with the Excessive Economic Power Decentralization Law. Nagano first became president of Fuji and then assumed the chairmanship of Nippon Steel Corporation when Yawata and Fuji joined again in 1970. An important leader of the business-industrial community, Nagano became chairman of the JAPAN CHAMBER OF COMMERCE AND INDUSTRY in 1969. Together with KOBAYASHI ATARU, SAKURADA TAKESHI, and MIZUNO SHIGEO, he has been recognized as one of the major powers in the postwar Japanese political and economic world. _Itō Hajime_

Naganuma case

(Naganuma Jiken). One of the most controversial legal cases in postwar Japan, centering on the question of the constitutionality of the SELF DEFENSE FORCES (SDF). The suit, initiated in July 1969, alleges that the SDF violates article 9 of the 1947 constitution of Japan, which contains an explicit RENUNCIATION OF WAR as a sovereign right of the Japanese people and prohibits the maintenance of military forces. Despite this ban, the Japanese government in 1954 established the SDF, whose air, land, and naval branches now make Japan a potentially significant military power in Asia.

The Naganuma case arose when the SDF began construction of a Nike antiaircraft missile launching site on a mountaintop that had been designated as a forest preserve near the town of Naganuma in Hokkaidō. Some 271 residents, including farmers who claimed that their lands would be adversely affected by the removal of trees and alteration of the watershed, filed suit to halt construction of the facility on the grounds that the very existence of the SDF was unconstitutional under article 9.

In September 1973 the Sapporo District Court agreed that the SDF was unconstitutional and barred the construction of the Nike facility. In August 1976, however, the Sapporo High Court reversed the decision on appeal. The High Court ruled that the constitutionality of the SDF was essentially a "political question," a matter for legislative judgment, since it involved the sovereign existence of the Japanese nation, and therefore was not justiciable by the courts. As of 1981, the case was on appeal before the Supreme Court. See also SUNAGAWA CASE; SUZUKI DECISION; CONSTITUTION, DISPUTE OVER REVISION OF. _Kenneth M. Tagawa_

Nagaoka

City in central Niigata Prefecture, central Honshū. Located on the river Shinanogawa, Nagaoka developed as a port and POST-STATION TOWN in the Edo period (1600–1868). With the opening of the oil fields here, machine and chemical industries developed. It is served by several important rail lines and highways. The fireworks at the Nagaoka festival (early August), the cherry blossoms and autumn foliage at Yūkyūzan Park, and several nearby hot springs attract visitors. Pop: 180,258.

Nagaoka Hantarō (1865–1950)

Japan's most eminent physicist before the age of quantum mechanics. Born in Nagasaki and a graduate of Tōkyō University. His research included work in the fields of electromagnetism, spectroscopy, and geophysics. He is known especially for his theory of atomic models, advanced in 1903. Nagaoka taught at Tōkyō University, was first president of Ōsaka University and president of the Imperial Academy. He was awarded the Order of Culture in 1937, the year of its inception. _Tanaka Akira_

Nagaokakyō

City in southwestern Kyōto Prefecture, central Honshū. The site of NAGAOKAKYŌ, the imperial capital from 784 to 794. Conveniently located between the cities of Ōsaka and Kyōto, it is undergoing rapid urbanization. Principal industries are machinery and electrical appliances. It is known for its beer and bamboo shoots. Of interest are the excavated remains of the ancient capital and Kōmyōji, a temple associated with HŌNEN, the founder of the Jōdo Buddhist sect. Pop: 71,447.

Nagaokakyō

Imperial capital from 784 to 794. With the enthronement of Emperor Kōnin (709–782) in 770, the desire grew to move the capital from HEIJŌKYŌ (now the city of Nara), where the older nobility and the Buddhist monasteries were entrenched. In 784 the new emperor, KAMMU, decided to move to Nagaokakyō (now the city of Nagaokakyō, Kyōto Prefecture). With easier access to the Inland Sea via the river Yodogawa, the new site was more convenient for transportation. It was also the base of the wealthy HATA FAMILY, relatives of the ambitious Fujiwara no Tanetsugu, who had originally proposed the site. Several misfortunes took place, including the assassination of Tanetsugu by jealous rivals in 785, and following the suggestion of WAKE NO KIYOMARO, it was decided to move the capital to HEIANKYŌ (now the city of Kyōto) in 794. Excavations since 1955 have yielded the remains of several government buildings.
—— Fukuyama Toshio, _Daigokuden no kenkyū_ (1955). _Kitamura Bunji_

Nagaragawa

River in central Gifu Prefecture, central Honshū. It originates in the mountain Dainichidake in the northwestern part of the prefecture, flows through the Nōbi Plain, past the cities of Mino and Gifu and enters Ise Bay. Together with the IBIGAWA and KISOGAWA, it is known for numerous floods. The water is used for irrigation. CORMORANT FISHING (ukai) is a famous tourist attraction and has been practiced since the Heian period (794–1185); it takes place from the middle of May to the middle of October every year. Length: about 120 km (75 mi).

Nagareyama

City in northwestern Chiba Prefecture, central Honshū, on the river Edogawa. In the Edo period (1600–1868) Nagareyama prospered as a river port. Rice and mirin (a sweet sake) are its main products. The construction of large housing complexes has made Nagareyama a residential suburb of Tōkyō. Pop: 106,635.

Nagasaki

Capital of Nagasaki Prefecture, Kyūshū. Its importance as a port dates from 1571, when the local daimyō ŌMURA SUMITADA opened it at the request of the Portuguese. During the 200-year-long period of NATIONAL SECLUSION, the island of DEJIMA, constructed in Nagasaki Bay in 1634–36, was the only port opened to foreign trade (see

NAGASAKI TRADE). In 1855–61, Japan's first modern shipbuilding yard, the NAGASAKI SHIPYARDS (now a part of Mitsubishi Heavy Industries, Ltd), was constructed here. On 9 August 1945 an ATOMIC BOMB was dropped on Nagasaki; destruction was almost total. The city has recovered since then as a center of shipbuilding and other industries affiliated chiefly with Mitsubishi. The port serves as a base for deep-sea fishing and as an entrepôt for marine products. Special local products include *karasumi* (dried mullet roe), *kamaboko* (boiled fish paste), tortoise-shell work, and *kasutera*, a kind of sponge cake. The Urakami district, remembered as a place where Christianity was secretly practiced in defiance of the Tokugawa shogunate's bans (see KAKURE KIRISHITAN), is the site of the Urakami Catholic Church, Peace Park, International Cultural Hall, and Nagasaki University. The Ōura district, a residential area for foreigners since the end of the Edo period (1600–1868), contains the Glover Mansion, the residence of the English merchant Thomas Blake GLOVER, and the Ōura Catholic Church, built in 1864. Other places of interest are Sōfukuji, an Ōbaku Buddhist temple built in 1629; the Meganebashi, a Chinese-style stone bridge constructed in 1634; the site where the TWENTY-SIX MARTYRS were killed in 1597; and the remains of the Dutch trading post on Dejima. The Okunchi Festival (October), kite flying (April), and PEIRON BOAT RACES (June) attract great numbers of visitors each year. Area: 239.68 sq km (92.52 sq mi); pop: 447,091.

Nagasakibana

Cape on southern Satsuma Peninsula, Kagoshima Prefecture, Kyūshū. Composed of volcanic rock. It offers a view of the mountain Kaimondake and the islands dotting the sea to the south. It is the northernmost limit of the wild Japanese sago palm. The Ryūgū Shrine is located here. Nagasakibana is part of Kirishima–Yaku National Park.

Nagasaki Flag Incident

(Nagasaki Kokki Jiken). One of the most serious diplomatic issues between Japan and the People's Republic of China in the period before Japan's formal recognition of the latter. On 2 May 1958 a Japanese man took down the national flag of the People's Republic of China at an exhibition of Chinese postage stamps and paper cuttings sponsored by the Japan–China Friendship Association (Nitchū Yūkō Kyōkai) at the Hamaya department store in Nagasaki. The culprit was arrested but was soon released. Shortly before this incident, the Japanese government had stated that since Japan had no formal diplomatic relations with the People's Republic, the Chinese flag was not protected by Japanese law. The incident underlined the fact that Japan had not yet officially recognized China and delayed progress in trade relations.

The Chinese flag had already been a point of contention in efforts to establish informal relations. During negotiations over the fourth Japan-China trade agreement (signed 5 March 1958), the right of Chinese trade representatives to hoist the flag at a headquarters to be established in Japan had been a disputed issue, and attempts at compromise led to a bitter series of charges and countercharges involving Japan, the People's Republic, and the Nationalist government in Taiwan. After the Nagasaki incident, the Chinese broke off trade negotiations as well as cultural and friendship exchanges, and it was more than two years before another Chinese trade delegation came to Japan. *KAMACHI Noriko*

Nagasaki Kaisho

(Nagasaki Meeting Place). Semiofficial merchant organization that monopolized overseas trade during the Edo period (1600–1868), when foreign trade was limited to the port of Nagasaki under the NATIONAL SECLUSION policy of the Tokugawa shogunate. Formed in 1604 by merchants from Sakai, Kyōto, and Nagasaki who were granted monopoly rights in the raw-silk trade (see ITOWAPPU), and known as the Shōnin Kaisho, it was later enlarged to include merchants from Ōsaka and Edo (now Tōkyō) and was called the GOKASHO SHŌNIN Kaisho. By 1698, when it was renamed the Nagasaki Kaisho, it not only controlled all goods brought by Chinese and Dutch traders—the only foreigners allowed to enter Japan—but also supervised the flow of gold and silver in foreign exchange and the financial administration of the city. In return for its privileges, the organization paid taxes (UNJŌ) to the shogunate and donated part of its profits to the residents of Nagasaki. Although it was nominally

Nagasaki —— Statue of Peace, Peace Park

The bronze Statue of Peace by Kitamura Seibō, cast in 1955 for the Nagasaki Peace Park. Located near the hypocenter of the area devastated by the atomic bomb, the park is a memorial to the victims of the bombing.

under the jurisdiction of the city commissioners *(machi bugyō)* of Nagasaki, the Kaisho, with several government officials on its staff, operated as a self-governing organ until it was dissolved in 1867. See also NAGASAKI TRADE.

Nagasaki Prefecture

(Nagasaki Ken). Located in northwestern Kyūshū and bounded on the north by the Genkai Sea and Tsushima Strait, on the east by Saga Prefecture and the Ariake Sea, on the south by the Amakusa Sea, and on the west by the East China Sea. The prefecture is composed of four hilly peninsulas (the Kita Matsuura, Nishi Sonogi, Nagasaki, and Shimabara peninsulas), and off-shore islands that include TSUSHIMA, HIRADOSHIMA, and the Iki and Gotō groups. The climate is generally mild because of its southerly location and warm ocean currents.

Because of its proximity to the Asian mainland, the Nagasaki area has long served as one of Japan's most important contact points with foreign cultures. After the TAIKA REFORM of 645 the islands of Iki and Tsushima were made into island provinces, and the peninsular area was part of Hizen Province. Following St. Francis XAVIER's arrival at the port of Hirado in 1550, the area was visited by numerous European missionaries and traders. A major uprising occurred on the Shimabara Peninsula in 1637 (see SHIMABARA UPRISING) following the suppression of Christianity by the Tokugawa shogunate. For most of the Edo period (1600–1868) the city of NAGASAKI was the only port open to foreign commerce. The present boundaries were established in 1883 after the Meiji Restoration. In 1945 Nagasaki was the second city, after Hiroshima, to suffer an atomic bomb attack.

The principal products of the prefecture are sweet potatoes, sardines, coal, and ships. Cattle are bred on Hiradoshima and the Gotō Islands. In fishing it is second only to Hokkaidō, 20 percent of its catches being obtained by dragnet fishing. Pearl and seaweed culture is also carried out. Coal began to be mined in the 18th century and flourished in the Meiji period (1868–1912), but many of the mines have been shut down.

Tourist attractions include Unzen–Amakusa, Saikai, Iki–Tsushima, and Genkai national parks; the remains of the Dutch trading post on the island of Dejima; and the Chinese temple Sōfukuji, in the city of Nagasaki. There are also sites associated with Christianity, such as the ruins of Hara Castle, the scene of the Shimabara Uprising. Area: 4,102 sq km (1,583 sq mi); pop: 1,590,554; capital:

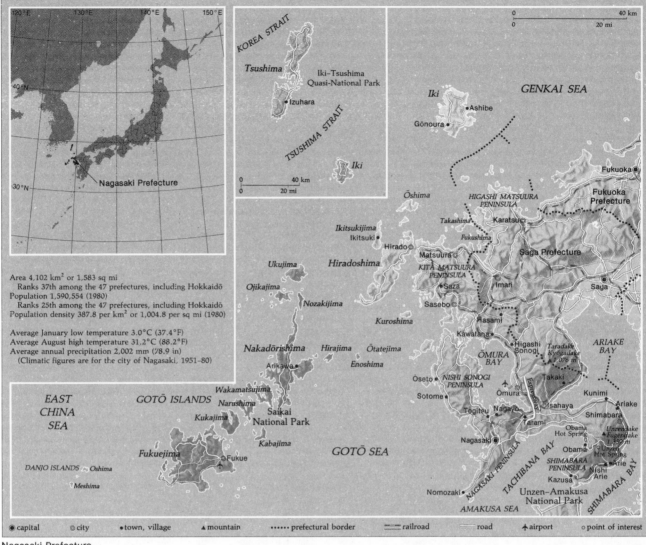

Area 4,102 km² or 1,583 sq mi
Ranks 37th among the 47 prefectures, including Hokkaidō
Population 1,590,554 (1980)
Ranks 25th among the 47 prefectures, including Hokkaidō
Population density 387.8 per km² or 1,004.8 per sq mi (1980)

Average January low temperature 3.0°C (37.4°F)
Average August high temperature 31.2°C (88.2°F)
Average annual precipitation 2,002 mm (78.9 in)
(Climatic figures are for the city of Nagasaki, 1951–80)

● capital   ◎ city   ● town, village   ▲ mountain   ••••• prefectural border   ═══ railroad   ═══ road   ✈ airport   ○ point of interest

Nagasaki Prefecture

Nagasaki. Other major cities include SASEBO, ISAHAYA, and ŌMURA.

Nagasaki school

(Nagasakiha). A school of artists active in Nagasaki from the 17th through the 19th centuries. Nagasaki was the only port open to foreigners during most of the Edo period (1600–1868); consequently, Nagasaki artists tended to concentrate on foreign subjects, such as the Dutch and Chinese residents of the city, sometimes borrowing technical and stylistic innovations from European or Chinese painting. Their art was multiform and subject to a variety of influences but may be divided into four main categories: woodblock prints created for the local tourist trade; official pictures painted by government artists to illustrate foreign objects imported into Japan; bird-and-flower paintings inspired by the Chinese artist SHEN NANPIN (Shen Nan-p'in; J: Chin Nampin) who taught in Nagasaki from 1731 to 1733; and works by individualist artists, often with Western techniques of shading and perspective. In addition, other types of art prevalent in Nagasaki included ŌBAKU SECT Zen paintings, *kanga* (Chinese painting), and BUNJINGA (literati painting).

Such diversity of styles and genres makes it difficult to establish in what measure any one of these stylistic traditions is present in a given painting or to classify individual artists by style. Instruction, friendships, and adoptions tended to cross school lines. Most of the Nagasaki painters drew freely from a potpourri of stimuli to make pictures of every conceivable type.

Woodblock Prints —— Known as Nagasaki *miyage* (souvenirs of Nagasaki), woodblock-printed pictures were popular as inexpensive mementos for travelers who wished to return home with a token of

the exotic city. Chief subjects were single or group studies of Dutch or Chinese traders, their great ships, and their exotic paraphernalia. Executed by amateurs, printed on low-grade paper, and colored by hand or with the use of a stencil, the untutored artlessness of early Nagasaki *miyage* communicates much charm. During the late Edo period these prints achieved a technical excellence that rivaled the best woodblock prints produced in Edo (now Tōkyō). Though few individual names emerged from the Nagasaki print tradition, a number of publishing houses became famous, chief among them Hariya, Toshimaya, Bunkindō, and Yamatoya.

Official Painters (Kara-e Mekiki) —— This is the branch of Nagasaki art specifically referred to by Japanese art historians as Nagasakiha. To meet the unique need to catalog foreign imports into Nagasaki, the government established a painting appraisal bureau in 1697 under the control of an official art appraiser (*kara-e mekiki*). His duties included making copies of imported paintings and other commodities for government records. The post continued with no major changes until it was abolished in 1870. The role of *kara-e mekiki* painters was analogous to that of the KANŌ SCHOOL painters: sanctioned by government patronage, they developed and were bound by a distinctive yet conservative style. The *kara-e mekiki* style at its best combined elements of traditional Japanese painting, Ming-dynasty decorative realism, and aspects of Western illusionism. The office was hereditary and claimed by four prominent families: Watanabe, Hirowatari, Ishizaki, and Araki. Each had its own distinctive character, Watanabe and Hirowatari conforming more to Chinese idioms, Ishizaki and Araki more to Western influence.

Shen Nanpin School —— The introduction of Chinese amalgams of European and Chinese stylistic elements profoundly affected the development of Western-style painting in Japan. The Chinese school most influential in this regard was that of Shen Nanpin, an artist relatively unknown in China. The art he taught had its roots in the long-established BIRD-AND-FLOWER PAINTING of China, which by the early 18th century had begun to show the effects of European stylistic influence. The rich, colorful, and, to the Japanese eye, extremely realistic paintings he created during his two years in Japan caused a sensation. Among the significant artists and later important transmitters of the style were KUMASHIRO YŪHI (1713–72), Sō Shiseki (1712–86), and Kakutei (b 1722).

Individualists—— The painters not hampered by the restrictions of the formal *kara-e mekiki* manner of painting were generally more daring and creative in their expression. The three most noted of the individualists were Wakasugi Isohachi (1759–1805), Araki Jogen (ca 1773–1824), and KAWAHARA KEIGA.

By the end of the Edo period, international treaties between Japan and the United States (1854), Britain (1854), and Russia (1855) opened other ports to foreign trade, and Nagasaki lost its prominence. The mystique of the foreigner, which had nurtured and sustained the tradition of the Nagasaki school, faded with the greater visibility of foreigners. See also WESTERN-STYLE PICTURES, EARLY.

■——Cal French, *Through Closed Doors: Western Influence on Japanese Art* (1977). Masanobu Hosono, *Nagasaki Prints and Early Copperplates* (1978). Kōbe Shiritsu Namban Bijutsukan, *Kōbe Shiritsu Namban Bijutsukan zuroku*, 5 vols (1968–72). Nagami Tokutarō, *Nagasaki no bijutsushi* (1974).   Cal FRENCH

Nagasaki Shipyards

(Nagasaki Zōsensho). Shipyard located in the city of Nagasaki, Kyūshū. Originally built by the Tokugawa shogunate with Dutch help in the years 1855–61, it was taken over by the new government after the Meiji Restoration of 1868 (see GOVERNMENT-OPERATED FACTORIES, MEIJI PERIOD). As part of the government's program of selling state enterprises to private interests (KAN'EI JIGYŌ HARAISAGE), the shipyard was leased to the entrepreneur IWASAKI YATARŌ in 1884 and sold to his firm, the MITSUBISHI Company, in 1887. Renamed the Mitsubishi Nagasaki Zōsensho in 1893, it was the largest privately owned shipyard in Japan until the end of World War II. It is now part of the MITSUBISHI HEAVY INDUSTRIES, LTD.

Nagasaki trade

Overseas trade centered in the port of Nagasaki from the first arrival of Portuguese ships in 1571 until the opening of Japan late in the Edo period (1600–1868). In a narrower sense the term refers to foreign trade after Japan was closed in 1639 by the NATIONAL SECLUSION policy of the Tokugawa shogunate. Before seclusion, trade in Nagasaki was virtually monopolized by the Chinese and the Portuguese, particularly the latter. Indeed, the Christian *daimyō* ŌMURA SUMITADA donated Nagasaki and its hinterland to Portuguese Jesuits in 1580. The city prospered as a center of missionary work and overseas trade until the national unifier TOYOTOMI HIDEYOSHI issued his ANTI-CHRISTIAN EDICTS in 1587 and took over the city. The Tokugawa shogunate also kept the city under its direct control and stationed a commissioner (Nagasaki *bugyō*) there to oversee the VERMILION SEAL SHIP TRADE. After its proscription of Christianity in 1639, the shogunate permitted only the Chinese and the Dutch to trade at DEJIMA, a man-made islet in Nagasaki Harbor (see also DUTCH FACTORY; DUTCH TRADE). For the next 200 years the administration of commerce was left largely to the NAGASAKI KAISHO, a semiofficial merchant organization that enjoyed exclusive rights to the Chinese raw-silk trade (see ITOWAPPU). Beside raw silk, the principal imports were silk fabric, herbs, sugar, and spices; exports included silver, copper, camphor, sulfur, and swords. The number of ships and the volume of trade were strictly regulated. With the signing of the ANSEI COMMERCIAL TREATIES in 1858 and the rescinding of the seclusion policy, Nagasaki lost its position as Japan's only international seaport.

Nagasawa, Kanaye (1853–1934)

Real name Isonaga Hikosuke. California winemaker whose career illustrates the Westernization of a *samurai* from the Satsuma domain (now Kagoshima Prefecture) late in the Edo period (1600–1868). He was born in Kagoshima, the son of Isonaga Magoshirō, superintendent of a gunpowder factory. Renamed Nagasawa before being sent abroad with other youths by the Satsuma government, he arrived in Great Britain in 1865, attended two years of school in Aberdeen,

Nagasaki Shipyards

Several ships under construction at the Nagasaki Shipyards of Mitsubishi Heavy Industries, Ltd.

Scotland, and went to London. Through Laurence OLIPHANT, member of parliament and former legation officer in Japan, Nagasawa met Thomas Lake HARRIS, an American mystic who invited him to the state of New York in 1867. As Harris's secretary, he rose to prominence in the Brotherhood of the New Life, Harris's utopian community, although it was never clear that he converted to Christianity. Nagasawa became manager of 2,000 acres near Santa Rosa when the group moved to California in 1875. Eventually inheriting the estate as sole owner, Nagasawa continued to run the community's winemaking ventures. He died on 1 March 1934, respected as a businessman, vintner, and horse breeder.   Joseph W. SLADE

Nagasawa Rosetsu → Rosetsu

Nagase & Co, Ltd

(Nagase Sangyō). Trading firm specializing in chemical goods. Nagase & Co was established in 1917 and has been under the management of the Nagase family ever since. It is the exclusive importer and sales agent for films and photographic materials from Eastman Kodak Co of the United States. It also has tie-up arrangements with General Electric Co of the United States and CIBA–Geigy A. G. of Switzerland, and is now becoming increasingly active in the field of plastics. It maintains eight offices and five local companies overseas. Sales for the fiscal year ending March 1982 totaled ¥475.5 billion (US $1.9 billion), and the company was capitalized at ¥5.2 billion (US $21.6 million). Corporate headquarters are located in Ōsaka.

Nagashino, Battle of

One of the decisive military encounters in the process of Japan's reunification in the late 16th century. On 29 June 1575 (Tenshō 3.5.21) the united forces of the hegemon ODA NOBUNAGA and the future shōgun TOKUGAWA IEYASU, said to number some 40,000 men, routed the inferior army of TAKEDA KATSUYORI, the *daimyō* of Kai, Shinano, and Suruga provinces (now Yamanashi, Nagano, and part of Shizuoka prefectures), who had laid siege to Ieyasu's fort at Nagashino in Mikawa Province (now Hōrai Chō, Aichi Prefecture). Katsuyori's defeat removed a dangerous threat from Nobunaga's eastern flank, freed him to mount an overpowering campaign against the adherents of the Buddhist Jōdo Shin sect (see IKKŌ IKKI) in the province of Echizen (now part of Fukui Prefecture) three months later, and helped him to consolidate his control over central Japan. Nobunaga's victory was due in great part to his force of 3,000 musketeers *(teppō ashigaru)*, who fought from behind entrenchments and palisades, inflicting terrible damage on Katsuyori's mounted knights; hence the Battle of Nagashino represents a change from the medieval to a more modern form of warfare (see FIREARMS, INTRODUCTION OF).   George ELISON

Nagata Masaichi (1906–   )

Film producer and owner of a professional baseball team. Born in Kyōto. He began to work for the Kyōto film studio Nikkatsu Productions (see NIKKATSU CORPORATION) in 1925 and founded his own company, Daiichi Eiga Sha, in 1934. He produced several masterpieces directed by MIZOGUCHI KENJI, such as *Naniwa erejii* (1936, Ōsaka Elegy) and *Gion no shimai* (1936, Sisters of the Gion). Apart from their professional work, Nagata had an intimate friendship with Mizoguchi. Nagata also produced KUROSAWA AKIRA's *Rashōmon* (1950), and *Shaka* (1961, Buddha), the first 70-millimeter film made in Japan. He received several imperial awards for his distinguished service in Japanese film production. His rather dictatorial manner and lack of sympathy toward labor, however, have often invited criticism not only from his employees, but also from the public. *ITASAKA Tsuyoshi*

Nagata Teiryū (1654–1734)

Also known as Taiya Teiryū or Yuensai. KYŌKA poet of the early part of the Edo period. The son of a pastry-shop owner in Ōsaka and elder brother of JŌRURI playwright KI NO KAION, he studied *haiku* and *kyōka* from an early age. He eventually became the first professional *kyōka* poet, training numerous disciples and popularizing *kyōka* in the Kyōto–Ōsaka area. Teiryū's *kyōka*, a skillful blend of the literary and the colloquial, are both amusing and delicate. Main collections are *Kyōka iezuto* (1729) and *Yuensai okimiyage* (1734).

Nagata Tetsuzan (1884–1935)

Lieutenant general of the Imperial Japanese Army and architect of the army's long-range military and industrial preparation for war. Born in Nagano Prefecture. Graduated from the Army Academy in 1904 and the Army War College in 1911. He was attached to several Japanese legations in Europe during and immediately after World War I. As a member of the army's special research committee to study the implications of that conflict he became impressed with the massive organization needed to wage modern war. He gained a reputation in the 1920s as an exceptionally brilliant strategist and was the first to articulate the concept of national defense mobilization, designed to put the Japanese army and nation on a total war footing in times of national emergency.

Promoted to major general in 1932 and appointed chief of the powerful Military Affairs Bureau (Gummukyoku) in 1934, Nagata was identified with the more pragmatic faction of the army, the TŌSEIHA (Control faction). His national planning ideas earned him the violent animosity of younger and more radical officers of the KŌDŌHA (Imperial Way faction), the faction insistent on "spiritual training." On 12 August 1935 he was assassinated by one of these Kōdōha officers, Lt. Col. Aizawa Saburō (1889–1936), who was executed after a military trial.

🔲——Mark Peattie, *Ishiwara Kanji and Japan's Confrontation with the West* (1973). Ben-Ami Shillony, *Revolt in Japan: The Young Officers and the February 26, 1936, Incident* (1973). *Mark R. PEATTIE*

Nagata Tokuhon (ca 1513–1630)

Physician. Also known as Kai no Tokuhon. Birthplace unknown. Nagata traveled through the country and treated the general public at a nominal fee. He is said to have been in the service of the Takeda family in Kai Province (now Yamanashi Prefecture) and to have treated a Tokugawa shōgun. He was the first in Japan to practice the basic medical treatments prescribed in the Han-dynasty Chinese medical book *Shang han lun,* such as inducing sweating and vomiting, and cathartic treatments. *YAMADA Terutane*

Nagato

City in northwestern Yamaguchi Prefecture, western Honshū, on the Sea of Japan. Nagato developed as a fishing port and market town during the Edo period (1600–1868). Fishing is still its chief industry. The island of Ōmijima off the coast is one of the most scenic spots in the Kita Nagato Coast Quasi-National Park. The Yumoto and Tawarayama hot springs are within the city limits. Pop: 27,576.

Nagato

A battleship of the Imperial Japanese Navy. Built as part of the so-called HACHIHACHI KANTAI (Eight Eight Fleet) program, it was the first battleship in the world to mount a 40 centimeter (15.8 in) main battery. Construction of the ship was begun at the Kure Naval Dockyard in 1917, and completed in 1920. It had a displacement of 43,000 tons, a top speed of 25 knots per hour, and a main battery of eight guns. The *Nagato,* a sister ship of the MUTSU, took part in the battles of MIDWAY, the PHILIPPINE SEA, and LEYTE GULF. It was seriously damaged in an air raid on Yokosuka naval port in July 1945. After the war it was used by the United States for nuclear bomb tests at Bikini Atoll in the Pacific. *ICHIKI Toshio*

Nagatoro

Gorge on the middle reaches of the river Arakawa, western Saitama Prefecture, central Honshū. It is characterized by exposed crystalline schist terraces. Nagatoro is designated a Natural Monument, and is part of the prefectural Nagatoro–Tamayodo Natural Park. Length: approximately 4 km (2.5 mi).

Nagatsuka Takashi (1879–1915)

WAKA poet and novelist. Born in Ibaraki Prefecture. He became a disciple of the poet MASAOKA SHIKI and strove to attain the ideal of objective photographic description *(shasei)* advanced by his teacher. He helped to fund the *waka* magazine *Ashibi* in 1903 with ITŌ SACHIO. He also wrote treatises on poetic theory. His *waka* reveal a delicate sensibility, finely tuned to the progression of nature. His masterpiece, the long novel *Tsuchi* (1910, The Earth), depicts the poverty-stricken life of tenant farmers in his native village seen against a background of the changing seasons. The work was highly praised by the novelist NATSUME SŌSEKI and is considered a classic of the "peasant literature" *(nōmin bungaku)* of the early 20th century. As a poet he is considered a member of the progressive *Araragi* group. His poetry is collected in *Nagatsuka Takashi zenkashū* (1951).

nagauta

(literally, "long song"). A major form of lyrical song *(utai-mono)* accompanied by SHAMISEN music, common in the KABUKI theater and in concerts. The earliest direct reference to *nagauta* is in the *Matsu no ha,* a 1703 collection of lyrics for *shamisen* songs. Though the term originally referred to music of the Kyōto–Ōsaka (Kamigata) area, *nagauta* developed primarily in the city of Edo (now Tōkyō) as kabuki dance music. *Shamisen* musicians were part of kabuki by the mid-17th century, though the specific use of the term Edo *nagauta* first appeared only in a kabuki poster of 1704. By the end of the 18th century *nagauta* became a major accompaniment genre for kabuki dances. In the 19th century it developed a tradition of non-danced concert pieces *(ozashiki nagauta)* which were performed in private mansions and now are heard in concert halls.

The standard *nagauta* ensemble today consists of several *shamisen* and singers plus hand drums *(ōtsuzumi and kotsuzumi),* the *taiko* stick drum, and either the NŌ-drama flute *(nōkan)* or a bamboo flute *(takebue or shinobue).* The drums and flute are known collectively as the *hayashi.* The *nagauta shamisen* is a middle-sized *(chūzao)* form. There may also be an obbligato *(uwajōshi)* shamisen with a capo *(kase)* attached to the fingerboard to accommodate higher pitches. The basic *nagauta* repertory contains over 100 pieces in both the dance and concert traditions. The kabuki dance form *(buyōji)* is basic to the structure of *nagauta* pieces although, like the sonata form in Western music, it is only a frame of reference upon which very different compositions can be created. Famous composers are Kineya Rokuzaemon IX (d 1819) who wrote the dance pieces *Oharame* (1810) and *Echigo-jishi* (1811); Rokuzaemon X (1800–1859), writer of the concert pieces *Aki no irokusa* (1845) and *Tsurukame* (1851); and Kineya Shōjirō III (1851–96), whose *Renjishi* (1872), *Genroku hanami odori* (1878), and *Kagamijishi* (1893) are popular on kabuki and dance stages as well as in concerts. Composition continues and *nagauta* is taught at the Tōkyō University of Fine Arts and Music as well as privately. See also KABUKI MUSIC.
🔲——Asakawa Gyokuto, *Nagauta no kiso kenkyū* (1955). William Malm, *Nagauta: The Heart of Kabuki Music* (1963). Tanabe Hisao, *Shamisen ongaku shi* (1963). *William P. MALM*

Nagaya no Ō, Rebellion of

(Nagaya no Ō no Hen). Political incident of the Nara period (710–794). Since the reign (672–686) of Emperor TEMMU, members of the imperial family had steadily gained political ascendance at the

court. By the time of Emperor SHŌMU (r 724–749), Prince Nagaya (676 or 684 to 729), a grandson of Temmu and descended from Emperor TENJI on his mother's side, had come to rival members of the FUJIWARA FAMILY in influence. In 729 a minor official of the Fujiwara faction secretly informed the emperor that the prince was plotting a rebellion. The emperor had the prince's residence surrounded, and the prince and his family were obliged to commit suicide.
KITAMURA Bunji

Nagayo Sensai (1838–1902)

Medical administrator. Born to a family of physicians in Hizen (now Nagasaki Prefecture). At the age of 16 he went to Ōsaka and became a pupil of OGATA KŌAN. After serving as president of Nagasaki Igakkō, a medical school, he visited Europe and the United States as a member of the IWAKURA MISSION (1871–73). Upon his return home he contributed to the founding of a modern medical system in Japan. He was responsible for the establishment of the Medical Affairs Bureau in the Ministry of Education, for the promulgation of the Vaccination Law, and for the drafting of a comprehensive medical law, the so-called Medical Order (Isei). He helped to set up the Tōkyō Igakkō (a predecessor of the medical faculty of Tōkyō University). He served as president of the school from 1875 to 1878 and director of the Bureau of Public Health in the Home Ministry.
ACHIWA Gorō

Nagayo Yoshirō (1888–1961)

Novelist, playwright. Born in Tōkyō. Son of the physician NAGAYO SENSAI. Graduate of Tōkyō University. Participated in *Shirakaba*, a coterie magazine founded in 1910 by MUSHANOKŌJI SANEATSU and other Peers' School (see GAKUSHŪIN UNIVERSITY) alumni. A typical spokesman for the liberal and humanistic philosophy of the group (see SHIRAKABA SCHOOL), he began writing plays and novels. Within the framework of a well-constructed plot, his works portray clashes between uncompromising idealists whose beliefs differ. Also known as a critic, Nagayo maintained his humanistic stance in the face of first the popularity of the so-called proletarian literature in the 1920s and later the coming of World War II. His works include *Kōu to ryūhō* (1916–17), a play, *Indara no ko* (1920), a collection of plays, *Takezawa sensei to iu hito* (1924–25), a novel, and *Waga kokoro no henreki* (1957–59), his autobiography.

nagegane

(literally, "invested silver"). Speculative investments in overseas trade made by Japanese merchants early in the Edo period (1600–1868). Wealthy merchants from the seaports of Hakata (now Fukuoka) and Nagasaki lent large sums of money individually or jointly to Portuguese and Chinese merchants, as well as to captains of Japanese overseas trading ships (see VERMILION SEAL SHIP TRADE), for their voyages and business transactions. The ships and cargo were put up as collateral. These loans were risky because of the possibility of shipwreck (in which case loans were cancelled) or bad faith on the part of the foreign traders. The merchants therefore charged very high interest rates, ranging from 35 to 110 percent. The term of the loans was six months, the time usually required for a round trip. The money used in these transactions was usually *chōgin*, or silver ingots.

naginata

A weapon with a wooden shaft approximately 1.2 to 2.4 meters (4–8 ft) in length and a curved blade usually 30 to 60 centimeters (1–2 ft) in length. The shaft butt is capped with iron. The term *naginata* also refers to the art of fencing with a simulated weapon composed of an oak shaft and a mock blade consisting of two strips of bamboo with a leather cap holding them together. The butt is capped with leather.

The *naginata* was the principal weapon of foot troops from the 11th century until well into the 15th century. It was the favorite weapon of Buddhist WARRIOR-MONKS. Early *naginata* tended to have shorter shafts and longer blades than those of the 17th century onward, when *samurai* women were trained in their use. Contrary to common belief, the *naginata* remained in the arsenal of men until the abolition of the feudal system following the Meiji Restoration (1868). Men's *naginata* had heavier blades and shafts than women's. During the Meiji period (1868–1912), *naginata* became primarily a form of physical exercise for women, although a few historical schools continued to have male mentors.

The All Japan Naginata Federation controls instruction and promotion in rank. *Kata* (form) receives great emphasis. In tournaments KENDŌ (fencing) equipment is worn but with two exceptions: the gauntlets have separate fingers for the index fingers, and the contestants wear *suneate* (shin guards). The cuts and thrusts are as in *kendō*, with the addition of cuts to the ankles and butt thrusts to the ribs. The Tendō school of *naginata* has the most adherents. This school uses oak substitutes for weapons and includes a wide variety of forms of weapons. The Tendō school alone has 160 *naginata* exercises.

──Roald M. Knutsen, *Japanese Polearms* (1963). Mitamura Kunihiko, *Dai Nippon naginata-dō kyōhan* (1939). Sonobe Shigehachi, *Kokumin gakkō naginata seigi* (1941). Zen Nihon Naginata Remmei, *Shashin to zukai ni yoru atarashii naginata* (1968).
Benjamin H. HAZARD

Nago

City on the island of Okinawa, Okinawa Prefecture. Principal products are pineapples, sugar cane, rice, beer, and cement. Nago was relatively untouched by World War II. Attractions include Nago Bay, Todoroki Falls, and the remains of Nago Castle. Pop: 45,994.

nago

A general term for low-status peasants who stood in a socially and economically dependent relationship to specific landowners. They were variously known as *myōshi, tsukurigo, hikan,* FUDAI, or *jige,* depending on the region. During the medieval period (13th–16th centuries), *nago* were serf-like peasants who worked the soil for such local landholders as MYŌSHU. During the Edo period (1600–1868) they were tenant cultivators in hereditary subordination to the landowners called HOMBYAKUSHŌ, to whom they owed labor services (in some areas they were permitted to substitute payment in goods). In return they received the use of small plots of land, separate dwellings, and common village property. In many cases *nago* were listed in the temple registers (*shūmonchō*) as members of their master's household; the master assured their livelihood, and they were required to obtain his permission to marry, to conduct funeral services, and so forth. With the development of a money economy, their numbers steadily declined. Some of them bought their way into the ranks of tenant farmers (MIZUNOMI-BYAKUSHŌ), while others chose to remain nominally *nago* to evade official responsibilities. Until recent times, the term *nago* continued to be used loosely in certain areas for hired help or menials in farming communities. See also OYAKATA AND HIKAN.

Nago Bay

(Nago Wan). Inlet of the East China Sea, on the western coast of the main island of Okinawa, Okinawa Prefecture. Nago, the main city in the north of the island, is on this bay, which forms part of the Okinawa Coast Quasi-National Park.

nagoshi

Annual rite of purification (*harae*) held at local Shintō shrines on the last day of the sixth month according to the lunar calendar. It is also called *minatsuki-barae,* borrowing the poetic synonym for the lunar sixth month, Minatsuki. Along with *ōharae* on New Year's Eve, *nagoshi* is one of two purificatory rites, observed by the imperial court since ancient times, which divides the year into equal segments. Today the rite of *nagoshi* takes different forms in various locales. A common practice on the observance of *nagoshi* is the rite of *chinowa*, in which the source of disease and defilement is believed to be eliminated by passing through a circle made of reeds. Another less common variation is to stroke the worshiper's body with a simply fashioned paper or straw doll (see KATASHIRO) to draw out any impurities and then to cast the doll into a stream. See also KEGARE; MISOGI.
INOKUCHI Shōji

Nagoya

Capital of Aichi Prefecture, central Honshū, on Ise Bay. The political, financial, and cultural center of the Pacific coastal area between Tōkyō and Ōsaka and the center of the CHŪKYŌ INDUSTRIAL ZONE,

Nagoya

Downtown Nagoya, with Maezu Park in the foreground and the Nagoya Television Tower in the distance.

it is the fourth largest city in Japan after Tōkyō, Yokohama, and Ōsaka.

Located on the fertile NŌBI PLAIN, Nagoya was settled early on; several mounded tombs (KOFUN) such as Shiratoriryō, said to be that of the mythic hero Prince YAMATOTAKERU, are located in its south central section. Toward the end of the medieval period (13th–16th centuries), it prospered as the seat of ATSUTA SHRINE, also connected with Prince Yamatotakeru. During the 16th century it was the military base of the Imagawa family, who built a castle, and was subsequently taken over by ODA NOBUNAGA. With the unification of Japan by TOKUGAWA IEYASU and the construction of a castle in 1609–14, Nagoya became the base of the Owari domain, one of the three successor houses (GOSANKE) of the Tokugawa family. Under the patronage of successive *daimyō*, the arts, particularly poetry, dance, and NŌ, prospered. Nagoya continued to be important in the modern era; it suffered considerable destruction during World War II but has been rebuilt with large-scale city planning.

Nagoya is preeminently a business-industrial city, with about 30 satellite cities within a 40-kilometer (25-mi) radius. Principal industries are transportation machinery, chemicals, steel, textiles, foodstuffs, and ceramic ware for export. It has traditionally been known for its *shippō* (CLOISONNÉ). The wholesale business, concentrated in the Chōjamachi area, takes up more than 90 percent of its total commerce. Its port facilities are among the largest in the country.

Nagoya Castle, rebuilt in 1959, is the chief tourist attraction. Other attractions are a television tower observatory, the Atsuta Shrine, and Ōsu Kannon, the popular name for the Shingon sect temple Shimpukuji. Recreational spots include the zoo and botanical garden at Higashiyama, the Peace Park, Tsuruma Park, and Nakamura Park. Educational institutions such as Nagoya University, the Prefectural Cultural Center, the Prefectural Art Museum, the Tokugawa Art Museum, the City Science Museum, and prefectural and city libraries are found in the city. The Ohoho Festival at the Atsuta Shrine (May) and the Nagoya Festival at the Tōshōgū Shrine (April) also draw visitors. Area: 325.97 sq km (125.82 sq mi); pop: 2,087,884.

Nagoya Castle

A castle located in the city of Nagoya; originally built in 1609–14 by the hegemon TOKUGAWA IEYASU, on the site of a smaller abandoned castle once occupied by ODA NOBUNAGA, to ensure the security of the Tōkai region in central Japan. It served as the residence of Ieyasu's ninth son Yoshinao, whose descendants (see GOSANKE) maintained control of the castle until the Meiji Restoration of 1868. The city of Nagoya grew up around the castle, which was considered an excellent example of late Momoyama architecture because of its lavish decoration and furnishings. The five-storied donjon was destroyed during World War II, but its exterior has since been reconstructed. Also reconstructed were replicas of its pair of famous golden *shachi* (dolphinlike sea creatures), almost 3 meters (10 ft) high and covered with gold scales, which now decorate the gable roof ends of the new ferroconcrete main keep. Three original corner turrets, the second front gate, and the stone foundation walls sur-

vived the war and have been designated Important Cultural Properties.

Nagoya Gen'i (1628–1696)

Physician. Also known as Nagoya Tansuishi. Regarded by many as the founder of *koihō*, the classicist school of traditional Chinese-style medicine. A native of Kyōto. A contemporary of Itō Jinsai, the Confucian scholar who proposed going back to the original teachings of Confucius, Nagoya advocated a return to classical Chinese medicine. He thus had a high regard for Chinese medical classics such as the *Shang han lun* and rejected the Chinese Jin-Yuan (Chin-Yüan) medicine on which the so-called latter-day school of medicine in Japan *(goseihō)* was based. See also MEDICINE: history of medicine. — YAMADA Terutane

Nagoya Railroad Co, Ltd

(Nagoya Tetsudō). Private railway company based in Nagoya. It boasts the second longest railway lines among private railway companies in Japan after KINKI NIPPON RAILWAY CO, LTD. Founded in 1894, it started operating electric streetcars in the city of Nagoya in 1898. It then extended its lines to the suburbs and absorbed other smaller lines in Aichi and Gifu prefectures to create a unified rail network in the Nagoya area. After World War II it diversified activities by creating subsidiary companies in bus transportation, department stores, housing development, and leisure. It is now the mainstay of the Meitetsu (Nagoya Railway) group, which numbers 270 companies in all. The company operates hotels on Saipan and Tinian in the Mariana Islands. In 1981 the total length of its railway tracks was 543.1 kilometers (337.5 mi); at the end of March 1982, annual revenue totaled ¥92.7 billion (US $385.1 million) and the company was capitalized at ¥29.7 billion (US $123.4 million). Corporate headquarters are located in Nagoya.

Nagoya University

(Nagoya Daigaku). A national, coeducational university located in Nagoya. Founded in 1881 as Aichi College of Medicine, it became the Aichi Prefectural College of Medicine in 1920, Nagoya National College of Medicine in 1934; Nagoya Imperial University in 1939; and Nagoya University in 1949. It has faculties of letters, education, law, economics, science, medicine, engineering, and agriculture, as well as the following research institutes: Institute of Environmental Medicine, Institute of Atmospherics, Water Research Institute, and Institute of Plasma Physics. Enrollment in 1980 was 7,184.

Naha

Capital of Okinawa Prefecture, on the island of Okinawa. A trading port of the kingdom of Ryūkyū (see OKINAWA) from early times, it served as a transit port for trade with Japan, China, and Southeast Asian countries. It became the prefectural capital in 1879, when Okinawa was incorporated into the Japanese prefectural system. Completely destroyed in World War II, Naha was under American military administration until 1972. Industries include tourism and small businesses. Local products are traditional Okinawan handcrafts such as porcelain, lacquer ware, *bingata* fabrics (see OKINAWAN TEXTILES), and *awamori* liquor. An international airport links Naha with other islands in the prefecture and with Japan proper and several foreign countries. Of interest are the gate called Shurei no Mon, the graves of the kings of Ryūkyū, and the stone pavement at Kanagusuku. Pop: 295,801.

naichi zakkyo

(mixed residence in the interior). A term used during the Meiji period (1868–1912) in reference to the opening of Japan to foreign residence. This was one of the most important, and symbolically one of the most emotional, issues in connection with revision of the so-called Unequal Treaties (see UNEQUAL TREATIES, REVISION OF).

Under the terms of the ANSEI COMMERCIAL TREATIES, which Japan concluded with Western nations in the 1850s, after 200 years of NATIONAL SECLUSION, foreigners were granted the right to reside in their own enclaves in some parts of the country, usually in cities and treaty ports where legations and consulates were established (see KYORYŪCHI). Within these enclaves they were free to engage in business, practice their religions, and own property. Most important, they enjoyed rights of extraterritoriality, so that all litigation concerning them was conducted in consular courts beyond the reach of Japanese law.

These arrangements were unsatisfactory for both foreigners and Japanese. The foreigners wished to escape the limits of their communities and enjoy similar freedoms throughout the country; it was they who pressed for *naichi zakkyo*. The Japanese, on the other hand, viewed extraterritoriality and other privileges as evidence that Westerners looked down on them as an inferior nation. They wished to end these prerogatives, and treaty revision became the main objective of Meiji diplomacy. It was also a domestic political issue, as opposition factions and members of the FREEDOM AND PEOPLE'S RIGHTS MOVEMENT combined their concern for people's rights with national rights.

It was clear that the most satisfactory solution to the question of treaty revision would be to open the country to foreign residence in return for the abrogation of extraterritoriality. But revision of the unequal treaties could be accomplished only through lengthy negotiations.

At first the foreigners were reluctant to surrender their privileges and hoped to extend them to the entire country, as they had done in China. They were openly scornful of the Japanese legal system and argued that their rights could never be protected under Japanese law. Eventually, however, as the Meiji government promulgated new civil and criminal codes and established a constitutional framework of government—all modeled on Western examples—Britain, the United States, and other nations one by one indicated readiness to relinquish their nationals' favored status.

The Japanese, for their part, were at first adamant against mixed residence. It became an emotional issue as nationalists and patriots recalled the tradition of their country as "the land of the gods," uncontaminated by the presence of aliens. The idea that foreigners might be allowed to live freely in the interior, owning land and engaging in business, was unthinkable. There were others, however, among whom BABA TATSUI was notable because he wrote about the subject in English, who conceded that if the Japanese wished to be treated as equals of Westerners, they must open their land to outsiders so long as the latter respected Japanese law.

The leaders of the Meiji government accepted as inevitable that foreigners must be permitted to reside and do business throughout Japan, but they were too timid at first to insist on the quid pro quo. Foreign Minister INOUE KAORU was willing to propose that Japan appoint foreign judges in Japanese courts to hear cases involving foreigners and seek Western approval of its domestic legal reforms before ending extraterritoriality. His successor, ŌKUMA SHIGENOBU, stiffened these terms but retained a provision for foreign judges. Foreign governments were willing to accept these proposals, but they were enormously unpopular in Japan. Domestic opposition was such that Inoue was forced from office in 1888 and Ōkuma was badly injured by a bomb in 1889. By then, however, most domestic opposition was directed at foreign judges, not foreign residence.

New treaties signed in 1894 (see ANGLO-JAPANESE COMMERCIAL TREATY) and subsequent years terminated extraterritoriality, and Japan was opened to foreign residence and commerce in 1899. The opening of Japan was to have far-reaching consequences because it brought capital and technology from abroad, which contributed greatly to the economic transformation of the country.

🕮——Hagihara Nobutoshi, *Baba Tatsui* (1967). Inoue Kiyoshi, *Jōyaku kaisei* (1955).   *Akira* IRIYE

naidaijin

1. (inner minister). In ancient times, an auxiliary government post (RYŌGE NO KAN), i.e., one not prescribed by the TAIHŌ CODE (701) as part of the RITSURYŌ SYSTEM of administration. FUJIWARA NO KAMATARI was the first to hold the post in 669. After the appointment of Fujiwara no Michitaka (953–995) as *naidaijin* in 989, the post became a permanent one, directly under the ministers of the right and left (*udaijin* and *sadaijin*).

2. (lord keeper of the privy seal). A post established in 1885, with the introduction of the cabinet system as a separate administrative office not of cabinet rank. The first *naidaijin* was SANJŌ SANE-TOMI, a courtier who had played an important role in the Meiji Restoration (1868). At first the post had little political significance, but with the passing of many of the Meiji oligarchs (GENRŌ), its holders gradually gained influence. In 1907, the Naidaijin Fu (Office of the Lord Keeper of the Privy Seal) was established. After the death of the last *genrō*, SAIONJI KIMMOCHI, in 1940, the politically astute *naidaijin* KIDO KŌICHI came to choose the prime ministers, a prerogative that formally belonged to the emperor. The post was abolished in November 1945.

Naikaku Bunko → Cabinet Library

naikan therapy

A rehabilitative and psychotherapeutic method of guided introspection developed by Yoshimoto Ishin (b 1916), a businessman and devout Buddhist. The term *naikan* (literally, "looking inward"), although divorced from religion, is rooted in the tenets of the JŌDO SHIN SECT (True Pure Land sect). It was first practiced in 1954 as corrective therapy for prison inmates and has since been expanded to treat mentally disturbed and physically ill patients and to promote moral discipline and revitalization in healthy adults and schoolchildren. Objective information regarding the success of *naikan* therapy is difficult to obtain, but the opinions expressed in professional circles—psychiatric, psychological, correctional—are sympathetic and positive.

Treatment lasts from one to two weeks. For best results, maximal isolation and immobility are imposed upon the client who is confined to a space just large enough to sit in, such as a corner of a room. The client is insulated from all external stimuli except for the counselor, who makes brief visits every hour or so to speak with him. During the waking hours, from dawn until nightfall, the client is supposed to make a constant effort to recollect and examine his past in accordance with a specific, threefold set of instructions. The client is advised to place himself in: (1) relation to a series of particular persons, most importantly his mother, who have played a significant role in his life; (2) in particular time intervals of his life, e.g., his school days; and (3) in relation to the questions he asks himself. What care (*sewa*) have I received? What have I done to repay (*okaeshi*) that care? What trouble (*meiwaku*) and worry (*shimpai*) have I caused others? The client is encouraged to remember concrete events rather than abstract impressions.

Naikan therapy, if properly conducted, should bring the client to a radical reevaluation of his self-image with a heightened awareness of his dependence upon the benevolence of and overwhelming debt to others, and a sense of irredeemable guilt for having so unjustifiably hurt them. Self-blame, gratitude, and humility are to replace punitive proclivities, rancor, and arrogance. Toward the final stage, the patient is expected to resolve to expiate his guilt by constructively working to repay the benefactors and serve society.

Naikan therapy has attracted the interest of cross-cultural researchers and therapists both in Japan and abroad because it is considered an exclusive product of Japanese culture and because its effectiveness is attributed to its appeal to certain Japanese core values. Most notable here are the moral value of self-examination (*jiko hansei*), an awareness of ON (indebtedness), the imperative of *ongaeshi* (repayment for an *on* debt), the need to avoid causing trouble (*meiwaku*) to others, and the importance of empathy or understanding (*omoiyari*) for the pain of others. These values become emotionally charged when locked, as in *naikan*, into the culturally stereotyped image of a nurturant, sacrificial, suffering mother (see CHILDHOOD AND CHILD REARING).

The cultural basis of *naikan* therapy is further found in the patterns of interaction between the counselor and client. The whole system of *naikan* is likened to a school rather than a clinic: the counselor and client are referred to as *sensei* (teacher) and *seito* (pupil), treatment as training or study, the completion of treatment as graduation. Stern discipline prevails in this "educational" atmosphere. At the same time, what impresses and disarms the client is the extraordinary humility on the part of the *sensei*. The hourly counseling begins and ends with the *sensei*'s deep bow; he or she never gives orders but politely and humbly requests the *seito* to follow his advice. This exemplary humility stimulates even greater humility on the part of the *seito*, which facilitates *naikan* reflection. In the course of the therapy the client may accumulate *on* debt to the counselor which motivates the debtor to complete the *naikan* course properly.

🕮——John I. Kitsuse, "A Method of Reform in Japanese Prisons," *Orient/West* (1962). Takie Sugiyama Lebra, "Culturally Based Moral Rehabilitation: The Naikan Method," in Takie Sugiyama Lebra, *Japanese Patterns of Behavior* (1976). Murase Takao, "Naikan Therapy," in William P. Lebra, ed, *In Culture-Bound Syndromes, Ethnopsychiatry, and Alternate Therapies* (1976). Okumura Nikichi,

Satō Kōji, and Yamamoto Haruo, ed, *Naikan ryōhō* (1972). Yoshimoto Inobu, *Naikan yonjūnen* (1965).

Takie Sugiyama LEBRA

Naikoku Kangyō Hakurankai → National Industrial Exhibition

Naimushō → Home Ministry

Naitō Jōsō (1662–1704)

HAIKU poet of the early part of the Edo period; one of BASHŌ's 10 principal disciples. Formerly a *samurai* of the Inuyama domain, Owari Province (now Aichi Prefecture), he became a priest in 1688 and joined Bashō's group the following year. He was the most faithful of Bashō's disciples, mourning the master's death for three years. Though he worked within a narrow scale, using only the random, everyday material of a simple life, his poetry is considered the finest expression of SABI, a concept of beauty that occupies a central place in Bashō's poetics. Some of his verses may be seen in the anthology *Sarumino* (1691), for which he wrote the postscript, and in the *Jōsō hokkushū* (1774). Among his prose works are the *Nekorobigusa* (1694), a moving essay written soon after Bashō's death, and the essay collection *Nembutsu sōshi* (1774).

Naitō Konan (1866–1934)

Scholar of Chinese history; original name, Naitō Torajirō. Born the son of a Confucian scholar in what is now Akita Prefecture, Naitō graduated from the Akita Normal School in 1885. He decided to become a journalist, and in 1887 he went to Tōkyō, where he joined the staff of the *Meikyō zasshi* (Journal of Enlightened Teaching). Three years later he joined the Seikyōsha, the nationalist organization founded by MIYAKE SETSUREI, and wrote for its journal, *Nihonjin* (The Japanese). He then worked for the newspapers YOROZU CHŌHŌ and *Ōsaka asahi shimbun*. In 1899 Naitō made the first of many trips to China; in 1907 he was invited to join the newly established seminar on Chinese history at Kyōto University and became a professor there in 1909. From then until his retirement in 1926, Naitō trained many scholars and helped to build up the university's strong tradition in East Asian studies. His interests in Chinese history ranged from ancient times through the Qing (Ch'ing) dynasty (1644–1912), and in his publications from 1914 onward he formulated a new theory of periodization analogous to that used for Europe. The so-called Naitō historiography (Naitō *shigaku*), later refined by his student and successor MIYAZAKI ICHISADA, was enormously influential among non-Marxist scholars and is still a principal feature of the "Kyōto school" of Asian studies. Naitō was also an expert on the history of Chinese painting, a collector of rare Chinese books, a skilled calligrapher, and a composer of Chinese poetry.

— Naitō Konan, *Naitō Konan zenshū* (Chikuma Shobō, 1969–76). Hisayuki Miyakawa, "An Outline of the Naitō Hypothesis and its Effects on Japanese Studies of China," *Far Eastern Quarterly* 14.4 (1955).

Naitō Torajirō → Naitō Konan

Nakabayashi Chikutō (1776–1853)

Artist in the BUNJINGA (literati painting) tradition. Born in Nagoya, the son of a physician. From the age of 15 Chikutō was patronized by Kamiya Ten'yū, a collector of Chinese paintings and calligraphy. When Chikutō was 20 he took up residence in a local temple and established a studio. At age 27 he went to Kyōto with friend and fellow painter YAMAMOTO BAIITSU, and there he joined the literati circle of the calligrapher and historian RAI SAN'YŌ.

As a theoretician Chikutō was conservative, professing strict adherence to Chinese literati theories and brush methods. He criticized popular art schools of his day for diverging from the proper Chinese literati spirit and he attempted to classify Japanese painters according to Dong Qichang's (Tung Ch'i-ch'ang) system of "Northern" and "Southern" schools (see NANGA).

Chikutō's paintings reflect his principles. They utilize restrained brushwork and are formal and academic rather than overtly expres-

sive, in harmony with his quiet, retiring nature. His style is largely based on early-17th-century Chinese interpretations of earlier artists' manners, but his works are generally more patterned and decorative than his Chinese sources. He is best known for his landscapes but also painted the "four gentlemen" (SHIKUNSHI) and birds and flowers. In addition, Chikutō published a number of painting manuals.

— Kanematsu Romon, *Chikutō to Baiitsu* (1910).

Patricia J. GRAHAM

Nakadai Tatsuya (1932–)

Actor. Real name Nakadai Motohisa. Born in Tōkyō, he joined the Haiyūza actors' training school in 1952 and performed his first stage role in 1954. His first movie appearance was a walk-on part in KUROSAWA AKIRA's *Shichinin no samurai* (1954, SEVEN SAMURAI). His true film debut was not until Inoue Umetsugu's *Hinotori* (1956, Fire Bird). He later appeared in a magnificent portrayal of the young protagonist in ICHIKAWA KON's *Enjō* (1958, Conflagration), the cinema version of MISHIMA YUKIO's novel *Kinkakuji* (Temple of the Golden Pavilion). He firmly established his position as a film actor in the lead role of KOBAYASHI MASAKI's five-part film, *Ningen no jōken* (1959–61, The Human Condition). Among other works by Kobayashi, Nakadai has starred in SEPPUKU (1962, Harakiri), *Kaidan* (1964, Kwaidan), and *Jōiuchi* (1967, Rebellion), which have all received acclaim abroad. Among works by Kurosawa Akira, Nakadai starred alongside MIFUNE TOSHIRŌ in *Yōjimbō* (1961, Bodyguard), *Tsubaki Sanjūrō* (1962), and *Tengoku to jigoku* (1963, High and Low). In Kurosawa's *Kagemusha* (1980), Nakadai himself played the lead. He is an adaptable actor, capable of playing all kinds of roles, whether villain, hero, or comic.

ITASAKA Tsuyoshi

Nakada Kaoru (1877–1967)

Scholar of the history of law. Born in Yamanashi Prefecture. A 1900 graduate of Tōkyō University, where he studied legal institutions of the Kamakura period (1185–1333), he joined its faculty in 1902 and became a full professor in 1911. Known primarily as the founder of the modern discipline of legal history in Japan, his interests extended to Chinese and European legal systems as well, but from 1925 onward he devoted most of his research to Japanese legal institutions of the premodern and early modern periods. He received the Order of Culture (Bunka Kunshō) in 1946. His writings include *Ōchō jidai no shōen* (1906, Shōen during the Late Heian Period) and *Meiji shonen no iriaiken* (1928, Commonage in the Early Meiji Period). The latter work has been used as a reference in settling commonage disputes.

UEDA Nobuhiro

Nakae Chōmin (1847–1901)

Materialist philosopher, political theoretician, and popular rights advocate of the Meiji period (1868–1912). Nakae Chōmin (original name Nakae Tokusuke) was born in Kōchi, the castle town of the Tosa domain (now Kōchi Prefecture), in 1847. His father, a low-ranking *samurai*, died while Chōmin was still a boy. Chōmin attended the domain academy, where he was trained in the Zhu Xi (Chu Hsi) school of Confucianism (SHUSHIGAKU). At the same time, he studied Wang Yangming Confucianism (YŌMEIGAKU) and learned Dutch with Hagiwara Senkei and Hosokawa Junjirō (1834–1923). In 1865 he was sent to Nagasaki to study French and subsequently made his way to the shogunal capital of Edo (now Tōkyō), where he served as interpreter for Léon ROCHES, the French envoy, in the closing years of the Tokugawa shogunate.

In 1871 Chōmin was sent to France by the new Meiji government and spent the next three years studying history, philosophy, and literature. Highly influenced by French and British liberal thought, he returned to Japan in 1874 and briefly served in the bureaucracy, first as head of the Tōkyō Foreign Language School and later as secretary of the GENRŌIN (Chamber of Elders). Policy differences with MUTSU MUNEMITSU forced him to resign his position in the Genrōin in 1877, whereupon he devoted himself to the private academy he had founded in 1874 and to his studies of Zen Buddhism and the Chinese classics.

In 1880 SAIONJI KIMMOCHI, whom he had come to know in France, returned to Japan and asked him to help in founding a newspaper. The result was the *Tōyō jiyū shimbun* (Oriental Free Press), in which Chōmin and Saionji urged the adoption of a parliamentary system of government and proclaimed the rights of the people.

With the demise of the newspaper under government pressure, Chōmin began to publish his own magazine, *Seiri sōdan* (Anecdotes on Statecraft). In it he published his translation of Rousseau's *Social Contract* in 1882.

Through his writings in the *Tōyō jiyū shimbun, Seiri sōdan,* and the Liberal Party (JIYŪTŌ) organ, the *Jiyū shimbun,* Nakae Chōmin became known as one of the leading liberals of his day and as the principal spokesman for the radical wing of the FREEDOM AND PEOPLE'S RIGHTS MOVEMENT. As the "Eastern Rousseau," his popular nickname, Chōmin found himself out of step with the conservatively inclined Meiji oligarchs. Like other supporters of the Jiyūtō, he was expelled from Tōkyō under the new PEACE PRESERVATION LAW OF 1887 (Hoan Jōrei). Moving to Ōsaka he founded the *Shinonome shimbun* (The Dawn News) and had a hand in organizing *sōshi shibai,* a kind of political street theater. It was at this time that KŌTOKU SHŪSUI became his student.

With the promulgation of the Meiji Constitution in 1889, Chōmin decided to enter politics, and succeeded in being elected to the first national Diet in 1890. His political goals were to form a united front of the popular parties against government power in order to continue the struggle for greater public rights in the newly established parliament. These goals were thwarted, however, when the Tosa branch of the Jiyūtō gave way to government bribery and pressure, and Chōmin, incensed at the duplicity of his allies, resigned his seat in the Diet.

Chōmin spent the next 10 years working at a variety of commercial jobs, none of which proved particularly successful. Dissatisfied with his life in the business world, he tried to reenter politics in 1898 with a new political party, the Kokumintō (National People's Party). But this venture also ended in failure, and in 1900 he was informed by his doctors that he had only a short time to live.

In the following year and a half Chōmin wrote his two most important philosophical works, *Ichinen yūhan* (A Year and a Half) and *Zoku ichinen yūhan* (A Year and a Half, Continued). In these works he expanded on the materialistic philosophical position he had first developed in *Rigaku kōgen* (An Exploration of the Principles of Philosophy), published in 1886. Contrasting the idealistic world of psychic images *(ishō setsu)* with a materialistic theory of substance *(jisshitsuron),* Nakae attempted to establish a philosophical system that could bridge the world of Tokugawa idealism to the scientific realism that he identified with the modern West. His final effort in this quest, *Zoku ichinen yūhan,* which was subtitled "No God, No Spirit," was completed a few days before his death in 1901, and constitutes what many scholars regard as the most important statement on Meiji materialism.

Chōmin was a prolific writer. In addition to *Rigaku kōgen, Ichinen yūhan, Zoku ichinen yūhan,* and numerous other books and articles on political and philosophical subjects, he published his major political study, *Sansuijin keirin mondō* (A Discussion on Politics by Three Intoxicated Men), in 1887. It was written in the form of a convivial conversation between the fictitious Professor Nankai—an idealistic political philosopher—and his two visitors, one a progressive gentleman scholar of so-called WESTERN LEARNING and the other a more nationalistic conservative. The book was an attempt by Chōmin to stimulate popular interest in sovereignty, parliamentarianism, and other questions of government. A complex thinker, Chōmin's philosophical materialism is often seen as a link between the 19th-century Japanese intellectual tradition and modern Western materialist doctrines such as socialism and Marxism, to which his disciple, Kōtoku Shūsui, was subsequently attracted.

◪ —— Works by Nakae Chōmin: *Nakae Chōmin shū* (Kaizō Bunko, 1929). *Chōmin senshū* (Iwanami Bunko, 1936). Works about Nakae Chōmin: Nobutaka Ike, *The Beginnings of Political Democracy in Japan* (1950). Kōtoku Shūsui, *Chōmin sensei* (1902). Hijikata Kazuo, *Nakae Chōmin* (1958). Kuwabara Takeo, *Nakae Chōmin no kenkyū* (1969). F. G. NOTEHELFER

Nakae Tōju (1608–1648)

Confucian scholar; founder of the Wang Yangming school (YŌMEIGAKU) of Confucianism in Japan. He was born the son of a farmer in Ōmi (now Shiga Prefecture) but was raised and educated by his grandfather who was a *samurai* retainer of a *daimyō* in Iyo (now Ehime Prefecture) in Shikoku. After a period of service with the same daimyō, Tōju returned to Ōmi in order to take care of his mother. Here he started a private school and taught the Confucian classics. He was admired for his exemplary lifestyle and respected for his learning; he came to be known as the Sage of Ōmi.

Tōju began his Confucian studies with the philosophy of Zhu Xi (Chu Hsi; see SHUSHIGAKU) but in his mid-30s turned his attention to the teachings of Wang Yangming. Zhu Xi taught that *li* (J: *ri*), the principle of all things, emanates from an objective, timeless Supreme Ultimate (taiji or t'ai chi; J: taikyoku). In contrast, Wang Yangming believed that *li* exists in the mind a priori and is known intuitively. The two schools came into conflict, the Zhu Xi school being officially endorsed by the Tokugawa shogunate, but Tōju continued to admire both philosophers. "The wisdom of the two men," he wrote, "consists in their embracing in their hearts the principle of heaven and in overcoming selfish desires. Neither of them would kill a single innocent person even if world conquest were at stake." As this statement indicates, Tōju's chief concerns were moral conduct and the pursuit of justice. Learning was to be pursued, not for worldly ends but for moral reasons. The virtuous life, he asserted, lay in following the dictates of one's conscience or what Wang Yangming called "intuitive knowledge" or "good knowledge" (liangzhi or liang-chih; J: ryōchi). Since good knowledge is inherent in everyone, all have an equal chance of becoming virtuous. In this sense, Tōju believed in the equality of men and women.

Good knowledge, Tōju further explained, was universal and eternal. It was identical with all principles of virtue and synonymous with the principles of heaven, the mind, and filial piety. He placed special emphasis on filial piety because he believed that it was a fundamental virtue that should and could be pursued by everyone.

Tōju, emphasizing unity of thought and action, believed that one's understanding of virtue must be put into practice. His philosophy, therefore, tended to foster an activist way of life and influenced many important thinkers and political leaders of Tokugawa Japan. At the end of the Edo period (1600–1868), proimperialist samurai known as *shishi* were influenced by the teachings of Tōju and his disciples and put their notions of justice into practice by working for the overthrow of the Tokugawa shogunate and the restoration of imperial rule. The most prominent of Tōju's disciples was KUMAZAWA BANZAN, who was actually more effective in disseminating Wang Yangming's philosophy than his teacher. *Okina mondō* (Dialogues with an Old Man) is Tōju's best known work.

◪ —— Galen M. Fisher, "The Life and Teaching of Nakae Tōju, the Sage of Ōmi," in *Transactions of the Asiatic Society of Japan* 36 (1908). Inoue Tetsujirō, *Nihon shushigaku no tetsugaku* (1933). Itō Tasaburō, ed, *Nakae Tōju, Kumazawa Banzan,* in *Nihon no meicho,* vol 11 (1976). *Tōju sensei zenshū,* 5 vols (Iwanami Shoten, rev ed 1940). Mikiso HANE

Nakagawa

River in Tochigi and Ibaraki prefectures, central Honshū, originating in the mountain Nasudake and flowing south past the city of Mito to enter the Pacific Ocean at the city of Nakaminato. It was formerly used for transportation. The water is utilized by Mito for drinking and by the city of Katsuta for industrial purposes as well as for irrigation. Length: 126 km (78 mi); area of drainage basin: 3,270 sq km (1,262 sq mi).

Nakagawa

River in southeastern Tokushima Prefecture, Shikoku, originating in the mountains on the border between Tokushima and Kōchi prefectures and flowing east into Kii Channel at the city of Anan. Cedar afforestation is in progress on the upper reaches, and mandarin oranges *(mikan)* are cultivated on the lower reaches. Dams and electric power plants are being constructed. Length: 125 km (78 mi); area of drainage basin: 874 sq km (337 sq mi).

Nakagawa Gorōji (1768–1848)

Involuntary resident in Russia and introducer of smallpox vaccination techniques into Japan. While serving as a guard-interpreter in the southern Kuril Islands in 1807, he was captured by Russian raiders and taken to Siberia. During the next five years he visited Irkutsk, surreptitiously destroyed maps and documents on Japan whenever the opportunity arose, and at Yakutsk observed the immunizing effects of smallpox vaccine while working as a doctor's assistant. Brought back to Japan in 1812 to be exchanged for Captain V. M. GOLOVNIN, a surveyor seized on Kunashiri (the southernmost Kuril island) the previous year, Nakagawa bolted from his captors. He subsequently wrote an account of Russia and put into practice the medical knowledge acquired there during the smallpox epidemics of 1824, 1835, and 1842. He was afterwards employed in the service of the Matsumae domain (now part of Hokkaidō).

John J. STEPHAN

Nakagawa Jun'an (1739–1786)

Physician and scholar of WESTERN LEARNING. Born to a family of physicians in the Obama domain (now part of Fukui Prefecture), in his youth he developed an interest in botany and mineralogy, and in 1764, with HIRAGA GENNAI, he invented a kind of asbestos cloth. He later became interested in Western medicine, and after studying the Dutch language with the physician Yasutomi Kiseki, he joined with MAENO RYŌTAKU, SUGITA GEMPAKU, and others in translating into Japanese the *Ontleedkundige Tafelen* (1734, Anatomical Tables), a Dutch version of the German work *Anatomische Tabellen* (1722) by Johann Adam Kulmus (1689–1745). Published in 1774 as *Kaitai shinsho* (New Book of Anatomy), this work laid the foundation for the study of European medical science in Japan. Jun'an also studied with the Dutch physician and botanist Carl Peter THUNBERG and became friendly with Izaak TITSINGH, the director of the Dutch trading post in Nagasaki.

Nakagawa Yoichi (1897–   )

Novelist, poet. Born in Kagawa Prefecture. Studied at Waseda University. Nakagawa began his career as a WAKA poet, in 1924 joining *Bungei jidai*, a coterie magazine that gave birth to the SHINKANKAKU SCHOOL. In 1925 he published two short stories, "Gozen no satsujin" and "Kōru butōjō," written in an elaborate and exotic style. A love story, *Ten no yūgao* (1938), was very popular on the eve of World War II. His postwar novels include *Shitsuraku no niwa* (1950) and *Tambi no yoru* (1957–58).

Nakagawa Zennosuke (1897–1975)

Legal scholar. Born in Tōkyō, he was graduated from Tōkyō University in 1921. The following year he was appointed to the law faculty of Tōhoku University, where he remained until his retirement in 1961. Thereafter he served as a professor at Gakushūin University and as president of Kanazawa University. A protégé of HOZUMI SHIGETŌ, Nakagawa made important contributions to the field of family law, and he played a leading role in the revision of the CIVIL CODE after World War II. His writings include *Mibunhō no kiso riron* (1939, Basic Theory of the Law of Domestic Relations), *Nihon shinzokuhō* (1942, Family Law in Japan), *Shinzokuhō* (1958, Family Law), and *Sōzokuhō* (1964, Inheritance Law). BAI Kōichi

Nakahama Manjirō (1827–1898)

Also known as John Manjirō or John Mung. Fisherman from Tosa Province (now Kōchi Prefecture) who lived for several years in the United States and later became an official of the Tokugawa shogunate and the Meiji government. In 1841 Manjirō and four others were shipwrecked on a deserted island believed to have been Torishima, some 570 kilometers (354 mi) south of Tōkyō. Four months later they were rescued by an American whaling ship, the *John Howland*. His fellow castaways disembarked in Hawaii, but Manjirō, whose intelligence had impressed the captain, William Whitfield, was invited to go to the United States. With Whitfield's support, he studied at a school in Fairhaven (near New Bedford), Massachusetts, and then worked at a cooperage and shipped on a whaling voyage before going to California in 1849 to prospect for gold. With his earnings he took passage on a mail boat and returned to Japan via Okinawa in 1851. Because of the shogunate's NATIONAL SECLUSION policy, Manjirō was at first subjected to interrogation by the Nagasaki commissioner, but the next year he was allowed to return to his home province, where he was employed by the *daimyō*.

When US Commodore Matthew C. PERRY arrived in Japan in 1853 to demand that the shogunate open the country to foreign trade, Manjirō was called into service as a translator; in 1855 he was made an instructor at the Nagasaki Naval Training Center (KAIGUN DENSHŪJO). In 1859, after Japan had opened its ports to trade with the United States, he published the first English-language phrasebook, *Eibei taiwa shōkei* (Shortcut to Anglo-American Conversation). In 1860 Manjirō acted as chief interpreter for the shogunate embassy to the United States to ratify the HARRIS TREATY of 1858 (see UNITED STATES, MISSION OF 1860 TO). In 1864 he was invited

by the government of the Satsuma domain (now Kagoshima Prefecture) to teach English, navigation, and whaling. After the Meiji Restoration of 1868, he was appointed by the new national government as an instructor at the Kaisei Gakkō (now Tōkyō University).

Nakahara Chūya (1907–1937)

Poet. Born in Yamaguchi Prefecture. Attended Ritsumeikan Middle School in Kyōto. Nakahara initially wrote *waka* poems. He was later attracted to the free-form poetry of the dadaist TAKAHASHI SHINKICHI. In 1924, he went to Tōkyō and became friends with the critic KOBAYASHI HIDEO and the poet Tominaga Tarō (1901–25), through whom he was introduced to the poetry of the French symbolists Rimbaud and Verlaine. He began experimenting with symbolist verse, writing such poems as "Asa no uta" (1926). His poetry collections include *Yagi no uta* (1934) and *Arishi hi no uta* (published posthumously in 1938).

Nakai Riken (1732–1817)

Neo-Confucian scholar of the Edo period (1600–1868). Born in Ōsaka, the son of Nakai Shūan, a Confucian scholar instrumental in founding KAITOKUDŌ, a school for commoners. With his older brother Chikuzan (1730–1804), Riken studied with Goi Ranshū (1697–1762) at the Kaitokudō. After their father's death, the two sons took on the management of the school. Riken later founded his own school, the Suisaikan, but after Chikuzan's death he returned to the Kaitokudō. Unlike his brother, who was extrovert, fond of literature, and interested in affairs of government, Riken was eccentric and preferred the sequestered life of a scholar. His teachings tended to draw on elements from different schools rather than depending solely on the Neo-Confucian (SHUSHIGAKU) tenets then dominant in Japanese scholarship.

Nakajima Atsushi (1909–1942)

Novelist. Born in Tōkyō. Graduate of Tōkyō University. Most of his writing was done during the 10 years that he taught at a girls' high school in Yokohama. Seeking a better climate for his asthma, he went for one year (1941–42) to Palau, Western Caroline Islands, at that time under Japanese mandate, as an official of the South Sea Islands Government Office. *Kotan* (1942), a set of stories he wrote during this time, was published in *Bungakukai*. His next work, *Hikari to kaze to yume* (1942), an account of Robert Louis Stevenson's final years in Samoa, gained him further recognition. *Riryō* (1943, published posthumously), a novel set in China during the early Han dynasty (206 BC–AD 8), perhaps best exemplifies Nakajima's qualities—elegance of language, erudition, and pessimism.

Nakajima Chikuhei (1884–1949)

Businessman and politician. A pioneer of Japan's aircraft industry; born in Gumma Prefecture and graduated from the Naval Engineering School. Realizing the future potential of airplanes while in the navy, he resigned from it in 1917 to establish the Airplane Research Institute. The institute later became the Nakajima Aircraft Co, the manufacturer of numerous military airplanes, including the Nakajima Model 5 and engines for the ZERO FIGHTER. Nakajima was elected to the House of Representatives in 1930 and became leader of one of the factions of the RIKKEN SEIYŪKAI in 1939. He served as railways minister (1937–39) and commerce and industry minister (1945). After World War II, in 1950, Nakajima Aircraft Co was split into 12 independent companies, 5 of which later merged to establish FUJI HEAVY INDUSTRIES, LTD, an automobile company that now makes Subaru. KOBAYAKAWA Yōichi

Nakajima Nobuyuki (1846–1899)

Politician. Born in Tosa Province (now Kōchi Prefecture). Nakajima joined the antishogunate movement of the 1860s, working for the KAIENTAI, a trading company organized by the Tosa activist SAKAMOTO RYŌMA to buy Western arms. After the Meiji Restoration (1868) he became governor of Kanagawa Prefecture (1874) and then a member of the GENRŌIN (Chamber of Elders), the protosenatorial body. His sympathies with the FREEDOM AND PEOPLE'S RIGHTS MOVEMENT eventually alienated Nakajima from the oligarchic government, however, and he joined the JIYŪTŌ (Liberal Party) at the time of its founding in 1881. He was chosen vice-president, but the following year he left to become president of the Rikken Seitō (Constitutional Government Party), a spin-off from the Jiyūtō. He was banished from Tōkyō under the newly enacted PEACE PRESERVATION LAW OF 1887 (Hoan Jōrei) for his political activities, but in the first Diet elections (1890) he was elected to the House of Representatives as a member of the Rikken Jiyūtō (later the Jiyūtō) and became the first speaker of the House. He left the Jiyūtō in 1892, was appointed ambassador to Italy the same year, and was made a member of the House of Peers two years later. His wife was KISHIDA TOSHIKO, an early feminist.

Nakajima Shōen → Kishida Toshiko

Nakajima Toshiko → Kishida Toshiko

Nakajō

Town in northern Niigata Prefecture, central Honshū. Nakajō developed as a market town and POST-STATION TOWN in the Edo period (1600–1868). With the discovery of natural gas, a chemical industry has developed. Agriculture is also active. Good skiing and swimming facilities are located here. Pop: 29,014.

Naka Kansuke (1885–1965)

Novelist; poet. Born in Tōkyō. Graduate of Tōkyō University, where he was a student of NATSUME SŌSEKI. In order to alleviate his family's financial difficulties after his father's death and his brother's mental illness, he wrote Gin no saji (1913; tr The Silver Spoon, 1976). This novel, which deals with the world of a little boy, is based on his own experiences as an introverted child of poor health who is fascinated with beauty and hungry for love. Through Sōseki's recommendation, it was serialized in the newspaper Asahi shimbun (April–June 1913; April–June 1915), and with this he achieved recognition as a novelist. Throughout his life, he remained outside the main literary currents, writing essays and short stories that reflected his stoic, reclusive life. Other works include Inu (1922), a novel, and Rōkan (1935), a collection of poems.

Nakama

City in northern Fukuoka Prefecture, Kyūshū, on the river Ongagawa. Formerly a farming village, Nakama developed rapidly in the middle of the Meiji period (1868–1912) with the opening of the CHIKUHŌ COALFIELD. Since the closing of the mines in 1964, enamel ware and electric appliance industries have been introduced. Housing projects have made it into a satellite city of Kita Kyūshū. Habu Park is noted for its 100 images depicting the disciples of Buddha. Pop: 48,647.

Naka Michiyo (1851–1908)

Historian. Born in the Morioka domain (now Iwate Prefecture). At the domain school he was considered a child prodigy and was adopted by one of his teachers, Naka Michitaka. After graduating from Keiō Gijuku (now Keiō University), he taught East Asian history and Chinese classics at various schools, including Tōkyō University and the Tōkyō Higher Normal School (later Tōkyō University of Education). Naka is remembered for having proven definitively that the traditional date (660 BC) for the accession of JIMMU, the legendary first emperor of Japan, was historically invalid (see KIGEN). In addition to ancient Japanese history, he wrote on the Yuan (Yüan; 1279–1368) and Qing (Ch'ing; 1644–1912) dynasties of China and on Korea and Mongolia.

Nakamigawa Hikojirō (1854–1901)

Businessman who laid the foundation of the MITSUI industrial and financial conglomerate (ZAIBATSU). Born into a samurai family of the Nakatsu domain (now part of Ōita Prefecture), Nakamigawa was a nephew of FUKUZAWA YUKICHI, the outstanding propagator of Western knowledge during the Meiji period (1868–1912). After studying at his uncle's school, Keiō Gijuku (now Keiō University), and in England, he entered government service in 1878 as a protégé of the statesman INOUE KAORU. Nakamigawa resigned his post when ŌKUMA SHIGENOBU was ousted from government in the POLITICAL CRISIS OF 1881, and in the following year he began publish-

ing the daily newspaper JIJI SHIMPŌ for Fukuzawa. As president of the San'yō Railway Company from 1887 to 1891, Nakamigawa introduced radical and innovative management policies. In 1891 he was appointed director of the Mitsui Bank and entrusted with the task of reorganizing the floundering Mitsui combine. Serving until his death as virtual leader of the entire Mitsui zaibatsu during its formative years, Nakamigawa carried out major reforms, modernizing Mitsui's management, abandoning its traditional dependence on government patronage, and expanding its investment in modern industry.

📖——Nihon Keiei Shi Kenkyūjo, ed, Nakamigawa Hikojirō denki shiryō (1969). Tsunehiko Yui, "The Personality and Career of Hikojirō Nakamigawa, 1887–1901," Business History Review 44 (Spring 1970). Steven J. ERICSON

Nakaminato

City in eastern Ibaraki Prefecture, central Honshū, on the Pacific. The city flourished as a transit port during the Edo period (1600–1868) for products being shipped from Sendai to Edo (now Tōkyō). It is a base for deep-sea fishing for bonito, mackerel, and tuna. Seafood processing and shipbuilding industries thrive. The beach at Ajigaura is popular with swimmers. Pop: 33,324

Nakamura

City in southwestern Kōchi Prefecture, Shikoku. Situated on the river Shimantogawa, Nakamura developed under the courtier Ichijō Norifusa (1423–80), who fled with his followers from Kyōto during the ŌNIN WAR. Place names taken from parts of Kyōto, like Kyōmachi and Gion, remain to this day. Rice, vegetables, fruit, lumber, and marine products are produced. Pop: 35,465.

Nakamura Chōhachi (1865–1940)

Roman Catholic priest active in the Japanese immigrant community in Brazil. Born in Nagasaki Prefecture and christened Domingos, Nakamura was assigned to Brazil as a missionary in 1923. He spent the rest of his life in the difficult task of evangelizing in remote areas and gained great respect among Japanese immigrants and native Brazilians alike. Church and civil leaders in the area where he lived have expressed hope of receiving official recognition of his work from the Vatican. SAITŌ Hiroshi

Nakamura Fusetsu (1866–1943)

Western-style painter; calligrapher. Real name Nakamura Sakutarō. Born in Tōkyō, he studied there with Koyama Shōtarō (1857–1916) and then in France with Jean-Paul Laurens. Upon his return to Japan in 1905 he joined the Taiheiyō Gakai (Pacific Painting Society). He often painted historical subjects, particularly from Chinese history, in a European academic style. He was such an accomplished calligrapher that the novelist MORI ŌGAI asked in his will that Nakamura write the inscription for his gravestone. In 1936 Nakamura established the Calligraphy Museum (Shodō Hakubutsukan) in Tōkyō, which houses a collection of over 10,000 items of Chinese calligraphy and related materials.

Nakamura Gakuryō (1890–1969)

Japanese-style painter. Real name Nakamura Tsunekichi. Born in Shizuoka Prefecture, he studied traditional TOSA SCHOOL painting with Kawabe Mitate (1837–1905). In 1912 he graduated from the Tōkyō Bijutsu Gakkō (now Tōkyō University of Fine Arts and Music). Later he became a member of the reorganized Nihon Bijutsuin (see JAPAN FINE ARTS ACADEMY) artist group. He is chiefly remembered for his copies of the wall paintings in the temple HŌRYŪJI in Nara, and for his murals in the main hall of the SHITENNŌJI in Ōsaka. For these accomplishments he received the Order of Culture and was made a member of the Japan Art Academy (Nihon Geijutsuin). Influenced by Western painting, particularly in his choice of bright colors, he nonetheless remained faithful to the YAMATO-E tradition.

Nakamura Hajime (1921–   )

Scholar of Indian philosophy and Buddhism. Born in Matsue, Shimane Prefecture, he graduated from Tōkyō University in 1936 and taught there from 1954 to 1973. With Indian philosophy and Buddhist studies as his point of departure, he produced a large volume of works in the field of comparative study of ideas. He was also active in the advancement of cultural exchange between Japan and other nations. His best-known work is *Tōyōjin no shii hōhō* (1948–49; tr *Ways of Thinking of Eastern Peoples: India, China, Tibet, Japan,* 1962–63). In 1973 he founded a private academy, the Tōhō Gakuin, for the study of East Asian thought. The following year he completed a three-volume dictionary of Buddhist terms, *Bukkyōgo daijiten.*

📖——Nakamura Hajime, *Nakamura Hajime senshū,* 23 vols (Shunjūsha, 1961–77).　　　　*Murakami Shigeyoshi*

Nakamura Kenkichi (1889–1934)

WAKA poet. Born in Hiroshima Prefecture. Graduate of Tōkyō University. From around 1909 he became a major contributor to *Araragi,* the influential *waka* poetry magazine founded in 1908, to which he submitted naturalist-style poems colored by a youthful romanticism. He later shifted to a more subjective and meditative style. His principal collections are *Rinsenshū* (1916) and *Keiraishū* (1931).

Nakamura Kusatao (1901–)

HAIKU poet. Real name Nakamura Seiichirō. Born in Fujian (Fukien), China, where his father was a diplomatic official. Graduate of Tōkyō University. In 1933 he joined *Hototogisu,* an influential modern haiku coterie originally founded by MASAOKA SHIKI in 1897. He later became disenchanted with the group's preoccupation with mere description of nature, and he left it to establish his own magazine *Banryoku* in 1946. In his later works, he attempted to evoke the whole of human existence. Principal collections are *Chōshi* (1936) and *Banryoku* (1941).

Nakamura Masanao (1832–1891)

Also known by his pen name, Nakamura Keiu. Born in Edo (now Tōkyō). Confucian scholar; best known for his translations of Samuel Smiles's *Self Help* (1871) and John Stuart Mill's *On Liberty* (1871). *Self Help (Saigoku risshi hen)* was widely read and was called "the bible of the Meiji era."

In addition to being a prodigious writer and translator, Nakamura was a prominent educator and thinker. In 1873 he founded the Dōjinsha school, which was on par with FUKUZAWA YUKICHI's Keiō Gijuku in its day, later headed what was to become Ochanomizu Women's University, and taught at Tōkyō University. A pioneer in women's education and in humanitarian causes, Nakamura was baptized on Christmas Day 1874, becoming the first prominent Meiji figure to become a Christian.

Nakamura's active humanism and belief that God's laws are indelibly inscribed upon each man's conscience can be traced to his background as a Confucian scholar. Nakamura entered the SHŌ-HEIKŌ, the official shogunate academy of Confucian studies, as the youngest student in its 240-year history and soon came under the influence of SATŌ ISSAI, who stressed the monistic intuitive YŌMEI-GAKU philosophy. In his search for the moral foundation for the West's superior strength Nakamura concluded that it was Christianity. Equating the traditional Confucian concept of *tendō* (the "Way of heaven") with the Christian concept of the "Laws of God," Nakamura maintained that Japan would become a strong and prosperous nation only if individual Japanese listened to God's voice within them and acted accordingly. Nakamura took the lead in the MEIRO-KUSHA, Japan's leading society of modernizers, in advocating moral development as the necessary prelude to significant institutional change.

📖——Jerry K. Fisher, "Nakamura Keiu: The Evangelical Ethic in Japan," in Robert J. Miller, ed, *Religious Ferment in Asia* (1974). Takahashi Masao, *Nakamura Keiu* (1966).　　*Jerry K. Fisher*

Nakamura Mitsuo (1911–)

Literary critic. Real name Koba Ichirō. Born in Tōkyō. Graduate of Tōkyō University. He began writing literary essays in his early twenties and gained recognition for his *Futabatei Shimei ron* (1936), a critical study of Japan's first modern novelist, FUTABATEI SHIMEI. From 1938 to 1939 he studied in France. After World War II, he established himself as a major critic. His 1950 book *Fūzoku shōsetsu ron* was widely acclaimed. In this polemic he asserted that modern Japanese novels were "distorted," tending to be no more than fictionalized autobiographies lacking in meaningful social criticism. Most of Nakamura's works are critical biographies of writers that emphasize their intellectual development. He received the Yomiuri Literary Prize in 1958 for his *Futabatei Shimei den* and again in 1964 for the play *Kiteki issei.* His other works include the critical studies *Tanizaki Jun'ichirō ron* (1954) and *Shiga Naoya ron* (1954). English translations of his works include *Contemporary Japanese Fiction* (1969) and *Modern Japanese Fiction* (1968).

Nakamura Shin'ichirō (1918–)

Novelist, poet, literary critic. Born in Tōkyō. Graduate of Tōkyō University. He was a member of the Matinée Poétique group, formed in 1942, which made a great contribution after World War II to new forms of poetry. A writer in the early wave of postwar literature, he established his name as a novelist with a set of five novels, reminiscent of the work of Proust, that begins with *Shi no kage no moto ni* (1946–47) and ends with *Nagai tabi no owari* (1952). Nakamura is also known for his numerous essays on 20th-century European literature. His principal works are *Kaiten mokuba* (1957), *Kūchū teien* (1963), both novels; and *Rai San'yō to sono jidai* (1971), a critical biography of the early 19th century scholar RAI SAN'YŌ.

Nakamura Tekisai (1629–1702)

Neo-Confucian scholar of the early part of the Edo period (1600–1868). Born into a wealthy merchant family in Kyōto, he studied Confucianism on his own. He led a reclusive life, devoting himself to the "investigation of things" (*kakubutsu kyūri*) that ranged from heavenly bodies to plants, animals, and weights and measures. Together with ITŌ JINSAI, he was considered the most prominent scholar of his time. See SHUSHIGAKU.

Nakamura Utaemon

A well-known family line of KABUKI actors, originally from the Kyōto-Ōsaka area. Utaemon I (1714–91) was famous for his *jitsuaku* (villainous *samurai*) roles. Utaemon III (1778–1838) surpassed Utaemon I, his father, in both skill and popularity, becoming one of the greatest actors of his time. Since he was not handsome, he did not perform romantic leads, but otherwise, Utaemon III brilliantly covered the entire range of male and ONNAGATA (female impersonator) roles. He was also a gifted dancer. His successor and pupil Utaemon IV (1798–1852) also was remarkably versatile, capable of playing any role in the kabuki repertory. He earned the nickname: "Kaneru" ("Versatile One"). In his prime, the popularity of Utaemon III exceeded that of Bandō Mitsugorō IV (1800–1863), a magnificent performer and a professional rival.

Throughout his long and distinguished career, Utaemon V (1865–1940) remained primarily an *onnagata.* After the death of Ichikawa Danjūrō IX (1838–1903; see ICHIKAWA DANJŪRŌ) and Onoe Kikugorō V (1844–1904; see ONOE KIKUGORŌ), his elegant, classical performances gave a strong sense of continuity to the then uncertain future of kabuki. He collaborated with TSUBOUCHI SHŌYŌ (1859–1935), a leading scholar of the Japanese theater, in presenting Shōyō's plays, which incorporated elements of Western theater, such as from the opera.

His son, Utaemon VI (b 1917), is a leading *onnagata* of the contemporary kabuki stage. Utaemon VI's deep concern for the preservation of the classical style in the kabuki theater is revealed clearly by his dedicated efforts to encourage the writing of new kabuki plays in a style and form more faithful to past practices. MISHIMA YUKIO, who wrote some of them, was one of his most ardent supporters. Utaemon VI also performs in the revival of those important kabuki plays that are rarely presented. These two artistic goals are largely promoted through his own loyal circle of devoted pupils and colleagues who, as a group, present special performances. Along with Onoe Baikō VII (b 1915), another celebrated *onnagata,* Utaemon VI has been designated one of the LIVING NATIONAL TREASURES by the Japanese government.

📖——Ihara Seiseien (Toshirō), ed, *Utaemon jiden* (1935). Kawatake Shigetoshi, *Kabuki meiyū den* (1956). Mishima Yukio, ed, *Rokusei Nakamura Utaemon* (1959).　　*Ted T. Takaya*

Nakano

City in northeastern Nagano Prefecture, central Honshū. It was under direct shogunate control during the Edo period (1600–1868).

Fruits, mainly apples, grapes, and peaches, are grown. Nakano is Japan's leading producer of *enokidake*, a kind of mushroom. It is also known for its handicrafts made of willow, akebia *(akebi)*, and wood. Pop: 39,318.

Naka no Ōe, Prince → Tenji, Emperor

Nakano School

(Rikugun Nakano Gakkō). Popular name given to the secret sabotage, propaganda, and intelligence program conducted by the Imperial Japanese Army during the Second Sino-Japanese War and World War II. Formed under the auspices of the Army Ministry's Military Service Bureau in 1938, the program took the cover name Kōhō Kimmu Yōin Yōseijo (Rear Service Personnel Training Center) and was loosely called a school by its members. It was first located in the Kudan district of Tōkyō. Moved to the western Tōkyō suburb of Nakano in 1940, the Rikugun Nakano Gakkō was assigned a commanding officer of the rank of major general. Students, selected from intellectually astute junior officers, followed an ambitious curriculum that included foreign languages, foreign cultures, cryptography, and radio engineering. Between 1938 and 1945, some 3,000 graduates took assignments in the United States, the Soviet Union, Germany, China (including Manchuria), India, and Southeast Asia. One alumnus, Lieutenant Onoda Hiroo (b 1922), returned to Japan in 1974 after a solitary 30–year war in the jungles on the Philippine island of Lubang.   John J. STEPHAN

Nakano Seigō (1886–1943)

Journalist and politician, widely known for his speeches denouncing political corruption and advocating spiritual individualism. Nakano was born in Fukuoka, the eldest child of a father who came from a lower *samurai* background. He graduated from Waseda University in 1909 (with a major in political science and economy) and joined the newspaper *Tōkyō asahi shimbun* as a correspondent. Nakano also wrote regularly for MIYAKE SETSUREI's journal, *Nihon oyobi nihonjin* (Japan and the Japanese), which was widely read and respected. In 1913 Nakano married Miyake's daughter, and in 1923 he joined forces with him in establishing a new journal, *Gakan* (Our View). In these journals, Nakano challenged the Europocentric view of the modern world and defended Japan's development within the Asian cultural context. He urged his readers to retain their cultural legacy of spiritual independence, selfless commitment, and the ideal of refusing to conform to external historical forces.

Nakano's basic ideas are set forth in a historical account of Meiji political and intellectual history, *Meiji minken shi ron* (Popular Rights during the Meiji Period), which he published in 1913. The origins of modern Japan, he argued, are found in the rise of the common people during the MEIJI RESTORATION (1868) and the unleashing of creative action by unique, nonconformist individuals. These two themes remained important in his thinking and writing throughout his career. He consistently advocated the importance of "popular nationalism" and, on this basis, criticized the dominance of politics by elites. He also referred often to the spirit of individualism exemplified in the philosophical tradition of Wang Yangming (J: Ō Yōmei; see YŌMEIGAKU) and embodied in such great historical figures as ŌSHIO HEIHACHIRŌ and SAIGŌ TAKAMORI. These men, he believed, were totally dedicated to the radical popular ideal that made possible opposition to conservative bureaucratic politics.

Nakano joined the political party movement to actualize within the context of the Diet some of the ideals he advocated. Beginning in 1920, he was elected eight times to the lower house from his home city of Fukuoka. He joined INUKAI TSUYOSHI's Reform Club (Kakushin Kurabu), then entered the KENSEIKAI party, and in 1927 its successor, the RIKKEN MINSEITŌ. His investigation of the TANAKA GIICHI cabinet's involvement in the assassination of the Chinese warlord ZHANG ZUOLIN (Chang Tso-lin) led to the dissolution of the cabinet in 1929. Later, as vice-minister of communications in the HAMAGUCHI OSACHI cabinet, he submitted legislation to establish government ownership of the telephone system.

Despite these concrete efforts, Nakano's political career was destined to end in bitter frustration. His idealistic populism and individualism could not be actualized within Diet politics, and he found himself increasingly isolated from the major factional alignments in the Rikken Minseitō. In 1932 he joined a splinter group called the National Alliance (Kokumin Dōmei), and in 1936, the

TŌHŌKAI, serving as president. Believing that Diet politics was hopelessly corrupt, Nakano was briefly attracted to what he believed to be an "idealistic individualism" in Hitler and Mussolini. Moreover, on the basis of this popular nationalism, which held that all societies in Asia had the right to develop their own distinctive cultural identities, Nakano endorsed the "liberation of Asia." Throughout these years he continued to speak out against bureaucratic insensitivity and arbitrary government.

Nakano openly criticized the government headed by TŌJŌ HIDEKI during World War II. He denounced the IMPERIAL RULE ASSISTANCE ASSOCIATION as being bureaucratic and not popular and condemned the government-controlled elections of 1942. In defiance of the government's suppression of speech and assembly, in a three-hour speech at Waseda University on 10 November 1942 Nakano entreated his young audience to retain as precious values spiritual autonomy, the capacity to resist, and the determination to oppose the despotic forces of bureaucracy in the name of an ideal. He reminded them of their individual potential to rise up alone in the universe *(tenka hitori o motte okoru),* saying that this was the foundation of their freedom.

In October 1943, suspected of plotting the overthrow of Tōjō, Nakano was arrested and jailed. A month later, placed under house arrest and forbidden to write for the press or deliver public speeches, he took his own life.

◼——Nakano Seigō, *Meiji minken shi ron* (1913). Inomata Keitarō, *Nakano Seigō no shōgai* (1964). Tetsuo Najita, "Nakano Seigō and the Meiji Restoration in Twentieth-Century Japan," in James Morley, ed, *Dilemmas of Growth in Prewar Japan* (1971).

Tetsuo NAJITA

Nakano Shigeharu (1902–   )

Poet, critic, and novelist; born and raised in the hamlet of Takaboko, Fukui Prefecture, the second son of a small farmer and petty government official. His first literary works were *tanka* (31-syllable WAKA poems in the classical five-line form), composed while he was a member of a student poetry association in the Fourth Higher School of Kanazawa in Ishikawa Prefecture. In April 1924 Nakano entered the German Literature Department of Tōkyō University. In the summer of 1925 he was admitted to the SHINJINKAI (New Man Society), Japan's first Marxist student organization. The experience of metropolitan life, as well as involvement with radical politics, led Nakano to turn away from classical poetic forms to the writing of lyric free verse and essays. His poems in the magazine *Roba* (Donkey), organized by Marxist students under the aegis of the poet MUROO SAISEI, won him encouragement from the writer AKUTAGAWA RYŪNOSUKE.

Nakano became a member of the Nihon Puroretaria Geijutsu Remmei (Japanese Proletarian Arts League) in 1926. After graduating from Tōkyō University in March 1927, he devoted himself to full-time work in the PROLETARIAN LITERATURE MOVEMENT. He was a founder and editor of the magazine *Puroretaria geijutsu* (Proletarian Arts), where he published his first short story, "Shōnen" (1927, The Boy). In March 1928 Nakano was elected to the standing committee of the newly formed NAPF (Nippona Artista Proleta Federacio) and to the editorial board of its magazine *Senki* (Battle Flag). That year he and the leftist critic KURAHARA KOREHITO engaged in a sharp debate in the pages of *Senki* on the nature of proletarian art. The first volume of Nakano's critical essays, *Geijutsu ni kansuru hashirigakiteki oboegaki*, was published by Kaizōsha in 1929; his first anthology of fiction, *Tetsu no hanashi* (Stories of Steel), was published in June 1930.

Nakano married the SHINGEKI (New Theater) actress Hara Masano in April 1930. In the summer of 1931 he formally joined the underground organization of the Japan Communist Party. That October the first anthology of his poetry, *Nakano Shigeharu shishū* (1935, Collected Poems of Nakano Shigeharu), was confiscated from the publisher by the police. In April 1932, after four previous short detentions, Nakano was arrested and held in prison for nearly two years. He was released with commuted sentence after making a minimal statement of ideological conversion (TENKŌ) in which he admitted being a Communist Party member and promised to withdraw. The theme of *tenkō* dominated Nakano's works from 1934 to 1936, particularly the celebrated novella *Mura no ie* (1935, The House in the Village). In December 1937, as the war in China intensified, Nakano was enjoined from publishing for one year. When the ban was lifted, he published the novel *Uta no wakare* (1939, Farewell to Song), describing student life in Kanazawa, the move to

Tōkyō, and his decision to turn from *tanka* to free verse. During the Pacific War, Nakano was under constant police surveillance. Resisting pressure to write prowar propaganda he limited his publications to several literary essays, including an excellent study of the *tanka* poet SAITŌ MOKICHI, *Saitō Mokichi nōto* (1940–41).

After the war's end, Nakano helped found the Shin Nihon Bungakukai (Society for a New Japanese Literature). He rejoined the Communist Party in November 1945. Between July 1946 and September 1947, Nakano directed a series of essays, *Hihyō no ningensei* (Humanness in Criticism), against ARA MASAHITO and HIRANO KEN of the Kindai Bungakukai (Modern Literature Association) in a politics and literature debate. The novella *Goshaku no sake* (Five Cups of Sake), an original critique of the postwar constitution and emperor system, appeared in January 1947. In April 1947 Nakano was elected Communist Party representative to the Diet and served for three years.

Nakano worked in Communist Party cultural activities throughout the 1950s and early 1960s while writing novels and numerous essays. The novel *Muragimo* (1954, Gut Feelings) recaptured Nakano's Shinjinkai experience, revealing his underlying sense of confusion in the face of the conflicting demands of his artistic sensitivity, his political commitments, and his filial duty to his father in the countryside. *Nashi no hana* (1957–58, Pear Blossoms), based on Nakano's rural childhood, won the Yomiuri Literary Prize in 1960. In 1964 Nakano was purged from the Communist Party along with dissidents who opposed the ban on Soviet partial nuclear testing. His long novel *Kō, otsu, hei, tei* (1965–69, A, B, C, D) is a retrospective examination of his relationship with the party.

■———Nakano Shigeharu, *Nakano Shigeharu zenshū*, 28 vols (Chikuma Shobō, 1976–80). *Brett DE BARY*

Nakanoshima Kin'ichi (1904–)

Composer, performer, and scholar of SŌKYOKU *koto* music. His father, a SHAKUHACHI player, was the eldest son of the Yamada-school KOTO musician Nakanoshima Shōsei (1838–94); his own earliest studies in *koto* were with his mother, who died when he was 10. After studies in *koto*, NAGAUTA, and *itchū-bushi* with various other teachers, he became head of the Nakanoshima line, and in 1937 was appointed a professor at the Tōkyō Music School (now Tōkyō University of Fine Arts and Music), where he has remained throughout his professional career. His many works for *koto* and other Japanese instruments are written in a forceful and sometimes contrapuntal style that incorporates elements of Bartok and Bach but displays a consummate understanding of native traditions.

Representative pieces are the *koto* solo *Mittsu no danshō* (1942) and the *shamisen* solo *Banshikichō* (1941). He frequently performs with his wife Keiko, daughter of the Yamada-school musician Imai Keishō (1871–1947); their sensitive, controlled playing can be heard on many recordings. Nakanoshima has performed abroad on several occasions, and has also edited all the classical Yamada-school works. *David B. WATERHOUSE*

Nakano Tomonori (1887–1965)

Businessman. Born in Tokushima Prefecture; graduate of Kyōto University. While serving as an assistant at the university, Nakano developed the Nakano cell for brine electrolysis. He established the NIPPON SODA CO, LTD, to make commercial use of the new technology. He later diversified into many other fields and developed a financial and industrial combine known as Nissō Kontserun (from the German *Konzern*) in 1937. After World War II, however, Nakano's business empire was forced to break up, and he remained relatively inactive during his last years. *UDAGAWA Masaru*

Nakano Ward

(Nakano Ku). One of the 23 wards of Tōkyō. On the Musashino Plateau. After the Tōkyō Earthquake of 1923, it developed rapidly as a residential community. A number of railway stations in the ward are surrounded by busy shopping centers. Pop: 345,575.

Nakano Yoshio (1903–)

Scholar of English literature and literary critic. Born in Ehime Prefecture. Graduate of Tōkyō University, where he later taught Elizabethan drama. He also wrote journalistic essays. Since 1953, when he gave up his university post, he has been an active critic on many social and political issues. His numerous translations of English works include *The Merchant of Venice, Gulliver's Travels,* and *The Moon and Sixpence.* Other works are *Erizabesu chō engeki kōwa* (1947), lectures on Elizabethan drama, and *Roka Tokutomi Kenjirō* (1972–74), a voluminous critical biography of TOKUTOMI ROKA, the Meiji-period (1868–1912) novelist.

Nakaoka Shintarō (1838–1867)

Antishogunate activist from the Tosa domain (now Kōchi Prefecture). The eldest son of a high-ranking village official, he became interested in the SONNŌ JŌI (Revere the Emperor, Expel the Barbarians) movement under the influence of his fencing teacher, TAKECHI ZUIZAN, who was the leader of the Tosa loyalist movement. In 1862 he went to Kyōto to join proimperial activists from all over Japan. After the COUP D'ETAT OF 30 SEPTEMBER 1863 expelled the radical loyalists from Kyōto, however, Tosa rejected extremism in favor of the more moderate MOVEMENT FOR UNION OF COURT AND SHOGUNATE. Nakaoka was obliged to quit his domain and join other activists in Chōshū (now Yamaguchi Prefecture), the center of the antishogunate movement. In 1864 he participated in the unsuccessful attempt to reestablish Chōshū's influence at the court (see HAMAGURI GOMON INCIDENT). Two years later he and SAKAMOTO RYŌMA, another activist from Tosa, succeeded in negotiating the SATSUMA–CHŌSHŪ ALLIANCE, a military coalition with the rival domain of Satsuma (now Kagoshima Prefecture). Allowed to return to Tosa, he organized a 50-man squad (the RIKUENTAI) to engage in antishogunate activities in Kyōto. Even after the shōgun TOKUGAWA YOSHINOBU formally returned his political mandate to the emperor in November 1867, Nakaoka demanded that the Tokugawa give up all their lands and offices. In December 1867 he and Sakamoto were killed by members of the Mimawari-gumi, a shogunate patrol squad in Kyōto. See also MEIJI RESTORATION.

Nakao Kumaki (1900–1975)

Leader of the Japanese immigrant community in Brazil. Born in Kumamoto Prefecture, Nakao emigrated to Brazil at the age of 14. While working as a farmer, he published a manual for writing letters in Portuguese in 1922. He helped found the Cotia Cooperative Society (founded in 1927), and later established the Jaguaré Fertilizer Company. He was the second president of the Japanese Culture Society of Brazil (Sociedade Brasileira de Cultura Japonesa) as well as the founder and director of the Center for Japanese-Brazilian Studies (Centro de Estudos Nipo-Brasileiros). *SAITŌ Hiroshi*

Nakarai Bokuyō (1607–1678)

Physician and poet of *haikai* (see HAIKU) and KYŌKA. Born in the city of Sakai in what is now Ōsaka Prefecture. Nakarai studied *haikai* under MATSUNAGA TEITOKU, founder of the Teimon school, and had several of his verses published in anthologies. He was called to Edo (now Tōkyō) to serve as physician to the shōgun's family. The sharp wit of his extemporaneously composed *kyōka* gained him considerable respect among a circle of prominent shogunate officials and their wives. His *haikai,* though noted for their buoyant and rhythmic style, show little depth of insight. He is chiefly noted for the posthumous collection *Bokuyō kyōkashu.*

Nakasendai Rebellion

(Nakasendai no Ran). Unsuccessful rebellion led by Hōjō Tokiyuki (d 1353) against Emperor GO-DAIGO and his KEMMU RESTORATION government in 1335; an attempt to restore the KAMAKURA SHOGUNATE, which had fallen in 1333. Remnants of the HŌJŌ FAMILY, who had been waiting for an opportunity, gathered under Tokiyuki and raised an army with the aid of the Suwa family of Shinano Province (now Nagano Prefecture). They occupied Kamakura briefly but were defeated by ASHIKAGA TAKAUJI. Tokiyuki managed to escape and was pardoned by Go-Daigo, but he was later killed in battle by Takauji, who had himself turned against the emperor late in 1335. The term *nakasendai* refers to Tokiyuki as heir to his father, HŌJŌ TAKATOKI, the last Kamakura regent; he was called *sendai* ("previous generation") in contrast to Ashikaga Takauji, who was called *kōdai* ("later generation").

Nakasendō

One of the five main highways (GOKAIDŌ) under direct control of the Tokugawa shogunate during the Edo period (1600–1868); also known as Kiso Kaidō or Kisoji. With 67 post stations along its 500-kilometer (315-mi) route, this road passed through the mountains of central Japan, starting at Nihombashi, the bridge in Edo (now Tōkyō) where all other highways converged, and ending slightly east of Kyōto at Kusatsu (in present Shiga Prefecture), where it joined the TŌKAIDŌ, the main coastal route between Kyōto and Edo. In contrast to the heavily traveled Tōkaidō, the mountainous Nakasendō had little traffic and, although longer by 20 kilometers (12.4 mi), had fewer streams to cross. Toll barriers (SEKISHO) were maintained at Usui (in present Gumma Prefecture) and at Kiso Fukushima (in present Nagano Prefecture).

Nakasone Yasuhiro (1918-   )

Prime minister since 1982. Born in Gumma Prefecture, Nakasone was elected to the House of Representatives in 1947 and has been returned to office in all subsequent elections. Appointed minister of transport in the Satō Eisaku cabinet, he subsequently held several ministerial posts, including that of director-general of the Defense Agency. In 1982 Nakasone was elected Liberal Democratic Party leader and consequently became prime minister.

Nakatsu

City in northern Ōita Prefecture, Kyūshū, on the Suō Sea. Nakatsu flourished as a castle town in the Edo period (1600–1868). Industrial products include steel tubes and porcelain ware. It is the birthplace of the scholar FUKUZAWA YUKICHI, whose former residence has been designated a historical site. The Taigadō is a hall that houses the paintings of IKE NO TAIGA. It is the gateway to the gorge known as YABAKEI. Pop: 63,942.

Nakatsukasa Naishi no nikki

(Diary of Nakatsukasa Naishi). Late 13th century. A personal account in the form of a diary by a woman in service at the imperial court. The work is usually attributed to a daughter of Fujiwara no Nagatsune. Her dates are not known, but from information contained in the diary she appears to have been a lady-in-waiting (naishi) under the Central Affairs Bureau (Nakatsukasa) and an attendant to the heir apparent, who later ascended the throne as Emperor FUSHIMI.

The entries are dated from 1280 to 1292, but it is questionable whether the entire work was written in diary sequence. From around 1288, the entries are more detailed, and it may be that the author began the writing of it from this time, with the earlier entries actually a memoir. This would account for some of the inaccuracies and discrepancies in the text. Certainly, the introductory remarks and the general melancholy mood of the work are much like the nostalgic reminiscences of an older person.

There are about 150 WAKA poems in the diary; these form the core of the work. The writer is particularly skillful in the use of the aesthetic sensibility known as MONO NO AWARE. She depicts a scene, creates a mood, and thus evokes a sympathetic feeling in her reader. Some of the scenes she portrays may be likened to monochrome paintings. "How pitiful, the evanescent fleeting bird's nest, on the lower branches of the pine, on the small isle of the lake!" or "Among the reeds, helpless, a drifting boat. How pitiful are those with no settled shelter!" The writer alludes to poems of the KOKIN-SHŪ and other imperial anthologies. Her prose, also, is in the tradition of the court ladies of the Heian period (794–1185).

The content of the diary focuses on life at the imperial court. Court dress, amusing pastimes, and various ceremonies are recorded in detail. Of particular interest are the ceremony of enthronement and the Daijōe (Harvest) festival. The diary fails to relate the major historical events occurring around this time, although it does mention the attempted assassination of the emperor.

The value of this diary does not lie in the historical information it contains or in the outstanding writing ability of the author. The *Nakatsukasa Naishi no nikki* is of interest because of its position in Japanese literature—it is one of the last of the diaries by court ladies—and also because it shows a transition to the view, prominent during the Kamakura period (1185–1333), that the world is ephemeral and transitory. See also NIKKI BUNGAKU.

———Ikeda Kikan, "Nakatsukasa no Naishi nikki kō," unpublished. Klaus Müller, tr, *Die Nakatsukasa no Naishi Nikki Zeit: Ein Spiegel Höfischen Lebens in der Kamakura-Zeit* (1965). Tamako Niwa, tr, "Nakatsukasa Naishi Nikki," PhD dissertation, Harvard University (1955). Tamai Kōsuke, "Nakatsukasa no Naishi nikki chūshaku," unpublished.   Tamako NIWA

Nakatsu Keikoku

Gorge on the upper reaches of the Nakatsugawa (tributary of the SAGAMIGAWA), northern Kanagawa Prefecture, central Honshū. Located downstream of Ochiai, it is noted for huge rugged rocks, spring foliage, and crimson autumn leaves. Length: approximately 4 km (2.5 mi).

Nakatsukyō

Gorge on the upper reaches of the Nakatsugawa (a tributary of the ARAKAWA), western Saitama Prefecture, central Honshū. Located within Chichibu–Tama National Park. Sheer cliffs of the Chichibu palaeolithic bed soar up on both banks. Crimson autumn leaves attract numerous visitors. Length: approximately 6 km (3.7 mi).

Nakaumi

Also called Nakanoumi and Chūkai. Lagoon located between Tottori and Shimane prefectures, western Honshū. It is a saltwater lake. Prawn and eel culture flourish. A project to reclaim 28 sq km (11 sq mi) of land for agricultural and industrial use is currently under way. Area: 98.5 sq km (38 sq mi); circumference: 84 km (52 mi); depth: 17.1 m (56.1 ft).

Nakaura Julião (ca 1570–1633)

One of the young envoys sent by the CHRISTIAN DAIMYŌ of Kyūshū on the MISSION TO EUROPE OF 1582. Born in Nakaura in the Ōmura domain (now part of Nagasaki Prefecture), he studied at the Jesuit seminary in Arima. The mission left for Europe in 1582, had a papal audience in 1585, and returned to Japan in 1590. Nakaura entered the Society of Jesus in 1591 and was ordained in 1608. Even when the Tokugawa shogunate intensified its persecution of Christianity after 1612, he continued his missionary activities. He died a martyr in October 1633.   Adriana BOSCARO

Nakayama Gishū (1900–1969)

Novelist. Real name Nakayama Yoshihide. Born in Fukushima Prefecture. Graduate of Waseda University. Nakayama gained recognition as a writer with his novelette *Atsumonozaki*, which won the 1938 Akutagawa Prize. His experience as a war reporter during World War II resulted in the short story "Teniyan no matsujitsu" (1948), a eulogistic account of two young intellectuals who died on the Pacific island of Tinian toward the end of the war. After 1950 he switched to historical novels, becoming a leading writer of that genre. He often took as subjects historical figures who fought for lost causes. Nakayama's humanity is reflected in his sympathy for the defeated. Other works include "Ishibumi" (1939), a short story based on his grandfather, and *Shōan* (1963), a historical novel on the 16th century warrior AKECHI MITSUHIDE that was awarded the Noma Prize.

Nakayama Ichirō (1898–1980)

Economist. Born in Mie Prefecture. After graduating from the Tōkyō University of Commerce (now Hitotsubashi University) in 1923, he studied under J. A. Schumpeter at Bonn University in Germany. Upon his return to Japan in 1929, Nakayama became a professor at his alma mater and taught economic theory. In 1949 he began a seven-year term as president of Hitotsubashi. He served from 1946 as member and later as chairman of the Central Labor Relations Commission. He also belonged to a variety of the government's economic and labor councils and committees, some of which he chaired. Nakayama contributed greatly toward the popularization of the general equilibrium theory of economics in Japan and the development of an econometric analysis of the Japanese economy. He trained a number of young economists, and his policies were important to Japan's postwar recovery and growth. Nakayama's major works on economics are found in *Nakayama Ichirō zenshū* (1973).

                    YAMADA Katsumi

Nakayama Miki (1798–1887)

Founder of the religious organization TENRIKYŌ. Born the eldest daughter of Maekawa Masanobu in the village of Sammaiden in Yamato Province (now the city of Tenri, Nara Prefecture). Although she was an unusually gentle and sensitive child by nature, her outlook on life was influenced by the pessimism of her family, devout followers of PURE LAND BUDDHISM. She became a pious seeker of the truth and, disillusioned with the human condition, decided to become a nun. However, at her parents' strong urging, she married Nakayama Zembei (1788–1853) of the village of Shōyashiki in 1810 at the age of 13.

The marriage was a turning point for her in that it led her to affirm the things of this world. She began to see the necessity of making man's earthly life less painful, and consequently devoted herself to the worship of Shintō deities and innumerable acts of compassion. Her moral and religious consciousness reached an extreme state when she was about 40. She claimed to have received a revelation from a deity, Tenri Ō no Mikoto, on 9 December 1838 (Tempō 9.10.23) and to have become the "Shrine of God" three days later, on 12 December 1838 (Tempō 9.10.26), when the Nakayama family accepted the god's request to have her become his abode. As part of her mission she directly began to give away her belongings to needy people, and continued to do so even after the death of her husband in 1853. Her family suffered great poverty as she went about her mission to spread the "divine wisdom" *(tenri)* that had been revealed to her. Some 20 years after her revelation, Miki began to work miracles of healing. She gained many followers, although her success also brought criticism and persecution, even imprisonment. She remained, nevertheless, firm in her purpose and wrote the *Mikagura uta* (Songs for the Sacred Dance) and the *Ofudesaki* (Tip of the Divine Writing Brush), both considered the scriptures of Tenrikyō. She also taught her disciples dances to perform before God. She left the corporeal world at the age of 90, as her disciples performed the *kagura-zutome* (salvation dance service) in the nearby main sanctuary. The founder of Tenrikyō is called Oyasama (Beloved Parent) by her followers, who believe that she eternally resides in the world, extending protection.

■——Byron H. Earhart, *The New Religions of Japan: A Bibliography of Western-Language Materials* (1970). Nakayama Shōzen, *Hitokotohanashi: Anecdotes on the Foundress and Her Disciples* (1964). Tenrikyō Church Headquarters, *Life of Oyasama, the Foundress of Tenrikyō* (1967). Tenrikyō Church Headquarters, *A Short History of Tenrikyō* (1967). Tenrikyō Church Headquarters, *Anecdotes of Oyasama, the Foundress of Tenrikyō* (1977).

Toyoaki UEHARA

Nakayama Shichiri

Gorge on the Mashitagawa (a tributary of the KISOGAWA), central Gifu Prefecture, central Honshū. Located between Gero Hot Spring and the town of Kanayama, it is a part of Hida–Kisogawa Quasi-National Park. The gorge was almost impassable in ancient days; now it is accessible in all seasons. Length: approximately 23 km (14 mi).

Nakayama Shimpei (1887–1952)

Composer. Born in Nagano Prefecture, and educated at the Tōkyō Music School. He leaped to fame with his song "Kachūsha no uta" (1914), as performed by the actress Matsui Sumako (1886–1919) in a musical drama based on Tolstoy's last novel, *Voskresenie* (1899, Resurrection). However, he became best known for his many melodies in the style of Japanese folk song, festival music, *kouta* chamber songs, and children's songs; and as such his "new folk songs" *(shimmin'yō)* were an important influence on popular commercial song (RYŪKŌKA) in the 1920s. Their lyrics were often by well-known poets, notably Noguchi Ujō (1882–1945), KITAHARA HAKUSHŪ (1885–1942), and SAIJŌ YASO (1892–1970). He also composed pieces for the dancer Fujikage Shizue (1880–1966). His songs as recorded on the Victor label by such singers as Ichimaru, Kouta Katsutarō, and Fujimoto Fumikichi, became immensely popular. They include: "Amefuri Otsuki san" (1919), "Sendō kouta" (1922), and "Susaka kouta" (1923).

■——Victor Records, *Nakayama Shimpei no min'yō*, JV–1024/5 (2-record set). *David B.* WATERHOUSE

Nakayama Sohei (1906–   )

Banker. Born in Tōkyō. After graduating from Tōkyō University of Commerce (now Hitotsubashi University), Nakayama joined the IN-DUSTRIAL BANK OF JAPAN, LTD, in 1929 and became chairman in 1968 after serving as vice-president and president. He concurrently served as director of the JAPAN DEVELOPMENT BANK and the JAPAN COMMITTEE FOR ECONOMIC DEVELOPMENT (Keizai Dōyū Kai). One of Japan's leading bankers, he played an important role in reorganizing the shipping industry and rescuing the Yamaichi Securities Co from bankruptcy. *ITŌ Hajime*

Nakayama Steel Works, Ltd

(Nakayama Seikōsho). Company engaged in the manufacture and sale of steel and secondary steel products. It was established in 1919. Under the brand name Three Stars, the company sells such products as galvanized and corrugated sheets, which are well known in Southeast Asia. It ranks seventh among Japan's blast furnace steelmakers, and is the top maker of checkered plate and light gauze steel. Future plans call for modernization of its rolling facilities as well as development of new products and types of steel. Sales for the fiscal year ending March 1982 totaled ￥115.7 billion (US $480.6 million), and the company was capitalized at ￥3.5 billion (US $14.5 million). Corporate headquarters are located in Ōsaka.

Nakayama Tadamitsu (1845–1865)

Court noble and activist in the movement to overthrow the Tokugawa shogunate and restore direct imperial rule. In 1858 Tadamitsu entered court service as an attendant. Both he and his father, Tadayasu (1809–88), were drawn to the SONNŌ JŌI (Revere the Emperor, Expel the Barbarians) movement, and in 1863 Tadamitsu gave up his rank and went to the Chōshū domain (now part of Yamaguchi Prefecture), the center of the imperial-loyalist movement. He participated in the Chōshū attacks on foreign ships in the Shimonoseki Strait (see SHIMONOSEKI BOMBARDMENT). Also in 1863, he joined a group of loyalists in the TENCHŪGUMI REBELLION, an attack on shogunate officials in Yamato Province (now Nara Prefecture). The rebels were quickly surrounded by shogunate troops, but Tadamitsu escaped to Chōshū. The following year he was murdered by members of a conservative clique, the so-called Zokurontō, who were opposed to Chōshū's involvement in national politics. See also MEIJI RESTORATION.

Nakayama Yoshihide → Nakayama Gishū

Nakaya Ukichirō (1900–1962)

Physicist. Internationally known for his research on snow. Born in Kaga, Ishikawa Prefecture, he graduated from Tōkyō University in 1925. He became interested in snow while a professor at Hokkaidō University and in 1938 produced the first laboratory-synthesized snow crystals. He served as director of Hokkaidō University's Institute of Low Temperature Science. He was also a noted essayist, whose works included *Fuyu no hana* (1938, Flowers of Winter). His *Snow Crystals: Natural and Artificial* was published in 1954.

Nakazato Kaizan (1885–1944)

Popular writer and author of the highly acclaimed multivolume novel *Daibosatsu Tōge* (1913–41). Real name Nakazato Yanosuke. Although Nakazato always stood outside the mainstream of the Japanese literary world and steadfastly maintained a critical stance toward the literary establishment and the government, he exerted a profound influence on the readers of his time and on popular writers of a later period.

Early Career——Born in Hamura, Kanagawa Prefecture (now part of suburban Tōkyō), Nakazato was very poor as a youth and was drawn to the FREEDOM AND PEOPLE'S RIGHTS MOVEMENT (Jiyū Minken Undō) and the ideas of UCHIMURA KANZŌ and other Christian thinkers. In 1903, he won a prize for a story he had submitted to a newspaper, and two years later, having become acquainted with the socialist writer KINOSHITA NAOE, became an editor at the socialist newspaper *Chokugen*. In the same year, he helped start a socialist literary journal, *Kaben*. At the same time he was attracted to Tolstoy and also began studying Buddhist philosophy, regularly practicing Zen meditation. Nakazato also came to be known as an outspoken pacifist poet. By the time he joined the staff of the newspaper MIYAKO SHIMBUN in 1906, he had already decided to dedicate himself to writing as a career. His story *Kōya no gijin* (1910), centering on the leader of a peasant rebellion, established his reputation as a writer.

Daibosatsu Tōge —— The first installment of the work that proved to be his masterpiece and, most would agree, the most successful work of POPULAR FICTION in Japan, appeared in the *Miyako shimbun* in 1913, but only with the appearance of a new series in 1925 in the *Tōkyō nichinichi* and other newspapers did it win nationwide popular acclaim. Started when the author was 28, the series was left uncompleted after the publication of the 32nd volume in 1941, when he had turned 57.

Daibosatsu Tōge (tr *Dai-Bosatsu Toge: Great Boddhisattva Pass*, 1929) is set against the turbulent political events of the 1850s and 1860s leading up to the MEIJI RESTORATION of 1868. The scene shifts constantly, and the cast of characters is equally far-ranging—swordsmen, shogunal retainers, masterless *samurai*, court nobles, doctors, merchants, peasants, pilgrims, thieves, ladies-in-waiting, nuns, *geisha*, and prostitutes—close to 100 in all. In this panoramic sweep one figure stands out, the master swordsman Tsukue Ryūnosuke. Against the larger backdrop of the conflict between proimperial forces and proshogunate forces, the author presents in Tsukue a protagonist who belongs to neither side, freely moving from one to the other. He kills and debauches without reason, and after losing his sight in an explosion, becomes even more vicious and nihilistic.

Daibosatsu Tōge lacks a unifying plot. It is instead a series of episodes, each bearing on the human cycle of life, suffering, death, and man's stubborn blindness to truth. The fates of female characters such as Ohama and Ogin, who are attracted to Ryūnosuke although he is a murderer, and Oyuki, who longs to be cut down by his sword, all show the power of karma. At the same time, by exploring the meaning of events like peasant uprisings, the author brings a historical depth to his work.

The Attraction of Tsukue Ryūnosuke —— Tsukue Ryūnosuke is the first character in popular Japanese literature to emerge as a fascinating individual. In contrast to the predominantly realistic approach of contemporary Japanese literature, which has generally focused on the angst of introverted intellectuals, Nakazato gives us an uninhibited man of almost limitless energy, who breaks taboos, cuts all bonds of family and home, and confronts the reader with a view of the dark depths of human nature. He differs from the ideal samurai in that for him, technical mastery of swordsmanship is completely unrelated to the samurai's traditional spiritual aspirations. Having given up all hope of self-knowledge, he is reduced to the most basic traits of a swordsman, living from impulse to impulse and moment to moment.

An important reason, perhaps, for the immense popularity of the *Daibosatsu Tōge* series during the 1920s was its timeliness: readers suffering from the post-World War I economic depression and the social unrest that followed the great Tōkyō Earthquake of 1923 felt that they could somehow identify with its amoral, nihilistic antihero.

Later Period —— In 1920 Nakazato resigned from the *Miyako shimbun*. He continued to work on *Daibosatsu Tōge* but scorned the commercialism of the publishing business and the exclusive nature of the Japanese literary world. He settled in his home town of Hamura, founded a school based on agrarianist principles, and embarked on travels throughout Japan. He also traveled to Korea, China, and the United States in the 1930s and recorded his impression of these journeys in two books. Nakazato never married, the reason being—it was said—he preferred work for mankind rather than for a wife and children. There were a number of women in his life, however. During World War II, when many writers willingly contributed their talents in support of the war effort, Nakazato refused to do so. He never abandoned his principles; Nakazato was a rare writer who chose to stand alone to the end. *ASAI Kiyoshi*

Nakazawa Dōni (1725–1803)

Teacher and propagator of SHINGAKU, the school of ethics directed at commoners. Born in Kyōto into a family of textile weavers. He succeeded to the family business, but in middle age he developed an interest in Shingaku, becoming a student of TESHIMA TOAN, a disciple of its founder ISHIDA BAIGAN. At Toan's behest in 1779 he went to Edo (now Tōkyō) to spread Shingaku teachings and to establish a school. He lectured widely in eastern Japan and won the admiration of a number of *daimyō* and other high-ranking *samurai* as well as commoners. He was even given permission by shogunal senior councillor MATSUDAIRA SADANOBU to lecture retainers of the shogunate. Dōni's success in propagating Shingaku was largely due to his informal and simple lecturing style and to his practical advice that the study of life itself was the highest form of learning. His major work is *Dōni ō dōwa* (1795–1810), a collection of talks.

Nakijin castle remains

(Nakijin Gusuku). Late-14th-century castle site at Nakijin, Okinawa Prefecture. Belonging to the kings of Sampoku, the northernmost of the three medieval Ryukyuan kingdoms (see OKINAWA: earliest times to 1945), the castle was strategically located on a hill overlooking a river. It consisted of a series of interlinking enclosures (*kuruwa*) surrounded by a stone wall. As a result of its trade contacts with the Ming dynasty (1368–1644) of China, Nakijin castle flourished for nearly a century, but in 1429 it was destroyed by Shō Hashi (see CHŪZAN'Ō), unifier of the Ryūkyūs. See also SHURI CASTLE REMAINS. *KITAMURA Bunji*

nakōdo

(go-between). A person who arranges marriages. His or her functions include introducing the parties, acting as intermediary in the preliminary negotiations, presiding over the marriage ceremonies, and maintaining a long-term relationship with the couple that may include dispute resolution. The *nakōdo* usually performs these functions with his or her spouse.

Social Context —— The continued existence of the *nakōdo* is due to the strong regard for social connections in Japan. Both social history (such as family background) and existing social networks are recognized as highly significant in defining the person. In the traditional social organization, the IE, or household, was the basic unit, and the individual was defined as a member of the *ie* rather than as an autonomous unit. Marriage (*engumi*) was regarded as a link between families, and it was considered essential that this take place between families of similar social status. In the premodern period, arranged marriages occurred predominantly among families of high status, such as nobles, *samurai,* or wealthy farmers. Among the lower classes, self-selection of marriage partners was more common; village youth groups or nightly visiting customs for young men frequently made go-betweens unnecessary. The use of *nakōdo* became widespread among all social classes only after the Meiji Restoration (1868). This was probably because of the function of the *nakōdo* as "guarantor" of continuing relationships in times of increasing mobility and migration from country to city. In addition, go-betweens are used in other social contexts in Japan, where face-to-face confrontations are generally avoided.

After World War II the new CIVIL CODE radically altered the marriage laws, defining marriages as a choice between individuals. However, a gap exists between law and practice, since even today there is a strong emphasis on the family unit, and the opportunities for finding a suitable partner are rather limited.

Love Marriage and Arranged Marriage —— Since the war, "love marriage" *(ren'ai kekkon)* has been on the increase. However, arranged marriage and love marriage are not totally contrasting institutions. They represent different kinds of introductions rather than different kinds of marriage. In the latter, as in the former, the partners find out about each other's background, either on their own or through mutual friends, and often ask an honorary go-between to preside at the marriage ceremony.

Arranged marriage *(miai kekkon;* see MIAI) is also changing in the direction of greater consideration of personal compatibility. Dating between the first formal meeting *(miai)* and the engagement, and greater consideration of the individual's wishes are all recent innovations in the arrangement process.

Most Japanese (98 percent) are married by the time they are 50. Roughly half of them, according to one survey, say they married through use of a *nakōdo.* But if one uses the term *nakōdo* in its broadest sense, including the honorary *nakōdo* in romantic marriages, the figure must be considerably higher than half. Again, in many instances there is not one go-between but several, who perform different functions at various stages. Most *nakōdo* are not professionals: they are usually older people who command respect—a teacher, a superior at work, or an elder relative.

Marriage Negotiations —— Marriage is a constant topic of conversation in Japan, and a potential *nakōdo* will obtain a great deal of information by means of informal gossip. He or she may also receive a request from someone in person or in the form of a letter accompanied by a photograph. At the initial stage the go-between decides on a "match" after weighing three major criteria: (1) family backgrounds; (2) earning potential of the male, since he will have the primary responsibility of supporting the family (important considerations include educational level, schools attended, and employment); and (3) personal characteristics.

Namahage

Namahage visiting a house in Oga, Akita Prefecture. With the wooden knife they threaten to cut off the excess flesh of lazy children.

After informally approaching one party, the *nakōdo* proposes the match to the other, usually making the first formal request in the form of a letter from the male to the female. The letter contains essential information about the potential groom as well as a photograph. If the girl and her family respond favorably, as a sign of good faith, each party will refrain from considering another offer until the proceedings are completed, one way or the other. The proposal may be rejected on grounds of inadequacy in any one of the three sets of criteria. In this phase of the negotiations either side may request more information from the *nakōdo* and may even employ a detective agency *(kōshinjo)*. Research may include examining HOUSEHOLD REGISTERS *(koseki)* and interviewing neighbors, former teachers, or employers. Negotiations are sensitive and if prospects seem positive, potentially damaging information will be withheld.

If the first two sets of criteria are met, the next step is to arrange a meeting between the prospective bride and groom. In a city, the *miai* may be a dinner party at a restaurant or a theater performance, attended by the *nakōdo* and a family member (usually a parent) from each side. In the country it may be a meeting at a restaurant or some scenic place.

After the *miai*, both parties must decide whether or not to continue negotiations. At this point the decision is theoretically left to the individuals involved, but subtle pressures operate on them to proceed. At the same time, it is acceptable to say no, and in fact many people go through several *miai*. If the proceedings continue beyond this point, the couple will commonly date. This indicates increasing commitment to the match and usually leads to the formal engagement *(yuinō)*. The *nakōdo* and his or her spouse officiate at an exchange of gifts and ritual objects that symbolize a long, fruitful union. They also officiate at the wedding.

If the go-between's functions have been purely ceremonial *(tanomare nakōdo)*, his or her relationship with the couple after the wedding will be ceremonial as well. In most cases, however, the go-between's responsibilities do not end with the wedding. If things go wrong, he or she may be called upon to mediate, or even to arrange for divorce. Although customs vary, the newlyweds are generally expected to visit the go-between on return from their wedding trip to express their thanks. They are also expected to keep in touch with the go-between in varying degrees: giving presents at appropriate seasons, paying respects at the New Year, or at the very least sending a New Year's card.

While the task of go-betweens is not easy, their efforts are acknowledged as socially valuable. See also MARRIAGE; WEDDINGS.
■——Robert Blood, *Love Match and Arranged Marriage* (1967). Tanizaki Jun'ichirō, *Sasame yuki* (1943–48), tr Edward G. Seidensticker as *The Makioka Sisters* (1957). Ezra Vogel, "The Go-Between in a Developing Society: The Case of the Japanese Marriage Arranger," *Human Organization* 20.3 (Fall 1961).   Jane BACHNIK

Nakoku

Small state in northern Kyūshū during the 2nd and 3rd centuries. According to the late 3rd century Chinese chronicle WEI ZHI *(Wei chih)*, Nakoku was located 100 *li* (values for the *li* mentioned in this chronicle are uncertain) southeast of ITOKOKU, the site of negotia-

tions between the Japanese state of YAMATAI and envoys from the Daifang (Tai-fang) Commandery, a Chinese colony in Korea. The country was ruled by an official called a *shimako* (or *jimako*), who was assisted by a *hinamori*, and with approximately 30 other countries recognized the suzerainty of a state (generally believed to be Yamatai) with a female ruler. The population numbered some 20,000 households *(ko)*, making it second in size only to that of Yamatai, which had 70,000 households.

Nakoku has been identified with Wa no Nakoku (the country of Na in Wa) mentioned in the Chinese *Hou Han shu* (History of the Later Han Dynasty [25–220]) and with the inscription on a gold seal (KAN NO WA NO NA NO KOKUŌ NO IN), thought to have been bestowed by the first emperor of that dynasty on the ruler of Nakoku, that was discovered near Fukuoka in 1784. If this is correct, it means that Nakoku had established hegemony in northern Kyūshū even before the 30 small countries were unified by Yamatai in the 3rd century. Nakoku is thought to be identical with Nanoagata or Nanotsu, places mentioned in the chronicle *Nihon shoki* (720), near Hakata, the city of Fukuoka.   KITAMURA Bunji

Nakoso no Seki

(Barrier of Nakoso). Originally called Kikuta no Seki, it was known as Nakoso (literally, "do not come") no Seki by the beginning of the Heian period (794–1185). Located near what is now the town of Iwaki in Fukushima Prefecture, it was one of the three ancient fortified barriers (the others were SHIRAKAWA NO SEKI and Nezu no Seki) built in northeastern Honshū in the 8th century to prevent southward incursions by the aboriginal EZO people. Nakoso no Seki acquired many historical and literary associations. In classical *waka* poetry it is one of the stock place names known as UTA MAKURA and instantly evokes in the reader the feelings of loneliness and desolation associated with military service or exile on a distant frontier.

namahage

A custom in which visitors, costumed as gods or demons called *namahage*, make the rounds of local households on the eve of Koshōgatsu (the 15th of the first month in the old lunar calendar; 15 January in the present calendar). Although the custom is found widely in Japan, its observance on the OGA PENINSULA in Akita Prefecture is especially famous and has become a tourist attraction. Two or three young men in the village, wearing fierce-looking masks and covered with straw capes, visit each house and ask whether there is a disobedient child or lazy person in the family. They are then plied with food and drink and sent away with money and ricecakes. The custom was originally observed around the first of the first month, and the *namahage* was supposed to represent a god who came from afar to bless and guard the villagers or promise a bumper crop.   INOKUCHI Shōji

namako → sea cucumbers

Namamugi Jiken → Richardson Affair

Namba Daisuke → Toranomon Incident

namban

(literally, "southern barbarian"). Term applied principally to the Iberian and Italian missionaries, merchants, and sailors who visited or worked in Japan in the 16th and 17th centuries, and to the European customs and products they introduced. The term originated in China, where all foreigners were regarded as barbarians. Hence, "southern barbarians" referred to the inhabitants of Vietnam, Laos, Cambodia, and other countries to the south of China. In the same way, the Japanese used the term in reference to the peoples of Siam (Thailand), Java, and the Philippines.

The Portuguese and Spaniards who reached Japan in the 16th century had sailed up from the south, either from Macao or the Philippines, and so by extension the term *nambanjin*, or "southern barbarian men," came to be applied to them as well (in distinction to the word *kōmōjin*, or "red-haired men," used in connection with the Dutch and English, who arrived in Japan early in the 17th century). The word *namban* was also used to describe the things introduced

Namban art

One of a pair of six-panel folding screens depicting the arrival of European traders (left) at a Japanese port and their reception by missionaries (right). Kanō school. Colors and gold leaf on paper. 182 × 371 cm. Early 17th century. Suntory Museum of Art, Tōkyō.

by the Europeans—*namban* ships, *namban* dress, *namban* cooking, etc. The Jesuit church built in Kyōto in 1576 was commonly called the Nambanji (Southern Barbarian Temple).

While the term *namban* was obviously not a complimentary epithet, it was not meant to be taken in its literal sense as derogatory. Toward the end of the 16th century, in fact, there was a short-lived craze in Japan for *namban* words, dress, and cooking. Nevertheless, in view of contemporary European eating and bathing habits, and of the fact that visiting sailors were far from being cultural representatives, the term had a certain validity. *Michael* COOPER

namban art

("southern barbarian" art). Art connected in any way with the European missionaries and merchants in Japan during the 16th and 17th centuries. This broad definition allows the inclusion of not only the works of Japanese artists painting in Western style, to which the term is often restricted, but also European imported art and traditionally executed Japanese screens depicting Europeans. Most of the *namban* art produced in Japan can be dated between 1590, when interest in things European reached its peak, and 1614, when missionaries were expelled from the country.

In the course of their missionary activities the Jesuits imported from Europe a large number of religious paintings to decorate their churches and to use as gifts. Owing to the subsequent anti-Christian persecution, most of these works were destroyed and only a few are now extant. These paintings also served as models for Japanese artists, although because of transport and financial problems the imported works were generally both small in size and indifferent in quality.

The arrival of the talented Italian Jesuit Giovanni Niccolo in 1583 enabled the Jesuits to organize courses on Western painting and engraving at their boys' school in Kyūshū. Niccolo taught art there until the expulsion of the missionaries, after which he continued teaching at Macao, where he died in 1626. The paintings produced by his students and other Japanese artists were for the most part copies of Western pictures and were often religious in theme. One of the best examples of this type is *Madonna of the Rosary* (color on paper, preserved at Kyōto University), comprising the madonna and child, four saints, and miniature illustrations of the 15 mysteries of the rosary. Despite the overcrowded composition and a certain stiffness in execution, the work demonstrates the remarkable skill of an unidentified Japanese artist painting in a still unfamiliar Western style.

But the majority of extant *namban* paintings produced by Japanese are secular in theme, many of them probably inspired by the portraits, atlases, and illustrated books known to have been brought back from Europe by the youthful envoys of the Christian *daimyō* of Kyūshū (see MISSION TO EUROPE OF 1582) on their return to Japan in 1590. Prominent among such works are the large sixfold screens portraying idyllic pastoral scenes with languid Western figures, of-

ten playing musical instruments in the foreground, and with lakes and mountains in the background. The colorful depiction of these exotic figures and settings made ideal decorations in the dimly lit rooms of mansions, but here again, artistic technique, especially plasticity and perspective, is often faulty. There are also various extant screens showing mounted Western warriors. One striking example of this type is an imaginary and highly colorful scene of the Battle of Lepanto, conveniently transposed to dry land. The composition is grossly overcrowded with elephants, chariots, prancing horses with noticeably foreshortened hindquarters, and crowds of soldiers with a forest of spears, but the unsatisfactory composition was probably thought to be offset by the exotic content of the work. Recent research has shown that the figures portrayed on this screen were copied from various European paintings and prints.

Few of these paintings are signed, although some of the best of them bear the seal of a certain Nobukata, about whom nothing is known. Not content with merely copying European works, Nobukata had the initiative to use a quasi-Western style of painting when he executed with considerable deftness portraits of Oriental subjects, such as Daruma and the Nichiren monk Nikkyō (1552?–1608).

Another type of painting inspired by imported European works is seen in screens depicting either maps of the world or bird's-eye views of Western cities. Some of the latter, for example those illustrating Rome and Lisbon, were copied with remarkable exactness. The world maps are also interesting in that they show the rapid growth of Japanese knowledge of world geography as a result of contact with Westerners.

In its broadest sense, the term *namban* art includes works that, although executed in traditional Japanese style, take Europeans as their principal theme. Of these, the best-known examples are the *namban* screens. Usually produced in pairs, about 60 of these six-panel screens have been cataloged, although the authenticity of many of them can be questioned. The left-hand screen of a typical pair shows the arrival of the Portuguese carrack at Nagasaki and the offloading of its cargo, while the right-hand screen depicts the Portuguese merchants and their servants walking through the streets of the port, often being greeted by black-robed missionaries. Variations on this theme in a few screens include imaginary views of a foreign port, probably Goa, and scenes of horse races. Most of the screens appear to have been painted by lesser members of the KANŌ SCHOOL; a screen now preserved in Kōbe bears the seal of Kanō Naizen (1570–1616), while another, in Ōsaka, is attributed to KANŌ MITSUNOBU. These fascinating works are for the most part to be found in Japan, for example at the Kōbe Municipal Museum of Namban Art, but some may be viewed abroad in museums in Lisbon, London, Boston, San Francisco, Washington, and elsewhere.

Namban motifs, including Europeans, Western ships, rosaries, and crosses, are to be found on contemporary lacquer ware, such as flasks, containers, and boxes, as well as on metal TSUBA, or sword guards. The copperplate illustrations found in some of the books published by the JESUIT MISSION PRESS can also be included in the wider definition of *namban* art.

Namban art, in the strict meaning of the term, that is, work done in Western style by Japanese artists, is of considerable interest in comparative art history, for this was the first time that a fusion of Western and East Asian art forms took place. That the promising work of Japanese artists remained undeveloped and immature is hardly surprising, given the short time during which this new art form was practiced in Japan. The expulsion of the missionaries and the subsequent closing of the country to Western influence brought this cultural experiment to an end and prevented its development into a mature and established art form.

■——Fernando G. Gutiérrez, "A Survey of Nanban Art," in Michael Cooper, ed, *The Southern Barbarians* (1971). Okamoto Yoshitomo, *Namban byōbu*, 2 vols (1970). Yoshitomo Okamoto, *The Namban Art of Japan* (1972).   *Michael* COOPER

Nambanji

(Southern Barbarian Temple). A Jesuit church built in Kyōto in 1576; construction was begun with the permission of the military hegemon ODA NOBUNAGA and work continued for a year. The church was dedicated to the Assumption of Our Lady and the official inauguration took place at Christmas 1576. The building was destroyed in 1588 on the orders of TOYOTOMI HIDEYOSHI. A contemporary fan painting by Kanō Motohide depicts the church as a three-story building in Japanese style. A metal European-style bell, bearing the Jesuit IHS monogram and the date 1577 (Tenshō 5), is preserved in the temple Myōshinji in Kyōto and is thought to have belonged to the church.   *Michael* COOPER

namban trade

(literally, "southern barbarian" trade). Trade conducted by Iberian merchants in Japan during the 16th and 17th centuries. It was carried on mainly by the Portuguese, who utilized their spacious carracks and their Macao entrepôt to supply the Japanese with Chinese silk in exchange for silver. A small trade was also conducted by Spanish merchants until 1624, when Spaniards were expelled from the country.

The first Europeans to reach Japan were three Portuguese traders who landed on Tanegashima, an island south of Kyūshū, in 1543. European merchants were subsequently allowed to enter the country freely and trade with little or no restriction. As a rule Kyūshū *daimyō* welcomed Portuguese trade, as the profits therefrom helped to finance the intermittent wars between the different domains. After experimenting with various Kyūshū ports, in 1570 the Portuguese sounded the Bay of Nagasaki, and this fine natural harbor became the headquarters of their commerce in Japan.

The Portuguese did not sell many European goods in Japan; for the most part they acted as middlemen between China and Japan. The Ming dynasty (1368–1644) had forbidden direct commerce between the two nations, and so the Portuguese were able to monopolize the Sino-Japanese trade. In Japan there was much demand for Chinese silk, which at that time was superior in quality to the local product. On account of their presence in Macao, the Portuguese were able to obtain Chinese silk at the semiannual Guangzhou (Canton) trade fair. Prices fluctuated, but the Portuguese could buy silk at Guangzhou for about 80 taels a picul (1 picul=60 kg or 133 lb) and sell it at Nagasaki for about 150 taels. The Chinese placed great value on silver, and the newly developed mines in Japan provided an ample supply. The ratio of the values of gold and silver was about 1:13 in Japan but about 1:6 in China, with the result that large profits could be made by the Portuguese in the exchange of Chinese silk for Japanese silver.

Portuguese merchants brought tin, lead, musk, and gold to Nagasaki and exported swords, lacquer ware, and *kimono,* but silk and silver were by far the most important commodities. To avoid glutting the market, the Portuguese laid down strict regulations governing the export of silk from Macao. The official carrack carrying silk to Nagasaki was limited to one a year and was placed under the command of a *capitão-mor,* or captain major, a crown appointment. The amount of silk to be sent to Japan was fixed annually and could total as much as 2,000 piculs. A system called the *armação* was developed by which Macao citizens were able to purchase a share in the trading venture. From the beginning of the 17th century the silk was sold in bulk to a consortium of Japanese merchants; this system was called *pancada* in Portuguese and ITOWAPPU in Japanese, and it guaranteed a fixed price for the coveted silk.

The military leaders TOYOTOMI HIDEYOSHI and TOKUGAWA IE-YASU had a personal interest in the silk trade, and this caused them

to moderate their stand against Christianity for fear of jeopardizing the lucrative commerce. Ieyasu's desire to foster this trade is well illustrated in the incident involving the carrack *Madre de Deus,* which was engaged in a running battle with Japanese forces at Nagasaki in 1610 (see MADRE DE DEUS INCIDENT). Despite this setback in Japanese-Portuguese relations, trade was resumed within two years, so eager were both the Macao and Japanese authorities to continue the silk trade. But Ieyasu's dependence on the Portuguese merchants was reduced by the arrival of Dutch traders in 1609. In 1614, in preparation for his showdown with the Toyotomi faction, Ieyasu issued a decree expelling missionaries from Japan but allowing Portuguese trade to continue.

Ieyasu's interest in foreign commerce was not shared by his two immediate successors, Hidetada and Iemitsu, both of whom displayed a deep antipathy toward Christianity and rightly suspected that Portuguese merchants were smuggling disguised missionaries into the country. As a result the Japanese authorities laid down increasingly strict regulations governing Portuguese trade. Dutch intervention also contributed to the decline of this trade. In 1603 the Dutch seized a richly laden carrack in Macao harbor only a day before it was due to sail to Japan. Because of these Dutch attacks on their shipping, the Portuguese were forced to use light galliots instead of the clumsy carrack on the Macao–Nagasaki run from 1618, and from then onward about half a dozen of these swift vessels carried the silk to Japan each year.

The end to the *namban* trade was occasioned by the SHIMABARA UPRISING of 1637–38. The difficulty experienced by the Japanese authorities in quelling this local uprising made the shogunal government apprehensive about the threat of Christianity and the possibility of intervention by European colonial powers. As a result, in 1639 the Portuguese were ordered to leave Japan. In the following year Macao sent a delegation to Nagasaki to plead for a resumption of commerce; by order of the Edo government some 60 members of the Portuguese delegation and of the mostly Asian crew were decapitated. Another unsuccessful attempt to resume the silk trade was made in 1647; this time the delegation escaped the fate of its predecessor and returned safely to Macao.

Namban trade, so colorfully depicted on painted screens of the period, was intrinsically an unstable enterprise, depending as it did on the rupture of Sino-Japanese relations. The establishment of an effective central government in Japan, the commencement of the anti-Christian persecution, and the intervention of the hostile Dutch all contributed to bringing this commerce to an end.

■——C. R. Boxer, *The Great Ship from Amacon: Annals of Macao and the Old Japan Trade, 1555–1640* (1963). Michael Cooper, "The Mechanics of the Macao–Nagasaki Silk Trade," *Monumenta Nipponica* 27.4 (1972). Okamoto Yoshitomo, *Jūrokuseiki Nichiō kōtsū shi no kenkyū* (1947). Takase Kōichirō, *Kirishitan jidai no kenkyū* (1977).   *Michael* COOPER

Nambara Shigeru (1889–1974)

Political scientist and educator. Born in Kagawa Prefecture. While a student at Tōkyō University, he was drawn to Christianity, in particular to the MUKYŌKAI (nonchurch) movement of UCHIMURA KANZŌ. He began his teaching career in 1921, lecturing on political science at his alma mater. As a Christian and a liberal, he put himself at great personal risk by speaking out against the militarist government during World War II. After the war, as president of Tōkyō University (1945–51) and a member of several government committees on educational reform, he vigorously defended academic freedom; he also criticized the policies of Prime Minister YOSHIDA SHIGERU and opposed any revision of the 1947 constitution. After his retirement he devoted himself to research, refining his theories on the relation between politics and religion. His works are collected in *Nambara Shigeru chosakushū,* 6 vols (1972–73).

Nambokuchō period → Northern and Southern Courts

Nambokuchō seijun ron

Historical debate *(ron)* over the question of imperial legitimacy *(seijun)* during the period of the NORTHERN AND SOUTHERN COURTS (Nambokuchō; 1336–92), when there occurred the only major dynastic schism in Japanese history.

Although the courtier-general KITABATAKE CHIKAFUSA, one of the early leaders of the Southern Court at Yoshino, forcefully argued the case for that court's legitimacy in his historical tract JINNŌ SHŌTŌ KI (1339–43, Chronicle of the Direct Descent of Divine Sovereigns), few others at the time seriously challenged the status of the Northern Court at Kyōto, which enjoyed the superior military support of the MUROMACHI SHOGUNATE (1338–1573). And after 1392, when the Yoshino cause was abandoned, there seemed little reason to regard the defunct Southern Court as anything more than one of history's losers.

The case for Southern Court legitimacy was renewed during the Edo period (1600–1868), especially by scholars of the MITO SCHOOL, who argued that Emperor GO-DAIGO and his successors as southern rulers had always retained possession of the IMPERIAL REGALIA (mirror, sword, and jewels), the unchallengeable symbols of imperial rank. Also behind the sentiment of the Mito scholars and others in favor of the Southern Court was admiration for the conduct of those loyalists, including KUSUNOKI MASASHIGE, who had fought most courageously and unselfishly for Go-Daigo.

The controversy reached a climax in 1911, when the government of Prime Minister KATSURA TARŌ became embroiled in a debate over the presentation of the Northern and Southern Courts period in history textbooks prepared by the Ministry of Education for primary schools. At issue was the use of the term "northern and southern courts" itself, since it was argued that there could be no division of Japan's imperial sovereignty as suggested by the simultaneous existence of two courts. Under pressure from all quarters (including Emperor MEIJI, who was a descendant of the northern line of emperors), the Katsura government decided in favor of southern legitimacy and decreed that henceforth the school texts should deal with the years 1336 through 1392 as "The Period of the Yoshino Court" (Yoshino jidai).

H. Paul VARLEY

Nambu Chūhei (1904–   )

Broad and triple jumper. Born in Hokkaidō. Graduate of Waseda University. Professor of Kyōto Industrial University. He set the world record of 7.98 meters (26 ft) in the broad jump in 1931, which remained unbroken as a Japanese record for 39 years until 1970. He won the gold medal in the triple jump in the Los Angeles Olympics in 1932 with a world record of 15.72 meters (51.6 ft).

TAKEDA Fumio

name cards

(meishi). A card printed with a person's name; place of employment, title, address, and telephone number are usually added. In Japan such cards are exchanged during introductory greetings at business and social occasions. Name cards with a person's name handwritten on Japanese paper were first used in Japan around the beginning of the 19th century. Western-style printed name cards were probably first used in the final years of the Tokugawa shogunate (1603–1867) by government officials who came into contact with foreigners at the time of the opening of Japan. During the Meiji period (1868–1912), various types of name card came into common use. Those used by women sometimes have rounded corners and are generally smaller than those used by men. In recent years many name cards have been printed from left to right rather than from top to bottom, and businessmen who meet often with foreigners generally use cards with the information printed on one side in English. Japanese customarily exchange name cards at their first meeting to establish relative status. The backs of name cards are also widely used to jot a message or a note of introduction to be delivered by a third person.

TSUCHIDA Mitsufumi

Namerikawa

City in eastern Toyama Prefecture, central Honshū. Situated on Toyama Bay, it was originally a prosperous fishing port. More recently its proximity to the city of Toyama has made it an industrial and residential suburb. Machine, textile, and pharmaceutical plants are located here. Stock farming and the cultivation of rice and tulips are also important. Pop: 30,744.

names

The four main types of proper name found in Japan—family names, men's names, women's names, and place names—each have their own peculiarities and are considered separately below; but when they are written in Chinese characters, as is usually the case, they have in common the fact that they present anyone who does not know the particular family, person, or place with the enormous problem of deciding on the most appropriate readings for the characters. The difficulty arises from the multiplicity of readings, both ON READINGS, based on Chinese pronunciations, and KUN READINGS, based on native Japanese words, that are available for each Chinese character used in names, and from the great number of combinations possible when, as happens with most names, they are written with two or more characters. A book of personal name readings, for example, lists 133 characters that have 10 or more possible name readings and, conversely, the common name elements taka and nori, are found written with 168 and 225 different characters, respectively. It is true that, since some readings and characters are much more commonly used in names than others, it is usually possible to arrive at a likely reading when faced with a name written in characters, and that in recent years a limit has been put on the number of characters available for use when registering the personal names of children. This limitation does nothing, however, to restrict the number of possible readings for the characters permitted for personal names, or to help with the problem of unpredictable readings and characters enshrined in many family names and place names. In short, personal knowledge is still the only sure guide to the correct reading of Japanese names.

People's Names —— The names of Japanese, like their postal addresses, go from the general to the particular and have the family name before the personal name, but in most other respects the modern Japanese usage of people's names closely resembles that found in the West. People have a family name and an official personal name, which is kept unchanged throughout their life. Nicknames and artistic or professional names corresponding to noms-de-plume are also often used. When a person is called by name in formal relationships outside the family circle, only his family name is used, either alone or, more often, with an appropriate suffix equivalent to Mr., Mrs., Miss, Dr, Professor, and so forth. When necessary to avoid confusion between two individuals with the same family name, it is possible to use only the first character of the full personal name as a short form, like the Western use of initials, e.g., Kindaichi Kyō (for Kyōsuke) and Kindaichi Haru (for Haruhiko). Within the family or among intimates, it is common to use an abbreviated form of the personal name with the familiar ending -chan, in very much the same way and with much the same feeling as name forms like Willy, Billy, and Lizzy.

Group (Clan and Family) Names —— In Japan up to the end of the 8th century, the two main types of name given to groups within society were UJI, to indicate lineage groups or clans, and KABANE, hereditary titles of nobility, each of which was at any one time borne by a number of uji and individuals and which indicated social standing according to the relationship with the imperial family or recognition of services performed for it. The kabane names and ranks varied from period to period, but there were eight in the system set up by the emperor TEMMU in 684. These were, in descending order, mahito, asomi (later pronounced ason), sukune, imiki, michi no shi, omi, muraji, and inaki (or inagi). Kabane were customarily used after the name of the uji or its geographical location and before the personal name in the case of an individual, e.g., Nakatomi no Muraji Kamako indicates one Kamako who belonged to the Nakatomi clan with the rank of muraji (another name for the person known to history as Nakatomi no Kamatari or FUJIWARA NO KAMATARI).

During the Heian period (794–1185) the usage of group names became much more complex. The court had granted clan and personal names in special circumstances: clans related to the imperial line that were given names included the Tachibana, Ariwara, Minamoto, and Taira. As time went on, the numbers of people using one or another of the names of such powerful clans grew enormously, and it became necessary to make internal distinctions. One way of doing this was by reference to the geographical location of the group. In the case of the Fujiwara, for example, groups within the great clan came to refer to themselves by the place within the capital of Kyōto where they had their residence, e.g., Ichijō (First Avenue), Nijō, Kujō. Or, if they were based in an outlying area, they used a new group name that combined one character of the clan name with one character of the name of the province where they were located. For example, the Fujiwara 藤原 group based in the province of Izu 伊豆 took the name Itō 伊藤 , using the on reading of fuji, and others from elsewhere coined names such as Katō 加藤 , Satō 佐藤 , Endō 遠藤 , and Kondō 近藤 in a similar way.

Then, from the middle of the period, military families who had settled in rural areas began to distinguish themselves from others of the same clan by using the name of their locality or lands, first as a kind of alternative name and then, from the 13th century onward, as their standard family name. All these kinds of name, both original and second-stage, had become wholly fixed in their usage by the early part of the 17th century, but they were still officially allowed only for the aristocracy, military families, and certain members of the lower orders, such as famous artisans or artists who were given special permission. Humbler individuals were referred to only by their personal names or, where necessary, by prefixes indicative of their trade or location.

Two years after the Meiji Restoration of 1868, however, anyone was allowed to take a family name, and in 1875 family names were made compulsory. This led to the appearance of family names of every conceivable kind. Most people adopted as their name one with which they had previously had some kind of association, but there were many instances of local officials giving whole hamlets the same surname, and of simple, illiterate people taking—or, again, being given by officials—the names of commercial products such as brands of tea, or of plants and animals. The frequent mistakes in the characters used to write some names have in many cases survived to the present day, adding to the confusion of Japanese name readings.

At the present time, the names Satō and Suzuki each account for more than 1.5 percent of the population, and other common family names are Tanaka, Yamamoto, Watanabe, Kobayashi, Saitō, Tamura, Itō, and Takahashi. Certain regional differences have been noted. Satō, for example, is commonest in Hokkaidō and the Tōhoku region; Suzuki in the area from Tōhoku through the Kantō to the central region; Tanaka in Kyūshū; and Yamamoto in southern Honshū and Shikoku. All kinds of character readings are to be found in family names; the most that can be said in making a choice is that, although there are many exceptions, on balance most family names have native Japanese readings rather than Sino-Japanese ones (on readings).

Personal Names——As in many societies, it was the custom in olden times in Japan not to call people directly by their true names, especially when referring to superiors, but to use instead their titles or indications of residence or direction that would identify them. It was felt that the name was indivisible from the person and that knowledge of another's true name gave one power over him. In the ancient court society of Japan, for example, for a man to ask a woman's true name equaled a proposal of marriage and for her to give it indicated acceptance. This is why some of the most famous women writers of the time are known, not by their real names, but by such sobriquets as MURASAKI SHIKIBU and SEI SHŌNAGON, which use court titles of male relatives and nicknames. Even today most countries generally refer to their dignitaries by title rather than by name, and this is especially true of Japan, where the personal name of the emperor, for example, is never used.

In naming children in modern Japan, consideration may be given to seniority in the case of brothers, or to the number of strokes in characters, as advised by fortune tellers on the basis of the characters of the family name; but in almost all cases characters (or the sounds of the names, when they are written in KANA) are chosen for their auspicious meanings and happy associations, that is, as talismans to invoke the health, strength, prosperity, beauty, elegance, or accomplishments of the child. Thus, in 1948 the most common names among males between the ages of 15 and 64 (assuming the most usual readings for the characters involved) were 清 Kiyoshi (purity), 茂 Shigeru (prosperity), 一郎 Ichirō (first male), 実 Minoru (achievement) or Makoto (truth)—both readings are common— 勇 Isamu (bravery), 三郎 Saburō (third male), 正 Tadashi or Masashi (rectitude), and 義雄 Yoshio (loyal male), in that order; and those for females of the same age group were 和子 Kazuko (peace), 文子 Fumiko (lettered), 久子 Hisako (long-lived), きよ Kiyo (purity), 静子 Shizuko (tranquil), and 幸子 Sachiko or Yukiko (good fortune).

The choice of characters permitted for use in personal names (though not their possible readings) was limited from 1 January 1948 to the 1,850 TŌYŌ KANJI (current-use Chinese characters), but in 1951 it was extended by the addition of 92 characters, to be used solely in personal names. In 1981 the number of these additional characters that can be used only for personal names was increased to 166. The chosen name and its written form, either Chinese characters or kana, have to be officially reported to the local government within 14 days of the birth of a child.

Men's Names——Until late in the 8th century, personal names derived from a wide range of objects, places, and characteristics associated with the individual and, in the case of men, usually ended in -maro or -ko. From that time men's personal names most often took the form of Japanese four-syllable readings of two-character combinations (e.g., Nari-hira; Michi-naga) or, less often, Japanese three-syllable readings for only one character (e.g., Kaoru; Susumu). The custom also arose of brothers having one character of their names in common and, from about the end of the 11th century, of sons using one of the characters in their father's name in the name they were given on reaching manhood. When a strong military society developed from the 12th century, a feudal lord or the dignitary in charge of the coming-of-age ceremony (GEMPUKU) would often grant the use of one of the characters of his own name instead, and this custom is continued today in the world of the arts, where a junior is often allowed the use of one of his teacher's name characters on achieving full status himself.

In premodern Japan, men of the upper ranks of society could have a variety of personal names. The main categories were: (1) yōmyō or dōmyō (child name). This was the name by which the child was usually known. In most periods and areas it was customarily given on or by the seventh day after birth and remained in use until superseded by other names at the coming-of-age ceremony held when the boy was about 15. Many child names ended in -waka, -maru, -maro, or -ō (e.g., Ushiwaka; Sakuramaru). Men of the lower classes normally used these child names throughout their lives. (2) tsūshō or yobina, zokumyō, kemyō (current name). This was the ordinary name by which a man would commonly be known (e.g., Tarō; Kazuma; Jirōzaemon) and was given him in the coming-of-age ceremony together with the jitsumyō (see below). The commonest tsūshō were those which, in origin at least, indicated the order of birth, as in the sequence Tarō (big male) or Ichirō (first male), Jirō, Saburō, and so forth, down to Jūrō, and then Yoichi for the 11th. The son of Tarō could be called Kotarō (Tarō, Jr), and his grandsons Magotarō (Tarō III), and then Hikotarō (Tarō IV). In some clans a personal name could be prefixed by a character indicating the lineage: Hei-, as in Heitarō, for a member of the Heike (Taira) clan, for example, and Gen-, as in Gentarō, for one from the Genji (Minamoto). (3) jitsumyō or nanori (true name). This was a formal adult name used in close association with the clan name: e.g., Minamoto no Shitagau (Shitagau of the Minamoto clan). A jitsumyō was felt to be so closely identified with the individual that other people would use it of him very rarely and not at all with reference to a superior person such as the emperor or their father. Upon the death of a distinguished person, his jitsumyō became known as an imina (taboo name).

In addition to these, many other types of name were, and still are, used in special circumstances. In imitation of Chinese practice, for example, scholars would often assume an elegant, formal name (azana) such as Bunrin or Shisei, consisting of two Chinese characters pronounced, naturally, in on readings. This same form was also found in Buddhist names: hōmyō (law names) like Saigyō and Dōgen were taken upon entry into the priesthood, and kaimyō (precept name) refers more exclusively to the posthumous name of a believer. Okurina (conferred name) is the posthumous title used of an exalted personage, the most frequent examples of which are the names used for emperors after their deaths and, in modern times, for their reign periods while they are still alive (e.g., Meiji; Taishō; Shōwa). At the other extreme, nicknames (adana) were not uncommon, used either alone or in conjunction with a tsūshō: e.g., Nossori Jūbei ("Plodder Jūbei"). Within this category could be included the yagō (house names) traditionally used by kabuki actors and families on the basis of shops or districts with which they were associated.

Finally, there was a host of literary and artistic names, of which some kinds are still to be found. Gō (pseudonym) or gagō (elegant pseudonym) were the types of name adopted by all Japanese writers and artists, often in bewildering succession. Hokusai, for example, was only one of more than 30 gō used by the artist. There are also some specific terms for particular types of gō: haimyō, for example, means a name taken by a haiku poet, and geimei (artistic name) the kind used by actors and all kinds of other entertainers.

Because of the cultural heritage from China, it is natural that Buddhist names and the vast majority of artistic and other assumed names should be read with on readings of the characters, and the formal, classical associations of such readings can still affect the reading of men's ordinary names on occasions. Most of these take the form of what were earlier tsūshō or jitsumyō, and although the latter most often have native kun readings as their official versions, it is not uncommon for the on readings of the same characters to be used sometimes instead. A man may, for example, be registered officially and be known among his familiars as Hideaki 英明 but he himself may frequently call himself Eimei, using *on* readings for the same characters as a more formal and academic alternative, when appropriate. Others may also choose to read the characters in this way as a solution to the problem of knowing which of the many Japanese readings should be used, or simply for brevity. Hence, the novelists Itō Hitoshi and Kikuchi Hiroshi are universally known as Itō Sei and Kikuchi Kan, respectively.

Most men's names at the present time are of two characters, but changes are inevitably taking place. For example, only 5 percent of men born in the period 1884–88 had one-character personal names, as opposed to 20 percent of those born 1929–33; conversely, 30 percent of the older group had names ending in *-rō*, but only 5 percent of the younger men have such names.

Women's Names —— Before the 9th century, women's names seem mostly to have ended in *-me*, *-iratsume*, or *-toji*, e.g., Shima-me, Hiro-toji. From then on, empresses, imperial princesses, and occasionally other senior court ladies had formal personal names like Sadako and Nobuko, which consisted of one character pronounced with a two- or three-syllable Japanese reading and followed by the suffix *-ko*. The taboos involved with this kind of *jitsumyō*, however, led also to the wide use of *yōmyō*, *tsūshō* (e.g., Murasaki Shikibu) and, later, to the use of various elegant names, many of them derived from the TALE OF GENJI. Among humbler women the *-ko* suffix was never used, but the 16th century saw the introduction of the prefix *o-* to indicate respect or affection. This developed more widely during the Edo period (1600–1868). Oda Nobunaga's sister, for example, was known as Oichi, and Toyotomi Hideyoshi's wife as Onene. Most women in this period had two-syllable names written with two *kana*, and until the Meiji Restoration, the sound and form of a woman's name showed her status immediately.

With the growth of a more classless and better educated society, however, there developed a great variety of women's names, with marked generation differences. For example, only 5 percent of women born in the years 1884–88 wrote their names wholly in Chinese characters and as many as 85 percent wrote them wholly in *kana*, but the corresponding figures for women born between 1929 and 1933 were 70 percent and 20 percent. The use of the formerly aristocratic ending *-ko* grew steadily from about 3 percent in the mid-1880s to 80 percent in 1935. This marks a very weakened appreciation of the respectful connotations of the ending, but some women, particularly among the intelligentsia, drop the *-ko* when giving their own name. The modern trend in women's names, then, is close to the ancient court practice in having most often two-syllable names plus the suffix *-ko*, or three-syllable elegant names like Harue with no suffix, both types being written either in *kana* or in characters of appropriately happy meaning.

Place Names —— Accounts of the origin of place names are a common feature of the earliest written works in Japan, dating from the 8th century, especially in those known as the FUDOKI. These gazetteers were compiled for each province on the orders of the emperor in 713, and those that survive explain the names by quoting local legends, mostly involving the descent of heavenly beings to the area. By so doing they invested the locality with divine associations and, conversely, gave the legends verisimilitude by the connection with existing place names. In the same year, the emperor also ordered that place names should be written with auspicious characters, and it is thought to be from this period too that the custom of normally using two Chinese characters for names began. Many rare characters and rare character readings still survive in place names, and since the majority of such names have also been taken into use as family names, their unusual characters and readings add greatly to the difficulties of reading and writing Japanese.

Japanese place names are of many different types and by no means are all their etymologies known for sure, but in general they can be said to have arisen from either geographical or historical causes; that is, they derived either from the countless natural features of the land itself, or from the inhabitants' activities during their history.

The names of geographical origin generally refer to such obvious features of the land as *kawa/-gawa* (river), *yama* (mountain), *saki* (cape), *tani* (valley), *no* (plain), *hara* (moor), *shima* (island), *hama* (beach), *tsu* (ford; harbor), and *kata/-gata* (beach; bay). These elements are often combined with each other or modified by descriptive prefixes, such as *ō* (large), *ko* or *o* (small), *hiro* (broad), *taka* (high), *naga* (long), *fuka* (deep), *nii* (new), and *yoko* (side), and the directional words *kita* (north), *minami* (south), *higashi* (east), *nishi*

(west), *kami* (upper), *naka* (middle), and *shimo* (lower), to form full place names, as in Nagasaki, Hiroshima, Yokohama, Niigata, and Ōtsu. Other elements of less obvious meaning within this type include: *hinata* (a south-facing slope), as in Kobinata; *ochiai* (a confluence of rivers), as in Shimo Ochiai; and *suka* (sandy bank/beach), as in Yokosuka.

History has left countless remains in Japanese place names. Some derive from the Ainu, although not many of them can be identified with certainty apart from those ending in *-betsu* or *-nai* in the northern parts of Japan; and at the other extreme, modern Tōkyō (eastern capital) was so called in contrast to its predecessor Kyōto (capital metropolis). (Both of these places, incidentally, are somewhat exceptional in having their names made up of *on* readings.) In between lie thousands of place names that bear witness to the use and development of the country by the Japanese. The reclamation of land, for example, is shown by such place names as Shinkai (newly opened up) and Shinden (new rice fields), often preceded by a name of the person responsible, and many place names—and, hence, family names—show religious associations by the use of such components as *kami* (god), *miya* (shrine), and *tera* (temple).

Administratively, the country is divided into prefectures *(ken)*, except in the case of Tōkyō, which is a *to* (metropolitan prefecture or metropolis); Ōsaka and Kyōto prefectures, called *fu* (urban prefectures); and Hokkaidō, in which *dō* (road; route; circuit) is used to designate the whole island. Smaller divisions consist of *shi* (city), *ku* (city ward), and *chō/machi* (district) in the case of urban areas; and of *gun* (rural district), *machi* (township), *mura* (village) and, sometimes, a smaller unit called *azana* (hamlet), which is usually abbreviated to *aza* before the name of the hamlet (e.g., *aza* Yoshida), or omitted altogether. The names of two or more adjacent local government areas are sometimes combined to form a name for the larger area. These combined names are usually written with one character from each of the two names, often using alternative *on* or *kun* readings of the characters: e.g., Keihin 京浜 is used for Tōkyō 東京 and Yokohama 横浜 together, and Keihan 京阪 for Kyōto 京都 and Ōsaka 大阪.

■ —— Araki Ryōzō, *Nanori jiten* (1959). I. V. Gillis and P. C. Pai, *Japanese Surnames* (1939). I. V. Gillis and P. C. Pai, *Japanese Personal Names* (1940). A. J. Koop and H. Inada, *Japanese Names and How to Read Them* (1923, reissued 1960). Yoshida Sumio, "Namae to sono moji," in *Bunkachō Kokugo Shirīzu VI: Kanji* (1974). P. G. O'Neill, *Japanese Names* (1972). Ōno Shirō and Fujiya Yutaka, *Nandoku seishi jiten* (1977). Herschel Webb, *Research in Japanese Sources: A Guide* (1965). Yamanaka Jōta, *Chimei gogen jiten* (1968). Yanagita Kunio, *Chimei no kenkyū* (1968).   P. G. O'NEILL

Nametoko

Gorge on the upper reaches of the river SHIMANTOGAWA (also called Megurogawa), southern Ehime Prefecture, Shikoku, between the city of Uwajima and the town of Matsuno. Surrounded by primeval forests, in which wild monkeys roam. It abounds with deep pools and waterfalls, including Yukinowanotaki. Part of Ashizuri–Uwakai National Park.

Namiki Gohei

The name of a succession of major dramatists in the KABUKI theater. Gohei I (1747–1808), a pupil of Namiki Shōzō I (1730–73), was already the foremost dramatist of the Kyōto–Ōsaka area by the age of 40 but he later moved to Edo (now Tōkyō). His plays are noted for their masterful blending of realistic characters and the logical consistency of their plots, elements then lacking in the Edo kabuki but generally adopted soon after his arrival.

At Ōsaka, Gohei I's outstanding works included *Kimmon gosan no kiri* (1778, Thief Goemon on the Temple Gate), *Keisei kogane no shachihoko* (1782, Stealing the Golden Fishscales), and *Kanjin kammon tekuda no hajimari* (1789, The Murder of a Foreign Emissary). In Edo, he continued his brilliant career with such memorable plays as *Godairiki koi no fūjime* (1794, Oman and Gengobei), *Sumida no haru geisha-katagi* (1796, Umegawa and Chūbei), and *Tomigaoka koi no yamabiraki* (1798, The Two Shimbei). He is credited with writing more than 110 *jidai-mono* (historical plays) and *sewa-mono* (domestic plays).

Namiki Gohei II (1768–1819) died about two years after assuming this name and is better remembered as Shinoda Kinji I. Gohei III

(1790–1855) is celebrated as the writer of the dialogue for Ichikawa Danjūrō VII's *Kanjinchō* (1840, The Subscription List), one of the greatest masterpieces in the kabuki repertory. See also KABUKI JŪHACHIBAN.

—— Kawatake Shigetoshi, *Kabuki sakusha no kenkyū* (1940). A. C. Scott, *Kanjinchō, a Japanese Kabuki Play* (1953), a translation of *Kanjinchō*.   *Ted T. TAKAYA*

Namiki Shōzō

The name of two important figures in the KABUKI theater. Shōzō I (1730–73), a leading dramatist from the Kyōto–Ōsaka area, is best remembered as the inventor of the revolving stage. He wrote some 100 works, mostly *jidai-mono* (historical plays). These dramas include *Keisei ama no hagoromo* (1753, The Feathery Garment from Heaven), *Sanjikkoku yobune no hajimari* (1758, The Beginning of Heavy Cargo Ships on the Yodo River), and *Sanzen-sekai yarikuri ōrai* (1772, Kin'emon, the Notorious Pirate).

Although Shōzō II (d 1807), a relative of Shōzō I, left no prominent kabuki plays, there is strong evidence that he might be the author of *Kezairoku* (or *Gezairoku*, 1801), a manual for kabuki playwriting, which is a rare and valuable source on this subject.

—— Earle Ernst, *The Kabuki Theatre* (1956). Kawatake Shigetoshi, *Kabuki sakusha no kenkyū* (1940). Kawatake Shigetoshi, *Nihon engeki zenshi* (1959).   *Ted T. TAKAYA*

Namiki Sōsuke (1695–1751?)

Also known as Namiki Senryū. A major dramatist of the PUPPET THEATER who wrote over 40 JŌRURI plays. During his successful career he often collaborated with other notable playwrights, including Takeda Izumo I (d 1747; see TAKEDA IZUMO), Izumo II (1691–1756), and Miyoshi Shōraku (1706?–72?). He worked at both the Takemotoza and Toyotakeza, the principal playhouses for the puppet theater in Ōsaka. His plays associated with Takemotoza include *Natsumatsuri Naniwa kagami* (1745, The Summer Festival in Naniwa), *Sugawara denju tenarai kagami* (1746, The Secrets of Sugawara's Calligraphy), *Yoshitsune sembonzakura* (1747, The Thousand Cherry Blossoms of Yoshitsune), and *Kanadehon chūshingura* (1748, The Treasure of Loyal Retainers).

He died while still writing *Ichinotani futaba gunki* (1751, The Chronicle of the Battle of Ichinotani). Completed by his collaborators, this play also became a perennial favorite.

—— Aubrey S. and Giovanna M. Halford, *The Kabuki Handbook* (1956). Wakatsuki Yasuji, *Ningyō jōruri shi kenkyū* (1943).   *Ted T. TAKAYA*

Nampo Jōmyō (1235–1308)

Monk of the RINZAI SECT of Zen Buddhism; also known as Nampo Jōmin, Nampo Shōmyō, or Entsū Daiō Kokushi. Born in Suruga Province (now Shizuoka Prefecture). He took holy orders at an early age after studying with Jōben of the temple Kenzuiji. He later studied at KENCHŌJI in Kamakura under the Chinese monk RANKEI DŌRYŪ. Between 1259 and 1260, Nampo traveled to Sung China, where he received instruction from Kidō Chigu (Ch: Xutang Zhiyu or Hsü-t'ang Chih-yü) of Kinzanji (Ch: Jingshansi or Ching-shan-ssu). Upon his return to Japan in 1267, he served as supervisor of the library of Kenchōji under Dōryū. In 1270 he went to Kōtokuji in Tsukushi (now northern Kyūshū); the following year he moved to Sūfukuji in DAZAIFU, and for the next 33 years he devoted himself to proselytizing in the northern Kyūshū area. In 1305, under imperial command he became the head of Manjuji in Kyōto. Two years later he was invited by the former regent Hōjō Sadatoki to become abbot of Kenchōji. Nampo laid the foundation for the subsequent rise of the Rinzai sect, and among his disciples were many notable monks, including SŌHŌ MYŌCHŌ. The Daiō subsect of the Rinzai sect began with him. He wrote a book called *Goroku* (Records of Sayings).

Namu Amida Butsu

Also known as the formula of the NEMBUTSU, this phrase literally means "I take my refuge in AMIDA Buddha." The recitation of *Namu Amida Butsu*, calling on Amida's compassion, is the fundamental practice in Pure Land teachings, along with faith in Amida Buddha, the essential key to ensuring birth in the Pure Land where attainment of Buddhahood is assured. As its recitation is easy to perform, it is considered by the Pure Land sects to be the practice most suited for the dull-witted people of an age far removed from the time of the historical Buddha Śākyamuni (see ESCHATOLOGY). Among the canonical sutras of PURE LAND BUDDHISM the Larger and the Smaller *Sukhāvatīvyūha* sutras also call for the practice of *nembutsu*, but the *Amitāyurdhyāna-sūtra* in particular calls for the recitation of the phrase.   *Robert RHODES*

Namu Myōhō renge kyo

Also known as *daimoku*. *Namu Myōhō renge kyo* is a phrase meaning "I take my refuge in the LOTUS SUTRA." Its recitation is the basic practice of the NICHIREN SECT. *Myōhō renge kyo* is not only the title of the Lotus Sutra but is held to be the essence of the reality the sutra reveals. The recitation of *Namu Myōhō renge kyo* is considered to lead a person to Buddhahood and to be the practice most suitable for followers of the Lotus Sutra during the degenerate age of *mappō* (see ESCHATOLOGY). Along with the *honzon* (object of worship) and the *kaidan* (ordination platform), it is one of the Sandai-hihō (Three Great Secret Dharmas) of the Nichiren sect.   *Robert RHODES*

Namura Shipbuilding Co, Ltd

(Namura Zōsensho). Company engaged in shipbuilding and the manufacture and sale of various steel products such as structures, frames, and bridges. It was established in 1911. In response to the worldwide demand for larger ships, it built a new shipyard, equipped with a computerized control system and a semitandem building dock at the city of Imari in Kyūshū in 1974. Sales for the fiscal year ending March 1982 totaled ¥32.8 billion (US $136.3 million) and the export ratio was 46 percent. In the same year the company was capitalized at ¥1.5 billion (US $6.2 million). The company has its headquarters in Ōsaka and maintains a representative office in London.

nanakamado

(mountain ash). *Sorbus commixta*. A deciduous tree of the family Rosaceae which grows wild in mountainous areas all over Japan and is known for its beautiful fall foliage and red fruit. It grows 7–10 meters (23–33 ft) high and has a diameter of 0.3 meters (1 ft). The bark is dark brown with gray tinges, has a rough surface, and gives off a peculiar smell. The branches are dark purplish red. *Nanakamado* has alternate compound leaves, each composed of 5–7 pairs of oblong leaflets with serrated edges. The flowering season is in July and the white florets are gathered on compound flower stalks at the ends of the branches. The berries that follow the flowers are round and become red as they ripen.

The wood is hard and the tree's name derives from the saying that even after putting it into a stove *(kamado)* seven *(nana)* times, it remains unburned. Related species found in Japan include the *sabiba nanakamado* (*S. commixta* var. *rufo-ferruginea*), which has brown hairs along the veins on the underside of the leaflets; the *urajiro nanakamado* (*S. matsumurana*), whose leaflets have white undersides; the *takane nanakamado* (*S. sambucifolia*) a shrub which grows wild in high mountains; and the *nankin nanakamado* (*S. gracilis*), whose leaf stalks characteristically develop stipules.   *MATSUDA Osamu*

Nanao

City in northern Ishikawa Prefecture, central Honshū, on Nanao Bay. A busy port from the Edo period (1600–1868), Nanao is today one of the major trading ports on the Sea of Japan. It imports a large amount of lumber from the Soviet Union. Lumber processing as well as brick and cement industries flourish. Wakura Hot Spring is located here. Pop: 50,394.

Nanatsugama

Sea caves in the city of Karatsu, northern Saga Prefecture, northwestern Kyūshū. Located along the Genkai Sea, they consist of seven basaltic caves in jointed columnar cliffs on the sea. The larger caves can be toured by excursion boats. Part of the Genkai Quasi-National Park.

nanga

("Southern painting"). Term used to refer to BUNJINGA, Japanese literati painting of the 18th and 19th centuries. The term originated with the Chinese expression *nanzonghua (nan-tsung-hua)*, meaning "Southern-school painting," which is pronounced *nanshūga* in Japanese. *Nanga* is an abbreviation of *nanshūga*, and has no counterpart in Chinese.

The term *nanzonghua* was first used by the Chinese painter-critic Dong Qichang (Tung Ch'i-ch'ang; 1555–1636). He traced the aesthetic lineage of literati painters of his day from the 8th-century painter-poet Wang Wei down through such artists as Dong Yuan (Tung Yüan) of the Five Dynasties (907–960), Mi Fu of the Northern Song (Sung) dynasty (960–1126), Huang Gongwang (Huang Kung-wang) of the Yuan (Yüan) dynasty (1279–1368), to Wen Zhengming (Wen Cheng-ming) of the Ming dynasty (1368–1644). In doing so, Dong loosely identified himself and other literati artists with what he called the "Southern school" and aligned the opposing academic tradition with the "Northern school." Dong's Northern-Southern distinction was based on an analogy with the Northern and Southern divisions of Zen (Ch: Chan or Ch'an) Buddhism and was not strictly geographical or clear-cut. But it did reflect general stylistic differences in Chinese landscape painting.

Japanese literati painters, who were mainly, but not solely, influenced by the landscape styles of the Chinese literati, were not well informed of the subtleties of this genealogy when they adopted the term *nanga*.

Nangakuha

("Southern Learning" school). The branch of Neo-Confucian studies (SHUSHIGAKU) founded in Tosa (now Kōchi Prefecture) around 1548 by a Zen Buddhist priest, Minamimura Baiken. It was at first guided by several priests, but later became completely secularized under TANI JICHŪ, who counted among his disciples NONAKA KENZAN and YAMAZAKI ANSAI. In contrast to other branches of Neo-Confucianism in Japan, the Tosa school placed special emphasis on translating theory into action and on defining the proper relationship of the emperor to the people *(taigi meibun)*. As the mainstream of Confucian learning in Tosa, it influenced the antishogunate restorationist (SONNŌ JŌI) movement of the late years of the Edo period (1600–1868).

naniwa-bushi

Also commonly known as *rōkyoku*. A type of narrative ballad rhythmically intoned to SHAMISEN accompaniment. Similar to GI-DAYŪ-BUSHI, KIYOMOTO-BUSHI, and other kinds of JŌRURI chant in its musical style, *naniwa-bushi* was a popular stage entertainment whose repertory consisted of embellished narratives taken largely from accounts of actual historical events, widely known stories, and traditional tales *(monogatari)*. These were performed by a solo chanter/narrator to the accompaniment of a single *shamisen* player.

An early form of STREET ENTERTAINMENT, with affinities to religio-secular chants of the 13th and 14th centuries, *naniwa-bushi* first developed in the Kansai (Ōsaka-Kyōto) region during the Edo period (1600–1868). It was originally performed by street musicians, who gradually moved indoors to small huts set up on the grounds of temples and shrines. From such humble origins *naniwa-bushi* came to be a feature attraction in hundreds of small YOSE (variety and vaudeville) halls and even in larger theaters by the late 1870s. *Naniwa-bushi*'s place in society rose with the quality of the stage on which it was performed. The influence of the phonograph record in the early 1900s also helped foster a "golden age" of *rōkyoku*. Three performers of the Meiji period (1868–1912) who did much to modernize the art were Tōchūken Kumoemon (1873–1916), Yoshida Naramaru II (1880–1967), and Shikishima Ōkura (1878?–1938).

Though it enjoyed great popularity along with KŌDAN and RAKUGO comic storytelling through the 1910s, the advent of motion pictures caused *naniwa-bushi*'s decline in the late 1920s. The upsurge in nationalistic fervor in Japan beginning in the mid-1930s, however, produced an unprecedented resurgence in *rōkyoku*'s popularity, aided by the further spread of records and radio. After World War II, *rōkyoku* once again went into decline with the development of new types of entertainment. It tended to draw fans more from the countryside than the cities and suffered from storyline as well as musical stagnation. *Rōkyoku* is rarely broadcast now over radio or television, and there are few performers who can match the sophistication and high quality of past masters such as Bekkōsai Toramaru I (1854?–94), Tenchūken Ungetsu I (1899–1945), Naniwa-tei Ayatarō (1888–1960), Suzuki Yonewaka (1899–1979), Hirosawa Torazō II (1899–1964), Tamagawa Katsutarō II (1898–1969), Kasugai Baiō (1905–74), and Mikado Hiroshi (b 1907).   NAGAI Hiroo

Naniwakyō

A capital city begun by Emperor TEMMU in about 683, and the site of a series of palaces; located in what is now Hōenzaka Chō in the city of Ōsaka. The sovereigns Kōgyoku (reigned 642–645 as Kōgyoku and 655–661 as SAIMEI) and KŌTOKU (r 645–654) had palaces in the neighborhood, which had been settled as early as the 5th century. The first large palace there with a conventional formal plan was built by Temmu in 679. It consisted of eight rather small ministry buildings in the administrative compound (chōdōin) and an uncrowded courtyard to the north that contained the Great Hall of State (DAIGO-KUDEN). The nature of the residential compound (dairi) and the southernmost forecourt is uncertain because of modern occupation of the site.

The palace was destroyed by fire in 686, but Empress JITŌ (r 686–697) rebuilt it, at least in part, and Emperor MOMMU (r 697–707) and Empress Genshō (r 715–724) both resided there. Emperor SHŌMU (r 724–749) began a new palace at Naniwakyō in 726. It was completed in 732, but the capital was there only from March 744 to February 745. It had a far more spacious chōdōin, comprising 12 large buildings, and a complex of several units to the north. The palace was allowed to deteriorate after the capital was moved to SHIGARAKI NO MIYA in February 745.

Although Temmu probably laid out the city—at least theoretically—in a square grid pattern with the palace at the north, it was largely unoccupied until the 8th century, and the plan remained asymmetrical. The capital is thought to have had 16 broad avenues (bō) running north-to-south, intersected by 12 others (jō) running east-to-west, 8 of them on the west and 4 on the east, although it is doubtful whether any grid pattern actually materialized. The outer dimensions of Naniwakyō were probably about four by three kilometers (2.5 by 1.9 mi). Shōmu expanded the city in 734 by combining two jō-and-bō blocks into one and adding a line of large blocks on the east and another row on the south. Only in the northwest are there any suggestions of a checkerboard scheme today.

■ ——Nakao Yoshiharu, "Naniwa no miya to Naniwakyō," in Ueda Masaaki, ed, *Tojō* (1976). Yamane Tokutarō, *Naniwa no miya* (1964).   J. Edward KIDDER, Jr.

Naniwa miyage

Book on the puppet plays (JŌRURI) of CHIKAMATSU MONZAEMON, written by his friend Hozumi Ikan (1692–1769) and published in 1738. Although Ikan was a Confucian scholar and a disciple of ITŌ TŌGAI, he is best remembered for this work, which provides commentary on the titles, difficult passages, and organization of nine of Chikamatsu's *jōruri*. The most notable feature of the book is the introduction in which Ikan recounts a dialogue between himself and Chikamatsu. It is the only record of Chikamatsu's personal view on *jōruri*: that the essence of truth in artistic endeavor lies somewhere between fiction and reality. Ikan selected the title *Naniwa miyage* (literally, "souvenir of Naniwa") because Naniwa (Ōsaka) was the birthplace of the *jōruri* genre. Ikan's son, who took the pen name CHIKAMATSU HANJI, became a famous *jōruri* playwright.

Nanjing (Nanking) Incident

(Nankin Jiken). 1. Clash between Chinese Nationalist (Guomindang or Kuomintang) soldiers and foreigners at Nanjing on 24 March 1927. The Nationalist army, attempting to suppress warlordism and unify China under the Nationalist Party, occupied Nanjing after the withdrawal of the warlord army of Zhang Zongchang (Chang Tsung-ch'ang; 1882–1932) on 23 March. Nationalist soldiers thereupon assaulted foreigners, looted foreign businesses and residences, and attacked the Japanese, American, and British consulates. Foreign casualties included six dead and several wounded. Fifty-two foreigners took refuge at a Standard Oil residence on the outskirts of the city. When Nationalist troops began to attack them, the USS *Noa* and the HMS *Emerald* shelled the Nationalists, allowing the group to escape to the ships. Fifty Japanese soldiers were landed to protect the withdrawal of Japanese nationals from the city, but they succeeded in avoiding clashes with Nationalist troops. The incident was the climax of xenophobia in the Nationalist Revolution, and it occurred during the struggle between moderates and radicals within the Nationalist Party. Although the Nationalists later claimed that communists trying to discredit the Nationalist leader CHIANG KAI-SHEK were behind the incident, it was apparently spontaneous. The Western powers and Japan demanded an apology, indemnities, and punishment for the perpetrators of the incident. In April 1928 the United States and China reached an agreement, and Japan, Britain, France, and Italy soon reached settlements as well.

2. Atrocities committed by the Japanese army against the civilian population of Nanjing and vicinity from December 1937 to January 1938, early in the SINO-JAPANESE WAR OF 1937–1945. Upon entering Nanjing on 13 December 1937 after a few days of fighting, the Japanese army began a wholesale murder of Chinese men on the pretext that they were Chinese soldiers trying to escape in civilian clothes. As discipline broke down among the Japanese troops, they began to kill civilians indiscriminately. According to estimates made at the Tōkyō WAR CRIMES TRIALS, about 42,000 civilians, mostly women and children, were killed in Nanjing, and over 100,000 civilians and prisoners of war in the vicinity of the city over the next six weeks. There were an estimated 20,000 rapes; 12,000 shops were looted; and a third of the city was destroyed by fire. The incident, committed with the sanction of officers, was the worst atrocity committed by Japanese military forces during World War II. The commander of the Japanese troops at Nanjing, Matsui Iwane (1878–1948), was sentenced to death for war crimes in 1948.

■——Works about the 1927 Incident: Dorothy Borg, *American Policy and the Chinese Revolution, 1925–1928* (1947, repr 1968). Etō Shinkichi, "Nankin jiken to Nichibei," in Saitō Makoto, ed, *Gendai Amerika no naisei to gaikō* (1959). Akira Iriye, *After Imperialism: The Search for a New Order in the Far East, 1921–1931* (1965). Works about the 1937 Incident: Robert J. C. Butow, *Tojo and the Coming of the War* (1961). Lloyd E. Eastman, "Facets of an Ambivalent Relationship: Smuggling, Puppets, and Atrocities during the War, 1937–1945," in Akira Iriye, ed, *The Chinese and the Japanese: Essays in Political and Cultural Interactions* (1980).

Robert ENTENMANN

Nanjō Bun'yū (1849–1927)

Eminent Buddhologist and Sanskrit scholar, born in Mino Province (now part of Gifu Prefecture). Following his ordination as a priest of the Ōtani branch of the JŌDO SHIN SECT, he went to England in 1876 to study Sanskrit Buddhist texts under Max Müller (1823–1900) at Oxford University. He published many texts and English translations. Returning to Japan in 1884, he taught at Tōkyō University and later served as president of Shinshū (now Ōtani) University. The most famous of his publications is a *Catalogue of the Chinese Translation of the Buddhist Tripiṭaka* (1883), commonly known as the Nanjō Catalogue.

Nanki Bunko

(Nanki Library). A collection of some 100,000 volumes assembled by successive generations of the Ki (Wakayama) branch of the Tokugawa family (see GOSANKE). Today it is one of the special collections of the University of Tōkyō Library. The Nanki Bunko was the first important gift of books to the university library after its destruction in the great Tōkyō Earthquake of 1923; it was donated by Tokugawa Yorimichi, who had maintained the collection as a public library at his residence in the Azabu section of Tōkyō. It contains histories, literary works, and maps, as well as descriptive works on Japanese aesthetics, theater, art, music, flower arrangement, and the tea ceremony. The name *nanki* ("southern wild ginger") was given to the library to distinguish it from the AOI LIBRARY, another Tokugawa collection of books. *Aoi* (wild ginger; *Asarum caulescens*) was the Tokugawa family crest.

Theodore F. WELCH

Nankoku

Also known as Nangoku. City in central Kōchi Prefecture, Shikoku. The prefecture's granary since ancient times, Nankoku was a pioneer in double-cropping. Vegetables and tobacco are cultivated in alternation with rice. It is known for its *onagadori* (a long-tailed Japanese fowl). Kōchi Airport is located here. Pop: 44,866.

Nansei Islands → Ryūkyū Islands

nanshinron → southern expansion doctrine

Nansō Satomi hakkenden

(1814–42, Satomi and the Eight "Dogs"). An illustrated historical romance by the celebrated early 19th-century GESAKU fiction writer Takizawa BAKIN in nine sections and 181 chapters describing how the fortunes of a warrior family, which fell in defeat in the Kakitsu Rebellion (1441), are revived with the aid of eight "dog" warriors (each of whose surnames begins with the Japanese word for dog) and a host of other loyal retainers. An epic work, it may be divided into three parts: establishment of the Satomi family in Kazusa (now part of Chiba Prefecture; chapters 1–14), assembly of the eight "dog" warriors under the Satomi banner (chapters 15–131), and the struggles of the Satomi against the combined forces of the shōgun's deputies in the Kantō (eastern Honshū) region (chapters 131–181). After a Satomi victory the eight warrior heroes and a family embassy go to Kyōto to pay respects to the emperor and shōgun and ask that Satomi patriarch Yoshizane's daughter, Fusehime, be recognized as a deity and a shrine constructed in her honor because of the many miracles she has performed. Each of the eight "dogs" is married to one of Satomi Yoshinari's eight daughters, and the Satomi clan flourishes in peace for generations thereafter.

Nansō Satomi hakkenden is classified as a YOMIHON ("reading book"), one of the major varieties of *gesaku* fiction usually serious and highly moral in tone that was popular in the mid-19th century. Like other *yomihon*, *Hakkenden* is written in a modified form of classical Japanese with some colloquial elements and a heavy sprinkling of Chinese constructions, roughly similar to that of the GUNKI MONOGATARI (military chronicles). Bakin uses a poetic rhythm of alternating clusters of five and seven syllables, the traditional meter of Japanese verse (see WAKA), ballad recitation, and the JŌRURI puppet theater. Various conventions and techniques of Japanese drama and Chinese colloquial fiction help impart an epic quality to the work.

In form and structure *Hakkenden* is historical romance of an allegorical nature. Into scenes and situations that invoke an imaginative recreation of actual historical happenings, Bakin weaves a complex allegory. His basic theme is restoration, with morality as its foundation and fate the force insuring that morality prevails. Good and evil, interwound like tangled strands of thread, are incarnated in characters who serve as emblems. Good is seen to benefit one's own progeny more than oneself, while evil deeds meet punishment in one's own lifetime. Good and evil both activate supernatural forces which exert an influence on the various turns of events.

Most of the characters strike one as more caricatures than as individually developed human beings. The heroes are largely exemplars of the warrior code (BUSHIDŌ), on which the work in total is a lofty discourse, and the heroines self-sacrificing paragons of virtue. Many modern readers regard this as a flaw in the romance. But Bakin's rich and inventive imagination and his ability to create fascinating incidents in which the heroes test their mettle and exercise their superhuman ability compensate for this weakness.

Bakin was the most articulate literary exponent of the Confucian and Buddhist idea that fate is linked to morality. *Hakkenden* embodies this concept in the imaginative structure of historical romance and takes a place with the TALE OF GENJI and other Japanese classics that deserve universal acclaim.

Leon M. ZOLBROD

Nan taiheiki → Imagawa Sadayo

Nantaisan

Also called Futarasan and Kurokamiyama. Conical volcano in the Nasu Volcanic Zone. It is within the borders of the city of Nikkō, western Tochigi Prefecture, central Honshū, dominating the north bank of Lake Chūzenji. Composed of andesite, it has highly developed radial drainages. Once a center for religious excercises of the SHUGENDŌ sect, the inner sanctuary of Futara Shrine is still on its summit. It is part of Nikkō National Park. Height: 2,484 m (8,148 ft).

nanten

(nandin). *Nandina domestica*. An evergreen shrub of the family Berberidaceae, found in mountainous areas of Kyūshū, Shikoku, and western Honshū, as well as central China and India. In Japan it is widely cultivated as an ornamental. Its dark brown trunks grow in clusters, usually reaching a height of 2 meters (7 ft) and occasionally 3 meters (10 ft). The large alternate pinnate leaves grow at the tips of the branches and bear tapered, leathery leaflets. In June small white flowers appear on long stalks and are followed in fall and winter by clusters of bright red berries. The wood is yellow. Numerous horticultural varieties have been developed, including *shironanten*, distinguished by its white berries; *fujinanten*, with lavender berries; and *kinshi nanten,* which has threadlike leaves. There are also varieties with mottled leaves.

Because its name suggests the expression *nan o tenzuru* (to overturn misfortune or adversity), *nanten* has traditionally been regarded as an auspicious plant. Paintings of *nanten* and daffodils, or *nanten* and pine, are displayed on festive occasions. It was said that warriors of old used to put its leaves in their armor and display branches in their homes to ensure victory. *Nanten* was also used as an alcove ornament for coming-of-age ceremonies (GEMPUKU), and pregnant women were known to place sprays of *nanten* under their coverlets for a safe delivery. Children were given chopsticks made of *nanten* in the belief that these would ward off illness. Even now, *nanten* leaves are used as garnishes for ceremonial presents of rice cooked with adzuki beans *(sekihan)* and fish.

The German physician Engelbert KAEMPFER, who visited Japan in 1690, was the first Westerner to describe the plant, but he died before publishing his description. His manuscript and drawings were later used by the Swedish naturalist Carl Peter THUNBERG, who visited Japan in 1775 and introduced the plant to Europeans as *Nandina.*
                                                                    MATSUDA Osamu

nanushi → shōya

Nan'yō

City in southern Yamagata Prefecture, northern Honshū. Grapes are cultivated in the city's hills. Winemaking, silk reeling, and the production of switchboards are its principal industries. The Akayu Hot Spring attracts visitors. Pop: 36,682.

Nanzan University

(Nanzan Daigaku). A private, coeducational university located in Nagoya. Its predecessor was Nanzan Foreign Language School, established in 1946. It was granted university status in 1949, and maintains faculties of letters, foreign languages, economics, business management, and law. It has the following research institutes: Anthropological Institute; Nanzan Institute for Religion and Culture. Enrollment in 1980 was 5,243.

Nanzenji

Head temple of the Nanzenji branch of the RINZAI SECT of ZEN Buddhism. Located in Sakyō Ward, Kyōto. Nanzenji was originally the detached palace (or villa) of the retired emperor KAMEYAMA. In 1291 he converted it to a Zen temple, naming it first Ryūanzan Zenrin Zenji and later Zuiryūzan Nanzenji. He appointed Mukan Fumon (1212–91) as its chief priest. Kameyama was a strong supporter of the temple, and it is said that he participated in its construction. This imperial patronage lent great prestige to Nanzenji.

In 1334 Emperor GO-DAIGO ranked Nanzenji first among the Five Temples (GOZAN) and installed as chief priest MUSŌ SOSEKI, who greatly contributed toward the prosperity of Nanzenji. Later, in 1386 the shōgun ASHIKAGA YOSHIMITSU elevated Nanzenji to a special rank above five newly designated Gozan temples, giving it preferential treatment in other ways as well until eventually the temple became an object of envy. In 1393 the warrior-monks of the temple ENRYAKUJI attacked Nanzenji and burned down many of the buildings. The temple was rebuilt by the shōgun Ashikaga Yoshimochi (1386–1428) but was again largely destroyed by fires in 1447 and 1467. During and after the Azuchi-Momoyama period (1568–1600), with the support and protection of the imperial court, TOYOTOMI HIDEYOSHI, and the Tokugawa shōguns, Nanzenji was again reconstructed. Most of the present buildings date from this period. At the time of the Meiji Restoration of 1868, the prestige of Nanzenji declined because of the suppression of Buddhism by the new government (see HAIBUTSU KISHAKU). In 1876 Nanzenji became the head temple of an independent branch, the Nanzenjiha, of the Rinzai Zen sect.

At present the main buildings of the temple are: a *butsuden* (Buddha hall), a *sōdō* (meditation hall), a *kuri* (monks' living quarters), two *hōjō* (abbot's living quarters), a *sammon* (main gate), a *chokushimon* (imperial gate), a *karamon* (Chinese gate), a *sōmon* (outer gate), and a bell tower.

The main gate, known as Tenka Ryūmon (Dragon Gate of the World), was constructed by TŌDŌ TAKATORA in 1628 and is in the Zen style. The gate is well known as a place where the legendary spy and bandit Ishikawa Goemon is said to have often hidden from his pursuers; Goemon's story is told in a famous *kabuki* play, with the main gate as one of the stage settings. Among the images in the sanctum of the gate is one of a crowned Śākyamuni Buddha. On the ceiling are drawings of Chinese phoenixes and celestial nymphs ascribed to KANŌ TAN'YŪ.

The *butsuden,* the main hall of the temple, lies beyond the main gate. The original hall was contributed by Toyotomi Hideyoshi but burned in 1895; the present hall dates from 1909. Inside the hall are images of Śākyamuni Buddha and two bodhisattvas: Monju (Skt: Mañjuśrī) and Fugen (Skt: Samantabhadra).

The two *hōjō* are known as the *daihōjō* (abbot's large living quarters) and *shōhōjō* (abbot's small living quarters); both have been designated national treasures. The *daihōjō* may be the original *seiryōden* (emperor's living quarters) built by Hideyoshi and later moved to Nanzenji, but there is contradictory evidence concerning this theory. The *daihōjō* preserves numerous murals and paintings, executed in a sumptuous style reminiscent of the Momoyama era (late 16th century), on screens and *fusuma* (paper sliding doors). In the Yanagi no Ma (Willow Chamber) there are famous paintings of a waterfall, mountains, and birds ascribed to KANŌ MOTONOBU, in addition to murals of willows; in the Jakō no Ma (Musk Chamber), paintings of pines and musk cats ascribed to KANŌ SANRAKU; in the Ohiru no Ma (Day Chamber), paintings of various Taoist immortals ascribed to KANŌ EITOKU; in the Nishi no Ma (West Chamber), paintings of pine trees and hawks ascribed to Eitoku or Kanō Munenobu (1514–62); and in the Tsuru no Ma (Crane Chamber), paintings of pine trees and cranes ascribed to KANŌ MITSUNOBU. There is also an image of KANNON (Skt: Avalokiteśvara). The *shōhōjō* is thought to have been brought from FUSHIMI CASTLE and is well known for its three Tora no Ma (Tiger Chambers): the paintings of tigers in these rooms, ascribed to Kanō Tan'yū, are of particular renown.

At Konchiin (a *tatchū,* or subsidiary temple, of Nanzenji) there are landscapes ascribed to the Chinese Emperor Huizong (Hui-tsung, 1082–1135) and an ink painting designated a national treasure, ascribed to MINCHŌ, a painter-priest. At one time there were nearly 100 *tatchū* at Nanzenji, but now there are just over 10. At Nanzen'in, another *tatchū* and the mausoleum of Emperor Kameyama, there is a statue of the emperor in a seated position; it was probably made around 1305. Nanzenji preserves many other works of art, such as an ink painting of Bodhidharma by SHŌKEI.

Nanzenji is also noted for its gardens. The garden of the *daihōjō* is composed of sand, stones, and pine trees. It is thought to have been designed by KOBORI ENSHŪ. The garden of Nanzen'in is preserved in the Kamakura style and is one of the most noted gardens in Kyōto today.
                                                                    Hoyu ISHIDA

Naobi no Kami

("The Rectifying Deities"; also called Naohi no Kami). A divine couple, Kamu Naohi no Kami and Ō Naohi no Kami, who appear in a myth on the origin of evil and purification in the two early chronicles KOJIKI (712) and NIHON SHOKI (720). When the deity Izanagi no Mikoto (see MYTHOLOGY) had returned from the Land of the Dead (Yomi no Kuni), he bathed in a river to purify himself of the pollution he had incurred there and gave birth to a series of deities. Among them were the two Rectifying Deities as well as Yaso Makatsuhi no Kami and Ō Makatsuhi no Kami, a divine couple born of the dust and filth of the netherworld, and Itsunome no Kami, the purifier.

Shintō theologians have engaged in controversy over the nature of these deities since the 18th-century scholar MOTOORI NORINAGA proposed a dualistic view of Shintō deities *(kami)* based on this myth. His idea of evil *kami* and righteous *kami* was refuted by HIRATA ATSUTANE, who insisted on a fundamental monistic view of *kami.* In the latter theology, so-called evil *kami* originated in Izanagi's wish to get rid of pollution and prevent evil from intruding into the world, and they were thus turned into scapegoats. Accordingly, evil *kami* and rectifying *kami* are fundamentally both sides of the same coin created by *kami* for human salvation. A Shintō soteriology has developed from these controversies in the modern times.
■——Nishida Nagao, *Nihon shintōshi kenkyū,* vol 1 (1978).
                                                                    Kyōko Motomachi NAKAMURA

Naoki Sanjūgo (1891–1934)

Novelist. Real name Uemura Sōichi. Born in Ōsaka. Attended Waseda University. He was an eccentric, as illustrated by his pen name,

Nara
Sarusawa Pond with the five-story pagoda of the temple Kōfukuji in the background.

Nara
Approach path to Kasuga Shrine. Donated by believers, the many stone lanterns are lighted twice a year, in February and August.

which he changed each year to reflect his age (Sanjūgo or "thirty-five" was the last). He first became known as a columnist for the magazine BUNGEI SHUNJŪ, writing scathing critical gossip about contemporary literary figures. After this he started writing historical fiction and popular novels, advocating that popular writing be valued more highly as literature. The year after Naoki's death, his friend KIKUCHI KAN, publisher of *Bungei shunjū*, established in his honor the Naoki Prize, one of Japan's two most prestigious literary prizes (the other being the Akutagawa Prize). His works include *Nangoku taiheiki* (1930–31) and *Nihon no senritsu* (1932).

naorai

(communion). SHINTŌ ceremony of communion between a god (KAMI) and human worshipers in which the participants share *sake*, rice, fish, and vegetables previously offered to and sanctified by the god. Etymologically *naorai* has been interpreted variously as a return to ordinary life from the state of *imi* (period of abstinence and purification) during religious observances, partaking of sacred meals together with the gods, or rectifying mistakes committed during a rite.

In the ancient past *naorai* formed a central part of a Shintō rite, although its practice varied from shrine to shrine. All participants, parishioners and priests alike, were required to purify themselves through abstinence and to observe various taboos prior to the rite. Food offerings were prepared with a purified fire and subsequently eaten by participants in front of the altar as a form of a common meal with the god. In modern usage, however, *naorai* marks the end of the rite and the subsequent festive banquet. The offerings are taken away from the altar at the end of the rite and the feast is often held in another room. The rules of abstinence are no longer ob-

served, and the participants return to daily life in the community. See also SHINTŌ RITES.   Kyōko Motomochi NAKAMURA

Naoshima Islands

(Naoshima Shotō). Group of islands in the central Inland Sea, off the city of Tamano, Okayama Prefecture, western Honshū. Administratively a part of Kagawa Prefecture. It consists of 27 islands centering about Naoshima. A Mitsubishi Metal Corporation copper smelting plant was established on the main island, Naoshima, in 1917. Globefish and yellowtail are cultivated in these islands.

Nara

City located in the northern part of Nara Prefecture, central Honshū, on the northern fringe of the Nara Basin. The capital of Japan from 710 to 784, Nara is today the seat of the prefectural government. Spared from destruction in World War II, it still preserves a large number of cultural relics, attracting a great number of tourists each year.

Natural Features——Hills of Plio-Pleistocene sedimentary rock run from north to west in the city area, separating Nara from the Kyōto Basin to the northwest. The city lies on the Yamato plateau in the east, and on its western fringes are found the steep slopes of the Kasuga fault scarp, with well-developed terraces, on which the city first grew. Nara has a continental climate, with the lowest mean temperature (−0.6°C or 30.9°F) coming in January and the highest (31.9°C or 89.4°F) in August. Annual precipitation is 1,390 millimeters, with the heaviest rainfall in the months of June, July, and September.

History——Constructed in the year 710 and patterned after the Tang (T'ang) dynasty capital of Chang'an (Ch'ang-an; modern Xi'an or Sian), the original city (HEIJŌKYŌ) measured 4.8 kilometers (3.0 mi) from north to south and 4.3 kilometers (2.7 mi) from east to west. Traces of the main streets, which were laid out in checkerboard fashion, can still be seen. In ancient Nara, which at one time boasted a population of 200,000, the Heijō Palace stood in the center of the northern part of the city, with such buildings as the Daigokuden, where the emperor had his office. Heijōkyō was later expanded to the east, where the KASUGA SHRINE and the large temples of KŌFU-KUJI and TŌDAIJI were situated. Recent excavations at various sites in the city, including the site of the imperial palace, have yielded new insight into life in ancient times. See also HISTORY OF JAPAN: Nara history.

With the transfer of the capital to NAGAOKAKYŌ in 784, Heijō-kyō fell into decline. The temples of Kōfukuji and Tōdaiji continued to wield power, however, especially in the Heian period (794–1185), operating large-scale manors (SHŌEN) and even establishing their hegemony over other temples in the area. Their powerful warrior-monks came into conflict with the TAIRA FAMILY, who set fire to Nara in 1180. In the Kamakura period (1185–1333) the city recovered its prosperity and achieved a larger population and size than ever before.

In the Edo period (1600–1868), Nara became a TENRYŌ or land under the direct control of the Tokugawa shogunate. Under shogunal protection, the production of Nara *sarashi* (linen) flourished until competition from cotton goods produced in other provinces brought about its decline. Toward the end of the Edo period, the town of Nara once again fell into decline. Even in the Meiji period (1868–1912), the city's population showed little increase. It was not until about 1955 that a population increase was registered, as Nara became a residential suburb of Ōsaka, 41.2 kilometers (25.6 mi) away.

Nara Today——The making of *sumi* (Chinese ink), begun in the Heian period, and of calligraphic brushes are the two most important industries today, with Nara supplying over 90 percent of the country's *sumi*. Other small-scale traditional crafts include sculpted dolls, lacquer ware, and *uchiwa* (fans).

The development of national highways connecting Nara with Ōsaka and Nagoya has led to the creation of new industries, including plastics, in the southern part of the city. The expansion of both the Japanese National Railways and private railway lines has greatly reduced the traveling time between Nara and Ōsaka. Large-scale residential projects completed in the hilly regions to the west of the city present a striking contrast to the ancient capital.

Rice, wheat, strawberries, and watermelon are grown in the southern urban area and tea and cucumbers are cultivated in the mountainous eastern area. Cattle-raising and dairy farming are also popular.

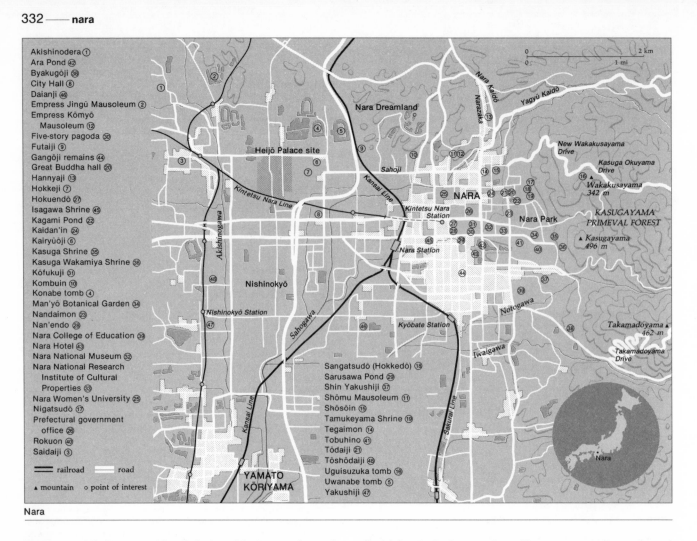

Akishinodera ①
Ara Pond ㊷
Byakugōji ㊳
City Hall ⑧
Daianji ㊻
Empress Jingū Mausoleum ②
Empress Kōmyō
  Mausoleum ⑫
Five-story pagoda ㉚
Futaiji ⑨
Gangōji remains ㊹
Great Buddha hall ⑳
Hannyaji ⑬
Hokkeji ⑦
Hokuendō ㉗
Isagawa Shrine ㊺
Kagami Pond ㉒
Kaidan'in ㉔
Kairyūōji ⑥
Kasuga Shrine ㉟
Kasuga Wakamiya Shrine ㊱
Kōfukuji ㉛
Kombuin ⑩
Konabe tomb ④
Man'yō Botanical Garden ㉞
Nandaimon ㉓
Nan'endo ㉘
Nara College of Education ㊴
Nara Hotel ㊸
Nara National Museum ㉜
Nara National Research
  Institute of Cultural
  Properties ㉝
Nara Women's University ㉕
Nigatsudō ⑰
Prefectural government
  office ㉖
Rokuon ㊵
Saidaiji ③

━━━ railroad   ━━━ road

▲ mountain   ○ point of interest

Sangatsudō (Hokkedō) ⑱
Sarusawa Pond ㉙
Shin Yakushiji ㊲
Shōmu Mausoleum ⑪
Shōsōin ⑮
Tamukeyama Shrine ⑲
Tegaimon ⑭
Tobuhino ㊶
Tōdaiji ㉑
Tōshōdaiji ㊽
Uguisuzuka tomb ⑯
Uwanabe tomb ⑤
Yakushiji ㊼

Nara

Tourism and Culture

Tourism and Culture——Nara Park, famed for its tame deer and set against the rolling hills of WAKAKUSAYAMA and KASUGAYAMA, is a favorite tourist spot. The deer are the guardians of Kasuga Shrine, the tutelary shrine of the FUJIWARA FAMILY. Other shrines and temples are scattered throughout the city, each with a number of national cultural treasures and structures. Kōfukuji is noted for its Muromachi-period (1333–1568) pagoda, SARUSAWA POND, and Buddhist sculpture. Tōdaiji is particularly known for its Great Buddha and Great Buddha hall, the largest wooden structure in the world, measuring 47.5 meters (156 ft) high. The SHŌSŌIN repository within its precincts houses numerous treasures, including artworks that found their way to Japan from Persia via China in the Nara period.

TŌSHŌDAIJI, located in the western part of the city, was established by the Chinese monk GANJIN in 759; the pillars and wooden figures in its temple hall exhibit influences from Greek art. YAKU-SHIJI, also in the western part of the city, is the headquarters of the HOSSŌ SECT. Its West Pagoda, whose reconstruction was completed in 1981, contrasts sharply with the almost 750-year-old East Pagoda. It is famous for its Yakushi trinity, housed in the Main Hall, and other fine early-Nara- and Heian-period Buddhist artworks.

Other institutions of note are the NARA NATIONAL MUSEUM, NARA NATIONAL RESEARCH INSTITUTE OF CULTURAL PROPERTIES, the YAMATO BUNKAKAN (a museum), Nara Women's University, and the Nara College of Education. Area: 212 sq km (131.73 sq mi); pop: 297,893.

TAKEHISA Yoshihiko

nara → oaks

Nara Basin

(Nara Bonchi). Also known as the Yamato Basin. In northern Nara Prefecture, central Honshū. One of several fault basins in the central Kinki (Kyōto–Nara–Ōsaka) region. Flanked by the Kasagi Mountains on the east and the Ikoma and Kongō mountains on the west, it consists of the flood plain of the river Yamatogawa and

alluvial fans in the lower regions. Numerous reservoirs are located in the basin, where the principal crops are rice, strawberries, and watermelons. A center of ancient culture, it has many historical tombs, palace sites, and temples, including HŌRYŪJI. Today it is a residential area, and industries are also developing. The major cities are Nara, Tenri, and Kashihara. Area: approximately 300 sq km (116 sq mi).

Nara Buddhism

A term referring to the six Buddhist sects officially recognized during the Nara period (710–794). They were introduced into Japan in the following approximate order: Sanron, Jōjitsu, Hossō, Kusha, Ritsu, and Kegon (see articles on the individual sects). The Kusha and probably the Jōjitsu as well were not truly independent sects with their own priesthood, but rather "text schools" that were concerned with the exegesis of the Kusharon (Abhidharmakośa) by Vasuban-dhu (ca 320–400) and the Jōjitsuron (Satyasiddhi) by Harivarman (ca 250–350). The study of the Kusharon was carried out by members of the Hossō clergy, the study of the Jōjitsuron by the Sanron clergy.

Only three of the original Nara sects survive today as religious bodies: the Hossō with its headquarters at the temples YAKUSHIJI and KŌFUKUJI, the Ritsu with its headquarters at TŌSHŌDAIJI, and the Kegon with its headquarters at TŌDAIJI. The Sanron sect, which was the major Buddhist school in the pre-Nara and early Nara periods, declined rapidly after the 9th century and disappeared entirely as an independent lineage in the 14th century. One hundred nineteen temples, mainly in the Nara region, are at present affiliated with one or another of the three surviving Nara sects.

Stanley WEINSTEIN

Nara history → history of Japan

Narai

District in the village of Narakawa, southwestern Nagano Prefecture, central Honshū. During the Edo period (1600–1868), Narai pros-

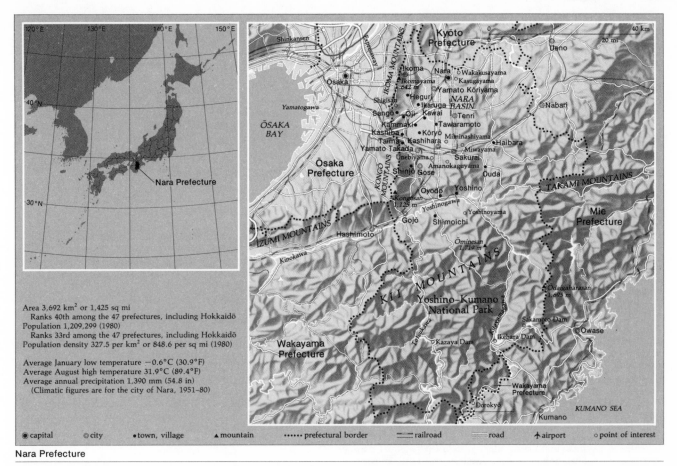

Area 3,692 km² or 1,425 sq mi
  Ranks 40th among the 47 prefectures, including Hokkaidō
Population 1,209,299 (1980)
  Ranks 33rd among the 47 prefectures, including Hokkaidō
Population density 327.5 per km² or 848.6 per sq mi (1980)

Average January low temperature −0.6°C (30.9°F)
Average August high temperature 31.9°C (89.4°F)
Average annual precipitation 1,390 mm (54.8 in)
  (Climatic figures are for the city of Nara, 1951–80)

◉ capital   ◎ city   ● town, village   ▲ mountain   ⋯⋯ prefectural border   ┅┅ railroad   ▬▬ road   ✈ airport   ○ point of interest

Nara Prefecture

pered as the POST-STATION TOWN in the exact middle of the 69 posts of the highway Nakasendō. Its Edo-period aura attracts many visitors.

Nara Kokuritsu Bunkazai Kenkyūjo → Nara National Research Institute of Cultural Properties

Nara Kokuritsu Hakubutsukan → Nara National Museum

Nara National Museum

(Nara Kokuritsu Hakubutsukan). A museum in Nara noted for its collection of Buddhist art; established in 1889 as the Nara Teikoku Hakubutsukan (Nara Imperial Museum) and known by its present name since 1952. On exhibit there are, in addition to the Buddhist images and Buddhist altar articles owned by the museum itself, various Buddhist art objects entrusted to it by ancient shrines and temples throughout the country, particularly those in the Kyōto–Ōsaka area. Each year in the autumn a special exhibition is held of imperial properties normally kept in the SHŌSŌIN art repository. In the museum's collection are a 12th-century handscroll of the type known as JIGOKU-ZŌSHI, the late-11th- or 12th-century mandala *Jōdo mandara-zu,* and the 9th-century seated sculpture of the Buddha Yakushi. The old main building of this museum, a representative Western-style building of the Meiji period (1868–1912), has been designated an Important Cultural Property. Also at the museum is the Hassōan, a tea ceremony house in the style of the Oribe school of TEA CEREMONY. *FUJIKAWA Kinji*

Nara National Research Institute of Cultural Properties

(Nara Kokuritsu Bunkazai Kenkyūjo). One of two national research institutes attached to the Agency for Cultural Affairs under the Ministry of Education; located in the city of Nara, with branches in the city of Kashiwara and the village of Asuka, all in Nara Prefecture. The institute employs a 70-member research staff and comprises

departments for the excavation and restoration of HEIJŌKYŌ, FUJI-WARAKYŌ, and other sites, and the study of documents from Japan's early historical and Nara (710–794) periods; three laboratories for research on ancient craft technologies and architecture; and the semiautonomous Asuka Historical Museum and Center for Archeological Operations, which offers training and assistance for excavations throughout the country. Journals published: *Nara kokuritsu bunkazai kenkyūjo gakuhō, Nara kokuritsu bunkazai kenkyū shiryō, Nara kokuritsu bunkazai kenkyūjo kijun shiryō, Asuka shiryōkan zuroku;* library resources: 41,729 volumes. See also TŌKYŌ NATIONAL RESEARCH INSTITUTE OF CULTURAL PROPERTIES.

Gina Lee BARNES

Nara period

The historical period beginning in 710, the year the capital was moved from FUJIWARAKYŌ to HEIJŌKYŌ (now the city of Nara), and ending in 784, when the capital was moved to NAGAOKAKYŌ. The 10 years at Nagaokakyō (784–794) are usually included in the Nara period, however, giving it an end-date of 794. The Nara period marked the height of the Chinese-inspired RITSURYŌ SYSTEM of government as well as the active introduction of other aspects of Chinese civilization (see SUI AND TANG [T'ANG] CHINA, EMBASSIES TO). Also, in order to make Buddhism the spiritual base of centralized political authority, provincial temples (KOKUBUNJI) were established throughout Japan. The Nara period saw the compilation of Japan's first chronicles, the KOJIKI (712) and NIHON SHOKI (720). Under the influence of Tang China, there was an efflorescence of the arts known as TEMPYŌ CULTURE. At the same time the final years of the Nara period witnessed the onset of the disintegration of the *ritsuryō* system as evidenced in the increase in poverty among the peasants and in the numbers of homeless wanderers, and the collapse of the *kōchi kōmin* system of public ownership of land. See also HISTORY OF JAPAN: Nara history.

Nara Prefecture

(Nara Ken). Located in the central part of the Kinki region in central Honshū, Nara Prefecture is landlocked and borders Kyōto Prefecture to the north, Mie Prefecture to the east, and Ōsaka and Wakayama prefectures to the west and south. Farming and forestry have long been its principal industries, although several other industries and land development projects have been recently established in the northern part.

Geography and Climate —— Apart from the NARA BASIN in the northern part, the prefecture is generally mountainous. The Median Tectonic Line runs through the central part of the prefecture to the east and west along the river Yoshinogawa. To the north of this line, graben basins and horst mountains alternately run north to south. From the west are located, respectively, the Ikoma and Kongō mountains, the Nara Basin, and the highland called Yamato Kōgen. To the south of the line are found steep young mountain ranges such as the KII MOUNTAINS. The principal rivers of the prefecture are, besides the Yoshinogawa, the YAMATOGAWA and TOTSUKAWA. Reflecting the complicated topography, the climate of Nara Prefecture varies greatly. The climate in the Nara Basin to the north is generally warm with low precipitation, hot summers, and cold winters, while the temperature is low and precipitation heavy in the southern mountainous district.

History —— As the site of the YAMATO COURT, which unified Japan from the 4th to the 7th century, the area flourished early on as the political center of ancient Japan; it was designated as Yamato Province in the ancient provincial system (KOKUGUN SYSTEM). The city of Nara was the country's capital and religious and cultural center during the Nara period (710–794), when it was known as HEIJŌKYŌ. After the capital was moved to HEIANKYŌ in 794, Nara was only briefly at the center of political events in the period of Northern and Southern Courts (1336–92). The present boundaries of Nara Prefecture were established in 1887.

Industries —— As evidenced by Jōmon (ca 10,000 BC–ca 300 BC) and Yayoi (ca 300 BC–ca AD 300) artifacts, farming in the Nara Basin dates back more than 2,000 years. Agriculture and forestry centering on the mountainous Yoshino district are the two main industries in the prefecture. The Nara Basin is noted for its rice and vegetables. Tea is grown on the Yamato Kōgen and persimmons in the valleys of the Yoshinogawa. The woodworking industry centers on the cities of SAKURAI and GOJŌ. Modern industries such as spinning, plastics, rubber, and electrical machinery are located in Nara, YAMATO KŌRIYAMA, and YAMATO TAKADA. Traditional products include lacquer ware, *sumi* (india ink), brushes, mosquito nets, *chasen* (bamboo whisks), *sōmen* (a kind of noodles), and Japanese paper (WASHI).

Tourism and Culture —— The prefecture has many historical sites and scenic views. The temples of TŌDAIJI, KŌFUKUJI, YAKUSHIJI, and TŌSHŌDAIJI; KASUGA SHRINE; the Heijō Palace site; and Nara Park are found in the city of Nara. HŌRYŪJI and TAKAMATSUZUKA TOMB are located in neighboring villages. The oldest road in Japan, the Yamanobe no Michi, is located in the eastern part of the Nara Basin. YOSHINO–KUMANO NATIONAL PARK, with such outstanding mountains and gorges as YOSHINOYAMA, ŌDAIGAHARASAN, ŌMINESAN, and the DOROKYŌ gorge attract visitors. Area: 3,692 sq km (1,425 sq mi); pop: 1,209,299; capital: NARA. Other major cities include KASHIHARA, Yamato Kōriyama, Yamato Takada, IKOMA, and TENRI.

Narashino

City in northwestern Chiba Prefecture, about 25 km (16 mi) east of Tōkyō. During World War II, Narashino was known as a military base. Since then it has become a bedroom community of Tōkyō. Chiba Institute of Technology, Nihon University, and several other institutions of higher learning are located here. Pop: 125,154.

Nara Women's University

(Nara Joshi Daigaku). A national women's university located in Nara, Nara Prefecture. Established in 1908 as the Nara Women's Higher Normal School, it attained its present status in 1949, and is now one of two national women's universities, along with OCHANOMIZU WOMEN'S UNIVERSITY. It has faculties of letters, science, and home economics. Enrollment was 1,519 in 1980.

Naraya Mozaemon

Name of successive heads of a merchant family of Edo (now Tōkyō) during the Edo period (1600–1868). The second Naraya Mozaemon was a poor wage laborer for a lumber merchant, but Mozaemon III (d 1714) amassed a great fortune, beginning with his profit from rebuilding the Tokugawa family shrine, the Tōshōgū at Nikkō, after an earthquake in 1683. He became official lumber purveyor to the shogunate and, with KINOKUNIYA BUNZAEMON, was reputed to be one of the two wealthiest merchants in Japan. His son Mozaemon IV (1695–1725; nicknamed Naramo) was better known for his extravagance, spending vast sums in the theater district and the YOSHIWARA pleasure quarter. When his favorite courtesan, Tamagiku, died, he spent lavishly to honor her memory, sponsoring JŌRURI and musical performances in the theaters and decorating the streets of Yoshiwara with lanterns during the Bon Festival. The family business survived until the end of the Edo period.

Narcotics Control Law

(Mayaku Torishimari Hō). A law enacted in 1953 to control the import, export, manufacture, compounding, distribution, receipt, and possession of narcotics in order to prevent injury to health arising from the use of narcotics for purposes other than medicinal or research and to provide measures to assist in the medical treatment of drug addicts. As a measure to treat drug addicts, the law provides that, by order of the governor, drug addicts may be medically examined by psychiatrists to determine the necessary treatment, and when necessary, they may be compulsorily hospitalized in "drug addict treatment institutions."

From the time immediately following World War II until the present, the criminal use of narcotics and stimulant drugs has decreased dramatically; at present, the rate of narcotics use has nearly leveled off. Recently, however, a trend of increased criminal use of stimulant drugs has been observed.

The use of opium poppies and related derivatives is controlled through the Opium Law (Ahen Hō) of 1954. The use of stimulant drugs is controlled through the Stimulant Drug Control Law (Kakuseizai Torishimari Hō). The use of poisons and deleterious substances is controlled by the Poisons and Deleterious Substances Control Law (Dokubutsu oyobi Gekibutsu Torishimari Hō).

SAWANOBORI Toshio

Narita

City in northern Chiba Prefecture, central Honshū. Narita developed as the home temple town (MONZEN MACHI) of Shinshōji. The construction of the New Tōkyō International Airport (popularly called the Narita Airport) in SANRIZUKA has led to the creation of new housing and industrial complexes. Shinshōji is its attraction, drawing some 10 million visitors annually. Pop: 68,416.

Narita Airport → New Tōkyō International Airport

Narita Tomomi (1912–1979)

Politician. Born in Kagawa Prefecture; graduate of Tōkyō University. Narita worked for what is now Mitsui Tōatsu Chemicals, Inc, but resigned to pursue a political career. In the second postwar election (1947) he was elected to the House of Representatives as a member of the JAPAN SOCIALIST PARTY. Ideologically aligned with its left wing, he became a secretary of the party in 1962 and party chairman in 1968, a position he retained until 1977.

Naruko

Also known as Narugo. Town in northwestern Miyagi Prefecture, northern Honshū. Naruko constitutes the southern half of the Kurikoma Quasi-National Park. Onikōbe and Narugo hot springs, Narugo Gorge, and ski resorts attract tourists. It is known for its Narugo *kokeshi* (dolls) and *narugo-nuri* lacquer ware. Pop: 12,066.

naruko

("bird rattles"). A type of KAKASHI or scarecrow used to frighten birds and animals away from crops. In ancient times they were also called "pulling boards" (*hikiita*). A series of small wooden boards with bamboo sticks attached are suspended from a long rope tied between two poles and fixed so that one end can be pulled from a distance to create a racket that scares away animals and birds. The job of shaking the rattles was most often given to children and the elderly.

NOGUCHI Takenori

Naruto Strait

Whirlpools created by tidal currents give Naruto Strait, literally "roaring gate," its name. The island of Awajishima can be seen in the background.

Naruse Jinzō (1858–1919)

Educator. A pioneer in higher education for women in Japan. Founder of JAPAN WOMEN'S UNIVERSITY (Nihon Joshi Daigaku). Born in what is now Yamaguchi Prefecture. He worked in several posts there, including that of elementary school principal. Later he became a Christian and engaged in missionary work in Kōriyama, Nara Prefecture, and Niigata. In 1890 he went to the United States to do research on education for women. After returning to Japan in 1894, he became principal of Baika Jogakkō (Baika Girls' School) in Ōsaka. In 1901 he founded Nihon Joshi Daigakkō, which later became Japan Women's University. As head of that school, he continued to work for the advancement of women's education in Japan.

Naruse Mikio (1905–1969)

Film director whose career extended from the latter part of the silent film era in the early 1930s to the postwar era of humanist social commentary in the 1960s. Naruse had an extremely melancholic view of human existence, and his films reflect this outlook. One of his most consistent themes is the entrapment of his characters through their internalization of Japanese social values. Perhaps because women are most often afflicted with this problem, they are generally the protagonists of Naruse's films.

Naruse's own life experiences bear some similarity to those of his heroines. Orphaned when he was very young, Naruse lived with his elder brother and sister until he went out to work for himself at the age of 15, cutting short his formal education out of financial necessity. When he was 21 a friend of the family helped him get a job at the Kamata studios of Shōchiku Motion Picture Company (see SHŌCHIKU CO, LTD), where he assisted with props. He saw many colleagues progress to director's status before him, but in the early 1930s he was at last directing short melodramas and comedies much like the silent films by OZU YASUJIRŌ.

Frustrated at Shōchiku, Naruse leaped at the chance to move to PCL, a small studio which later became part of the Tōhō studios (see TŌHŌ CO, LTD), in 1934 and make talkies. With the international success of his film *Tsuma yo bara no yō ni* (Wife! Be Like a Rose!) in 1935, Naruse married his leading lady, Chiba Sachiko, and began writing films to suit her bright vivacious personality. But they did not suit the melancholy Naruse, nor did the marriage, and what ensued was a slump of 15 years during which Naruse could not produce a box-office success. His first film after this slump to gain much favorable criticism was *Meshi* (1951, Repast), which was based on a novel by HAYASHI FUMIKO about a childless marriage on the verge of crisis. With more adaptations of Hayashi's work Naruse found his element, and success. *Inazuma* (1952, Lightning), *Bangiku* (1954, Late Chrysanthemums), *Hōrōki* (1962, A Wanderer's Notebook, or Lonely Lane) and the phenomenally successful *Ukigumo* (1955, Floating Clouds) all portray lower- and lower-middle-class women who fight to maintain their integrity and financial independence.

Naruse's cinematic style was simple, usually in confined working-class Japanese houses, requiring minimal camera movement. Unlike many directors, he hated working on location, and avoided it at all costs. Naruse was primarily concerned with character revelation through slow, almost dramaless stories; hence the actors and the script were of prime importance. Naruse's camera treatment of even his favorite actress, TAKAMINE HIDEKO, shows a lack of involvement perfectly coordinated with the matter-of-fact grimness of his films. Often criticized for the lack of action in his films, Naruse achieved instead a deeply moving yet antidramatic form, in which a shifting glance can carry as much meaning as a murder.

——Audie Bock, *Japanese Film Directors* (1978).

Audie BOCK

Narushima Ryūhoku (1837–1884)

Journalist, essayist, critic. Real name Narushima Korehiro. Born in Edo (now Tōkyō), son of a Confucian scholar. While serving the Tokugawa shogunate in various posts, he wrote a collection of anecdotes about Edo's red-light district that he later used in the first part of his major work *Ryūkyō shinshi* (1859–60). After the Meiji Restoration (1868) he declined a position offered by the new government and traveled instead to Europe (1872–73). After his return he became an influential figure in early Meiji-period journalism as editor-in-chief of *Chōya shimbun*, an antigovernment newspaper. Although he wrote in a rather old-fashioned kind of KAMBUN, he did not hesitate to satirize contemporary society and government, especially the bureaucracy. The second part of *Ryūkyō shinshi*, completed in 1874, treats with a sharp sense of irony the social and psychological changes wrought by the Meiji Restoration. The third part, written two years later, was censored by the government, and only its preface survives. His other works include *Kōsei nichijō* (1881–84), a travel diary of his European tour.

Naruto

City in northeastern Tokushima Prefecture, Shikoku, on the Naruto Strait. Naruto developed in ancient times as a port linking Shikoku with Ōsaka and Kyōto. Salt fields were developed in the Edo period (1600–1868). Today it has pharmaceutical and chemical industries, sea bream fishing, and *wakame* (seaweed) cultivation. Ferry service connects the city with the Ōsaka–Kōbe area, and Naruto is scheduled to be one point on a Honshū–Shikoku bridge. The Naruto whirlpools can be seen from Naruto Park. Pop: 63,422.

Naruto Strait

(Naruto Kaikyō). Narrow strait between the island of AWAJISHIMA and the city of Naruto, Tokushima Prefecture, northeastern Shikoku, connecting the eastern Inland Sea and the Kii Channel. Well known for the many whirlpools created by its rapid tidal currents and the resulting differences in water level; the currents reach a speed of 18.5 km (11.5 mi) an hour at high tide. Marine products include sea bream and *wakame*, a kind of seaweed. One section of a bridge connecting Honshū with Shikoku is being built over the strait. Width: 1,300 m (4,264 ft); deepest point: 85 m (279 ft).

Nasu

Town in northern Tochigi Prefecture, central Honshū, between the two mountains Nasudake and Yamizo. Principal industries are lumbering, woodworking, dairy farming, and stone quarrying. A cluster of hot springs, golf links, and skiing grounds are among its tourist attractions. Pop: 26,824.

Nasudake

Also called Chausudake. Composite volcano in the NASU VOLCANIC ZONE, northern Tochigi Prefecture, central Honshū. The highest peak in the Nasu Volcanic Group. It is composed of andesite, and gas rises from its crater. Nasu Hot Springs is on its slopes. Climbing and skiing are available. Part of Nikkō National Park. Height: 1,917 m (6,288 ft).

Nasu Kōgen

Highland, on the eastern slope of the mountain NASUDAKE, northern Tochigi Prefecture, central Honshū. Area of rice cultivation and dairy farming. Also a resort area, with golf links and ski grounds. Numerous villas have been built here recently. A toll road leads up to the highland. Hot springs include Nasu Yumoto, Shin Nasu, and Ōmaru. Part of Nikkō National Park. Elevation: 340-400 m (1,115-1,312 ft).

Nasu no Yoichi (fl late 12th century)

Warrior who fought on the side of the Minamoto in the TAIRA–MINAMOTO WAR (1180-85). He is known solely for a feat of archery recounted in the 13th-century war chronicle HEIKE MONOGATARI: during the Battle of Yashima (1185) the Taira tied a fan to the mast of a small boat in the offing and challenged the Minamoto, who were massed on the beach, to shoot it down. Nasu no Yoichi succeeded with his first arrow, winning the admiration of even the Taira. This story has long been a favorite subject in the performing arts, notably in HEIKYOKU recitation. *Barbara L. ARNN*

Nasu Volcanic Zone

(Nasu Kazantai). Volcanic zone running from the southeast coast of Sakhalin to the island of Rishiri near the northwestern tip of Hokkaidō and through western Hokkaidō, the central Tōhoku Region, and northern Kantō Region, ending at ASAMAYAMA on the border between Gumma and Nagano prefectures—more than 1,000 km (621 mi). Major volcanoes include YŌTEIZAN, HAKKŌDASAN, IWATESAN, ZAŌZAN, BANDAISAN, NASUDAKE, NANTAISAN, and AKAGISAN. The zone includes the great caldera lakes of Shikotsu, Tōya, Towada, and Tazawa and has many hot spring spas. It forms the nucleus of numerous national and quasi-national parks.

National Aerospace Laboratory

(Kōkū Uchū Gijutsu Kenkyūjo). Government research center administered by the SCIENCE AND TECHNOLOGY AGENCY. Located in the city of Chōfu, Tōkyō Prefecture. Established in 1955, it conducts a wide range of research in technology for aircraft, rockets, and aerospace in general. It publishes the *Technical Report of the National Aerospace Laboratory* and the *Technical Memorandum of the National Aerospace Laboratory*.

national anthem

The de facto Japanese national anthem is "Kimigayo" (His Majesty's Reign).

Basil H. Chamberlain, author of *Things Japanese,* translated the anthem as follows:

Kimi ga yo wa	Thousands of years of happy reign be thine;
Chiyo ni yachiyo ni	Rule on, my lord, till what are pebbles now
Sazare ishi no	By age united to mighty rocks shall grow
Iwao to nari te	Whose venerable sides the moss doth line.
Koke no musu made	

The words of the song are from a WAKA in the 10th-century anthology KOKINSHŪ. The author is unknown. The poem became popular in various genres of vocal music, such as JŌRURI, KOUTA, and BIWA singing, and eventually the first line of the *Kokinshū* version, *waga kimi wa* (my lord . . .), was changed to the now traditional, *kimi ga yo wa* (my lord's reign . . .). In 1870 an Englishman named John W. Fenton who was a military music teacher in the Satsuma domain set this poem to music in the hope of composing a national anthem, but his version was later discarded as not suitably dignified. In 1880 a committee appointed by the Imperial Household Ministry to select a musical score for the "Kimigayo" poem accepted the tune submitted by Hayashi Hiromori. It was performed for the emperor on his birthday, 3 November 1880. From this point on "Kimigayo" enjoyed a kind of semiofficial status. In 1893 the Ministry of Education made it the ceremonial song to be sung in elementary schools on national holidays. Soon it was sung at state ceremonies and sports events. However, "Kimigayo," which has been popularly identified as the national anthem for many years, has never been officially adopted as such. *Yukihisa SUZUKI*

National Archives

(Kokuritsu Kōbunshokan). Official depository for records of the Japanese government. It opened on 1 July 1971 after 10 years of planning following the recommendation in 1961 of the Japan Science Council that all government archives be gathered and preserved in one location. The National Archives, therefore, concerns itself with the gathering, preservation, processing, organizing, and servicing of the official documents, both domestic and foreign, that had previously been maintained by the CABINET LIBRARY (Naikaku Bunko) and by each government ministry since the Meiji Restoration (1868). Housed in a building located in the Kitanomaru Park area of the Imperial Palace grounds in Tōkyō, the Kōbunshokan presently houses and administers the 520,000 items of the Cabinet Library (which still retains its name). In addition, the Kōbunshokan contains the archival documents of the Office of the Prime Minister and the growing collection of prewar documents previously held by the government ministries themselves. *Theodore F. WELCH*

National Association of Commercial Broadcasting in Japan

(Nihon Minkan Hōsō Remmei). A nationwide organization of commercial radio and television stations. It was founded in July 1951, roughly the same time as commercial broadcasting began in Japan, and by 1979 there were 109 affiliated broadcasting companies (see BROADCASTING, COMMERCIAL). This association concerns itself with a wide range of problems common to commercial broadcasting companies, conducts promotional campaigns to acquaint the public with its activities, and seeks to promote goodwill among its affiliated member stations. It engages in the following kinds of activities: the establishment of broadcast ethics in accordance with existing broadcast codes; investigation and research in broadcast technology and operations; overseeing the proper handling of materials under copyright; and providing instruction and handling public relations about commercial broadcasting. *Nozaki Shigeru*

National Atlas of Japan

(Nihon kokusei chizu). First published by the GEOGRAPHIC SURVEY INSTITUTE in 1977. Contains important information concerning Japan's natural resources, society, economy, and culture provided by various government departments, universities, and research institutes. It is the first full-scale atlas compiled and published by a Japanese government agency and follows the basic format found in the national atlases of other nations. It is available in Japanese and English editions. *SHIKI Masahide*

national banks

(kokuritsu ginkō). Private banking facilities established in accordance with the National Bank Ordinance (Kokuritsu Ginkō Jōrei) of 1872 and converted into ordinary commercial banks between 1883 and 1899. Patterned after the US National Bank Act, the National Bank Ordinance called for the issue of convertible national bank notes to replace nonconvertible government notes (DAJŌKAN SATSU) and to supply capital for industrial development (see SHOKUSAN KŌGYŌ). But certain requirements of this ordinance, such as the convertibility of notes into specie, made this an unattractive form of investment, and only four national banks were established under the original regulations. The Meiji government revised the ordinance in 1876, authorizing the use of pension bonds (KINROKU KŌSAI) issued under the measures for compulsory commutation of *samurai* stipends (CHITSUROKU SHOBUN) as banking capital and abolishing the specie reserve requirement for note issue. While sacrificing the convertibility of notes, these amendments provided former samurai with a profitable outlet for their bonds. As a result, many new national banks were established. Although they contributed to the capitalization of pension bonds, their large issue of nonconvertible paper currency added to the inflationary crisis of the late 1870s, prompting the government to stop licensing new national banks after the founding of the 153rd Bank in 1879. After the establishment of the BANK OF JAPAN under the MATSUKATA FISCAL POLICY, the government in 1883 again revised the National Bank Ordinance, stipulating that the notes issued by each national bank be redeemed within 20 years of the bank's founding, at which time it was to be converted into an ordinary commercial bank. Accordingly, the last of the national banks, the 153rd Bank, became an ordinary commercial bank in 1899. *TANAKA Akira*

national defense

The Japanese equivalent of the English "national defense" is *kokubō,* a broad term, including the maintenance and strength of mili-

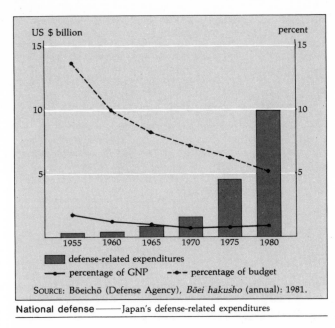

US $ billion ... percent

defense-related expenditures
percentage of GNP — percentage of budget

SOURCE: Bōeichō (Defense Agency), *Bōei hakusho* (annual): 1981.

National defense——Japan's defense-related expenditures

National defense

International Comparison of Defense Expenditures

	Defense expenditures (US $ billion)	Per capita defense expenditure (US $)	Percentage of budget	Percentage of GNP (1979)
Soviet Union	148.00[1]	574[1]	Unknown	11–13
United States	142.70	644	23.3	5.2
China	56.94	56	18.0[2]	9.0
West Germany	25.12	410	22.2	3.3
United Kingdom	24.45	437	10.7	4.9
Saudi Arabia	20.70	2,518	28.1	15.0
France	20.22	374	17.5[2]	3.9
Japan	8.96	75	5.2	0.9
Italy	6.58	124[2]	8.2[2]	2.4
Netherlands	5.24	374	7.3	3.4

[1] 1978.
[2] 1979.

SOURCE: Bōeichō (Defense Agency), *Bōei hakusho* (annual): 1981.

tary forces, as well as certain nonmilitary aspects of a nation's security posture, such as attitude to defense, economic strength, political stability, and the international environment. *Kokubō* is thus far less specifically military in connotation than the word normally used for "defense," *bōei,* as it appears in such terms as Defense Agency (Boeichō).

From the years immediately following Japan's surrender in 1945, through the development of the cold war, to the tensions of the present day, the international environment has changed profoundly. For Japan, which has been extraordinarily dependent on imported raw materials and exports for its recovery and prosperity, the maintenance of a peaceful world has been a matter of the highest priority. In concert with the other members of the industrially advanced West, Japan has seen that the increasing complexity and growing diversity of "threats" to the peace call for an increased attention to questions of national defense.

Japan has applied strict self-limitations with respect to the maintenance of peace through the use of military force, and, for the purpose of safeguarding national security, places the greatest emphasis on the combination of the United States Japan Security Treaty (see UNITED STATES–JAPAN SECURITY TREATIES), peaceful diplomacy, overseas economic relations of mutual interdependence, and cultural exchange. (For the situation before World War II, see MILITARISM; ARMED FORCES, IMPERIAL JAPANESE.)

Evolving Attitudes——It is said that General Douglas MacArthur, the supreme commander of the Allied forces (see SCAP) occupying Japan after World War II, intended to dismantle completely the old military forces and military industries and to transform Japan into "the Switzerland of the Far East" (see OCCUPATION). However, the development of the cold war and the war in Korea radically altered the situation, and the need arose not only to prevent Japan from slipping into the Eastern Bloc, but also to have the Japanese themselves participate in their country's defense. Thus in 1950, after the outbreak of the Korean War, a NATIONAL POLICE RESERVE of 75,000 men was formed. In 1952 Japan regained full independence; at the same time the United States–Japan security treaties, which had been concluded in 1951, became effective. With the addition of maritime and air forces, the National Police Reserve developed into the NATIONAL SAFETY FORCES in 1952, which two years later were reorganized as the SELF DEFENSE FORCES.

The basic framework of the military component of national defense, consisting of the Self Defense Forces plus the United States–Japan security treaties, has remained down to the present time. In the early days of the cold war the United States requested a considerable degree of Japanese rearmament or at least a substantial strengthening of the Self Defense Forces, but Prime Minister YOSHIDA SHIGERU was opposed on the grounds that such action would "suppress the economy and make for domestic instability." He consistently promoted a policy of "inexpensive defense" and reliance on the United States.

The Basic Policies for National Defense declared by the KISHI NOBUSUKE cabinet in 1957 recognized this policy in its fundamental points, and Japan has subsequently pursued and achieved economic development through a policy of peaceful coexistence and promotion of an international environment favorable to free trade. It has engaged in economic exchanges with both China and the Soviet Union under conditions of an "equidistant diplomacy." Current national defense issues involve increased military activities by the Soviet Union in waters near Japan, American requests for greater defense efforts, economic cooperation with and aid to developing countries, and the maintenance of stable supplies of natural resources. See also INTERNATIONAL RELATIONS.

National Defense Policy——The NATIONAL DEFENSE COUNCIL's basic policy for national defense, established in 1957, begins with a statement of objectives: to preserve the country's peace and independence, which are founded on democratic principles; to deter indirect or direct aggression; and to repel aggression if it should occur. Four means to achieve the objectives are given: international cooperation; stabilization of public welfare; a gradual increase in defense capabilities; and a defense system centered on the security treaties. The Liberal Democratic Party, which since then has continued to direct the Japanese government, adheres to this policy.

Additional policies elaborated in consonance with the above have been adopted. These include: the HIKAKU SANGENSOKU (the three nonnuclear principles of not manufacturing, possessing, or introducing into Japanese territory nuclear weapons, as approved by the Diet in 1972); a prohibition on the dispatch of troops overseas, first stated in 1954; a prohibition against conscription, first given concrete expression in the House of Representatives by the head of the Legislative Bureau in 1970; the three principles regarding the export of arms explained before the House of Representatives by Prime Minister SATŌ EISAKU in 1967 as the official government policy (see ARMS EXPORT, THREE PRINCIPLES OF); and the maintenance of a "strictly defensive posture" *(senshu bōei),* a peculiarly Japanese term signifying a passive defense strategy. The strategy, elaborated as defense policy in the 1970 defense white papers, included the concepts of keeping military capabilities to a minimum level necessary for self-defense; the ruling out of "preventive" attacks on other countries; eschewing strategic bombers, strategic missiles, and attack aircraft carriers; and the statement that in cases of infringement of Japanese territorial waters, air space, or even land, no weapons would be fired until there was an armed attack by the intruder. Each of these policies has been criticized, and in the late 1970s and early 1980s the strict interpretation of the 1970 defense white paper doctrine has been less in favor.

National Defense Policies of the Major Political Parties

Since the end of World War II, it has been generally true among the industrially advanced Western nations that, despite often bitter disputes on domestic policies between the government and opposition parties, a broad consensus has existed on matters of foreign relations and national defense policy. In contrast, in Japan there has been relatively little difference among Japanese political parties on domestic policies, but major gaps have existed in the fields of diplomacy and defense. Ever since the creation of the National Police Reserve, the Liberal Democratic Party has continued in the seat of political power, and therefore this party's thinking on national defense has come to constitute national defense policy. However, the discrepancy between the government and the opposition parties on matters of national defense has acted to hinder the formation of a popular consensus.

Although the details of each party's policy have changed slightly from time to time, the following discussion focuses on the fundamental attitudes of the five major parties concerning the Self Defense Forces and the United States–Japan security treaties.

The Liberal Democratic Party: Possession of the minimum necessary levels of self-defense capability should be allowed as a nation's right. The provisions of the security treaties, including the stationing of US military forces in Japan, are considered indispensable to national defense.

The Japan Socialist Party: Until the joint Upper and Lower House General Election of June 1980, the Self Defense Forces had been considered unconstitutional and the party had called for their dismantling, with consideration for the effects such action would cause and a proposal to create a national police force, or "peace brigades for national construction." The JSP had also called for a proclamation of peace and neutrality and the replacement of the security treaties with a United States–Japan nonaggression treaty. In the 1980 elections, however, the JSP took the position of affirming the present status of both the Self Defense Forces and the security treaties.

Kōmeitō (Clean Government Party): For many years the party platform of the Kōmeitō was to reorganize the Self Defense Forces into a national police reserve force and to annul the United States–Japan security treaties by mutual agreement. In October 1981, however, it decided to recognize the Self Defense Forces as conforming to the constitution as long as they limited their duty and weaponry to the defense of Japanese territory, and to accept the security treaties, given the present circumstances.

Democratic Socialist Party: Adhering to the principle of a "strictly defensive posture" and of maintaining the Self Defense Forces as required, the party recognizes the function of the United States–Japan security treaties. At the same time it suggests improvements regarding its implementation.

Japan Communist Party: Dismantle the Self Defense Forces in two stages. First, reduce in size and reeducate personnel, and second, assist personnel to find new employment. The security treaties should be annulled after the one-year notice period and a nonaggression treaty signed.

Japanese-American Relations —— As has been noted, the cold war and the Korean conflict greatly altered the policy of the United States toward Japan and its armed forces, leading to the conclusion of the security treaties in 1951. The treaties not only stipulated joint defense against a military attack but also called for economic cooperation between the two countries. Revised in 1960 and 1970, they continue to the present and constitute the core of Japanese-American relations with respect to national defense. They have also contributed in many ways to Japan's economic development and, by extension, to the development of its defense base.

With the enunciation of the so-called Nixon Doctrine in 1969, and the American decision to withdraw military support from South Vietnam, voices have been raised as to the treaties' reliability. These doubts have been reinforced by economic troubles in the United States and the difficulties it has had in meeting its far-flung military commitments, especially after such incidents as the Soviet invasion of Afghanistan and the hostage crisis in Iran in 1979. At the same time, there are segments of public opinion that oppose the treaties for such reasons as the presence of American troops in Japan, apprehension lest Japan be drawn into an unwanted conflict, and fears of Japanese involvement in American global strategy.

American pressure on Japan to expand its defense expenditures, largely dormant until late 1979, has increased considerably, and Japan has shown a far more positive response to Western requests that the nation play a bigger role in international security efforts. See also UNITED STATES AND JAPAN.

Public Attitudes in Japan to National Defense —— The majority of Japanese hold the view that Japan's national defense should be achieved through a combination of diplomacy, economic power, military capability, and other factors. Especially among progressive intellectuals and students, opposition to the Self Defense Forces and the United States–Japan security treaties is widespread (see PEACE

MOVEMENT). In addition to concern over Japanese involvement in American strategy, reasons for such opposition would include a general aversion to military matters stemming from the bitter experience of war and defeat and regret over the violence inflicted on various Asian peoples. The constitutional issues raised by article 9 of the 1947 CONSTITUTION forbidding the employment of belligerent actions as a means of national defense is a further factor.

Nevertheless, it would appear that the Japanese are gradually moving to a more pragmatic or realistic position, especially in the wake of such incidents as the MiG-25 Incident of 1978 (in which a Soviet Air Force pilot seeking asylum flew deep into northern Japanese territory and landed almost undetected), the increased activity and strength of Soviet air and naval units near Japan, the American disposition to pull back from Asia after the Vietnam War, and the invasion of Afghanistan in 1979.

Regular and extensive public opinion surveys have borne out this change in attitudes since 1977. By 1980 national attitudes toward the Self Defense Forces had seemed overwhelmingly positive, with over 86 percent acceptance. The United States–Japan security treaties provoke little overt opposition, and are generally accepted. Public opinion does not, however, reflect any desire to expand drastically the Self Defense Forces, and remains heavily opposed to the introduction of nuclear armaments.   MUTSU Gorō

National Defense Academy

(Bōei Daigakkō). School to train officers of the SELF DEFENSE FORCES; located in Yokosuka. Begun as the National Safety Academy (Hoan Daigakkō) under the jurisdiction of the Safety Agency, it assumed its present name in 1954, when the Safety Agency became the Defense Agency. It is the equivalent of the prewar imperial ARMY ACADEMY and imperial NAVAL ACADEMY. It offers university-level courses in the natural sciences, engineering, liberal arts, and social science. Postgraduate courses have been given since 1964. About 530 students are admitted each year. From their second year they are divided according to their branches of service. After graduation they receive about a year of military cadet education, together with ordinary university graduates, at the military cadet schools of the Land, Air, and Maritime Self Defense Forces.

IWASHIMA Hisao

National Defense College

(Bōei Kenshūsho). Institution for education and research on national security problems. Starting as the National Safety College (Hoan Kenshūsho) under the jurisdiction of the Safety Agency in 1952, it assumed its present name when the agency became the Defense Agency in 1954. Two-thirds of the students are uniformed men of the rank of colonel and the rest are young civilians, drawn from the Defense Agency and other ministries and agencies of the Japanese government. It is the equivalent of the United States National Defense University, Washington DC, formerly known as the National War College. In 1972 the National Defense College absorbed the War History Institute of the Defense Agency, which had responsibility for editing a history of the Pacific War. The National Defense College has three departments: Education, Research, and Military History.   IWASHIMA Hisao

National Defense Council

(Kokubō Kaigi). Cabinet body in charge of matters related to national defense. Established in 1956 and modeled on the National Security Council in the United States. Its members are the prime minister (chairman), the vice-prime minister, the ministers of foreign affairs and finance, the directors general of the Defense and Economic Planning Agencies, and others appointed by the prime minister. The prime minister is obliged to consult the council on all matters relating to defense, including basic defense policy, national defense programs, policies on defense-related industries, and decisions on emergency military action.   MUTSU Gorō

National Defense Women's Association → Dai Nippon Kokubō Fujinkai

National Diet Library

(NDL; Kokuritsu Kokkai Toshokan). Japan's largest library, formed by combining the former Imperial Library with the libraries of the upper and lower houses of the Diet. The merger of staff, books, and functions took place as a result of the promulgation of the National Diet Library Law of February 1948. Modeled after the Library of Congress of the United States, the NDL serves first the informational needs of the national legislators. The library not only provides legislators with materials and space for reading books, it also responds to their research requests and initiates investigation into areas of ongoing foreign and domestic concerns of the legislature. It provides, upon request, drafts, analyses, and evaluations of proposed legislation. In fulfilling its secondary purposes, the library, through its 30 agency library branches, assists the executive and judicial branches of government in the exchange and loan of materials in their collections, while coordinating acquisitions activities to minimize needless duplication. Cooperative research effort and the creation of specialized bibliographies of use to particular agencies form still other elements of its function of service to national and local public bodies. This feature of close cooperation among government libraries is rarely seen elsewhere in the world. The tertiary purposes of the library lie in the extension of services to scholars and the general citizenry of Japan. Beginning with the legal provisions of mandatory deposit in the library of all Japanese publications, and including the receipt of foreign publications through purchase, gift, and exchange, the public has access to a wide range of informational resources. Readers may go directly to the library for in-house use of the collections, they may have material photocopied, or they may borrow from the collections via the interlibrary loan program established in cooperation with other libraries. The NDL also fulfills an important role as a bibliographic center and as a central library for the preparation of cataloging records for use by other libraries in Japan and abroad. Printed catalog cards for depository books have been issued since 1950. The library also exchanges government documents and represents Japan in international library affairs.

In 1970 the total number of books exceeded 2.5 million, and periodicals were in excess of 24,000 titles. In the same year, $4.5 million was the total NDL budget, of which $500,000 was spent for books. In 1981 the total budget had risen to just over $40 million, and the number of books to 4.2 million. The library's permanent quarters next to the Diet is a six-story concrete structure containing 49,587 square meters (569,000 sq ft) of floor space. See LIBRARIES.

Theodore F. WELCH

National Federation of Regional Women's Organizations → Chifuren

national flag

(kokki). The national flag of Japan has a crimson disc, symbolizing the rising sun, in the center of a white field. It is popularly known as the Hinomaru (Sun Flag). The design has long been a popular one, although it is not known when it was first used. It is said that at the time of the MONGOL INVASIONS OF JAPAN (1274 and 1281) the priest NICHIREN presented a rising-sun flag to the shōgun. After Emperor GO-DAIGO was driven from the throne and the capital in 1336, his loyalist forces all used a similar banner. The Sengoku-period (1467–1568) warriors TAKEDA SHINGEN, UESUGI KENSHIN, and DATE MASAMUNE adopted it as their emblem on the battlefield; and the national unifier TOYOTOMI HIDEYOSHI used it in his INVASIONS OF KOREA IN 1592 AND 1597. The Tokugawa shogunate (1603–1867), too, adopted the flag for its ships in the early 1600s; and as growing numbers of Western vessels appeared in Japanese waters in the mid-19th century, the shogunate decreed, on the suggestion of SHIMAZU NARIAKIRA, that all Japanese ships fly flags with the rising sun on a white field for identification. The flag was flown on the KANRIN MARU, the ship that carried the shogunate mission of 1860 to the United States to ratify the HARRIS TREATY. It was not until 27 January 1870, however, that the new Meiji government officially designated it as the national flag of Japan. Yukihisa SUZUKI

national health insurance

(kokumin kenkō hoken). The Japanese national health insurance system is applicable to persons without company or other medical coverage, such as the self-employed and farmers, housewives and children, and the elderly. Workers in enterprises with less than five employees may also be covered, as can resident foreigners. The current system defrays some 70 percent of a person's medical and related expenses. Coverage is upon application made at one's local municipal office. Payments made into the system are relatively low, and many of the insured have little or no income. Hence, the system is continually in financial difficulty, a situation aggravated by the recent trend to exempt the elderly from paying medical fees. A solution that has been strongly advocated is to increase government subsidies.

Japan's first national health insurance law was passed in 1938. This was intended primarily to improve conditions in agricultural and fishing villages following years of economic depression. The insurers then were national health insurance unions established voluntarily by local communities. In 1948, a revision of the law replaced union management of the system by public operation under the local communities. A new national health insurance act was promulgated in 1958 requiring local governments to operate the system, thus achieving a nationwide dissemination of medical insurance. See also MEDICAL AND HEALTH INSURANCE.

NIWATA Noriaki

national income

(kokumin shotoku). The value of final goods and services produced in a nation over a specified period of time. National income can be estimated in two equivalent ways. The incomes side approach aggregates incomes earned by individual households and corporations, while the product side approach aggregates value added (value of final product less cost of inputs) across productive activities. The most common national income measures used in international comparison are gross national product (GNP, value added by a country's citizens) and gross domestic product (GDP, value added within a country's borders).

Size and Structure of Japanese National Income—Japan's GDP in 1978 was ¥205 trillion (US $974 billion), the third highest in the world after that of the United States and the Soviet Union. Japan has occupied this rank since 1968. Although its GDP was still far below that of the United States (US $2.1 trillion), in 1978 it was higher than that of West Germany (US $639.2 billion), France (US $470.5 billion), and the United Kingdom (US $308.2 billion). In 1978 Japan's per capita GDP was ¥1.78 million (US $8,458) compared with US $9,602 in the United States, US $10,426 in West Germany, US $5,514 in the United Kingdom, and US $8,827 in France.

Japan's swift rise to become the third largest economy in the world was accomplished through spectacular economic growth from 1955 through the end of the 1960s. The nation's average annual growth rate of some 10 percent during this period was about double those of Western nations. See ECONOMIC HISTORY: contemporary economy.

Table 1 compares average real growth rates of key indicators for leading industrial countries. As is clear from the table, economic growth rates began to slow in the early 1970s, a trend that is particularly pronounced in the case of Japan. The absolute size of Japan's growth rate, however, still remains high.

The growth of Japan's national income can best be understood by examining its structure from three perspectives: the types of goods produced, the distribution of incomes, and the composition of spending. Production figures provide an industry-by-industry breakdown of national income and reflect changes in the INDUSTRIAL STRUCTURE. In the postwar period, the share of total production provided by primary industries (agriculture, forestry, and fishing) declined, while the shares of secondary (manufacturing) and tertiary (service) industries increased. In 1977, for example, the breakdown of the GDP was 4.9 percent primary, 36.3 percent secondary, and 58.8 percent tertiary. Comparable figures for 1950 were 26 percent, 31.8 percent, and 42.3 percent, respectively. (Methods of calculating these figures differ slightly over the two periods, so some caution is in order in interpreting these and subsequent data.)

National income can also be analyzed according to its distribution among the various factors of production, i.e., wages, salaries, profits, and rent. The share of employee compensation (wages and salaries) has been steadily increasing, while that of income from unincorporated enterprises has been declining. The share of income from unincorporated family enterprises is much higher in Japan than in other advanced countries. This share, however, dropped from 39.8 percent in 1952 to 17.8 percent in 1977. The share of employee compensation, on the other hand, grew from 47.6 percent to 67.8 percent over the same period.

From expenditure data, one can learn the share of the national income directed to consumption and that directed to savings or investment. Japan's income statistics show an extraordinarily high

National income —— Table 1

	Gross domestic product (GDP)		Private final consumption expenditure		Gross fixed capital formation	
	1965–70	1970–76	1965–70	1970–76	1965–70	1970–76
Japan	12.4	5.1	9.9	5.9	18.3	3.1
United States	3.2	2.6	3.9	3.2	1.5	0.0
United Kingdom	2.4	2.0	1.9	1.8	3.9	0.7
France	5.3	3.9	4.9	4.6	6.6	3.3
West Germany	4.5	2.3	4.6	2.7	3.4	−1.2
Italy	6.1	3.0	6.3	2.8	8.1	−0.1

Average Real Growth Rates of Japan and Other Major Countries (in percentages)

SOURCE: Economic Planning Agency, *Annual Report on National Accounts* (annual): 1979.

National income —— Table 2

International Comparison of Final Household Consumption Expenditures, 1975 (in percentages)

	Japan	United States	United Kingdom	Italy	Sweden	Australia
Food, beverages, and tobacco	28.9	17.9	31.2	36.0	28.6	26.2
Clothing and footwear	8.0	7.3	8.6	8.4	7.3	8.4
Gross rent, fuel, and power	15.7	19.6	19.2	13.2	20.3	16.7
Furniture, furnishings, and household operation	6.7	7.6	7.2	5.9	6.8	9.2
Medical care and health expenses	9.5	10.8	1.0	8.4	4.1	6.1
Transportation and communications	8.5	15.2	13.4	10.7	14.5	15.4
Recreation, entertainment, education, cultural services	8.1	8.6	10.0	5.5	8.9	6.7
Other goods and services	14.6	13.0	9.4	12.0	9.5	11.3
Total	100.0	100.0	100.0	100.0	100.0	100.0

SOURCE: United Nations, *Yearbook of National Account Statistics* (annual): 1976. Economic Planning Agency, *Annual Report on National Income Statistics* (annual): 1978.

level of savings and investments, a fact that was instrumental in the nation's rapid growth. The share of domestic capital formation rose from 20 percent in the late 1950s to 30 percent and higher in the 1960s and 1970s. Although the ratio slipped during the OIL CRISIS OF 1973, it has since recovered.

Table 1 shows that the growth trends of Japan's private consumption expenditure and gross fixed capital formation (i.e., investment) changed substantially between the late 1960s and the early 1970s: throughout the former period, investment grew faster, but consumption took the lead in the latter period.

Complementary Structure and Economic Growth —— A major reason behind the growth of the Japanese economy has been the complementary structure of the national income: the aggressive promotion of industrialization through technological innovation in the production sphere has been supported by massive investment and heavy savings in the area of expenditures. The large-scale investments of the postwar era have been, at least partially, a continuation of a pre–World War II trend. The prewar period also saw the accumulation of technologies, knowledge, education, and experience in the process of industrialization. Postwar growth, however, has been spurred by the rapid expansion of heavy and chemical industries. The share of light industries such as textiles, foodstuffs, and sundries, which was overwhelming in the prewar and early postwar periods, gave way to heavy manufacturing and chemical processing.

Especially interesting, however, are the changes in saving behavior which supported this transformation of production. The ratio of savings to national income is exceptionally high in Japan compared with other countries. Gross savings of course rose rapidly during the high-growth period, along with the large gains in income. But even the savings ratio grew, from 24.4 percent in 1965 to 32.5 percent in 1970. The ratio declined during the oil crisis, but only because of a sharp drop in corporate savings (household savings rose during the crisis, because of fears of unemployment).

The household savings ratio stood at 22.2 percent in 1977, a figure slightly higher than that in the high-growth period. The figure is exceptionally high compared to Western countries: the comparable figures are 7 percent for the United States, 11 percent for Great Britain, and 15 percent for West Germany. There are several reasons for the extraordinarily high savings ratio in Japan's household sector. One is that incomes have grown at a faster rate than in the West; another is that a major portion of wage and salary income is composed of annual and semiannual bonuses (see BONUS). In addition, relatively poor social security protection necessitates the accumulation of cash reserves for emergency use. Finally, the absence of consumer financing forces substantial savings before the purchase of such large-scale real assets as housing. See also CONSUMPTION AND SAVING BEHAVIOR.

National income accounts also contain information on the composition of household consumption expenditures (see Table 2). The greatest intercountry differences are seen in food, beverages, and tobacco, the share of which tends to decline in direct proportion to the rise in per capita income. The share of clothing and footwear, on the other hand, is more or less equal, regardless of income. In contrast, the share of rent, fuel, and power tends to rise with income.

Seen as a whole, the composition of consumption expenditure in Japan is standard. Differences in life modes and customs between countries become evident only when expenditures are analyzed closely. The data in Table 2 show a comparatively low level of transportation and communication costs in Japan, reflecting relatively low automobile-related expenses (due to the nation's limited area, poor roads, and well-developed public transportation system). Overall, Japan's expenditure mix most resembles Italy's, except in the area of recreation and education.

The Public Sector in National Income —— It is widely believed that the Japanese government has played a key role in the growth of the economy. One measure of this is the extent to which the gov-

National income —— Table 3

		Composition of Government Final Consumption Expenditure by Purpose, 1975 (in percentages)					
	Japan[1]	United States	United Kingdom	Italy	Sweden[2]	Australia[1]
General public services	27.2	15.0	13.7	27.5	14.8	20.0
Defense	8.7	30.0	22.1	15.8	14.2	13.7
Education	37.8	26.2	23.3	32.7	22.0	30.1
Health	4.1	2.3	21.0	5.5	23.8	20.1
Social security and welfare services	4.7	7.0	6.1	6.8	12.1	2.9
Housing and community development	5.1	3.3	2.6	2.8	1.7	1.6
Other community and social services	1.6	3.3	2.1	0.8	5.7	3.7
Economic services and other purposes	10.9	12.3	9.1	8.1	5.7	8.0
Total	100.0	100.0	100.0	100.0	100.0	100.0

[1] Fiscal years.
[2] 1974.
SOURCE: United Nations, *Yearbook of National Account Statistics* (annual): 1976. Economic Planning Agency, *Annual Report on National Income Statistics* (annual): 1978.

ernment has helped encourage investment. The ratio of investment expenditure by the government to gross national expenditure is high (9 percent in 1975) compared to the average of about 3 or 4 percent for other industrial countries. The need for strong government support to spark economic growth and to augment limited social overhead capital is the primary reason for high public sector investment in Japan. However, the share of government consumption expenditure in national income is lower in Japan (10 percent) than in other industrial countries (generally about 20 percent). Demand for government services tends to increase with income, so government consumption expenditure is expected to increase.

Table 3 gives an international comparison of government spending (there are considerable institutional differences between nations, so only general features can be inferred from these statistics). As is clear from the table, defense spending is exceptionally low in Japan. This is because Japan's postwar CONSTITUTION renounces war, so that the legal status of even modest defense expenditures is often uncertain. The share of defense spending declined in the 1970s.

Spending for general public services, on the other hand, is comparatively high in Japan. General services include basic outlays for administration, foreign affairs, law enforcement, and public safety. The share of this category tends to fall as the government's per capita spending rises, and this tendency is expected to be repeated in Japan. The high level of spending for housing and community development is explained by the poor condition of housing and regional sanitation systems. As the nation develops, increasing amounts of money have been committed to improving living conditions. Spending on education, social security, and welfare services has likewise increased.

The wide differences in health-related expenditures among the various countries, on the other hand, reflect differences in combinations of public and private health services. Both Tables 2 and 3 shed light on this issue. The shares of health and social security and of welfare services in final government consumption expenditure in Table 3 and that of medical care and health expenses in final household consumption expenditure in Table 2 vary widely from country to country because of differences in income levels and medical insurance systems. Japan belongs to a group of countries, including the United States and Italy, where household shares are very high. In countries such as Great Britain and Sweden, where socialized medicine is practiced, government shares are much higher. See also HEALTH CARE SYSTEM; MEDICAL AND HEALTH INSURANCE.

Transfer Payments in National Income —— Most of national income accrues to those who have directly earned it (e.g., employees and corporations), but some is transferred to others. Income received without direct provision of productive services is called transfer income. Transfer income comprises (1) property incomes, such as interest, dividends, and rent; (2) transfers to and from the government via direct taxes and SOCIAL SECURITY PROGRAMS; (3) transfers in the form of insurance benefits; and (4) grants-in-aid in the form of welfare payments.

The share of transfer incomes in total national income in Japan has been steadily increasing in recent years, from 35.5 percent in 1970 to 42.1 percent in 1977. Of the above-mentioned categories, property income comprises the largest share, followed by direct taxes and social security payments. These two categories together accounted for 84 percent of all transfer payments in 1977. Property incomes accounted for 48 percent of the total, and of this, interest payments were the large majority. Moreover, the interest payment share of property income rose from 85 percent in 1970 to 90 percent in 1977. This indicates that households have been steadily shifting their assets from cash deposits to time deposits, long-term bonds, and debentures.

Income transferred between the household and government sectors grew to an impressive 36 percent of total transfer income in 1977. The share of social security payments and social benefits made to households by the government, for example, grew from only 6 percent in 1965 to 9.8 percent in 1977, showing that income redistribution is steadily increasing. Although the share of government-household transfers is still low on an international scale, it is expected to continue its expansion.

■■ —— Economic Planning Agency, Government of Japan, *Annual Report on National Accounts* (annual; title before 1979, *Annual Report on National Income Statistics*). Kazushi Ōkawa et al, ed, *Chōki keizai tōkei*, vol 1, *Kokumin shotoku* (1974).

MIYAZAWA Ken'ichi

National Industrial Exhibition

(Naikoku Kangyō Hakurankai). Name of a series of five exhibitions of domestic products, sponsored by the Meiji government between 1877 and 1903 as part of its SHOKUSAN KŌGYŌ (Increase Production and Promote Industry) policy. Although the first exhibition displayed mostly industrial crafts, such as textiles, paper, and china, successive exhibitions increasingly included machines, reflecting the advancement of Japanese industry. Along with the prefecture-sponsored kyōshinkai (competitive exhibitions) begun in 1880, the National Industrial Exhibitions helped develop and propagate industrial technology. Prefectural governments, newspaper companies, and chambers of commerce assumed responsibility for organizing these exhibitions after 1903.

National Institute for Research Advancement

(Sōgō Kenkyū Kaihatsu Kikō; often known as NIRA). This institute was established by special legislation in March 1974, and receives funds, which it in turn invests, from national and local governments and from the private sector. A target of ¥30 billion (about US $125 million) had been set; nearly ¥17 billion (about US $72 million) was raised by the end of March 1979. Operating costs of the institute are covered entirely by interest on the fund's investments. The institute's goal is to accelerate implementation of comprehensive research and development on various social problems. NIRA had engaged in 190 research projects by the end of March 1979, including its own projects and those which it commissioned from other public and private research organizations. Results appear in government publications; NIRA also sponsors seminars and symposia to facilitate communication regarding research. Already completed have been projects concerning energy, tasks for the 21st century, and urban problems. NIRA is carrying out a joint research project on atomic energy with the Rockefeller Foundation.   *Hirata Masami*

nationalism

(kokka shugi; minzoku shugi). A shared devotion and loyalty to one's nation. As Boyd C. Shafer has put it, nationalism is "that sentiment unifying a group of people who have a real or imagined common historical experience and a common aspiration to live together as a separate group in the future." Japanese nationalism germinated from an elitist patriotism felt by a handful of extraordinary individuals who, as "men of determination" *(shishi)* late in the Edo period (1600–1868) and as political leaders in the Meiji period (1868–1912), stressed the national welfare over private interests, particularly in defending Japan from foreign aggression. As society grew more integrated in the late 19th century, nationalist feelings spread broadly to the public and took two main forms.

One was statism *(kokka shugi),* or nationalist loyalties focused on the state. Statism demanded that all Japanese subjects obey and serve the state as the highest object of their allegiance. They were expected to serve in the armed forces, pay taxes, and wholeheartedly back the state's goals at home and abroad. Statist nationalism posited an organic state, as defined in 19th-century Germany, with an existence of its own separate from parties, monarchs, voters, or political institutions.

The other main form of nationalist feeling was ethnic or popular nationalism *(minzoku shugi),* with allegiance centering on the Japanese as a people. Popular nationalists felt an unbreakable bond with fellow Japanese because of their shared history, customs, religions, language, and gene pool. Popular nationalism stressed horizontal webs of loyalty to other Japanese rather than vertical filaments of allegiance to an impersonal state. Whereas statism often placed concrete demands for service on the individual, popular nationalism usually involved more sentiment than program.

Japanese nationalism reached its zenith of intensity during 1937–45, when an extreme form of statism—ULTRANATIONALISM—came to the fore. Although they are now generally detached from formal obligations to the state, nationalist feelings of cultural and ethnic identity have continued to bind the Japanese people to one another since World War II.

Premodern Patriotism——Since early times the Japanese have been conscious of their own distinctiveness in relation to their East Asian neighbors. The chief components of this separateness have included Japan's geographic isolation, its monolingual culture, its relatively great ethnic homogeneity, its people's strong ties to the soil, common beliefs in the gods of Shintō, and an EMPEROR who simultaneously propitiated the gods, legitimized the state, and symbolized the people. These elements of cohesiveness served as preconditions for later patriotic feelings of loyalty to the land and all its people.

Such emotions in old Japan surfaced most regularly during political or diplomatic crises. When Mongol forces invaded Kyūshū in 1274 and 1281 (see MONGOL INVASIONS OF JAPAN), they provoked terror throughout the country and fulfilled the bleak forecasts of the Buddhist prophet NICHIREN. Although this patriotic priest helped make people more conscious of being Japanese, he was primarily a religious reformer, not a secular ideologue. Internal strife in the early 14th century led a court historian, KITABATAKE CHIKAFUSA, to expound theories of imperial uniqueness that proved useful 600 years later to the apologists for Japan's empire in East Asia. But however strong their rejection of Chinese learning or their devotion to fellow inhabitants, Japanese patriots expressed no clear conception of nation or of the commonweal before Japanese feudalism began to weaken in the late 18th century.

By then Japanese society was slowly undergoing a change from a feudal social structure to a more open status hierarchy based on vertically organized interests of wealth and talent. Internally hierarchical groups such as joint-stock companies, small manufacturing enterprises, early agricultural producers' cooperatives, and even nascent political parties after 1868 began to compete for places on a status ladder presuming inequality but also mobility. (This arrangement has only recently yielded to the looser class system of contemporary capitalism.)

When these vertically arranged groups vied with one another for predominance, they naturally trumpeted their own partisan interests for political or economic advantage. In response, Japanese patriots in the mid-19th century began to speak out on behalf of the whole society, since patriotism above all appeals to the common good of all who share the same country, as opposed to narrower interests rivaling one another for status. Patriotism is holistic and all-inclusive within a country's borders, as it tries to surmount private, selfish advantage by directing attention to the shared interests of all of a country's subjects or citizens.

Patriots and Nationalists, 1850–1890——The agents that catalyzed Japanese patriotism in the mid-19th century included strong military, diplomatic, and economic pressures from Europe and America; discontent with the TOKUGAWA SHOGUNATE's shabby treatment of the throne; a recrudescence of anti-Chinese nativist ideas, especially among scholars of National Learning (KOKUGAKU), of whom MOTOORI NORINAGA was the most important. Others, like AIZAWA SEISHISAI and YOSHIDA SHŌIN, flaunted the xenophobic slogan Revere the Emperor, Expel the Barbarians (SONNŌ JŌI), an elitist perception of the national interest during the foreign policy crisis of the 1850s. In this fashion they transfigured "free-floating" fief loyalties, in Albert M. Craig's phrase, into sentiments attached to the nation as a whole.

Even more to the point, patriotic loyalties expressed by a few farsighted statesmen helped to sanction new leaders and reform programs after the MEIJI RESTORATION of 1868. In their drive to enrich the country and strengthen the army (FUKOKU KYŌHEI), government officials erected a strong, efficient state. The espousal of nationalist sentiments spread from a small band of selfless patriots to the public at large, coinciding with the rise of powerful and effective institutions of central government. The integration of Japanese society after 1868 through the development of media, education, and a single national market helped every adult Japanese to understand the common national interest.

Statist Nationalism, 1890–1945——In the late 1880s ITŌ HIROBUMI and others created for the Meiji government a full-dress CONSTITUTION, giving permanent and codified structure to informal procedures evolved since 1868 by the new leaders. They also defined allegiance to the state as the citizen's highest duty. The IMPERIAL RESCRIPT ON EDUCATION, issued in 1890, was the sacred scripture of this new statism, known as *kokka shugi.* Soon the legal scholars HOZUMI YATSUKA and UESUGI SHINKICHI and the philosopher INOUE TETSUJIRŌ echoed MOTODA NAGAZANE's defense of state power. Government-sponsored Shintō festivals, ceremonies honoring the emperor, and homiletic ethics texts in the schools after 1903 helped to spread the statist version of nationalism to every family.

This indoctrination took place just as the Meiji hierarchy of competing interests began to give way to the social relations of enterprise capitalism, particularly during and after World War I. New formulations of nationalism stressing myths of social harmony and Japanese uniqueness appeared, now that Japan was growing more like other modern industrial societies. Political leaders like TANAKA GIICHI and patriot-scholars like ŌKAWA SHŪMEI extended these doctrines of state loyalism while Japan lapsed into economic and diplomatic peril in the 1920s and 1930s. Statism was magnified into ultranationalist dogmas once politics fell under strong military influence in the late 1930s. The government handbook KOKUTAI NO HONGI (Cardinal Principles of the National Essence), published in 1937, announced that the "individual is an existence belonging to a State" and "is fundamentally one body with it." Such doctrines evaporated in the rubble of military defeat in August 1945.

Popular Nationalism, 1890–1945——Equally strong in the late 19th century were sentiments focused on the nation as a people *(kokumin shugi).* The antigovernment FREEDOM AND PEOPLE'S RIGHTS MOVEMENT of the late 1870s was followed in 1887 by the *Nihon dōtoku ron* (Discourse on Japanese Morality) of NISHIMURA SHIGEKI, who wrote not to praise the state but to build character among the people. Even less ambiguously, men such as KUGA KATSUNAN, MIYAKE SETSUREI, OKAKURA KAKUZŌ, and SHIGA SHIGETAKA debated what it meant to be Japanese in a world of sharply divergent and conflicting cultures.

Popular nationalists with conservative predilections, especially the Nation of Essence and Japanism movement, attacked the government for its halfhearted treaty revision efforts after 1887. Less respectable were rightist groups such as the GEN'YŌSHA and the AMUR

RIVER SOCIETY, whose nationalist dreams embraced a far more aggressive policy abroad than the state intended. Some members of these societies defined the dreams as PAN-ASIANISM, variously seeking cultural, political, or even militantly anti-Western affinities with Asian neighbors. The SINO-JAPANESE WAR OF 1894–1895 and the RUSSO-JAPANESE WAR a decade later helped to disseminate nonofficial nationalism of this conservative sort to citizens who believed that their state was not standing up to the Western powers—especially when each conflict ended in diplomatic embarrassment for Japan after a brilliant military success.

On the left were popular nationalists of even greater stature. The socialist KŌTOKU SHŪSUI, soon to be falsely denounced and executed for lese majesty, advocated patriotic devotion to the common good under a benevolent throne. The early socialist ABE ISOO and the Christian spokesman UCHIMURA KANZŌ both labored to align their beliefs with their feelings of patriotism, as did the folklore specialist YANAGITA KUNIO after World War I. Like their counterparts on the right, these men felt no less loyal to the nation for all their stiff opposition to the government ruling them.

Popular nationalism in the 1920s and 1930s, expressed by such liberal activists as YOSHINO SAKUZŌ and SAIONJI KIMMOCHI, resisted absolute allegiance to the state but usually accepted the institutions of government. National reconstructionists, such as KITA IKKI, attacked the programs, personnel, and institutions of the state as they struggled to build a "just society." Even more quixotic were the romantic agrarian nationalists GONDŌ SEIKYŌ and TACHIBANA KŌZABURŌ, who decried centralized rule and advocated a primitive farm communalism as the shared sentiment binding the Japanese people in one nation.

Most treatises on KOKUTAI, the national essence, were linked before World War II with statist ideas, whereas nation-centered thinking generally stressed the happiness and welfare of the people. If statist and popular nationalism were never entirely distinct, neither were they functionally equivalent. Except for anarchists and certain communists, nearly all modern Japanese political thinkers have been nationalists in that they have felt deep emotional attachment to their fellow countrymen. As the ideology of the ruled, not the rulers, popular nationalism was usually more idealistic and less specific than the statist doctrines of the authorities. The force and direction of these two forms of nationalism were very different: statism was aggressive and centripetal, popular nationalism defensive and politically centrifugal.

For most popular nationalists the emperor symbolically unified the people, just as he capped the statist vision of the well-ordered polity. But to statists the emperor's exalted role was in good part a modern, political/legal function specified in constitutional writ, whereas most popular nationalists venerated the emperor because of his unique historical role as chief priest of Shintō and intercessor with the gods on behalf of the people. It seems very likely that the country's capacity for national mobilization in the late 1930s and early 1940s was enhanced because the state fitted itself to the ethnopsychological inclinations of common Japanese to identify with one another as a people under a sacerdotal throne, rather than because the state extracted unyielding popular devotion to itself as sovereign. Statism in its ultranationalist form won out during World War II mainly because of the economic and diplomatic emergency facing Japan, the unique constitutional position of the military beyond civilian control, and the overriding need to mobilize for a war of national survival. Yet not even the massive indoctrination campaigns of the government toward its own people during wartime healed the cleavage between statist and popular nationalism.

Postwar Nationalism——Since 1945 Japanese politicians, businessmen, and intellectuals have periodically debated what it means to be Japanese. Because of the defeat in the war loyalties to the state have been muted, but affinities with fellow Japanese remain strong and meaningful. Economic prosperity and international peace have kept threats to the nation at their lowest level in two centuries. The main framework for discussing Japanese nationalism has been the extraordinary internationalization of cultural life since 1945. Japanese now question what it means to be Japanese, not in isolation or quarantine from other countries but in constant interaction with the outside world. Japanese nationalism, never an absolute allegiance even in its prewar statist versions, has come to compete vigorously with other claims on the individual's loyalty, both transnational (sports, jazz, art, world peace) and subnational (company, school, family). Literature and the arts have grown so cosmopolitan, and with them styles and tastes in the marketplace, that some critics have found it hard to separate modernity from Japaneseness.

Yet few Japanese, however free from provincial prejudices, forget that their distinctive social structure makes them still feel remarkably different from other peoples. Social rather than political attributes have been the paramount elements of postwar Japanese notions of separateness. Statist nationalism has given few hints of revival in the period since 1945. But its potential for future mischief in a worldwide economic or military crisis, according to some writers, is reinforced by the persistence of the imperial throne as a rallying point of loyalties. As the country moves toward the 21st century, new definitions of Japanese nationalism will have to be developed to accommodate the nation's continuing need for psychic security amid constant change.

——Delmer M. Brown, *Nationalism in Japan* (1955). T. R. H. Havens, *Farm and Nation in Modern Japan: Agrarian Nationalism, 1870–1940* (1974). Kinoshita Hanji, *Nihon no uyoku* (1953). Masao Maruyama, *Thought and Behaviour in Modern Japanese Politics* (1963). Kenneth B. Pyle, *The New Generation in Meiji Japan* (1969). Richard Storry, *The Double Patriots* (1957). Takeda Kiyoko, *Dochaku to haikyō* (1967). George M. Wilson, *Radical Nationalist in Japan: Kita Ikki, 1883–1937* (1969). T. R. H. HAVENS

Nationality Law → Japanese nationality

National Japanese Language Research Institute

(Kokuritsu Kokugo Kenkyūjo). A national institute for scientific research on all matters concerning the Japanese language. Located in Kita Ward, Tōkyō.

The National Japanese Language Research Institute was established on 21 November 1948 for the scientific study of the Japanese language and of the linguistic life of the Japanese people. Its members belong to the civil service and are appointed by the Agency for Cultural Affairs, which also determines its budget; before June 1958, it was directly under the Ministry of Education. Its full-time staff of 77 carries out research in the areas of linguistic structure, linguistic activity, and linguistic change and also does work in linguistic education, quantitative linguistics, and Japanese language teaching.

The institute publishes *Kokugo nenkan*, a yearbook listing all publications related to the Japanese language published in Japan, and has published more than 70 volumes of scientific research. Of particular note are the *Nihon gengo chizu* (Linguistic Atlas of Japan) in six volumes (1966–74) and the *Okinawago jiten* (Dictionary of the Okinawan Language; 1st ed 1963, 5th ed 1976). Pioneering in the field of sociolinguistics, the institute has published seven volumes since 1950 detailing sociolinguistic surveys conducted throughout Japan. The use of a computer has also allowed statistical studies of the Japanese lexicon and of the use of Chinese characters in magazines and newspapers. Willem A. GROOTAERS

National Land Agency

(Kokudochō). An auxiliary organ of the Prime Minister's Office established in 1974 in conjunction with the enactment of the National Land Use Law (Kokudo Riyō Keikaku Hō). The agency is empowered to formulate basic land-use plans, while coordinating urban planning, water resources management, and regional land development. It is headed by a director-general appointed by the prime minister. See also LAND PROBLEM.

National Mobilization Law

(Kokka Sōdōin Hō). Legislation for mobilizing Japan's civilian society and economy during World War II. It provided the overall legal authority for deploying "manpower and material resources for the highest and most efficient development of the total power of the state in time of war."

The Kokka Sōdōin Hō, which replaced earlier statutes controlling the munitions industries, was drafted by the Planning Board of the first KONOE FUMIMARO cabinet soon after Japan went to war with China in July 1937 (see SINO-JAPANESE WAR OF 1937–1945). Although the proposed law was similar to those recently passed with little opposition in France and Britain, the bill was attacked as unconstitutional when it was introduced to the 73rd Diet in January 1938. Under pressure from the military, legislators finally approved the law without amendment on 24 March 1938. It was officially promulgated on 1 April and took effect on 5 May.

Twenty-five of its 50 articles provided for controls on civilian organizations, labor, industrial and consumer commodities, corporations, contracts, prices, and the news media. The law empowered the government to subsidize war production and indemnify manufacturers for losses caused by mobilization. It also contained 18 articles setting penalties for violations.

Wartime restrictions were not imposed by IMPERIAL ORDINANCE (chokurei), without coming before the Diet, but each had to be sent for "advice" to a 50-person mobilization screening council representing business, party politics, the bureaucracy, and the armed forces. Few such orders were issued before 1941; until then the state was still primarily the chief customer, rather than designer, of the economic buildup that remained under the leadership of private industry. But citizens' daily lives were already straitened by "spiritual mobilization," propaganda, censorship, and forced savings campaigns. The national muster was speeded by Konoe's NEW ORDER MOVEMENT in the fall of 1940, which placed tighter controls on labor and community organizations under the Kokka Sōdōin Hō.

The 7 December 1941 (8 December in Japan) attack on Pearl Harbor was the decisive event for Japan's overall mobilization. Shortly before, the 76th Diet had revised the Kokka Sōdōin Hō to expand the state's powers. Preparations for an all-out war grew intense: civilian factories were turned into war plants, control boards were set up in a dozen key industries, a labor registry was established, and eight major plans for raising output were announced. The full authority of the Kokka Sōdōin Hō was brought to bear on the society as well as the economy during 1942–45. The mobilization foundered not so much because it was tardy but because of incomplete integration, growing scarcity of natural resources after 1942, and the simple fact that the imperial forces were losing the war. The law was formally abolished on 29 September 1945.

——T. A. Bisson, Japan's War Economy (1945). Jerome B. Cohen, Japan's Economy in War and Reconstruction (1949). Hara Akira, "Senji tōsei keizai no kaishi," in Iwanami kōza: Nihon rekishi, vol 20 (Iwanami Shoten, 1976). T. R. H. Havens, Valley of Darkness: The Japanese People and World War Two (1978). Japan Times & Mail, The National General Mobilization Law (1940).

T. R. H. HAVENS

National Museum of Ethnology

(Kokuritsu Minzokugaku Hakubutsukan). Located in the city of Suita, Ōsaka Prefecture, the museum was established in 1974 and opened to the public in 1977. It offers up-to-date ethnographic information, based on field research, on the world's peoples and societies. The museum's collection includes articles of daily life as well as materials related to religion and art. Exhibits are divided into geographical areas corresponding to Oceania, the Americas, Europe, Africa, West Asia, Southeast Asia, and East Asia. Special cross-cultural exhibits deal with overall themes such as music and linguistics. The museum features a Videotheque, consisting of audiovisual equipment that automatically selects, presents, and returns video cassette tapes upon request of the viewer. FUJIKAWA Kinji

National Museum of Modern Art, Tōkyō

(Tōkyō Kokuritsu Kindai Bijutsukan). Located in Kitanomaru Park, Chiyoda Ward, Tōkyō, the museum collects, preserves, and exhibits outstanding works of modern art and related reference materials. The museum was first opened in 1952 in the Kyōbashi section of Tōkyō under the auspices of the Ministry of Education. In 1969 it was moved to its present building, designed by Taniguchi Yoshirō and donated by ISHIBASHI SHŌJIRŌ. The Film Center was opened in 1970 in the original building in Kyōbashi.

The museum has a collection of some 3,000 works in the fields of Western-style painting, Japanese-style painting, sculpture, prints, and crafts. Among these are YOKOYAMA TAIKAN's Metempsychosis, FUJITA TSUGUHARU's Street in Paris, Sugai Kumi's Motorway in the Morning, MUNAKATA SHIKŌ's Crowd of Excited Women, and OGIWARA MORIE's Woman. Special exhibitions of Japanese and Western art are held in the first floor gallery, and works from the museum's collection are exhibited on the second through fourth floors.

The Crafts Gallery was opened in 1977. It is housed in the former administrative headquarters of the Old Imperial Palace Guard, a Western-style Meiji-period (1868–1912) building which has been designated as an Important Cultural Property. The gallery has a collection of some 600 items, including works by such representative contemporary craftsmen as TOMIMOTO KENKICHI, HAMADA SHŌJI, SERIZAWA KEISUKE, and Matsuda Gonroku.

The Film Center, originally the Film Library within the National Museum of Modern Art, is the only national film institute. It owns approximately 6,000 Japanese films and 569 foreign ones. It collects and preserves films and other related materials and carries out film-related research; the center also has a daily film showing. In addition to its exhibits, the museum sponsors various lectures and issues a yearly report and monthly periodical, Gendai no me (Today's Focus).

National Museum of Western Art

(Kokuritsu Seiyō Bijutsukan). Located in Ueno Park in Tōkyō. A collection of European art, the basis of which is the large group (over 400 items) of French paintings and sculpture of the 19th and 20th centuries collected by the late Matsukata Kōjirō. These objects were held in France during World War II and were declared French property by the San Francisco Peace Treaty but were subsequently given to Japan by the French government. Rodin, Bourdelle, and Maillol are well represented in the sculpture section. Since its opening in 1959, the museum has broadened its collection to include works of earlier centuries by artists from Italy, Holland, Flanders, Spain, and England. The museum's main building was designed by Le Corbusier; the annex, which opened in 1979, was designed by MAEKAWA KUNIO. See also MUSEUMS. Laurance ROBERTS

national parks and quasi-national parks

These terms denote scenic or historical land declared public property by the Japanese government with a view to preservation and development for purposes of recreation and culture. National parks (kokuritsu kōen) are administered by the Environment Agency of the Prime Minister's Office, and quasi-national parks (kokutei kōen) are administered directly by the prefectural governments under the supervision of the Ministry of Public Welfare. National parks, along with quasi-national and prefectural parks, represent a concerted effort to protect Japan's environment which began in the 1930s and gained momentum in the 1950s. The first national parks were the Inland Sea and the Unzen (now Unzen-Amakusa) national parks, established on 16 March 1934. Attempts are being made to protect and preserve a wide variety of land, including mountains, plateaus, valleys, volcanoes, rivers, islands, coastlines, forests, and wildlife. In 1980 there were 27 national parks and 51 quasi-national parks, at least one in virtually every prefecture around the country. National parks are generally much larger than quasi-national and prefectural natural parks.

National Personnel Authority

(Jinjiin). Independent agency of the Japanese government responsible for the administration of the national civil service. It was established in 1947 under the National Civil Service Law (Kokka Kōmuin Hō) at the recommendation of the Supreme Commander for the Allied Powers (SCAP) as a part of the democratization of the bureaucracy and improvement of personnel management. First called Rinji Jinji Iinkai, it was renamed the Jinjiin in 1948.

It acts as a board of equity, ensuring that recruitment is impartially made on the basis of merit and that disciplinary actions are fairly taken. It advises the government and the Diet on setting wages for civil servants, who are restricted in their rights to collective bargaining and strikes; its annual recommendations are based on comparative wage surveys (see NATIONAL PERSONNEL AUTHORITY RECOMMENDATIONS). The agency is composed of three full-time commissioners, who are appointed by the cabinet with the approval of the Diet, and an Executive Office, which has five bureaus and other organs.

National Personnel Authority recommendations

(Jinjiin kankoku). Recommendations made to the cabinet and Diet on matters concerning all national employees by the NATIONAL PERSONNEL AUTHORITY (NPA; J: Jinjiin), an administrative organ set up in conjunction with the National Civil Service Law of 1948 (Kokka Kōmuin Hō). Since by law public employees have neither collective bargaining rights nor the right to strike, the NPA, acting on their behalf, issues advisory opinions on the revision of labor conditions

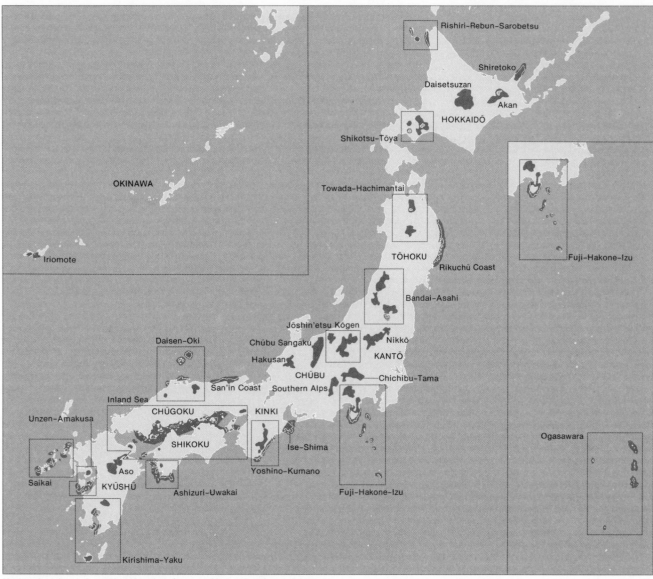

Rishiri-Rebun-Sarobetsu
Shiretoko
Daisetsuzan
Akan
HOKKAIDŌ
Shikotsu-Tōya
Towada-Hachimantai
TŌHOKU
Rikuchū Coast
Bandai-Asahi
Fuji-Hakone-Izu
Jōshin'etsu Kōgen
Chūbu Sangaku
Nikkō
Daisen-Oki
Hakusan
KANTŌ
Chichibu-Tama
CHŪBU
San'in Coast
Southern Alps
Inland Sea
Unzen-Amakusa
CHŪGOKU
KINKI
Ogasawara
SHIKOKU
Ise-Shima
Saikai
Aso
Yoshino-Kumano
KYŪSHŪ
Ashizuri-Uwakai
Fuji-Hakone-Izu
OKINAWA
Iriomote
Kirishima-Yaku

National parks and quasi-national parks ———— National parks as of 1983

that affect some half million national employees. The standards for change prescribed by the law are the cost of living, the scale of wages for private enterprise, and other important factors. For that reason, the NPA carries out periodic cost-of-living surveys and wage surveys of jobs by type in the private sector. When conditions arise that necessitate a wage increase of 5 percent or more, the NPA is obliged by statute to recommend a revision of the wage scale for national employees. Thus, when there is a change of 5 percent or more in the cost of living or when circumstances result in a differential of 5 percent or more in wages relative to the private sector, the NPA issues an advisory report. Despite the existence of this advisory board, however, the government virtually ignored its recommendations and failed to implement any change until 1953. No reports were issued thereafter until 1959. Between 1960 and 1967 the NPA's recommendations were carried out, though tardily and under less than perfect conditions. This slowness to act, which reflected both the government's financial state and its wage policies, led public employees to demand collective bargaining rights and the right to strike. Since 1970 the government has implemented most NPA advisory reports. Generally, the NPA makes its recommendations in August, and they are retroactive to April after they go into effect. For local public employees *(chihō kōmuin)*, there is the National Personnel Commission, or Jinjiin Kai, which handles similar problems. Its role is much like that of the NPA, and it often joins in the NPA's advisory opinions. See also PUBLIC EMPLOYEES.

KURITA Ken

National Police Reserve

(Keisatsu Yobitai). Forerunner of the SELF DEFENSE FORCES. When the Korean War began in June 1950 and the main strength of the United States Forces stationed in Japan was dispatched to the Korean peninsula, the Supreme Commander for the Allied Powers, Douglas MACARTHUR, ordered the Japanese government to form a National Police Reserve of 75,000 men to fill the gap. From the time the order was issued on 8 July 1950 to the end of the year, the National Police Reserve gradually took over the job of maintaining public peace and order. The contradiction between the National Police Reserve and article 9 of the 1947 CONSTITUTION, which prohibits rearmament, became a controversial issue. In 1952 it was reorganized into the NATIONAL SAFETY FORCES, which later became the Self Defense Forces.

HATA Ikuhiko

"national polity" → kokutai

National Public Safety Commission

(Kokka Kōan Iinkai). The governmental body responsible for the administration and coordination of police activities throughout Japan, and for the supervision of Japan's law enforcement agency, the National Police Agency (Keisatsuchō). The commission was established in 1947 with the specific purpose of guaranteeing the neutrality of the police in politics and preventing government misuse of police powers. It was to do this by insulating the police from political pressure and by ensuring the maintenance of democratic methods of administration within the police forces. At the same time a public safety commission (kōan iinkai) was established in each prefecture to supervise its police. Prefectural public safety commission members are appointed by the governor with the consent of the prefectural assembly. They are independent from the National Public Safety Commission but keep close contact with it and with the commissions of other prefectures.

The National Public Safety Commission is an external organ of the Prime Minister's Office (Sōrifu), and consists of a chairman who holds the rank of minister of state and five members, all appointed by the prime minister. It operates independently of the cabinet, but liaison and coordination with the cabinet are facilitated by the chairman's membership in that body.

The major tasks of the National Police Agency, which is attached to and controlled by the commission, include the general determination of overall standards and policies for Japan's police forces, criminal investigations, scientific crime detection, and coordination and communication between local police forces. In case of a national emergency, the agency assumes command of the prefectural police forces. See POLICE SYSTEM.

National Safety Forces

(Hoantai). Forerunner of the SELF DEFENSE FORCES. Originally called the NATIONAL POLICE RESERVE, together with a maritime force founded in April 1952, it was put under the newly founded National Security Agency in August 1952 and renamed the National Safety Forces. In 1954 it was reorganized into the Self Defense Forces.   HATA Ikuhiko

National Salvation Association

(Ch: Chongguo Renmin Jiukuo Hui or Chung-kuo Jen-min Chiu-kuo Hui). Part of the growing Chinese protest against Japan's aggression in North China, the All China Federation of National Salvation Associations, commonly referred to as the National Salvation Association, was founded in Shanghai in May 1936 by noncommunist intellectuals and politicians who opposed the Guomindang (Kuomintang; Nationalist Party) government's policy of fighting Chinese communists instead of the Japanese. The association became the leader of the National Salvation Movement, a proliferation of organizations and demonstrations which was sparked by the DECEMBER NINTH MOVEMENT (1935) in Beiping (Peiping; now Beijing or Peking). On 15 July 1936 several leaders of the National Salvation Association published an open letter, "A Number of Essential Conditions and Minimum Demands for United Resistance to Invasion." The letter, directed primarily at the Guomindang, called for an immediate end to civil war between the Guomindang and the Chinese Communist Party, the release of political prisoners, and the formation of a coalition government to resist Japan.

Communist support for the association's aims and a strike in Japanese-owned cotton mills in Shanghai provided the pretexts for the Guomindang to arrest seven prominent leaders of the association in November 1936. The arrests became infamous throughout China, and pressure increased on CHIANG KAI-SHEK, leader of the Guomindang, to adopt a policy of resistance to Japan.

The National Salvation Movement achieved its aim by July 1937, when along with other factors, it forced Chiang to implement a united front policy against Japanese aggression (see SINO-JAPANESE WAR OF 1937–1945). The same month the Guomindang released the association leaders. The growth and activities of the National Salvation Movement elicited sharp resentment in Japan, adding to popular sentiment in support of Japanese military ambitions in China.

National Science Museum

(Kokuritsu Kagaku Hakubutsukan). Museum in Ueno, Tōkyō, in which materials concerning natural science are studied, collected, and displayed. In addition to carrying out educational activities, it functions as a research center for the study of the natural history of the Japanese archipelago. Started in 1877 as the Kyōiku Hakubutsukan, it acquired its present name in 1949. Besides the main building, there are separate buildings for natural history, the technical arts, physical science, and technology. Educational and research programs on conservation and ecology are carried out at the museum's nature study park in Minato Ward, Tōkyō.   FUJIKAWA Kinji

National Seclusion

(Sakoku). Policy (1639–1854) adopted by the Tokugawa shogunate (1603–1867) to legitimize and strengthen its authority both domestically and in East Asia. The main elements of the policy were the exclusion of Catholic missionaries and traders, the proscription of Christianity in Japan, and the prohibition of foreign travel by Japanese. The seclusion was not total, because Dutch, Chinese, and Koreans were permitted access to Japan; moreover, designated officials and traders from the domains of Satsuma (now Kagoshima Prefecture) and Tsushima were allowed to go to the Ryūkyūs and to Korea, respectively. The Korean trade in Japan, however, was confined to Tsushima, and the only Japanese port open to the Dutch and Chinese was the shogunate-controlled city of Nagasaki.

The seclusion policy was enunciated in five directives issued by the shogunate's senior councillors (rōjū) in Edo (now Tōkyō) to its two commissioners (bugyō) in Nagasaki between 1633 and 1639. The term sakoku itself did not come into use until early in the 19th century, when a Nagasaki scholar of WESTERN LEARNING coined it for the title of his translation of a portion of Engelbert KAEMPFER's History of Japan.

Since the Meiji Restoration (1868), there has been a continuing debate over the meaning of the word sakoku. Initially the term was used in a derogatory sense by those who felt that Japan had been forcibly "closed" by the shogunate and had fallen behind the West until forcibly "opened" again by Commodore PERRY in 1853. This view emphasized the shogunate's fear of Christian ideas and of foreign intervention and saw the "Sakoku edicts" as the culmination of a series of ANTI-CHRISTIAN EDICTS dating back to 1587. According to this view, Japan was willing to sacrifice Western trade to ensure ideological orthodoxy.

Later Japanese historians challenged the importance of the anti-Christian motive, stressing instead economic and political factors. They viewed the Sakoku policy as the final act in creating unchallenged shogunate control over the country and saw it primarily in domestic terms, giving little attention to foreign relations. More recent studies have attempted to show that foreign relations, especially in East Asia, played a significant role in the shogunate's decision to close the country.

Even if one rejects the anti-Christian motive as the primary concern, the issue of Christianity was still quite important to Japanese leaders. The first edict prohibiting Christianity was issued by TOYOTOMI HIDEYOSHI in 1587 and later elaborated by the Tokugawa shogunate in decrees of 1612 and 1614. However, many Christians survived by being discreet, and the shogunate made only an occasional show of force, for example in 1622, when 55 Christians were executed.

The situation changed in 1623, when TOKUGAWA IEMITSU became shōgun. Persecutions increased as more vigorous anti-Christian officials, such as Takenaka Uneme no Shō (Nagasaki bugyō, 1629–33), were named to important posts and new practices of surveillance and torture were initiated. The shogunate was thus already attempting to eliminate Christianity in Japan even before the first Sakoku edict of 1633.

Foreign trade, the other major issue of the Sakoku edicts, had also been the subject of restrictive regulations for many years. However, whereas the shogunate's policy regarding Christianity was primarily a domestic concern, its foreign trade policy had both domestic and foreign aspects.

Domestically, the shogunate's greatest concern was to prevent the daimyō in southwestern Japan from offering a challenge to its power. Some of these daimyō had traded actively with foreigners, and a few had even become Christians to facilitate trade. The earliest effort to control this trade was the VERMILION SEAL SHIP TRADE licensing system, adopted in the 1590s and used by Tokugawa leaders until 1635. In 1609 the shogunate, in a further restrictive measure, ordered the daimyō to surrender all ships with a capacity of over 500 KOKU (1 koku = about .28 cubic meters or 10 cubic feet). This measure was taken so that no daimyō could pose a military threat to the shogunate, but also because the shogunate wanted to limit the daimyō's profits from overseas trade. In 1616 the shogunate again restricted the daimyō's economic benefits by limiting all foreign trade, except that with the Chinese, to the ports of Nagasaki and Hirado.

The other major domestic concern involving foreign trade related to Japanese merchants in large cities. The first significant policy regarding these merchants was the creation of the ITOWAPPU rawsilk monopoly system in 1604. Originally applied to the purchase of raw silk from Portuguese ships by designated merchants of Nagasaki, Sakai, and Kyōto, the system was expanded to include Chinese ships as well in 1631. In the same year, a further restriction on foreign trade was employed when the shogunate established the HŌ-SHOSEN system, which required a permit from the *rōjū* in addition to the vermilion seal needed previously. By supporting monopolistic *itowappu* merchants, the shogunate was able to control this emerging class and even use it to buttress its own power base.

In foreign affairs as well, the shogunate used trade, and the diplomacy surrounding it, to legitimize and strengthen its power. The China-centered tribute system had traditionally been the apparatus for both legitimation and foreign trade in East Asia, but before the beginning of the Edo period (1600–1868) the TALLY TRADE between China and Japan had been terminated. The Ming dynasty of China had severed relations because of WAKŌ (Japanese pirate) raids and refused to resume them after Hideyoshi's INVASIONS OF KOREA IN 1592 AND 1597. Hence the shogunate's early efforts to regularize trade with China failed.

With the establishment of trading factories by the Dutch in 1609 and the British in 1613, and the growth of private Chinese trade, the shogunate no longer needed the sanction of the Ming government to conduct trade in East Asia. By the 1620s, it was unwilling to compromise its growing independence for the minor benefits of direct relations with the Ming; it desired legitimation through foreign trade and diplomacy but would not submit to tributary status to accomplish this.

The Tokugawa regime thus turned to two smaller powers in East Asia, the Ryūkyūs and Korea, to help bolster its position at home. The Ryūkyūs, at the time of the establishment of the shogunate, paid tribute to both China and Japan. In 1609 it came under the control of the Satsuma domain, and in the following year the Ryukyuan king was forced to make a tribute mission to Japan to help legitimize Tokugawa rule. The shogunate allowed trade between Satsuma and the Ryūkyūs to continue throughout the Edo period, fully aware that considerable unsanctioned trade was carried on in the islands with the Chinese, who after 1635 were supposed to be confined to Nagasaki.

The Koreans also sent a full mission to Japan in 1607, thus helping the Tokugawa shōgun to legitimize his rule. A considerable trade developed between the two countries, with the SŌ FAMILY, the daimyō house of Tsushima, placed in charge. The trade prospered to the point that it is estimated that its volume surpassed Nagasaki's. Both the trade and the tribute missions continued throughout the Edo period.

The shogunate did not intend to cut itself off from all foreign trade but merely desired to set its own guidelines. The British departed on their own in 1623, and the Spanish were expelled in the following year, so that by the time of the first Sakoku edict in 1633, Japan was trading with the Dutch at Hirado, the Portuguese at Nagasaki, the Koreans through Tsushima, the Ryukyuans through Satsuma, and the Chinese at various Japanese ports.

The first Sakoku edict was issued on 6 April 1633 (Kan'ei 10.2.28). The 17 articles in the directive can be divided into three sections, covering the coming and going of Japanese overseas, the search for Christian converts and missionaries, and the regulation of foreign trade. All ships and Japanese subjects were forbidden to leave Japan for a foreign country without a valid *hōsho* license; all Japanese living abroad were to be put to death if they tried to return to Japan, except for those who had resided abroad for less than five years and had been unavoidably detained. Concerning Christianity, the Nagasaki *bugyō* was to investigate all those suspected of being Christians, and a reward was offered to any informer who revealed the location of a BATEREN (foreign priest). When a foreign ship arrived, it was to be guarded by ships belonging to the Ōmura domain (now part of Nagasaki Prefecture) while a report was sent to Edo. Any foreigner who helped a *bateren* or any other proscribed foreigner was to be imprisoned at Ōmura, and, finally, a strict search was to be made for *bateren* on all ships entering Japan. The last section dealt with foreign trade, more specifically with the operation of the *itowappu* system in Nagasaki.

The second Sakoku edict, dated 3 July 1634 (Kan'ei 11.5.28), was basically the same as the directive of 1633. The third Sakoku edict, of 12 July 1635 (Kan'ei 12.5.28), was similar to the previous two but more specific in its prohibitions. The dispatching of ships abroad was absolutely forbidden. Moreover, if a Japanese was caught trying to leave or return to Japan, he was to be executed, and both the ship and its captain were to be detained pending charges.

The fourth Sakoku edict, issued on 22 June 1636 (Kan'ei 13.5.19), contained 19 articles. The previous travel restrictions were repeated, and new ones, concerning the offspring of "southern barbarians" (Portuguese and Spanish), were added. None of these offspring was allowed to remain in Japan, upon threat of execution, and Japanese who had adopted such offspring were to be handed over, together with the children, to the Portuguese for deportation. The reward for informing on a *bateren* was increased, and foreign trade regulations were explained in greater detail, with a few minor changes made as to how and when to sell raw silk.

The last of the Sakoku edicts, issued on 4 August 1639 (Kan'ei 16.7.5) in the aftermath of the SHIMABARA UPRISING (1637–38), contained only three articles. It stated that in light of the continued arrival of *bateren*, the formation of groups by Christian believers to plot against the shogunate, and the smuggling of items to help the hiding priests and their followers, Portuguese ships would no longer be allowed to enter Japanese ports. Any ship disobeying this order was to be destroyed and its crew and passengers executed.

The shogunate demonstrated that it intended to enforce this prohibition when in 1640 it arrested 74 people who sailed from Macao to Nagasaki to reopen relations with Japan. Sixty-one were executed, and the remaining 13 Chinese crew members were allowed to return to Macao.

The shogunate also transferred the Dutch from Hirado to the man-made island of DEJIMA in Nagasaki Harbor in 1641. DUTCH TRADE regulations would undergo some minor changes during the Edo period, and Chinese merchants would come under tighter control, but the fundamental guidelines were established by 1641. After this, apart from the Ryukyuan and Korean trade, the only foreign trade allowed was that of the Dutch and Chinese at Nagasaki.

Over the next 200 years, the Portuguese, British, Americans, and Russians attempted unsuccessfully to alter the seclusion policy. However, this policy, which in the 1630s had been a rational attempt to legitimize and strengthen shogunate authority, had by the early 19th century become more a burden than an asset. The PHAETON INCIDENT of 1808, in which a British warship sailed into Nagasaki Harbor in defiance of shogunate orders, demonstrated that regulations had become quite lax. On the theoretical level, however, national seclusion continued to be championed by scholars of the nationalist MITO SCHOOL. It was only with the arrival of Perry in 1853 that the shogunate was forced to rethink its seclusion policy and indeed to justify its own existence. National Seclusion was formally brought to an end by the KANAGAWA TREATY of 1854 and the ANSEI COMMERCIAL TREATIES of 1858. See also HISTORY OF JAPAN: Edo history.

📖——Asao Naohiro, *Sakoku*, in *Nihon no rekishi*, vol 17 (Shōgakukan, 1975). Charles Boxer, *The Christian Century in Japan, 1549–1650* (1951). Iwao Seiichi, *Sakoku*, in *Nihon no rekishi*, vol 14 (Chūō Kōron Sha, 1971). Ronald Toby, "Reopening the Question of Sakoku: Diplomacy in the Legitimation of the Tokugawa Bakufu," *Journal of Japanese Studies* 3.2 (1977).　　　Lane R. EARNS

National Service Draft Ordinance

(Kokumin Chōyō Rei). An imperial ordinance promulgated in July 1939 on the authority of the NATIONAL MOBILIZATION LAW to draft the civilian population; it was issued to ensure an adequate supply of labor for strategic industries during wartime. Enforcement of ordinance particulars was left to the discretion of the minister of welfare. No exemptions were allowed, except in cases of illness or physical handicap. Under the ordinance 1,610,000 men and women were drafted, and 4,500,000 workers were reclassified as draftees. With the deterioration of Japan's military position in World War II, the ordinance was subsumed under the more comprehensive Kokumin Kinrō Dōin Rei (National Labor Service Mobilization Law) of March 1945 (abolished in October 1945).

National Space Development Agency of Japan

(Uchū Kaihatsu Jigyōdan). Government agency established in 1969 to develop a space exploration program. Headquarters are in Tōkyō. The agency operates a rocket launching site on the island of Tanegashima, south of Kyūshū, and carries out the development and testing of satellites. The Tsukuba Space Center in Ibaraki Prefecture, which tracks the flight of satellites after launching, is also under its supervision. Following the successful launching in 1975 of Engineering Test Satellite I (nicknamed *Kiku*), the agency has continued the development and launching of satellites for various purposes. See also SPACE TECHNOLOGY.

National Spiritual Mobilization Movement

(Kokumin Seishin Sōdōin Undō). Movement formed in 1937 as a part of the National Mobilization (Kokka Sōdōin) Movement to rally the nation for an all-out effort for victory in the war against China (see SINO-JAPANESE WAR OF 1937–1945). Representatives from 74 national organizations, including the Japan Red Cross, the Military Reserve Association, the Japan Association of Shintō Priests, and various labor and womens' groups, assembled at Prime Minister KONOE FUMIMARO's official residence in October 1937 and became incorporated as the Central League of the Spiritual Mobilization Movement. The organization, under the direction of Admiral Arima Ryōkitsu (1861–1944), had few concrete programs and simply appealed to the masses for patriotic support of the effort in China.

As the "China Incident" broadened into a full-scale war, in an attempt to bolster the movement, Konoe added 19 organizations to the league and appointed cabinet vice-ministers Ishiwata Sōtarō (1891–1950) and Hirose Hisatada (1889–1974) to the board of governors. Still, the movement relied mostly on the well-worn slogans of "national unity," "virtuous perseverance," and "loyalty and patriotism."

The HIRANUMA KIICHIRŌ cabinet, which took office in January 1939, reorganized the movement "to prepare the nation for the task of building a new order in East Asia." General ARAKI SADAO, who was minister of education, chaired the Central Commission to Strengthen Spiritual Mobilization. Under Araki the movement stressed practical steps to promote the "unity of mind and matter" in constructing the "new order." These measures lacked imagination and style, however, consisting mostly of campaigns to conserve gasoline and electricity, to encourage savings, or to cooperate with the government in keeping prices down. Although the spiritual mobilization campaigns were publicly criticized as superficial and vague, especially by army factions and the so-called revisionist bureaucrats (shinkanryō) who urged institutional reform and political reorganization to meet the challenges of the war in China, the conservative Hiranuma preferred to rely on psychological campaigns rather than implement radical reforms.

Although never given the wholehearted support of all ruling circles, the Spiritual Mobilization Movement succeeded in reaching the masses through public rallies, radio programs, and printed matter. The neighborhood associations called TONARIGUMI, established in 1938 to inculcate correct moral attitudes, became formal local control organizations by September 1940.

📖——Gordon Berger, *Parties Out of Power in Japan, 1931–1941* (1977). Richard Yasko, "Hiranuma Kiichirō and Conservative Politics in Pre-War Japan," PhD dissertation, University of Chicago (1973). Yokusan Undō Shi Kankōkai, ed, *Yokusan kokumin undō shi* (1954).   Richard YASKO

National Sports Festival

(Kokumin Taiiku Taikai, commonly referred to as Kokutai). Begun in 1946. One of the representative amateur sports events in Japan jointly sponsored by the JAPAN AMATEUR SPORTS ASSOCIATION, the Ministry of Education, and the local prefectural government where the festival takes place. The site is selected from among the prefectures annually. The festival actually consists of three seasonal meets, winter, summer, and fall, and the games are played in two major divisions, one for adults and the other for those under 18. The festival covers some 30 different sports, including traditional Japanese martial arts, a high school baseball tournament, and mountaineering.   TAKEDA Fumio

National Tax Tribunal

(Kokuzei Fufuku Shimpanjo). Tribunal that reviews and rules on requests for review of dispositions based on the laws concerning national taxes under article 78 of the National Tax Common Provisions Law (Kokuzei Tsūsoku Hō).

The National Tax Tribunal is affiliated with the National Tax Agency. The president of the tribunal is appointed by the director of the agency subject to the approval of the minister of finance, but he is given independence in the exercise of his authority. In addition to the main tribunal office in Tōkyō, there are 13 branch offices, one each in Tōkyō, Ōsaka, and in the other regional national tax office

jurisdictions. A total of 242 national tax adjudicators and their assistants were employed as of 1979.

Most requests for review that come to the tribunal concern dispositions (rectifications, decrees, and delinquency dispositions) made by a head of a district TAX OFFICE. Taxpayers can request review of rectifications of their blue returns (a blue form upon which some income tax reports are made), but in general, requests for review of other dispositions cannot be made without first declaring an objection to the head of the district tax office. The direct request for review must be made within two months of learning of the disposition and then the actual review must be requested within one month of receiving approval to proceed.

Requests for review are made to the branch office of the tribunal, whose jurisdiction encompasses the jurisdictional area of the district tax office that made the disposition. Three national tax adjudicators or assistants sit in conference to make the ruling. When a request for review involves particularly important legal problems, however, the matter may, upon the judgment of the president of the tribunal, be transferred from the branch office to the main office for review and ruling. In general, review involves only a review of the pertinent documents, but on application of the person requesting review, an opportunity for oral presentation is granted. In all cases, the ruling is made in the name of the president of the tribunal.

When the requirements preceding requests for review have not been fulfilled, as, for example, when the deadline for requesting review has passed, the request will be dismissed (kyakka). If the request for review is groundless, a ruling of rejection (kikyaku) will be handed down; and if the request proves to have proper justification, a ruling cancelling all or part of the original disposition will be made. If the person requesting the review is dissatisfied with the ruling of the tribunal, he may seek cancellation of the original disposition by bringing suit in a district court.

The president of the National Tax Tribunal is given considerable independence in the exercise of his authority. However, he must present his ideas in advance to the director of the National Tax Agency when he makes a ruling based on an interpretation of the law that differs from the interpretations in the circulars issued by the director, or when he makes a ruling that will clearly become an important precedent. At such times, the director gives direction to the president based on the decision of the National Tax Review Commission, except in such cases where the president of the tribunal has accepted the contention of the person requesting review and the director has recognized the president's ideas as appropriate. The National Tax Review Commission is a consultative organ established in the National Tax Agency to prevent the director of the agency from being arbitrary in the exercise of his authority in these matters and to protect the independence of the National Tax Tribunal. The National Tax Review Commission consists of up to 10 members named by the minister of finance. See also TAX LAW.

                                  KANEKO Hiroshi

National Treasures

(Kokuhō). The designation given by the Japanese government to a group of objects of exceptional historical and artistic importance in order to ensure their preservation. National Treasures were originally given recognition under the Preservation of Ancient Shrines and Temples Law (Koshaji Hozon Hō) of 1897 and later under the Preservation of National Treasures Law (Kokuhō Hozon Hō) of 1929. Since there was a need for the improvement of protective measures in the aftermath of World War II, the Law for Protection of Cultural Assets (Bunkazai Hogo Hō) was promulgated in 1950 (revised in 1954 and 1975). This abandoned the designations previously given to National Treasures and substituted the term "Important Cultural Properties" (Jūyō Bunkazai), with a new selection from among these objects to be advanced to the status of National Treasures.

At the time of the Meiji Restoration of 1868, the sudden enthusiasm for modernization, combined with anti-Buddhist sentiment, threatened the very existence of what are now notable monuments among the officially recognized National Treasures of the country. At one point, buildings such as the KŌFUKUJI pagoda in Nara and HIMEJI CASTLE in what is now Hyōgo Prefecture were bid for at auction for the scrap value of their component materials, but they were saved only because the cost of dismantling them would have been prohibitive. In response to this danger, the new central government issued a proclamation for the protection of ancient shrines and temples as early as 1871.

One of the most effective advocates for the preservation of Japan's antiquities in the late 19th century was the young Bostonian Ernest F. FENOLLOSA, who had been invited in 1878 by Tōkyō University to teach philosophy. Partly as a result of his efforts and those of his colleague OKAKURA KAKUZŌ, the Preservation of Ancient Shrines and Temples Law was passed in 1897. Items chosen for protection were listed under such headings as painting, calligraphy, and works of decorative art (kōgei, literally, "industrial arts"), from which swords were separated later as a distinct category.

This law did much to preserve the buildings and art works belonging to ancient religious institutions, identifying items of special cultural significance and providing funds and guidance for their protection. However, art objects of national importance belonging to government agencies or owned by corporations or individuals were not covered, and broader legislation was needed to prevent the dispersal of such objects, and particularly, to guard against their exportation to foreign countries. Consequently, the Preservation of National Treasures Law was passed in 1929 to take the place of the older law and to expand the definition of what constituted a National Treasure.

The air raids of World War II destroyed many objects designated as National Treasures and many others were threatened by the general destitution of the immediate postwar years. When, as a result of inadequate safety measures in the use of artificial lighting, a fire destroyed many of the early-8th-century Buddhist wall paintings at the Nara temple HŌRYŪJI in 1949, the Diet took the disaster as an occasion to enact the Law for the Protection of Cultural Assets of 1950. This act, which made use of the term "cultural assets" (bunkazai) law for the first time, was founded on a fundamental revision of the concept of appropriate governmental participation in the preservation of cultural assets, both tangible and intangible.

The cultural properties of special historical and artistic value listed in this legislation include buildings, paintings, sculpture, the decorative arts, calligraphy, books, old documents, and other tangible objects. It also listed, for the first time, Intangible Cultural Assets (Mukei Bunkazai): matters of interest to students of folklore and anthropology and those concerned with the preservation of traditional skills in the areas of theater, music, weaving, dyeing, and the ceramic arts, to name only a few. The term "National Treasure" was reserved for special application in this new legislation and the intangible assets to be preserved were ascribed merely to "bearers of important cultural assets," but the publicity generated by the selection of these people resulted in the popular expression LIVING NATIONAL TREASURES (Ningen Kokuhō).

As an indication of the degree of selectivity used in the application of the term "National Treasure" in the new legislation, it should be noted that in 1981 there were 1,759 paintings listed as Important Cultural Properties but only 151 as National Treasures. Selection is made in a quasi-legislative fashion. One of the many departments of the Agency for Cultural Affairs of the Ministry of Education produces a draft motion that the minister of education presents to the Committee for the Protection of Cultural Assets. The motion, if accepted, is then referred to various subcommittees of specialists, who are required to arrive at a unanimous decision before favorable action can be taken and reported to the minister of education.

The activities of the Committee for the Protection of Cultural Assets are followed with wide and respectful public interest, a notable change from the days when government action was needed to prevent the private dismantling of what are now recognized as some of Japan's greatest treasures.

—— Barbara Adachi, The Living Treasures of Japan (1973). Bunkachō, ed, Kokuhō jiten (Benridō, 1976). Bunkachō, ed, Kokuhō jūyō bunkazai sōgō mokuroku: Bijutsu kōgeihin hen (Daiichi Hōki Shuppan, 1980). Rekishi hyakka, vol 9 of Nihon kokuhō jiten (Shin Jimbutsu Ōrai Sha; winter 1980). Lloyd CRAIGHILL

national wealth

(kokufu). Stocks of goods accumulated over time for production and consumption. National wealth is a measure of assets (a stock concept), which generate national income (a flow concept). Before World War II, government agencies conducted eight surveys of national wealth to determine the state of its assets and help to formulate economic policy; the ECONOMIC PLANNING AGENCY has conducted such surveys every five years since 1955.

The precise definition of national wealth has varied over time, but in the 1970 survey it was defined as all tangible assets at least one year old, excluding art objects and items worth less than

¥10,000 (US $28 in 1970). National wealth thus consists of tangible fixed assets such as buildings and structures (roads, harbors, and other facilities), machinery and apparatus, vessels, rolling stock and transportation equipment, tools and accessories, plants and animals; inventories of raw materials, finished and unfinished work, and merchandise; and foreign assets minus foreign liabilities. National wealth excludes land and other endowed natural resources, intangible assets, and assets used for national defense. The survey covers the public sector (the central and local governments), the enterprise sector (including private, state, and local government enterprises), the nonprofit organization sector, and the household sector. In addition to the information on the central government's wealth, the estimate is based on samples of local governments, corporate enterprises, and household wealth.

The national wealth survey distinguishes between gross asset value and net asset value. The gross asset value is roughly the replacement value and is obtained by multiplying the value of the asset at the time of acquisition (taking into account depreciation) by the appropriate inflation factor. The net asset value is the replacement value minus capital consumption allowance.

According to the 1970 survey, the national wealth in terms of gross asset value reached ¥300 trillion (US $838 billion), in a year when the gross national product reached approximately ¥70 trillion (US $195 billion). Tangible fixed assets constituted 90 percent of national wealth, inventory assets 9 percent, and net foreign assets 1 percent. The four largest items among tangible fixed assets were buildings (32 percent of national wealth), household assets (24 percent), structures (14 percent), and machinery and apparatus (11 percent). In terms of ownership, the enterprise sector accounted for 45 percent, the household sector 38 percent, the public sector 12 percent, and the nonprofit organization sector 4 percent.

Of the gross asset value of the enterprise sector, 83 percent belonged to the private enterprise sector, in which industries with the greatest gross asset value were manufacturing (44 percent of the private enterprise sector); wholesale and retail (14 percent); and agricultural, forestry, and fishery (12 percent). The gross value of household assets divided into 37 percent for residential structures and 63 percent for durable and semidurable goods. The net asset value, ¥160 trillion ($447 billion), was distributed somewhat differently from the gross asset value.

—— Keizai Kikaku Chō, ed, Kokufu chōsa hōkoku (1970).
KOGIKU Kiichirō

Natori

City in central Miyagi Prefecture, northern Honshū, 11 km (7 mi) south of Sendai. Natori developed as a POST-STATION TOWN on the highway Ōshū Kaidō. Fishing and farming are its principal occupations, although the city serves today as one of the satellite cities of Sendai. The largest mounded tomb (KOFUN) in northeastern Japan, the Raijinyama Tomb, and several other kofun attest to early settlement of the area. Pop: 49,716.

Natsuigawa

River in southeastern Fukushima Prefecture, northern Honshū, originating in the central Abukuma Mountains and flowing southeast to enter the Pacific Ocean at the city of Iwaki. The river is part of a prefectural natural park. Length: 67 km (42 mi).

Natsume Sōseki (1867–1916)

Novelist and scholar of English literature. Real name Natsume Kinnosuke; born in Tōkyō. With rare insight, Sōseki scrutinized Japan's "civilization" and the psychology of intellectuals caught between the contradictions of life in a backward country during modern times. At first his style was florid and pedantic, combining the traditional haibun (essay style employed by HAIKU poets, usually studded with haiku) and kambun (Chinese prose) styles with European modes of expression. Eventually he developed a more colloquial and flexible prose style better suited to examine the depths of human psychology. In terms of literary achievement and influence, Sōseki ranks with MORI ŌGAI (1862–1922) as a major figure in modern Japanese literature.

Biography —— The eighth and last child of Natsume Kohyōe Naokatsu and his wife, Chie, Sōseki was sent to a foster home immediately after birth. He was brought back to his parents once but eventually was adopted by his foster family, the Shiobara. Because of discord between his foster parents and changes in the Natsume family's situation, Sōseki went back and forth between the two houses for his whole childhood. The death of his mother in 1882, when he was 15, and of his two oldest brothers in 1887 intensified his sense of insecurity. His early education included intensive studies in classical Chinese. By the time he entered the English department of Tōkyō University, he had already decided to become a scholar of English literature. There he began to compose haiku under the influence of MASAOKA SHIKI (1867–1902), who had entered the university at the same time to major in Japanese literature. When he graduated, Sōseki was tormented by "a feeling of insecurity, as if deceived by English literature," but stayed on two more years for graduate work. In 1895 he taught at Matsuyama Middle School, Ehime Prefecture, and in the following year at the Fifth Higher School in Kumamoto Prefecture.

Sōseki went to England as a government student in 1900. There he suffered serious bouts of depression as a result of solitude and poverty, but from these torments he gradually formed the framework of his work *Bungakuron* (1907, Literary Theory), which was based on "the resolution to think of oneself first." On returning home in 1903, he replaced Lafcadio HEARN at the First Higher School and at Tōkyō University and lectured on literary theory and literary criticism.

During that period Sōseki continued to contribute haiku, *renku* (haiku-style linked poetry), *haitaishi* (poetry similar to *renku* but with a set theme), and *shaseibun* (literary sketches) to the haiku periodical HOTOTOGISU, founded by his friend Masaoka Shiki and later headed by TAKAHAMA KYOSHI (1874–1959). In the meantime, the first part of his novel *Wagahai wa neko de aru* (1905; tr *I Am a Cat*, 1961), which was completed in December 1904, was well received by members of *Hototogisu* and printed in the January issue of that periodical. This inspired Sōseki to write more fiction. While the novel continued in installments, Sōseki wrote short stories, including "Rondon tō" (1905, Tower of London). His 1906 works *Botchan* (Little Master; tr *Botchan*, 1972) and *Kusamakura* (Grass Pillow; tr *The Three-Cornered World*, 1965) established his reputation as a novelist. In 1907, deciding to devote himself entirely to writing, he quit all his teaching jobs and joined the newspaper *Asahi shimbun*. During the time he worked for the *Asahi*, he wrote approximately one full-length novel per year.

In the summer of 1910, while at Shuzenji spa, he vomited blood from a gastric ulcer and remained bedridden until the following year. During his illness he wrote *Omoidasu koto nado* (Things I Recall, Etc), which probes his experiences on the brink of death. For the remaining four years of his life, Sōseki continued to write despite his illness. He also took a strong interest in the new literary generation and supported the members of the SHIRAKABA SCHOOL and *Shinshichō* group. In Sōseki's later years AKUTAGAWA RYŪNOSUKE, KUME MASAO, Matsuoka Yuzuru (1891–1969), and others became staunch followers of his literary principles; they created a literary circle called "the Sōseki mountain range" by later generations. When Sōseki died in 1916, the obituaries in the press were much longer than those of General ŌYAMA IWAO, who had died at the same time.

Works —— *I Am a Cat* (1905), a humorous narrative, written from the viewpoint of a cat, is a biting satire on human lives distorted by a "civilized" society. While *I Am a Cat* was being published in installments, Sōseki wrote the seven short stories collected in *Yōkyoshū* (1906). These are mostly fantasies in a restrained and elegant style, which contrasts with the wordiness of *I Am a Cat*. *Uzurakago* (1906, Quail Basket), the collection of fictional works after *Yōkyoshū*, includes *Botchan, Kusamakura,* and *Nihyakutōka* (The Typhoon; tr *Nihyakutoka*, 1918). Journeys and idealized main characters are themes common to these works. The adventures of *Botchan* appealed to popular tastes. The above works, along with *Nowaki* (1907, The Tempest), are generally classified in the early period of Sōseki's literary life.

Sōseki's major literary interests began to develop in the works published in installments by the *Asahi shimbun,* and gradually his writings assumed a distinctive character. The first installment novel, *Gubijinsō* (1907; tr *Red Poppy*, 1918), criticizes modern civilization through its portrayal of various types of youths. This motif is continued in his other Meiji-period works, especially *Sanshirō* (1908; tr *Sanshirō*, 1977) and *Sorekara* (1909; tr *And Then*, 1978). *Sanshirō,* utilizing the "stream of consciousness" technique, with which he had already experimented in *Kōfu* (1908, The Miner), studies the shifting psychological state of the main character Sanshirō. At the same time it shows the bewildering array of social relationships in life with its

Natsume Sōseki

Sōseki as photographed in September 1912, shortly before he began writing the novel *Kōjin* (The Wayfarer).

depiction of an individual among intellectuals of different ages in a modern city. The bitterness of lost love that the modern youth Sanshirō tastes contrasts with the absurdity of the youthful experiences recalled by his mentor Hirota. This contrast demonstrates Sōseki's understanding of the changing times.

Nagai Daisuke, the main character of *Sorekara,* seems a further development of Sanshirō, this time in the role of a lover. But Daisuke also possesses Hirota's clear view of civilization. After a reunion with a woman he once loved who is now married to someone else, Daisuke becomes involved in an illicit relationship. The experience threatens his intellectual purity to the point of destruction. Sōseki here seems to equate morality with the established social order, whose norms inhibit human nature.

Sōseki's middle period also includes *Mon* (1910, The Gate; tr *Mon,* 1972). At this time he also wrote a group of short pieces on dreams and psychology. These include "Bunchō" (1908; tr "The Paddy Bird," 1951), "Yumejūya" (1908; tr "Ten Nights of Dreams," 1974), and "Eijitsu shōhin" (1910, Spring Day's Small Pieces). In these pieces Sōseki's style became even more polished and versatile.

The serious illness at Shuzenji marked the beginning of Sōseki's late period. His criticisms of civilization in the middle period are somewhat softened, while the analyses of the thinking of intellectuals are extremely thorough. In such characters as Sunaga Ichizō in *Higansugi made* (1912, Until after the Equinox), Nagano Ichirō in *Kōjin* (1913; tr *The Wayfarer,* 1967), and Sensei in *Kokoro* (1914, The Heart; tr *Kokoro,* 1957), Sōseki intensifies his examination of the solitary, intense, and even occasionally demented mind. With this shift in emphasis, the youths of the Sanshirō type, such as Tagawa Keitarō, Nagano Jirō, and other earlier narrators, became less important. Like Sensei, the protagonist in *Kokoro,* Sōseki remained interested in portraying the plight of his contemporaries who lived isolated from the world while still uniquely and ineluctably tied, by love or hate, to their time, the Meiji era.

The next work, *Michikusa* (1915; tr *Grass on the Wayside,* 1969), further develops the theme of an intellectual's sufferings in the context of changing human relationships. This novel contains striking autobiographical elements and shows the author's attempt to criticize himself. The shifting between a subjective examination of the self and an objective view of others, is further developed in Sōseki's final and unfinished work *Meian* (1916; tr *Light and Darkness,* 1971). The main characters, Tsuda Yoshio and Onobu, represent a new type of husband and wife who are tied together by what they believe to be love. Their love is gradually transformed by their relations with others. The novel breaks off when Tsuda leaves for a spa after his illness to meet his old lover. In this dramatization of inevitable crises in ordinary human relationships, Sōseki reached the peak of his creative powers. *Meian* surveys transitions in the age and changes in social class and measures the influences of these social and historical factors on the human consciousness. With its grand scope *Meian* demonstrates the potential of the Meiji-period novels analyzing the state of society. Sōseki died just before completing this project. While working on *Meian,* he composed a poem in classical Chinese every day. It is said that these poems express the idea of *sokuten kyoshi* ("become one with heaven, liberated from the self"), which he longed for in his later years. See also the section

on Natsume Sōseki and Mori Ōgai in LITERATURE: modern fiction.
🔖——*Sōseki zenshū,* 16 vols (Iwanami Shoten, 1965). *Sōseki bungaku zenshū,* 11 vols (Shūeisha, 1967). Etō Jun, *Sōseki to sono jidai* (1970). Komiya Toyotaka, *Natsume Sōseki* (1938).

UCHIDA Michio

nattō

Food product made by fermenting steamed soybeans with the *nattō* bacillus for several days. The bacillus breaks up the protein in the soybeans, leaving it soft, sticky, and brown. A valuable source of protein, vitamin B_2, and enzymes, *nattō* was first made in the later part of the Edo period (1600–1868). It is usually eaten mixed with minced scallions *(negi),* mustard, raw egg, and soy sauce as a side dish for rice. Being easily digested, *nattō* is also used as a baby food.

ŌTSUKA Shigeru

natural disasters

The most destructive of natural disasters in Japan are EARTHQUAKES. The TŌKYŌ EARTHQUAKE OF 1923 alone left over 100,000 dead and tens of thousands injured. In Japan's recorded history there have been 17 earthquakes that caused at least 1,000 deaths each, and 7 that caused over 5,000 deaths. In most of these cases the major destruction was caused by fires or tidal waves that followed the tremors. The most destructive natural disasters, after earthquakes, are the numerous autumn TYPHOONS. The typhoon which struck Ise and Ōsaka bays on the Pacific coast of western Honshū in 1959 left 5,041 people dead or missing. Damage was increased by the onslaught of huge waves upon the cities of Ōsaka and Nagoya. Although there were no large-scale disasters in the 1970s, annual damage attributed to natural disasters was estimated at between ¥480 billion (US $1.7 billion) and ¥1.45 trillion (US $5.1 billion), and the average number of dead or missing persons was 250 per year.

In 1962 the government passed the Basic Disasters Prevention Law (Saigai Taisaku Kihon Hō). This was supplemented in 1978 by enactment of the Large-scale Earthquake Special Measures Law (Daikibo Jishin Taisaku Tokubetsu Sochi Hō) and the Active Volcano Special Measures Law (Katsudō Kazan Taisaku Tokubetsu Sochi Hō).

🔖——Kokudochō, ed, *Bōsai hakusho* (annual). Satō Takeo et al, *Saigairon* (1964).

JIMBO Genji

natural features → Japan

naturalism

(shizen shugi). A significant Japanese literary movement begun around 1906 and lasting through the 1920s. Strongly influenced by its late 19th-century European model, naturalism in Japan stood in opposition to subjectivism, imaginative escapism, and classicistic posturing by earlier Meiji period (1868–1912) writers, and sought to depict modern society and the lives of the men and women who compose it as objectively and truthfully as the subject matter of science is studied and presented.

In the beginning, Japanese naturalists borrowed freely from the works of the French naturalists, namely Flaubert, the Goncourt brothers, Maupassant, and above all Zola. Even before the publication of TAYAMA KATAI's *Futon* (1907, The Quilt), which is regarded as one of the first and most important works of Japanese naturalism, such writers as KOSUGI TENGAI, NAGAI KAFŪ, OGURI FŪYŌ, and KUNIKIDA DOPPO had written novels and short stories that adhered, at least in part, to the principles formulated by their European forerunners. In these very early efforts, care was taken to write in a style marked by an objective, detached method of narration and scholarly care in documentation of historical background. Their subjects, for the most part, were drawn from the lower strata of society and no detail of their sordid, unhappy lives was spared.

In these early works of Japanese naturalism, as in those of their French predecessors, emphasis was placed on the social environment of the characters and the totally subordinate relation of the individual human beings to it. In these works, there is a pervading sense of the control exerted over the actions and destinies of the characters by impersonal social, economic, and biological forces. Human free will is shown as weak and almost completely ineffectual.

Although many such works, adhering to the principles laid out by Zola, were published in Japan before the Russo-Japanese War of 1904–05, it was not until SHIMAZAKI TŌSON's *Hakai* (1906; tr *The Broken Commandment,* 1974) and Katai's *Futon* that Japanese naturalism took its own shape and set its own course. In the two above works and others, what the authors wanted was not merely realism and objectivity in style as much as simple "naturalness" in opposition to what they saw as overuse of flowery language and plot contrivances by mainstream writers of the day. They wanted genuine heartfelt sentiment and expression, and above all preferred unabashed confession to purge their main character—often the author himself, thinly disguised—of all that is not well. In time, owing to the confessional nature of these and similar works, Japanese naturalist fiction came to be known as the *watakushi shōsetsu* or I-NOVEL.

The main characteristics of Japanese naturalism as seen in the works of such writers as Tōson, Katai, IWANO HŌMEI, and TOKUDA SHŪSEI are: (a) emphasis on simple family situations rather than on heroism or historic events; (b) the complete avoidance of didacticism or artificiality in dialogue and the use of dialect where appropriate; (c) the avoidance of monologues and asides; (d) the avoidance, as much as possible, of obvious plot contrivance; and (e) "confession," or outpouring of the innermost feelings of the main character.

Although naturalism in Japan was overwhelmed by the overriding element of confession and went the way of the I-novel, the naturalist emphasis on genuineness of expression and respect for the individual experience was not forgotten. Perhaps more than any other literary movement, naturalism left an indelible mark on modern Japanese fiction.

James T. KENNEY

naturalization

(kika). The process whereby one who is not a Japanese citizen ("an alien") acquires Japanese citizenship. The permission of the minister of justice must be obtained for naturalization. Application for citizenship can be made through the district legal affairs bureau *(chihō hōmukyoku)* that has jurisdiction over the area in which the applicant resides. The application requires submission of documents certifying that the applicant meets certain qualifications for naturalization. When application is made on behalf of an alien under 15 years of age by a legal representative, documents that certify the applicant's competency must also be submitted.

Under the provisions of the Nationality Law (Kokuseki Hō) of 1950, an alien who desires to be naturalized must fulfill the following requirements: he or she must have maintained a domicile *(jūsho)* in Japan for five or more consecutive years; be at least 20 years old and legally competent according to the law of his or her native country; be of good character; have sufficient means to support himself or herself; have no other citizenship or surrender any other citizenship upon acquiring Japanese citizenship; and never have plotted or advocated the overthrow of the constitution or government of Japan and never formed or belonged to a party or other organization that has plotted or advocated the overthrow of the constitution or government of Japan.

The minister of justice may grant exceptions to the above requirements in the following cases. The five-year residency requirement is reduced to three years for the husband of a Japanese citizen, the natural child of a Japanese citizen, or the natural child of someone born in Japan. The residency requirement is eliminated in the case of a person born in Japan whose natural father or mother was born in Japan.

The residency, age, and self-support requirements may be eliminated for: the wife of a Japanese citizen, the natural child of a Japanese citizen who has a domicile in Japan, the adopted child of a Japanese citizen who has resided in Japan for one year or more and was a minor according to the law of his or native country at the time of adoption, or someone who has lost Japanese citizenship (except for those previously naturalized in Japan) and has a domicile in Japan.

The minister of justice, with the approval of the Diet, may also grant citizenship to an alien who does not fulfill any of the above requirements if that person has rendered especially meritorious service to Japan.

The minister of justice informs the applicant by public notice in the OFFICIAL GAZETTE *(Kampō)* when citizenship has been granted. The citizenship is effective from the date of issue of the public notice. See also FOREIGNERS, LEGAL STATUS OF.

Akira SAKAI

natural monuments and protected species

(tennen kinembutsu). The Japanese term *tennen kinembutsu* usually translated as "natural monument," has a wider range of meaning than any one English equivalent. In the strict sense it refers to natural objects and phenomena (including species of animals and plants) characteristic of, or peculiar to, Japan that have been designated for preservation under the CULTURAL PROPERTIES LAW of 1950 or similar local laws. These include certain geological or mineral formations and areas, other than national parks, of special historic, scenic, or scientific interest, all of which would be referred to as natural monuments in English, as well as certain species of animals and plants found only in specific areas of Japan, which, being protected by law, would be called protected species in English. The term is also used loosely to refer to any such natural objects or species whether designated by law or not. This article is limited to a discussion of legally protected natural monuments and species.

Natural monuments and protected species are classified into two categories: those designated for preservation by the national government under the Cultural Properties Law and those set aside for protection by the laws of local public bodies such as prefectures, cities, towns, and villages.

Particularly important and scientifically valuable natural properties have been designated as *tennen kinembutsu* according to the provision of art. 69 of the Cultural Properties Law. These include animals (along with their natural habitats and breeding or migration grounds), plants (together with their indigenous locations), and geologic and mineral formations (including sites with specific natural phenomena).

Article 80 of the law provides protection for the designated monuments or species. Changes in existing conditions, or acts affecting the preservation of the monuments or species come under the purview of the director-general of the Agency for Cultural Affairs. Any violation of the provisions of this article may lead to a sentence of up to five years imprisonment, with or without hard labor, a heavy penalty for cultural laws of this kind. The law also provides that expenditures made by local governments for the investigation, protective propagation, or restoration of *tennen kinembutsu* or the purchase of land for their protection may be subsidized by the national treasury.

Protected areas. Areas of specific interest that have been set aside as *tennen kinembutsu* are classified under a number of official designations such as Nature Protection District, Primeval Forest, and Shrine Forest. Nature Protection Districts include Lake TOWADA, the river OIRASEGAWA, the Kurobe gorge (see KUROBE KYŌKOKU), the Oze, Torishima, and Kushiro bogs, and the island of Minami Iōjima (see IŌ ISLANDS). Primeval Forests include the Daisetsuzan area in Hokkaidō, with its forests of Yeddo spruce *(Picea jezoensis)* and Sakhalin fir *(Abies sachalinensis);* the SARUGAWA Headwaters Primeval Forest; and the Maruyama Primeval Forest of broad-leaved trees, including the *katsura (Cercidiphyllum japonicum).* Also noteworthy are the Kasugayama Primeval Forest in Nara, a temperate-zone forest, and the Aso Kitamukidani Primeval Forest of chinquapin *(Pasania cuspidata)* and *tabu no ki (Machilus thunbergii).* One Shrine Forest is the Miyazaki Kashima Forest, a temperate-zone forest in the Shimo Shinakawa District, Toyama Prefecture.

Animals. Indigenous species of Japanese wildlife designated as protected species include the *Amami no kurousagi* (see RABBITS), the *meguro* (Bonin honeyeater), and the giant salamander (see SALAMANDERS). Though not indigenous species, the Japanese crested ibis, short-tailed albatross, the Japanese crane, and the Japanese stork are limited in distribution to certain areas. Other *tennen kinembutsu* include cranes and their migration grounds in Kagoshima Prefecture, the natural habitat of SEA BREAMS in the waters of Taino-ura in Chiba Prefecture, and the breeding grounds of HORSESHOE CRABS in the waters around the city of Kasaoka, Okayama Prefecture. Naturalized species include the magpie and turtle dove and domestic birds and animals, such as certain varieties of fowl, the Misaki horse bred in Toimisaki in Miyazaki Prefecture (see HORSES), Mishima cattle bred in Mishima, Yamaguchi Prefecture (see CATTLE), and the long-tailed cock bred in Kōchi Prefecture.

Plants. Certain rock-zone flora found in specific locations, such as the group of plants of the Ishimakiyama limestone zone indigenous to the city of Toyohashi, Aichi Prefecture, and the Apoidake alpine plant group in Hokkaidō, are also counted as *tennen kinembutsu.* The boundary zones of distribution of certain plants found only in limited areas, such as the southern boundary zone of the Ehime iris (native to Numata Nishi District in the city of Mihara in

Hiroshima Prefecture) and the southern boundary zone of species of iris (native to the town of Kurino in Kagoshima Prefecture) are also classified as *tennen kinembutsu.* A great number of very old or very large individual trees have also been designated as natural monuments.

Geologic formations that have been designated as national monuments include the group of cirques (deep steep-walled basins) at YAKUSHIDAKE, the limestone cave known as AKIYOSHIDŌ in Yamaguchi Prefecture, and the upthrust coasts of Kisakata in Akita Prefecture. A number of unique mineral formations and fossil sites have also been designated.

➤——Bunkachō Bunkazai Hogobu, ed, *Tennen kinembutsu jiten* (1981). Bunkazai Hogo Iinkai, ed, *Tokubetsu shiseki tennen kinembutsu zuroku* (1963). SHINADA Yutaka

natural resources

One of the most remarkable aspects of the post-World War II "economic miracle"—Japan's rapid economic growth after 1955—is that Japan is very poor in natural resources. The epithet "poor little Japan" is a fitting one in terms of energy resources and almost all of the major materials needed for modern industry. Japan's industrial complex, the third largest in the world after the late 1960s, has been built on one of the weakest resource bases of all the industrialized nations. Despite great efforts to increase the domestic production of key raw materials, Japan's overall dependence on imported raw materials stood at roughly 90 percent in 1980 and continues to grow each year. Barring some major technological breakthrough, such as a successful program for the separation and use of hydrogen from the seas, there is little likelihood that Japan will be able to reduce its dependency on imported materials. Any significant expansion in production of most raw materials appears to be both economically and geologically impossible.

Though Japan is surprisingly rich in the variety of her resources (it is sometimes called a "museum of minerals"), the size and quality of most of the deposits limit production to small fractions of the nation's requirements. The degree of dependency on foreign sources can be illustrated by the following figures from the 1970s: petroleum, 99.8 percent; coking coal, 88 percent; bauxite, 100 percent; uranium, 100 percent; nickel, 100 percent; iron ore, 99.4 percent; copper, 76 percent; and lead, 46 percent. Japan also relies on outside sources for 100 percent of its raw cotton, wool, and rubber, as well as large and growing amounts of forest products, agricultural commodities, and even some varieties of seafood. The large increase in Japan's dependency on foreign sources is almost exclusively due to the exceptionally high rate of economic and industrial growth since the mid-1950s. In almost all cases, domestic resources were inadequate or barely adequate before rapid growth, and Japan had no other choice but to turn to foreign sources. And, in many cases, imported raw materials were of a better quality and cheaper than the domestic products. Even in the case of coal, one of the resources in relative abundance, domestic production has dropped by more than half because of the high cost and low quality in comparison to imported coals, especially coking coal.

The explosive growth of industry along with the demands of the new affluent society has put a heavy strain on energy sources in Japan. In addition to the annual industrial growth rates of 20 percent or better during some years, most Japanese families were able to purchase refrigerators, washers, and television sets, among other appliances. This too has greatly increased the demand for energy. Periodic shortages along with sharp rises in production costs have made the energy industries a top priority for government planning and support.

Coal——Japan's coal reserves were estimated at about 8 billion metric tons in 1975, tiny in comparison to the USSR or the United States but relatively abundant compared to most Japanese resources. Annual production in the late 1970s was about 19 million metric tons, down sharply from the 50 to 55 million metric tons of the 1950s and 1960s. The largest and most productive fields are poorly located at opposite ends of the country in Hokkaidō and Kyūshū, at considerable distances from the industrial heartland that stretches from the Tōkyō area to Kōbe. Transportation costs from the mines to the major markets add considerably to the relatively high costs of production. Until very recently the Chikuhō fields of Kyūshū produced the largest volume of coal because of generally better quality, closeness to tidewater, and closer proximity to Japan's major centers of heavy industry. With the exhaustion of many of the richer and more accessible seams, the center of production has shifted to the

Ishikari and associated fields of Hokkaidō. Other important coal fields are at Jōban, well situated northeast of the Tōkyō metropolitan markets and Ube in westernmost Honshū across from the industrial complexes of the Kita Kyūshū area.

Japanese coal is generally low-grade bituminous and is low in heating value. High-grade coking coal supplies are negligible and virtually all the nation's needs must now be imported. Coal seams are generally thin, deep below the surface, badly broken, steeply inclined, and plagued by inflammable gases. Mechanization is difficult and expensive and working conditions in many of the mines are very hazardous. High costs of production, relatively dangerous operations, loss of life in mining disasters, bitter labor-management strife, and competition from oil and other energy sources have all led to a sharp drop in production and in the number of mines and miners. The coal-mining labor force dropped from about 244,000 in 1960 to roughly 23,000 in 1975 and the number of operating mines declined from 682 to 39. The rationalization program that has closed marginal mines and where possible mechanized operations did result in a sharp rise in productivity, but the market for domestic coal has continued to slump and the future of the industry is much in doubt even with government subsidies and the sharp increase in the cost of petroleum. Plans call for an annual output of about 20 million metric tons in the 1980s. Some Japanese coal companies are looking to new or expanded joint ventures with foreign producers to increase the import of higher-grade, cheaper foreign coal. Stockpiles of domestic coal continue to plague the industry. Any major program to replace oil with coal would add enormous costs to the economy, and production levels like those in the United States would soon exhaust Japan's reserves. See COAL; MINING.

Petroleum and Natural Gas —— Japan's petroleum refining industry is the third largest in the world, and virtually all crude oil must be imported, primarily from the Middle East, with smaller flows from Indonesia and China. The paucity of crude oil and the recent sharp increases in price have been especially troublesome to Japan because of its unusually heavy dependence on petroleum, about 75 percent of the energy supply, in comparison with most other major industrial nations. The largest part of the trickle of domestic oil comes from the Niigata fields located along the northwest coast of Honshū. Other smaller and scattered fields are located mainly in northern Honshū and Hokkaidō. The newest and apparently most productive field is the Aga Oki offshore development about 11 kilometers (7 miles) off the coast of Niigata Prefecture. Several groups of companies are now test drilling for offshore fields along the continental shelf between Hokkaidō and Kanazawa. While there is little hope for any new and large onshore discoveries, there is continued optimism over offshore exploration along the continental shelf. Agreements reached with South Korea in the late 1970s may open large areas to offshore exploration, possibly as a cooperative effort between the two nations. Japanese rigs have been exploring off the northeast coast of China and there has been great interest in Japan over the possibility of major joint ventures along the shelf of the Yellow Sea and the East China Sea.

Small natural gas fields and wells are scattered about, with the largest concentrations in Hokkaidō, northern Honshū, and the Chiba area in close proximity to the huge markets of the Kantō area. A natural gas pipeline now connects the Niigata fields with Tōkyō and petroleum pipelines are planned or under construction in northern and central Honshū to tie the producing area with the major markets along the Pacific coast from Sendai to the Kōbe area. As in the case of the coal industry, most of Japan's increased demand for petroleum and liquefied gas will have to come from foreign sources. Joint development programs with petroleum surplus countries, such as Japan's participation in the offshore area between Kuwait and Saudi Arabia, have high priority with both private industry and governmental agencies in Tōkyō. See PETROLEUM; PETROCHEMICAL INDUSTRY.

Hydroelectric Power —— High and rugged terrain, generally abundant precipitation, and fast flowing streams have made it possible for Japan to develop one of the world's largest hydroelectric industries. While hydroelectric plants are found throughout the country, the heaviest concentrations are located in central Honshū close to the center of the industrial belt between Tōkyō and Kōbe. In the past, because of Japan's rugged topography, short, swift streams, and narrow valleys, most hydroelectric plants were of rather small scale and used the natural flow of the stream to generate electricity. It was therefore necessary to supplement production with thermal power during periods of low water, usually in the winter, and during peak load periods in the summer. A few large-scale

plants, dams, and reservoirs were built after World War II, but few such sites are available because of the country's geography. Hydroelectric plants produced the largest share of Japan's electricity in the past, but less than a quarter in 1980. The enormous growth in demand for electricity in the postwar era and the high cost of constructing dams and hydroelectric facilities led to an accelerated program for the development of thermal power—accounting for nearly 70 percent of the total output of electricity by 1980. The future of the hydroelectric industry is unclear. While possibly half of the hydroelectric potential remains to be developed, the remaining sites are in more marginal locations, and the costs of constructing plants, reservoirs, and transmission facilities will be much higher than for those sites already developed. Further hydroelectric construction will depend in large part on the relative cost of competing sources of energy, especially oil and nuclear power. See DAMS.

Nuclear Power and Alternative Sources —— Japan is among the leading nations in the development of nuclear power plants. Given the enormous growth in demand for energy, the lack of oil, the high cost of coal, and marginal quality of potential hydroelectric sites, nuclear power seemed to many to offer the greatest hope for easing Japan's energy crisis. Though Japan lacks uranium ore and must import its nuclear fuel from abroad, the hope for cheap power from a relatively small volume of fuel led the nation's planners to embark on a major program in the construction of nuclear plants. Some 14 atomic reactors had been built by 1978 and seven more were in various stages of construction. The Japanese government's long range economic planning projected a nuclear energy industry that would increase its proportion of the nation's electricity output from less than 5 percent in the early 1970s to one-quarter by 1985 and more than one-third by 1990. The construction of nuclear power plants has stalled, however, and the very future of the industry is in considerable doubt. Sharp increases in the cost of construction, growing concern about the safety of atomic reactors, defects in equipment and subsequent shutdowns, and growing resistance from many communities to the building of plants has resulted in at least a temporary moratorium on expansion of the industry. The near disaster at the Three Mile Island nuclear power plant in Harrisburg, Pennsylvania, in 1979 added new fears about the safety of the industry in general and US equipment and technology in particular. The Japanese nuclear industry relied heavily on American-designed reactors, and there is growing debate over whether Western European technology may be safer and more appropriate to Japanese needs.

Assuming the development of plants that will reach safety levels acceptable to the government and the public, nuclear energy could become a major growth industry again. If the industry is revitalized, Japan is planning an expansion of its uranium enrichment and reprocessing capability and eventually the development of fast breeder reactors.

Although only a small fraction of the nation's energy can be met through alternative energy sources, research and development is proceeding in several areas. These include solar, geothermal, gasification and liquefaction of coal, and the separation and use of hydrogen from the sea. When and if any of these new sources become major factors in Japan's energy production depends on the success of future technology and the relative costs of production. See NUCLEAR ENERGY POLICY; ENERGY INDUSTRIES.

Metals and Minerals —— As in the case of energy sources, Japan's metal resources have become almost totally inadequate for the world's third largest industrial complex. The magnitude of the demand for metals can perhaps best be measured in terms of industrial production and world ranking. Japan is the leading shipbuilder, in some years responsible for better than half of all the world's new tonnage, and surpassed the United States in the production of automobiles in 1980 with an output of over 11 million vehicles. It ranks third in steel production with a 1977 production of 102 million metric tons and a capacity of 140 million metric tons, just behind the USSR and the United States. Japan is also the world's largest exporter of steel and automobiles, and on a per capita basis produces more steel than either the USSR or the United States. One can add to the above the world's third largest aluminum industry with a production of over 1 million metric tons per year, a consumer durables industry which has made it possible for most Japanese homes to have color television sets, refrigerators, electric washing machines, sewing machines, and vacuum cleaners at a household diffusion rate second only to the United States. A significant portion of many of the durables is also exported. The size of Japan's deposits of metal ores makes it literally impossible to reduce the dependence on overseas supplies. Short of a great depression or some other catastrophe,

Japan's needs for imported metals will be much larger in the future than in the 1970s, even with a slower industrial growth rate than in the past. One study by the Ministry of International Trade and Industry forecast Japan's 1980 demand at 30 percent of all raw materials and mineral fuels entering international trade.

Taking the steel industry as a key example, Japan is dependent on imported iron ore for over 99 percent of its requirements. With a 1974 production of about 102 million metric tons of crude steel, imported iron ore amounted to about 125.5 million metric tons of the total 126.2 million metric tons consumed in Japanese blast furnaces. Imported iron ore comes from several sources with Australia and Brazil being the major ones. Of the total consumption of just over 65 million metric tons of coking coal, about 58 million metric tons were imported, a foreign dependency rate of about 88 percent. The bulk of the ferro-alloys that went into the steel also came from foreign sources. Dependency on scrap iron was only about 9 percent as the Japanese steel industry includes an unusually large number of giant blast furnaces, about 60 in all, with the emphasis on pig iron production for the oxygen converters that now produce most of Japan's steel. As one of the most affluent countries in the world, Japan also generates a large volume of scrap.

As part of the nation's program to produce as much domestic material as possible, Japan has developed three sources of iron for its steel industry. These include iron ore, pyrite cinder, and native iron sands. Most of the domestic iron ore, about 600,000 metric tons per year, comes from small mines scattered from Hokkaidō through Tōhoku to central and western Honshū and northern Shikoku. The ore is of rather low grade and requires beneficiation to upgrade it for the blast furnaces. Iron pyrite cinder is a by-product of the sulfuric acid industry, and the annual output, though small like iron ore, represents a minor saving in imports. Iron sands have also contributed a tiny fraction of the steel industry's iron. In the case of all three domestic sources, the reserves simply cannot add any significant amount to the iron supply. The estimated reserves of iron ore, about 70 million metric tons, is roughly equal to a year's production in the United States. See IRON AND STEEL; IRON AND STEEL INDUSTRY.

Other Metals and Minerals —— More than 1 million metric tons of aluminum is produced in Japan; production is totally dependent on imported materials, with Australia as the largest supplier of bauxite. Even in the case of copper and zinc, two metals in which Japan was in the past self-sufficient, foreign resources are now necessary to maintain current production. More than 75 percent of the raw materials used in the production of copper is imported, with the two largest suppliers of ore being the Philippines and Canada. The zinc industry imports 55 percent of its raw materials, primarily from Peru, Canada, and Australia. Domestic supplies of lead amount to about 45 percent of demand with Canada as the major source of imports. Foreign dependency on nickel is complete, and only minor fractions of demand for antimony, mercury, chromium, molybdenum, and magnesite are supplied from domestic mines. Phosphate rock is also a major deficiency in Japan's resource base. Deposits of sulfur and sulfide ores, limestone, and graphite are abundant and are important basic materials for many industries including Japan's large and diversified chemical industries. See NONFERROUS METALS INDUSTRY.

Wood and Pulp —— Japan's forests cover about 60 percent of the land area and comprise one of the nation's major resources. With Japan's range in climatic zones, from Hokkaidō with long, cold, snowy winters in the north to the subtropical south, many different forest types are represented. Species such as spruce, larch, and fir are found in Hokkaidō and northern Honshū. Conifers and broadleaf mixed forests are dominant in central Honshū and include chestnut, birch, maple, pine, hemlock, and cedar; southern Japan has a broadleaf evergreen cover with camphor, live oak, and palms. Groves of bamboo are common in the warmer zones.

The forests supply materials for homes, utensils, furniture and, largely in the past, charcoal. Lumber supplies have grown tight and wood products are relatively expensive, forcing Japan to look to outside sources for about 60 percent of its lumber by the late 1970s. The forests also supply a large volume of wood for one of the world's largest producers of pulp, paper, rayon, and other products. As in the case of lumber and plywood, domestic production is no longer adequate and imports now loom large, comprising roughly 10 percent of consumption. Imports of wood products and pulp come mostly from North America, Southeast Asia, and the Soviet Union.

In addition to supplying materials for construction and manufacturing, Japan's forests are a valuable resource in protecting the nation's soils, rivers, and reservoirs and in preventing floods and erosion. With the growth of affluence and the booming tourist industry, forest lands have become increasingly valuable as parks and scenic spots.

While the Japanese have traditionally been more aware of forest conservation than most of their neighbors in Asia, the heavy demands on the forest have led to overcutting and have created serious problems in some areas, especially Hokkaidō. New and expanded programs of reforestation are needed for both future supplies of wood and watershed and soil protection. Any major expansion of wood and pulp production would result in heavy environmental damage to Japan, and wood imports seem to be a permanent part of the long and growing shipping list. See FORESTRY.

Prospects —— Virtually all of Japan's natural resources are of such a small size as to make it impossible to expand production without exhausting or seriously depleting them in a very brief period of time. One estimate of Japan's total practical coal reserves is 3.25 billion metric tons; if they were mined at the current rate of production in the Soviet Union, they would be exhausted in about five years. Compared to the other two super-industrial powers, the United States and the Soviet Union, Japan's resource base is pitifully weak and fragile. In short, Japan's position vis-à-vis natural resources is that of an almost totally "have-not" nation. In terms of key materials and fuels, more than 90 percent must be imported. Japan can best be described as an "international workshop." There is no possibility of economic survival without continued access to foreign resources on a global scale. No single nation or area could possibly supply the variety and volume of materials needed by Japan.

Throughout the postwar era, Japan's policy has been to expand and diversify its sources of raw materials and fuels. The programs have generally been successful, and Japan imports materials from all corners of the world. In the case of coking coal, for example, closer ties with Australia and Japanese investments in that country have resulted in a major expansion of Australian coking coal exports to Japan, until they equal coal imports from the United States.

Many people in Japan are hoping for major increases in imports of materials from China, including petroleum, which could help lessen the nation's dependency on Middle Eastern crude oil, which stands presently at about 85 percent. Sino-Soviet tensions have raised interesting questions for Japan in terms of Siberian or Chinese materials and energy. After many long and difficult negotiating sessions with Moscow, promising programs for joint Japanese-Soviet development of Siberian resources have been suspended, at least for the foreseeable future. Greater access to China and Siberia, two of the most promising areas with large surpluses of materials, will depend to a major degree on future political relations between Moscow and Beijing (Peking) and their respective views on Japanese joint ventures with the other.

Another major aspect of Japan's search for resources is its increasing participation in overseas resource development projects, either unilaterally or in cooperation with other industrialized nations, to help develop basic resource industries and export capability. Investments and exports of technology to Southeast Asia, the Middle East, Latin America, and Africa have become an important part of Japan's search for materials, especially over the past decade.

Finally, Japan's extraordinary industrial growth took place during a period of expanding trade along with an abundance of relatively cheap raw materials and fuels. The supply situation has grown tighter and the cost of many key materials has risen sharply, especially since the early 1970s. The quadrupling of crude oil prices by the OPEC nations was a severe blow to the Japanese economy, and continuing price increases pose a severe threat to future economic growth. Whether Japan can afford to increase its imports in the future, at the high rates now charged, is a serious problem for the nation's planners. Tighter supplies and increasing competition for these materials is one of Japan's most serious challenges in the coming decades. International competition for scarce or expensive resources is growing, not only from the rich industrialized nations but also from such nations as South Korea and Taiwan. Both are increasingly competitive with Japanese industry, and each requires larger and larger amounts of imported materials.

■ ——Isaiah Frank, ed, *The Japanese Economy in International Perspective* (1975). International Society for Educational Information, *Atlas of Japan: Physical, Economic and Social* (1970). Japan Institute for International Affairs, *White Papers of Japan, 1971–72* (1973). Kawata Publicity, *Japan's Iron and Steel Industry* (1976). Saburō Ōkita, *Japan in the World Economy* (1975). The Oriental Economist, *Japan Economic Yearbook* (annual). Tsuru Shigeto et al, *Nihon keizai chizu* (1954). Glenn T. Trewartha, *Japan: A Geography*

(1965). Akira Watanabe, *The Geography of Japan* (1957). The Yano Tsuneta Memorial Society, *Nippon: A Charted Survey of Japan* (annual).   Robert B. HALL

natural sciences

(shizen kagaku). Natural science in Japan faced a critical time of change in the latter half of the 19th century, particularly after the Meiji Restoration in 1868. Before 1868, under the NATIONAL SECLUSION policy of the Tokugawa shogunate, the development of traditional science as well as of WESTERN LEARNING followed what may be called an indigenous pattern. With the opening of the entire country to foreign influences, science developed more freely and began to parallel modern Western science in content and quality.

Chinese Influences——It goes without saying that natural science as it is understood in the West did not exist in ancient Japan. It was only in the 7th century, when cultural influence from China became stronger, that science in its present sense came into being. It was an exact copy of Chinese science and included mathematics, astronomy, and medicine—subjects common in most ancient cultures. Medicine and astronomy were usually associated with fortune-telling and magic and covered a broader range of subjects than what is considered to be science today.

The curriculum of studies at the Japanese court, like its bureaucratic system, was a small-scale replica of the Chinese mode. Students were obliged to read Chinese classics, such as the *Zhou bi suanjing (Chou pi suan-ching)* for astronomy and the *Jiu zhang suanshu (Chiu chang suan-shu)* for mathematics. Minor Korean influences were reflected in some texts. The courses were initially conducted by Korean immigrants (see KIKAJIN). They were eventually succeeded by native Japanese, but it is highly doubtful that anything resembling a systematic course of studies was established.

Toward the close of the 9th century, it was decided to stop sending embassies to China (see SUI AND TANG [T'ANG] CHINA, EMBASSIES TO). The Chinese system remained in form only, and astronomy, mathematics, and other studies as well as connected offices became the hereditary prerogatives of certain families.

Parallel to this development of scientific studies was the development of Buddhist influence throughout the ancient and medieval periods. Among Buddhist monks, studies that were distinct from Chinese court culture were introduced through the sutras. In medicine, for example, the notable doctors were Buddhist monks. Tantric Buddhism, which held *genshō riyaku* ("doing good in the present life") as its motto, was introduced to Japan, and the monks doubtless used their knowledge of herbs as a way of spreading their religion. In astronomy and calendrical science, the monks made horoscopes according to Indian astronomical illustrations contained in the Chinese text *Xiuyaojing (Hsiu-yao-ching)*. Indian astronomy was in competition with traditional Chinese calendrical science for predicting solar and lunar eclipses.

Introduction of Western (Namban) Culture——The culture that had been imported from China during the 7th–9th centuries was assimilated into a distinctive Japanese style. Other than this, little occurred in the sciences until the 16th century, when Jesuit missionaries arrived in Japan. Unlike the case in China, however, the scientific knowledge introduced by the Jesuits did not have a great impact in Japan. Matteo Ricci (1552–1610) and his fellow missionaries sought to influence the Chinese court with their knowledge of Western astronomy and succeeded in converting traditional Chinese calendrical science into Western-style calculation. This was not the case with Japan: the missionaries who came to Japan some 30 years earlier than Matteo Ricci's visit to China had no intention of influencing Japan with their knowledge of astronomy. Moreover, in Japan court astronomy was not at the center of the governmental system as it was in China, and so the Jesuits did not consider astronomy as an important means of converting the Japanese. It should also be noted that 16th-century Western astronomy was not much more advanced than Chinese or Japanese astronomy. Western astronomy had some influence, however, especially navigational astronomy.

In medicine, new methods of surgery were introduced. Western surgery became the major current in surgical practice, though it should be added that 16th-century surgery was concerned primarily with staunching bleeding and stemming infection.

Early Edo Period——In the early Edo period (1600–1868), feudal rule was established, and Confucianism was welcomed among the ruling *samurai* class. In astronomy, the Shoushi (Shou-shih) calendar of the Yuan (Yüan; 1271–1368) dynasty was adopted with some alterations to form a new Japanese calendar, the Jōkyōreki, which was adopted in 1684, effective 1685. Solar and lunar eclipses were predicted according to Japanese methods of calculation. However, at least until the first half of the Edo period, calendrical science depended mainly on traditional Chinese astronomy.

In the field of medicine, Jin –Yuan medicine, therapeutic methods used in China during the Jin (Chin; 1125–1234) and the Yuan dynasties, was widely used. At the beginning of the 18th century, a more clinically centered medicine was used, which marked a departure from Chinese methods. See also MEDICINE: history of medicine.

In the end of the 17th century and the beginning of the 18th, mathematics was developed by men such as SEKI TAKAKAZU, who created their own schools. Going beyond practical mathematics these scholars of WASAN (Japanese traditional mathematics) solved geometric problems using algebraic formulae. *Wasan* attracted many who enjoyed mathematics simply as an intellectual game, especially in the 19th century.

It was against this background that Western astronomy became the focus of interest. Since astronomical phenomena are universal and have an objectivity of their own, it was easier to compare the accuracy of astronomical methods, such as the prediction of solar eclipses. It was because of this that the Jesuits had been able to convince the Chinese of the superiority of Western astronomical methods. This was now realized by the Japanese, who had regarded China as their model. Throughout the Edo period, the Japanese, who were traditionally receptive to foreign cultures, were to ponder whether Western or traditional Chinese knowledge was superior.

As for astronomy, the Japanese now decided that Western science was much more advanced. For this reason, in 1720, the eighth shōgun, TOKUGAWA YOSHIMUNE, abrogated the law banning Chinese literature about the West, especially Christianity, which had been enforced throughout the first half of the 17th century. Dutch books on science were also permitted to enter Japan.

The cancellation of the law did not mean that the shogunate now encouraged the study of natural science; it was the shogunate's intention to keep a monopoly on Western knowledge. Nonetheless, many scholars were inspired to study Dutch, and it was through their acquaintance with Western astronomy that they became convinced of the superiority of Western science.

Modern Science and Western Learning——The names Copernicus, Galileo, Kepler, and Newton always come to mind in talk about men who shaped the mainstream of modern science. The Copernican theory was introduced into Japan by Motoki Yoshinaga (1735–94), a translator who worked with Dutch merchants in Nagasaki. Motoki translated a Dutch book on Copernicus and published it as *Oranda chikyū zusetsu* in 1771. The original book contained some passages concerning the relationship between Christianity and Copernicus, and thinking that the theory had something to do with Christianity—then banned in Japan—Motoki excised all the parts dealing with the religion. In 1774 Motoki translated another work, Willem J. Blaeu's *Tweevoudigh Onderwijs van de Hemelshe en Aardsche Globen* and published it as *Tenchi nikyū yōhō*. Blaeu had introduced the Copernican theory in his work, but Motoki referred to it simply as the heliocentric theory and avoided a complete translation. The Copernican theory was presented in full scale with the translation in 1792–93 of a Dutch version of George Adams' *Treatise Describing and Explaining the Construction and Use of New Celestial and Terrestrial Globes* (1766).

The Chinese literature on Western knowledge that came to Japan contained no reference to the Copernican theory. This was mainly because the Jesuits who went to China consciously distorted Copernicus's teachings, and as a result his name was not associated with the heliocentric theory. In Japan, therefore, it was not the astronomers, but the Dutch translators who came to know and accept the Copernican theory.

There are three ways of viewing the Copernican theory. The first is from a purely astronomical point of view. In China, Copernicus was introduced solely as a specialist in astronomy. Copernican astronomy, however, was not taken seriously in Japan. The second is from the cosmological or geometrico-morphological viewpoint. Heliocentrism, obviously, is the basic tenet of "cosmological Copernican theory." The third is from the viewpoint of physics and dynamics. In the Chinese cultural sphere the process of *qi (ch'i; J: ki)*, the energy in motion in the universe, was more important than the form or structure of the universe. In fact, in Chinese cosmology, there was a tradition of looking down upon morphological theory and of placing emphasis on function and force working in the universe. Thus in Japan, too, "heliocentric theory" was translated as *chidōsetsu*, or the moving earth theory. The structural or spatial relationship between the sun and the earth was not important. Rather, the Japanese (and the Chinese) were fascinated by the analysis of the dynamics based on the polar concept, the concept of earth-heaven or motion-motionlessness, stemming from the *yin-yang* philosophy of traditional China. The term "moving earth theory" was coined by SHIZUKI TADAO, a student of Motoki. The term was later exported to China and the Chinese cultural sphere, and even today, it is used to express the Copernican or heliocentric theory.

Galilean theory was not introduced to China by the Jesuits because of its conflict with Christianity. It failed to influence Japan directly, because by the time the Japanese started reading Dutch books in the latter half of the 18th century, Galileo's name had been absorbed into Newtonian mechanics. Shizuki was the first to introduce Newtonian mechanics in Japan, as well as in Asia. He had already written books introducing Western science, but he decided to translate John Keill's *Introductiones ad veram Physicam et veram Astronomiam* (London, 1739), not only because Keill's book had become available to the Japanese in Dutch translation, but also because it included the philosophical arguments following the establishment of Newtonian mechanics. Shizuki was interested in finding a metaphysical basis for Newtonian mechanics in East Asian philosophy and hoped to formulate an original natural philosophy that would combine both *ki* (ch: *qi*) monism and Newtonianism. Newtonian physics was far beyond his understanding, and he found it impossible to fit neatly together the principles of the *Yi jing (I ching)*, *ki* monism, and Newtonianism.

In both China and Japan, where the universe was viewed in more relative terms than in the West (see NATURE, CONCEPT OF), the Copernican theory was accepted without much opposition; it was simply a shift in emphasis. In contrast, Newtonianism was too heterogeneous to be grasped within the scope of traditional scholarship. Finding that Newtonian physics lacked a metaphysical foundation and only described phenomena, Shizuki attempted to introduce the idea of *ki* monism into Newtonian physics, but it simply did not work. Newtonianism tried to reduce everything to particles and their motion, and a reductionist principle was utterly alien to East Asian thought. Furthermore, the *Yi jing* and *yin-yang*, which formed the philosophical foundation of traditional East Asian science in the Edo period, played a decorative rather than a functional role. Thus the attempt to use traditional metaphysics as the basic principle for modern Western science ended in failure.

At the same time the reductionist method of Newtonianism was useful in explaining individual phenomena. Again, there existed a hierarchy of theory and application in Newtonianism, and this hierarchical view of scholarship in terms of theory and application was to be taken up by later scholars of Western studies, especially professional physicians. Physicians, unlike astronomers and translators in government, were relatively free agents. In Japan, as a group they were the only scientific professionals. The kinds of modern scientists and technologists who were beginning to emerge in the West were completely unknown in 18th- and 19th-century Japan. Among the physicians were many translators of books on modern science. In their translations, especially in the prefaces, they emphasized that physics was the basis of all science, including medicine, and explained the relationship between theory and application. That is, they explained that physics was the basis of physiology, that physiology was the foundation of medicine, and that the knowledge of practical cures was based on them all. It is doubtful whether such a view was fully understood by their readers. Actually, for all practical purposes what physicians practicing Western medicine needed was enough knowledge of physics and chemistry to prepare medicinal compounds.

From the point of view of natural history, Western studies did not strongly impress the Japanese; natural history was merely a matter of certain differences between East and West. However, the emphasis of natural philosophy on hierarchy, universality, and methodology was welcomed as something that had not existed in traditional science. The scholars of Dutch learning gave it the name *kyūri* (Ch: *qiongli* or *ch'iung-li*, "to understand the principle"). It was a direct translation of the Dutch term *natuur kunde* (nature physics). The word already existed in the vocabulary of Zhu Xi (Chu Hsi) philosophy and must have been chosen by the scholars because they wanted to take part in the respect and authority enjoyed by the Zhu Xi school (see SHUSHIGAKU). Their choice of *kyūri* was also an indication that they correctly understood the idea of natural philosophy in Western science.

After the middle of the 18th century physicians led the way in studying Western science. They first looked to anatomy. In Chinese medicine, physiology and pathology were explained in terms of *ki* (ch: *qi*), the energy that permeated the universe. There was no need for an accurate science of anatomy and there was no solidist tradition. In the *koihō* or classicist school of medicine in Japan, however, the necessity for taking a solidist approach was perceived and autopsies were carried out. In 1774 SUGITA GEMPAKU, the scholar of Western learning, published a translation of a Dutch textbook of anatomy, but it was more to advertise the superiority of Western medicine than for practical application. The translation also served as a catalyst for Japanese medicine to change from the *ki* theory of pathology to a solidist pathology.

Learning, then, was primarily concerned with medicine, but in the middle of the 19th century, as foreign ships approached Japanese shores and the necessity for national defense increased, the emphasis shifted to military technology. The samurai class, especially, began to study Western firearm technology as a necessary part of its profession.

Science after the Meiji Restoration——With the Meiji Restoration, Japan embarked on a program of Westernization. The idea of modernizing science and technology had already been present in the tradition of Western learning, but its application was not systematic. The feudal lords of several domains, such as Satsuma (now Kagoshima prefecture), tried to update their armies toward the end of the Edo period, but these efforts were sporadic and undertaken at individual initiative. Under the new Meiji government scientific education was institutionally organized. The term for science was *kagaku* instead of *kyūri*. *Kagaku* originally meant the study of every branch of learning and did not imply any specialization. This term was used first in a written plan of INOUE KOWASHI, who became minister of education in 1893. He wrote, "first study language, then study *kagaku*," meaning that one should study Western languages and then master specific disciplines in the original language. As opposed to *kyūri*, which was a cognitive term, *kagaku* was an institutional one and reflected well the basic intent of the Meiji government's policy. In other words, Western science during the 18th and the 19th century had been accepted by scholars of Western learning as a form of natural philosophy, while for Meiji policymakers, who were much more interested in its specific application, it was a means to an end. In the early 19th century, some scholars had already held that Confucian studies lost out to Western studies because they were not specialized, and Meiji leaders hoped to learn from this. First, a modern school system was established, and colleges offering courses to train specialists were founded. This approach was characteristic of Western scientific education at the time.

The Meiji government stopped supporting traditional studies such as astronomy, *wasan,* and Chinese medicine (*kampō;* see MEDICINE: traditional medicine). It invited Western lecturers, sent students abroad, and had them teach specialized courses when they returned to Japan. Until 1880, basic projects were initiated by the government, mainly to meet the requirements of a modern nation. These projects were carried out by Japanese who had been educated by foreign teachers and by the foreign teachers themselves and included the measurement of Japanese longitude and latitude, installation of nationwide communication lines, the making of sea charts, geological surveys, and the establishment of railroads. By the latter half of the 1880s, the first generation to receive a proper college education and to enter the scientific profession had come of age.

The scientists of the first generation were not capable of basic research; they were rather administrators who worked to establish the infrastructure of higher education and research. The only research that reached international standards was that undertaken during their studies abroad. In contrast, the second generation who received their education under the new system experienced the frustration of not being able to find proper research facilities or posts.

In Japan, as in the United States, during the two world wars scientific research was carried out by universities, companies, and government. Of these only the laboratories at national universities enjoyed high prestige. Professors could detach themselves from educational duties to concentrate on research. The INSTITUTE OF PHYSICAL AND CHEMICAL RESEARCH (Rikagaku Kenkyūjo), which was founded in 1917 on the model of the Kaiser Wilhelm Akademie in Germany, is still considered the ideal research institution.

During World War II, science in Japan suffered from being cut off from foreign sources of information. The Japanese military and government, which had previously relied on foreign technology, had to depend solely on Japanese scientists and technologists. Research funds were increased and in a sense for the first time technologists and scientists were given an opportunity to express their identity as a group. However, as Japan's war position deteriorated, scientific research came to a virtual standstill.

Science in the Postwar Era—— Under the OCCUPATION, the SCIENCE COUNCIL OF JAPAN was established with the guidance of Harry C. Kelly (1908–76), assistant head of the Science and Technology Section of SCAP (the headquarters of the Allied Occupation in Japan). Members elected from the scientific community at large sat on the council. The Japanese scientific world, which had remained inactive long after the war, only started to recover in the latter half of the 1950s. In the 1960s, stimulated by technological innovation abroad and rapid economic growth at home, the Japanese scientific community expanded greatly. Several Western nations decreased their budget for scientific research in the latter half of the 1960s, but West Germany and Japan slowly increased their scientific budgets.

One characteristic of scientific research in Japan is that research funds come mostly from private investment. This is because companies were reorganized and expanded greatly after the war, and military research was forbidden under the 1947 constitution. After the 1973 oil crisis, research investment by private companies temporarily decreased, but investment by the public sector has steadily increased. In Japan, unlike the United States and Soviet Union where projects such as space research are promoted for national prestige, research has centered on projects with high economic returns. However, rapid economic growth in the beginning of the 1970s has led to environmental problems such as pollution. The opinion that scientific research should not be left in the hands of the private sector and that a comprehensive science policy should be thought out is gaining support. See also ASTRONOMY; BIOLOGY; CHEMISTRY; EARTH SCIENCES; MEDICINE: medical research; and PSYCHOLOGY IN JAPAN.

—— Shigeru Nakayama, *A History of Japanese Astronomy: Chinese Background and Western Impact* (1969). Shigeru Nakayama, *Characteristics of Scientific Development in Japan* (1977). Shigeru Nakayama, "Japanese Scientific Thought" in *Dictionary of Scientific Biography* 15 (1978). S. Nakayama, D. Swain, and E. Yagi, *Science and Society in Modern Japan* (1974). E. Smith and Y. Mikami, *A History of Japanese Mathematics* (1914). M. Sugimoto and D. Swain, *Science and Culture in Traditional Japan, A.D. 600–1854* (1978). *Shigeru* NAKAYAMA

nature, concept of

The basic, etymological meaning of the Japanese word *shizen*, which is used to translate the English word "nature," is the power of spontaneous self-development and what results from that power. The Chinese characters for the Japanese term *shizen* literally mean "from itself thus it is." It expresses a mode of being rather than the existence or "nature" of objects in the natural order.

The term *shizen*, if understood as a general expression encompassing heaven and earth, including mountains, water, animals, and plants, cannot be found in ancient Japanese. This was not due to any lack of a capacity for abstract thought on the part of the Japanese people in ancient times, but because their chief concern was to recognize each and every phenomenon as a manifestation of the KAMI (god or gods) behind it. It was hard for them to think of the everflowing wind and the immovable mountains as all belonging to the same general classification of nature. It is safe to say that the "articulated" thought process of the Japanese (which is reflected in their polytheism) tied up with their aesthetic sensibility to separate the universe into its elements and, consequently, to forestall simplified generalizations about it. If we insist, however, on finding generic terms for nature in the ancient literature, we can offer comprehensive expressions like *ametsuchi* (heaven and earth) and *ikitoshi ikerumono* (living things).

In the mythology of the NIHON SHOKI (720) nature and man are related as if in one family. The first offspring of Izanagi and Izanami were neither *kami* nor human but islands and land masses. Human beings do not stand opposed to nature as in Western thought. Neither are they superior to it. Their lives are embedded in it.

This classical idea may be seen expressed in various Japanese cultural forms such as Zen paintings, literati art works, the tea ceremony, and flower arrangement, all of which had their roots in Chinese culture and thought. In nature, subject and object become fused into one reality, a fact that also served as a reason for the frequent use in poetry of the various seasonal flowers, animals, and sights.

The idea of nature as so many expressions of the power of spontaneous self-development is also found in medieval Japanese Buddhism. When salvation was viewed as a necessity consequent upon "the vow of the Tathagata, and not as a result of the practitioner's exercises," *shizen*-nature became SHINRAN's (1173–1263) *jinen*, another expression for the impersonal being of the formless Amitābha Buddha (AMIDA). (*Jinen* and *shizen* are different readings of the same Chinese characters.)

Attempts to understand nature according to laws were made in later periods. In the Edo period, YAMAGA SOKŌ (1622–85) wrote of the inevitability of nature, by which he meant that the universe, by necessity, is as it is. MIURA BAIEN (1723–89) and ANDŌ SHŌEKI (1703?–62), tried to describe the universe as an orderly whole in terms of law. But this was not yet a conception in abstract terms. It was only after the beginning of the Meiji period (1868–1912) that the Western concept of nature signifying the natural order came to be attached to the term *shizen*. *IMAMICHI Tomonobu*

nature in Japanese religion

There is in Japan no specific social institution or segment of people devoted to beliefs and practices venerating nature, so it is misleading to speak of "nature worship"or a "religion of nature" in Japan. Nevertheless, the peculiarly Japanese appreciation of nature has played an extremely important role in the cultural and religious life of the Japanese people. This appreciation is found in both SHINTŌ and BUDDHISM, as well as in popular religious practices, and has been a major source of inspiration in literature and the arts in general. No English term adequately describes the many aspects of the religious appreciation of nature in Japan, and even in borrowing the English word "nature," we must be sure not to impose certain Western philosophical and religious notions upon the concrete details of the Japanese tradition. The most important of these, in contrast to the Japanese view, is the Western, especially Christian, tendency to place God above man and nature and to place man outside nature.

In Japanese the word most frequently used to refer to nature is *shizen*, and in the modern usage it may refer to the physical world or the entire created world. The term is an ancient compound of two Chinese characters read *ziran (tzu-jan)*, meaning "naturalness" or "spontaneity," which appeared in Chinese writing as early as the *Daodejing (Tao-te ching)*, a famous Chinese Taoist text attributed to the legendary Laozi (Lao-tzu; ca 6th century BC). In both the Chinese and Japanese world views, there is less distance between man and the divine realm than in the Western (Judeo-Christian) monotheistic tradition, and nature is elevated to a very lofty position. Nature is seen in terms of the divine or sacred, and a major thrust of Chinese and Japanese culture has been to consider man's proper place as being within the lap of nature.

Even before Chinese literary and philosophical traditions reached Japan in the mid-6th century, some features of the Japanese appreciation of nature were already in strong evidence. From prehistoric times the Japanese people seem to have venerated KAMI or gods, which most often were seen as the sacred powers within nature. In the KOJIKI and NIHON SHOKI, two early semimythological chronicles of Japanese history, the *kami* are portrayed as taking an integral part in the creation of the Japanese islands. Rituals were closely related to the passing of the seasons, especially to the cycle of rice agriculture (see AGRICULTURAL RITES). As Shintō developed into a more highly organized religion there emerged more formal festivals for honoring the New Year and the various stages of rice agriculture from transplanting to harvesting and also festivals related to other aspects of the natural economy, such as fishing. On a mundane level, enthronement ceremonies for a new emperor have been timed to coincide with the natural cycle of the rice harvest. Thus religion in early Japan was already closely attuned to the powers and patterns of nature, even though a specific "nature religion" did not emerge.

Religious celebration of the sacred power of nature and specific natural objects in Japan was never divorced from an aesthetic appreciation of nature. As early as the 8th century, the sacredness and beauty of mountains, streams, and other natural objects was lauded in the MAN'YŌSHŪ, the first great anthology of Japanese verse. In later works, such as the early-11th-century TALE OF GENJI, sensitivity to the nuances of nature in its seasonal cycles is one of the main thematic elements. Landscape painting, too, has always enjoyed the highest reputation in China and Japan. Not only Taoist influence, but also Buddhist, particularly Zen influence, is seen in much of the painting and poetry extolling the sacred beauty of the landscape. The Japanese Buddhist emphasis upon man's enlightenment within the realm of nature, or even through the power of naturalness, may be a reflection of indigenous Japanese views of nature. Both Shintō and Japanese Buddhism feature rites of purification and asceticism in natural surroundings such as sacred mountains, waterfalls, and sea water (see MISOGI). Even Confucian notions of man's subservience to heaven (Ch: *tian* or *t'ien;* J: *ten*) may be supported by ancient Japanese agricultural notions of indebtedness to the bountifulness of nature.

Although views of nature differ somewhat in Shintō and Buddhism, and from age to age, some general patterns cut across several traditions and various periods. First, nature is revered for its sacredness and beauty in its own right, not through secondary importance as a creation of divinities. Second, nature is revered not so much as an abstract entity but more concretely in terms of specific mountains, trees, and streams in particular locales. Third, both humans and *kami* are understood as dwelling within nature, rather than above or outside it; ideally human beings and *kami* participate cooperatively in the joyous celebration of the harmony and fruitfulness of nature. Fourth, although nature has its dark side, with calamities and disasters, this is just one aspect of a duality also reflected in the ambiguous character of human motivation and even in malevolent deities. Such principles as these have seldom been written down in the Japanese tradition because, as Shintō writers like to emphasize, they are more readily experienced as directly perceived sentiments than as logically demonstrated propositions.

While the principles listed above constitute the traditional ideal of nature in Japan, this ideal, like so many others, has not always been realized. In fact, since the late 19th century, when industrial development expanded rapidly, pollution has become an increasingly serious problem, especially because industrial wastes in Japan are concentrated over such a small land and sea mass.

Non-Japanese are apt to ask how such pollution is allowed to occur if the Japanese ideal of nature has been so high. The answer is not altogether clear; nevertheless, we can suggest some changed factors in the modern setting that help explain this contradiction. For one thing, Japanese people have become increasingly separated from the agricultural cycle, there now being relatively few full-time farmers. Generally speaking, the agriculturally based Shintō appreciation of nature is much diminished in modern Japan. Thus, as in most technologically developed countries, nature has become desacralized in Japan. However, if the sacred aspect of nature is on the wane, the aesthetic ideal of natural beauty is still very much alive. Many urban Japanese still idealize the beauty of nature, but in compartmentalized pockets, as any visitor to Tōkyō who has escaped the noise and air pollution of a crowded street to relax in a tea garden tucked away in a wooded corner of the city can attest.

The aesthetic appreciation of nature in Japan, with its roots in the religious celebration of nature, is still prominent in modern Japan. The writing and reading of poetry praising natural beauty is a popular pastime for many modern Japanese. Similarly, such arts as the TEA CEREMONY, flower arranging (*ikebana),* and cultivating dwarf trees (BONSAI) flourish as popular hobbies. These arts are a living testimony to the rich Japanese tradition of venerating nature, and many persons outside Japan have adopted these arts as a means of expressing their own aesthetic appreciation of nature.

■——H. Byron Earhart, "The Ideal of Nature in Japanese Religion and Its Possible Significance for Environmental Concerns," *Contemporary Religions in Japan* 11.1-2 (1970). William R. LaFleur, "Saigyō and the Buddhist Value of Nature," *History of Religions* 13.2 (1973), 13.3 (1974). Tsuda Sōkichi, "Outlook on Nature," in Tsuda Sōkichi, *An Inquiry into the Japanese Mind as Mirrored in Literature,* tr Matsuda Fukumatsu (1970). H. Byron EARHART

Naumann, Edmund (1854–1927)

German geologist; known as the father of Japanese geology. One of the first teachers of geology at Tōkyō University (1875–85), Naumann conducted geological surveys in many parts of Japan. He is famous for his identification of the FOSSA MAGNA (Great Fissure Zone), which vertically divides the main island of Honshū southwest to northeast. At Naumann's suggestion, the Ministry of Agriculture and Commerce in 1878 established a geology department (now the GEOLOGICAL SURVEY OF JAPAN). Entering its employment, he created the basis for geological mapmaking in Japan. His major work was *Geologische Arbeiten in Japan* (1901).

Naval Academy

(Kaigun Heigakkō). School to train officers of the Imperial Japanese Navy. Founded in Tsukiji, Tōkyō, in 1869 and moved to Etajima in

Hiroshima Prefecture in 1888. The academy was closed in 1945 when the navy was disbanded after World War II. Students took the academy's entrance examinations after finishing four years of middle school in the pre-1945 educational system and studied for three or four years. Upon graduation they became midshipmen, candidates for the rank of ensign, attaining that rank after a period of active duty and an overseas cruise. ICHIKI Toshio

Naval General Staff Office

(Gunreibu). Highest military organization of the Imperial Japanese Navy. It became independent of the General Staff Office in 1893. The chief of the Naval General Staff Office was directly subordinate to the emperor and was in charge of the planning of national defense and strategy. See also ARMED FORCES, IMPERIAL JAPANESE.

HATA Ikuhiko

Navy Ministry

(Kaigunshō). Cabinet ministry from 1872 to 1945. The Navy Ministry and the ARMY MINISTRY (Rikugunshō) were established in April 1872 under the DAJŌKAN system of government to replace the Ministry of Military Affairs (Hyōbushō), which was dissolved at that time. Initially the ministry was in charge of both administration and command of the navy, but in May 1893, when the Naval General Staff (Kaigun Gunreibu) was established as a separate organ of command, the ministry was left with only administrative functions. It was abolished in November 1945 and replaced by the temporary Demobilization Ministry (Fukuinshō), which supervised the repatriation of Japanese military forces. See also ARMED FORCES, IMPERIAL JAPANESE.

nawabari

A figurative term meaning domain, territory, sphere of influence; literally, "rope stretching." Derived from the folk custom of land demarcation by stretching a straw rope along boundaries. In ancient times, straw rope was used to delineate an area that was supposed to be a sacred area of the gods. The rope served as a talisman against the invasion of evil spirits as well as a means of demonstrating the occupation of territory by the god.

From the Kamakura period (1185–1333) onward, *nawabari* signified the location of a military camp or the area in which a castle was to be built. *Nawabari*—along with other terms such as *shima* (island) and *niwaba* (garden)—has been used since the Edo period (1600–1868) by YAKUZA (gangsters) and gamblers to refer to their territory. The concept of *nawabari* is also important in business and bureaucratic organizations. IWAI Hiroaki

Nawa Nagatoshi (?–1336)

One of the heroes of the KEMMU RESTORATION and the paradigm of loyalty to the emperor in prewar Japanese historical writing. Nagatoshi was a member of a powerful warrior family in Hōki Province (now Tottori Prefecture). In 1333, when Emperor GO-DAIGO escaped from his exile on Oki Island and landed in Hōki, Nagatoshi organized forces that helped to destroy the regime of the HŌJŌ FAMILY. For his role in restoring the emperor to his throne in Kyōto, Nagatoshi was appointed to important posts in the Records Office (Kirokusho) and the Office of Imperial Guards (Musha-dokoro), two vital organs of Go-Daigo's restoration government. When ASHIKAGA TAKAUJI turned against Go-Daigo and attacked Kyōto in 1336, Nagatoshi was one of the loyalist generals who chased him to Kyūshū; when Takauji returned later in the year, Nagatoshi again fought in defense of the emperor, this time at the cost of his life. After the Meiji Restoration of 1868, the Nawa Shrine in Tottori Prefecture was built in his honor. The play *Nawa Nagatoshi* (1913) by KŌDA ROHAN is another monument to his memory.

Naya Sukezaemon → Ruson Sukezaemon

Nayoro

City in northern Hokkaidō. One of the most important cities of the Nayoro Basin. Products include potatoes, medicinal herbs, and dairy goods. Paper and lumber factories are located here. A unit of the Ground Self Defense Force is stationed in the city. Pop: 35,031.

nayosechō

A kind of land register used in premodern Japan. In the Kamakura (1185–1333) and Muromachi (1333–1568) periods, *nayosechō* were ledgers prepared for the purpose of tax collection by estate (*shōen*) proprietors. Based on land surveys conducted by these proprietors, the *nayosechō* documented the types and sizes of fields and the amounts of tax to be levied, according to the names of the local landholders (MYŌSHU), who were responsible for the payment of the taxes. In the Edo period (1600–1868) the term came to refer to basic ledgers used to assign the annual tax to the farmers within a village. These were prepared by village officials based on the *kenchichō* (land survey ledger) and recorded the type, size, and yield of each piece of cultivated land within the village according to names of the owners.   *UEDA Nobuhiro*

Naze

City on the island of Amami Ōshima in the Amami Islands. Administratively a part of Kagoshima Prefecture, Kyūshū. It is the administrative, economic, and cultural center for the Amami Islands. Its subtropical climate is suited for growing bananas, papaya, and pineapples. Ōshima *tsumugi*, a silk weave, is a well-known local product. Pop: 49,023.

nazo nazo → riddles

NCR Japan, Ltd

(Nippon NCR). Company engaged in the manufacture and sale of cash registers and other business machines. Established in 1920. It also engages in the import and sale of computers made by National Cash Register (NCR) of the United States, which holds 70 percent of its stock. Its cash registers have contributed to the modernization of shop management in Japan. The company began to diversify its business during the 1960s to include accounting machines, adding machines, and data processing equipment. In the 1970s it developed and started selling electronic cash registers. Sales for the fiscal year ending November 1981 totaled ¥69.7 billion (US $311.5 million) and the export ratio was 10 percent. In the same year the company was capitalized at ¥8 billion (US $35.7 million). Corporate headquarters are located in Tōkyō.

Nebuta Festival

(Nebuta Matsuri, or Neputa Matsuri). One of many festivals held during, and associated with, the BON FESTIVAL season. The most famous Nebuta festivals are held in the cities of Aomori and Hirosaki in Aomori Prefecture. Between 1 August and 7 August large floats are carried or rolled on wheels through the city in the evening, with the townspeople singing and dancing to musical accompaniment. The floats have enormous paper images of popular or legendary characters and are lit from the inside, making them glow eerily in the dark. After the procession the floats are thrown into a river or the sea. The festival originated in a kind of purification rite in which paper images of human beings, straw boats, paper lanterns, or other objects were cast away on a river as a means of sending away illness or bad fortune (see TANABATA FESTIVAL). Such festivals, which can be found all over Japan, are called *nemurinagashi* (literally, "floating away sleep"). There is no doubt a connection between the name Nebuta and the "*nemuri*" (sleep) of this word.   *INOKUCHI Shōji*

negi → Welsh onion

negoro-nuri

(Negoro lacquer). A type of lacquer ware characterized by a red lacquer surface rubbed to reveal an underlying layer of black. The term *negoro-nuri* is derived from lacquer ware made and utilized from the end of the 13th century onward by the priests of Negoroji, a temple in Kii Province (now Wakayama Prefecture). These were originally monochrome lacquer wares, but with repeated handling the surface layer of red was worn away in uneven patches, producing a striking contrast of red and black lacquer. The simplicity of shape, the quality of the lacquer and, above all, the irregularly worn surface of the lacquer and the contrasting colors became highly prized and widely imitated. The term *negoro-nuri* has been ex-

tended to include lacquer ware in which this surface effect is deliberately rather than randomly achieved. Although the term is derived from the distinctive lacquer ware of Negoroji, wares of a similar type were made before the founding of the temple in 1140 and after its destruction in 1585. There are no surviving lacquer wares from the Negoroji itself. See LACQUER WARE.   *Julia HUTT*

neighborhood associations

Informal, quasi-governmental, or mandatory neighborhood associations have played an important role in Japanese society at various times in its history. GONINGUMI (literally, "five-man groups") were established throughout the country during the Edo period (1600–1868); first utilized as a mechanism for social control, they later developed into vehicles for local self-help and self-governance. The *goningumi* lost their legal status after the Meiji Restoration (1868), but informal ties remained. New associations, called CHŌNAIKAI (neighborhood associations) emerged after 1920, and these were made mandatory by the government in 1940. At the same time, smaller groups called TONARIGUMI (neighbor groups) were also established; both were used for social control, mobilization, and such functions as rationing. Both *tonarigumi* and *chōnaikai* were abolished by Occupation authorities after World War II, but unofficial associations once again operate in many traditional urban areas and rural towns; these serve a number of social functions and tend to be closely aligned with conservative political parties.

nekki

Children's game for two or more players. A tree branch or bamboo root, cut to a length of about 30 centimeters (1 ft) with one end sharpened, is driven into the ground. Players attempt to knock down the stick by tossing their own sticks against it. Iron spikes are also used. This game has been played since ancient times and is said to have originated from the practice of driving into the earth the *nekki*, the piece of wood used to support the traditional New Year's pine and bamboo decoration (*kadomatsu*). Because of the danger of injury from the sharp spikes, the game was sometimes forbidden to children.   *SAITŌ Ryōsuke*

nembutsu

The invocation NAMU AMIDA BUTSU (I take my refuge in the Buddha AMIDA [Skt: Amitābha]), uttered in the hope of rebirth into Amida's Pure Land. This modern conception of *nembutsu* describes but one form of what was once a varied practice. In addition to this invocational *nembutsu* (*shōmyō nembutsu*), there were also contemplative *nembutsu* (*kannen nembutsu*; the practice of envisioning the characteristics of a Buddha) and meditative *nembutsu* (*okunen nembutsu* or *rikan*; meditation on Buddha-nature or the spiritual qualities of a Buddha). Moreover, *nembutsu* were sometimes directed to Buddhas other than Amida and to goals other than Pure Land rebirth, such as the cancellation of bad karma or the immediate realization of enlightenment.

Nembutsu focusing on Amida became an important practice in China soon after the introduction of Buddhism there in the 1st century AD. By the 9th century, Pure Land devotion and the cultivation of all varieties of *nembutsu* flourished in China and were brought from there to Japan by the founders of the Tendai sect. About the middle of the Heian period (794–1185), a richly ceremonial contemplative form of *nembutsu* gained popularity among the aristocracy and clergy of Japan. In 985 the most comprehensive treatment of *nembutsu* in Buddhist literature, the ŌJŌYŌSHŪ (Essentials of Pure Land Rebirth) was composed by the Tendai monk GENSHIN (942–1017). He taught that the highest form of *nembutsu* was the *nembutsu-zammai* (Skt: *samādhi*) of the Tendai school, a highly disciplined practice combining both meditative and invocational *nembutsu* with the goal of enlightenment rather than rebirth, but he also urged simple invocational *nembutsu* as a means to Pure Land rebirth for those incapable of *nembutsu-zammai*. Genshin's teachings were the point of departure for HŌNEN (1133–1212), who formulated and popularized the modern notion of *nembutsu*. In 1175 Hōnen broke away from the Tendai order, asserted the independence of the Pure Land movement, and taught that the simple utterance of the Buddha's name was the only path to salvation. The JŌDO SECT and the JŌDO SHIN SECT founded by SHINRAN took *nembutsu* as their primary religious exercise.   *Allan A. ANDREWS*

nembutsu odori

A folk dance expressing the joyfulness of those whose faith assures them salvation, through the chanting or singing of the Buddha AMIDA's name (see NEMBUTSU) or the Buddhist hymns (WASAN). Reputedly started by the monk KŪYA (903–972), the *nembutsu odori* spread widely during the Kamakura period (1185–1333), through the efforts of IPPEN (1239–89), the founder of the JI SECT of PURE LAND BUDDHISM. This dancing and chanting is said to free performers from wordly distractions, and it has also been performed to pacify the spirit of the dead at the BON FESTIVAL or to ward off evil. Its impact on Japanese traditional dance and FOLK PERFORMING ARTS in general is significant. OKUNI of Izumo (fl ca 1600), a *nembutsu odori* dancer, is reputed to be the founder of KABUKI.　　　*Misumi Haruo*

Nemuro

City in eastern Hokkaidō. It was developed in the early Meiji period (1868–1912) by colonist militia (TONDENHEI) and their families. A base for fishing in the northern seas, it has one of the largest catches of salmon, trout, and crab in Japan. Tangle is gathered on the coast. Dairy farming is a more recent development. Pop: 42,881.

Nemuro Peninsula

(Nemuro Hantō). Located in eastern Hokkaidō. Extending northwest into the Pacific Ocean, it has a hilly terrain with extensive grazing grounds. The surrounding waters are rich with salmon; the city of Nemuro, a leading urban area, is a major center for the processing of marine products. NOSAPPUMISAKI, a cape at the eastern tip of the peninsula, offers excellent views of the HABOMAI ISLANDS.

Nemuro Strait

(Nemuro Kaikyō). Strait between eastern Hokkaidō and the island of Kunashiri. Its narrowest section, the Notsuke Channel (narrowest point 16 km or 9.9 mi), is shallow and unfit for navigation by large ships. The strait freezes over in parts during the winter. The fishing ports of Nemuro and Shibetsu are located along this strait. Length approximately 120 km (74.5 mi).

nenchū gyōji → festivals

nengajō → New Year's cards

nengō

(era names; also called *gengō*). Official names or slogans, usually of good omen, applied to reigns or parts of reigns in China and the countries that adopted its writing and calendrical systems. Analogous (though unofficial) American examples include "The New Deal" and "The Great Society." In Asia they were traditionally used for dating events (see PERIODIZATION; CALENDAR, DATES, AND TIME). Although some Japanese sovereigns have reigned under only one era name (*issei ichigen;* a practice followed uniformly since 1868), most changed their *nengō* periodically for various reasons. The first Japanese era name was Taika (Great Change), instituted in 645 to memorialize the coup d'etat of that year and the ensuing administrative reforms (see TAIKA REFORM) during the reign of Emperor KŌTOKU, who in 650 changed the era to Hakuchi (White Pheasant) in celebration of the auspicious discovery of an albino of that species. Since 701 *nengō* have been used without interruption in Japan, the only country where they survive. The practice has come under criticism from time to time since the Meiji period (1868–1912), but its continuance was assured in 1979 by vote of the Diet.

nengu

(literally, "annual tribute"). The basic land tax collected from the peasantry by the proprietors of estates from the latter half of the Heian period (794–1185), and later by feudal lords (*daimyō*) during the period of warrior rule (1185–1868).

With the gradual breakdown of the RITSURYŌ SYSTEM of administration and the rise of large private estates (SHŌEN) in the 10th century, the statutory taxes (SO, YŌ, AND CHŌ) were diverted from the central government. The grain tax (*so*) was still nominally paid

Nembutsu odori

Dancers at a *nembutsu odori* held on the island of Sado in Niigata Prefecture. In this version of the dance, believed to date back at least 300 years, participants strap stone images of the bodhisattva Jizō to their backs. Brought from the nearby temple Daikōji, these images are thought to grant the prayers of the dancers.

to the imperial treasury, but the handicraft textile tax (*chō;* now called *zōkuji*) and the corvée labor tax (*yō;* now BUYAKU) were taken over by the *shōen* proprietors. As they acquired additional civil and tax immunities (FUYU AND FUNYŪ), the proprietors came to control the grain tax (now called *nengu*) as well.

Nengu was in principle collected from all MYŌSHU, the peasant-cultivators with certain rights (*shiki*) to land. They delivered the produce to *shōen* officials (SHŌKAN), who in turn forwarded it to the proprietor (RYŌSHU) with a document accounting for all tribute collected. *Nengu* was usually paid in the form of rice (from wet fields) or soybeans (from dry), but in later centuries it was sometimes paid in money.

During the Kamakura period (1185–1333), the land stewards (JITŌ) appointed to the estates by the shogunate appropriated much of the *nengu*, although they were not legally empowered to collect it. There are records of frequent clashes between proprietors and stewards over these fiscal rights. In the succeeding Muromachi period (1333–1568), the provincial governors (*shugo*) who had become great regional lords (SHUGO DAIMYŌ) usually siphoned off half of the *nengu* through the *shōen* system (see HANZEI; SHITAJI CHŪBUN). As they gained complete political control over their domains (see ICHI-EN CHIGYŌ), however, these regional lords (now SENGOKU DAIMYŌ) carried out land surveys and devised their own systems of taxation.

In 1582 the national hegemon TOYOTOMI HIDEYOSHI undertook a systematic land survey (see KENCHI) with an eye to completely reorganizing the tax-collection system. Each parcel of land was evaluated according to its yield in terms of *koku* (1 *koku* = about 180 liters or 5 US bushels) of rice. The combined assessment figure (KOKUDAKA) was determined for each village and the tax base determined accordingly. The peasant cultivators (HYAKUSHŌ) were taxed directly, two-thirds of their crop going to the government. A rice surcharge (*kuchimai*) was also levied, at a rate of 2 *shō* (about 3.6 liters or 3.3 quarts) per *koku*. The basic outlines of Hideyoshi's tax system were to remain in force through the Edo period (1600–1868) and beyond, until the enactment of the LAND TAX REFORM OF 1873–1881.

The nomenclature of land taxes varied greatly from period to period. During the Edo period, for example, the basic tax levied on rice was known as *honnengu* or HONTO MONONARI, and the surcharge as KUCHIEI AND KUCHIMAI. Miscellaneous taxes on forest, field, and marine products were known collectively as KOMONO-NARI, temporary taxes as UKIYAKU, taxes on merchants and fishermen as UNJŌ or MYŌGAKIN, and additional taxes on villages (varying according to the rice yield) as *takagakari mono*. The basic land tax was generally paid in rice, although in shogunate-held domains (TENRYŌ) it could be paid in either money or grain.

The basis for assessment also varied widely according to period. During the Edo period two methods were employed. The earlier method, called KEMI or *sebiki kemi*, based assessment on an annual inspection of yield per *tan* (1 *tan* = about 0.1 hectare or about 0.25 acre). It was replaced by the less burdensome JŌMEN assessment, which relied on the average yield over several years and was fixed

Nemuro——Nemuro Harbor

The city of Nemuro sits on the Nemuro Peninsula at the extreme eastern tip of Hokkaidō. Its proximity to the rich fishing grounds of the northern Pacific Ocean makes it an ideal port for the fishing boats that pack its harbor.

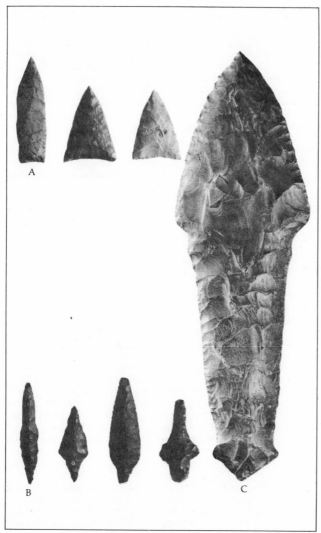

Neolithic period——Stone tools

A: Three arrowheads excavated from the Fukkirizawa site, Aomori Prefecture. 3 cm (right). Incipient Jōmon. B: Four arrowheads excavated from the Terashita site, Aomori Prefecture. 3.6 cm (right). Final Jōmon. C: Spearhead excavated from the Kasaneishidaira site, Fukushima Prefecture. 21 cm. Early Jōmon. Keiō University, Tōkyō.

for a period of 3 to 10 years. Once the tax base was established, the local shogunal intendant (DAIKAN) notified each village in writing of its tax quota. The share of individual cultivators was determined by the villagers themselves at a meeting. Taxes were delivered to the *nanushi,* one of the three leading village officials *(murakata san'-yaku),* at a specified time. They were then forwarded to the *daikan* or the domainal lord, who acknowledged receipt with a document *(nengu kaisai mokuroku).*   ŌGUCHI Yūjirō

nenki

In legal history a term generally meaning period or era, a person's age, or a period of time from a certain point in the past until the present. From the last of these senses it took on—from the end of the Heian period (794–1185) through the Muromachi period (1333–1568)—the more specific meaning of a period of limitation of rights regarding real estate. Also known as *nenjo,* this period of limitations was fixed by the GOSEIBAI SHIKIMOKU, the fundamental code of the Kamakura shogunate (1192–1333), at 20 years. When suits involving land ownership were contested in the courts of the Kamakura shogunate and it was proven that the land in question had either been occupied by one party or not occupied by the other party for a period of 20 years, it was usual to hold under the *nenki* law that the current state of possession remain unchanged, regardless of the contestant's claim to the original title. However, the *nenki* law was not applied to lawsuits regarding the seizure of estates by military stewards (JITŌ), or lands owned by shrines or temples.

It is thought that the Kamakura shogunate enacted the *nenki* law mainly in order to protect its direct vassals by guaranteeing their current landholdings and to prevent the regime from being undermined by numerous lawsuits regarding landownership that arose in the wake of the JŌKYŪ DISTURBANCE of 1221. The *nenki* was thus essentially a part of the *samurai* code (BUKEHŌ) but was later used by some estate proprietors. In the Muromachi period (1333–1568) a similar system was adopted in the legal code of the imperial court nobility *(kugehō).*

Nenki also refers to a land trade in use from the Kamakura period through the Edo period (1600–1868), also called *nenki uri* and *nenki kokyaku.* Under this system a piece of land was purchased for a fixed number of years, at the end of which it was automatically returned to the seller. A similar system to this was *honsen-gaeshi* (or *hommono-gaeshi*), which differed from *nenki uri* in that the land sold did not return to the seller unless he bought it back. These two terms were often used indiscriminately. Both were frequently used as methods of establishing collateral for credit.   UEDA Nobuhiro

nenkō system → seniority system

Neo-Confucianism → Confucianism; Shushigaku

neolithic period

(shinsekki jidai). The Jōmon period (ca 10,000 BC–ca 300 BC) is considered to be Japan's neolithic period or "new stone age" because it possessed at least two artifacts common to other neolithic cultures: pottery (see JŌMON POTTERY) and polished STONE TOOLS. However, agricultural village life—another trait often used to define neolithic cultures—was not typical of the Jōmon period, which was mainly characterized by a hunting and gathering way of life. See also HISTORY OF JAPAN: prehistory.   Peter BLEED

Nerima Ward

(Nerima Ku). One of the 23 wards of Tōkyō. Residential district. Recreational facilities include Shakujii Park and Toshimaen Amusement Park. Pop: 564,140.

Netherlands and Japan

The Netherlands boasts the longest history of uninterrupted relations with Japan of any Western nation. For more than 200 years, relations between the Netherlands and Japan were of a very special nature: during the period of strict NATIONAL SECLUSION under the Tokugawa shogunate (1603–1867), the Dutch and the Chinese were the only foreigners allowed into Japan. The tiny Dutch outpost in

Nagasaki served as Japan's single source of knowledge of Europe and the rest of the Western world.

Premodern Period—— Although several Dutchmen had arrived earlier on Portuguese ships, the first encounter between the Netherlands and Japan may be said to have taken place when the Dutch ship LIEFDE was shipwrecked off the coast of Bungo Province (now Ōita Prefecture), Kyūshū, in 1600. Communications with its captain, Jacob Quaeckernaeck, eventually led to formal relations between the newly formed Dutch East India Company and the Tokugawa shogunate. In 1609 a representative of the Dutch fleet under Admiral Verhoeff submitted a message and gifts from the stadholder (later prince) Maurits to TOKUGAWA IEYASU, then retired at Sumpu (now the city of Shizuoka). This permitted the opening of a DUTCH FACTORY at Hirado (near Nagasaki). After an incident in 1628, in which captain HAMADA YAHYŌE and his crew were seized by Dutch authorities in Taiwan, the factory was temporarily closed for four years (1628–31).

As the Tokugawa shogunate gradually strengthened its strictures against Catholic missionaries, the Dutch hoped to avail themselves of new opportunities. Following successive National Seclusion edicts, however, the factory buildings at Hirado were destroyed in 1641 and the personnel ordered to move to DEJIMA, an island in Nagasaki Harbor. The Dutch conducted trade from Dejima until 1860. From 1641 to 1847 the number of Dutch ships visiting Nagasaki totaled 606, an average of 3 per year. They brought silk, textiles, hides, and dyes in exchange for bullion, coins, and camphor. This pattern of DUTCH TRADE (Oranda bōeki) was maintained while the shogunate's policy on the permissible amount of cargo and number of ships changed several times. On the other hand, the Dutch East India Company was forced to undergo reorganization because of financial problems, and in 1799 it was dissolved. There was a marked decrease in the number of Dutch ships arriving in Nagasaki, but a new head of the Dejima post, Hendrik DOEFF, distinguished himself with his diplomatic skills in several incidents, including the visit of the Russian Nikolai REZANOV in 1804 and the arrival of the *Phaeton*, a British man-of-war flying Dutch colors (see PHAETON INCIDENT).

After the Netherlands recovered the East Indies colonies, which it had lost during the Napoleonic wars, regular voyages were resumed between the East Indies and Nagasaki. In 1840 Philipp Franz von SIEBOLD, a doctor who had been deported from Japan at the end of 1829 for possessing maps and other contraband articles, proposed to the newly ascended King William II to advise the shogunate to open the country to trade. Four years later the frigate *Palembang* entered Nagasaki with William's message. The shōgun refused to reply. In 1852, under instructions from his government, the head of the Dejima factory presented the draft of a trade treaty, but this too was ignored.

While the Netherlands attempted the OPENING OF JAPAN through the established customary channels, the United States chose to persuade Japan by a show of arms; it succeeded in 1854 in opening the country. In 1858 the ANSEI COMMERCIAL TREATIES were signed. A Dutch-Japanese Treaty of Amity was concluded in 1856, followed by a supplementary treaty the following year, permitting trade at the Dutch factory and the lifting of all restrictions on the number of ships and volume in trade. A treaty of commerce and friendship was signed in 1858. The first diplomatic representative, Jan Hendrik DONKER CURTIUS, took up his duties in Edo (now Tōkyō); the factory at Dejima was designated a vice-consulate in 1860.

Even after the enactment of the national seclusion policy, the interpreters (ORANDA TSŪJI) at Dejima had used Portuguese in speaking to the Dutch. In due course they took up the study of the Dutch language. Dutch studies, or Rangaku, initially confined to language study, were later to include various Western disciplines transmitted through the medium of the Dutch language. From the times of ARAI HAKUSEKI, a Confucian scholar and shogunate adviser, and the eighth shōgun TOKUGAWA YOSHIMUNE (1684–1751), who relaxed restrictions on the import of Chinese translations of Western works, Rangaku gradually became more familiar to Japanese intellectuals. Two works published in Japanese, *Kaitai shinsho* (A New Book of Anatomy) of 1774 and *Rangaku kaitei* (A Ladder to Dutch Learning) of 1788, promoted this trend. In the first half of the 19th century Rangaku developed into Yōgaku (see WESTERN LEARNING) with official sponsorship. In 1862 NISHI AMANE, TSUDA MAMICHI, ENOMOTO TAKEAKI, and others were sent to the Netherlands to study. They were to contribute significantly to the politics, education, and military affairs of Japan in the years to follow.

KANAI Madoka

Modern Period—— The Netherlands Trading Company (Dutch: Nederlandsche Handel-Maatschappij; NHM), founded in 1824 under the sponsorship of King William I, attained a dominant position in Dutch trade with the Far East, especially with the Netherlands East Indies. In 1859 Albertus J. Bauduin (1829–90) arrived in Nagasaki as its agent. In 1863 he was also appointed as Dutch consul, and he later represented Switzerland and Denmark as well. He stayed in Nagasaki until 1868, then moved to Hyōgo (now Kōbe), where he remained until 1874. Thanks to his activities, Dutch-Japanese trade developed in a spectacular way; their historical relations with Japan also gave the Dutch a major advantage over their competitors. In 1862, for example, the Japanese government ordered a propeller-driven steamship through NHM. This vessel, built at Dordrecht and christened *Kaiyō maru*, was delivered at Yokohama on 1 May 1867. It became the flagship of the shogunate navy but ran aground in a heavy storm off Hokkaidō the following year. After the MEIJI RESTORATION of 1868 other nations gained precedence over the Netherlands, and in the early 1880s the trading post at Kōbe was closed. In 1919 the NHM again opened a branch in the same city, but this time for banking only.

In the 1860s and 1870s several Dutch physicians contributed much to the development of Japanese medicine, continuing a tradition established in the premodern period. Among them were Dr Koenraad W. Gratama (1831–88), who taught at Nagasaki, Edo (now Tōkyō), Yokohama, and Ōsaka (1866–71); Dr A. J. C. Geerts (1843–83), Gratama's successor in Nagasaki, who established laboratories for chemistry and hygiene in Tōkyō, Kyōto, and Yokohama; and Dr Christiaan J. Ermerins (1840–79), who taught medicine at Ōsaka Medical School from 1871 until 1878. In the field of hydraulic engineering, Cornelis J. van Doorn (1837–1906) and Johannes DE RIJKE were active in Japan in the last quarter of the 19th century.

From the end of the Meiji period (1868–1912), relations between Japan and the Netherlands became complicated by the existence of the Dutch colonial empire in Southeast Asia and Dutch fears of Japanese economic and territorial expansion. In 1899 the Japanese in the Netherlands East Indies legally acquired the status of "Europeans"; in 1912 a commercial treaty was concluded by which their activities in trade, industry, shipping, and immigration were regulated according to the so-called most-favored-nation principle. Until the world economic crisis of 1929, there were no special problems, but in the 1930s relations rapidly deteriorated because of the unfavorable trade balance and—after the occupation of the Netherlands by Nazi Germany during World War II—because of Japanese demands for oil, rubber, and other strategic goods.

Immediately after the Japanese attack on Pearl Harbor in 1941, the Netherlands government in exile declared war upon Japan. Japanese attacks upon the Netherlands East Indies began in January 1942; with the capitulation of Java (9 March 1942), the conquest of the Dutch colonies in that part of the world was complete. All Dutch and Indonesian personnel of the Royal Netherlands Indies Army, as well as all Dutch civilians and a large number of Eurasians, were interned in camps in the East Indies, Singapore, Thailand, and Burma, as well as in Japan proper. The harsh treatment of the prisoners in these internment camps has brought about lingering anti-Japanese feelings in a considerable section of the Dutch population. Although leaders of the Indonesian nationalist movement, like SUKARNO, assisted Japan in its war efforts, their demands for permission to use the Indonesian flag and to sing their national anthem were turned down by the Japanese. As late as September 1944, independence was promised to the Indonesians. It is significant that the inhabitants of the Indies were denoted as "natives" (genjūmin) by the Occupation authorities; only toward the end of the war were they officially called Indonesians (indoneshiajin).

In September 1951 the Netherlands was one of the 48 nations that signed the SAN FRANCISCO PEACE TREATY, officially terminating the state of war with Japan. In 1955 Dutch exports to Japan totaled only 37 million Dutch florins (Dfl; US $390,400), but by 1978 this amount had grown to Dfl 641 million (US $6.6 million). In the same period the value of Japanese goods exported to the Netherlands rose from Dfl 67 million (US $707,500) to Dfl 2.6 billion (US $26.4 million).

Cultural exchange between the two countries is promoted by the Netherlands–Japan Association in The Hague and the Japan-Netherlands Associations in Tōkyō, Ōsaka, and Nagasaki. Scholarly interest in Japan is furthered by the Netherlands Association for Japanese Studies, a chapter of the European Association for Japanese Studies. The activities of the Society for the Study of Historical Relations between Japan and the Netherlands (Nichiran Kōshō Shi

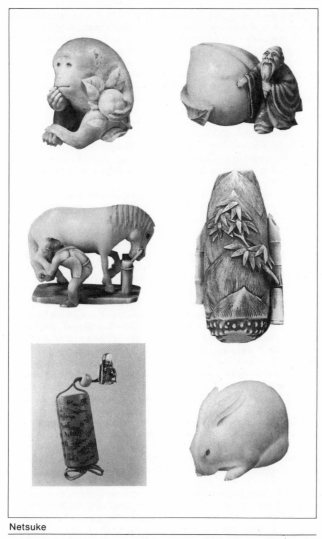

Netsuke

Clockwise from top right: Chinese sage with peach by Nagai Rantei (23 mm), bamboo shoot (52 mm) and rabbit (38 mm) by Kaigyokusai, a *netsuke* attached to an *inrō* (10 cm), horse and farrier (26 mm) by Nagai Rantei, and monkey (33 mm) by Kaigyokusai. Ivory. Late 18th–19th century. Tōkyō National Museum.

Kenkyūkai) and the Society for the Study of Materials for Dutch Learning (Rangaku Shiryō Kenkyūkai) are centered around the Japan–Netherlands Institute (Nichiran Gakkai), established in Tōkyō in 1975. In the spring of 1980 a cultural agreement between the Netherlands and Japan was concluded.

📖 ———John Z. Bowers, *Western Medical Pioneers in Feudal Japan* (1970). Charles Ralph Boxer, *Jan Campagnie in Japan, 1600–1850* (1936, rev ed 1950). Grant G. Goodman, *The Dutch Impact on Japan, 1640–1853* (1967). Kanai Madoka, ed, *Sakoku: Japan's Seclusion Policy, 1633–1853*, Acta Asiatica 22 (1972). J. P. Kleiweg de Zwann, *Völkerkundliches und Geschichtliches über die Heilkunde der Chinesen und Japaner mit besonderer Berücksichtigung holländischer Einflüsse* (1917). *Frits Vos*

netsuke

A piece of sculptured wood or ivory used to secure a cord carrying personal belongings to the sash *(obi)* which acts as a belt on traditional Japanese dress. Traditional Japanese dress for men and women had very few places in which to keep small personal objects. Women kept things in their sleeves, but men had no equivalent in which to carry essentials such as seal cases (INRŌ), tobacco pouches, purses, pipes in cases, and small writing kits, known as *yatate*. Things like this were called *sagemono* ("hanging objects"), and the logical place to hang these things was from the sash. To hold the cord in place, a toggle was fitted at the other end. This toggle was called a *netsuke*.

This practice of hanging personal possessions from a cord was not unique to Japan; evidence of similar practices has been found in many other cultures, most relevantly in China. The earliest Japanese pictures of *sagemono* in use are to be found in illustrated handscrolls of the Kamakura period (1185–1333), but it was not until the 17th century that *netsuke* became widely used and produced with a certain amount of artistic intention. The first mention of a *netsuke* maker is in the woodblock-printed encyclopedia *Kimmō zui* (1690), which notes that "craftsmen in horn" made among other things *netsuke* and *ojime;* these were the bead-like sliders which pulled together the double cord to which the *netsuke* and *sagemono* were attached. Here "horn" is illustrated by a tusk of ivory. Other organic materials, such as wood, small gourds and nutshells were probably also used, as well as small items of personal use like seals. The earliest specially made *netsuke,* to judge from the illustration in *Kimmō zui,* were flattish turned discs of ivory called *manjū,* after the flat round rice cake. Some makers of lacquered *inrō* may also have provided matching lacquer *netsuke* as early as the 17th century; these would probably have been in the shape of small boxes.

Netsuke were produced in the greatest numbers during the Edo period (1600–1868). During the latter part of this period, the merchant classes (CHŌNIN) gained in status and wealth, although they continued to rank well below the *samurai* in the feudal class system. Thus they were restricted to a fairly rigorous dress code, which included a ban on ostentatious clothing. (Jewelry as such was not worn in Japan at the time, and there was a marked lack of interest in precious stones and metals and in unnecessary personal adornment such as rings, necklaces, and brooches.) *Netsuke,* however, were not considered in this light.

Two other developments were of seminal importance to the growing use of *netsuke:* the widespread acceptance and use of tobacco and an increasing interest in Chinese carved toggles and seals. Tobacco smokers needed a place to keep their smoking paraphernalia, and a cord from the sash made a great deal of sense for this purpose. There was a long tradition of hardstone and ivory seals and toggles in China, and the early part of the 18th century saw the opening of Japan to many Chinese books and imported goods after a ban of some 80 years. This Chinese influence is apparent both in the themes and the materials that appear in the *netsuke* of this period, notably in an increased fashion for ivory, which had not been much used in Japan until then, especially for carving, for the native sculptural tradition had nearly all been in wood and lacquer. The earliest discernible themes in *netsuke* reflect this Chinese influence, generally consisting of tall figures, carved in ivory or wood up to about 15 centimeters (6 in) high. For the most part, they have two holes bored into them in the back, through which the cord is passed. The subjects of these were either Taoist or Buddhist figures, or the Chinese or Dutch merchants who came to Nagasaki. The Chinese are often represented as effete, and the Dutch as large-nosed clowns, but this is in keeping with the generally humorous approach of the *netsuke,* which also portray Japanese subjects in a ludicrous vein. These early types seem to belong to the period from about 1730 to 1780.

The earliest *netsuke* carvers appear to have been amateurs. The first detailed account of *netsuke* producers is in the book *Sōken kishō* (1781) by Inaba Tsūryū, an Ōsaka sword merchant. Curiously, it is almost the last account until the 20th century. Inaba mentions 57 *netsuke* craftsmen, mainly in Ōsaka, Kyōto, and Edo (now Tōkyō), but also in a number of provincial areas, particularly places near Nagoya. Many of these must have been professionals, although Inaba reserves the greatest praise for an amateur carver, Yoshimura Shūzan (d 1776). Yoshimura fits into the Chinese ideal of the gentleman artist, and his works were generally Chinese figures in delicately painted wood. Painting of *netsuke* remained a comparative rarity except in the rather folklike pieces resembling simple dolls made at Nara and other provincial centers. The preferred effect was always for natural, polished wood or ivory, which gained softness and patina from rubbing against the dress. This is still a desired quality among collectors.

Only about a third of the makers mentioned in the *Sōken kishō* have left signatures which can be found on extant *netsuke,* supporting the view that 18th-century *netsuke* tended to be unsigned. This did not mean, however, that the carvers had no personal pride in their work. Rather, it reflects the tradition of anonymity in Japanese arts and crafts that had existed from the 7th century onward and that was beginning to break down in the mid-Edo period as people began to feel a greater sense of individuality. By the early 19th century, in common with other crafts such as sword accoutrements, it was becoming usual rather than exceptional for *netsuke* to be signed.

What is clear from the *Sōken kishō* is that by the late 18th century a confident, more compact style had developed.

Viewed in terms of Japanese art history, the *netsuke* thus fill what might otherwise be viewed as a mysterious gap in sculptural activity. For while Japanese sculptors produced such truly monumental achievements as the grand Buddhist sculptures of the Kamakura period and the smaller but very refined Zen portrait figures and NŌ masks of the Muromachi period (1333–1568), there is apparently very little sculptural achievement on the same scale from the 16th century onward. In fact, the *only* large-scale sculpture was that in Buddhist temples, and once this tradition had run out of vitality, there was no means of expression of reasonable size for carvers. The Tokugawa shogunate added to the dilemma by banning architectural decorative carving in all but the largest official buildings. Many Buddhist sculptors were producing miniature, portable shrines for private devotions by the 17th century. These shrines show the same assiduous care for tiny detail that was to become such an important aspect of the *netsuke*. Sometimes the deities set in them were only 10 centimeters (4 in) high, yet carved in amazing detail with the many symbolic attributes of, for example, the bodhisattva KANNON. Thus there developed a tradition for making miniature *netsuke*. The names of some schools of *netsuke* carvers are associated with BUDDHIST ART.

Other craftsmen who also converted into *netsuke* makers were the mask makers (the Deme family in Edo were such) and the makers of carved red lacquer in imitation of an admired Chinese technique. The ivory tradition, not an important part of Japanese culture until the 18th century, was confined until then to very minor areas of production. These included the turned roller ends for hanging scrolls and handscrolls, personal seals carved with the owner's name in relief, and plectra for musical instruments. But from such objects as these must have developed the craft of ivory carving in miniature. The craftsmen who turned ivory on the lathe must be presumed to have been the first makers of the aforementioned *manjū*. The seal makers were probably the first to do actual carvings in the round, if they followed the Chinese tradition of turning the handle of a seal into a small carving of, for example, a *shishi* (a mythological lion dog). Certainly the *Kimmō zui* suggests that this happened as early as the late 17th century.

Similarly, the makers of plectra for musical instruments produced off-cuts of triangular sections that were frequently used for *netsuke* carving, and many earlier *netsuke* are of a noticeably flattened conical shape. (One of the flat sides would lie very comfortably against the hip.) These craftsmen, too, probably turned to carving.

The great age of *netsuke* in terms of production, quality, and artistic achievement was the first half of the 19th century. In place of the earlier scholarly slant, *netsuke* became more humorous, and there was more variation both in subjects and materials used. Carvers were taking more trouble with their work, sometimes taking as long as two months to complete their finest pieces. Such *netsuke* must have been expensive, but there was a significant market for them among the rich merchant class, whose obligatory dress code, as noted above, made *netsuke* a useful but unobtrusive symbol of wealth.

The characteristics of *netsuke* of this period are small size, intricacy, and compactness. Instead of the long, rather relaxed sculptures of Chinese figures found in the 18th century, there is an emphasis on native subjects of all kinds such as craftsmen, entertainers, legendary figures from Japanese history, mythical creatures, animals and birds, and even representations of objects, such as tiles, tea bowls, or even hanging paintings. Ingenuity was admired above everything, and the smaller the *netsuke* and the more complicated its detail, the more it was admired. To this period belong the carvings of Chinese palaces, shown inside clam shells, and the *manjū netsuke* engraved with an entire map of Japan or a complete list of the post-station towns of the highway TŌKAIDŌ on a curved surface 2 or 3 centimeters (about 1 in) across. These tendencies seem particularly associated with the slick, rather superficial tastes of the great cities of Edo and Ōsaka, and the former gradually became dominant in quantity of carvers, of whom Hōjitsu (d 1872) is a typical example. However, perhaps the most highly skilled of all the carvers is Kaigyokusai of Ōsaka (1813–92), who specialized almost entirely in ivory.

The end of Japan's NATIONAL SECLUSION in the 1850s had negative results for *netsuke*. Japanese tastes were for a time confused by the vast influx of Western innovations, and this did little for an art such as *netsuke*, which relied heavily on traditional artistic values. *Netsuke* became very popular among foreigners, being both amusing and easy to transport. Large collections of *netsuke* were amassed in Europe and America. To meet this new demand, large amounts of inferior *netsuke* were produced for the undiscriminating foreign buyer, usually in ivory or cheap substitutes, and this practice has continued ever since. Many *netsuke* must have been destroyed, along with much of the city of Edo, in the great Ansei fire of 1857. To replace them, large quantities of cheaply made *netsuke* were produced, without much regard for artistic standards and dominated by the easily made *manjū* shape. Finally, the market which had existed for high-quality *netsuke* was affected by changes in Japanese dress. Dress codes disappeared with the abolition of the official class system by the Meiji government and Western clothes became increasingly popular. To be sure, this was part of a general decline in traditional crafts, as craftsmen turned their skills toward more exportable products.

However, there was a continued, if small, demand for fine *netsuke* in the Meiji period (1868–1912). This can be regarded as part of a self-conscious urge late in the 19th century to preserve traditional crafts in such institutions as the Tōkyō School of Fine Arts (now Tōkyō University of Fine Arts and Music). During this period *netsuke* carvers also started making *okimono* (ornaments), which tended to be larger, naturalistic works in ivory very much slanted toward the Western market. These *okimono* are at their best very fine indeed, and it is clear that the opportunity to carve larger objects was a welcome relief to highly skilled sculptors who until then had been restricted to the miniature. In fact, the desire to break away from the *netsuke* is already clear in the late Edo period. Minwa of Edo, for example, in the late 18th century, produced some excellent small portrait sculptures over 15 centimeters (about 6 in) high; Toyomasa of Tamba (now part of Kyōto and Hyōgo prefectures) and others carved "false swords" in wood; and Kaigyokusai made tea scoops and even sword hilts. Although *okimono* are very Westernized in taste, the best of them are now seen as true descendants of the *netsuke* tradition.

The *netsuke* tradition has continued ever since and still produces masterpieces of miniature carving, but these *netsuke* have become an art form in themselves and do not have the same feeling as those made for use. Within the last 20 years several American and European carvers have begun making them.

One of the most appealing aspects of *netsuke* is the variety of its subjects. There are, however, a few consistent design elements. To carry out their practical function, there were definite limits to the possible size of the *netsuke*, which ranged from 2.5 to 15 centimeters (1 to 6 in). Anything larger would be too cumbersome, while anything smaller would not effectively do the job. *Netsuke* were generally three-dimensional carvings (*katabori*) of a human being, a deity or mythical creature, or apparition, an animal, plant, or architectural fantasy. The holes for the cord were either bored into a flat back, or created by aspects of the design such as limbs or branches.

The common *manjū netsuke* were either engraved, inlaid, or carved in semirelief. A variation of the *manjū*, the *kagamibuta* ("mirror lid") *netsuke*, was a *manjū* case, into which was fitted a decorated metal plate. The plate was held in position by the cord, which was looped through a hole in the plate. This type of *netsuke* was produced in large quantities in the late 19th century, particularly in Tōkyō, by makers of sword trappings who had lost most of their business following the edict of 1876 (HAITŌREI) banning the wearing of swords by civilians.

Masks were popular subject material for *netsuke*, particularly in Edo. These were from a variety of sources—ceremonial Buddhist *bugaku* (GAGAKU) and *gigaku* masks, Nō drama masks, and the carvers' own imaginations. Some *netsuke* had a practical use in addition to securing the cord to the sash. The earliest of these were seals, and flint and tinder sets, but later on, small knives, ashtrays, watches, sundials, and tea ceremony utensils were made as *netsuke*.

The materials used in *netsuke* varied a great deal. Because of the function of the *netsuke*, lighter, organic materials were preferred to hardstones. All kinds of wood were used, including some hardwoods probably imported from China or Southeast Asia. Ivory was increasingly popular, and all varieties were used, the most prized being the tusks of the narwhal and of the Southeast Asian elephants. Lacquer was popular, and other organic materials included nuts, coral, antler, horn, amber, and a fossilized sea pine called *umimatsu*. Eyes were often inlaid with tortoise shell, glass, amber, metal, horn, or ebony.

Identifying the creator of any Japanese work of art can be difficult, and *netsuke* are no exception. Signing *netsuke* was not a consistent practice, and often a master would sign works by students. A master's studio would use his name on all its products. Added to this are the great numbers of fakes. For the amateur collector the safest course is to choose by quality alone, and to take professional advice on the question of antiquity.

■——Richard Baker and Lawrence Smith, *Netsuke: The Miniature Sculpture of Japan* (1976). Raymond Bushell, *The Netsuke Handbook of Ueda Reikichi* (1961). Raymond Bushell, *Collectors' Netsuke* (1972). Neil Davy, *Netsuke* (1974).   *Lawrence* SMITH

Nevskii, Nikolai Aleksandrovich (1892–1945)

Russian philologist who specialized in Japanese, Ainu, and Ryukyuan languages and cultures. Born in Yaroslavl and graduated from the Oriental Languages Department of St. Petersburg University, Nevskii came to Japan in 1915 and studied under the folklorists YANAGITA KUNIO, ORIKUCHI SHINOBU, and KINDAICHI KYŌSUKE. For the next 14 years, while supporting himself as a Russian language instructor, he conducted ethnographical surveys throughout Japan and Taiwan and collected material on Tangut sources in Peking. Unlike his friend and fellow orientalist Serge ELISSÉEFF, who emigrated after the October Revolution, Nevskii tried to come to terms with the Soviet regime. In 1929 he returned to Russia, leaving behind a Japanese wife and daughter. With the help of a successful classmate, Nikolai KONRAD, he became an instructor of Japanese at Leningrad University and continued his Tangut research at the Oriental Institute and Hermitage Museum. In 1937 at the height of Stalin's purges, Nevskii and his wife (who had rejoined him) were arrested as spies. They both died in 1945 at separate camps. Officially rehabilitated in 1957, Nevskii posthumously received the Lenin Prize in 1962 for his Tangut studies. His work on Ainu folklore and on Miyakojima (an island in the Ryūkyū Archipelago) is highly regarded in both Japan and the USSR.

■——L. L. Gromkovskaya and E. I. Kychanov, *Nikolai Aleksandrovich Nevskii* (1978). Katō Kyūzō, *Ten no hebi* (1976).   *John J.* STEPHAN

new industrial cities

(*shin sangyō toshi*). Areas designated according to the 1962 Act for the Development of New Industrial Cities. The areas were chosen in order to promote local industry and to check the concentration of people and industries in large cities. Public funds were used to improve basic facilities and to introduce new industries, but the results have not been as good as anticipated, creating pollution, among other problems. The 15 designated zones are Dōō (central Hokkaidō), Hachinohe, Sendai Bay, Jōban–Kōriyama, Niigata, Matsumoto–Suwa, Toyama–Takaoka, Okayama Kennan (southern Okayama Prefecture), Tokushima, Tōyo (eastern Ehime Prefecture), Shiranui–Ariake–Ōmuta, Ōita, Hyūga–Nobeoka, Akita Bay, and Nakaumi.

NISHIKAWA Osamu

New Liberal Club

(Shin Jiyū Kurabu; NLC). Political party founded by six Diet members from the LIBERAL DEMOCRATIC PARTY on 25 June 1976. The first chairman was KŌNO YŌHEI and the first secretary-general was Nishioka Takeo—both younger members of the House of Representatives. An initial NLC "boom" saw total members increase to 23 in the next elections for each House, and the party was also successful in electing local assembly candidates. The "boom" collapsed following Nishioka's bolting from the party in a dispute with Kōno, and only 4 of 31 candidates won seats in the 1979 elections for the House of Representatives. The party's conservative "new liberalism" espouses a modest welfare state within a free economy, with a general appeal to the urban middle class. As of 1980 the Shin Jiyū Kurabu held two seats in the House of Representatives.

Lee W. FARNSWORTH

"New Order in East Asia" → Tōa Shinchitsujo

New Order Movement

(Shin Taisei Undō). A generic term popularized in 1940 and 1941 to describe a series of domestic reform proposals in Japan. Although the term was used loosely to refer to political, economic, cultural, journalistic, and many other reforms, its usage was most commonly and widely adopted in the context of political reform plans.

In one sense, the calls for a new political order (*seiji shin taisei*) reflected the culmination of the "reformist" impulses that underlay more than a quarter century of attacks on the efficacy and morality of the early 20th-century political system under the Meiji Constitution. In fact, however, the major forces active in the movement in 1940 merely constituted a conglomeration of conventional interest groups, whose demands for greater political influence had been redefined in terms of the necessity for Japan to strengthen its capacity to deal with the international crises in East Asia and Europe.

For example, within the lower house of the Diet, many members of the major parties—the RIKKEN SEIYŪKAI and RIKKEN MINSEITŌ—urged the creation of a new political party to restore the influence they had gradually lost during the 1930s. Minor parties and factions of the Diet likewise agitated for a new party to provide them with the political power they had hitherto been unable to acquire through the competitive electoral process. Outside of the Diet, a number of reformist groups advocated the creation of a new parliamentary party that would oust the existing parliamentary forces from the Diet and install a reformist coalition in control of the lower house and the cabinet. A number of other political leaders, such as ARIMA YORIYASU and Kazami Akira (1886–1961), sought through the creation of a new political party to enhance the influence of vocational and agrarian guilds in the face of the dominance of big business and landlord pressure groups. At the same time, the Home Ministry—particularly the Local Affairs Bureau—hoped to establish stronger administrative controls over the local affairs of the villages, towns, and cities under its jurisdiction, while the Imperial Army was equally eager to mobilize new political support groups for its programs of armaments development and the creation of a "national defense" economy. By the spring of 1940, each group was seeking to advance its respective interests through reforms it declared to be essential for coping with Japan's protracted military conflict in China and the new range of opportunities and dangers emanating from the outbreak of World War II in Europe.

The key political figure in harmonizing these conflicting domestic political demands and orienting them toward a strengthening of Japan's international capabilities was KONOE FUMIMARO. Throughout his career, and particularly as prime minister from June 1937 to January 1939, Konoe had attempted to ensure that the many conflicting political demands of Japan's ruling elite groups did not impede the stability of the Japanese government or its international position. He likewise had long sought to mitigate the possibility that the advent of mass society and mass politics would undermine the state's control over the citizenry or the ruling elite's control over the institutions of the state. By June of 1940 Konoe was once again prepared to serve as prime minister, and he concluded that the position he was about to assume must be strengthened institutionally to obtain the compliance of other elite groups and the citizenry with the economic and military policies he envisioned for Japan's expansion in East and Southeast Asia.

In short, Konoe began considering concrete methods that would allow the prime minister to *enforce* "national unity." He drew heavily upon the "reformist" ideas developed at that time by his "brain trust," the SHŌWA KENKYŪKAI, an organization of intellectuals, bureaucrats, and journalists established in 1933. Ultimately, Konoe's plans for a new political order relied primarily on draft proposals formulated by Yabe Teiji, a Tōkyō University political scientist and prominent member of the Shōwa Kenkyūkai.

While many groups sought to expand their influence through political reform, they were not eager to surrender any of their existing power to a strengthened prime minister's office, and as the nation was enmeshed in military operations against China, Konoe was reluctant to provoke any disruptive political turmoil with his plans for sweeping reform. By late June, however, he had apparently concluded that the war in China was on the verge of diplomatic settlement. Thus, for the first time, he publicly declared himself willing to lead a broad reform movement to establish a new political order. Although he was not explicit about the details of his plan at the time, his principal goals were to strengthen the prime minister's prerogatives and create a new mass political support group for his domestic and foreign policies. Eager to benefit from the popular Konoe's patronage, the advocates of a new political party restated their demands in terms of the creation of a new wartime popular organization (*kokumin soshiki*) and new political order, while bureaucratic and military programs for local political mobilization also took on the rubric of the new political order.

Between late August and early October of 1940, Konoe as prime minister had representatives of each major political interest group meet together to hammer out the details of the new political order under his guidance. On 12 October 1940 the new popular organization which was to be a central component of the new order was launched officially as the IMPERIAL RULE ASSISTANCE ASSOCIATION (Taisei Yokusankai). However, the New Order Movement encountered three serious barriers that ultimately destroyed it.

First, although many groups assumed a positive attitude toward Konoe's reform program in the hope of expanding their influence, none of them was in fact willing to surrender any of its prerogatives. Thus, for example, all of the political parties and factions in the lower house formally dissolved their organizations between July and August, in the expectation that their actions would lead Konoe to install them in positions of leadership in his new popular organization. However, as it became evident to major party leaders that they would enjoy less, rather than more, political influence under the new system, their attitudes became increasingly cautious and finally hostile. Similarly, Home Ministry and army supporters of the new order endorsed Konoe's plans only to the extent that their own purposes could be advanced, and they stoutly resisted any diminution of their existing influence.

Second, the reforms proposed under the new political order—particularly those pertaining to a strengthening of the prime minister's post vis-à-vis other organs of the state—were perceived by many conservatives, such as HIRANUMA KIICHIRŌ, as violating the spirit of the Meiji Constitution and providing an overconcentration of state power in the hands of one man and his political support group.

Finally, as the promise of an early diplomatic settlement of the war with China proved to be illusory, Konoe himself became increasingly reluctant to provoke a major political upheaval at home through the forceful implementation of his new order program.

By early 1941, Konoe had abandoned all of the controversial features of the new political order, and the Imperial Rule Assistance Association had been converted from a vanguard of political reform to the status of a nonpartisan, nationwide organization for promoting citizen backing for established government programs. Despite sporadic subsequent efforts by reformist groups to reinfuse the organization with partisan qualities, the entire New Order Movement actually had a very minimal impact on the powers of the prime minister and on the allocation of political power among the nation's political elite groups. Major party leaders, businessmen, and conservative bureaucrats and ideologues proved to be successful defenders of the political system developed under the Meiji Constitution.

The failure of the new order movement to "reform" the political system revealed the vitality and strength of the conservative forces on the eve of the Pacific War and determined the essential contours of the wartime political system under which Japan fought. At the same time, the political battles over the new order question in 1940–41, and again whenever the "reformist" camp sought to extend its influence during the war, indicated that beneath the façade of "national unity," controversy and competition persisted throughout the war and were central elements of the political landscape during this period.

◼———Gordon Mark Berger, *Parties Out of Power in Japan, 1931–1941* (1977). Imai Seiichi and Itō Takashi, ed, *Kokka sōdōin (2): Gendai shi shiryō,* 44 (1974). Kinoshita Hanji, *Shin taisei jiten* (1941). Konoe Fumimaro, *Ushinawareshi seiji,* ed Godai'in Yoshimasa (1946), tr as *Memoirs of Prince Konoye* in *Pearl Harbor Attack: Hearings Before the Joint Committee on the Investigation of the Pearl Harbor Attack,* Part 20 (1946). Nihon Seiji Gakkai, ed, *Nempō seijigaku, 1972: "Konoe shin taisei" no kenkyū* (1973). Yabe Teiji *Konoe Fumimaro,* vol 2 (1952). Yokusan Undō Shi Kankō Kai, ed, *Yokusan kokumin undō shi* (1954).   *Gordon M. BERGER*

new religions

"New religions" is the customary English translation for the Japanese term *shinkō shūkyō* (newly arisen religions) as well as its abbreviation *shin shūkyō* (new religions). The term is not a precise category but a general label, probably developed first by journalists, to refer to the increasing number of new religious groups founded in the early decades of the 20th century. Because journalists and intellectuals have often used the label disparagingly to refer to pseudoreligious and even fraudulent groups, the kind of religious movements that are the subject of this article usually prefer not to be known as new religions. These movements either emphasize their roots in prior traditions or refer to themselves as lay movements. There

have been various attempts to classify these movements under such headings as messianic, nativistic, millenarian, utopian, revitalistic, eschatological, faith healing, or crisis cult; however, there is no one such category into which all of them will fit. Ill defined and unsatisfactory as it is, the term "new religions" will be used in this article to refer to the many new religious movements which have arisen in Japan outside organized SHINTŌ and BUDDHISM starting in the early 19th century. Generally, in contrast to the established religions *(kisei shūkyō)* of Buddhism and Shintō, these emerged among the common people and were often founded by charismatic or purportedly semidivine leaders.

Social and Religious Background——— In Japanese religious history Buddhism and Shintō represent the mainstream of formally organized religion, with clearly identifiable ecclesiastical structures: priesthood, institutions and buildings, regular rituals, formal writings, and doctrines. (Participation in Christianity has never been numerically comparable to participation in Shintō and Buddhism.) In addition to formally organized religions, the two Chinese philosophical and religious traditions of Taoism and Confucianism exerted considerable influence upon thought and social institutions, but rarely assumed the form of organized religions. Even more important for understanding the background of the new religions is the wealth of beliefs and practices that existed informally outside organized religions. This unsystematized wealth of religious phenomena may be called "popular religion" in the sense of elements of organized religions which filter down to the people and are transmitted from generation to generation without direct contact with the organized religions. (Examples of this are recitations of the name of Amida Buddha or the title of the Lotus Sutra as an act of faith and petition for help, practices which originated within Buddhism but may be performed by any person regardless of affiliation with any particular Buddhist sect.) One may also speak of FOLK RELIGION in the sense of beliefs and practices which emerged from folk traditions, such as rice-transplanting ceremonies and shamanistic practices. The new religions are distinguished from older traditions, specifically the "established religions," because they developed new socioreligious organizations (with priesthood, buildings, rituals, etc). The distinction between the new religions, and popular and folk religion, is not so sharp; the latter have usually been unsystematic oral traditions taken for granted by the people at large. What made the new religions conspicuous is their claim to be fully organized and legitimate religions, on a level with Buddhism and Shintō.

The new religions have drawn upon all the previous religious traditions of Japanese history. One element of Japanese Buddhism frequently taken over by the new religions has been the memorial ritual for the dead, which the new religion REIYŪKAI, for example, has treated as an essential religious ritual for modern man. An aspect of Shintō that has carried over into the dynamics of many new religions is the view of the world as inhabited by KAMI (deities), to which man should be responsive; this is the indirect source of the "revelations" received by many founders of new religions. The popular teachings of Neo-Confucianism, with their emphasis on family stability and social responsibility as a kind of cosmic obligation, have penetrated the teachings of a number of new religions. Even Taoism, which is perhaps the most inconspicuous of all Japanese traditions, provided a host of cosmological notions from which some new religions have drawn; KONKŌKYŌ's founder took one Taoist divinity (Konjin) previously considered to be malevolent, and through the revelation that Konjin was a benevolent deity, organized a new faith. Probably the best example of popular religion's influence upon the new religions is the widespread faith in the Lotus Sutra and the accompanying practice of reciting the title of the Lotus Sutra (in the chant NAMU MYŌHŌ RENGE KYŌ, or variations thereof). This faith and practice, originally developed by the Nichiren sect of Buddhism and then adopted popularly, is central to such new religions as Reiyūkai, RISSHŌ KŌSEIKAI, and SŌKA GAKKAI. Folk practices such as shamanism, which had never been systematized or institutionally organized, also exerted tremendous influence upon the new religions, and sometimes experiences of shamanistic possession constituted the founding event or revelation of a new religious movement.

Thus, the new religions are not "new" in the sense of introducing elements never before seen within Japanese religious history. Rather, we might say that they are largely made up of "renewed" elements from previous traditions. The new religions emphasize the recovery and restoration of these basic elements in their proper practice and interpretation, particularly as they are relevant to the contemporary world. Some social scientists have seen this reinterpretation of traditional values within a new socioreligious organization as an attempt to revitalize the earlier world view.

It appears that at the time these new religions started up in numbers, organized religion had become so formal and out of touch with the common people that they were ready to join new movements that were more vital. The stage was partially set during the first half of the 17th century, when the Tokugawa government required family membership in a local Buddhist temple as a means of enforcing the ban on Christianity (see TERAUKE). In functional terms, local temples served as an arm of the government, with families being required to report all occasions such as births, weddings, and deaths to their "parish" temple. With rare exceptions for Shintō services, all funerals had to be conducted by Buddhist priests. This led to the almost universal custom of having a Buddhist altar in main households and observing regular memorial services for family ancestors, with hereditary affiliation of families to "parish" temples. All this increased the financial wealth and ecclesiastical strength of Buddhist temples and denominations but did not necessarily enhance the spiritual enthusiasm of the people for Buddhism.

Affiliation to Buddhism was by family blood line; affiliation to Shintō, the other major established religion, was mainly by family residence. By the Edo period (1600–1868) it was customary for families living in the district around a local shrine to be considered as parishioners (ujiko). It was considered obligatory for parishioners to contribute to the upkeep of their local Shintō shrine and to participate in its festivals, just as they expected to have their newborn children blessed symbolically as children of the UJIGAMI, or local tutelary deity. Local Shintō shrines were very much a part of village life, often with rotating lay leadership; larger shrines had professional priests and less contact with the common people.

Thus, established religion in the Edo period operated mainly in terms of hereditary and residential ties. A family took care of its ancestors with the help of Buddhism, sought tutelary help for its residence through Shintō, made special requests at particular shrines and temples, and accepted many of the moral ideas of Neo-Confucianism. At the same time, families and individuals believed in and practiced many aspects of popular religion and folk religion, such as recitation of Buddhist formulas and exorcism by shamans.

During the same period, however, the social fabric that supported this complex religious world view began to change, and this set the stage for the emergence of new religious movements. Increasingly, patterns of life that in former times had been the privilege of the nobility and the warrior class came to be imitated and modified by the common people. For example, farmers began to own their own tools and animals and develop a greater sense of autonomy. In turn this shifted agriculture away from a dependence on kinship to a tenant-farmer relationship. At about the same time the notion of "family"—with specific ancestors, a Buddhist family altar (butsudan), and formal Buddhist services for funerals and memorials—formerly the practice of the warrior class, became widespread among farmers. The Edo period also saw a greater use of money by a larger group of people, in conjunction with the rise in commercial operations. All these trends were accompanied by considerable population shifts, and the total effect was to weaken the ties to local Buddhist temples and Shintō shrines, both of which were based on a more stable, sedentary social grouping. By the 16th and 17th centuries, pilgrimages had become popular among the common people, stimulated by such factors as greater ease of travel and the rise of a money economy. Pilgrim associations and similar grassroots organizations (KŌ) were ways in which local people could draw together for social and religious communion in addition to family participation in Buddhist temples and Shintō shrines. The kō were a form of transition from family and village units of participation in religion to the pattern of nationwide participation eventually seen in the new religions. It is no accident that new forms of social organization and the new religions both arose first in the areas of most rapid economic growth, especially in southwestern Japan. These social and economic changes helped set the stage for the emergence of the new religions, in that they tended to weaken family and village ties, and prompted people—both individuals and families—to form social and religious groups apart from strictly hereditary and territorial considerations.

Early Development of the New Religions —— The emergence of the new religions is often discussed in terms of three main periods: from the early to late 19th century, when the first such groups appeared; from the late 19th century through the early decades of the 20th century, when dynamic movements such as ŌMOTO arose; and after World War II, when radically different conditions helped

groups such as Risshō Kōseikai and Sōka Gakkai achieve phenomenal growth.

The first identifiable new religion, Nyoraikyō, was founded in 1802, and a number of other new religions appeared in quick succession: KUROZUMIKYŌ in 1814, TENRIKYŌ in 1838, and other groups throughout the 19th century. Although these movements easily attracted popular support, the government frowned on them and obstructed or even suppressed them, occasionally jailing the founders. Many of the 19th-century movements were related to pilgrimage associations and large Shintō shrines. These groups functioned by accepting the affiliation with recognized Shintō (and occasionally Buddhist) institutions, and by the late 19th and early 20th centuries the government had conceded to 13 movements the status of officially recognized sect (SECT SHINTŌ; Kyōha Shintō). These included Kurozumikyō, Tenrikyō, and Konkōkyō.

Because they were so closely related to Shintō, some scholars have not wanted to include these early movements in the category of "new religions," preferring to reserve the label for movements which broke more sharply with established traditions. Be that as it may, it is well to recognize that the 19th-century movements included some with Buddhist derivations, such as Nyoraikyō and Hommon Butsuryūshū (the latter founded in 1857) and the Tenrikyō, although officially recognized as a Shintō sect, actually displayed diverse influences. These early movements constituted a transitional stage between the less organized pilgrimage associations or other grassroots organizations, and the sophisticated 20th-century movements which had access to mass media.

Tenrikyō, the first new religion to achieve a large membership and organizational strength, is a good example of these 19th-century movements. The founder of Tenrikyō, NAKAYAMA MIKI (1798–1887), was a pious and hardworking farm wife who received a divine revelation in the form of "permanent" possession by a kami who claimed to be the true original kami. This new divinity, Tenri Ō no Mikoto, ordered her to spend the rest of her life spreading the message of this revelation of "divine wisdom" (tenri). She quickly gained followers who sought her out for protection against diseases and aid in safe childbirth.

Nakayama Miki's success in attracting a following brought her harassment by the government and even imprisonment; under pressure from the authorities, this movement had to accept supervision from other religious bodies. Even though it was granted relatively independent status as an official sect of Shintō in 1908, Tenrikyō did not achieve real independence until after 1945. Tenrikyō's founder, like those of other new religions, was seen as a living god (IKIGAMI), and therefore her life and actions became divine models for her religion and its members. Another common aspect of these early new religions was an attempt to recover traditional religious values that had been neglected. Nakayama Miki criticized selfishness and attempted to restore the harmony that once existed between mankind and heaven (or God the Parent), a restoration that would lead to a joyous life (yōkigurashi). This distinctive faith was so successful that before long it included hundreds of thousands of members, and its founding site became the present city of TENRI, a center for religious pilgrimage and the location of TENRI UNIVERSITY.

The Twentieth Century —— The 19th-century movements built on previous traditions, either through the coalescing of a loose pilgrimage group or through rapid mobilization following a founding figure's revelation. The divine or charismatic character of a founder was transmitted to the next leader; organization might be carried out by an aide of the founder or a later leader. These new religions did not depend upon participation through hereditary or residential affiliation but actively sought new members on the strength of the religion's ability to relieve human suffering.

The late 19th century and early decades of the 20th were the second major period in the formation of new religions. The movements that arose in the 20th century are not fundamentally different from their 19th-century predecessors, but they developed more rapidly and extensively and made greater use of the mass media to recruit members. For example, TANIGUCHI MASAHARU, who founded SEICHŌ NO IE in 1930, gained support for his movement through his success as a publisher of a popular spiritual magazine. His autobiography, which has continued to be a best seller on the Japanese market, is an illustration of the role of both the mass media and capitalistic enterprise in the new religions of the 20th century.

Taniguchi had been active in Ōmoto before founding Seichō no Ie, and the founder of Ōmoto, DEGUCHI NAO (1837–1918), had been active in Konkōkyō before starting her own movement. Once a number of new religions had developed in the 19th century, it became a frequent pattern for spiritually talented persons to gain experience in an existing new religion before being inspired to found their own. Ōmoto is an instructive example, because it both links the 19th and 20th centuries and shows the development of a rather simple movement steeped in folk practices to an internationally oriented and complex new religion. Deguchi Nao was a woman of rather poor but pious upbringing who received her revelation through possession by a *kami* in 1892. Leaving Konkōkyō, she actively began to minister to the sick and spiritually troubled through her own mixture of elements borrowed from Konkōkyō and folk religious practices. The real organization of this movement—in fact its second founding—was brought about by Deguchi Nao's son-in-law Deguchi Onisaburō (1871–1948), who had his own experience of possession and instruction in Shintō rituals. He expanded Nao's rather utopian vision into a more highly organized and intellectually phrased message and went so far as to advocate a world family system under one religious vision. The movement attracted large numbers of followers, and at the same time came under suspicion from the state. Deguchi Onisaburō traveled to Manchuria and actively promoted European ties, teaching Esperanto to his followers and publishing extensively in Esperanto as part of his claim to a religious message bridging East and West. He also claimed to support the national goals of the Japanese imperial government, but nevertheless the authorities chose twice to prosecute Ōmoto, alleging that it was a dangerous religious sect engaging in treasonous activities. In spite of government oppression of this sort, the 19th-century movements held their own or grew in influence while other movements arose, such as Reiyūkai (1923) and Seichō no Ie (1930).

The third period in the development of new religions is characterized by the radically different social and political conditions present after World War II and an explosive proliferation of new religions. There was general demoralization owing to defeat and some disenchantment with the involvement of Shintō and Buddhism in the war effort. There had been a mass exodus from the bombed cities to the countryside, and then a return to the rebuilt cities. There was now a definite shift from an agricultural-rural to an industrial-urban lifestyle. Changed political conditions made it possible to organize religious movements with a freedom never before possible. In the decades prior to World War II the government's suppression of all suspicious social and religious movements had become much more oppressive, but with the end of the war the government halted all religious oppression. Although freedom of belief had been promised in the 1889 Meiji Constitution, it was not until 1945 that complete freedom of religion was attained. The result of all these changes was that religious movements could develop any teachings and form any desirable organizational ties they wished. Members of Sect Shintō could shed their official affiliation and become independent. Any movement claiming to be religious could register with the government as a "religious juridical person" and become exempt from paying taxes on religious income.

Two new religions that experienced some of the most remarkable growth in the postwar period had been founded just before World War II. Both these movements, Risshō Kōseikai and Sōka Gakkai, have their roots in the Nichiren tradition of Buddhism. Risshō Kōseikai is famous for its success with the *hōza* system of gathering small groups of people under leaders to discuss religious issues and problems in daily life; more recently it has distinguished itself in international peace and interreligious discussions. Claiming more than 4 million members, it is the second largest new religion.

Sōka Gakkai, officially a lay movement of the Nichiren Shōshū Buddhist sect, is the largest contemporary new religion, claiming more than 6 million members. This movement, which had its formal beginnings in 1930, was fairly small through World War II, when it was persecuted by the government for refusing, on the religious grounds of exclusive faith in the Nichiren tradition, to participate in Shintō support for the war effort. After the war, the general director, Toda Jōsei (1900–1958), had to rebuild the organization almost from scratch; he led an all-out recruiting drive, which by 1958 had boosted membership to 750,000 families. Sōka Gakkai entered the political arena and began mobilizing its membership to vote for local and national candidates; in 1964 under the leadership of its third president, IKEDA DAISAKU, it formed a political party, KŌMEITŌ (the Clean Government Party), which has had remarkable success in getting its candidates elected. Charged in 1969 with interfering with the publication of anti-Sōka Gakkai materials, Kōmeitō was officially separated from Sōka Gakkai. It continues to be a major political force. Sōka Gakkai expanded its social agencies in the late 1960s and early 1970s, opening a number of its own schools and founding Sōka University.

Sōka Gakkai is a good example of how traditional Nichiren Buddhism, particularly faith in the Lotus Sutra, can be adapted to modern times, since this devotion is the common faith which links its new voluntary organizations in the solving of immediate problems in daily life. Like some other new religions, it has been active in Europe and North and South America, where it is usually known as Nichiren Shōshū.

Significance of the New Religions —— New religions as a whole have permanently changed the overall pattern of Japanese religion. In addition to the two traditional established Japanese religions of Shintō and Buddhism, and the more recently accepted Christianity, the new religions now represent a major force by virtue of the sheer number of such organizations and the size of their memberships. New religions are reaching the status of "established religions," because of their history of a century or so and their sophisticated organizational structure. The large new religions, with extensive publication facilities, cultural organizations, elaborate peer and interest groups, and even school and university organizations, are full-fledged institutions of the complex modern Japanese society. In 1951 many of the new religions formed the Shin Nihon Shūkyō Dantai Rengōkai (Union of New Religious Organizations of Japan) to facilitate cooperation on such issues as the promotion of freedom of religion.

Social scientists have generally interpreted Japanese new religions in a theoretical framework which identifies the origin of such movements at times of social disorder—as in the Meiji period (1868–1912) and immediately after World War II—and tries to explain the believers' motivation in terms of socioeconomic deprivation. It is often pointed out that new religions emerged during periods when family structure seemed to be weakening and that the new religions provided a substitute for the large extended family. They also aimed to relieve immediate human problems. These theories, however, do not account for the positive enthusiasm and creativity that have been the hallmarks of the successful new religions. Actually, family devotions and family transmission of new religions have been influential in both the new and old religions, providing a continuity of traditions.

There has been a history of public controversy about the new religions. They are praised for retaining traditional values or damned for retaining "anachronistic superstitions." They are often attacked for their sophisticated use of the mass media, or for commercialism. They are alternately lauded for their warm and personal discussion groups and criticized for continuing to foster a conforming mentality devoid of the idea of individual responsibility. The new religions either enlighten politics with high ideals or manipulate power in the name of religion. But criticisms and praise can be aimed at old, established religions as well. All this ambivalence and questioning occurs because the role of religion in modern life has not been sufficiently explained. The latest position is that in a modern, secular society religious people (especially inspired ones like the founders) are "disturbed" or "abnormal"—another inadequate theory. It appears that the new religions will be an indelible part of the Japanese religious scene for the foreseeable future. The new religions are a good example of how one culture is attempting to make traditional values relevant to the modern world. See also MISOGIKYŌ; SPIRIT OF JESUS CHURCH; HOLY SPIRIT ASSOCIATION FOR THE UNIFICATION OF WORLD CHRISTIANITY.

—— H. Byron Earhart, *The New Religions of Japan: A Bibliography of Western-Language Materials* (1970). Hori Ichirō et al, ed, *Japanese Religion* (1972). H. Neill McFarland, *The Rush Hour of the Gods: A Study of the New Religious Movements in Japan* (1967). Murakami Shigeyoshi, *Nihon hyakunen no shūkyō—haibutsu kishaku kara sōka gakkai made* (1968).   H. Byron EARHART

news agencies

The history of news agencies in Japan begins in the early part of the Meiji period (1868–1912). Japan's first contact with a foreign news agency took place in 1871 when Denmark's Great Northern Telegraph completed a telegraphic line via Shanghai to Nagasaki. The *Japan Mail*, an English-language newspaper in Yokohama, gained access to this new line by contract with Reuters and began featuring world news. Japanese-language newspapers translated articles from the *Japan Mail* for later release until the Naigai Tsūshinsha (Domestic and Foreign News Agency) concluded the first direct agreement between a Japanese news agency and a foreign one, Reuters, in 1893.

The first news agency in Japan, the Jiji Tsūshinsha (no connection with the present Jiji Tsūshinsha or JIJI PRESS), was established in 1888 by Mitsui & Co upon the urging of the Japanese government.

By this move, the government hoped to control the flood of antigovernment rhetoric arising out of the FREEDOM AND PEOPLE'S RIGHTS MOVEMENT (Jiyū Minken Undō) which had gained momentum throughout the country in anticipation of the opening of a national Diet. The resulting news agency is said to have released government statements, tending to take a progovernment stance. About this time newspapers began to concentrate more on news reportage and less on opinion statements, a trend that served to increase the importance of news agencies. Many new agencies appeared in the ensuing years, and by 1926 the news agencies based in Tōkyō alone numbered 33.

Two important agencies were the Nihon Dempō Tsūshinsha (Japan Telegraphic News Agency) and the Nihon Shimbun Rengōsha (Japan Associated Press). The Japan Telegraphic News Agency was founded in 1907 by MITSUNAGA HOSHIO. Its financial stability was ensured by its activities as an advertising agent, and it entered into agreements with the Wolff Agency of Germany and United Press. The Japan Associated Press was founded in 1926 by eight influential newspapers which pooled funds to form a joint news agency. Both its operational methods and its name were modeled after the Associated Press and it established ties with both the Associated Press and Reuters.

As World War II drew near, the Japanese government, feeling the need for controls on speech, made plans to create a single government news agency, and in 1936 the Japan Telegraphic News Agency and the Japan Associated Press were combined to form the DŌMEI TSŪSHINSHA (Dōmei News Service) with the advertising section of the Telegraphic News Agency remaining intact; it later became DENTSŪ, INC, Japan's largest advertising agency. All other news agencies were disbanded. Following the war, the staff of the Dōmei agency created the KYŌDŌ NEWS SERVICE (Kyōdō Tsūshinsha) and the Jiji Press. These two firms are the largest news agencies in Japan. Also active are the Radio Press (RP) translating important news from foreign short-wave broadcasts as well as many specialized agencies distributing news in particular fields. See also INTERNATIONAL COMMUNICATIONS.

—— Tsūshinsha Shi Kankōkai, Tsūshinsha shi (1968). Imai Sachihiko, Tsūshinsha (1973). *Arai Naoyuki*

newspapers

In Japan, newspapers may be divided into those published only in morning or evening editions, and those published in both morning and evening editions. These newspapers are distributed nationally, by geographical bloc or prefecture, or by region and city.

Besides general news-oriented papers, there are special interest newspapers which are devoted to economics, sports, book reviews, industry, and trade. Other newspapers address readers such as women, students, or children. In addition, political parties and labor unions publish newspapers for members, not necessarily for profit. The frequency of publication of these specialized newspapers varies widely, from daily editions to monthly editions.

History —— From the beginning of the 17th century through the middle of the 19th century printed handbills with or without pictures were sold in big cities at the time of a major event. These papers were called *yomiuri* ("read and sell"; referring to the custom of selling the handbills by reading them aloud), or KAWARABAN ("tile-block printing"; referring to the use of clay printing blocks engraved with characters and pictures).

The first modern newspaper was the *Nagasaki Shipping List and Advertiser* published twice a week beginning in 1861 by the Englishman A. W. Hansard in Nagasaki. In November of the same year, Hansard moved the paper to Yokohama and renamed it the JAPAN HERALD. In 1862 the Tokugawa shogunate began publishing the KAMPAN BATABIYA SHIMBUN, a translated and re-edited edition of *Javasche Courant*, the organ of the Dutch government in Batavia (now Djakarta). These two papers were published by and for foreigners, that is, they were papers containing only foreign news. Newspapers covering domestic news were first started by the Japanese in Edo (now Tōkyō), Ōsaka, Kyōto, and Nagasaki in 1868. YANAGAWA SHUNSAN's *Chūgai shimbun*, typical of these early papers and a model for later newspapers, carried domestic news as well as abridged translations from foreign papers. The first Japanese daily paper, the YOKOHAMA MAINICHI SHIMBUN was launched in 1871. The *Tōkyō nichinichi shimbun* (predecessor of the MAINICHI SHIMBUN), the YŪBIN HŌCHI SHIMBUN (predecessor of the HŌCHI SHIMBUN), and the oldest existing local newspaper, the *Kōchū shimbun* (predecessor of the *Yamanashi nichinichi shimbun*), were all begun in 1872.

Most papers published at this time were referred to as "political forums," because they demanded the establishment of a Diet and printed political opinions at the time of the FREEDOM AND PEOPLE'S RIGHTS MOVEMENT (Jiyū Minken Undō). However, after the issuance of the imperial decree announcing the establishment of the Diet, the newspapers virtually became organs of the newly formed political parties and mainly carried items critical of the government. The readers came mostly from the ranks of the former *samurai* class and intelligentsia. These newspapers were called *ōshimbun* (large newspapers). *Koshimbun* (small newspapers) were popular newspapers containing local news, human interest stories, and light fiction. They were easy to read, full of homiletic moralizing, and carried articles catering to the rather plebeian tastes of the masses. The YOMIURI SHIMBUN, which began publishing in 1874, is a typical example.

Partially because strong government pressure caused the *ōshimbun* to fail, new newspapers printing impartial news started springing up around 1880. The ASAHI SHIMBUN was launched in 1879 in Ōsaka, and the JIJI SHIMPŌ in 1882 in Tōkyō. Both *ōshimbun* and *koshimbun* began carrying more news. The first full-scale commercial newspaper published for the newly emerging urban working class, the YOROZU CHŌHŌ, was started by KUROIWA RUIKŌ in 1892. Around this time NEWS AGENCIES were also formed. With the sudden increase in circulation made possible by the widespread use of rotary presses and the growth of advertising, Japanese newspapers became large capitalistic enterprises. Newspapers merged, leading to a decrease in their number, and the gap between *ōshimbun* and *koshimbun* widened. The PRESS LAW OF 1909 detailed conditions and procedures for the issuance of newspapers and magazines, restricted the content of articles, and provided for the punishment of violators. This law remained in effect without modification until 1945.

In the general atmosphere of TAISHŌ DEMOCRACY of the late 1910s to mid 1920s, newspapers came out in favor of democratic campaigns such as the MOVEMENT TO PROTECT CONSTITUTIONAL GOVERNMENT. The *Asahi shimbun* of Ōsaka was subjected to pressure from the government for the use of an expression interpreted by the authorities as slander against the emperor, in connection with its news coverage of the RICE RIOTS OF 1918. In response, a number of staff journalists resigned and the *Asahi* printed a letter of explanation. This case highlights the intensified government control over speech and thought at the time. From about this time major newspapers endeavored to expand news coverage and modernize equipment. After the Tōkyō Earthquake of 1923 the *Asahi* and *Mainichi* became the two largest national newspapers, virtually dominating the Japanese newspaper industry, and the *Yomiuri shimbun*, saved from bankruptcy by SHŌRIKI MATSUTARŌ in 1924, rose to third place on the strength of its sensational articles.

With the growing militarism in Japan early in the 1930s, freedom of the press began to be curtailed. The press was placed under the complete control of the government and military authorities and was used as a propaganda organ from the outbreak of the Sino-Japanese War in 1937 (see SINO-JAPANESE WAR OF 1937–1945) until the end of World War II in 1945. Newsprint was rationed, and many newspapers were forced to merge. The number of newspapers dropped from 848 in 1939 to 54 in 1942.

After World War II, although SCAP (the headquarters of the Allied Occupation of Japan) abolished all wartime laws and regulations controlling the press, reports inimical to the Occupation were suppressed by rigid censorship. Newspapers were encouraged to launch so-called "democratizing" drives to eliminate employees who had cooperated with the government's militaristic policies, and the managements of some 44 papers were replaced. New newspapers sprang up in various places. With the development of the cold war, however, an about-face in Occupation political policy frustrated this "democratizing" drive and some 700 press workers suspected of being communist sympathizers were discharged during the infamous RED PURGE of 1950. A number of new papers, unable to compete with their established counterparts, bowed out of the scene one after the other.

Free competition among newspapers revived after the lifting of controls on newsprint in 1951. The system of morning and evening editions of the same paper and monopoly dealerships, which had been suspended, also revived, and major papers started printing local editions, adding to the already severe competition. Technological innovations in the 1960s and 1970s, such as Chinese character teletypes, monotypes, facsimiles, computer typesetting, and computerized layout systems, greatly facilitated newspaper production.

Newspapers as Mass Media —— The opinion-making activity of Japanese newspapers gradually declined as the papers became interested in profits and had to respond to a broader readership. The heavy pressures from the government and the military authorities which forced newspaper management to maintain strict editorial impartiality and nonpartisanship also weakened the papers' capacity for strong editorial policy, and the general papers have never revived the lively political forums of the 19th century. When weekly magazines, comic magazines, and television became popular after World War II, general newspapers (some evening papers excepted) were not looked to for entertainment, so they began to concentrate on news and advertising. Furthermore, progress in broadcast media such as radio and TV deprived the newspapers of their edge on prompt reporting, which forced the press to turn to in-depth articles and news commentary, albeit politically neutral.

Circulation —— According to statistics of the JAPAN NEWSPAPER PUBLISHERS AND EDITORS ASSOCIATION, the total circulation of daily papers as of October 1980 was 46,391,096, or an average of 1.29 newspapers per Japanese household. General papers accounted for 88.3 percent, and sports papers for 11.7 percent. Morning papers accounted for 52.3 percent, evening papers 4.9 percent, and morning-evening papers 42.8 percent. If the morning and evening editions of the same paper are counted as two, Japan would rank second in the world in 1978 in per capita circulation of newspapers (558:1,000).

Most Japanese general papers come out in both morning and evening editions, and 92 percent are delivered directly to the readers' homes through monopoly dealerships. The five major daily general papers, the *Asahi shimbun, Mainichi shimbun, Yomiuri shimbun,* SANKEI SHIMBUN, and NIHON KEIZAI SHIMBUN, which have sufficient resources to maintain a nationwide delivery network, account for 52.1 percent of the entire circulation of daily general papers. The readers of these national papers are concentrated in and around large cities like Tōkyō and Ōsaka, where publishing offices are located; many prefectural papers enjoy more than 50 percent of the newspaper circulation in their areas.

Monopoly Dealerships —— Early in their history, newspapers were sold on consignment to bookstores, but the *Tōkyō nichinichi shimbun* initiated a home delivery system which was soon followed by other papers, and newspaper dealers specializing in delivery set up businesses throughout the country. The *Hōchi shimbun* started exclusive dealerships in 1903 to distribute only its own papers nationwide. The dealers were not only responsible for delivery but also acted as subscription salesmen. News of the resulting increase in circulation for the *Hōchi* prompted other papers to set up their own news dealerships, and the system of monopoly newspaper dealerships peculiar to Japan was created in 1930. However, poor working conditions, chronic labor shortages, and rising labor costs are making maintenance of this sales system very difficult. Excessive badgering of potential readers by rival dealerships has drawn strong criticism from the public.

Journalists —— Would-be journalists in Japan are selected from among new university graduates through examinations conducted by the individual newspaper companies. The examinations are notoriously difficult and many hundreds of applicants may compete for a single job. Once accepted, however, newspapermen can look forward to lifetime employment; they rarely move on to other companies. Japanese companies more often than not shift newspapermen to administrative positions by the time they become senior reporters, leaving actual reporting and editing activities to underlings. Unlike the custom in the West, it is considered undesirable for newspapermen to remain "in the field." However, many newspaper companies have created a new position called "editorial committee member," so that veteran reporters may continue news-gathering activities while enjoying the status and compensations that go with administrative positions. See also INTERNATIONAL COMMUNICATIONS; FREEDOM OF SPEECH, REGULATION OF; NEWSPAPERS, LOCAL; NEWSPAPERS, NATIONWIDE.

◼ —— Arai Naoyuki, *Shimbun sengo shi* (1979). Haruhara Akihiko, *Nihon shimbun tsūshi* (1969). Inaba Michio and Arai Naoyuki, ed, *Shimbungaku* (1977). The Japan Newspaper Publishers and Editors Association, ed, *The Japanese Press* (annual). The Japan Newspaper Publishers and Editors Association, ed, *Nihon shimbun nenkan* (annual). *ARAI Naoyuki*

newspapers, local

(chihōshi). Local newspapers in Japan consist primarily of prefectural and regional papers. The majority of these newspapers got

New Tōkyō International Airport

View of the main runway and the north and south wings of the passenger terminal; below the latter can be seen the control tower.

their start during the time of the political and social movements that sprang up in the Meiji (1868–1912) and Taishō (1912–26) periods. Most of the present prefectural papers came into existence with the system established by the government in 1942 of one paper to a prefecture. Regional papers like the HOKKAIDŌ SHIMBUN, SANKEI SHIMBUN, CHŪNICHI SHIMBUN, and the NISHI NIPPON SHIMBUN have sales territories that extend over several prefectures. The largest of these papers, like the *Chūnichi* have a million or more readers, while most of the prefectural papers generally have between 100,000 and 300,000 subscribers.

Readers in any given prefecture usually subscribe to only one local newspaper; in cases where they do subscribe to two papers, one of the national newspapers (see NEWSPAPERS, NATIONWIDE) is usually their other choice. The appeal of local newspapers is of course that they treat subject matter closer to the lives of the readers in a particular locale than that found in the giant national dailies. Since the late 1960s, however, national newspapers began making advances into the territory of local and regional papers, and the market is rapidly changing. On the other hand, local newspapers have been strong in their coverage of such issues as local environmental problems and movements to revive local culture. See also NEWSPAPERS. *HAYAKAWA Zenjirō*

newspapers, nationwide

(zenkokushi). A general term for the three major national dailies, the ASAHI SHIMBUN, YOMIURI SHIMBUN, and MAINICHI SHIMBUN, all of which have nationwide distribution. All three newspapers started in Ōsaka in the 1870s and 1880s offering entertainment features and news to the masses as so-called small newspapers (*koshimbun*; see NEWSPAPERS) in contrast to the so-called large newpapers (*ōshimbun*) which concentrated on political issues. During the period of the Sino-Japanese War of 1894–95 and Russo-Japanese War of 1904–05, they made impartiality and neutrality their motto, and went on to overtake the "large newspapers" by devoting their energies to news coverage rather than propaganda, thus becoming "mass newspapers," each with readerships of over a million. The great Tōkyō Earthquake of 1923 dealt a destructive blow to Tōkyō-based newspapers and allowed the Ōsaka-based dailies to become national newspapers with large nationwide circulations.

From their very first editions, all three papers offered feature articles, serial novels by well-known writers of the day, sensational news reportage, and sports coverage. They also devoted space to items on hobbies, women's topics, and family columns, thus creating a content with appeal to a mass audience.

In recent years the big national dailies have expanded their operations to include radio and television programming. Competition for readers has led to various innovations, and recently they have begun making inroads into the sales of local newspapers. See also NEWSPAPERS; NEWSPAPERS, LOCAL. *HAYAKAWA Zenjirō*

New Tōkyō International Airport

(Shin Tōkyō Kokusai Kūkō). International airport located some 66 kilometers (41 mi) east of Tōkyō in the city of Narita, Chiba Prefec-

New Year——Kadomatsu

A pair of *kadomatsu* in front of a doorway in the Gion district of Kyōto. The arrangement consists of pine and bamboo (the latter cut diagonally at the top). The ornamental kale and dwarf bamboo leaves at the bottom are not typical of all areas of Japan. Straw tassels *(shimekazari)* hang over the door.

New Year——Joya no kane

New Year's eve at Chion'in, Kyōto. Monks from the temple, surrounded by spectators, are engaged in tolling the bell 108 times. The number 108 refers to the Buddhist teaching that human beings are plagued by 108 earthly desires; with each toll of the bell, one is dispelled.

ture. Also known as Narita Airport. Replacing Tōkyō International Airport (Haneda Airport) as the international airport serving Tōkyō, the airport opened in May 1978.

Haneda Airport had registered a sharp increase in the volume of passengers and air freight in the early 1960s, and because it was judged inadequate for the volume of traffic expected in the near future even with expansion, studies for the construction of a new international airport were initiated in 1962. In 1966 the New Tōkyō International Airport Authority was created and charged with the construction, management, and operation of a new airport at Narita. Construction work on the airport began in 1969, but its completion was delayed from 1971 to 1975 and its opening to 1978 because of fierce opposition to the airport from a coalition of local inhabitants and students (see CITIZENS' MOVEMENTS).

Located at some distance from central Tōkyō, the New Tōkyō International Airport is connected with Tōkyō by the Japanese National Railways' Narita line and the private Keisei line. An expressway between the airport and Tōkyō is used by limousine buses. Check-in procedures can also now be completed for many flights at the Tōkyō City Air Terminal in central Tōkyō.

The New Tōkyō International Airport's main runway measures 4,000 meters (13,120 ft) in length. The airport has a total area of 550 hectares (1,358.5 acres). Future plans call for the construction of a parallel runway of 2,500 meters (8,200 ft) and a crosswind runway of 3,200 meters (10,496 ft), with the area of the airport to be expanded to 1,065 hectares (2,630.6 acres) to accommodate the new facilities. At present, 33 airlines from 30 countries are utilizing the airport,

with approximately 180 flights landing and departing from the airport each day. The airport annually handles some 8,200,000 passengers and 480,000 metric tons (529,104 short tons) of air freight.

New Trunk Line → Shinkansen

New Woman's Association → Shin Fujin Kyōkai

New Year

(Shōgatsu). New Year observances are the most important and most elaborate of Japan's annual events. Though customs differ by locality, at this time homes are decorated, and the holidays are celebrated by family gatherings, visits to shrines or temples, and formal calls on relatives and friends. In recent years the New Year festivities have been officially observed from 1 January through 3 January, during which time all government offices and most companies are closed.

Preparations for seeing in the New Year were originally undertaken to greet the TOSHIGAMI, or deity of the incoming year. These began on 13 December, when the house was given a thorough cleaning. More recently this cleaning has been performed closer to the end of the month. The house is then decorated in the traditional fashion: A sacred rope of straw *(shimenawa)* with dangling white paper strips *(shide)* is hung over the front door to demarcate the temporary abode of the *toshigami* and to prevent malevolent spirits from entering. It is also customary to place *kadomatsu,* an arrangement of tree sprigs, especially pine branches, bamboo stalks, and in some areas, plum branches, at the gateway to ensure prosperity and good health for the coming year. A special altar, known as a *toshidana* (literally, "year shelf"), is piled high with flat, round rice cakes *(kagamimochi),* bottles of rice wine *(sake),* persimmons, and other foods in honor of the *toshigami.*

YEAR-END FAIRS *(toshi no ichi)* are held toward the end of December for purchasing these holiday items. By New Year's Eve the *toshiki* (literally, "year wood"; fuel offered to the *toshigami* for use during the season) has been stacked, NEW YEAR'S CARDS *(nengajō)* written and sent, the *mochi* (rice cakes made of pounded glutinous rice) made, and the traditional holiday dishes *(osechi ryōri)* prepared.

In recent years, the flurry of activity in preparation for the traditional religious and familial rites has tended to be overshadowed by secular activities such as *bōnenkai* (literally, "forgetting-the-year parties"), Christmas parties, and, after the New Year, *shinnenkai* (new year parties), all of them generally excuses for much eating and drinking (see also ENKAI). Children also look forward to receiving money (OTOSHIDAMA) from family and neighbors.

New Year's Eve —— The night before New Year's is called Ōmisoka; in the past, days were reckoned from sundown to sundown so that Ōmisoka was actually part of New Year's Day. Families formally sat down to a traditional New Year's meal on this night. Nowadays many people visit Buddhist temples to hear the temple bells rung 108 times at midnight *(joya no kane)* to dispel the evils of the past year or watch this event on television. It is also customary to eat *toshikoshi soba* (literally, "year-crossing noodles") in the hope that one's family fortunes will be lengthened and extended like the long, thin noodles.

On New Year's Eve in some areas, visits by the *toshigami* are enacted by costumed performers who go from house to house performing the pony dance *(harukoma-mai)* or lion dance (SHISHI-MAI), or who masquerade as comics or devils (see NAMAHAGE).

New Year's Days —— The first day of the year *(ganjitsu)* is usually spent with members of the family. Although religious observances vary according to the period and the region, on this day it is customary, especially in rural areas, for the head of the household or the designated *toshiotoko* (literally, "year man") to rise before dawn and draw from the well the first water *(wakamizu)* of the New Year. He then makes tea or a special soup called *zōni,* or heats the bath with this water, sets out a traditional holiday breakfast from the prepared *osechi ryōri,* and makes an offering to the *toshigami.* Traditionally, the *toshiotoko* was the man of the house, but, with the weakening of belief in the *toshigami,* it has become customary to relegate these preparations to an older son or the women of the family.

In both urban and rural areas people throng to Buddhist temples and Shintō shrines in vast numbers on New Year's Day, often wearing their best *kimono.* On these visits, known as *hatsumairi* or *hatsumōde* (literally, "first visit"), prayers are offered for the good fortune of the family. According to official statistics, some 71,000,000 people visited temples and shrines over the three-day New Year holiday in 1981. The three most popular places were the Meiji Shrine in Tōkyō (with 3,600,000 visitors), the Kawasaki Daishi, a temple in Kawasaki, Kanagawa Prefecture (with 2,900,000 visitors), and the Shinshōji, a Buddhist temple at Narita in Chiba Prefecture (with 267,000 visitors).

In the Imperial Palace, at dawn or early on the morning of 1 January, the emperor performs the rite of *shihōhai* (worship of the four quarters), in which he does reverence in the directions of various shrines and imperial tombs and offers prayers for the well-being of the nation. Once the *shihōhai* is completed, the New Year celebrations may begin at the palace and shrines. On 2 January the public is allowed to enter the inner palace grounds; the only other day this is possible is the emperor's birthday.

On the second and third days of the New Year holidays, friends and business acquaintances visit one another to extend greetings (*nenshi*) and sip *toso*, a spiced rice wine. The second, fourth, or eleventh day formally signals the start of such traditional domestic chores as sewing and ropemaking, of doing the first calligraphy of the year (*kakizome*), of striking the first hoe (*kuwazome*) in tilling the fields, of fishing, and of other kinds of work. These are all marked by observances or celebrations of a symbolic nature; the actual work begins later. For example, most office workers will visit their office on the fourth but not actually start work until the following day. On the seventh a special gruel containing seven kinds of herb called *nanakusagayu* is eaten. On the seventh or fifteenth, depending on the area, the *kadomatsu* and *shimenawa* are taken down and set aflame as a beacon fire to light the gods' way back. On the sixteenth young apprentices (as well as daughters-in-law and servants) are given a special holiday (*yabuiri*) to visit their parental homes. The sixteenth is also called Hotoke Shōgatsu, the first day in some regions for holding Buddhist observances. On the twentieth, or Hatsuka Shōgatsu, final holiday and other observances are held in some areas.

Ōshōgatsu and Koshōgatsu

Shōgatsu refers to the first month of the year as well as the period of the New Year's holidays. The events described above concern what is commonly referred to as Ōshōgatsu (literally, "Big New Year"). There is, however, another traditional New Year's called Koshōgatsu (literally, "Small New Year"). The former follows the date calculated by the Gregorian calendar, and the latter is set according to the lunar calendar. Koshōgatsu thus starts with the first full moon of the year on about 15 January and is largely observed in the rural areas of Japan.

The Ōshōgatsu celebration centers around the events welcoming the *toshigami*, but the main events of the Koshōgatsu are rites and practices praying for a bountiful harvest. In the early Japanese language the word *toshi*, meaning year, was synonymous with *ine*, or rice plant, and in an agricultural society like Japan the *toshigami* took on the character of agricultural deities. The *mayudama*, for example, is a colorful holiday decoration made by hanging small, cocoon-shaped rice cakes or dumplings and an assortment of talismans from the branches of a bamboo or willow; it is hung in doorways and rooms as a token of request for a plentiful silkworm cocoon crop. The *mochibana* is a decoration made of ring-shaped rice cakes hung on a tiny willow branch; it is placed on the *kamidana*, or god shelf, near the miniature shrine. The *awabo hiebo* is yet another talismanic decoration made from branch cuttings fashioned to resemble ripe heads of rice. Other rites include *niwataue* and *taasobi*, in which the entire rice-growing cycle from planting to harvest is symbolically acted out.

Prayer is the principal element in most of the observances celebrating the beginning of work in a new year. However, *torioi*, a Koshōgatsu rite in which children beat the ground with sticks and recite a chant to drive off harmful birds, and *narikizeme*, in which the trunks of fruit trees are ritually slashed with a stick to ensure a plentiful fruit crop, are quite clearly magic rituals. Auguries, such as *kayuura*, are performed to divine whether the year's harvest will be rich or poor. In *kayuura* a length of bamboo is cut into 12 (13 in a leap year) pieces, each representing a month of the year, and boiled in gruel. The pieces are then split open; the amount of liquid absorbed into the hollow section of each piece foretells the crop for that month. Several games played at New Year's, such as SUGO-ROKU (a kind of parcheesi), *karuta* (see PLAYING CARDS), and HANE-TSUKI (shuttlecock and battledore) are also sometimes augural in nature. INOKUCHI Shōji and Stanley WEINSTEIN

New Year's cards

(*nengajō*). Japanese send New Year's greeting cards to virtually all of their relatives, friends, and acquaintances, and businesses, too, send out cards to their customers. The Japanese New Year's card fulfills much the same function as the Western Christmas card, but the Japanese send them out in much greater quantities, a single individual's mailing often numbering in the hundreds. The card itself also differs from the Christmas card. Instead of being folded and placed in an envelope it is typically made from a regular government-issued postcard. There is, nevertheless, considerable variety or even creativity in what appears on the card. Many families design their own postcards and have them printed. Cards posted between 15 and 28 December are held by the post office and delivered together on 1 January. One type of government-issued New Year's card is printed with lottery numbers, which may enable the recipient to win various prizes. The government also issues special New Year's postcards sold at one yen above the regular price, the extra money going to charity.

The custom of sending Christmas cards has also gained some popularity among young people in Japan, but has by no means affected the practice of sending New Year's cards. Traditionally New Year's, the most important holiday in Japan, is a time when people visit each other to celebrate the happy occasion, to thank each other for the past year's favors, and to solicit good will for the coming year. Because of the difficulty of paying visits to all but a limited number of relatives and friends, the custom of sending New Year's cards, which came into vogue late in the 19th century, made it possible to extend greetings to virtually all those in one's social network. New Year's cards mailed out each year number in the billions for the whole of Japan. Harumi BEFU

New Zealand and Japan

While two New Zealand brothers owned a small paddle steamer going daily between Yokohama and Tōkyō as long ago as 1868, for the next 80 years personal, commercial, and official contacts between New Zealand and Japan were only intermittent and never close. Japanese ships escorted New Zealand troops to the Middle East in 1915, and in 1928 Japan became the first country with which New Zealand concluded a commercial treaty in its own right. But these instances were exceptional in a pattern of relations that, on the New Zealand side at least, was tinged with suspicion. Although critical of Japanese aggression against China in the 1930s, New Zealand's part in the Pacific War was relatively small, since its forces were most active in the Middle East and Europe. After the war New Zealand's proposals for a restrictive peace settlement with Japan did not prevail, and on 28 April 1952, when the San Francisco Peace Treaty came into effect, the New Zealand mission in Japan, previously accredited to the Supreme Commander for the Allied Powers (SCAP), became New Zealand's first legation in Japan. Later that year, the Japanese established a legation in Wellington.

In the decade following ratification of the peace treaty, Japan and New Zealand entered upon an increasing variety of dealings together. Contracts were extended between officials and businessmen; and first steps were taken in cultural and sporting exchanges. New Zealand worked hard for Japan's admission to the United Nations.

On both sides there was a clear desire at the governmental level to transcend the difficulties of the past; while their wartime animosities toward Japan had not been completely set at rest, most New Zealanders now looked toward Japan without hostility and with growing curiosity and expectation. In September 1958 a treaty of commerce was signed, and in 1962 the New Zealand government took what was at the time the bold course of establishing most-favored-nation trading relations with Japan, the first such step taken by one of Japan's former adversaries. It opened the way to a vast expansion of Japanese manufactured goods on to the New Zealand market and fed the expectations on New Zealand's part of growing benefits in its economic and other dealings with Japan.

In the next decade, these expectations were substantially fulfilled. Among New Zealanders, interest in things Japanese continued to grow. At the highest level, contact was maintained through exchanges of visits by the prime ministers of the two countries and other ministers, and in a number of international settings, particularly in Asia, New Zealand and Japan became accustomed to consulting and working together. But it was in the area of trade that the true sinew of the relationship lay. In the years between 1962 and 1972, the annual level of trade grew from a few million dollars to almost 500 million dollars. Since the two economies are largely complementary, each can offer things that the other needs. New Zealand has been able to supply large quantities of farm and forestry products, while Japan has provided many of the sophisticated manufactures that New Zealand needs.

Since the mid-70s, old settings have been expanded and new contexts created. The New Zealand–Japan Educational Exchange Agreement signed in 1974, the Japan Advisory Committee established in 1975, and the New Zealand–Japan Parliamentarians' Association of 1977 are giving New Zealanders and Japanese enhanced opportunities to work together. Some 2,000 young New Zealanders are studying Japanese each year, and growing numbers now have the opportunity to study in Japan. Trade has continued to grow and in 1978 totaled over 800 million dollars, divided about equally. Japan is now New Zealand's most important trading partner.

Nevertheless, an element of strain and uncertainty has developed between the two countries, and issues patiently but unprofitably discussed over many years have now become problems which may well impair the relationship in the years to come. In the years since 1962, New Zealand has persistently tried to persuade Japan to liberalize its system governing imports of agricultural and forestry products, only to be frustrated by the Japanese agricultural system which, in the interest of self-sufficiency, keeps prices high and demand relatively low and treats imports simply as a means of regulating the system. In the years until 1976 New Zealand's painstakingly presented arguments achieved virtually no results, and for certain agricultural products, particularly butter, milk powder, and beef, sales fluctuated wildly.

Early in 1976 New Zealand made a decisive change in its strategy. In a series of exchanges, it sought better access to various sectors of the Japanese market, again without success, and then announced that until some satisfactory response had been made, Japanese fishing boats would not be licensed to fish in New Zealand's waters, which had recently been vastly extended by changes in the international law of the sea. In June 1978 it was announced that an agreement substantially satisfactory to New Zealand had been reached, and that Japanese fishing boats would be licensed to take a specified tonnage from New Zealand's extended economic zone. Since the terms of the agreement have been kept secret, it is difficult to assess to what extent New Zealand's requests for improved access for its agricultural and forestry products have been or are likely to be met. Nevertheless, the agreement has served ostensibly to take the strain out of relations between New Zealand and Japan.

The recent airing of complaints is likely to inject some caution into future dealings between the two countries, but Japan will inevitably be of great importance to New Zealand—as a major power, as a trading partner, and as a source of influence and leadership in Southeast Asia and the Pacific Basin. Relations between Japan and New Zealand have come a long way since the chilly and suspicious days before World War II. But a great deal needs still to be done by New Zealand—to extend contacts with Japan, to enhance New Zealand's commercial efforts there, to make New Zealanders and Japanese better known to one another.

📖——Graham Kitson, "Perspective on New Zealand–Japan Trade and Economic Relations," *Asia Pacific Forum* (March 1978). Paul Knight, "New Zealand Beef Exports to Japan," *Asia Pacific Forum* (March 1978). Tom Larkin, *New Zealand and Japan in the Post-War World* (1969). M. P. Lissington, *New Zealand and Japan 1900–1941* (1972). John Mowbray, "Trade Relations between New Zealand and Japan," *Asia Pacific Forum* (February 1976). B. E. Talboys, "New Zealand's Case for Improvements in the Economic Relationship with Japan," *Asia Pacific Forum* (February 1976).　　T. C. LARKIN

Neyagawa

City in northeastern Ōsaka Prefecture, central Honshū, on the river Yodogawa. The area was formerly known for its rice and lotus roots *(renkon)*; however, the establishment of machine, textile, and chemical factories and the growth of residential areas have made it a satellite city of Ōsaka. Of interest are Jōmon (ca 10,000 BC–ca 300 BC) and Yayoi (ca 300 BC–ca AD 300) period archaeological sites, in the eastern section, and a branch temple of the Narita Fudōsan (SHINSHŌJI). Pop: 255,864.

Nezame monogatari emaki

Illustrated handscroll (EMAKIMONO) in the brightly-colored *tsukuri-e* style; dated to the second half of the 12th century. The single surviving scroll, measuring 25.6 by 508.28 centimeters (10 by 200 in), in the collection of the Yamato Bunkakan in Nara, contains four pictures with four garbled and fragmentary sections of text.

The 11th-century novel *Nezame monogatari* (The Tale of Nezame), better known as YORU NO NEZAME, is heavily dependent on the TALE OF GENJI in style and construction. The main elements of the plot are the unhappy love affair of the heroine, Nezame, with her sister's husband; Nezame's flight from an infatuated emperor; and finally, the romantic adventures of her son Masako no Kimi and the emperor's daughter. All existing texts are lacking much of the last part of the story. Since this is the part covered by the surviving portions of the *emaki,* the scroll has literary as well as artistic importance.

The first illustration shows three children in a spring garden playing flutes under willow and flowering cherry trees, while two ladies sit listening in a house to the left. The two following illustrations also show the houses and gardens of elegant ladies whom Masako no Kimi visits, in late spring and summer respectively. In the latter picture the characters can barely be seen through the doors of the house, but their feelings are suggested by the verdant green of the garden plants. The final picture shows an interior scene in muted colors, implying quiet pathos. The former emperor, now in retirement, receives a letter from Nezame, whom he had believed dead.

The pictures are strongly reminiscent of the GENJI MONOGATARI EMAKI (*Tale of Genji* scrolls). The *tsukuri-e* painting technique, using brilliant, opaque colors, is similar in all respects but one: in the garden scenes, the background is not painted over but instead is decorated with various forms of gold and silver leaf, as in the calligraphic sections of the *Genji* scrolls. The emphasis placed on elements of natural scenery, which are treated in a highly decorative manner, is a major characteristic of *Nezame.* The figures are much smaller than those in *Genji,* and in many cases they are shown from the back, revealing only robes and hair. The perspective is extremely high, giving a bird's-eye view of the interiors (FUKINUKI YATAI). Its exaggerated style suggests that the *Nezame monogatari emaki* should be dated somewhat later than the *Genji monogatari emaki.* Its lavishly decorative quality is in keeping with the spirit of the final days of the Fujiwara period (894–1185).

📖——Shirahata Yoshi, ed, *Nezame monogatari emaki,* in vol 17 of *Nihon emakimono zenshū* (Kadokawa Shoten, 1965).

Sarah THOMPSON

Nezamenotoko

Scenic gorge on the river KISOGAWA, Nagano Prefecture, central Honshū. Consists of huge granite rocks that have been eroded into strange shapes. The view from the temple Rinsenji is particularly fine. The area is claimed to be associated with the legend of Urashima Tarō, a fisherman who visited a palace in the sea and returned after an absence of many years.

Nezu Art Museum

(Nezu Bijutsukan). Located in Tōkyō. The collection of the late NEZU KAICHIRŌ, it opened to the public in 1940 but was evacuated during World War II and escaped the destruction suffered by the estate property in the bombing of May 1945; it is now shown in a building erected in 1955. The Japanese section includes paintings, calligraphy, ceramics, lacquer, and metalwork; the Chinese section has bronzes, paintings, sculpture, lacquer, and ceramics. Among the best-known Japanese paintings in the collection are the 13th- or early-14th-century *Nachi no taki* (Nachi Waterfall) and a KŌRIN masterpiece—the famous pair of sixfold screens with irises on a gold ground. There is a particularly choice group of Japanese ceramics, including many tea-ceremony objects. The Chinese bronze vessels of the Shang (2nd millennium BC) and the early part of the Zhou (Chou; 1027 BC–256 BC) dynasties form a group unique for their size and exuberant decoration. There is also a distinguished group of Chinese paintings from the Song (Sung; 960–1279) and Yuan (Yüan; 1279–1368) dynasties. The museum has published a wide range of catalogs. See also MUSEUMS.　　*Laurance* ROBERTS

Nezu Kaichirō (1860–1940)

Businessman and politician. Born in Yamanashi Prefecture. He became president of TŌBU RAILWAY CO, LTD, in 1905, and brought prosperity to the company by extending the line to Nikkō and Kinugawa and developing the land alongside it. Nezu also managed several other railroad companies and industries. He was elected to the House of Representatives in 1904 and later served in the House of Peers. He established several academic and cultural institutions, including the Musashi Higher School (now Musashi University). His large art collection served as the basis for the NEZU ART MUSEUM in Tōkyō.   MAEDA Kazutoshi

nezumi → rats and mice

nezumimochi

(Japanese privet). *Ligustrum japonicum.* An evergreen shrub of the olive family (Oleaceae) which grows wild in mountainous areas of central and western Honshū. It is also planted as a hedge. It stands about 2 meters (7 ft) in height, has gray bark, numerous branches, and elliptical opposite leaves with leathery, glossy surfaces. In the summer, conical flower stalks appear on the tips of the new branches, producing dense clusters of small white blossoms. These are followed by oblong fruits, which ripen to a purplish black color.   MATSUDA Osamu

NGK Insulators, Ltd

(Nippon Gaishi). Leading manufacturer and distributor of electrical insulators, also engaged in the manufacture and sale of corrosion-resistant chemical equipment, environmental control equipment, and special inorganic materials. NGK Insulators was established in 1919 and first exported insulators to the United States and Canada in 1930. It now exports insulators to more than 110 countries. In 1954 NGK first exported a complete factory for the manufacture of insulators to India. Currently NGK has sales and service centers in the United States, Canada, and Belgium. Locke Insulators, Inc, was established in 1974 jointly by NGK (as majority shareholder) and General Electric Company, USA, as NGK's production base in North America. In 1977 NGK established NGK–Baudour, S.A., in Belgium as its production base in Europe. By 1965 NGK had already initiated successful commercial production of porcelain insulators and bushing shells for 500-kilovolt electric power transmission. Steady and rigorous research and development efforts are now being made to meet the needs of the electric power industry for the approaching age of ultrahigh voltage (1,000 kilovolts and above) power transmission. NGK has also branched out into corrosion-resistant chemical equipment (1922), beryllium products and new ceramics (1958), and environmental control equipment (1962). Sales for the fiscal year ending March 1982 were ¥121.7 billion (US $505.6 million), of which insulators and related products accounted for 60 percent and other products 40 percent. In the same year the company was capitalized at ¥11.1 billion (US $46.1 million). Its head office is located in Nagoya.

NHK

(Nippon Hōsō Kyōkai; Japan Broadcasting Corporation). The national public broadcasting system in Japan. In contrast to the commercial broadcasting system, which operates on revenue from advertisers, NHK's financing depends solely on revenue from reception fees paid by families with one or more television sets.

Broadcasting in Japan began in 1925, when the Tōkyō Broadcasting Station was incorporated to offer broadcasting service to subscribers in the Tōkyō area. Two similar stations were established that same year in Ōsaka and Nagoya. These three stations were combined in 1926 to form Nippon Hōsō Kyōkai, forerunner of the present NHK, which monopolized broadcasting in Japan until the end of World War II. NHK was put under direct control of the Supreme Commander for the Allied Powers (SCAP) during the American Occupation, and was reorganized as a special public corporation to serve the whole nation in accordance with the BROADCASTING LAW enacted in 1950. The new law included provisions for commercial broadcasting, which began in 1951, stripping NHK of its status as the sole broadcasting station in the country. Regular telecasts were begun in February 1953.

The operation committee is the highest decision-making organ, consisting of 12 regular members, who are appointed by the prime minister with the approval of the Diet. The highest ranking officer responsible for the management of daily operations is the chairman of the board, who is appointed by the operations committee. The budget and administration of NHK are also subject to the approval

of the Diet, and public control over NHK is exercised solely through the Diet.

At present NHK conducts nationwide and local broadcasts through two television, one FM radio, and two AM radio channels. NHK also conducts international broadcasts for a composite total of nearly 40 hours a day in 21 languages to 18 broadcast zones throughout the world. NHK maintains stations in various locations in Japan and branches in key foreign cities. NHK is currently staffed by approximately 16,000 people.

📖 ──NHK, Radio and TV Culture Research Institute, ed, *50 Years of Japanese Broadcasting* (1977).   GOTŌ Kazuhiko

NHK Spring Co, Ltd

(Nippon Hatsujō). Producer of plate springs, sheet springs, and other types of springs. Established in 1936, this firm is currently one of the three major spring manufacturers in the world. It has production bases in Brazil, Thailand, Spain, and Taiwan and sales companies in the United States. It also supplies technological assistance to the Philippines and Iran. The company is currently tackling the problem of reducing the weight of its products to conform to the government's energy-saving policies. Sales for the fiscal year ending March 1982 totaled ¥91.9 billion (US $381.8 million), and the company was capitalized at ¥7.6 billion (US $31.6 million). Corporate headquarters are located in Yokohama.

Nichibei Shūkō Tsūshō Jōyaku → Harris Treaty

Nichibei Washin Jōyaku → Kanagawa Treaty

Nichiei Dōmei → Anglo-Japanese Alliance

Nichiei Tsūshō Kōkai Jōyaku → Anglo-Japanese Commercial Treaty of 1894

Nichii Co, Ltd

Major retailer ranking fifth in the Japanese supermarket industry. Established in 1963 through the merger of four clothing companies, Nichii has diversified its sales to include foodstuffs, sundry goods, and housewares. The company quickly became known as a mass sales firm concentrating on household items, and was able to grow rapidly. The Nichii group consists of four divisions which manage mass sales, department stores, voluntary projects, and specialty stores. Sales totaled ¥490.9 billion (US $2.1 billion) in the fiscal year ending February 1982, with 42.5 percent generated by clothing, 30 percent by household items, 25.8 percent by foodstuffs, and 1.7 percent by other products. In the same year the company was capitalized at ¥10 billion (US $42.5 million). Corporate headquarters are located in Ōsaka.

Nichimen Co, Ltd

(Nichimen Jitsugyō). A general trading company (*sōgō shōsha*) engaged in exports and imports, domestic wholesaling, plant engineering and construction, and real estate. One of the nine leading Japanese trading firms, it is a principal member of the SANWA BANK, LTD, group. Nichimen's predecessor, Nippon Menka Kaisha (Japan Cotton Trading Company), was established in 1892 and became one of the nation's biggest importers of raw cotton. Nichimen assumed its current name in 1957, when the Japanese economy was shifting its emphasis from light industry to heavy and chemical industries. Through extensive diversification into nontextile fields the company upgraded itself to a general trading company. It has approximately 80 branches and liaison offices overseas, all linked by a computerized communication system. The company is also involved in about 100 joint ventures overseas. Future plans call for the promotion of more offshore business and the expansion of plant engineering and construction projects. Sales for the fiscal year ending March 1982 totaled ¥2.9 trillion (US $12 billion), distributed as follows: metals and fuel 32.5 percent; machinery and construction 27.1 percent; foodstuffs 14.4 percent; textiles 11.7 percent; chemical and synthetic resins 9.3 percent; lumber, paper, pulp, and others 5 percent. The export ratio was 24.6 percent. Capitalization stood at ¥11.4 billion (US $47.4 million) in the same year. The company's main offices are located in Tōkyō and Ōsaka. See also GENERAL TRADING COMPANIES.

Nichiren

Detail of a late-13th-century Buddhist painting. The figure here is said to be Nichiren. Colors on silk. Myōhokkeji, Mishima, Shizuoka Prefecture.

Nichinan

City in southern Miyazaki Prefecture, Kyūshū, on the Hyūga Sea. A former castle town, the city is noted for its early harvest rice, peas, paprika, and shaddock. It is also a fishing base for bonito and tuna. Its pulp industry utilizes the cedars that grow in the city. Nichinan is a part of the Nichinan Coast Quasi-National Park, whose attractions include Udo Shrine and a cactus park. Pop: 52,949.

Nichiō (1565–1630)

Buddhist priest of the NICHIREN SECT and founder of the FUJU FUSE SECT. Born in Kyōto, Nichiō became a monk at the temple Myōkakuji in Kyōto and in 1592 became its abbot. In 1595 he objected to the Nichiren sect's participation in an interdenominational Buddhist service that the hegemon TOYOTOMI HIDEYOSHI proposed to hold to commemorate his deceased kin and the recent completion of the great Buddha image at the temple Hōkōji. He based his objection mainly on the Nichiren tradition that a believer in the truth of the LOTUS SUTRA as interpreted by NICHIREN should neither receive offerings from nonbelievers, such as Hideyoshi, nor give to them (fuju fuse; literally, "not giving, not receiving"). Finding that the majority were willing to compromise and conform to Hideyoshi's order, Nichiō left his temple and secluded himself in the countryside until Hideyoshi's death in 1598. The intransigent attitude of Nichiō and his followers continued to divide Nichiren sectarians, however, and in 1599 the future shōgun TOKUGAWA IEYASU summoned both parties for a debate in his presence. During the debate Nichiō dared to challenge the notion of the ultimate supremacy of secular power and was sent into exile on the island of Tsushima by Ieyasu. Even after his return to Kyōto in 1612 and until his death, he continued to criticize compromisers in the sect. In 1691 the Fuju Fuse sectarians were outlawed by the shogunate; they survived as a clandestine group until 1876, when the ban was lifted. *TSUCHIDA Tomoaki*

Nichiren (1222–1282)

Buddhist monk. Founder of the NICHIREN SECT (also known as the Hokke or Lotus sect) of Buddhism; one of the leaders of the "new Buddhism" of the Kamakura period (1185–1333).

Nichiren was born in the seaside village of Kominato in Awa Province (now part of Chiba Prefecture); his father was probably a low-level estate overseer involved in fishing. Sent at the age of 12 to a nearby TENDAI SECT temple, Kiyosumidera, for his education, Nichiren underwent a crisis stemming from doubts about the efficacy of Pure Land (Jōdo) beliefs (see PURE LAND BUDDHISM); he prayed to Kokūzō, an esoteric bodhisattva enshrined at Kiyosumidera, and received a vision in which Kokūzō bestowed wisdom on him. Ordained at the age of 16 as Zeshōbō Renchō, he embarked on an extended tour of study at the major centers of Buddhist learning in the Kansai area, especially at Mt. Hiei (Hieizan; see ENRYAKUJI), and included stays at Onjōji (see MIIDERA) and Mt. Kōya (see KŌYASAN), returning around 1253. His early works show a devotion to esoteric Tendai and SHINGON SECT teachings (see also ESOTERIC BUDDHISM) as well as to theories of absolute monism derived from

Tendai HONGAKU (original enlightenment) ideas, a growing faith in the LOTUS SUTRA (Skt: *Saddharmapuṇḍarīka-sūtra*; J: *Myōhō renge kyō* or *Hokkekyō*), one of the most widely venerated of Mahāyāna Buddhist scriptures, and a strong dislike for Pure Land Buddhism.

On 2 June 1253 Nichiren preached against the Jōdo and ZEN sects at Kiyosumidera. Traditionally regarded as the founding of the Nichiren sect, this denunciation and a subsequent quarrel with the local magnate Tōjō Kagenobu, a Pure Land devotee, over control of the Kiyosumidera led to Nichiren's expulsion from Awa the following year. Settling in Kamakura, Nichiren gradually turned away from his esoteric Buddhist faith toward early Tendai theories: on this basis he developed an increasingly exclusive faith in the supremacy of the Lotus Sutra with its doctrine of universal salvation and the eternal Buddha Śākyamuni, whom he hailed as "lord, teacher, and parent." Stimulated perhaps by the Pure Land belief in the efficacy of the NEMBUTSU, the invocational recitation of the name of the Buddha AMIDA (Skt: Amitābha), as a means of securing birth in Amida's Western Paradise, Nichiren evolved a similar belief in the practice called *daimoku* (title), a chanting recitation of the phrase NAMU MYŌHŌ RENGE KYŌ ("I take my refuge in the Lotus Sutra") as an invocation affirming the devotee's belief and conferring salvation and which Nichiren took as the object of his worship *(honzon)*. Nichiren held that the *daimoku* of the Lotus Sutra contained all the merits of that sutra, as well as all the merits of all the scriptures and virtues of the Buddha; all these merits are spontaneously yielded to the person who, as he later wrote, "receives and keeps" the *daimoku*. He also developed his early idea of "blasphemy" (heresy, unbelief in the Lotus Sutra), according to which even silence or tolerance in the face of such blasphemy was taken as complicity in the sin. Based on this idea, Nichiren completed in 1260 his RISSHŌ ANKOKU RON (A Treatise on Pacifying the State by Establishing Orthodoxy), which held the Jōdo movement responsible for recent disasters and other calamities if this were not done. Presented to Hōjō Tokiyori (1227–63), the de facto head of the Kamakura shogunate, it led to attacks on Nichiren and his exile to Izu in 1261.

Nichiren's life in Izu is not well documented. His surviving works show his increasing doubts about esoteric Buddhism and the organization of his so-called "five principles" *(gogi)* as the rationale of his belief, namely: (1) the teaching (the Lotus Sutra); (2) the capacities of its recipients; (3) the time (the degenerate third age of Buddhism known as *mappō*, or "the latter doctrine," which was commonly reckoned to have begun in 1052; see ESCHATOLOGY); (4) the country (Japan); and (5) the order of propagation or (in later writings) the teacher (Nichiren). Nichiren also felt a growing sense of his mission as the persecuted ascetic *(gyōja)* of the Lotus Sutra, the messenger of the Buddha in the latter days.

Released from exile at Izu in 1263, he returned to Kamakura, making two trips to Awa in 1264 and 1266, on the first of which his old enemy Tōjō Kagenobu nearly succeeded in having him assassinated. The arrival in Japan of the first Mongol embassy in 1268 (see MONGOL INVASIONS OF JAPAN) built up his hopes for the fulfillment of his predictions of foreign invasions made in the *Risshō ankoku ron*. His expanded denunciations of the Jōdo, Shingon, and other sects and of such prominent monks as Ninshō (1217–1303) of the RITSU SECT embroiled him in lawsuits, while his aggressive behavior and the arming of his followers finally led to his arrest and near execution at Tatsunokuchi near Kamakura in September 1271.

After being held for several weeks under arrest, Nichiren was banished to the island of Sado. Deserted by most of his followers and expecting imminent death, Nichiren sought during his confinement to justify his suffering and his seeming failure as retribution for his own past sins and as the fulfillment of scriptural prophecies concerning those who propagate the Lotus Sutra in the degenerate age of *mappō*. This period marked a critical point in Nichiren's religious life. The most notable of his apologetic works from this time is the *Kaimoku shō* (1272, Opening the Eyes), which Nichiren evidently wrote as a last testament for his followers. Specifically, during this period Nichiren began to identify his mission with the roles of two bodhisattvas in the Lotus Sutra: Jōfukyō (Skt: Sadāparibhūta), who was persecuted in the distant past for his preaching, and Jōgyō (Skt: Viśiṣṭacaritra), the leader of a huge number of bodhisattvas, disciples of the Buddha from incalculable past aeons who were summoned from under the earth to preach the Lotus Sutra. Nichiren believed that the *mappō* age was the time appointed for Jōgyō and his followers to appear to preach the ultimate truth of the Lotus Sutra. It was also at this time that Nichiren began to defend in formal terms his long-standing tactic of aggressively criticizing the "blasphemies" of others; even many of his followers had come to doubt this policy of *shakubuku* (literally, "break and subdue"), which had brought about his persecution. Against this, Nichiren contended that *shakubuku* was a more appropriate tactic for the degenerate *mappō* age than the tolerant policy of accepting the relative truth in other teachings (*shōju*, "gather and accept") as a basis for conversion.

During his detention, Nichiren also began to compose his distinctive MANDALA (written in Chinese characters) which arrange Buddhas, bodhisattvas, and other deities around the *daimoku* of the Lotus Sutra. He continued to write out these mandalas and distribute them to his most faithful followers as objects of worship and protective amulets during his last years.

The miseries of his exile in Sado were partially alleviated by Nichiren's successes in debating with local monks and in gaining new converts. After 1272 he also began to receive visits from his disciples, who had begun to regroup after the recent persecution, and he became more optimistic about his mission.

The new optimism is seen in several works, notably the *Kanjin honzon shō* (The Object of Worship in Contemplation), his most sophisticated work, which he composed for his inner circle of disciples in the spring of 1273; it expounds Nichiren's interpretation of *ichinen sanzen* (three thousand realms in one thought), the Tendai theory of reality; the Buddha's Pure Land in this world; the object of worship; and the reinterpretation of *mappō* as the age in which the Buddha's ultimate teaching would appear. Nichiren continued to develop this last theme in his subsequent writings.

Nichiren's proselytizing activities proved so successful that his enemies attempted to suppress his Sado following, apparently without success. A movement to secure Nichiren's release finally succeeded and he left Sado on 28 April 1274.

After a two-month stay at Kamakura, trying unsuccessfully to persuade the authorities that only the exclusive adoption of his religion could repel the Mongols, Nichiren left Kamakura and settled at Minobu in Kai Province (Yamanashi Prefecture), where he remained until his death eight years later. Surrounded by many disciples there, he directed his increasingly far-flung and often persecuted followers by means of a voluminous correspondence. His writings and teachings from this period show a number of distinct characteristics. He attacked Tendai figures, especially later esoteric writers like ENNIN. There is a sense of his having transcended his Tendai origins through belief that his doctrine, having been hidden until this later age, came directly from the Buddha. His work conveys a strong interest in the unfolding of Buddhist history and what he saw as his catalytic role in it. Nichiren clearly sets down his "four maxims" (*shika kakugen*) denouncing other sects: reciting the name of Amida leads to everlasting hell; followers of Zen are devils; Shingon will be the ruin of the country; and members of the Ritsu sect are traitors. The *daimoku* is the quintessential expression of Lotus Sutra teachings. Nichiren summed up his beliefs in what he called the "three great secret doctrines" (*sandai hihō*): i.e., (1) the object of worship (*honzon*, defined either as Śākyamuni Buddha or the impersonal truth itself); (2) the ordination platform *(kaidan)*, a center for Nichiren's faith which he never defined but was probably meant to parallel the Tendai center at Mt. Hiei (Hieizan); and (3) the *daimoku* of the Lotus Sutra. He believed in the inevitability of a Mongol victory over Japan as a condign punishment for the unbelief of the Japanese people. The failure of the two invasions (1274 and 1281) was a great disappointment to him.

In his earlier years Nichiren conceived of salvation in terms of the present world, which he identified with the Pure Land of the Buddha. Although he never completely abandoned the ideal of "becoming a Buddha in one's present body" (SOKUSHIN JŌBUTSU), derived from Tendai and Shingon beliefs, his later works, perhaps reflecting his persecutions and his failure to convert the authorities, tended to emphasize future rebirth in *Ryōzen jōdo* (The Pure Land of the Spiritual Mountain), an idealization of Mt. Gṛdrakūṭa, where the Lotus Sutra was preached.

Repeatedly ill from 1278, Nichiren left Minobu in October of 1282 to visit a hot spring but got no further than Ikegami (now in Ōta Ward, Tōkyō), where he died on 21 November.

Nichiren has always remained an ambivalent and controversial figure and his teachings and reputation have often been distorted by later writers, especially by those who have mistakenly seen him as an ultranationalist devoted to the emperor. His own loyalty was ultimately to the transcendent truths of the Lotus Sutra to which the

political order was supposed to conform. His religion, a fusion of several elements of old and new Buddhism (with an increasing preponderance of the latter), was upheld by his magnetic personality and clearly filled a need among lower-level warriors, from whom he drew many of his followers and who saw in him a master not unlike their military leaders. His frequently intemperate language and reputation as a fanatic must be balanced against his scholarship and his genuine concern for his followers.

——Anesaki Masaharu, *Nichiren the Buddhist Prophet* (1916, repr 1966). Asai Yōrin, *Nichiren shōnin kyōgaku no kenkyū* (1973). Nichiren, *Nichiren shōnin ibun*, 4 vols (1952–59). Miyazaki Eishū et al, ed, *Kōza Nichiren* (1972). Tokoro Shigemoto, *Nichiren no shisō to Kamakura bukkyō* (1965). H. G. LAMONT

Nichiren sect

One of the new Buddhist sects of the Kamakura period (1185–1333), founded in 1253 by the Tendai monk NICHIREN. Also known as the Hokke or Lotus sect. Based on exclusive faith in the LOTUS SUTRA (Skt: *Saddharmapuṇḍarīka-sūtra*), a widely venerated Mahāyāna Buddhist scripture known in Japan as the *Myōhō renge kyō* or *Hokekyō*, it is noted for its practice of chanting the *daimoku* (title) of that scripture, NAMU MYŌHŌ RENGE KYŌ ("I take my refuge in the Lotus Sutra"), as an invocation containing the merits of the Buddha and his entire teaching. This article deals with the Nichiren or movement in a broad sense and not merely with the Nichiren sect centered at Minobu in Yamanashi Prefecture, which has used that name since 1876.

Basic Doctrines and Controversies ——The Nichiren movement is so sharply divided into various branches that a common statement of belief is not easy to formulate; certain doctrines are common to most sects, but the sects frequently interpret them in different ways.

In common with certain aspects of TENDAI SECT teachings, the Lotus Sutra is declared to be the supreme scripture of the Buddha which was preached during the fifth and last period of his life and which abolished all previous "expedient" teachings. The first half of the scripture (the *shakumon* or "manifestation doctrine") reveals the attainment of Buddhahood by all beings; the second half (the *hommon* or "fundamental aspect") reveals the eternal nature of the Buddha. For the Nichiren sect the *hommon* is the more important. The metaphysical teaching of the Lotus Sutra is the Tendai monistic concept of "three thousand realms in one thought" *(ichinen sanzen)*; this is not to be used as an abstract object of meditation but is contained in the *daimoku* of the Lotus Sutra which, when chanted with faith, yields all the merits of Buddhahood to even the simplest believer.

The Lotus Sutra, though preached in the Buddha's time and circulated since then, is to have its true meaning revealed only in the current age on the basis of "five principles" *(gogi)*: (1) its "teaching" is the highest; (2) the "faculties" of beings are now lowly and therefore need this highest teaching; (3) the "time" is *mappō* (see ESCHATOLOGY), the third and most degenerate age of Buddhism starting in 1052, the age designated by the Buddha as the time when the Lotus Sutra would be propagated; (4) the "country," namely Japan, will be the center of propagation; and (5) the "order of propagation" or later the "teacher," namely the bodhisattva Jōgyō (Skt: Viśiṣṭacaritra), is a disciple of the eternal Buddha, whose reincarnation is Nichiren (some groups such as the "Fuji branch" hold Nichiren to be the true eternal Buddha). The essence of the Lotus Sutra is now revealed in "three great secret doctrines" *(sandai hihō)*: (1) the *honzon* or object of worship, the nature of which has been debated but which is most commonly a mandala in Chinese characters showing buddhas, bodhisattvas, and other deities arranged around the *daimoku* or a statue of Śākyamuni Buddha (with or without the Buddha Tahō; Skt: Prabhūtaratna) attended by Jōgyō and three other companion bodhisattvas; (2) the *kaidan* or "ordination platform," meant as a replacement for the Tendai center at Mt. Hiei (see HIEIZAN); and (3) the title or *daimoku*. Only briefly mentioned by Nichiren, the location of the *kaidan* has been claimed by various temples, and many writers, especially after the 16th century, hold it to be an abstract ideal.

Faith in the Lotus Sutra is to be shown by the aggressive refutation of other beliefs (*shakubuku*, "break and subdue"), a practice which deliberately courts persecution to expiate past sins. This is known as "reading the Lotus Sutra with one's body" (*shikidoku*). Likewise, one is, in theory, supposed to reject donations to or from unbelievers (*fuju fuse*, "not receiving, not donating"), for any such tolerance for a wrong faith is seen as complicity in blasphemy against the true teaching. Salvation is variously characterized as "becoming a Buddha in one's present body" (SOKUSHIN JŌBUTSU) or rebirth in the Pure Land of the eternal Buddha (Ryōzen Jōdo, "the Pure Land of the Spiritual Mountain").

Just before his death in 1282, Nichiren chose six senior monks as his spiritual heirs: Nichiji (1250–?), Nitchō (1252–1317), Nikō (1253–1314), Nikkō (1246–1333), Nichirō (1245–1310), and Nisshō (1236–1323); except for Nichiji, who went to the Asian mainland in 1295, these monks, together with Nichiren's old warrior disciple Toki Tsunenobu (known as Nichijō; 1216–99), founded the original lineages in the Kantō region. This lack of a single leader, the ambiguities of Nichiren's teachings and the early lack of a complete standard canon of his writings, the influx of Tendai ideas, especially HONGAKU (original enlightenment) monism, the tendency to create exclusive secret doctrines or "oral transmissions" supposedly from Nichiren himself, and temperamental differences among the disciples made schisms almost inevitable.

The schisms in the movement developed in two phases, first in the Kantō area and then in Kyōto once the sect expanded there. The first schism was the withdrawal of the rigorist Nikkō from Minobu to form his own group, the "Fuji branch," near Mt. Fuji. Although the other Kantō groups also quarreled among themselves, none of their schisms remained as permanent as the original one between themselves and the Fuji branch which developed its own doctrines.

The Kantō lineages in general expanded their activities into Kyōto from the 14th century, but it was the disciples of Nichirō, in particular, who created branches in Kyōto: Nichizō (1269–1342) established the Shijō lineage at Myōkenji with a rigorist offshoot at Myōkakuji (1378), and Nichijō (1298–1369) of Honkokuji established the Rokujō lineage. From these lineages new schisms arose, all based on variants of one doctrine: whereas the Kantō lineages (except for the Fuji branch) upheld the unity *(itchi)* of the *hommon* and the *shakumon* and were thus Itchi factions, four important groups around Kyōto proclaimed variants of the idea that the *hommon* is substantially superior to the *shakumon*. The Shōretsu (superior-inferior) factions were: the Myōmanji group (1384) of Nichijū (1314–92), the Honjōji group (1404) of Nichijin (1335–1414), the Hachibon (eight chapters) or Honryūji branch (1415) of Nichiryū (1384–1463), and the followers of Nisshin (1444–1528), who seceded in 1522. These factions have all remained permanent subsects to this day, despite attempts at healing the Shōretsu–Itchi dispute in 1466 and 1564.

Climax and Decline—— Despite these internal divisions and repeated attacks by the jealous soldier monks of Mt. Hiei, the Nichiren sect counted about half the populace of Kyōto as adherents in 1469. Allied to the district organizations of the cities (MACHISHŪ), it became an autonomous power around Kyōto (1532–36) as the Hokke Insurrection (see TEMMON HOKKE REBELLION) expanded to nearby provinces. This movement was crushed in 1536 when monk armies from Mt. Hiei destroyed the Nichiren establishments in Kyōto. Even after the sect was allowed to rebuild its temples, it never regained its former power, and its general decline in the Kansai region was hastened by persecutions under military dictator ODA NOBUNAGA.

The persecutions of the 16th century caused many Nichiren leaders to renounce the militant tactics of earlier centuries. The one exception to this trend was the FUJU FUSE SECT started in 1595 by NICHIŌ, who called for a strict observance of Nichiren's principle of neither accepting from nor donating to unbelievers. This refusal of even government offerings led to persecutions, and the last Fuju Fuse groups were forced underground in 1691 and only reemerged in 1876.

The strict government control of religious bodies and the policy of forbidding religious conversions made moderation and compromise the only viable policy; the energies of the sect were largely turned toward Tendai scholarship, theoretical debates on *hongaku* monism, monastic observances, education in sectarian seminaries *(danrin)*, and the publication of historical, biographical, and bibliographical works.

Many of these activities, which have continued to influence modern Nichiren scholarship and doctrine, were far removed from the life of the ordinary believer; however, the sect was able to draw patronage from the flourishing merchant class through cults of various deities associated with the sect—cults which promised benefit in this life through the display of sacred objects and through lay confraternities (kōchū) organized for pilgrimages. Despite such popular activities, the religious practices of the sect as with most other tradi-

tional Buddhist sects tended to ossify into "funeral Buddhism," especially in the latter part of the Edo period (1600–1868).

Modern Period (1868–): "Nichirenism"—— The Meiji period (1868–1912) brought few changes to the established Nichiren sect apart from the forced separation of Shintō from Buddhism and some nominal sectarian reorganization: the old Kantō Itchi factions united as the smaller "Nichiren sect" (1876) in Minobu, the Shōretsu factions remained independent with new names, and the Fuju Fuse splinter groups reemerged (1876). Except for a brief government-ordered wartime reorganization (1939–46) these divisions remain today with few changes.

The real power of the Nichiren movement shifted in modern times to lay-oriented movements largely outside the traditional sects and generally labeled "Nichirenism" *(Nichiren shugi)*. These movements took several forms. Popular religious organizations arose, characterized by faith healing and the promise of benefit in this life, shamanistic practices, in many cases ancestor worship, strong group-consciousness, and more or less aggressive proselytization. With the exception of the SŌKA GAKKAI, which is tied to the Nichiren Shō sect (True Nichiren sect), few have strongly defined doctrines. Partially descended from the old Edo lay confraternities, these groups can be traced back as far as the Hommon Butsuryū Kō, founded in 1857, and are best represented now by the REIYŪKAI, founded in 1925, and its most popular offshoot, the RISSHŌ KŌSEIKAI, founded in 1938, and by the Sōka Gakkai, founded in 1930.

Most Nichiren groups, including those mentioned above, when politically active, have been relatively conservative and nationalistic. Nichiren himself valued Buddhist orthodoxy above the claims of the state, and a number of older sects as well as new groups have endured persecution for their exclusive Buddhist beliefs, for example, from extreme Shintō-oriented nationalists in the 1930s and 1940s. Many Nichiren believers have attempted to read an emperor-centered right-wing nationalism into Nichiren's religion. This tendency is represented by men such as Tanaka Chigaku (1861–1939), founder of the Kokuchūkai (National Pillar Society) in 1914. This type of "Nichirenism" had an effect on nationalist writers such as KITA IKKI (1883–1937) and some military leaders such as ISHIWARA KANJI (1889–1949). In most extreme forms it virtually dissolved Nichiren's faith into right-wing emperor-worship by declaring the emperor to be the *honzon* or object of worship. Left-wing or Marxist Nichiren writers like Senō Girō (1890–1961) have also appeared, but their following has been relatively small and their devotion to Nichiren has in many cases decreased in proportion to their leftist tendencies.

Admiration for Nichiren as a person or historical figure can be seen in numerous leading writers in modern Japan, including those who do not share Nichiren's religious views. Much of this admiration stems from Nichiren's position as an "outsider," defying authority in the name of a transcendent ideal. Thus even a Christian like UCHIMURA KANZŌ (1861–1930) saw in Nichiren's self-exile at Minobu an admirable retreat from official entanglements. The socialist writer KŌTOKU SHŪSUI (1871–1911) saw Nichiren's defiance in revolutionary terms.

Tanaka Chigaku's voluminous writings converted a number of intellectuals and writers to Nichiren's faith, but not a few of these formed their own distinctive views: thus TAKAYAMA CHOGYŪ (1871–1902), the "Nietzsche of Japan," converted to Nichiren's faith without accepting Tanaka's interpretations. In the field of literature, MIYAZAWA KENJI (1896–1933) was also an admirer of Tanaka, and his works describe the hard lot of Japanese peasants from an aesthetic perspective tinged with Nichiren's ideas.

Japan's defeat in 1945 led many Nichiren believers and organizations, in common with other Japanese, to embrace antinuclear pacifism. One notable instance is the Nihonzan Myōhōji (Daisōga) founded by Fujii Nittatsu (b 1885). Fujii, a Nichiren missionary on the Asian mainland, and his group formerly supported Japanese expansionism but after 1945 turned their energies to world peace.

It is clear that the Nichiren movement cannot simply be dismissed as "militaristic" or "nationalistic," an epithet still casually given to it by some writers. Its turbulent history has left it sharply divided yet has also endowed it with a range of thought which has allowed it to appeal to wide segments of Japanese society and thus to expand beyond traditional sectarian institutions in a way unparalleled by any other Buddhist sect.

▬——Risshō Daigaku Nichiren Kyōgaku Kenkyūjo, ed, *Nichiren kyōdan zenshi* (1971). Shigyō Kaishū, *Nichirenshū kyōgaku shi* (1972). Tokoro Shigemoto, *Kindai shakai to Nichiren shugi* (1972).

H. G. LAMONT

Nichiro Gyogyō Kaisha, Ltd

A company engaged primarily in whaling and fishing for salmon and trout in the Sea of Okhotsk and other northern waters, Nichiro Gyogyō was founded in 1907 and incorporated in 1914. It later absorbed a large number of other firms to become the largest Japanese concern active in these waters. After World War II the company's facilities in Siberia, the Kurils, and Sakhalin were seized by the Soviet Union (see TERRITORY OF JAPAN). It resumed fishing in 1952, and has since developed new fishing grounds off the west coast of Africa. It is also involved in joint ventures promoting the development and import of marine products. Sales for the fiscal year ending November 1981 totaled ¥209.9 billion (US $938.1 million), of which fresh and frozen fish constituted 50 percent; frozen food 19 percent; canned fish 12 percent; and feedstuff, dairy products, and others 19 percent; in the same year capitalization stood at ¥8.2 billion (US $36.6 million). Corporate headquarters are located in Tōkyō.

Nichiro kyōyaku → Russo-Japanese agreements of 1907–1916

Nichiro Senso → Russo-Japanese War

night schools

(yagaku). Secondary schools, colleges, and universities that offer coursework at night. Since compulsory education in Japan extends through middle school, nighttime middle-school education is not sanctioned by the SCHOOL EDUCATION LAW OF 1947. Nevertheless, such schools have been established for the benefit of those children who begin working at an early age. The number of night schools at this level reached a peak of 71 in 1953 with 3,118 students; since then the number of students and schools has declined annually.

At the high school level, part-time instruction can also be arranged during the daytime, but it is usually given at night. In many cases, these programs are administered in conjunction with regular full-time high schools. The duration of study is four or more years, and the curriculum and the degree received upon graduation are the same as in regular schools. Nighttime high school programs also reached a peak in 1953 and have declined since; enrollment in 1978 was less than 4 percent of the total number of high school students.

Colleges and universities have also established divisions that conduct evening courses for credit. The duration of instruction is four or five years. Of 431 universities and colleges, 62 have evening divisions, of which 77 percent are private schools; of 515 junior colleges, 113 have evening divisions, of which 72 percent are private schools. Most evening courses are offered in the fields of literature, economics, commerce, law, and a few of the physical sciences. Night school students composed 8 percent of total college and university enrollment in 1978.   *Saitō Kenjirō*

nihommachi

Japanese communities in Southeast Asia in the 16th and 17th centuries. The growth of the VERMILION SEAL SHIP TRADE, especially in the first half of the 17th century, took Japanese to almost every part of Southeast Asia. At the same time, various edicts against Christianity, beginning in 1585, caused the exodus of many Japanese Christians. The earliest attested Japanese settlement overseas was in Dilao (now part of Manila), Philippines, which is said in early-17th-century records to have had a Japanese population of some 3,000, the largest known. The second in size appears to have been in Ayuthia (now Ayutthaya), Thailand; there, forming a self-governing community of some 1,500, the Japanese settlers were active in trade and, under the leadership of YAMADA NAGAMASA, prominent in local politics. Other *nihommachi* were located in San Miguel (now part of Manila), Philippines; Tourane (now Da Nang) and Faifo, Vietnam; and Pnompenh and Ponhealu, Cambodia. Strictly speaking, the term *nihommachi* applies only to these seven communities, but many Japanese residents were also present in Tainan, Taiwan; Batavia (now Djakarta, Indonesia) and Macao, and it is sometimes loosely applied to them as well. With the implementation of the NATIONAL SECLUSION policy by the Tokugawa shogunate in the 1630s, these overseas communities lost contact with Japan and

Nihonga

Detail of the painting *Merciful Mother Kannon (Hibo Kannon)* by Kanō Hōgai. A major example of *nihonga*, this work also shows Hōgai's interest in incorporating Western techniques such as the use of chiaroscuro. Ink and colors on silk. 196.0 × 86.4 cm. 1888. Tōkyō University of Fine Arts and Music.

gradually lost their identity, although small numbers of descendants of the Japanese settlers were reported in various parts of Asia in the 18th century.

Nihommatsu

City in central Fukushima Prefecture, northern Honshū. It developed as a castle town in the Muromachi period (1333–1568) and later became a POST-STATION TOWN on the highway Ōshū Kaidō. A once prosperous silk-reeling industry is being replaced by the furniture industry. Attractions are the site of the old castle, now a park, Adachigahara plateau, supposedly the site of the devil's den mentioned in a Nō play by the same name, and a chrysanthemum and lantern festival, both held in October. The city is the gateway to the mountain ADATARASAN and the DAKE HOT SPRING. Pop: 33,639.

Nihon

An influential Meiji-period (1868–1912) newspaper launched by KUGA KATSUNAN in 1889 on the day the Constitution of the Empire of Japan was promulgated. It championed NIHON SHUGI (literally "Japanism"), the term for a kind of Japanese nationalism that sprang up in the late 19th century in reaction to the growing tide of Westernization that followed the Meiji Restoration. Its major contributors included journalists like MIYAKE SETSUREI and HASEGAWA NYOZEKAN and men of letters like MASAOKA SHIKI. *Nihon* opposed the ideas of INOUE KAORU and other Meiji oligarchs about Westernizing the Japanese government. Stressing the importance of native Japanese traditions, it advocated democracy by means of a people-oriented constitutional system. More than 20 issues of the paper were judged unfit for publication and suppressed by the authorities. After Kuga fell ill in 1906, *Nihon* passed to other hands and became affiliated with the RIKKEN SEIYŪKAI, one of the major political parties of the time. It ceased publication in 1914.

Nihon Bijutsuin → Japan Fine Arts Academy

Nihon Bungaku Hōkokukai

(Patriotic Association for Japanese Literature). Society created during World War II to mobilize Japanese writers and to propagate a Japan-centered view of the world through literature. Organized in 1942 with the aid of the government's intelligence bureau, it had more than 3,000 members, led by such writers as KUME MASAO, Nakamura Murao (1886–1949), YOSHIKAWA EIJI, and KIKUCHI KAN. It published a newsletter, *Bungaku hōkoku* (Serving the Country through Literature), and held two annual Great Asian literary congresses with delegates from Asian countries and territories then controlled by Japan. It also sponsored public lectures and publication of anthologies of nationalistic poems and war novels. The society was disbanded after Japan's defeat in 1945.   James R. MORITA

Nihon Cement Co, Ltd

(Nihon Semento). Formerly known as Asano Cement. A major cement manufacturer, the company is based on a government-built cement factory bought by ASANO SŌICHIRŌ in 1884. It has shown leadership in cement production in terms of scale, equipment and technology, quality, distribution system, and pollution control. In recent years it has developed an energy-saving suspension preheater kiln with completely computerized operation control. Besides various types of cement, the product line includes building and construction materials, steel, and industrial equipment, as well as Asano Clean Set, an effective agent for rapidly hardening soft soil, which can also be used for treating sludge and other industrial wastes. Nihon Cement also involves itself in feasibility studies, raw material surveys, plant designing, and the supervision of plant construction and operation both at home and abroad. Sales for the fiscal year ending March 1982 totaled ¥176 billion (US $718.8 million), of which cement accounted for 80 percent and other products 20 percent. The company was capitalized at ¥10.8 billion (US $44.1 million) in the same year. Corporate headquarters are located in Tōkyō.

Nihon daijisho

Japanese-language dictionary compiled by the novelist YAMADA BIMYŌ (1868–1910) and published in 1892–93 in 12 volumes. It was, with ŌTSUKI FUMIHIKO's *Genkai* (1889–91), the first lexicon of the Japanese language to employ a modern format. Although the quality of its definitions is uneven, the indication of the accent for word was an important innovation.   Uwano Zendō

Nihondaira

Upland between Shimizu and Shizuoka cities, central Shizuoka Prefecture, central Honshū. Near the top of Udosan (307 m or 1,007 ft). Known for its panoramic view, especially of Mt. Fuji (Fujisan) and Miho no Matsubara, a grove of pine trees. A popular recreation and resort area. Largely covered by tea plantations. The center of Nihondaira Prefectural Natural Park.

nihonga

(Japanese-style painting). Comparatively little is known of the Japanese artists who were active during the third quarter of the 19th century and whose careers spanned the end of the Edo period (1600–1868) and the early part of the Meiji period (1868–1912). Artistic distinctions among the traditional schools of painting had been minimized by the versatility and technical skill of artists whose choice of style was largely determined by the subject matter painted, the disposition or purpose of the commission, and the preferences of the patron. In Kyōto, remarkable correlation existed between the taste of the court and the townsmen. The more innovative artists sought new ideas from ancient paintings stored in local temples and shrines and from chance examples of Western art that became more accessible with the opening of Japan to foreign trade starting in 1858.

Shiokawa Bunrin (1808–77) and Kishi Chikudō (1826–97) occasionally succeeded in synthesizing the traditional with the new, but many others who dabbled in Western art, such as MORI KANSAI, KŌNO BAIREI, and KAWABATA GYOKUSHŌ, did so out of a spirit of experimentation and perhaps a desire to cater to the public taste for exotica. At this time most painters were too rooted in their traditions to be profoundly moved by their limited exposure to Western art.

During the last quarter of the 19th century, the art derived from the traditional schools of painting came to be known collectively as *nihonga* (Japanese-style painting), as distinct from the new school of painting modeled upon European oil painting, termed YŌGA (Western-style painting). The official encouragement of *yōga* and the indiscriminate enthusiasm for Western culture during the early Meiji period posed less of a threat to the survival of the traditional artists than the political, economic, and social policies of the Meiji government, which drastically altered the fabric of their lives and their sources of patronage. The most adversely affected were the official KANŌ SCHOOL and TOSA SCHOOL artists who, deprived of their sinecures and stipends, had difficulty reestablishing themselves because their academic painting had ceased to enjoy critical or popular esteem. HASHIMOTO GAHŌ and others relied upon compatriots in government to secure them positions as antiquarians, restorers, and draftsmen in the army, navy, education and home ministries. By contrast, literati painting (BUNJINGA) artists such as TAZAKI SŌUN, TANOMURA CHOKUNYŪ, and TOMIOKA TESSAI were much in vogue with bureaucrats who prided themselves on their knowledge of Chinese culture. SHIBATA ZESHIN and other able artists had been able to resume their careers soon after the period of political turmoil that culminated in the Meiji Restoration (1868), but their development was inhibited by critics, at home and abroad, who decried the intrusion of Western motifs and admonished them to conform to native traditions.

It was because of the close ties that existed between the court, artists, and entrepreneurs that the MARUYAMA-SHIJŌ SCHOOL, the Kishi school, and other Kyōto schools of painting were able to weather the Meiji Restoration and that their successive heirs continued to dominate the Kyōto art world. The Shijō-school painter Shiokawa Bunrin persuaded connoisseurs, collectors, scholars, antiquarians, and artists to form the Jounsha (later named the Kōso Kyōkai). This organization held its first exhibition in 1868 and for a short period sponsored a cooperative gallery. Its members worked actively with local officials to help revitalize the major art industries and to establish the Kyōto Exposition, which from 1871 on regularly featured the accomplishments of leading artists and craftsmen. Tanomura Chokunyū, Kōno Bairei, and artists from all factions helped the governor of Kyōto establish, in 1880, the Kyōto Prefectural Painting School (Kyōto Fu Gagakkō), the first art school to offer training in both Japanese and Western-style painting as well as a design course for craftsmen. Chokunyū, Bairei, Chikudō, Kansai, and other prominent painters taught there, but it was their private schools, and those of the next generation of artists, such as TAKEUCHI SEIHŌ, that attracted pupils as gifted as NISHIYAMA SUISHŌ, UEMURA SHŌEN, HASHIMOTO KANSETSU, and TSUCHIDA BAKUSEN. Not until the end of the Meiji period did artists of the caliber of MURAKAMI KAGAKU, DŌMOTO INSHŌ, and FUKUDA HEIHACHIRŌ emerge from the Kyōto Prefectural Painting School, which was by then called the Kyōto Municipal College of Painting.

In Tōkyō, the situation of traditional artists had been exacerbated by the termination of the old SANKIN KŌTAI system, the collapse of the shogunate, and the intrusive role of the new Meiji bureaucrats. Kawase Hideharu (1841–1907), SANO TSUNETAMI, Kuki Ryūichi (1852–1931) and other officials who had been involved in Japan's participation in national and international expositions decided to form, in 1879, an art organization of a semiofficial nature known as Ryūchikai (Dragon Pond Society; after 1886 it was renamed the Nihon Bijutsu Kyōkai, the Japan Fine Arts Association), which sponsored a series of exhibitions of ancient and modern art with such diverse aims as reviving interest in native arts, providing artists with new sources of inspiration, raising the level of public taste, and encouraging the development of an export trade that could capitalize on the European and American craze for japonaiserie. In their eagerness to garner prizes for Japan, they disrupted the intimate relationship between artists, craftsmen, and patrons that had made Japanese art such an integral part of the decor and daily life of the people.

The conservative faction in the Ministry of Education, led by Kuki Ryūichi and HAMAO ARATA, was implacably opposed to Western-style painting and since 1882 had successfully thwarted plans to establish an art school that might be dominated by *yōga* artists. Through the help of Ernest FENOLLOSA and OKAKURA KAKUZŌ, and assisted by KANŌ HŌGAI and HASHIMOTO GAHŌ, they established in 1887 the Tōkyō Bijutsu Gakkō (now Tōkyō University of Fine Arts and Music; opened 1889), where they sought to train artists exclusively in traditional techniques and to create a new art that would combine what they considered to be the best features of oriental and Western art. They fostered a new type of *nihonga* that was akin to Pre-Raphaelite painting in its eclecticism, preoccupation with technique, and with religious, moral, and literary values. It is best exemplified by the early works of their ablest pupils, SHIMOMURA KANZAN, HISHIDA SHUNSŌ, and YOKOYAMA TAIKAN.

Political pressures forced Okakura in 1896 to expand the curriculum to include *yōga* and to engage KURODA SEIKI, who used the preparations for the Paris Exposition of 1900 to conspire with francophile officials to force Okakura's resignation from the school and to oust Kuki from his position as director of the Imperial Museum and vice-president of government expositions. The majority of the staff left with Okakura to form the private JAPAN FINE ARTS ACADEMY (Nihon Bijutsuin), whose fortunes fluctuated during the waning years of Meiji because of Okakura's extended absences abroad. After the academy was reorganized in 1914 by Taikan and Kanzan, its exhibition (Inten) became the focus for many talented artists. Their main competitors were the new leaders of the Tōkyō Bijutsu Gakkō, such as TERAZAKI KŌGYŌ, Kawabata Gyokushō, and his pupil HIRAFUKU HYAKUSUI; their close associates in the Nihon Bijutsu Kyōkai; and the major Kyōto artists. The intense factionalism that prevailed was based upon politics and personalities rather than artistic differences, which were often more varied within a group than between groups.

In 1907 the Ministry of Education established an official annual art exhibition, the BUNTEN, with competitions and official recognition in both *yōga* and *nihonga*. Soon representation at the Bunten and receipt of its coveted awards became the major criteria for a successful artistic career. In the *yōga* division, the quest for recognition led to an increase in the size of paintings, a brightening of the palette, more intricate compositions, and more "edifying" subjects with sentimental appeal. The result was an academic art of great charm and technical refinement that drew its subject matter and stylistic inspiration from the entire spectrum of Japan's artistic heritage. *Nihonga* was so self-consciously intent upon asserting the achievements of the past that it remained curiously remote from the dynamism that wrought such a profound transformation of Japan during the Meiji era.

📖 ——Frederick Baekeland, *Imperial Japan: The Art of the Meiji Era (1868–1912)* (1980). Kawakita Michiaki, *Gendai no nihonga,* vol 9 of *Genshoku gendai Nihon no bijutsu* (1980). Kobayashi Tadashi, *Nihon Bijutsuin,* vol 2 of *Gendai Nihon no bijutsu* (1979). *Meiji no nihonga,* no. 17 of *Nihon no bijutsu* (September 1967).

Ellen P. CONANT

Nihon Gakujutsu Kaigi → Science Council of Japan

Nihon Gakujutsu Shinkōkai → Japan Society for the Promotion of Science

Nihon Gakushiin → Japan Academy

Nihon Geijutsuin → Japan Art Academy

Nihongi → Nihon shoki

Nihon Ginkō → Bank of Japan

Nihon hyōron

(Japan Review). A general-interest magazine. Publication began in 1926 when the magazine was first put out by the Nihon Hyōronsha as a financial journal, *Keizai ōrai.* Its name was changed to *Nihon hyōron* in 1935. Following the lead of CHŪŌ KŌRON and KAIZŌ, it became a general-interest magazine. During World War II, however, the name was changed to *Keizai hyōron,* and for a time it went back to being a financial journal. Following the war it shifted back to a general-interest format and attracted attention by focusing on reportage of current events. In 1951 it was suppressed by the authorities as a result of articles criticizing OCCUPATION policies. It resumed publication in 1956, but failed after putting out two issues.

Nihonjin

Magazine of criticism. First published in April 1888 by MIYAKE SETSUREI, SHIGA SHIGETAKA, and the other organizers of the group known as the SEIKYŌSHA. It was first edited by the members of the group in cooperation but later principally by Miyake. The title of the magazine, *Nihonjin* (The Japanese), indicates the traditionalism of the editors, who were against the uncritical Westernization popular during the early part of the Meiji period (1868–1912) and who stressed the Japanese national values that had been formed in the course of the country's long history. The conservative ideas and attitudes of the editors of the magazine included elements of such disparate ideologies as nationalism, liberalism, and socialism. The magazine not only stressed traditionalism by declaring the inherent value of the state itself, but called for the autonomous reform of Japanese society without slavishly imitating the West; it also criticized the social ills produced under the capitalist system. Because of its strong criticism of the government, publication of the magazine was frequently prohibited, and there were two periods in which it changed its name to *Ajia* (Asia). The periods in which the magazine was published as *Nihonjin* were from 1888 to 1891, 1893 to 1895, and 1895 to 1906. In 1907 the magazine changed its name to *Nihon oyobi nihonjin* (Japan and the Japanese) when reporters from the newspaper *Nihon* (Japan) joined the staff. At times publishing twice a month and at times once a week, *Nihonjin* (including its issues as *Ajia*) published 826 issues before ceasing publication on 1 September 1923.

📖 ——Kenneth B. Pyle, *The New Generation in Meiji Japan: Problems of Cultural Identity, 1885–1895* (1969). *YAMARYŌ Kenji*

Nihon keizai shimbun

Japan's largest financial and business trade newspaper. In 1876 MASUDA TAKASHI, general manager of Mitsui Bussan (now MITSUI & CO, LTD), launched a business weekly, the *Chūgai bukka shimpō.* The paper became a daily in 1885, and then in 1889 the name was changed to *Chūgai shōgyō shimpō.* It was divested from Mitsui and came under a privately managed partnership. In 1911 the Chūgai Shōgyō Shimpōsha was organized as a company to run the paper. In 1942 it absorbed two other business papers, the *Nikkan kōgyō shimbun* and the *Keizai jiji shimpō,* along with a handful of trade journals to form the *Nihon sangyō keizai shimbun.* The *Nikkan kōgyō* went independent again in 1945, and in 1946 the company and paper took the present name of *Nihon keizai shimbun.*

Having a long history and an established reputation as an economic trade paper, the *Nihon keizai shimbun* experienced rapid growth in conjunction with Japan's high economic growth rate in the 1960s. Over the years it has continued to specialize in business news—much like the *Wall Street Journal.* It is one of the most influential financial news publications in Japan. It has offices in Tōkyō, Ōsaka, Nagoya, and Sapporo. News is gathered from bureaus scattered around the country as well as from some 20 overseas bureaus. It has special contractual agreements with various international wire services including the Associated Press and United Press International, and foreign newspapers like the *Financial Times.* The company also publishes the *Nikkei ryūtsū shimbun,* the *Nikkei sangyō shimbun,* magazines, and books. In 1979 it was capitalized at ¥800 million (US $3.6 million). Circulation was 1.8 million in 1979.

Nihon Kiin

Leading organization of Japan's professional GO players. Established in 1924 through a merger of several major *go* groups, it acts to advance and popularize the game, and exerts a strong influence on amateurs. The word *kiin* dates from the Edo period (1600–1868), when it referred to prominent family lines (IEMOTO) that held government sanction to issue rankings of *go* players. Today the association's main activities include organization of professional matches and tournaments with newspaper and television support, issuance of rankings, publication of *go* literature, and introduction of the game to foreign audiences. There are more than 300 branch organizations and a membership of approximately 300 professionals which accounts for 80 percent of the nation's top players. The head office is located in Chiyoda Ward, Tōkyō. *HAYASHI Yutaka*

Nihon Kirisuto Kyōdan → United Church of Christ in Japan

Nihon Kirisutokyō Rengōkai → Christian Churches, Japan Association of

Nihon kiryaku

(Outline Record of Japan). Also known as *Nihon kirui* and *Hennen kiryaku*. A history of Japan in 34 chapters, of unknown authorship, compiled late in the Heian period (794–1185). Written in annalistic form, it covers the history of Japan from the mythological age of the gods to the reign of Emperor Go-Ichijō (1016–36). The section on the mythological period is taken in its entirety from the NIHON SHOKI (720). *Nihon kiryaku* is useful as a supplement to the RIKKO-KUSHI (Six National Histories), supplying additional information.

G. Cameron HURST III

Nihon Kyōsantō → Japan Communist Party

Nihon Mingeikan → Japan Folk-Craft Museum

Nihon Minkan Hōsō Remmei → National Association of Commercial Broadcasting in Japan

Nihon Minshutō

(Japan Democratic Party). Conservative party formed in November 1954 in opposition to the Liberal Party led by YOSHIDA SHIGERU, who was then prime minister. Not to be confused with the MIN-SHUTŌ (Democratic Party). The party drew its 140 members from three conservative groups: the Japan Reform Party (Nihon Kai-shintō), the Japan Liberal Party (Nihon Jiyūtō), and the anti-Yoshida faction of the Liberal Party. HATOYAMA ICHIRŌ was president, SHI-GEMITSU MAMORU vice-president, and KISHI NOBUSUKE party secretary. With the resignation of the Yoshida cabinet after a no-confidence vote in December 1954, Hatoyama formed his first cabinet. In the general election of February 1955 the Nihon Minshutō became the dominant party, and Hatoyama formed his second cabinet. A month after the merger of the left and right factions of the Japan Socialist Party in October 1955, the Nihon Minshutō merged with the LIBERAL PARTY (Jiyūtō) in the so-called *hoshu gōdō* (conservative merger) to form the LIBERAL DEMOCRATIC PARTY (Jiyū Minshutō). See also POLITICAL PARTIES. HARADA Katsumasa

Nihon Montoku Tennō jitsuroku → Rikkokushi

Nihon Musantō

(Japan Proletarian Party). Left-wing political party formed in March 1937, with Katō Kanjū (1892–1978) as chairman and SUZUKI MOSA-BURŌ as secretary general; it was made up mainly of labor union members. Katō won a seat in the lower house of the Diet in the general election held the following month. The party failed in its effort to create a popular front against the government's militaristic and inflationary policies, largely because of ideological differences with the moderate SHAKAI TAISHŪTŌ (Socialist Masses Party), the only other socialist party with any influence. In December 1937 the government arrested the leaders of the Nihon Musantō in the POPU-LAR FRONT INCIDENT, and the party was disbanded.

Nihon Nōsan Kōgyō

Leading formula-feed manufacturer in Japan; also produces pork and poultry products. Established in 1931, it doubled its businesses by merging with the feed companies of the Mitsubishi and Tōkyū groups in 1971. Plans call for diversification of its product line and the use of new technology to improve productivity. Sales for the fiscal year ending May 1982 totaled ¥162 billion (US $684 million) and the company was capitalized at ¥5.9 billion (US $24.9 million). Corporate headquarters are located in Yokohama.

Nihon Radiator Co, Ltd

A large manufacturer of heat-related automobile parts affiliated with NISSAN MOTOR CO, LTD, the Nihon Radiator Co was established in 1938. In 1964 Nissan invested in the company, which became its sole supplier of radiators, car heaters, and mufflers. Some 80 percent of the total sales of the company now go to Nissan. A subsidiary operates in California. Sales for the fiscal year ending March 1982 totaled ¥125 billion (US $519 million); capitalization stood at ¥3.7 billion (US $15.4 million) in that year. Corporate headquarters are located in Tōkyō.

Nihon rettō kaizō ron

(plan for the remodeling of the Japanese archipelago). An economic development plan proposed in 1972 by Prime Minister TANAKA KA-KUEI. The proposal was initially put forth in Tanaka's best-selling book by the same name, published a month before he became prime minister.

The goal of the plan, one of a series promoting the decentralized development of Japan, was to deconcentrate industry from the heavily populated and polluted Tōkyō–Ōsaka industrial belt. Regional industrial centers were to be built, linked by superhighways and high-speed trains. The entire plan would have taken more than a decade to complete and would have involved massive public expenditures. The initial enthusiasm for the plan helped bring Tanaka to power.

Critics argued that the plan would spread pollution throughout the country, undermine agricultural production, and increase Japanese dependence on imported raw materials and food. Real estate speculation based on the plan pushed land prices to unprecedented levels, and the recession following the OIL CRISIS OF 1973 led to the scuttling of the plan. See also COMPREHENSIVE NATIONAL LAND DEVELOPMENT PLAN.

Nihon Rōmanha

(Japanese Romantic school). A nationalistic literary movement active in the mid-1930s through World War II; also the name of the magazine published by the same group. Heavily influenced by the aesthetics of German romanticism (as expressed, for example, in the works of Friedrich Schlegel), it advocated patriotism and sought to instill pride in the native literary tradition by urging people to read the Japanese classics. The movement's principal organizers were YASUDA YOJŪRŌ, Nakatani Takao (b 1901), and KAMEI KATSU-ICHIRŌ; its membership included such notable writers as DAZAI OSAMU and SATŌ HARUO.

The Nihon Rōmanha grew out of an earlier literary movement centered around the magazine *Kogito,* first published in 1932. Organized by Yasuda Yojūrō, Nakajima Eijirō (1910–45), Tanaka Katsumi (b 1911) and other former classmates at the Ōsaka Higher School, the *Kogito* group stood in opposition to the Marxist literature that had been in the ascendency in the 1920s and early 1930s and advocated returning to the Japanese classics. This classical movement, fueled by political uncertainties and the highly publicized TENKŌ, or forced ideological conversion, during the 1930s of a large number of leftist writers, soon developed into a larger romantic movement, represented by the Nihon Rōmanha.

The magazine *Nihon rōmanha* was first published in 1935 as a forum for a growing number of young authors interested in bringing about a revival of Japanese classical literature. By the time its final issue was brought out in 1938, more than 50 noted writers had joined the movement, including DAN KAZUO, ITŌ SHIZUO, NAKA-GAWA YOICHI, and HAGIWARA SAKUTARŌ. The movement had a great impact on young intellectuals during the war years, who were surrounded by social and political uncertainties and who faced the prospect of violent death.

Following Japan's defeat in 1945, the Nihon Rōmanha movement came under heavy criticism for its support of Japanese militarism through literature. However, in recent years there has been a cry for the revival of Japanese romanticism; in 1979 a new magazine *Rō-manha* was published. Started by Yasuda, Nakatani, Asano Akira, and others from the prewar group, the new Rōmanha denies all postwar criticism of the movement and promises to carry out its original mission of looking to the Japanese classics as a source for a new literature.

——Hashikawa Bunzō, *Nihon rōmanha hihan josetsu* (1965). Takeuchi Yoshimi, *Kokumin bungaku ron* (1954). Yasuda Yojūrō, *Nihon rōmanha no jidai* (1969). HASHIKAWA Bunzō

Nihon Rōnōtō

(Japan Labor-Farmer Party; also called Nichirōtō). "Proletarian" party founded by the moderate wing of the RŌDŌ NŌMINTŌ in December 1926. Attempting to distinguish itself from its parent party and another major leftist rival, the SHAKAI MINSHŪTŌ (Socialist People's Party), it claimed to offer the sole practical socialist alternatives to the Diet's "bourgeois" policies. This program won to its ranks two moderate socialist groups, the anticommunist factions of the Nihon Nōmin Kumiai (Japan Farmers' Union) and the leftist and centrist factions of the SŌDŌMEI.

While striving throughout 1927 to organize a united noncommunist front of left-wing parties, the Nihon Rōnōtō campaigned for tenant rights, reduction of utility rates, and Japan's noninvolvement on the China mainland. This program won it only one seat in the 1928 election, despite the implementation that year of universal manhood suffrage. Later in 1928 it strove to expand its power by creating a new party for leftists who had survived the government's banning of the Rōdō Nōmintō and mass arrest of communists in the MARCH 15TH INCIDENT. The resulting merger of the Nihon Rōnōtō with the Nihon Nōmintō (Japan Farmers' Party), some local labor parties, and the remnants of the Rōdō Nōmintō led to the formation in December 1928 of yet another ephemeral left-wing party, the Nihon Taishūtō (Japan Masses Party). See also HISTORY OF JAPAN: Taishō and early Shōwa history.

Nihon ryōiki

Also called *Nihon reiiki*. The earliest Japanese collection of *setsuwa* (Buddhist moral tales; see SETSUWA BUNGAKU). Compiled around 822 by Kyōkai (also known as Keikai), a Buddhist priest of the temple YAKUSHIJI in Nara. The 116 tales depict intervention in human affairs by supernatural elements. The Buddhist message of cause and effect is the shared theme and the major source of unity in the work. The full title is *Nihonkoku gempō zen'aku ryōiki* (or *reiiki; A Record of Miraculous Instances in Japan of Virtue and Vice Rewarded in This Present Life*).

The *Ryōiki* is written entirely in the hybrid form of Chinese known as HENTAI KAMBUN. Plots develop quickly, dialogue is uncomplicated, and structure elementary. The simple stories generally fit into two categories: Buddhist stories such as those about men reborn as cows or sent to the Land of the Dead because they violated the Buddhist law, and non-Buddhist stories such as that of Sugaru of Chiisakobe, ordered to catch the Thunder God by Emperor Yūryaku.

As Kyōkai mentions in his preface, the *Ryōiki* was inspired by such Chinese writings as the *Mingbaoji (Ming-pao-chi)*. It also contains stories and quotations derived from various Buddhist writings. The *Ryōiki* reveals contemporary religious trends and portrays the ordinary life of the people. It had a significant role in the history of Japanese literature and an extensive influence on later *setsuwa* collections such as the *Konjaku monogatari* (ca 1120), as well as on other genres.

📖——Yoshiko Kurata Dykstra, "A Study of the *Nihonkoku genpō zen-aku ryōiki*," PhD dissertation, University of California, Los Angeles (1974). Kyōko Nakamura, *Miraculous Stories from the Japanese Buddhist Tradition* (1973).　　Yoshiko Kurata DYKSTRA

Nihon sandai jitsuroku → Rikkokushi

Nihon Sankei

(The Three Views of Japan). Refers to the three most famous scenic spots in Japan. They are the group of islands called MATSUSHIMA in Miyagi Prefecture, the pine tree covered sandbar known as AMANOHASHIDATE in Kyōto Prefecture, and the island of ITSUKUSHIMA in Hiroshima Prefecture, with its Shintō shrine gateway in the Hiroshima Bay.

Nihon Shakai Shugi Dōmei

(Japan Socialist League). Confederation of socialist organizations formed in December 1920 by YAMAKAWA HITOSHI, SAKAI TOSHIHIKO, and other leftist leaders; Japan's first alliance of socialist, anarchist, and labor groups. The previous year had witnessed a growth in trade union organization as well as a resurgence of socialist activity. Growing contacts between the two movements prompted a call from the SHINJINKAI and other left-wing intellectual groups for an all-encompassing union of labor and socialist organizations. The resulting Japan Socialist League, with 3,000 members, organized groups and lecture meetings throughout the country, but because of the heterogeneous character of its membership, the organization suffered from a lack of ideological unity and an inability to go beyond mere propaganda work. The alliance was also subject to heavy government suppression and forced to disband in May 1921. After its dissolution, communists and anarchists began to break away from the socialist movement.

Nihon Shakaitō → Japan Socialist Party

Nihon shihon shugi hattatsu shi kōza

(Lectures on the History of the Development of Japanese Capitalism). Landmark collection of works by Marxist scholars who supported the JAPAN COMMUNIST PARTY line; published in seven volumes by Iwanami Shoten from 1932 to 1933. With the aim of clarifying the nature of Japan's coming revolution, which was believed to be imminent in view of the worldwide economic crisis, the authors, under the direction of NORO EITARŌ, HIRANO YOSHITARŌ, YAMADA MORITARŌ, and Ōtsuka Kinnosuke (1892–1977), made historical analyses of various aspects of Japanese capitalism. The writers sought to prove that the revolution would be a "bourgeois-democratic" upheaval by pointing out the feudal character of Japanese capitalism. From the title of this collection, the coterie of scholars who subscribed to this viewpoint came to be known as the KŌZAHA ("Lectures" faction). Publication of the work intensified the continuing dispute over revolutionary strategy between supporters of the Communist Party position and its opponents, the so-called RŌNŌHA, who centered on the magazine *Rōnō* (Labor-Farmer) and, stressing the bourgeois character of Japanese capitalism, argued that the impending revolution would be a socialist one. See NIHON SHIHON SHUGI RONSŌ.

Nihon shihon shugi ronsō

(the debate on Japanese capitalism). Pre-World War II debate among Japanese Marxian economists concerning the nature and degree of capitalist development in Japan. Although certain parts of this debate began in the early 1920s and continued well into the postwar period, the full-scale debate can be said to extend roughly from 1927 to 1937, beginning with the establishment of the journal *Rōnō* (Labor-Farmer) and ending with the mass arrests of Marxian university professors between 1936 and early 1938. The debate divided the majority of Marxian economists into two predominant schools of thought: the KŌZAHA ("Lectures" faction) and RŌNŌHA (Labor–Farmer faction), so called because of publications associated with each group. The two groups differed over their views of the level of capitalist development in Japan. The Kōzaha stressed what it considered to be the essentially feudal or "semifeudal" aspects of post-Meiji Japan, while the Rōnōha stressed the characteristics Japan shared with the more advanced capitalist nations. From this difference of interpretation the debate extended to such issues as agricultural development, landlord-tenant relations, wages and employment, and the changing industrial structure. By focusing the attention of so many Marxian economists and economic historians on the question of Japan's development in this way, the debate decisively influenced both the course of development of Marxian economics in Japan and the general analysis of Japanese capitalist development throughout the prewar and early postwar periods.

Central Issues of the Debate——The main question addressed by the debate was whether to characterize Japan's economic development as purely capitalist in nature, or as a kind of partial capitalist development resting on, and in some sense being determined by, a feudal or semifeudal base. Both schools took the England described by Marx as their model of capitalist development and found Japan backward in comparison.

The debate emerged from their different interpretations of this "backwardness." To Kōzaha writers, the tenacity of feudal or at least "semifedual" relations within the country prevented Japan from developing in what they considered to be the usual way. In their view, the MEIJI RESTORATION of 1868 had simply brought about a reconstitution of the feudal land system under an absolutist monarchy supported by a sociopolitical stratum of feudal landlords and bourgeois capitalists. The Rōnōha, on the other hand, saw the Meiji Restoration as marking the end of feudalism in Japan and as the beginning of full-scale capitalist development and thought that any backward characteristics would disappear in time. In a sense, the Kōzaha saw anything that deviated from what they considered the classic model of capitalist development as feudal or semifeudal, stressing these "unique" characteristics and deemphasizing the general processes of capitalist development within the country, whereas the Rōnōha stressed the general character of Japanese development and tended to minimize the long-term significance of the particularities of Japan's historical circumstances.

Although both groups recognized the development of industry and large industrial houses after the Meiji Restoration, the debate focused more on the analysis of the agricultural sector as the key to understanding Japan's development. To the Kōzaha, the rural areas in particular were characterized by feudal or semifeudal landlord-tenant relations, and the consequent high rents and low standard of living of tenants were to be explained by noneconomic coercion rather than by the market phenomena and capitalist motivations that would characterize agriculture within a fully capitalist economy. Rōnōha writers, on the other hand, tended to explain the high rents and poor conditions of rural areas by the relative backwardness of the industrial sector which had not as yet expanded fast enough to absorb the agricultural labor force, resulting in intense competition on the part of small farmers and tenants wanting to maintain their plots of land at any cost. They denied that relations in agriculture were even "semifeudal" in nature. To them, Japan was without doubt a capitalist country, and capitalism, almost by definition, required the dissolution of the agricultural labor force into wage-labor and the overcoming of all feudal characteristics. Above all, they criticized the Kōzaha's failure to see the expansion of capitalism, rather than rural landholding patterns, as the determining force behind the development of modern Japan.

Unfortunately, neither group was able to substantiate theoretically its position by applying a Marxian analysis of the worldwide and sectoral unevenness of capitalist development to a specific historical case. The Kōzaha viewpoint was posited more as a "model," with little theoretical explanation, for a "feudal" economy that certain writers considered not to have changed substantially since the Kamakura period (1185–1333), despite the country's industrialization during the late 19th and early 20th centuries and its entry into the world economy. Even key terms like "semifeudal" were left vague and unexplained without being justified as theoretically meaningful concepts. The Rōnōha was able to point out important weaknesses in the Kōzaha's arguments and bring original ideas into the discussion, particularly with regard to agrarian problems, but their arguments lacked consistency, and they, too, were never able to analyze Japan's specific historical circumstances in a comprehensive, systematic way.

Historical Context of the Debate——Part of the explanation for the strengths and deficiencies in the Kōza and Rōnō arguments lies in the particular way in which the debate emerged. Because of the highly politicized nature of the academic world during this period, the course of the debate was often dictated by political affiliation and external pressures (Comintern directives, government repression, and so on) rather than by economic theory alone.

The history of the debate is intimately tied to changes within the JAPAN COMMUNIST PARTY (JCP) during this period. In 1922 the "Draft of the Japan Communist Party Program," also known as the Bukharin Thesis, represented the party's position; this was an early form of the Kōzaha-type argument. By 1924 the JCP had divided into two opposing groups, the Reconstruction (Saiken) and Dissolution (Kaitō) factions, whose different analyses of the level of Japan's political development were direct forerunners of the arguments expanded in the debate on Japanese capitalism.

The Reconstructionists held that Japan was much like feudal Russia in its stage of development and advocated the formation of a vanguard party capable of promoting the two-stage (bourgeois and socialist) revolution that Japan required. In 1926 they were able to "reconstruct" the JCP along these lines, and although they incorporated certain Dissolutionist-type ideas concerning the extent of capitalist development into the "1927 Thesis" of the JCP, severe criticism from the Comintern drove them to return to a strict "feudalist" type of analysis in their more representative "1932 Thesis." Writings supporting the positions adopted by the JCP with the "1932 Thesis" were collected into the 1932–33 NIHON SHIHON SHUGI HATTATSU-SHI KŌZA (Lectures on the History of the Development of Japanese Capitalism), the seven-volume lecture series (kōza) by which this school of thought came to be known. (See COMINTERN 1927 THESIS; COMINTERN 1932 THESIS).

The Dissolution group believed that Japan had already undergone considerable capitalist development and would therefore need only a one-stage (proletarian) revolution. To achieve this they advocated dissolving the party in order to work through mass movements. In 1927 members of the Dissolution group began publishing the journal Rōnō, from which the school of thought derived its name, and with this the full-scale debate had begun.

The Kōza position came to be exemplified in the works of such scholars as NORO EITARŌ, HATTORI SHISŌ, YAMADA MORITARŌ, and HIRANO YOSHITARŌ and the aforementioned lectures series which they and others edited. Representative writers of the Rōnōha came to include KUSHIDA TAMIZŌ, SAKISAKA ITSURŌ, Tsuchiya Takao (b 1917), and other authors whose articles appeared in the journal Rōnō edited by ARAHATA KANSON, INOMATA TSUNAO, SUZUKI MOSABURŌ, YAMAKAWA HITOSHI, and others. The writings of both schools include a good deal of original empirical research, for example, that of Yamada on the very low ("semi-servile") wages paid in a wide range of industries, and the investigations of Kushida, Tsuchiya, and others into various forms of landholding and landlord-tenant relations. Historical periods of particular interest to these schools include the late Edo and early Meiji periods, as well as the years during which the debate took place.

Postwar Significance of the Debate——The 1930s brought an end to the debate as most of the participants were subjected to threats, firings, and arrest; however, the immediate postwar period brought a renewed interest in Marxian economics, and with this came a variety of attempts to analyze Japan's new economic circumstances. Initially these were outgrowths of the prewar positions; the so-called "Neo-Kōza" writers, for example, tried to combine a Kōza-type argument for the prewar period with a Rōnō-type explanation for the postwar years. Both Rōnō and Kōza positions subsequently underwent considerable change, turning the discussion in new directions. One school, originated by UNO KŌZŌ, attempted to understand the specificity of Japanese development within the world economy using a "stages theory" approach and stimulated new investigations into important theoretical, methodological, and historical questions.

More generally, the proliferation of individual studies and lines of argument within Marxian economics since the 1950s stands in sharp contrast to the unified schools of the prewar years, and the distance of these arguments from early Rōnō and Kōza positions might give the impression that the prewar debate was inconsequential, at best, to the development of a systematic analysis of Japanese capitalism. However, the fact that postwar studies are able to be conducted at a more sophisticated level than the prewar debate ever achieved is in large part due to the research and discussion that had already taken place. Above all, the arguments of the prewar Rōnō and Kōza schools are suggestive, if not conclusive, interpretations of important historical and theoretical issues regarding the analyses of uneven development in general and Japan's development in particular. The debate not only posed these questions but also began to point out characteristics of the Japanese economy and its historical development that would later be the subject of more detailed empirical studies and more comprehensive theoretical analyses of Japanese capitalist development within a world context.

Donna L. DOANE

Nihon shoki

(Chronicle of Japan). Oldest official history of Japan covering events from the mythical age of the gods up to the reign of the empress JITŌ (r 686–697). According to its sequel, the Shoku nihongi (797), the Nihon shoki was completed on 1 July 720 (Yōrō 4.5.21). The Shoku nihongi also recounts that Prince TONERI, a son of Emperor TEMMU, was ordered to compile the Nihon shoki and that upon its completion he presented 30 volumes plus 1 volume of genealogical charts. Although the official name of the work was Nihongi, the 8th-century anthology MAN'YŌSHŪ and the Koki (ca 738), a commentary on the TAIHŌ CODE, refer to it as the Nihon shoki.

Compilation——The process of compilation may be said to have begun in the 10th year of the reign of Temmu (681), when Prince Kawashima (657–691), a son of the former emperor TENJI, and 11 others were ordered to draw up an official copy of the genealogy of the imperial family (see TEIKI) and various other ancient records. In 714 Ki no Kiyohito (d 753) and Miyake no Fujimaro were added to the team.

Of the 30 volumes in the Nihon shoki, the first and second deal with mythical times and are known as "Jindaiki." Volumes 3 to 30 cover events from the reign of Emperor JIMMU until that of Jitō in chronological order. The *Nihon shoki* differs from the earlier KOJIKI in that it includes sections from the Chinese historical work WEI ZHI *(Wei chih)* and the Korean works *Paekche ki, Paekche pon'gi,* and *Paeckche sinch'an.* Perhaps in an attempt to give a wider perspective, it also includes quotes from the IKI NO MURAJI HAKATOKO NO FUMI, an account by an official who visited Tang (T'ang) China, and the *Ilbon segi* (J: *Nihon seiki*), a history by the Korean monk Tohyŏn (J: Dōken) from the kingdom of Koguryŏ. The accounts from volume 14 onward become increasingly detailed, volume 28, for example, being entirely devoted to the JINSHIN DISTURBANCE of 672.

Another point of contrast between the *Nihon shoki* and the *Ko-jiki* is the former's emphasis on recent events as opposed to the detailed treatment of mythical events in the latter. Written in classical Chinese, the individual chapters of the *Nihon shoki* differ in vocabulary, evidence that many people participated in the project. FUJIWARA NO FUHITO, a powerful figure in the government, is also thought to have played a central role in compiling the work.

The use in the title of "Nihon," a term used since the late 7th century to refer to Japan in the context of foreign relations, and the work's considerable coverage of dealings with China and Korea reveal the compilers' desire to establish a sense of national identity. It must be remembered, however, that the tendency of the ruling class to view SILLA (as Korea was then called) as a tribute-paying barbarian kingdom distorted the chronicle's presentation of Korean-Japanese relations. The *Nihon shoki* also contains references to events occurring close to the time of its completion. For example, in the section dealing with the genealogy of Emperor Tenji, the emperor's daughter Princess Abe (the future Empress Gemmei; 661–722, r 707–715) is recorded as having "later established a capital in Nara," conclusive proof that it was she who moved the capital to HEIJŌKYŌ in 710. Moreover, the section dealing with the introduction of Buddhism during the reign of Emperor KIMMEI cites a passage from the *Konkōmyō saishōō kyō,* a collection of Buddhist texts newly translated into Chinese by the Tang scholar Yijing (I-ching) in 703.

Commentaries —— Upon its completion, the *Nihon shoki* was read widely by government officials and intellectuals. There are indications that during the Nara period (710–794) the history was taken up in lectures and studies, and there is definite evidence that lectures on the *Nihon shoki* were held on at least six separate occasions during the Heian period (794–1185). *Hizen no Kuni fudoki* and *Bungo no Kuni fudoki,* gazetteers from the mid-8th century, both contain sections based on passages from the work. In addition, the *Koki* and annotations in the *Man'yōshū* include quotes from the *Nihon shoki,* indications that the work had a wide audience. The genealogical work SHINSEN SHŌJIROKU, dating from 815, makes special mention of whether or not its information agrees with the *Nihon shoki.*

Several ancient manuscript copies of the *Nihon shoki* survive. The one from the private collection of Sasaki Nobutsuna (1181–1242) is a partial copy of the first volume, made, it is believed, sometime during the late Nara or early Heian period. Other copies dating from the Nara and Heian periods are the Inokuma, Shitennōji, Tanaka, and Iwasaki manuscripts.

Commentaries on the *Nihon shoki* abound. The SHAKU NIHONGI was compiled in the late 13th century. Beginning in the Kamakura period (1185–1333) and lasting into the Muromachi period (1333–1568), the *Nihon shoki* came to be viewed increasingly as a Shintō sacred text; commentaries from these times include Imbe no Masamichi's *Nihon shoki kuketsu* and ICHIJŌ KANEYOSHI's *Nihon shoki sanso.* It was not until the Edo period (1600–1868), however, that strictly academic research on the history appeared, notably *Nihon shoki tsūshō* by TANIGAWA KOTOSUGA and *Shoki shikkai* (or *Shoki shūge*) by Kawamura Hidene (1723–92) and his son Masune. SUZUKI SHIGETANE's commentary on the mythical sections, *Nihon shoki den,* and BAN NOBUTOMO's exegesis of volume 28, *Nagara no yamakaze,* are also worthy of note.

—— Kojima Noriyuki, *Jōdai Nihon bungaku to Chūgoku bungaku* (1962). Mishina Shōei, *Nihon shoki Chōsen kankei kiji kōshō* (1962). *Nihon shoki,* in *Nihon koten bungaku taikei,* vols 67–68 (Iwanami Shoten, 1967). *Nihon shoki,* tr W. G. Aston as *Nihongi* (1896). Tsuda Sōkichi, *Tsuda Sōkichi zenshū,* vol 1 (Iwanami Shoten, 1936). *UEDA Masaaki*

Nihon shugi

(Japanism). A nationalistic ideology that emerged in the late 1880s; it opposed democracy, socialism, individualism, and other Western concepts and sought to preserve traditional Japanese values and institutions. It was originally advocated by intellectuals like INOUE TETSUJIRŌ and TAKAYAMA CHOGYŪ in reaction to the policy of Westernization the government had pursued since the MEIJI RESTORATION of 1868. Stressing the uniqueness of Japan's national polity (KOKUTAI) and the supremacy of the state, Japanism was part of the conservative backlash among intellectuals and government leaders that found its definitive expression in the IMPERIAL RESCRIPT ON EDUCATION of 1890. After being temporarily eclipsed by liberal currents in the Taishō period (1912–26), it reemerged during the upsurge of ULTRANATIONALISM in the 1930s. *TANAKA Akira*

Nihon Shūkyō Remmei → Japan Federation of Religions

Nihon Tenji Toshokan → Japan Braille Library

Nihon Tetsudō Kaisha

(Japan Railway Company; became Nihon Tetsudō Kabushiki Kaisha in 1893). The first and, until its nationalization in November 1906, the largest private railway company in Japan; founded in November 1881 by a group of nobles and former *samurai* led by the statesman IWAKURA TOMOMI with funds from the Fifteenth National Bank or "peers' bank." Japan's first railways had been built by the government, previous attempts at private development having failed owing to the difficulty of raising capital. In 1880, however, the government cancelled its immediate railway construction plans in accordance with its new retrenchment policy (see MATSUKATA FISCAL POLICY), triggering a concerted movement by members of the former ruling class to found a private joint-stock railway company with enough government support to ensure the successful floating of its shares. Adopting the name Japan Railway in line with their original aim of building a nationwide railway network, the company promoters obtained permission from the government to build lines from Tōkyō to Takasaki and Aomori. Because the promoters aimed at securing a source of income for the nobles and former samurai—a major government objective—and proposed to build lines originally slated for construction by the state, they received generous terms of assistance from the government, including an interest subsidy and a profit guarantee. The Tōkyō–Takasaki line was completed in 1884 and the Tōkyō–Aomori line in 1891, the government having been entrusted with construction and operation of the lines. The company recorded excellent business results and served as a catalyst for the private railway boom of the late 1880s. In February 1898 the firm was hit by the so-called Nittetsu Strike, the biggest labor strike during the Meiji period (1868–1912). The government purchased Nihon Tetsudō under the Railway Nationalization Law of 1906, and the company's lines became the Japanese National Railways' Tōhoku trunk line, Takasaki line, and so on.

—— Hoshino Takaaki, "Nihon tetsudō kaisha to Daijūgo Kokuritsu Ginkō," *Musashi daigaku ronshū,* 17 (June 1970) and 19 (August 1971 and March 1972). *Steven J. ERICSON*

Nihon University

(Nihon Daigaku). A private coeducational university with central administrative offices in Chiyoda Ward, Tōkyō. It was founded as Nihon Hōritsu Gakkō (Nihon Law School) in 1889 by Yamada Akiyoshi (1844–92), KANEKO KENTARŌ, and YAMAGATA ARITOMO. In 1903 the school was reorganized and adopted its present name, and in 1920 it received university status. Since World War II it has expanded its faculties and campuses throughout Japan and is now the largest private university in the country. There are faculties of law, arts and sciences, political science and economics, commerce, fine arts, science and technology, engineering, industrial engineering, medicine, dentistry, and agriculture and veterinary medicine. University affiliates include a correspondence division, a two-year junior college, 21 research institutes including the Atomic Research Energy Institute, the Shimoda Institute of Marine Research, the Human Science Laboratory, the Law Institute, the Economic Science Research Institute, Judicial Institute and Research Institute of Agriculture and Veterinary Medicine, 11 senior high schools, 3 junior high schools, and 1 kindergarten. Enrollment was 72,545 in 1980.

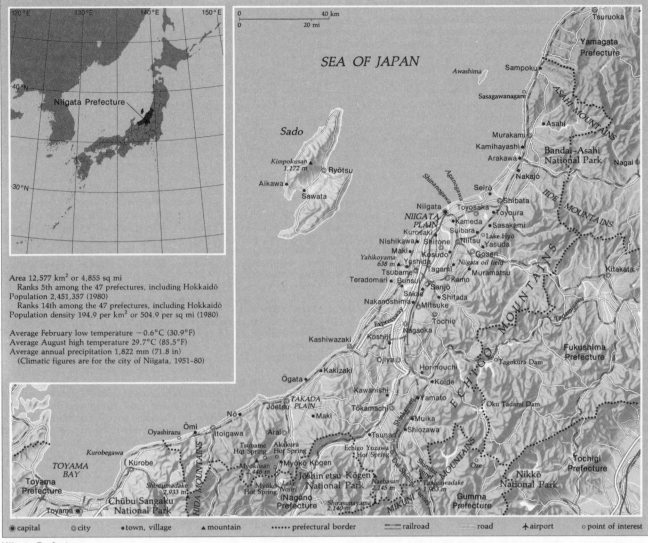

Area 12,577 km² or 4,855 sq mi
  Ranks 5th among the 47 prefectures, including Hokkaidō
Population 2,451,357 (1980)
  Ranks 14th among the 47 prefectures, including Hokkaidō
Population density 194.9 per km² or 504.9 per sq mi (1980)

Average February low temperature −0.6°C (30.9°F)
Average August high temperature 29.7°C (85.5°F)
Average annual precipitation 1,822 mm (71.8 in)
  (Climatic figures are for the city of Niigata, 1951–80)

| ⊚ capital | ◎ city | ● town, village | ▲ mountain | ••••• prefectural border | ▭▭ railroad | ▭▭ road | ✈ airport | ○ point of interest |

Niigata Prefecture

Niichi Suto → General Strike of 1947

Niigata

Capital of Niigata Prefecture, central Honshū, on the Sea of Japan. During the Edo period (1600–1868) it was a prosperous port for transshipping rice from northern Honshū to Ōsaka. With the signing of the ANSEI COMMERCIAL TREATIES (1858), it was opened to foreign trade. Still the largest port in the Hokuriku region, it also has chemical, oil-refining, machinery, textile, and lumber industries. The Niigata Festival (in August) is known for its spectacular fireworks at Bandai Bridge. Pop: 457,783.

Niigata Engineering Co, Ltd

(Niigata Tekkōsho). Manufacturer of ship engines, industrial machine tools, and rolling stock. It was established in 1895 as an iron works, producing and repairing oil-drilling equipment for the NIPPON OIL CO, LTD, in Niigata Prefecture. The company later began production of railway cars and gasoline motors, becoming independent of Nippon Oil in 1910. Operations were later expanded to include the production of machine tools, cast products, and high-speed diesel engines. After World War II, advanced technology was introduced from the United States, Great Britain, and West Germany to make Niigata Engineering a comprehensive machinery maker. The company exports oil and chemical plants to the Middle and Near East, Latin America, Southeast Asia, and Africa. It has joint venture subsidiaries in Saudi Arabia and Indonesia, which engage in the construction and maintenance of industrial plants, and

has sales companies in the Netherlands, Hong Kong, and Singapore. Sales for the fiscal year ending March 1982 totaled ¥177.3 billion (US $736.5 million); the export ratio was 33 percent and capitalization stood at ¥16.3 billion (US $67.7 million) in the same year. Corporate headquarters are located in Tōkyō.

Niigata Plain

(Niigata Heiya). Also known as Echigo Plain. Located in central Niigata Prefecture, central Honshū. This flood plain with deltas of the rivers SHINANOGAWA and AGANOGAWA borders the Sea of Japan. The long, flat, and low coast has sand dunes and sand banks along the seashore, while the interior of the plain is marshy. From the Edo period (1600–1868) its numerous lakes have disappeared through flood control and land reclamation projects. In 1922 a project to shorten the course of the Shinanogawa was completed. This plain yields the richest harvest of rice in Japan, and tulip bulbs and pears are now also grown. The region is, moreover, a source of natural gas. Most of the cities in the prefecture are located on the plain, the largest being NIIGATA. Area: approximately 2,000 sq km (772 sq mi); length: 100 km (62 mi); width: 10–30 km (6–19 mi).

Niigata Prefecture

(Niigata Ken). Located in central Honshū and bounded on the north by the Sea of Japan, on the east by Yamagata Prefecture, on the south by Fukushima, Gumma, and Nagano prefectures, and on the west by Toyama Prefecture. The border areas are all covered by mountain ranges, and foothills and plateau areas cover most of the interior section. The major level areas are located along the coast. The island of SADO in the Sea of Japan is administratively a part of

Niigata and one of the largest of Japan's offshore islands. The climate is noted for its heavy snowfall, especially in the interior mountain valleys.

Parts of the Niigata region were occupied by EZO tribesmen as late as the 7th century, but they were gradually conquered or pushed farther north by the advancing forces of the central government. The mainland portion of Niigata constituted Echigo Province after the TAIKA REFORM of 645, while Sado was designated a separate province. The Echigo area fell under the rule of various warlords, including the Uesugi family, after the Heian period (794–1185) and was divided into numerous domains in the Edo period (1600–1868). The discovery of gold deposits on Sado led the Tokugawa shogunate to take direct control over the island. The prefecture's present name dates from 1871; the current boundaries were established in 1886.

Niigata remains one of Japan's major rice-producing areas; forestry is also important. Large-scale industries, which include chemicals, machine production, and oil refining, are of recent development. The *sake*, textile, and furniture industries are active. The country's largest reserves of petroleum and natural gas are located here.

Sado's rugged scenery and distinctive folk culture attract visitors. The mountains of Niigata proper belong to the Jōshin'etsu Kōgen, Chūbu Sangaku, Bandai–Asahi, and Nikkō national parks. Well-known hot spring resorts include Echigo Yuzawa, Myōkō, Akakura, and Tsubame. Area: 12,577 sq km (4,855 sq mi); pop: 2,451,357; capital: Niigata. Other major cities include NAGAOKA, JŌETSU, SANJŌ, and KASHIWAZAKI.

Niihama

City in eastern Ehime Prefecture, Shikoku, on the Hiuchinada, an inlet of the Inland Sea. From the 17th century, Niihama prospered as a port for shipping copper ore from the Besshi Copper Mine (closed in 1973; see BESSHI COPPER MINE LABOR DISPUTES). In the early part of the Meiji period (1868–1912) chemical, metal, and machine industries affiliated with the Sumitomo ZAIBATSU developed here. More recently, a petrochemical industrial complex has been constructed. Pop: 132,352.

Niijima Jō (1843–1890)

Also known as Joseph Hardy Neesima. The first ordained Protestant Japanese Christian and recipient of a degree (BS, Amherst College, 1870) from a Western institution of higher learning; founder of Dōshisha (now DŌSHISHA UNIVERSITY) in Kyōto in 1875.

Niijima was born in Edo (now Tōkyō), where his father, a *samurai,* was secretary to the *daimyō* of Annaka domain (now part of Gumma Prefecture). Chosen to study Dutch, he went on to the shogunal naval school (Gunkan Sōrenjo); later he taught himself algebra, geometry, and the rudiments of navigation.

Chinese translations of biblical excerpts from the Books of Genesis and John and of Elijah C. Bridgman's *Historical Geography of the United States of America* aroused his curiosity about the world and the concept of an authority higher than that of his parents and ancestors or his domain. Determined to venture abroad, in 1864 he made his way to the treaty port of Hakodate where he secretly boarded a ship. He arrived in Boston in July 1865 aboard *The Wild Rover.* The ship's owner, Alpheus Hardy, a devout Christian and trustee of Phillips Academy in Andover, Massachusetts, and Amherst College, arranged to send him to both these institutions.

Niijima was baptized at Andover in 1866, graduated from Amherst in 1870, and entered Andover Theological Seminary. In 1872 the Japanese minister to Washington, MORI ARINORI, persuaded him to lend his services as interpreter to the IWAKURA MISSION to the United States and Europe. Niijima wrote the official reports on education and then returned to Andover to complete his theological training. At the 65th annual meeting of the Congregational mission board at Rutland, Vermont, in October 1874 he made a ringing appeal for funds to start a Christian school in Japan and obtained pledges of $5,000.

Niijima was well received on his return to Japan, 10 years after his departure. The government leader KIDO TAKAYOSHI smoothed the way for the establishment of a school in Ōsaka, but because of opposition by the governor the decision was made to try Kyōto. In view of the city's Buddhist and imperial connections this was a bold move. The new school, named Dōshisha, grew rapidly, especially after attracting the "Kumamoto Band," a group of young Christians who had left the KUMAMOTO YŌGAKKŌ in Kyūshū, and by the mid-1880s permanent brick buildings were being built.

In 1884 he journeyed again to Europe and America. Returning to Kyōto he strove to elevate Dōshisha to university status (which it finally attained in 1912). Publicized in TOKUTOMI SOHŌ's *Kokumin no tomo* and other publications, Niijima's appeal drew national as well as local support, including more than token contributions from many Meiji leaders. The year before his death, Amherst College honored him with an LLD, the first given a Japanese. He died in January 1890 in Ōiso and was buried on Nyakōji, a hill on the eastern rim of Kyōto.

A "doer" rather than a "thinker," Niijima combined the zeal for reform of New England Congregationalism and the discipline of samurai tradition with a sincerity that was rarely doubted; in spite of poor health he was tireless in traveling, preaching, and planning mission strategy.

— A. S. Hardy, *Life and Letters of Joseph Hardy Neesima* (1891).   Otis CARY

Niimi

City in northwestern Okayama Prefecture, western Honshū. A castle town in the Edo period (1600–1868), Niimi is now an important railway center. Limestone quarrying and cement making are its principal industries. Farm products include tobacco, vegetables, and beef. Pop: 28,933.

Niinamesai

An annual rite, performed from ancient times in the 11th month and now observed on 23 November, in which the emperor makes an offering of the newly harvested rice to the deities of heaven and earth *(tenjin chigi),* expresses his gratitude to them for having protected the crops, and then partakes of the rice offering in communion with the deities. According to the *Nihongi* or NIHON SHOKI (720, Chronicle of Japan), the Niinamesai (Festival for the New Tasting), also called the Shinjōsai, had its origin in mythical times. It was supposedly first performed by the divine imperial ancestress, the sun goddess AMATERASU ŌMIKAMI, using rice newly harvested from the sacred fields in heaven. The Niinamesai is similar to the DAIJŌSAI in that it is an offering from the new harvest to all the deities of heaven and earth but differs from the latter in that it is an annual rite, whereas the Daijōsai is held only at the accession of a new emperor. Hence the Niinamesai is omitted during the year that a Daijōsai is held. The observance of the Niinamesai was discontinued during the Ōnin War (1467–77), which ravished Kyōto, and was not formally resumed again until 1739.

The basic ritual consists of the presentation by the emperor of the new rice and other offerings at a special hall (Shinkaden) in the palace; it is repeated in the morning of the 24th and then followed by a feast called Toyo no Akari no Sechie. Similar offerings are simultaneously presented on the emperor's behalf at the Ise Shrine and all former national shrines *(kampeisha)* and provincial shrines *(kokuheisha).* November 23, the day on which the Niinamesai is observed, was chosen in 1948 as the date of a new national holiday, Labor Thanksgiving Day (Kinrō Kansha no Hi). The autumn festival *(akimatsuri),* widely celebrated in rural Japan to offer thanks to the agricultural deities, is a popular expression of the imperial Niinamesai. See also KANNAMESAI.   Stanley WEINSTEIN

Niitsu

City in central Niigata Prefecture, central Honshū. During the Muromachi period (1333–1568) Niitsu prospered as a castle town of the UESUGI FAMILY, and in the Edo period (1600–1868) as a market town. Its once rich oilfields have been depleted, and it now grows rice, fruit, and saplings. Pop: 62,283.

Niiza

City in southern Saitama Prefecture, central Honshū. A copper-rolling center since the Edo period (1600–1868), Niiza began developing other industries from 1960. It is rapidly becoming a residential suburb of Tōkyō. The Zen Buddhist temple Heirinji here is noted for its stand of ancient trees. Pop: 119,312.

Niji no Matsubara

Pine grove located in the city of Karatsu, Saga Prefecture, Kyūshū. Facing Karatsu Bay, the area is famous as a scenic spot because of its beautiful pine trees and sand. It is said that the lord of Karatsu

Castle planted the trees in the early part of the Edo period (1600–1868). Length: approximately 5 km (3 mi).

Nijō Castle

Residential castle located in the city of Kyōto. Construction began in 1569 by the warload ODA NOBUNAGA and was completed by TOKUGAWA IEYASU, the founder of the Tokugawa shogunate. It was to serve as a residence during visits by the shōgun to the capital. It is a representative example of the plains castle (hirajiro; see CASTLES); rectangular in layout, its main compound (hommaru) is distinctive in being built on a slightly raised earth bank. The main keep came from FUSHIMI CASTLE at the time of its demolition by the Tokugawa, but it was destroyed by fire in 1750. The castle is a fine example of 17th-century architecture. The mansion-style buildings of the Ninomaru Palace in the secondary compound (ninomaru) are representative of the popular SHOIN-ZUKURI style of architecture and have been designated a National Treasure. Nijō Castle is famous for its creaking floor boards, said to chirp like nightingales as a warning against would-be silent attack. It is also known for the beautiful design of its garden.

Nijōgawara no rakusho

("Nijōgawara Scribblings" or "Lampoons"). A set of 88 lines of satirical verse that were posted by an anonymous author at the intersection of Nijō (Second Avenue) and the Kamo riverbed (kawara) in Kyōto in September 1334 (Kemmu 1.8). Although brief, the Lampoons are an invaluable commentary on the state of confusion and social flux into which Kyōto was thrown after the destruction of the Kamakura shogunate (1192–1333) and during the effort of Emperor GO-DAIGO to restore imperial rule (see KEMMU RESTORATION). Go-Daigo's government, staffed mainly by courtiers, proved singularly inept in dealing with the fundamental needs and demands of what had become a warrior society. If we are to believe the Nijōgawara Lampoons, the restoration government could not even maintain order in the capital, where samurai and others from different regions of the country were congregating in increasingly greater numbers. Lawlessness was rife, and both courtiers and warriors made spectacles of themselves as they sought to ape each other's ways. Above all, according to the Lampoons, the old social statuses and distinctions were being rudely upset, especially by the rough samurai parvenus from the Kantō region who were intruding so conspicuously upon the traditional world of courtier elegance and privilege. The Nijōgawara Lampoons are contained in the chronicle KEMMU NENKAN KI; an English translation may be found in David John Lu, ed, Sources of Japanese History, vol 1 (1974).   H. Paul VARLEY

Nijō Tameyo (1250?–1338)

Poet and leader of the dominant conservative poetic faction at court. Tameyo succeeded his father Fujiwara no Tameuji as head of the senior Nijō branch of the Mikohidari family of court poets and critics descended from FUJIWARA NO SADAIE (Teika; 1162–1241). He and his supporters were politically allied with the Daikakuji line of emperors, which in the late 13th century alternated with the Jimyōin line in supplying occupants for the throne. In both politics and poetry Tameyo and his faction were bitterly opposed by the allied Kyōgoku and Reizei factions, the two junior family lines descended from the same forebears as the Nijō. The poetic differences were fundamental and pointed, the Kyōgoku–Reizei poets practicing and advocating new styles and much greater freedom of diction and expression than their opponents.

In 1303 Tameyo was given the honor of appointment as sole compiler of the 13th imperial anthology, Shin gosenshū (1303, New Later Collection). His fortunes went down with the accession of Emperor Hanazono (1297–1348; r 1308–18), and when, further, his arch enemy KYŌGOKU TAMEKANE (1254–1332) was appointed compiler of a new imperial anthology by the retired emperor Fushimi (1265–1317; r 1287–98), he responded with a series of outraged but ultimately ineffective protests to the throne. When in 1318 Emperor GO-DAIGO ascended the throne, Tameyo came into his own again, becoming at the age of 68 the elder statesman of court poetry and enjoying considerable prestige by virtue of the position he occupied. In the same year he was appointed by Go-Daigo to compile his second imperial anthology, the Shoku senzaishū (Collection of a Thousand Years, Continued), which he completed probably in 1320. This gave him the rare distinction of compiling two imperial an-

thologies, as well as an opportunity for revenge against Tamekane by including none of his poems. However, with the exile of Go-Daigo in 1331 for plotting against the military government, the Nijō party were put down once more, and Tameyo is said to have escaped the political turmoil by going into seclusion at the famous Buddhist monastery atop Mt. Kōya (Kōyasan), far from the capital.

Though an important and prominent figure among his contemporaries owing to his inherited status as doyen of court poets, Tameyo was ungifted and uninspired. Believing that he was preserving the orthodox tradition, he advocated a bland, inoffensive style of tedious mediocrity. His poetic treatises, Waka teikin shō (Notes on Poetry for Beginners), completed in 1326, and Waka yōi jōjō (A List of Cautionary Pointers for Poetic Composition), of uncertain date, merely reiterate some of the oft-repeated prescriptions of his forebears, adding nothing new or original. However, because of the complete dominance of the Nijō faction from the mid-14th century onwards, the large number of 177 of his poems are included in imperial anthologies. He left no personal collection.
━━ ———Robert H. Brower and Earl Miner, Japanese Court Poetry (1961).   Robert H. BROWER

Nijō Yoshimoto (1320–1388)

Courtier and statesman; scholar and authority on traditional customs and practices; poet and theoretician, particularly of renga (linked verse). Yoshimoto was the son of the regent and minister of the left, Nijō Michihira. He served at court first under Emperor GO-DAIGO (1288–1339; r 1318–39) but when Go-Daigo fled to Yoshino south of the capital and set up the Southern Court, Yoshimoto remained in Kyōto where he served under successive emperors of the northern line. He rose to the junior first court rank, became inner minister and head of the Fujiwara family, and was four times regent. During the period of dynastic schism between the NORTHERN AND SOUTHERN COURTS, when court culture and learning were at a low ebb, Yoshimoto stands out as a scholar and authority ranking in importance with ICHIJŌ KANEYOSHI (1402–81) and SANJŌNISHI SANETAKA (1455–1537) as a custodian and transmitter of traditional aristocratic culture.

Yoshimoto wrote several works of importance on court custom and ceremonial, but he is best known for his contributions to poetry. As a high noble and courtier he was almost as a matter of course an important patron of classical poetry, sponsoring various poetic gatherings and competitions and supporting the conservative Nijō school of poets hereditarily allied with the Jimyōin, or northern line, emperors. He appears first to have studied under Nijō Tamesada and later to have become a pupil of the important conservative poet TON'A (1289–1372). In addition to his participation in and sponsorship of poetry contests and the like, he wrote important treatises of conservative Nijō poetics, particularly Gumon kenchū (1363, Sage Replies to Ignorant Questions) and Kinrai fūtei shō (1387, Notes on Poetic Styles of the Recent Past). More than 60 of his poems are found in imperial anthologies beginning with the 17th, the Fūgashū (ca 1346, Collection of Elegance).

It was as a renga poet and theoretician that Yoshimoto was best known to posterity, however. He was from the outset more interested in linked verse than in the traditional 31-syllable genre, and he appears to have begun his study of it at a young age. He became a pupil of the renga master GUSAI (1281?–1375?), thereby putting himself under the tutelage of a member of the commoner class. With Gusai's collaboration and assistance, Yoshimoto compiled the TSUKUBASHŪ, a collection of superior renga verses, and his influence with the sovereign gained for the collection official status equivalent to an imperial anthology of classical poems. In 1372 he codified a set of rules for linked verse known as Renga shinshiki (1372, New Rules of Renga) or Ōan shinshiki (New Rules of the Ōan Era), for which he also obtained imperial sanction amounting to quasi-legal status. By this means he succeeded in establishing universal rules for linked verse, which had until then been composed under an anarchy of different sets of rules varying from place to place and from school to school. Yoshimoto also wrote several important treatises on renga: Renri hishō (ca 1349, Secret Notes on the Principles of Linked Verse); Tsukuba mondō (1357–72, Questions and Answers on the Art of Renga); Kyūshū mondō (1376, Questions and Answers from Kyūshū); Renga jūyō (1379, Ten Styles of Renga); and Jūmon saihi shō (1383, Top Secret Notes on Ten Questions). His renga poetics are in essential agreement with the poetics of traditional court poetry of the conservative school.   Robert H. BROWER